BLUEWATER

New Bluewater Minnow

The all new Bluewater Minnow has been developed with the toughest of Bluewater species in mind. With many conventional lures the action can quickly become untuned with knocks and bumps but this new in-mould bib and body will ensure the lure will track true and straight time and time again without the need for adjustment.

The new design also allows for exceptional speed to chase the fastest pelagic species with it comfortably holding in at 8 knots.

The Ghost Mould Innovation features colours and designs never seen before in Bluewater lures, these colours will mirror the most predominant baitfish across both the Pacific and Indian Oceans as well as some more wild and unpredictable colours that will entice the toughest predatory fish.

LIVEGLO
FLUORESCENT TECHNOLOGY

LENGTH MM	WEIGHT GMS	DIVING DEPTH	HOOK SIZE
160	38	3mt/12ft	2/0
200	64	3mt/12ft	4/0

+12
3mt/12ft

Minnow STD Series

Minnow Pro Series

The Pro Series range of Bluewater Minnow lure colours, feature an abalone shell foil and laser insert, that makes for a realistic finish that has proven very effective on all pelagic species.

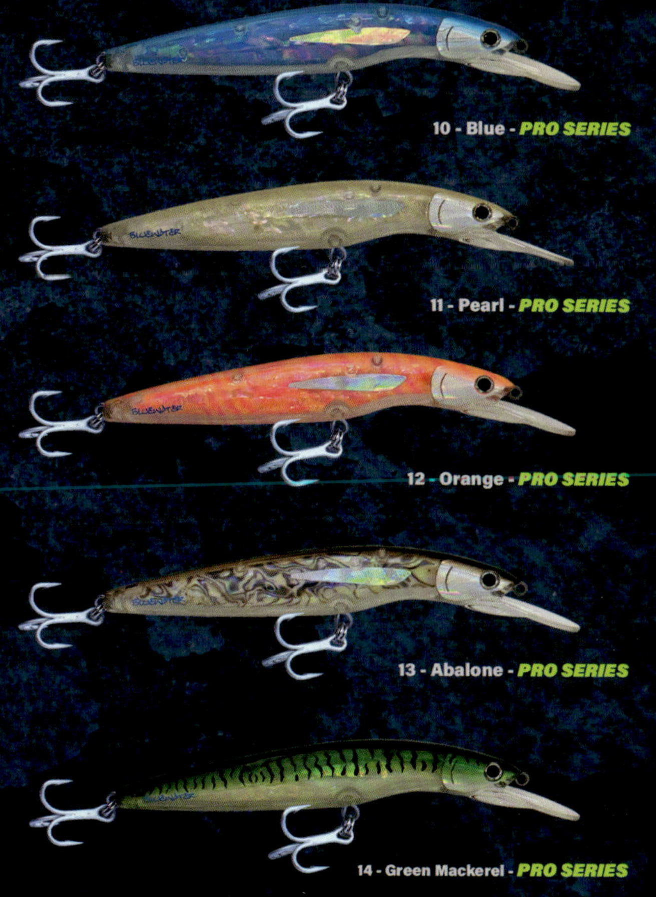

FISHERMAN'S GATEWAY BYNOE HARBOUR

DRIVE IN, FLY IN OR BOAT IN!

Crab Claw Island Resort is a picturesque coastal retreat nestled within Bynoe Harbour, a little over an hour's drive from Darwin.

Visitors can access some of the best fishing and crabbing in the NT in the pristine harbour, nearby Fog Bay and the Arafura Sea.

Bynoe Harbour is the perfect place for the experienced fisho or the first timer hoping to make it onto the brag board.

The sealed boat ramp allows you to quickly launch your boat, with plenty of parking for your car and trailer. The ramp is near our cabins making it easy to launch and retrieve as the tide allows.

Crab Claw Island Resort has the perfect balance of fishing, fun and relaxation.

RELAX AND STAY WITH US

Our cabins are affordable, comfortable and accommodate between four and six people, perfect for singles, couples, groups and families.

SCENIC BEACHFRONT CABINS are perched over our private beach just metres from the water's edge.

SPACIOUS FAMILY CABINS provide additional room and bedding options to comfortably accommodate families and groups.

QUIET RETREAT CABINS are nestled among lush vegetation overlooking one of our swimming pools.

SECLUDED TWO-BEDROOM VILLAS contain one double and two single beds in each room with a large shared bathroom.

NO BOAT, NO WORRIES!

You can hire one of our four Quintrex Renegades. Choose from either a 4.6m side console with a Yamaha 60hp, or 4.2m tiller steer with a Yamaha 50hp which are available for full or half day hire. Each boat comes with its own icebox, shade and all the necessary safety equipment. We will even launch and retrieve for you.

www.crabclawisland.com.au

INTO

GETTING THERE

Located 105km from Darwin CBD, the drive to Crab Claw is mostly sealed with 11km of well maintained graded dirt road.

Travel outbound on the Stuart Highway, turn right onto Cox Peninsula Road, proceeding 50km and turning left onto Fog Bay Road.

You will come to our Crab Claw Island Resort sign, make a right and you will find us.

Visitors are advised to look out for wildlife and exercise caution when travelling at dusk and dawn.

RECHARGE AT BREEZES RESTAURANT

The resort's Breezes Restaurant includes a well stocked licenced bar with panoramic views and fresh ocean views.

We are open for breakfast, lunch and dinner and welcome resort guests and day visitors.

Enjoy a great range of a la carte classics, sit back and relax with an icy cold drink.

Unwind and cool off in one of our two refreshing saltwater pools located amongst the tropical gardens. The pools are fenced, with child safety gates.

Ph: 08 8978 2313

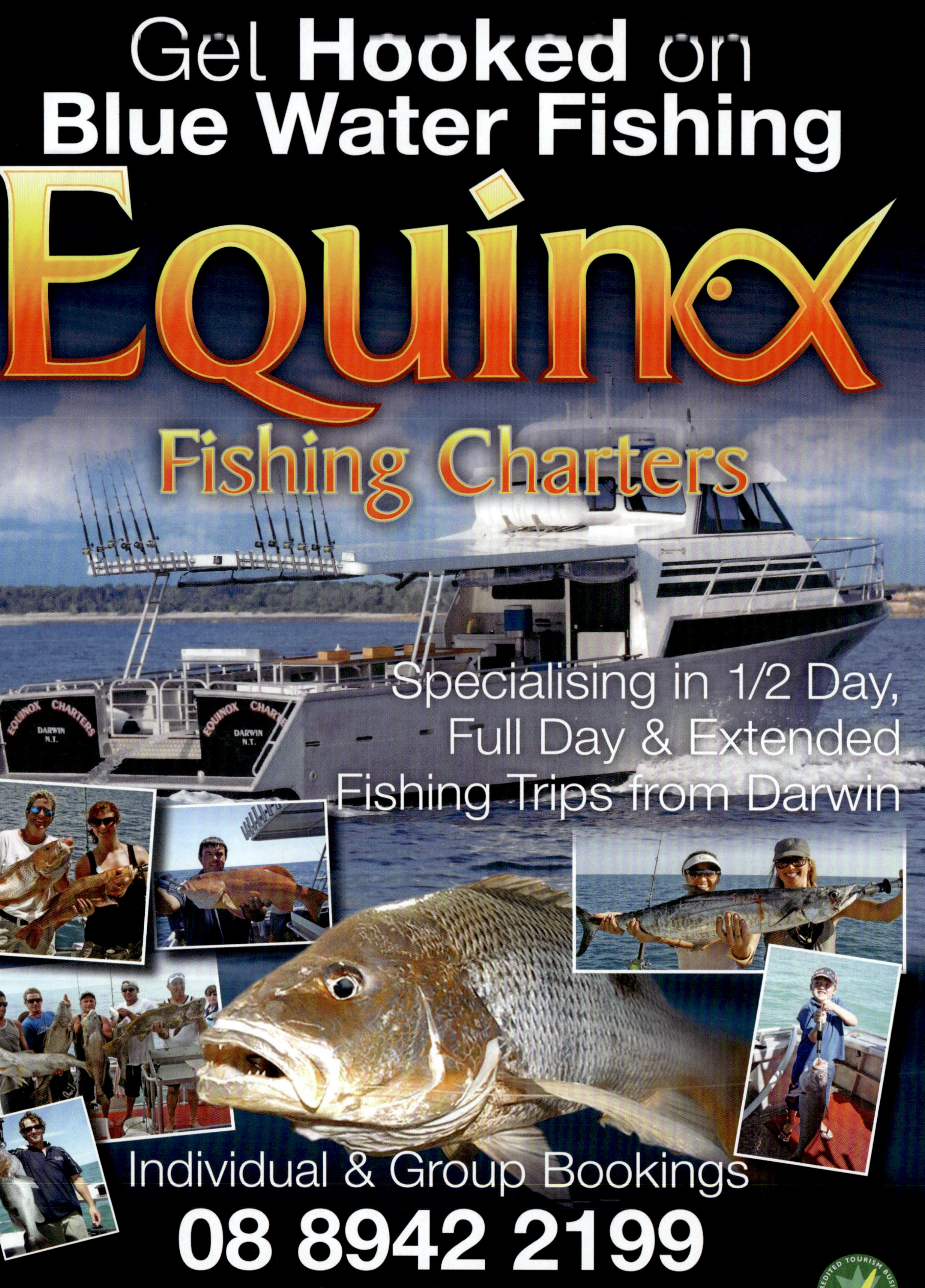
Get Hooked on
Blue Water Fishing
Equinox
Fishing Charters
Specialising in 1/2 Day,
Full Day & Extended
Fishing Trips from Darwin
Individual & Group Bookings
08 8942 2199
www.equinoxcharters.com.au
ACCREDITED TOURISM BUSINESS
AUSTRALIA

Family Owned and Operated!
We Do Deals!
CRAIG'S
FISHING WAREHOUSE
Darwin's BIG Tackle Store
Check Out Craig's Custom Shop Online
www.craigsfishingwarehouse.com.au
Psycho Bling
'Pearl Jam' Reidy's Big B52
The Classic Green Bling
Craig's Bling Pink Camo Pro-Fish Cap
Classic Barra "Bling"
Custom Reidu's
Green Bling 17a Bomber
Craig's FISHING WAREHOUSE
Phone: (08) 8947 4867
Email: sales@craigsfishingwarehouse.com.au
Cnr Stuart Hwy/Berrimah Rd - Truck City, Berrimah
"So much more than a Tackle Store!"
'Get it at Craig's'

The regional colour code ...

South-West WA

Israelite Bay to Albany 40-42
Albany to Bunbury 42-43
Leeman to Port Denison 54-55
Mandurah (Peel Inlet, Murray River) 44-45
Perth (Swan River) 48-49
Rockingham (Cockburn Sound) 46-47
Rottnest Island 50-51
Yanchep to Jurien Bay 52-53

North-West WA

Carnarvon 61
Dampier-Karratha 70-71
Exmouth 65-67
Kalbarri-Geraldton 56-57
Montebello Islands 72
Ningaloo 62-65
Onslow (Mackerel Islands, Ashburton River) 68-69
Pardoo-Cape Keraudren 78-79
Port Hedland 75-77
Port Smith 80-81
Point Samson-Cossack 73-74
Quobba (The Ledge, Camp Rock, Korean Star) 62-63
Shark Bay (Denham, Steep Point, Dirk Hartog Island) 58-61

The Kimberley

Admiralty Gulf (Mitchell River, Cassini Island) 95
Broome (Dampier Peninsula) 83-85
Brunswick Bay (Prince Regent River) 92-93
Derby (Fitzroy River, King Sound) 88-90
King Sound ('Thousand Island Coast') 86-87
Napier Broome Bay (Kalumburu, Drysdale River) 97
Ord River (Wyndham, Kununurra) 100-105
Ord to Cape Londonderry (Berkeley, King George Rivers) 98-99
Vansittart Bay (Truscott Airstrip) 96
Walcott Inlet (Doubtful Bay, Secure Bay) 90-91
York Sound (Prince Regent, Roe, Moran Rivers) 92-93

Northern Territory

Adelaide River (Saltwater Arm, Goat Island) 140-141, 182-183
Borroloola (Rosie Creek to Calvert River) 198
Bynoe Harbour (Indian Island, Crab Claw Resort) 142-150
Cape Hotham (Ruby Island) 138-139
Cox Peninsula (Tapa, Turnbull Bays, Woods Inlet) 120-121
Cobourg Peninsula (Port Essington, Black Point) 166-167
Croker Region (New Year, Oxley Islands, Wiligi) 169
Daly River (Channel Point, Red Cliff, Cape Ford) 174-178
Darwin Harbour (cyclone and WWII wrecks) 109-128
Dundee Beach 151-154
East Alligator River 189
Engineered Artificial Reefs 158-159
Fenton Patches Artificial Reef System 118-119
Finniss River to Moyle River 160-161
Gove Peninsula (Nhulunbuy) 170-171
Groote Eylandt 162
Gunn Point 132-136
Kakadu Billabongs (Yellow Water, Red Lily, 4-Mile) 190
Katherine (Knotts Crossing, Flora River, Nitmiluk) 174-175
Lee Point Artificial Reef System 112
Limmen Bight River (Limmen Fishing Camp) 199
Mary River (Shady Camp, Corroboree, Hardies) 184-187
McArthur River (King Ash Bay, Vanderlin Islands) 198-199
Mini Mini (Endyalgout Island) 168
Peron Islands (Channel Point, Point Blaze) 156-157, 160
Robinson River (Wearyan River, Calvert River) 202
Roper River (Roper Bar, Tomato Island, Port Roper) 191-195
Saltwater Arm, The Narrows (Adelaide River) 140-141
Shoal Bay (Buffalo Creek, King Creek, Howard River) 129-131
South Alligator River (Nourlangie Creek) 188, 190
Tiwi Islands (beach camps by permit) 163-165
Towns River 196
Vanderlin Islands (Centre Island) 198, 200-201
Vernon Islands (Leaders Ck Fishing Base) 134, 136-137
Victoria River 180-181

North Queensland

Aurukun (Archer, Watson, Ward Rivers) 215
Burketown (Albert, Leichardt, Nicholson Rivers) 204-205
Bamaga/Seisia (Jardine River, The Tip) 222-225
Bathurst Bay 234-235
Cairns (Barron River to Russell River) 240-246
Cooktown & Daintree (Endeavour, Annan Rivers) 236-241
Jackey Jackey (Escape River) 226-227
Karumba (Norman, Bynoe, Flinders Rivers) 206-207
Kirke River (Love River) 214
Kowanyama (Mitchell, Coleman Rivers, Topsy Creek) 212
Lakefield (North Kennedy, Bizant, Normanby Rivers) 230-233
Lockhart River (Lloyd Bay, Chili Beach) 228
Mapoon (Wenlock, Ducie Rivers) 218-219
Normanton (Norman River) 206-207
N-W Cape rivers (Skardon, Jackson, Doughboy, Cotterell) 220-221
Pormpuraaw (Chapman, Edward, Mungkan) 213
Port Douglas (Dickson Inlet) 242
Port Stewart 229
S-W Cape York rivers (Gilbert, Nassau, Staaten) 208-211
Weipa (Mission, Embley Rivers) 216-217
Vrilya Point (Crystal Creek, Number 2) 221-222

Central Coast and SEQ

Ayr-Bowen (Burdekin River, Cape Upstart, Dingo Beach) 264-269
Bundaberg (Burnett, Kolan Rivers, Baffle Creek) 307-308
Brisbane (Bribie, Moreton & Stradbroke Islands) 315-319
Ingham (Palm Islands, Cattle Creek) 254-256
Innisfail (Johnstone, Tully, Hull, Murray Rivers) 247-250
Hervey Bay (Fraser Island, Great Sandy Strait) 306-311
Hinchinbrook (Herbert River, Lucinda) 251 253
Gladstone (Curtis Island to Turkey Beach) 296, 302-303
Mourilyan & Tully 248-249
Maryborough (Mary River, Great Sandy Strait) 309-310
Mackay (Seaforth, Sarina, Cape Palmerston) 276, 280-289
Proserpine (Proserpine River, Repulse Inlet) 274-275
Rockhampton (Fitzroy River, Coorooman Creek) 299-300
St Lawrence (West Hill, Styx, Hoogly, Waverley Rivers) 290-291
St Helens 278-279
Stanage Bay (Clairview) 292-295
Sunshine Coast (Caloundra, Mooloolaba, Noosa) 312-314
Townsville (Ross, Bohle, Haughton, Barratta Rivers) 257-263
Town of 1770 (Round Hill Creek, Baffle Creek) 305
Tweed/Qld border (Tallebudgera Creek, Nine Mile Reef) 320-325
Yeppoon (Corio Bay, Coorooman Creek, Keppel Isles) 296-298
Whitsunday Islands (Airlie Beach) 272-273

New South Wales

Ballina (Richmond River, Evans Head) 326-327
Batemans Bay (Clyde River) 359
Bermagui (Wallaga Lake) 361
Brunswick Heads/Byron Bay 324-325
Broken Bay (Hawkesbury, Cowan, Berowra) 348-349
Coffs Harbour (Solitary Islands) 331
Camden Haven 338-339
Eden (Twofold Bay, Green Cape) 363
Forster-Tuncurry (Wallis Lake) 340-341
Jervis Bay (Ulladulla, St George's Basin) 358
Kempsey (Macleay River, South West Rocks) 334-335
Lake Macquarie 346-347
Merimbula (Pambula, Wallagoot Lake, Bega River) 362
Myall Lakes 341
Nambucca Heads (Nambucca, Bellinger Rivers) 332-333
Narooma (Moruya River, Tuross Lake, Montague Island) 360
Newcastle (Hunter River) 344-345
Nowra (Shoalhaven River) 357
Port Macquarie (Hastings River) 336-337
Port Stephens (Karuah River) 342-343
Red Rock (Corindi River, Wooli River) 330
South West Rocks (Macleay River) 335
Sydney (Sydney Harbour, Botany Bay, Port Hacking) 348-355
Taree (Manning River) 338-339
Tweed Heads (Nine Mile Reef, South Reef, Black Rock) 320-321
Yamba-Iluka (Clarence River, Sandon River) 328-329
Wollongong (Lake Illawarra) 356

Victoria

NSW border to SA border 364-367

South Australia

Vic border to WA border 368-373

Stocked Dams

Awoonga 377
Barambah 381
Borumba 313
Boondooma 381
Bundoora 294
Burdekin Falls 375
Callide 379
Cania 378
Clarrie Hall 320
Coolmunda 380
Copeton 383
Cressbrook 379
Eungella 377
Gregory 302
Glenbawn 384
Glenlyon 382
Hinze 374
Julius 378
Keepit 384
Kinchant 377
Koombooloomba 247
Kununurra 375
Lenthall 302
Leslie 382
Manton 378
Maraboon 383
Maroon 379
Monduran 379
Moondarra 378
Moogerah 382
Mulwala 374
Pindari 383
Proserpine (Peter Faust) 376
Samsonvale 381
Somerset/Wivenhoe 380
St Clair 384
Teemburra 376
Theresa Creek 289
Tinaroo 376
Windamere 345
Wuruma 279

Landbased Spots

Northern Territory 193
NT Barra Floodways 197
Norwest 94
North Queensland 247
SEQ/Northern NSW 322
Sydney 350

General Information

Baits 25
Barra Bible 30-31
Barra Rivers 172-173
Boats & Vehicles 37
Cast Nets 24
Ciguatera 312
Cherabin 22
Fish ID 11-21
Habitat Restoration 38
Lobsters 22
Lures & Tackle 26-29
Mud crabs 32-33
Oysters 23
Rods & Reels 36
Redclaw, Marron 25
Spanish Mackerel 273
Squid & Octopus 35
Stingers 278
Stocked Waters 372-384
Tides & Weather 34

Visit web links at the top of Page 10 for fishing regulations.

The latest fishing regulations

NT ... www.nt.gov.au/marine
Qld ... www.daf.qld.gov.au/business-priorities/fisheries/recreational
NSW ... www.dpi.nsw.gov.au/fishing/recreational/fishing-rules-and-regs
Vic ... www.vfa.vic.gov.au/recreational-fishing
SA ... www.pir.sa.gov.au/fishing
WA ... www.fish.wa.gov.au/fishing-and-aquaculture/

Sea rescue radio

Volunteer marine rescue groups monitor radio VHF Channel 16. Check with your local group regarding other radio frequencies and channels.

NT's $10k barra aren't hard to find

Top Enders are a lucky mob. Not only do they have all the best fish, but a lure or bait cast into Territory waters can hook up to an instant $1,000,000 prize.

If you didn't already know, the Northern Territory releases around 100 tagged barramundi each year across the Top End, and each fish is worth $10,000 to its captor.

Several fish are eligible to win a single $1m grand prize.

It's an annual promotion called Million Dollar Fish.

Every year MDF gets better. In a first for the event, organisers released an extra 12 tagged fish just before Christmas 2021, and provided GPS marks for each fish's location.

Landbased anglers have caught many of the tagged fish.

Barramundi survive tagging well. Proof is in the MDF results, with several of each season's tagged fish recaptured every year since the event began in 2015.

Tagged fish from prior seasons have been caught, and while they may no longer be eligible for prizes they show that the tagged barramundi remain present for some time.

MDF winners

There was a myth that MDF barramundi eligible for the $1m prize were meteries. This is not true. For example, in 2021 none of the $1m fish were over a metre when released.

It is also untrue that tagged fish are not available in remote parts of the Top End, as Darwin, Kakadu, Katherine, Arnhem Land and the Tiwi Islands all receive tagged fish.

Not only are the tagged fish spread far and wide, one fish eligible for the million dollar prize may be released in each of those regions.

Meanwhile, fishing across Australia develops. More artificial reefs have been built around the mainland coast, and structure has been installed in dams too.

Fish passages have been built at barriers on rivers to restore fish migration. Parts of the mighty Murray River are being resnagged, and lost southern shellfish reefs are being recreated thanks to proactive organisations like Ozfish.

There are lucrative fishing competitions across the nation for tournament anglers and family fishos.

In northern Australia, the fishing opportunities are better than they have been in years.

Fishing has been one of the activities less affected by the COVID19 pandemic. Some bush camps have closed however, so check before travelling.

Don't forget to register at **www.milliondollarfish.com.au**

Matt Flynn

North Australian FISH FINDER 14th edition
Published: 2022
The Editor's Office Pty Ltd,
PO Box 272, Huonville, Tas, 7109.

For editorial and advertising matters contact the publisher by email
fishfindermaps2@gmail.com

WARNING

Access to spots described in this book may be affected by COVID19 restrictions, closures, quarantine regulations, lockdowns and the like. Check before planning a trip.

Some species of fish are subject to temporary fishing bans and/or location closures to rejuvenate stocks. Spots listed in this book may not be fished for the described species when bans are in place - check your local regulations before fishing.

The maps and GPS data in this book are provided only to illustrate fishing and diving spots. Basic chart information is provided only to illustrate fishing and diving areas.

THIS BOOK IS NOT TO BE USED FOR LAND OR SEA NAVIGATION. COMPLETE MAPS AND NAUTICAL CHARTS MUST BE USED WHEN NAVIGATING.

Ongoing negotiations from Aboriginal land and sea rights court cases, as well as changing legislation, land holdings and creation and management of marine parks, means land/sea access and fishing regulations may differ from what is printed in this book. Visit government and Aboriginal land council websites for the latest information before fishing.

No responsibility will be taken for misadventure arising from use of information in this guide. No warranty is provided in relation to the information, including accuracy, reliability, completeness or suitability, and no liability is accepted, including without limitation, liability in negligence, for any loss, damage or costs, including consequential damage, relating to any use of this guide.

GPS co-ordinates provided may be subject to typographical or other error. Co-ordinates may mark hazardous reefs and as such should only be approached during good conditions.

Waves may break unexpectedly over submerged reefs.

UNMARKED HAZARDS, INCLUDING ROCKS, SHIFTING SANDBANKS, SUBMERGED TREES AND MORE MAY EXIST IN ALL WATERWAYS.

Crocodiles inhabit northern waters, including beaches, offshore islands, harbours, inland waterholes, creeks and rivers ... sometimes they are even on roads ... do not take risks.

Marine park sanctuaries are illustrated with approximate boundaries - refer to state or federal park maps for the latest detailed boundaries and other zones and conditions. GPS data for wrecks and other features in no-fishing sanctuaries is provided for divers. Be sure to know marine park zone boundaries and rules before fishing.

Some wharves are subject to security zones. These zones may change at short notice. Check with local port authorities before fishing near wharves. Be sure also to understand navigational law when using shipping channels.

Some aerial photography in this book was provided under licence by Qld, WA, NT and NSW government departments. These departments give no warranty in relation to the data.

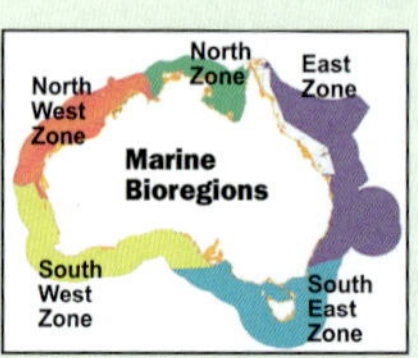

Federal Marine Park Zones

Federal marine parks cover Commonwealth waters, extending to the outer limits of the Exclusive Economic Zone 200 nautical miles from shore. These zones add to the complex network of state government zones, which include no-fishing areas and areas with useage restrictions. Most federal zones are outside areas commonly fished by recreational fishermen and are not shown in this book. Visit **https://parksaustralia.gov.au/marine/** for detailed information.

Please report errors or updates by email to fishfindermaps2@gmail.com. Errors and update notices are available online at **www.fishfinderbooks.com/upd.html**

To use waypoints in this book, set your GPS unit to **degrees and minutes** (d.mm.mmm). Use the datum **WGS 84**. GPS waypoints printed with the word 'Chart' are taken from official digital charts and are supplied as useful reference points, or to mark interesting features, and may not necessarily be good fishing spots. Other GPS data comes from many sources - no guarantees are made to the usefulness of any supplied GPS data.

1 fathom = 1.829m (6 feet)

Some images in this book may be digitally altered to make fish look better, but not bigger.

FISH FINDER generally uses gazetted place names. Unofficial names are, where possible, enclosed in apostrophes.

Many fish pictures in this book were taken in the Top End ... Australia's Fishing Territory

Cover images: Robert 'Buzzdog' Busby with NT barramundi, Glen Cowling with NQ red emperor, Dennis Smart with NT longtail tuna

SHANE COMPAIN

Barramundi

It is not until you catch a barramundi (*Lates calcarifer*) that you can truly appreciate these magnificent fish. The "barra" is heavy-shouldered and covered in a thick layer of skin and scales that has a metallic sheen in sunlight. With its mouth closed it is a streamlined fish, but the huge mouth opens to bucket-like proportions, easily inhaling large fish and other aquatic creatures. It lives in fresh and saltwater, hits lures hard and leaps when hooked. In dams they grow to 44kg+, but 4kg to 12kg is the average size. They are superb table fish. The barra follows bait schools using tidal currents in rivers and across flats. It will also rest in snags, ready to ambush passing bait. Finding bait is the key to catching them. Fish snags, eddies and tidal drains where bait congregates, and present lures or livebaits realistically. Barra are targeted during the "run-off" when wet season floodwater flows into rivers and out of coastal creeks, but they can be caught all year, especially in warm weather. Queensland's stocked dams provide good fishing, while the NT's floodplain rivers are an exciting wild fishery. Several NT rivers, Darwin and Bynoe Harbours, Fog Bay and Shoal Bay, have been closed to netting to allow barra sportfishing to thrive. WA bought out Broome's barra netters in 2013 and Queensland announced three area net closures in 2015.

See also the Barra Bible within.

Golden snapper (fingermark)

The golden snapper (*Lutjanus johnii*), called fingermark bream on the East Coast, and more rarely, spotted-scale sea perch, is one of Australia's great sportfish. They are found in creeks, harbour arms and over inshore reefs. Small "goldies" feed on estuary rockbars, while bigger fish prefer coastal reefs and wrecks. They are caught to 12kg on the East Coast and to about 8kg off the NT and WA. They reach about as far south as Hervey Bay in Queensland and Onslow in WA. Where the water is clear, big fish are easier to tempt at night. Livebait is helpful, especially live squid. Always use fresh bait, with freshly netted sardines or herring being among the best bait. In shallow water, golden snapper will take minnow-style lures and soft plastics. Jigs work well at times. Over shallow reefs the fish can sometimes be berleyed up from the bottom. Golden snapper bite best in the warmer months, and usually bite more strongly on the slack of big tides. Small fish will move in schools over mudflats and along beaches on an incoming tide. Big fish can be found on reefs to about 70m, but also in shallow areas. Research shows they grow slowly and are vulnerable to overfishing. They are susceptible to barotrauma, so fishing should stop when bag limits are reached. They are among the best tropical table fish.

MATT WEST

KIMBERLEY FISHING CHARTERS

Queenfish (skinny)

The queenfish, leatherskin or skinny (*Scomberoides commersonnianus*) is probably the most exciting fighting fish readily available to northern landbased anglers. They range from about Exmouth, WA, to the NSW/Qld border. They are abundant, take lures and baits, run hard and leap repeatedly. Queenfish like inshore reefs, headlands, sandbars and estuaries, and are often found in tidal rips. They grow to about 14kg, but average around 4kg. Bigger fish are found in areas with no gill nets. They respond to surface lures. When they are shy, try a small lure and light trace. They are tasty if eaten fresh. To make pickled fish, soak the diced flesh in a mix of lemon juice, vinegar, chilli, onion and spices. A small oceanic form of queenfish is a popular billfish swim-bait.

Threadfin and blue salmon

The threadfin, king or golden salmon (*Polynemus sheridani* - below right) and the smaller blue salmon (*Eleutheronema tetradactylum* - below left) are unusual fish that frequent shallow estuaries, rivers, creeks and beaches. Blue salmon are caught offshore on occasions. Threadfin salmon use whisker-like fins to herd prawns. They may ignore lures when feeding this way. A small livebait or fly presented in the salmon's path might be taken. A salmon's presence is betrayed by flurries of prawns and baitfish in the shallows, and they can often be sight-fished. When not fixated on prawns they will readily take lures and livebaits. Salmon usually fight hard and fast. They are good to eat, especially if bled and iced on capture. Golden salmon grow to 40kg. Blue salmon are far smaller. Threadfin are an important fish in the Norwest, including along WA's Eighty-Mile Beach. Big threadfin are caught on the Queensland coast as far south as Brisbane, particularly in Rockhampton's Fitzroy River. In recent years the NT's Shady Camp coast has produced many big fish. Net bans off Broome, WA, have seen a resurgence in salmon numbers.

'AGENT86'

GAVIN HOULT

Trevally

There are many types of trevally found in Australian waters. There are 23 species off Australia's East Coast alone. Internationally, they are generally known as "jacks". Trevally are found in a variety of marine habitat, from offshore reefs to tidal flats and creeks. They can live in landlocked freshwater lagoons. They are found singly and in schools. All trevally are tough customers, fighting long and hard. The largest is the giant or lowly trevally (*Caranx ignobilis* - picture H) which can be silver, brassy or black, with small spots. It grows to a back-breaking 80kg. Its northern range is from central WA to central NSW, with the biggest fish found on remote reefs, usually on points facing the current. Casting large poppers is an exciting way to catch them, but heavy spinning tackle is needed to land them. The golden trevally (*Gnathanodon speciosus* - G) is common around tropical reefs and flats. Juveniles are silver/yellow with black bars. Adults grow to 1.2m and have only faint bars. The golden trevally has an extendable, soft mouth that is different from the hard mouths of most trevally. It is reputedly the best-eating of all trevally. The turrum or gold-spotted trevally (*Carangoides fulvoguttatus* - I) is an elongated trevally, as is the bludger (*Carangoides gymnostethus* - K) and tille trevally (*Caranx tille* - E). The turrum has dark spots on the body.

The brassy, or tea-leaf trevally (*Caranx papuensis* - F) has small black spots above and below its lateral line, with a narrow white outer edge to its lower caudal fin. "Brassies" are one of the more common trevally in northern waters and are good sport. Other common trevally include bigeye (A), cale (C), bumpnose, barcheek, bluefin (D), black and diamond trevally (*Alectis indica* - J) and the similar pennant fish (*Alectis ciliaris*). Juvenile pennant fish have long filaments trailing from the dorsal and anal fins, resembling a box jellyfish in the water. The longfin trevally (*Carangoides armatus*) is another similar species.

Most trevally take lures and baits, and fish from a school may pursue a lure or hooked fish. In tropical waters, trevally schools are sometimes found feeding much like tuna schools, with birds overhead and a lot of surface activity. Large trevally are found around reefs during big tides, especially reefs rising out of deep water, as the fish hang in current rips on reef edges. Big trevally will also cruise shallow flats and reefs. Enjoyable sight-fishing can be had over clear flats and reef. Trevally are acceptable table fare if eaten fresh, although some species, such as the bludger, are dark fleshed and poor. Most fishermen return them to the water. They are a nuisance when taking baits intended for better-tasting reef fish. This should not distract from their sporting value. The unrelated permit (*Trachinotus falcatus* - B) has the typical trevally shape, and is regarded for its fighting ability. It feeds over shallow flats and can be sight-fished, being a trophy species among fly fishermen. Southern dart (*Trachinotus russeli*), found in the surf, are much like permit in shape. In southern waters the silver trevally (*Pseudocaranx georgianus* - L) reigns, and is a popular catch from the surf, rocks and jetties. It is called skippy in WA. Small trevally make a useful livebait for big spanish mackerel.

'AGENT86' PICTURE
K

L
TOM CLANCY
PICTURE

A
'AGENT86' PICTURE

Jewfish/mulloway

Northern Australia has the fast-growing black jewfish (*Protonebia diacanthus* - A). Their size, commonly 10kg+, and table quality, make them popular. They are targeted on coastal reefs and wrecks, but also inhabit tidal rivers and creeks. They are usually caught on bait, but will take lures. The scaly jewfish or river croaker (*Nibea squamosa*) reaches 80cm, has a blunt snout and often has bony lumps on the dorsal fin and tail. The soldier croaker (*Nibea soldado*) reaches 60cm and has a high arched back. The little jewfish (*Johnius vogleri*) reaches 30cm and has a dark stripe on the second dorsal. In southern waters, the mulloway (*Argyrosomus hololepidotus* - B) is caught. It has pearly spots along its lateral line. It is the biggest Aussie jewfish, frequenting surf beaches and headlands, visiting river mouths in floods when bait is flushed out. Black jewfish and mulloway overlap around Gladstone, Qld, and Carnarvon, WA. Significant restrictions apply to taking black jewfish in Queensland.

B
FISHABOUT

'AGENT86' PICTURE

Longtoms

Longtoms are common across northern Australia. There are fresh and saltwater species. They attack lures, but hook-ups are rare because of their toothy jaws. Longtoms are reasonable table fish. Oceanic longtoms will sometimes come leaping into a spread of trolled lures, perhaps attracted by noise from the boat.

Coral trout

Coral trout are possibly Australia's most highly-regarded reef fish. They support a lucrative live fish seafood export industry. They are caught around coral and rocky reefs in tropical waters, from shallow foreshores to the wide shoals. They are also found over rubble. They take live and dead baits, and lures, with a preference for large fish-flesh baits. The biggest coral trout, to about 28kg, come from remote waters. Though superb table fare, coral trout are a ciguatera toxin risk. In offshore waters the common coral trout (*Plectropomus leopardus* - D) is usually the prevailing species. It has a blue ring around its eye. In coastal waters, around rocky foreshores and shallow reefs, the bar-cheeked coral trout (*Plectropomus maculatus* - C) is found. Arguably the most striking variety is the footballer trout (*Plectropomus laevis* - A) which has two colour types - one with broad black and white stripes and yellow fins, and one with the familiar blue spots, but with four broad stripes (as pictured). The body colour of the "spotted footballers" varies. Another species, usually found on more remote coral reef lagoons and reef slopes, is the passionfruit trout (*Plectropomus areolatus* - E). Vermicular trout (*Plectropomus oligacanthus* - F) have lines on their face and are comparatively rare. The coronation trout is a different fish (*Variola loutiare* - B) and smaller than most coral trout. The coral rock cod (*Cephalopholis miniata* - not pictured) has a similar shape and colour to coral trout, but with a rounded tail. In southern waters, the harlequin fish (*Othos dentex*) looks somewhat like a coral trout.

A
ARAFURA BLUEWATER CHARTERS

B
ARAFURA BLUEWATER CHARTERS

C
WARREN JEFFERY PICTURE

D
GREG REYNOLDS PICTURE

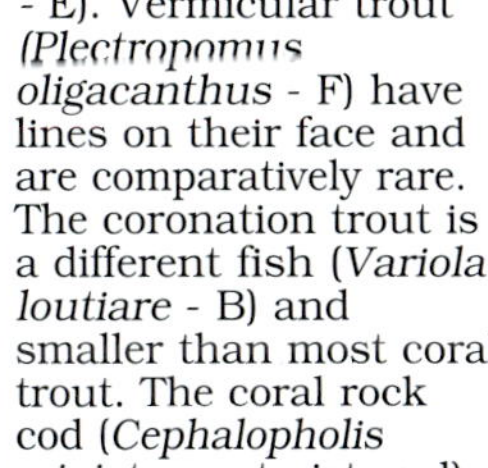
E
HARRY DELIOS PICTURE

F
ARAFURA BLUEWATER CHARTERS

Parrot, tuskfish (bluebone), baldchin

This group includes several similar-looking fish, all being part of or related to the wrasse family. Parrot fish, with beak-like mouths, are mostly herbivorous and not often caught by anglers. Wrasses with peg-like teeth, variously called tuskfish, bluebone and groper by fishermen, are caught across the north. WA's baldchin groper is a slow-growing wrasse found between Dunsborough and Coral Bay. It reaches about 7kg. It is a popular catch and subject to significant fishing restrictions, especially at the Abrolhos Islands. The blackspot tuskfish (pictured) and blue tuskfish are common on northern coastal reefs. They will move into shallow water with the tide, including tidal creeks, to feed on shellfish and crabs. In northern NSW and Queensland, the venus tuskfish is a popular catch. In southern waters there are many wrasse, including the blue groper. Northern tuskfish are good table fish, but some of the southern wrasse are not so good. They all bite well on crab baits, but also take squid, prawns and fish flesh. They will also take lures, particularly jigs.

ROSA ARKAM-LOVASI PICTURE

Barracuda

There are 26 species of barracuda worldwide, and some of the biggest ones live in Australia's northern waters, in estuaries and offshore. Despite their fearsome appearance 'cuda are distantly related to the humble mullet. Barracuda often leap when hooked, but the fight is usually short. They sometimes form large schools around reefs and can be a nuisance. Barracuda take lures and baits but are poor eating. Avoid their sharp teeth. They can smell odd and are better in the water than an esky. In southern waters a similar but unrelated species is the barracoutta. The southern 'coutta is a popular food fish in Tasmania, but in other states is generally considered a nuisance, as they sometimes appear in numbers and steal baits. Southern 'coutta have bony flesh.

TRUE BLUE BONEFISH

Red bass

The red bass (*Lutjanus bohar*) is red with a brown to black colour on its back. Grooves run from the eyes to the nostrils. This thickset, powerful fish grows to 75cm. It is known to reach 50 years of age. It occurs throughout northern Australia on reasonably deep grounds, but may be caught on surface lures on the edges of some reefs. It is a commercial fish in some parts of the world, but in Australia is a considered a high ciguatera toxin risk.

BRADEN MENZIES

Nannygai

Several somewhat similar red reef fish are caught in tropical waters. The most popular is the large-mouthed nannygai, also called saddletail snapper (*Lutjanus malabaricus*, picture A). Large specimens are usually found in deep water near coral reefs, but they are caught on shallow reefs in some areas, and over rubble, particularly in depressions in the seabed and on "fern grounds". Use sonar to find schools. This species sometimes schools with the small-mouth nannygai, also called crimson sea perch (*Lutjanus erythropterus*, B), which has a smaller mouth and more rounded head. The largemouth nannygai is the superior eating fish. Other red reef fish are the paddletail (C), Indonesian snapper and red emperor. Paddletail are a ciguatera risk.

Mangrove jack

The mangrove jack (*Lutjanus argentimaculatus*) is one of Australia's favourite fish. Jack specialists cast lures to snags and rockbars in creeks, along rocky foreshores, and over shallow reefs in estuaries. If you are not quick after the hook-up they will swim into a snag. They fight hard and are good to eat. Remote sandy creeks are the best place to find them, but the busy East Coast still has good jacks on jetty pylons and rock walls in suburban creeks. They have been caught as far south as Eden, NSW, and Geraldton, WA. Jacks move onto offshore reefs as they age, growing to around 20kg, where they are usually caught at night. Despite their reputation for living on snags, studies have shown they can be highly mobile, moving along many kilometres of coastline. They are aggressive lure takers but can be fussy, especially in heavily fished areas. If jacks are lure-shy, try using livebait.

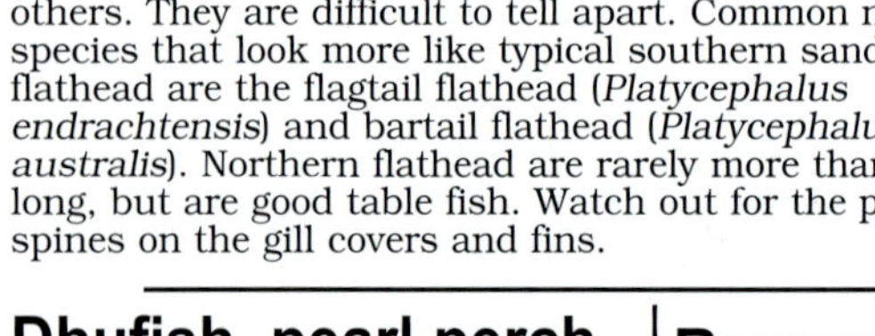

'Reddies'

Indonesian snapper (*Lutjanus bitaeniatus*) are common across the north. In NT waters they are usually dubbed "reddies" or "redfish", often caught alongside similar juvenile smallmouth and largemouth nannygai (above). They have white borders on the anal and pelvic fins. Good eating.

TRUE BLUE BONEFISH

Bonefish

The bonefish (*Albula vulpes*) is found across northern Australia. They are at their best on the flats inside Ningaloo Reef. A superb sportfish on fly.

Rays & sawfish

Stingrays, shovelnose sharks and sawfish are common in remote northern Australia. All Australian sawfish species are protected, including the freshwater sawfish. Sawfish grow to 7.6m and are quick to take a bait intended for other fish. If you hook a big one, cut the trace - it is safer for you and the sawfish. In remote northern estuaries, shovelnose sharks are common and can be seen browsing sandflats at high tide, with fins out of the water. They grow large and are powerful fighters when hooked. There are several stingray varieties in northern waters, all must be handled carefully because they have a venomous spine on their tail. Picking them up by placing thumb and finger in the ears is not safe. Stingray stings often occur when fishermen are wading in muddy water to collect bait. The pain is excruciating. Stingrays and shovelnose sharks are fine table fare if you skin them.

'Rock flathead'

Several species of flathead are caught in northern Australia but are rarely targeted. Many are spiky-looking fish when compared with typical southern flathead, and are dubbed "rock flathead". Rock flathead include fringe-eye flathead (*Cymbacephalus nematophthalmus*), crocodile fish (*Cymbacephalus beauforti*), and tasselsnout flathead (*Thysanophrys cirronasa*). There are others. They are difficult to tell apart. Common northern species that look more like typical southern sand flathead are the flagtail flathead (*Platycephalus endrachtensis*) and bartail flathead (*Platycephalus australis*). Northern flathead are rarely more than 50cm long, but are good table fish. Watch out for the painful spines on the gill covers and fins.

'AGENT86' PICTURE

Dhufish, pearl perch

Glaucosoma species are superb table fish. The WA dhufish *(G. hebraicumis)* is best known and grows to 25kg. It is found from Esperance to Shark Bay, WA. They visit inshore reefs, but are usually caught in deeper water. The pearl perch or "pearly" *(G. scapulare)* is found on central east coasts reefs out to 200m. The threadfin pearl perch *(G. magnificum*, at left) is found across northern Australia. Another northern species found mostly west of Darwin is the deepsea dhufish *G. buergeri*.

Barramundi cod

This fish (*Chromileptes altivelis)* is instantly identifiable, looking like a cross between a barramundi and a malabar cod. This species matures as a female before changing sex to male, with females being sexually mature about 40cm. They grow to 70cm and 5kg and live to depths of about 40m. Barramundi cod are found mainly on the Great Barrier Reef but also inhabit NT and northern WA inshore reefs. They are delicious, and coveted in the live fish trade. In some areas they have become rare and are protected.

CHRIS RAINBIRD PICTURE

Marlin, sailfish and swordfish

Of the various billfish, tropical inshore waters have mainly sailfish (*Istiophorus platypterus* - C) and black marlin (*Makaira indica* - B), often well within reach of trailerboats. Blue marlin (C) and striped marlin are found further offshore. Sailfish are the fastest recorded fish, and they grow fast too, almost 2m in a year. They reach 90kg, but the usual size is 10kg to 30kg. WA's Broome and the NT's Fog Bay and Groote Eylandt have prolific sailfish grounds, where schools (pods) of sailfish rise to baits, but there are other good northern locations, including around the Kimberley's Cassini Island, and off WA's Pilbara coast. Small black marlin and sailfish are caught within reach of trailer boats along the East Coast, with Cape Bowling Green near Townsville among the top spots. East Coast fishing is seasonal as the black marlin move up and down the coast. Giant black marlin are fished primarily by a fleet based in Cairns, where fish over 1000-pounds (454kg) are caught from September to December. The WA coast has readily accessible large blue marlin and black marlin where the Continental Shelf hugs the coast near Exmouth Peninsula. Marlin fishing is highly visual and exciting. Fishers use baits of whole fish rigged to swim or skip behind a boat, as well as lures and teasers to help raise fish to the surface. Sailfish enthusiasts use comparatively light tackle and small skipping baits such as garfish. Crews watch the "spread" behind the boat carefully, looking for fish rising to baits. Billfish are usually around baitfish congregations. With some rare exceptions, landbased billfishing is limited to locations bordering deep, clear water. The broadbill swordfish (*Xiphias gladius* - D) is an unrelated deepwater species of billfish that may appear almost anywhere there is 200m or more of water. A reliable fishery has been found off Tasmania and Victoria. Squid rigged with cyalume sticks are generally used for bait, and the fish can be targeted in daylight hours in sufficiently deep water.

JONAH YICK PICTURE

FISHING CAIRNS

Milkfish & giant herring

The milkfish (*Chanos chanos* - above) is a powerful fish of inshore waters, but it only takes bread baits and flies. Float a bread bait into a bread berley trail and hang on! Similar looking is the giant herring (*Elops hawaiensis* - below), another powerful coastal dweller. It readily takes lures. Both are bony and poor table fare.

TRUE BLUE BONEFISH

Moonfish, batfish

The plate-like silver "moonie" or nine-spined batfish (*Zabidius novemaculeatus*) and the large teira batfish (*Platax teira* - below) are considered bait-stealers. The teira batfish has deeper dorsal and ventral fins and a darker coloration than the "moonie". "Moonies" are OK to eat. Teira batfish are not so good.

Jobfish

Most "jobfish", also called "snappers", belong to the genus *Pristipomoides*. An exception is the green jobfish (*Aprion virescens*). They are usually caught in the 80m to 120m zone, but green jobfish can be found on reef edges. Species include the rusty, rosy, ruby, ornate and golden-eye jobfish, and sharptooth, flame and goldband snappers (pictured). They fight all the way up in deep water and are good table fish.

TREVOR DURLING

Mahi-mahi (dolphin fish)

Dolphin fish, dorado or mahi-mahi are the names for two similar species, both caught offshore, usually near flotsam, buoys or FADs. Mahi-mahi grow fast, up to 7cm a week, to 1kg in six months and 10kg in a year. They reach 2m and 40kg. They spawn constantly and rarely live more than two years. If eaten fresh they are superb. In the tropics they occur all year, but in sub-tropical waters are summer fish. Their colours can vary from gold to brilliant blue.

ARAFURA BLUEWATER CHARTERS

Cobia (black kingfish)

Cobia (*Rachycentron canadum*) are found along much of Australia's coastline. They grow to about 70kg and are often found in inshore waters where reef meets sand. They are found in open water. They congregate near shipping pylons and other obstructions, with the channel markers in Brisbane's Moreton Bay producing some huge fish. The Quobba to Ningaloo coast in WA produces big cobia for landbased fishos. The NT's Fog Bay produces plenty of cobia, but they are less often seen in the more turbid Darwin and Bynoe Harbours. Cobia often accompany marine animals such as manta rays and whales. Casting lures at a passing manta sometimes finds a fish. The cobia's unusual profile, dark colour and habit of swimming with pectoral fins spread out horizontally makes the fish look like a shark in the water. Cobia are partial to crab baits, and fresh fish flesh. They are an excellent table fish if bled and iced on capture.

'AGENT86'

Grunter

There are two grunter, or javelin fish, found in the north, the barred grunter (*Pomadasys kaakan* - A) and the smaller spotted grunter (*Pomadasys argenteus* - B). In some areas, such as the southern Gulf of Carpentaria, and along the East Coast from Mackay to Gladstone, this species has a huge following. And yet, in much of the far north, grunter are ignored. Small fish congregate at times, and are nuisance bait pickers, but the big fish are good sport. Grunter, called ock-ock in the Territory because of the noise they make when landed, are usually caught on flesh baits, although they will grab a lure on occasion. They are common in bays, estuaries and coastal rocky reefs. Larger fish move from coastal reefs into creeks and estuaries when a food source is available, such as prawns, usually after heavy rain. In recent times, big fish seem to have taken up permanent residence in Gladstone Harbour, possibly as a result of deepwater dredging. Grunter are often found alongside golden snapper (fingermark). The larger of the two grunter species grows to 6kg. They are found from WA's Shark Bay (rarely) across the north to the NSW border. Some of the best grunter fishing is had out of Karumba in the lower Gulf of Carpentaria.

ANGLERS ADVANTAGE

Flag

The small colourful snappers common across the north coast are generally called "flag" by recreational fishermen. The spanish flag, or stripey (A) is abundant, found over most shallow rocky reefs. The brownstripe snapper (B) is also called a "flagfish". The five-lined snapper (C) is an attractive, small species that forms large schools in clear coral reef waters. Flags take most baits. Large spanish flag are worth eating. The smaller ones are great livebaits for big mackerel, and work well as cut flesh baits for coral trout.

MATT FLYNN PICTURES

Tripletail

The tripletail (*Lebotes surinamensis*) occurs in tropical seas. While rarely caught they are not particularly rare, and would be caught more if targeted. They have unusual habits, staying near floating debris in open water and estuaries. Juvenile fish swim on their side and look like a leaf. Tripletail grow to 24kg, but a fish over 4kg is big in Australia. They take small baits and lures, fight hard and are good tucker. They have been caught as far south as Georges River, NSW. They are sometimes confused with barramundi.

MELITA ROGERS

ARAFURA BLUEWATER CHARTERS

Sea bream

Several varieties of "sea bream" are found on deep northern reefs. These include the Robinson's sea bream (above), collared sea bream, Japanese sea bream, and mozambique large-eye bream. These are top table fish. The collared sea bream can have an iodine taint, presumably from their local diet - this can be detected by running a hand down the fish and smelling your skin. Fish that do not smell of iodine are good to eat.

WARREN JEFFERY PICTURE

Cod and groper

In the tropics, "cod" or "groper" is a name applied collectively to fish with a head making up almost a third of the body, with cavernous mouth, spiky front dorsal fin, sharp gill covers, squat body and thick patterned skin. These include the flowery cod (*Epinephelus fuscoguttatus* - A), rankin cod (*Epinephelus multinotatus* - B), gold-spot or estuary cod (*Epinephelus coioides* - C), malabar or blackspot cod (*Epinephelus malabaricus* - D), groper (*Epinephelus lanceolatus* - E) and chinaman cod or Charlie Court (*Epinephelus rivulatus* - F). There are many more. Cod readily grab baits and lures. Smaller cod are good to eat. They are abundant in the north. Most species in NSW are protected. Very large fish are protected in some states.

AGENT86 PICTURE

ARAFURA BLUEWATER CHARTERS

'AGENT86' PICTURE

F

D

GAVIN HOULT

Emperor

Trickies, piggies, norwesters and sweetlip are the names used by fishermen to describe a group of fish that are a huge part of the tropical bluewater scene. The most important are the red emperor (*Lutjanus sebae* - A), redthroat or sweetlip emperor (*Lethrinus miniatus* - B) blue-lined emperor or tricky snapper (*Lethrinus laticaudis* - C), longnosed emperor (*Lethrinus olivaceus* - D), spangled emperor or norwest or yellow snapper (*Lethrinus nebulosus* - E), and orange-finned or buffalo emperor (*Lethrinus arythracanthus* - F). These tasty fish frequent coral reefs, rocky reefs and patchy sand and rubble areas. They take most baits and can often be caught in numbers. Drift fishing over suitable flat ground can work well, and once fish are found it is a simple matter to take the boat back over a spot for another drift. Red emperor are usually found in water 30m or more deep, often in small schools, although they enter reef shallows in some areas. They bite well at night. Fishermen can expect to tangle with reds of more than 15kg in some places, but the average size is 3kg. Most species of emperor are prized for their looks and eating quality. The spangled emperor is widely distributed, being found from Perth to Sydney. It is common on or near shallow tropical coral reefs, particularly in the north-west. In some areas it can be caught from beaches. In the NT, red emperor are commonly found on clear bluewater reef and rubble areas, well away from the turbid water of floodplain river outlets. The most common NT emperor species is the tricky snapper. It grows to about 4kg, averaging 1-2kg, and occurs in big numbers across a variety of habitat. It is good to eat. The streamlined longnosed emperor likes reefs where the water is clear, which in the Top End means in sand/reef areas well away from rivers. Buffalo emperor are usually caught singly on deep reefs.

Wahoo

Wahoo are near the top of the offshore light-tackle sportfish list, being one of the fastest fish in the sea. They are found from WA's Rottnest Island and across the north to about Montague Island in NSW. They grow over 2m and more than 60kg. Wahoo are good to eat. They can be distinguished from spanish mackerel by their unusual tail and broad verticle bars, most visible when the fish are first caught. Wahoo are most common in deep blue water off the Great Barrier Reef and WA, but they are also caught on the NT's widest reefs. They are happy to destroy carefully prepared marlin baits and are regarded as a pest when fishermen chase billfish.

Mackerel

Spanish or narrow-barred mackerel (*Scomberomorus commerson* - A), shark mackerel (*Grammatorcynus bicarinatus* - B), broadbar or grey mackerel (*Scomberomorus semifasciatus* - C), spotted mackerel (*Scomberomorus munroi* - D) and school mackerel (*Scomberomorus queenslandicus*) are common across northern Australia. In the NT they move closer to the coast in the dry season (winter), but are available all year. They appear at different times along Australia's east and west coasts. Fishing in the early morning and late afternoon is usually best. Find bait to find mackerel. Where the water is cloudy they are more likely to be taken near the surface during daylight. They are caught on live or dead baits and cast or trolled lures. Live fish baits and lures rigged on downriggers account for spanish mackerel to 35kg. Baits of small reef fish will entice big mackerel. Surface teasers run near lures will help excite fish into striking. Troll lures fast. If arches appear on sonar at midwater try dropping a bait or jig down to them. Big mackerel make long runs when hooked, and will jump if a shark is in pursuit. They have sharp teeth, so use wire traces. Mackerel can be filleted or cut into cutlets, to grill or fry. Bleed and ice them on capture for best results.

TACKLE WORLD COOLALINGA

Maori sea perch

Lutjanus rivulatus is also called blubberlip snapper because of its plump lips. Adults are brownish grey/green with small white spots, and blue lines on the head. Juveniles have three to eight brown bars on their sides. They occur on bluewater tropical reefs of WA, NT and Qld. Adults live in deeper waters (50–100m) and they are also found on shallow coral reefs and flats. Juveniles sometimes occur in shallow waters near estuaries. They live alone or in small groups and are carnivores, feeding on fishes, cephalopods and crustaceans. They grow to about 11kg and are good to eat, but have been associated with ciguatera poisoning. Gutting them can be a smelly business, presumably because they eat a lot of shellfish.

Leatherjackets, triggerfish

A variety of leatherjackets and triggerfish occur across Australia, usually on reefs less than 100m deep, but some live in the open sea. The "trigger" is the first dorsal spine, which the fish uses to lock itself into holes. In the tropics triggerfish are a ciguatera risk. They are a popular food fish in southern waters, but considered a nuisance by many. They should be gutted when caught, and the skin removed. They have strong jaws and sharp teeth which can cut through hooks. They take most baits.

FISHABOUT TOURS

ARAFURA BLUEWATER CHARTERS

Chinaman fish

This heavily-built, powerful fish is readily identifiable by the deep pits ahead of its red eyes. *Symphorus nematophorus* prefers bluewater drop-offs near reefs, especially those 40m+ deep, but inhabits some shallower reefs. Colour ranges from brown-blotched orange to red, depending on size and location. Young fish have horizontal stripes. They are usually caught from 4-8kg, but fish to a metre long are quite common. They take most baits and fight hard. The firm, tasty flesh carries a risk of ciguatera poisoning, but some people eat them in the NT and WA. The species usually occurs singly. It is found from the Ryukyu Islands to the Malay Peninsula, New Guinea and right across northern Australia, generally on clear bluewater reefs.

A 'AGENT86'

B TREVOR DURLING

BRADEN MENZIES PICTURE C

Tuna

Mackerel tuna (A) and longtail tuna (B) are the common species in far northern inshore waters, with the much larger yellowfin tuna more abundant on the east and west coasts. Other species that may be encountered in the north are dogtooth (C) and bigeye tuna. In the south, bluefin tuna rule, along with striped tuna and albacore. In the Northern Territory, many fishos chase longtail tuna, a small but hard-fighting species that averages about 8kg, and is abundant in coastal waters. The schools move quickly from place to place, busting up on the surface as they chase bait. Look for seabirds that follow the schools. The trick is to put the boat near the fish and cast small chrome lures, jigs or even painted sinkers, and retrieve them fast. Trolling works when the schools are bold, but the fish are more often flighty, which means long-distance casting is the best method. The fighting endurance of these small tuna is exceptional. Longtails make reasonable table fare if bled promptly. Some people find the sliced raw flesh delicious with a dipping sauce. Mackerel tuna and bonito are arguably the least palatable of the tunas, but they make great bait. Yellowfin and albacore are arguably the best tuna to eat, with albacore dubbed "the chicken of the sea".

Sharks

Australian waters are home to many sharks, big and small. In Australia there are 28 varieties of whaler shark alone. Common northern sharks include hammerheads, winghead (right), tiger, sicklefin lemon, blacktip, whitetip, bull, tawny nurse and spinner. Sharks know fishing boats provide easy meals, and you will soon tire of loosing fish to them, even in rivers, where bull sharks are common. Sharks can be good sport, and small varieties such as the blacktip are good to eat if bled on capture. Otherwise, it is best to release them, as sharks have become rare across much of the world. Some species, such as the speartooth shark, are protected.

OBSESSION FISHING SAFARIS

'AGENT86'

Blue bastards & brown sweetlip

The blue bastard (*Plectorhinchus caeruleonothus* - left) is found across northern Australia. It was named as a separate species in 2015, being previously confused with painted sweetlip. The blue bastard is more thickset than painted sweetlip. Juveniles are brown with horizontal stripes. This species has gained fame as a flats fly fishing target. The similar painted sweetlip (*Diagramma labiosum*) is also called blackall, mother-in-law fish and slatey bream. Adult fish are slate grey in colour, while younger fish have yellow or orange spots. The body to the tail tapers more than the blue bastard. The brown sweetlip (*Plectorhinchus gibbosus* - right) is another common fish of tropical estuaries and coastal reefs. All these fish are of dubious eating quality.

GAVIN HOULT PICTURE

Sooty grunter

Several species of freshwater grunters, also called black bream, sooties, khaki, leathery or coal grunters, are found across tropical Australia. The Burdekin River marks the southern limit of their wild range in Queensland. They are native inhabitants of rivers, but have been stocked in dams, where they soon grow bigger and fatter than they ever did in the waters from where they originally came. The largest species, popular with fishermen, is *Hephaestus fuliginosus.* Fish to 7kg have been caught in Queensland dams, but a 4kg fish is big. Any sooty over 1kg will put up a real battle. They are usually found near submerged timber or undercut banks, where they take small lures and baits. They strike hard. Sooties are hardy fish that tolerate a variety of water conditions, although they prefer clear, flowing sandy streams, and are abundant in the pristine freshwater reaches of North Queensland and Top End rivers. They feed on prawns and small fish, but their diet also includes weeds, falling fruit and pandanus nuts. Opinions vary on their table quality. Those fish that have been eating vegetation can have an offensive smell when opened up.

'AGENT86' PICTURE

Saratoga

Two species of saratoga (*Scleropages leichardti* and *Scleropages jardini*) inhabit the freshwater reaches of rivers, and are stocked in dams. They like cover and are usually found near aquatic plants. They take surface lures in wild strikes. If barramundi are quiet, put on a small surface lure and fish for saratoga. Bass lures are effective, including weedless lures, where the hook is shielded from snags. Fly gear works well. In the NT, Manton Dam, the Mary River system and Kakadu NP billabongs are hotspots. On Cape York Peninsula the Jardine River and its associated billabongs hold saratoga, as do some other Cape rivers. In SEQ and NSW saratoga are found in stocked dams. They incubate young in their mouths. They are poor table fare.

ROZA ARKAM-LOVASI PICTURE

CODY MCINTOSH PICTURE

Powertails

Catfish have an image problem in Australia. In some parts of the world, notably the USA, they are prized fish. Australian species do all the right things - they grow large, fight hard and even cook up quite well, and yet almost no Aussie fishermen like them. Perhaps calling them "powertails" might make them more popular. Northern Australia has several species of salmon-tailed and eel-tailed catfish. The most commonly caught are the lesser salmon catfish (*Neoarius graeffei*) found in fresh and brackish water from the NT to NSW; the common and widely distributed salmon catfish (*Neoarius leptaspis*); the shovelnosed catfish or silver cobbler (*Neoarius midgelyorum*) from the western Top End and Kimberley; and the eastern shovelnosed catfish (*Neoarius paucus*). These species are usually caught in rivers and estuaries, but are sometimes found far offshore. Salmon-tailed catfish are strong fish. Big ones pull harder, dare we say it, than barramundi. In WA's Kimberley the shovelnose catfish grows to 30kg and provides good sport in Lake Kununurra and Lake Argyle, where the species supports a commercial fishery. There are also several species of eel-tailed catfish (also called tandans) which live in fresh and saltwater habitats, but these are not often caught. Eel-tailed freshwater catfish are protected in many areas as their numbers have declined. Their round nests can be seen in some clear, shallow rivers. Catfish have dorsal and pectoral fins with sharp poisonous spines, and must be handled with care.

MATT FLYNN PICTURE

Ox-eye herring

These are called tarpon in Australia, but they don't grow huge like the famous American sportfish. *Megalops cyprinoides* is found in tropical fresh and salt water. They take lures and are spectacular, if miniscule, fighters. Tarpon provide fun when barra are quiet. The larger fish are found in estuaries.

JUSTIN JONES PICTURE

Sleepy cod

These fish are abundant in tropical dams and waterholes. They take lures and are good to eat, but rarely grow much over 1kg.

Mouth almighty

These small fish are common in tropical freshwater dams and waterholes. They'll grab a lure almost as big as themselves, and are a good livebait for big barra.

ROZA ARKAM-LOVASI PICTURE

Archer fish

The archer fish (*Toxotes jaculatrix*) is well known for being able to shoot down an insect with a squirt of water. They are better known among fishermen for grabbing lures nearly as big as the fish. They put up a spirited battle for a species that rarely grows more than 500g. Small archer fish can be seen patrolling the water's surface in back eddies. They are easily caught on a small hook or lure and make a good barramundi bait, alive or dead. Archer fish are OK to eat but are usually returned to the water.

GAVIN HOULT PICTURE

Jungle perch

Kuhlia rupestris has a cult following because it is found in gin-clear rainforest streams. It was once found as far south as northern NSW. Rivers of remote North Queensland now have the best fishing, with the biggest fish, to 50cm, in the more remote pools. They are also found in tidal reaches of rivers, where they breed. They take small lures and baits. In 2014 jungle perch were reared at a research facility at Bribie Island. These were released into a Gold Coast hinterland stream, and a stream near Mackay. It is believed that weirs and other river obstructions, rather than overfishing, depleted jungle perch numbers in populated areas. They are found in other countries.

FISHING CAIRNS

Tailor

Pomatomus saltatrix is found in southern Australia from Exmouth, WA, to Fraser Island, Qld. They are seasonal visitors of surf beaches and rock washes, but also visit estuaries. Hotspots include Queensland's Fraser Island and WA's Kalbarri. Tailor take baits and lures. Their teeth can cut nylon line, so use ganged hooks or wire. Tailor taste good if bled, iced and eaten fresh. They reach about 8kg. Small fish are called "choppers", big fish are "greenbacks".

Yellowtail kingfish

Seriola lalandi is found as far north as Exmouth, WA, and Gladstone, Qld, usually close to coastal reefs and headlands, and around islands. In Victoria, the Rip at the mouth of Port Phillip Bay is a good spot. The Sydney Harbour entrance also produces good fish. In South Australia there is an unusual annual run of big fish in shallow Coffin Bay. They are now showing up in southern Tasmania. Kingfish grow to 70kg and are strong fighters. Despite their aggression, big kingfish can also be fickle. If they don't take lures, try livebait such as squid. They are renowned for swimming into reefs when hooked. Small fish are good tucker if eaten fresh.

MATT FLYNN

Silver drummer

There are several species of light-coloured drummer, with a similar fish called buffalo bream in WA. *Kyphosus sydneyanus* is the largest, found from Fraser Island, Qld, south to Shark Bay, WA. Silver drummer are mainly herbivores that occasionally take tiny baits of weed or bread. They make a poor meal but expect a tough fight if you hook one.

Black drummer

"Pigs" or black drummer (*Girella elevata*) occur from about Noosa, Qld, south to Apollo Bay, Victoria, and northern Tasmania. They like the wash of reefs and headlands, and jetties. They take weed and prawn baits. Pigs are only OK to eat if cleaned promptly. They fight hard.

FISHABOUT TOURS

Australian salmon

Australian salmon (*Arripis trutta*) form huge schools. They are often found near shore. Adults frequent surf beaches and headlands, while juveniles enter estuaries. There are eastern and western sub-species. They take lures and baits. Salmon grow to 10kg and fight hard. The flesh is best suited for fish cakes. The similar but much smaller tommy ruff frequents WA and SA waters.

Flathead

Australia has several flathead species. The biggest is the dusky flathead, found mainly within eastern and south-eastern estuaries. The smaller bar-tail flathead is common in the north, while tiger and bluespot flathead are prevalent in deeper southern waters. There are other species and some are hard to tell apart. Flathead lie in sand or mud, or on rocks, waiting to ambush bait. Sandflat channels and tidal drains are good spots to try. Drift fishing works well. Lures and livebaits will take "lizards". Flathead are good to eat. Big fish are often returned to the water to breed. Handle them carefully as they have sharp gill spines.

Luderick

Girella tricuspidata frequents headlands, rock walls and piers of south-east Australia in season. Weed baits presented on a light line with a float work best. Gut and ice luderick quickly to obtain the best eating quality.

Pink bream (snapper)

The famous Aussie "snapper" *Pagrus auratus* is actually a sea bream, related to tarwhine and black bream. Real snapper are *Lutjanids*, but the snapper tag is likely stuck with this fish forever. Snapper are found in southern waters from about Karratha in WA to Townsville in Queensland. They were popular in South Australia, but a ban was introduced after stocks in the Gulfs declined. WA's Shark Bay has its own snapper population. Snapper are usually caught from boats, but catches are made from rock and beach, usually after rough weather. Berleying works well. Fish at dusk, dark or dawn for best results. Schools appear to migrate along a coastline, visiting a feeding ground, before moving on. Some areas have winter and summer runs. They grow to 20kg, but are usually much smaller. Snapper are a good food fish.

Flatfish

Sole and flounder are found around Australia. Large specimens are more common in southern waters. They have a small mouth and are usually taken as by-catch by whiting anglers. Flounder can be speared by wading sandflats on calm nights with a floodlight. The light is shone ahead and the flounder are seen in the sand, speared and placed in a floating tub. Check local regulations before spearing. Flathead and crabs are also easily speared - again, check regulations before fishing. Flounder and sole are highly regarded as food fish.

FISHABOUT TOURS

Bream and whiting

These are arguably Australia's two most commonly caught fish. Bream species include northern pikey bream, yellowfin bream (bottom right), of which there are several species, and southern black bream. Bream are found around structure such as pylons, oyster racks and rock walls, but are also caught over flats and in the surf. There are several species of sand whiting (below left), and they are found mostly on flats. Queensland's Moreton and Hervey Bays, Pumicestone Passage, Jumpinpin and WA's Shark Bay are great whiting spots, as are SA's gulf and Melbourne's bay beaches. Bream and whiting take worm or peeled prawn baits, tiny crabs and small lures. In the south, king george whiting inhabit coastal waters around seagrass beds and take baits of pipi or squid.

SHANE CURRY PICTURE

TOM CLANCY

Freshwater cod

The murray cod (*Maccullochella peelii peelii*) was once supreme in Australia's inland waters, but became scarce soon after white settlement. They have been making a comeback in the Murray River, but environmental events affect their numbers. Dawn and dusk in summer are the best fishing times. Diving lures or baits should be cast near snags for best effect. Surface lures work well at times. Cod grow to at least 110kg, but very large fish are hard to find. They are widely protected and usually released. Special cod fishing rules apply in some areas. The Mary River cod (*Maccullochella peelii mariensis*) occurs naturally only in the Mary River system in south-east Queensland. The protected Clarence River or eastern cod (*Maccullochella ikei*) once lived in the Clarence, Richmond and Brisbane River systems, but was near extinction by the end of the 1930s. The Mann-Nymboida catchment of the Clarence River has a remaining wild population. The protected trout cod (*Maccullochella macquariensis*) is found in the Murray River from Yarrawonga to Barmah Forest and in Seven Creeks near Euroa in Victoria. Restocking of all freshwater cod species is under way. They have been successfully stocked in many dams.

Silver perch

Silver perch (*Bidyanus bidyanus*) have done well as a stocked dam fish, but wild stocks in the Murray River are scarce. These fish have small mouths and are not as keen on lures as bass and yellowbelly, but they will take a small bait or fly. They grow to about 8kg. Large fish may become vegetarian. The similar **macquarie perch** was once quite common, but is now only found as wild stock in Lake Dartmouth on the Mitta Mitta River in Victoria and the Yarra River. Stocking is under way.

Australian bass

The bass (*Macquaria novemaculeata*) is possibly our most popular freshwater sportfish, supporting a competition circuit. Bass share traits with barramundi, as they need access to saltwater to breed and they hit surface lures hard. Bass have become the mainstay of freshwater stocking in NSW and southern Queensland east of the Dividing Range. Victoria is also stocking bass. These fish thrive but can't breed in dams, and much of their natural river habitat has been made unsuitable by weirs. In summer, try casting lures near cover in the mornings and evenings. In dams, use sonar to find congregations of fish, and drop jigs or baits. Bass are good to eat, but are usually released. They grow to 4kg, but a 2kg fish is a good bass. A similar species, the estuary perch, is found in the tidal sections of many NSW and Victorian rivers.

TOM CLANCY

TOM CLANCY PICTURE

Yellowbelly

Also called callop and golden perch, yellowbelly (*Macquaria ambigua*) were once restricted to the Murray-Darling basin, but the stocking of this fish in dams has been successful. These fish can not usually breed in still waters, so stocking must be ongoing. Wild stocks in the Murray River have suffered from habitat changes and the introduction of carp, but as yellowbelly can withstand poor water conditions, including high salinity, wild stocks are still about in reasonable numbers. Spawning in spring and summer is set off by increased daylight and rising water levels, and they will travel hundreds of kilometres upstream to spawn. They usually feed near the bottom and can be caught on baits of worms, shrimps or yabby, but they will hit lures hard. Look for them around snags. Fishing in the warmer months is usually most productive. As a freshwater fish, their eating quality is good. A 2kg wild perch is a good fish but they reach a football-shaped 10kg+ in impoundments. A much touted 25kg fish from Kow Swamp is now thought to have been a murray cod.

TOM CLANCY PICTURE

Trout

Trout need cool water, which limits their range to NSW, Victoria and Tasmania, with a few fish in SA and WA. Some waters are stocked, but the best hold wild stocks. Brown, brook and rainbow trout are in Australia, with browns most common. Fly fishing for trout is considered challenging, but trout are easy enough to catch. They take lures, and can't resist earthworm baits. They are quite good to eat, especially smoked. Atlantic and chinook salmon are stocked in some Australian waters.

Carp

The carp (*Cyprinus carpio*) is good sport but poor table fare. They are hardy and almost any stream or lake can support them. This is a declared noxious fish that must not be returned to the water. Unfortunately the warm, turbid and still waters of the Murray River and its tributaries have proved ideal habitat for them. Most baits will take carp, including bread, corn and sandwich meat. Peak fishing is in summer. Carp grow to 20kg, and are powerful fighters.

TOM CLANCY

Redfin

The much-loved feral fish *Perca fluviatilis* is one of the best freshwater table fish and good sport if you can find big ones, but plagues of small fish are more common. They are an aggressive lure-taker. Use worms or shrimp for bait.

TOM CLANCY

Catch giant freshwater prawns

The giant freshwater prawn, or cherabin, is a vital part of northern ecosystems, and of great interest to fishermen.

Not only are these large prawns prolific at times, they grow as long as a forearm, although much of that is the two long pincers.

They are found across northern Australia and are easily caught in baited pots.

Like barramundi, the cherabin *Macrobrachium spinipes* migrates from fresh to salt water each year.

Considerable cherabin research has been undertaken in the Top End's Daly/Katherine River system.

It was shown that cherabin reproduce along the entire waterway.

However, the larvae needed to migrate from fresh to salt water within seven days of hatching to survive.

This requirement may apply to other northern rivers.

A researcher set traps at 22 Daly River sites each day, and the cherabin were counted, weighed, measured and sexed to estimate changes in abundance over time, and determine patterns of reproduction.

Very few reproductive or berried females were observed outside the Build-up and wet season months, meaning reproduction was highly seasonal.

The females bred throughout the river, up to 400km from the river mouth.

Larvae hatched in the Katherine River tributary more than 400km upstream from the Daly mouth could only reach the estuary in time to survive during large wet season floods.

Giant freshwater prawn (cherabin)

DARWIN TAXIDERMY

The annual cherabin journey began when waterflow increased with the monsoon.

At the end of the wet season, during the run-off months, juvenile cherabin the size of a thumb migrated back upstream.

For about 30 days in April and May, they were observed in numbers, with at times millions of juveniles moving back up the river at night.

The research suggested that large wet season flows were critical for the survival of larvae that hatch well upstream, and that bigger flows probably increase cherabin populations.

Because cherabin are critical food for fish such as barramundi and other wildlife, damming or water extraction from northern rivers could have severe consequences on the ecosystem.

Cherabin are usually targeted with baited traps.

Rules apply to the design of traps, primarily to prevent turtles from being trapped and drowned.

Flesh baits work well, but chicken pellets and meat-free baits attract fewer pests, particularly crocodiles.

If cherabin are around in numbers, pots can be checked every hour. If numbers are low, leave pots overnight.

Cherabin are active at night, and can be seen in shallows as their eyes glow red in a torch beam, as do barramundi and crocodile eyes.

A bait can be staked in shallows to attract cherabin for netting or spearing, where it is legal, but be wary of crocodiles.

Small live cherabin are great barramundi bait.

They are also good to eat, try them boiled, grilled or fried.

Surrounded by rock lobsters

Rock lobsters are found right around the Australian coastline. They are often incorrectly called crayfish.

The northern varieties are known collectively as tropical spiny lobsters, but are commonly called "painted crays".

Lobsters found most often in northern Australia are the **painted lobster** (*Panulirus versicolor*), **ornate lobster** (*Panulirus ornatus*), **long-legged lobster** (*Panulirus longipes*) and **two-spined lobster** (*Panulirus penicillatus*).

The painted lobster can be identified by the light stripes down its legs, while the ornate lobster has a less striking pattern, with blotches on its legs.

The two-spined lobster has two pairs of spines joined at their bases between the antennae. The long-legged lobster has a light line down each of its dark, unusually long legs.

Tropical lobsters have been found as far south as Sydney, NSW, and Albany, WA.

Tropical lobsters go through several free-swimming larval stages, sometimes being swept hundreds of kilometres away from the spawning site by ocean currents, before finally settling on the bottom at just under a year of age in waters of about 5m to 17m deep.

To the south, in Western Australia, the main species is the **western rock lobster** (*Panulirus cygnus*). This looks like the ornate rock lobster, but is only found as far north as Exmouth, WA.

WA's western rock lobster population fluctuates considerably, depending on the strength of the Leeuwin Current, and the frequency and intensity of westerly winds.

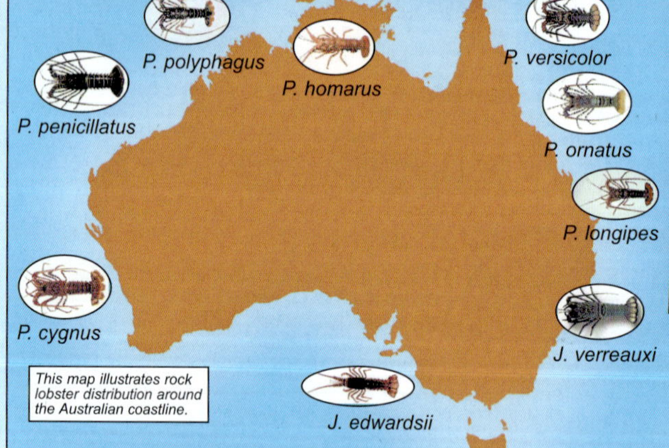

This map illustrates rock lobster distribution around the Australian coastline.

In years when the Leeuwin Current is flowing strongly, a higher proportion of larval lobster return to the coast.

Westerly winds also help more larval lobster reach coastal reefs.

On the south-east coast the **eastern rock lobster** (*Jasus verreauxi*) is found roughly from Tweed Heads in NSW to Port MacDonnell, SA.

The **southern rock lobster** (*Jasus edwardsii*) is found south of Cape Leeuwin, WA, and Sydney, NSW.

While southern lobsters readily enter baited pots, northern varieties are far less inclined to do so, even though they do eat meat. The most effective collection method for northern varieties is to snorkel and pull them out of their lairs.

RICK TRIPPE PICTURE

Ornate lobsters

Tropical rock lobsters can also be collected by torchlight over sand near shallow reefs at night at low tide, and may be found in the early morning.

In North Queensland there is a live export industry for lobsters taken by divers. The main market is China and most of the catch is taken within the Great Barrier Reef Marine Park.

Lobsters are subject to intensive commercial and recreational harvest.

Strict rules apply to catching them in all states, but especially so in southern states.

Tropical lobsters are not considered as tasty as southern lobsters, or mud crabs, but no one knocks them back.

Boiling them in salt water, then chilling the meat, is arguably the best way to process them.

Huge wild oysters of the North

The large and delicious tropical blacklip oyster is abundant across northern Australia.

This premium shellfish has long been sought for its size and flavour.

Being also hardy and fast growing, it has become the subject of a budding aquaculture industry.

While the blacklip oyster *Saccostrea echinata* is abundant in some areas, you will not find them everywhere, even in remote regions.

They don't thrive in turbid waters, which is why there are none in places like Darwin Harbour.

Instead, they are found in numbers on coastal rocks outside of muddy estuaries where the water is clearer.

Once you find a patch it is easy enough to knock them off the rocks with hammer and chisel or screwdriver.

There is a rock oyster found in Darwin Harbour and it is a small species related to the Sydney rock oyster.

The large pearl oyster *Pinctada maxima* is found across northern Australia. It inhabits specific areas, prefering areas of flat bottom and high current flow in water less than 50m deep.

Collecting Kimberley blacklip oysters

It was historically harvested by divers but the pearl industry now grows their own.

North Australian waters never had the massive shellfish reefs typical of southern waters before European settlement because most of the northern coast is a "depositing shoreline" with lots of mud, and suitable hard coastal substrate for large oyster reefs is not in abundance.

Where there are rocky reefs in the Far North the attached life is mostly encrusting soft corals and hard corals, particularly sponges.

There are relatively few shellfish in Darwin Harbour due to the extreme conditions of big tides and natural silt.

Most of the harbour's shellfish are associated with mangrove habitat, with snails and bivalves being the main species. The "longbum" (*Telescopium telescopium*), a large marine snail, is the main shellfish exploited by humans around Darwin.

A once popular shellfish, as revealed by vast quantities of shell in Darwin-region middens, was the roughback cockle (*Anadara granosa*).

This is no longer found in the harbour, possibly because of natural changes to habitat.

When exploring the remote north, keep in mind that Aboriginal land extends down to the intertidal zone where blacklip oysters are found.

Australia's once massive southern oyster reefs were mined for lime and otherwise overharvested.

They soon disappeared after white settlement.

Today, these oyster reefs are being restored thanks to restoration projects by organisations such as Ozfish.

Restoration of these reefs is likely to boost fish stocks.

Oyster reefs will also improve water quality, as oysters are highly effective filter feeders, each one "cleaning" up to 50 litres of water a day.

Throwing a cast net

Check local regulations before cast-netting

Method 1

With the attached rope coiled around your right hand extend the cast net as shown here

With your forefinger extended and your thumb and middle finger forming an 'O', push downward with your left hand

Stop 80cm above the leadline. You have now divided the lower net into two parts, one each side of your forefinger

While gripping the top of the net, take half with your right hand from underneath. The other half remains gripped in your left hand

One half is in each hand

With the palm of your left hand facing away from your body, place the half of the net in that hand into your right hand and grip firmly

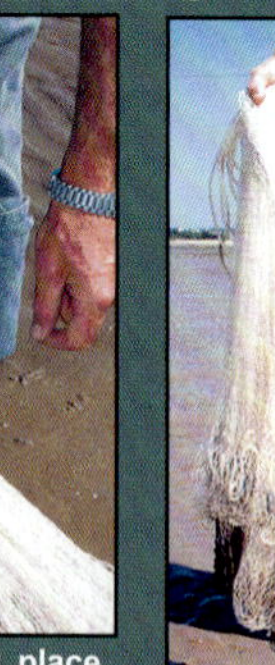
Suspend the net in your right hand

Take the leadline in your left hand

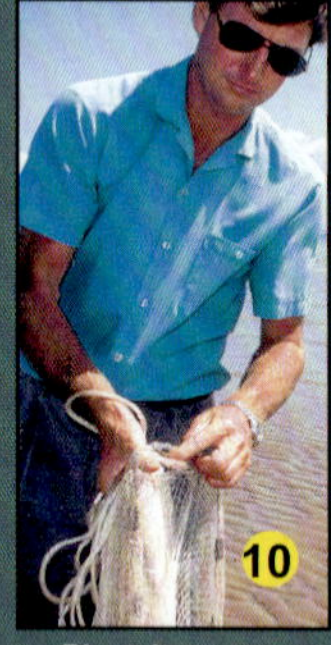

Place it over your right-hand thumb. Grasp the front of the net with your left hand 20cm above the leadline, then gather 70cm of leadline from the front of the net in your left hand. You are ready to throw

Swing your body through 90 degrees as you cast in an underhand motion. *Pictures courtesy NT FISHERIES*

Method 2

Method 1 shown at the top keeps the net off the thrower and is therefore cleaner, drier and keeps any trapped stinger tentacles off the thrower. It also achieves good distances. Method 2 however is usually the easiest to learn. Note that smaller nets are easier to cast. Method 1 is demonstrated by PHIL HALL and Method 2 is demonstrated by GEORGE VOUKOLOS Jr.

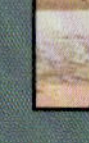

Check local regulations before using a cast net!

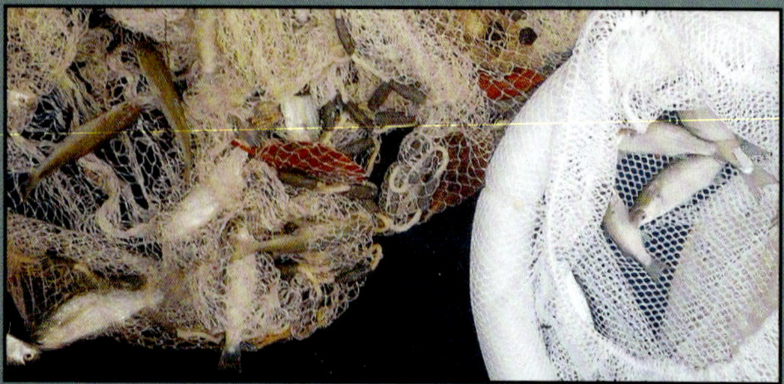

Fresh is best

Mullet

Mullet are found around Australia. There are about 80 species worldwide.

Most live in saltwater, but some can live in freshwater.

They must be gathered in traps or nets as most mullet won't take a bait.

They are a hardy livebait. When dead, the cut fillets make a durable, oily deadbait. Large mullet are a good trolled bait for billfish and mackerel.

Barramundi will take large mullet, while juvenile (poddy) mullet are ideal for flathead, threadin and blue salmon, jacks, golden snapper, jewfish and more.

Most mullet species form schools, but the large diamond-scale mullet *Liza vaigiensis* is often seen singly or in pairs.

The popeye mullet *Rhinomugil nasutus* is conspicuous in tropical estuaries, swimming in schools with its head out of the water, using its split eyes to watch above and below. The popeye is a great bait, but hard to net because of its excellent eyesight.

At low tide in estuaries subject to large tidal flow, mullet mill around before moving with the tide. Anglers should be busy with cast nets before the tide turns.

In southern waters the yellow-eye mullet will take small meat baits, and is a good mulloway bait.

Sardines & Herring

Sardines and herring are baitfish of vital importance to the northern fishery.

Herring have a dark marking on the back of the fin whereas sardines have a black spot at the front of the fin where it joins the body. Herring tend to live near structure, not forming surface "bait balls". Sardines form schools.

When sardines are in the shallows the schools ripple the surface, where they can be cast-netted.

Around wharves these baitfish can be caught with tiny bait jigs.

Three important species of northern sardines are in the genus *Sardinella*, often called green-backed sardines. *Sardinella gibbosa* is the largest, reaching 70g. It is called goldstriped sardine.

Sardinella albella and *Sardinella brachysoma* are smaller sardines, weighing up to about 40g.

Sardines and herring do not live long, so populations fluctuate between good and bad years.

In southern waters the pilchard or bluebait *Sardinops sagax* is a hugely important baitfish. It is generally used as a bought packet bait for salmon, tailor and mulloway.

Keeping bait alive

Mullet are tough fish that usually survive being collected with a cast or drag net. They are hardy in a bait tank.

Sardines and herring are more fragile. They can be netted, but catching them with bait jigs minimises damage. They are difficult to keep alive in a bait tank, probably dying from osmotic shock after scales have rubbed off.

The "solution" is to dilute livetank seawater with fresh, to reduce osmotic potential.

Live saltwater prawns are great bait and can usually be kept alive in a bait tank for extended periods.

A mesh bait-keeper net hung in the water is the best way to keep bait alive. Using fine livebait hooks to minimise damage.

Freshwater shrimp

In south-eastern Australia, freshwater shrimp are hugely abundant at times, and easily harvested for bait.

There are three species in the Murray/Darling system. *Paratya australiensis* is most common. It is found in Queensland, NSW, Victoria, Tasmania and SA. It can tolerate salinity and can live in estuaries.

Shrimp are prime bait and can be caught in traps or nets, but check local gear laws first. Shrimp are omnivorous and many baits will lure them, including cheese. Put traps in slow-flowing water near vegetation.

The length of adult shrimp is 3cm to 4cm. Shrimps are difficult to keep alive for long but they work well as deadbait. Use fine-gauge hooks to minimise damage to the shrimp so that it keeps kicking for as long as possible.

Shrimp are most active in warm weather. Eggs are carried under the female's tail in August and September. They hatch in late spring to early summer. Because they have a short life cycle, shrimp numbers fluctuate with annual seasonal conditions.

Prawns

In muddy northern estuaries prawns can be harvested with cast nets, drag nets or scoop nets, where regulations allow. They are usually abundant in the wet season. Most fish will not refuse a live or fresh prawn bait.

Southern prawns are usually taken at night using a light and scoop night.

Dead prawns work well on bream and whiting. Peel them first for better results.

Squid

Squid are found in most coastal waters and are a great live, dead or cut bait. A live squid will tempt snapper, kingfish and mulloway when nothing else will. Squid are easily caught on jigs at night under lights, or at dawn and dusk. See Page 35. They are widely available as a frozen bait product.

Garfish

Garfish are caught in shallow waters around Australia. They make ideal skipping baits for sailfish, and can be used whole on ganged hooks for tailor, mulloway,, kingfish and more.

Gar can also be cut up for small bottom baits.

Where legal, these fish can be collected with a cast net. Otherwise, catch them with very light line and tiny hooks baited with squid.

Use berley to bring garfish to the boat.

Worms & Nippers

Worms and nippers can be pumped from mudflats with a bait pump.

Bait worms include tubeworms, squirtworms and bloodworms. They can be dug in some areas, but check regulations. Seagrass rafts often contain worms that are useful bait.

Beach worms stick their heads out of the sand when a fish carcass is placed in the wash of surf beaches, but grabbing them and pulling them out is tricky.

Other useful baits are the small crabs and shellfish found on foreshores. Crabs are ideal for tuskfish and big bream.

Pipis can be found on surf beaches by digging one's toes into the sand.

Cunjevoi, found on ocean rocks, has a flesh that is good bait for drummer.

For herbivores such as luderick, green and brown weed are the ideal bait, but careful bait presentation is critical.

Freshwater crays - yabbies, marron, gilgies

The most important of Australia's freshwater crayfish is the abundant ***redclaw crayfish*** (*Cherax quadricarinatus* - pictured) a tropical species native to Queensland.

It is now widely distributed across northern Australia and has found its way into overseas waterways, where it has become a feral pest.

Fortunately they are a tasty pest, making a great meal, and the smaller ones are also a good livebait.

The redclaw is identifiable by a red strip on the outside of the claws in males.

The male is larger than the female, reaching 25cm in length and 600g.

Redclaw live in ponds, creeks, rock pools and fast flowing rivers in tropical and subtropical regions.

They can tolerate a broad temperature range and poor water quality. They are omnivorous.

Redclaw are commercially farmed.

In the wild, they are easily caught with baited traps.

The most abundant southern cousin of the redclaw is the ***common yabby*** (*Cherax destructor* and *Cherax albidus*).

The yabby is native to NSW, Victoria and South Australia, including throughout the Murray-Darling system.

Yabbies were stocked into WA farm dams in 1932, and some Tasmanian dams also have them.

Redclaw crayfish

Eating redclaw

Freshwater crayfish such as redclaw should be purged in a bin of freshwater before cooking. The water will turn brown as their waste is released. You may wish to change the water once or twice. Boil them whole in salt water, or grill. While freshwater crayfish taste fine on their own, the cooked flesh can be removed from the tails and used in salads or sandwiches. Crayfish are excellent bait for many freshwater fish. Use them whole as a livebait, or use the tail for deadbait.

They are variable in colour, often with a bluish hue. They grow to 30cm, but are usually 10cm to 20cm. They can survive dry periods by burrowing in mud, a habit that destroys earthen dam walls.

Like redclaw, the yabby is easily caught in a trap. They are good to eat.

The large ***Murray crayfish*** (*Euastacus armatus*) is found in the Murray and Murrumbidgee Rivers and tributaries.

Adults grow to 2kg, making this the second largest freshwater crayfish species in the world. Despite its wide distribution in Australia it is no longer abundant and most states have significant fishing restrictions for them.

In WA, a large freshwater crayfish called ***smooth marron*** *(Cherax cainii)* is popular with fishermen. The related ***hairy marron*** *(Cherax tenuimanus)* is endangered.

Marron are the third largest freshwater crayfish in the world, growing to 38cm and an impressive 2kg. Marron were originally only found between WA's Harvey and Albany, but have since been introduced to rivers and dams between Hutt River, north of Geraldton, to east of Esperance.

Marron prefer sandy areas with structure, where organic matter accumulates.

WA has freshwater crayfish called ***koonacs*** (*Cherax plebejus* and *Cherax glaber)*. Koonacs grow to 20cm.

They live further inland than marron, inhabiting ephemeral rivers and swamps.

WA also has freshwater crayfish called ***gilgies***.

There are two species, *Cherax quinquecarinatus* and *Cherax crassimanus*.

Gilgies are found in most streams, rivers and irrigation dams in the south-west, often alongside marron.

Gilgies can burrow to escape droughts. They have a wider distribution than marron, but reach only 13cm.

In Tasmania, the ***giant freshwater crayfish*** (*Astacopsis gouldi*) reaches 80cm and 5kg.

It is the world's biggest freshwater crayfish and is protected.

MODEL	LENGTH	WEIGHT	DIVING DEPTH	ACTION
SUSP	120mm	23gms	3mt/10ft	SUSPEND
+3	120mm	23gms	1mt/3ft	WOBBLE
+6	120mm	23gms	2mt/6ft	WOBBLE
+10	120mm	23gms	3mt/10ft	WOBBLE
+15	120mm	23gms	5mt/15ft	WOBBLE
+20	120mm	23gms	7mt/20ft	WOBBLE

Bibbed lures and depth ratings

Some bibbed-minnow lures are supplied in a range of models that swim at different depths. One of the best examples, and a popular lure for targeting barramundi, is the Classic 120.

The table above shows the depths that each Classic 120 model dives too.

Depth labels are rubbery, as various factors affect lure depth, such as how much line is let out when trolling, the troll or retrieve speed, the line thickness, and the height the rod is held.

For trolling northern rivers for barramundi, the +10 model is most popular, along with shallower models for when fish feed near the surface. Deeper models are useful in dams.

As well as a range of depths, lures are sold in a huge range of colours, shapes and sizes.

All this can be overwhelming for a newbie fisho looking at a tackle shop's lure wall.

Understanding lure colour is a science in itself, as colours soon disappear as a lure dives. For example, a lure that is bright red near the surface becomes drab as it dives down.

Lure size, contrast, swimming vibration and flash are arguably more important than colour.

Nonetheless, in barramundi fishing, bright green lures have a strong following, as well as gold or metallic lures that flash as they swim. Barramundi can find lures at night, with lure size, vibration and silhouette being factors to consider when fishing in darkness.

Most bibbed minnows float until retrieved, when they dive. Suspending lures neither float or sink and therefore have a particularly realistic presentation. Sinking minnows, though effective, don't float away from snags when the retrieve is stopped, so they tend to get stuck on structure.

In bluewater fishing, the ability of a lure to swim fast can be critically important.

Thankfully, the most successful lures are well known and tend to dominate tackle shop displays and fisho banter, which helps makes lure choice easier.

Surface swimmers

There are many surface lures. The **Killalure 2 Deadly** is an innovative design by NT fishing guide Lance Butler. It can be fished like a normal diving lure, with a wiggle and rolling action, or it can be blooped like a popper. This makes it deadly on barramundi. It is also effective lure when chasing northern pelagics such as trevally, queenfish and spanish mackerel. It is supplied in 60mm, 80mm and 120mm sizes.

Verticle jigs

Verticle timber stands hold big fish such as barramundi and cod, where jigs like this **Reidys Rattler** work well. Just drop the lure and raise and lower the rod. Strong hooks ensure you stay attached.

Shallow runners

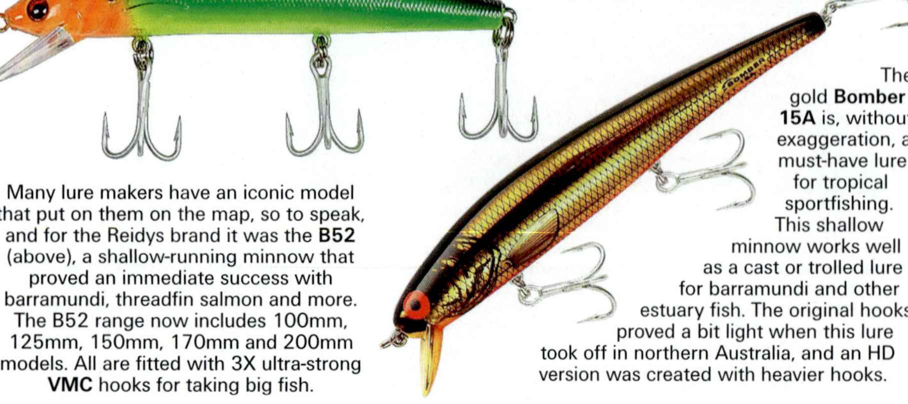

Many lure makers have an iconic model that put on them on the map, so to speak, and for the Reidys brand it was the **B52** (above), a shallow-running minnow that proved an immediate success with barramundi, threadfin salmon and more. The B52 range now includes 100mm, 125mm, 150mm, 170mm and 200mm models. All are fitted with 3X ultra-strong **VMC** hooks for taking big fish.

The gold **Bomber 15A** is, without exaggeration, a must-have lure for tropical sportfishing. This shallow minnow works well as a cast or trolled lure for barramundi and other estuary fish. The original hooks proved a bit light when this lure took off in northern Australia, and an HD version was created with heavier hooks.

Handbody Barramundi & Estuary Lures

Choosing

You will find impressive lure wall displays in Australia's northern tackle shops.

The huge selection might appear bewildering, but if you are chasing barramundi it is not difficult to choose the right lures.

A handful of lure types will cater for most fishing situations in rivers, bays, tidal creeks and billabongs.

Tropical predators, including barramundi, threadfin salmon, queenfish, tripletail, trevally, cod and mangrove jacks, will take the same lures, especially in the smaller sizes.

Some large barramundi lures can be trolled fast and double as lures for bluewater fish such as mackerel.

Dual-purpose lures are helpful because tackle boxes can run out of space.

The bibbed minnow is the most popular lure style for barramundi trolling and casting. Bibbed minnows are made in a range of shapes, sizes and swimming depths.

Soft plastic shads, with their waggling tails, also work well.

They come in a vast range of shapes and sizes.

Soft plastics work particularly well on barramundi in freshwater locations, and during the wet season run-off season.

Vibes are hugely popular. Never leave a barra hotspot that seems quiet until you have tried a vibe.

Surface lures such as poppers and dog-walkers work well on barramundi at night, or when they are boofing bait at the surface.

Poppers also work on pelagic fish such as queenfish and trevally.

A point to consider when buying lures is quality. Many cheap "bargain bin" lures will not stand up to big fish.

Floating and sinking minnows

Most bibbed minnows float until retrieved. They dive to a depth largely determined by the size of the bib.

Floating models are good for casting over rocks and other snags.

They will rise when the retrieve is stopped, allowing an angler to work a lure close to fish-holding structure.

A big-bibbed minnow works well over snags, as it tends to swim head-down, with the bib bumping over snags, keeping hooks clear.

Sinking minnows are harder to fish because they sink into snags, unless used skillfully.

Nonetheless, sinking lures can be effective when snags are too steep or deep for floating-diving lures.

A weighted trace can sink a floating lure where a snag or riverbank is deep and instant diving ability is required. A small barrel lead crimped on the leader will suffice, and the lure will often be taken as it descends.

Depth of dive is the main consideration when choosing bibbed minnows.

The lure's rated depth should match the depth you are fishing.

Shallow-diving minnows and surface lures are essential for barramundi fishing, as barra often

your lures

feed at or near the surface. These lures are handy for fishing flats and shallow weedbeds.

Barramundi will often feed in a few inches of water, and lures that swim just under the surface are an important part of the arsenal.

Soft plastics

Soft plastic lures are popular because they are effective.

They sometimes get strikes when hardbody lures do not. The wriggling tail seems to switch predators on.

They can be worked deep or shallow, and they can also be worked up and down as a jig.

Soft plastics are bought either assembled on a jig head, or the lure and jig head are bought separately.

Mixing and matching jig heads on lure bodies can make a big difference.

Often, the lightest possible jig heads, such as resin heads, allow the most realistic presentation.

Most soft plastics have a single hook. The hook-up rate is lower than with hardbody lures, but fish will hit a soft lure multiple times.

Vibes

These combine the best of soft and hardbody lures and can be incredibly effective, especially on barramundi. They can be jigged, cast or trolled.

Prawns

These lures are usually very light and must be cast on an ultra-light threadline outfit. They often work when all else fails.

Jigs

These are dropped and jigged back, or jigged up and down on the spot.

They are effective on barramundi when used next to verticle timber.

They can also work well in the bluewater, cast or trolled like other lures. They tend to foul snags because they have no bib and the underslung hooks are exposed.

Retrieving a lure

Ultra-slow retrieves along the bottom or surface can entice reluctant barramundi into biting.

Other days a fast or twitchy retrieve might be needed.

With pelagic fish, retrieve fast.

Lure presentation can make the difference between a strike, or no strike. Try everything, but be sure to give slow a go for barramundi.

Leader material

Wire leaders are usually only needed when fishing for toothy predators such as mackerel. For other fish, including barramundi, a hard nylon leader material is used.

A 30kg nylon leader line is adequate for big barramundi, but go lighter when fishing for smaller fish.

Where fish are shy or the water is clear, use fluorocarbon leader, which has low visibility under water.

Prawns, Vibes & Soft Plastic Lures

Glow *Gold glitter* *Glow tiger*

Prawn imitations will take fish when no other lure will, and they are especially effective on barramundi, threadfin salmon, jacks, snapper, bream and more. These **Gillies Shrimp** have a realistic look

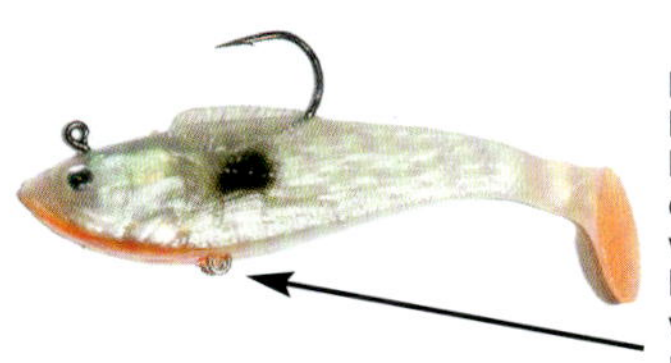

Reidys Rubbers have a spare loop for a dropper hook, which improves hook-up rates where snags are not an issue

Jig heads come in a variety of shapes and sizes for unrigged plastics. Usually the lightest weight that can be comfortably fished works the best

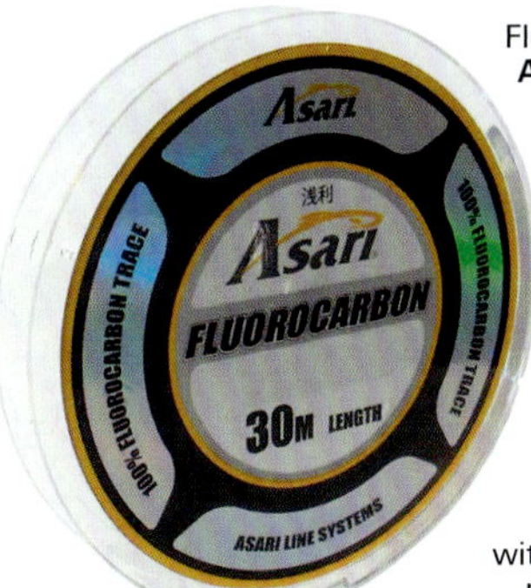

Fluorocarbon leader by **Asari** has low visibility and is useful when fishing clear water or where fish see a lot of lures and have become educated. Otherwise, use a hard nylon leader material as it may resist abrasion better than fluorocarbon. Wire trace is only required when targeting fish with sharp teeth, such as mackerel and sharks

Soft plastic lures such as these by **YUM** work well when fishing for barramundi. They tend to get hit more but the single hooks on most soft plastics bring a lower hook-up rate than lures armed with treble hooks. A treble hook can be added to some soft plastics to improve the hook-up rate, but the trade-off is getting snagged more often. Some lures are sold pre-rigged with lead jig heads, which saves rigging time

Pearl white *Ayu* *Blue pearl*

Reidys Fish Snakz

Karens pearl *Rainbow trout* *Red head* *Gold* *Sunset* *Pretty fish*

Gillies Vibe

Blue shad *Hot orange*

Vibes are a great all-rounder

A vibe is a style of soft plastic lure that can be cast, trolled or jigged. Vibes in northern Australia went from virtually unknown to hugely popular in a short space of time. They also work well on temperate freshwater species such as yellowbelly, redfin and cod. The advantage of these lures is that they are versatile, and will often get a strike when other lures fail. They can be dropped straight down alongside verticle timber or undercut banks and jigged, or cast at fallen trees or rockbars and retrieved. They can even be trolled. Their fast swimming action and soft plastic body gives them some sort of appeal that fish respond too. They have perhaps only one disadvantage, being easily snagged if treble hooks are used. Fishing methods can be altered to minimise snagging. Some of the **Reidys Fish Snakz** and **Gillies Vibe** range are shown above

Slippery around snags

Some hardbodied lures are designed to bump over snags. The combination of big bib at the front and high anchor point makes them swim head down and bum up, keeping the hooks clear of snags. Most times anyway. A great snag troller for barramundi, yellowbelly and cod is **JJ's StumpJumper**, sold in various sizes, colours and bib styles

Scum Frog weedless lure

Weedless lures are useful when fish are hiding among snags and weeds. Barramundi in billabongs will often reside in weeds during the day, entering open water at night. Saratoga feed around weeds, especially lilly pads. There are various weedless lure systems, and all involve covering the hook point in a manner that stops weed catching, but still allowing the fish to impale itself when it bites. Naturally, such a system misses a few fish, but it is a trade-off worth making because you can put lures where the fish are. **Reidys Weedies** lures are shown at left

A **Gillies Wobbler** ... a type of spoon

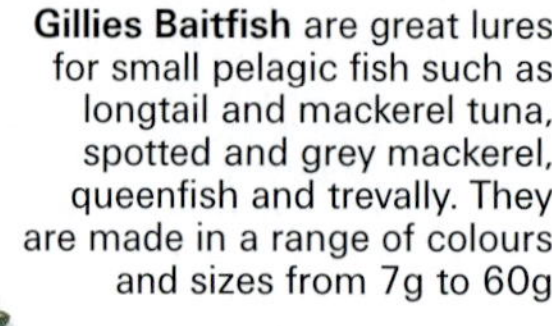

Gillies Baitfish are great lures for small pelagic fish such as longtail and mackerel tuna, spotted and grey mackerel, queenfish and trevally. They are made in a range of colours and sizes from 7g to 60g

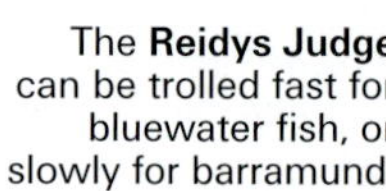

The **Reidys Judge** can be trolled fast for bluewater fish, or slowly for barramundi

Lures with moulded-in bibs tend to withstand being hit by big fish

The **Bluewater Minnow** is made in 120mm, 160mm and 200mm sizes

The **Reidys Blooper** (A) and **Reidys J Walker** (B) are made in different sizes for bluewater and freshwater fishing. The **Killalure Cone Popper** (C) is an effective surface lure for big barramundi and giant trevally

Hawaiian links ... arguably the best of the snap links

Snap links ... handy but prone to twist open on big fish

The **Classic Bluewater P163 Rocket Popper** has a tail weight that makes it cast like a rocket

Essential Items

Long-handled, sturdy fish grips are essential for handling big fish like barramundi securely and safely. The fish can be held in the water at arm's length. If lifting a fish that will be released, be sure to support it by the body while using the lip grip. Studies have shown that suspending fish by the lip can cause severe damage

Small ball sinkers are ideal for livebaiting or threading onto a trace to make a floating lure sink, but do not let children handle lead sinkers

Wire trace is required for sharp-toothed predators

Long-nosed, long-handled stainless pliers help safely remove lures with multiple treble hooks from struggling fish, or fish with a hook located well inside the jaw. Some pliers double as crimpers

Crimps are used on heavy nylon leaders when knots are unsuitable. Also used with wire traces. Stainless crimping pliers are required to apply them

Small, heavy gauge hooks are ideal for reef fishing, as they handle both large and small fish

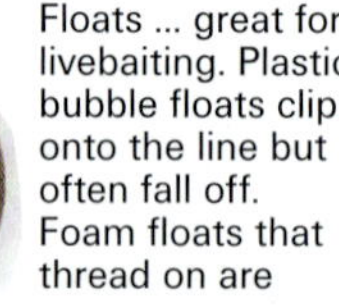

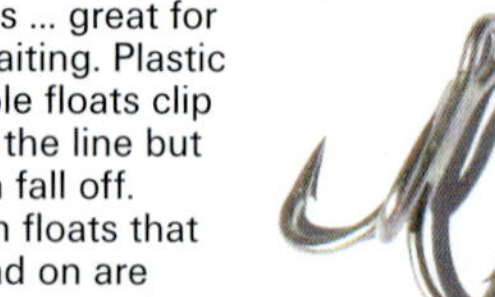

Large-gape, fine-gauge hooks such as these 7/0 Suicides (below) are ideal for livebaiting as they lessen damage to baitfish

Floats ... great for livebaiting. Plastic bubble floats clip onto the line but often fall off. Foam floats that thread on are more secure

Treble hooks (below) such as these VMC 6X-strong are ideal replacements for rusted or inferior hooks on barramundi lures

Gillies Species Packs provide essential tackle items needed to chase smaller fish such as bream, whiting, salmon and flathead

Rod tips can fail when miles from home. Always carry spares and hot melt glue to repair them

Your essential

Catching large fish is more enjoyable with the right gear, and quality tackle is less likely to let you down when you are travelling, and many miles from a tackle shop.

Most fishing, either up north chasing barramundi, or fishing the southern surf for salmon and tailor, can be done with 10kg to 20kg braided line.

For bottom fishing over reefs, 25kg to 50kg nylon lines are the norm.

For barramundi fishing in rivers and estuaries, 10kg to 15kg main lines and nylon leaders of 20kg to 50kg are generally used.

When using ultralight lures for estuary fish such as jacks and bream, low-visibility fluorocarbon (clear) leaders work well.

Wire traces are used when toothy fish such as mackerel may be encountered.

Ultralight gear is used to fool fish in clear water, or when they are reluctant to bite.

Barramundi slow down during cool weather, and lures well presented on light leaders are more likely to get a strike in such conditions.

Check out Page 36 for advice on choosing rods and reels.

There is a good spread of essential items listed above. Be sure to also have on your northern tackle checklist: *camera, sunscreen, insect repellent, and cool clothing, a good hat, and water bottles.*

Bluewater Lures

Pelagic fish are more likely to take lures that are moving fast.

Slow lures will attract attention but mackerel and tuna may just follow behind and not strike them.

Lures for pelagic fish must therefore be capable of swimming fast without blowing out of the water.

They also must be able to withstand being chewed by mouths full of sharp teeth, and be able to hold together through extended battles.

Up north, some barramundi lures will double as mackerel lures.

Examples are the Reidys Judge and Classic 120.

Here's a brief description of lures for bluewater fishing.

Bibbed minnows: These are much the same as the minnows shown on previous pages, but not all bibbed minnows that are great freshwater lures can be trolled fast enough for bluewater fishing. Some will blow out the water, or produce too much drag.

Deep divers usually have larger bibs and generally have to be trolled more slowly, but some modern bib designs can be trolled fast.

The best bibbed minnows swim true after a mauling, but some, particularly timber lures, often require retuning of the bib or line-attachment eye after a big fish is caught.

Bluewater Gear

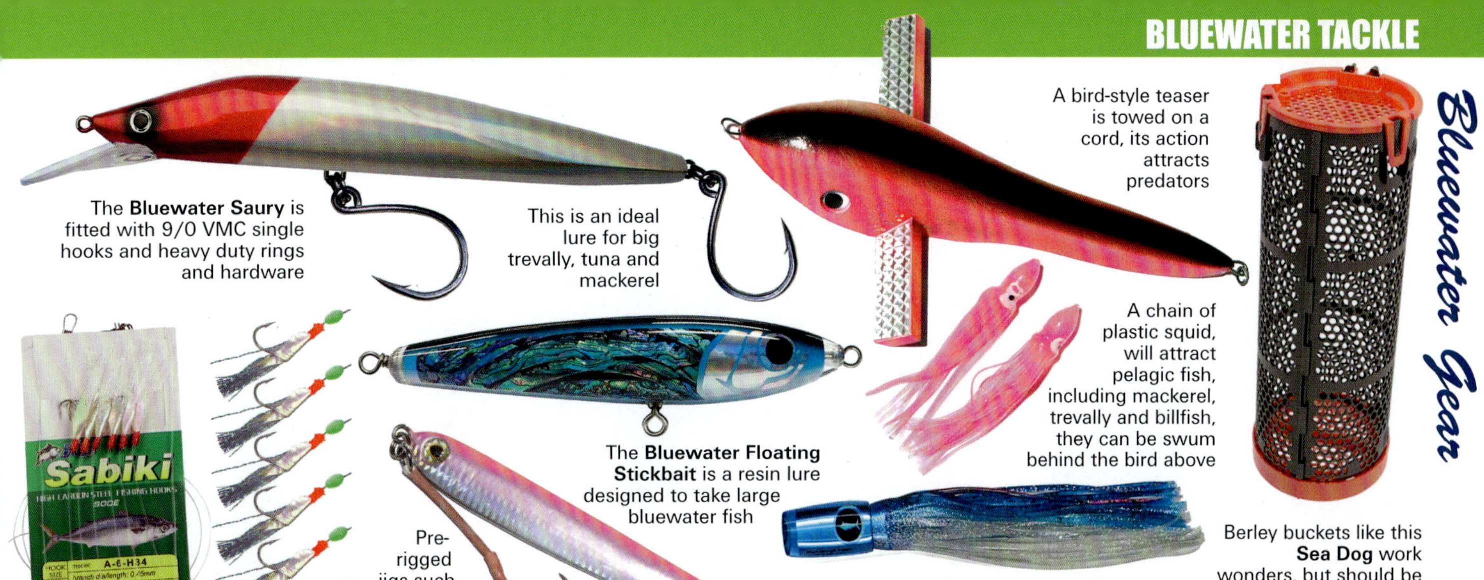

The **Bluewater Saury** is fitted with 9/0 VMC single hooks and heavy duty rings and hardware

This is an ideal lure for big trevally, tuna and mackerel

A bird-style teaser is towed on a cord, its action attracts predators

A chain of plastic squid, will attract pelagic fish, including mackerel, trevally and billfish, they can be swum behind the bird above

The **Bluewater Floating Stickbait** is a resin lure designed to take large bluewater fish

Pre-rigged jigs such as these by **Sabiki** are ideal for catching baitfish

A **Reidys** metal knife jig

Pusher-style trolling lures come in plunger or pop head designs and a range of colours. They take marlin and sailfish, tuna, wahoo, mackerel and mahi mahi

Berley buckets like this **Sea Dog** work wonders, but should be attached to small boats with a breakaway line in case a shark or crocodile takes interest

Essential Items

As well as a filleting knife (grey handle), you should carry a quality fish skinning knife (white handle) and a sharpener

All boaters need a good landing net. Up north, you need a strong net with an oversize pouch because the fish encountered tend to be big. A knotless soft net (pictured) improves the survival rate of released fish, and also doesn't entrap hook barbs as easily as fibre mesh does

Braid scissors ... required for easy trimming of modern fishing lines

Almost all fishing today is done with low-stretch braided line. Nylon monofilament lines that older fishos grew up with are now used primarily as leader material. Braided lines have a smaller diameter than nylon, meaning they are less affected by the current. Their low-stretch quality means bites are keenly felt, even in deep water. Braid of 15kg breaking strain in a quality brand such as **Fins** will cater for most saltwater fishing situations

A fabric-mesh floating keeper net (below) hung over the side of the boat will keep bait alive for long periods and is especially effective for sardines and herring that do not usually last long in a bucket, even with aeration. Fabric nets do not rust like wire bait pots. Be sure to buy a net that has mesh fine enough to retain your intended bait. Also be sure to pull the net in before you move the boat to the next fishing spot. Very large tubular nets are made called 'keep nets' which are used in some countries to retain a catch of large fish until it can be weighed at the end of a competition. These could have application as bait keepers in Australian fishing

fishing tackle check-list

The minnows shown above can be trolled fast and can withstand substantial punishment.

Spoons, slugs and slices: These simple lures are shiny pieces of metal with a hook attached.

The metal may be solid and straight (a slice or slug), or a thin curved plate (a spoon or wobbler), and the lure might also be adorned with additional feathers, fabric, plastic or other material.

These are cheap, durable lures that work well in a variety of situations.

When chasing schools of pelagic fish, use the smallest metal slices or slugs that can be cast the distance.

Spoons and slices generally work best with a fast retrieve. They can also be dropped down and jigged back up.

Jigs: Jigs are usually dropped to the bottom and retrieved in a manner that might entice a fish to strike.

These lures include weighted feathers, metal slices, vibes and soft plastics.

Jigging has become popular with reef fishermen, especially when there are a lot of bait pickers around, because bigger fish tend to take the jigs.

Surface lures: Surface lures work well on many pelagic fish, and they provide an exciting added visual aspect to fishing.

Surface lures include poppers, pushers, bloopers and dog walkers.

Poppers bloop or skip along the surface, depending on their design.

True bloopers have a cup-faced head.

Fast surface lures have an angled head and can skim along the surface.

Dog walkers zig-zag across the surface much like a popeye mullet.

Poppers are particularly effective on queenfish and trevally.

Pushers are specialist billfish lures consisting of a resin or rubber head and plastic skirt. They bob and dive in an enticing fashion when trolled.

Paravanes and downriggers: These are used to take trolled lures and baits deep.

They are effective when pelagic fish are feeding at midwater. Paravanes are attached to the line and should be rigged with wire so they don't get bitten off. Most downrigger weights are dropped by winch on a cable with the fishing line attached to a release clip.

Tackle boxes: Buy a big tackle box with separate trays, so that treble hooks on lures don't become entangled.

Using sonar to target fish

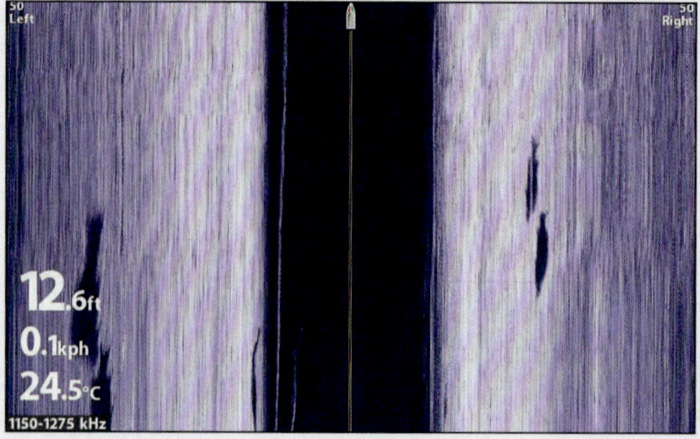

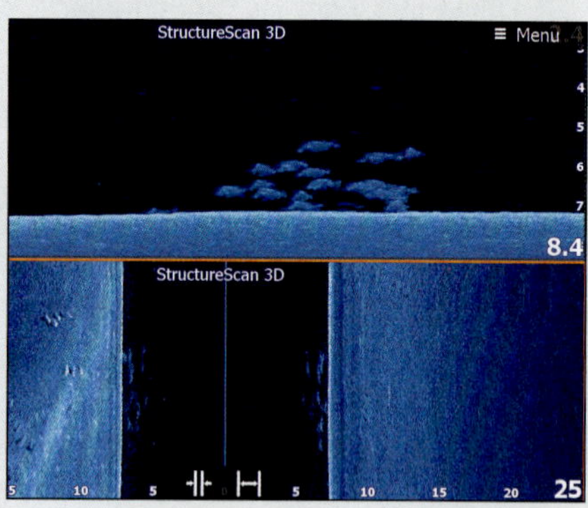

***LEFT:* Zooming in on a barramundi shadow *CENTRE:* A crocodile as seen on sidescan *RIGHT:* Baitfish at midwater, and their shadow**

Most fishing in far northern Australia is done in shallow water, where sidescan and downscan sonar works best.

Sonar definition is now so good that the outlines of fish can sometimes be seen and species identified.

Barramundi are an easy fish to identify because of their distinctive shape, and their habit of resting in a head down position.

Single fish can be seen moving with the current at midstream or resting on the bottom, and lures placed accordingly.

Groups of fish can be seen among snags or over rockbars.

Crocodiles can be seen lying on the bottom or at midwater, sometimes as a shark cruises by.

It is almost as enjoyable watching the sonar screen as it is catching fish.

As sidescan reveals fish that are hiding within by structure, a skipper can decide whether it is worth investing time working a snag pile.

Champion fishos use sidescan to follow barramundi up rivers with the tide.

Sidescan reveals where fish are located, and allows accurate placement of lures.

There's no longer any need to lose lures just to probe a snag pile to see if fish are there.

Sonar will also depict individual billfish out on the bluewater, giving fishermen some idea where to set baits or lures.

Are spanish mackerel or tuna near the surface, the sea floor or somewhere between?

The fish arches will tell the story.

Another feature of modern sounders is the ability to accurately map the bottom.

A skipper can easily create his or her own mini charts, and do it in real time.

FISH FINDER TM started making micro charts several years ago, using third party software and a laptop computer.

Today, all the number-crunching is done for the user by Lowrance units.

Detailed micro charts can be used to advantage in many types of fishing.

A good fisherman can still catch fish without sidescan or downscan, but skilled use of sonar can make a huge difference to a fishing day, or a competition outcome.

There is also great enjoyment to be had in seeing what fish are under the boat, even if they aren't biting.

The Wet is playtime

The Top End's wet season was once a dreaded time of year.

'The Wet' was so poorly regarded the NT tourist commission changed the name to 'tropical summer'.

Before roads were sealed it was right to fear the Wet, as travellers could be bogged for weeks. Today, most roads to fishing spots are sealed. Floods still block roads, but the water soon drops.

The Wet is a great time to chase barramundi. The run-off from monsoonal rain is when maturing barra from billabongs go downstream, and young barra go upstream. Fishermen catch them along the way. You don't even need a boat, as barramundi can be caught from floodways along roads.

The Wet, from about Christmas to April, is also a great time to experience the Top End. The rain brings cool spells, and nature glows green. Along the floodplain rivers, nature is supercharged.

You will find the best wet season fishing spots in this book.

When fishing floodways, keep in mind the ever-present crocodile danger, and also passing vehicles.

About barra

Northern Territory research shows that most barramundi make predictable movements through the year. Importantly though, they don't all march to the same drum.

Some fish move far up and down rivers over a short space of time, while others sit on a favourite snag for years.

Barramundi are often recaught near where they were tagged.

Other things you should know ...

Barramundi like warm water. Aquaculture studies show they feed and grow best when the water is between 25C and 36C. At 22C or below and above 38C their feeding is significantly affected. Quick falls in temperature may put them off the bite. In cool weather look for warm water.

Barramundi are voracious feeders, and are usually found where food is abundant.

Barramundi like cover, including timber, weeds, bankside vegetation and rockbars, but they also move up waterways with the tide, following bait schools. They can be found on calm tidal flats, in tiny mud snake drains in tidal creeks, and in eddies.

On the coast, barra prefer calm, shallow water, usually on the sheltered insides of coves. They like murky water along shorelines, and will use clearer water, often defined by a colour change, to feed.

They are often more active at night. The rise and fall of the moon and cloud cover can affect activity.

Barramundi usually feed by ambush, often at the surface, rising slowly under a baitfish before inhaling it in a gulp of water. They will approach prey very slowly, and an ultra-slow lure retrieve can be effective.

Barramundi behaviour changes with tides. On outgoing tides they may hang near drains where bait is leaving. Or they may rest on the river bed. On incoming tides they move upstream, following or looking for bait. They will move into mangroves with the rising tide, making it much harder to catch them.

In freshwater, with no tidal influence, they are arguably less predictable. However, fish seen at midwater or above on sonar may be feeding.

In waterholes, high temperatures and rain-driven debris can lower oxygen levels. These conditions are typical of the late Build-up just before the wet season breaks.

Barra will become sluggish and may even die in these conditions.

They often rest at an angle in a nose-down position. This can be seen on sonar. They may not be actively feeding, but a lure pulled past their nose might get hit.

In recent times, barramundi have been targeted in competitions when they are resting on the bottom of rivers, even in full current at midstream.

Fishermen have used sonar to locate them, and then made accurate casts to induce a strike.

Areas of mud bank indented with cone-shaped nose marks, visible at low tide, may be holding spots for barra.

Barramundi prefer the muddy rivers and creeks of the tropical north, from the Ashburton River near Onslow, WA, to the Mary River, at Maryborough, Queensland.

Rivers with large floodplains are ideal habitat, and these are found across the Top End, with some Queensland rivers draining into the Gulf of Carpentaria also prolific.

Clear, sandy tropical creeks usually have smaller numbers of barra than muddy waterways.

Barra can locate prey in muddy water, and at night.

While they have keen eyesight, they can sense vibration to locate prey.

Night fishing can be effective with surface lures.

Run-out tides are often best for barramundi fishing. Work creek mouths and drains. When fishing an incoming tide, work the eddies, ridges along mudflats or foreshores, rock outcrops and flats and channel edges.

At low tide, fish holes.

Trophy barramundi are caught by moving up a river or creek as big barra follow big mullet upstream.

Barramundi will cruise open water at night near wharf lights, they may loiter next to or swim along a shadow, waiting for bait.

In tidal rivers, barramundi are often found among submerged timber. Some snag piles get their own names during fishing competitions.

Rockbars are always good places to troll for barramundi, as are any bumps on the bottom.

During the wet season, the fish move over floodplains, returning as rivers fall below the banks.

Floodplain creek mouths and their colour changes can fish well, but the presence of bait is important.

In lagoons, barra will rest among lillies and weedbeds, sometimes in the sunny shallows. Use weedless lures to get close to the fish.

Pandanus root clumps are hiding places for barra.

Horizontal fallen trees, including mangroves, are good spots to try.

Pockets of still water along the banks of rivers hold fish, including around tussocks. Listen for telltale "boofs" or flurries of bait as barra feed.

Rock walls are another good spot. Trolling river rock walls is popular in Queensland.

Sight fishing over flats can be exciting.

Some anglers like fishing small tides because of the clearer water, but others like big tides because it gets bait schools balled up and moving.

Bigger tides often see the fish feeding more aggressively, especially during the warming weather of the Build-up.

RAIN DEPENDANT RIVERS
FRESHWATER
ESTUARY
MARINE
BEST
BEST
FAIR
DECEMBER
JANUARY
FEBRUARY
MARCH
APRIL
MAY
JUNE
JULY
AUGUST
SEPTEMBER
OCTOBER
NOVEMBER
DARWIN BREEDING SEASON
LARVE
hatch 1.5 mm; high tide washes eggs and larvae into coastal swamps and creeks where they grow 20 mm in the first month
ADULT
spawning around river mouths early in the wet season
ADULT
maturing males move downstream at the beginning of the wet season
JUVENILES
grow to 30 cm in their first year, migrate upstream into freshwater reaches at the end of the wet season
SEX REVERSAL
males turn into females - 3-5 years
SUB ADULT
three years old, sexually mature, grows to 58 cm
ADULT
sexually mature at four years of age. 69 cm returns to estuary

Catching

Mud crabs have possibly the sweetest meat in the sea, yet they are usually abundant and easily captured.

Queensland ramp surveys revealed that mud crabs are the most popular catch among boaters.

"Muddies" maintain numbers even where fishing pressure is moderately high, thanks to their prolific breeding ability and fast growth rate.

They have considerable seasonal variations in numbers, partly because the larvae are at the whim of ocean currents, which distribute them along the coast. Other factors such as rainfall likely affect spawning and survival of young crabs.

Mud crabs are synonymous with the tropics, but they are sometimes found well south of their usual range.

The normal range is between Exmouth Gulf in WA to the Bega River in NSW, but they have been found as far south as Wilson Inlet, WA.

The NT's Darwin Harbour has a particularly healthy crab fishery thanks to ideal habitat and commercial restrictions.

The largest and arguably sweetest Australian mud crab is the green or brown *Scylla serrata*, also called giant mud crab. The smaller, orange-red *Scylla olivacea* is common in some areas, particularly in the WA Kimberley. *Scylla olivacea* has been dubbed the "rambo crab" because it is aggressive.

The green crab forms by far the bulk of the commercial catch.

Mud crabs grow and reach sexual maturity quickly.

Most of the mud crab's life cycle is in inshore waters, but females migrate offshore in summer with their eggs, carrying up to two million at a time. Egg-laden females have been found 30km offshore in 300m of water.

Currents bring the crab larvae back into estuaries.

Orange mud crab

Green mud crab

Mud crabs mature in their second year, at between 130mm and 170 mm across the shell. The crab's shell can reach an impressive 240mm wide in their three to four-year lifespan, with some crabs weighing 2kg+.

South-East Asian studies suggest mud crabs live in mangrove forests at a density of 16 to 46 crabs per hectare.

Studies have found that 50 per cent of material in a crab's gut is usually molluscs, 20 per cent is crustaceans, and the remaining 30 per cent is debris. In crabs where the gut is less than 50 per cent full, inorganic material makes up most of the content.

In the Far North, mud crabs are usually targeted in the cooler months, but in their southerly range the warmer months can be productive.

Where they are abundant they can be easily caught, either by walking the mangroves and picking them up, or hooking them out of their holes. Australian fishos tend to use baited traps or dillies, depending on what local regulations allow.

Mud crabs prefer fresh fish baits, but crabs are attracted to most flesh baits, including chicken carcasses, beef bones, kangaroo, mutton and so on.

Mud crabs can be caught on any tide.

Cooking crabs

Mud crabs are one of the best seafoods to make an impressive presentation, using the legs and claws as a garnish. A claw protruding from a bisque or salad rarely fails to impress. Crabs can be steamed, boiled or poached. First, wash the crab(s) and place in a freezer or ice slurry for 40 minutes to kill them - this is humane, and it also makes the meat more tender. If boiling, use salted water in a large pot. Adding a dash of vinegar may make the meat easier to remove from the shell. Bring the pot to the boil and put the crab(s) in. Bring to the boil again and cook for up to 12 to 20 minutes, depending on the size of the crabs. Once cooked, place the crabs into a salted ice slurry. When cool, clean them in the slurry. Let the pieces drain dry. Season with lemon, pepper, garlic, chilli and onion if required. If the crab is to be finished after initial cooking by barbecuing or frying, do not overcook the crab in the first stage.

Building tides, coming off neaps, are perhaps ideal, but spring tides can be good for crabbing, with crabs moving up creeks with the first push.

On big tides, tie pots to mangroves to stop them washing away, and put the pots in eddies and gutters.

Ensure floats on ropes are

Tied crabs stay in one piece

Some top crab-tiers use bare feet to do this, which allows the tier to use the big toe to hold the final knot as you tie the cord off. Fishermen who follow these steps carefully should be able to tie big tropical mud crabs without incident. The area at the back of the crab where our model's foot sits is the safe part of the crab. (1) Lay 80cm of string over the claws and pull it back under the front of the shell. Then wrap it back under the base of claws and then bring the string forward and around the pinchers (2) using the spine on each pincher as a guide to hold the string. Do one claw at a time if it is easier. With the claws pulled back hard take one end of the string back to the base of one of the two rear swimming legs. It may now help to flip the crab (3). Bring the string back around from the outside of the swimming leg to and around the base of the other swimming leg. Pull the string back up to the top of the shell to the other end of the string and tie a secure knot (4) and the job is done. Practise on a crab that has been in an icebox, as cold slows them down.

male crab

immature female

mature female

Press here to check if crab is 'full' ... if the shell flexes it is an 'empty' crab

a feed of 'muddies'

big enough to resist being pulled under by current.

Mangroves with arched roots are a habitat of mud crabs, but steep muddy banks, rock walls and mudflats are all worth a try.

Retrieve pots every half-hour or so for best results if there is good tidal movement. Leave longer during small tides.

The longer pots are in the water, the more likely they will be interfered with by predators, including crocodiles, groper, sharks and other crabbers.

At night, use glow sticks or reflectors to mark pots.

Scylla serrata moves far up tidal rivers and creeks after long periods without rain, and moves back down and even outside rivers to the flats when heavy rains set in.

Collapsing mesh-covered pots are handy for storage.

In WA, crab pots or traps are illegal. Open dillies are used. These can be worked fast.

To hook crabs, look for holes along muddy banks and around mangroves.

A piece of stout wire or steel with a U-bend at the end is carefully pushed down and behind the crab, and it is pulled out.

A crab with a shiny new shell may be recently moulted and lacking meat. Press on the shell near the flipper. If it is soft release the crab.

Worn claws and attached shellfish suggest a full crab.

Learn to tie crabs. This stops them throwing claws.

Store live crabs in a cool, damp hessian bag.

Put crabs on ice to make them docile.

These crab-handling pliers make it much easier to remove stubborn crabs from nets. Fingers are kept well clear of the powerful claws.

At northern tackle shops or contact the maker shanedoevy@hotmail.com or visit his online store **http://stores.ebay.com.au/doev557**

Blue swimmer and sand crabs

Australia's blue swimmer crabs (mostly *Portunus armatus*), are also called 'blue manna' or 'sand crabs'. They occur right around the Australian mainland. They reach 22cm across the shell, 1kg in weight and 80cm claw span. Though having less meat than mud crabs, the flesh is highly regarded. They live in estuaries, sheltered bays and offshore waters to 50m deep. By day, they usually hide in sand, waiting for a passing meal. At night they are more mobile. They prefer sandy seagrass areas. In WA blue crabs are a popular target around Perth, Shark Bay, Exmouth and Port Hedland. South Australia's two gulfs produce premium crabs, as do some NSW estuaries and Victoria's Gippsland lakes. They show up in many other places. They are usually caught with baited drop dillies or scoop nets, depending on the depth fished and local regulations. Blue crab runs tend to be seasonal, in the warmer months in southern waters, although they can be caught all year. Closed seasons and bag limits apply, check local laws. There are four known species of blue swimming crabs in Asia-Pacific waters. Two are known to occur around Darwin, but it is safe to safe they are of little interest in the NT thanks to the ready supply of big mud crabs. The sand crab (*Ovalipes australiensis* - above far right) reaches 15cm shell width. It inhabits southern waters from Fraser Island, Queensland, to Perth, WA. They move in big numbers at times and are edible.

Pots and dillies

Drop dilly

Fold-up trap

Collapsible trap

Know your mud crabs

The green mud crab *Scylla serrata* (left) is the largest and tastiest mud crab. It forms 99 per cent of the NT and Qld commercial catch. It prefers saline waters. It has green or greenish-blue claws. It grows to an impressive 28cm carapace width and may exceed 3kg.

The orange mud crab *Scylla olivacea* grows to 18cm carapace width. Its aggression has earned it the nickname 'rambo crab'. It tolerates brackish water. It seems dominant in WA's Kimberley region and is caught alongside *Scylla serrata* in some areas.

Scylla paramamosain is an Asian species found in sandier areas near mangroves. It reaches only 15cm across the carapace. It has orange and green claws and sharp frontal teeth. This and *S. tranquebarica* (right) are probably not found in Australia.

The purple mud crab *Scylla tranquebarica* is an Asian species that grows to a carapace width of 20cm. It has purple claws, however Australia's *Scylla serrata* can also have a purplish hue.

PARAMAMOSAIN & TRANQUEBARICA PHOTOS: Queensland Museum

Tides are much bigger in northern Australia

The tidal range in Australia's north is far greater than the south, but not uniformly so. From Torres Strait to the west end of Arnhem Land the spring range is about 3m, falling to 2.6m at Port Essington on Cobourg Peninsula, but increasing westward. At St Asaph Bay on Melville Island, north of Darwin, the range is 4.2m. Darwin's mean spring range is 7.3m. It can reach 9.1m.

At Wyndham, at the west end of the apex of Cambridge Gulf in the WA Kimberley, the range is 7m, and further along at Collier Bay and King Sound, the biggest tides in Australia have a spring range to 11m, with a mean spring range of 10.3m at Derby township.

Going west the spring range falls until North West Cape at Exmouth. It is 8.53m at Broome (West Kimberley), and 5.8m at the Pilbara's Port Hedland, with 5.48m at Cossack and 4.1m at Fortescue. South of North West Cape the spring range becomes less. It is 1.8m at Maud Landing, 1.52m at Carnarvon, and at Geraldton it is only .76m.

To the south, as far as Leeuwin and along the western south coast as far as Eucla, the range is only .75m, the smallest tides in Australia. Going further to the east along the south coast the range increases. It is 1.67m at Port Eyre, 1.8m at Streaky Bay, Coffin Bay, Port Lincoln and at Cape Willoughby, on the east end of Kangaroo Island. The range increases beyond this as the tidal wave moves up the narrowing Spencer and St Vincent Gulfs in South Australia.

Further along the SA coast and into Victoria it is 1.52m at Port Macdonnell, but diminishes to .91m at Portland and Warrnambool, and then increases again, with 1.52m at Apollo Bay and 1.58m at Port Phillip Heads. It is 2.43m at the entrance to Corner Inlet, but only .91m at Lakes Entrance and at the Snowy River mouth.

The range is 1.52m at Jervis Bay, 1.8m at Sydney Heads, diminishing to 1.53m at Fort Denison, within the harbour, 1.67m at the entrances to the Clarence Richmond Rivers, and 2m at the Brisbane bar.

It is 3.35m at the entrance of Maryborough's Mary River, and 3.65m at Sea Hill, Keppel Bar. Broad Sound, where north and south floodstreams meet, has the greatest range on the East Coast, where the spring rise in the Sound may be from 7.31m to 9.14m.

A far smaller tidal range is experienced north of Broad Sound until approaching the tip of Cape York Peninsula.

In the Gulf of Carpentaria, the range varies and is quirky, sometimes affected by the wind, surprising boaters.

The weather bureau image depicts tidal range across Australia, with red showing greatest movement.

Northern weather, and why fishos love cyclones

Tropical weather patterns are different to weather in southern Australia, and understanding it is a critical part of successful and safe northern fishing.

During summer, tropical weather can be severe, changing quickly, and creating hazardous conditions.

The weather bureau offers ever-expanding online services that make it easy to see what is happening.

Fishos can watch storm fronts on radar in real time (see picture), and view latest rainfall and water level data for favourite rivers. This information is important in deciding when and where to go fishing.

North of about Broome in the west and Cairns in the east, the "wet tropics" have two distinct seasons, the dry season, about May to September, and the wet season, about November to March. The Dry and the Wet.

There are also two recognised periods in the year between the Dry and the Wet. These are the Build-up (September onward) and the Build-down (March onward).

The Build-up is a period of intense storms, while the Build-down is the famous "run-off" period. Both are prime times for barra fishing.

The mid-year dry season brings blue skies, little rain and steady winds. The wind is from high-pressure systems over the mainland, setting up an easterly airflow. In the far north, the dry season wind usually picks up in the morning and blows most of the day. In some areas there is a noon lull and a change to an afternoon onshore "sea breeze". This is caused by land warming, forcing hot air to rise and cool sea air to fill the vacuum over land in the afternoon. Heavy monsoonal rain usually starts in December, and by this time 4WD excursions should be clear of boggy areas and river crossings.

The monsoon brings westerly winds, storms, rough seas and the threat of cyclones.

The intensity of each wet season is tied to La Nina and El Nino world weather patterns. La Nina years are usually much wetter, and barramundi fishing much better.

Cyclones usually occur from November to April. Several cyclones can form each year. Winds may exceed 240km/h. Lingering "near-miss" cyclones and low pressure systems are welcomed by fishermen because associated flooding ensures good barramundi fishing.

Visit **www.bom.gov.au** before fishing and check the weather radar for storm fronts. The "current observations" pages reveal wind conditions at various coastal weather stations. River heights and rainfall pages provide additional invaluable information.

Understanding Australian fishing weather

South-West Western Australia: Given the generally exposed nature of this coastline to the open ocean, with a lack of significant estuaries and harbours, boaters are reliant on good weather to go bluewater fishing.

The south-west region has a Mediterranean climate, with hot, dry, windy summers and mild, reasonably wet winters, with autumn and spring being transition months.

The climate is influenced by the sub-tropical ridge of high pressure. For much of the year the ridge is to the south, when easterly to south-easterly winds prevail.

During winter, cold fronts deliver rainfall. Rain averages four days out of every seven during winter but flooding is rare in Perth.

There are extended dry periods during summer, during which time creeks and minor rivers stop flowing. Fish such as bream will make their way up rivers at this time.

Summer sea breezes are strong in the south-west, dubbed "The Doctor" in Perth. Summer winds are mainly easterly but are varied in the warmer months by sea breezes, and in the cooler months by westerlies that bring the bulk of annual rainfall.

Despite gales in winter, average wind speeds in winter are considerably lighter than in summer.

Some of the most popular gamefish arrive off Perth in summer, during the windy season.

South Australia: This state is dry, with median annual rainfall from about 100mm east of Lake Eyre to more than 1000mm on the Mount Lofty Ranges.

Even the mighty Murray River ceases to flow in dry conditions, although this is largely because of water use in agriculture.

South Australia's gulf waters have a moderating influence on temperatures along their coasts. The gulfs also have sheltered waters, at least in comparison with open ocean, with Kangaroo Island shielding the Gulf of St Vincent from the ocean.

The seasonal variation of SA weather is controlled by the position of the subtropical ridge of high pressure.

During the warmer half of the year, November to April, this ridge is located south of the continent. High pressure systems generally move east along the ridge but are often positioned south of the Great Australian Bight. Consequently, the most frequent airstream across the state during this period is from south-east to east.

Although cold fronts associated with southern low pressure systems penetrate the ridge during summer, they generally don't produce rain.

Warm moist tropical air can move into SA from the north in summer, bringing thunderstorms.

In autumn the subtropical ridge moves north and remains over the continent for most of May to October.

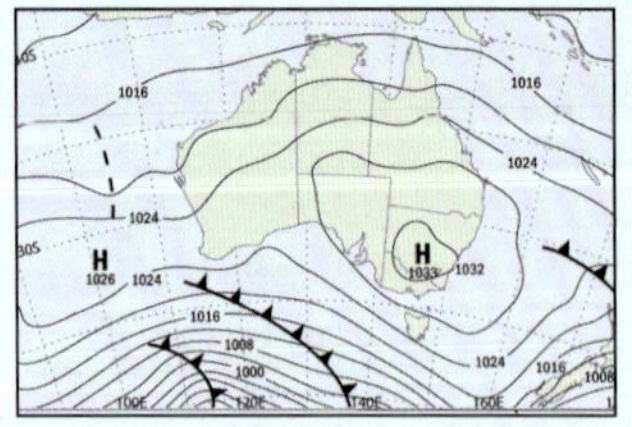

During this period the most frequent winds are from the north-west to south-west. Fronts associated with depressions, travelling eastwards across the ocean during winter, bring gales that are a hazard for boaters.

Because South Australia is largely flat, dry and hot, trout exist only in a very few waters.

Victoria: Victoria has a range of different climate zones, from the hot, dry Mallee region of the northwest to the alpine snowfields in the northeast.

Median annual rainfall ranges from less than 250mm in parts of the Mallee to more than 1800mm over mountainous regions.

The Great Divide mountains in Victoria reach 1986m at Mt Bogong. There are several peaks in excess of 1500m in northeast Victoria.

The Great Divide extends westwards almost to the South Australian border.

To the west and north of the Great Divide the land flattens out to the hot, dry inland plains. The coastal strip, south of the ranges, is generally wetter, except in the far east where the Strzelecki Ranges shelter the East Gippsland District from moisture-laden westerly winds.

The climate changes across the state are reflected by marked changes in vegetation.

High rainfall and low temperature have allowed trout to flourish in some parts of Victoria.

New South Wales: This state is entirely within a temperate zone. The climate is generally mild, but very high temperatures occur in the northwest and very cold temperatures on the Southern Tablelands.

The Great Dividing Range, running north to south in the east of NSW, has a large impact, creating four distinct climate zones; the coastal strip, the highlands, the Western Slopes and the flatter country to the west.

The coastal strip is influenced by the warm Tasman Sea, which in general keeps the region free of extremes of temperature, and provides rainfall, the annual median of which ranges from 750mm in the south to 2000mm in the north.

The mountains of the Great Divide reach a height of 2228m at Mt Kosciuszko, with NSW's high areas producing cold water for trout fishing.

Travelling from east to west across the range, the elevation increases away from the coastal plain, and west of the divide it gradually descends onto the Western Plains. On the western slopes the rainfall gradually decreases. The varied climate across the State is reflected by changes in vegetation.

Mild winters on the north coast favour boating.

Drought: Poor rainfall has major ramifications for fisheries, including dams and the Murray/Darling system, and coastal waters.

Weather Websites & Apps

Weather forecasts, rain radars, road reports, beach and harbour webcams and regular social media reports help fishermen ascertain conditions.

The joy of squidding

Squid are abundant, fun to catch and good to eat. They also make great bait, so there's every reason to chase them.

Australia has several squid species. "Calamari squid" refers to squid with full-length fins, while "arrow squid" have fins extending only partly down the body.

The southern calamari (*Sepioteuthis australis* - pictured) is a large squid found from Brisbane across the southern coast to Ningaloo, WA.

It is abundant in the two South Australian gulfs and Melbourne's two large bays.

Its colour quickly changes from orange-brown, to white with black bands, to almost transparent. It has diamond-shaped fins that extend down the body, widest at mid-way along. The mantle reaches 50cm. It lives over reef, sand and seagrass in shallow, inshore waters. It is active at night, but is often caught at dawn and dusk. It forms small schools.

In northern waters, this species is replaced by the northern calamari, also called bigfin reef squid, or tiger squid (*Sepioteuthis lessoniana*).

This squid has fins that extend the length of the body, the widest point being closer to the rear of the body. It may have black bands, with iridescent marks on the mantle. The mantle reaches 40cm.

It is found across the northern coast from about NSW to Shark Bay, WA. It moves onto shallow reefs at night but may be seen along foreshores in the day, sometimes in just a few inches of water.

Find them by spotlighting shallows at night.

There are several arrow squid species. They occur in schools and are usually most active at night. It is believed they go deeper on bright moonlit nights.

Red arrow squid (*Nototodarus gouldi*) occur in huge numbers south of Fraser Island, Queensland, and Shark Bay, WA. Other species are found in northern waters.

In oceanic waters, Australian fishermen may encounter the large diamondback squid (*Thysanoteuthis rhombus*). These have a diamond-shaped fin which extends right along the body. The body reaches 1m and they weigh up to 20kg. They are found in tropical and sub-tropical waters, usually near the surface of open ocean waters.

Squid and cuttlefish expel purple/bluish ink. Let them squirt their ink before bringing them aboard.

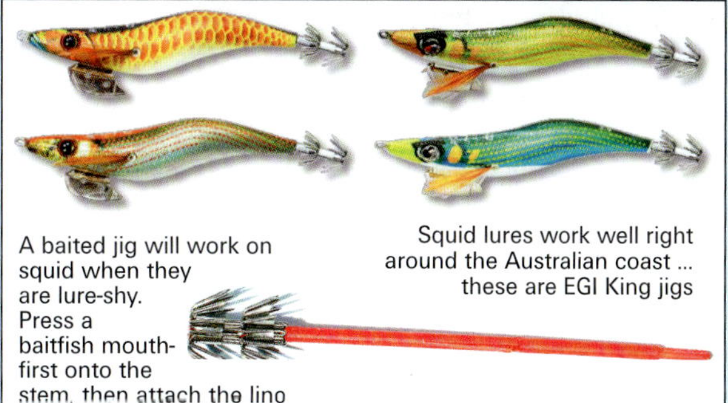

A baited jig will work on squid when they are lure-shy. Press a baitfish mouth-first onto the stem, then attach the line

Squid lures work well right around the Australian coast ... these are EGI King jigs

Octopus

Octopus are of little interest to most Aussie fishermen, yet are common and make a great meal. They are good bait.

The common octopus (*Octopus tetricus*) grows to an impressive arm span of up to 2m.

It has a white eye pupil and orange-rust red arms and can change the colour of its skin, normally mottled brown, to imitate seaweed. It is found in subtropical eastern Australia. A related species lives at similar latitudes in WA.

It is usually found on tidal rocky shores, but spends much of its life over soft sediment. It emerges at night to feed on crabs and shellfish. Its lair is surrounded by rubble, often with the drilled shells of its prey.

The southern keeled octopus (*Octopus berrima*) is common in shallow coastal waters of south-eastern Australia.

It is cream to light brown with a skin-keel around the mantle edge. It has an arm span to 50cm. It exists in southern Australia. It is most common in sand and seagrass in shallow waters. It hides in the sand during the day, or uses rocks or rubbish to shelter.

The hammer octopus (*Octopus australis*) is similar, but lives in the subtropical waters of South-East Queensland and central NSW.

The white-striped octopus (*Octopus ornatus*) has one of the widest distributions, thanks to its planktonic hatchlings. The arms are pink to red with paired white spots, with short white stripes on the mantle. It reaches an armspan of 2m, and is found from northern NSW north to Perth, WA. It is mainly found on coral reefs. Its lairs are verticle holes, and it forages over reef flats or on sand/gravel at low tide at night.

The veined octopus (*Octopus marginatus*) is widespread in the Indian Ocean. It has branching dark brown veins over the mantle and down the arms, with a white to cream wedge under each eye. Its armspan is up to 50cm. It lives in sandy, muddy and shelly habitats from shallows to 200m.

It emerges at dusk and dawn to forage. It can bury itself in sand or mud.

The pale octopus (*Octopus pallidus*) lives in the same areas as the southern keeled octopus. It lacks the skin ridge keel. It has a solid body and short, stout arms. It has spikes of skin over the body. Its armspan is to 60cm. It is common over sand in bays and coastal waters of Victoria, SA and Tasmania out to 600m. It feeds on crustaceans and shellfish. It hides in daylight.

The **blue-lined and blue-ringed octopus** comprise small species often found in rock pools. When disturbed they display blue markings. They have a deadly bite and should not be touched.

Cuttlefish

There are 10 known cuttlefish (*Sepia* species) in Australian waters. They have a white oval-shaped "cuttlebone" inside, often seen washed up on beaches.

Australia has the world's largest cuttlefish, the giant cuttlefish (*Sepia apama*), which has a mantle to 50cm, and weighs up to 5kg.

It is found in southern waters from Brisbane, Queensland, to Shark Bay, WA. It can quickly change colour. It lives on reefs, seagrass beds, and over sand and mud out to 100m. In SA's Spencer Gulf it forms a dense breeding school near Whyalla from May to August. Other species are found in northern waters.

Cleaning cuttlefish can be messy. Grasp the internal cuttlebone and twist it towards yourself. The cuttlebone will cut through the hood and come away. Pull the intestinal sac and legs away. Place the hood flat down, skin-side up, and separate the skin from the flesh, peeling the skin back. Cut the hood up for cooking. You can cook cuttlefish without peeling off the skin, but the skin turns dark purple.

Catching

Squid are easily caught using squid lures or baited jigs. They are most active at dawn, dusk and night and are attracted to light, especially around wharves and jetties. In some areas cast nets or spears can be used to catch them. Check local laws first. Octopus can be caught by searching for them at low tide, or using octopus traps. Check regulations. Cuttlefish will on occasion take squid jigs but are usually an incidental catch.

Cooking

Squid, cuttlefish and octopus make a fine meal. A squid's head should be pulled away and the remaining innards and transparent 'quill' removed from the body. This leaves a cone-shaped white body that can be cut into the familiar 'calamari rings'. Crumbing or battering and frying is popular - cook quickly on high heat for a tender result. Soaking in milk overnight may help tenderise squid. Cuttlefish are messy to prepare and should be cut into strips. Octopus has a strong following among some chefs, and is pickled by culinary enthusiasts. It is chewy but tasty.

Choosing a rod-reel combo

A quality reel enhances the fishing experience. It also won't let you down when you are miles from home.

In tropical marine waters reels must resist corrosive salt, heat and humidity and the forces applied by big fish.

Some models made for the USA market are freshwater reels. These will corrode.

Reels shown here are suitable for saltwater fishing.

Cheap gear can ruin a trip, as spare parts are not readily available in remote areas. Buy quality gear and look after it.

A good reel, properly maintained, is easy to cast, essential when lure fishing.

A smooth drag allows you to better appreciate a battle with a big fish, and with less chance of the line breaking.

The Curado 150DC is the go-to barra baitcaster, with digital backlash control

Shimano's SLX150DC is a cheaper baitcaster alternative, also with digital backlash control

Shimano Stradic's is a popular high performance light spinning reel

Shimano's Saragosa spinning reels are built for tackling larger fish

Baitcasters: Among barramundi fishos, the "baitcaster" reel rules.

They are designed to cast lures with ease and accuracy.

Baitcasters are overhead reels. They sit on top of the rod, which allows your thumb to easily apply spool pressure.

A baitcaster works by releasing line from a revolving spool, a system which offers excellent line control when casting and playing fish, as thumb pressure can be applied.

When matched with a pistol grip rod, a baitcaster reel gives effortless one-handed casting.

Some right-handed fishermen learn to use left-handed baitcaster reels, as the rod then does not have to change hands after casting.

If you plan to cast lures all day, choose a small, low-profile baitcaster.

If trolling, a heavier reel with more line capacity might be warranted, but will be less enjoyable to cast all day.

The downside of a baitcaster is that it requires casting practise, and most trips usually involve untangling a "bird's nest" or two when a cast goes awry. Backlash controls help alleviate this problem.

Baitcasters can be difficult to cast into the wind, and they don't work as well with ultralight lures. They require regular maintenance for flawless operation.

For barramundi fishing, baitcaster outfits are usually loaded with 10kg to 15kg line.

Spinning reels: The "eggbeater" or spinning reel is an alternative to the baitcaster.

Eggbeaters are better for casting ultra-light lures and fine-line "finesse" fishing.

An eggbeater is mounted under the rod. They are easy to use because, when casting, line is simply pulled in loops from the front of the spool. The finger control required to cast accurately is easy to master.

While you don't see many eggbeaters used among serious barramundi enthusiasts, they work perfectly well on most species of fish.

High-quality eggbeaters can handle sailfish and small marlin.

They are available in a range of sizes.

Medium-sized eggbeaters work well as an all-round reel.

Reel sizes are best discussed with tackle shop staff when matching a reel with a rod.

Keep in mind that it is better to be "over-gunned" than under-gunned when fishing remote areas, where the chance of hooking big fish is higher.

Boating reels: Reels used for bottom fishing and trolling tend to be heavy-duty overhead designs.

Winches and handlines are popular with some reef fishermen, but heavy-duty rods and reels have a greater following. Overhead reels used for bottom fishing can double as trolling reels.

In deep water, electric reels are worth the expense, because pulling rigs up in more than 70m of water soon becomes tiresome.

Reels can be customised.

Improved drag washers are available, or you can improve the washers yourself.

Handle knobs are changeable on many reels.

Line: A reel's line capacity is important when chasing powerful pelagic fish, especially from land.

Also, although fish like barramundi or freshwater cod rarely take much line in a fight, repeated snags through the day can soon diminish the quantity of line on a small baitcaster reel, so a reasonable line capacity is useful.

For barramundi, 10kg to 15kg braid is popular. For bread and butter fishing, 4kg to 6kg outfits are popular, using nylon or braided line.

Always carry extra line.

Rods: While a single rod and reel outfit might handle a variety of fishing, having specific outfits for each style of fishing can make the experience more enjoyable.

Fishing from shore requires a longer rod that can cast well and keep line above rocks or breaking waves. In boats, shorter rods are convenient.

Lure fishing for speedsters such as tuna requires a high-speed reel that can retrieve lures fast, and a powerful rod that casts well.

If pulling lures behind a boat (trolling) is the style of fishing you prefer, then short rods and large reels with extra line capacity can be used, as casting is not required.

For reef fishing with bait, or jigging, a powerful rod and reel helps an angler haul reef fish in before sharks strike.

For saltwater fly fishing, a freshwater trout outfit will not suffice. Specialist fly gear is needed.

Most rods today are made from carbon fibre, which is light and powerful. Fibreglass rods still have a following, and they withstand rough handling.

Rod (groin) buckets are useful when chasing big fish, or when surf fishing.

Don't underestimate the humble handline for bottom fishing from a boat. With gloves, the tug-of-war with a big fish can be fun.

With all gear, remember that quality is felt long after price is forgotten.

Rock fishing essentials

Travelling fishos who intend to go rock fishing must carry extra gear to enjoy safe and enjoyable fishing.

Long rods and line strong enough to handle big fish in the surge zone are just the start.

A long-handled gaff, or a three-pronged gaff on a rope with inward facing hooks that is sent down the line, are absolute musts, so that fish can be pulled safely from the danger zone.

In some localities where rock fishing is popular and king waves occur, anchor points have been installed so fishermen can attach themselves to minimise the chance of being washed away.

To make use of anchor points fishermen must carry a suitable lanyard.

Surprisingly few rock fishermen use anchor points, or wear slimline life jackets, perhaps because it appears "uncool".

As a result, rock fishing has become one of Australia's most dangerous sports. Every year fishermen are swept away to their deaths.

Many good rock spots require walking and/or climbing, so travel light. Shoe crampons can be useful in some areas, and a liability in others.

Rock fishing in much of northern Australia and the Queensland coast tends to be safer, as the waters are more sheltered, lacking the large swells produced by open ocean.

The biggest seas and most dangerous rock fishing spots are in WA, NSW and Victoria, and in SA, outside the two gulfs.

Beach and bank launching

Boat ramps are almost everywhere, but there are fishing spots that require beach or bank launching. A large 4WD vehicle is usually required to do this.

It is easy to get into difficulty, especially on beaches, where wave action washes sand away from the wheels. Never attempt a risky launch without a back-up vehicle.

Unsealed boat ramp

Keep tides in mind. A firm sandy bank launch at high tide might become a mudflat at low tide, and the launch slope and sand hardness may be different as the tide changes. Boaters must also consider the weather. It might be calm when the boat goes in, but what will it be like later retrieving in wind and waves?

Done carefully, with partially deflated tyres, large trailer boats can be launched from beaches.

Some fishos prefer to use small inflatable boats or cartoppers, and launch by hand or with a quad bike.

Extendable trailer drawbars and oversize jockey wheels can assist bank launching.

Mooring boats near camp sites requires cares, as large tides can hang a boat on the bank, or lift an anchor. Wading to moored boats is unwise in crocodile country.

Camping basics

Choosing a camping rig depends on where you are going and how often you will move.

Fast movers need a simple rig that sets up and pulls down quickly.

Some camper-trailers have a dinghy rack. There are also specialist vehicle roof racks for dinghies.

If you plan to go off the beaten track, be sure your camper-trailer or van is designed for rough roads. If it is not, grief awaits.

If heading north, a simple mesh tent with removable rain cover is ideal for tropical camping, where coastal temperatures are mild at night and hot in the day. Mesh tents allow breezes through while keeping out flying and crawling insects.

Buy a tent with midge mesh. Get a large size that fits table and chairs.

A large tarp gives shade and keeps dew off at night.

One-man mesh mozzie dome tents are ideal for sleeping in boats.

Enclosed tents are better for southern areas where cold and rain is likely.

In the tropics, a fridge or icebox is essential for perishables.

Remote camping requires self-sufficiency. **A detailed packing list is essential.**

Carry spare parts, including extra fishing gear.

Fishing remote country

The family sedan will safely get you to many fishing hotspots, including far-northern locations such as Weipa, Cooktown, Karumba, Darwin, Kakadu, Wyndham, Derby, Kununurra and Broome.

Sealed roads now lead to concrete boat ramps on most major waterways.

Much of the once infamous Cape York Peninsula road to Weipa is now sealed.

Nonetheless, a 4WD vehicle is often needed to go off the beaten track, and better handles muddy, sandy boat ramps, beach and bank launches, and unsealed roads.

A 4WD is also needed to access wet season fishing spots during flooding.

Driving through water crossings has long been part of the wet season fishing experience, and a high-clearance 4WD with snorkel is best for the job.

The toughness of a 4WD transmission is best for towing.

Some of the best fishing spots require sand driving.

Soft sand, rocky tracks and steep hill climbs require low-range gearing.

For long-distance touring it is best to use a large vehicle.

Diesel engines are more economical and reliable.

Older vehicles may represent excellent value, but buy a model with a good reputation.

Consider modifications such as a suspension lift, strong roof rack with dust cover, snorkel, bullbar, spotlights and heavy duty towball mount.

In Australia's heat, when towing heavy loads, often into strong headwinds, a vehicle's cooling system must be in good order.

Camping on the Karunjie Track, Pentecost River, WA

Boats

For corrugated dirt roads and tight bush tracks, a 3.5m to 3.7m cartopper dinghy or punt, mounted on a sturdy roof rack that allows easy loading, is hard to beat.

With a cartopper, there is no trailer to catch trees on tight tracks.

A solid dinghy will fish most rivers, billabongs and bays.

You might be able to nip out to a nearby island.

The downside is that dinghies are uncomfortable, even unsafe, in poor weather.

Cartoppers are a nuisance if you move camp each day or two, as you must repeatedly pull the boat down and set it up. But cartoppers can be driven into places bigger boats will not easily go.

Canoes and foldup boats are not recommended in northern waters, because large crocodiles may attack small boats.

While a "12-foot tinny' is versatile, boats of between 4m and 5.2m offer more scope for adventure, and this is the size-range generally chosen by dedicated barramundi fishos.

These boats can go further than cartoppers, and travelling is safer and more comfortable. Bigger boats carry more camping gear and supplies. Weekend trips may require sleeping space.

Alloy is the best hull material as it is light, strong, and resistant to knocks against rocks. Alloy boats are also easily customised.

All hulls require careful trailering over rough roads, with careful attention paid to hull supports.

Thick plate-alloy hulls are better for rough-road trailering, but must be well mounted on the trailer.

Trailers

To tow a boat where there are unsealed, corrugated roads you need a tough trailer. Few standard factory trailers are suitable.

The trailer must be correctly sprung. Dinghy trailers are often oversprung, sending extra shock through the boat.

Springs have to work hard, so carry spare springs and tools to replace them.

The boat must have a dust cover. Wrap the outboard motor in plastic wrap or a cover to keep road dust out.

The outboard leg will require a steel support with thick chafe resistant padding.

Heavy objects should be removed from a boat for towing as they can damage the hull.

Small outboard motors and batteries should be secured in the vehicle. If you plan to tackle tight bush tracks you may need an offroad trailer hitch instead of a towball.

A trailer should have ground clearance like the vehicle.

A trailer that takes the same rims and tyres as the vehicle lessens the need for spares.

When driving corrugations check the trailer for loose bolts every 50km, particularly on spring U-bolts. Carry spares.

Consider an auxiliary motor. A 5hp motor can get you home in most conditions.

An electric motor with GPS functionality allows easy "anchoring" with the spot lock, and auto-piloted trolling.

A bow headlight is useful at night. A sonar/GPS unit is almost essential.

Safety gear should include a VHF radio and satellite phone.

Carry extra drinking water.

Restoring our waterways

Aquatic habitat across Australia is being restored.

Removal of man-made fish passage barriers has become critically important as climate change amplifies periods of drought.

Barriers include dams, weirs, floodplain levee banks, road culverts and fords on public and private land.

Even stream height gauges can present a barrier.

Recent fish passage restoration projects include the Mackay-Whitsunday Fish Barrier Prioritisation Survey, which identified 9676 potential fish barriers.

The barrier sites have been prioritised and restoration projects planned, with some already completed.

South-East Queensland's Bremer River is an example of what can be done.

Berrys Weir was a 2.4m barrier blocking 41km of the river to fish migration.

The barrier impacted bass, sea mullet and long-finned eels, among other species.

A 33-ridge fishway was constructed at the weir, the largest rock ramp fishway built in Australia.

Fish, including reintroduced Mary River cod, can now negotiate the river.

Up to 4075 fish a day were recorded migrating upstream across the Bremer fishway.

These included juvenile sea mullet at 316 fish a day, freshwater mullet at 266 fish a day, and empire gudgeon at 2020 fish a day. While mullet and gudgeon are not sportfish for most of us, they form the diet of larger fish.

Fishways allow passage of juvenile diadromous species.

Diadromous fish spawn in an estuary, migrate to freshwater as juveniles, using freshwater as nursery habitat to grow quickly, then move back to the estuary to spawn.

Tedlands Creek fishway at Koumala

PICS COURTESY CATCHMENT SOLUTIONS

Bremer River fishway in South-East Queensland

Barra from Boundary Creek fishway

Shellfish Reef Projects

Lost shellfish reefs are being restored around Australia. Massive southern oyster reefs were mined for lime after white settlement, destroying the reefs. New reefs are being created using a bed of crushed rock. Fishing is often allowed on the reefs, but with special rules, such as no anchoring. There are shellfish reef projects at:

*Oyster Bay, Albany, WA.
*Gulf of St Vincent, SA.
*Port Phillip Bay, Victoria.
*Sydney Harbour, Brisbane Water, Hastings River and Macleay River, NSW.
*Bribie Island, Moreton Bay and Noosa River, Queensland.

Also in Queensland, the Tedlands Creek rock ramp fishway at Koumala recorded 5327 fish a day ascending the fishway, with barramundi recorded at 5.25 fish a day.

The barra were from 31-89mm in length. The more juveniles that make it upstream into wetlands, the more adult fish will make it back to the estuary.

Access to wetlands increases survival of fish, as it does for crustaceans such as giant freshwater prawn (cherabin).

A Boundary Creek cone fishway in the Rocky Dam Creek catchment recorded 1360 fish a day ascending to upper reaches. This included 28 barra a day from 25mm to 108mm in length. Tarpon (oxeye herring) were recorded at 7.39 fish per day.

Mackay's Gooseponds rock ramp fishway had 30,000 fish cross it on its biggest day, and averages 28,000 daily.

Queensland's Catchment Solutions' spokesman Matt Moore said Gooseponds had the best result of any fishway he had trapped.

Also in Queensland recently, a fishway was installed at Murray Creek near Mt Ossa, north of Mackay, and another at Sandy Creek south of Mackay.

Barrier removal projects have occurred in other states.

A Victorian study in 1999 found the state's Murray-Darling drainage alone had 310 stream gauges, 504 dams and weirs, 228 fords, 17 culverts and 86 natural fish barriers. The state's south-east waterways had 397 gauges, 535 dams and weirs, 210 fords, 31 culverts and 120 natural fish barriers.

Recent NSW projects include fishways on Karuah River, Wolli Creek, Warren Weir, Guningbar Creek, Duck Creek, Crooked Creek, Bumbuggan Creek and Island Creek.

The need to provide fish passage was recognised early in Australia, with the first recorded fishway built in 1913. A total of 44 fishways were built in NSW by 1985.

Unfortunately most early fishways were poorly built or designed.

The Far North benefits from wet season flooding can breach barriers for extended periods, however road crossings and weirs still limit passage during years of below average rainfall.

Resnagging the mighty Murray River

They might be a nuisance when your lure hooks them, but snags are critically important habitat.

The Murray River's lower reaches through South Australia are being restored with resnagging projects.

The river was historically de-snagged to help boats navigate, and to reduce flood damage. Habitat loss from the removal of snags contributed to declines in native fish populations.

Snags increase habitat for bacteria, algae, micro-organisms, invertebrates and crustaceans, and indirectly support water birds and marsupials.

Snags create food sources for native fish and support breeding by providing additional surfaces for eggs to be attached. Small native fish can take refuge from predators among snags.

Snags that are located near each other support localised groups of native fish, which is expected to create more resilient overall populations, especially important during challenging climatic conditions.

South Australia's resnagging project had introduced 47 snags into the river by 2021. In 2019, the pilot project added 24 snags at two sites - four snags at the initial test site downstream of Lock Four near Bookpurnong, and 20 snags downstream of Lock 3 near Banrock Station wetland.

In 2020 alone, 23 new snags were added, including 13 downstream of Lock Three near Overland Corner, and 10 downstream of Lock Four near Bookpurnong.

Snags adjacent to Banrock Station were found to have golden perch, silver perch, unspecked hardyhead, rainbowfish, cod, bony herring and Australian smelt.

Snag materials were sourced through the Katarapko Floodplain Project.

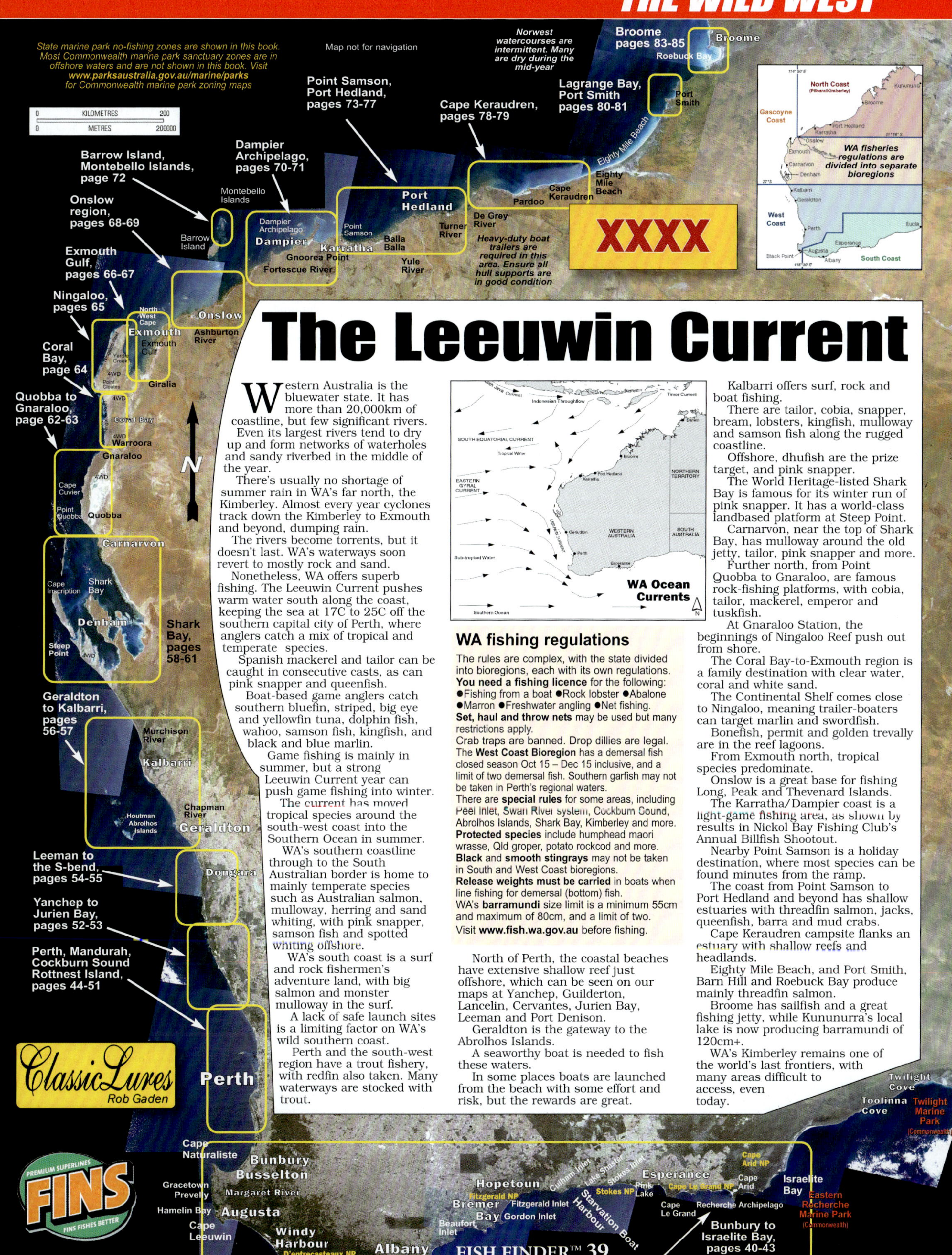

The Leeuwin Current

Western Australia is the bluewater state. It has more than 20,000km of coastline, but few significant rivers.

Even its largest rivers tend to dry up and form networks of waterholes and sandy riverbed in the middle of the year.

There's usually no shortage of summer rain in WA's far north, the Kimberley. Almost every year cyclones track down the Kimberley to Exmouth and beyond, dumping rain.

The rivers become torrents, but it doesn't last. WA's waterways soon revert to mostly rock and sand.

Nonetheless, WA offers superb fishing. The Leeuwin Current pushes warm water south along the coast, keeping the sea at 17C to 25C off the southern capital city of Perth, where anglers catch a mix of tropical and temperate species.

Spanish mackerel and tailor can be caught in consecutive casts, as can pink snapper and queenfish.

Boat-based game anglers catch southern bluefin, striped, big eye and yellowfin tuna, dolphin fish, wahoo, samson fish, kingfish, and black and blue marlin.

Game fishing is mainly in summer, but a strong Leeuwin Current year can push game fishing into winter.

The current has moved tropical species around the south-west coast into the Southern Ocean in summer.

WA's southern coastline through to the South Australian border is home to mainly temperate species such as Australian salmon, mulloway, herring and sand whiting, with pink snapper, samson fish and spotted whiting offshore.

WA's south coast is a surf and rock fishermen's adventure land, with big salmon and monster mulloway in the surf.

A lack of safe launch sites is a limiting factor on WA's wild southern coast.

Perth and the south-west region have a trout fishery, with redfin also taken. Many waterways are stocked with trout.

WA Ocean Currents

WA fishing regulations

The rules are complex, with the state divided into bioregions, each with its own regulations.

You need a fishing licence for the following: ●Fishing from a boat ●Rock lobster ●Abalone ●Marron ●Freshwater angling ●Net fishing.

Set, haul and throw nets may be used but many restrictions apply.

Crab traps are banned. Drop dillies are legal.

The **West Coast Bioregion** has a demersal fish closed season Oct 15 – Dec 15 inclusive, and a limit of two demersal fish. Southern garfish may not be taken in Perth's regional waters.

There are **special rules** for some areas, including Peel Inlet, Swan River system, Cockburn Sound, Abrolhos Islands, Shark Bay, Kimberley and more.

Protected species include humphead maori wrasse, Qld groper, potato rockcod and more.

Black and **smooth stingrays** may not be taken in South and West Coast bioregions.

Release weights must be carried in boats when line fishing for demersal (bottom) fish.

WA's **barramundi** size limit is a minimum 55cm and maximum of 80cm, and a limit of two.

Visit **www.fish.wa.gov.au** before fishing.

North of Perth, the coastal beaches have extensive shallow reef just offshore, which can be seen on our maps at Yanchep, Guilderton, Lancelin, Cervantes, Jurien Bay, Leeman and Port Denison.

Geraldton is the gateway to the Abrolhos Islands.

A seaworthy boat is needed to fish these waters.

In some places boats are launched from the beach with some effort and risk, but the rewards are great.

Kalbarri offers surf, rock and boat fishing.

There are tailor, cobia, snapper, bream, lobsters, kingfish, mulloway and samson fish along the rugged coastline.

Offshore, dhufish are the prize target, and pink snapper.

The World Heritage-listed Shark Bay is famous for its winter run of pink snapper. It has a world-class landbased platform at Steep Point.

Carnarvon, near the top of Shark Bay, has mulloway around the old jetty, tailor, pink snapper and more.

Further north, from Point Quobba to Gnaraloo, are famous rock-fishing platforms, with cobia, tailor, mackerel, emperor and tuskfish.

At Gnaraloo Station, the beginnings of Ningaloo Reef push out from shore.

The Coral Bay-to-Exmouth region is a family destination with clear water, coral and white sand.

The Continental Shelf comes close to Ningaloo, meaning trailer-boaters can target marlin and swordfish.

Bonefish, permit and golden trevally are in the reef lagoons.

From Exmouth north, tropical species predominate.

Onslow is a great base for fishing Long, Peak and Thevenard Islands.

The Karratha/Dampier coast is a light-game fishing area, as shown by results in Nickol Bay Fishing Club's Annual Billfish Shootout.

Nearby Point Samson is a holiday destination, where most species can be found minutes from the ramp.

The coast from Point Samson to Port Hedland and beyond has shallow estuaries with threadfin salmon, jacks, queenfish, barra and mud crabs.

Cape Keraudren campsite flanks an estuary with shallow reefs and headlands.

Eighty Mile Beach, and Port Smith, Barn Hill and Roebuck Bay produce mainly threadfin salmon.

Broome has sailfish and a great fishing jetty, while Kununurra's local lake is now producing barramundi of 120cm+.

WA's Kimberley remains one of the world's last frontiers, with many areas difficult to access, even today.

Cape Arid/Le Grand NP beach launches

- Thomas Fishery, soft sand, 4WD only, narrow track in, closed in winter in after rain.
- Barrier Anchorage, soft sand, 4WD only, tide dependant, summer only.
- Thomas River beach launch, soft sand, 4WD only.
- Seal Creek beach launch, soft sand, 4WD only, tide dependant.
- Poison Creek beach launch, soft sand, 4WD only, gravel track in, closed after winter rain.
- Duke of Orleans Bay, boat ramp.
- Lucky Bay, 4WD beach launch.
- Cape Le Grand Beach, 4WD beach launch.

No firearms or dogs allowed in the national parks.

Surf and salmon

The Great South-West

White sand, spectacular headlands and shallow inlets make up the coast west of the WA/SA border through to Perth. This is a dry region and the sea is clear and rarely discoloured by floodwater. The Southern Ocean rises out of deep water to meet a rugged coast that is swept each year by the warm Leeuwin Current from the west, which accounts for much of the seasonal aspects of the fishing. Near the WA/SA border the Nullabor Plain presents a cliff face to the ocean, with very little access to the water. Not until Esperance is there civilisation, with family holiday facilities. In recent times WA dhufish, Norwest blowfish and blacktip reef sharks have appeared off Esperance, while yellowtail kingfish and mulloway seem to be increasing in number. Conversely, pink snapper seem less common at inshore spots where they were once regularly caught, suggesting that local waters might be warming. The main species targeted in the south-west are still salmon, where large specimens of the WA subspecies are dubbed "blackbacks". When salmon are running the water goes dark with fish, and they are caught one after another. The salmon run extends to Perth when the water is cool enough, but some south-west areas, notably Esperance and Bremer Bay, have salmon all year. Also in the estuaries are spotted, sand and yellowfin whiting, yellow-eye mullet, black bream, tarwhine, flathead, flounder, silver trevally, gar and herring. In the surf, mulloway are found all year, although salmon, mullet and herring are the more usual catch. Snook, breaksea cod, leatherjackets, harlequin fish, queen snapper (blue morwong), and samson are found offshore. In the more remote areas blue groper grow large, and offshore are red bight snapper, also known as nannygai. Despite being a dry part of the world, trout and redfin are found in some south-west streams, but the bream fishing in the inlets is far more reliable, with trophy black bream caught each year. Just within the SA border is Yalata, home of some of the country's best mulloway beaches. Along the Great Australian Bight there is limited fishable access to the coast for more than 500km. If you are fit, you can do the steep climb down the cliff to Toolinna Cove, about 400km west of the SA/WA border, which might produce big salmon, mulloway, trevally or sharks. Otherwise, the first area of great interest to fishos travelling west is the Israelite Bay region and Cape Arid National Park, 150km west of Esperance.

Israelite Bay

This area requires high-clearance 4WD and self-sufficiency. Tyres must be deflated for the sand tracks. Never drive over seaweed piles, as bogging is inevitable. Beach launching within the shallow bay is only for cartoppers or kayaks. Bigger boats are better off launched elsewhere within Cape Arid NP. Israelite Bay is sheltered and shallow and has good whiting fishing, but beach fishing is better on the deeper 40-Mile Beach north of the bay, or around Point Malcolm 25km to the south. Salmon is the main species, usually all year, with silver trevally, herring, mullet and mulloway all a chance. Storms can carpet the area with weed, making access hard. The Eastern Group of Islands are 10km and 25km out. For visitors who drive in from Esperance via Fisheries Rd (the usual route), the last fuel outlet is Condingup, 80km from Esperance. There are shaded camp sites near Israelite Bay and at Point Malcolm. More coastal camps are to the south-west at Seal and Jorndee Creeks, and Thomas Fishery. Heading north-east from Israelite Bay, well organised 4WD fishos can travel via the beach at low tide about 120km north to Point Culver, where there is more good surf fishing. A track leads up the cliffs and back to the highway. A Commonwealth marine sanctuary applies wide of Israelite Bay.

Wharton

Wharton lies about half way between Cape Arid and Esperance, on the Duke of Orleans Bay off Orleans Bay Rd, near the mouth of the Dailey River. The bay has a caravan park and reasonably sheltered beach launching, and there is no shortage of reef within 10km of Wharton, including Bay Rock, Dodd Rock and John Island within the bay. Three island groups lay within 15km of the launch site. For landbased fishos, there are many tracks leading off the main roads to scenic and fishable coastal access points. Dunns

Esperance Landbased

A 415m public jetty was opened in 2021 following the demolition of the once popular Tanker Jetty in 2019. The new jetty produces skippy, herring, squid, snook, gar, flathead and more. For surf fanatics, Roses Beach, about 35km west of town, is one of the best local beaches for big salmon. Other salmon spots include West Beach, Chapmans Point, Stockyards and Salmon Beach. Salmon are about all year, but Sept/Oct and just before Easter produce the biggest fish. Herring are all year but best in summer. Winter full moons are best for gummy sharks, while mulloway are best on new or full moons all year. Kingfish are a regular catch off the rocks, with king george whiting on coastal grounds, and mullet along sheltered beaches in autumn/winter. Rock fishing in this region is dangerous.

Esperance GPS Marks

There are many worthwhile lumps and bumps near Esperance. The first 12 marks are within 30km of the boat harbour. Fishing reefs around the islands is a good starting point.
Note that reefs may break unexpectedly.

a. Tuesday Rock 33 54.205S 121 50.345E
b. Bail Rock 33 51.582S 121 59.531E
c. Pot Rock 33 54.538S 121 54.495E
d. Sweep Rock 33 53.189S 122 00.398E
e. Sunday Patch 33 55.797S 121 49.790E
f. Dolphin Rock 33 54.999S 122 00.876E
g. Black Island Nth 33 54.326S 121 59.833E
h. 29m Ground 33 57.712S 121 56.024E
i. 'Wonky Finger' 33 56.192S 122 02.912E
j. Time Rock 33 57.703S 122 02.298E
k. Douglass Patch 33 58.419S 121 49.791E
l. Douglass West 33 58.557S 121 48.446E

Off map ...

Sunk Rocks 34 00.058S 121 46.654E
Hendy East 34 03.069S 121 54.767E
Beagle Reef Nth 34 00.829S 121 58.157E
Beagle Reef Sth 34 01.657S 121 57.826E
Smiths Rock Sth 34 04.027S 121 51.865E
Leg of Lamb Bank 34 04.075S 121 49.595E

Esperance Artificial Reef

A. The reef consists of 'Apollos', 'Abitats' and 128 reef dome modules. It was installed in 31m of water 8km east of Esperance in 2018.
Approx 33 52.263S 121 58.834E

Rocks, about 20km west of Wharton, produces salmon and mulloway. Wharton Beach and its nearby rocks fish well. Just 20km east is Alexander Bay, with good rock and beach fishing. Kennedys Beach and Tagon Point 38km east of Wharton fish well for trevally, salmon, sharks and mulloway. The Thomas River has bream. It flows into Yokinup Bay, where salmon and mulloway are caught in the surf, at the start of Cape Arid NP. Poison Creek beach between Cape Arid and Cape Pasley is renowned for big salmon. It can be reached by 4WD track, and then by driving on the beach. Sharks, mulloway and tailor patrol gutters at night.

Esperance

The town has sheltered boat launching facilities with good spots nearby. The beach fishing is incredible when big salmon are running. The fish bite all year, but are usually best around Sep/Oct and just before Easter as they migrate back and forth. Otherwise, herring, trevally, mullet and whiting are the main surf catch. Boaters will find spotted whiting, squid, pink snapper and herring. Samson and kingfish are commonly caught. A seaworthy trailerboat gives access to the Recherche Archipelago, keeping in mind the powerful Southern Ocean. Expect unexpected wave breaks over reefs. Rock fishing is good at many locations, but dangerous. Some sites west of the town have anchor points installed, and lifejacket hire is available from Tackle World in Esperance. Launching is easy at Bandy Creek Boat Harbour. The town ramp is good, but is exposed to easterly weather. A new public jetty was built in 2021 to replace the historic Tanker Jetty, and it fishes well for gar, salmon, herring, whiting, mullet and squid. The road follows the coast west of Esperance and gives access to good fishing at West Beach, Chapmans Point, Hughes Step, Salmon Beach, Fourth Beach and Nine Mile Beach. East of Esperance is Cape Le Grand National Park, a large area with good rock and beach fishing. Beach launching is possible in calm weather. Landbased spots in Cape Le Grand NP include Lucky Bay, Rossiter Bay, Hellfire Bay and Thistle Cove. A Commonwealth marine sanctuary applies to the Tory Islands, 45km south-east of Esperance.

Stokes Inlet

This 6km-long inlet is 80km west of Esperance, with the first campsite about 4km from the highway. It is a worthwhile stop for those who love black bream. Other species are available when the inlet opens to sea. Floodwater from the Young and Lort Rivers open the entrance after high rainfall. The estuary is up to 10m deep.

Hopetoun

The location in the middle of nowhere makes this town of 300 attractive to touring fishermen. It is 585km from Perth, 258km from Albany and 239km west of Esperance. Another attraction is the feature-rich bottom within 12km south-south-east of the jetty and boat ramp. Beware the drying reef south-west of the ramp. Local species include queen and pink snapper, samson, kingfish, and harlequin fish. Quoin Head to the west of Hopetoun, is accessible by rough 4WD track, with good rock fishing for large fish. Nearby Mason Bay also fishes well. Munglinup Beach is protected by reef. It has camping and 4WD beach launching, though the beach is 2WD accessible. Just 7km west of Hopetoun is the 5km-long Culham Inlet, which has black bream, but the Phillips River is more reliable. Starvation Boat Harbour, 40km east of Hopetoun, is not much of a boat harbour, but an east-facing beach, with camping at the north end. Beach launching is in good weather only.

Bremer Bay

This area has some of the best beach and rock fishing in the south-west, and excellent bream fishing in the Bremer River's Wellstead Estuary. A 4WD is needed to reach the best surf spots. For the family fisho, Short Beach is has a sealed road and good salmon fishing. Fosters and Reef Beaches require high-clearance 4WD, with salmon and trevally. Many rock platforms in this area drop into deep water and can produce samson, kingfish, pink snapper and mulloway. There is a boat ramp in the lower Bremer River at Muirs Point. The estuary entrance beach has mulloway when the bar opens. There is a marina boat ramp at Fishery Beach. A 4WD track leads 17km north of Bremer township to Gordon Inlet, with bream in the upper river for cartopper and canoe fishos. Further north, beach launching is inside Point Ann at Cheadanup, located on the rabbit proof fence. This is part of Fitzgerald River National Park. It is about 180km by road between Albany and Bremer Bay, with public launch sites at Two People's Bay, Cheynes Beach, and Cape Riche.

The Salmon Migration

Two Australian salmon species migrate along the east and west coasts each year. *Arripis truttacea* occurs off WA, SA, Victoria and Tasmania. Spawning is in southern WA in the Esperance/Albany region from March to April. Juveniles are carried east on the Leeuwin Current in early winter. They arrive in SA nurseries from July to September. Juveniles are also found in WA waters. Mature salmon migrate back from SA to WA waters, though some adults remain in SA. If Perth waters cool enough, salmon reach the metropolitan area, especially around Rottnest Island, about May. Eastern salmon (*Arripis trutta*) occur in NSW, Victoria and Tasmania. Juveniles are found in sheltered coastal waters and estuaries, mainly in the southern part of the species range. East Coast fish spawn in coastal waters from November to February. The East Coast fish travel at least as far north as Sydney. In Victoria and Tasmania there is an overlap of both species.

Albany

Albany (see map next page) is a popular fishing location because it offers safe sea access for boaters, and has beaches facing in different directions, allowing anglers to fish out of prevailing winds, with relatively sheltered water near the town. There is a summer prawn and blue crab run. An annual salmon run occurs on scenic beaches, and the fish will bite until anglers are exhausted. Sadly, rock fishing off Albany combines big waves and smooth, slippery rocks, a fatal recipe. Boat launching is at the town ramp, Frenchmans Bay, Emu Point, Misery Beach and Lower King. A few of Albany's better spots are:

- Bornholm Beach, accessible via rough 4WD track, produces salmon and herring.
- Shelley Beach, accessible by 2WD, has mostly salmon;
- Mutton Bird Island, most species, can be reached by 2WD to the carpark, and 4WD beyond.
- Torbay Inlet, black bream.
- Salmon Holes, one of the best salmon spots near Albany in late summer and autumn, accessible by 2WD. Avoid the rocks, people have drowned there.
- Frenchman Bay, a good spot to take the boat, beach launching.
- Princess Royal Harbour, most species for small boat fishos.
- Oyster Harbour, bream in the snaggy King and Kalgan Rivers.
- Middleton Beach; easy access to salmon fishing from town.
- Two Peoples Bay, boat launching in calm weather.
- The Sand Patch, landbased reef fishing for most species, a long walk down steep stairs located next to the local prison.
- Normans Beach, salmon. Fishermen must park and walk.
- Cheyne Beach, one of the best salmon beaches.

Albany also has the HMAS *Perth* artificial reef for divers, and there are several natural reefs in and near King George Sound.

Albany Offshore Marks

The inside of the islands are reasonably sheltered. Beware breaking waves over reefs.

GPS Marks

a. Gio Batta Patch 35 02.852S 117 59.725E
b. 18m reef 35 03.955S 117 58.053E
8m rise 35 02.972S 117 56.773E
c. Michaelmas Reef 35 02.906S 118 00.395E
d. Herald Rocks 35 01.630S 118 02.320E
e. 22m reef 35 01.984S 118 03.723E
f. East Shoal 35 05.943S 118 03.219E and also West Shoal 35 05.956S 118 02.469E
g. Breaksea West 35 03.736S 118 04.713E

Wrecks

A. HMAS *Perth*, buoyed, diving only.
B. *Cheynes III*, buoyed, diving only.

Shellfish Reef Restoration

In 1791 an early explorer named Oyster Harbour for the number and size of its oysters. By the late 1800s they were gone, from over-harvesting, poor water quality and disease. An ongoing project is now restoring the oyster reefs, reconstructing them with limestone rock rubble. Local fishing is expected to improve markedly as the reefs grow.

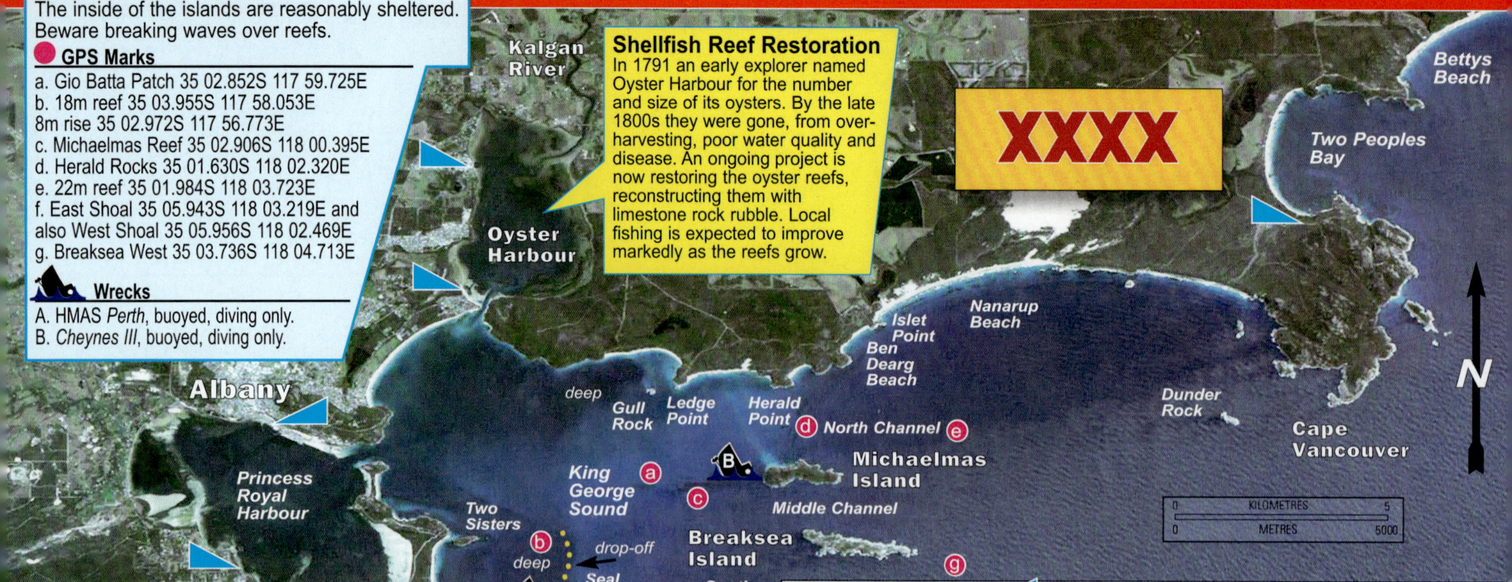

Map not for navigation.
Beware waves breaking over submerged reefs

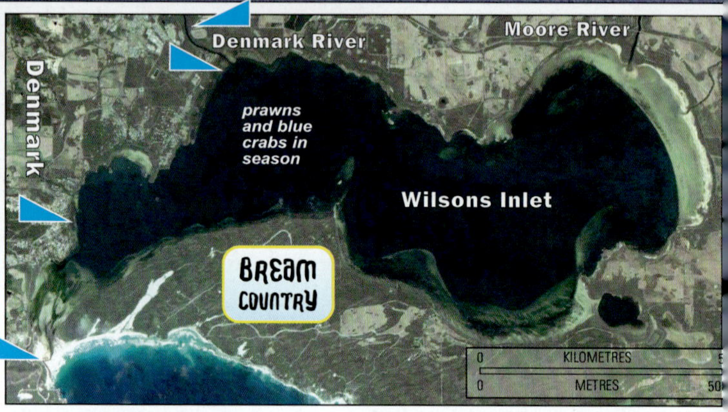

Denmark

The main feature here is Wilson Inlet, fed by the Little, Denmark and Hay Rivers. Boat ramps are on the west bank near the sea entrance, one of these being a sand launch into the sea just inside Wilson Head. Wilson Inlet is a large waterway that produces pink snapper, spotted whiting and bluespot flathead, as well as mullet, bream, tarwhine and crabs. Pink snapper fish well when the bar opens in winter. The inlet has good runs of prawns and blue crabs. Launching is at Rivermouth Caravan Park, Inlet Drive, and Denmark River, South Coast Highway, east of the traffic bridge, and off Minsterly Road. Hay River is best for quality bream. Ocean Beach outside the inlet has superb salmon fishing in late summer and autumn, as well as mulloway and pink snapper. It can be reached by 4WD when the inlet is closed. The rocks at the western end produce large fish, including samson and kingfish. Beach launching is possible at Ocean Beach, Madfish Bay, Peaceful and Parry Beach in good conditions.

Other spots include:

- McGeary's Rock (Ocean Beach) 11km south of Denmark, along Ocean Beach Rd. Drive past the main carpark, up the hill and take the second turn on the left. Sand whiting, mulloway, trevally, sampson, herring and salmon. Beach launching in good conditions.
- Flat Rock (Ocean Beach). Park in the main carpark, walk to the beach, turning right towards the rocks and take the track behind the rocks. Trevally, herring, whiting, salmon.
- Lights Beach. Beach and rock fishing. Drive 8km along Ocean Beach Rd, turning right onto Lights Rd for about 5km then turn left to the beach. Trevally, herring and salmon.
- Elephant Rocks (William Bay). Good here for spotted whiting. Go west on the South Coast Hwy for 14km and turn left into William Bay Rd. Turn left at the carpark, right after 50m and into the carpark. Walk 500m along the trail to the Elephant Cove. Most species.
- Waterfall Beach and Madfish Bay is a safe, scenic spot. Turn left at William Bay carpark, then a gravel road to Waterfall Beach. About 1km further is Madfish Bay. Herring, spotted and sand whiting, and trevally. Salmon from February to May. Snorkelling at Greens Pool. Boat launching in good conditions.
- Parry Beach is about 25km west, of Denmark along the South Coast Hwy. Beach and rock fishing by 4WD. Most species, including mulloway, samson and sharks. Beach launching in good conditions. Camping available, call Denmark Shire (08 9848 0300).
- Hilliers Beach, Parry Beach Rd. Drive past the holiday park turn-off, continue 300m then park and walk to beach. Herring, trevally and whiting.
- Boat Harbour (4WD only) is a scenic spot. About 30km west of Denmark, along the South Coast Hwy, turn left and travel 10km along a rough track. There is a protected bay with a surf beach and exposed reef. Most species.
- Peaceful Bay. This is 44km west of Denmark. Take Peaceful Bay Rd to the beach and turn left onto the beach, for herring, whiting, salmon and rock fish. Boat launching.
- Conspicuous Beach 51km west of Denmark for herring, sand whiting and salmon.

Walpole-Nornalup

Walpole has a large inlet which has two main parts, separated by a channel. There is a private ramp at Rest Point, with public launch sites at Walpole town jetty, Coalmine Beach and Nornalup. The shallow estuary tailor, herring, flathead, juvenile salmon, tarwhine, cobbler and flounder. The system is fed by the Frankland, Deep and Walpole Rivers, which have bream, with redfin and occasional trout in the upper Frankland. Shore fishing is best at Coalmine Beach and the west shore, and on the west side of the sea entrance at Skippy Rock. Sea access from the estuary is possible by boat in good conditions, but is often dangerous. West of Walpole a road leads to Mandalay Beach carpark. This deep beach has mulloway, salmon, tailor and sharks, as well as smaller species. East of Walpole, big fish can be caught at Conspicuous Beach, accessible by 2WD. To the east, Peaceful Bay community has a boat ramp and reef fishing nearby for samson, groper, kingfish, snapper, blue morwong and more. Irwin Inlet flows into the bay and has bream, as does its Kent River. Further east, Parry Beach has camping, 4WD beach launching and beach/rock fishing, with deeper water at adjacent Mazzoletti Beach.

Windy Harbour

Boats launch from the beach, where there is camping. To the west 40km is the pristine Broke Inlet, a pristine 4500ha expanse of water scenic water. It has quiet camping spots, accessible by 4WD. The inlet is fed primarily by the Shannon River, which is closed to fishing. The inlet's 4km long entrance usually only opens in winter, and the exposed surf beach outside can be productive.

Augusta

For the touring fisho, Augusta has a large estuary, worthwhile rivers, and safe launching into the sea through a big marina inside Cape Leeuwin. There are reef grounds extending south-east from Cape Leeuwin, keeping in mind the Ngari Capes Marine Park sanctuary. Hardy Inlet is fed by the Blackwood and Scott Rivers. A dinghy gives access to the estuary's bream, spotted and yellowfin whiting, trevally, flathead, cobbler, herring, mullet, flounder, prawns and blue crabs. The Blackwood River has some huge bream, along with whiting, but light tackle and fresh or live bait is a must. Sea-run trout are a chance, with mostly redfin far upstream. Beach fishing east of the inlet entrance is good, with 4WD tracks leading through to Windy Harbour, with creek mouths along the way. Salmon are the main catch in late summer/autumn. In poor weather some beaches north of Augusta offer shelter. Spots include:

- Colour Patch, near the shops at the estuary mouth - whiting, flathead, bream, trevally, herring.
- Ellis St Jetty, as above, with mulloway at night.
- Ringbolt Bay, squid, whiting, herring.
- Deepdene - 4WD track off Cosy Corner Rd, beach fishing.
- Hamelin Bay, north of Augusta, fish the beach by 4WD or travel further to Caves Rd.
- Skippy Rock, trevally, herring, samson, kingfish and snapper.

KILOMETRES 0 5
METRES 0 5000
N
Blackwood River
Scott River
Molloy Island
Thomas Island
Hardy Inlet
Swan Lake
Augusta

Offshore
Reef extends from Cape Leeuwin just 7km south of the sea entrance. Chart AUS116 reveals plenty of ground to explore.

Cape Leeuwin, East Flinders Bay and Flinders Island Sanctuary Zones exist in this area within the **Ngari Capes Marine Park.**

Maps not for navigation

Public boat ramps are located within the marina rock walls, providing safe launching

Yallingup

The township has a van park and shop. Torpedo Rocks south of Yallingup is a productive platform, but dangerous. Smiths Beach has salmon in autumn, mulloway in winter and big tailor in summer. Canal Rocks is more sheltered, with herring and trevally, and there is a boat ramp. Wyadup Rocks is accessible by sealed road. It is not safe, but offers the chance of tuna. Further south, Injidup Point has smaller species, and requires care. Further south a 4WD track passes good beaches, with Moses Rock a highlight, the platforms reachable after a long walk. Samson are a chance here. Yallingup has a small sanctuary under the Ngari Capes Marine Mark, with a larger Indijup sanctuary off Cape Clairault to the south.

Cape Naturaliste

Rock fishing on the west side of the cape is good, but dangerous. A long-handled gaff allows safer landing of fish. Samson, salmon, kingfish, tuna and sharks are all here. A rough track follows the coast. Sugarloaf Rock is one of the better spots. There is good fishing off the rocks between Sugarloaf Rock and the Cape itself. The Sugarloaf track off the Cape Naturaliste Rd is accessible by 2WD, but most other tracks in this area need 4WD. For boaters, Wright Bank off the point has dhufish, pink snapper, queen snapper and breaksea cod. Around Cape Naturaliste and entering Geographe Bay, the rocky point around Bunker Bay is reasonably sheltered and good for autumn salmon. This area is also worthwhile for boaters, launching from Dunsborough. An artificial reef installed 7km off Dunsborough in early 2014 (see diagram) has pink snapper, samson, dhufish and more. A sister reef was installed off Bunbury. Watch for bonito and tuna. The HMAS *Swan* dive wreck lies 6.7km to the west of the artificial reef, part of the Ngari Capes Marine Park, which includes sanctuary zones, with a larger Commonwealth zone 40km west of Cape Naturaliste. Dunsborough has small beaches and rocky areas that fish well for salmon and herring in autumn. Tailor and trevally also show up. Try Casle Bay an Meelup. At Wonnerup crabs and squid are caught in the estuary. The beach has herring, trevally, whiting and flathead.

Busselton

The shallow beach is good for spotted and yellowfin whiting, flathead and flounder. Boaters chase crabs and squid in the shallows. Busselton's long jetty is famous, with bluefin and yellowfin tuna, bonito, samson fish and mulloway all possible, with john dory around the pylons. The end of jetty is a sanctuary. The Capel River river mouth has mulloway after rain. The river has small bream, with tailor at the mouth. Peppermint Grove Beach south of Capel River produces tailor, whiting, herring, flathead, flounder and trevally. Forrest Beach has most surf species, with mulloway after rain opens up the creeks.

Bunbury

There is an artificial reef 5km off Point Casuarina, installed in 2014. The Cut at the mouth of Leschenault Inlet has landbased fishing for small mulloway, tailor, herring and salmon. The inlet has blue crabs in summer, with spotted whiting, bream, flounder, flathead and herring. Harbour breakwaters have tailor and mulloway, with bream and whiting in the harbour. Mulloway at night. Preston and Collie Rivers have bream. The Collie has small mulloway. Back Beach, south of the harbour breakwaters, has herring and tailor, with salmon in autumn.

Ngari Capes Marine Park

Sanctuary zones apply from Busselton south to around Augusta. See the latest online sanctuary zone maps at **www.fish.wa.gov.au**

Bunbury & Dunsborough Artificial Reefs

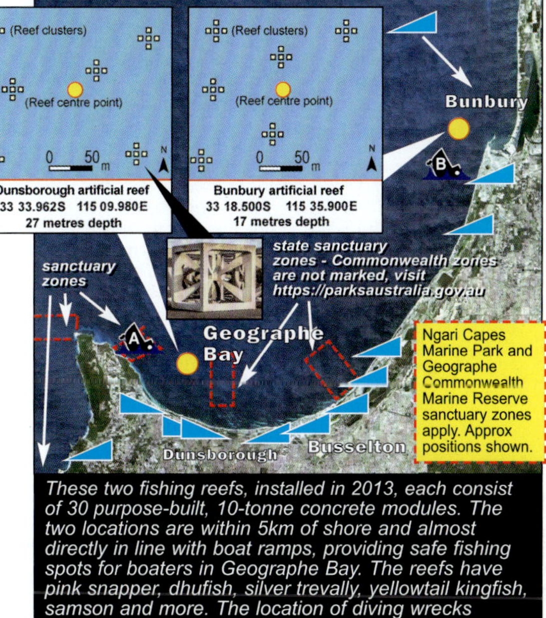

These two fishing reefs, installed in 2013, each consist of 30 purpose-built, 10-tonne concrete modules. The two locations are within 5km of shore and almost directly in line with boat ramps, providing safe fishing spots for boaters in Geographe Bay. The reefs have pink snapper, dhufish, silver trevally, yellowtail kingfish, samson and more. The location of diving wrecks HMAS Swan (A) and Lena (B) are also shown.

Margaret River region

North of Augusta, Hamelin Bay, Prevelly, Gracetown and Canal Rocks are popular destinations for boaters. Gracetown's Cowaramup Bay is picturesque and has a van park, beach launching and good grounds nearby. Beaches and rocks in this area have tailor, salmon, herring, trevally and groper, but care is required on the rocks. Note that Kilcarnup Sanctuary Zone exists north of Cape Mentelle, with the Cape Freycinet Zone about 15km to the south. A larger sanctuary zone exists wide of Cape Freycinet under the South West Commonwealth Marine Reserve.

Key to Map

Hotspots

1. San Remo to Mandurah. Beach has tailor, salmon in season, Mulloway in deep gutters and whiting and herring during day.
2. Peel Inlet Mouth: whiting, herring, tailor and salmon in season. Pink snapper in storms.
3. Halls Head: long beach with herring and whiting in the day and big mulloway and tailor at night. Salmon in season. Expect to lose rigs on the reef.
4. Falcon Bay: a popular spot to take children as it is protected and has herring, yellowfin and sand whiting. The point reef areas have tailor, salmon.
5. Dawsville Cut: herring, yellowfin and KG whiting and tailor inside, with herring, tailor and salmon at the ocean end. Pink snapper in storms. There are many jetties and platforms.
6. Tims Thicket: First accessible beach in the metro area, a 4WD is best or park and walk down. Good salmon in season, also tailor, herring and whiting. Yelloweye mullet at times.
7. White Hills: 4WD essential. Variety of species. Herring and whiting in day. Popular for salmon. Tailor in evenings, with mulloway. Snapper in storms.
8. Point Grey: a great summer spot for surface luring yellowfin whiting. Ideal flat for scooping blue crabs.

Launch sites

Ramps can be used on most tides.

1. Mary St Lagoon, multi-lane, large carpark, fish cleaning.
2. Waterside Cres, single lane, reasonable carpark.
3. Multi-lane ramp, reasonable parking off Dampier Ave.
4. Shallow sand ramp, Olive Rd.
5. Rees Place, in canal area, multi-lanes, large carpark, $10 fee, washdown available
6. Leprechaun ramp: multi-lanes, good parking, off Estuary Rd.
7. Park Ridge, single lane off Estuary Rd, limited parking.
8. Coondanup, single lane, Birchley Rd.
9. Nairn's ramp: Nairn Rd, multi-lanes, small carpark, finger jetty.
10. Riverside Dve, Furnissdale Rd, small ramp, finger jetties.
11. Batavia Quays, multi-lane, jetty.
12. Culeenup Rd, Yunderup/North Rd intersection, one lane.
13. Wharf Cove, off Camarri Way, multi-lanes, large carpark.
14. Murray Bend, Ravenswood Rd, one lane.
15. Mandurah Quays, one lane, finger jetty, often gated.
16. Melros Beach, off Melros Beach Rd, beach launch, 4WD.
17. Avalon Beach, corner of Yeedong Rd and Avalon Pd, beach launch, 4WD.
18. Mandurah Ocean Marina, off Breakwater Pde, single lane, good parking, fish cleaning.
19. Pinjarra boat ramp: off Henry St, single lane, reasonable parking.
20. Mariners Cove, off Waterlily Dve, good parking, finger jetty.

Wrecks

A. Mandurah Artificial Reef - see next page.

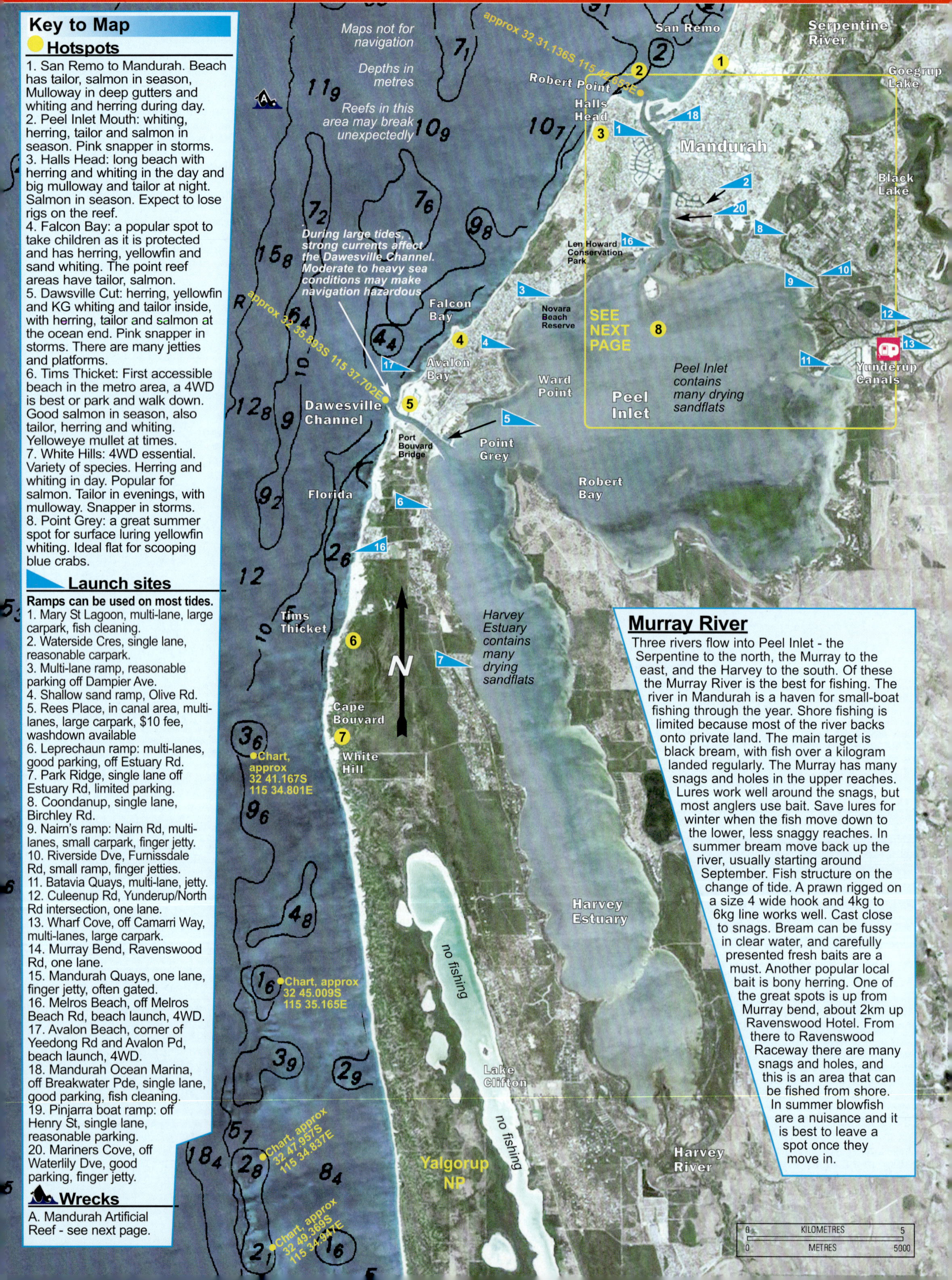

Maps not for navigation
Depths in metres
Reefs in this area may break unexpectedly
approx 32 31.136S 115 42.653E
San Remo
Serpentine River
Goegrup Lake
Robert Point
Halls Head
Mandurah
Black Lake
Len Howard Conservation Park
During large tides, strong currents affect the Dawesville Channel. Moderate to heavy sea conditions may make navigation hazardous
approx 32 35.893S 115 37.702E
Falcon Bay
Novara Beach Reserve
SEE NEXT PAGE
Avalon Bay
Ward Point
Peel Inlet
Peel Inlet contains many drying sandflats
Yunderup Canals
Dawesville Channel
Port Bouvard Bridge
Point Grey
Robert Bay
Florida
Tims Thicket
Harvey Estuary contains many drying sandflats
N
Cape Bouvard
White Hill
Chart, approx 32 41.167S 115 34.801E
Harvey Estuary
no fishing
Chart, approx 32 45.009S 115 35.165E
Lake Clifton
no fishing
Chart, approx 32 47.957S 115 34.837E
Yalgorup NP
Harvey River
Chart, approx 32 49.369S 115 34.947E
KILOMETRES
METRES
5000

Murray River

Three rivers flow into Peel Inlet - the Serpentine to the north, the Murray to the east, and the Harvey to the south. Of these the Murray River is the best for fishing. The river in Mandurah is a haven for small-boat fishing through the year. Shore fishing is limited because most of the river backs onto private land. The main target is black bream, with fish over a kilogram landed regularly. The Murray has many snags and holes in the upper reaches. Lures work well around the snags, but most anglers use bait. Save lures for winter when the fish move down to the lower, less snaggy reaches. In summer bream move back up the river, usually starting around September. Fish structure on the change of tide. A prawn rigged on a size 4 wide hook and 4kg to 6kg line works well. Cast close to snags. Bream can be fussy in clear water, and carefully presented fresh baits are a must. Another popular local bait is bony herring. One of the great spots is up from Murray bend, about 2km up Ravenswood Hotel. From there to Ravenswood Raceway there are many snags and holes, and this is an area that can be fished from shore. In summer blowfish are a nuisance and it is best to leave a spot once they move in.

Mandurah Artificial Reef

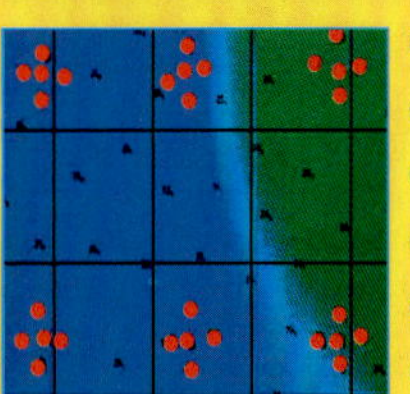

Cluster 1	32 31.532S 115 34.931E
Cluster 2	32 31.532S 115 34.979E
Cluster 3	32 31.534S 115 35.028E
Cluster 4	32 31.585S 115 34.931E
Cluster 5	32 31.587S 115 34.979E
Cluster 6	32 31.588S 115 35.026E

This reef consists of 30 concrete modules of 3sqm each, spread over 4ha in clusters of five. It is similar to the Bunbury/Dunsborough reefs to the south. The Mandurah reef is 9km from the Dawesville Cut and 12km from the Mandurah estuary entrance, in 25m of water, on flat sand. Expect to catch pink snapper, dhufish, trevally, baldchin, samson fish, tailor and more.

Special rules

Mandurah waters fall into the West Coast Bioregion and special rules are in place to combat overfishing. The demersal finfish season closes from October 15 through to December 15 in an area from just south of Shark Bay through to Black Point, near Augusta. During this period the taking of demersal species is prohibited. If you catch a demersal finfish during this period it must be returned to the water. Visit **www.fish.wa.gov.au** for details.

Crabs

Blue swimmer crabs are found throughout Peel and Harvey estuaries and around Mandurah. In deep water the best technique is to use a drop net baited with fresh mullet. Leave the net on the bottom for 3-6 minutes then retrieve in a swift smooth motion. Scooping for crabs is popular on the flats during day and night, but wear shoes to protect feet from glass, crab claws and cobbler stings. A large crabbing closure, including estuaries and open sea, from about Fremantle to Bunbury, applies from Sept 1 to Nov 30. A large area around Cockburn Sound is closed to crabbing all year. Check the WA Fisheries website for closure area limits and any changed or new restrictions.

5 knots within all canals

Local species advice from Tuckeys Tackle

- **Herring:** caught all year with small hooks and berley cages.
- **Mackerel:** caught when waters start reaching 22C, the James Service and Five Fathom Bank are great trolling areas.
- **WA dhufish:** found on deep reefs off Mandurah and also the James Service and Five Fathom Bank. Use octopus or mullet baits, metal jigs and soft plastics.
- **Mulloway:** try deep gutters off Mandurah beaches and rock walls, they are a viable lure target in canals and marinas.
- **Pink snapper:** caught on the James Service and Five Fathom reefs using unweighted pilchards. Use a berley trail at anchor. Caught off the ends of Mandurah and Dawesville channels during storms.
- **Salmon:** the run lasts from Easter to June/July. Bait and lures.
- **Samson fish:** on most reefs off Mandurah. Five Fathom and James service reefs produce big ones.
- **Skippy:** *In the Mandurah and Dawesville channels, landbased and boat fishing. Use berley at the Five Fathom and James Service Reefs.
- **Tailor:** popular in summer on the beaches, many school sized (30-40cm) tailor, with bigger fish in winter. Also caught in the Peel and Harvey estuary by trolling small lures.
- **Yellowfin whiting:** Peel and Harvey estuaries hold huge numbers in summer. Also found in the Dawesville channel and the flats around the Old Traffic Bridge.
- **KG whiting:** found in Dawesville Cut when the water turns dirty, larger fish on reefs. Use squid bait.
- **Squid:** found in the shallows of the Dawesville and Mandurah channel around weedbeds. Use a small jig (size 2.0-2.5) as they can be spooky on bigger jigs.
- **Black bream:** popular in Murray and Serpentine Rivers, canals and marinas. River prawn baits work best, and lures.
- **Prawns:** both river prawn and Mandurah king prawns after big rains. Fish either side of old or new traffic bridges on foot or by boat.

Key to Map

Hotspots

1. Peel Inlet mouth to Mandurah foreshore: Rocky foreshore has herring, yellowfin and king george whiting, crabs in the day, cobbler at night. Wade with a crab scoop during summer for blue crabs.
2. Port Mandurah Canals: best fished by small boat for big yellowfin whiting and small mulloway. Crabs.
3. Old Traffic Bridge: fishing platforms underneath. Herring, tailor, yellowfin and king george whiting, tarwhine and crabs are regular catches. Cobbler at night. Mulloway too, but these are usually lost in the pylons. During the prawn run scoop nets and lanterns are used to catch big king prawns that run out with the tide.
4. Waterside Canals: best fished with a boat for whiting and crabs. Mouth has small tailor. Crabs. Cobbler at night.
5. Bypass Bridge: This bridge was also built with fishing platforms. Crabbing is popular using drop nets, and king prawns can be scooped on the outgoing tides under the lights at night. Herring, tailor and whiting at times.
6. Scoop crabs from shore here - usually best during summer. Use shoes to protect feet from glass. Floating tub to put crabs in. Other locations are Cox Bay near Falcon, Dawesville and Coodanup.
7. Serpentine River: crabs can be found a long way upstream. Some big black bream - try early morning or late afternoons near snags, and move quietly.
8. Murray River: A big river with excellent crabbing along its tidal areas, along with most local fish species. Try using fresh local prawns or live yabby baits around the tree snags, and small soft plastic lures. See text on previous page.
9. Flathead along edges in late summer.

GPS Beware breakers on reefs

There are two north-south reef formations off Mandurah that are of special interest to boaters.

James Service Reef 32 27.100S 115 39.781E
This mark is 10km from the Mandurah Channel. It is part of the north-south Murray Reefs that extend 15km north to Warnbro Sound.

Five Fathom Bank 32 27.778S 115 36.873E
This formation starts north of Cape Bouvard and extends north past Mandurah to Rottnest Island. The mark is 10km from Mandurah Channel.

Perth

Local fishos have the Swan and Peel Inlet estuaries, ocean beaches, inshore reef, Rottnest Island, FADs, and deep sea fishing. Seasonality differs each year with the Leeuwin Current. Tropical fish such as spanish mackerel arrive and linger with warm water. View the current at the Weather Bureau website, or ask tackle shops about its status. Big snapper are often caught in close after storms. Rays and sharks are a pest on beaches and groynes, along with norwest blowies. Perth winds can be strong, with the reliable afternoon south-wester dubbed "The Doctor".

Key to Map

Hotspots

1. Stragglers: Exposed reef. King george whiting, herring and big skippy. Tailor in white water and samson fish in deeper water nearby.
2. Woodmans Point and Coogee jetties: snapper, salmon in winter, with mackerel, sharks, herring in summer. Also mulloway, sand and king george whiting, skippy and tailor. AT publication, Woodmans Point's Ammo Jetty was to be restored. Squid can be caught from local weedbeds in boats.
3. Reefy area, good for most species.
4. Safety Bay to Warnbro Sound: Sand and king george whiting, tailor, herring, squid and crabs caught from shore.
5. Becher Point: beach has summer tailor. Herring, sand whiting and the occasional mulloway also turn up.
6. Secret Harbour is the start of a long line of beaches stretching south to Mandurah. Tailor, herring, whiting and mulloway. During the day sand whiting can be a pest. For bigger yellowfin whiting, fish with bloodworms early in morning. Winter sees mullet taking small baits, and herring and tarwhine.
7. Golden Bay: beautiful beach with big tailor on summer afternoons.
8. Singleton Beach: summer tailor, fish deeper gutters before dark and fish with pilchards. Whiting, herring, tarwhine and mullet can be caught, mulloway to 25kg.
9. Madora Beach is perhaps the best for mulloway close to Perth. Use cut fish fillet in the gutters on a rising tide after dark. Mulloway to 30kg are taken, plus tailor, herring and whiting.
10. Five Fathom Bank runs to the north and south west of Garden Island. Dhufish, snapper, samson, trevally, KG whiting and lobsters. In summer spanish mackerel and yellowfin tuna.
11. Tailor around white water.

Launch Sites

1. Cockburn Power Boats Association near Woodmans Point and next to the Cockburn Power Boat Club, Jervoise Bay Cove (off O'Kane Court), multi lanes with two jetties. Protected by groyne. Popular for fishing the top of Cockburn Sound. Plenty of parking.
2. Challenger Beach: Handy location but shallow and unprotected, suits smaller boats.
3. Kwinana Beach, Wells Rd: shallow, with groyne, T-jetty, difficult in wind. Ample parking.
4. Rockingham: Two ramps near each other. Good access to the bottom of Cockburn Sound and safe launching conditions during south-west winds. Limited parking, fees apply.
5. The Causeway: Excellent ramp on west side of Garden Island Causeway. Fees apply.
6. Safety Bay: Two-lane ramp with jetty, end of Carlisle St. Bottom is sand.
7. Safety Bay Rd next to Bent St. Jetty.
8. Safety Bay Rd near Donald Dve. Ends in sand.
9. Port Kennedy ramp, ample parking.
10. Ramp on west side off Mary St, on east bank in Mandurah Ocean Marina.
11. Inside canal at Waterside Dve.

CHARTED SHOALS, 37km west of Warnbro Sound
32 18.401S 115 21.645E and 32 19.574S 115 19.974E
32 23.647S 115 18.992E and 32 25.066S 115 19.029E

Cockburn Sound

The 10km-long Garden Island barrier creates the relatively calm waters of Cockburn Sound where snapper, king george whiting, herring and squid are caught on the sheltered east side, with dhufish, samson, tailor and salmon on the western reefs. The deeper channels on the east side have snapper and mulloway after dark. Most of Garden Island is Navy land and off limits, but some of the island is a nature reserve, with beach access for boaters. Fishermen visiting Carnac Island to the north may observe sea lions on the beach. The seagrass beds on the east side produce squid and herring, with the ocean side producing samson, dhufish and snapper. Mewstone and Rowboat Rocks to the north-east of Carnac Island hold herring, trevally, king george whiting, samson and tailor. Big tailor inhabit the white water around the rocks. The local Gravel Patches have snapper, with many boats anchored over these areas each evening. The snapper sometimes aggregate in big schools. Several boat ramps give access to the Sound. Sea conditions depend on time of year, with winter being calmer between gales. The Sound is reasonably comfortable in all winds except strong northerlies.

Key to Map

Hotspots (next page)

NOTE: Seasonal snapper closure applies See map next page.

1. The big industrial jetties are usually off limits to anglers. The structures attract herring, trevally and tailor, big snapper and mulloway after dark. Security regulations around wharves can change - check before fishing near them.
2. Herring Bay has herring, flounder and more. Requires caution in boats.
3. Sulphur Bay has snapper, trevally, king george whiting, salmon in May, tailor and squid.
4. Buchanan Bay is good squid country. To the south, Colpoys Point has snapper in season. The reefs between Garden Island and Carnac have herring, and sandy spots have whiting.
5. The Causeway can only be fished by boat. Fish the channels through the archways for trevally, tailor, bonito, king george whiting, tarwhine, herring, squid.
6. Cockburn Power Boats Assoc: Fish the groyne for herring, trevally, squid. Quality pink snapper at times.
7. ASI Groyne: Trevally, tarwhine, herring, tailor and bonito. Use strip baits or pilchards after dark for mulloway or pink snapper. Rays are a problem.
8. Challenger Beach: This is surrounded by industrial area but still worth fishing for herring and tailor, especially during afternoon seabreeze. During the day - sand whiting, big flathead and flounder. Power station outlet has tailor.
9. Kwinana Jetty is on Wells Rd near the boat ramp. Bread and butter species.
10. Rockingham's public jetties have pink snapper. Use pilchards or strip baits on heavy lines after dark for snapper and occasional mulloway. During the day herring, slimy mackerel, yellowtail, squid.

Wrecks

The sunken barge in front of the Alcoa refinery is a snapper hotspot with fish to 13kg in summer.

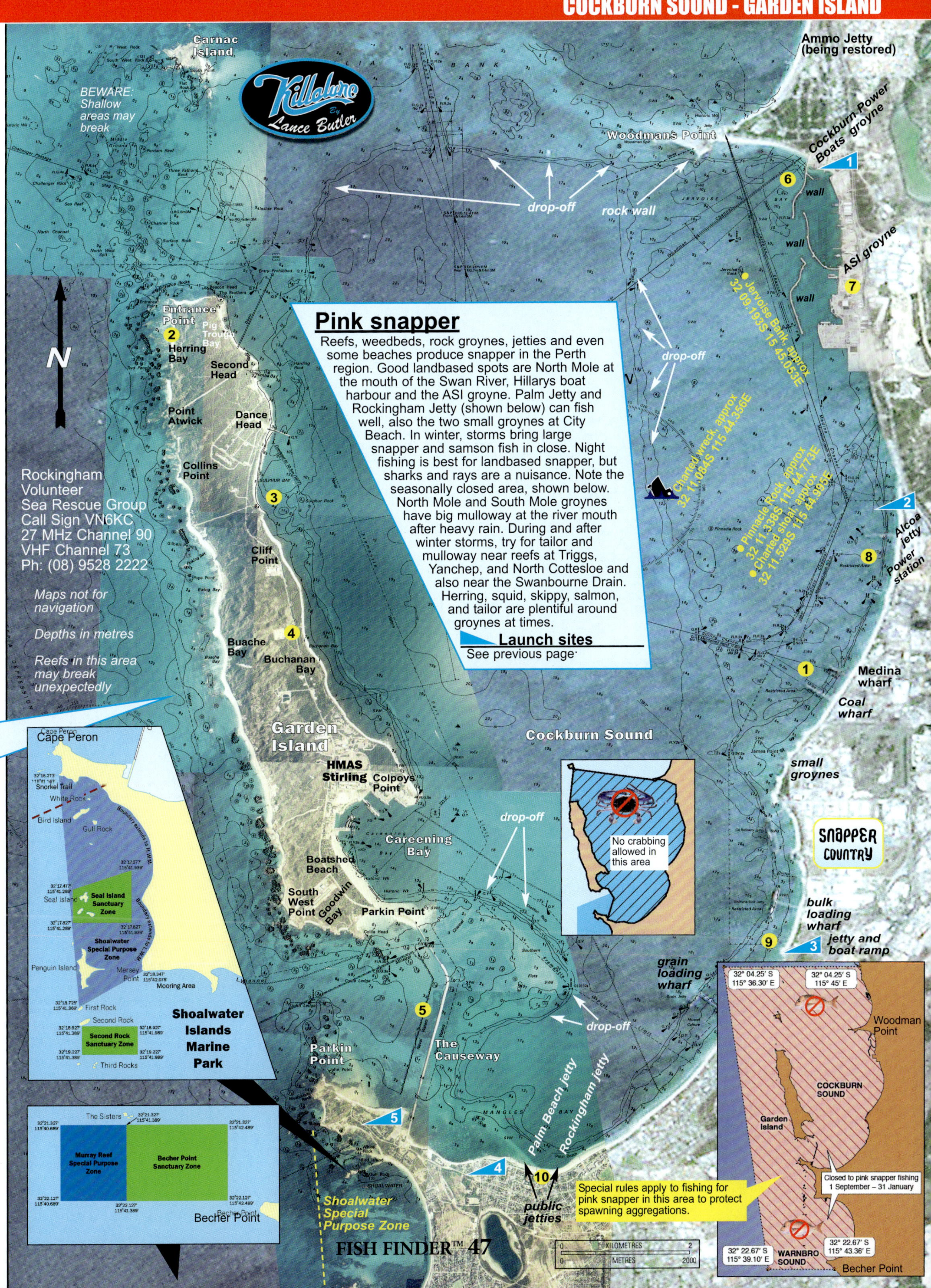

Pink snapper

Reefs, weedbeds, rock groynes, jetties and even some beaches produce snapper in the Perth region. Good landbased spots are North Mole at the mouth of the Swan River, Hillarys boat harbour and the ASI groyne. Palm Jetty and Rockingham Jetty (shown below) can fish well, also the two small groynes at City Beach. In winter, storms bring large snapper and samson fish in close. Night fishing is best for landbased snapper, but sharks and rays are a nuisance. Note the seasonally closed area, shown below. North Mole and South Mole groynes have big mulloway at the river mouth after heavy rain. During and after winter storms, try for tailor and mulloway near reefs at Triggs, Yanchep, and North Cottesloe and also near the Swanbourne Drain. Herring, squid, skippy, salmon, and tailor are plentiful around groynes at times.

Launch sites

See previous page

WA Artificial Reefs

Reefs have been installed off Bunbury, Dunsborough, Esperance, Exmouth, Mandurah, Ocean Reef and Perth. A major natural oyster reef has been restored in Oyster Harbour at Albany, with expansion of the reef area set to continue. These artificial reefs are in addition to annual FAD deployments.

Fremantle Harbour

The mouth of the Swan River has mulloway and snapper on occasions, but the main catch is bream, whiting, cobbler, flounder and flathead. Chopper tailor appear in summer. Prawns and blue crabs in season. Bream are in the far upstream reaches of both the Swan and the Canning Rivers. Mussels are abundant in the system, but eating them is not recommended.

Key to Map

Hotspots

MAP ON LEFT: 1. Fishing allowed on south side of the port. Herring, yellowtail, slimy mackerel and skippy. Big mulloway after dark in autumn.
2. South Mole: Herring, and skippy during the day. Use berley. Tailor in late arvo from the rocks.
3. North Mole: In daylight, herring, skippy. Early morning and late arvo, tailor and bonito. After dark, sharks, mulloway and stingrays.
4. Old Power Station: The coast to South Beach has shore spots to fish for herring, skippy and squid. Near the old power station there are fishable rock areas. Small groyne and beach has herring, tailor and big sand whiting.
5. Fremantle Boat Harbour: Fish the groynes on the seaward side. Skippy, herring and sand whiting in daytime, in the arvo, tailor. Weedbanks just out from the sailing club have squid and king george whiting.
6. Fremantle Traffic Bridge: Access by walkway out to centre pylons and climbing to platforms. Tarwhine and bream near pylons on prawn or mussel baits. Tailor and mulloway after dark, incoming tides. King prawns on outgoing tides after dark in autumn. Small samson fish and pink snapper caught here.
7. Stirling Bridge: Fish from shore under the pylons - herring, tailor and flathead. Spinning with small lures and jigs works well.
MAP ON RIGHT: 8. landbased fishing Mindarie rocks and marina walls.
9. Rock and beach fishing at Burns Beach. Burns Rocks are exposed reefs 1km offshore - mixed species.
10. Landbased fishing from rock walls at Hillarys marina. Also small rock groynes along beach just south of the boat harbour.
11. Good fishing at Trigg Beach and off rocks to the north.
12. City Beach - two small rock groynes.
13. Cottlesloe rock groyne. Reef on south side of groyne. Another rock groyne is further south opposite Beach St.
14. The Narrows - big mulloway and other species near bridge pylons, easily accessible. Flats nearby have whiting, flathead and flounder.
15. Deep Water Point: good area for most fish, and crabs.
16. Upper reaches best for bream in summer.
17. Mulloway off groynes after rain, north groyne (North Mole) best for other species.
18. Various jetties exist from Swan River entrance to along the suburban foreshores. Good ones are Jo Jo's Jetty in Nedlands (end of Broadway Dve), Point Walter Jetty, Claremont Jetty (end of Jetty Rd), East St Jetty in East Fremantle, and Deepwater Point Jetty, The Esp, Mt Pleasant.

Prawns

Thousands of people go prawning each season in the Swan-Canning and Peel-Harvey estuaries. Millions of prawns have been stocked into these waters. On calm summer evenings, during the dark phases of the moon between October and February, prawning lights illuminate the estuaries as people chase western river prawn (*Metapenaeus dalli*) and the larger western king prawn (*Penaeus latisulcatus*). There is a closed season for prawning in the Swan-Canning and in parts of the Peel-Harvey system, with a different season on the Serpentine, Murray and Dandalup Rivers. A prawn's life cycle is dominated by the moon. Prawns grow rapidly, moulting shells to coincide with the full moon (and high tides) each month. After reaching maturity, growth and moulting slows. Live river prawns are almost translucent, having blue tips and a greasy feel. King prawns are cream in colour, with brown body markings and blue legs and tail fins. While a river prawn spends its life in rivers or estuaries, a king prawn goes through larval stages in the ocean, and settles in estuaries. During spring, river prawns reach about 5cm at 10 months. King prawns do not achieve this until Jan/Feb, but can reach 8cm by late summer. A prawn caught further north in Shark Bay measured 24.4cm. Prawns can be legally taken using a single hand-dip net, a single hand-scoop net or single hand-throw net, although many local area restrictions apply. Visit **www.fish.wa.gov.au** for details.

Launch sites

1. Ocean Reef Boat Harbour, via Boat Harbour Quays off Ocean Reef Rd. Multi-lanes, fees apply.
2. Hillarys Boat Harbour, Northside Dve at intersection of Hepburn Ave, Whitfords Ave and West Coast Dve. Multi-lanes, fees apply.
3. Multi-lane ramp off Riverside Rd, Fremantle, fees apply, limited parking.
4. Good ramp off Burke Dve.
5. Two small ramps close by - JH Abrahams Reserve, and Matilda Bay, both off Hackett Dve.
6. Small ramp off Mill Point Rd.
7. Maylands, Clarkson Rd.
8. Ramp in green area off Great Eastern Hwy, Abernethy Rd.
9. Good ramp accessed via freeway overpass at the end of Gentilli Way.
10. Pay ramp and parking at Deep Water Point. Upgraded in 2018. Good fishing spots nearby.
11. Small unsealed launch site.
12. Claughton Reserve ramp, 5am to 10pm.
13. Pickering Park, unsealed.
14. Ramp in park off Swan St, Guildford. Open 5am to 10pm.
15. Balbuk Way, Rivervale. Two lanes, waterski area is nearby.
16. Coode St, South Perth. Affected by sand, high tide only.
17. Mosman Bay, Johnston St.
18. Cockburn Power Boats Association.

Reef Towers

Two towers were installed in January 2017 south of Rottnest Island in an area called 'The Paddock'. The towers differ from the concrete reefs off Dunsborough, Bunbury and Mandurah. The 12.5m high upper part of the towers concentrates baitfish, attracting pelagic fish and some demersal species. Expect yellowtail kingfish, salmon, spanish mackerel, tuna, pink snapper, dhufish, baldchin groper, mulloway and more.

Tower 1 32 07.527 115 27.013 - 44.3m
Tower 2 32 07.461 115 26.978 - 45m

Swan River

Black bream are a popular target in the Swan River. Bream and other marine fish move upriver in summer and downriver during winter when it rains. In parts of the river they can be caught all year. During the big tides of August and September, sea water is pushed far into the system and from September to November bream, mulloway, tailor, flathead, flounder and whiting move upstream. In summer, bream can be found above the Causeway. Places to fish include East Fremantle, Point Walter, Mosman Park, the old Swan Brewery site and Canning Bridge. The secret to successful fishing, especially with bigger bream, is to fish light, and use little, if any, weight on the line. Night fishing improves the odds. Baits can be rigged under a small float for snaggy areas. Small lures work well at times and are a good way to beat the abundant blowfish. Try light resin heads on tiny soft plastic lures. Fish around snags, pylons and mussel banks. Bream like structure, but will move onto sandbanks to feed. In winter, try Blackwell Reach and Mosman's where the water is deep, as freshwater flow often sits on top. For year-round fishing try from East Perth to Garratt Road Bridge. The best time to fish is early mornings and evenings and the change of tide.

Mulloway are reasonably common in the river and are sometimes caught in large sizes. Livebait is important for success. One of the best spots is The Narrows. September-January is the peak mulloway period. Flathead are another favourite and are caught upstream to Guildford, but more often in the lower reaches. Yellowfin whiting are found in the Swan in small numbers, with East Fremantle arguably the best spot. Fresh or live bloodworms are the best bait. For chopper tailor, fish from Maylands to Fremantle with bait or lures. Mullet can be caught using light tackle and a piece of compressed bread on a hook. Other local fish are skippy, grunter, herring and flounder. There are public jetties throughout the system.

Surf and beach

Skippy, tailor, salmon, herring, whiting and mulloway are caught in the surf. For sand whiting, fish the beach gutters between Swanbourne and Trigg. Also try around Mettams Pool and Watermans Beach. South of the Swan River try along Kwinana to Rockingham, Secret Harbour and Golden Bay. Whiting are found close to shore. Mornings and afternoons are best and the strong daily sea breeze doesn't put fish off. On beaches fish the incoming tide. At East Fremantle, try fishing an evening outgoing tide in winter.

North Metro Artificial Reef

North Metropolitan Artificial Reef is 7km from Ocean Reef and 11km from Hillarys. There are 292 concrete modules of two designs to 1.8m high, in a zig-zag pattern, over a 400m by 250m area, in 27m of water.

Throw nets

Throw nets are not permitted in the Swan and Canning Rivers.

Bream

In the Swan and Cannings Rivers only two bream over 40cm may be taken.

MAAC Blue Water Open Fishing Classic

This annual competition is held in February and is the largest competition in the Perth metropolitan area. The first competition was in 1985. It now attracts hundreds of competitors, with prizes totalling more than $40,000. For information visit **www.maac.com.au**

Fremantle Volunteer Sea Rescue

Call Sign VN 6DI 27 MHz
Channel 88 and 90
VHF Channel 16 and 73

Garfish ban

Taking *southern sea garfish* is prohibited in waters between 31° south (just north of Lancelin) and 33° south (near Myalup), to protect breeding fish following a decline in the stock. The smaller species *robust garfish* may still be taken from within this area.

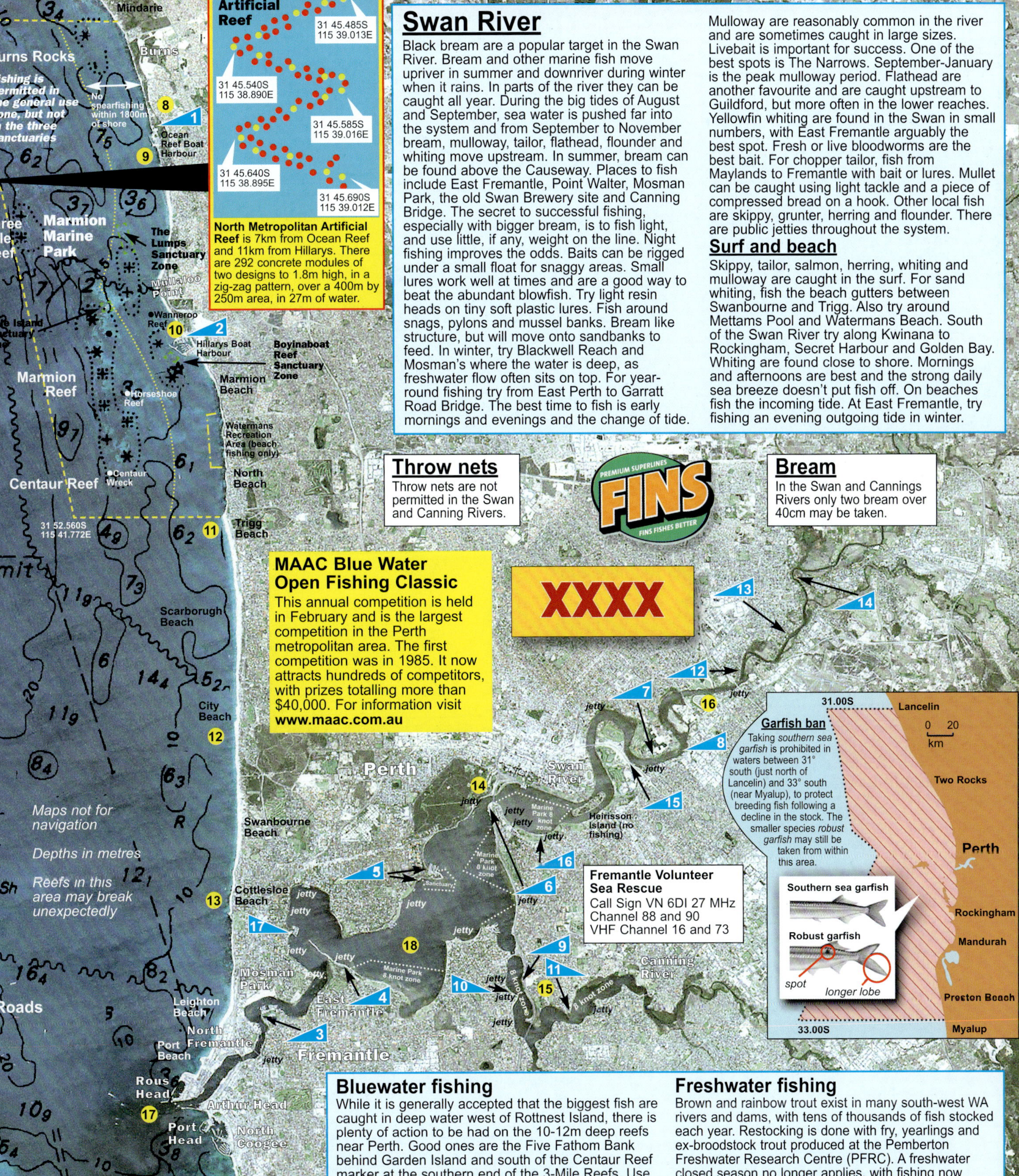

Bluewater fishing

While it is generally accepted that the biggest fish are caught in deep water west of Rottnest Island, there is plenty of action to be had on the 10-12m deep reefs near Perth. Good ones are the Five Fathom Bank behind Garden Island and south of the Centaur Reef marker at the southern end of the 3-Mile Reefs. Use berley to get the fish in close and biting in this clear, shallow area. Expect to catch king george whiting, snapper, dhufish, yellowtail kingfish, samson fish, spanish mackerel, pike, breaksea cod, harlequin fish, skippy, salmon, sharks and rays. Squid and cuttlefish are usually abundant. West of Rottnest Island there are several FADs that hold dolphin fish. As they are from 37km to 55km out from Perth boat ramps, a seaworthy boat is a must. See page 50 for FADs.

Freshwater fishing

Brown and rainbow trout exist in many south-west WA rivers and dams, with tens of thousands of fish stocked each year. Restocking is done with fry, yearlings and ex-broodstock trout produced at the Pemberton Freshwater Research Centre (PFRC). A freshwater closed season no longer applies, with fishing now permitted all year, but a freshwater licence is required for anyone older than 16 who is fishing south of Greenough. Fishers may take four fish (combined) of rainbow trout, brown trout and freshwater cobbler. Trout have a minimum size of 30cm. Redfin perch have no size limit. There are no other bag or size limits for WA freshwater fish. Redfin perch are a popular fish caught in most WA trout waters, but should not be released. The Shannon River is closed to all fishing.

FADs

Official FADs are installed in waters 100m to 200m deep up to 60km off Perth, west of Rottnest Island, near an ocean trench. They are installed for the game fishing season each summer, and are usually in place from November to May. Dolphin fish (mahi mahi) are the main catch, with yellowfin tuna, cobia, wahoo, marlin, trevally and mackerel. Approach quietly and respect other FAD users. The FADs are retrieved each winter for maintenance. Perth Game Fishing Club supplies the GPS marks each year ... visit **www.pgfc.com.au** for more information.

The Wreck Graveyard

Several vessels have been scuttled west of Rottnest Island. The *Derwent* wreck, at approx 32 03.516S 115 12.207E, 22km west of the island, lies in almost 200m. Ask Perth tackle shops for GPS data for others. Most are historic sites and can not be fished.

Cray Pot Floats

Cray pot floats are a navigational hazard during the lobster season. These are seen along much of the west coast. Avoid entangling the ropes with fishing gear, as lost hooks are a risk to cray crews.

Rottnest Island

With its rock ledges, weedbeds, sheltered coves and clear water, Rottnest Island is a popular boating and fishing destination. It is just 18km from Perth. Rottnest has some of the southern-most tropical coral reef in Australia. There are 135 species of tropical fish on the island's reefs, compared to 11 along the metro coastline. Overall, 450 fish species are found in Rottnest Island waters. Migrating whales pass through the area on their way to and from northern breeding grounds. To conserve this special environment, sanctuary zones, no boating areas, speed limits and other guidelines are in place. The island is so popular that an annual ballot system is run to allocate accommodation during holidays. Visit **www.rottnestisland.com** for details. A raft of local regulations are intended to preserve Rottnest's environment. Everyone entering the Rottnest Island Reserve, including the marine reserve, must pay an admission fee. The Rottnest Island Authority manages moorings and jetty pens on the Island. Visit **www.rottnestisland.com/boating/** for details.

Fishing

Fishing gear can be hired or bought at Rottnest Malibu Diving, the General Store in Thomson Bay, and the Geordie Bay Store. The local fish include reef dwellers, seagrass inhabitants and pelagic species. The dhufish is king of the reefs, mostly taken from deeper waters. King wrasse, silver drummer, red-lipped and dusky morwong, black-spot goatfish, leatherjackets, breaksea cod and sweep are plentiful. Samson and yellowtail kingfish appear from time to time. The seagrass hosts sand and king george whiting, cobbler and flathead. Migratory fish include herring, tailor, salmon and trevally. Lobsters, octopus, cuttlefish and squid inhabit inshore reefs. Spearguns, gidgies and net fishing are prohibited in the Marine Reserve. For the latest information visit **www.fish.wa.gov.au**

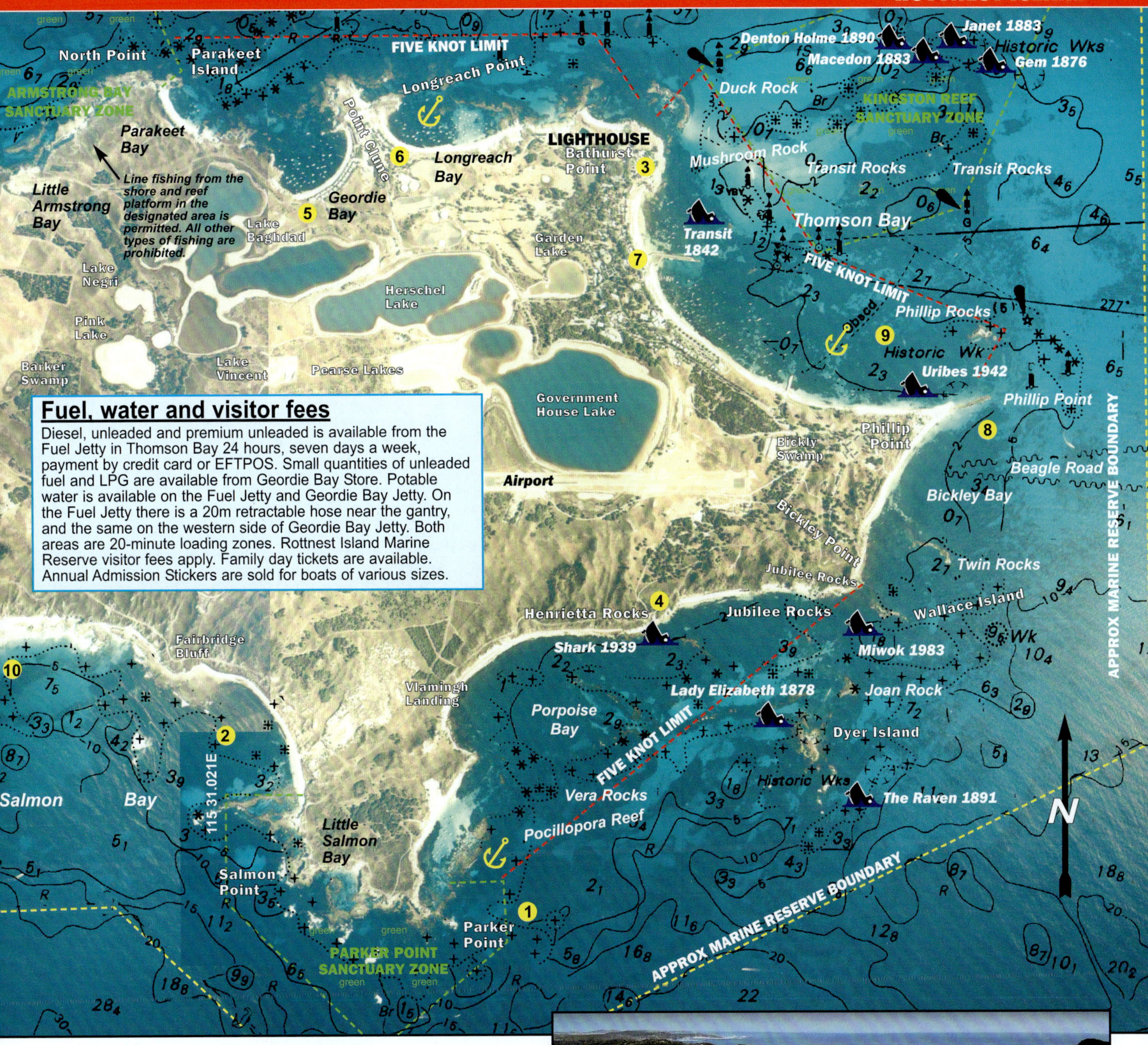

Fuel, water and visitor fees

Diesel, unleaded and premium unleaded is available from the Fuel Jetty in Thomson Bay 24 hours, seven days a week, payment by credit card or EFTPOS. Small quantities of unleaded fuel and LPG are available from Geordie Bay Store. Potable water is available on the Fuel Jetty and Geordie Bay Jetty. On the Fuel Jetty there is a 20m retractable hose near the gantry, and the same on the western side of Geordie Bay Jetty. Both areas are 20-minute loading zones. Rottnest Island Marine Reserve visitor fees apply. Family day tickets are available. Annual Admission Stickers are sold for boats of various sizes.

Key to Map

Hotspots

TIPS: Use small baits on light tackle from shore, as the fish encountered will usually be small. A favourite is whitebait presented on a set of small ganged hooks. Berley can be effective, especially for herring and trevally - try a mix of pollard and tuna oil or crushed pilchards. Boat fishermen should use heavier gear as bigger fish are found in the deeper water. Caution is required navigating around the island as there are reefs and often a heavy swell.

1. Parker Point: The area outside the sanctuary produces tailor, herring and trevally. Troll the deep water outside the sanctuary for yellowfin tuna, yellowtail kingfish and shark mackerel. Berley can attract monster samson fish to the boat.
2. Salmon Point to Fairbridge Bluff (outside sanctuary) - herring, trevally, whiting, tarwhine.
3. Bathurst Point is a good place to fish before catching the ferry at Thomsons Bay nearby. Herring can be abundant when using berley.
4. Henrietta Rocks has herring and trevally: use small baits with berley.
5. Geordie Bay is the second-most popular mooring area after Thomsons Bay. It has accommodation and is crowded during the summer holiday period. Herring and sand whiting are caught from shore and from moored boats.
6. Point Clune to Longreach Bay has mostly herring from the beaches and reefs. Some trevally and king george whiting are taken here.
7. Thomson Bay is the main settlement and the ferry landing. The ferry jetty has herring, , trevally, whiting and squid. Herring are common around Thomson Bay.
8. Phillip Point has a reef with tailor: fish from a boat and cast into the white water. From shore there are herring, trevally and some tailor.
9. Squid, whiting and herring in the anchorage.
10. Herring, trevally, sand and king george whiting and some salmon in autumn.
11. Charlotte Point to Armstrong Point is a good area for smaller species such as herring, skippy, tarwhine, sand whiting and occasional king george whiting.

Rottnest Island
NATHAN MAHNEY

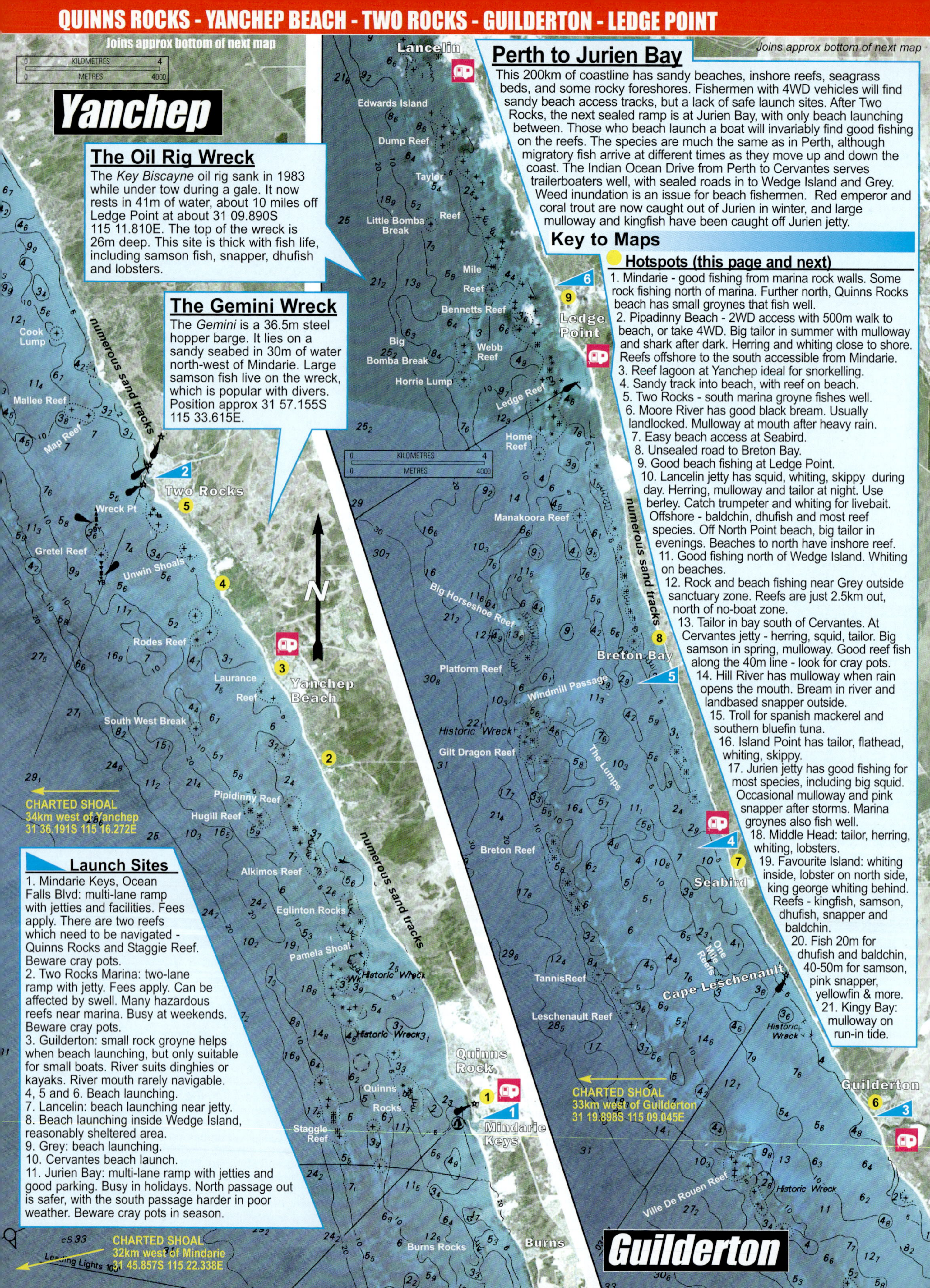
QUINNS ROCKS - YANCHEP BEACH - TWO ROCKS - GUILDERTON - LEDGE POINT
Joins approx bottom of next map
Yanchep
The Oil Rig Wreck
The Key Biscayne oil rig sank in 1983 while under tow during a gale. It now rests in 41m of water, about 10 miles off Ledge Point at about 31 09.890S 115 11.810E. The top of the wreck is 26m deep. This site is thick with fish life, including samson fish, snapper, dhufish and lobsters.
The Gemini Wreck
The Gemini is a 36.5m steel hopper barge. It lies on a sandy seabed in 30m of water north-west of Mindarie. Large samson fish live on the wreck, which is popular with divers. Position approx 31 57.155S 115 33.615E.
Perth to Jurien Bay
This 200km of coastline has sandy beaches, inshore reefs, seagrass beds, and some rocky foreshores. Fishermen with 4WD vehicles will find sandy beach access tracks, but a lack of safe launch sites. After Two Rocks, the next sealed ramp is at Jurien Bay, with only beach launching between. Those who beach launch a boat will invariably find good fishing on the reefs. The species are much the same as in Perth, although migratory fish arrive at different times as they move up and down the coast. The Indian Ocean Drive from Perth to Cervantes serves trailerboaters well, with sealed roads in to Wedge Island and Grey. Weed inundation is an issue for beach fishermen. Red emperor and coral trout are now caught out of Jurien in winter, and large mulloway and kingfish have been caught off Jurien jetty.
Key to Maps
Hotspots (this page and next)
1. Mindarie - good fishing from marina rock walls. Some rock fishing north of marina. Further north, Quinns Rocks beach has small groynes that fish well.
2. Pipadinny Beach - 2WD access with 500m walk to beach, or take 4WD. Big tailor in summer with mulloway and shark after dark. Herring and whiting close to shore. Reefs offshore to the south accessible from Mindarie.
3. Reef lagoon at Yanchep ideal for snorkelling.
4. Sandy track into beach, with reef on beach.
5. Two Rocks - south marina groyne fishes well.
6. Moore River has good black bream. Usually landlocked. Mulloway at mouth after heavy rain.
7. Easy beach access at Seabird.
8. Unsealed road to Breton Bay.
9. Good beach fishing at Ledge Point.
10. Lancelin jetty has squid, whiting, skippy during day. Herring, mulloway and tailor at night. Use berley. Catch trumpeter and whiting for livebait. Offshore - baldchin, dhufish and most reef species. Off North Point beach, big tailor in evenings. Beaches to north have inshore reef.
11. Good fishing north of Wedge Island. Whiting on beaches.
12. Rock and beach fishing near Grey outside sanctuary zone. Reefs are just 2.5km out, north of no-boat zone.
13. Tailor in bay south of Cervantes. At Cervantes jetty - herring, squid, tailor. Big samson in spring, mulloway. Good reef fish along the 40m line - look for cray pots.
14. Hill River has mulloway when rain opens the mouth. Bream in river and landbased snapper outside.
15. Troll for spanish mackerel and southern bluefin tuna.
16. Island Point has tailor, flathead, whiting, skippy.
17. Jurien jetty has good fishing for most species, including big squid. Occasional mulloway and pink snapper after storms. Marina groynes also fish well.
18. Middle Head: tailor, herring, whiting, lobsters.
19. Favourite Island: whiting inside, lobster on north side, king george whiting behind. Reefs - kingfish, samson, dhufish, snapper and baldchin.
20. Fish 20m for dhufish and baldchin, 40-50m for samson, pink snapper, yellowfin & more.
21. Kingy Bay: mulloway on run-in tide.
Launch Sites
1. Mindarie Keys, Ocean Falls Blvd: multi-lane ramp with jetties and facilities. Fees apply. There are two reefs which need to be navigated - Quinns Rocks and Staggie Reef. Beware cray pots.
2. Two Rocks Marina: two-lane ramp with jetty. Fees apply. Can be affected by swell. Many hazardous reefs near marina. Busy at weekends. Beware cray pots.
3. Guilderton: small rock groyne helps when beach launching, but only suitable for small boats. River suits dinghies or kayaks. River mouth rarely navigable.
4, 5 and 6. Beach launching.
7. Lancelin: beach launching near jetty.
8. Beach launching inside Wedge Island, reasonably sheltered area.
9. Grey: beach launching.
10. Cervantes beach launch.
11. Jurien Bay: multi-lane ramp with jetties and good parking. Busy in holidays. North passage out is safer, with the south passage harder in poor weather. Beware cray pots in season.
CHARTED SHOAL 34km west of Yanchep 31 36.191S 115 16.272E
CHARTED SHOAL 32km west of Mindarie 31 45.857S 115 22.338E
CHARTED SHOAL 33km west of Guilderton 31 19.898S 115 09.045E
KILOMETRES
METRES
numerous sand tracks
Cook Lump
Mallee Reef
Map Reef
Two Rocks
Wreck Pt
Gretel Reef
Unwin Shoals
Rodes Reef
Laurance Reef
Yanchep Beach
South West Break
Pipidinny Reef
Hugill Reef
Alkimos Reef
Eglinton Rocks
Pamela Shoal
Historic Wreck
Quinns Rocks
Quinns Rocks
Mindarie Keys
Staggie Reef
Burns Rocks
Burns
Leading Lights
Lancelin
Edwards Island
Dump Reef
Taylor Reef
Little Bomba Break
Mile Reef
Bennetts Reef
Big Bomba Break
Webb Reef
Horrie Lump
Ledge Reef
Ledge Point
Home Reef
Manakoora Reef
Big Horseshoe Reef
Platform Reef
Windmill Passage
Breton Bay
Historic Wreck
Gilt Dragon Reef
The Lumps
Breton Reef
Seabird
One Mile Reefs
TannisReef
Cape Leschenault
Leschenault Reef
Historic Wreck
Guilderton
Ville De Rouen Reef
Historic Wreck
N
Guilderton

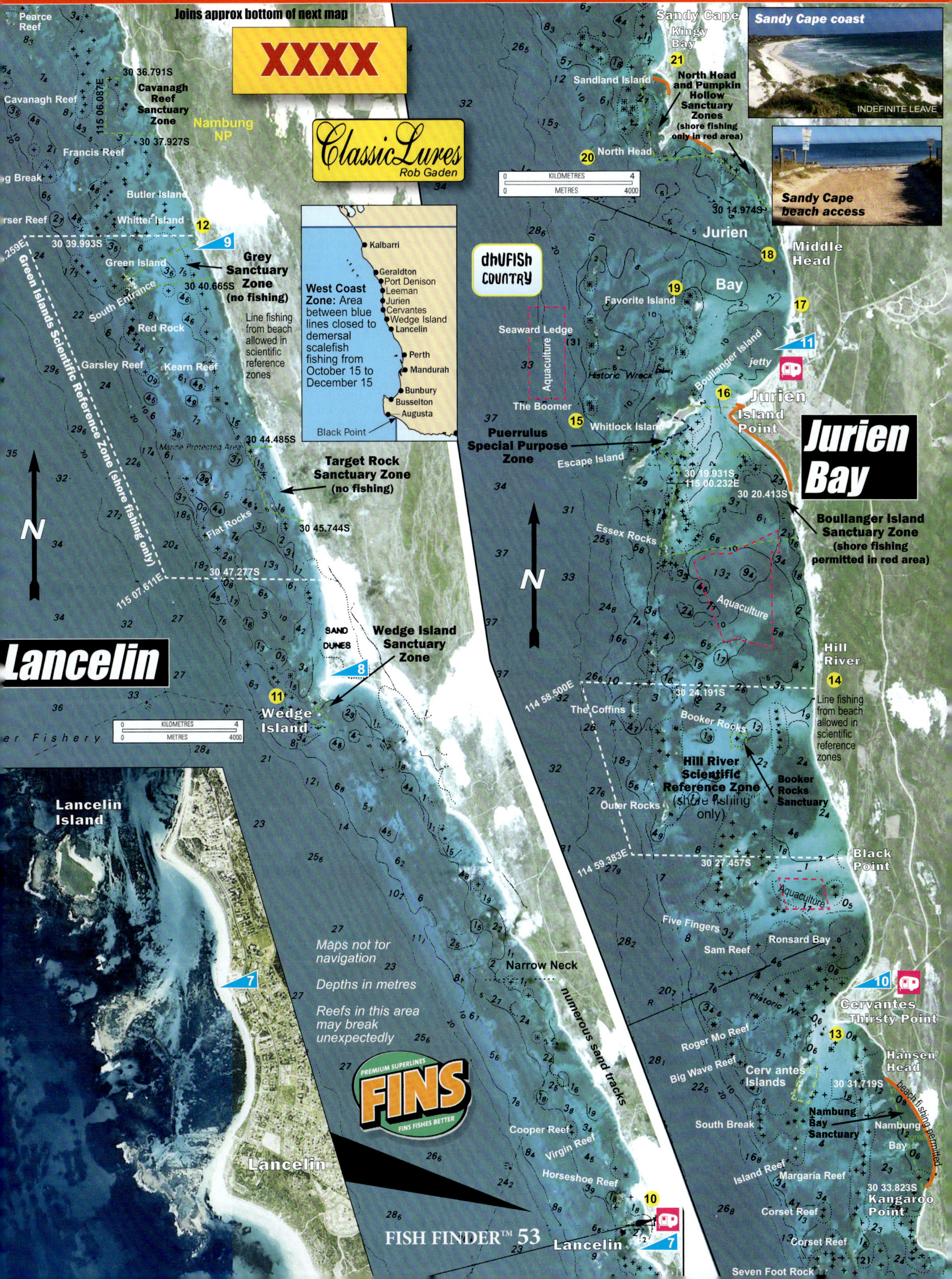
Joins approx bottom of next map
XXXX
Classic Lures
Rob Gaden
Sandy Cape coast
INDEFINITE LEAVE
Sandy Cape beach access
Pearce Reef
Cavanagh Reef
30 36.791S
Cavanagh Reef Sanctuary Zone
115 06.087E
30 37.927S
Nambung NP
Francis Reef
Butler Island
Whitter Island
30 39.993S
Green Island
Grey Sanctuary Zone (no fishing)
30 40.665S
Line fishing from beach allowed in scientific reference zones
South Entrance
Red Rock
Garsley Reef
Kearn Reef
Green Islands Scientific Reference Zone (shore fishing only)
30 44.485S
Target Rock Sanctuary Zone (no fishing)
30 45.744S
Flat Rocks
30 47.277S
115 07.611E
SAND DUNES
Wedge Island Sanctuary Zone
Lancelin
Wedge Island
KILOMETRES
METRES
Lancelin Island
Lancelin
West Coast Zone: Area between blue lines closed to demersal scalefish fishing from October 15 to December 15
Kalbarri
Geraldton
Port Denison
Leeman
Jurien
Cervantes
Wedge Island
Lancelin
Perth
Mandurah
Bunbury
Busselton
Augusta
Black Point
dhufish country
Maps not for navigation
Depths in metres
Reefs in this area may break unexpectedly
FINS
PREMIUM SUPERLINES
FINS FISHES BETTER
Narrow Neck
numerous sand tracks
Cooper Reef
Virgin Reef
Horseshoe Reef
Lancelin
FISH FINDER™ 53
Sandy Cape
Kingy Bay
Sandland Island
North Head and Pumpkin Hollow Sanctuary Zones (shore fishing only in red area)
North Head
30 14.974S
Jurien Bay
Middle Head
Favorite Island
Seaward Ledge
Aquaculture
Historic Wreck
The Boomer
Boullanger Island
jetty
Jurien
Island Point
Whitlock Island
Puerrulus Special Purpose Zone
Escape Island
30 19.931S
115 00.232E
30 20.413S
Jurien Bay
Boullanger Island Sanctuary Zone (shore fishing permitted in red area)
Essex Rocks
Aquaculture
Hill River
Line fishing from beach allowed in scientific reference zones
114 58.500E
30 24.191S
The Coffins
Booker Rocks
Hill River Scientific Reference Zone (shore fishing only)
Booker Rocks Sanctuary
Outer Rocks
114 59.383E
30 27.457S
Black Point
Aquaculture
Five Fingers
Sam Reef
Ronsard Bay
Cervantes
Thirsty Point
Historic Wk
Roger Mo Reef
Big Wave Reef
Cervantes Islands
Hansen Head
30 31.719S
Nambung Bay Sanctuary
Nambung Bay
beach fishing permitted
South Break
Island Reef
Margaria Reef
30 33.823S
Kangaroo Point
Corset Reef
Corset Reef
Seven Foot Rock

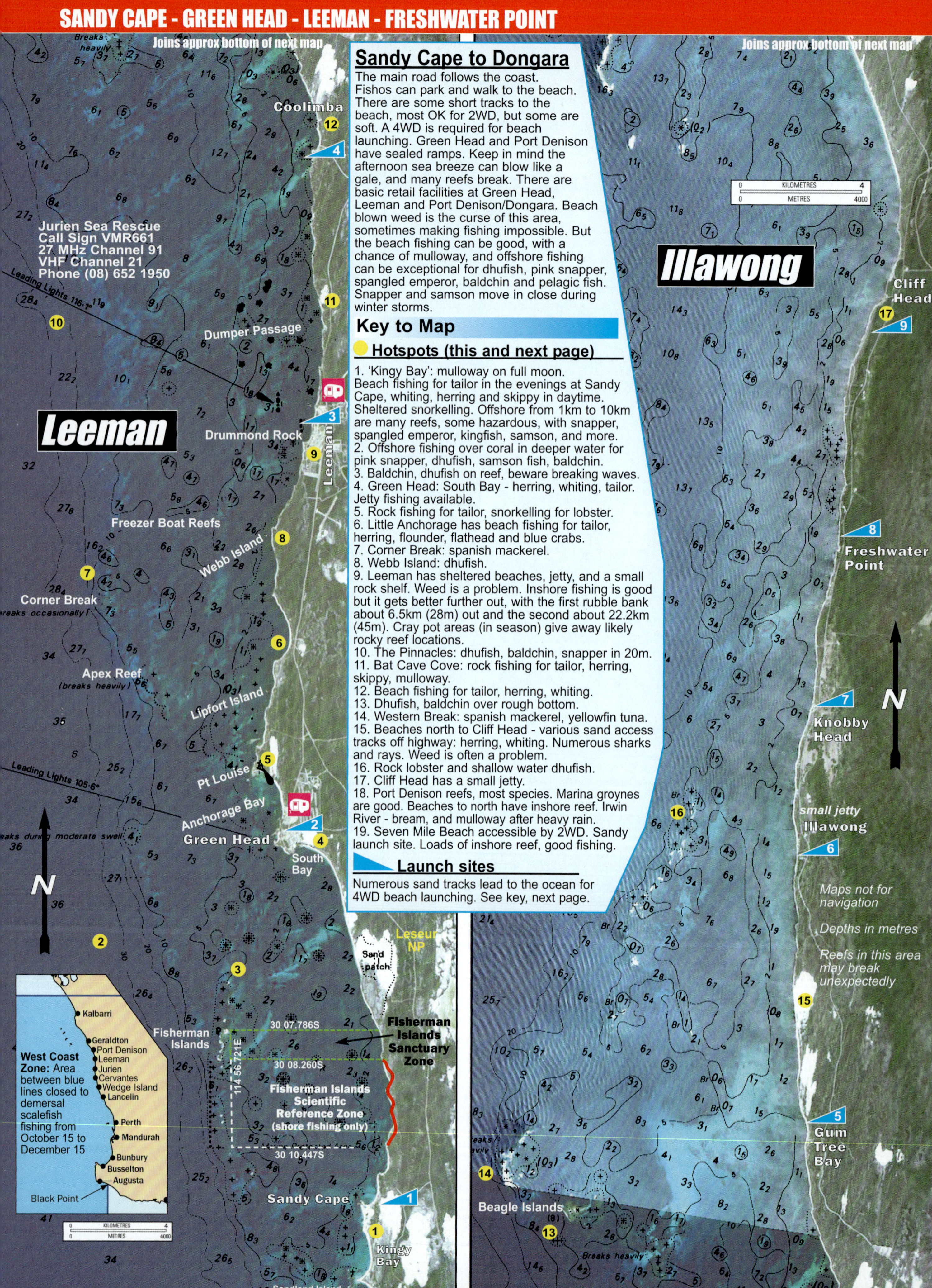

SANDY CAPE - GREEN HEAD - LEEMAN - FRESHWATER POINT
Joins approx bottom of next map
Sandy Cape to Dongara
The main road follows the coast. Fishos can park and walk to the beach. There are some short tracks to the beach, most OK for 2WD, but some are soft. A 4WD is required for beach launching. Green Head and Port Denison have sealed ramps. Keep in mind the afternoon sea breeze can blow like a gale, and many reefs break. There are basic retail facilities at Green Head, Leeman and Port Denison/Dongara. Beach blown weed is the curse of this area, sometimes making fishing impossible. But the beach fishing can be good, with a chance of mulloway, and offshore fishing can be exceptional for dhufish, pink snapper, spangled emperor, baldchin and pelagic fish. Snapper and samson move in close during winter storms.
Key to Map
Hotspots (this and next page)
1. 'Kingy Bay': mulloway on full moon. Beach fishing for tailor in the evenings at Sandy Cape, whiting, herring and skippy in daytime. Sheltered snorkelling. Offshore from 1km to 10km are many reefs, some hazardous, with snapper, spangled emperor, kingfish, samson, and more.
2. Offshore fishing over coral in deeper water for pink snapper, dhufish, samson fish, baldchin.
3. Baldchin, dhufish on reef, beware breaking waves.
4. Green Head: South Bay - herring, whiting, tailor. Jetty fishing available.
5. Rock fishing for tailor, snorkelling for lobster.
6. Little Anchorage has beach fishing for tailor, herring, flounder, flathead and blue crabs.
7. Corner Break: spanish mackerel.
8. Webb Island: dhufish.
9. Leeman has sheltered beaches, jetty, and a small rock shelf. Weed is a problem. Inshore fishing is good but it gets better further out, with the first rubble bank about 6.5km (28m) out and the second about 22.2km (45m). Cray pot areas (in season) give away likely rocky reef locations.
10. The Pinnacles: dhufish, baldchin, snapper in 20m.
11. Bat Cave Cove: rock fishing for tailor, herring, skippy, mulloway.
12. Beach fishing for tailor, herring, whiting.
13. Dhufish, baldchin over rough bottom.
14. Western Break: spanish mackerel, yellowfin tuna.
15. Beaches north to Cliff Head - various sand access tracks off highway: herring, whiting. Numerous sharks and rays. Weed is often a problem.
16. Rock lobster and shallow water dhufish.
17. Cliff Head has a small jetty.
18. Port Denison reefs, most species. Marina groynes are good. Beaches to north have inshore reef. Irwin River - bream, and mulloway after heavy rain.
19. Seven Mile Beach accessible by 2WD. Sandy launch site. Loads of inshore reef, good fishing.
Launch sites
Numerous sand tracks lead to the ocean for 4WD beach launching. See key, next page.
Jurien Sea Rescue
Call Sign VMR661
27 MHz Channel 91
VHF Channel 21
Phone (08) 652 1950
Leeman
Illawong
Coolimba
Dumper Passage
Drummond Rock
Freezer Boat Reefs
Webb Island
Corner Break
Apex Reef
(breaks heavily)
Lipfort Island
Pt Louise
Anchorage Bay
Green Head
South Bay
Leseur NP
Sand patch
Fisherman Islands
Fisherman Islands Sanctuary Zone
Fisherman Islands Scientific Reference Zone (shore fishing only)
30 07.786S
30 08.260S
30 10.447S
114 56.721E
Sandy Cape
Kingy Bay
Sandland Island
Leading Lights 116.1°
Leading Lights 105.6°
West Coast Zone: Area between blue lines closed to demersal scalefish fishing from October 15 to December 15
Kalbarri
Geraldton
Port Denison
Leeman
Jurien
Cervantes
Wedge Island
Lancelin
Perth
Mandurah
Bunbury
Busselton
Augusta
Black Point
KILOMETRES
METRES
Cliff Head
Freshwater Point
Knobby Head
small jetty
Illawong
Gum Tree Bay
Beagle Islands
Breaks heavily
Maps not for navigation
Depths in metres
Reefs in this area may break unexpectedly
N

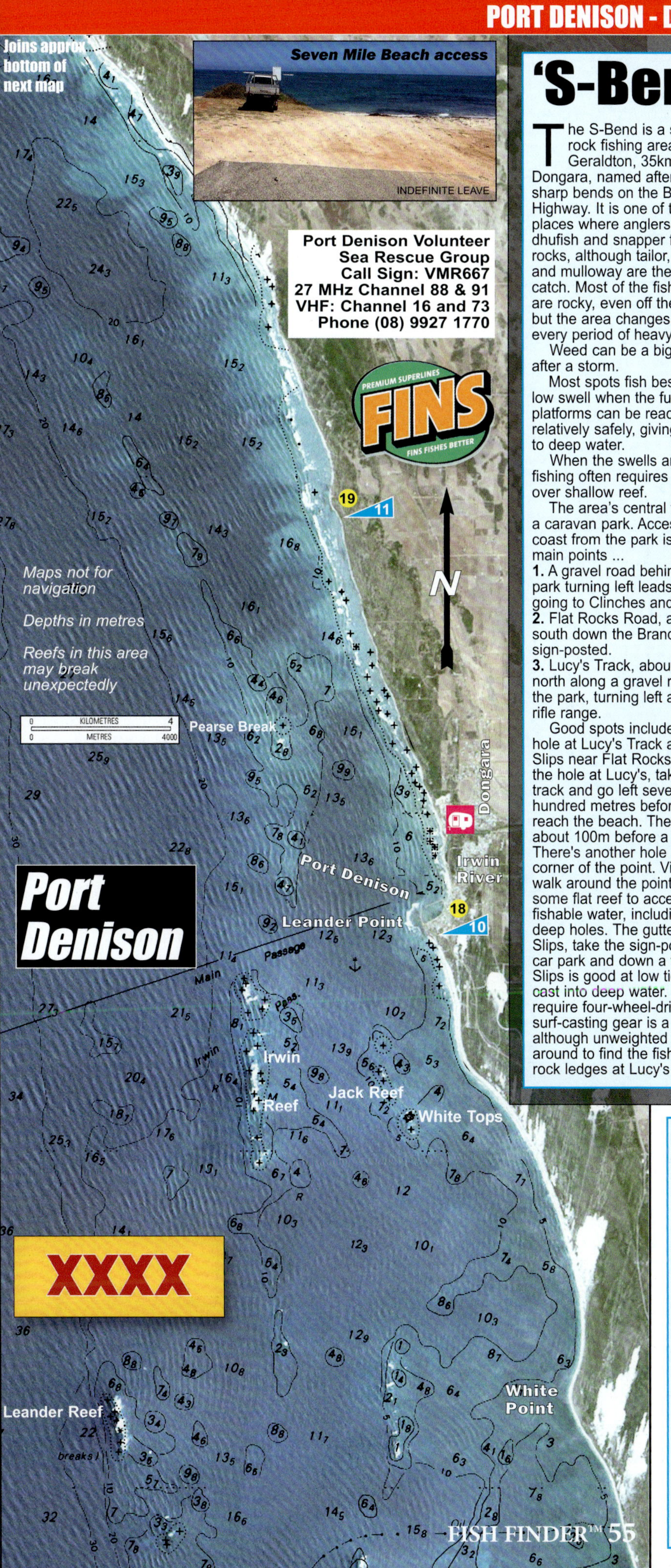

'S-Bend'

The S-Bend is a surf and rock fishing area south of Geraldton, 35km north of Dongara, named after two sharp bends on the Brand Highway. It is one of the few places where anglers can take dhufish and snapper from the rocks, although tailor, herring and mulloway are the usual catch. Most of the fishing spots are rocky, even off the beaches, but the area changes after every period of heavy weather.

Weed can be a big problem after a storm.

Most spots fish best during a low swell when the furthest platforms can be reached relatively safely, giving access to deep water.

When the swells are up, fishing often requires casting over shallow reef.

The area's central feature is a caravan park. Access to the coast from the park is via three main points ...

1. A gravel road behind the van park turning left leads to a track going to Clinches and Duncans.
2. Flat Rocks Road, about 3km south down the Brand Hwy. It is sign-posted.
3. Lucy's Track, about 5km north along a gravel road from the park, turning left along the rifle range.

Good spots include the main hole at Lucy's Track and The Slips near Flat Rocks. To get to the hole at Lucy's, take the track and go left several hundred metres before you reach the beach. The hole is about 100m before a point. There's another hole at the corner of the point. Visitors can walk around the point past some flat reef to access more fishable water, including two deep holes. The gutter past the flat reef is shallow but can hold tailor. To get to The Slips, take the sign-posted Flat Rocks turn-off to the beach and go north through the car park and down a track for a few hundred metres, or walk from the car park. The Slips is good at low tide with a low swell, when fishermen can stand on the reef and cast into deep water. This is a dhufish spot. There are other tracks in this area and they require four-wheel-drive. Deflation of tyres may be required if the sand is soft. Good surf-casting gear is a must. Lure fishing is often more practical in the snaggier areas, although unweighted baits or floats can be used in appropriate conditions. Move around to find the fish - they are sometimes found biting in only one or two areas. The rock ledges at Lucy's and Flat Rocks are dangerous in a swell, so take care.

S-Bend
Flat Rocks
Fingers
Dhu Hole
KILOMETRES
METRES
Kingy Hole
S-Bend Caravan Park
Back Beach
sand tracks
Brand Highway
Duncans
Clinches
Slips
Red Emperor Road
Flat Rocks
Flat Rocks Road
Secret Men's Business

Beach launching

Launching boats from sand is required to access reefs along much of this coast, away from the sealed ramps at Green Head or Port Denison. Afternoon sea breezes can make launch and retrieval difficult. Pay attention to weather forecasts. A second vehicle is useful in case of problems. Some fishos launch inflatables by quad bike.

Launch sites

1. Beach launching at Sandy Cape. Relatively sheltered bay. The road in is gravel and OK for 2WD but beach access is 4WD only. The camp sites are large, with private, bins, toilets, caretaker. To access, when driving to Jurien Bay, at the T-junction turn right to Green Head. There is then a signposted road to the left.
2. Two boat ramps at Green Head, one near the jetty and the other (shallow) at South Bay. Navigation out to sea requires care because of reefs.
3. Leeman town ramp (shallow) and Sea Rescue Ramp. Avoid low tide, and watch for reefs.
4, 5, 6, 7, 8, 9. Beach launching via tracks, exposed.
10. Port Denison: good ramp inside marina. Hazardous reef outside - stay to the right of the cardinal mark when leaving the ramp. Avoid heavy weather.
11. Beach launch at Seven Mile Beach.

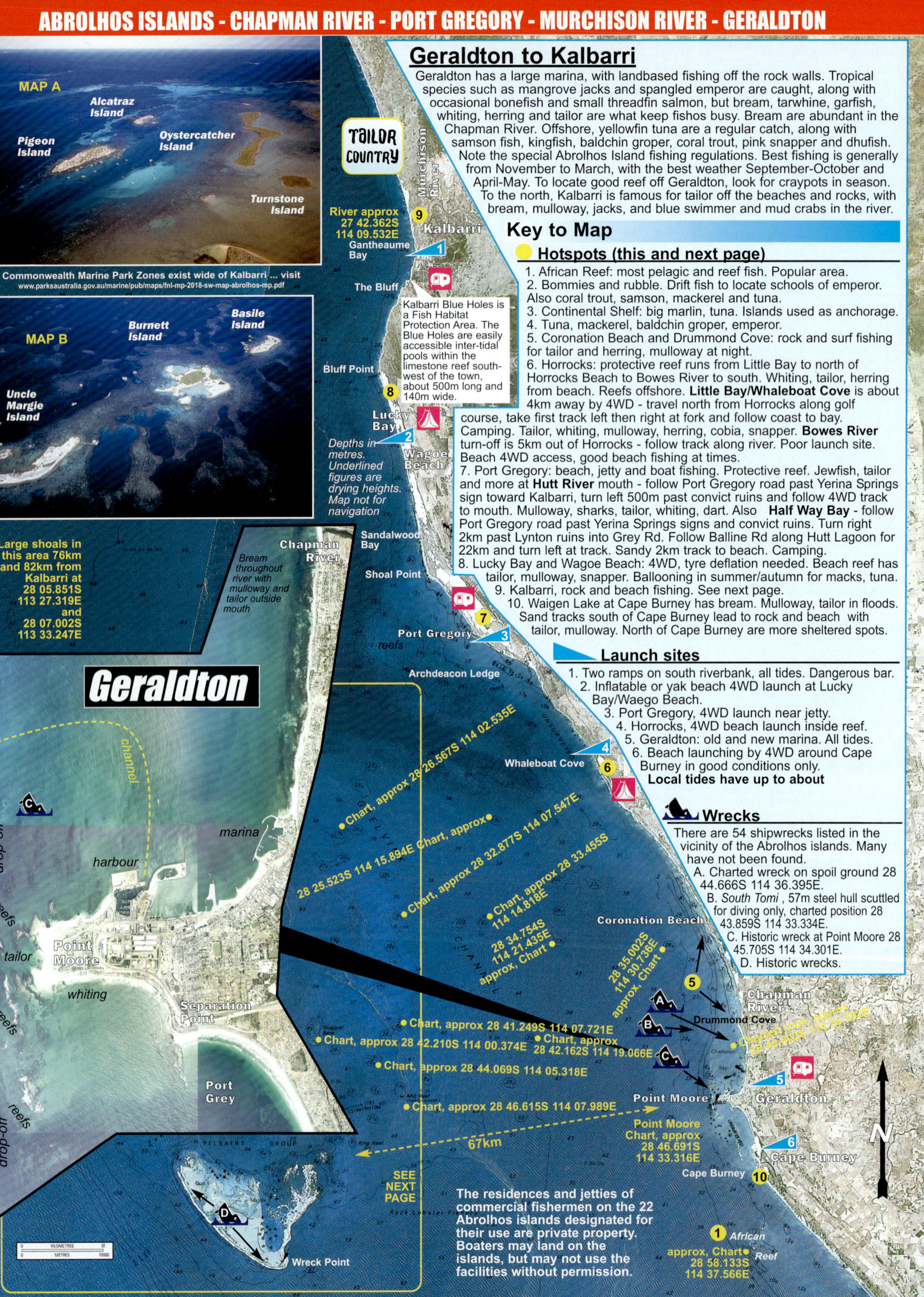

Geraldton to Kalbarri

Geraldton has a large marina, with landbased fishing off the rock walls. Tropical species such as mangrove jacks and spangled emperor are caught, along with occasional bonefish and small threadfin salmon, but bream, tarwhine, garfish, whiting, herring and tailor are what keep fishos busy. Bream are abundant in the Chapman River. Offshore, yellowfin tuna are a regular catch, along with samson fish, kingfish, baldchin groper, coral trout, pink snapper and dhufish. Note the special Abrolhos Island fishing regulations. Best fishing is generally from November to March, with the best weather September-October and April-May. To locate good reef off Geraldton, look for craypots in season. To the north, Kalbarri is famous for tailor off the beaches and rocks, with bream, mulloway, jacks, and blue swimmer and mud crabs in the river.

Key to Map

Hotspots (this and next page)

1. African Reef: most pelagic and reef fish. Popular area.
2. Bommies and rubble. Drift fish to locate schools of emperor. Also coral trout, samson, mackerel and tuna.
3. Continental Shelf: big marlin, tuna. Islands used as anchorage.
4. Tuna, mackerel, baldchin groper, emperor.
5. Coronation Beach and Drummond Cove: rock and surf fishing for tailor and herring, mulloway at night.
6. Horrocks: protective reef runs from Little Bay to north of Horrocks Beach to Bowes River to south. Whiting, tailor, herring from beach. Reefs offshore. **Little Bay/Whaleboat Cove** is about 4km away by 4WD - travel north from Horrocks along golf course, take first track left then right at fork and follow coast to bay. Camping. Tailor, whiting, mulloway, herring, cobia, snapper. **Bowes River** turn-off is 5km out of Horrocks - follow track along river. Poor launch site. Beach 4WD access, good beach fishing at times.
7. Port Gregory: beach, jetty and boat fishing. Protective reef. Jewfish, tailor and more at **Hutt River** mouth - follow Port Gregory road past Yerina Springs sign toward Kalbarri, turn left 500m past convict ruins and follow 4WD track to mouth. Mulloway, sharks, tailor, whiting, dart. Also **Half Way Bay** - follow Port Gregory road past Yerina Springs signs and convict ruins. Turn right 2km past Lynton ruins into Grey Rd. Follow Balline Rd along Hutt Lagoon for 22km and turn left at track. Sandy 2km track to beach. Camping.
8. Lucky Bay and Wagoe Beach: 4WD, tyre deflation needed. Beach reef has tailor, mulloway, snapper. Ballooning in summer/autumn for macks, tuna.
9. Kalbarri, rock and beach fishing. See next page.
10. Waigen Lake at Cape Burney has bream. Mulloway, tailor in floods. Sand tracks south of Cape Burney lead to rock and beach with tailor, mulloway. North of Cape Burney are more sheltered spots.

Launch sites

1. Two ramps on south riverbank, all tides. Dangerous bar.
2. Inflatable or yak beach 4WD launch at Lucky Bay/Waego Beach.
3. Port Gregory, 4WD launch near jetty.
4. Horrocks, 4WD beach launch inside reef.
5. Geraldton: old and new marina. All tides.
6. Beach launching by 4WD around Cape Burney in good conditions only.

Local tides have up to about

Wrecks

There are 54 shipwrecks listed in the vicinity of the Abrolhos islands. Many have not been found.

A. Charted wreck on spoil ground 28 44.666S 114 36.395E.
B. *South Tomi* , 57m steel hull scuttled for diving only, charted position 28 43.859S 114 33.334E.
C. Historic wreck at Point Moore 28 45.705S 114 34.301E.
D. Historic wrecks.

The residences and jetties of commercial fishermen on the 22 Abrolhos islands designated for their use are private property. Boaters may land on the islands, but may not use the facilities without permission.

Rock, river and reef

The Geraldton to Kalbarri coast has great rock fishing, while the Abrolhos Islands have the southernmost coral reefs in the Indian Ocean. The Continental Shelf drops away just a few kilometres from the islands.

Geraldton is the usual base for Abrolhos expeditions, about a 70km run to the Pelsaert Group. The Abrolhos consists of 122 low-lying limestone islands in three groups - Pelsaert, Easter and Wallabi - across about 100km of ocean. Some islands are the homes of lobster fishermen.

The Leeuwin Current is an important feature. There is an overlap of tropical and temperate species. The coral reefs have baldchin groper, dhufish, pink snapper and coral trout. On the Continental Shelf blue and black marlin, wahoo, dolphin fish and sailfish are found.

Good fishing exists within the islands at African Reef, Mid Reef and various other reefy patches. Coastal species include kingfish, cobia, samson, trevally, bream, tailor, whiting and jewfish. Mackerel are caught from the rocks.

Kalbarri has beach and rock fishing for tailor, dart, whiting and mulloway. The upper Murchison River is usually just dry with pools. When a cyclone passes, it is a torrent. The tidal section has jacks, giant herring and trevally, with bream and whiting the main target, along with blue swimmer and mud crabs. A reliable spot for bream is around the island near the boat ramp. Landbased tailor and mulloway fishing attract people to Kalbarri. The river mouth is dredged to allow lobster boats to pass, but it is a risky crossing.

TOM LEUSHUIS

Murchison River mouth, with the estuary immediately inside shown below

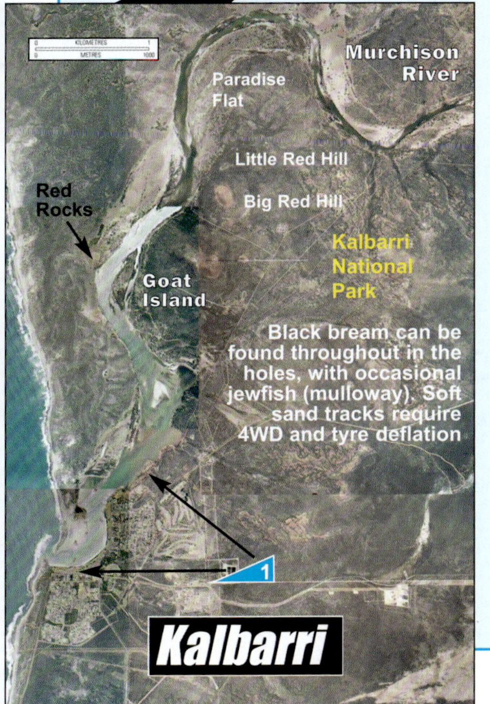

Tailor central

Kalbarri has several nearby rock and beach fishing hotspots - see the map to the right.

Some of the out-of-town rock spots, such as Goat Gulch, require long walks and specialist rock fishing gear and great caution. These spots can be fished by boat in calm weather.

Trophy tailor can be caught at the town.

Oyster Reef has great fishing, eclipsed only by the rock at the river mouth which cops the full swell. It has big tailor, but is a dangerous spot, although long casts from the beach will reach it.

A boat can access Oyster Reef by staying behind the wash. Or just walk the beach.

Wittecarra Creek and Red Bluff Beach are popular tailor spots. Chopper tailor tend to inhabit Kalbarri in summer, with greenbacks in winter. Fish the holes inside the reefs, or in gutters. High tides and dusk/dawn are best.

Jewfish are often caught when tailor have been running. The river mouth sandbar area is the best place, when the water is dirty after rain.

Sand Patch - 27 36.236S 114 07.946E, shallow reef near shore for winter snapper.

Baldface - 27 28.894S 114 04.436E, winter dhufish grounds, also samson fish and tropical reef species.

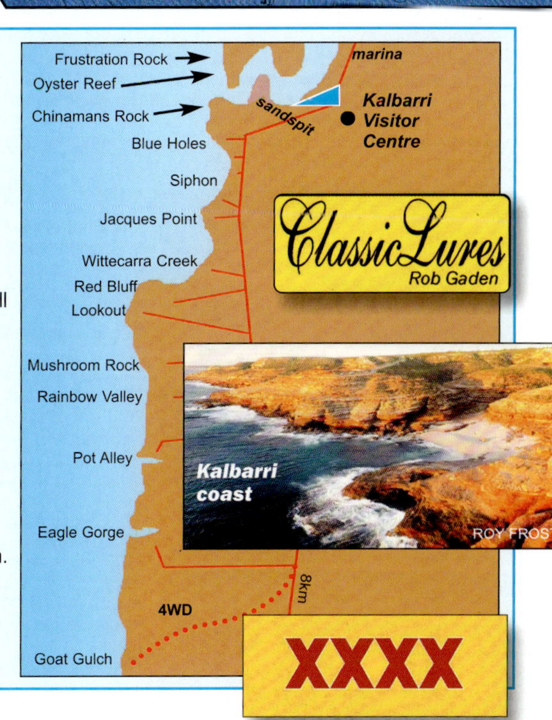

Sand and seagrass

Shark Bay, 400km north of Geraldton, is best known for its pink snapper, whiting and squid. The bay is easily fished, with reasonably sheltered waters and concrete boat ramps at the township of Denham, and at nearby tourist stop Monkey Mia. The marine habitat is mostly shallow sandflats, channels and seagrass beds, with coral in some areas. Clear water and calm sandy beaches are the norm. There are 12 types of seagrass and this supports about 12,000 dugongs and a healthy fish, crab and tiger shark population. The area is a marine park with some no-fishing zones and special regulations, mostly governing the taking of Shark Bay pink snapper, which surprisingly don't intermix with the pink snapper stocks outside the bay. Other fish caught include whiting, bream, garfish, tailor, squid, mackerel, trevally, queenfish and mulloway. The local emperor are called black snapper or piggies. These and tuskfish are found on the shallow reefs, with red emperor, dhufish and pelagic fish out wide. Ocean access is gained by launching from the beach inside Steep Point at Shelter Bay and travelling through the passage. A ferry is available to Dirk Hartog Island. The best boating time is between June and October, when winds are lighter and temperatures milder. Strong winds blow in summer.

Steep Point and False Entrance

The Steep Point rock ledge is a famous landbased spot - whales swim by and big mackerel, billfish, cobia, kingfish, snapper and more are caught from the rocks. Cliff gaffs are required. Balloon fishing methods are used for pelagic fish, as prevailing winds blow out from the rocks, but lure and bait casting works. Good footwear is a must and wearing a life preserver is recommended - for some reason, fishermen rarely do. Even with a life preserver, it is a long swim to safety. False Entrance is an alternative camping and fishing spot near Steep Point. The rock platform itself is rougher than Steep Point. Gaffing is harder as the cliffs at False Entrance are higher than the lowest Steep Point ledge. The beach at False Entrance is a superb spot for tailor, with mulloway in the evenings. False Entrance is on the same track as Steep Point, being just 7km from the signposted junction. Camping was being managed as part of Edel Land National Park at publication. For bookings visit **https://parks.dpaw.wa.gov.au/park-stay**. Boats are launched at Shelter Bay, which is a mooring area with several nearby campsites. Book permits well in advance or you will likely miss out. Fires or pets are not permitted, and visitors must be self sufficient.

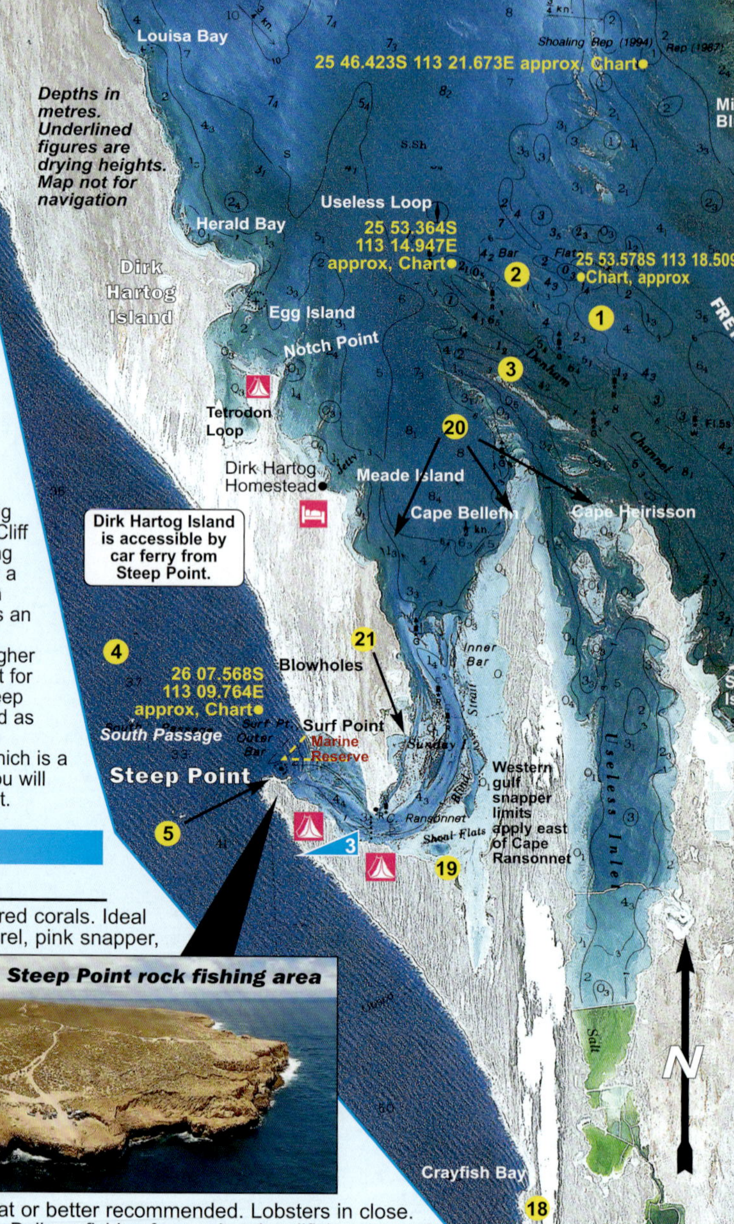

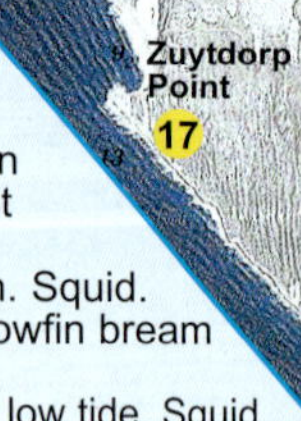

Key to Map

Hotspots

1. Bar Flats: Large area of deeper channels and seagrass beds with scattered corals. Ideal for small craft from 5m up. Fish with a floating pilchard at anchor for mackerel, pink snapper, black snapper (grass emperor).
2. Bar Flats Coral: shallow corals. Fish quietly at anchor, a great spot for baitcasting and lure fishing. A good area for fly-fishing. Snapper, tuskfish, coral trout, sea perch, mackerel, garfish etc.
3. Denham Channel: Drift fish on an incoming tide, best in the evening. Deep channel with scattered corals. Pink snapper, black snapper, mackerel. Tuna in the winter months.
4. Bottom fishing: red emperor, samson, trout, rankin cod, snapper - 6m boat or better recommended. Lobsters in close.
5. Steep Point: 4WD only. One of the best landbased fishing locations in WA. Balloon fishing for mackerel, sailfish, tuna and occasional marlin from rock platform at the point, mostly in summer. The point itself is usually in the lee of summer winds. Good beach fishing from the nearby sandspit to Monkey Rock for tailor, cobia and snapper. Mulloway and whiting from sandspit. Whiting and buffalo bream (drummer) off the beaches. Sharks in the evening. Squid from rock points. Crayfish in season. Good bottom fishing off the cliffs. Area can be dangerous for small craft because of the bar at the entrance, which breaks right across in heavy weather. Sandy access tracks require 4WD and tyre deflation. 4WD boat launching at Shelter Bay, which also has the best campsites. Visit **www.steeppoint.com.au** for local fishing tours.

Steep Point rock fishing area

BEN DURNIN

Bottle Bay

MATT FLYNN

Monkey Mia

MATT FLYNN

Giraud Point

AGENT86

6. White Island: Snapper schooling grounds. Special snapper rules apply in this region. Squid.
7. The area is dotted with small islands and rocky outcrops. Good fishing for tailor, yellowfin bream and tuskfish in the summer. Mackerel and pink snapper most of the year.
8. Lagoon Point: All vehicles. Fish incoming tide. Whiting in winter, tailor all year. Mussels at low tide. Squid.
9. Little Lagoon: All vehicles. Whiting, flathead all year.
10. Monkey Mia: All vehicles. Mulloway in the evening at sandspit east of ramp. Tailor in summer.
11. Red Cliff Bay: All vehicle access. Whiting, bream, flathead at high tide. Blue crabs.
12. Snapper around rough bottom. Squid.
13. Eagle Bluff: All vehicles. Fish high tide for school shark, tuskfish and tailor.
14. Nanga: All vehicles. Whiting, flathead at high tide.
15. Baba Head: 4WD. Bream, tailor, flathead, squid. Coastal camps available at Tamala Station.
16. Kangaroo Island: 4WD. Crabs, tailor. Snapper, tuskfish at bar south of island. Prawns on evening outgoing tide.
17. False Entrance: 4WD. Rock fishing from the southern point. Surf fishing to the north of the bay.
18. Crayfish Bay: 4WD. Rock fishing. Snapper, tuskfish. Access for divers in good weather.
19. Blind Inlet has sight-casting for bonefish.
20. Spangled emperor, pink snapper off rocky points.
21. Spangled emperor, pink snapper, tuskfish.
22. Pink snapper, jewfish.
23. Gladstone camp site has toilets. Boat needed for good fishing, beach launching. Limited firewood. Yaringa Station Homestead is opposite turn-off to Gladstone.

BEN DURNIN

Shelter Bay

Launch sites

1. Denham sealed launch site, most tides. 2. Monkey Mia sealed launch site, most tides. 3. Beach launching near Steep Point at Shelter Bay, 4WD only. 4. Big Lagoon beach launch. 5. Whalebone beach launch. 6. Nanga Bay Resort. 7. Giraud Point beach launch. **Local tides have up to about 1.3m movement.**

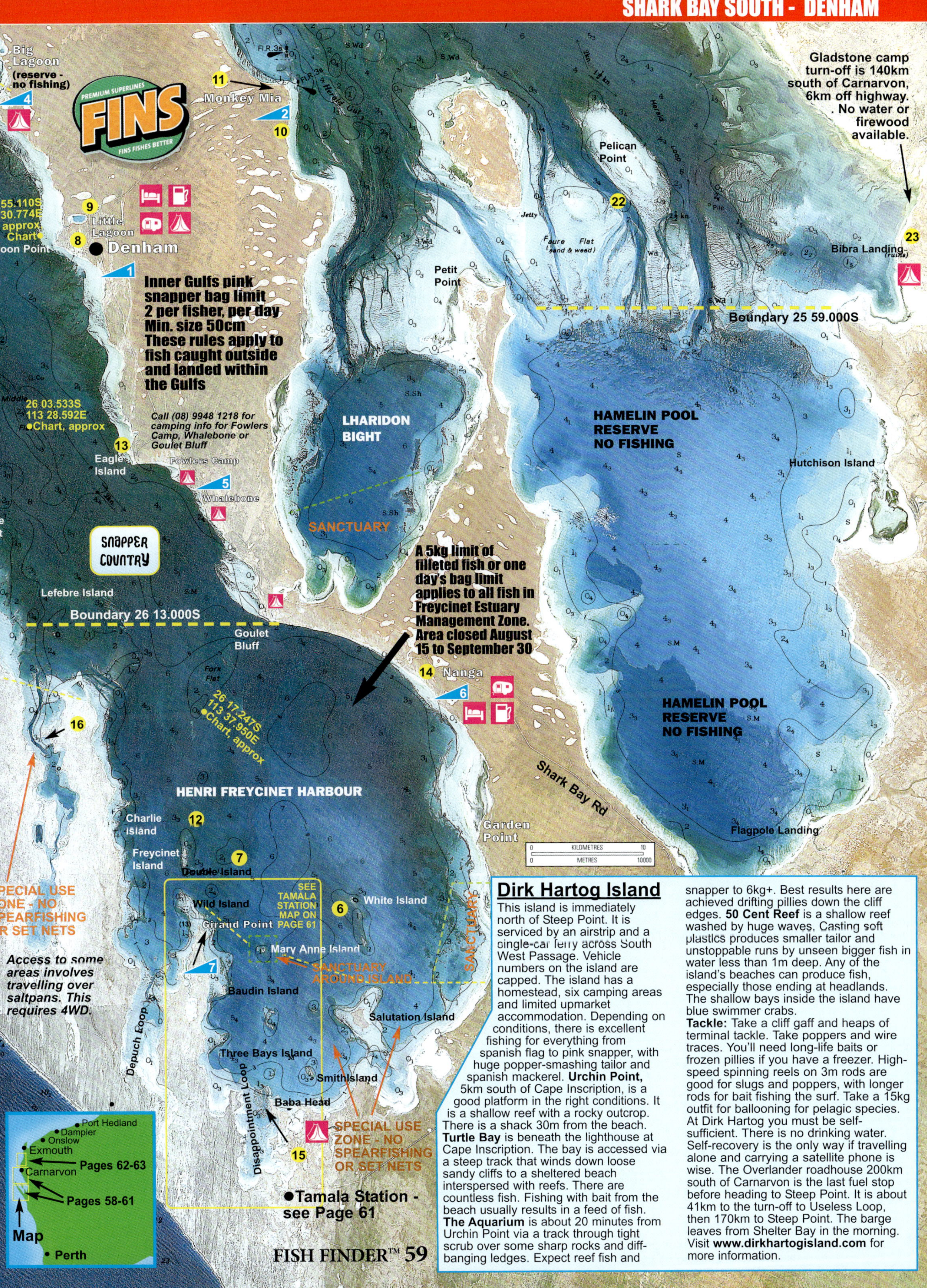

Dirk Hartog Island

This island is immediately north of Steep Point. It is serviced by an airstrip and a single-car ferry across South West Passage. Vehicle numbers on the island are capped. The island has a homestead, six camping areas and limited upmarket accommodation. Depending on conditions, there is excellent fishing for everything from spanish flag to pink snapper, with huge popper-smashing tailor and spanish mackerel. **Urchin Point,** 5km south of Cape Inscription, is a good platform in the right conditions. It is a shallow reef with a rocky outcrop. There is a shack 30m from the beach. **Turtle Bay** is beneath the lighthouse at Cape Inscription. The bay is accessed via a steep track that winds down loose sandy cliffs to a sheltered beach interspersed with reefs. There are countless fish. Fishing with bait from the beach usually results in a feed of fish. **The Aquarium** is about 20 minutes from Urchin Point via a track through tight scrub over some sharp rocks and diff-banging ledges. Expect reef fish and snapper to 6kg+. Best results here are achieved drifting pillies down the cliff edges. **50 Cent Reef** is a shallow reef washed by huge waves. Casting soft plastics produces smaller tailor and unstoppable runs by unseen bigger fish in water less than 1m deep. Any of the island's beaches can produce fish, especially those ending at headlands. The shallow bays inside the island have blue swimmer crabs.

Tackle: Take a cliff gaff and heaps of terminal tackle. Take poppers and wire traces. You'll need long-life baits or frozen pillies if you have a freezer. High-speed spinning reels on 3m rods are good for slugs and poppers, with longer rods for bait fishing the surf. Take a 15kg outfit for ballooning for pelagic species. At Dirk Hartog you must be self-sufficient. There is no drinking water. Self-recovery is the only way if travelling alone and carrying a satellite phone is wise. The Overlander roadhouse 200km south of Carnarvon is the last fuel stop before heading to Steep Point. It is about 41km to the turn-off to Useless Loop, then 170km to Steep Point. The barge leaves from Shelter Bay in the morning. Visit **www.dirkhartogisland.com** for more information.

Mulloway town

Carnarvon, 900km north of Perth, is home to year-round mulloway (jewfish) and tailor fishing. Blue crabs, mud crabs and prawns are found around mangroves near the town, with a mix of tropical and sub-tropical species out wide. Threadfin salmon are caught in the coastal shallows in winter. Some of the best spots are ...

- Pelican Point sandspit: big tailor at dusk.
- Remains of One-Mile Jetty. The jetty was destroyed by a cyclone in early 2021. What remains of the structure will likely hold mulloway schools just as the original jetty did. Also expect snapper, tailor, bream, sharks, garfish and squid in this area. Best May to August.
- Miaboolya Beach: 2WD access. Mulloway and tailor.
- Gascoyne River mouth: mulloway, tailor, whiting, jacks, flathead in tidal water. The upper freshwater reaches are unproductive, much of it flowing underground under a wide sandy river bed.
- Fascine River mouth (old southern outlet of Gascoyne River mouth): golden trevally and flathead, incoming tide. Fascine rock wall is a good fishing platform for jacks, bream, cod, trevally.
- Teggs Channel and Massey Bay: blue crabs and mackerel, with whiting and flathead in nearby creeks.

Shark Bay is famous for its pink snapper, best between March and September. Trevally and queenfish are best between April and July. Mulloway are best near full tide at dawn, with tailor at dusk rising tide.

Northern Shark Bay has excellent fishing around the islands, which provide lee shores. However strong winds tend to blow from September to February for days at a time, making boating difficult.

Key to Map

Hotspots

1. Broadhurst Corals: Shallow corals similar to Bar Flats Coral on previous page. Mixed species.
2. 80 Acres: Shallow corals ... tuskfish, mackerel, black snapper. Big mackerel, spangled emperor off Cape Peron North. Fishing for pink snapper is not permitted in the eastern bay.
3. Big Lagoon entrance: 4WD only. Snapper on rising tide at bar at the mouth, bream in lagoon below reserve area. Main lagoon is sanctuary.
4. Bottle Bay: 4WD only. Reef fish at high tide. Tailor in evening. Also Gregories. Camping areas. Soft sand requires tyre deflation.
5. Peron North: 4WD only. Balloon fish for mackerel, tailor in the evening. Oysters at the base of the red sand hills. Beach fishing for big queenfish, small snapper and piggies, occasional mulloway.
6. Levillain Shoal: Productive all year. Broken ground with corals. Can be rough with moderate winds on an incoming tide. Only for experienced boaters ... usually no radio contact available. Pink snapper from June to August, sweetlip, coral trout, sea perch, tuskfish, mackerel all year. Good anchorage south at Withnell Point.
7. Best fishing is ocean from False Entrance to Cape Inscription, larger boats only. Good fishing close to Cape Inscription for pink snapper and emperor.
8. Carnarvon: Vicinity of former One-Mile Jetty has mulloway, tailor, mackerel, trevally, threadfin salmon. Fishing by boat, mulloway near end of old jetty structure - use live tailor for bait. Nearby river mouth accessible by track and fishes well for flathead, whiting, jacks, threadfin salmon.
9. Bush Bay camp site: beach launch and toilets. Bream, flathead, whiting, longtom in creeks along coast. Bigger fish in channels out front, including spangled emperor. Camps can be among mangroves but king tides can be a problem. Busy during holidays. Out of phone range.
10. Herald Bluff: old pearling camp, 4WD only. Good whiting in winter. Mud crabs in the mangroves and school sharks at Guichenault Point.
11. Mackerel, wahoo on drop-off, big tailor in edge washes.

Wrecks

A. Whaling Barge: 24 54.442S 113 37.085E, 1.16km from lead light, snapper and mulloway at night, 6m deep.
B. The Tyres artificial reef: 25 02.788S 113 32.390E Tyre reef and sunken trawler sitting on sand, 14m deep. Best fishing at dawn and dusk. Most local species.
C. *Gudrun* historic wreck, sunk 1901. No fishing sanctuary and dive site.

Reefs

a. The Banks ... sloping coral bottom, mixed reef fish, approx 24 58.834S 112 30.636E. Mixed fish.
b. Ballast Ground: 24 53.767S, 113 36.027E, undulating weed-covered bottom, 8m deep. Snapper, emperor.

Launch sites

1. Two-lane concrete ramp, Harbour Rd, with toilets, cleaning table.
2. Monkey Mia ramp (see page 59), all tides.
3. Beach launching at Gregorys, Sth Gregorys, Bottle Bay.
4. Beach launching at Herald Bight.
5. Denham ramp (see page 59), all tides.

Local tides have up to about 1.72m movement.

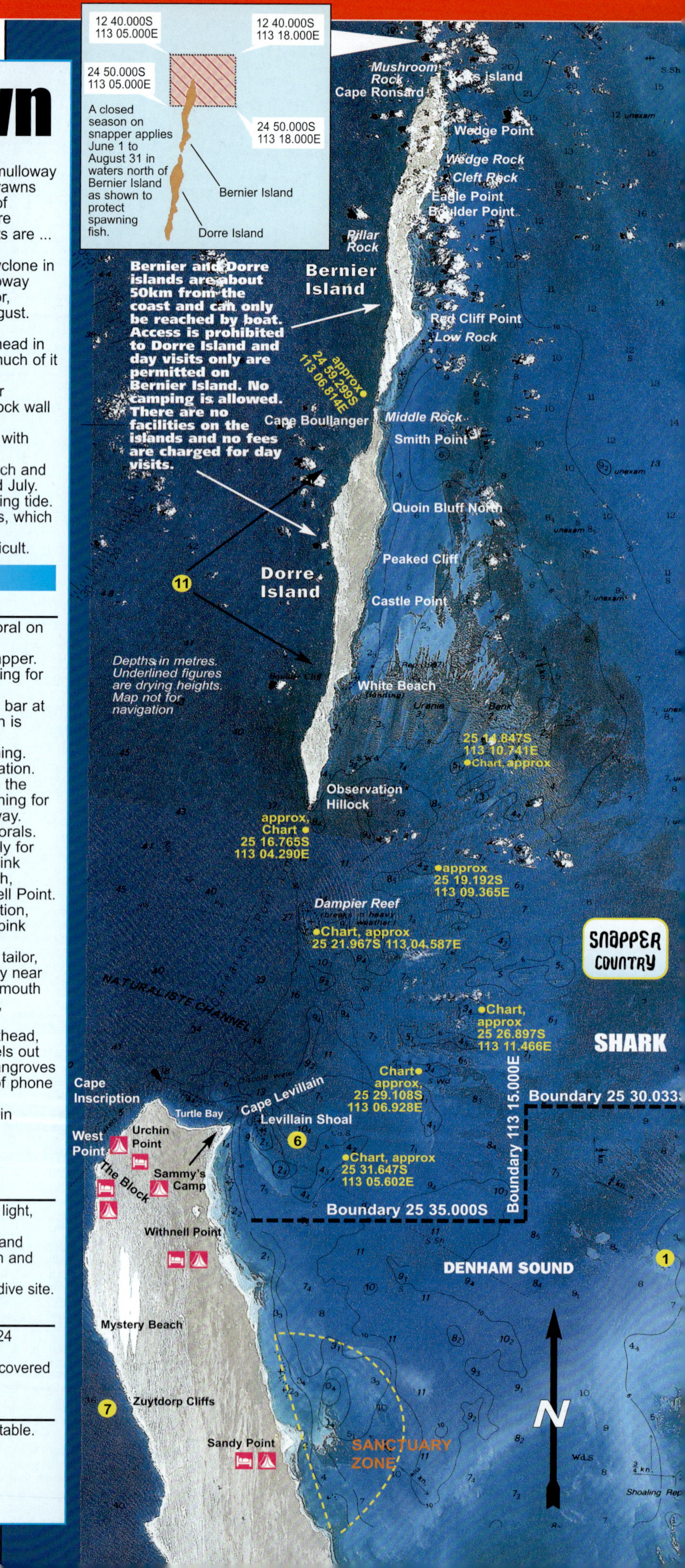

12 40.000S 113 05.000E
12 40.000S 113 18.000E
24 50.000S 113 05.000E
24 50.000S 113 18.000E
A closed season on snapper applies June 1 to August 31 in waters north of Bernier Island as shown to protect spawning fish.
Bernier Island
Dorre Island

Bernier and Dorre islands are about 50km from the coast and can only be reached by boat. Access is prohibited to Dorre Island and day visits only are permitted on Bernier Island. No camping is allowed. There are no facilities on the islands and no fees are charged for day visits.

Depths in metres. Underlined figures are drying heights. Map not for navigation

SNAPPER COUNTRY

Classic Lures
Rob Gaden
Killalure By Lance Butler
Gascoyne River (intermittent waterway)
24 52.289S 113 37.362E approx. Chart
Blowfish Banks
Miaboolya Beach
Miaboolya Creek
Crab Creek
Point Whitmore
Carnarvon
The Fascine
Babbage I
Oyster Creek
Gascoyne Road
Elbow Shoal
Grey Point
Gascoyne River mouth, showing the timber groynes and Whitmore Island
An artificial reef was to be deployed off Carnarvon at publication. Visit www.fish.wa.gov.au for details.
Bush Bay camp turn-off is 33km south of Carnarvon, with 8km track from highway. No water, some firewood, toilets.
Carnar-fin
Carnarvon has an annual May-June fishing competition. For details visit www.carnar-fin.org.au
Bush Bay
Greenough Point
Boundary 25 16.100S
EASTERN GULF ZONE
Boundary 113 31.000E
SANCTUARY ZONE
Cape Peron Flats
BAY
SPECIAL USE ZONE - NO SET NETS OR SPEARFISHING
Unsurveyed
Cape Peron North
SPECIAL USE ZONE - NO SPEARFISHING OR SET NETS
Broadhurst Bight
HERALD BIGHT
Bottle Bay
Jimmys Bay
Gregories
18 Mile
Sth Gregories
Cattle Well
Brockman Bay
Guichenault Point
4WD
Eastern Gulf closed May 1 to July 31
HOPELESS REACH
Boundary 25 37.920S
SANCTUARY ZONE
Boundary 25 45.920S
Red Cliff Bay
Tamala Station Map
Tamala was closed at publication, citing difficulties with its camping licence. A Tamala spokesman said a reopening date was not known.
GIRAUD POINT
HONEYMOON BAY
DOUBLE BEACH
LITTLE NANNAS
TEA TREE WEST
TEA TREE
NANAS
SHELL BEACH
THREE BAYS NORTH
THREE BAYS
SNAPPER BAY
OUT CAMP
SNAPPER ROCKS
TENT LANDING
CAMP 7
KEENYS CAMP NORTH
KEENYS CAMP
PRICKLY POINT
TO DENHAM
Tamala Station has coastal camping for fishermen, with beach launching. Sites are exposed, so bring your own shade.
www.tamala.com.au
XXXX

Remote coral beach camping

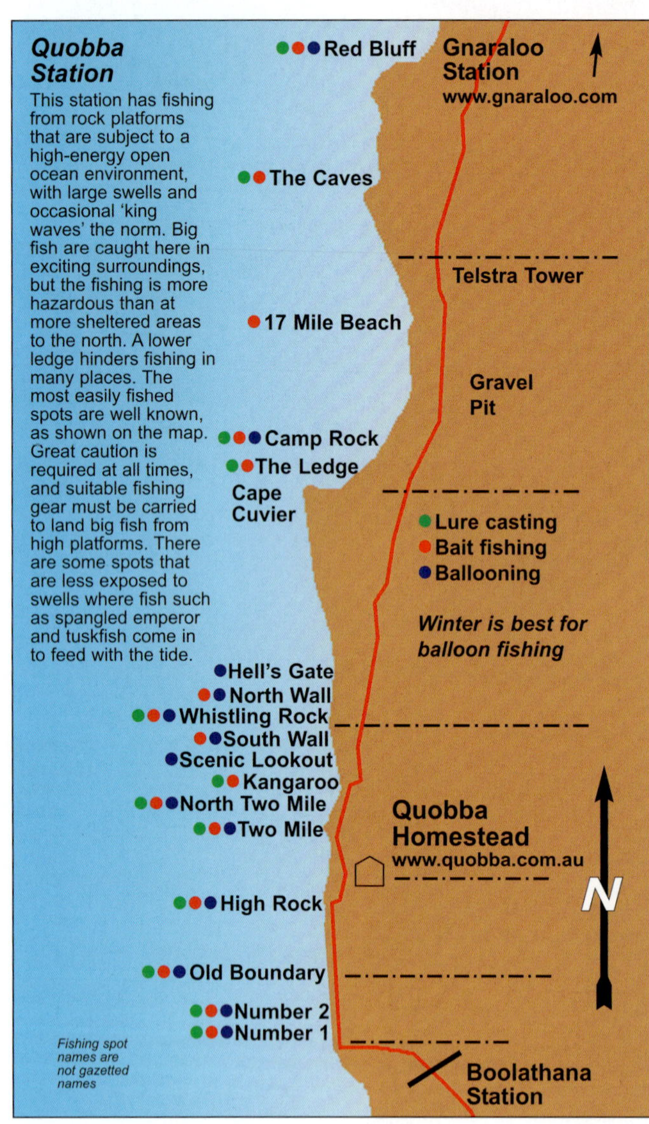

Camp names are not gazetted names

gap in reef · lagoon · Locked boundary gate · To Coral Bay · 33km to Warroora Homestead · 14-Mile Camp · 4WD · 2WD · fringing reef · lagoon · rubbish pit · N

Beach Fishing Only

gap in reef · Sandy Point · 4WD · fringing reef · lagoon

Pelican Sanctuary Zone

Pelican Point · No access · 4WD · Maggies

Beach Fishing Only

Elles Beach · Nev's Corner · Stevens · 4WD · Wedding Hill · Black Moon Cliff · Veronica's Vista · Sasha Belle's Spot · rubbish pit · Bulbarli surfing · Nick's Camp · The Laqoon · sandy crossing 4WD only · rubbish pit · Nolan's Nook · Amhurst Point · 15km to Minilya-Learmonth Rd

Warroora Homestead
www.warroora.com

Warroora Station

Though there are coral lagoons further south, the coastline along Warroora Station marks the southern point where fringing coral reef and inner lagoons dominate the coast. This station has mainly beach and coral reef lagoon fishing. Boaters can beach launch and go offshore through gaps in the fringing reef when conditions are suitable. Beach camps that were once run by the station are now run by Parks and Wildlife. There is a private campground near the station, about 1.5km from the beach. Visitors should bring drinking water. Non-potable water is available at the homestead. Quad bikes and motorbikes are not allowed on the station.

Coral lagoon fishing

Spangled emperor are caught from the beaches inside the lagoons, as well as tuskfish, queenfish and trevally. Tiger squid hunt in the shallows and can be sight-fished from beaches in daylight calm weather.

Beach camp bookings

For beach camp bookings visit Parks and Wildlife at **https://parks.dpaw.wa.gov.au/site/warroora-coast**

The Quobba-Ningaloo coast has some of Australia's best beach camps for fishing, surfing and snorkelling.

Station-owned camps extend north from Quobba Station at the south, to just south of Yardie Creek. Further north, the beach camps are run by WA Parks and Wildlife.

The camps are basic but beautiful, with ocean views over coral bays, providing easy access to beach fishing and snorkelling.

Some camps have vehicle access for beach launching.

Ningaloo is Australia's largest fringing coral reef, at 260km long.

It is just 100m offshore at its closest point and less than 7km at its furthest.

The Continental Shelf lies just 18.5km out.

Ningaloo Marine Park, opened in 1987, covers 4000sq km, from Amherst Point in the south to Bundegi Reef in Exmouth Gulf to the north. The park extends about 18.5km to sea.

A sandy coastal track runs through pastoral stations from Quobba to Coral Bay, but thoroughfare access is blocked.

Camping and accommodation is at Quobba Station, Gnaraloo and Warroora stations.

In recent times, Parks and Wildlife has been taking control of some beach camps.

The Ningaloo region has beach, reef, flats and offshore game fishing. The beaches produce queenfish, golden and giant trevally and spangled emperor within the reef lagoons, with a chance of permit, bonefish and cobia.

Out wide are emperor, cod, tuskfish, coral trout, mackerel, trevally and more.

With the Continental Shelf coming close to the mainland, trailerboaters have a rare chance to catch blue and black marlin, sailfish, wahoo, dolphin fish, mackerel and broadbill swordfish.

Fishing charter boats work from Coral Bay and Exmouth.

Fishermen can have a fine time using a dinghy or yak at Ningaloo during calm weather. To go outside the reef requires a seaworthy boat.

On the stations, drivers must stick to tracks to prevent dune erosion. Visitors must bring fuel, food and water. Some areas require portable toilets.

A compressor for reinflating tyres is needed for sand driving.

Be prepared for private station fishing bag limits, imposed to enhance sustainability.

Parts of Ningaloo, including some beaches, are sanctuaries. Some sanctuaries allow beach fishing within.

Getting there: The Quobba-Ningaloo region is 700km north of Perth, and 130km north of Carnarvon. To reach Quobba, take the Blowholes Road turn-off 30km north of Carnarvon on the Great Northern Hwy.

A 4WD vehicle is needed for many coastal camp sites.

To reach Warroora Station, from the north take the Warroora Northern access 15km south of the Coral Bay turn-off.

If coming from Carnarvon, turn left at the Lyndon Crossing Rest Area and drive 23km to the homestead.

Visitors can fly in to Learmonth Airport, 37km south of Exmouth. Coaches also service this area.

Seasons: Most visitors come between April and November. High temperatures, strong winds and cyclones discourage summer visits, but good fishing is had all year.

Bait and Tackle: A good surf rod is a must for beach and rock fishing, together with some chrome lures for distance casting.

Ballooning rigs are used to get baits out from the rocks. Ganged hooks and pilchard baits work well on tailor, mackerel and the like.

Boat fishing requires everything from handlines to trolling and spinning rods.

Launching: There are sealed ramps at Bundegi (north of Exmouth), Tantabiddi Creek and near Coral Bay. Beach launching can be done in some spots, and is the only way south of Yardie Creek.

The gaps between reefs leading to the ocean can be treacherous.

*Outside of the protected lagoons, rock fishing is dangerous and has claimed lives.

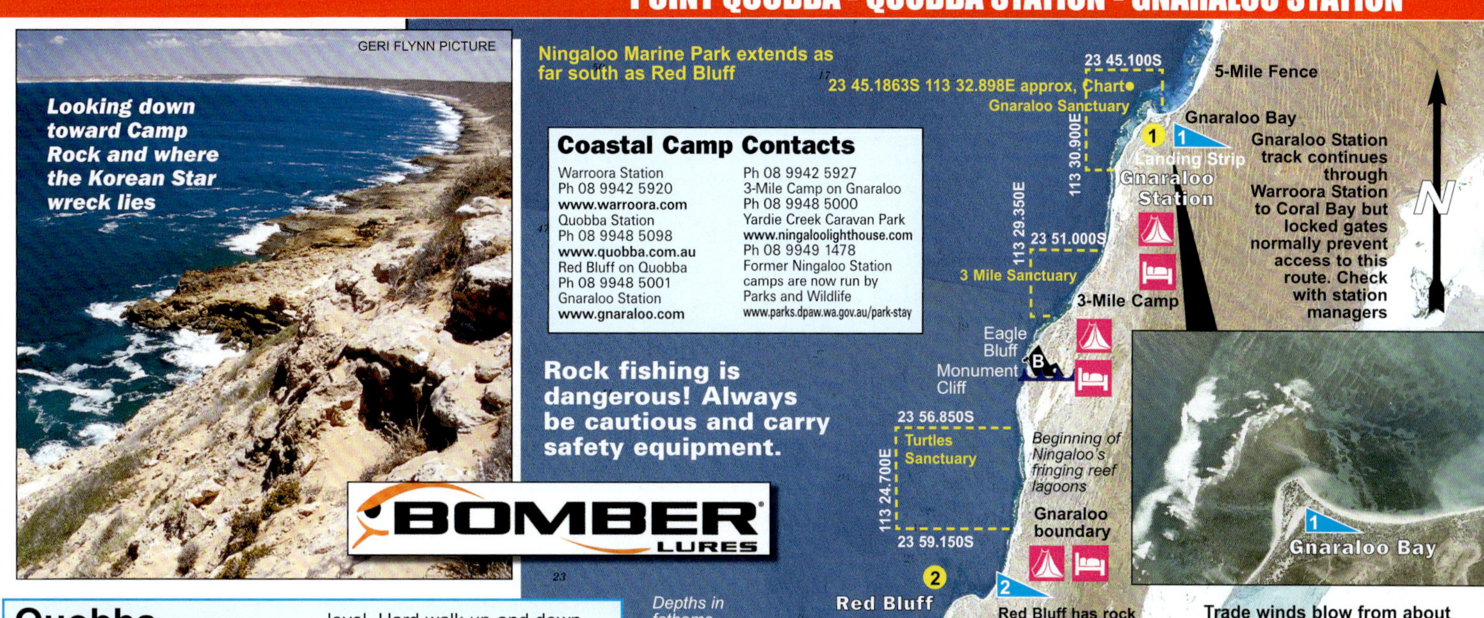

Quobba

Rock and beach meets open ocean here, offering spectacular but potentially dangerous fishing. Large fish, sharks and even humpback whales swim close to shore. Some areas have good rock platforms, with deep water close in, but much of the coast has a low ledge that makes fishing difficult. Ballooning is popular when the wind blows off shore. The Caves, The Ledge, Camp Rock and the *Korean Star* wreck (A) site are good spots, but there are others. Don't ignore the shallow lagoons, as tuskfish and spangled emperor feed in close. Off the ledges, spanish mackerel, kingfish, trevally, queenfish, cod, mulloway, cobia and tailor are caught. The road north of Quobba is rough and tracks require 4WD. Red Bluff and 3-Mile surf camps are popular stays, but 3-Mile is in a sanctuary. The *Magnolia* wreck (B) is worth a snorkel. Gnaraloo has a sheltered coral bay with a firm beach launch.

Key to Map

Hotspots

1. Gnaraloo Bay: area outside sanctuary has pelagic and reef fish in close. Rough road. Reasonably protected firm beach launch. Swimming, accommodation and great snorkelling.
2. Red Bluff: camping, beach and rock fishing. Mainly a surfing area but there is good fishing here when conditions are bad elsewhere.
3. The Ledge: good fishing position, flat rock 6m above sea level. Hard walk up and down. All species. Nearby *Korean Star* wreck (A) and Camp Rock is easier - steep 4WD track descends cliff.
4. High Rock: Platform 10m above water level. Popular spot for ballooning, bottom fishing and spinning. Tailor, trevally, queenfish, mackerel, and tuna. Safety rail erected, but is a dangerous area.
5. The Boundary: rocky platform 5m above sea level fishing into deep snaggy water. Good ballooning location with offshore wind, and reef fish.
6. Point Quobba: sheltered bay and beach, shallow reefs. Night fishing for spangled emperor, shark, reef fish. Tailor, whiting, queenfish, squid, trevally during day. The FHPA boundaries extend from the reef just north of the lagoon and adjacent marine waters, south to, and including, Black Rock. Fishing is prohibited in the 'restricted' area but permitted in the FHPA, subject to Gascoyne region rules.
7. Shoals: excellent fishing in calm weather.

Launch sites

1. Gnaraloo: good 4WD beach launch, beware breakers nearby. Cabins and camps, road in is sandy and rough. Ph (08) 9942 5927. **www.gnaraloo.com**
2. Red Bluff: camping and 4WD beach launching for small boats in calm weather. Ph (08) 9948 5001. **www.quobba.com.au**
3. 4WD beach launch south of blowholes. Quobba Station to north has accommodation and 80km of coastline. Ph (08) 9948 5098.

Trade winds blow from about mid September to mid February, making it hard to fish. Late in February the hot easterlies arrive. April/May is comfortable, with often gentle breezes. June/July and August are quiet at times, with some strong south-easters. Winter weather is usually created by the top of the fronts that bring cold weather to southern states, so it pays to watch these fronts.

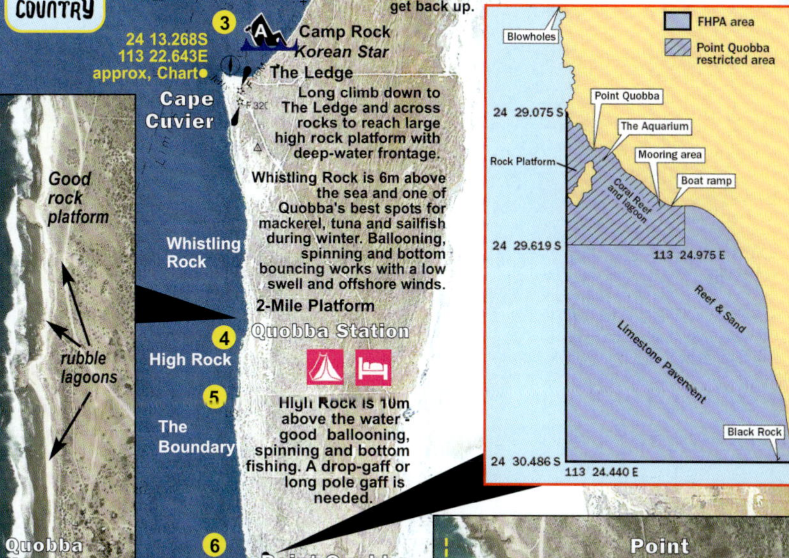

Looking towards Cape Cuvier, with The Ledge to the bottom left. Most fish species can be caught from the rocks, and whales will swim past a few metres out from where fishermen stand

Ningaloo Reef, showing the inner lagoon and the outer drop-off

Exmouth Gulf flats cobia caught on fly

WWW.TRUEBLUEBONEFISH.COM.AU

Joins bottom of next page

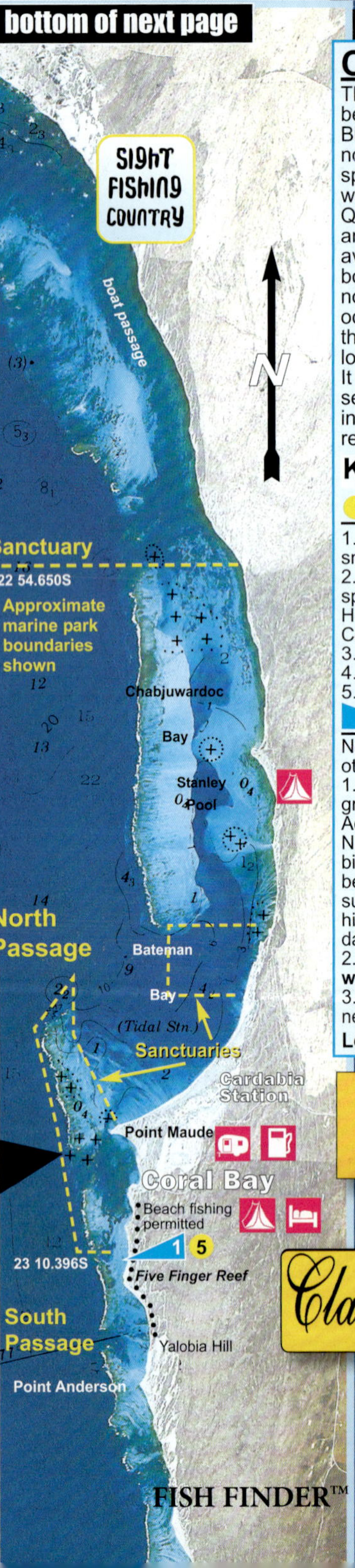

Coral Bay

This small tourism-based community lies next to a stunning beach, with clear blue water and endless inshore coral reef. Bills Bay (Town Bay) is a sanctuary but visitors may fish just north of and south of the bay. Boaters will find ample fishing space outside the protected zones. Snorkelling and even wading here reveals big spangled emperor in close. Queenfish, trevally, tuskfish, permit and occasional bonefish and tiger squid can be caught in the lagoons. The species available outside the reef are too many to list. To take a boat outside there are two main options. North Passage north of Point Maud is a wide, deep passage to the ocean. Boaters can generally navigate across the bay to this passage at high tide but otherwise must take a longer route along a channel marked through the coral. It is wise to mark your route for the return trip. The second option is South Passage. This is a narrow gap in the reef that is unsafe in poor weather, and is not recommended. Winter brings more calm spells.

Key to Map

Hotspots

1. Gnaraloo: sandy beach with coral shallows. Superb snorkelling and reasonable lagoon fishing.
2. Coral Bay: beach fishing outside sanctuaries - mainly spangled emperor. landbased fishing off rocks at Monk Head boat ramp. The Continental Shelf starts 46km from Coral Bay, but runs as close in as 10km further north.
3. Beach fishing at Warroora - private camps.
4. Bruboodjoo - camping, snorkelling, beach fishing.
5. Landbased fishing off boat ramp rock walls.

Launch sites

Note: Waves can break in the reef passages, and over other reefy areas. Boating caution is required.

1. Coral Bay, concrete boat ramp and finger jetty on a groyne island near Monk Head, 1.5km south of township. Access via Banksia drive, turn east of the Backpackers Ningaloo Club on the way into town and follow the bitumen road. A channel runs out from the ramp. Stay between the markers as coral outcrops reach the surface. North Passage is reasonably safe but best near high tide. Navigation at night or in bad weather is dangerous. Avoid South Passage in poor conditions.
2. Beach launching and fishing at Warroora Station. **www.warroora.com**
3. Good beach launch at Gnaraloo, but waves often break nearby. **www.gnaraloo.com**

Local tides have up to about 1.5m movement.

Air access to this region, 1200km north of Perth, is via Learmonth Airport, 37km south of Exmouth

Coral Bay Sea Rescue monitors radio messages in this area. Boat hire and fishing charters are available.

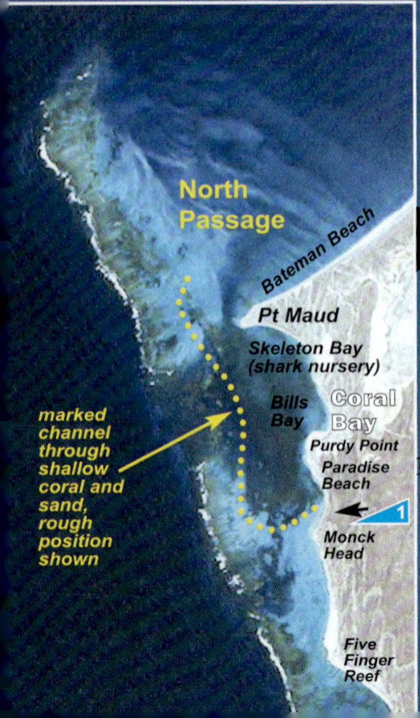

WWW.CORALBAY.ORG

Coral Bay ramp

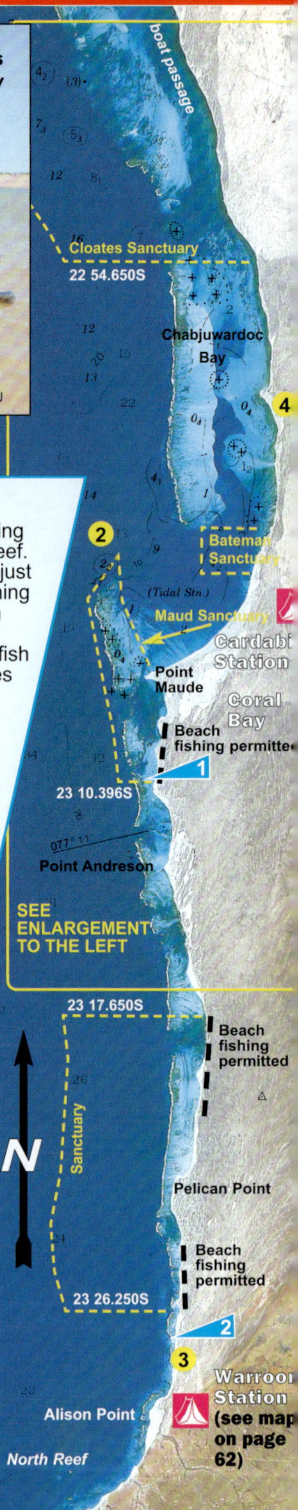

Map not for navigation. Depths in fathoms. Underlined figures are drying heights.

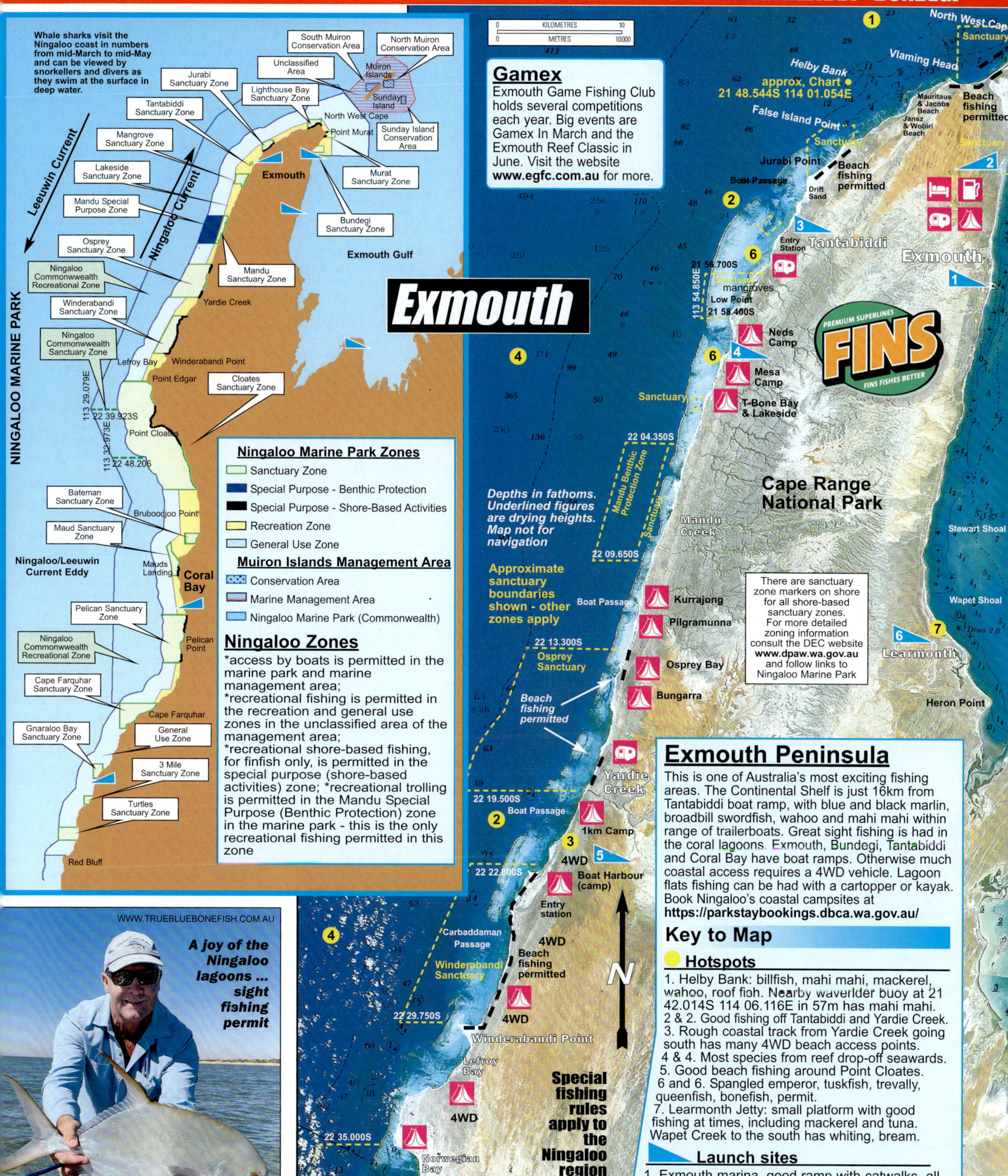

Exmouth

Gamex

Exmouth Game Fishing Club holds several competitions each year. Big events are Gamex In March and the Exmouth Reef Classic in June. Visit the website **www.egfc.com.au** for more.

Ningaloo Zones

*access by boats is permitted in the marine park and marine management area;
*recreational fishing is permitted in the recreation and general use zones in the unclassified area of the management area;
*recreational shore-based fishing, for finfish only, is permitted in the special purpose (shore-based activities) zone; *recreational trolling is permitted in the Mandu Special Purpose (Benthic Protection) zone in the marine park - this is the only recreational fishing permitted in this zone

Exmouth Peninsula

This is one of Australia's most exciting fishing areas. The Continental Shelf is just 16km from Tantabiddi boat ramp, with blue and black marlin, broadbill swordfish, wahoo and mahi mahi within range of trailerboats. Great sight fishing is had in the coral lagoons. Exmouth, Bundegi, Tantabiddi and Coral Bay have boat ramps. Otherwise much coastal access requires a 4WD vehicle. Lagoon flats fishing can be had with a cartopper or kayak. Book Ningaloo's coastal campsites at **https://parkstaybookings.dbca.wa.gov.au/**

Key to Map

Hotspots

1. Helby Bank: billfish, mahi mahi, mackerel, wahoo, roof fish. Nearby waverider buoy at 21 42.014S 114 06.116E in 57m has mahi mahi.
2 & 2. Good fishing off Tantabiddi and Yardie Creek.
3. Rough coastal track from Yardie Creek going south has many 4WD beach access points.
4 & 4. Most species from reef drop-off seawards.
5. Good beach fishing around Point Cloates.
6 and 6. Spangled emperor, tuskfish, trevally, queenfish, bonefish, permit.
7. Learmonth Jetty: small platform with good fishing at times, including mackerel and tuna. Wapet Creek to the south has whiting, bream.

Launch sites

1. Exmouth marina, good ramp with catwalks, all tides, 2.5km south of town.
2. Raised (sandproofed) ramp and finger jetty at Bundegi, useable most tides, but exposed.
3. Tantabiddi, from .5m tide up for big boats, smaller boats most tides, two finger jetties.
4. Neds Camp, beach launch.
5. Beach launching only south of Yardie Creek.
6. Beach launching near Learmonth jetty.
7 & 7. Beach launching cartoppers/yaks.

Local tides have up to about 1.69m movement.

Charlie Court

Muiron Islands Management Area

Approximate marine park boundaries shown

King Reef

This artificial reef was installed in 2018 just 6.45km north-east of Exmouth ramp at **21 54.938S 114 11.235E** It comprises six steel units and 49 concrete modules. Forty fish species were seen soon after deployment.

Depths in metres. Underlined figures are drying heights. Map not for navigation

ENLARGEMENT NEXT PAGE

Exmouth Gulf Station - *coastal day access available for a fee. Phone 08 9942 5936*

Bullara Station - *coastal access and camping available. Phone 08 9942 5938 www.bullarastation.com.au*

Giralia Station - *coastal access and camping available. Phone 08 9942 5937 www.giraliastation.com.au*

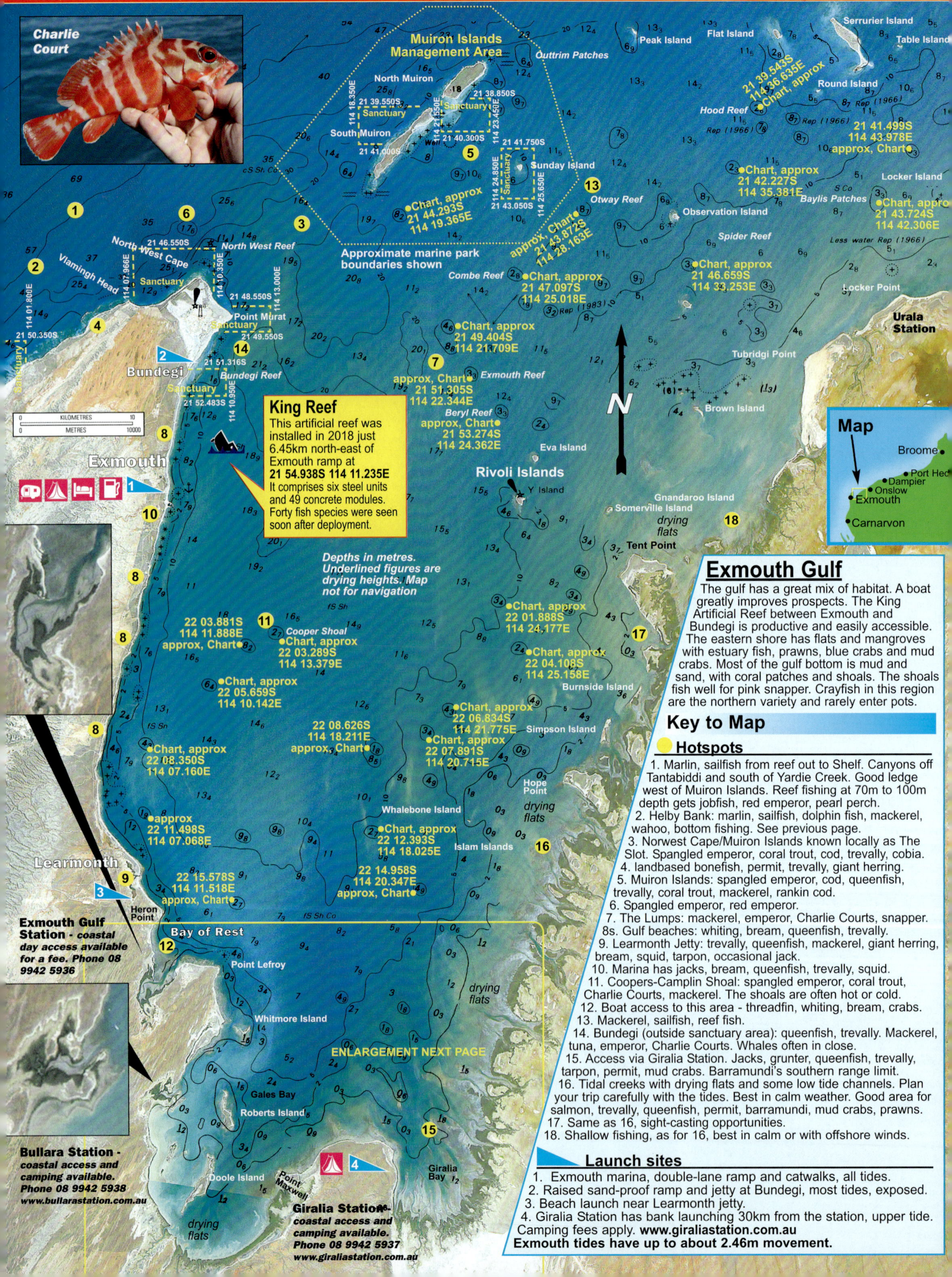

Exmouth Gulf

The gulf has a great mix of habitat. A boat greatly improves prospects. The King Artificial Reef between Exmouth and Bundegi is productive and easily accessible. The eastern shore has flats and mangroves with estuary fish, prawns, blue crabs and mud crabs. Most of the gulf bottom is mud and sand, with coral patches and shoals. The shoals fish well for pink snapper. Crayfish in this region are the northern variety and rarely enter pots.

Key to Map

Hotspots

1. Marlin, sailfish from reef out to Shelf. Canyons off Tantabiddi and south of Yardie Creek. Good ledge west of Muiron Islands. Reef fishing at 70m to 100m depth gets jobfish, red emperor, pearl perch.
2. Helby Bank: marlin, sailfish, dolphin fish, mackerel, wahoo, bottom fishing. See previous page.
3. Norwest Cape/Muiron Islands known locally as The Slot. Spangled emperor, coral trout, cod, trevally, cobia.
4. landbased bonefish, permit, trevally, giant herring.
5. Muiron Islands: spangled emperor, cod, queenfish, trevally, coral trout, mackerel, rankin cod.
6. Spangled emperor, red emperor.
7. The Lumps: mackerel, emperor, Charlie Courts, snapper.

8s. Gulf beaches: whiting, bream, queenfish, trevally.

9. Learmonth Jetty: trevally, queenfish, mackerel, giant herring, bream, squid, tarpon, occasional jack.
10. Marina has jacks, bream, queenfish, trevally, squid.
11. Coopers-Camplin Shoal: spangled emperor, coral trout, Charlie Courts, mackerel. The shoals are often hot or cold.
12. Boat access to this area - threadfin, whiting, bream, crabs.
13. Mackerel, sailfish, reef fish.
14. Bundegi (outside sanctuary area): queenfish, trevally. Mackerel, tuna, emperor, Charlie Courts. Whales often in close.
15. Access via Giralia Station. Jacks, grunter, queenfish, trevally, tarpon, permit, mud crabs. Barramundi's southern range limit.
16. Tidal creeks with drying flats and some low tide channels. Plan your trip carefully with the tides. Best in calm weather. Good area for salmon, trevally, queenfish, permit, barramundi, mud crabs, prawns.
17. Same as 16, sight-casting opportunities.
18. Shallow fishing, as for 16, best in calm or with offshore winds.

Launch sites

1. Exmouth marina, double-lane ramp and catwalks, all tides.
2. Raised sand-proof ramp and jetty at Bundegi, most tides, exposed.
3. Beach launch near Learmonth jetty.
4. Giralia Station has bank launching 30km from the station, upper tide. Camping fees apply. **www.giraliastation.com.au**

Exmouth tides have up to about 2.46m movement.

Where records fall

Exmouth Game Fishing Club has had almost 150 gamefish records in state, national and international categories, covering 28 species, a fine illustration of the local fishing quality.

Despite a lack of significant nearby rivers, Exmouth offers rich variety, from sight fishing sandy flats inside reef lagoons, to deep-sea trolling for all six species of billfish over the Continental Shelf, with coral reef fishing in between.

The eastern gulf flats are sheltered in easterly winds. This area marks the southern limit for WA's barramundi.

The gulf produces tropical reef fish, as well as occasional southern species such as tailor and pink snapper.

The Continental Shelf is at its closest point to the Australian mainland on the north-west end of the Exmouth Peninsula.

This is perhaps WA's prime billfish area, with big black and blue marlin caught in summer, and sailfish all year, with a gulf sailfish run in October-November.

Known billfish grounds include the drop-off directly out from Tantabiddi boat ramp northwards, and offshore from the Muiron Islands.

Prawns, crabs and lobsters

With so many sportfish available, Exmouth's crustaceans are sometimes overlooked.

Exmouth Gulf produces blue swimmer crabs well over legal size, unlike waters further north where blue crabs are usually smaller.

The gulf's blue crab movements seem hard to predict, unlike the more predictable seasons further south. Tackle World Exmouth said local blue crabs can move two or three times a year. Staff know when crabs are running because crabbing gear starts selling. Dropping nets from boats in 4m to 6m of water seems to work best.

The gulf also produces mud crabs. These are found mainly around mangrove creeks in the eastern gulf, but they show up elsewhere.

Prawns are abundant in the gulf, but the times when they are accessible to recreational fishing methods is not easy to determine.

Rain is an important local driver to prawn abundance, and when they are about they can be seen leaping when a boat moves through the shallows. Local prawn species are bananas, brown tigers, endeavours and western kings.

Exmouth's North West Cape is where the range of northern and southern rock lobsters species intersect, with western rock lobster and painted rock lobster both found in this region. Only western rock lobsters commonly enter baited pots.

Sailfish, mahi mahi, cobia, wahoo, spanish mackerel and longtail tuna are encountered in these areas.

Good reef fishing is had around North West Cape, with boaters catching mainly spangled emperor, rankin cod, tuskfish and pelagic fish.

North West Cape's oyster rocks are a well-known haunt of oversize trevally. These are taken on poppers near sunrise and sunset. Queenfish and permit are also caught.

Rankin cod inhabit offshore reefs, along with coral trout.

On the 100m line, jobfish, red emperor, chinaman and pearl perch are caught. The small "Charlie Court" cod is popular with Exmouth visitors because of its abundance near shore, and its eating quality.

Dinghy anglers generally target inshore reefs from Bundegi to Point Murat, where humpback whales give the odd scare as they surface.

Further offshore, on a series of sand ridges, sailfish are prolific, usually chasing bait schools entering and leaving the gulf with the tides.

The Muiron Island area is popular with local charter boats, which target both reef and pelagic fish.

Note the sanctuary zones.

On the east side of the gulf the shallow creeks and flats have jacks, threadfin salmon, trevally, queenfish, permit, bonefish and bream.

While the Ashburton River north of Onslow is regarded as the southern limit of the barramundi's range, they can be found in the shallows on the east side of Exmouth Gulf in summer.

The southern gulf can be accessed through a private station for a fee.

Diving and snorkelling is popular around Exmouth because of the clear water and spectacular coral reefs.

Exmouth has good facilities, including a large marina with protected boat ramp.

There are sealed ramps at Bundegi, north of Exmouth, and Tantabiddi, on the ocean side of the peninsula.

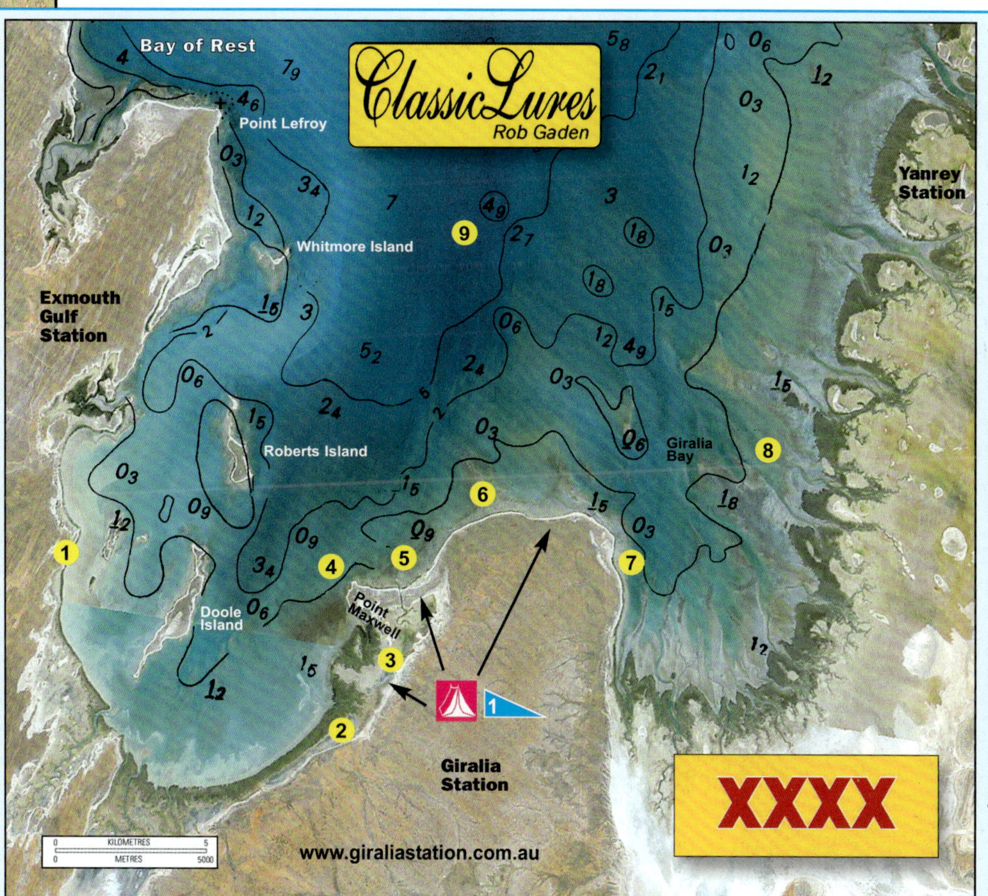

Key to Map

The Giralia Station coastline has landbased fishing at high tide, and is well suited to to dinghy or yak fishing, although northerly winds will make the southern gulf rough. Beach launching is required.

Hotspots

1. Shallow prawning area.
2. 'Three Creeks' - these small creeks are accessible from half tide up, with shallow flats out the front to keep in mind when returning by boat. Jacks, threadfin salmon, cod, bream, whiting, flathead.
3. 'First Creek' - flathead, whiting, bream, cod, threadfin salmon, jacks.
4. Troll Point Maxwell for mackerel around high tide. Tuskfish and cod over the shallow reef.
5. Good launching spot once tide rises. Bream, whiting, threadfin salmon, jacks, flathead in the creek at high tide.
6. Queenfish and trevally from beach at high tide, as well as bream, flathead, salmon and whiting.
7. Most local species in this area.
8. Threadfin salmon, barramundi, cod, mud crabs along the eastern mangrove shoreline and inside the creeks. Careful trip planning with the tides is required because of the extensive drying flats. Best in warm calm or westerly weather.
9. Grunter, cod, coral trout, snapper on patches in lower gulf. Mackerel and tuna schools, watch for birds.

Launch sites

1. 4WD beach launching near campsites on upper tide.

Exmouth tides have up to about 2.46m movement.

Visit Exmouth Game Fishing Club for more information www.egfc.com.au

The Mackerel Islands

Onslow gets less fishing pressure than other Norwest communities. The wide reefs have a mix of southern and tropical reef fish, with pink snapper, coral trout, various emperor, cod and pelagic fish all a chance on the same day. There is a good run of spanish mackerel, hence the name "Mackerel Islands", as well as big trevally and queenfish. Coral around the various islands provides world-class diving opportunities. A track runs along the Ashburton River's freshwater and saltwater reaches, and boats can be bank-launched at unofficial camp sites. This is the start of the barramundi's WA range. The Ashburton's tidal water has threadfin salmon, flathead, whiting, jacks and mud crabs, with a chance of a barramundi in summer. For dinghy fishermen, the creeks around Onslow are small and tide dependent, but have jacks, mud crabs, salmon and occasional barra. Offshore fishing is the main attraction, the shallow coastal reefs have coral trout, tuskfish, rankin cod and spangled emperor, with red emperor, cobia and wahoo also showing up out wide. Some locals fish the old gas wells - these have been cut down, but structure left on the seafloor can be worth fishing. The Mackerel Islands Group comprises 10 islands. Thevenard and Direction Islands have accommodation. Thevenard is 6km long and 1.5km wide, surrounded by stunning coral. If staying on Thevenard, trolling near the cabins works well, and big mackerel have been caught from the beach. Sandy Cays near the back of Thevenard has queenfish and mackerel. Just 22km north-east of Thevenard is Airlie Island, which has unlimited queenfish and trevally - the west-side sandbar fishes well on a falling tide. At 26km north of Thevenard, Rosily Cays and Rosily Shoals fall away into deep water and have red emperor, big mackerel and GTs. Large trailer boats are needed for these spots. It is a long run out to deep water from Onslow, but past the 50m contour fishos will find billfish, dolphin fish, wahoo, tuna and big reef fish. Near the Onslow Channel, beware Ward Reef at approx 21 36.584S 115 04.531E. For those with long-range boats, the Montebello Archipelago is 150km north-east of Onslow, with shallow-water sportfishing.

GPS

Brewis Reef 21 29.822S 114 54.771E
Sultan Reef 21 24.738S 115 05.819E
Taunton Reef 21 18.529S 115 13.073E
Rosily Cays 21 15.743S 115 01.059E
Rosil Shoals 21 19.725S 114 59.105E

Shoals 15km or less from Onslow

Hastings Shoal 21 34.155S 115 03.577E
Saladin Shoal 21 34.253S 115 01.849E
No Name Shoal 21 33.147S 115 06.505E
Gorgon Patch 21 33.147S 115 06.505E
Weeks Shoal 21 31.237S 115 05.593E
Koolinda Patch 21 33.578S 115 05.514E

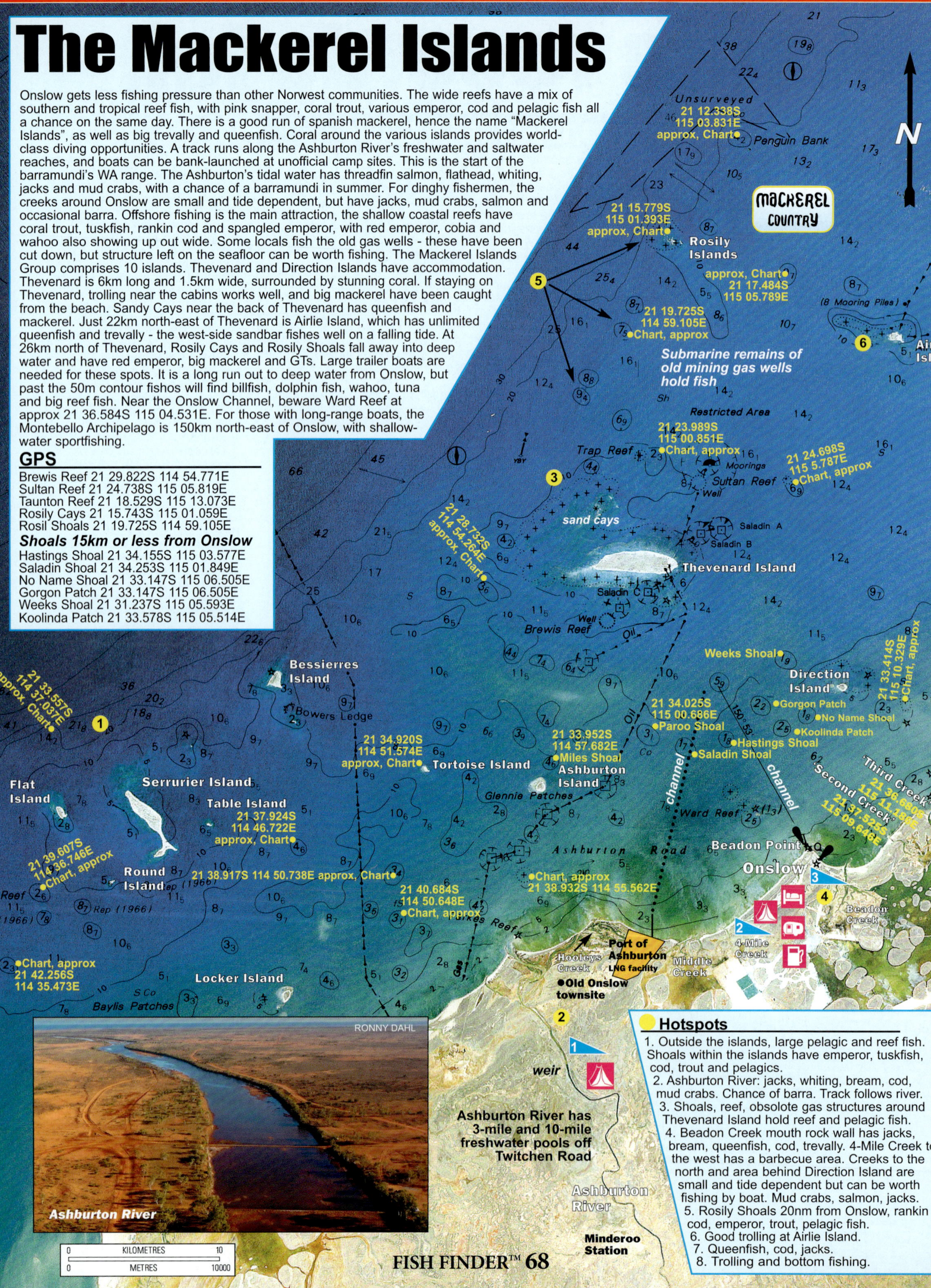

Ashburton River

Hotspots

1. Outside the islands, large pelagic and reef fish. Shoals within the islands have emperor, tuskfish, cod, trout and pelagics.
2. Ashburton River: jacks, whiting, bream, cod, mud crabs. Chance of barra. Track follows river.
3. Shoals, reef, obsolote gas structures around Thevenard Island hold reef and pelagic fish.
4. Beadon Creek mouth rock wall has jacks, bream, queenfish, cod, trevally. 4-Mile Creek to the west has a barbecue area. Creeks to the north and area behind Direction Island are small and tide dependent but can be worth fishing by boat. Mud crabs, salmon, jacks.
5. Rosily Shoals 20nm from Onslow, rankin cod, emperor, trout, pelagic fish.
6. Good trolling at Airlie Island.
7. Queenfish, cod, jacks.
8. Trolling and bottom fishing.

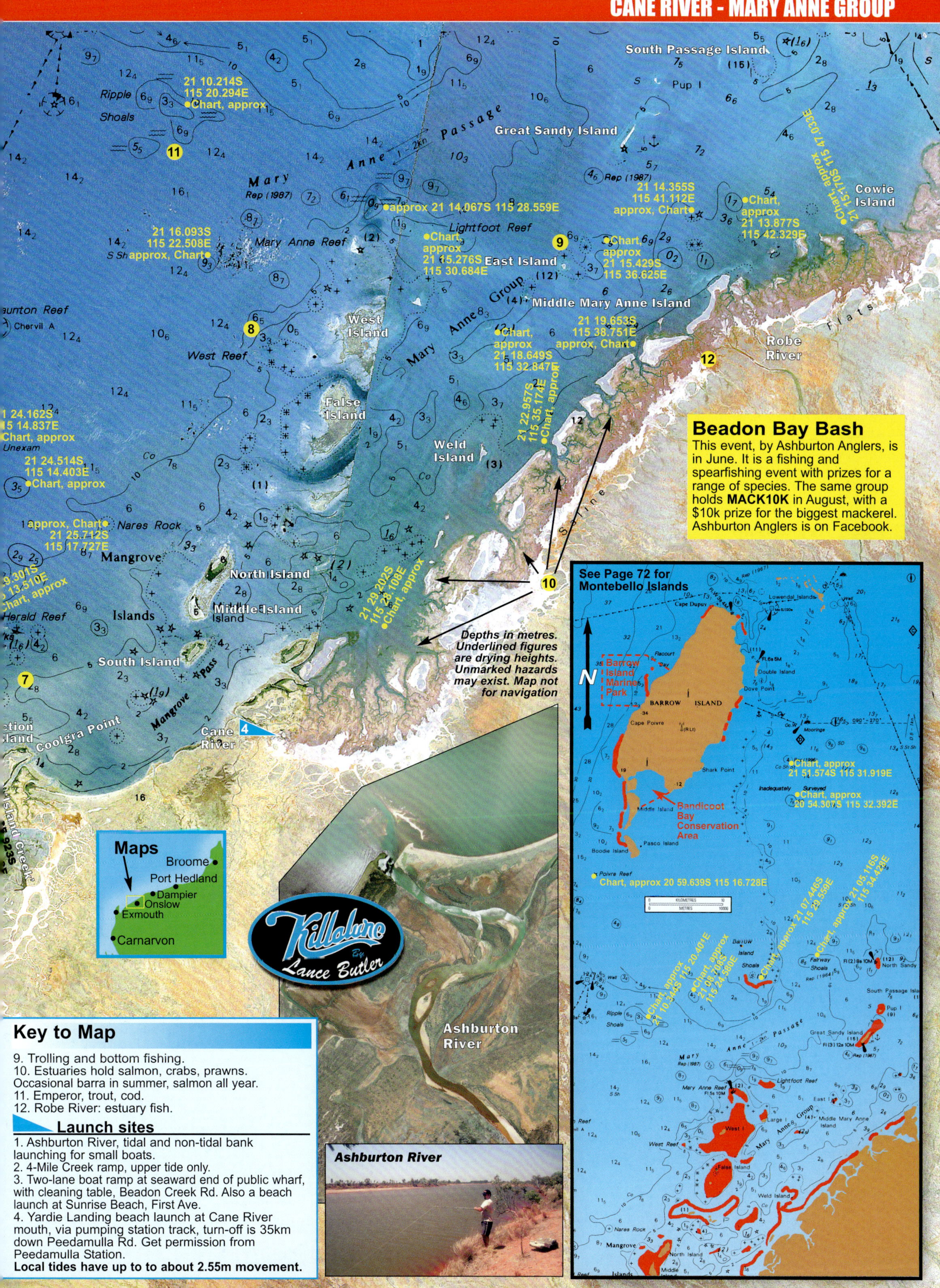

Beadon Bay Bash

This event, by Ashburton Anglers, is in June. It is a fishing and spearfishing event with prizes for a range of species. The same group holds **MACK10K** in August, with a $10k prize for the biggest mackerel. Ashburton Anglers is on Facebook.

Key to Map

9. Trolling and bottom fishing.
10. Estuaries hold salmon, crabs, prawns. Occasional barra in summer, salmon all year.
11. Emperor, trout, cod.
12. Robe River: estuary fish.

Launch sites

1. Ashburton River, tidal and non-tidal bank launching for small boats.
2. 4-Mile Creek ramp, upper tide only.
3. Two-lane boat ramp at seaward end of public wharf, with cleaning table, Beadon Creek Rd. Also a beach launch at Sunrise Beach, First Ave.
4. Yardie Landing beach launch at Cane River mouth, via pumping station track, turn-off is 35km down Peedamulla Rd. Get permission from Peedamulla Station.

Local tides have up to to about 2.55m movement.

Ashburton River

Cleaverville launch site

PETER FAULKNER

Cleaverville Creek

JOURNEYMAN

The shallow island coast

This shallow coast has more than 40 islands, with a great many reefs and shoals. The local estuaries are small but can provide good sport. There are few launch sites, and long distances must be travelled by sea to reach some of the more worthwhile grounds. Estuary species caught here include threadfin and blue salmon, queenfish, trevally, jacks, with occasional barramundi in summer, and mud crabs. Spanish mackerel, big trevally and sailfish are common around the outer islands, while the reefs hold tuskfish, coral trout, and various cod and emperor species. Further offshore the sky is the limit, with the Montebello Islands 130km west of Dampier a drawcard for those with larger boats. Coastal camp sites have no shade and campers must be self sufficient. Dampier's Burrup Peninsula is scenic, and its shallow bays are worth a cast or two. In Karratha, Nickol Bay Fishing Club is an active group, hosting an annual Billfish Shootout. For details visit http://ansa.karratha.com

Key to Map

Hotspots

1. Islands - sand, rock and coral shallows. Queenfish, big trevally. Also tuskfish, trout, cobia, cod, flag, spangled emperor.
2. Sight casting for various species.
3. Queenfish, trevally, mackerel.
4. Reef fish, sailfish, mackerel, tuna.
5. Blue and threadfin salmon, barramundi, grunter, whiting, bream. Shallow. Cod, trevally, jewfish, flathead near Fortescue mouth. River mouth is shallow at low tide.
6. Good trolling and reef fishing.
7. Reef fishing, big pelagic species.
8. Reef fish, mackerel.
9. Sailfish offshore (best July/Oct), and mackerel. Close in to the islands queenfish, big trevally in tidal rips.

10&10. Creeks have barra, salmon, grunter, jacks, mud crabs. Enter and explore at high tide.

11. Jewfish in deep water at entrance hole, salmon.
12. Threadfin salmon over a metre long are caught on Nickol Bay flats, and in and around the tidal creeks.
13. Reef fish, occasional sailfish. Trevally, queenfish, mackerel at island.
14. Reef fishing over Madelaine Shoal (just off map), big sailfish, small black marlin, cobia on outer island tip, queenfish, trevally, mackerel inside.

Launch sites

1. Fortescue River: firm bank launch, 24km off highway, large camping area with no shade, mouth shallow at low to mid tide.
2. Gnoorea Point and 40-Mile Beach, 13km off highway (turn-off is 32km south of the Karratha Rd turn-off on the highway). Firm but exposed beach launch with bush camp sites.

3a. Hampton Harbour has four lanes. Beware shallow reefs when leaving the harbour. Sams Island is a restricted area and speed limits apply. Useable most tides.

3b. Multi-lane ramp on Ian Williams Crescent.

4. Back Beach: open water with groyne, upper tide.
5. Cleaverville 4WD creek bank launch, 26km off highway. Sheltered. Camping.
6. Burrup Peninsula beach launches ... beware tidal flats during big tides: *Hearson Cove. *Cowrie Cove. *Withnell Bay.
7. Boat ramps at Cossack and Point Samson - see Pages 73-74.

Local tides have up to about 4.57m movement.

NBSC Billfish Shootout

This billfish competition is held by Nickol Bay Sportfishing Club, with 40+ teams competing for $30,000+ in prizes. It is usually held mid year. For more information visit the club's website at **www.ansa.karratha.com** or call 08 9183 8883.

Karratha Back Beach ramp

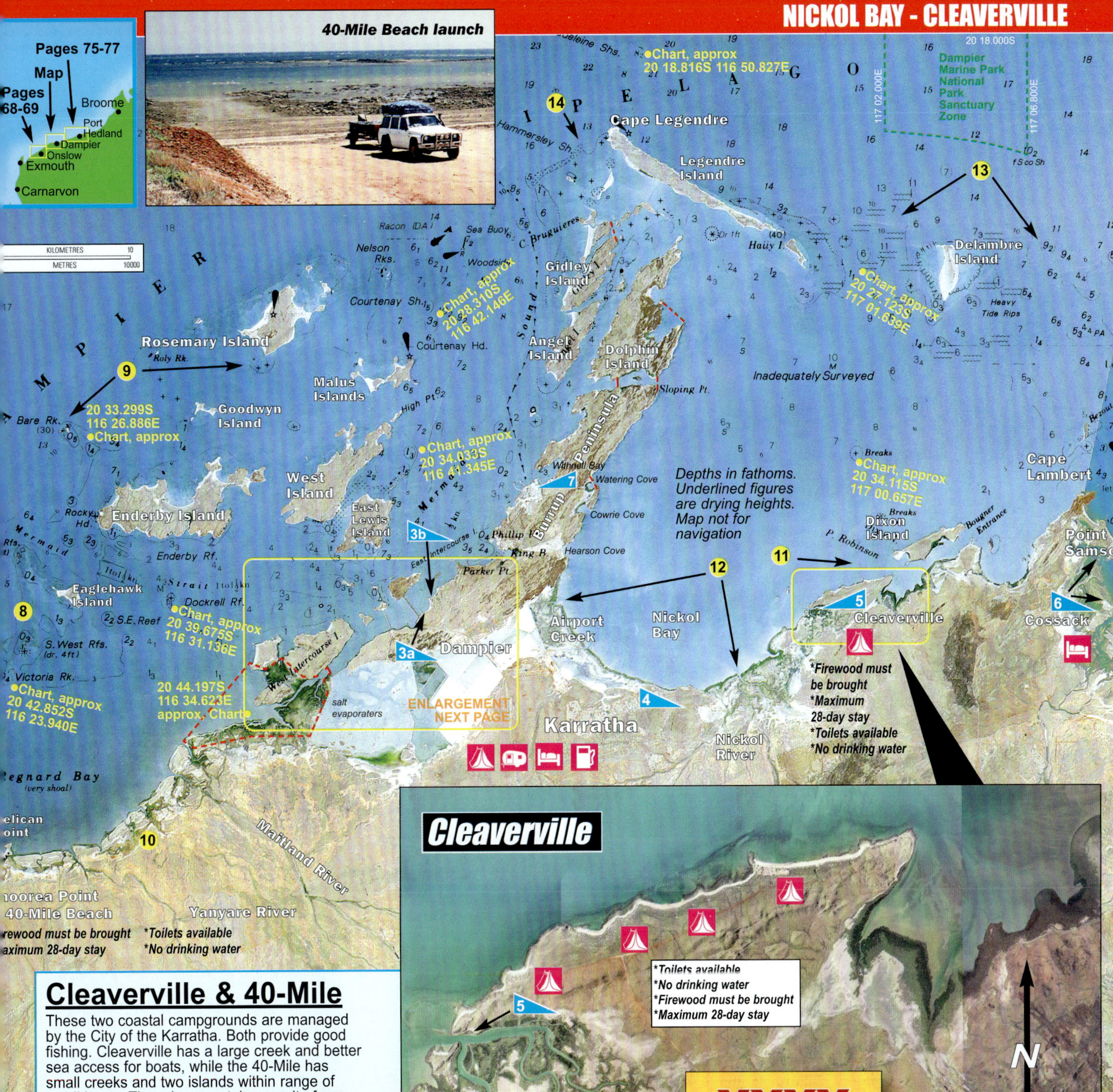

Cleaverville & 40-Mile

These two coastal campgrounds are managed by the City of the Karratha. Both provide good fishing. Cleaverville has a large creek and better sea access for boats, while the 40-Mile has small creeks and two islands within range of small boats. There is a caretaker on site from May 1 to September 30 and camp fees apply only during this period. At the time of writing the rates were $16 a night, or $92 a week. Fires are permitted but wood must be brought in. There are rubbish bins and sullage disposal pits. Shade is limited, so bring a tarpaulin or awning. Keep in mind the area has large tides with up to 5m movement. Afternoon sea breezes can be strong. Offshore fishing can be productive over the shallow reefs, with mackerel, trevally and a variety of tropical reef fish. Threadfin and blue salmon, jacks, cod, queenfish and mud crabs are the main catch in the creeks, with a chance of creek barramundi in summer, and tiger squid in calm weather.

Cleaverville

This beachside campground 26km east of Karratha is popular with boat and landbased anglers. The highway turn-off is signposted, with a 13km run on a gravel road to the campground. This area is most popular in winter. There are several kilometres of secluded sites, almost all with sea views. A 4WD vehicle is not necessary for camping, with many sites accessible in 2WD vehicles, however some sites are on soft sand. There is a firm beach launch into the creek suitable for most trailer boats, but it has a shallow gradient and is best on the upper tide. The creek contains a good depth of water for the most part, with patches of oyster rock. Proceed with caution. The ledge just down from the ramp drops into deep water and is good for landbased fishing. There are rocky points along the coast that can be used by landbased anglers near high tide. Boaters can fish in the creek when the wind is up or head out of the mouth when conditions allow.

40-Mile

This campground is a 40-minute drive west of Karratha on an unsealed road off the highway. The 4WD beach launch is reasonably firm but very exposed. There are several small creeks to the east and west to explore on the upper tide. Boaters can visit North-East and South West Regnard Islands, which are about 9km and 12km out. Regnard Bay is very shallow, with reef fishing improving for bigger fish from about 12km out. Mainly queenfish, trevally and salmon are caught off the beach, with tuskfish, flag and cod on the inshore reef grounds.

The northern Montebello Islands, looking south

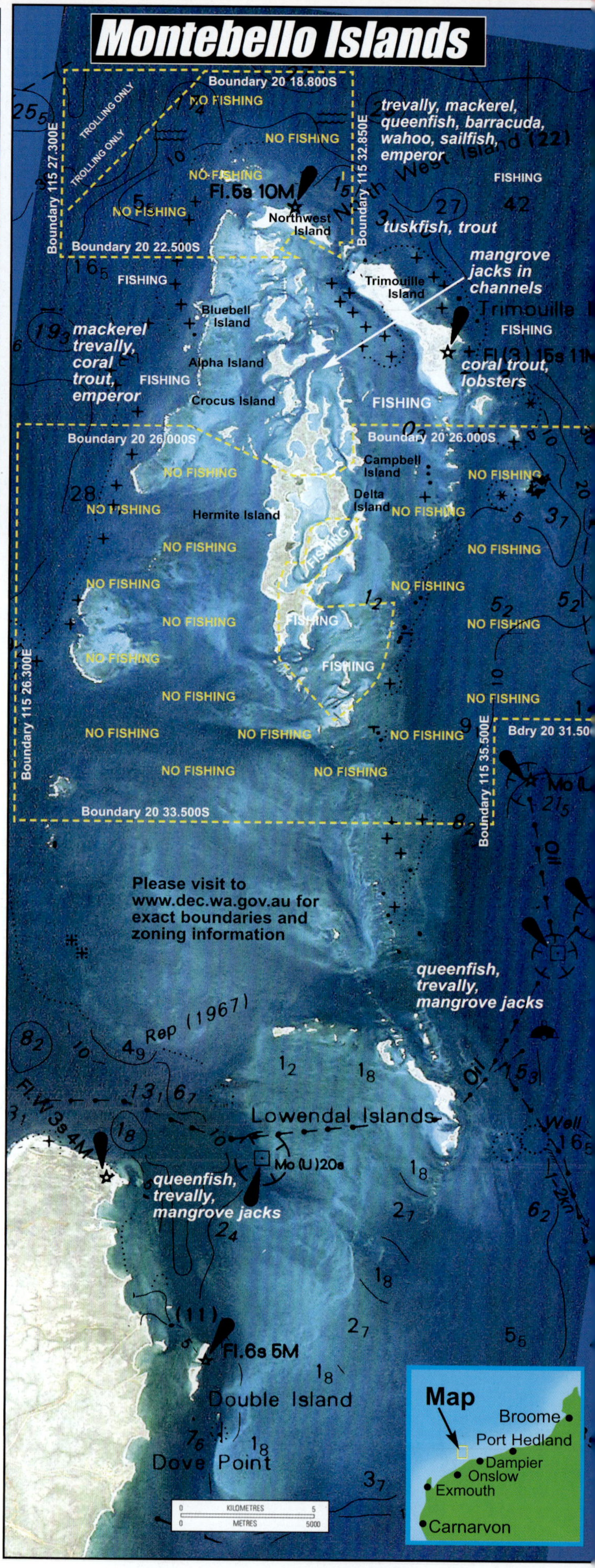

COL ROBERTS PICTURE

265 islands

The Montebello Islands consist of 265 low sand, limestone and sandstone islands with convoluted shorelines dissected by channels, lagoons and intertidal bays.

The islands are about 140km north-east of Onslow, 120km west of Dampier, within reach of large trailer boats with sufficient fuel capacity, yet far enough to minimise fishing pressure.

The best option for smaller boats is to launch at Fortescue River mouth and travel the 90km to the islands.

Part of the area's attraction is its biodiversity, with extensive mudflats, seaweed/seagrass beds and mangrove communities.

The Montebello and Barrow Islands Marine Park sanctuary zones form a large portion of the area. In these areas fishing is not permitted - be sure to get a detailed zoning map at www.parks.dpaw.wa.gov.au before fishing.

The islands gained notoriety as the first site for British atomic bomb testing between 1952 and 1956.

Three bombs were exploded - the first on the HMS *Plym* – a frigate anchored in 12m of water just off Trimouille Island.

The crater can still be seen on a depth sounder and in aerial photos today.

The second bomb was detonated on Trimouille Island and the third on Alpha Island.

Derelict metal structures such as the observation posts are still radioactive and signs warn visitors not to spend more than an hour a day on the affected islands.

The Lowendals are a scattered group of islands between the southern end of the Montebellos and north end of Barrow Island.

This area is shallow and mostly uncharted, with numerous sandbars and reefs. It is ideal terrain for trevally, queenfish, shark mackerel and tuna, however overnight anchorages around the islands are limited.

The main island is in a restricted area because of shipping and oil pipelines.

The best option is to travel further to the north and be based at the Montebellos, which offer more protection and fishing options.

No matter which way the wind blows there is always somewhere to fish in the lee at the Montebellos.

If the wind is from the east (mostly May-Sept) then the western side can be targeted.

Conversely if the wind is from the west (Sept-April) then the east side can be targeted, or alternatively between the various islands.

The islands have many deep channels. home to big mangrove jacks, coral trout, spanish flag and spangled emperor.

Also within the island chain are numerous coral bommies, many of which contain lobsters.

To top off the buffet, mud crabs are also found.

Offshore, the reefs are home to coral trout, trevally, mackerel, barracuda etc.

If weather permits Tryal Rocks, located about 18km off the north-west tip, offers great trolling for spanish mackerel, wahoo and sailfish.

Tryal Rocks is the site of Australia's first recorded shipwreck.

In 1622 the *Tryal* struck a reef that now bears the ship's name, resulting in a large loss of life.

Most local charter boats concentrate on fishing the offshore reefs for species such as red emperor, coral trout and rankin cod.

Montebello Islands

Boundary 20 18.800S
Boundary 20 22.500S
Boundary 115 27.300E
Boundary 115 32.850E
TROLLING ONLY
NO FISHING
Fl.5s 10M
Northwest Island
trevally, mackerel, queenfish, barracuda, wahoo, sailfish, emperor
North West Island (22)
FISHING
tuskfish, trout
mangrove jacks in channels
Trimouille Island
Trimouille I
Bluebell Island
Alpha Island
Crocus Island
mackerel trevally, coral trout, emperor
coral trout, lobsters
Boundary 20 26.000S
Campbell Island
Delta Island
Hermite Island
Boundary 115 26.300E
Boundary 115 35.500E
Bdry 20 31.50
Boundary 20 33.500S

Please visit to www.dec.wa.gov.au for exact boundaries and zoning information

queenfish, trevally, mangrove jacks
Rep (1967)
Lowendal Islands
Mo (U) 20s
Fl.W 3s 4M
queenfish, trevally, mangrove jacks
Fl.6s 5M
Double Island
Dove Point
KILOMETRES
METRES

Map
Broome
Port Hedland
Dampier
Onslow
Exmouth
Carnarvon

Pilbara

There are few towns on the Pilbara coast, and most are mining communities. Fly-in fly-out mine employment keeps the permanent local population small.

One town is a bit different. The small community of ***Point Samson*** has a marina, van park, motel, shop, and not much else. It has a boat ramp suitable for large trailer boats and is within sight of the impressive Cape Lambert ore-loading jetty.

Nearby is ***Cossack***, next to Butcher Inlet, south of Point Samson. It has a boat ramp, an old stone wharf and historic buildings.

Wickham is nearby, but Point Samson and Cossack are far enough from Karratha and Dampier to escape the bigger crowds.

Most visitors come to the Pilbara during the calmer and cooler winter, but summer visitors catch barra.

Cossack has the best estuaries nearby. Point Samson's causeway over the local creek can fish well.

Be aware that Point Samson has a small sanctuary.

Trolling the Point Samson reef towards the Cape Lambert pier (outside the sacntuary) gets tuna, mackerel, queenfish and golden trevally.

Trolling the rock walls outside Point Samson produces barracuda, queenfish, tuna, trevally, cod, jacks and barra. Tuna feed in shallow water near the marina at times.

There are three creeks within 22km east of Point Samson. They are at 20 44.222S 117 21.520E, 20 44.239S 117 22.969E and 20 43.966S 117 26.263E.

Sherlock River mouth is 37km from Point Samson at 20 42.351S 117 33.039E. Enter creeks on a rising tide.

Cossack's stone wharf can fish well for tuskfish, jacks and bream, with a chance of barra, salmon and mud crabs.

Offshore from Point Samson and Cossack, the target species are emperors, particularly red and long-nosed emperor, various cod, and spanish mackerel. Bring all the gear you need as there are few local services.

Dampier/Karratha: The best reef fishing starts about 37km miles off Dampier.

It is about 45km to Madeleine Shoals, a serious proposition, located just outside the archipelago at about 20 19.263E and 116 50.481E and about 20 18.636S 116 50.972E. Other spots include the reefs around Roly Rock, at about 20 29.970S 116 30.155E. The drop-off along the outside of Rosemary Island is worth fishing.

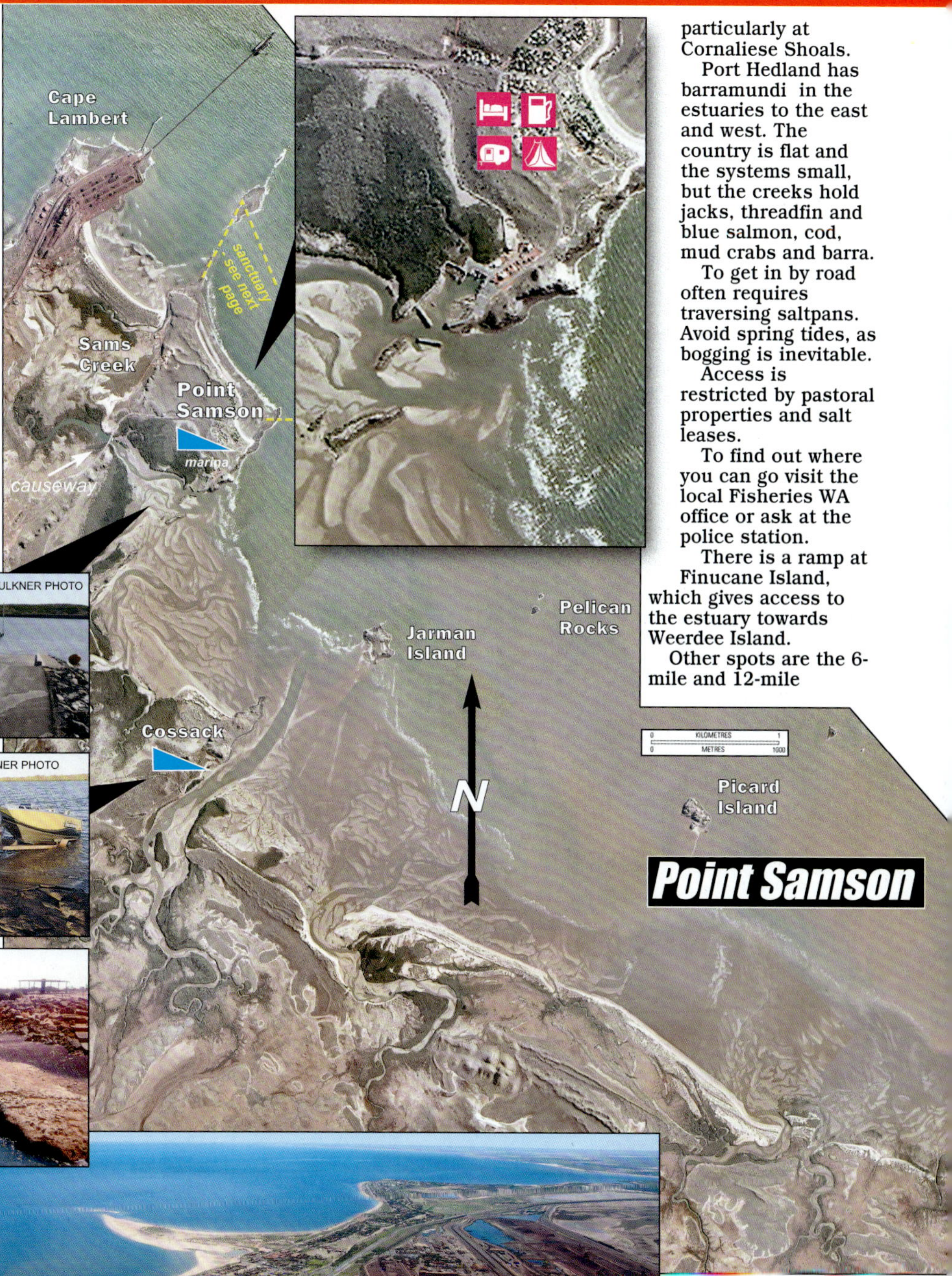

Cape Lambert

Sams Creek

Point Samson

sanctuary see next page

marina

causeway

PETER FAULKNER PHOTO

Point Samson ramp

PETER FAULKNER PHOTO

Cossack ramp

Port Hedland harbour entrance

Cossack

Jarman Island

Pelican Rocks

N

Picard Island

KILOMETRES 0 1

METRES 0 1000

Point Samson

Port Hedland

Port Hedland: The town is quite stark but has good fishing and a protected dual-lane ramp. The channel pylons extending out to sea hold pelagic fish. There is a lengthy spoil bank created by seabed being pumped from the main shipping channel. Here anglers can park vehicles and fish for blue salmon during their annual winter run, as well as queenfish.

The holes created by dredging and ship propellers near the wharves are home to large black jewfish. These bite best at night.

There are billfish off Port Hedland, particularly at Cornaliese Shoals.

Port Hedland has barramundi in the estuaries to the east and west. The country is flat and the systems small, but the creeks hold jacks, threadfin and blue salmon, cod, mud crabs and barra.

To get in by road often requires traversing saltpans. Avoid spring tides, as bogging is inevitable.

Access is restricted by pastoral properties and salt leases.

To find out where you can go visit the local Fisheries WA office or ask at the police station.

There is a ramp at Finucane Island, which gives access to the estuary towards Weerdee Island.

Other spots are the 6-mile and 12-mile estuaries, or Port Hedland harbour. Six-Mile Creek is reached by a short track off the main road.

Balla Balla: This is a popular remote spot. Access is over a 21km unsealed road, with the highway turn-off directly opposite the Whim Creek Hotel, an hour's travelling time south-west of Port Hedland. There is a muddy launch site.

To avoid being bogged, plan a trip on rising neap tides and retrieve near high tide.

The options out of Balla Balla include the DePuch and Forestier Island group for mackerel, trevally, queenfish and black jewfish. The estuaries have cod, jacks, mud crabs and threadfin salmon.

For those with larger craft, the offshore waters around Geographe Shoals are a pelagic and reef fishing hotspot.

Point Samson regional chart GPS marks with distances

Tessa Shoals, 22km to 30km
20 29.986S 117 20.306E
20 29.556S 117 22.503E
20 28.990S 117 24.763E
20 30.310S 117 21.457E
No Name Shoal, 32km
20 24.949S 117 22.277E
20 24.890S 117 21.265E
20 24.753S 117 23.076E
Charted wreck, 28km
20 29.624S 117 24.970E
Delambre Reef, 24km
20 26.367S 117 14.350E
No Name Shoal, 28km
20 24.382S 117 09.690E
Channel Shoal, 24km
20 27.666S 117 19.431E

The Yule River mouth ... plenty of good holes on the bends, but be in place before low tide, or risk stranding

Hotspots

1. Scattered reef 50m from shore with natural rock groyne running out from beach holds tuskfish: use local black crabs for bait gathered at night by torch. Squid trapped in pools at low tide.
2. Coral trout, tuskfish near channel.
3. Reef has coral trout, queenfish, lobsters.
4. Rocks around Bezout Island have big tuskfish and other fish.
5. Crayfish, trevally along Hat Rock and Picard Island drop-offs.
6. Mackerel around Pelican Rocks.
7. Big oysters on rocks off north tip.
8. Deep water off north of Delambre Island has big pelagic fish - troll deep lures or use live bait.
9. Shallow reef has lobsters, tuskfish.
10. Sandy beach with coral shallows: great snorkelling.
11. Salmon, barra, queenfish.
12. Marina rocks outside creek fish well on outgoing tide for most species.

Kunmunya and **Samson II** wreck sites - no fishing allowed within 500m of 20 25.81S 117 12.80E

Point Samson Reef NO FISHING ZONE extends almost 1km to sea

Delambre Island
tidal rips
Bezout Island
wharf
Dixon Island
causeway
Pelican Rocks
Jarman Island
Hat Rock
Picard Island
Harding River
Point Samson

RECREATIONAL AND COMMERCIAL FISHING ACTIVITIES PROHIBITED
20°36.277'S 117°11.589'E
20°36.678'S 117°11.205'E
20°37.884'S 117°12.460'E
20°37.907'S 117°11.936'E

Butcher Inlet, adjacent to Cossack

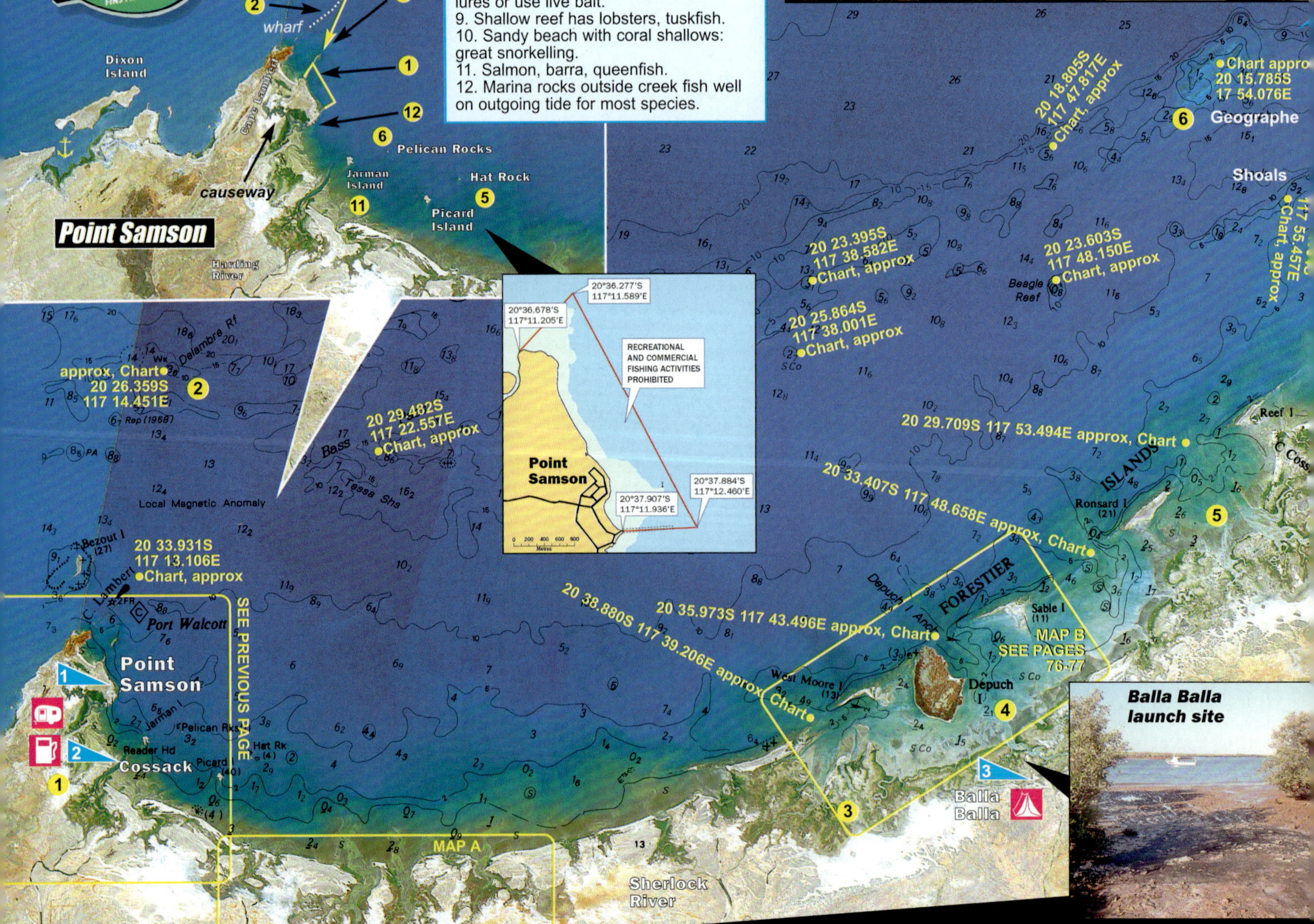

20 18.805S 117 47.817E Chart, approx
20 15.785S 117 54.076E Chart approx
Geographe Shoals
117 55.457E Chart, approx
20 23.395S 117 38.582E Chart, approx
20 23.603S 117 48.150E Chart, approx
Beagle Reef
20 25.864S 117 38.001E Chart, approx
20 26.359S 117 14.451E approx, Chart
Delambre Rf
20 29.482S 117 22.557E Chart, approx
Bass
Tessa Shs
Local Magnetic Anomaly
20 33.931S 117 13.106E Chart, approx
Bezout I
C Lambert
Port Walcott
SEE PREVIOUS PAGE
Point Samson
Cossack
Jarman I
Pelican Rks
Reader Hd
Hat Rk
Picard I
20 29.709S 117 53.494E approx, Chart
Reef I
C Cossigny
ISLANDS
Ronsard I
20 33.407S 117 48.658E approx, Chart
FORESTIER
Depuch Anch
Sable I
MAP B SEE PAGES 76-77
20 35.973S 117 43.496E approx, Chart
20 38.880S 117 39.206E approx, Chart
West Moore I
Depuch I
Balla Balla
MAP A
Sherlock River

Balla Balla launch site

Port Hedland

There is summer barramundi fishing in the estuaries, but salmon, jacks, trevally, queenfish and mud crabs are more commonly caught. Boaters will find top-notch pelagic and bottom fishing offshore, with bigger fish generally caught on the wider reefs. Black jewfish are in the port and at nearby Balla Balla. Big tides require careful trip planning.

Key to Map

Hotspots

1. Butcher Inlet, estuary fish. There are low tide holes, but it is not navigable at low tide. Summer best for barramundi, winter for salmon. Also mud crabs, bream, jacks, tuskfish, cod, queenfish.
2. Spangled emperor, coral trout, chinaman fish, emperor, cod, mackerel and trevally. Also painted crayfish and occasional sailfish.
3. Estuaries west of rocky Depuch Island offer good fishing. Trevally, queenfish, salmon, jewfish, cod. Lobsters around islands. Sherlock River mouth can fish well.
4. Balla Balla Creek: Access is over a 21km unsealed road, turn-off is opposite Whim Creek Hotel. To avoid being bogged, launch and retrieve at high tide. Trevally, queenfish, salmon, jacks, cod. Jewfish near mouth. Barramundi in summer, and mud crabs. There are spots where keen fishos can pitch tents, but it is not a great camping area.
5. Jacks, mud crabs, barramundi, salmon. Barramundi best from September to April. Not navigable at low tide. See following pages.
6. Geographe Shoals: pelagic and reef fish.
7. Estuaries, queenfish off Cape Thouin.
8. Reef fishing, mackerel, sailfish.
9. Channel markers hold pelagic fish. They are numbered in groups of two with the highest (46) closest to shore. Further out the distance between them doubles. Mackerel are caught from 42 onwards. Try 24 and 14 for big queenfish, trevally.
10. Finucane Island: To reach the island, follow the signs to Wedgefield (Industrial Area) from the North West Coastal Highway. Turn left at the Finucane Island Road (second street on the left). Follow this road until the rail crossing before BHP Iron Ore and turn left. Turn next left to ramp. Mackerel, threadfin and blue salmon, whiting, cod, tarpon, barramundi.
11. Spoil Bank is opposite hospital in Sutherland St. Salmon, queenfish, mackerel. 4WD required to access north end of bank.
12. Port Hedland has several handy landbased fishing spots. The Community Park area has fishing along Cemetery Beach. Big salmon, bream, queenfish and whiting can be caught on this strip. The rocks near the playground are good at high tide. Also the rocks at Cooke Point. Follow sand tracks to beach from corner of Dempster and Goode St. Pretty Pool is a tidal inlet, 8km from the town centre. Access is through sandhills adjoining Cooke Point Caravan Park, or via Styles Road and Matheson Dve. Mud crabs can be caught some distance from the creek mouth. Beware stonefish. Just out of town, the Four-Mile Creek access is a right turn off Styles Road. The road follows a sandhill to the foreshore. Further travel possible by 4WD. Care required on big tides as flats will be awash. Six-Mile Creek turn-off is 1km north of the saltworks entrance, then drive 3km.

Launch sites

1. Port Samson, good site for offshore trips. Van park.
2. Cossack, upper tide.
3. Balla Balla Creek 4WD launch: upper tide only.
4. Finucane Island, Boat Ramp Rd. Also Boodarrie Landing, high tide.
5. Town ramp. Also 4WD launch (5a) at 6-Mile Creek.
6. Bank launches: tracks affected by tide. Seek local information.

Local tides have up to about 6.81m movement.

Geos GPS

74km west of Port Hedland
20 13.920S
117 55.430E
20 14.840S
117 54.120E
20 20.100S
117 47.430E
20 18.810S
117 50.560E
20 17.730S
117 50.270E

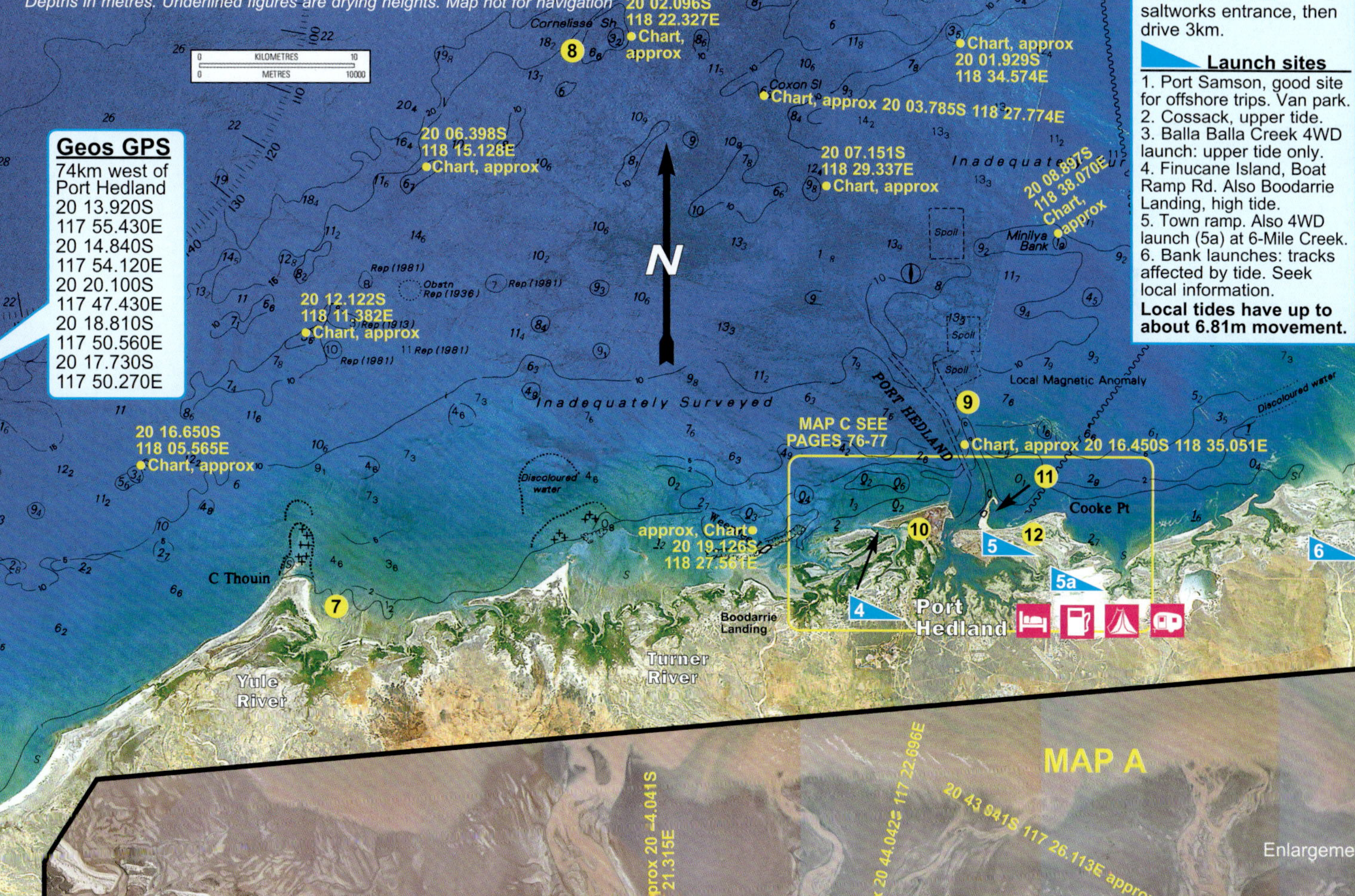

Port Hedland Bluewater Classic

This Port Hedland Game Fishing Club event is held about August each year and attracts an impressive list of prizes and categories. Email fishing@phgfc.com.au

KILOMETRES
METRES
West Moore Island
West Moore Island
West Moore Island Fishing Lodge
Depuch Island
creek
see picture at right
Flats and channels always changing
drying flats
West Moore Island
MAP B
Flats and channels always changing
drying flats
drying flats
rocks
barra trolling edge
Finucane Island
Weerdee Island
Oyster Inlet
Downes Island
West Creek
Flats and channels always changing
Boodarrie Landing
South West Creek
Turner River
Classic Lures
Rob Gaden

Balla Balla

This large tidal creek is 95km west-south-west of Port Hedland, with the turn-off opposite the Whim Creek Hotel, which was closed at publication. Careful trip planning is required as low tides here leave vast drying flats. Rocky patches near the 4WD launch site (1) have deep water nearby, holding jacks, jewfish, cod, salmon and mud crabs. The upper creek has jacks and occasional barra. There is a trolling edge (2) downstream of the launch site. The area around Spot 3 is good for mackerel, queenfish, trevally and tuskfish. Spot 4 (inside creek) holds water at low tide and has a large rockbar with deep water and two shallow rockbars. The hole at the south end of Depuch Island (5) has barra and jewfish in dirty water, use livebait. When crabbing, be sure to place dillies where they won't wash away in tidal currents. It is a 40km run out to the best reef spots as the inner coast is shallow, but the fishing can be exceptional, with red emperor, coral trout, spanish mackerel and more.

The eastern side of De Puch Island

Balla Balla River

Port Hedland

The local creeks are subject to a tidal range to about 7m. From September to February barramundi fire up, but salmon, cod, jacks, trevally and queenfish are the main catch through the year. Barramundi tend to peak just before Christmas. Mud crabs and blue swimmer crabs are caught in the creeks. Some creeks have track access and bank launching, but this is reliant on tides. Tracks over tidal flats are often not useable during and after big tides or heavy rain. For boaters, creeks further afield are worth exploring and many have fishable holes at low tide - livebaiting the holes usually works well. Jewfish are caught in deep water around the port, but keep in mind that anchoring is not permitted in shipping channels and boats may not obstruct a ship in any way. The best reef fishing is a 40km run from the port as the inner waters are shallow. Launch sites are at Finucane Island and Port Hedland.

Key to Map

Hotspots

1. Spoil Bank: deep water off sand. Salmon, queenfish, bream, flathead, whiting, barra.
2. Hole at creek mouth: salmon on rising tide.
3. Oyster Inlet: fishes well for tuskfish. Mackerel, queenfish on a rising tide.
4. Rock outcrop at end of Six Mile Creek road, good lure-casting spot.

Further afield, off map ...

Yule River mouth and associated fishable creek systems are inside Cape Thouin 40km west of Port Hedland.

False Cape Thouin has a large tidal creek system 25km west of Port Hedland.

There are two good creeks fishable by boat 25km and 30km east of Port Hedland.

Maps not for navigation

MAP C

North Point
spoil bank
1
Cooke Point
Flats and channels always changing
Port Hedland
Pretty Pool
Nelson Point
Stingray Creek
Burgess Point
wharf
Anderson Point
Smith Point
Lumsden Point
bank launch
4
rocks
Six Mile Creek
South Creek
South East Creek

Port Hedland GPS

Minilya Bank 20 08.936S 118 38.176E, 18.5km from port
Charted rise 20 07.117S 118 29.354E, 24km from port
Charted rise 20 06.565S 118 26.498E, 26km from port
Charted rise 20 06.158S 118 27.019E, 26km from port
Charted rise 20 05.563S 118 25.190E, 30km from port
Wreck 20 02.400S 118 22.145E, 20nm from port
Cornelisse Shoal 20 02.101S 118 22.598E, 37km from port
South of Cornelisse 20 03.734S 118 20.981E
South of Cornelisse 20 03.892S 118 20.631E
Charted rise 20 02.213S 118 25.435E, 37km from port
Charted rise 19 57.719S 118 33.791E, 38.8km from port
Charted rise 20 07.861S 118 25.322E, 26km from port
Charted rise 20 01.925S 118 34.529E, 32km from port
Little Turtle Island 20 01.101S 118 48.536E, 42km from port
North Turtle Island 19 53.329S 118 53.882E, 60km from port
Cape Thouin rise, 20 12.092S 118 11.594E, 43km from port
Geographe Shoals 20 15.687S 117 54.215E, 74km from port
Beagle Reef 20 23.642S 117 48.216E, 84km from port

Remote Cape Keraudren & Pardoo Station

Cape Keraudren camp and Pardoo Station are two boating access points along this otherwise mostly inaccessible coastline.

Pardoo Station has a tidal creek bank launch. There are five creeks west of Pardoo Creek that can fish well. Offshore fishing, though shallow, is good for tuskfish, emperor, trout and pelagics.

The station has 16km of shallow beaches and rock foreshore, with access to three creeks. Queenfish, trevally, salmon and cod are the main catch, with a chance of a barramundi.

From Pardoo it is a 47km run to the De Grey mouth, or further to Bedout Island, north of the De Grey, where the fishing can be superb.

At De Grey River mouth, barramundi, threadfin and blue salmon, jewfish, jacks and mud crabs are available. The freshwater hole at the highway usually only holds jacks, tarpon and barra after a big rainy season, just after floodwaters have fallen.

The small Condon and Mulla Mulla Down Creek estuaries have jacks, cod, bream, salmon and mud crabs. Condon produces barra on an incoming tide during the warmer months.

Mulla Mulla Down Creek has trevally, mackerel, queenfish and barracuda. Golden snapper and jewfish are also caught. Try fishing the three small rock islands, mostly covered at high tide, about 200m out from the Mulla Mulla Down Creek mouth.

Pardoo van park has camping, cabins and a restaurant, but the nearest fuel is 40km away. The station is 13km off the highway on an unsealed road. It is closed from December to March. Details at www.pardoostation.com.au

Permission is rarely given to traverse De Grey Station to visit De Grey River mouth, so access is by sea from Pardoo or Port Hedland.

Cape Keraudren Nature Reserve is a public camping area 14km off the Great Northern Highway. There is a concrete ramp, best used towards the top of the tide, although a very low tide will expose a smooth rock ledge where small boats can be launched into the channel.

If the wind makes retrieving a boat difficult at the ramp, 4WD vehicles can use the soft sandy bank of the creek on the upper tide.

There are trevally, queenfish and mackerel on the inshore rocks, and offshore fishing for reef species, mainly tuskfish and coral trout.

The water is shallow until about 26km out, and then drops away slowly.

The 80-Mile Beach Caravan Park is 250km north of Port Hedland, with the turn-off about 25km west of Sandfire roadhouse. The beach, actually 220km long, has mostly threadfin salmon, queenfish, catfish and sharks. Sanctuaries exist off the map, for details visit www.parks.dpaw.wa.gov.au/park/eighty-mile-beach

This shallow region has big tides and drying flats. Low tides can see the water recede for a kilometre or so. Surf rods and livebaits, or pilchards, are generally used to catch salmon.

Beach launching is possible in calm weather near high tide.

Cape Keraudren campground near high tide
Hotspots
1. Big trevally, queenfish around island. Shallow, exposed area.
2. Reef west of Bedout Island has spangled and red emperor, tuskfish, trout, mackerel. Reds are on rubble in more than 20m depth. Queenfish, trevally off island. Beware reefs.
3. De Grey River has salmon, jacks, queenfish, cod and some barramundi. Access is by sea from Port Hedland or Pardoo Station.
4. Queenfish, trevally in calm weather. Sight-fishing.
5. Condon and Titchilla estuaries. Headlands and islands fish at high tide - queenfish, trevally, mackerel. Barra at Titchilla.
6. Pardoo Creek has jacks, crabs, prawns, salmon, occasional barra. Local beaches have queenfish, salmon and trevally, with tiger squid in close in calm weather.
7. Threadfin salmon, cod, crabs, trevally inside estuary. Good trolling outside. Best reef fishing starts about 15km offshore.
8. Reef fishing over shoals, also mackerel, sailfish.
9. Rocks worth a cast on incoming tide, trevally, barra.
10. Reef - snapper, emperor.
Key to Map
Launch sites
1. Port Hedland, 73km away.
2. Pardoo Station: camping, creek launches, accomm, meals. Phone (08) 9176 4930. No fuel.
3. Cape Keraudren concrete ramp, mid-tide up. Rock shelf at dead low tide. Local tides move up to about 7.3m.
Good reef fishing begins 15km north of Cape Keraudren
Depths in metres. Underlined figures are drying heights. Map not for navigation
Eighty Mile Beach Caravan Park is 97km from Cape Keraudren
19 55.000S
119 47.000E
119 52.500E
Cape Kurtamparanya Sanctuary Zone
Solitary It.
Low cliffs of red sandstone
SEE ENLARGEMENT
19 58.000S
119 38.000E
Pananykarra Sanctuary Zone
Low Cliffs
19 57.400S
119 43.000E
Cape Keraudren
This area is part of Eighty Mile Beach Marine Park
26km
landbased fishing allowed
STEPHEN YATES
Low tide at Cape Keraudren ramp
Sanctuary zones are shown for the Eighty Mile Beach Marine Park. For detailed zoning information visit www.dpaw.wa.gov.au
camp sites
rock shelf
rocks
dries
dries
Pardoo Creek
Pardoo Station
Very sandy
Lighthouse Island
'Baked Bean Creek'
Mt Blaze
Tidal Area
Banningarra Creek
o not cross flat n tide over 6.5m
More creeks and estuary and rock shelves
Cape Keraudren
main road
Ranger HQ
KILOMETRES
METRES
Pardoo launch site
XXXX

Port Smith entrance

Tidal lagoon

Port Smith has protected beach launching into a sandy tidal estuary. The estuary is well-suited to cartopper dinghies and yaks, but bigger boats can be launched at high tide, giving access to bluewater fishing outside the estuary.

Port Smith is 23km down an unsealed road off the Great Northern Highway, 160km south of Broome. It is a pleasant location, with Port Smith Lagoon Caravan Park offering camping, retail and fuel.

The estuary is subject to huge tides. It dries at low tide to leave a hole near the entrance and an expanse of sand. The hole is the spot to fish until the tide comes in.

Big tuskfish cod are caught along the rocky edges of the entrance on an incoming tide. They rarely refuse fresh crab baits.

The sandbar at the entrance has queenfish, and the lagoon has mud crabs, cod, jacks and salmon.

While Port Smith gets fishing pressure during the tourist season, the offshore waters are only lightly fished. It is a long run to deep water, with 20m depth 35km from Port Smith's entrance. The shallow inshore reefs have tuskfish, emperor, coral trout, mackerel and trevally.

There is no formed boat ramp, with boaters launching over reasonably firm sand. It is possible to launch a portable boat near low tide, with care, but high tide is easier.

Fresh water for washdowns is a limited local resource, so try not to get too much salt water on the launch vehicle.

There is a sandy 4WD track leading to the entrance channel shore. The track has soft sand and requires tyre deflation.

Nearby Gourdon Bay is a beautiful spot just a short drive from the caravan park.

There are 4WD tracks to Cowrie Creek and the Saddle Hill Cliffs. Permits are needed for these areas, details at www.karajarri.com

Be sure to take repellent if camping as the sandflies are friendly.

Further north, Cape Bossut is at the south-western extremity of La Grange Bay. The bay's estuaries have jacks, grunter, pikey bream, salmon and mud crabs. Small creeks towards the ends of the bay produce some barramundi. Permission is needed to access Bidyadanga, also known as La Grange.

North of Port Smith is Barn Hill Station, which has a van park and beach launching.

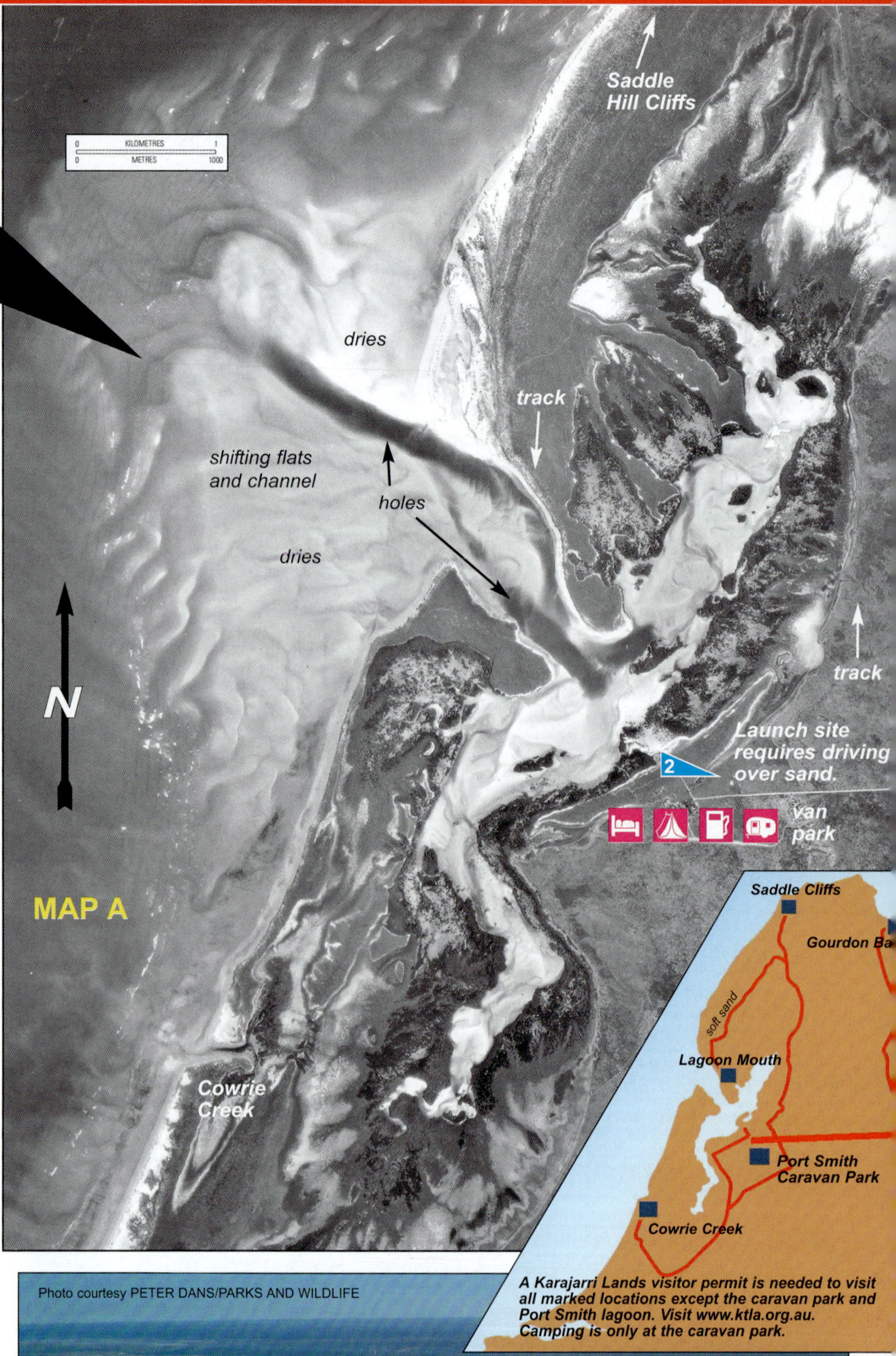

MAP A

Saddle Hill Cliffs

KILOMETRES 0 1
METRES 0 1000

dries

track

shifting flats and channel

holes

dries

N

track

Launch site requires driving over sand.

2

van park

Cowrie Creek

Saddle Cliffs

Gourdon Ba

soft sand

Lagoon Mouth

Port Smith Caravan Park

Cowrie Creek

A Karajarri Lands visitor permit is needed to visit all marked locations except the caravan park and Port Smith lagoon. Visit www.ktla.org.au. Camping is only at the caravan park.

Photo courtesy PETER DANS/PARKS AND WILDLIFE

MAP B

Creeks inside Cape Bossut, 30km south-west of Port Smith

Cowrie Creek

Key to Map

Hotspots

1. Troll for pelagic fish around headland. Tuskfish, spangled emperor, coral trout, cod over rough bottom - 32km by sea from Port Smith.
2. Same as Spot 1, but 13km from Port Smith.
3. Salmon, queenfish, mud crabs.
4. Good fishing in Port Smith. Tidal lagoon mostly empties at low tide. Strong currents on big tides, fish channel edges for tuskfish (bluebone). Mackerel, queenfish, trevally out wide.
5. Gourdon Bay is a beautiful place to fish at high tide. Shallow reefs outside, beaches and headlands. End of track is sandy.
6. Reef and pelagic fish.
7. Beach and boat fishing at Barn Hill Station. Shallow reef offshore.

Launch sites

1. Bidyadanga: permission needed to enter. Phone (08) 9192 4009.
2. Port Smith: firm beach launch at high tide. Caravan park nearby.
3. Gourdon Bay. Permit needed for access. Cartopper or kayak launch.
4. Beach launching at Barn Hill Station. Nearby Eco Beach has a paid beach launching service.

LaGrange Bay has up to about 9.5m tidal movement.

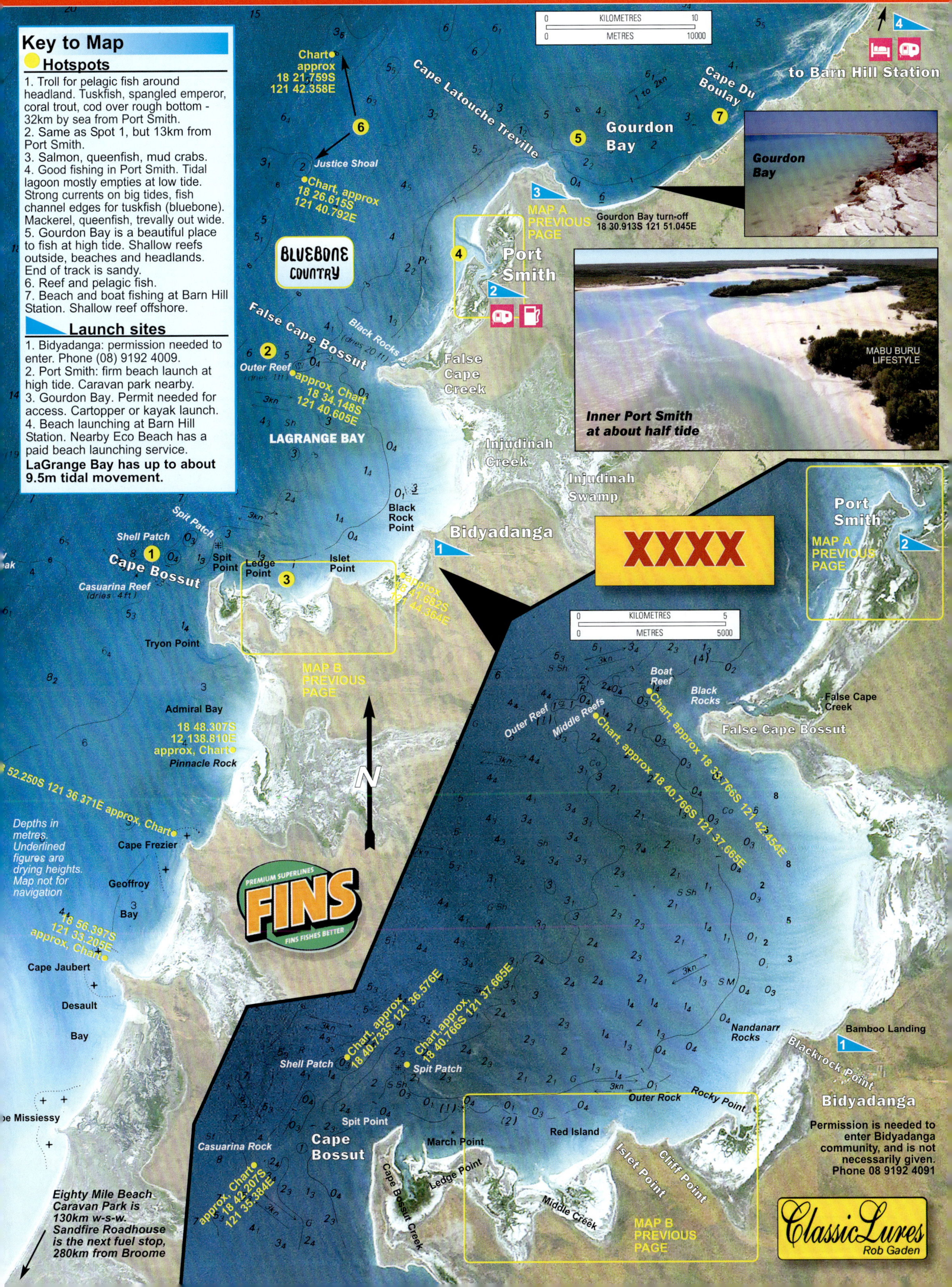

Gourdon Bay

MABU BURU LIFESTYLE

Inner Port Smith at about half tide

Permission is needed to enter Bidyadanga community, and is not necessarily given. Phone 08 9192 4091

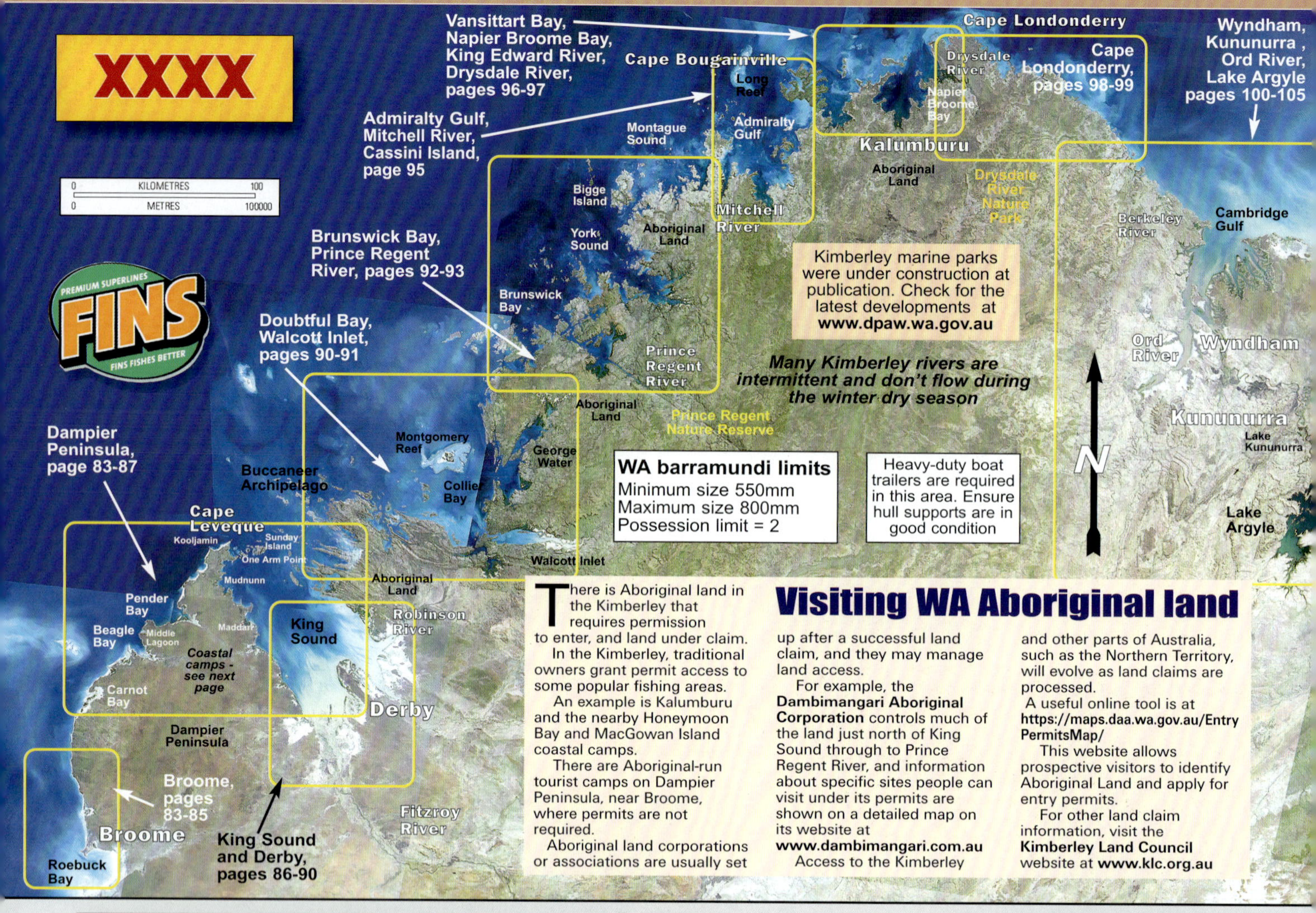

Vansittart Bay, Napier Broome Bay, King Edward River, Drysdale River, pages 96-97
Admiralty Gulf, Mitchell River, Cassini Island, page 95
Cape Londonderry, pages 98-99
Wyndham, Kununurra, Ord River, Lake Argyle pages 100-105
Brunswick Bay, Prince Regent River, pages 92-93
Doubtful Bay, Walcott Inlet, pages 90-91
Dampier Peninsula, page 83-87
Broome, pages 83-85
King Sound and Derby, pages 86-90
Coastal camps - see next page

Kimberley marine parks were under construction at publication. Check for the latest developments at www.dpaw.wa.gov.au

Many Kimberley rivers are intermittent and don't flow during the winter dry season

WA barramundi limits
Minimum size 550mm
Maximum size 800mm
Possession limit = 2

Heavy-duty boat trailers are required in this area. Ensure hull supports are in good condition

Visiting WA Aboriginal land

There is Aboriginal land in the Kimberley that requires permission to enter, and land under claim.

In the Kimberley, traditional owners grant permit access to some popular fishing areas.

An example is Kalumburu and the nearby Honeymoon Bay and MacGowan Island coastal camps.

There are Aboriginal-run tourist camps on Dampier Peninsula, near Broome, where permits are not required.

Aboriginal land corporations or associations are usually set up after a successful land claim, and they may manage land access.

For example, the **Dambimangari Aboriginal Corporation** controls much of the land just north of King Sound through to Prince Regent River, and information about specific sites people can visit under its permits are shown on a detailed map on its website at **www.dambimangari.com.au**

Access to the Kimberley and other parts of Australia, such as the Northern Territory, will evolve as land claims are processed.

A useful online tool is at **https://maps.daa.wa.gov.au/EntryPermitsMap/**

This website allows prospective visitors to identify Aboriginal Land and apply for entry permits.

For other land claim information, visit the **Kimberley Land Council** website at **www.klc.org.au**

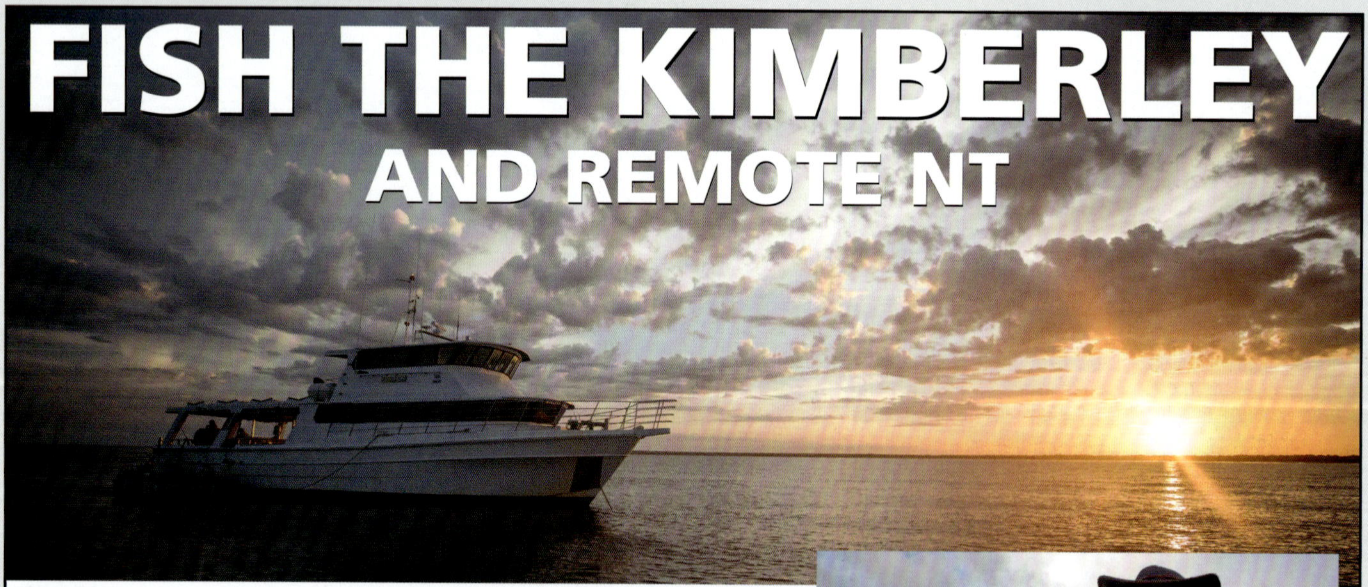

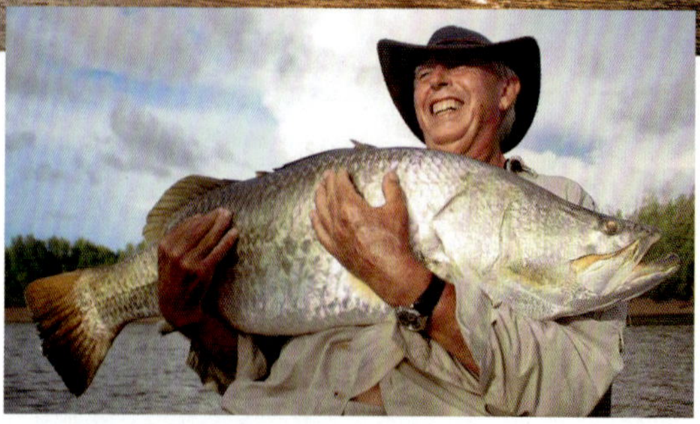

Remote coastal bush camps

The remote Dampier Peninsula, north of Broome, has coastal camps offering various levels of comfort, with red cliffs, white sand and blue water providing a memorable backdrop to the fishing.

The once famously rough Cape Leveque Road is now sealed, but tracks to some coastal camps require 4WD, and beach launching of boats is the norm.

There is endless adventure for hardcore fishing fanatics. Huge tides, numerous reefs and shallows, and long distances must be taken into account.

The peninsula is known for threadfin salmon, queenfish, mackerel, jacks and tuskfish. The western peninsula provides mainly a bluewater experience, with mud crabs and occasional barramundi in the bigger creeks.

Long-distance trips should be done with two boats and a satellite phone.

Small tides provide safer sea conditions. Mostcreeks dry at low tide.

Alcohol is not sold on Dampier Peninsula.

Some camps may be closed because of the COVID19 pandemic, check availability before planning a trip.

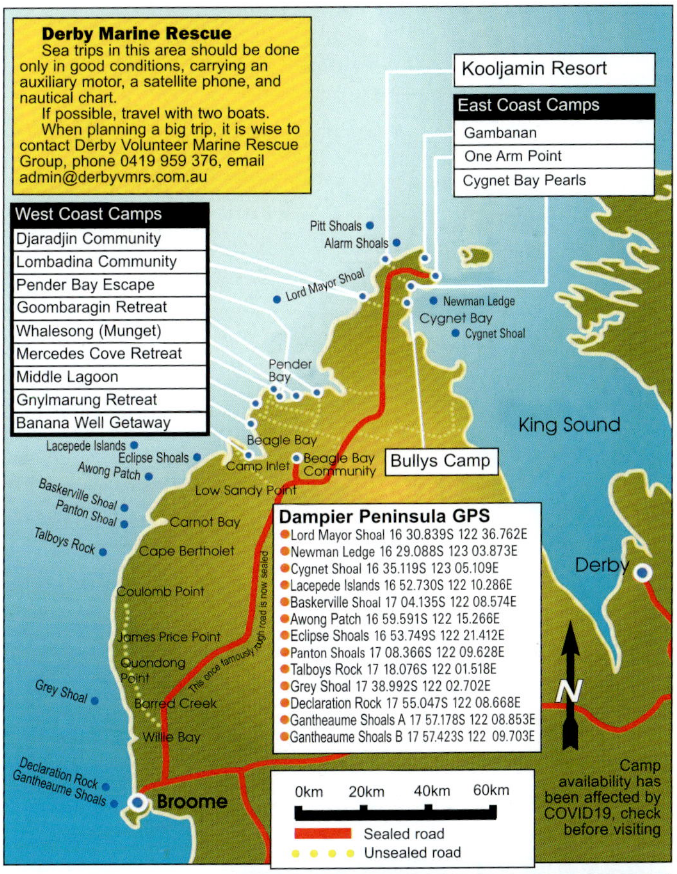

Derby Marine Rescue
Sea trips in this area should be done only in good conditions, carrying an auxiliary motor, a satellite phone, and nautical chart.
If possible, travel with two boats.
When planning a big trip, it is wise to contact Derby Volunteer Marine Rescue Group, phone 0419 959 376, email admin@derbyvmrs.com.au

West Coast Camps
- Djaradjin Community
- Lombadina Community
- Pender Bay Escape
- Goombaragin Retreat
- Whalesong (Munget)
- Mercedes Cove Retreat
- Middle Lagoon
- Gnylmarung Retreat
- Banana Well Getaway

Kooljamin Resort

East Coast Camps
- Gambanan
- One Arm Point
- Cygnet Bay Pearls

Bullys Camp

Dampier Peninsula GPS
- Lord Mayor Shoal 16 30.839S 122 36.762E
- Newman Ledge 16 29.088S 123 03.873E
- Cygnet Shoal 16 35.119S 123 05.109E
- Lacepede Islands 16 52.730S 122 10.286E
- Baskerville Shoal 17 04.135S 122 08.574E
- Awong Patch 16 59.591S 122 15.266E
- Eclipse Shoals 16 53.749S 122 21.412E
- Panton Shoals 17 08.366S 122 09.628E
- Talboys Rock 17 18.076S 122 01.518E
- Grey Shoal 17 38.992S 122 02.702E
- Declaration Rock 17 55.047S 122 08.668E
- Gantheaume Shoals A 17 57.178S 122 08.853E
- Gantheaume Shoals B 17 57.423S 122 09.703E

0km 20km 40km 60km
Sealed road
Unsealed road

Camp availability has been affected by COVID19, check before visiting

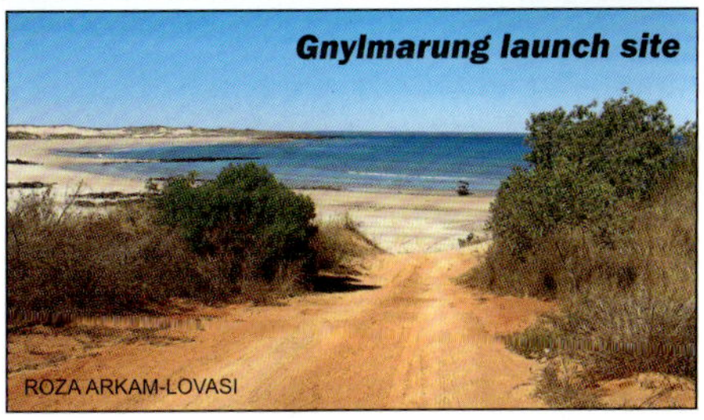

Gnylmarung launch site

ROZA ARKAM-LOVASI

Banana Well Getaway: A good choice for fishermen, being on the southern shore of Beagle Bay, with tidal creeks nearby. Probably the best camp on the western peninsula for barramundi and mud crabs. Houses, cabins and tent sites. Phone 08 9192 4040
www.bananawellgetaway.com.au

Gnylmarung Retreat: On the north side of Beagle Bay, on Middle Lagoon Road, 30km off the Cape Leveque Road. Cabins and camp sites, with water, beach launch, solar showers and laundry. Bluewater fishing for mainly queenfish, trevally, mackerel, coral trout, tricky snapper and tuskfish.
Ph: 08 9192 4097
www.gnylmarung.org.au

Middle Lagoon: Heading north, the Middle Lagoon turn-off is on the left after Beagle Bay, with 32km of unsealed road to the camp. Cabins and camps, a shop, some phone reception and free wireless. Bluewater fishing for mainly queenfish, trevally, mackerel, coral trout, tricky snapper and tuskfish.
Ph: 08 9192 4002
www.middlelagoon.com.au

Mercedes Cove: On the southern entrance to Pender Bay, with beach launch. Cabins and tents.
Phone 08 9192 4687
www.mercedescove.com.au

Goombaragin: This camp is located inside Pender Bay, being the nearest camp to the bay's large creek. All sorts of fish move up the creek with the tide in surprisingly clear water. There are tents, chalets and camp sites, with beach launching for small boats.
Ph: 08 9195 2200
www.goombaragin.com.au

Pender Bay Escape: Eleven beachfront camps, open all year. Also an air-con ensuite cabin. Phone 0429 845 707 or email penderbay@bigpond.com
Pender Bay Escape is on Facebook.

Kooljamin: A resort at the tip of the peninsula at Cape Leveque. Camping and accommodation, a restaurant, water, and 4WD launch. Excellent bluewater fishing in wild country. Airstrip available. (08) 9192 4970
www.kooljaman.com.au

Gumbanan Bush Camp (Kimberley Outback Xposure): Near One Arm Point. Camps and safari tents. Shallow around the camp but a good base for exploring exciting spots in northern King Sound. Ph: 0414 357 624
Gumbanan is on Facebook.

Whalesong (Munget): This is a cafe and campground on southern Pender Bay, looking over cliffs. Beach launching and bluewater fishing.
Phone 08 9192 4000
www.whalesongcafe.com.au

Cygnet Bay Pearls: Accommodation with restaurant and boat ramp. Camping, caravan, tents and shacks. Sheltered beach launching into northern King Sound. For careful boaters, there are big trevally and mackerel in this area.
Phone 08 9192 4283
www.cygnetbaypearlfarm.com.au

Bullys Camp, Djoodoon: A basic but likeable camp on Cygnet Bay. Turn right north of the Lombadina turn-off on the Cape Leveque Road. The camp is down 9km of sandy track.
Phone 08 3132 4359

Broome

The town has a new jetty and associated rock walls which are good fishing locations at high tide.

The big shipping jetty nearby is still a great fishing platform but access has been closed to much of its length.

Barramundi, queenfish, tuskfish, mackerel, gar, bream and trevally are all caught from the jetties.

At night, barramundi lurk around the jetty pylons. Look for them where shadows and illuminated areas meet.

Fishing improved in Roebuck Bay after gill nets were removed.

Dampier Creek produces barramundi, salmon and mud crabs.

Broome's offshore waters are famous for sailfish, with spectacular action at the annual billfish competition.

There are spangled emperor, trout and tuskfish on the reefs, with salmon, barramundi, tripletail, jewfish and mud crabs throughout the estuaries.

The Fitzroy River is within easy driving distance, with tidal and freshwater barramundi fishing.

The south-west side of Dampier Peninsula has a track up to Barred and Willie Creeks and beyond, while the sealed main road up the peninsula leads to coastal camps.

Dampier Peninsula estuaries generally have good water clarity despite huge tides. Watch rays, sharks and fish swim up creeks with the tide.

The clear water suits lure fishing. Dinghies are fine in the estuaries, but shallow water, wind and big tides can quickly bring seas up.

Broome is a base for remote Kimberley and Rowley Shoals long-distance charters.

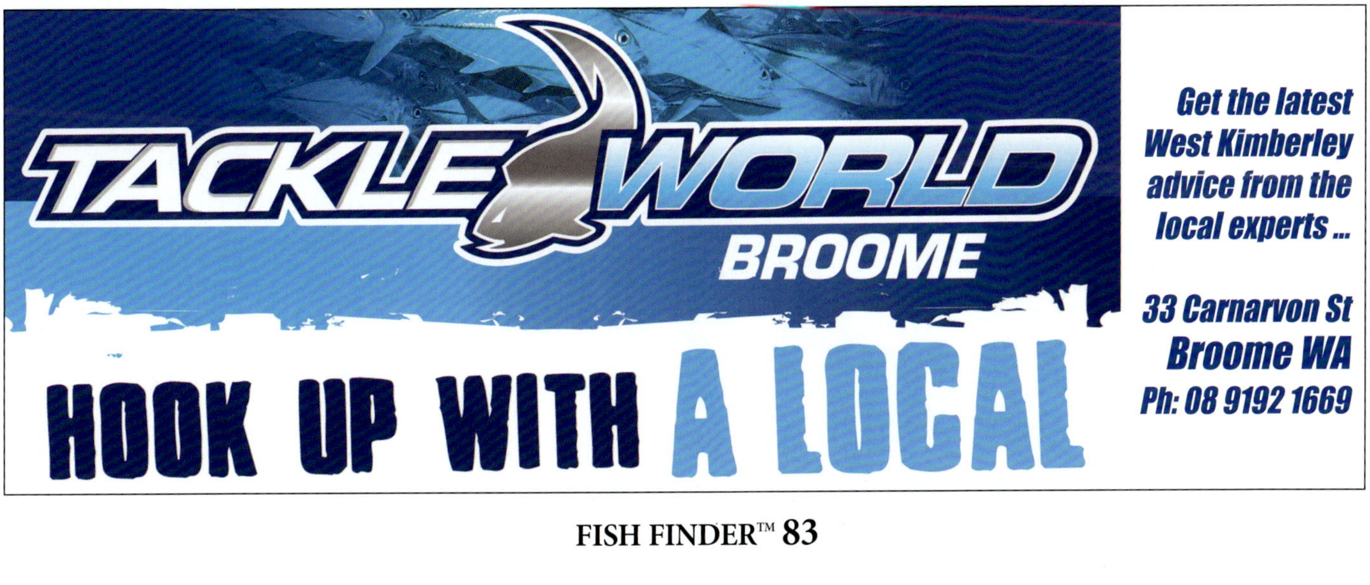

Salmon & sailfish

Broome is known for its reliable sailfish grounds and healthy stocks of salmon, barramundi and jewfish in net-free Roebuck Bay.

The bay's gill net licences were bought back in 2013 and local anglers now say threadfin salmon and barramundi fishing has improved greatly, with gillnet bycatch species such as queenfish and tripletail also improved.

The salmon "season" runs from May to September. In the warmer months, barramundi are the main target.

Pods of sailfish are raised reliably off Broome, supporting a major annual competition. The sailfish sometimes come in close to Willie Creek and Barred Creek on the Dampier Peninsula, accessible to small boats and even kayaks.

Broome sailfish are best pursued just after neap tides when the water is clearer. The main grounds are usually the 16-24 mile areas to the north-west ranging from 280 to 320 degrees off Gantheaume Point, where there is an undulating sea floor.

Close to Broome, Roebuck Deep has some of the deepest near-shore water in far northern Australia, with steep drop-offs, holes and ledges.

Jewfish are caught at the Jew Hole, about 200m off the Old Entrance Point boat ramp, as well as at the anchorages off Town Beach, and Black Ledge. The south side of Roebuck Deep has reef fish.

There are salmon, barra, jacks, tuskfish and mud crabs in local creeks, with the town's Dampier Creek the main attraction, followed by Crab Creek, reached by a road that follows the bay's foreshore to "Little Crab Creek".

The port jetty has barra, queenfish, mackerel, tuskfish and trevally. Big tides and the jetty's height make it challenging to fish, and in recent years only some of the walkway has been open. A smaller jetty and groyne has been built at Town Beach, with good fishing near high tide.

South of Broome, unsealed roads off the Great Northern highway go to Eco Beach, Barn Hill Beachside Station Stay and Port Smith Lagoon Caravan Park. Eco Beach offers trips to coastal Jacks Creek, while beach launching gives access to shallow coastal reefs at Barn Hill in good weather. More sheltered fishing is found in Port Smith tidal lagoon.

North of Broome is the excellent Dampier Peninsula, with several coastal camps.

A tidal range exceeding 9m must be taken into account around Broome.

Key to Map

Hotspots

1. Mackerel, reef fish. 2. Sailfish. 3. Mackerel, reef fish. 4. 'The Caves': mackerel, reef fish, cobia, sailfish. 5. Mackerel on reef edges. 6. Sailfish wide of creek mouths, usually mid-year. Also tuna. 7. Salmon, barra, tripletail. 8. Queenfish, trevally at mouth. Anchorage within. 9. Good reef fishing. 10. Mackerel, reef fish. 11. Sailfish over shoals. 12. Jacks Creek north of Eco Beach, jacks, barra, queenfish, salmon. Further is Yardoogarra Creek, with similar fishing. 13. Tuskfish, mackerel. 14. Estuary fish in tiny Crab Creek. Turn-off on highway. 15. Mackerel. 16. Reef fish.

Launch sites

All are tide dependent. 1. Two ramps, upper tide. See next page. 2. Beach launching inside point. 3. Ramp near van park. 4. Ramp on foreshore 3.8km west of Crab Creek. 5. Soft sand launch into 'Little Crab Creek'. 6, 7, 8. Bank/beach launches by 4WD. 9. Beach launch at Barn Hill. Paid launch service at Eco Beach. 10. Sandy launch into tidal lagoon.

Local tides may exceed 9m movement.

Broome jetty and boat ramps

Hotspots

1. Jewfish and golden snapper school along here, best at night.
2. Jew hole. Fish turn of tide and neap tides.
3. Mixed reef fish and jewfish along the drop-offs. Large golden snapper at night.
4. Reef fish, trevally. Shallow water makes it fishable in a reasonable current when deeper areas are unfishable.
5. Mackerel and cobia at Escape Rock drop-off.
6. Tuna shoals move through channel.
7. Trevally and mackerel among bommies.
8. Jetty: mackerel, reef fish, including tuskfish. Barramundi on surface at night in summer on livebait and lures. Deep-diving lures, or sinking lures, needed because of height of jetty.
9. Tuskfish, golden snapper and spanish flag.

Key to Map

10. Creek fishes best for barramundi Sept to April. Salmon, grunter and mud crabs in dry season.
11. Occasional trevally, queenfish, salmon off Cable Beach on rising tide. Tuna close inshore.
12. Town beach jetty and rock wall. Most species.
13. Golden snapper, jewfish.
14. Mackerel between Whale Rock and headland.
15. Mixed reef fish.

Launch sites

1 and 2. Two ramps, with new boating facility planned for this site. Old ramps are exposed, upper tide only, and many locals beach-launch from Gantheaume Point (3). Ramp 4 is town boat ramp, often covered in sand. Ramp 5 is near high-tide only. **Local tides have up to about 9.34m movement.**

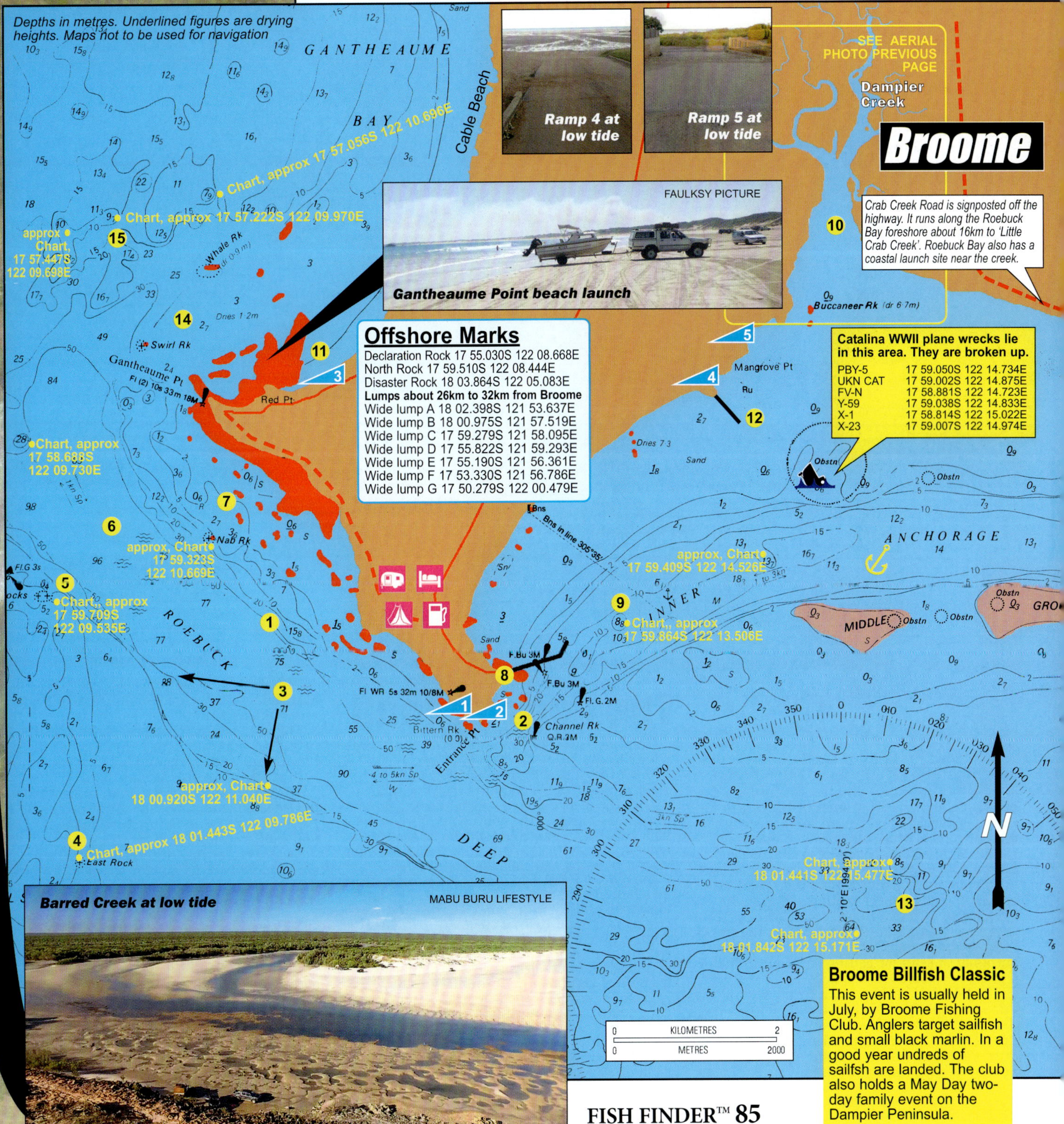

Depths in metres. Underlined figures are drying heights. Maps not to be used for navigation

GANTHEAUME BAY

Cable Beach

Ramp 4 at low tide

Ramp 5 at low tide

SEE AERIAL PHOTO PREVIOUS PAGE

Dampier Creek

Broome

FAULKSY PICTURE

Gantheaume Point beach launch

Crab Creek Road is signposted off the highway. It runs along the Roebuck Bay foreshore about 16km to 'Little Crab Creek'. Roebuck Bay also has a coastal launch site near the creek.

Chart, approx 17 57.056S 122 10.696E

Chart, approx 17 57.222S 122 09.970E

approx Chart, 17 57.447S 122 09.698E

Chart, approx 17 58.688S 122 09.730E

approx, Chart 17 59.323S 122 10.669E

Chart, approx 17 59.709S 122 09.535E

approx, Chart 18 00.920S 122 11.040E

Chart, approx 18 01.443S 122 09.786E

approx, Chart 17 59.409S 122 14.526E

Chart, approx 17 59.864S 122 13.506E

Chart, approx 18 01.441S 122 15.477E

Chart, approx 18 01.842S 122 15.171E

Offshore Marks

Declaration Rock 17 55.030S 122 08.668E
North Rock 17 59.510S 122 08.444E
Disaster Rock 18 03.864S 122 05.083E
Lumps about 26km to 32km from Broome
Wide lump A 18 02.398S 121 53.637E
Wide lump B 18 00.975S 121 57.519E
Wide lump C 17 59.279S 121 58.095E
Wide lump D 17 55.822S 121 59.293E
Wide lump E 17 55.190S 121 56.361E
Wide lump F 17 53.330S 121 56.786E
Wide lump G 17 50.279S 122 00.479E

Catalina WWII plane wrecks lie in this area. They are broken up.

PBY-5	17 59.050S 122 14.734E
UKN CAT	17 59.002S 122 14.875E
FV-N	17 58.881S 122 14.723E
Y-59	17 59.038S 122 14.833E
X-1	17 58.814S 122 15.022E
X-23	17 59.007S 122 14.974E

Whale Rk, Swirl Rk, Gantheaume Pt, Red Pt, Nab Rk, Buccaneer Rk, Mangrove Pt, ANCHORAGE, INNER, MIDDLE, ROEBUCK DEEP, Entrance Pt, Bittern Rk, Channel Rk, East Rock

KILOMETRES 0 – 2
METRES 0 – 2000

MABU BURU LIFESTYLE

Barred Creek at low tide

Broome Billfish Classic

This event is usually held in July, by Broome Fishing Club. Anglers target sailfish and small black marlin. In a good year undreds of sailfish are landed. The club also holds a May Day two-day family event on the Dampier Peninsula.

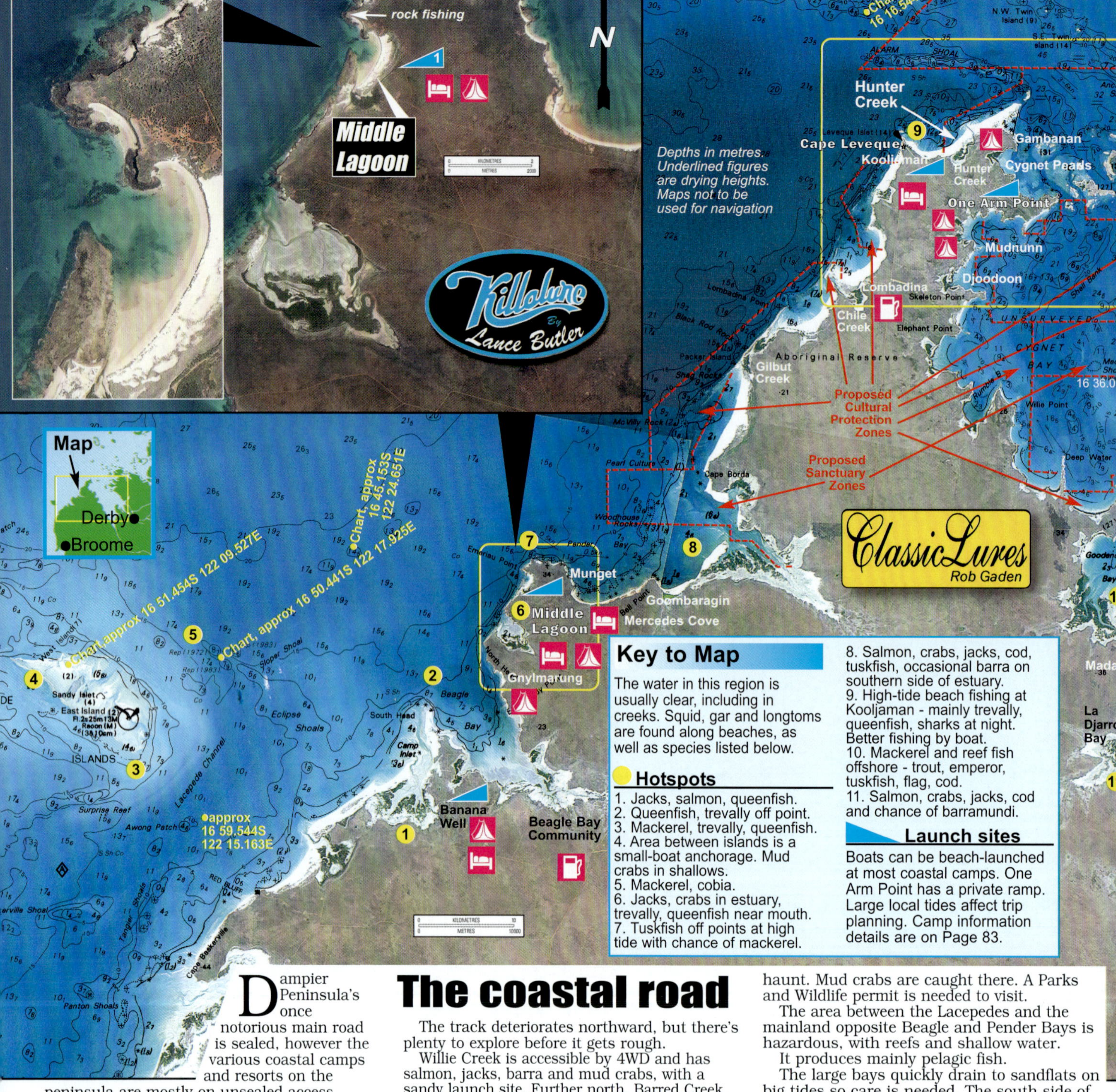

The coastal road

Dampier Peninsula's once notorious main road is sealed, however the various coastal camps and resorts on the peninsula are mostly on unsealed access tracks of varying quality and 4WD is required in many spots, especially for boat launching.

The peninsula's west coast is shallow and sandy, with clear water even during big tides.

Salmon, queenfish, trevally, jacks, tuskfish and mud crabs are the main catch from the foreshores, with trout, flag, spangled emperor, tricky snapper, cod and mackerel on the reefs.

Ballooning gear or long-distance casting outfits are useful for getting baits out to the fish on the shallower beaches.

The Coastal Track: A track turns west off the Cape Leveque Road and then runs north along the coast. This is Manari Road, with Willie Creek, Barred Creek, Quondong Point, James Price Point and Coulomb Point along the way. See the previous Broome pages.

The track deteriorates northward, but there's plenty to explore before it gets rough.

Willie Creek is accessible by 4WD and has salmon, jacks, barra and mud crabs, with a sandy launch site. Further north, Barred Creek mouth has rocks on the north bank, fishable at high tide. Beach launching is done on the south bank. A look over Cape Boileau reveals a startling vista of blue sea, red cliffs and white sand.

Quandong Point and James Price Point have headland fishing at high tide, best in the late afternoon and early morning. Hermit and ghost crabs are a great bait for tuskfish.

After Coulomb Point the track gets rougher and creek crossings are affected by the tide.

A beach launch gives access to estuaries from Cape Bertholet to Carnot Bay.

Offshore are the Lacepede Islands, low, sand cays about 110km north of Broome opposite Pender Bay. The waters are shallow sand and reef, best known for pelagic fish.

An anchorage exists between the two main islands, Middle and West, and is a queenfish haunt. Mud crabs are caught there. A Parks and Wildlife permit is needed to visit.

The area between the Lacepedes and the mainland opposite Beagle and Pender Bays is hazardous, with reefs and shallow water.

It produces mainly pelagic fish.

The large bays quickly drain to sandflats on big tides so care is needed. The south side of Pender Bay has mangrove foreshores that can fish well around high tide.

From Pender Bay to Cape Leveque are shallow offshore reefs with spangled emperor, flag, trout and tuskfish, but new marine park zones proposed at publication may limit inshore fishing.

Kooljaman resort is at the tip of the peninsula, accessed by the main peninsula road. A 4WD sand track follows the beach almost to Hunter Creek, which has crabs and jacks. Beach fishing here is not outstanding but boaters can do well.

Off One Arm Point, the Sunday Island group has big trevally in the tidal rips, but restrictive zonings were planned at publication, check before fishing.

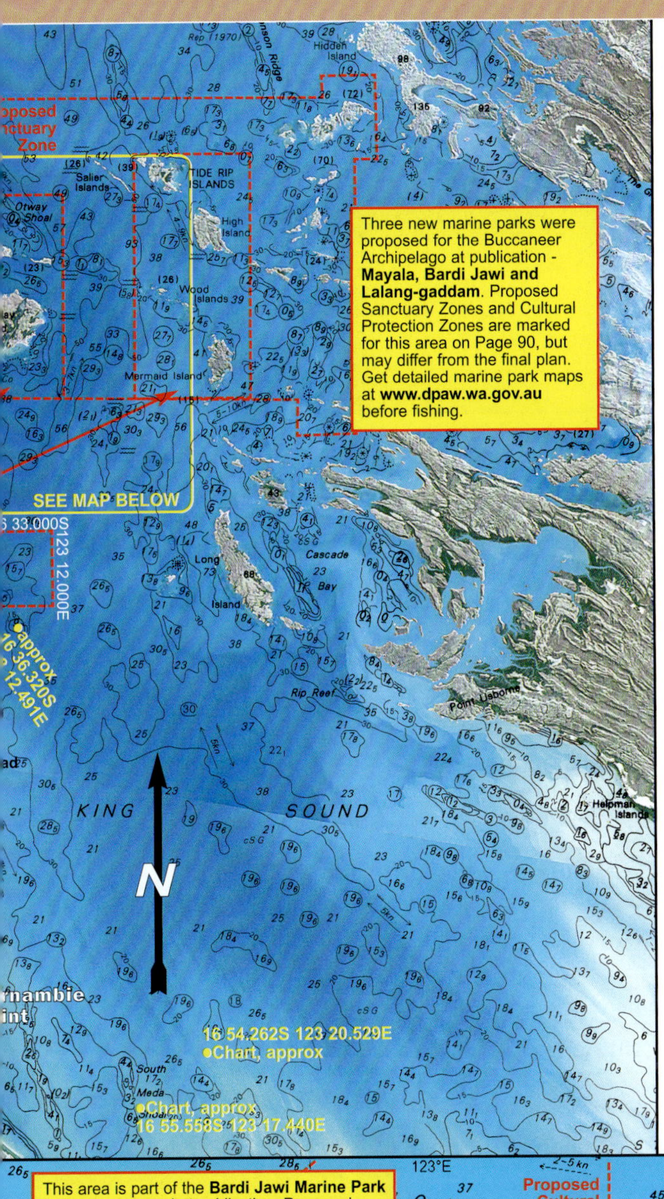

Endless islands

Appropriately known as the "Thousand Island Coast", the north of King Sound, in the vicinity of Koolan Island to Walcott Inlet, is one of the great cruising areas of the Kimberley.

The tides are huge, with up to 12m movement creating turbulent seas even without wind.

A popular pastime in Buccaneer Archipelago is reef fishing for big golden snapper.

The best tides for this are between neaps and springs.

Popular areas for golden snapper include Cockatoo, Irvine and Koolan Islands. Expect to catch tuskfish, coral trout, spangled emperor, golden snapper, jacks, cod and loads of trevally. See Pages 90-91.

Three new marine parks were planned for this area at publication, with some areas no longer accessible to fishermen.

Talbot and Dugong Bays: Talbot and Dugong Bays are among the most scenic waterways. They are south-east of Koolan Island.

A feature of this area are the Horizontal Waterfalls, tidal pinch rapids where water is forced through two gaps, an awesome sight. Boats can travel through the gaps, although the second-most narrow gap is not recommended except at the tidal turn when the water is slow.

Both Talbot and Dugong Bays have numerous waterfalls.

Extensive reef systems are uncovered towards low water which require careful navigating within Talbot Bay.

Many reefs are not marked on charts. Both bays have deep channels and produce reef fish, but note the sanctuary zones.

The estuaries contain threadfin salmon, barramundi and jacks.

Kingfisher Islands: Further to the east of Talbot Bay are the Kingfisher group of islands.

Big golden snapper inhabit the channel and drop-off, although the islands are best known for prolific queenfish and mega trevally, particularly at the eastern channel entrance, but note the sanctuary zone around the northern Kingfisher Island and associated islets.

Secure Bay: To the south is Secure Bay, aptly named as it affords protection to boats by way of encircling escarpments.

Secure Bay is two bays in one with access to the southern-most system through a narrow gap in the ranges. Enter at the turn of the tide, as whirlpools are common during tidal movement.

The southern-most bay is like a giant amphitheatre, bordered by sandstone and dolerite hills and a huge sandspit.

Secure Bay has good fishing for barra, jacks and smaller golden snapper. The rocky islands at both entrances hold big trevally and queenfish.

Walcott Inlet: About 20km north of Secure Bay, Walcott Inlet is an inland sea of 60km in length, into which the Charnley, Calder and Isdell Rivers flow.

It has a treacherous entrance channel, with tidal rips and whirlpools. The main body of water is a sanctuary, but fishing is permitted in the rivers, where barramundi are usually abundant.

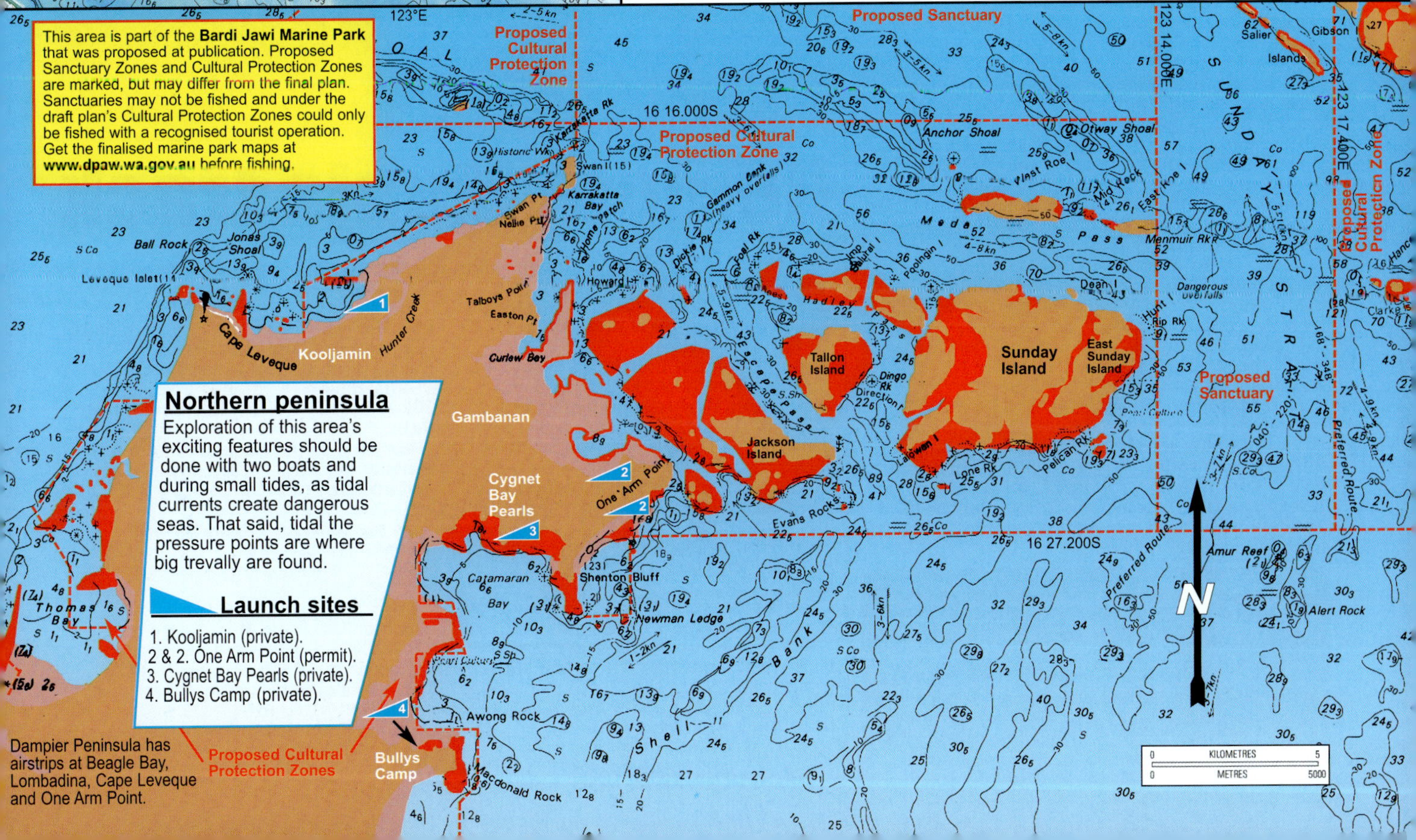

This area is part of the **Bardi Jawi Marine Park** that was proposed at publication. Proposed Sanctuary Zones and Cultural Protection Zones are marked, but may differ from the final plan. Sanctuaries may not be fished and under the draft plan's Cultural Protection Zones could only be fished with a recognised tourist operation. Get the finalised marine park maps at **www.dpaw.wa.gov.au** before fishing.

Northern peninsula

Exploration of this area's exciting features should be done with two boats and during small tides, as tidal currents create dangerous seas. That said, tidal the pressure points are where big trevally are found.

Launch sites

1. Kooljamin (private).
2. & 2. One Arm Point (permit).
3. Cygnet Bay Pearls (private).
4. Bullys Camp (private).

Dampier Peninsula has airstrips at Beagle Bay, Lombadina, Cape Leveque and One Arm Point.

Proposed Cultural Protection Zones

Proposed Sanctuary

Proposed Cultural Protection Zone

Cape Leveque · Kooljamin · Hunter Creek · Gambanan · Cygnet Bay Pearls · One Arm Point · Shenton Bluff · Newman Ledge · Awong Rock · Bullys Camp · Macdonald Rock · Thomas Bay · Tallon Island · Jackson Island · Sunday Island · East Sunday Island · Anchor Shoal · Otway Shoal · Evans Rocks · Alert Rock · Amur Reef · Salier Islands · Gibson · Pelican Rk · Lone Rk · Dingo Rk · Swan Pt · Nellie Pt · Talboys Point · Easton Pt · Curlew Bay · Catamaran Bay · Jones Shoal · Ball Rock · Leveque Islet · Shell Bank · Meda Pass · Menmuir Rks · Dean I · Hunt I · Preferred Route · Sunday Strait

16 16.000S · 16 27.200S · 123°E · 123 14.000E · 123 17.400E

KILOMETRES 0 5 · METRES 0 5000

Big tides and barramundi

The town of Derby is on a peninsula to the north of the Fitzroy River mouth, next to the shallow expanse of King Sound. The port, encompassing the jetty and boat ramps, is connected to the town via a causeway. The town is surrounded by vast mudflats.

May River
POSITIVE FISHING

Tides reach an astounding 11m+, depending on the time of year, draining much of King Sound dry.

Large barramundi are caught around Derby in the Fitzroy River, usually by casting livebaits into holes. Derby has two boat ramps, one at the jetty and one in a creek south of the jetty.

If you miss the tide, mud awaits.

Derby is a launch site for those doing long Kimberley voyages.

Make your first trip on neap tides, as King Sound chops up fast on big tides.

The May, Meda and Robinson rivers feed into Stokes Bay on the east side of King Sound. To the north around Port Usborne and Kimbolton, the topography changes from featureless to scenic ranges, with semi-enclosed estuaries.

Calder River freshwater mixes with turbid tidal water

Fitzroy River: To the south of Derby is the mouth of the Fitzroy River. The river is wide but shallow, with vast sandbars and shifting channels. The saltwater reaches form pools at low tide. Access is by sea from Derby on big tides, unless you get track access permission from Yeeda Station.

Boaters who fish the low tide pools should keep in mind the tidc comes in fast. Don't stray far from your boat.

A great spot is Telegraph Pool. It is influenced only by big tides, when the fish actively feed. At Pelican Pool and Sawfish Point, where there is full tidal influence, boat anglers can walk the pools at low tide for barra. Tracks follow the river, but Yeeda Station limits access.

Tumblegoodire, Willuns and Willare pools are above tidal influence.

Other pools exist all the way up to Fitzroy Crossing, with the Myroodah Crossing to Fitzroy Barrage region (Liveringa Station) having barra holes.

Geike Gorge near Fitzroy Crossing can fish well, especially after a big Wet.

On the east side of the river is Yeeda Cuttings, great for barra. It is tidal with a channel to the river. There are tidal creeks south of Derby, including Alligator and Ask Creeks, but accessing them involves traversing saltpans, with bogging risks.

Estuaries north-west of Derby at Doctors Creek and across the sound at Fraser River and the Huon River opposite Valentine Island have barra, but are best for mud crabs. Valentine Island has salmon.

Point Torment: Point Torment is about 50km north of Derby. Derby Visitor Centre has an access map.

This 4WD track should not be used during tides of 10m or more as the saltpan gets boggy. Salmon, barra, jewfish, snapper and crabs are caught.

The same species are at Black Rocks, opposite the lighthouse, south of Point Torment. It is shallow.

To the east of Point Torment is Stokes Bay. An estuary on the south side called Blue Holes has clean water behind rockbars. The holes have snapper, cod and jewfish. Reach it off the Point Torment track.

Further east are the May and Meda rivers, with barra. The Robinson River was part of a proposed sanctuary at publication. To access this area, contact Meda Station.

Access beyond is restricted by a military area. There are good estuaries between Robinson River mouth and Helpman Islands, including a rockbar, but access is by sea.

On the opposite (western) side of King Sound, Goodenough and Disaster Bays have barra, snapper, salmon and crabs.

Cassini Island

Parts of the Kimberley flow reasonably clear water even during the region's big tides.

There are offshore grounds with blue water and billfish, and islands with white beaches.

Cassini Island, north-west of Long Reef, is such a spot. It has red cliffs and caves, with white sandy coves dropping off into clear water.

Cassini has marlin to the west, and sailfish all around, even in the southern anchorage. Humpback whales visit from June to November.

Local reefs hold big trevally, mackerel, coral trout, cod and other reef fish.

Oliver Rock, 8.3km west of Cassini at 13 58.565S 125 33.595E, is an exciting destination where you can see big mackerel, trevally, cobia and sharks chase lures.

Dotted around this area are many isolated spots that are rarely fished, but note the sanctuary around nearby Long Reef.

Getting there: See Page 95. The nearest reasonable launch site is Kalumburu, for an island-hopping return trip of about 300km, although the rough Port Warrender track does give access to a beach launch, for a 140km return sea trip. A safer option is a tour from Mitchell River with a local mothership operator, after flying in by helicopter.

Cassini Island

Calder River at low tide
ROZA ARKAM-LOVASI PICTURES

Munja Track

Remote Munja track

Mt Elizabeth Station, about 30km off the Gibb River Road, has historically offered access to the Munja Track, a 4WD destination for adventurous fishos.

At publication, this 220km track was closed as new access arrangements were planned by traditional owners.

The track goes to Walcott Inlet, with good barra fishing in the Calder River.

See the map on Page 91.

A week is needed to travel the track, see the local sites and do some fishing and camping at the river.

The Munja Track has in the past included the Bachsten Creek Bush Camp.

The track requires high-clearance 4WD and careful driving.

The first 60km of track is average, with creek crossings. There is a steep jump-up at 66km that requires extreme care, and it takes about four hours to drive the first 70km.

After the first 70km the trip onward to Bachsten Creek Bush Camp is slower.

Not far from the camp is a freshwater hole. Beyond the hole is Bachsten Falls, Honeycomb Caves, The Rockhole, Harro's Lookout and Wren Gorge.

After Bachsten camp is a six-hour, 70km drive to Walcott Inlet and Calder River.

The river's coffee-coloured tidal water is home to plenty of big barramundi.

There are crocodiles, so fish and camp with care.

As the water is usually turbid, livebaiting works best.

The river is filled with mullet so catching bait is easy.

Local tides can be huge.

Some 4WD know-how, spare parts, and sufficient water and food supplies are needed to do the Munja Track.

***Mount Elizabeth Station**
Phone (08) 9191 4644
www.mtelizabethstationstay.com.au

KILOMETRES 0 10
METRES 0 10000
King Sound
PROPOSED MAIYALAM MP SANCTUARY ZONE BOUNDARY
123 41.000E
16 55.000S
Stewart River
Robinson River
STOKES BAY
Stokes Bay
UNSURVEYED
Depths in metres. Underlined figures are drying heights. Maps not to be used for navigation
Point Torment was named after biting bugs! Carry repellent.
Reference point, approx 17 02.321S 123 45.741E
Meda River
saltflats
Point Torment
Black Rocks Lighthouse
Valentine Island
Hutton River
Derby Sea Rescue
Ph 0419 959 376
admin@derbyvmrs.com.au
Australia's Biggest Tides
The highest Australian tides and the second highest tides in the world happen near Derby, WA, in late March and again in late April. The tides peak at 11.8m and drop to about 1.5m at low tide. Vast flats are exposed at low tide. Never walk far from your boat at low tide.
Doctor's Creek
May River
Mary Island North
Mary Island South
Fraser River
Map
Derby
Broome
Birdwood Downs Station offers accommodation and meals, located off the Gibb River Road east of Derby. It has no water access but is a useful base for fishing the nearby May and Fitzroy Rivers and Derby's King Sound.
www.birdwooddowns.com
Phone (08) 9191 1275
Depths in metres. Underlined figures are drying heights. Map not to be used for navigation
Derby
drying flats
saltflats
Ask Creek
Alligator Creek
The Telegraph Pool on the Fitzroy River
Large tides demand that launching and retrieving boats is carefully planned. Large areas become mudflats at low tide, so ensure you have ample time to arrive at your fishing spot.
Sawfish Point
Yeeda River
Yeeda Cuttings
These spots require permission from Yeeda Station. They can otherwise be reached by boat from Derby during suitable tides.
Wilhems Pool
Tumblegoodire Pool
Willare Pool
Tidal Fitzroy River ... some areas drain dry
Key to Map
Hotspots
Yeeda Station has advised it is limiting access to its Fitzroy River tracks. Most spots can be reached by sea from Derby on suitable tides.
1. Old highway crossing (Langi Pool) good spot for barra just after wet season. Barra around old bridge, shallow in places.
2. Telegraph Pool. Accessible only on big tides, when it fishes best.
3. Barra in Snag Pool. Tidal, with little water at low tide.
4. Barra in Milli Milli Pool.
5. Barra in Pelican Pool. Little water at low tide. Good area for collecting bait. Fast tidal run.
6. Yeeda Cuttings is good barra country. Fast run on large tides.
7. The May River turn-off is 22km up the Gibb River Rd from Derby, turn left, and then another 12km in. When you get to the second gate, you can go left to The Sandpit or right to Meda Rocks and toward the mouth. Beware crocs. The May is usually better on big tides as neaps don't leave much water. Trolling in the pools is good after the Wet. Contact Meda Station on (08) 9191 4730 for permission to visit.
8. Good reef fishing at times off Black Rocks. Large rocks in flowing tidal water.
9. Shallow at entrance. Jewfish, barra, golden snapper, mud crabs.
10. Salmon on south side of Valentine Island. Salmon, jewfish, golden snapper and mud crabs in both creeks.
11. Salmon, mud crabs. Shallow at low water with sandbars.
12. Barra, salmon in Alligator Creek.
13. Blue Holes: golden snapper, salmon, jewfish. No road access over 10m tides. Exposed reef at low tide can be crossed about three hours before high tide.
14. Small tidal creek - barra, salmon on live bait. Drains at low tide. Mud crabs.
15. Meda River best just after wet season for barra.
Launch sites
1. Derby boat ramp, near the jetty with sealed parking. This region has huge tides and launching is best done on a rising tide.
2. Bank launching at Blue Holes. Do not use after heavy rain or 9m-plus tides.
Derby's huge tides move up to about 11m. Plan trips accordingly.
Contact Liveringa Station for permission to enter the area upstream (off map) from Myroodah Crossing to Fitzroy Barrage, phone (08) 9191 4757

Bluewater fuel stop

A resort on Cockatoo Island, with accommodation, ice, fuel and beer sales, gives long-range boaters a handy base from which to explore this wild region.

Visiting the island by boat is tide dependent. Safe anchorage is usually on the south side of the island, but there were no moorings available at the time of publication. Fuel is sold from a barge in a nearby creek. Visitors can enjoy a swimming pool and order food. There is a charter boat available and a helipad. Call before visiting on 08 9191 4621.

Boaters will find no shortage of fish around the islands and reefs, keeping in mind the huge tides that flow here, and the marine park zones.

Estuary fishing in this region is good. Three major rivers enter the east end of Walcott Inlet, the Calder, Charnley and Isdell. The Munja Track leads to the Calder River, via Mount Elizabeth Station, see Page 88. The station is 30km off the Gibb River Road, with the turn-off about 70km after the Kalumburu Road intersection, 345km from Derby. Access fees apply. Visitors must be self-sufficient and vehicles set up for rough, rocky roads with jump-ups. The track was closed at publication, check before leaving.

Calder River: This has barra and jewfish on the rockbars. Fishing the muddy bank is possible in places. Cartoppers can be launched. A few kilometres above the Calder/Charnley junction is a rockbar on the Charnley, the tidal limit. A pool above the rockbar, inundated on spring tides, is a barra spot. A creek on the south-west side flows from a spring all year.

Isdell River: To the west of the Calder is Isdell River. An anchorage is just inside the mouth. Upstream are freshwater pools with barra, jacks and sooty grunter, especially just after the Wet. Springs run all year. The area between the Isdell and Calder/Charnley junction is dominated by sandbars and rocky outcrops. The channels and rockbars produce barra, salmon and jewfish on livebait.

To the west of the Isdell, Walcott Inlet opens out into a large bay which is a sanctuary. To the north is a slender island, with an anchorage between it and the mainland. Note the large sanctuary area, introduced in late 2016.

There is no road access other than by 4WD to the Calder River, as described. A rough road exists to the south-eastern end of Secure Bay, but it is a defence area and entry permission is difficult to obtain.

Some anglers charter helicopters to fish the Charnley River rockbar. The helicopters are usually available from April to September.

Doubtful Bay: This is one of the most scenic Kimberley locations. The bay has a big estuary, with islands and headlands, particularly at the entrance. Note the sanctuary zones.

The southern Doubtful Bay entrance is bordered by Raft Point and Steep Island, prime areas for queenfish, trevally and golden snapper. The best spot is the reef that extends north from Raft Point, where currents converge.

At the southern end of the bay is a mangrove creek which can be negotiated through a rock and island-strewn channel. Care needs to be exercised in this passage, which has jacks, snapper and jewfish. Once through the passage, the area opens and is an ideal anchorage.

The eastern arm contains rockbars, ideal spots for barra, while the southern arm terminates at a sloping rock face which flows freshwater during and just after the wet season. Note the sanctuary area.

The next system north is Red Cone Hill, named after a hillock which rises from the mangroves. This is a sanctuary. The east arm ends at a persistent waterfall.

Sale River: To the north is the most scenic river of Doubtful Bay, the Sale. It has red and orange ochre cliffs along its tidal length. About 15km upstream, where salt meets fresh, is an amphitheatre which doubles as an anchorage. Rockbars prevent further upstream access on neap tides. You can go further on spring tides, but must leave on time. Upstream the river forms freshwater pools. There are sandy areas and percolating freshwater springs. Downstream on the Sale there are no significant rockbars. Instead the river has sandbars at low tide, and side creeks.

George Water: Northern Doubtful Bay opens into George Water. To the east is Gibson Creek. Care is needed here, as it almost dries at low tide. On the west side is Barlee Impediment, with barra, jacks and snapper. George Water narrows into a rocky passage known as Glenelg River mouth. Take great care navigating. The Glenelg is famous for crocodiles and rarely visited, but is a barra hotspot.

There is no road access to Doubtful Bay. The only way to visit is by boat, floatplane or helicopter. There are no facilities.

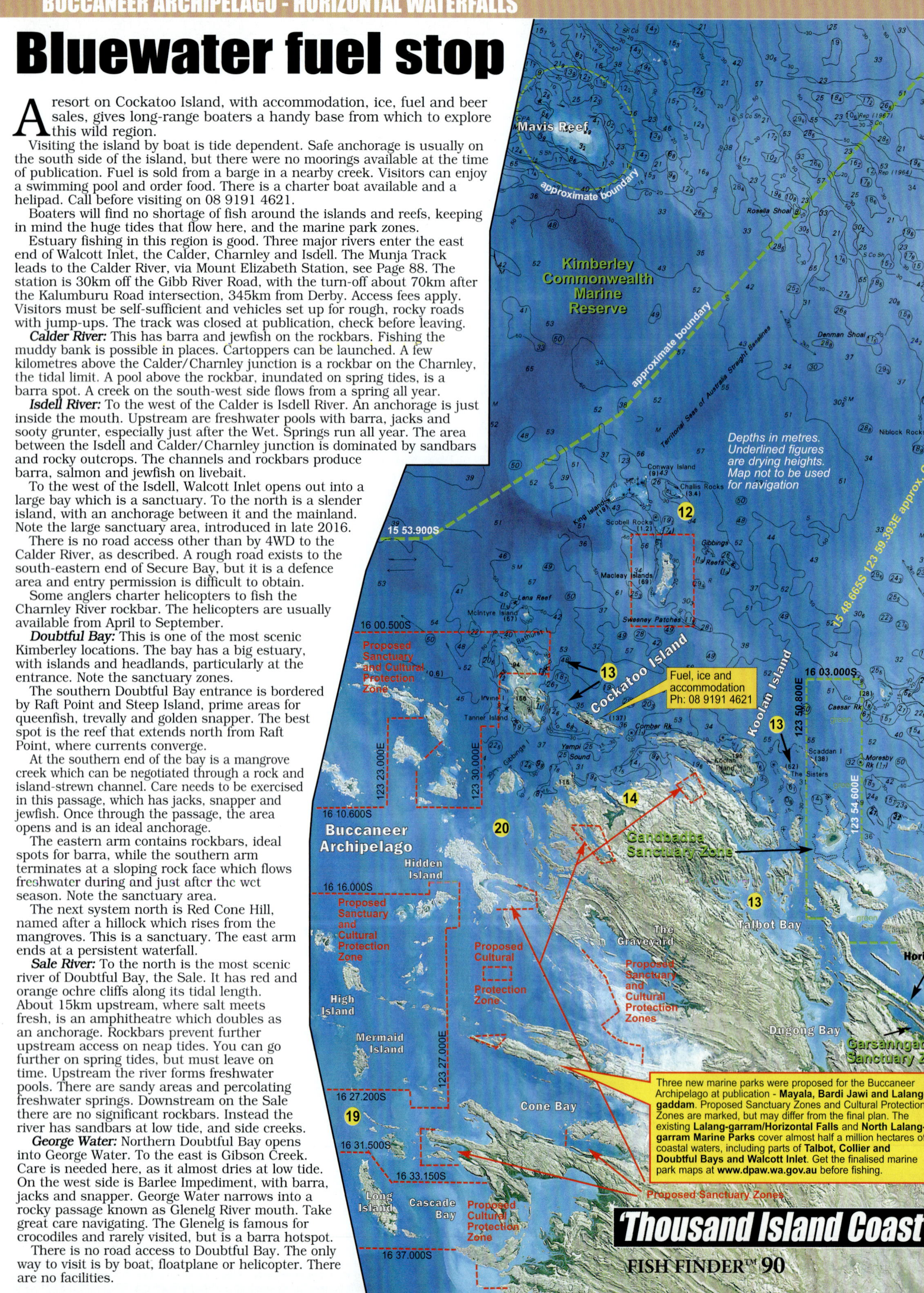

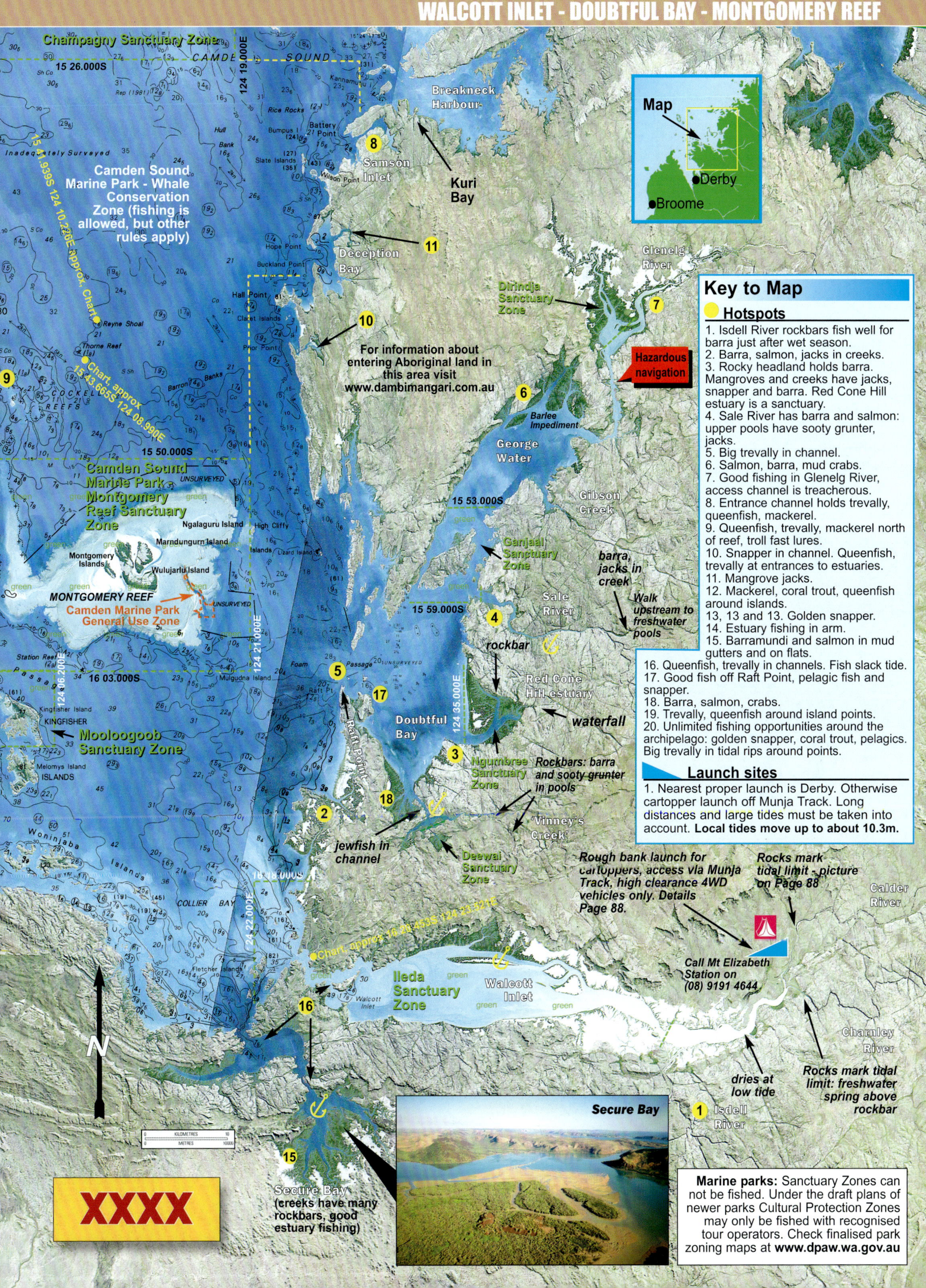

Champagny Sanctuary Zone
CAMDEN SOUND
15 26.000S
124 19.000E
Breakneck Harbour
Kuri Bay
Samson Inlet
8
Camden Sound Marine Park - Whale Conservation Zone (fishing is allowed, but other rules apply)
11
Deception Bay
Map
Derby
Broome
Glenelg River
Dirindja Sanctuary Zone
7
Key to Map
Hotspots
1. Isdell River rockbars fish well for barra just after wet season.
2. Barra, salmon, jacks in creeks.
3. Rocky headland holds barra. Mangroves and creeks have jacks, snapper and barra. Red Cone Hill estuary is a sanctuary.
4. Sale River has barra and salmon: upper pools have sooty grunter, jacks.
5. Big trevally in channel.
6. Salmon, barra, mud crabs.
7. Good fishing in Glenelg River, access channel is treacherous.
8. Entrance channel holds trevally, queenfish, mackerel.
9. Queenfish, trevally, mackerel north of reef, troll fast lures.
10. Snapper in channel. Queenfish, trevally at entrances to estuaries.
11. Mangrove jacks.
12. Mackerel, coral trout, queenfish around islands.
13, 13 and 13. Golden snapper.
14. Estuary fishing in arm.
15. Barramundi and salmon in mud gutters and on flats.
16. Queenfish, trevally in channels. Fish slack tide.
17. Good fish off Raft Point, pelagic fish and snapper.
18. Barra, salmon, crabs.
19. Trevally, queenfish around island points.
20. Unlimited fishing opportunities around the archipelago: golden snapper, coral trout, pelagics. Big trevally in tidal rips around points.
Launch sites
1. Nearest proper launch is Derby. Otherwise cartopper launch off Munja Track. Long distances and large tides must be taken into account. Local tides move up to about 10.3m.
10
For information about entering Aboriginal land in this area visit www.dambimangari.com.au
Hazardous navigation
9
Chart approx 15 43.655S 124 08.990E
6
Barlee Impediment
George Water
15 50.000S
Camden Sound Marine Park - Montgomery Reef Sanctuary Zone
Gibson Creek
15 53.000S
Ganjaal Sanctuary Zone
barra, jacks in creek
Ngalaguru Island
Marndungurn Island
Montgomery Islands
Wulujarlu Island
MONTGOMERY REEF
Camden Marine Park General Use Zone
Sale River
15 59.000S
4
Walk upstream to freshwater pools
rockbar
5
16 03.000S
124 21.000E
124 06.200E
17
Red Cone Hill estuary
124 35.000E
waterfall
Raft Point
Doubtful Bay
Mooloogoob Sanctuary Zone
KINGFISHER
3
Ngumbree Sanctuary Zone
Rockbars: barra and sooty grunter in pools
18
2
'Vinney's Creek'
jewfish in channel
Deewai Sanctuary Zone
Rough bank launch for cartoppers, access via Munja Track, high clearance 4WD vehicles only. Details Page 88.
Rocks mark tidal limit - picture on Page 88
Calder River
Chart approx 16 29.453S 124 23.321E
Ileda Sanctuary Zone
Walcott Inlet
Call Mt Elizabeth Station on (08) 9191 4644
16
Charnley River
N
dries at low tide
Rocks mark tidal limit: freshwater spring above rockbar
Secure Bay
1
Isdell River
15
Secure Bay (creeks have many rockbars, good estuary fishing)
XXXX
Marine parks: Sanctuary Zones can not be fished. Under the draft plans of newer parks Cultural Protection Zones may only be fished with recognised tour operators. Check finalised park zoning maps at www.dpaw.wa.gov.au

Travelling the Kimberley

Most of the Kimberley coast is impossible to reach by vehicle and difficult even by boat. Broome, Derby, Wyndham and Kununurra are the only easy boating access points.

A mothership charter is the best way for fishermen to explore this region. The ideal time to fish is just after the wet season when waterfalls are flowing.

Heli-fishing is another exciting option.

The Kimberley has opportunities for boaters who have long-range fuel capability and who plan trips carefully.

Fuel is available in very few places outside the towns, the most noteable being Kalumburu.

Fuel drops can be arranged at remote Truscott Airstrip. Cockatoo Island has a boat refuelling point.

Expect strong tidal currents as this region has some of the biggest tides in the world.

Anchoring overnight in the Kimberley requires care because of the big tides. A boat left high on the sand could be stranded for two weeks during a diminishing tidal cycle.

There are unexpected reefs and rockbars.

Read the water and slow down, use your eyes and watch the sounder.

Crocodiles are found throughout, including on islands, and they can behave aggressively around boats.

To enjoy this area, be prepared.

Some areas see few boats, although yachts and tourist boats visit regularly in the dry season.

It is safer to travel the Kimberley with another boat.

Take a satellite phone and radio and tell someone of your trip plan.

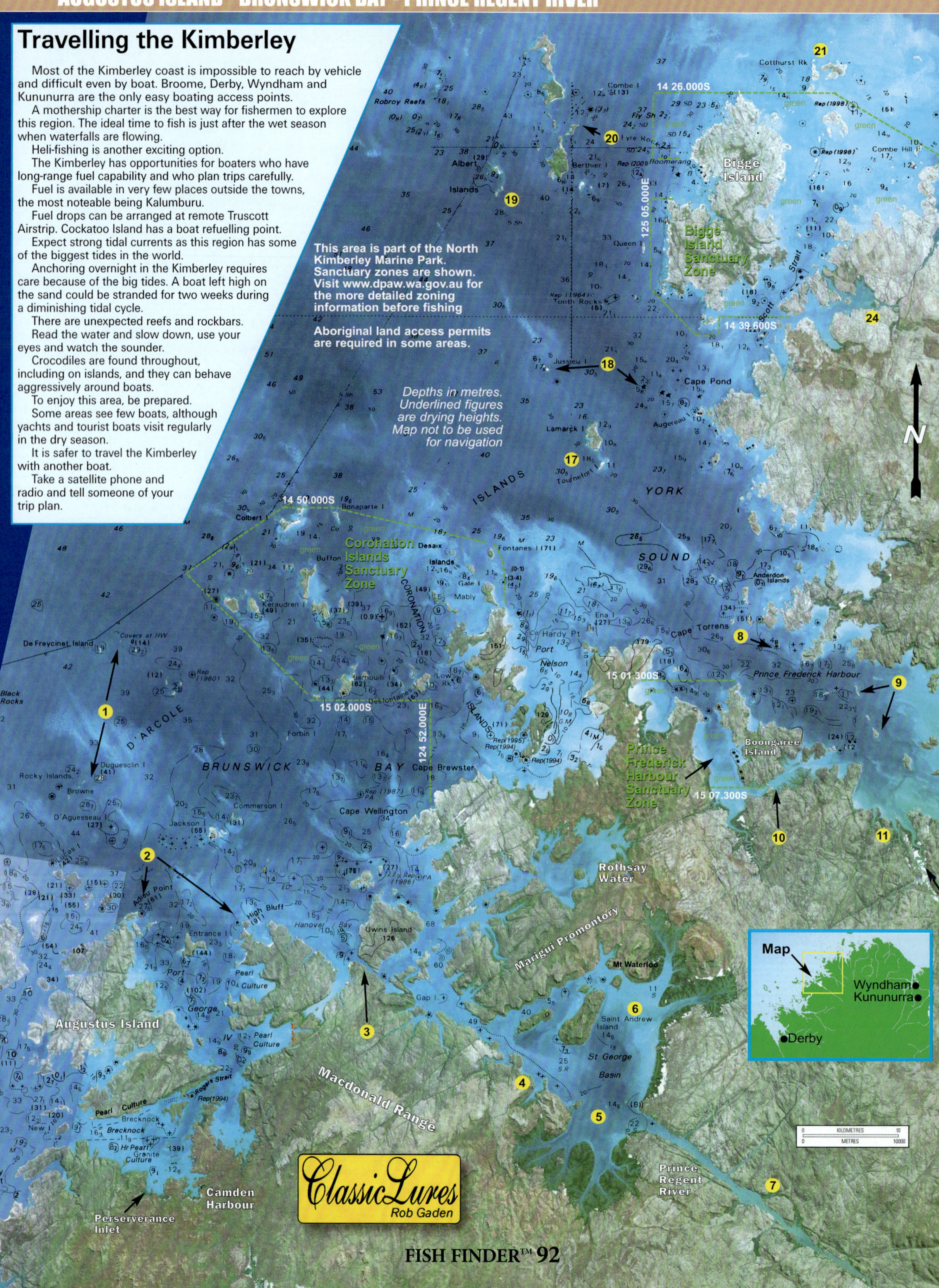

Remote and rugged

The major feature of the Brunswick Bay region is Saint George Basin and the scenic Prince Regent River.

Access can be gained by navigating either to the north or south of Uwins Island, although care needs to be exercised if taking the southern route, as the current that emanates from Munster Water is impressive.

The channel between the island and the mainland has trevally, queenfish and reef fish.

It is worth spending time in Saint George Basin before entering Prince Regent River.

Imposing Mt Trafalgar and Waterloo, as well as Saint Andrew and Saint Patrick Islands, make for a spectacular backdrop.

There is good golden snapper fishing along the channel edges, while the mudflats to the north and south of the basin are excellent for barra and threadfin.

Prince Regent River: This should only be navigated on an incoming tide, as it contains many reefs and sandbars.

This is a long river that basically runs in a straight line through rock.

The main features of the Prince Regent are King's Cascade waterfall and Camp Creek falls.

Try all the creek junctions and rockbars for barramundi and jacks.

There is a great fishing pool and rockbar 30km upstream from the mouth at the limit of tidal influence.

The freshwater reaches hold barra, jacks and sooty grunter.

Back towards the mouth, Camp Creek is a good location to pot mud crabs.

Prince Frederick Harbour is one of the most picturesque in the Kimberley, with the Hunter River the big attraction. Other major rivers are the Roe and Moran, as well as numerous estuaries, many without European names.

Hunter River: This is located on the northern side of the harbour. It has striking red cliffs and escarpments.

Casting to rocks at the base of the cliffs and to gutters which form near low tide is productive for barra and threadfin salmon.

Located at the north-eastern extremity is spectacular Hunter Falls, which requires a long walk upstream from the rockbar where salt merges with fresh.

There are many small rockbars in the river which hold barra. But the Hunter is also known for its prolific threadfin salmon fishing.

Opposite the Hunter River on the south-western side of the harbour is Boongaree Island.

Good fishing can be had for jacks, golden snapper, cod and jew in the channel.

At one point the channel plummets down deep and this is a prime black jewfish location.

Note the sanctuary zones on one side of the island and at the mouth of the Hunter River.

In Prince Frederick Harbour proper, there are small islands, reefs and sandbars which produce trevally, queenfish and mackerel in the dry season.

There are many other estuaries which see very little amateur fishing.

Roe River: The Roe and the short stretch of tidal water that exists at the mouth of the Moran before coming to an impenetrable rock face is mostly discoloured and studded with numerous sand and mudbars.

Nonetheless, salmon and barra are there. Use bait for best results. Beyond the Moran/Roe junction at the upper limits of tidal influence the river forms freshwater pools.

Access can be gained by anchoring a dinghy at the limits of tidal influence and walking along the bank edges. Here barramundi, jacks and sooty grunter provide good sport.

Montague Sound: This is rarely fished, as most boats pass through the area on the way to the Hunter River and Prince Regent Rivers to the south and Admiralty Gulf and Napier Broome Bay to the north.

As a consequence the area has seen little fishing pressure and is hardly explored in sportfishing terms.

Good anchorages exist at Coombe Hill Island and in Swift Bay. The Montalivet Islands to the north were used as an airforce early warning base during World War II.

Excellent pelagic fishing exists among these islands and at Wolf Rock to the north-east.

There are many small islands and reefs in this area which hold huge schools of trevally and queenfish. Most reef fish can be caught along the drop-offs and pinnacles, with the deeper water generally holding the bigger fish.

There are some protected beaches and bays in which to anchor or camp, although care needs to be exercised, as many big crocodiles inhabit this area, and the islands.

Getting there: There is no road access or facilities. Visitation is restricted to long-range charter boats. Helicopters operate out of Kununurra) to Mitchell Falls from April to September.

Anglers can fly by light plane from Broome, Derby or Kununurra to the Mitchell plateau airship and then transfer to a helicopter for a 20-minute transfer to a charter boat at the Hunter River.

Not only do anglers view the magnificent Mitchell Falls, but they also cut out enormous travelling times from Broome or Wyndham.

Kuri Bay has a privately-run pearling company, which does not sell fuel or provisions.

Key to Map

Hotspots

1. Big mackerel and trevally around these islands.
2. Trevally and queenfish around the points.
3. Trevally, queenfish in channel.
4. Golden snapper in estuary and near headland.
5. Barra and salmon on flats and in creeks.
6. Barra and salmon on flats and in creeks.
7. Prince Regent River has several feeder creeks and waterfalls that hold barra during and just after the wet season. Freshwater pools can be found 30km upstream from the river's mouth into Saint George Basin. The biggest, the impressive Kings Cascade Waterfall, is 20km from the mouth.
8. Queenfish, trevally on south of island near rocks.
9. Queenfish, trevally around all islands in central harbour.
10. Deep hole has jewfish and golden snapper. Barra and mangrove jacks on nearby rockbar.
11. Good creek for barra and salmon.
12. Barra and salmon.
13. Barra and salmon.
14. Moor boat here and walk to pools above rocks for barra, jacks and sooty grunter. Spend only an hour at high tide, or be stranded.
15. Barra, salmon best upstream.
16. Good barra and salmon fishing off head.
17. Big golden snapper, saddletail snapper, coral trout in deeper water near islands. Mackerel, trevally in shallower water. Big saddletail found on quite shallow reefs at times. Unrealised sailfish grounds may exist in these waters.
18. Good trolling for trevally, queenfish, mackerel.
19. Mackerel, trevally and reef fish.
20. Troll for mackerel.
21. Trevally, queenfish, mackerel around islands.
22. Good area for jacks, salmon, barra. Useful anchorage.
23. Queenfish, trevally.
24. Jacks, barra, salmon.
25. Most pelagic fish.

Launch sites

1. The nearest launch site is Derby, about 330km one way. Distances, large tides, changing weather and potential breakdowns must be taken into account when travelling this area. Satellite phones are a must.

Norwest landbased fishing

KUNUNURRA

After the wet season, Kimberley river crossings produce barramundi, but keep in mind the ever-present crocodiles.

1. Dunham River, Ord River junction. Only a few kilometres out of Kununurra, turn north off the highway at the tourist signs on the west side of the Kununurra Diversion Dam. Follow the track for 200m and turn off, again heading north prior to the ramp at Lion's Park. Follow it for about 2km until the end. Find your way down to the junction. Seasonal variations in flow determine fishability. Following first rains the dirty water can be unproductive. Barramundi, sooty grunter, tarpon, catfish, shark. Beware crocodiles.

2. Ivanhoe Crossing. The most popular landbased spot near Kununurra. Follow Ivanhoe Road north out of town for about 10km. The crossing is a barrier during dry season flows, with fish congregating below the structure. Once wet season flows push over, the bigger barramundi gather. Crocs.

3. Tarrara Bar. About 40km out of town on the Carlton Hill Road. Turn off on a track to the left just past the beginning of Carlton Hill Station. It is about 2km from there. The river is quite fast and deep, with sections of slower water to fish from rock faces. Barramundi, tarpon and sooty grunter. Beware crocodiles.

4. Skull Rock boat ramp. This is a few kilometres further along the Carlton Hill Road from Tarrara Bar turn-off. The ramp turn-off is signposted. There are fewer options here than other Ord River spots but sooty grunter are under the trees, with the odd barramundi.

5. Mambi Island boat ramp. This is about 60km from Kununurra along the Parry's Creek/Valentine Springs Road. The turn-off to the boat ramp is signposted. Long bank access. Shallow, but good fish have been caught here. Beware crocodiles.

6. Goose Hill Creek. From Kununurra the creek is just less than 20km further along the Parry's Creek road from the Mambi boat ramp turn-off. The turn-off to the right is not signposted but is easily seen, if you pass Goose Hill Community you have gone too far. Fishing is off a high bank and landing fish is tricky. Beware crocs. Changed annual waterflows can move the channel too and away from the bank. Best tide is debatable. Main fish are big barramundi, with sharks and catfish.

7. Spillway Creek. About 55km from Kununurra on the road to Lake Argyle. Generally it is a gentle flow but can rise considerably when rain overflows the lake. In high flows the rock is unstable, approach edges at your peril. During low flows the creek is safe enough. Mainly sooty grunter.

8. Pentecost River. About 15km of the river is acccessible from either Wyndham or the Gibb River Road. The rough Karunjie Track runs along the river. There are many places along its length to fish. The further upstream you are the higher the tide needed to reach it and the longer it takes to get there. Barramundi and threadfin salmon, with some jewfish.

9. Keep River. Travel through Kununurra and north along Weaber Plain Road, turning off onto the Legune road once you have passed over the main drain. From there the road heads through the Cave Springs Gap and back into the NT. Once you get to the river, head north along the track on its western bank. There are many turn-offs along the track that go to the river. All spots fire at different times. Main fish are barramundi, threadfin and jacks. Beware crocodiles.

Gnylmarung, Dampier Peninsula, north of Broome
ROZA ARKAM-LOVASI

DERBY/WYNDHAM

Landbased fishing in this area is made challenging by huge tides.

1. Wyndham recreational fishing jetty. This has a floating section that moves up and down with the tide. Main fish are jewfish, mud crabs, barramundi and catfish.

2. Fitzroy River. Various pools offer landbased fishing, keeping in mind the crocodile danger. The Telegraph Pool is probably best, fishing well when big tides breach the pool, but you need permission from Yeeda Station to go in by road.

BROOME

1. Old Broome Jetty: Unfortunately only some of the walkway has been open in recent times. The jetty is easily accessible, but is a high platform. Fish around the turn of high tide for trevally, queenfish, tuskfish, mackerel and tuna. Garfish form dense schools and big sharks pass by. Barramundi at night in the shadows. Use jigs or a lure with a big bib to "grab" the water when fishing from such a height, or use livebait.

2. Gantheaume Point: Short walk from car park, ballooning during dry season when easterly winds are blowing. Catch gar for bait and balloon for mackerel, trevally.

3. Port Smith: cliffs to the north of Port Smith are accessed via sandy 4WD track. Balloon or cast to pelagic fish that travel along the cliffs. Best on spring high tides.

4. Dampier Peninsula. The track up the west side gives landbased access to headlands and beaches, fishable at high tide. Species include salmon, queenfish, trevally, tuskfish and even mud crabs around the rocks. The northern peninsula has various camps with landbased fishing.

5. New Town Jetty. Broome's Town Beach has a new jetty, part of an overall foreshore development. The jetty is tide dependent. The nearby rock-barrier foreshore also fishes well at high tide.

KARRATHA - DAMPIER

1. Kaiser Marina breakwall, Dampier. On the west side of Hampton Harbour the wall is a popular spot. The area is shallow and best fished near high tide. Mangrove jacks and more off the rocks.

2. Hampton Harbour breakwall and jetty, Dampier. The wall surrounding Hampton Harbour marina fishes well at the top of the tide. For queenfish, use small chrome slices.

3. Hearson's Cove, Dampier (Burrup Peninsula). The rocks at the north-east end of Hearson's Cove are worth a look. Like many local spots they are best fished on a high tide. Lures and bait can be used here. Soft sand here, 4WD recommended.

4. Withnell Bay rocks, Dampier (Burrup Peninsula). The rocky outcrops in Withnell Bay are good landbased platforms and produce variety. This area is shallow and best at high tide. Withnell Bay is accessed off the Burrup road. The turn-off is sign-posted just before the gas plant.

5. Karratha back beach. The rocky shore that runs east-west from Karratha back beach boat ramp fishes well at high tide. Salmon, with barra in the warmer months. The mangroves have mud crabs.

6. Cleaverville Creek rock ledge. Turn-off on the Karratha to Roeburn toad. The ledge at the mouth of Cleaverville Creek is a good location. The relatively deep drop-off and rocky bottom holds fish on all tides. The area produces some big barramundi.

7. Johns Creek marina breakwall, Point Samson. A prime landbased spot, with barramundi at the top of spring tides in summer. Also jacks, bream, barracuda, cod and more. The breakwalls on both sides of the marina can be fished. The creek side of the breakwall has mud crabs.

8. Cossack Creek wharf. Fish the old wharf at high tide. Baits and lures can be used. Cossack Creek turn-off is on the Roeburn to Point Samson road. The flow here on big tides makes fishing difficult.

9. Johns Creek bridge culvert, Point Samson. The bridge culvert at John's Creek just before Point Samson is worth fishing. It can be fished before and after the high tide but is shallow at low tide. Barramundi, salmon, queenfish and jacks. As the tide runs out predators lay in wait for bait to be flushed out of the culvert.

PORT HEDLAND

1. Spoil Bank. The big sandspit straight out from town produces salmon, queenfish and other species.

2. Finucane Creek. The area near the boat ramp is a good barramundi spot.

3. Six-Mile Creek. Easily reached ledge can be fished at mid tide for barramundi, salmon, jacks, queenfish and more.

4. Outlying creeks. Access is possible over tidal claypan tracks, and the timing has to be right or bogging results - avoid the period during and shortly after big tides. Barramundi, threadfin salmon, grunter and jacks can be had.

ONSLOW

1. Ashburton River has access points where landbased fishing can be had. Bread and butter species, and threadfin salmon, jacks, giant herring, with occasional barramundi. High tide is best.

2. The Beadon Creek rock wall can produce good fishing on big tides. Queenfish are usually reliable, with trevally, cod and jacks. Tracks to nearby creeks provide limited shore fishing.

EXMOUTH

The calm beaches and saltwater lagoons of Ningaloo produce a variety of fish in shallow, clear water. Spangled emperor come in close, especially at night, and bonefish, permit, queenfish, trevally and even squid can be sight fished. Some areas are sanctuaries.

Here's some of the best landbased spots near Exmouth.

1. Learmonth Jetty. Located south of Exmouth town centre near the airport. It is only a small jetty but has a variety of species year round, including queenfish, mackerel, trevally, squid and shark. The beaches either side have bream, whiting, flathead and blue crabs. Great for families.

2. Bundegi Flats. Located north of Exmouth town centre, north of the sanctuary zone. On a rising tide you can walk out to the channels and target queenfish, trevally and at times see large schools of milkfish. Great for flyfishing or light spinning.

3. Exmouth town beach. Fish the high tide. In winter the whiting are great here. Bream, flathead and queenfish too. Schools of hardiheads are smashed by trevally and queenfish.

4. Various access points along the west side of the cape. Spangled emperor on the rising tide, or at dawn and dusk. Great for casting poppers or soft plastics for targeting trevally, queenfish, cod and more. Catch tuskfish with fresh prawn baits.

5. Sandy Bay in the Cape Range National Park, 80km from the township. Wonderful white sandy beach produce various sportfish. Great for families, swimming and snorkelling too.

6. Oysters. Access road at the tip of the cape. Renowned area for chasing large giant trevally from shore. Also cobia, giant herring, large queenfish, cod, spangled emperor, shark mackerel and longtail tuna.

SHARK BAY

1. Landbased fishing for whiting can be done almost anywhere in Shark Bay, with large squid off beaches that are near weedbeds. In some areas pink snapper can be caught from shore. Also gar, tailor and emperor. However the best landbased fishing is at **Steep Point**, one of WA's best rock fishing platforms, with large pelagic and reef fish. Specialist gear is needed, and 4WD. Bookings required through Parks and Wildlife.

SHARK BAY TO PERTH

1. Kalbarri has good beaches and rock platforms locally and along much of the nearby coast. Expect big tailor and mulloway, with bream in the river. The better ocean ledges produce pink snapper, dhufish and more.

2. The S-bend region has excellent rock and beach fishing, with good spots near the caravan park. Dhufish from shore are a possibility, but tailor and mulloway are more common.

3. The beaches and small jetties **through to Perth** are readily accessible and can produce good fishing. Many beaches are affected by seaweed, which can occur in such quantities it makes fishing impossible. Tommy ruffs (herring), yellowtail kingfish, mulloway, tailor, salmon, whiting, squid, sharks and rays are all caught.

A final frontier

Admiralty Gulf is bounded by a peninsula starting around Cape Voltaire in the west, and by a peninsula ending at Parry Harbour on the north-eastern extremity. This is one of the Kimberley's great fishing regions.

To the south are the Mitchell and Lawley Rivers. This is a spectacular area, with bauxite-laden escarpments along the edge of the Mitchell Plateau and Mitchell, Mertens and Surveyors Falls.

The Mitchell Plateau is one of the few places on the Kimberley coast with 4WD access. Drivers can get to Port Warrender near Crystal Head and Walsh Point, on rough tracks.

Long Reef: This reef appears at first glance to be a sandflat in the middle of nowhere. It was known for superb pelagic fishing, with big trevally, queenfish and sharks milling around the sandspit at certain stages of the tide. It became a sanctuary as part of the North Kimberley Marine Park and fishing is no longer allowed.

Cassini Island: To the west of Long Reef is Cassini Island, one of the best fishing locations in the Kimberley. The north and south ends produce mackerel, trevally, barracuda, reef fish and sailfish. Marlin to the west. Waves break over reefs at the north end. To the south are the Institut islands, with good fishing.

Mitchell River: One of the Kimberley's best barramundi rivers, but hazardous, with rocks everywhere. Barra congregate near the rock islands, rockbars and low tide gutters. The rockbars at the upper end of tidal influence (downstream of Mitchell Falls) are great for barra and jacks. On big tides the river dirties.

Lawley River: The Lawley and adjacent estuaries are popular with 4WD fishers who launch boats at Walsh Point. There are tourist camps opposite Myers Island and on One Tree Beach. The Lawley River rockbar at the limit of tidal influence holds barra, as do snags and rocks downstream. To the north and east are small estuaries and rock outcrops with good fishing. Waters around Myers, Malcolm and Steep Head Islands have trevally, queenfish and mackerel.

Parry Harbour: Parry Harbour has a good anchorage. It lacks significant creeks, although the shallow mudflats at the southern end hold big threadfin. At the entrance to the harbour, Fury Rock and a lump about one nautical mile north are good for mackerel and trevally.

Getting there: The Port Warrender road (4WD only) starts 63km north of King Edward River Homestead, turn-off on the Gibb River-Kalumburu Road. There is a bush airstrip at Mitchell Plateau. No provisions are available. Drysdale River Homestead is 97km south of the Port Warrender road turn-off. It sells fuel and limited provisions. A long sea trip from Kalumburu is an option.

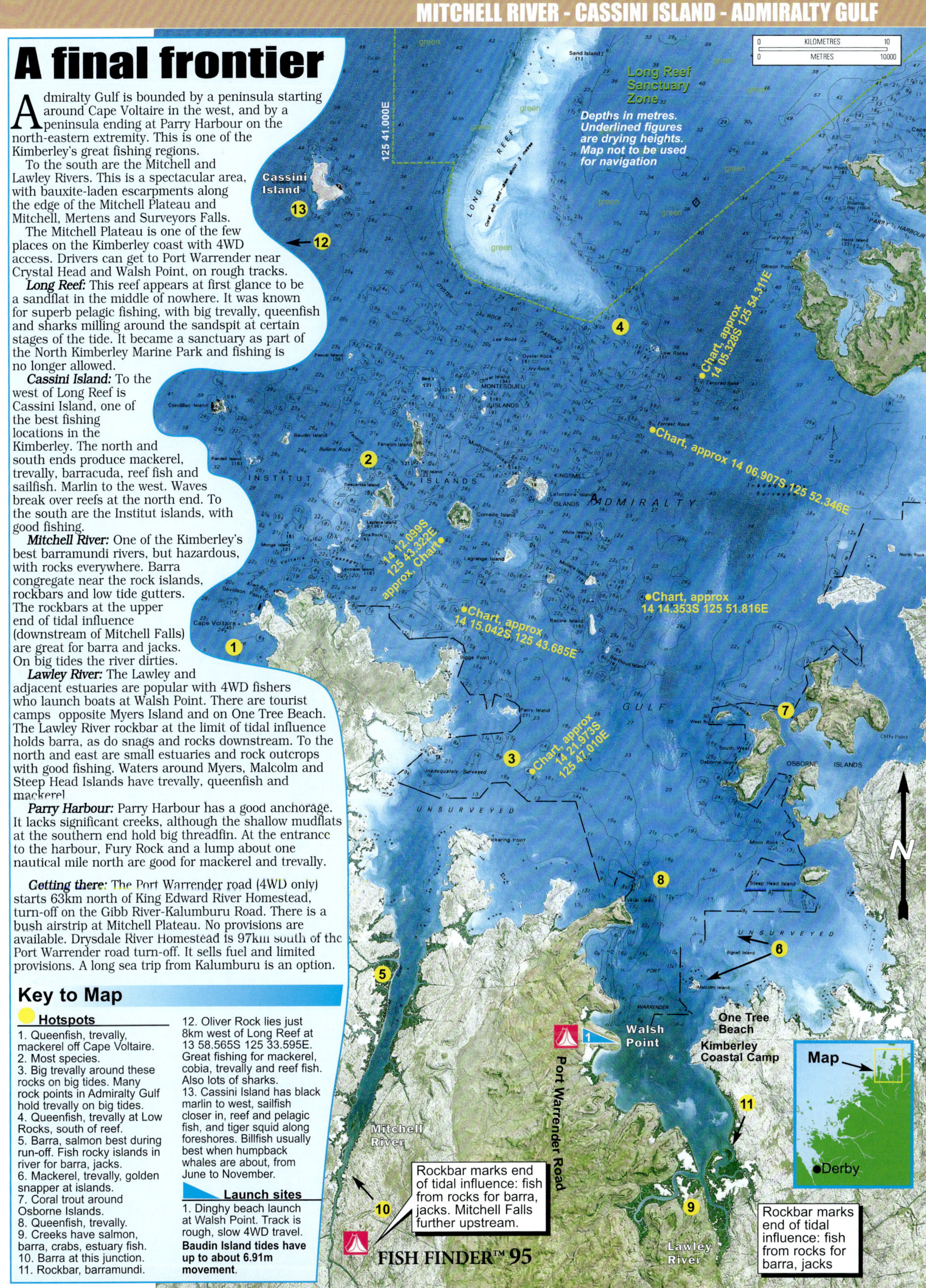

Key to Map

Hotspots

1. Queenfish, trevally, mackerel off Cape Voltaire.
2. Most species.
3. Big trevally around these rocks on big tides. Many rock points in Admiralty Gulf hold trevally on big tides.
4. Queenfish, trevally at Low Rocks, south of reef.
5. Barra, salmon best during run-off. Fish rocky islands in river for barra, jacks.
6. Mackerel, trevally, golden snapper at islands.
7. Coral trout around Osborne Islands.
8. Queenfish, trevally.
9. Creeks have salmon, barra, crabs, estuary fish.
10. Barra at this junction.
11. Rockbar, barramundi.
12. Oliver Rock lies just 8km west of Long Reef at 13 58.565S 125 33.595E. Great fishing for mackerel, cobia, trevally and reef fish. Also lots of sharks.
13. Cassini Island has black marlin to west, sailfish closer in, reef and pelagic fish, and tiger squid along foreshores. Billfish usually best when humpback whales are about, from June to November.

Launch sites

1. Dinghy beach launch at Walsh Point. Track is rough, slow 4WD travel.

Baudin Island tides have up to about 6.91m movement.

Key to Map

Hotspots

1. Mackerel, trevally off headland.
2. Trevally, queenfish.
3. Trevally, queenfish.
4. Most reef fish available on Waratah Shoal.
5. Golden snapper.
6. Numerous rockbars in Rocky Cove: jacks.
7. Jacks, golden snapper, barra.
8 and 8. Barra, salmon.
9. Good fishing for mackerel, trevally, queenfish, barracuda, reef fish.
10. Queenfish, coral trout, tuskfish.
11. Queenfish, trevally.
12. Queenfish, trevally, on east side of Eclipse Islands.

Launch sites

See next page. Nearest launch site is Kalumburu. Fuel drops can be arranged at Mungalalu-Truscott, phone (08) 9161 4004. Long distances and big tides apply in this region.

Refuel boats at Truscott

Vansittart Bay and Napier Broome Bay can be accessed through the Aboriginal community of Kalumburu, which has fishing camps and basic accommodation.

Two large rivers, the King Edward and the Drysdale, enter Napier Broome Bay, adding to the attraction of this great fishing area.

Mungalalu-Truscott is a former WWII airstrip to the east of Vansittart Bay that is now an operating airbase.

Fuel drops can be arranged at the nearby barge landing, phone 08 9161 4004 for details.

The ability to organise fuel drops allows extended boating trips to be planned.

Vansittart Bay: At the entrance to this bay are the Eclipse Islands, which are surrounded by shallow sandbars and reefs, home to a variety of pelagic fish.

Middle Rock, located between the Eclipse and Mary Islands, holds big trevally.

A pearling farm is located in Freshwater Bay.

Large schools of queenfish and trevally work tidal rips off headlands at the entrance, as well as at Red Island near Cape Bougainville. About 4km offshore is Bougainville Reef, which is a prime mackerel hotspot from around May to September. It is also a good area for reef fishing.

Towards the southern end of Vansittart Bay the water shallows noticeably.

Care is required when navigating, with rocks and reefs everywhere.

Waratah Shoal is a top lump for golden snapper, nannygai and red emperor, although sharks are a nuisance.

There are creeks at the bottom of the bay, but they drain near low tide.

Most of the creeks have rockbars, sandbars and mangrove jacks. Barramundi are about but not abundant.

While much of the Kimberley is swept by tides to 11m, the area around Truscott is affected by smaller tides.

This is a remote region and fishermen must carry adequate fuel, water and safety gear.

Note that in a boating emergency there is a manned airstrip at Troughton Island north of Vansittart Bay (off map).

Drysdale River mouth

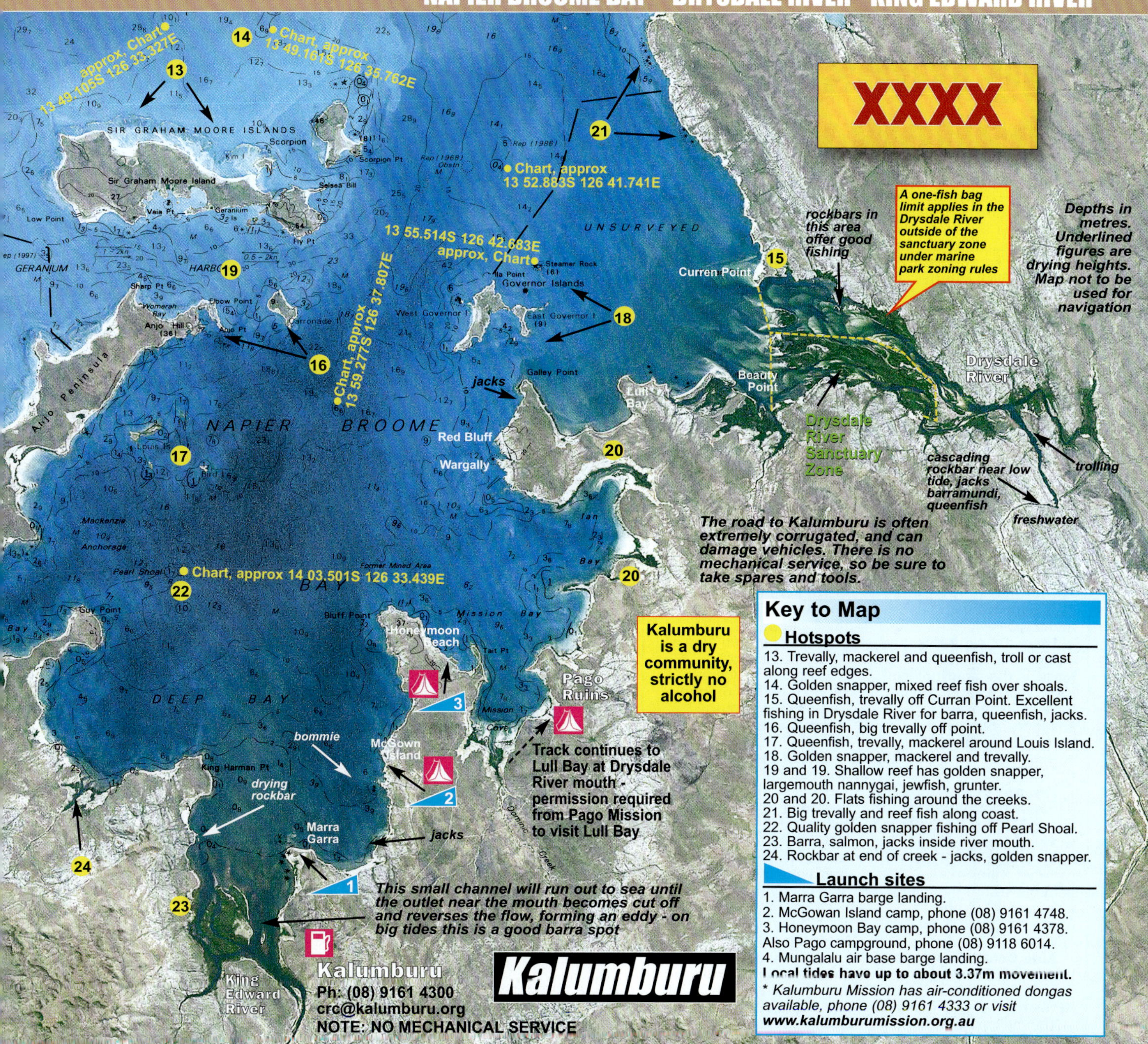

Pristine coastal camps

Napier Broome Bay can be reached by the unsealed road to Kalumburu. It is 550km from Kununurra and 650km from Derby.

There are coastal camps, and a van park at Kalumburu.

Entry permits were $50 a vehicle at publication, which can be purchased when you arrive at the Community Resource Centre, Uraro Store or at the coastal camps.

You'll also need a permit to enter Aboriginal Land from www.daa.wa.gov.au

Fishermen may only keep fish to eat during their stay.

A one-fish limit applies at Drysdale River outside of the sanctuary.

In and around the bay, expect to catch golden snapper, largemouth nannygai, tuskfish, jacks, jewfish, coral trout and pelagic fish.

Big milkfish can often be seen crusing the surface.

The Gibb River-Kalumburu road into Napier Broome Bay is for 4WD. The road is normally open from April to November, depending on weather.

Kalumburu: The township has fuel, food and basic accommodation. Kalumburu has an airstrip 2km from town.

There is a landing at West Bay, which adjoins the Mungalalu-Truscott airstrip. For fuel drops call 08 9161 4004 or visit www.mtairbase.com.au

King Edward River: During the dry season the river recedes into billabongs.

During and just after the wet season, when the river is flowing, barra fishing can be had from rocks on the lower reaches.

Dinghies can be launched at Longini landing north of Kalumburu.

North and south of the landing are rockbars. Cast shallow to medium-running lures towards the rocks and back eddies.

The King Edward mouth is a mangrove delta with sandbars and rocks, with navigation difficult near low water.

Near Kalumburu, boats can be launched at the barge landing, or from McGowans and Honeymoon Bay camps to the north, and at Beauty Point near the Drysdale River mouth, after taking a 4WD track past Pago Mission and across saltflats. Permission is required to go north of Pago.

Drysdale River: This is a big system by Kimberley standards, but it drains fast after the wet season.

The mouth is a vast sandflat and mangrove island delta with rocky islands, progressing to sandstone canyons upstream. It is has relatively clean water, even on big tides. It is known for jack fishing, but has barramundi.

The upstream end of tidal influence, known as "Barra Patch", produces quality fish during the warm Build-up (Sept-Nov).

Note the sanctuary zone.

Golden snapper and jewfish are on deeper reefs wide of the mouth, with queenfish, trevally and croal trout on rocky points.

Big tides and shallow water

Cape Londonderry is the northern-most tip of the Kimberley, with the coastline shown extending south-east to the Ord River mouth's Cambridge Gulf.

This area is best known among fishermen for its two rivers, the King George and the Berkeley, although there are other gems, mainly small estuaries.

The water is shallow around Cape Londonderry and the gap between the Cape and Stewart Island (about 7.4km offshore) should only be navigated at high tide and in calm weather.

The reefs around Cape Londonderry are part of a North Kimberley Marine Park sanctuary and can no longer be fished.

There are estuaries outside the sanctuary, towards the mouth of the King George River, which have jacks, golden snapper, bream and barra. Most can only be entered near the top of the tide.

Faraway Bay: A retreat named Faraway Bay is about 27km to the west of the King George River mouth. This is a place you can take your spouse fishing without complaint. It is useful to know its location in case of an emergency.

King George River: This has one of the most beautiful waterfalls in the Kimberley.

The falls are about 12km upstream of the mouth, preventing further tidal access upstream. As such, the system is relatively small, and it also experiences the smallest tidal range in the Kimberley.

The stone-lined river contains mangrove jacks and golden snapper, which respond well to lures cast in tight among the mangroves.

The best barramundi fishing comes from the area adjacent to a second, smaller waterfall in the eastern arm, and the mouth of a small creek at the mouth.

Offshore, Lesueur Island (which has a lighthouse) is a mecca for queenfish, trevally and mackerel and offers good bottom fishing.

Working further to the south-east along the coast are more small estuaries with jacks and limited barra. There are no substantial systems until the Berkeley River.

Offshore, Reveley and Uncle and Aunt Islands are home to big snapper and nannygai.

Berkeley River: The Berkeley (Page 100) is a popular barra river, best just after the wet season.

Local boaters undertake the 150km journey from Wyndham boat ramp.

It is also a heli-fishing destination, reached by air from Kununurra in 75 minutes.

There is a luxury lodge located at the mouth.

In the wet season, helicopters land and fish from the rockbar where the fresh meets salt (19km upstream) as well as the billabongs.

There are numerous sandbars offshore from the Berkeley mouth, making access difficult at low tide.

Within the river, boaters fish the main rockbar and then hike upstream to sample the billabongs.

At peak flood times during the wet season, the rocks on the eastern side of the mouth area produce big barra, but the bite is of short duration.

Otherwise the mangroves inside the mouth are good near low tide. The rockbar just inside the mouth of the first creek to the west also produces.

Leaving the Berkeley there are two systems worth trying towards the Ord River.

The first is around Buckle Head and the second is inside a bay to the north-west of Thurburn Bluff. Both can be difficult at low tide.

Getting there

Other than by flying to a private airstrip, or flying in by helicopter, the only access is by sea.

The Berkeley River is within medium boat range from Wyndham.

Travellers need to be self sufficient.

Travel with another boat, and carry extra fuel, water and spares. Check in with the local sea rescue before leaving.

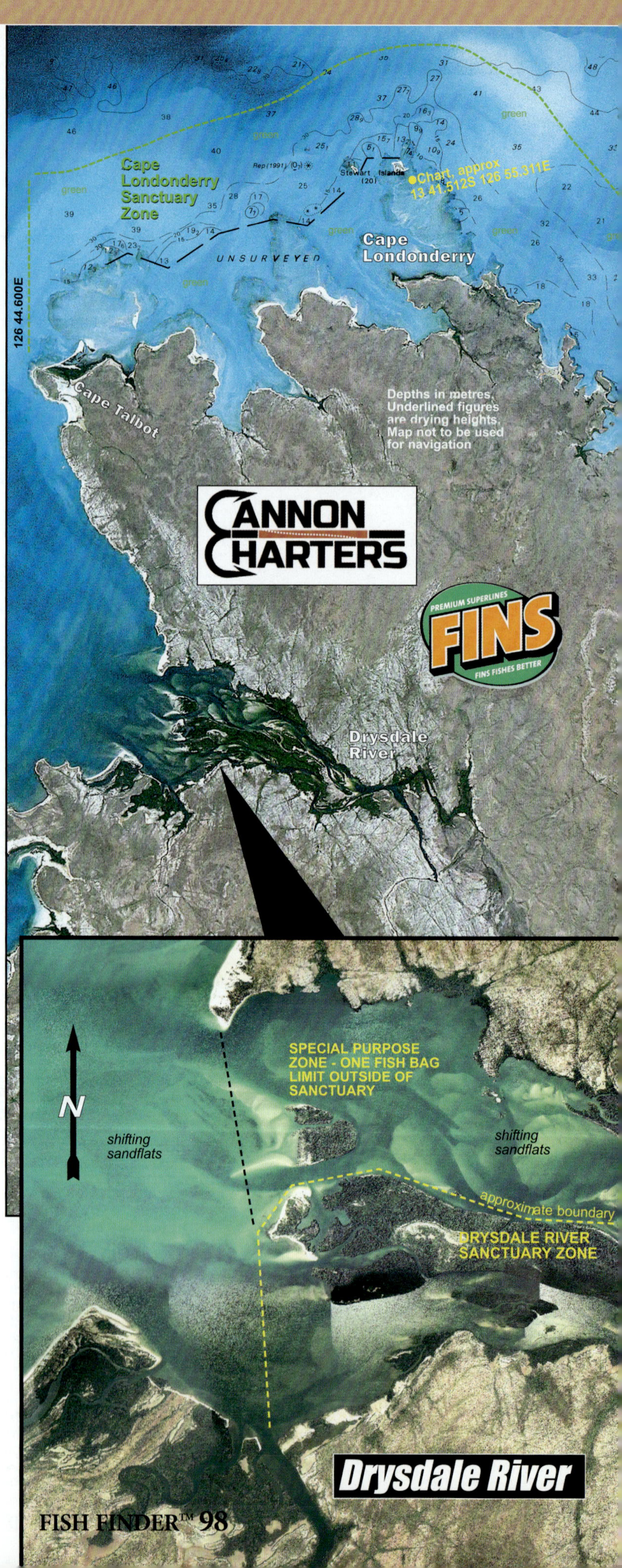

Hotspots

1. Big trevally around island edges.
2. Sandy creeks have mostly jacks, cod. High tide fishing. Golden snapper outside creeks.
3. Trevally, queenfish along reef edge.
4. Good fishing for trevally, mackerel and reef fish.
5. Mangrove jacks, some barra.
6. Barra where creek enters King George River.
7. Waterfall pool holds barra.

Key to Map

Launch sites

1. Wyndham is the nearest launch site. Strong tides, long distances, wind and lack of facilities must be taken into account in this area. Cape Londonderry is particularly hazardous, especially when wind and tide are opposed.

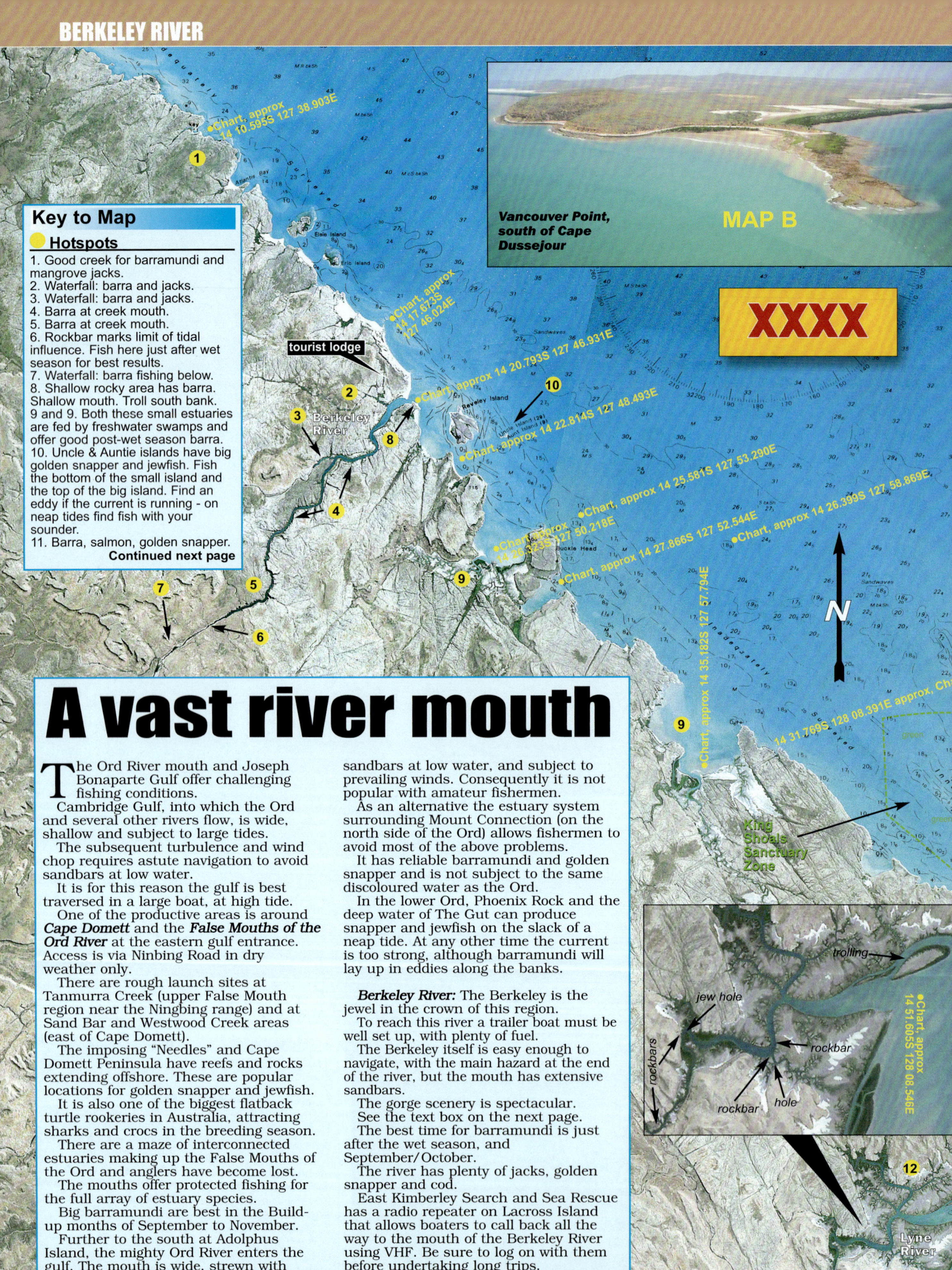

Key to Map

Hotspots

1. Good creek for barramundi and mangrove jacks.
2. Waterfall: barra and jacks.
3. Waterfall: barra and jacks.
4. Barra at creek mouth.
5. Barra at creek mouth.
6. Rockbar marks limit of tidal influence. Fish here just after wet season for best results.
7. Waterfall: barra fishing below.
8. Shallow rocky area has barra. Shallow mouth. Troll south bank.
9 and 9. Both these small estuaries are fed by freshwater swamps and offer good post-wet season barra.
10. Uncle & Auntie islands have big golden snapper and jewfish. Fish the bottom of the small island and the top of the big island. Find an eddy if the current is running - on neap tides find fish with your sounder.
11. Barra, salmon, golden snapper.

Continued next page

A vast river mouth

The Ord River mouth and Joseph Bonaparte Gulf offer challenging fishing conditions.

Cambridge Gulf, into which the Ord and several other rivers flow, is wide, shallow and subject to large tides.

The subsequent turbulence and wind chop requires astute navigation to avoid sandbars at low water.

It is for this reason the gulf is best traversed in a large boat, at high tide.

One of the productive areas is around ***Cape Domett*** and the ***False Mouths of the Ord River*** at the eastern gulf entrance. Access is via Ninbing Road in dry weather only.

There are rough launch sites at Tanmurra Creek (upper False Mouth region near the Ningbing range) and at Sand Bar and Westwood Creek areas (east of Cape Domett).

The imposing "Needles" and Cape Domett Peninsula have reefs and rocks extending offshore. These are popular locations for golden snapper and jewfish.

It is also one of the biggest flatback turtle rookeries in Australia, attracting sharks and crocs in the breeding season.

There are a maze of interconnected estuaries making up the False Mouths of the Ord and anglers have become lost.

The mouths offer protected fishing for the full array of estuary species.

Big barramundi are best in the Build-up months of September to November.

Further to the south at Adolphus Island, the mighty Ord River enters the gulf. The mouth is wide, strewn with sandbars at low water, and subject to prevailing winds. Consequently it is not popular with amateur fishermen.

As an alternative the estuary system surrounding Mount Connection (on the north side of the Ord) allows fishermen to avoid most of the above problems.

It has reliable barramundi and golden snapper and is not subject to the same discoloured water as the Ord.

In the lower Ord, Phoenix Rock and the deep water of The Gut can produce snapper and jewfish on the slack of a neap tide. At any other time the current is too strong, although barramundi will lay up in eddies along the banks.

Berkeley River: The Berkeley is the jewel in the crown of this region.

To reach this river a trailer boat must be well set up, with plenty of fuel.

The Berkeley itself is easy enough to navigate, with the main hazard at the end of the river, but the mouth has extensive sandbars.

The gorge scenery is spectacular.

See the text box on the next page.

The best time for barramundi is just after the wet season, and September/October.

The river has plenty of jacks, golden snapper and cod.

East Kimberley Search and Sea Rescue has a radio repeater on Lacross Island that allows boaters to call back all the way to the mouth of the Berkeley River using VHF. Be sure to log on with them before undertaking long trips.

Key to Map

Hotspots

12. Good estuary fishing in this system. The rockbar in the upper reaches of the most southerly arm fishes well.
13. Golden snapper, jewfish, salmon.
14, 14 and 14. Barramundi fishing good at times. Also salmon.
15. Jewfish hole to 38m - fish 15m mark.
16. Ord False Mouths offer excellent fishing. Live bait best in turbid water.
17. Golden snapper in channel along island.
18. Trevally, queenfish off rocks. Fathom Rock has big golden snapper in deep water on turn of neap tides.

Launch sites

1. Access via Ninbing Road. Strictly dry weather only. Otherwise Wyndham is the nearest launch.

Local tides have up to about 7.56m movement.

The second inlet east of Cape Domett ... like most estuaries in this area, it is a maze of shallow channels at low tide

MAP A

One of the false mouths of the Ord ... note the sandflat

MATT FLYNN PICTURE

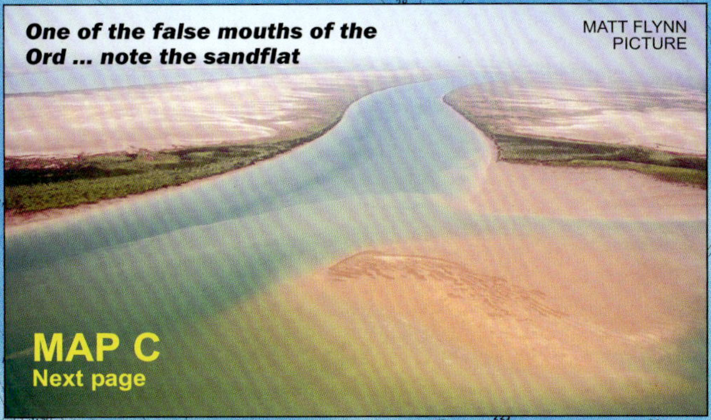

MAP C
Next page

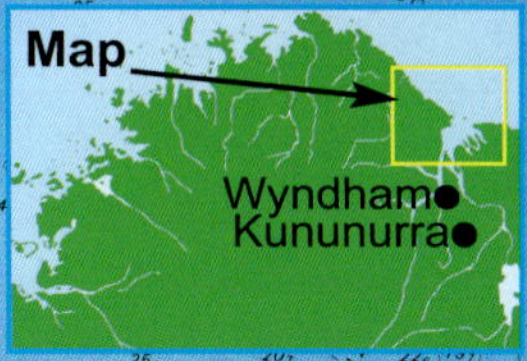

The Berkeley River Trip

It is about 150km from the Wyndham ramp to Berkeley River, with another 25km to travel to the top rockbar. Leave Wyndham on the high tide and travel with the tide. Travelling against the tide will use extra fuel. If the tide is low at Berkeley River mouth, enter from the south of Revely Island and watch for sandbars. On low tides it is not possible to enter from the north. If sleeping in the boat, moor near the top of the river as there are fewer bugs. If beach camping keep in mind that many crocodiles exist here and they may come up the beach. In case of emergency there is a resort near the mouth, with the resort boats usually visible. A favourite stopping spot with locals is about 1km down from the main rockbar, on the left side heading upstream. It is a spring waterfall, which has a rock pool. While the Berkeley River is a remote area, you can expect to see other boats during holiday periods. Skippers should log in with East Kimberley Sea Rescue at Wyndham ramp before leaving. The best chance of calm weather is during the Build-up and just after the wet season. Sometimes mornings provide a period of calm. If the wind comes up do not try to make the trip in a day. There are many places to stop and wait until the wind drops.

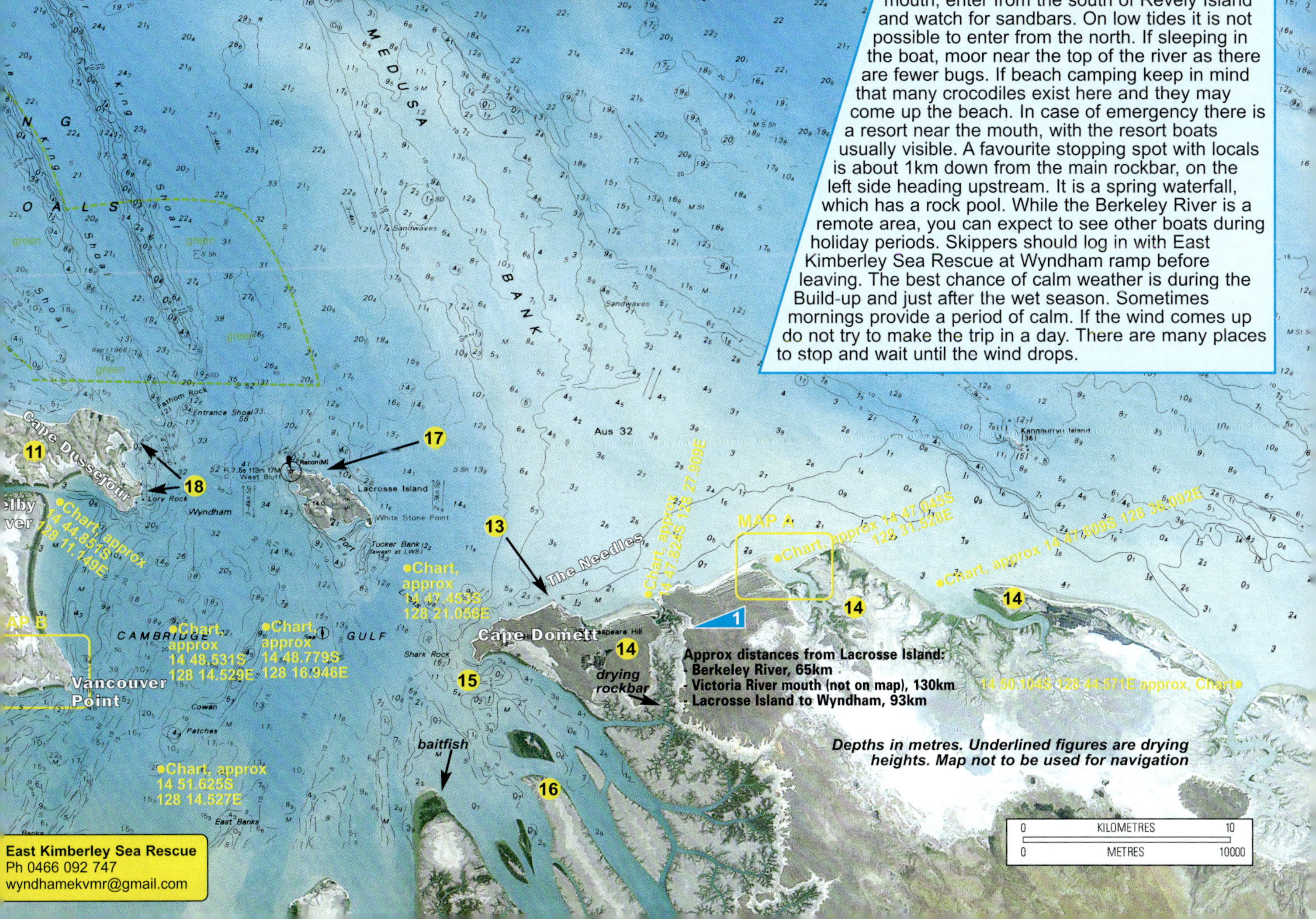

Approx distances from Lacrosse Island:
- Berkeley River, 65km
- Victoria River mouth (not on map), 130km
- Lacrosse Island to Wyndham, 93km

Depths in metres. Underlined figures are drying heights. Map not to be used for navigation

East Kimberley Sea Rescue
Ph 0466 092 747
wyndhamekvmr@gmail.com

ORD RIVER - PENTECOST RIVER - KING RIVER - PARRY CREEK

Darwin
Kununurra
Maps

Large crocodiles occur throughout the Ord River region

Thompson River
rockbar
rockbars
Ina Island
Australind Bank

MAP C ON PAGE 101

False Mouths

FALSE MOUTHS ON PAGE 105

Barramundi, estuary fish
Agnew Point
Malcolm Creek
Nicholls Point
rocks
Ord River
Mermaid Point
submerged rockbar - good fishing

False mouths of the Ord River. All this area and seaward good for estuary fishing. Fish snags for barra on neaps

deep a
shalle
roc
submerged rockbars
rockbars
rockbar

False Mouths of the Ord River goo for general estuar fishing and mud crabs - cast lures to snags and rockbars on neap tides or fish drains on bigger tides

Mission Station Reserve

East Kimberley Sea Rescue
Ph 0466 092 747
wyndhamekvmr@gmail.com

Patrick River
gravel bar
rockbar
Warambur Creek

Unmarked hazards, including rocks, reefs, sunken trees, may exist in all waterways

Large tides must be taken into account when travelling through the Ord River and its tributaries

Adolphus Island
Sphinx Rock 15 08.145 128 12.524E bottom fishing on still of tide
Channel Rock
The Gorge
Fairfax Island
Lower Ord Boundary
Bluff Head
Scott Point
East Arm
approx 15 10.180S 128 13.427E

Barra, jacks, golden snapper in these creeks, which are not subject to the same currents as the main river

DICK PASFIELD PICTURE

Lake Kununurra

15 18.435S 128 04.008E approx
Forrest River
rocks
Hay Point
Otway Island
Pender Point
Sellers Creek
Panton Island

Barra at creek mouth

Barra at creek mouth

approx 15 19.973S 128 07.639E

Pentecost River near Home Valley Station

VINC BROZE PICTUR

West Arm
Parry Creek

Wyndham boat ramp is useable on most tides, and has a floating pontoon. Launch on the high tide if travelling seaward, to take advantage of the outgoing tide. **Local tides have up to about 8.46m movement.**

tidal pool

wharf
Wyndham
Echo Point
Collins Creek
The Gut
King River

King River: mud crabs, some estuary fish

Barramundi at Goose Hill Creek and Collins Creek junction after Wet

Mattress Island (barra fishing)
Ord River
Goose Hill Creek
Abercorne Creek
Mambi (signposted)
Nyia Creek
rocks
Durack River
barra at crossing
N
Parry Creek road may be closed in wet conditions
Barra
rockbar
rockbars
billabongs

Lake Argyle

N

0	KILOMETRES	10
0	METRES	10000

Home Valley Homestead
Pentecost River
Bindoola Creek

(barra fishing after Wet from crossing, and downstream)

Salmond River
Pentecost River
tourist lodge

0	KILOMETRES	25
0	METRES	50000

ck to Cape Domett

Tanmurra Creek launch: rough bank launch at high tide only. Track impassible after heavy rain

WA's barramundi country

The Ord River flows freshwater all year from Lake Argyle, although the 1000sqkm lake, built in 1972, has reduced the total amount of water flowing down the river. The lake was built to create a vast irrigation area around Kununurra.

The Ord is a huge nursery area for barramundi, and it produces some big fish.

Popular locations include Echo Point, Collins and Goose Hill Creek junctions and Mattress Island, as well as the snags and weedbeds from House Roof Hill to Sandy Creek.

Upstream, signposted camp sites at Mambi and Skull Rock are good for fishos with cartoppers. Around Kununurra, Tararra Bar, Ivanhoe Crossing and the outfall gates of the Diversion Dam all produce barra.

Lake Kununurra, within the town, has silver cobbler (catfish), sooty grunter, cherabin, red claw and barramundi. Barramundi stocking has been a great success, with 120cm fish regularly taken.

Situated 70km east of Kununurra is the vast ***Lake Argyle***, supporting a commercial fishing industry which harvests silver cobbler.

In keeping with the size of this impoundment, the catfish grow to an impressive 40kg. Isolated barramundi captures were recorded in years past, presumably from escaped farm fish. These captures created intense interest, but a stocking plan has not been implemented.

Below Lake Argyle there are sooty grunter and the occasional barramundi in what the locals refer to as “the spillway”, which is crossed by the access road leading to the dam wall.

On the west side of Cambridge Gulf are productive estuary and river systems, including the ***Helby***, ***Lyne*** and ***Thompson***. The waters are often turbid, but these spots fish well, and mud crabs are abundant.

In the area around Wyndham, ***Parry Creek*** has big barra. So do the major systems to the south, the ***Durack***, ***Salmond*** and ***Pentecost***, set in picturesque rocky country. These can be most easily fished by helicopter from Home Valley Station. The Oombulgurri road crossing over the Durack produces barra during the wet season on big tides.

The Pentecost can be reached via the Gibb River Road at the crossing near Home Valley Station or upstream towards El Questro Station and downstream along the old Wyndham Karunjie Road. Home Valley runs helicopter fishing tours to local rivers.

Keep River is accessible from Kununurra, just across the WA-NT border on the unsealed Weaber Plain/Keep River Road. A 4WD dry season track runs with the river from the crossing on the main road down to a launch site, with spots along the bank used for bush camping. The Keep River has many rocky areas, making navigation difficult, but good barramundi and jacks are there to be caught.

Getting there: Kununurra and Wyndham have year-round access via the Great Northern and Duncan Highways. Kununurra has jet flights and accommodation. It is about an hour run in a vehicle to Wyndham, which has a concrete ramp that is subject to chop and great tidal flow, but it is suitable for all trailer boats.

Access to the lower Ord is via the old Parry Creek-Kununurra Road, which can be weather dependent. Access to ***Cape Domett*** is via the 150km ***Ninbing Road*** by 4WD, strictly dry weather only, with ***Tanmurra Creek*** bank launch along the way and a beach launch at the end of the track near Cape Domett, a remote area with many crocodiles and sandflies but huge fishing and crabbing potential.

Keep River

The launch site is reached by a track off the unsealed Weaber Plain/Keep River Road from Kununurra. The access track follows the river. It requires 4WD and is only useable in dry weather. The river is very rocky in parts and caution is required. Much of the river drains at low tide. There is excellent fishing for barramundi, salmon and jacks. Fishing is arguably best on neap tides when the water clears.

Keep River ... rocky!

Ord's False Mouths

This area comprises four arms, of which three are interconnected by channels. Access is by launching from Wyndham. The distance to the first mouth is about 67km from the ramp, so fuel demands are high.

The most northern arm has a very rough, high-tide bank launch at the top of ***Tanmurra Creek***, reached by a track off the Ningbing road.

Access through the False Ord mouths is best done on a high or rising tide, as there are sandbanks out front. These sandbanks can be hard to see and some rise quickly out of deep water, so watch your sounder and the water.

Be cautious when the wind and tide are running as waves tend to stand up, making it a bad place to get stuck. Other hazards include hard-to-see rockbars at the end of some creeks.

Log in with the East Kimberley Sea Rescue when departing Wyndham.

The False Mouths are subject to large tidal movements which make it difficult to fish when the current is ripping. The easiest tides to fish are just after neaps, with two to four metres of movement, when water clarity is at its best. A noon low tide is useful, as there will be easy access over sandbars at the mouths on the morning high tide, and an incoming tide in the afternoon to help navigate out.

The best fishing tends to be about an hour either side of low tide.

Always carry extra fuel in case conditions change. Once inside the False Mouths there is a maze of creeks and

Wyndham

Wyndham and Kununurra are gateways to WA's best barramundi fishing. Wyndham is on the lower reaches of the lower Ord River system. Kununurra, on the Ord's freshwater reach, is a different environment. Both locations are barramundi hotspots. The Ord River around Wyndham is mostly shallow estuary, with numerous tributaries. Below Echo Point the river is driven by huge tides over shallow mud and sandbanks, and while this means the lower Ord is muddy, barramundi love it. The water sometimes looks like liquid mud off Wyndham boat ramp, but there is good green water to be found at the mouths of some creeks that feed the main estuary. In contrast, the upper Ord near Kununurra is fed by a constant flow of freshwater from Lake Argyle, a dam many times the size of Sydney Harbour. The river above Mattress Island is quite clear and sandy, with barramundi and sooty grunter. Big barra are best targeted at night in the clear water, but become easier to catch during the wet season. There are camp sites at Skull Rock and Mambi on picturesque parts of the river. Camping is good, with grassy banks, shade trees and white sand, but beware crocodiles. The river at the camps is shallow, with some deeper areas upstream from Skull Rock. Cherabin are usually around. Fishing near Kununurra is good just after the wet season at the river crossings, where barramundi congregate. Lake Kununurra has become an excellent big-barra spot, thanks to stocking. There are other big rivers near Wyndham, as demonstrated by the view from the town's Five Rivers Lookout. The King River is a popular destination for diehard barra fishos, but for a new visitor, Parrys Creek, just north of the town boat ramp, is easier to fish. Locals fish the mouth of Parrys by boat, and the top of the creek from the bank, after driving down a rocky track through the back of the port. Livebait works best in the turbid waters. During the Build-up to the wet season and the wet season proper, big barramundi are usually biting well. Exploration around Wyndham will reveal some "secret" billabongs. Outside Kununurra are the tidal reaches of the Keep River. The road to the Keep is strictly 4WD, and impassible after heavy rain. Wyndham and Kununurra otherwise have sealed road access, providing barramundi fishing opportunities all year. The Ord River is also the gateway to the remote East Kimberley coast, a paradise for the well-prepared adventurer.

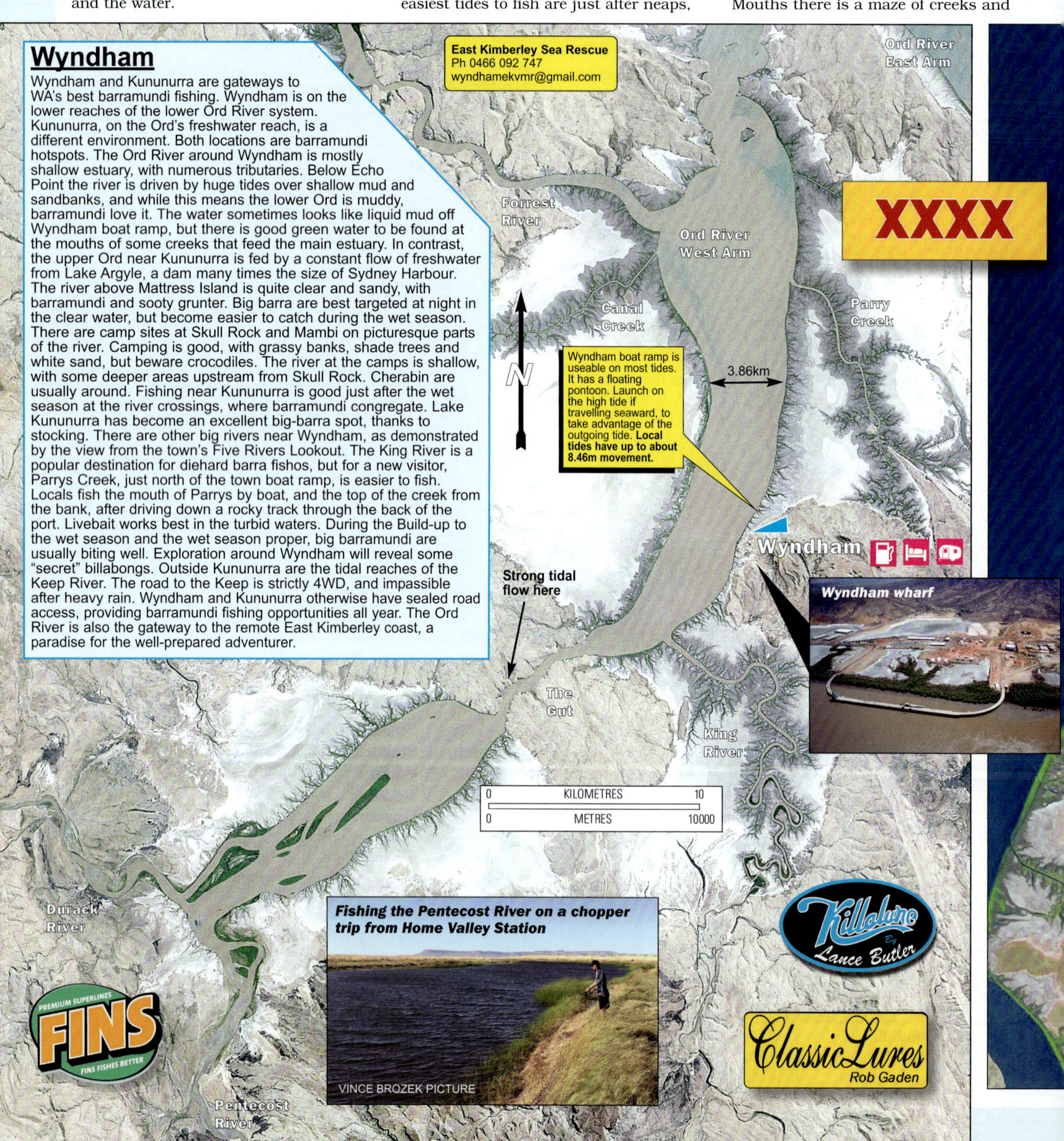

for remote adventure

offshoots. Without a GPS plotter it would be easy to become lost.

With so many creeks to choose from it can be difficult to decide where to fish.

Some creeks are fairly bare of structure so the few snags or rockbars available usually have fish on them.

The best method to fish hidden snags is to drive around at low tide to and mark them on GPS. Then fish them on the incoming tide.

Hardman River, just to the south of the first False Mouth entrance, is always worth a fish, as it has rockbars and usually has good snag structure.

Livebaiting is probably the most effective method in the False Mouths, but casting or trolling lures can produce fish.

At low tide small creeks and mud gutters drain into the bigger systems, and flicking soft plastics and shallow lures into the outflows is effective for barramundi and threadfin salmon. Other species include fingermark or golden snapper (fingermark), mangrove jack, jewfish, estuary cod, blue salmon, javelin fish (grunter), queenfish, trevally, groper and, of course, powertails (catfish).

There are some holes within the False Mouths and these are good areas to target bigger golden snapper and barramundi.

Jewfish also reside in these holes, and sometimes show up in shallow water.

Mud crabs are found throughout and are easily targeted by placing dillies near rockbars, snags, overhanging banks and mud drains, or follow the first push of tide in, working the dillies as you go.

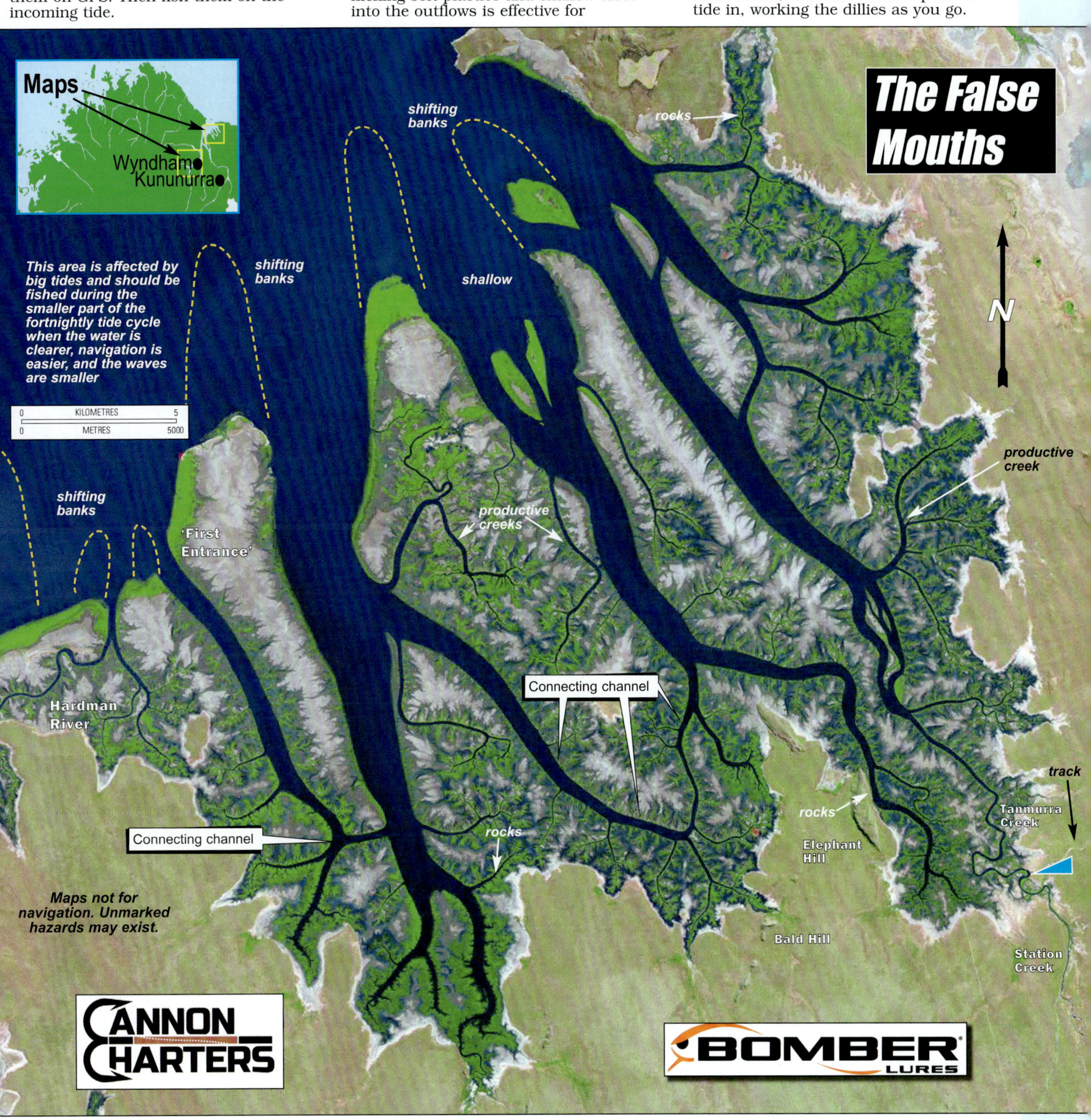

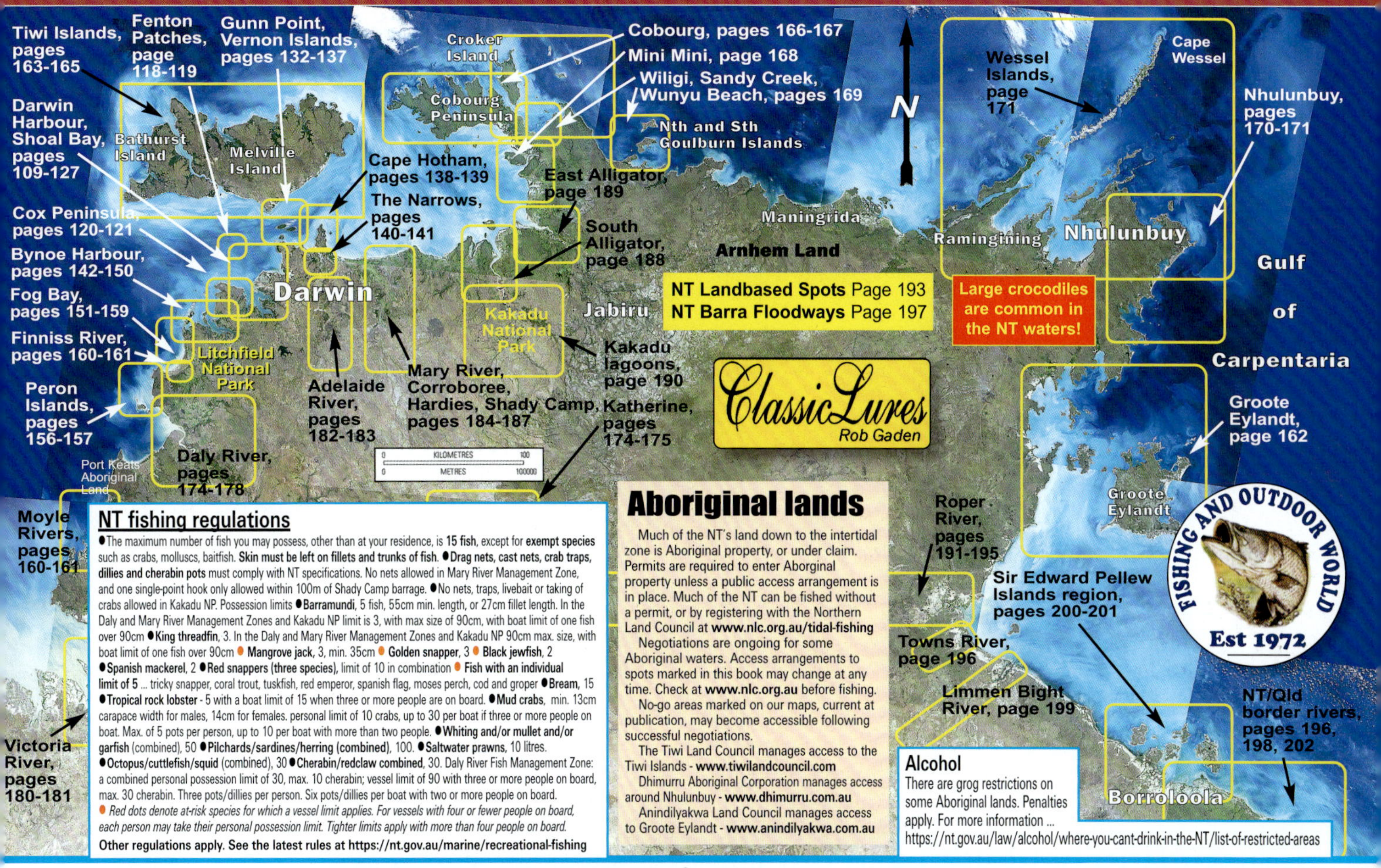

Tiwi Islands, pages 163-165
Fenton Patches, page 118-119
Gunn Point, Vernon Islands, pages 132-137
Croker Island
Cobourg Peninsula
Cobourg, pages 166-167
Mini Mini, page 168
Wiligi, Sandy Creek, Wunyu Beach, pages 169
Nth and Sth Goulburn Islands
Wessel Islands, page 171
Cape Wessel
Nhulunbuy, pages 170-171
Darwin Harbour, Shoal Bay, pages 109-127
Bathurst Island
Melville Island
Cape Hotham, pages 138-139
The Narrows, pages 140-141
East Alligator, page 189
Maningrida
Ramingining
Nhulunbuy
Cox Peninsula, pages 120-121
Bynoe Harbour, pages 142-150
Fog Bay, pages 151-159
Darwin
South Alligator, page 188
Arnhem Land
Gulf of Carpentaria
NT Landbased Spots Page 193
NT Barra Floodways Page 197
Jabiru
Kakadu National Park
Finniss River, pages 160-161
Litchfield National Park
Kakadu lagoons, page 190
Peron Islands, pages 156-157
Adelaide River, pages 182-183
Mary River, Corroboree, Hardies, Shady Camp, pages 184-187
Katherine, pages 174-175
Groote Eylandt, page 162
Port Keats Aboriginal Land
Daly River, pages 174-178
Moyle Rivers, pages 160-161
Roper River, pages 191-195
Groote Eylandt
Sir Edward Pellew Islands region, pages 200-201
Towns River, page 196
Limmen Bight River, page 199
Victoria River, pages 180-181
NT/Qld border rivers, pages 196, 198, 202
Borroloola

0 KILOMETRES 100
0 METRES 100000

Large crocodiles are common in the NT waters!

NT fishing regulations

● The maximum number of fish you may possess, other than at your residence, is **15 fish**, except for **exempt species** such as crabs, molluscs, baitfish. **Skin must be left on fillets and trunks of fish.** ● **Drag nets, cast nets, crab traps, dillies and cherabin pots** must comply with NT specifications. No nets allowed in Mary River Management Zone, and one single-point hook only allowed within 100m of Shady Camp barrage. ● No nets, traps, livebait or taking of crabs allowed in Kakadu NP. Possession limits ● **Barramundi**, 5 fish, 55cm min. length, or 27cm fillet length. In the Daly and Mary River Management Zones and Kakadu NP limit is 3, with max size of 90cm, with boat limit of one fish over 90cm ● **King threadfin**, 3. In the Daly and Mary River Management Zones and Kakadu NP 90cm max. size, with boat limit of one fish over 90cm ● **Mangrove jack**, 3, min. 35cm ● **Golden snapper**, 3 ● **Black jewfish**, 2 ● **Spanish mackerel**, 2 ● **Red snappers (three species)**, limit of 10 in combination ● **Fish with an individual limit of 5** ... tricky snapper, coral trout, tuskfish, red emperor, spanish flag, moses perch, cod and groper ● **Bream**, 15 ● **Tropical rock lobster** - 5 with a boat limit of 15 when three or more people are on board. ● **Mud crabs**, min. 13cm carapace width for males, 14cm for females. personal limit of 10 crabs, up to 30 per boat if three or more people on boat. Max. of 5 pots per person, up to 10 per boat with more than two people. ● **Whiting and/or mullet and/or garfish** (combined), 50 ● **Pilchards/sardines/herring (combined)**, 100. ● **Saltwater prawns**, 10 litres. ● **Octopus/cuttlefish/squid** (combined), 30 ● **Cherabin/redclaw combined**, 30. Daly River Fish Management Zone: a combined personal possession limit of 30, max. 10 cherabin; vessel limit of 90 with three or more people on board, max. 30 cherabin. Three pots/dillies per person. Six pots/dillies per boat with two or more people on board.

● *Red dots denote at-risk species for which a vessel limit applies. For vessels with four or fewer people on board, each person may take their personal possession limit. Tighter limits apply with more than four people on board.*

Other regulations apply. See the latest rules at https://nt.gov.au/marine/recreational-fishing

Aboriginal lands

Much of the NT's land down to the intertidal zone is Aboriginal property, or under claim. Permits are required to enter Aborginal property unless a public access arrangement is in place. Much of the NT can be fished without a permit, or by registering with the Northern Land Council at **www.nlc.org.au/tidal-fishing**

Negotiations are ongoing for some Aboriginal waters. Access arrangements to spots marked in this book may change at any time. Check at **www.nlc.org.au** before fishing.

No-go areas marked on our maps, current at publication, may become accessible following successful negotiations.

The Tiwi Land Council manages access to the Tiwi Islands - **www.tiwilandcouncil.com**

Dhimurru Aboriginal Corporation manages access around Nhulunbuy - **www.dhimurru.com.au**

Anindilyakwa Land Council manages access to Groote Eylandt - **www.anindilyakwa.com.au**

Alcohol

There are grog restrictions on some Aboriginal lands. Penalties apply. For more information ... https://nt.gov.au/law/alcohol/where-you-cant-drink-in-the-NT/list-of-restricted-areas

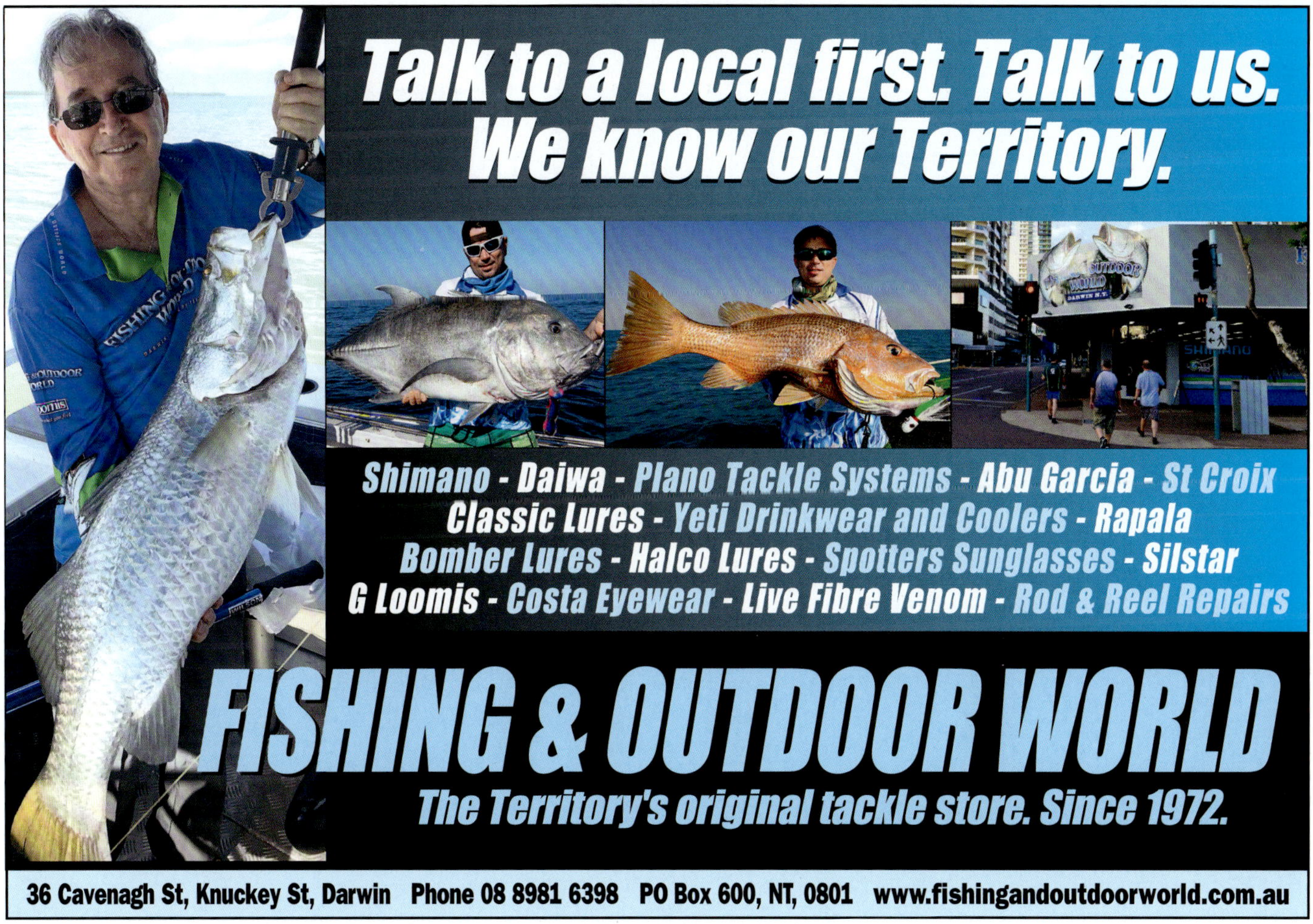

Your safety in the harbour is important to us, please avoid the shipping channel where possible!

Darwin Harbour Shipping Channels
(shown in Yellow)

LANDBRIDGE DARWIN PORT

Large vessels can only navigate inside the channels and cannot stop or turn to avoid collision without risk to their safety.

Anytime you are in the shipping channel, you are required by law to clear well in advance of large vessels using the channels. The master of a vessel must not anchor or permit the vessel to be anchored:

1) In a shipping channel except in an emergency; or

2) In a manner that is likely to obstruct or impede the safe passage or navigation of another vessel or create a hazard to the safe passage, navigation or operation of another vessel.

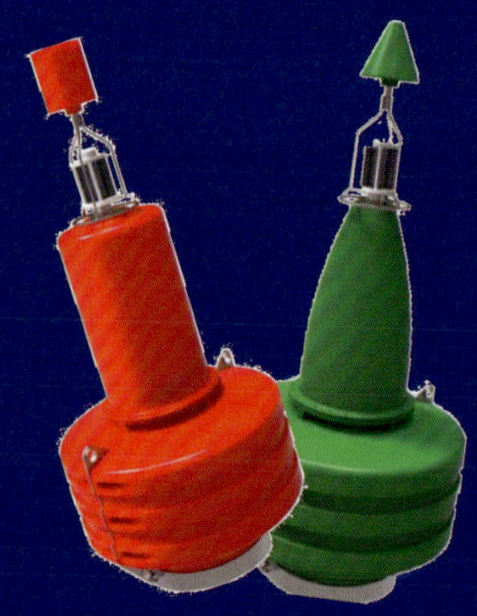

www.darwinport.com.au

Fishing Territory

With a Million Dollar Fish tagged barramundi competition, a large area of gillnet-free coastline, and a long-established and expanding artificial reef network, Darwin has arguably Australia's best capital city fishing.

Artificial reef clusters were installed at sites just 5km off Lee Point from 1996, and there are older artificial reefs within Darwin Harbour.

There are also WWII and cyclone wrecks and rocky reefs.

The harbour's artificial reefs are the "junk" variety, being mostly scuttled hulls.

Lee Point's three artificial reef sites are made from a mix of components, see Page 112. The first item was a huge bottlewashing machine.

Much more followed, with the nearby Rick Mills Memorial Reef made from mining equipment, hulls and shipping containers.

The Tipper Reef consists mainly of steel ore tippers, installed in 1999.

The 16m steel *Kay-Lee* hull was added later. In 2014 a steel pontoon and gangway from nearby Cullen Bay was added.

Large concrete culverts surround the reef sites.

The Lee Point reefs have been a great success, possibly because of their location between fertile Shoal Bay and Darwin Harbour.

Inside the harbour, the impressive *Medkhanun 3*, a 25m illegal foreign fishing vessel, was sunk with funds from gas firm Conoco Phillips.

There is an artificial reef off East Point called the *DSAC Barge*, and a larger site within the harbour based around the scuttled *Ham Luong* and *Song Saigon* refugee boats.

The part-salvaged remains of WWII ships like the *Peary*, *Mauna Loa*, *Zealandia* and *Meigs* still fish well.

Other wrecks include the *Kelat* and *Bellbird*.

Cullen Bay

Darwin has marinas at Cullen Bay, Tipperary Waters and Bayview Haven. Cullen Bay marina lock is opened at regular intervals, with the lockmaster called on VHF Channel 11. For those who don't catch a fish, Cullen Bay has restaurants overlooking the marina.

Ferries: A ferry service runs from Cullen Bay to Mandorah on the other side of Darwin Harbour. The ferry leaves from a pontoon outside the lock. Mandorah has a jetty where barra, mackerel, queenfish, trevally and sharks are caught.

Mindil Beach: North-east of Cullen Bay is Mindil and Vesteys Beach. Outside the marina is a low-tide sandbar near which queenfish, mackerel and tuna are caught in the dry season. The mouth of the creek near the casino is good for collecting mullet. Baitfish can be seen from the footbridge over the creek.

Rock walls: The external rock walls hold salmon, queenfish, trevally and barra, usually on a rising tide, and are good spots for landbased fishing for blue salmon, queenfish, trevally and bream. Fishing is not allowed inside the marina.

Superb habitat

Darwin Harbour is home to more than 400 species of finfish, five species of dolphin, four species of turtle, dugongs, many species of sharks and rays, several marine and land snakes, two species of large mud crab (and other crabs), prawns, shellfish, coral and more.

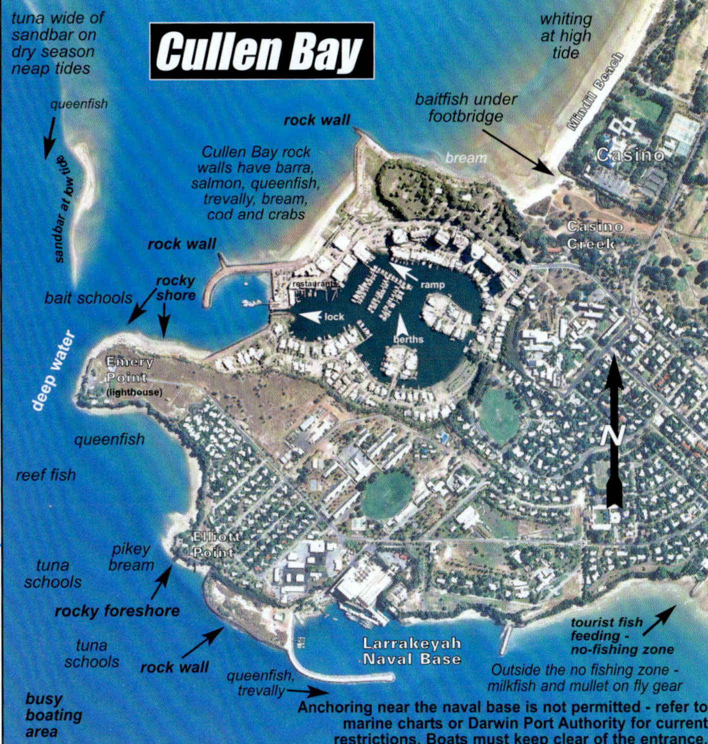

Harbour spots and shipping channels

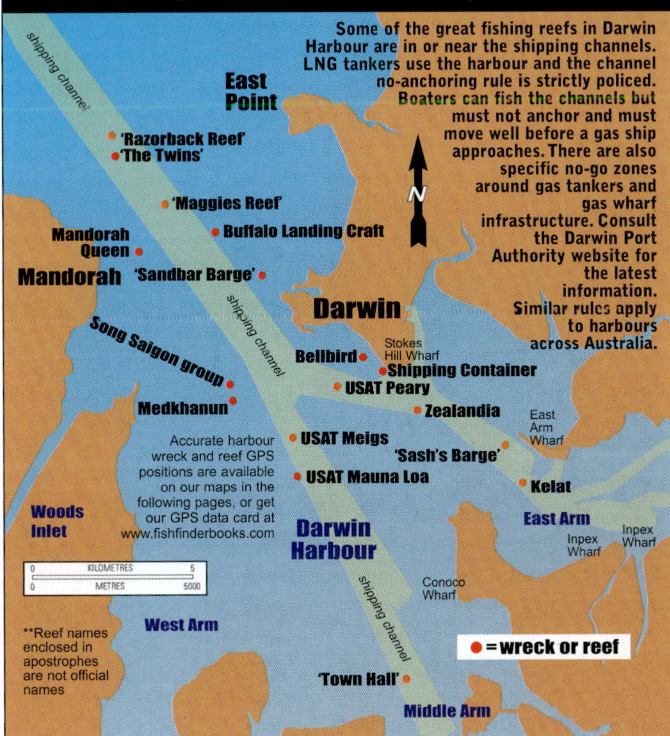

Much of the harbour's natural reef is worth fishing.

Deep rocky areas off Larrakeyah, the "Six Mile" and Channel Rock are among the best spots, but with gas freighters and other ships using the harbour, skippers must not anchor in the shipping channel or otherwise obstruct ships.

Skippers must move on sighting an approaching ship, well before it draws near.

Night lights are important when fishing the busy harbour.

Harbour arms

Darwin has three large arms, East, Middle and West Arm. There is a small central arm dubbed "Little West Arm".

The arms are shallow, mangrove-lined waterways, swept by huge tides, with large areas of dry mud and sandflat during big low tides.

The harbour and Bynoe Harbour to the south-west are lined by productive mangrove forest.

Barramundi, blue and threadfin salmon, queenfish, trevally, golden snapper, cod, jacks, jewfish, grunter, pikey bream, tripletail, milkfish, flathead and whiting are abundant.

Big mud crabs and a seemingly infinite supply of prawns are present.

Fishing the harbour is about the tides, which cycle roughly fortnightly between large "spring" tides and small neap tides. On big tides, barra fishos cast lures to draining mud gutters, and fish low-tide holes.

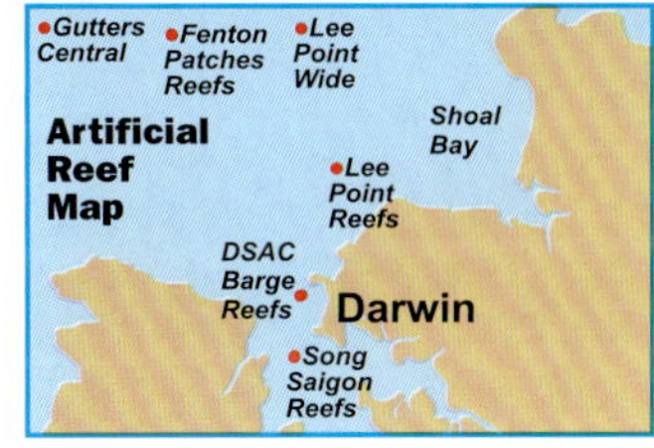

At high tide, fish move into mangroves to feed.

Small neap tides clear the turbid waters, when flats sight-fishing and deepwater or night bottom fishing works well.

The harbour has pelagic fish, mainly in the dry season, including longtail tuna, various mackerel and trevally species, queenfish, and occasional cobia.

Offshore

The first offshore artificial reef was installed 35km off Darwin in 1988 at the Fenton Patches, see Pages 118-119. This was the *Marchart 3* rig tender, still a great fishing spot today.

More scuttled hulls, concrete pipes, tyres and even bus shelters were used to create several more sites all about a nautical mile (1.85km) apart.

More recently, custom-built sites made from concrete modules were installed about 10km east and 12km west of the original Fenton reefs.

The Fenton reefs are mackerel hotspots, and produce big jewfish, golden snapper, redfish, cod, trout and trevally.

Black marlin and sailfish have also been caught.

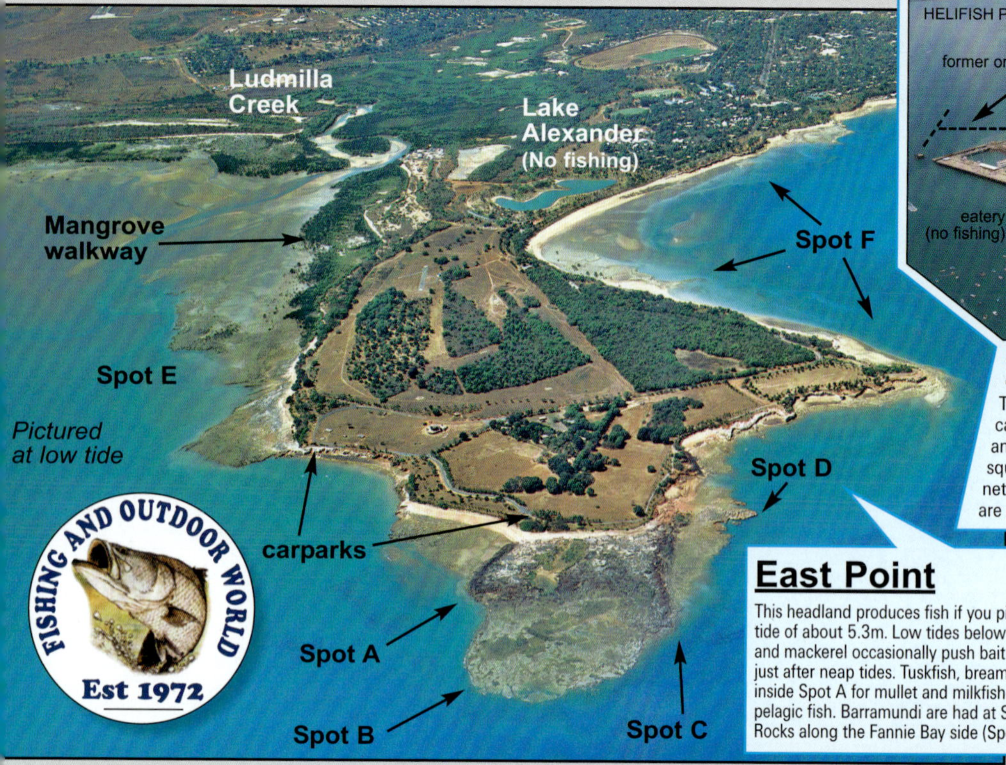

Ludmilla Creek
Lake Alexander (No fishing)
Mangrove walkway
Spot F
Spot E
Pictured at low tide
Spot D
carparks
Spot A
Spot B
Spot C
FISHING AND OUTDOOR WORLD Est 1972

HELIFISH PICTURE
former ore wharf remains
eatery (no fishing)
fishing platform

Darwin wharves during a fishing protest - these huge structures attract fish

Stokes Hill Wharf

The wharf has a fishing platform with artificial reefs in easy casting distance. Barramundi, queenfish, trevally, jewfish, cod and squid are caught here and along most of the wharf. Live squid or herring are great bait and can be caught with cast nets or jigs. Fishing is easier on neap tides and slack tide. Barra are under lights at night. **The eatery end is a no-fishing zone.**

East Point

East Point rocks are part of a marine reserve and a 30cm minimum fish size applies

This headland produces fish if you pick the right tides and fish early or late. Fish from Spot A on a high tide of about 5.3m. Low tides below 2m suit the ledges at Spot B. Pelagics such as queenfish, trevally and mackerel occasionally push bait up against the rocks at Spots B, C and D in the cool months, best just after neap tides. Tuskfish, bream, cod and snapper are also caught. Berley bread from the beach inside Spot A for mullet and milkfish. Long-distance lure casting or drifted balloon baits work best for pelagic fish. Barramundi are had at Spot E on low tides, and off the mangrove walkway at half tide. Rocks along the Fannie Bay side (Spot F) have blue salmon, bream and occasional barra at high tide.

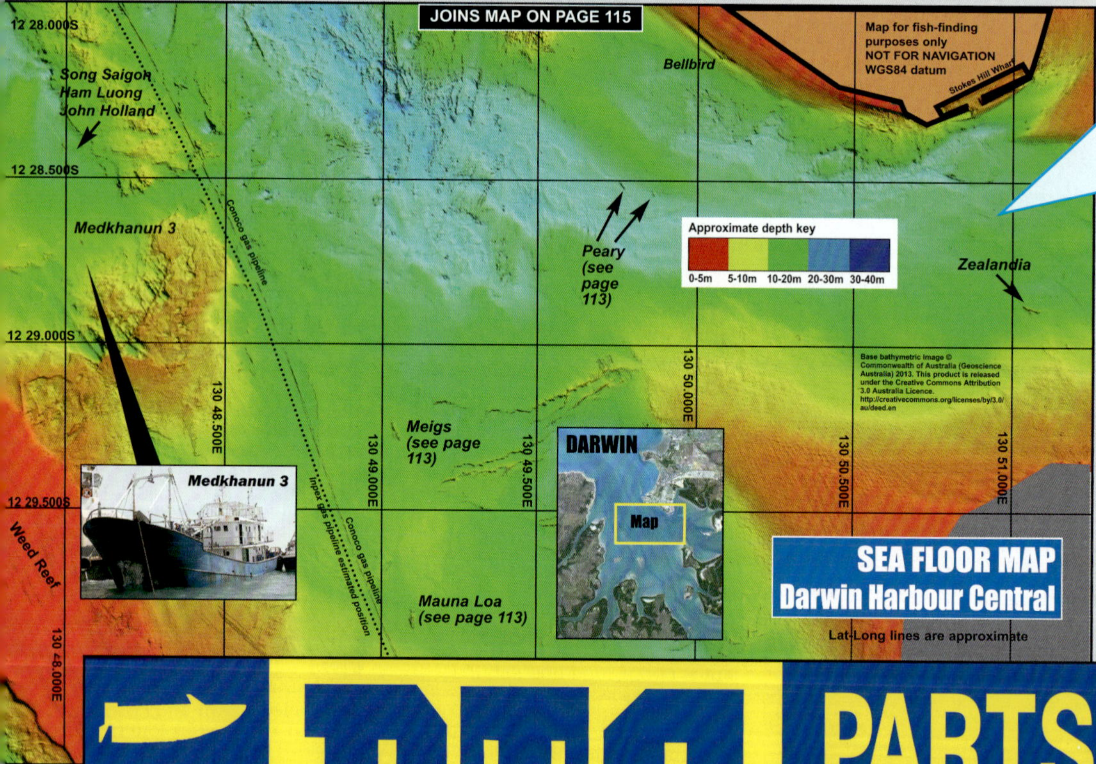

JOINS MAP ON PAGE 115

12 28.000S
Song Saigon
Ham Luong
John Holland
12 28.500S
Medkhanun 3
Conoco gas pipeline
12 29.000S
12 29.500S
Weed Reef
Bellbird
Map for fish-finding purposes only
NOT FOR NAVIGATION
WGS84 datum
Stokes Hill Wharf
Peary (see page 113)
Approximate depth key
0-5m 5-10m 10-20m 20-30m 30-40m
Zealandia
Meigs (see page 113)
Mauna Loa (see page 113)
130 48.000E
130 48.500E
130 49.000E
130 49.500E
130 50.000E
130 50.500E
130 51.000E
DARWIN
Map
Medkhanun 3
Base bathymetric image © Commonwealth of Australia (Geoscience Australia) 2013. This product is released under the Creative Commons Attribution 3.0 Australia Licence. http://creativecommons.org/licenses/by/3.0/au/deed.en

SEA FLOOR MAP
Darwin Harbour Central

Lat-Long lines are approximate

Central Harbour

The central area of Darwin Harbour contains several World War II and 1974 Cyclone Tracy wrecks, as well as artificial reefs. All are of interest to fishermen. There are also patches of rocky reef. Wreck and reef fishing must be done at the turn of the tide, or during neap tides, otherwise the tidal current tends to be too strong. Golden snapper, jewfish, tuskfish, flag, redfish and cod are the main species caught. Night fishing works well. Keep in mind that boaters must move long before a ship nears, and anchoring is not permitted in the shipping channel. Drifting and jigging lures over the various spots allows fishermen to move on quickly if a ship appears. The gas pipelines are worthwhile spots to drop baits or jigs, with some parts of the pipe showing higher profile than others.

Darwin Metro

Barramundi nets were banned in Darwin Harbour and nearby Shoal Bay in 1997. All other gill nets were removed in 2007. Commercial crabbing is not permitted in harbour waters. Queenfish, trevally, barramundi, salmon, golden snapper, cod and mud crabs are abundant. Whiting, bream, jacks and flathead are common, but not often targeted. Stokes Hill and Mandorah wharves, Mindil Beach, East Point, Nightcliff and Lee Point foreshores and Cullen Bay's rock walls are the main landbased fishing areas, with Nightcliff and Lee Point best at high tide, and parts of East Point good on lower tides. Tuna and mackerel are best in the dry season. Barramundi are caught all year, but are best in warm, calm weather. The Lee Point Artificial Reef System is a highlight for boaters, being easily accessible, with big jewfish, mackerel and more. The mangrove-lined harbour arms are unlocked in the following pages.

Key to Map

Hotspots

1. Fish landbased from Lee Point on early morning big high tides for queenfish, trevally, blue salmon, whiting. Limited low tide fishing on Shoal Bay side. For boaters, fish reef drop-offs for mackerel in arvos from May/Sept on building tides - berley garfish for live/dead bait.
2. Fish the junction drop-off with livebait on last of outgoing tide for barra. Landlocked at low tide.
3. Queenfish, barra, salmon, whiting, jacks in Rapid Creek. For barra, fish first incoming tide at night. A rockbar is located off the bike track.
4&4. Nightcliff rocks hold barra in calm weather, morning high tides. Salmon, mud crabs in mangroves.
5. North side of East Point has barra, queenfish. Fish low rising tide in calm September/October weather.
6. East Point has trevally, queenfish, tuskfish. Mullet, whiting off beach. Tuna/mackerel in dry season.
7. Barra at Casino Creek mouth in wet season. Mullet.
8. Rock patches near museum - barra, cod in calm weather. Mullet, garfish schools at high tide.
9. Bream off Larrakeyah foreshores in dry season. Rock wall has deep water. Mostly queenfish, trevally.
10. Fish from rock embankment for queenfish during morning/afternoon high tide.
11. Rock walls - barra, queenfish, salmon, cod, crabs.
12. Barra, salmon, mud crabs in both creeks. Fish draining gutters on falling tide, mangrove edges on rising tide. Use shallow lures or livebait.
13. Queenfish off sandbar in dry season.
14. Ludmilla Creek - turn off before East Point gate. Dinghy bank launch. Barra, salmon.
15. Barra under lights behind base of wharf.
16. Milkfish on bread baits - use bread berley.
17. As big tides rise barra move from channel edge to mangrove edge. Premium spot for Sept/Oct late arvo rising tides. Watch for bait, move boat onto flat and near mangroves as tide rises. Use livebait and shallow lures. Also snapper, grunter, bream, salmon, flathead.

Wrecks

A. Wreck in creek exposed at low tide.
B. *Bellbird* trawler, 12.28 139S 130.50 089E, 12m.
C. Submerged freight container, 12 28.424S, 130 50.301E, jewfish. Others may exist nearby.
D. 'Bottlewasher', 12 18.140S, 130 51.776E.
E. Small barge, 12 26.906S 130 48.610E, 22m.
F. DSAC Barge, 12 24.625S, 130 48.181E, 17m.
G. 'Tipper Reef' - ore tippers near a 16m steel fishing boat *Kay-Lee*, 12 17.967S 130 50.386E.
H. 'Old Mick Clancy Reef' - concrete yacht hull, broken up, 12 17.990S 130 50.467E.
I. 'MV Dodgy', 12 18.451S 130 48.864E. Other reef components at 12 18.458S 130 48.859E
J. *Rick Mills Reef*, 12 18.451S 130 48.872E.
K. 'Van Bruggen's Dream', steel yacht, part of Rick Mills Reef, 12 18.495S 130 48.923E.
L. Two hulls, Rick Mills area, position unknown.
J. Dakota plane, no anchors, 12 25.514S 130 48.104E.
K. Steel yacht hull, 12 17.945S 130 50.451E

Useful GPS

a. Angler Reef, 12 18.860S, 130 52.270E, reef and pelagic fish. Anchor or troll. See map Page 117.

Public launch sites

1. Nightcliff (Casuarina Dve), best above 3.5m tide. Do not back vehicle down onto the sand.
2. Trailer Boat Club (for members), above 2.5m.
3. Vesteys Beach (Atkins Dve), above 3.5m.
4. Doyles ramp (Conacher St), above 2.5m.
5. Dinah Beach (Frances Bay Dve), above 2.2m.
6. Cullen Bay all-tide toll ramp. Exit via lock.

Local tides have up to about 7.42m movement.

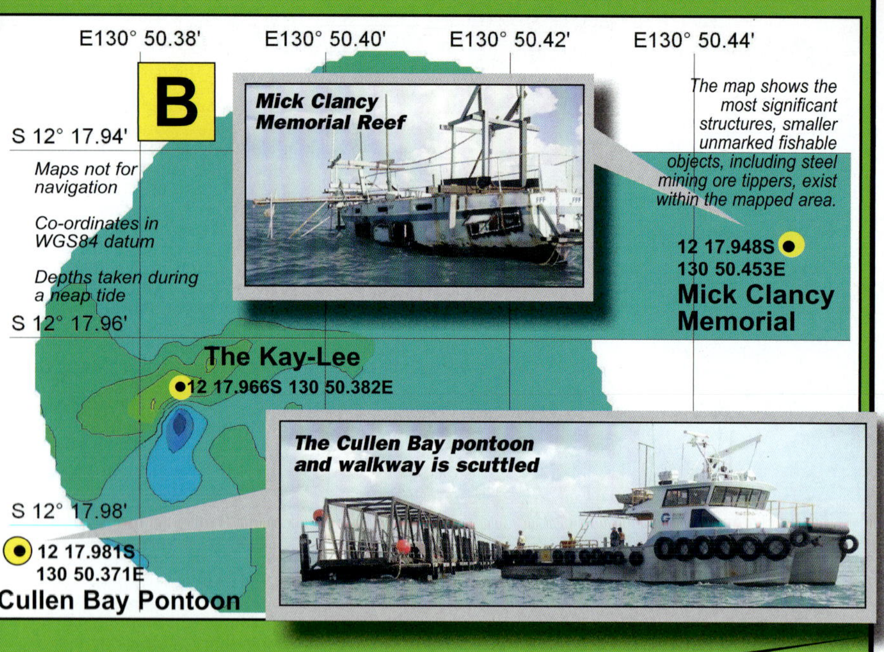

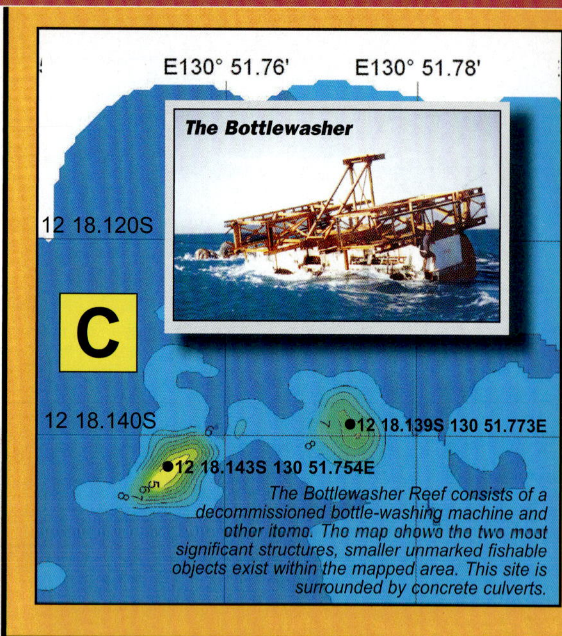

Three great sites

Lee Point Artificial Reef System includes concrete culverts, hulls, shipping containers, a pontoon and walkway, a bottle-washing machine, ore tippers, and more.

Various components make up each of the three sites. Six hundred concrete culverts were installed in 2011. The culverts surround the Rick Mills Memorial and Bottlewasher Reef sites. The culverts were each 6m long, enough to form a 3.6km line. By comparison, the *USS Oriskany*, an aircraft carrier billed as the world's largest man-made reef, is only 276m long.

A pontoon and gangway were added in 2014.

Jewfish, golden snapper, cod, flag, mackerel and trevally are the common catch, with best fishing usually at the turn of the tide.

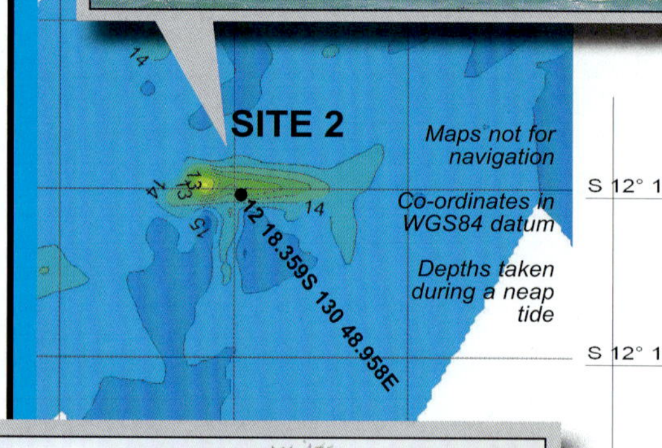

Concrete culverts

SITE 4
12 18.433S 130 48.817E

SITE 1 - Rick Mills Memorial Reef
12 18.460S 130 48.879E

A

Other fishable objects exist within the mapped area. The map shows the most significant structures. The central Rick Mills site is surrounded by culverts

SITE E
shipping containers
12 18.479S 130 48.832E
12 18.481S 130 48.829E
12 18.480S 130 48.846E
12 18.489S 130 48.847E

SITE 3
12 18.490S
130 48.920E

FISHING AND OUTDOOR WORLD Est 1972

E130° 48.82' E130° 48.84' E130° 48.86' E130° 48.88' E130° 48.90' E130° 48.92' E130° 48.94' E130° 48.96' E130° 48.98'

S 12° 18.40' S 12° 18.42' S 12° 18.44' S 12° 18.46' S 12° 18.48' S 12° 18.50'

The Van Bruggen's Dream

MV Dodgy and volunteers

USS Peary

The USS *Peary* (right) is a deep wreck by Darwin Harbour standards, at almost 30m. It has jewfish and golden snapper. The wreck is in two separate sections, easily located using GPS and sounder. The *Peary* sank during a Japanese air attack in WWII, and it was not until several years after the war that it was found. Like all the WWII wrecks it was extensively salvaged in the 1960s and now has a low profile. Anchor on a high point at the turn of the tide, or on neap tides, for best results.

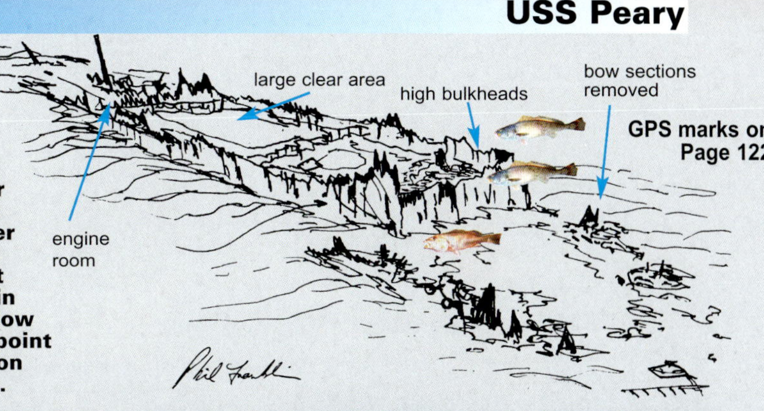

GPS marks on Page 122

USAT Mauna Loa

The *Mauna Loa* transport ship (above) was sunk in 1942 in almost 20m of water. It was extensively salvaged in the 1960s. This is a reasonably reliable jewfish wreck, but like any wreck the fish aren't always there. Jewfish are usually at the bow, which points to Middle Arm. Jewfish schools can occasionally be seen on sonar hovering over the wreck.

Medkhanun 3

The *Medkhanun 3* is a 25m illegal foreign fishing vessel scuttled in Darwin Harbour in 2007 to complement the nearby *Song Saigon/Ham Luong* artificial reef site. The wreck sits on its side south of the other reefs. It displays a huge profile on sonar. The *Medkhanun 3* is now a great fishing wreck, with big jewfish, cod and snapper. LNG company ConocoPhillips donated $10,000 to have the vessel cleaned up for sinking.

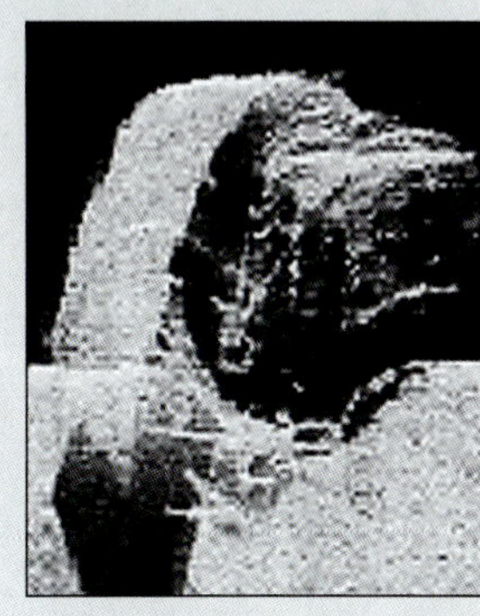

USAT Meigs

GPS marks on Page 122

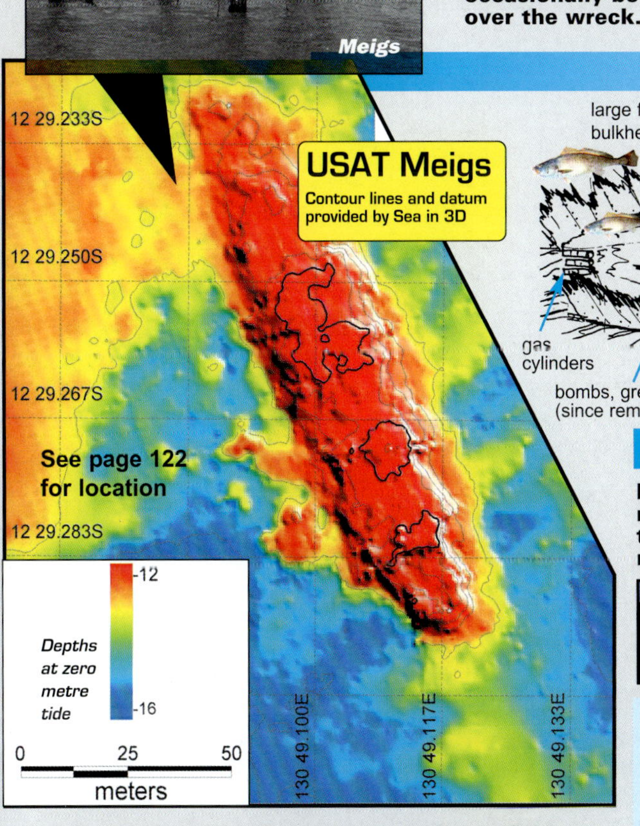

The USAT *Meigs* (above) was sunk in a WWII air attack in 1942. It protruded from the water until it was extensively salvaged. The low-profile remains now cover a large area of mud and sand, with the bow facing Middle Arm. Jewfish, golden snapper, moonfish, cod and flag can be caught.

Ellengowan

Most of the Ellengowan has rotted or sunk into mud, leaving the engine and boiler. But the remains still attract jewfish.

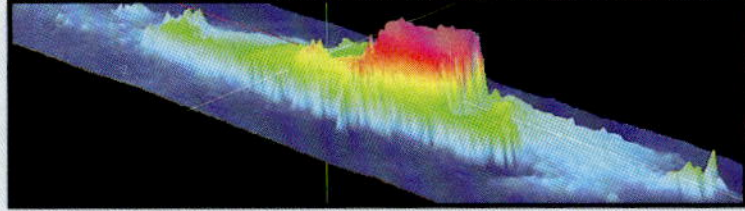

Sandbar barge

Not much is known about this small hull, which sits in deep water off the Cullen Bay sandbar. It is worth trying for cod, snapper, jewfish and occasional cobia.

Darwin Princess

This ferry sunk outside the harbour in 1974's Cyclone Tracy. The nearby *Booya* wreck is protected, but the *Princess*, lying upside down, can be fished. It is not considered a great spot.

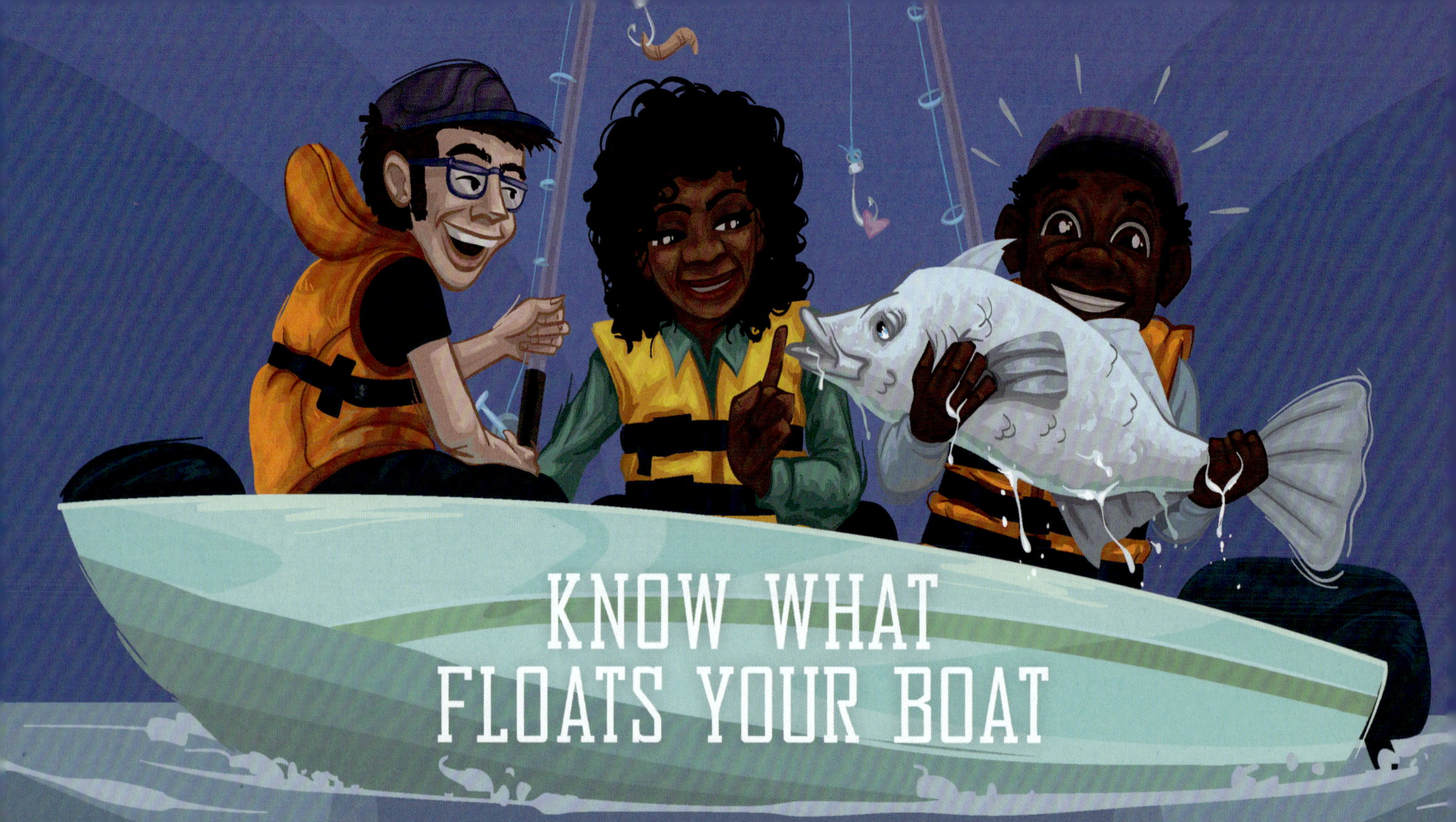

KNOW WHAT FLOATS YOUR BOAT

MINIMUM SAFETY EQUIPMENT

To be carried on board:

		Inland waters	Intermediate waters	Open waters
	One approved **personal flotation device** for each person on board	✔	✔	✔
	One **anchor** fitted with not less than 3 metres of chain shackled between the anchor and rope of not less than 50 metres overall length	✔	✔ (Two if vessel is over 10 metres in length)	✔ (Two if vessel is over 10 metres in length)
	Two paddles or oars fitted with rowlocks for all vessels under 5 metres in length unless fitted with an auxiliary means of propulsion	✔	✔	✔
	One bailer (fitted with lanyard) or **bilge pump**. A bilge pump is required for all vessels with covered bilges.	✔	✔	✔
	Fresh drinking water in a leak proof container (two litres for each person on board)	✔	✔	✔
	One **waterproof torch**	✔	✔	✔
	Two **red flares**	-	✔	✔
	Two **orange smoke signals**	-	✔	✔
	One **V distress sheet**	-	✔	✔
	Portable fire extinguisher (one if the vessel is between 5 and 10 metres in length / two if the vessel is over 10 metres in length. Not required for vessels under 5 metres.)	-	✔	✔
	Two 9L buckets with lanyards for vessels over 10 metres in length	-	✔	✔
	One **compass or operational GPS**	-	-	✔
	Electronic or paper chart for the area of intended operation	-	-	✔
	One **lifebuoy** (for vessels over 10 metres)	-	-	✔
	One **registered EPIRB**	-	-	✔

Categories of Water

Inland Waters - Non tidal rivers, lakes, dams and billabongs.

Intermediate Waters - All tidal rivers, declared sheltered waters areas and all other coastal waters up to 2 nautical miles from the coastline.

Open Waters - Means beyond intermediate waters.

Find out what floats your boat at www.marinesafety.nt.gov.au or call 08 8924 7100

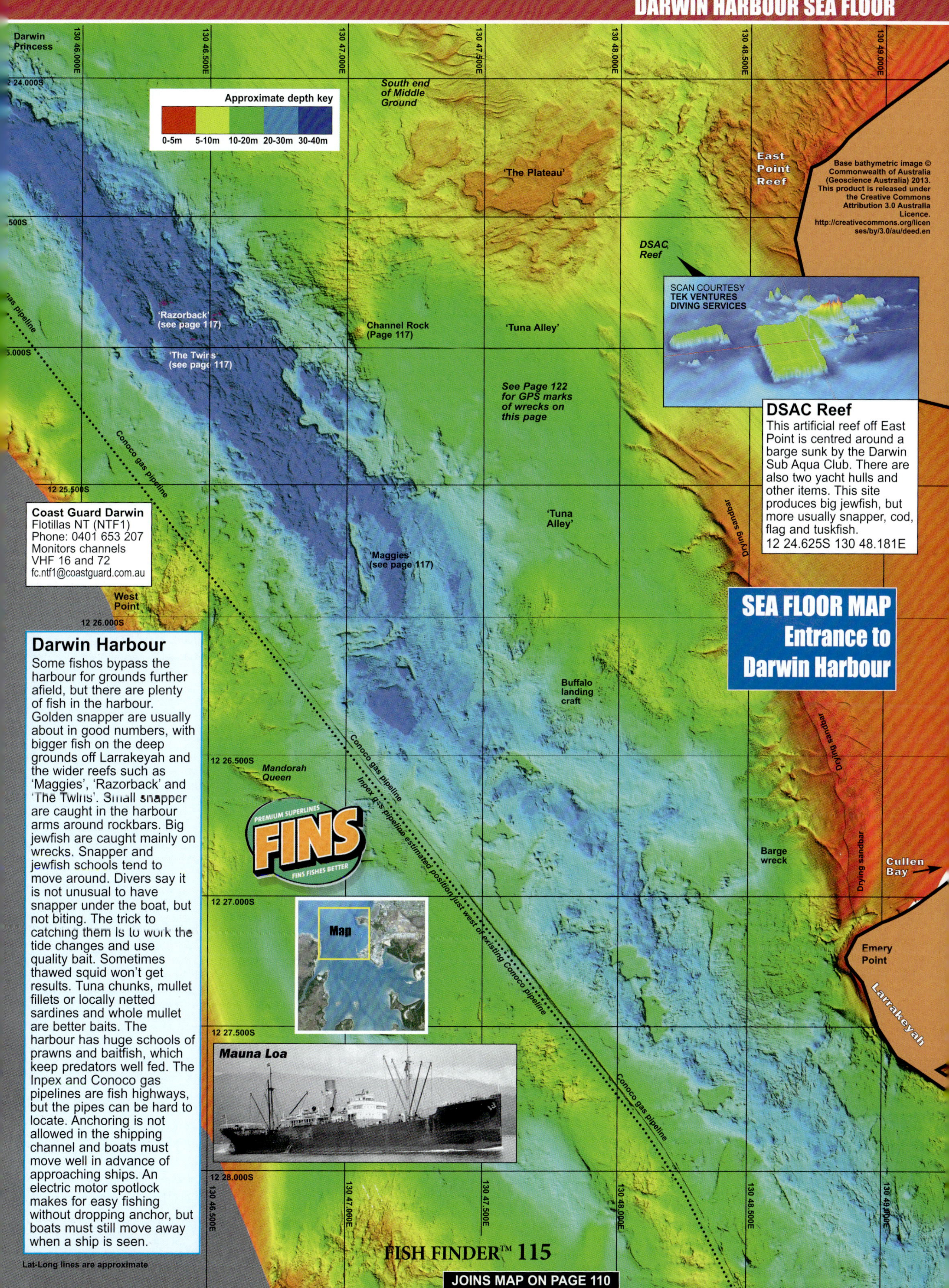

DSAC Reef

This artificial reef off East Point is centred around a barge sunk by the Darwin Sub Aqua Club. There are also two yacht hulls and other items. This site produces big jewfish, but more usually snapper, cod, flag and tuskfish.
12 24.625S 130 48.181E

SEA FLOOR MAP
Entrance to Darwin Harbour

Coast Guard Darwin
Flotillas NT (NTF1)
Phone: 0401 653 207
Monitors channels VHF 16 and 72
fc.ntf1@coastguard.com.au

Darwin Harbour

Some fishos bypass the harbour for grounds further afield, but there are plenty of fish in the harbour. Golden snapper are usually about in good numbers, with bigger fish on the deep grounds off Larrakeyah and the wider reefs such as 'Maggies', 'Razorback' and 'The Twins'. Small snapper are caught in the harbour arms around rockbars. Big jewfish are caught mainly on wrecks. Snapper and jewfish schools tend to move around. Divers say it is not unusual to have snapper under the boat, but not biting. The trick to catching them is to work the tide changes and use quality bait. Sometimes thawed squid won't get results. Tuna chunks, mullet fillets or locally netted sardines and whole mullet are better baits. The harbour has huge schools of prawns and baitfish, which keep predators well fed. The Inpex and Conoco gas pipelines are fish highways, but the pipes can be hard to locate. Anchoring is not allowed in the shipping channel and boats must move well in advance of approaching ships. An electric motor spotlock makes for easy fishing without dropping anchor, but boats must still move away when a ship is seen.

JOINS MAP ON PAGE 110

NATIONAL SHIPWRECK DATABASE

SS Zealandia

This 125m Australian steamship was sunk during a Japanese air attack on Darwin in 1942. After she sank her masts were well clear of the water. The ship was extensively salvaged in 1960, leaving a substantial mound of wreckage and cargo. The bottom profile is better than most of the salvaged wartime wrecks, often with bait balls showing on sonar, yet this site does not seem to produce jewfish like other harbour wrecks. However, the *Zealandia* usually has cod, trout, redfish, flag and golden snapper, with occasional trevally and mackerel.

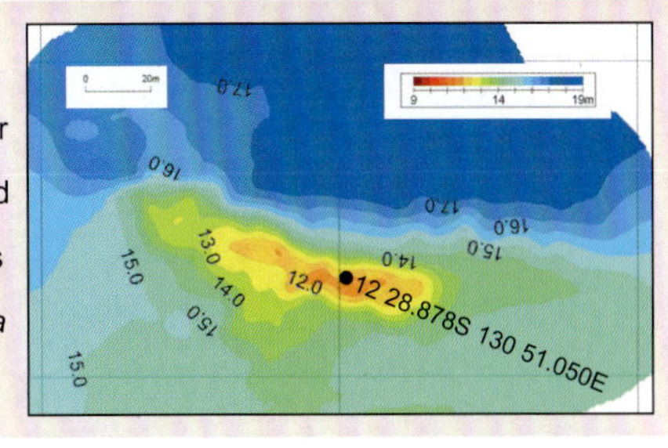

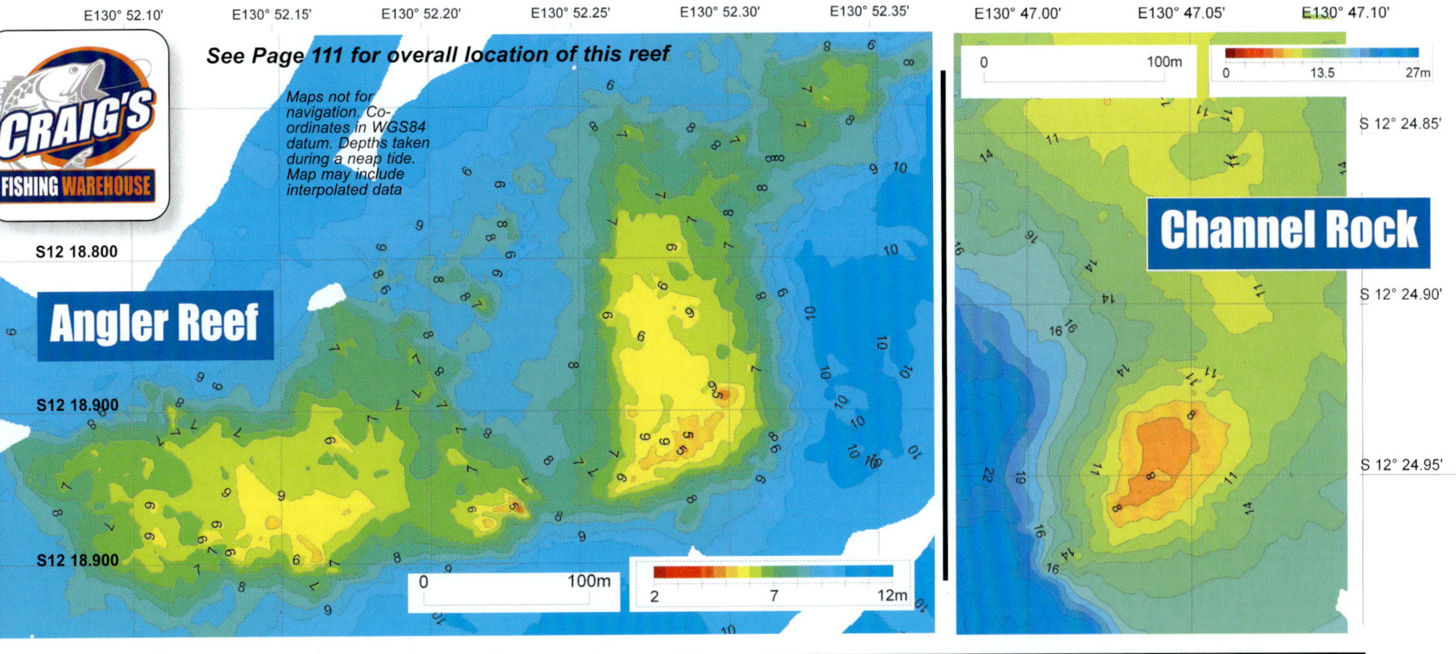

Six-Mile grounds for small boats

The deep "Six-Mile Grounds", located between Cox Peninsula and Channel Rock, are arguably the best natural reef fishing areas in Darwin Harbour.

The reefs are near enough to Darwin for small boats to fish in reasonable conditions, although it can quickly get rough during big tides.

Some of the best reefs are in the shipping channel, which means anchoring is not permitted. These reefs can be fished by drifting or using electric motor "spotlocks".

Even without anchoring, it is a legal requirement that ships are not obstructed, which means moving well in advance of a ship's approach.

The two reefs shown (right) are in deep water by Darwin standards, with "Razorback" sitting in 40m, coming up to 30m. "Maggies" is an extended ridge that comes up from 34m to 28m.

These depths were taken during neap tides.

"The Twins" is a broad reef consisting of two peaks.

Fish the turn of the tide, as these reefs are affected by strong currents, which can make it hard to hold a bait on the bottom. The fish usually bite best near the turn of the tide when the current goes slack.

Don't discount bigger tides, as jewfish are often caught when the the strong tidal flow ebbs.

On smaller tides snapper, redfish, grunter, flag and cod are caught. Mackerel are about in the dry season, along with tuna.

To catch mackerel during the day, drop livebaits of reef fish down to midwater or the bottom during neap or building tides.

Mackerel can also be caught by trolling at dawn and dusk.

Night fishing is productive for golden snapper.

Channel Rock (see map above right) is a prominent underwater feature at the entrance to Darwin Harbour.

It rises from 24m to 8m, creating tidal upwellings.

The highest part of the reef has a shipping marker nearby.

North of the rock is deep reef.

This area is affected by strong currents.

Use your boat lights at night. Keep watch at all times when fishing, as this is a busy shipping and boating area.

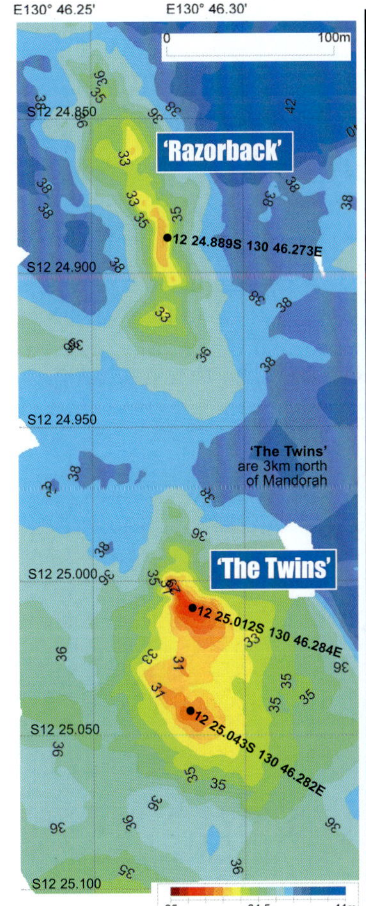

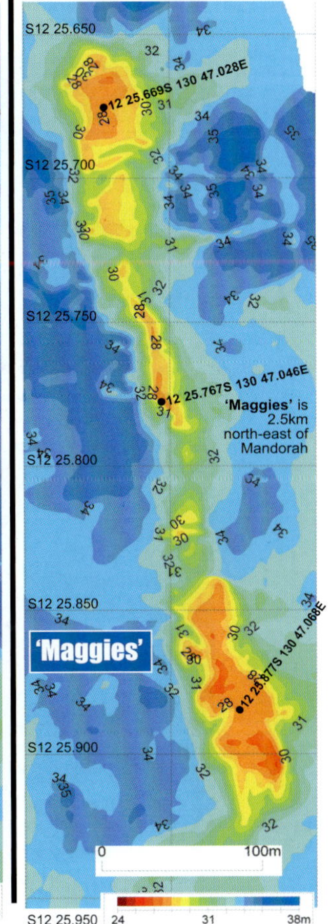

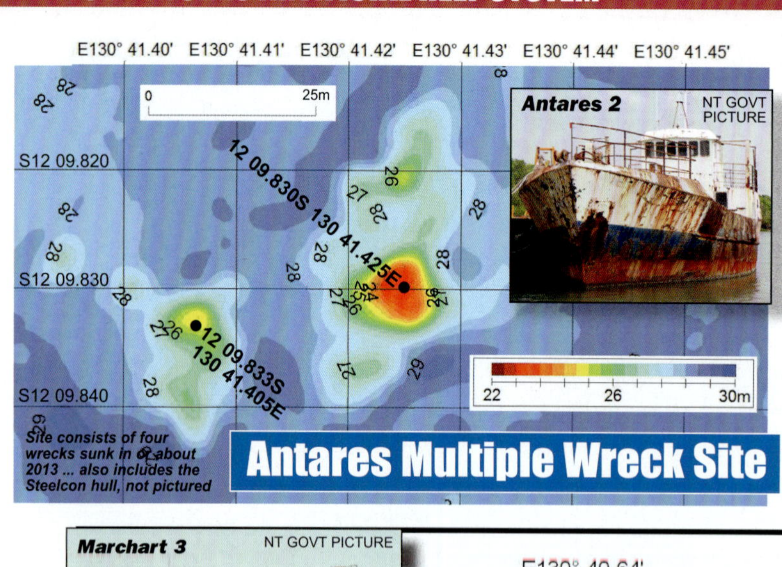

Amelia C ... lies next to the Antares 2, both sitting upright

Merindah Pearl ... now sitting upright about 100m north of Amelia C and Antares 2

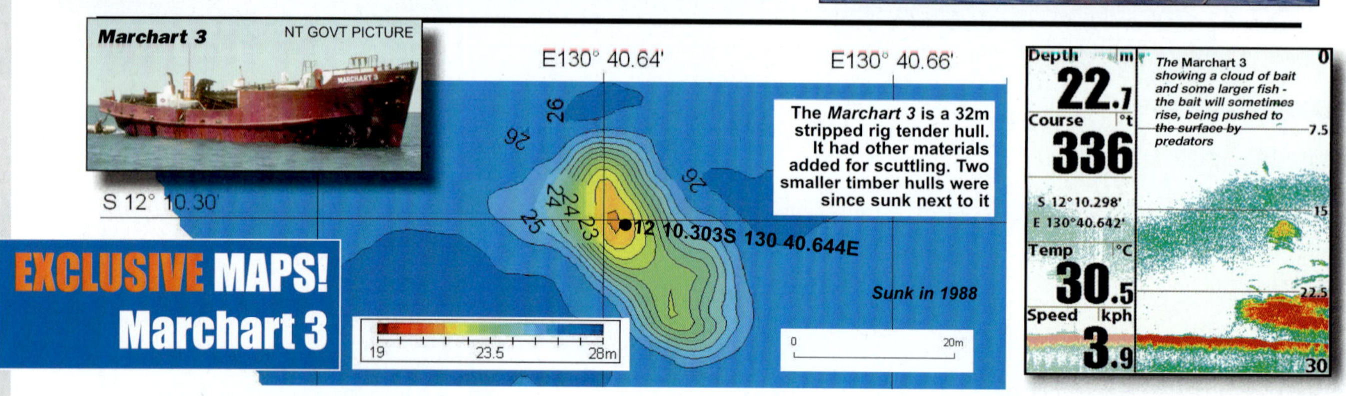

The *Marchart 3* is a 32m stripped rig tender hull. It had other materials added for scuttling. Two smaller timber hulls were since sunk next to it

The Marchart 3 showing a cloud of bait and some larger fish - the bait will sometimes rise, being pushed to the surface by predators

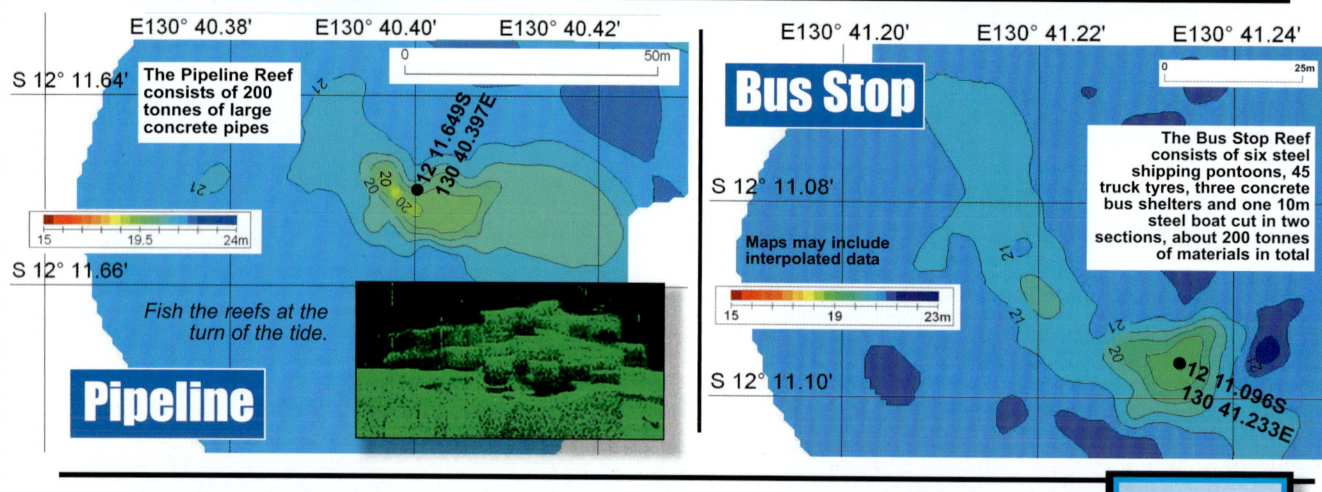

The Pipeline Reef consists of 200 tonnes of large concrete pipes

Fish the reefs at the turn of the tide.

The Bus Stop Reef consists of six steel shipping pontoons, 45 truck tyres, three concrete bus shelters and one 10m steel boat cut in two sections, about 200 tonnes of materials in total

Maps may include interpolated data

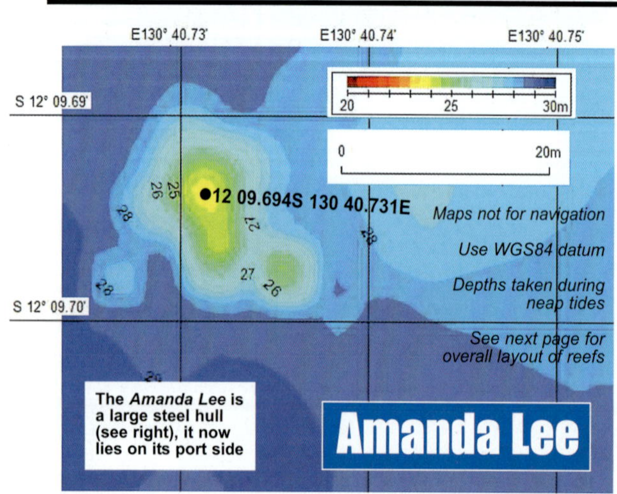

Maps not for navigation

Use WGS84 datum

Depths taken during neap tides

See next page for overall layout of reefs

The *Amanda Lee* is a large steel hull (see right), it now lies on its port side

The Amanda Lee was scuttled in 2011

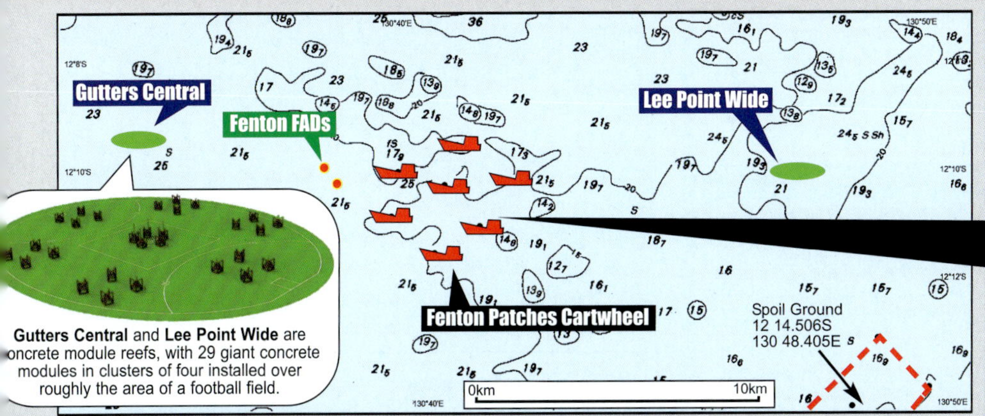

Gutters Central and Lee Point Wide are concrete module reefs, with 29 giant concrete modules in clusters of four installed over roughly the area of a football field.

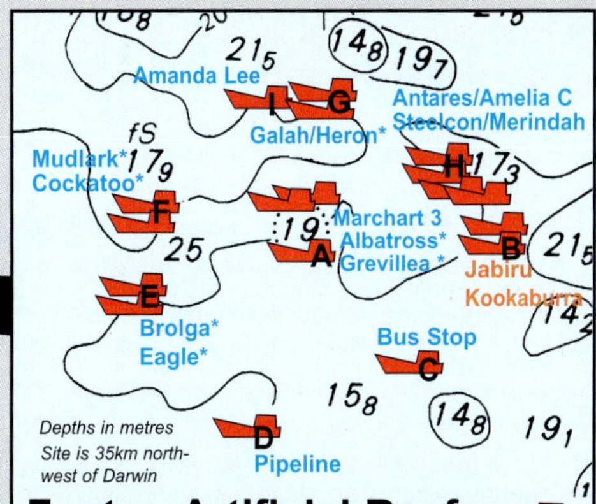

Fenton Artificial Reefs

A. *Marchart 3* and *Albatross*/Grevillea** (three hulls) 12 10.303S 130 40.644E 12 10.288S 130 40.578E
B. *Jabiru/Kookaburra* exact position unknown
C. *Bus Stop* 12 11.096S 130 41.233E
D. *Pipeline* 12 11.649S 130 40.397E
E. *Brolga*/Eagle** 12 10.999S 130 39.529E
F. *Cockatoo*/Mudlark** 12 10.099S 130 39.730E
G. *Galah*/Heron** 12 09.700S 130 40.764E
H. *Antares/Steelcon Merindah Pearl/Amelia C* 12 09.833S 130 41.405E 12 09.830S 130 41.425E
I. *Amanda Lee* 12 09.694S 130 40.731E

Location of timber *Jabiru/Kookaburra* hulls not known. Hulls marked with* have broken apart and/or shifted.

Fenton FADs

Fenton FAD 1 - 12 10.290S 130 38.544E
Fenton FAD 2 - 12 10.013S 130 38.232E

Engineered Reefs

Gutters Central - 12 09.459S 130 34.655E
Lee Point Wide - 12 10.083S 130 47.033E

See Page 158-159 for more FAD and reef detail.

Australia's best offshore reefs

The Fenton Patches Artificial Reef System is a unique fishing area 35km north-west of Darwin.

The patches are a series of shoals. The first wreck scuttled at the shoals was the steel rig tender *Marchart 3*, in 1988.

More structures were added in successive years, with the *Marchart 3* at the centre and other items located in a rough cartwheel pattern around it, about 1.85km apart.

Two reefs, *Pipeline* and *Bus Stop*, consist of pipes, concrete, tyres and more.

The 18m steel trepang boat *Amanda Lee* was added to the existing *Galah/Heron* timber hulls site in 2011. The *Antares 2, Amelia C, Merindah Pearl* steel trawlers and *Steelcon* hull form the largest site, most sunk in 2013.

Today the original *Marchart 3* still stands proud and produces plenty of fish.

In 2019 two engineered artificial reefs were installed 10km to the east and 12km to the west of the original Fenton reefs.

These two new sites include 29 custom concrete modules that are each 5m tall by 4m wide, set in clusters of four.

As well as the artificial reefs, this region has natural reef and two FADs.

The wrecks produce big black jewfish, golden snapper, redfish, trevally, cod, coral trout, mackerel and trevally, as well as occasional sailfish and black marlin.

Night fishing for jewfish and snapper can be more productive than day fishing.

Though the water is only around 20m deep, strong currents demand heavy sinkers. Strong tackle is needed to get fish in before sharks pounce.

Woods Inlet

Hotspot by ***Rick Huckstepp***

Woods Inlet is the first major offshoot on the eastern side of Darwin Harbour. I have a philosophy that the first creek or tributary in any major estuary fishes better than those further inland. Woods Inlet is no different.

Key to Map

1. A rockbar runs almost north/south and dries at spring low water. There are other small individual rocks scattered in the area, so caution should be exercised when approaching. At a 1.9m low tide as per the tide chart, there is .5m of water on the eastern side of the rocks which will be visible above the surface. This area is worth investigating when a spring tide drops to the point where the rocks start to become visible and also during September and October when barra gather to spawn during neap tides. The rocks will not protrude through the surface on a neap tide low water. Use shallow lures.
2. This area is an ordinary muddy bank at low tide. The end of the expansive flat that stretches from Talc Head meets the mangroves at this point and on tides other than neaps, fish will gather along this edge. The ideal time to look for them is on the last of the run-out and the first half hour of the run-in tide.
3. This big flat is a threadfin salmon haunt and anglers should look here on neap tides. Start at the bottom of the tide and drift over the flat as the water rises. A bamboo pole will alleviate the necessity to run the outboard motor. Undulations on the flat muddy bottom will hold the fish. Threadfin salmon will give away their presence when their dorsal and tail fins cut the surface. Barra will be at the front of the tide, sometimes in water so shallow they swim on their sides. The barra will be swimming for the protection of the mangroves at the back of the flat.
4. The top of the main watercourse of Woods Inlet is shallow. A mud islet is in the middle and the water behind holds mangrove jack and golden snapper snags. Barra can be caught in the gutters running into this deeper water.
5. A rockbar exists at this location. Take care during low tides. It is worth fishing for barra that are exiting the draining system.
6. This drain is a barramundi haunt. The upstream side of the gutter is the deepest and where most fish will be located.
7. This area dries in many places on spring lows. The muddy bottom will impede travel on the spring low. When the tide is down to 2m, prawns are flushed from the backwaters and you will find salmon feeding on them.
8. A mudbank separates the deeper channel on the east side of Woods Inlet from one not so deep on the west side. The west side will have about 0.7m of water in it on a 1.9m low tide. Fish the gutters.
9. This is the largest creek in Woods Inlet and the first you come to when travelling upstream on the eastern side. The second gutter on the left hand side when travelling up it is just west of where the creek branches into a fork. Cast into this gutter and then anchor in the gutter and cast to the centre of the creek. A gravel bed exists here and fish will forage on it as the tide turns. Barra, trevally, whiting and flathead can be caught here. Lead and copper cable on the bottom of the creek is a legacy of WWII.

Talc Head and Mica Beach

PIC A - see next page

Charles Point ... rough when wind and tide are opposed. No anchoring or alighting permitted under Kenbi rules

Tapa Bay central reef

Point Margaret ... much of this area is Aboriginal land that can not be fished above mean low tide

West Point and Mandorah wharf, which is to be redeveloped with associated rock walls

Harney Beach rocks - troll current rips for queenfish and trevally. No anchoring or alighting under Kenbi land claim

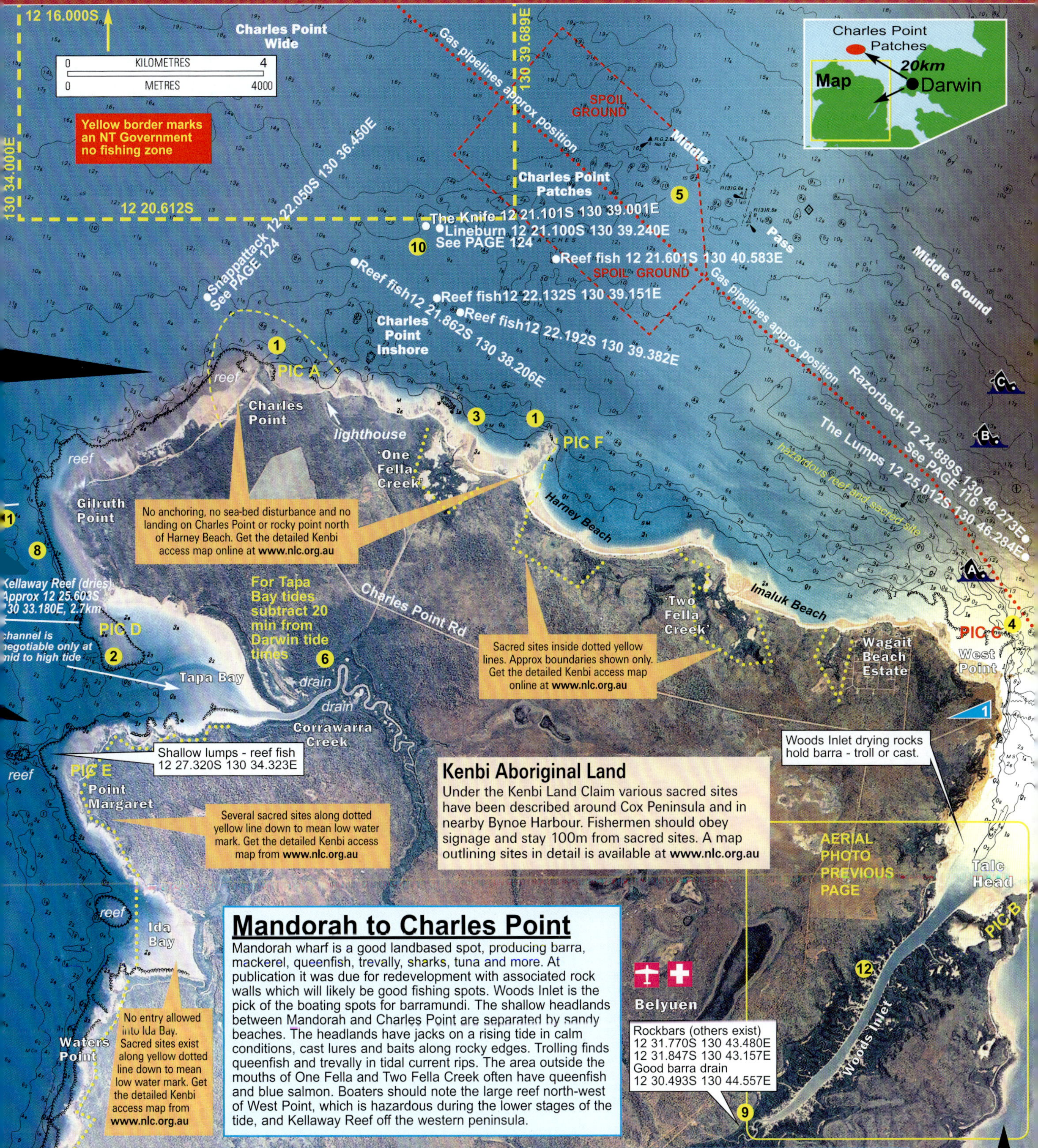

12 16.000S
130 39.689E
130 34.000E
12 20.612S

KILOMETRES 0 4
METRES 0 4000

Yellow border marks an NT Government no fishing zone

Charles Point Wide

Charles Point Patches
20km
Map
Darwin

Gas pipelines approx position
SPOIL GROUND
Middle
Pass
Middle Ground

Charles Point Patches
The Knife 12 21.101S 130 39.001E
Lineburn 12 21.100S 130 39.240E
See PAGE 124
Reef fish 12 21.601S 130 40.583E
SPOIL GROUND
Snappattack 12 22.050S 130 36.450E
See PAGE 124
Reef fish 12 21.862S 130 38.206E
Reef fish 12 22.132S 130 39.151E
Reef fish 12 22.192S 130 39.382E
Charles Point Inshore
Gas pipelines approx position
Razorback 12 24.889S 130 46.273E
See PAGE 116
The Lumps 12 25.012S 130 46.284E
hazardous reef and sacred site

PIC A
Charles Point
lighthouse
One Fella Creek
PIC F
Harney Beach
Gilruth Point
Kellaway Reef (dries) Approx 12 25.603S 130 33.180E, 2.7km
PIC D
channel is negotiable only at mid to high tide
Tapa Bay

No anchoring, no sea-bed disturbance and no landing on Charles Point or rocky point north of Harney Beach. Get the detailed Kenbi access map online at **www.nlc.org.au**

For Tapa Bay tides subtract 20 min from Darwin tide times

Charles Point Rd
Two Fella Creek
Imaluk Beach
Wagait Beach Estate
PIC C
West Point

Sacred sites inside dotted yellow lines. Approx boundaries shown only. Get the detailed Kenbi access map online at **www.nlc.org.au**

drain
drain
Corrawarra Creek

Shallow lumps - reef fish 12 27.320S 130 34.323E

PIC E
Point Margaret

Several sacred sites along dotted yellow line down to mean low water mark. Get the detailed Kenbi access map from **www.nlc.org.au**

Woods Inlet drying rocks hold barra - troll or cast.

Kenbi Aboriginal Land

Under the Kenbi Land Claim various sacred sites have been described around Cox Peninsula and in nearby Bynoe Harbour. Fishermen should obey signage and stay 100m from sacred sites. A map outlining sites in detail is available at **www.nlc.org.au**

AERIAL PHOTO PREVIOUS PAGE

Talc Head
PIC B
Ida Bay
Waters Point

No entry allowed into Ida Bay. Sacred sites exist along yellow dotted line down to mean low water mark. Get the detailed Kenbi access map from **www.nlc.org.au**

Mandorah to Charles Point

Mandorah wharf is a good landbased spot, producing barra, mackerel, queenfish, trevally, sharks, tuna and more. At publication it was due for redevelopment with associated rock walls which will likely be good fishing spots. Woods Inlet is the pick of the boating spots for barramundi. The shallow headlands between Mandorah and Charles Point are separated by sandy beaches. The headlands have jacks on a rising tide in calm conditions, cast lures and baits along rocky edges. Trolling finds queenfish and trevally in tidal current rips. The area outside the mouths of One Fella and Two Fella Creek often have queenfish and blue salmon. Boaters should note the large reef north-west of West Point, which is hazardous during the lower stages of the tide, and Kellaway Reef off the western peninsula.

Belyuen

Rockbars (others exist)
12 31.770S 130 43.480E
12 31.847S 130 43.157E
Good barra drain
12 30.493S 130 44.557E

Woods Inlet

N

Key to Map

Hotspots

1 and 1. Shallow headlands. Troll current rips for queenfish, trevally, barracuda, cast for jacks, barra. No anchoring or landing allowed above mean low water mark, see NLC website.
2. Reef edges - barra, salmon, jacks.
3. Outside creek mouth, barra, blue salmon, queenfish. Kenbi sacred sites apply to creeks, see map on NLC website.
4. West Point - queenfish in tidal rip. Jacks on reef edge on rising tide.
5. Snapper, jewfish over rubble and small ridges. Fish turn of tide.
6. Barra at small creek mouth.
7. Small coral trout around lumps.
8. Jacks against rocks on rising tide.
9. Mud crabs on first push of big tides.
10. Jewfish, snapper, cod.
11. Area wide of Gilruth Point known as 'The Farm'. Start at 12 24.645S 130 31.597E for reef fish.
12. Barra on mud drains on falling tide. Fish week days when fewer boats about.

Wrecks

A. NR *Diemen*, Cyclone Tracy trawler wreck, now covered by sand, 12 25.596S, 130 45.917E, depth 8m. May uncover after storms. Beware stonefish.
B. *Darwin Princess*, Cyclone Tracy wreck lying upside down, 12 23.888S 130 45.925E, jewfish, snapper - beware ships in this area.
C. *Booya*, Cyclone Tracy wreck and no fishing sanctuary - stay at least 150m away from 12 23.381S 130 46.281E. Can be dived with registered dive operators.

Nearest launch sites

1. Mandorah public ramp. Darwin boaters usually launch their boats from city ramps and travel across the harbour.

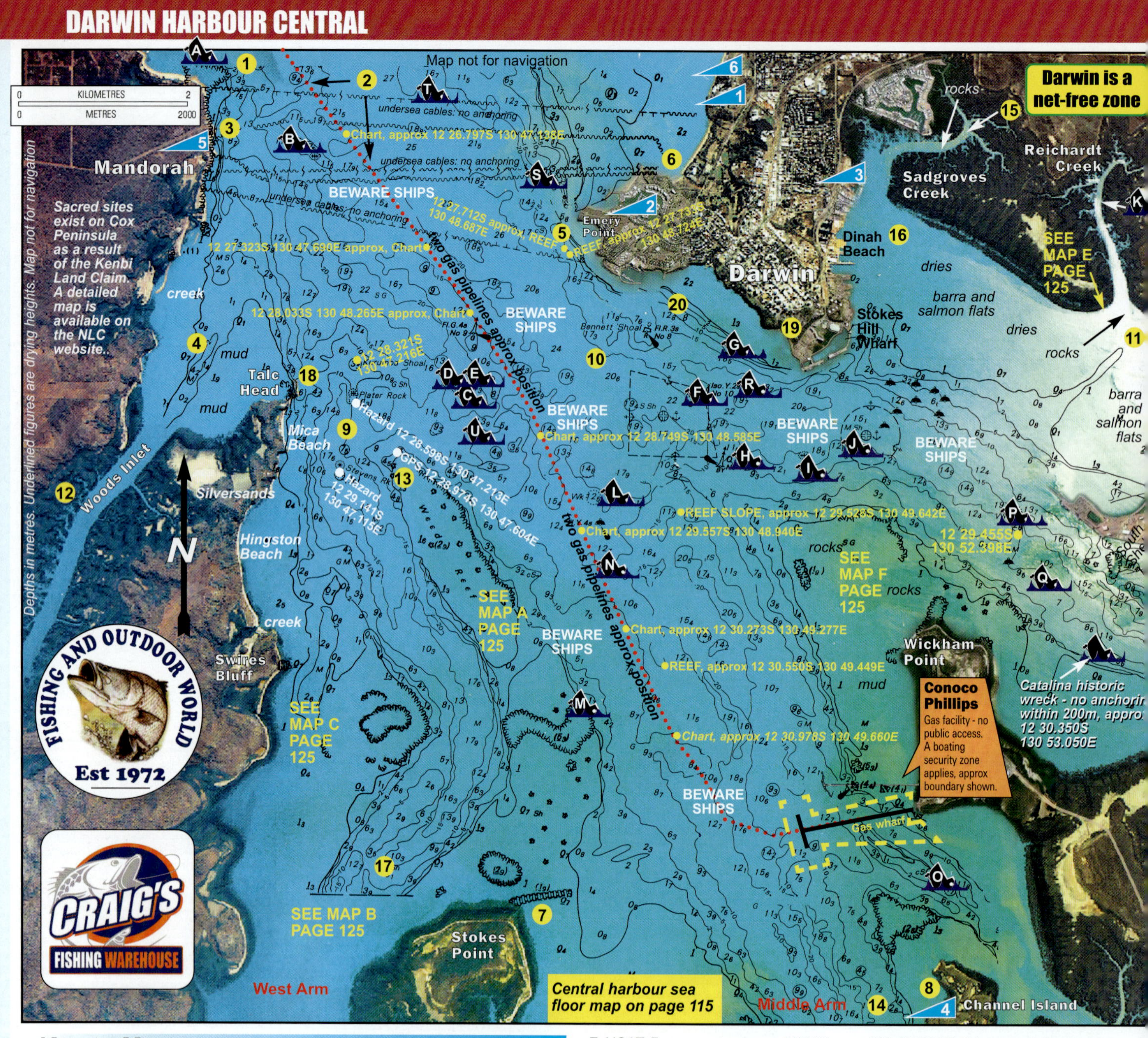

Key to Map

Hotspots & hazards

1. Rip off West Point has queenfish. Jacks against rocks on rising tide.
2. Inpex and Conoco rock-covered underwater gas pipelines: reef fish.
3. Mandorah wharf - trevally, queenfish, mackerel, tuna, barra. Rock walls to be installed here.
4. Drying rock patches hold barra.
5. Rough, deep bottom s-w of Emery Point has reef fish, snapper at night.
6. Good fishing area, baitfish often at creek mouth near the bridge.
7. Stokes Point rocky flat holds barra, salmon, cod in calm weather.
8. Landbased barra fishing off Channel Island rocks, long walk required.
9. Navigation hazards: Plater Rock and Stevens Rock become drying pinnacles towards low tide.
10. Longtail tuna schools in dry season - look for birds and surface activity.
11. Troll dual creek mouth for queenfish, salmon, barracuda on high tide. Fish low tide for barra.
12. Barra on mud drains, outgoing tide.
13. Weed Reef dries at mid-low tide. Trevally, queenfish on upper tide. Bommies and drop-off at northern tip.
14. Town Hall Hole has large jewfish, cod, snapper. Fish turn of neap tides.
15. Low tide hole, livebait for barra.
16. Mudflat edge has barra, salmon, snapper and queenfish, best Sept-Nov. Bait moves over flat on run-in tide. Move to mangrove edge as tide builds.
17. Deep rock patches, reef fish.
18. Barra where rocks meet mud near low tide in calm weather. Prawns in large mud drain on nearby flat.
19. Good landbased fishing for queenfish, trevally, barra. Use livebait.
20. Milkfish and mullet - use bread bait and berley. **Note:** Doctor's Gully has a fish-feeding tourist attraction with a no-fishing zone around it.

Wrecks in WGS84

A. NR *Diemen* (just off map), trawler sunk by Cyclone Tracy, 12 25.596S 130 45.917E, 8m and sometimes visible at low tide, mostly covered in sand. Occasional barramundi.
B. *Mandorah Queen*, ferry sunk by Cyclone Tracy, sits at bottom of deep sandbar (hull) with only a small still portion exposed, 12 26.563S 130 46.698E, 17m, jewfish.
C, D and E. The *Ham Luong, John Holland Barge, Song Saigon* are a grouped artificial reef. Use position 12 28.481S, 130 48.091E to locate the group, in about 20m of water.
F. USAT *Peary*, part-salvaged WWII wreck, reef fish, occasional big jewfish, 12 28.521S 130 49.788E, at 28m. Mini map page 113.
G. *Bellbird*, trawler sunk by Cyclone Tracy, 12 28.136S 130 50.090E, sits upside down at 12m, reef fish, schools of baitfish.
H. *British Motorist* (rubble only), approx 12 28.967S 130 50.336E, 16m.
I. *Landing Barge* 12 29.155S 130 50.712E. Reef fish.
J. *Zealandia*, part-salvaged WWII wreck, 12 28.883S 130 51.048E 18m, cod, snapper. Mini map page 113.
K. *Chang 1028* (east side of Reichardt Creek), exposed low tide.
L. USAT *Meigs*, part-salvaged WWII wreck, 12 29.269S 130 49.109E (DGPS) 18m, small reef fish, jewfish.
M. *Yu Han 22*, engine block exposed near low tide, 12 31.002S 130 49.035E (**TAKE CARE:** waypoint is 50m north-east of hazardous reef.)
N. USAT *Mauna Loa* (part-salvaged WWII wreck) 12 29.815S 130 49.162E rubble at 17m, jewfish usually at southern end of wreck, but sometimes swim around the general area at midwater.
O. *Ellengowan* (not much left) approx 12 32.274S 130 52.103E, 12m, snapper, jewfish, barra.
P. Small steel barge 12 29.346S 130 52.381E, 24m, wreck lies near reef in deep water. Snapper, jewfish.
Q. *Kelat*, coal barge, 12 29.910S 130 52.660E, mostly rubble, 12m, reef fish.
R. Sunken freight containers, 12 28.424S 130 50.301E, jewfish.
S. Small barge, jewfish, cod, snapper 12 26.906S 130 48.610E, 22m.
T. Amphibious landing craft, snapper, 12 26.278S 130 47.888E, 23m.
U. The 25m steel *Medkhanun* was scuttled in 2007. Lies on its side with a high profile on the sounder, approx 12 28.722S 130 48.142E, 18m. Jewfish, snapper. See page 113.

Launch sites

1. Doyles ramp (Conacher St, next to ski club), exposed, useable above 2.5m tide.
2. Cullen Bay toll ramp, all tides, sea entry through lock. VHF channel 11.
3. Dinah Beach ramp and pontoon, sheltered, use above 2m tide, best Darwin ramp, lacks parking on weekends.
4. Channel Island ramp (25km west of Palmerston), most tides, beware rocks and currents on big tides.
5. Mandorah public ramp.
6. Vesteys Beach, upper tide, exposed.

Local tides have up to about 7.42m movement.

East Arm boat ramp has a pontoon and loading platforms

HELIFISH PICTURE

Key to Map

Hotspots

1. Fish East Arm rock walls by boat for barra, jacks, bream. Best at night at high tide. During daylight use tiny lures and light leaders. No fishing from wharf. Darwin end of rock wall has queenfish and trevally in the incoming tidal rips, troll or jig.
2. Barra and salmon can be trolled in Myrmidon Creek but watch the rock bottom. Trevally often patrol the mouth.
3. The 9m-deep rocky reef in the mid-harbour at approx 12 30.121S 130 53.832E has snapper, grunter, bream, cod.
4. Trolling and casting for barra, salmon.
5. Drift the upper reaches on the first of the incoming tide and toss shallow lures.
6. Small ledge runs along the left as you go upstream. Anchor on the ledge as the tide starts to leave the mangroves. Berley for bream and snapper. In the Wet, salmon haunt the mudflat at the mouth. Rocks on the upstream side of the mouth hold jacks. The barra in the upper reaches sit along the bank.
7. Small rocks along eastern shoreline. Worth fishing if egrets are nearby.
8. Large rockbar on north shore just west of bridge and boat ramp fishable from shore at low tide for barra, jacks, snapper. Ramp has a fishing jetty. Jacks around bridge pylons.
9. Shallow creeks. Use an electric motor to manoeuvre through shallows while you fish the creek mouths.
10. Troll mouth on a 1.5m low for barra.
11. Creek fishes well at times for mud crabs. Further up is an area of oyster rocks, one patch of which has deep water around it. Fish it for barra. Rocky bottom.
12. Barra, salmon around flats.
13. Hudson Creek - troll the channel edges at the mouth for barra at low tide. Note that an old concrete landing lies in a hazardous position about midstream in the upper creek, see map.
14. Creek has bream, barra, snapper. Troll rocky upper reaches and wider stretches where rock gives way to mud. During the Build-up there is a barra on most drains. In the dry season there is sight-fishing inside the mouth with barra, salmon, trevally and queenies - a sandbar protrudes almost all the way across from half tide.
15. Good trolling inside and around the mouth. Bait fish the rocky areas and banks for snapper, barra and cod.
16. Rocks exist throughout upper Elizabeth River, hazardous at lower stages of tide. See next page for detail. Good fishing for snapper, bream, jacks, crabs and barra.
17. Fish near rocks inside island near creek mouth at low tide.
18. Fish creeks and drains for barra.

Catalina wrecks

The Catalinas are seaplane wrecks, sunk during WWII. Most of these "flying boats" still present a fair lump on the bottom and hold snapper, jewfish, cod and nightfish.

A. Catalina, 12 29.788S 130 54.521E
B. Catalina, 12 29.745S 130 53.817E
Catalinas C and D no longer accessible.

Launch sites

1. East Arm ramp, west of Hudson Creek, pontoon, loading platforms, most tides. Landbased fishing around carpark rock walls, see pic above left.
2. Palmerston ramp, with fishing jetty, pontoon and more, next to Elizabeth River bridge, useable most tides, see pic below.

Large concrete former barge landing in middle of side creek surrounded by various debris, navigation hazard at approx 12 28 228S 130 56.809E

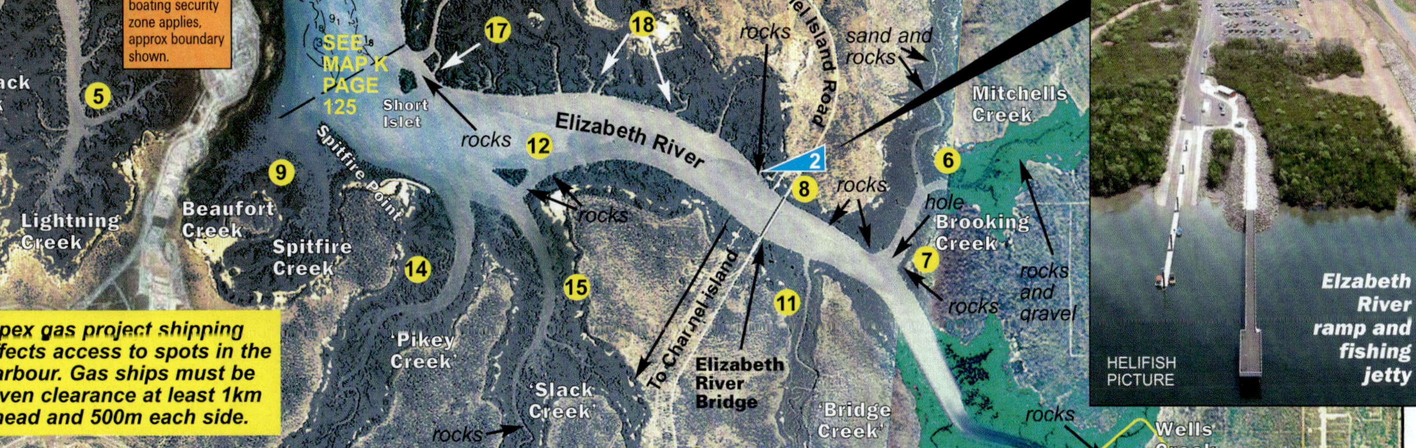

Inpex gas project shipping affects access to spots in the harbour. Gas ships must be given clearance at least 1km ahead and 500m each side.

HELIFISH PICTURE

Elzabeth River ramp and fishing jetty

Darwin Harbour

The harbour's three arms form a vast expanse of mangroves, tidal creeks, drying flats and reef, swept by tides of 7m+, and flushed with annual monsoonal rainfall. Darwin and Palmerston lie on the northern side, and most of the harbour shoreline is undeveloped. The harbour's WWII and cyclone wrecks have jewfish, golden snapper, cod, tuskfish, flag and redfish. Barramundi fishing has become hugely popular since commercial barramundi netting was stopped in 1997, and all other gill nets removed in 2007. There are several long concrete boat ramps, but access is problematic on the lowest tides, so trips must be planned accordingly. Like most of the harbour arms, East Arm (above) is lined with mangroves and offers good mud drain, rockbar and flats barramundi fishing, especially during the warm Build-up. Tidal creeks produce barramundi, blue and threadfin salmon, jewfish, bream, snapper, queenfish, jacks, grunter, trevally, barracuda and mud crabs. Drift quietly over flats during neap tides and you will see fish. Barramundi and other fish move into the mangroves with the rising tide. Rock walls or headlands washed by strong currents often have queenfish and trevally in the rips. Fish close to the walls with small lures and light leaders for barra, snapper, bream and jacks. Lucky anglers will catch coral trout and cobia in Darwin Harbour, as well as longtail tuna and spotted, grey and spanish mackerel. Night fishing is productive. A 2004 Darwin mud crab competition recorded an *average* weight per crab of 1.6kg, and excellent catches continue today. There is a run of prawns during and after each wet season but they are generally small. Landbased fishing can be had from wharves and rocky foreshores, usually at high tide. Increased shipping has changed aspects of harbour use, as boaters must give right of way to ships well in advance. Skippers should also check marine notices before fishing at **https://nt.gov.au/marine/marine-safety/notice-to-mariners**

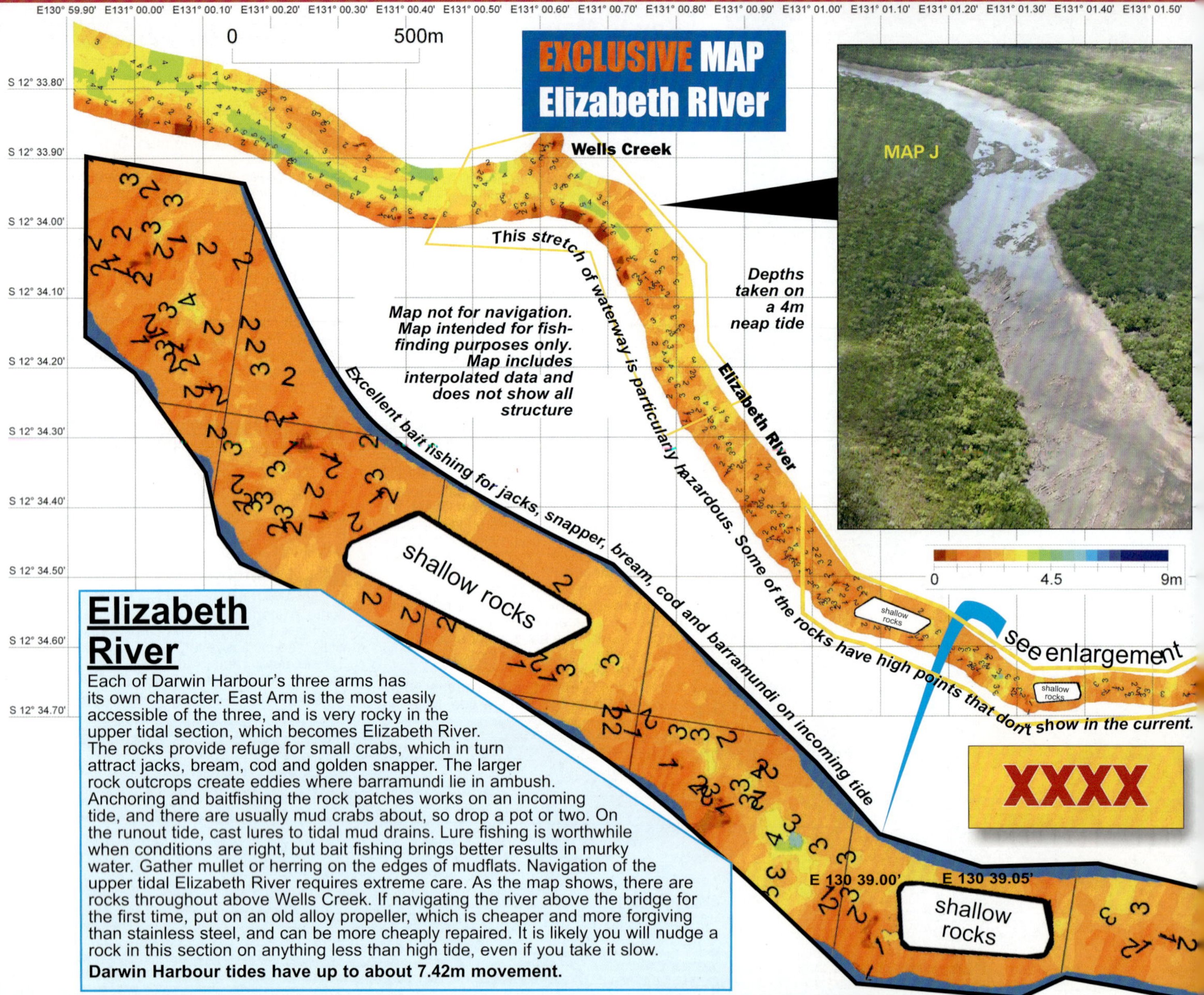

EXCLUSIVE MAP Elizabeth River

Wells Creek

MAP J

This stretch of waterway is particularly hazardous. Some of the rocks have high points that don't show in the current.

Depths taken on a 4m neap tide

Map not for navigation. Map intended for fish-finding purposes only. Map includes interpolated data and does not show all structure

Excellent bait fishing for jacks, snapper, bream, cod and barramundi on incoming tide

shallow rocks

see enlargement

Elizabeth River

Each of Darwin Harbour's three arms has its own character. East Arm is the most easily accessible of the three, and is very rocky in the upper tidal section, which becomes Elizabeth River. The rocks provide refuge for small crabs, which in turn attract jacks, bream, cod and golden snapper. The larger rock outcrops create eddies where barramundi lie in ambush. Anchoring and baitfishing the rock patches works on an incoming tide, and there are usually mud crabs about, so drop a pot or two. On the runout tide, cast lures to tidal mud drains. Lure fishing is worthwhile when conditions are right, but bait fishing brings better results in murky water. Gather mullet or herring on the edges of mudflats. Navigation of the upper tidal Elizabeth River requires extreme care. As the map shows, there are rocks throughout above Wells Creek. If navigating the river above the bridge for the first time, put on an old alloy propeller, which is cheaper and more forgiving than stainless steel, and can be more cheaply repaired. It is likely you will nudge a rock in this section on anything less than high tide, even if you take it slow.

Darwin Harbour tides have up to about 7.42m movement.

Charles Point hotspots

IMPORTANT! These three fishing spots are near a reef closure zone - know your zones before fishing. See the map on Page 121 for more information.

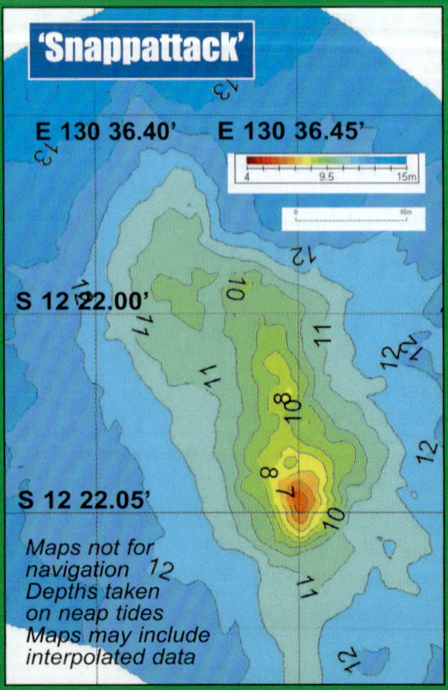

'Snappattack'

Maps not for navigation. Depths taken on neap tides. Maps may include interpolated data

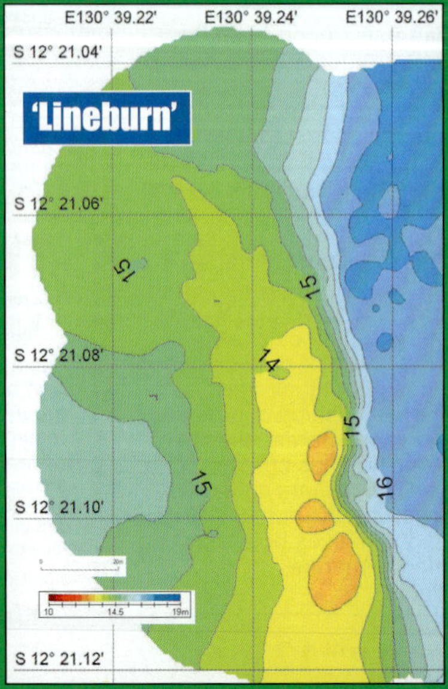

'Lineburn'

EXCLUSIVE MAPS 'The Knife'

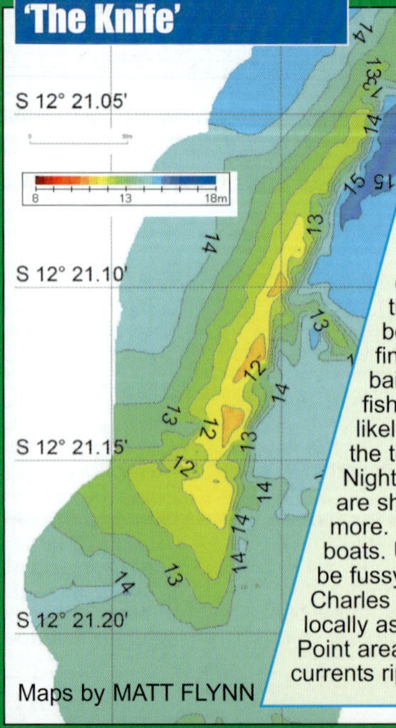

Charles Point Patches is a large area of reef and sand/mud/rock bottom 22km w-n-w of Darwin. Most of the patches do not rise much from the seabed. At times this area holds schools of big black jewfish. Blue salmon and golden snapper are also encountered, along with goldspot cod, grunter, flag, redfish and passing pelagic fish. Patches of reef can be found by looking for tidal current lines and mud boils. Move around until you find a spot that is showing fish or bait schools on the sounder. If no fish can be found, anchor on a likely spot and wait, as the turn of the tide is often when fish bite. Night fishing is best. Three spots are shown here, but there are many more. If in doubt, look for other boats. Use fresh bait, as jewfish can be fussy. Further west, going around Charles Point, is more reef, known locally as 'The Farm'. The Charles Point area can chop up badly as tidal currents rip around the point.

Maps by MATT FLYNN

MATT FLYNN PICTURES

MAP A: Weed Reef in central Darwin Harbour. MAP B: Looking towards Stokes Point and West Arm from the gap in Weed Reef on a .1m low tide. INSET BELOW: Plater Rock near Talc Head on a .3m spring low tide 12 28.598S 130 47.213E

MAP B

MAP C

MAP C: Looking from Swires Bluff to the gap between Weed Reef and Stokes Point, outside West Arm: MAP J: Elizabeth River upstream, with MAP K showing where it enters the harbour

difficult to proceed further except at high tide

MAP K

MAP E: Reichardt and Bleesers Creeks on a .1m low tide

MAP D

Beware patches of drying rock 'The Sirens' in the Middle Arm shallows, between Channel Island and Haycock Island. These sit just below the surface at various stages of the tide. They are at approx 12 34.993S 130 55.112E with another patch at 12 34.743S 130 54.575E. See Map G above right.

The harbour's West Arm has substantial drying sandbars and rock extending from Stokes Point and again 2.5km offshore at 12 31.122S 130 48.790E and 12 31.085S 130 47.458 which can catch unwary boaters. See Map C on this page.

MAP F: Looking over Wickham Point to East Arm Port

MAP L: Pioneer Creek, looking upstream towards the many rockbars

MAP O

MAP O: 'Three Ways' near the top of 'Little West Arm'

MAP N: Far up West Arm.
MAP M: The rocky Pioneer Creek.
MAP Q: Looking up the western leg of West Arm

MAP M

MAP G: Middle Arm's Haycock Reach

MAP H: Middle Arm near Middle Arm boat ramp, which is 800m from the visible pumping jetty

MAP I: These two rockbars are south of Middle Arm boat ramp at about 12 41.311S 130 57.568E and 12 41.724S 130 57.467E
MAP P: The two eastern legs of West Arm ... shallow and almost impossible to access on a spring low tide

MAP P

MAP Q

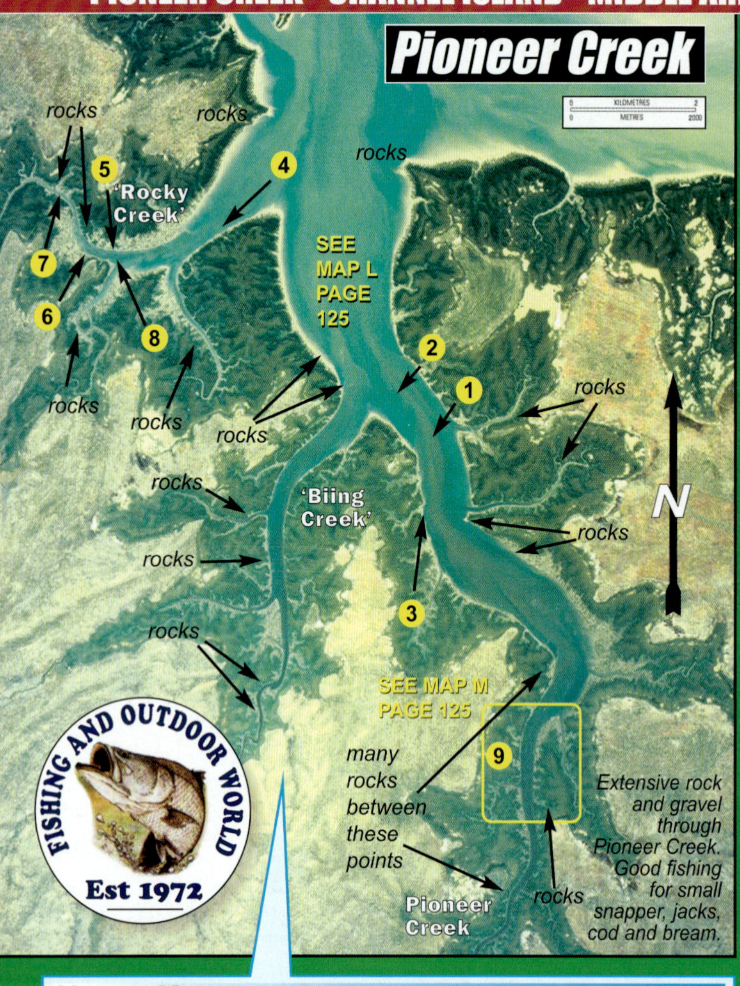

Key to Map

Hotspots

1 & 2. Two rockbars extend across the main creek. They can be found on the sounder at about 12 38.036S 130 53.109E and 12 37.701S 130 52.895E. Beware flats.
3. This rockbar is visible on the downstream side of a gutter. The rocks protrude up through the mangroves on the point and are high and dry at all tides. Anchor upstream on a runout tide, and cast for snapper and jacks. Barra may be in the gutter as the tide gets low.
4. Two distinct humps running at right angles to the shoreline can be found here using a sounder. They rise up from the bottom about 2m on the sounder. On spring low tides they are only 10m out from the shoreline and are ideal staging areas for most estuary species on the ebbing tide. Try trolling over the lumps with lures at various depths.
5. Gutters on the inside of the bend are good salmon and barra haunts.
6. A hazardous rockbar in this area.
7. Travelling upstream, look for timber structure. Ideal for barramundi, jacks and salmon.
8. There are some serious bommies midstream and on low tide, take care not to collide with them.
9. Excellent fishing at times around the rocks.

Launch sites

1. See the Darwin Harbour Middle Arm map (next page) for the nearest public boat ramp.

Channel Island

Channel Island, at the top of Darwin Harbour's Middle Arm, has good land-based fishing (1). Queenfish and barramundi are the main catch on lures, with cod, golden snapper, mangrove jacks and bream on bait. The rocky area under the bridge (2) fishes well at times for trevally, queenfish and jacks. Livebait is most effective.

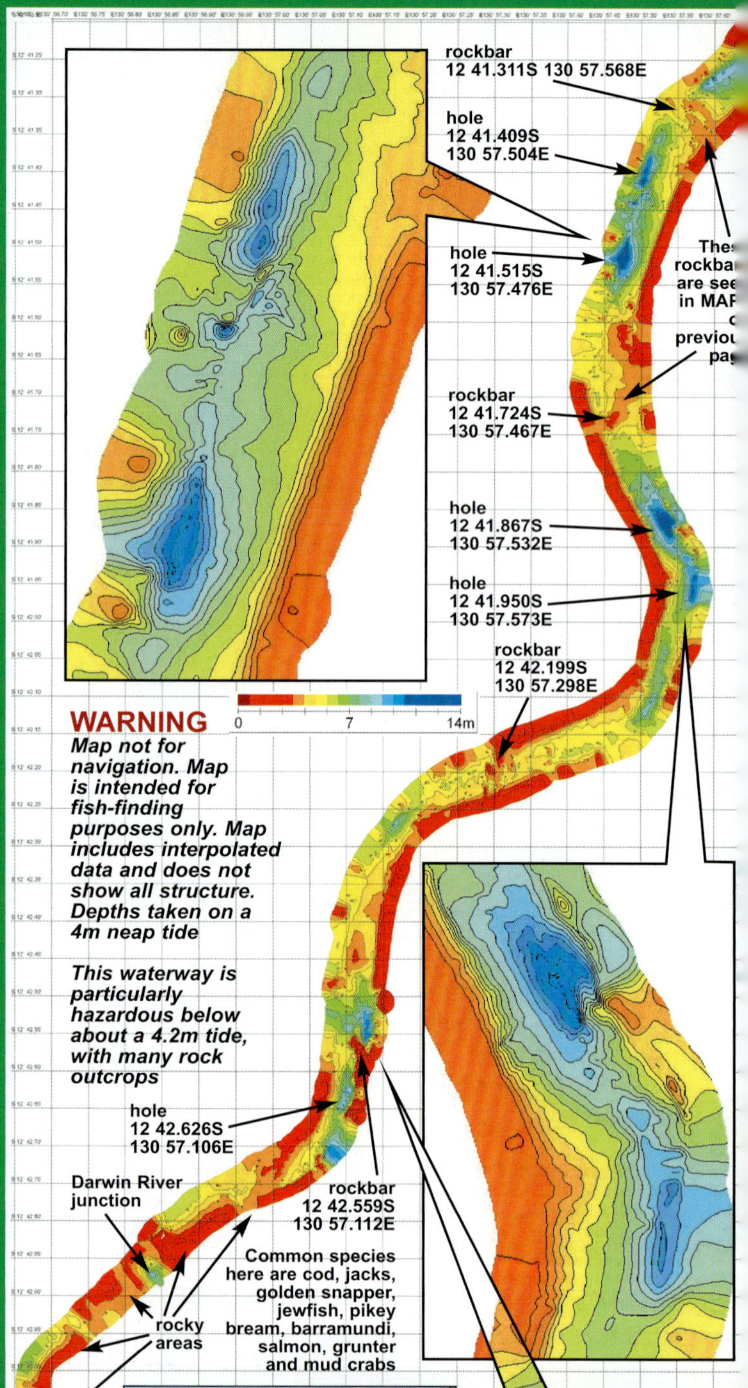

rockbar 12 41.311S 130 57.568E
hole 12 41.409S 130 57.504E
hole 12 41.515S 130 57.476E
These rockbars are seen in MAP ... previous page
rockbar 12 41.724S 130 57.467E
hole 12 41.867S 130 57.532E
hole 12 41.950S 130 57.573E
rockbar 12 42.199S 130 57.298E
hole 12 42.626S 130 57.106E
rockbar 12 42.559S 130 57.112E
Darwin River junction
rocky areas
Southport

0 7 14m

WARNING

Map not for navigation. Map is intended for fish-finding purposes only. Map includes interpolated data and does not show all structure. Depths taken on a 4m neap tide

This waterway is particularly hazardous below about a 4.2m tide, with many rock outcrops

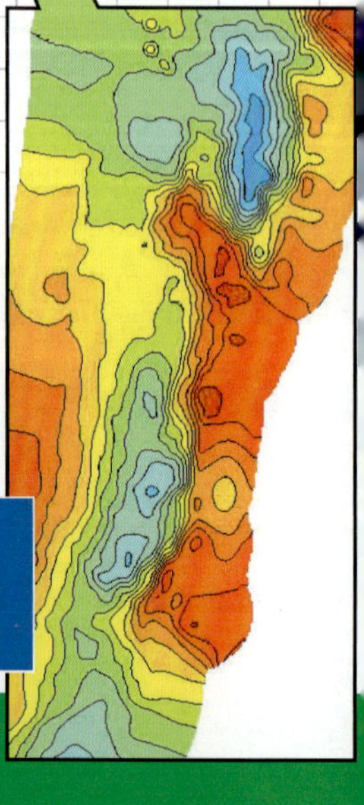

Common species here are cod, jacks, golden snapper, jewfish, pikey bream, barramundi, salmon, grunter and mud crabs

Rock patches hold barramundi near low tide and golden snapper at high tide

NTMAG EXCLUSIVE MAPS
Middle Arm by Matt Flynn

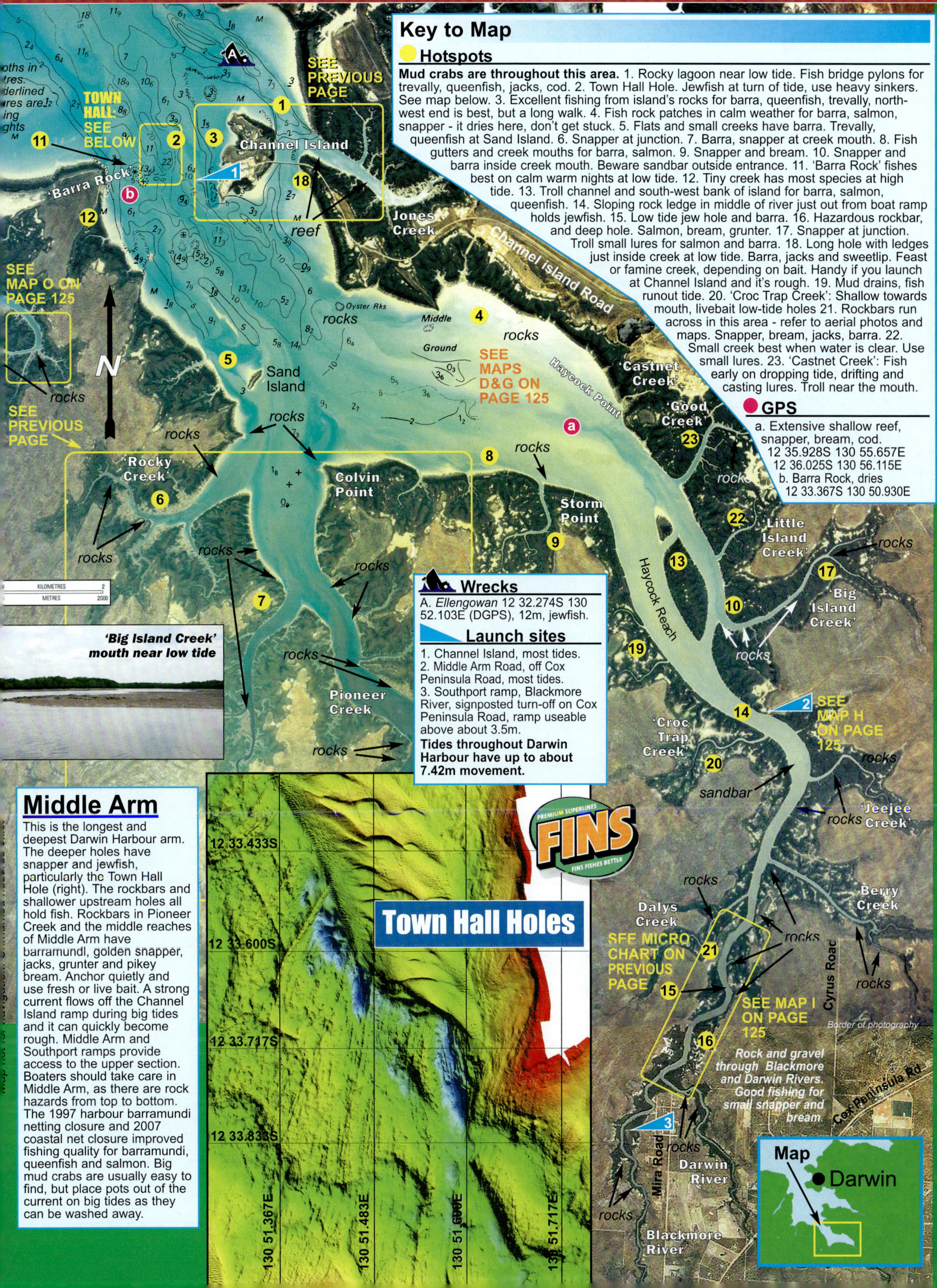

Key to Map

Hotspots

Mud crabs are throughout this area. 1. Rocky lagoon near low tide. Fish bridge pylons for trevally, queenfish, jacks, cod. 2. Town Hall Hole. Jewfish at turn of tide, use heavy sinkers. See map below. 3. Excellent fishing from island's rocks for barra, queenfish, trevally, north-west end is best, but a long walk. 4. Fish rock patches in calm weather for barra, salmon, snapper - it dries here, don't get stuck. 5. Flats and small creeks have barra. Trevally, queenfish at Sand Island. 6. Snapper at junction. 7. Barra, snapper at creek mouth. 8. Fish gutters and creek mouths for barra, salmon. 9. Snapper and bream. 10. Snapper and barra inside creek mouth. Beware sandbar outside entrance. 11. 'Barra Rock' fishes best on calm warm nights at low tide. 12. Tiny creek has most species at high tide. 13. Troll channel and south-west bank of island for barra, salmon, queenfish. 14. Sloping rock ledge in middle of river just out from boat ramp holds jewfish. 15. Low tide jew hole and barra. 16. Hazardous rockbar, and deep hole. Salmon, bream, grunter. 17. Snapper at junction. Troll small lures for salmon and barra. 18. Long hole with ledges just inside creek at low tide. Barra, jacks and sweetlip. Feast or famine creek, depending on bait. Handy if you launch at Channel Island and it's rough. 19. Mud drains, fish runout tide. 20. 'Croc Trap Creek': Shallow towards mouth, livebait low-tide holes 21. Rockbars run across in this area - refer to aerial photos and maps. Snapper, bream, jacks, barra. 22. Small creek best when water is clear. Use small lures. 23. 'Castnet Creek': Fish early on dropping tide, drifting and casting lures. Troll near the mouth.

GPS

a. Extensive shallow reef, snapper, bream, cod.
12 35.928S 130 55.657E
12 36.025S 130 56.115E
b. Barra Rock, dries
12 33.367S 130 50.930E

Wrecks

A. *Ellengowan* 12 32.274S 130 52.103E (DGPS), 12m, jewfish.

Launch sites

1. Channel Island, most tides.
2. Middle Arm Road, off Cox Peninsula Road, most tides.
3. Southport ramp, Blackmore River, signposted turn-off on Cox Peninsula Road, ramp useable above about 3.5m.

Tides throughout Darwin Harbour have up to about 7.42m movement.

'Big Island Creek' mouth near low tide

Middle Arm

This is the longest and deepest Darwin Harbour arm. The deeper holes have snapper and jewfish, particularly the Town Hall Hole (right). The rockbars and shallower upstream holes all hold fish. Rockbars in Pioneer Creek and the middle reaches of Middle Arm have barramundi, golden snapper, jacks, grunter and pikey bream. Anchor quietly and use fresh or live bait. A strong current flows off the Channel Island ramp during big tides and it can quickly become rough. Middle Arm and Southport ramps provide access to the upper section. Boaters should take care in Middle Arm, as there are rock hazards from top to bottom. The 1997 harbour barramundi netting closure and 2007 coastal net closure improved fishing quality for barramundi, queenfish and salmon. Big mud crabs are usually easy to find, but place pots out of the current on big tides as they can be washed away.

Town Hall Holes
12 33.433S
12 33.600S
12 33.717S
12 33.833S
130 51.367E
130 51.483E
130 51.600E
130 51.717E

West Arm

The upper arm is shallow, with rocky patches. First-timers should explore it carefully on a rising tide as it is difficult to impossible to navigate on big low tides and stranding is possible. This arm can be worth the extra travel from Darwin ramps as there are good trolling and drain-fishing opportunities, depending on the tides. Fish the rock patches with fresh or live bait for barra, snapper, cod, jacks, salmon and bream. Nearby "Little West Arm" is shallow and has rocky areas, especially near the top of "Skeg Creek". West Arm often has of salmon and barra, and the mud crabs are usually big.

Key to Map

Hotspots

1. Fish rocks for jacks, barra, snapper.
2. Barra, salmon, snapper.
3. Fish here if birds are feeding. Troll rocky bottom at low tide. If there are no fish they will often be in the creek on opposite (No 10). Upstream of creek 3 is good for drift-and-cast.
4. A rockbar crosses here. Barra, jacks.
5. Fish gutters on run-out tide.
6. Extensive rocky areas good for barra, salmon, jacks, golden snapper.
7. Good spot for barra, salmon.
8. Hole, barra, occasional jewfish.
9. "Rocky Road" ... the top of "Skeg Creek" narrows, with rocks either side and on bottom, visible at mid-low tide. A hazardous rock exists just before 90 degree bend. Top tinny spot, push right up with the tide and livebait. Also crabs.
10. Barra, salmon at mouth.
11. Drift and cast along here.

Launch sites

Nearest site is Channel Island. Otherwise Darwin ramps. Carry enough fuel and water as help might not be at hand on week days. The distance from Dinah Beach ramp to Stokes Point is 15km.

Not to be used for navigation

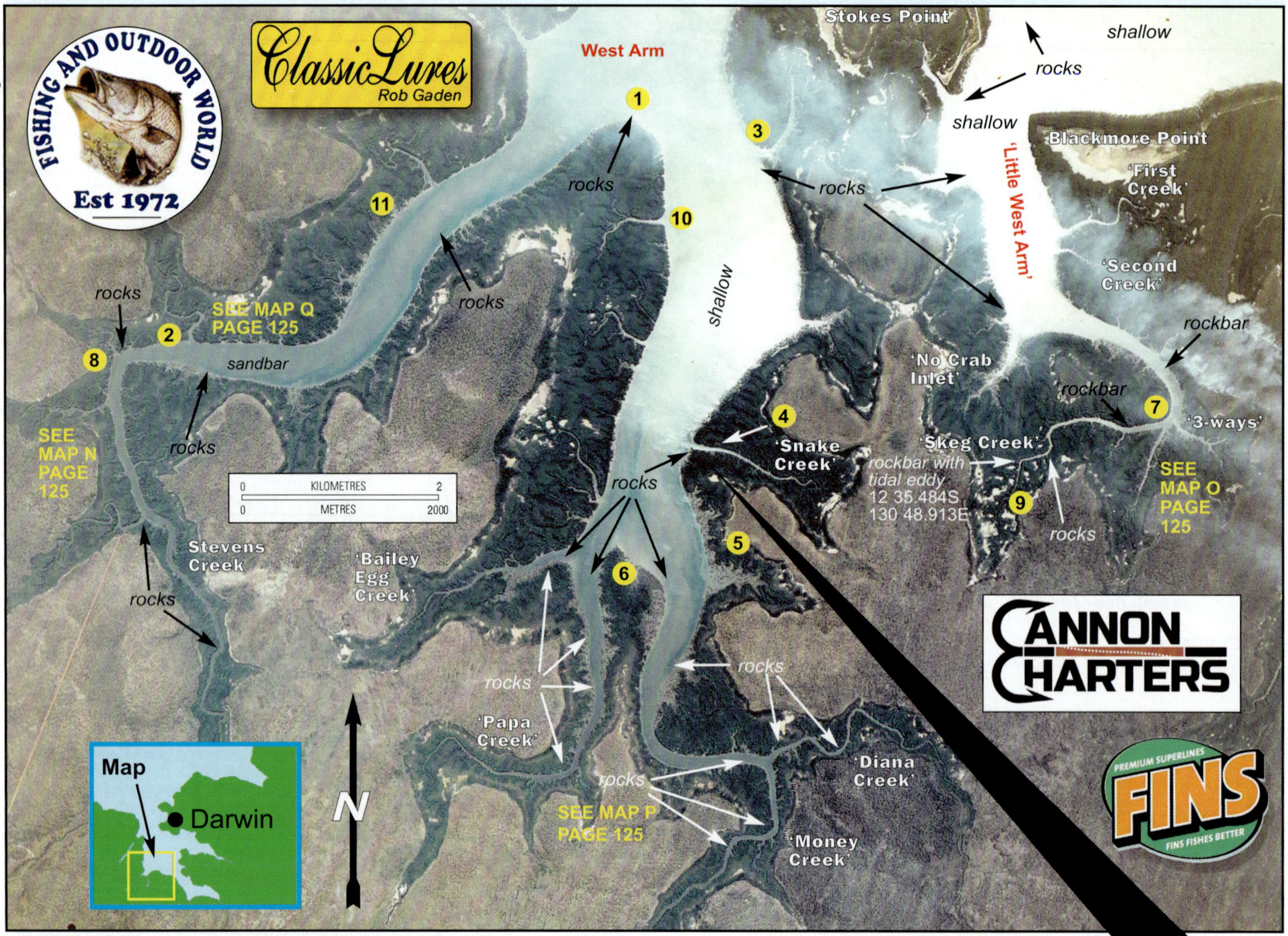

Stokes Point
West Arm
shallow
rocks
Blackmore Point
'First Creek'
'Little West Arm'
'Second Creek'
rockbar
'No Crab Inlet'
'3-ways'
'Snake Creek'
'Skeg Creek'
rockbar with tidal eddy 12 35.484S 130 48.913E
sandbar
SEE MAP Q PAGE 125
SEE MAP N PAGE 125
SEE MAP O PAGE 125
SEE MAP P PAGE 125
Stevens Creek
'Bailey Egg Creek'
'Papa Creek'
'Diana Creek'
'Money Creek'
KILOMETRES 0 2
METRES 0 2000
Map
Darwin
N

A West Arm side creek rockbar shown at low tide, with a high-tide micro chart at right

A closer look on a higher tide ... once submerged it becomes a hazard

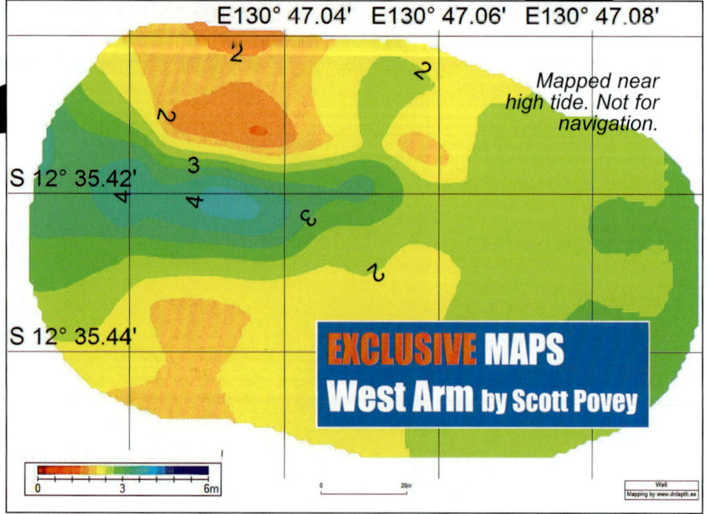

Shoal Bay and The Rock on a spring low tide

Metro barra

Shoal Bay is a broad expanse of mangrove-fringed turbid shallow water, immediately north of Darwin's northern suburbs.

The bay has a large wetland catchment and is a nursery area that attracts big barramundi.

Shoal Bay dries on low tides, leaving pools and channels.

The Build-up before the Wet is the best barra fishing period. The creeks can be good in the wet season, but watch the weather.

The big-barra spots are The Rock, King Creek mouth, the first rockbar in King Creek, the first junction inside Meckit Creek, Buffalo Creek near the ramp and upstream at the "Green Creek" outlet, as well as Howard River rockbar, and "Spot 6".

The Rock, at the entrance to Hope Inlet, is best on week days when there are fewer boats. Fish neap and building tides in calm weather, when the water clears.

Night fishing is usually good.

In creek holes, use live mullet on an unweighted or lightly weighted rig at low tide.

"Locking in" at low tide and fishing holes on foot is popular, but watch the incoming tide. During spring tides, the run-in tide moves fast.

Outer Shoal Bay surprises with tuna schools and loads of blue salmon. Early in the year prawns are thick. Crabbing is usually very good.

Creeks usually have enough water to fish at low tide, but travelling outside on less than about a 4.5m tide can be a nightmare, and you'll become stranded if the tide falls. Don't leave the ramp on a falling tide.

The rockbar just up from Buffalo Creek ramp produces big fish from the bank.

The bay also has sand whiting and bream. Catch them using peeled prawn baits.

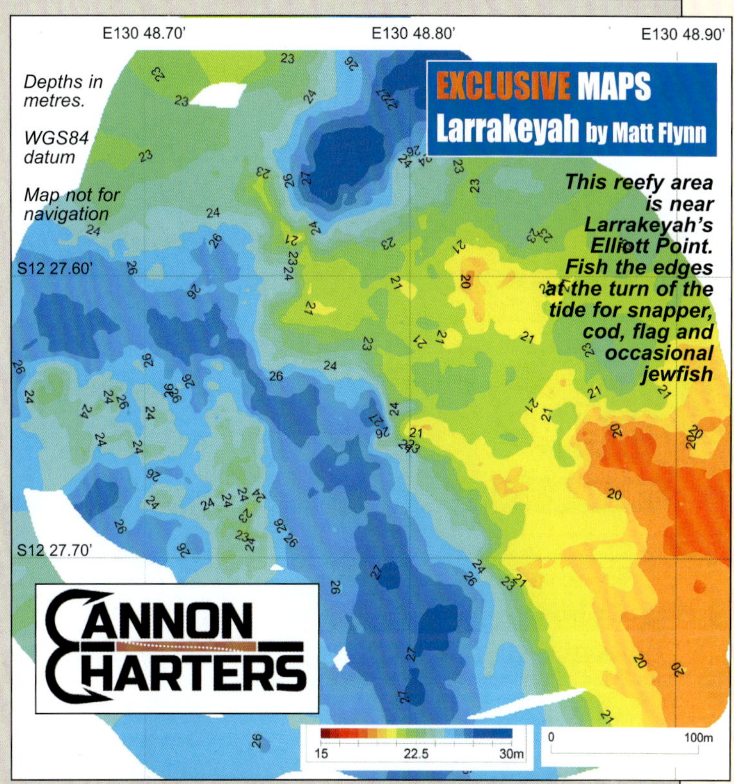

CBD reef fishing

You don't have to travel far from Darwin's CBD to catch reef fish such as golden snapper, jewfish, redfish, cod, tuskfish, tricky snapper and coral trout.

While you might think places near the city might be fished out, reef fish move in and out of the harbour all the time, replenishing stocks.

Divers report plenty of fish on local reefs even when fishos can't find any action.

As well as artificial reefs and wrecks, there is substantial broken bottom in the harbour, some of it located in deep water off Larrakeyah (above) next to the city.

Strong currents flow here so fish the turn of the tide, using the freshest bait you can find. Heavy sinkers may be required.

At slack water soft plastic jigs can work well. Night fishing can produce excellent results, especially on smaller tides, but keep an eye out for boat traffic.

If you have an electric motor, use the "spotlock", which allows moving the boat around quickly without needing to pull up an anchor.

Surprise catches happen in the harbour, including occasional large cobia, spanish mackerel and tripletail.

Trolling the Six Mile area with fast-swimming lures before dawn can net big spanish mackerel in the dry season, with the fish going deep in daylight.

Deep reefs around the Six Mile Buoy and Channel Rock fish well, buy keep in mind that boats may not anchor in the shipping channel, nor can they obstruct a ship in any way.

Darwin Harbour is a special place, as well as fish it is home to five species of dolphin, four species of turtle, dugongs, several species of sharks and rays, and more.

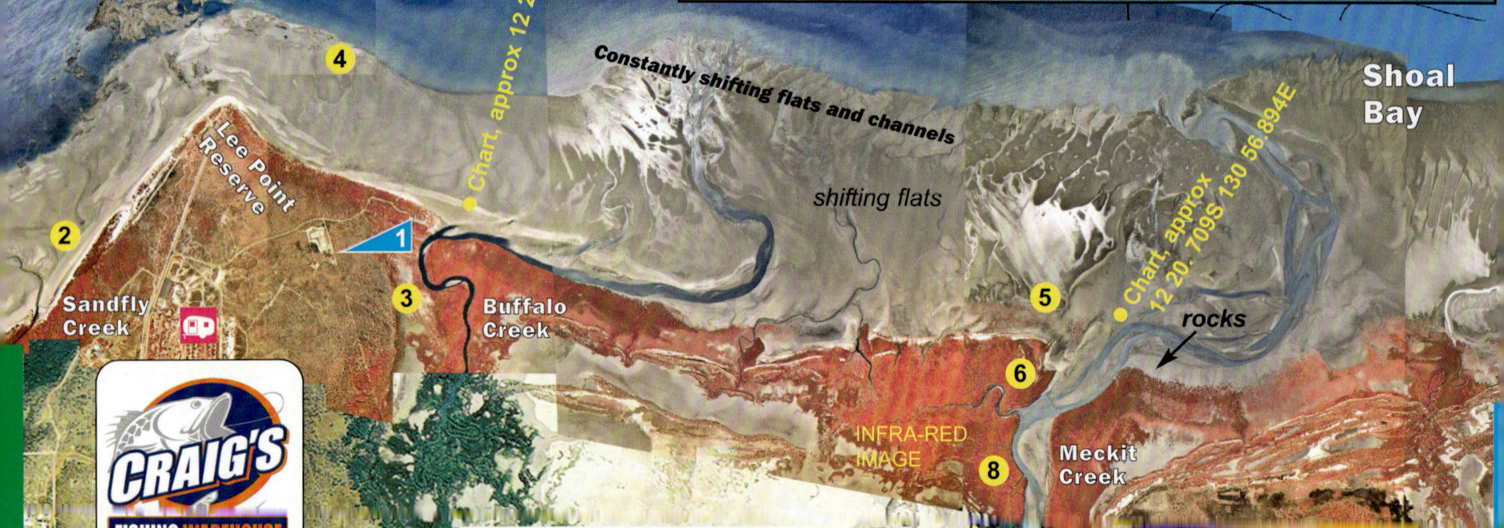

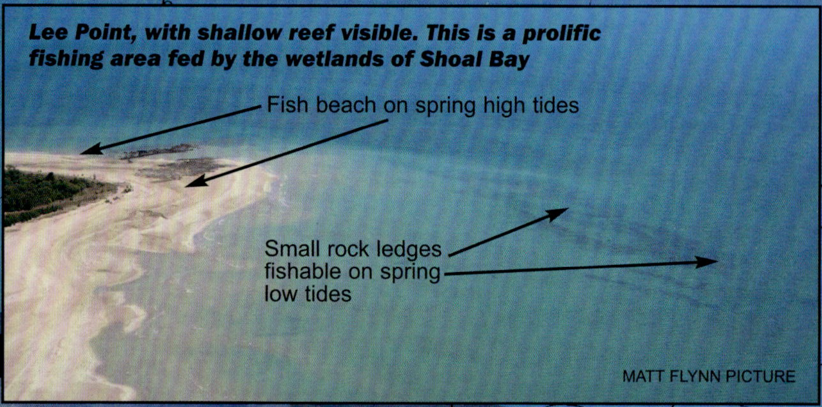

Key to Map

Hotspots

1. Lee Point rocks: queenfish, trevally, blue salmon, occasional barra. Best fishing off beach on spring high tides.
2. Sandfly Creek mouth can fish for whiting, salmon, occasional barra in wet season.
3. Buffalo Creek, big barra and blue salmon. Fish from sandy bank near mouth or rockbar just upstream from ramp near low tide. Cast poppers at night. Beware crocs. Boaters can fish low-tide holes with livebait and lures. Baitfish gather near the "green" waste water outflow upstream on the west bank.
4. Fish rock edges on spring low tides for most species. Whiting along beach.
5. Abundant prawns about February to March. Beware stingers.
6. Fish junction for barra at low tide.
7. Mack Attack 12 18.533S 130 54.062E - lump that holds school and spanish mackerel, occasional reef fish. Troll fast lures over the top of the main lump. Look for sea birds to locate tuna in the dry season.
8. Drift and cast early incoming tide. Big barra will stalk baitfish near clumps of submerged timber.

Launch sites

1. Buffalo Creek public ramp. Useable most tides, but creek mouth navigable above about 4m (less for small boats). Difficult area when rough.

Local tides move up to about 7.42m.

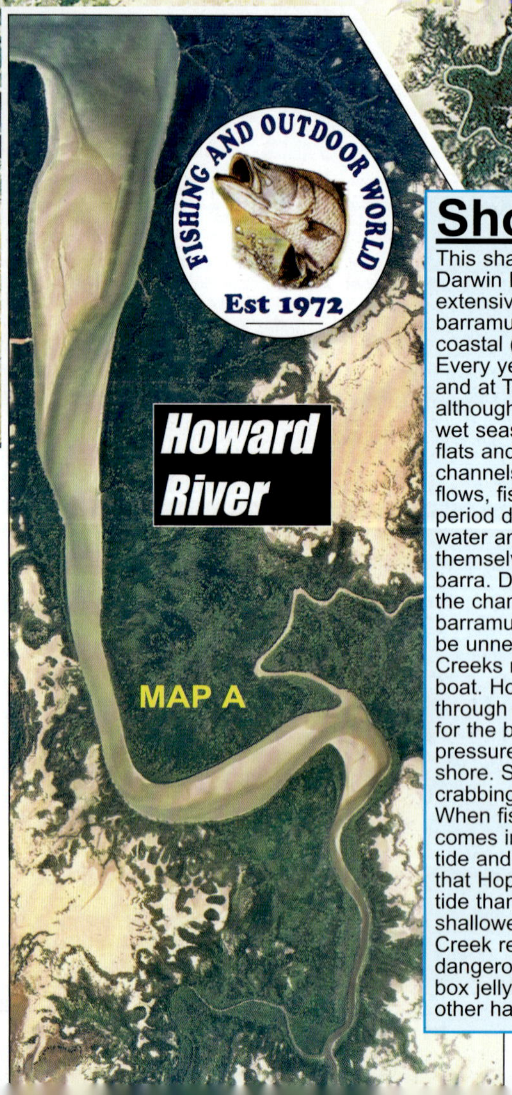

Shoal Bay

This shallow bay produces bigger barramundi than nearby Darwin Harbour presumably because it is a fish nursery with extensive wetlands behind the tidal creeks. A 1997 ban on barramundi nets in the bay and subsequent buyback of coastal (non-barra) gill net licences ensures quality fishing. Every year 10kg+ barra are caught in numbers in the creeks and at The Rock. The best fishing is usually Oct-Nov, although good fishing can be had during and just after the wet season, during calm spells. The bay becomes drying flats and shallow channels as the tide falls, and the channels change with each year or big storm. When run-off flows, fish the top of the creeks, especially 'Spot 6'. The period during and just after neap tides provides clearer water and the best lure fishing. Some boaters lock themselves into low tide holes on big tides to livebait for barra. During spring tides, walking the low-tide flats next to the channels and holes and casting lures produces barramundi, although the "quicksand" feel of some flats can be unnerving. Blue salmon are abundant. King and Meckit Creeks run through Navy property and can only be fished by boat. Howard River has a large rockbar accessible by 4WD through a reserve. Buffalo Creek is the main access point for the bay, with a tide-restricted ramp. Despite heavy fishing pressure, "Buff Creek" produces great barra each year from shore. Shoal Bay's creeks are closed to commercial crabbing, but the flats are not. Crabbing is usually excellent. When fishing the bay on foot keep in mind that the tide comes in about two hours after the scheduled Darwin low tide and it can come in fast, so stay near your boat. Note that Hope Inlet images shown above were taken on a higher tide than the other images - Hope Inlet is as shallow, if not shallower, than the rest of the bay. The entrance to Buffalo Creek requires about 4.5m of tide to enter and can be dangerous in strong winds. Shoal Bay waters are thick with box jellyfish at times. Stonefish, stingrays and crocodiles are other hazards for anyone entering the water.

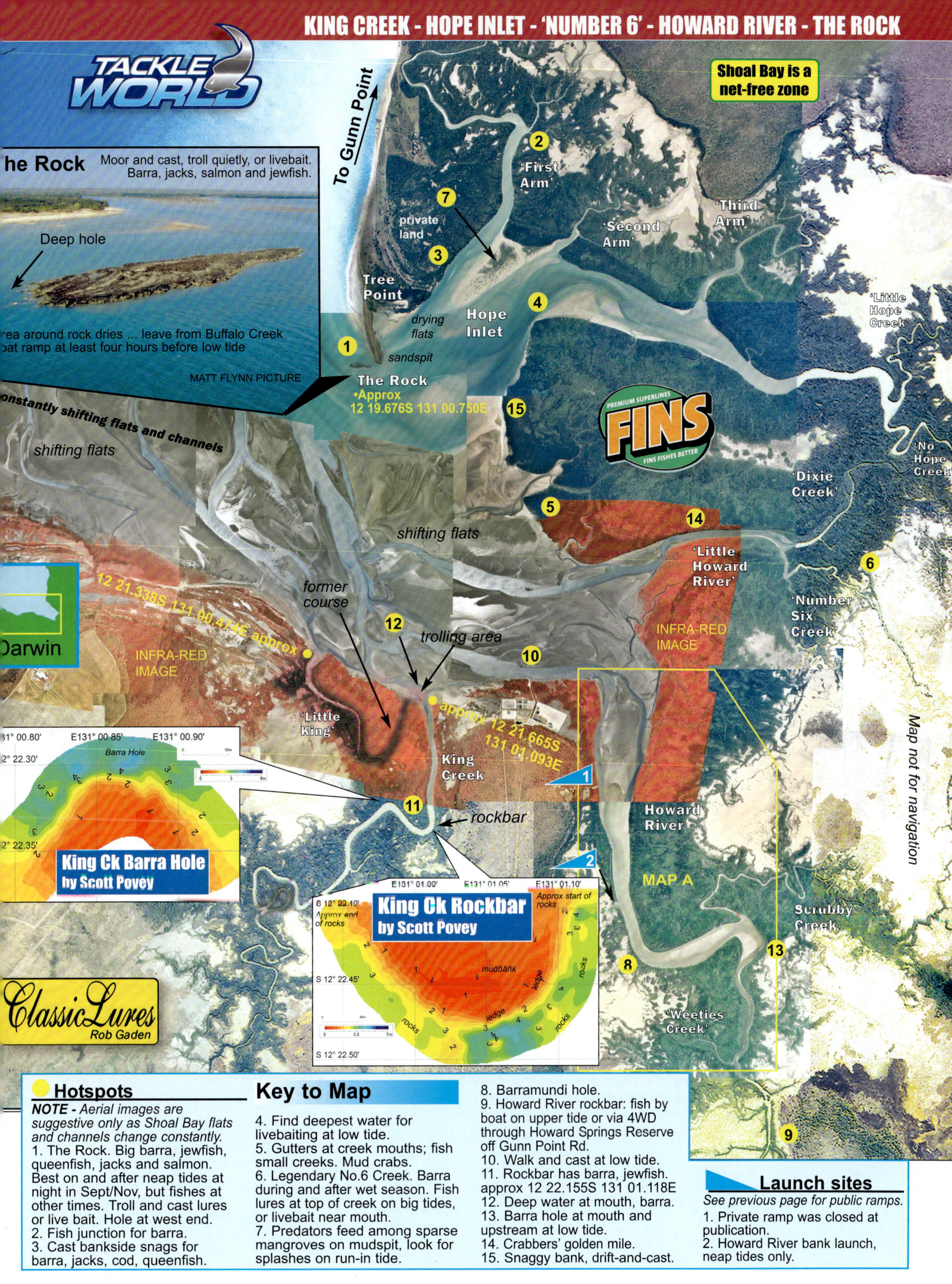

KING CREEK - HOPE INLET - 'NUMBER 6' - HOWARD RIVER - THE ROCK
TACKLE WORLD
To Gunn Point
Shoal Bay is a net-free zone
The Rock
Moor and cast, troll quietly, or livebait. Barra, jacks, salmon and jewfish.
Deep hole
Area around rock dries ... leave from Buffalo Creek boat ramp at least four hours before low tide
MATT FLYNN PICTURE
'First Arm'
private land
'Second Arm'
'Third Arm'
Tree Point
drying flats
Hope Inlet
'Little Hope Creek'
sandspit
The Rock
•Approx
12 19.676S 131 00.750E
constantly shifting flats and channels
shifting flats
FINS
'No Hope Creek'
'Dixie Creek'
shifting flats
'Little Howard River'
Darwin
12 21.338S 131 00.474E approx
former course
trolling area
'Number Six Creek'
INFRA-RED IMAGE
INFRA-RED IMAGE
'Little King'
approx 12 21.665S 131 01.093E
King Creek
King Ck Barra Hole
by Scott Povey
Barra Hole
rockbar
Howard River
MAP A
Map not for navigation
King Ck Rockbar
by Scott Povey
Approx end of rocks
Approx start of rocks
mudbank
ledge
rocks
Scrubby Creek
'Weeties Creek'
ClassicLures
Rob Gaden
Hotspots
NOTE - Aerial images are suggestive only as Shoal Bay flats and channels change constantly.
1. The Rock. Big barra, jewfish, queenfish, jacks and salmon. Best on and after neap tides at night in Sept/Nov, but fishes at other times. Troll and cast lures or live bait. Hole at west end.
2. Fish junction for barra.
3. Cast bankside snags for barra, jacks, cod, queenfish.
Key to Map
4. Find deepest water for livebaiting at low tide.
5. Gutters at creek mouths; fish small creeks. Mud crabs.
6. Legendary No.6 Creek. Barra during and after wet season. Fish lures at top of creek on big tides, or livebait near mouth.
7. Predators feed among sparse mangroves on mudspit, look for splashes on run-in tide.
8. Barramundi hole.
9. Howard River rockbar: fish by boat on upper tide or via 4WD through Howard Springs Reserve off Gunn Point Rd.
10. Walk and cast at low tide.
11. Rockbar has barra, jewfish. approx 12 22.155S 131 01.118E
12. Deep water at mouth, barra.
13. Barra hole at mouth and upstream at low tide.
14. Crabbers' golden mile.
15. Snaggy bank, drift-and-cast.
Launch sites
See previous page for public ramps.
1. Private ramp was closed at publication.
2. Howard River bank launch, neap tides only.

The small hole at the end of the southern Blue Hole

The outer Blue Hole at Gunn Point, showing the southern entrance at low tide

The outer Blue Hole has two large bommies that can catch boaters

LEFT: This creek is located at the end of the beach next to Gunn Point

This Gunn Point creek is a popular spot. It fishes best near high tide. Note the rock ledge near the mouth

The low-tide rip outside the outer Blue Hole's exit channel holds queenfish and trevally

This patch of mangroves and rocks outside Leaders Creek is dubbed 'Pussycat Island' by locals

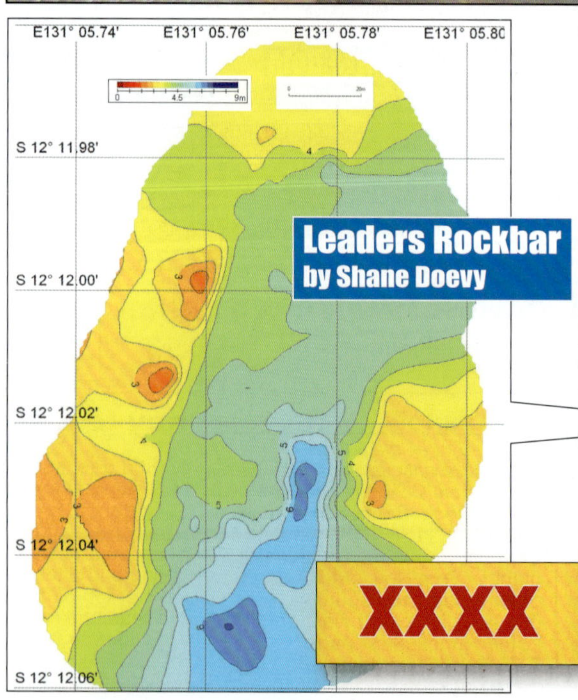

Key to Map

Hotspots

1. Big barramundi around rocks in Sept/Oct during calm weather.
2. Salmon, queenfish, whiting.
3. Troll along edges for queenfish, trevally.
4. Blue Holes - jacks, queenfish, flag.
5. Small creek holds salmon and barra.
6. Snapper, mangrove jacks on bait.
7. Small blue hole - interesting fishing for queenfish, trevally, jacks.
8. See map below for Leaders Creek spots.
9. Adelaide River Artificial Reef is a 10km run from Leaders Creek mouth at 12 07.587S 131 11.545E. Snapper, jewfish.

Wrecks and reefs

A. Adelaide River Artificial Reef 12 07.587S 131 11.545E.

Launch sites

1. Leaders Creek Fishing Base offers a range of services, including a secure trailer enclosure. About 2.5m tide needed to pass a rockbar below the ramp.
2. Saltwater Arm public ramp, 17km off Gunn Point Rd. About 2.8m tide needed to pass rockbar just downstream of ramp.

Gunn Point

This area is owned by the NT Land Corporation and is a popular dry season 4WD camping and fishing destination. Only road-registered vehicles can use the beach via three designated access points. Camping must be at least 10m back from the cliff edges and is not permitted on the beach. The beach has whiting, salmon, queenfish, trevally and occasional barramundi at high tide. Boating access is either from Darwin or nearby Leaders Creek. The reef edges troll for queenfish, trevally, jacks, trout and flag. The reef plateau has three Blue Holes, the largest being 3.7km long. These always hold navigable water but are almost landlocked at low tide, with water flowing hard from the exits. The smallest Blue Hole can be reached at low tide by mooring at the western end of the inner hole and walking, but beware stonefish. Casting lures or trolling the Blue Holes yields queenfish and trevally, with small coral trout, tuskfish, jacks, cod and flag

Barramundi can be sight-fished in the mangroves around high tide. Keep in mind when planning a Blue Holes trip you can not easily enter or leave the holes until high tide, so you must spend a day on the water, or get in and out around high tide. Skilled boaters can use the inner hole exit as outlined on Page 134. Smaller Blue Holes exist on the nearby Vernon Islands.

Leaders Creek

This is a good fishing/crabbing creek and it has the nearest launch site to the Vernon Islands, Blue Holes and Adelaide River Artificial Reef. The creek produces big jewfish and barramundi, mostly caught by trolling near the mouth. It is closed to commercial crabbing. Take care when travelling from the mouth around Glyde Point and to Fright Point as there are reefs.

Getting there

Take the Stuart Hwy from Darwin to the Howard Springs Rd, then turn down Gunn Point Rd. The ramp turn-off is about 44km further on. Leaders Creek Fishing Base has boat hire, accommodation, supplies and trailer storage. For more info on Gunn Point access and camping visit www.gunnpoint.com.au

Key to Map

Hotspots

1. Lots of snaggy corners and mangrove roots, ideal for bream and snapper on bait.
2. A nice eddy forms here on the incoming tide and barra, queenies and trevally use it to hold up. Troll either bank with small diving lures.
3. Jacks live here. Livebaits of prawns or small fish floated among the rocks will produce smashing hits from mangrove jacks.
4. The mouth of this creek is a good place to baitfish on the incoming tide. Anything may grab a bait cast into the shadows of the mangroves. There is a small sandbar with some standing dead timber outside the mouth where golden snapper can be trolled.
5. Trolling along this section of bank is productive on the incoming tide. Shallow lures fished in a couple of metres of water or less produce barra and salmon.
6. It is shallow just outside the mouth on the depicted side of the creek. When the tide comes in it washes over the mudflats and seems to dump a lot of food into the channel, as fish congregate here. Anchor on the edge of the discoloured water and fish baits.
7. This is roughly where the big jewfish are caught. Use your sounder to locate the channel, bait up with pilchards or squid, and be patient.
8. A deep ledge runs along this bank. Troll deep divers for barramundi and jewfish.
9. The outside of this bend is another good spot for bait fishing. Jewfish on pilchards. Big barra and jewfish on livebaits.
10. The deepest water in the creek can be found here. If you are prepared to work through the catfish, you will find jewfish. Some nice salmon are in this hole from time to time.

Looking across the low tide reef flat from the inner Blue Hole

The inner Blue Hole, showing the eastern entrance at low tide ... note the shallow bits!

Leaving the inner Blue Hole at low tide ...

The channel is shallow and flows hard. Not a place for the inexperienced. Trim motor up. Unmarked hazards may exist.

1 Approaching the eastern exit to the inner Gunn Point Blue Hole, noting the white water pushing up on a rock ledge to the right ...

Pictures taken near the end of the runout of a .77m low tide

2 Pushing past the rock ledge, with the water starting to boil as it is flows into the small channel ...

3 Looks pretty straightforward, keeping to the left ...

4 Moving faster now, still keeping to the left ...

5 Hang on, is that a huge bommie we are rushing towards?

6 Arrrrghhhhhhh!!!

7 There's deeper water on the right side!

Photos by MATT FLYNN
NAVIGATION by DENNIS 'AGENT86' SMART

8 Passing the bommie ... and the final few metres of channel leading out to sea are easier. Vernon Islands here we come!

Fishing the bigger tides

The Vernon Islands are three small islands 50km north-east of Darwin, near Gunn Point.

The islands belong to the Tiwi Aboriginal people.

Fishing is permitted in this area.

The islands rise steeply out of deep water between the mainland and much larger Melville Island to the north.

East Vernon Island and North West Vernon Island are covered with mangroves, most of which becomes inundated on big tides.

South West Vernon Island has terrestrial trees at its centre, with mangroves on its coastline.

All three Vernon Islands are about 7km in length.

The channels between the mainland and islands form part of Clarence Strait.

The 45m deep South Channel flows between the mainland and South-West Vernon Island. This is the narrowest channel, being only 1km wide.

Howard Channel, on the south side of North-West Vernon Island, reaches 68m deep and is 3.5km wide.

Between Melville and North-West Vernon Island lies North Channel, which reaches 48m and is known for its pelagic fish hotspots, Oliver and Smith Reefs.

Many boaters fish this area only on small tides, because big tides create strong currents that form whirlpools and messy seas, especially when wind and tide are opposed. However, this area is known for pelagics such as GTs, brassy trevally, queenfish and mackerel, and

MATT FLYNN PICTURE

A .77m low tide reveals the coral drop-off along the inner South West Vernon Island

these fish, particularly trevally and queenfish, bite well on big tides, especially building tides after neaps when water clarity is better.

Big trevally love the rips around reefs, and jacks and trout can be targeted along the coral walls on a spring low tide.

An added benefit of fishing this area during big tides is the interesting scenery revealed at low tide.

During big tides, you must choose your weather and travel in a seaworthy boat.

A suggested big-tide trip is to leave Buffalo Creek or Nightcliff ramp as a spring high tide rises, pass over the Gunn Point reef plateau into the inner Blue Holes on the high tide, and fish the outgoing tide in the inner Blue Hole, probing the mangroves and snags, and then moving into the hole itself with the tide to fish the rock-coral edges.

Skippers can either await the tide's return or leave carefully through the fast-flowing exit channel and fish the South Vernon Island edges at low tide.

It is then possible to fish the western outflow on the outer hole for trevally and queenfish, and enter the hole through the outflow as the tide rises.

FISH FINDER fished the Blue Holes and south edge of the South Vernon Island with Dennis "Agent86" Smart on a huge tide, from a .77m low up to 7.56m.

Water clarity was good enough to flick lures in the Blue Holes and along the island reef edges. We found barra, jacks, coral trout, tuskfish and pelagic fish.

So don't dismiss the Vernons on big tides, but take care with trip planning and the weather.

Crocodiles and stonefish also show up here, so take care on shore.

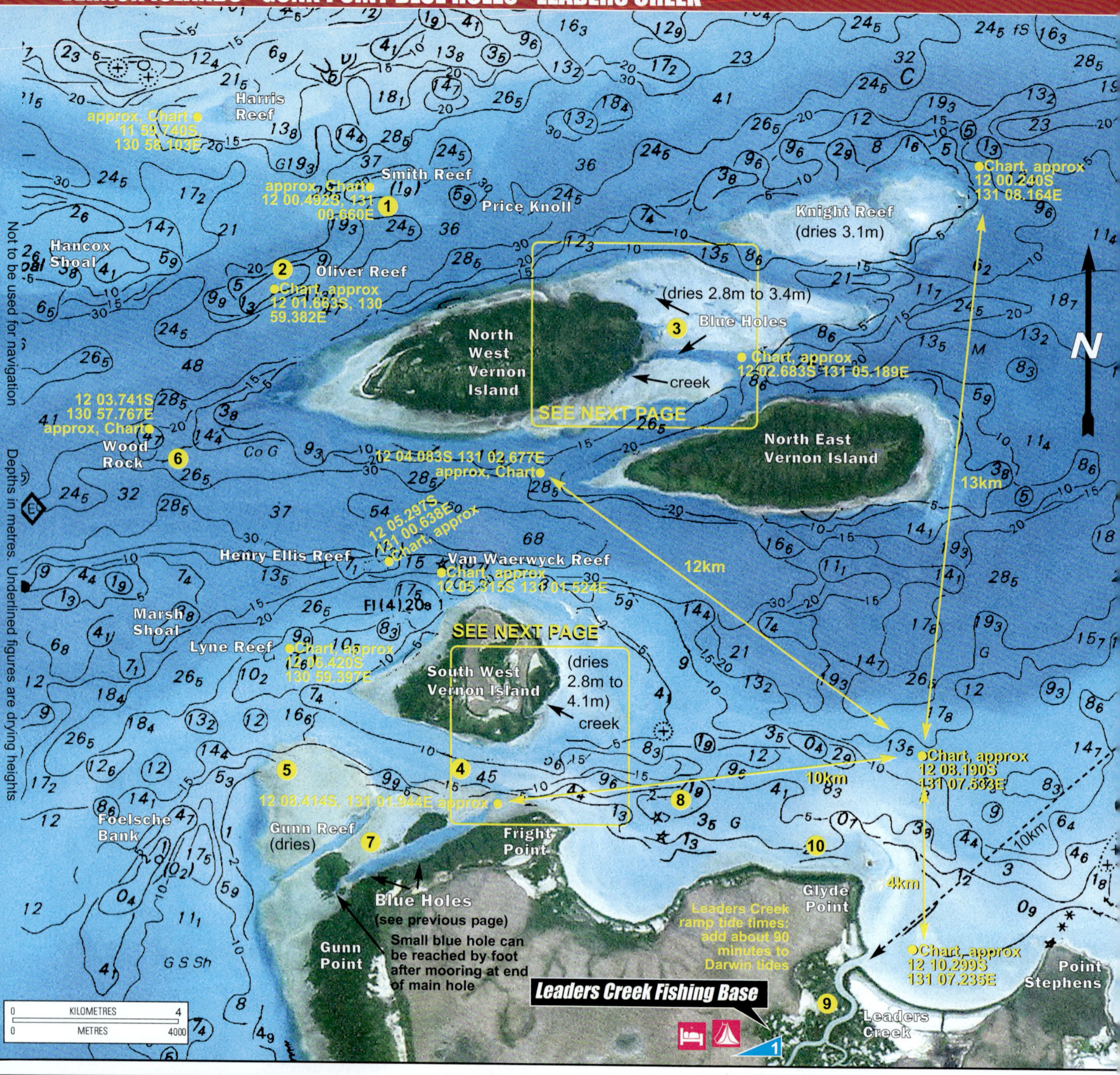

Coral gardens next to a Gunn Point Blue Hole ... stonefish country!

Key to Map

Hotspots

1. Smith Reef rises abruptly out of deep water. Fish here for trevally using poppers and diving lures. Works best on small to medium tides coming off neaps.
2. Oliver Reef. Trevally, queenfish.
3. North West Vernon Blue Hole. A small creek exists at the top of the hole. Enter on top of tide. You will become landlocked until the tide comes back in, but be sure second tide is high enough to leave! Fishes well for trevally, queenfish, mangrove jacks. Fish north wall of Blue Hole for coral trout.
4. Deep channel holds large jewfish, golden snapper, saddletail snapper. Fishing is easier on neap tides, but slack of big tides can fish better. Usually best just before wet season.
5. Gunn Point reef good area to troll for queenfish and trevally. Reef fish.
6. Snapper and reef fish on neap tides.
7. Gunn Point blue holes. As with North West Vernon Blue Hole, enter on high tide, fish the low. Mixed reef fish, trevally, queenfish.
8. Snapper along edges.
9. Leaders Creek has jewfish in deeper holes, barra, jacks, salmon, crabs. Snapper, blue salmon off Glyde Point. Creek has 24-hour secure trailer enclosure business, camping and boat hire.
10. Most species at top of big tides.

Wrecks and reefs

A. Adelaide River Artificial Reef 12 07.587S 131 11.545E, jewfish, snapper, cod, trevally, catfish.

Launch sites

1. Leaders Creek: follow the Gunn Point road and turn at the sign. **Tides are about 90 minutes behind Darwin, with 2.8m of water needed to pass a rockbar downstream from the ramp.**

STRONG CURRENTS AND DRYING REEFS MAKE THIS AREA HAZARDOUS

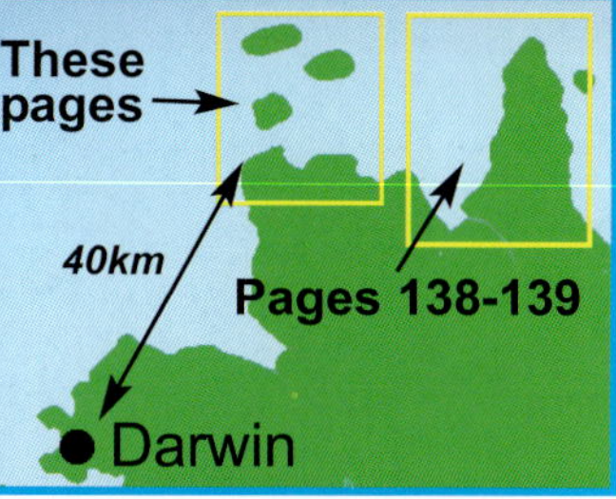

Unique islands

The Vernon Islands/Clarence Strait region is an interesting area, easily fished by trailerboats.

The islands and reefs have near-verticle sides, separated by deep channels.

Strong currents in the channels tend to concentrate bait schools and pelagic fish, including trevally, queenfish and mackerel, into specific areas.

Pelagic fish move away from the reefs during neap tides, and gather at the reefs on bigger tides.

Try fast trolling with poppers or high-speed lures, and keep a lookout for birds hovering over fish. Fish the sandbars (covered at high tide) at the end of South West Vernon Island for queenfish.

Jigging works well on spanish mackerel, which tend to go deep as the sun rises.

Good bottom fishing can be had for golden snapper, jewfish and redfish in the channels.

Move until you find fish.

The deep channels can only be bottom-fished at the turn of neap tides. Try drift-fishing.

The Blue Holes on the islands produce queenfish, jacks, cod, tuskfish and trevally.

The islands are pretty much inundated by big tides and the many small creeks are fascinating to explore and fish, but be sure to leave before the tide falls too low.

Jacks are a highlight in the creeks. Groper and sickle-fin lemon sharks add excitement.

Crayfish can be found on the reef flats at night.

Anglers can get to the Vernon Islands by boat from Darwin, or tow a boat to Leaders Creek Fishing Base.

It becomes rough in this area when wind and tide are opposed. Take extra fuel, at least 100m of anchor rope, and a spare anchor.

Cape Hotham

The peninsula is accessible by sea only, usually by launching from Leaders Creek or Saltwater Arm boat ramps. Its location between the mouth of the Adelaide River and the floodplain creeks of Chambers Bay means its coastline receives a high nutrient load each wet season. Not surprisingly, the area offers exceptional fishing. Large barramundi are caught along the foreshores and in the creeks, with jewfish and golden snapper on the shallow reefs. Mud crabs are usually abundant. Threadfin and blue salmon are ever-present. The creeks on the cape are small, but big enough to explore in a trailer boat. The entrance to most requires at least 3m of tide. Anchoring at the creek mouths on an early outgoing tide usually sees barramundi and threadfin salmon feeding aggressively, especially during the warmer months. On the west side, 'Chad's Creek' mouth usually has bait schools during the wet season, but even the tiny trickle down the beach from 'The Marsh' attracts barra, which can be seen loitering around mangrove roots. On the east side of the peninsula, 'Camp Creek' has a sandspit that is an exposed but popular camping spot for boaters, with good fishing through to the beginning of Chambers Bay, where there are oyster rock patches. All the eastern creeks will produce barra, queenfish, salmon and mud crabs. Keep in mind that going around the cape is dangerous in any sort of bad weather, as the wind and tide are often opposed.

Key to Map

Hotspots

1. Large reef area holds snapper, jewfish, cod, redfish, queenfish, trevally. Calm weather only, easier on small tides. Often dangerous seas.
2 and 2. Steep drop-off from reef plateau holds fish. Plateau itself has some sight fishing when tide just covers it, mainly queenfish and trevally, barra, salmon, bream in mangroves.
3. 'Chad's Creek' has salmon, barra, crabs and queenfish. Fish on outgoing tide, ideally about a 2.6m low. Troll mangrove edge for salmon and barra from mid tide up. Sight fishing on neaps.
4 and 4. Reef fish along edges.
5. 'Crab Creek' has a deep hole on the first bend inside. Livebait for barra, salmon, cod. Good crabbing. Accessible from about mid tide.
6. Sight fishing shallow mouth of 'Jacks Creek' for salmon, barra, with jacks inside. Shallow.
7. 'Camp Creek' has a large sandbar with a couple of trees. Accessible from about mid tide.
8. 'Two Creeks' is a dual creek mouth. Queenfish, barra, jacks and crabs. Good fishing off lagoon sandbar at mouth. Accessible from about mid tide.
9. 'Ruby' and 'Last' creeks have barra, salmon, crabs. Accessible from mid tide.
10. Golden snapper, jewfish, salmon around rock outcrops. Sight fishing on small tides.
11. Queenfish around shallow reefs on big tides.
12. Tiny, hidden outlet of 'The Marsh' holds barra in the mangroves during and just after wet season. Sight fishing around mangroves. Beware rocks near Escape Cliff.
13. Ruby Jew Hole - big jewfish and snapper.
14. Large area of drying rocks at west end of Chambers Bay, big barramundi in calm weather, cod, salmon, bream and other species.

Launch sites

Saltwater Arm and Leaders Creek have concrete ramps, or launch from Darwin.

Melville Island
Vernon Islands
This page
Darwin

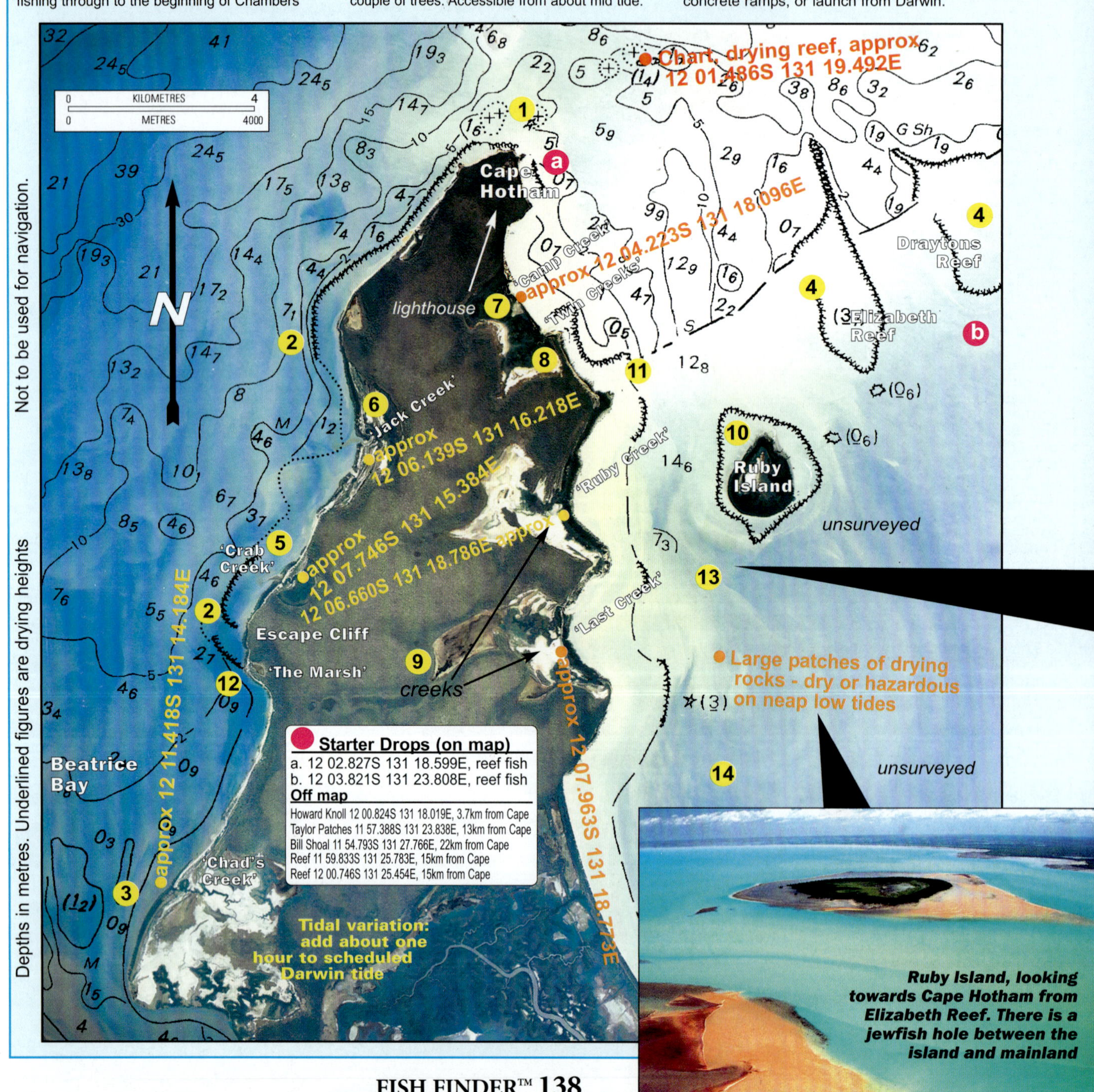

Ruby Island, looking towards Cape Hotham from Elizabeth Reef. There is a jewfish hole between the island and mainland

MATT FLYNN PICTURE

'Crab Creek' ... the picture above right was taken from the hole inside the mouth

'Twin Creeks' ... the dual mouth is on the east side of Cape Hotham

The Cape Hotham shoreline was subject to a land/sea claim at publication, check the latest access status with the Northern Land Council before fishing.

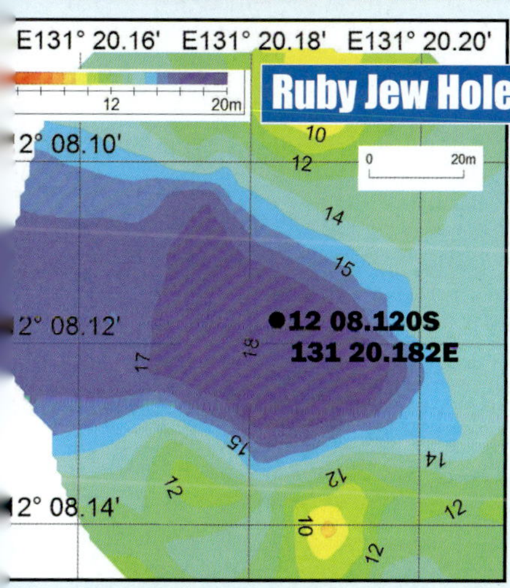

'Camp Creek' on the west side of Cape Hotham with 'Twin Creeks' at the distant end

'Chad's Creek' on the south-west side of Cape Hotham ... probably the best barra creek on the peninsula

'Jack Creek' on the upper west side of Cape Hotham, ... shallow, but good for jacks, crabs and barra

MATT FLYNN PICTURE

The outlet to 'The Marsh'

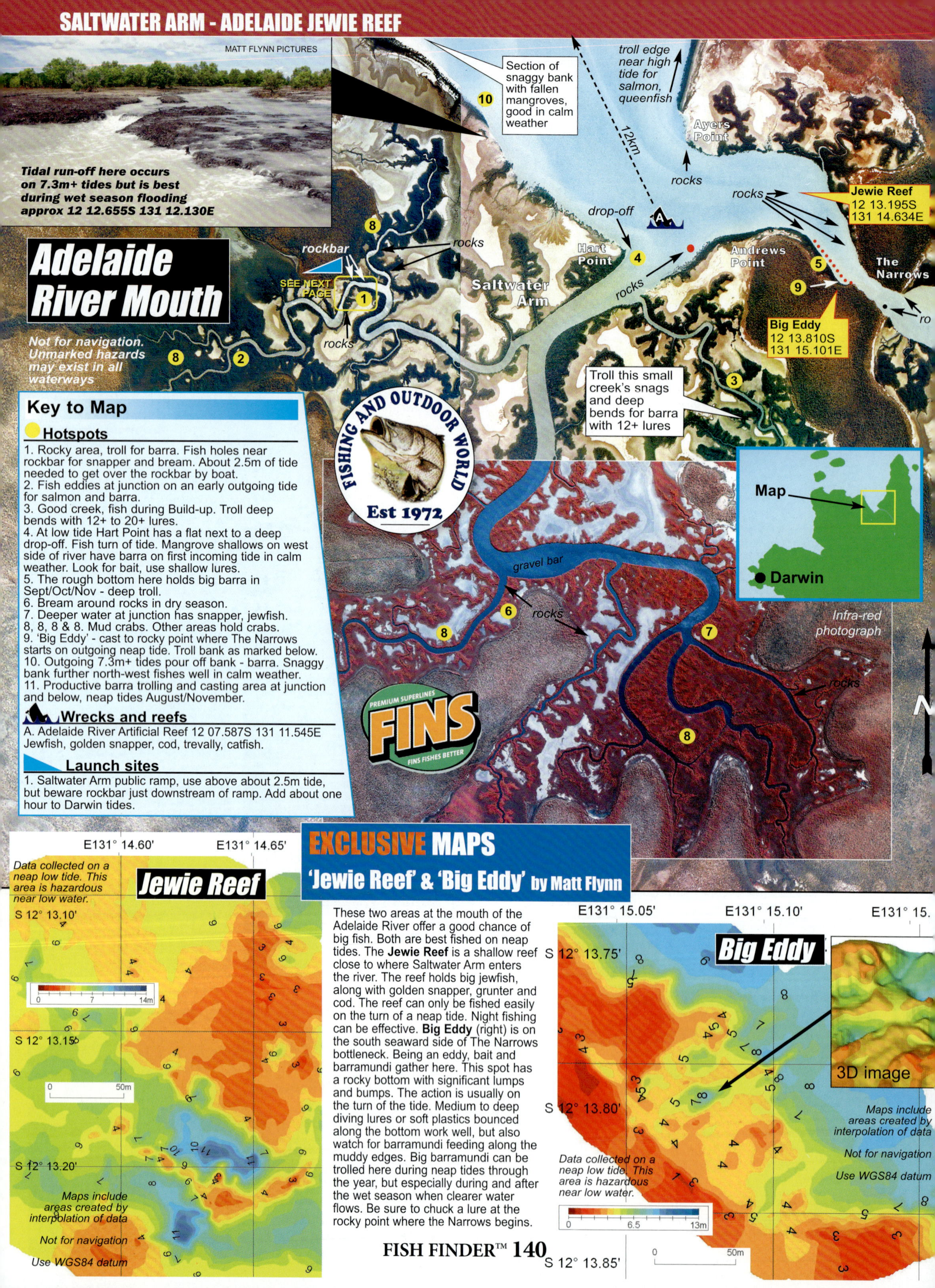

Key to Map

Hotspots

1. Rocky area, troll for barra. Fish holes near rockbar for snapper and bream. About 2.5m of tide needed to get over the rockbar by boat.
2. Fish eddies at junction on an early outgoing tide for salmon and barra.
3. Good creek, fish during Build-up. Troll deep bends with 12+ to 20+ lures.
4. At low tide Hart Point has a flat next to a deep drop-off. Fish turn of tide. Mangrove shallows on west side of river have barra on first incoming tide in calm weather. Look for bait, use shallow lures.
5. The rough bottom here holds big barra in Sept/Oct/Nov - deep troll.
6. Bream around rocks in dry season.
7. Deeper water at junction has snapper, jewfish.
8, 8, 8 & 8. Mud crabs. Other areas hold crabs.
9. 'Big Eddy' - cast to rocky point where The Narrows starts on outgoing neap tide. Troll bank as marked below.
10. Outgoing 7.3m+ tides pour off bank - barra. Snaggy bank further north-west fishes well in calm weather.
11. Productive barra trolling and casting area at junction and below, neap tides August/November.

Wrecks and reefs

A. Adelaide River Artificial Reef 12 07.587S 131 11.545E Jewfish, golden snapper, cod, trevally, catfish.

Launch sites

1. Saltwater Arm public ramp, use above about 2.5m tide, but beware rockbar just downstream of ramp. Add about one hour to Darwin tides.

EXCLUSIVE MAPS
'Jewie Reef' & 'Big Eddy' by Matt Flynn

These two areas at the mouth of the Adelaide River offer a good chance of big fish. Both are best fished on neap tides. The **Jewie Reef** is a shallow reef close to where Saltwater Arm enters the river. The reef holds big jewfish, along with golden snapper, grunter and cod. The reef can only be fished easily on the turn of a neap tide. Night fishing can be effective. **Big Eddy** (right) is on the south seaward side of The Narrows bottleneck. Being an eddy, bait and barramundi gather here. This spot has a rocky bottom with significant lumps and bumps. The action is usually on the turn of the tide. Medium to deep diving lures or soft plastics bounced along the bottom work well, but also watch for barramundi feeding along the muddy edges. Big barramundi can be trolled here during neap tides through the year, but especially during and after the wet season when clearer water flows. Be sure to chuck a lure at the rocky point where the Narrows begins.

Adelaide River Mouth

The river is a gill net free zone. It produces good fishing, but don't expect to work it out in a day. It is a turbid river, and the best fishing is usually restricted to neap tides and the wet season when floodwater clears the tidal section. The early Build-up is a good time to fish, before big rainstorms muddy the water. The rocks either side of The Narrows, particularly the downstream southern corner at 'Big Eddy', produce good fish. The three Wilshire Creeks fish well for big barramundi on neap tides. Troll bumps and snags, and watch for fish on sonar. On bigger tides cast to eddies and draining gutters. The area along the dotted line at Spot 5 is a good trolling run for big barramundi, and the small rock patches just inside and south of the Saltwater Arm junction are holding spots for smaller fish. The shallow reefs just outside The Narrows are renowned for black jewfish, but are only easily fishable on the turn of small tides. Outside the Adelaide River mouth on the west bank are tidal run-offs that drain on tides bigger than 7.3m - barra will sit along the edge near the draining water. The small flat and deep drop-off on the corner of Hart Point holds barra near low tide. Saltwater Arm (SWA) is a hugely popular crabbing spot, but the local crocodiles have become trained crab-bait stealers. The SWA ramp gives good access to Cape Hotham to the north, with Adelaide River Artificial Reef just 12km north-north-west from the entrance to Saltwater Arm.

Cape Hotham tides have up to about 4.47m movement.

This micro chart depicts the area immediately above and below the Saltwater Arm (SWA) boat ramp.

This is part of a large arm off the southern side of the Adelaide River mouth. The rockbar below the ramp can be negotiated on reasonably low tides with great care. The chart shows the shallowest spots.

This ramp is the gateway to several hotspots. The Narrows, the three Wilshire creeks, Cape Hotham, Ruby Island Jew Hole, and even the Chambers Bay creeks are accessible from this ramp.

The rocky area above and below the ramp can fish well when boat traffic is low. There are often mullet in the eddy near the ramp. On week days when boat traffic is low landbased fishos can catch golden snapper, pikey bream, cod, crabs and jacks, though the fishable area of bank at the ramp is small, and there are crocodiles.

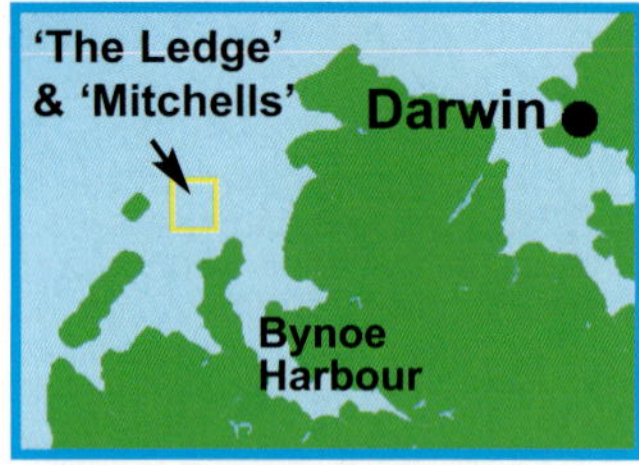

Bynoe Harbour

Simply called "Bynoe" by locals, this net-free mangrove-lined harbour is only 36km south-west of Darwin.

What makes Bynoe great is the unspoilt habitat and rich species mix. In a day, boaters can chase reef fish such as jewfish and golden snapper, mangrove dwellers such as barra and salmon, and pelagics such as mackerel and queenfish.

Bynoe's shores are largely undeveloped, with only the tiny Crab Claw Resort on the southern shore, and a pearling operation and shacks on the north shore.

Gill nets were removed in 2010, leaving everything except mud crabs to recreational fishermen.

The layout of the harbour, with the 17km-long Indian Island running down the middle, and islands at the harbour mouth, means Bynoe usually has a sheltered place to fish. There is a large network of tidal creeks.

Let's divide Bynoe into three parts:
1. The sea entrance, Port Patterson.
2. The outer (Grose) islands.
3. Inner harbour and creeks.

The sea entrance: Outside Bynoe is a complex area called Port Patterson, with two channels roughly split by the drying Middle Reef, as shown on the map on Page 144.

The channels average about 20-30m deep. Thrings Channel runs along Cox Peninsula to the east, with West Channel on the west side of Middle Reef. The channels have variable bottoms, with mud, sand and rock and drying reefs. Boaters must study Chart AUS29 before visiting this area.

Big tides sweep the region. On a big tide, with current and wind opposed, it gets rough. If coming around by sea from Darwin, the worst conditions are usually off Charles Point, with standing waves and sloppy seas.

West Channel, which runs out to Fish Reef, holds some of the best bottom fishing grounds, but Thrings Channel is the first encountered when coming in by sea from Darwin, and is worth a drop or two.

Of note is Kellaway Reef, a drying rocky reef that sits on the edge of Thrings Channel, with a steep drop-off. Kellaway is known more as a navigation hazard than a fishing spot. It often breaks.

There are lumps in Thrings Channel that hold big golden snapper, but most fishos go past Middle Reef to the West Channel reefs, or on to Fish Reef.

Middle Reef is a flat, drying rock plateau running 4km north-south and 2km east-west. It drops away on a shallow gradient. In calm weather it can be almost invisible, a significant navigation hazard. The main sandbar area is a sacred site.

Just 4km south of the sandspit is Moira Reef. This area has queenfish.

Most people who come to this area want to catch reef fish. Famous spots such as "The Ledge", "Mitchells Reef", the drop-off near Simms Reef and grounds around Fish Reef produce big goldies and jewfish, along with redfish, trout, tuskfish and cod.

While there are acres of reef, the biggest fish tend to be found where sloping reef meets a sand/mud bottom at 20m+. That said, some skippers target big golden snapper on the shallowest reefs around Quail Island in the Build-up, and on big tides.

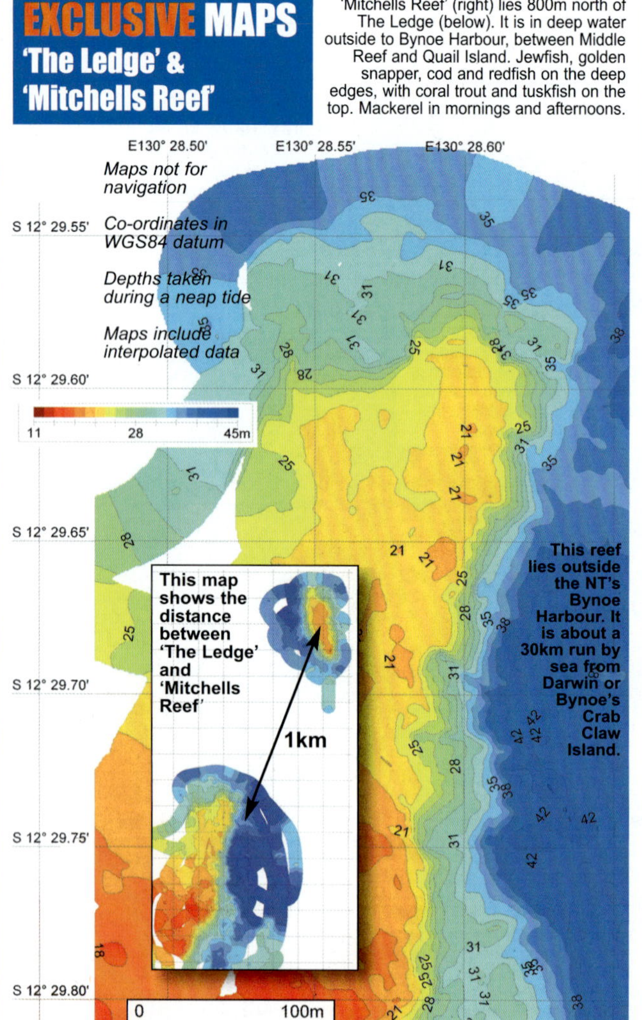

'Mitchells Reef' (right) lies 800m north of The Ledge (below). It is in deep water outside to Bynoe Harbour, between Middle Reef and Quail Island. Jewfish, golden snapper, cod and redfish on the deep edges, with coral trout and tuskfish on the top. Mackerel in mornings and afternoons.

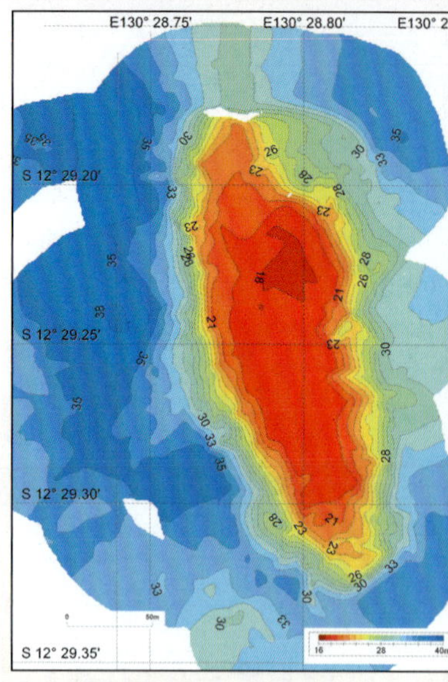

Grounds near Simms Reef are easy to access for small boats, being just over a 20km run, in reasonably sheltered waters, from the "Six Pack Creek" boat ramp on Bynoe's southern side, and Crab Claw Island.

"The Ledge" and "Mitchells Reef" produce consistent fishing. They are a 24km run from the Keswick Point launch site on the north shore. Reefs like these, bordering deep water between Quail Island and Middle Reef, can be prolific. In a day you might see sharks such as tigers, hammerheads, wingheads, sicklefin lemons, tawny nurse, spinners, blacktips and bulls, so there must be plenty of food.

Shallower water produces more tuskfish, trout, flag and cod. Spearos find big snapper on the shallow reefs. Redfish (Indon snapper) are abundant on the deeper Port Patterson reefs. They are small but good to eat. Spanish flag are also common.

Fishing is tide dependent, sometimes with no action until the fish decide to chew.

Port Patterson holds mackerel, mainly in dry season months, and it pays to float out a pilchard or live flag bait while reef fishing. Mornings and late arvos are best, and shallow or deep water can produce big fish.

Mangrove jacks are found throughout. They push hard up against the drying reefs and rocky foreshores as the tide comes in. Cast small lures into the shallows.

Small reef fish can be trolled along the foreshores where submerged rocks meets sand. Or anchor the boat, throw berley, and let fish come to you.

The inner harbour: Within Bynoe Harbour are reef ledges bordering the channel that have jewfish and snapper.

Another good spot for jewfish is just off **Crab Claw Island Resort**. The resort had a steel jetty, which was demolished. The remains were sunk in deep water nearby as an artificial reef. Fish the turn of the tide, using large, fresh baits and heavy line to pull the fish from the structure.

Crab Claw Island Resort has a boat ramp and accommodation. It is in an ideal position on the southern shore. Also nearby is Sandpalms Resort.

Indian Island, which divides the harbour into two, has sandy beaches with mudflats at low tide, the beaches being divided by small rock headlands.

Estuary fishing is centred mainly on the southern side of Bynoe Harbour in "Mackenzie Inlet", "Madford Inlet", and Milne Inlet. Not only does the south side of Bynoe Harbour have great creeks, it is also better sheltered from dry season south-easters. It is serviced by concrete ramps. Sandpalms Resort is located conveniently a short drive from the Milne Inlet ramp.

Some fishos like the eastern end of Bynoe where the harbour divides into Annie and Charlotte Rivers.

Unlike Darwin Harbour, where boat numbers can make tidal drain fishing a first-in, best-served situation, there is rarely a problem finding gutters to yourself in Bynoe.

Most southern Bynoe creeks have rockbars or rock and gravel patches, upon which small snapper, grunter, cod, bream and flathead will reside.

Use a cast net to catch local herring, sardines or mullet for bait.

A highlight of Bynoe is the flats fishing. The area inside the southern end of Indian Island is a good place to start. The channel on the south-west side of the island is shallow, but rocky outcrops along the shores are well worth a cast. Keep in mind this area can dry at low tide.

Boaters with an electric motor or pole will find barra, salmon, queenfish and brown sweetlip cruising the flats. Barra will sit in groups, as well as singly, under fallen trees, and near stumps and mangrove roots.

To the north of Bynoe lies Turnbull Bay, with good barra fishing. Turnbull is only a 6km run from Keswick Point launch site on Bynoe's northern shore.

To the south is the Finniss River freshwater ramp on Hardcastle road, a short drive from **Sandpalms** resort.

The outer islands: The islands outside Bynoe Harbour produce good fish. Bare Sand Island (Woolbechik) has an anchorage, a sandy channel on the south shore. The channel is usually accessed from the seaward side, but can be reached from the Bynoe side when the tide permits.

Further south-west are Grose and Beer Eetar Islands. Dum in Mirrie is surrounded by drying reef flat, which extends to the mainland near Native Point, where Fog Bay begins. The reef extends out to Roche Reefs in Fog Bay. Much of Roche Reefs dries, but the edges produce fish, and being shallow, it can be fished on big tides.

Hazards: Bynoe is a pearl farming area. Rafts are marked, but almost impossible to see at night, save for lights that might mark boundaries.

Like all Top End waters, Bynoe Harbour has box jellyfish, stonefish and crocodiles.

Boat retrieval is mostly impossible on spring low tides.

Aboriginal Land: Kenbi Land Claim conditions require that boaters stay away from some areas. Most areas are marked on our maps. A detailed map is available at **www.nlc.org.au.**

BYNOE WIDE - MIDDLE REEF - FISH REEF - LORNA SHOAL - BASS REEF

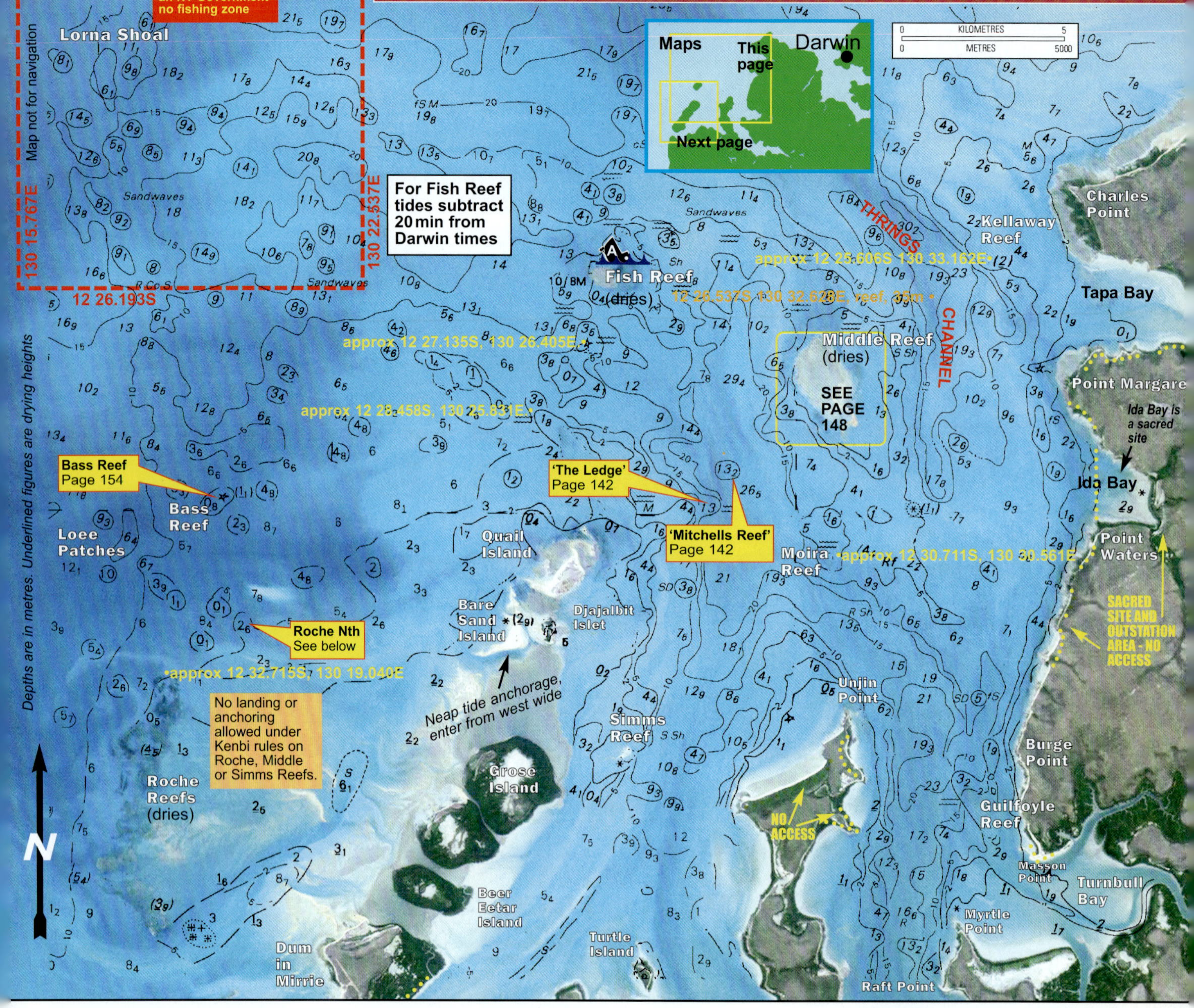

Red border marks an NT Government no fishing zone

12 19.655S

12 26.193S

130 15.767E

130 22.537E

Map not for navigation

Depths are in metres. Underlined figures are drying heights

For Fish Reef tides subtract 20min from Darwin times

Maps | This page | Next page | Darwin

KILOMETRES 0 5 | METRES 0 5000

Lorna Shoal · Sandwaves · Fish Reef (dries) · Middle Reef (dries) · SEE PAGE 148 · THRINGS CHANNEL · Kellaway Reef · Charles Point · Tapa Bay · Point Margaret · Ida Bay · Ida Bay is a sacred site · Point Waters · SACRED SITE AND OUTSTATION AREA - NO ACCESS · Moira Reef · Unjin Point · Burge Point · Guilfoyle Reef · Masson Point · Turnbull Bay · Myrtle Point · Raft Point · Simms Reef · Turtle Island · Beer Eetar Island · Grose Island · Dum in Mirrie · Bare Sand Island · Djajalbit Islet · Quail Island · Bass Reef · Loee Patches · Roche Reefs (dries) · NO ACCESS · N

approx 12 25.606S 130 33.162E

12 26.537S 130 32.528E, reef, 35m

approx 12 27.135S, 130 26.405E

approx 12 28.458S, 130 25.831E

approx 12 30.711S, 130 30.561E

approx 12 32.715S, 130 19.040E

Bass Reef Page 154

'The Ledge' Page 142

'Mitchells Reef' Page 142

Roche Nth See below

No landing or anchoring allowed under Kenbi rules on Roche, Middle or Simms Reefs.

Neap tide anchorage, enter from west wide

Charles Point to Roche Reefs

This area has reef, pelagic and foreshore fishing, accessible by trailer boat from Darwin or Bynoe Harbour launch sites. The first notable mark after travelling around Charles Point from Darwin is Kellaway Reef, which breaks and is a navigation hazard. Just 5.5km south-west, is the large drying Middle Reef, which extends from a flat rocky plateau at the north to a sandbar at the south, another navigation hazard. The sandbar part of the reef is a sacred site. Between Middle Reef and Quail Island is an area of deep sloping rock ledges (some marks provided) through West Channel. Jewfish, redfish, cod, tuskfish, trout, flag and big golden snapper are caught here, with mackerel and tuna in the dry season. Shallow Bass Reef holds jewfish, golden snapper and spanish mackerel. The shallow reefs around Quail Island have trevally on spring tides. Lumps and ledges around drying Fish Reef (which has a lighthouse), produce snapper, spanish flag and jewfish, with queenfish and mackerel on the troll. Loee Patches is a useful area during big tides when strong currents make other places difficult to fish. Roche Reef edges fish best in the dry season for mackerel, trevally, blue salmon and queenfish, with jewfish and golden snapper in the warmer months. As with most reef fishing areas, the turn of the tide is usually best, although different spots may fish at different stages of the tide.

Launch sites

Fishermen can launch in Darwin and travel around Charles Point. Ensure your fuel will cover the trip home if the weather turns bad. It is perhaps safer to trailer a boat to Bynoe Harbour's sheltered launch sites. To access Roche Reefs, launch from the Dundee Beach ramp in Fog Bay.

NOTE: If leaving by boat from Darwin travel around Charles Point in good conditions only, preferably at slack tide. Avoid when wind and tide are opposed. Approach shallow reef waypoints with caution in good conditions. Kenbi rules apply in this area, be sure to get the detailed Kenbi map from the NLC website before fishing. Anchoring or alighting is not permitted on Simms, Middle or Roche Reefs, Turtle Island, Charles Point or between Dum in Mirrie and Beer Eetar Islands. The northern beaches are off limits on Indian Island, as are Quail Island and Djajalbit Islet.

Wrecks

A. SS *Brisbane*, historic wreck site, broken up and part-exposed on Fish Reef at low water. Good fishing at times - jacks, flag, snapper, cod.

Key

Orange waypoint, bottom-fishing spot. Also see micro charts on Page 142.

Yellow waypoints, approx positions to assist in finding locations.

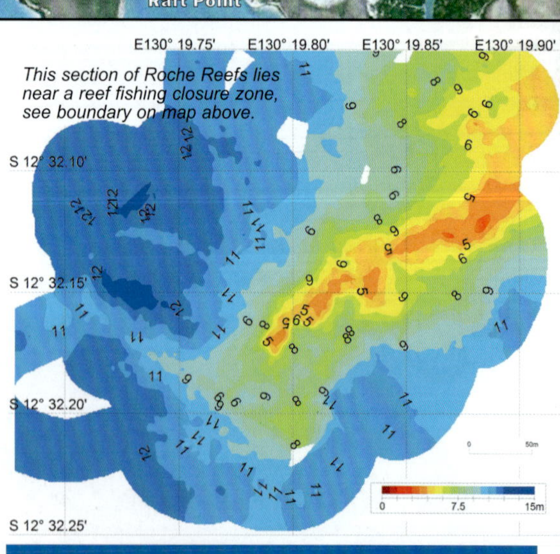

EXCLUSIVE MAPS Roche Reefs North

Key to Map

Hotspots

1. Troll edges for queenfish, mackerel and trevally. Reef fishing on medium tides.
2. Fish patches of rock. Trevally, queenfish, cod, snapper and blue salmon.
3. Bare Sand Island channel approach: good trolling for mackerel, queenfish.
4. Queenfish and blue salmon move in with the tide. Neap tide anchorage, overnight stopover point for weekenders and fishing competitions.
5. Waterfalls off reef on falling spring tides. Casting and trolling for queenfish, trevally, jacks.
6. Creeks good for crabs, barra and salmon.
7. Roche Reefs ... shallow reef, flag, snapper, queenfish, trevally. Berleying near the reef is fun as you can often see the fish. If you are in the shelter of the reef note that waves will ultimately break over the reef with the rising tide. No anchoring or alighting allowed under Kenbi.
8. Fish in channel on large incoming tides. Mostly dries at low tide, but holds some water.
9. Mud crabs in mangroves - high tide only.

Under the Kenbi Land Claim over Cox Peninsula and Bynoe Harbour some areas have no access and some have access with restrictions as marked. A detailed map showing sacred site locations is available at www.nlc.org.au

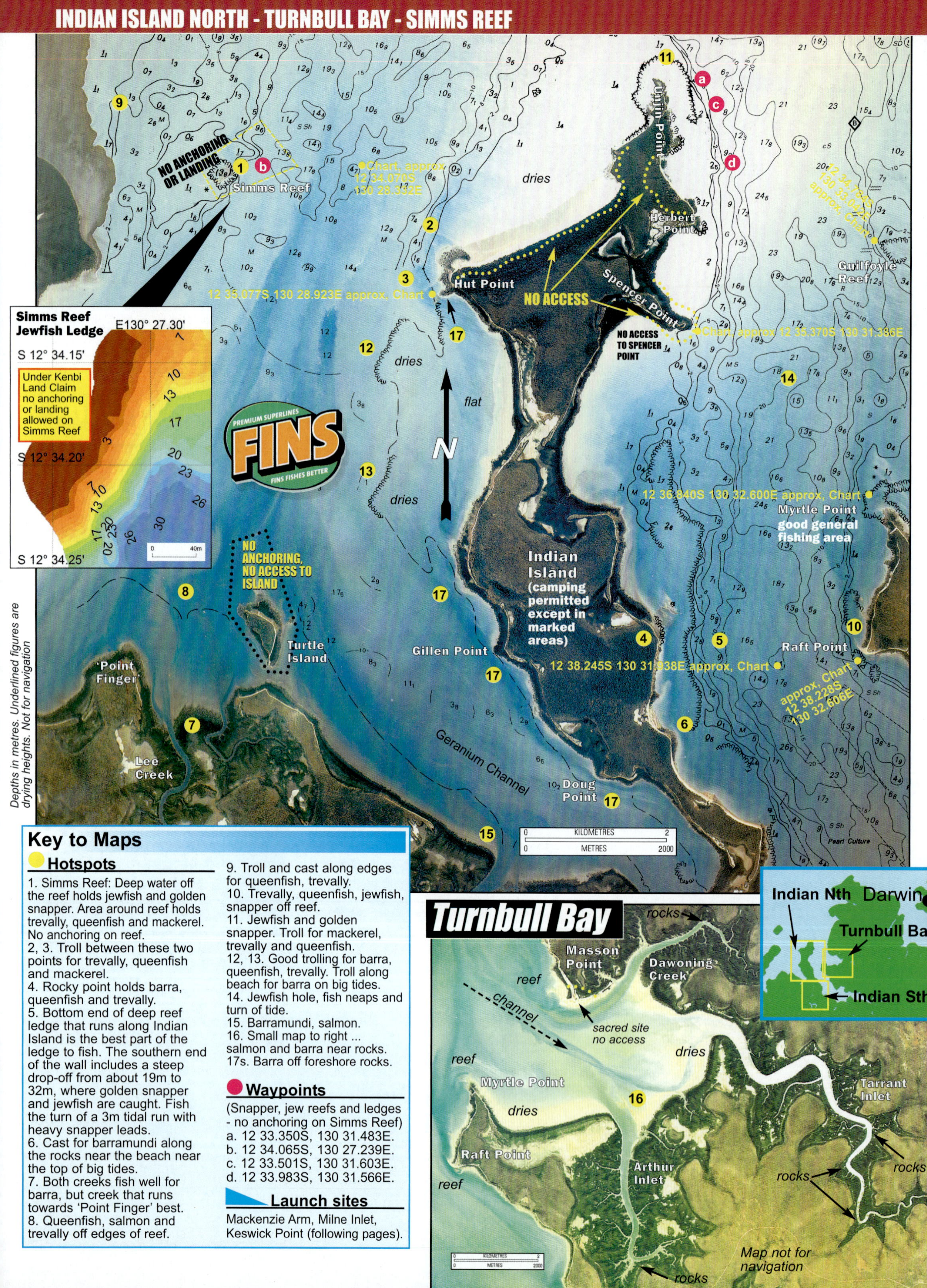

INDIAN ISLAND NORTH - TURNBULL BAY - SIMMS REEF
Simms Reef Jewfish Ledge
E130° 27.30'
S 12° 34.15'
S 12° 34.20'
S 12° 34.25'
Under Kenbi Land Claim no anchoring or landing allowed on Simms Reef
NO ANCHORING OR LANDING
Simms Reef
Chart, approx 12 34.070S 130 28.332E
12 35.077S 130 28.923E approx, Chart
Hut Point
NO ACCESS
Herbert Point
Spencer Point
Chart, approx 12 35.370S 130 31.386E
NO ACCESS TO SPENCER POINT
Urijn Point
12 34.752S 130 33.043E approx, Chart
Guilfoyle Reef
dries
flat
12 36.840S 130 32.600E approx, Chart
Myrtle Point good general fishing area
NO ANCHORING, NO ACCESS TO ISLAND
Turtle Island
Indian Island (camping permitted except in marked areas)
Gillen Point
12 38.245S 130 31.938E approx, Chart
Raft Point
approx, Chart 12 38.228S 130 32.606E
'Point Finger'
Lee Creek
Geranium Channel
Doug Point
Depths in metres. Underlined figures are drying heights. Not for navigation
FINS
Key to Maps
Hotspots
1. Simms Reef: Deep water off the reef holds jewfish and golden snapper. Area around reef holds trevally, queenfish and mackerel. No anchoring on reef.
2, 3. Troll between these two points for trevally, queenfish and mackerel.
4. Rocky point holds barra, queenfish and trevally.
5. Bottom end of deep reef ledge that runs along Indian Island is the best part of the ledge to fish. The southern end of the wall includes a steep drop-off from about 19m to 32m, where golden snapper and jewfish are caught. Fish the turn of a 3m tidal run with heavy snapper leads.
6. Cast for barramundi along the rocks near the beach near the top of big tides.
7. Both creeks fish well for barra, but creek that runs towards 'Point Finger' best.
8. Queenfish, salmon and trevally off edges of reef.
9. Troll and cast along edges for queenfish, trevally.
10. Trevally, queenfish, jewfish, snapper off reef.
11. Jewfish and golden snapper. Troll for mackerel, trevally and queenfish.
12, 13. Good trolling for barra, queenfish, trevally. Troll along beach for barra on big tides.
14. Jewfish hole, fish neaps and turn of tide.
15. Barramundi, salmon.
16. Small map to right ... salmon and barra near rocks.
17s. Barra off foreshore rocks.
Waypoints
(Snapper, jew reefs and ledges - no anchoring on Simms Reef)
a. 12 33.350S, 130 31.483E.
b. 12 34.065S, 130 27.239E.
c. 12 33.501S, 130 31.603E.
d. 12 33.983S, 130 31.566E.
Launch sites
Mackenzie Arm, Milne Inlet, Keswick Point (following pages).
Turnbull Bay
rocks
Masson Point
Dawoning Creek
reef
channel
sacred site no access
dries
Myrtle Point
Tarrant Inlet
Raft Point
Arthur Inlet
Map not for navigation
Indian Nth
Darwin
Turnbull Bay
Indian Sth

Under Kenbi Land Claim guidelines camping is permitted on most of Indian Island. Get the detailed Kenbi access map at the Northern Land Council (NLC) website.

Indian Island

Bynoe Harbour was closed to barramundi netting in 2010. During suitable tides, barra, salmon and other species can be seen cruising the flats, usually near mangrove roots. Use small prawn imitation lures or shallow minnows. The creeks and sheltered area inside Indian Island have good barra fishing. 'Six Pack' and 'Bennett Creeks' have rock patches with snapper, barra, salmon, cod and jacks. Both sides of Indian Island have small rock outcrops which provide lure-casting opportunities, depending on the weather and tide. Flats fishing is best on building neap tides in warm weather, when there is little wind. Mud crabs are usually plentiful, especially in the dry season, with prawns best in Feb/March. Boat ramps at Mackenzie Arm, Milne Inlet and Crab Claw Island (off map) give easy access to Indian Island.

Key to Map

Hotspots

1. Barra, salmon on flat, sight casting.
2. Jacks, bream, golden snapper on rockbar at mid tide.
3. Jacks, snapper along rock edge.
4. Good barra drains, cast shallow lures on start of an outgoing tide.
5. Barra hole at creek junction - livebait at low tide.
6. Barra, snapper, bream and jacks on rocky patches.
7. Snapper, queenfish, grunter around small foreshore rock outcrops. Beware shallow rocky areas in the middle of the waterway.
8. Snapper, bream, jacks around rocky patches on incoming tide.

Launch sites

1 and 2. Public ramps. Useable over about 2m tide but beware rocks.
3. Private ramp with camping, phone (08) 8978 2700.
Ramps reached via unsealed roads off Fog Bay Rd, which is sealed.

War Wrecks

Several WWII aircraft wrecks exist in and around Bynoe Harbour. These include a USAAF Warhawk and RAAF Spitfire (both off Gilruth Point), a RAAF Vultee Vengeance (1.4km n-w of Dum in Mirrie Island), a RAAF Wirraway (at Milne Inlet) and a Mitchell Bomber (off Bare Sand Island). While these wrecks are not fishing spots, components may be visible at low tide, adding some interest for those visiting the area. Bynoe's aircraft and Darwin Harbour's shipwrecks are a reminder of the NT's wartime heritage. There are likely still undiscovered war wrecks in Darwin waters.

Boating safety equipment in the NT

Boats must carry two orange smoke flares, two red flares, an EPIRB and a V-sheet if operating in the NT's intermediate or open waters, which includes most waters you are likely to fish.

It is wise to carry a marine radio at all times.

VHF is the frequency of radio commonly used in recreational boating, and waterproof handheld and fixed VHF units are affordable.

A marine radio provides not only an added level of safety in areas visited by few boats, but allows skippers to communicate with other skippers and monitor communications between boats.

An operator qualification for VHF can be obtained with Charles Darwin University or the Seafood and Maritime Industries Training (SMIT).

Coast Radio Darwin monitors VHF Channel 16 for emergency calls.

Coast Radio also broadcasts weather reports over VHF Channel 67 at 8.03am and 6.03pm every day.

Mobile phone coverage is limited to non-existent at most Top End fishing locations.

A phone booster aerial can increase range on a boat but the extended range will not be sufficient to be relied on in emergencies.

A satellite phone provides insurance against breakdowns when travelling to remote areas, but it is not a substitute for a marine radio or EPIRB in an emergency.

Other legally required boating equipment includes an approved flotation device for each person on board, and an anchor fitted with not less than 3m of chain and rope of not less than 50m.

Two anchors are required if a boat is over 10m in length, but it is wise for any seagoing vessel to carry a spare anchor, chain and rope.

Boats under 5m must carry two oars fitted with rowlocks, unless the boat is fitted with auxiliary propulsion.

Boats must also have a bailer fitted with lanyard, or a bilge pump.

A bilge pump is required for all vessels with covered bilges.

Fresh drinking water must also be carried, with at least 2L for each person on board.

A waterproof torch and a fire extinguisher is required if a boat is between 5m and 10m in length, along with a compass or GPS unit and electronic or paper chart for the area of operation.

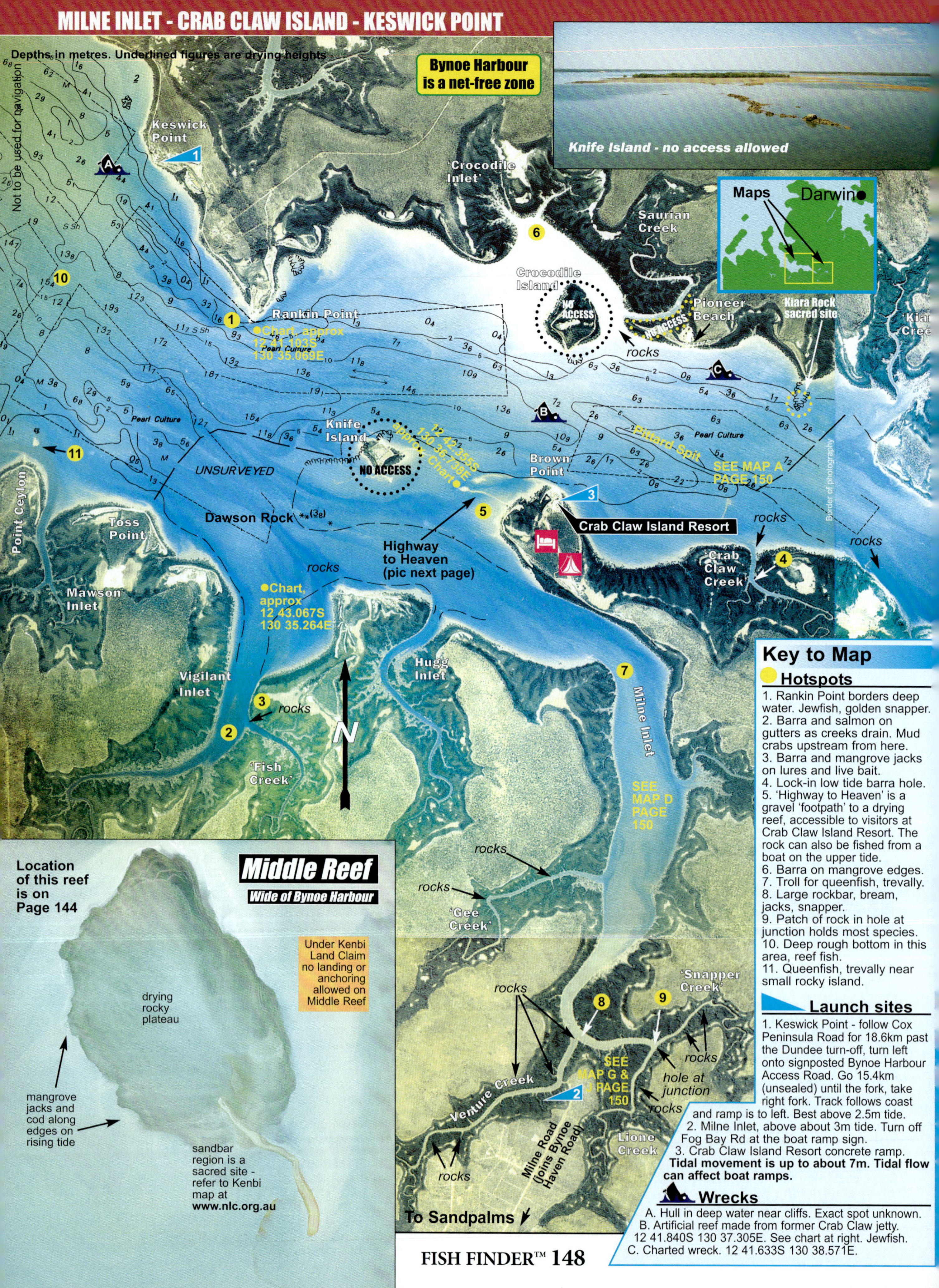

MILNE INLET - CRAB CLAW ISLAND - KESWICK POINT
Depths in metres. Underlined figures are drying heights
Not to be used for navigation
Bynoe Harbour is a net-free zone
Knife Island - no access allowed
Maps
Darwin
Keswick Point
'Crocodile Inlet'
Saurian Creek
Crocodile Island
NO ACCESS
Pioneer Beach
Kiara Rock sacred site
Rankin Point
Chart, approx 12 41.103S 130 35.069E
Pearl Culture
rocks
Knife Island
12 42.355S 130 36.739E approx Chart
Brown Point
Pittard Spit
SEE MAP A PAGE 150
UNSURVEYED
Dawson Rock
Crab Claw Island Resort
Point Ceylon
Toss Point
Mawson Inlet
Highway to Heaven (pic next page)
Crab Claw Creek
Chart, approx 12 43.067S 130 35.264E
Hugg Inlet
Vigilant Inlet
'Fish Creek'
N
Milne Inlet
SEE MAP D PAGE 150
'Gee Creek'
'Snapper Creek'
hole at junction
SEE MAP G & I PAGE 150
Venture Creek
Milne Road (joins Bynoe Haven Road)
Lione Creek
To Sandpalms
Middle Reef
Wide of Bynoe Harbour
Location of this reef is on Page 144
Under Kenbi Land Claim no landing or anchoring allowed on Middle Reef
drying rocky plateau
mangrove jacks and cod along edges on rising tide
sandbar region is a sacred site - refer to Kenbi map at www.nlc.org.au
Key to Map
Hotspots
1. Rankin Point borders deep water. Jewfish, golden snapper.
2. Barra and salmon on gutters as creeks drain. Mud crabs upstream from here.
3. Barra and mangrove jacks on lures and live bait.
4. Lock-in low tide barra hole.
5. 'Highway to Heaven' is a gravel 'footpath' to a drying reef, accessible to visitors at Crab Claw Island Resort. The rock can also be fished from a boat on the upper tide.
6. Barra on mangrove edges.
7. Troll for queenfish, trevally.
8. Large rockbar, bream, jacks, snapper.
9. Patch of rock in hole at junction holds most species.
10. Deep rough bottom in this area, reef fish.
11. Queenfish, trevally near small rocky island.
Launch sites
1. Keswick Point - follow Cox Peninsula Road for 18.6km past the Dundee turn-off, turn left onto signposted Bynoe Harbour Access Road. Go 15.4km (unsealed) until the fork, take right fork. Track follows coast and ramp is to left. Best above 2.5m tide.
2. Milne Inlet, above about 3m tide. Turn off Fog Bay Rd at the boat ramp sign.
3. Crab Claw Island Resort concrete ramp.
Tidal movement is up to about 7m. Tidal flow can affect boat ramps.
Wrecks
A. Hull in deep water near cliffs. Exact spot unknown.
B. Artificial reef made from former Crab Claw jetty. 12 41.840S 130 37.305E. See chart at right. Jewfish.
C. Charted wreck. 12 41.633S 130 38.571E.

Upper Bynoe

Tidal creeks, flats, channels and rockbars here produce barramundi, blue and threadfin salmon, queenfish, trevally, golden snapper, bream, jacks, jewfish, cod, brown sweetlip and mud crabs. All can be encountered in a day's fishing. There are gravel patches and oyster rock throughout, as well as deep reef ledges west of Crab Claw Island. Access is easy, thanks to public ramps on the southern side of the harbour off Fog Bay Rd. Crab Claw Island Resort has a ramp in the central harbour and the north shore has a launch site at Keswick Point. Neap tides are best for flats fishing. On big tides look for bust-ups around islands and points, where queenfish and trevally chase bait. Skippers should note that there are flats and rocks in unexpected places, and oyster rafts. Keep in mind the presence of crocodiles, stonefish, box jellyfish and stingrays when collecting bait.

SEE MAPS I and K PAGE 150

rock patches throughout

Fog Bay Road

Charlotte River

Strangman Creek

'Cecil Creek'

'Elmer Creek'

Under the Kenbi Land Claim over Cox Peninsula and Bynoe Harbour some areas have no access and some have access with restrictions as marked. A detailed map showing sacred site locations is available at www.nlc.org.au

rocks

shallow

Charlotte River

SEE MAP B AT RIGHT

'Fudd Creek'

Annie River

SEE MAP C PAGE 150

Rocky Creek

Basedow Creek

KILOMETRES 0 – 2
METRES 0 – 2000

Key to Map

Hotspots

1. Fish run-offs on the flats during receding tide and fish nearby small creek for barra, salmon.
2. Reefy area holds mixed fish.
3. Deeper water holds snapper and salmon at high tide.
4. Rocky area: snapper, salmon, bream and barra.

Launching at Keswick Point

Sheltered spots for small boats

Bynoe Harbour has a variety of fishing thanks to its great combination of flats, creeks, deep main channel, rocky reefs, rockbars and mangrove forest.

The flats tend to carry clearer water than Darwin Harbour, making the fish easier to see, improving prospects for fly and lure fishermen.

However, seeing barramundi and threadfin resting in the shallows and catching them are two different things. A careful approach and good presentation are often required for success. Small lures are recommended, especially vibes and prawn imitations, with fluorocarbon leaders. Livebait such as mullet and sardines is usually easy to find.

There is an artificial reef just off Crab Claw Island that produces king-size jewfish and golden snapper.

There is usually somewhere to fish in comfort out of the wind, but expect dry season south-easterlies and big tides to make the central harbour rough.

Also watch for storms from October, approaching dark stormfronts usually forewarn of trouble.

Crab Claw Island Resort, on Bynoe Harbour's southern shore, has elevated cabins, an open-air restaurant, campground and boat ramp, in a handy central location. This is the only development on the southern side.

A short drive from the Milne Inlet ramp is Sandpalms Resort, which has accommodation, a restaurant and bar, fuel and most supplies that fishermen need.

Looking south over the Charlotte and Annie junction in Bynoe Harbour

Walking the 'Highway to Heaven' at Crab Claw Island ... the low-tide gravel bar leads to a drying rock that is a casting platform, but watch the tide

Crab Claw Jetty

Contour lines and datum provided by Sea in 3D - for more maps visit www.users.bigpond.com/seain3d

130 37.25 E
130 37.26 E
130 37.27 E
130 37.28 E
130 37.29 E
130 37.30 E
130 37.31 E
130 37.32 E

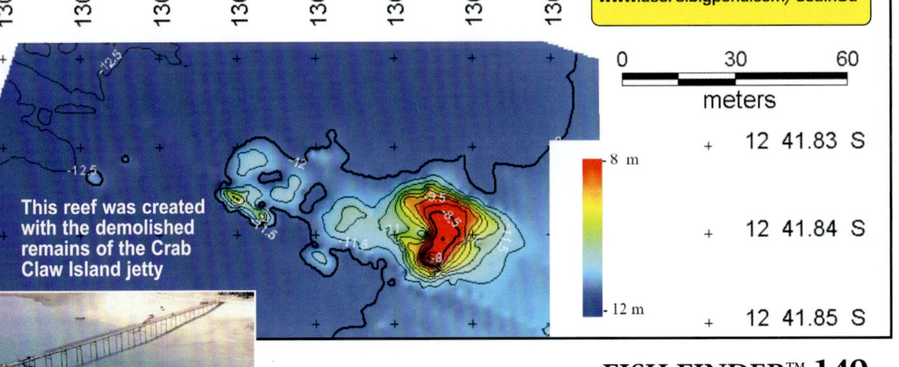

This reef was created with the demolished remains of the Crab Claw Island jetty

BYNOE HARBOUR AT LOW TIDE

MAP D: Looking up Milne Inlet at low tide

MAP E: Phoenix Inlet barra hole at low tide

See Pages 148-149 for this overall map area. MAP A: Looking from the south side of Bynoe Harbour towards Crocodile Island, with Crab Claw Island visible to the far left. This image, taken on a .13m low tide, shows sandbars that can catch unwary boaters. MAP B is on Page 149 (previous page). MAP C: The lower Charlotte River. MAP I: The upper tidal reaches of the Charlotte River just above the main rockbar on a .13m low tide. MAP G: The Milne Inlet boat ramp, with a rockbar at the creek junction immediately downstream

MAP H: Phoenix Inlet mouth at low tide

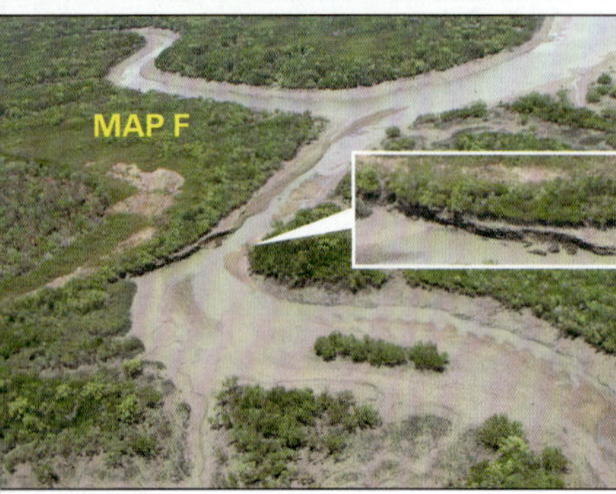

MAP F: This rockbar, off Mackenzie Arm, fishes on neap tides for bream and jacks. See Page 148.

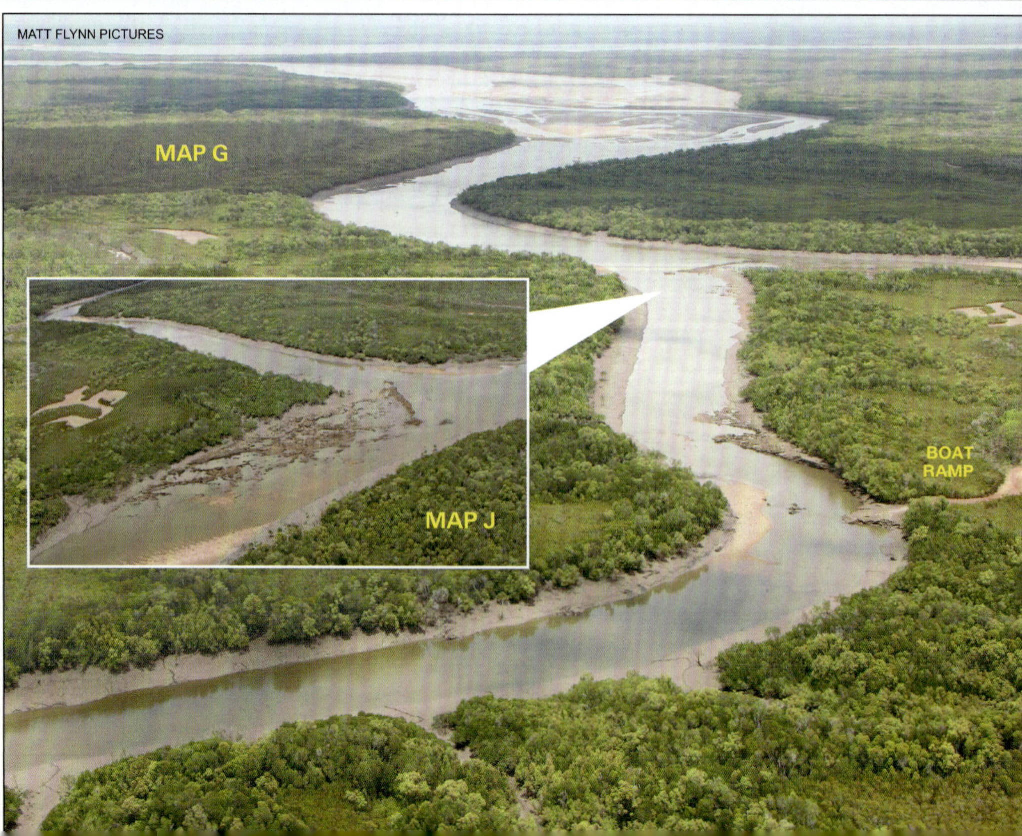

Dundee for bills and barramundi

Rock patches south of Dundee ramp produce large barra at high tide, usually in the early morning

The Dundee Beach ramp, often affected by sand, was to be upgraded in late 2022

RHONDA LEBROCQUE

Dundee Beach is the gateway to Fog Bay, 65km south-west of the NT capital city of Darwin.

The bay has coastal rock patches, shallow reefs, sailfish grounds and an offshore artificial reef, all supercharged each wet season by floodwaters from the Finniss and "Little Finniss" Rivers.

In a single day a well-organised crew can catch sailfish, reef fish and barramundi.

The bay can be fished on bigger tides than grounds off Darwin, as Fog Bay is less impacted by tidal currents.

There's plenty of fishing in close, but for those who venture about 70km out, are big red emperor, huge mangrove jacks and largemouth nannygai.

Pelagic fish are found throughout, with spanish mackerel caught in close during the dry season. To the south are the Peron Island grounds, and to the north is the entrance to Bynoe Harbour.

For landbased fishermen, the Dundee rocks produce barramundi, blue salmon, goldspot cod, golden snapper, jacks, trevally and queenfish.

For boaters, sailfish are a major fishery, with multiple hookups possible. Black marlin from 150kg down to 1kg are caught, suggesting a spawning ground is near.

There are cabins, camping and retail at the local lodge, with B&B-style accommodation also available in the area.

Bynoe Harbour arms and the freshwater section of the Finniss River extend behind Fog Bay.

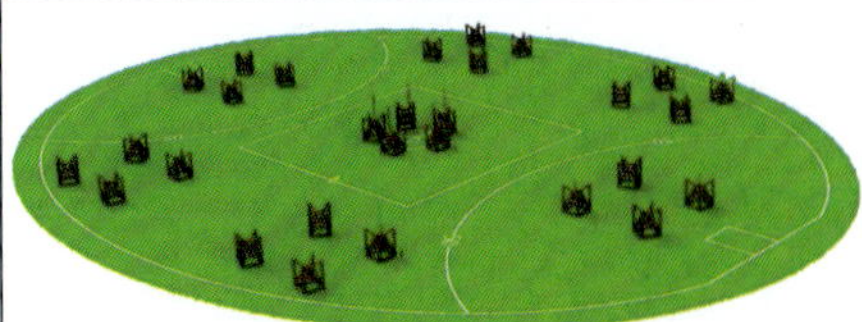

It is 20km from the Dundee Beach boat ramp to **Dundee Wide Artificial Reef**, where 29 concrete modules are installed in clusters of four over roughly the area of a football field, about 16m deep. **12 44.445S 130 10.387E**

Public boat ramps service Bynoe Harbour's Mackenzie and Milne Inlet arms, along with a ramp on the nearby freshwater section of the Finniss River at Hardcastle Rd, with accommodation at nearby Sandpalms Resort.

The tidal range in this area reaches 7m+ and there are drying reefs and flats, so boating must be undertaken with care.

Troll the foreshore rocks

Fishermen who use the boat ramp at Fog Bay's Dundee Beach tend to head wide to outlying reefs, or south to the Finniss River.

Yet there is good fishing to be had near the ramp along the beaches and headlands.

The rocks immediately south of the ramp hold large saltwater barramundi.

These barra can be fished landbased or by trolling close in calm conditions around high tide.

For yakkers and dinghy fishos, north of the ramp up to the Bynoe Harbour entrance are four rock outcrops along the beach that produce queenfish, salmon, barra, trevally, cod, and golden snapper.

The edges of these rocks can be fished in a dinghy during suitable weather, ideally if the wind is blowing offshore.

The secret to success is to be on the water very early, before the sun rises, during an incoming tide.

MATT FLYNN PICTURE

'Tamar Creek' at low tide ...the two rocky patches to the north troll well at high tide in calm weather

The water must be high enough to allow trolling and casting against the rocks. Use shallow to medium depth minnow lures on light rods and get in as close as conditions safely allow.

The rocks B and C on the map are usually where the action is. The photo of Tamar Creek shows rock patches B and C in the distance, exposed by the low tide.

Trolling along the sand/rock edge with lures that swim near the bottom will catch snapper and cod.

When the tide runs out troll Tamar Creek mouth.

The rock headland marked A can be reached on foot via the beach and is a great platform near high tide.

Queenfish, brassy trevally, blue and threadfin salmon, golden snapper, mangrove jacks and occasional barramundi can be expected.

Big jewfish have been caught from shore, so anything is possible.

Once the trolling run to headland C is complete, it is only a short run out to the shallow Roche Reefs and Loee Patches, where much the same species can be encountered, along with a good run of big spanish mackerel during the dry season months, and also queenfish and trevally.

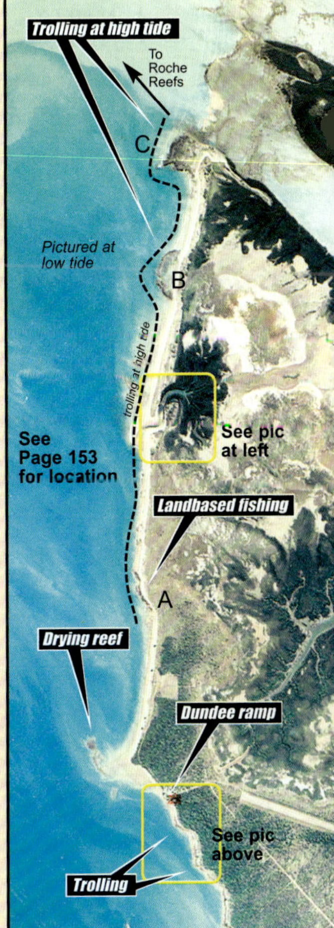

Looking n-w from Madford Inlet towards Grose Island

The south edges of Roche Reefs at low tide

Stingray Head, located between the Lodge of Dundee and Finniss River

Reef between Patterson Point and Warrmali Island, with Roche Reefs to the left, pictured at low tide

Dundee Beach

Fog Bay has patches of drying rock, the locations of which should be noted before boating. There are significant patches near Dundee boat ramp, and another is encountered when heading towards Roche Reefs. Fog Bay is a prolific area with jewfish, golden snapper, barramundi, blue and threadfin salmon, queenfish, cod, trevally, spanish mackerel and more. Large barramundi are caught on the coastal rocks north and south of the boat ramp during calm early morning high tides, especially in warm weather before the monsoon. The inner edges of Roche Reefs can be fished in small boats and produce mackerel, trevally and snapper in just a few metres of water, with sight-fishing on neap high tides. No anchoring or alighting is allowed on Roche Reefs under Kenbi rules. The entrance to Bynoe Harbour between the mainland and the first island dries and should only be navigated on the upper tide. Rocky headlands just south of Dundee boat ramp can be trolled at high tide for cod and barra. Just 4km south of the ramp is "Fog Rock", a small drying reef at 12 46.242S 130 20.938E, always worth a cast. At the far south end of Fog Bay, rocks inside Point Jenny are a big barra hotspot in the Build-up, but at publication access was only permitted to the mean low water mark. Dundee Jewfish Reef near the ramp (see chart at right) has blue salmon and jewfish, but is now overshadowed by the Dundee Wide Artificial Reef 20km out, made up of concrete modules spread in clusters of four over a football field-sized area. Fog Bay is known for its sailfish, with numbers varying each year with bait abundance. The 'Witch's Nose' at 12 41.378S 130 06.816E is a good sailfish starting point. Fog Bay's widest grounds produce big red emperor, nannygai, mangrove jacks and more.

Key to Map (next page)

Hotspots

1. High-tide trolling along rocks for queenfish, barra, snapper, blue salmon, trevally, cod.
2. Good land-based ledge at high tide.
3. Troll creek mouth for queenfish, trevally.
4. Shallow estuary with gutters. Barra, salmon, crabs.
5. Barra and crabs.
6. Fish rocks south of ramp for salmon, barra.

Wrecks and reefs

A. 20km from boat ramp to Dundee Wide Artificial Reef, 12 44.445S 130 10.387E, approx 16m deep.

Launch sites

1. Dundee ramp is concrete, but lower section affected by sand at times. Upgrade planned at publication. Add about 30 minutes to Darwin tides. Some fishos travel by 4WD on the beach from Stingray Head to fish or launch off the bank at Finniss River mouth, but this is partly private land and access could close at any time.

GPS waypoints

a. 12 39.182S 130 20.099E, 9m, mackerel, queenfish.
b. 12 40.926S 130 19.741E, reef (dries).
c. Dundee Jew Reef, best at night. Map at right.
d. 12 43.686S 130 20.683E, reef dries, queenfish, salmon, snapper around edges.

IMPORTANT PICTURE FOR DUNDEE NEWBIES!

Looking south towards the Lodge of Dundee at low tide ... note the drying reefs just offshore from the boat ramp

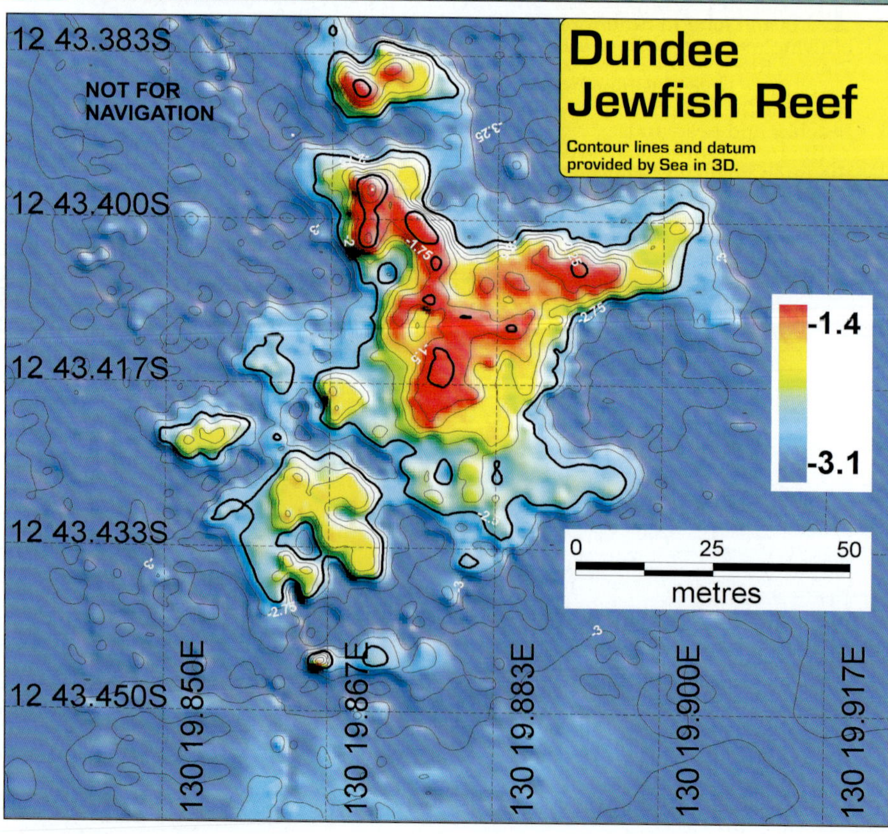

Dundee Jewfish Reef

Contour lines and datum provided by Sea in 3D.

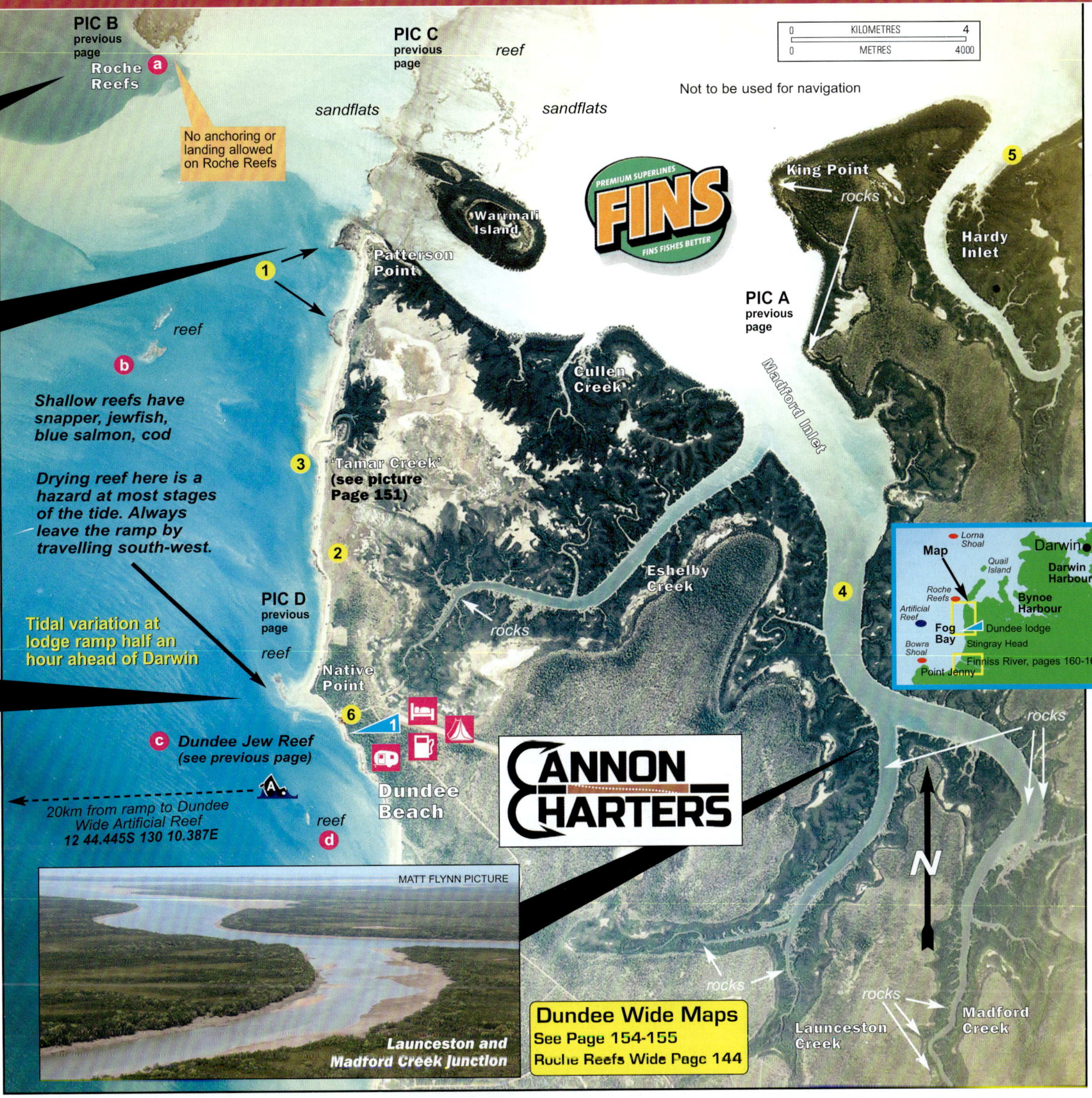

KILOMETRES 0 4
METRES 0 4000

Not to be used for navigation

PIC B previous page

(a) Roche Reefs

No anchoring or landing allowed on Roche Reefs

PIC C previous page

reef

sandflats

sandflats

PREMIUM SUPERLINES FINS FINS FISHES BETTER

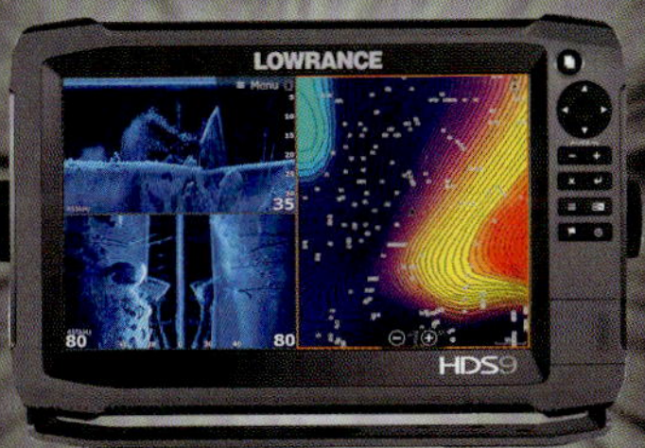

King Point

rocks

(5)

Hardy Inlet

Warrmali Island

(1)

Patterson Point

PIC A previous page

reef

(b)

Cullen Creek

Madford Inlet

Shallow reefs have snapper, jewfish, blue salmon, cod

(3) 'Tamar Creek' (see picture Page 151)

Drying reef here is a hazard at most stages of the tide. Always leave the ramp by travelling south-west.

(2)

Eshelby Creek

(4)

Map: Loma Shoal, Quail Island, Darwin, Darwin Harbour, Roche Reefs, Artificial Reef, Bynoe Harbour, Fog Bay, Dundee lodge, Bowra Shoal, Stingray Head, Finniss River, pages 160-161, Point Jenny

PIC D previous page

reef

rocks

Tidal variation at lodge ramp half an hour ahead of Darwin

Native Point

(6)

rocks

(c) Dundee Jew Reef (see previous page)

CANNON CHARTERS

20km from ramp to Dundee Wide Artificial Reef 12 44.445S 130 10.387E

Dundee Beach

reef

(d)

N

MATT FLYNN PICTURE

Launceston and Madford Creek Junction

rocks

rocks

Dundee Wide Maps See Page 154-155 Roche Reefs Wide Page 144

Launceston Creek

Madford Creek

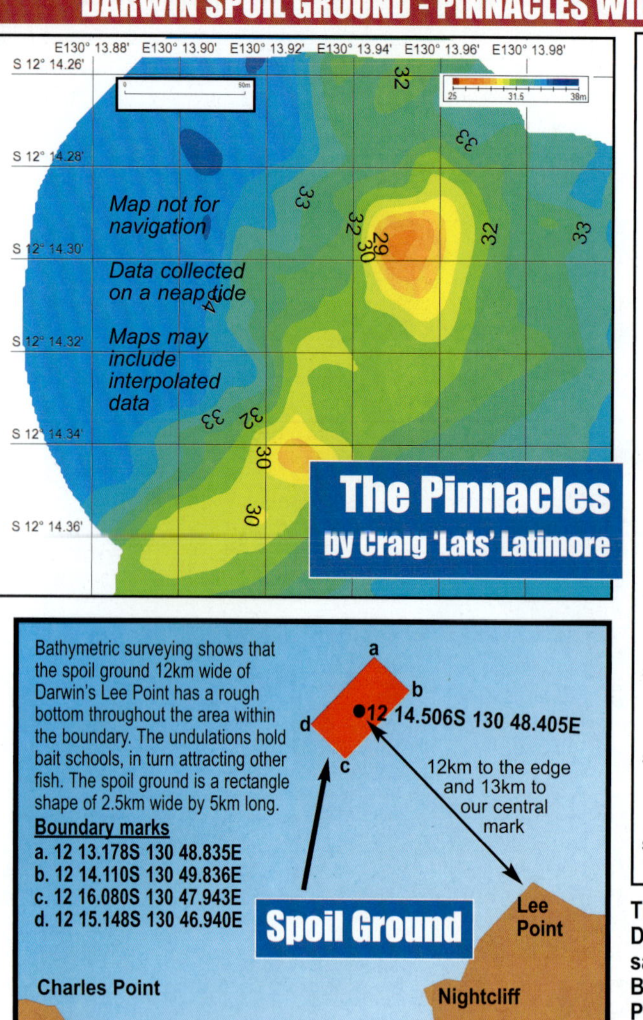

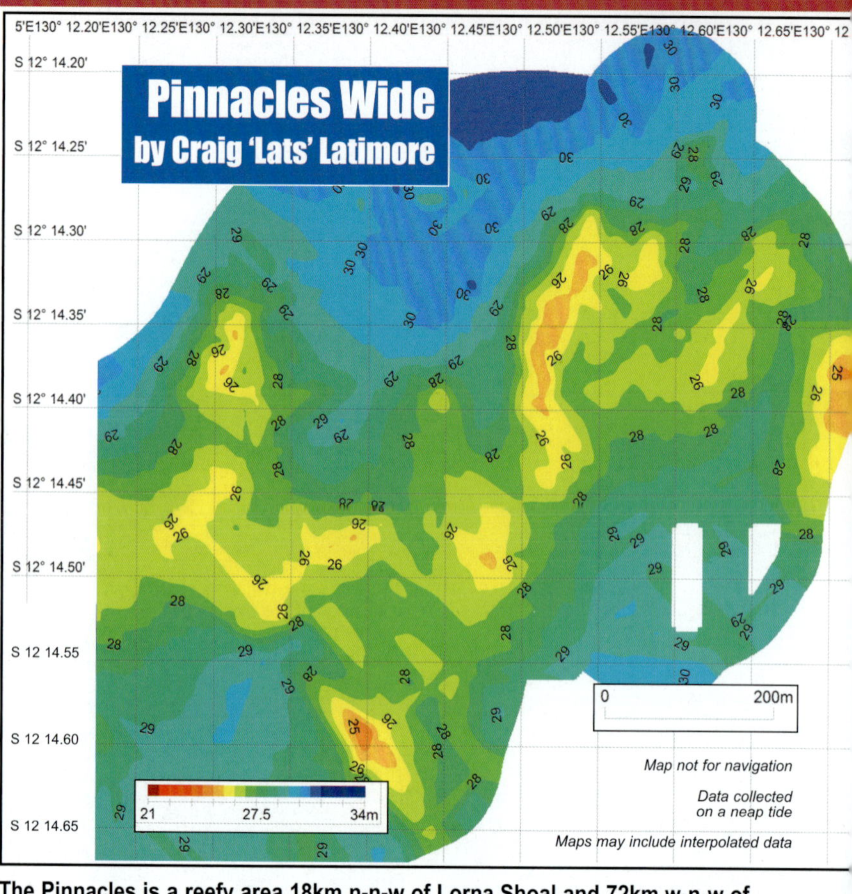

The Pinnacles is a reefy area 18km n-n-w of Lorna Shoal and 72km w-n-w of Darwin. It is known for spanish mackerel, but also produces reef fish. Expect sailfish on smaller tides when the water clears. The Pinnacles is 40km from Bare Sand Island anchorage outside Bynoe Harbour. Just 15km west of the Pinnacles is another reef area at 12 14.449S 130 03.502E, as shown on Chart AUS309. The reefs shown on the two micro charts here are 2.6km apart. LEFT: Darwin's Spoil Ground is the dredgings produced from Inpex gas pipeline work.

Bass Reef

This shallow rocky reef extends north from islands outside Bynoe Harbour through to Lorna Shoal. The reef is about 60km by sea from Darwin, or 45km from Bynoe Harbour boat ramps, or 22km from the Lodge of Dundee in Fog Bay. Bass Reef is popular with Darwin trailerboaters who use the Bare Sand Island natural anchorage for overnight stays, from which it is only 10km. Bass Reef and Loee Patches to the south-west are useful spots during bigger tides as the area is less affected by currents than deeper reefs. Bass Reef is popular with spearfishermen, as it is shallow and reasonably clear during neap high tides. The reef is best known for quality golden snapper and spanish mackerel, but it also has jewfish, cod, flag, tuskfish and coral trout. The reef produces big fish despite being shallow. Jewfish are best on big tides. The reef is a navigation hazard towards low tide. Beware breaking waves. Trolling and bait fishing works well, with mackerel best in mornings and afternoons. A great way to fish is to anchor and berley - expect to see snapper, mackerel, sharks and more in the berley trail. Travelling to Bass Reef from Darwin requires some planning with the tides and wind as the Charles Point area can be rough when wind and tide are opposed.

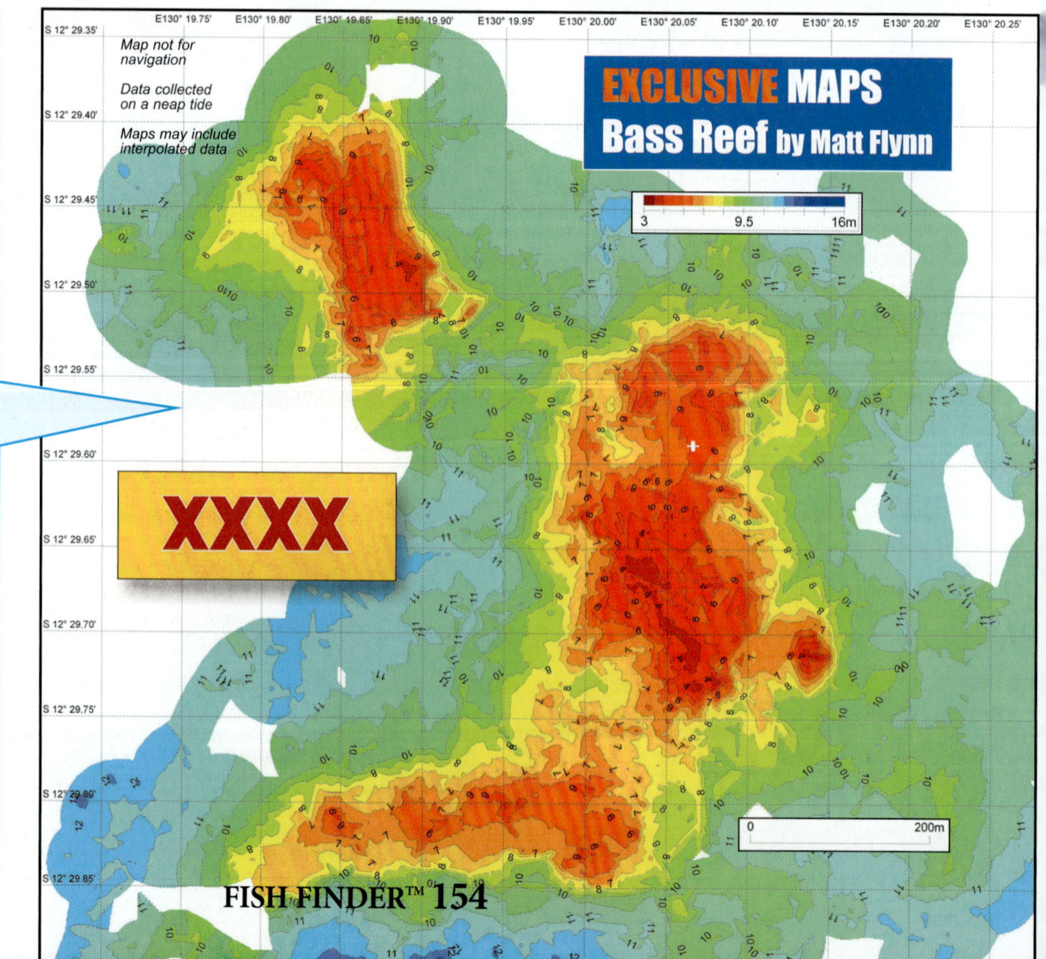

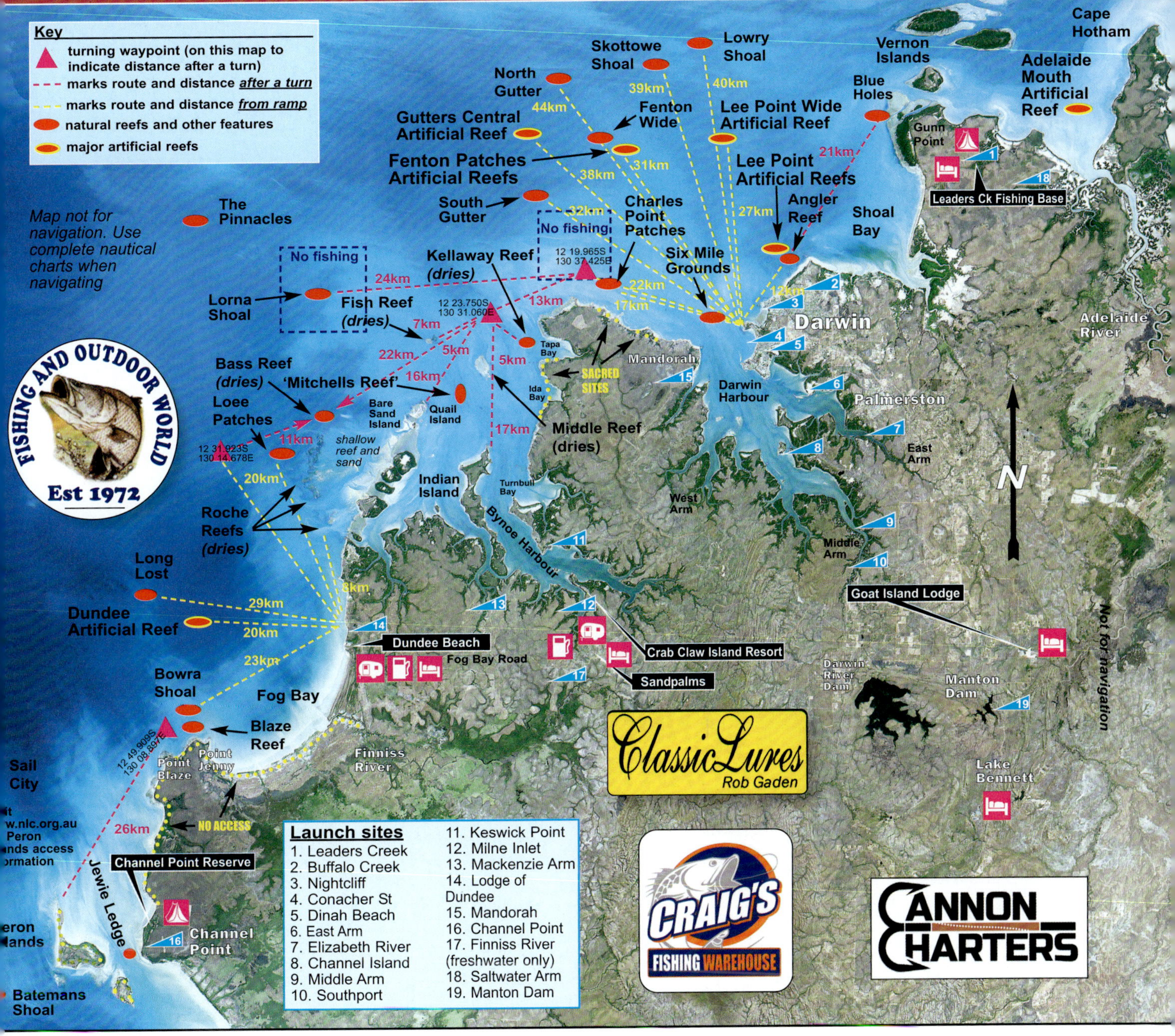

Key
- turning waypoint (on this map to indicate distance after a turn)
- marks route and distance *after a turn*
- marks route and distance *from ramp*
- natural reefs and other features
- major artificial reefs

Map not for navigation. Use complete nautical charts when navigating

Skottowe Shoal
Lowry Shoal
Cape Hotham
Vernon Islands
Adelaide Mouth Artificial Reef
North Gutter
Blue Holes
Gunn Point
39km
40km
44km
Fenton Wide
Lee Point Wide Artificial Reef
Gutters Central Artificial Reef
21km
Fenton Patches Artificial Reefs
31km
38km
Lee Point Artificial Reefs
Leaders Ck Fishing Base
South Gutter
Charles Point Patches
32km
27km
Angler Reef
Shoal Bay
The Pinnacles
No fishing
12 19.965S 130 37.425E
No fishing
Kellaway Reef (dries)
Six Mile Grounds
24km
22km
Lorna Shoal
Fish Reef (dries)
12 23.750S 130 31.060E
13km
17km
12km
Darwin
7km
Adelaide River
22km
5km
Tapa Bay
Mandorah
5km
Bass Reef (dries)
16km
SACRED SITES
'Mitchells Reef'
Ida Bay
Darwin Harbour
Loee Patches
Bare Sand Island
Quail Island
Palmerston
12 31.923S 130 14.678E
11km
shallow reef and sand
17km
Middle Reef (dries)
East Arm
20km
Indian Island
Turnbull Bay
N
Roche Reefs (dries)
West Arm
Bynoe Harbour
Middle Arm
Long Lost
8km
Goat Island Lodge
29km
Dundee Artificial Reef
20km
Dundee Beach
Crab Claw Island Resort
Fog Bay Road
23km
Sandpalms
Not for navigation
Bowra Shoal
Fog Bay
Darwin River Dam
Manton Dam
Blaze Reef
12 49.909S 130 09.897E
Point Blaze
Point Jenny
Finniss River
Sail City
Lake Bennett
26km
NO ACCESS
...t w.nlc.org.au Peron ...nds access ...ormation
Channel Point Reserve
Jewie Lodge
...eron ...ands
Channel Point
Batemans Shoal

FISHING AND OUTDOOR WORLD Est 1972

Launch sites
1. Leaders Creek
2. Buffalo Creek
3. Nightcliff
4. Conacher St
5. Dinah Beach
6. East Arm
7. Elizabeth River
8. Channel Island
9. Middle Arm
10. Southport
11. Keswick Point
12. Milne Inlet
13. Mackenzie Arm
14. Lodge of Dundee
15. Mandorah
16. Channel Point
17. Finniss River (freshwater only)
18. Saltwater Arm
19. Manton Dam

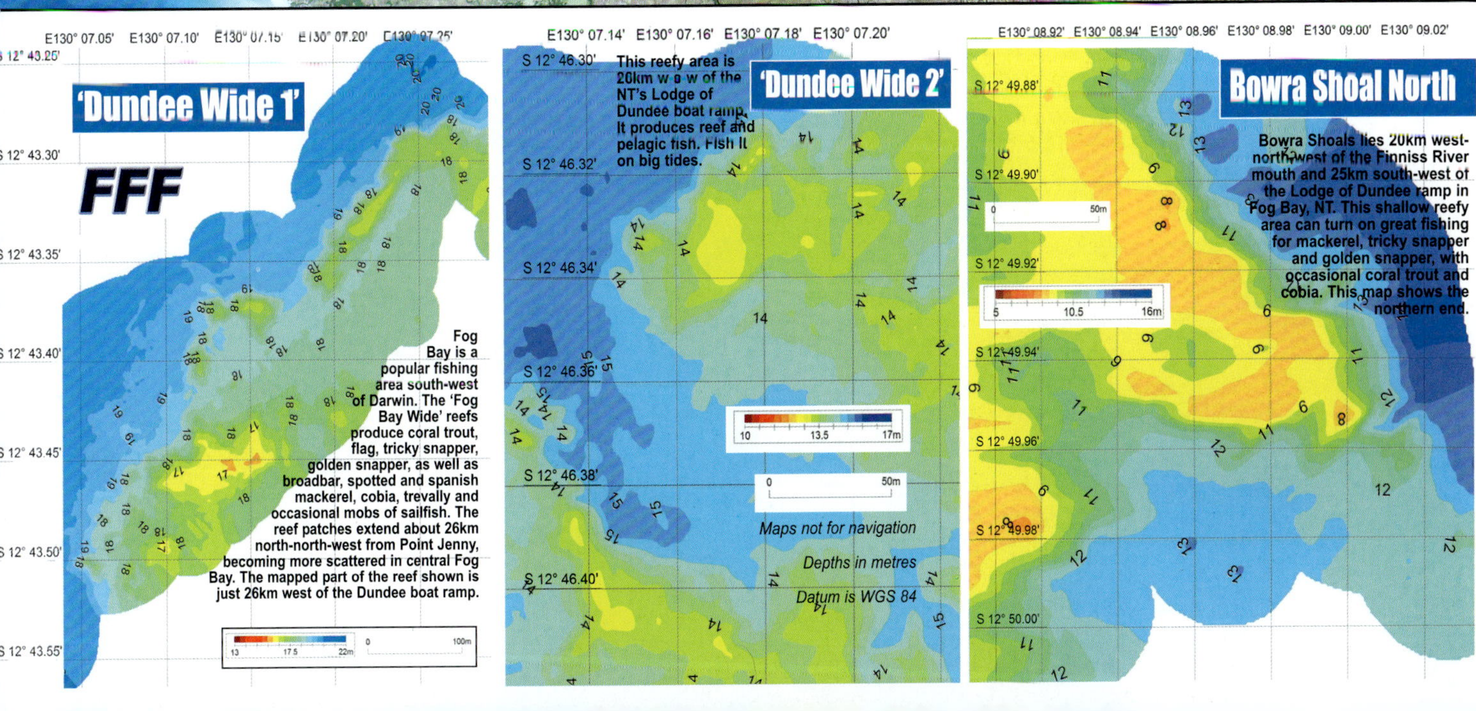

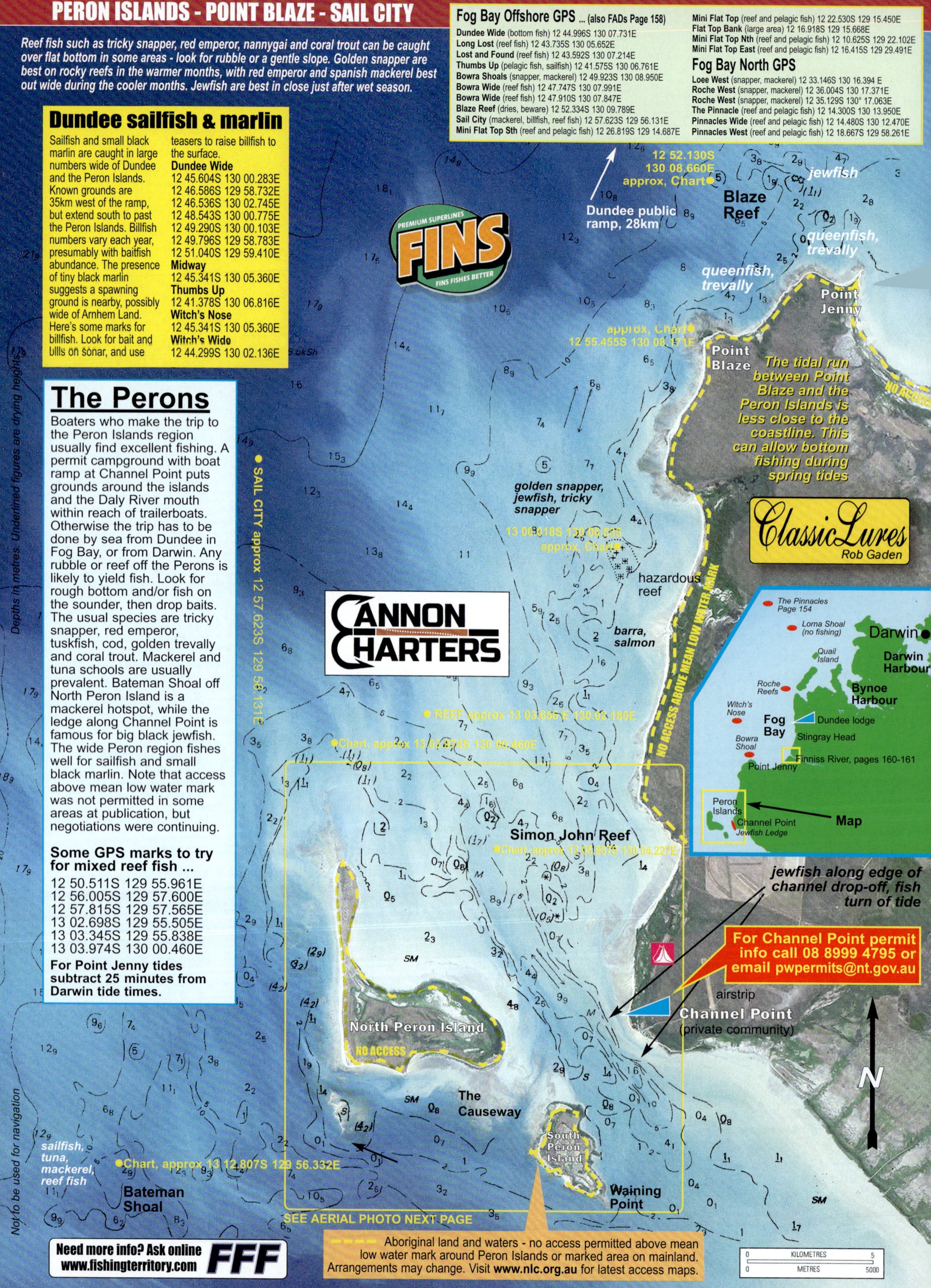
PERON ISLANDS - POINT BLAZE - SAIL CITY
Reef fish such as tricky snapper, red emperor, nannygai and coral trout can be caught over flat bottom in some areas - look for rubble or a gentle slope. Golden snapper are best on rocky reefs in the warmer months, with red emperor and spanish mackerel best out wide during the cooler months. Jewfish are best in close just after wet season.
Fog Bay Offshore GPS ... (also FADs Page 158)
Dundee Wide (bottom fish) 12 44.996S 130 07.731E
Long Lost (reef fish) 12 43.735S 130 05.652E
Lost and Found (reef fish) 12 43.592S 130 07.214E
Thumbs Up (pelagic fish, sailfish) 12 41.575S 130 06.761E
Bowra Shoals (snapper, mackerel) 12 49.923S 130 08.950E
Bowra Wide (reef fish) 12 47.747S 130 07.991E
Bowra Wide (reef fish) 12 47.910S 130 07.847E
Blaze Reef (dries, beware) 12 52.334S 130 09.789E
Sail City (mackerel, billfish, reef fish) 12 57.623S 129 56.131E
Mini Flat Top Sth (reef and pelagic fish) 12 26.819S 129 14.687E
Mini Flat Top (reef and pelagic fish) 12 22.530S 129 15.450E
Flat Top Bank (large area) 12 16.918S 129 15.668E
Mini Flat Top Nth (reef and pelagic fish) 12 10.625S 129 22.102E
Mini Flat Top East (reef and pelagic fish) 12 16.415S 129 29.491E
Fog Bay North GPS
Loee West (snapper, mackerel) 12 33.146S 130 16.394 E
Roche West (snapper, mackerel) 12 36.004S 130 17.371E
Roche West (snapper, mackerel) 12 35.129S 130° 17.063E
The Pinnacle (reef and pelagic fish) 12 14.300S 130 13.950E
Pinnacles Wide (reef and pelagic fish) 12 14.480S 130 12.470E
Pinnacles West (reef and pelagic fish) 12 18.667S 129 58.261E
Dundee sailfish & marlin
Sailfish and small black marlin are caught in large numbers wide of Dundee and the Peron Islands. Known grounds are 35km west of the ramp, but extend south to past the Peron Islands. Billfish numbers vary each year, presumably with baitfish abundance. The presence of tiny black marlin suggests a spawning ground is nearby, possibly wide of Arnhem Land. Here's some marks for billfish. Look for bait and bills on sonar, and use teasers to raise billfish to the surface.
Dundee Wide
12 45.604S 130 00.283E
12 46.586S 129 58.732E
12 46.536S 130 02.745E
12 48.543S 130 00.775E
12 49.290S 130 00.103E
12 49.796S 129 58.783E
12 51.040S 129 59.410E
Midway
12 45.341S 130 05.360E
Thumbs Up
12 41.378S 130 06.816E
Witch's Nose
12 45.341S 130 05.360E
Witch's Wide
12 44.299S 130 02.136E
The Perons
Boaters who make the trip to the Peron Islands region usually find excellent fishing. A permit campground with boat ramp at Channel Point puts grounds around the islands and the Daly River mouth within reach of trailerboats. Otherwise the trip has to be done by sea from Dundee in Fog Bay, or from Darwin. Any rubble or reef off the Perons is likely to yield fish. Look for rough bottom and/or fish on the sounder, then drop baits. The usual species are tricky snapper, red emperor, tuskfish, cod, golden trevally and coral trout. Mackerel and tuna schools are usually prevalent. Bateman Shoal off North Peron Island is a mackerel hotspot, while the ledge along Channel Point is famous for big black jewfish. The wide Peron region fishes well for sailfish and small black marlin. Note that access above mean low water mark was not permitted in some areas at publication, but negotiations were continuing.
Some GPS marks to try for mixed reef fish ...
12 50.511S 129 55.961E
12 56.005S 129 57.600E
12 57.815S 129 57.565E
13 02.698S 129 55.505E
13 03.345S 129 55.838E
13 03.974S 130 00.460E
For Point Jenny tides subtract 25 minutes from Darwin tide times.
Depths in metres. Underlined figures are drying heights.
Not to be used for navigation
SAIL CITY approx 12 57.623S 129 56.131E
12 52.130S 130 08.660E approx, Chart
Dundee public ramp, 28km
Blaze Reef
jewfish
queenfish, trevally
queenfish, trevally
Point Jenny
approx, Chart
12 55.455S 130 08.171E
Point Blaze
The tidal run between Point Blaze and the Peron Islands is less close to the coastline. This can allow bottom fishing during spring tides
NO ACCESS
golden snapper, jewfish, tricky snapper
13 00.018S 130 06.836 approx, Chart
hazardous reef
barra, salmon
NO ACCESS ABOVE MEAN LOW WATER MARK
REEF approx 13 03.656 E 130 02.180E
Chart, approx 13 03.974S 130 00.460E
Simon John Reef
Chart, approx 13 05.987S 130 04.227E
jewfish along edge of channel drop-off, fish turn of tide
For Channel Point permit info call 08 8999 4795 or email pwpermits@nt.gov.au
airstrip
Channel Point (private community)
North Peron Island
NO ACCESS
The Causeway
South Peron Island
Waining Point
sailfish, tuna, mackerel, reef fish
Chart, approx 13 12.807S 129 56.332E
Bateman Shoal
SEE AERIAL PHOTO NEXT PAGE
Aboriginal land and waters - no access permitted above mean low water mark around Peron Islands or marked area on mainland. Arrangements may change. Visit www.nlc.org.au for latest access maps.
KILOMETRES
METRES
The Pinnacles Page 154
Lorna Shoal (no fishing)
Quail Island
Darwin
Darwin Harbour
Roche Reefs
Bynoe Harbour
Witch's Nose
Fog Bay
Dundee lodge
Stingray Head
Bowra Shoal
Finniss River, pages 160-161
Point Jenny
Peron Islands
Map
Channel Point
Jewfish Ledge
N
FINS
CANNON CHARTERS
ClassicLures Rob Gaden
Need more info? Ask online www.fishingterritory.com
FFF

HELIFISH PICTURE

The area inside Point Jenny, at the far south of Fog Bay, provides some shelter from bad weather. This area is Aboriginal property to the mean low water mark

Reef at Point Blaze is a navigation hazard. This area is Aboriginal property to the mean low water mark

Remote camping

Channel Point Coastal Reserve campground, located on the mainland inside the Peron Islands, 130km south-west of Darwin, gives access to prime reef and barramundi hotspots.

An exposed, tide-dependent concrete ramp leads to prolific waters around the two islands, as well as the Anson Bay coastline and the mouth of the mighty Daly River to the south, and the rocky reefs off Point Blaze to the north.

There is no need to travel far for good fishing, as a long shallow ledge that runs along the coast just off the Channel Point community, is a black jewfish hotspot. The ledge is easily located on sonar.

To the south, the Anson Bay foreshore and creeks hold barramundi, threadfin and blue salmon and mud crabs, but watch the tide as this area dries.

Just 30km north of Channel Point is the beginning of a series of reefs that extend north of Point Blaze.

Wide grounds in this area are known for spanish mackerel and sailfish. Any rough bottom is likely to produce golden snapper, cod, coral trout, flag, golden trevally and more.

To visit the reserve, you must have a permit, even if not staying overnight. It is usually only accessible in the dry season, from May to November. By road you travel to the reserve either via Litchfield National Park using sealed roads from Batchelor, or via Cox Peninsula road and an unsealed road in Litchfield National Park. Once in Litchfield NP, turn west off the sealed Park Road just north of Wangi Falls, then travel 67km along the Marrindja, Labelle/Twin Hills unsealed road to the reserve. To make a booking, visit **https://nt.gov.au/leisure/parks-reserves/rules-and-permits/permits-for-parks/bookings-channel-point**

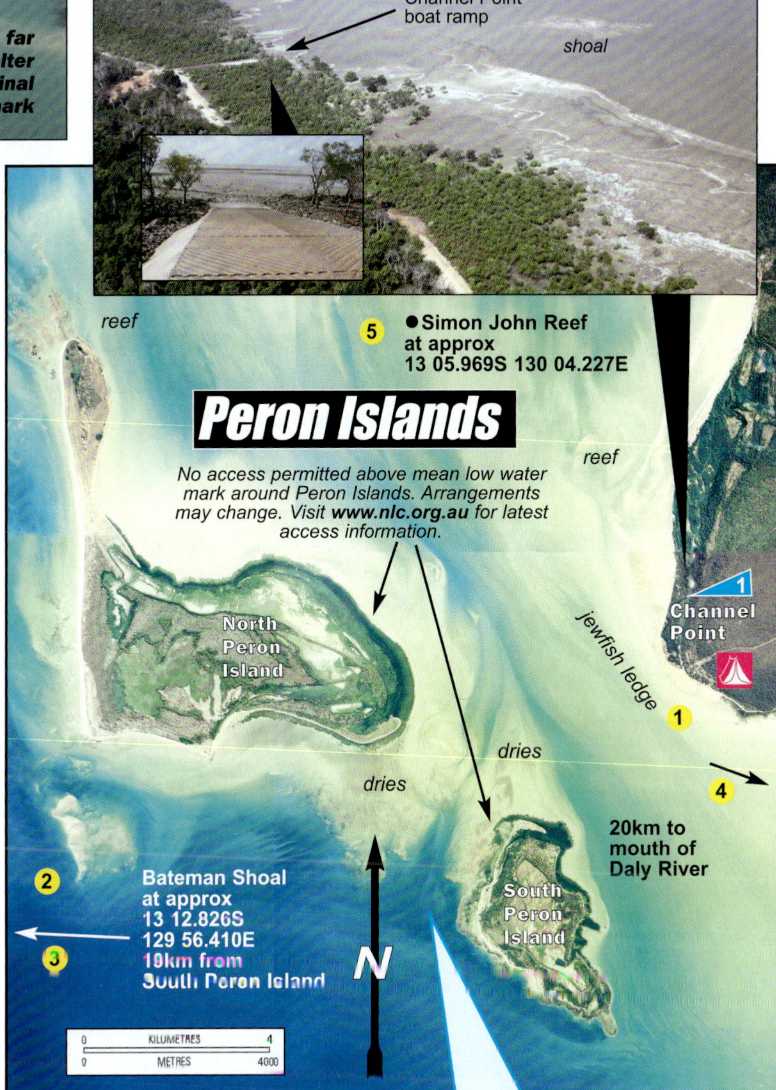

The gap between the Peron Islands on a spring low tide

Key to Map

Hotspots

1. The long drop-off along Channel Point produces large black jewfish. They usually bite best at the turn of the tide. Also golden snapper. Fishing at night with fresh bait brings best results. Catfish and small sharks can be a nuisance.
2. Queenfish off sandbar. Troll the current rips.
3. Mackerel and reef fish at Bateman Shoal. Find the deeper edges for better fishing. Top of the shoal has mostly bar-cheeked coral trout, cod and tuskfish.
4. Anson Bay flats through to the Daly River mouth have barramundi, salmon and mud crabs. Shallow, travel on a rising tide. Reynolds River (off map) has good barramundi run-off fishing during and just after wet season flooding.
5. Jewfish, golden snapper, tricky snapper, coral trout, tuskfish, queenfish, trevally around shallow reefs, best on bigger tides. Reasonably sheltered area but current rips through.

Launch sites

1. Channel Point, good ramp and camp. Permit fees and conditions apply, call (08) 8999 4795. Exposed ramp requires about 4m+ of water to launch. It is the closest public ramp to the Reynolds and Moyle Rivers.

Four engineered reefs

The largest single artificial reef deployment in the southern hemisphere took place in Northern Territory waters in late 2019.

Four custom-built reef sites were installed in the Greater Darwin region, each site consisting of 29 large concrete reef modules.

The individual modules stand 5m tall and 4m square at the base, weighing 24 tonnes each.

They are clustered in groups of mostly four modules.

Each site covers an area of 2.5ha, about the size of a football oval.

Two reefs are located east and west of the existing Fenton Patches Artificial Reef System, one is wide of popular Dundee Beach, and one is west of Cape Hotham, wide of the Adelaide River mouth.

Darwin waters are already well served with artificial wrecks and reefs, courtesy of the Bombing of Darwin Harbour in 1942, and Cyclone Tracy in 1974.

There are several long-established and productive artificial reefs.

Historically, the artificial reefs have been constructed using "materials of opportunity", such as decommissioned ships, trawlers, concrete pipes, culverts and discarded plant machinery.

The common euphemism for such installations is "junk reef".

More recently, artificial reef construction around the world has taken on a more scientific focus, with consideration given to specific construction materials and designs.

Such engineered reefs should last longer and improve fishing to a greater extent than junk reefs.

NT Fisheries says the four new reef complexes were engineered to suit their locations.

The concrete modules include internal caves, cryptic habitat and vertical relief that creates water upwellings.

In 2018, the Territory Government investigated possible locations for the new reefs, considering things such as water depth, commercial vessel traffic, existing fishing infrastructure and community feedback.

Ensuring safe clearance for commercial vessels meant the reefs had to go into a sufficient water depth, generally only found further off the coast.

Before the deployment, physical studies of the potential sites were conducted using sediment grabs, Baited Remote Underwater Video Systems (BRUVS) and bathymetric surveys to validate the suitability of sites and provide a baseline from which to reference future monitoring.

The new reefs were expected to take up to three years to become fully productive, which is late in 2022.

A variety of reef-associated species will benefit, including black jewfish, cod, groper and coral trout. There will also be species that remain adjacent to structures, such as snapper and emperor, along with pelagic fish such as mackerel and tuna.

The new reefs are suited to a range of fishing techniques.

Darwin's long-established junk reefs fish well for variety of fish.

The species mix tends to be somewhat site specific.

Some locations fish better than others for certain species, such as jewfish.

In Darwin Harbour, the degraded and/or partly salvaged remains of various WWII and cyclone wrecks still fish well today, even though many of the war wrecks have been extensively salvaged and have only a small remaining bottom profile.

For those with small boats, the Lee Point artificial reef system is productive and accessible from Darwin boat ramps.

Fishing artificial reefs is easier during smaller tides, as large tides bring strong currents and often rougher conditions.

Boaters can either drop a reef anchor onto a structure and pull up tight, if conditions allow, or drop a sand anchor near the reef and drift back to the site by letting out anchor rope.

If pulling up tight, beware a rising tide, which will gradually tighten the anchor rope and could cause a boat to go bow under.

"Spotlocking" with an electric motor is an ideal way to fish over wrecks and reefs, as it allows moving around without the need to pull up the anchor each time.

It is not uncommon to lose a stuck anchor when fishing artificial reefs.

Be sure to have adequate chain to guard against rope chafing, and always carry a spare anchor, chain and rope.

Reef fish tend to bite on the turn of the tide.

Move your boat if you don't get bites as bait placement can make a big difference to success when fishing wrecks and concrete modules.

Fish will often be at the part of the reef that is facing the current, or around bait congregations.

While bottom fishing, drop an unweighted bait out behind the boat for pelagic fish such as mackerel.

Berley can bring fish to the boat, but it also attracts sharks.

Sharks have become familiar with fishing boats at regularly visited spots such as artificial reefs, and they can make it impossible to land a fish, in which case it is best to move on.

If you want to catch a big jewfish, try fishing Darwin's artificial reefs or wrecks at night, and use a fresh piece of fish fillet for bait. You will need heavy tackle to pull big jewfish away from the structure.

Divers also use the artificial reefs, so watch for dive flags and keep clear.

***

GPS marks for Territory reefs, rockbars, FADs and more are in this book, or get these marks and hundreds more on the *NT Fishing GPS Data Card,* available at www.fishfinderbooks.com

The card's data can be downloaded onto most GPS units, saving hours of keying input.

Territory FADs

Topwater Fish Attracting Devices (FADs) have been installed in Top End waters.

NT Fisheries deployed five FADs off Darwin and Dundee Beach in September 2018.

The FADs were marked with yellow buoys and a flashing light.

These FADs attract both baitfish and large pelagic fish.

Note that they can break free from moorings. Never tie your boat up to a FAD.

The five marks are ...

Fenton Patches 1	12 10.290S 130 38.544E
Fenton Patches 2	12 10.013S 130 38.232E
North Gutter 1	12 05.459S 130 34.057E
North Gutter 2	12 05.200S 130 33.740E
Dundee Beach	12 40.000S 130 10.000E

NT GOVERNMENT PICTURE

Wharf platform has nearby reef

Darwin's landbased fishos are well catered for with 15 concrete reef modules installed off a public fishing platform at Stokes Hill Wharf.

Boat fishermen are excluded from the area, giving exclusive reef access for landbased anglers.

The components, pictured being installed below, were designed to combine the best features of a natural reef with caves, vertical relief and upwelling of water flow to create new habitats.

The site was originally occupied by timber hulls scuttled to provide good fishing from the public platform. These hulls degraded over time.

The new custom reefs produce cod, snapper and jewfish, with pelagic fish such queenfish and trevally also showing up. Squid and herring can also be caught in the area.

Barramundi are present near the surface around the wharf structure at night but are difficult to catch. A drop gaff is required to land big fish.

for bluewater fishermen

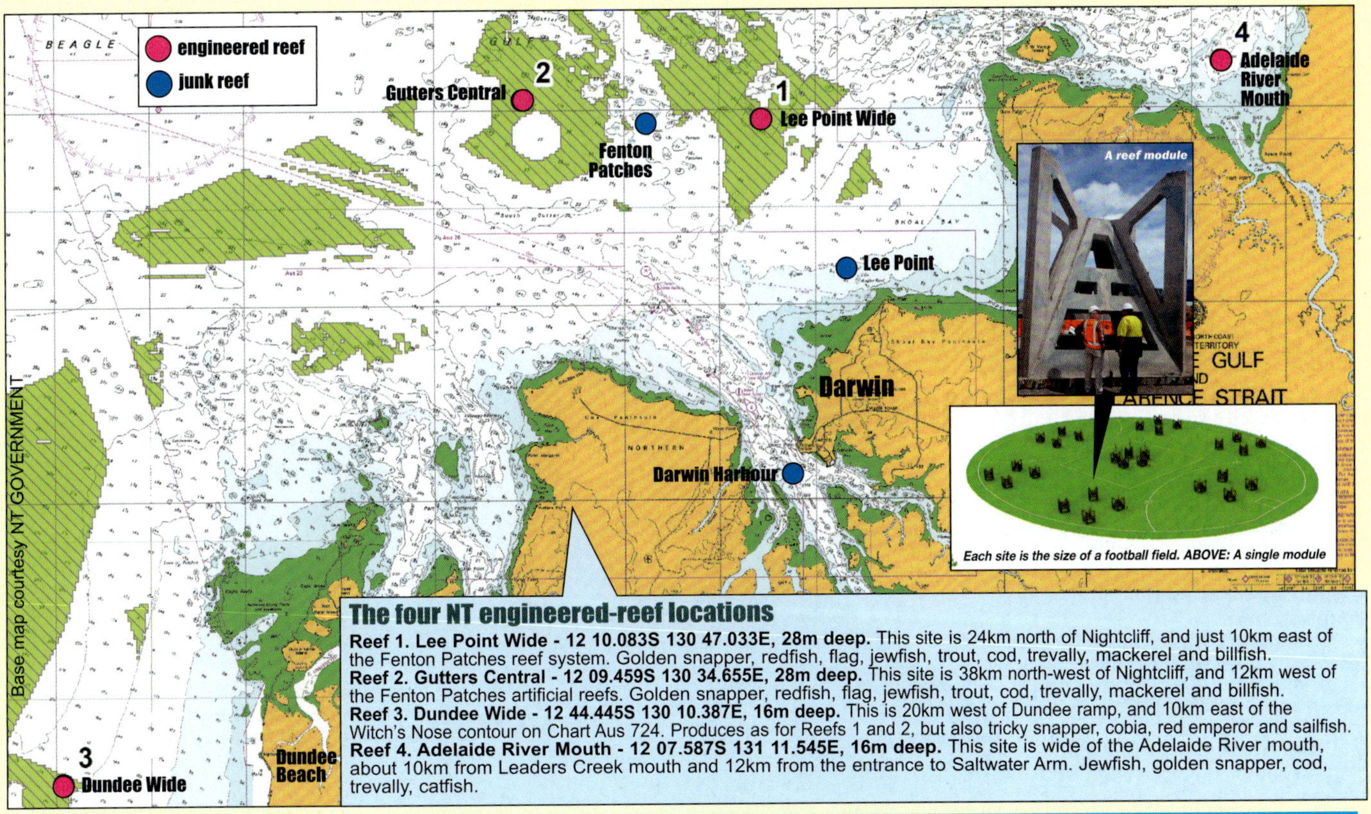

engineered reef
junk reef

2 Gutters Central
Fenton Patches
1 Lee Point Wide
4 Adelaide River Mouth
Lee Point
Darwin
Darwin Harbour
3 Dundee Wide
Dundee Beach

A reef module

Each site is the size of a football field. ABOVE: A single module

Base map courtesy NT GOVERNMENT

The four NT engineered-reef locations

Reef 1. Lee Point Wide - 12 10.083S 130 47.033E, 28m deep. This site is 24km north of Nightcliff, and just 10km east of the Fenton Patches reef system. Golden snapper, redfish, flag, jewfish, trout, cod, trevally, mackerel and billfish.
Reef 2. Gutters Central - 12 09.459S 130 34.655E, 28m deep. This site is 38km north-west of Nightcliff, and 12km west of the Fenton Patches artificial reefs. Golden snapper, redfish, flag, jewfish, trout, cod, trevally, mackerel and billfish.
Reef 3. Dundee Wide - 12 44.445S 130 10.387E, 16m deep. This is 20km west of Dundee ramp, and 10km east of the Witch's Nose contour on Chart Aus 724. Produces as for Reefs 1 and 2, but also tricky snapper, cobia, red emperor and sailfish.
Reef 4. Adelaide River Mouth - 12 07.587S 131 11.545E, 16m deep. This site is wide of the Adelaide River mouth, about 10km from Leaders Creek mouth and 12km from the entrance to Saltwater Arm. Jewfish, golden snapper, cod, trevally, catfish.

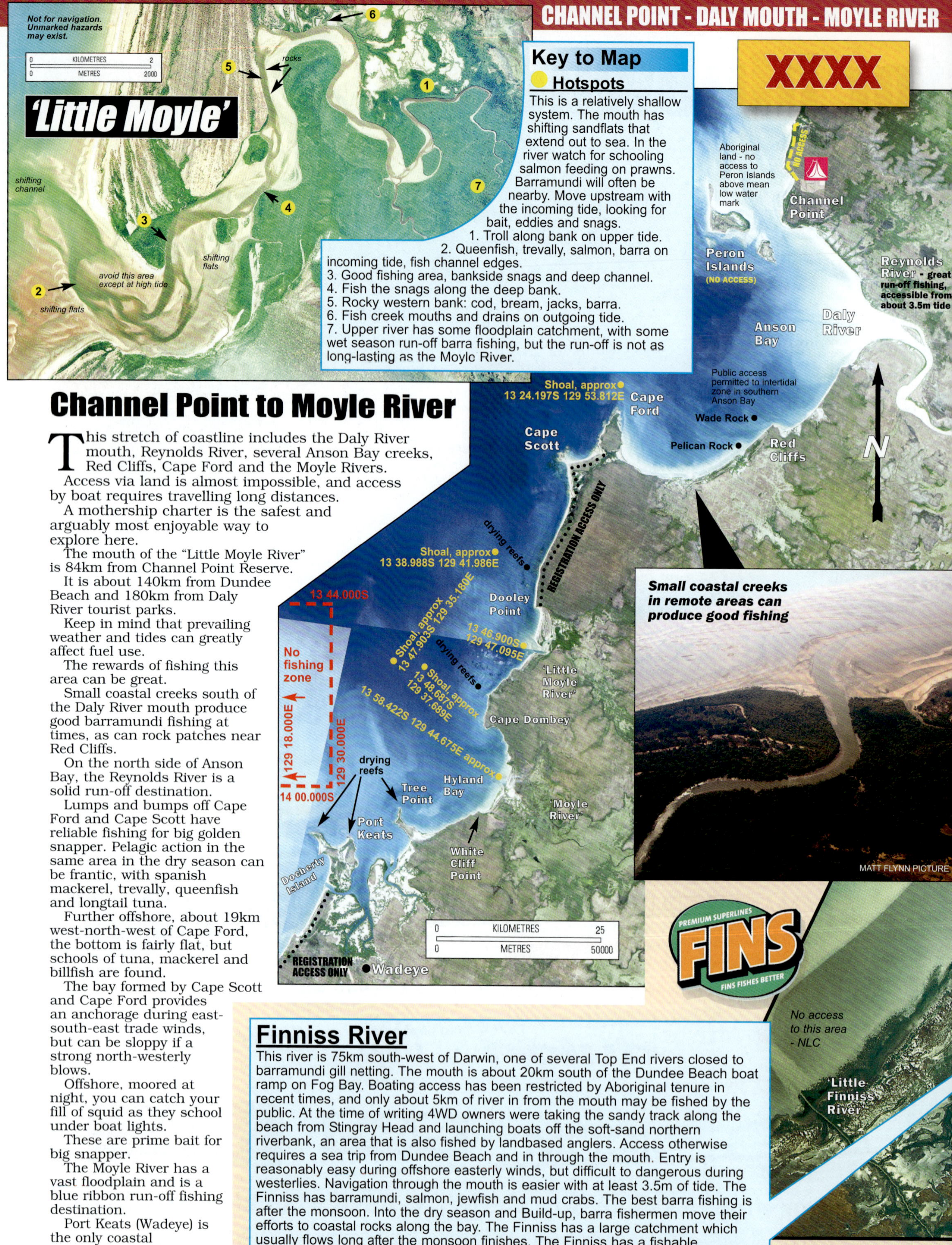

Key to Map

Hotspots

This is a relatively shallow system. The mouth has shifting sandflats that extend out to sea. In the river watch for schooling salmon feeding on prawns. Barramundi will often be nearby. Move upstream with the incoming tide, looking for bait, eddies and snags.

1. Troll along bank on upper tide.
2. Queenfish, trevally, salmon, barra on incoming tide, fish channel edges.
3. Good fishing area, bankside snags and deep channel.
4. Fish the snags along the deep bank.
5. Rocky western bank: cod, bream, jacks, barra.
6. Fish creek mouths and drains on outgoing tide.
7. Upper river has some floodplain catchment, with some wet season run-off barra fishing, but the run-off is not as long-lasting as the Moyle River.

Channel Point to Moyle River

This stretch of coastline includes the Daly River mouth, Reynolds River, several Anson Bay creeks, Red Cliffs, Cape Ford and the Moyle Rivers.

Access via land is almost impossible, and access by boat requires travelling long distances.

A mothership charter is the safest and arguably most enjoyable way to explore here.

The mouth of the "Little Moyle River" is 84km from Channel Point Reserve.

It is about 140km from Dundee Beach and 180km from Daly River tourist parks.

Keep in mind that prevailing weather and tides can greatly affect fuel use.

The rewards of fishing this area can be great.

Small coastal creeks south of the Daly River mouth produce good barramundi fishing at times, as can rock patches near Red Cliffs.

On the north side of Anson Bay, the Reynolds River is a solid run-off destination.

Lumps and bumps off Cape Ford and Cape Scott have reliable fishing for big golden snapper. Pelagic action in the same area in the dry season can be frantic, with spanish mackerel, trevally, queenfish and longtail tuna.

Further offshore, about 19km west-north-west of Cape Ford, the bottom is fairly flat, but schools of tuna, mackerel and billfish are found.

The bay formed by Cape Scott and Cape Ford provides an anchorage during east-south-east trade winds, but can be sloppy if a strong north-westerly blows.

Offshore, moored at night, you can catch your fill of squid as they school under boat lights.

These are prime bait for big snapper.

The Moyle River has a vast floodplain and is a blue ribbon run-off fishing destination.

Port Keats (Wadeye) is the only coastal community in this area.

Finniss River

This river is 75km south-west of Darwin, one of several Top End rivers closed to barramundi gill netting. The mouth is about 20km south of the Dundee Beach boat ramp on Fog Bay. Boating access has been restricted by Aboriginal tenure in recent times, and only about 5km of river in from the mouth may be fished by the public. At the time of writing 4WD owners were taking the sandy track along the beach from Stingray Head and launching boats off the soft-sand northern riverbank, an area that is also fished by landbased anglers. Access otherwise requires a sea trip from Dundee Beach and in through the mouth. Entry is reasonably easy during offshore easterly winds, but difficult to dangerous during westerlies. Navigation through the mouth is easier with at least 3.5m of tide. The Finniss has barramundi, salmon, jewfish and mud crabs. The best barra fishing is after the monsoon. Into the dry season and Build-up, barra fishermen move their efforts to coastal rocks along the bay. The Finniss has a large catchment which usually flows long after the monsoon finishes. The Finniss has a fishable freshwater section (off map) accessible from Hardcastle Rd, off Fog Bay Rd. The turn-off is signposted. Beware crocodiles throughout this area.

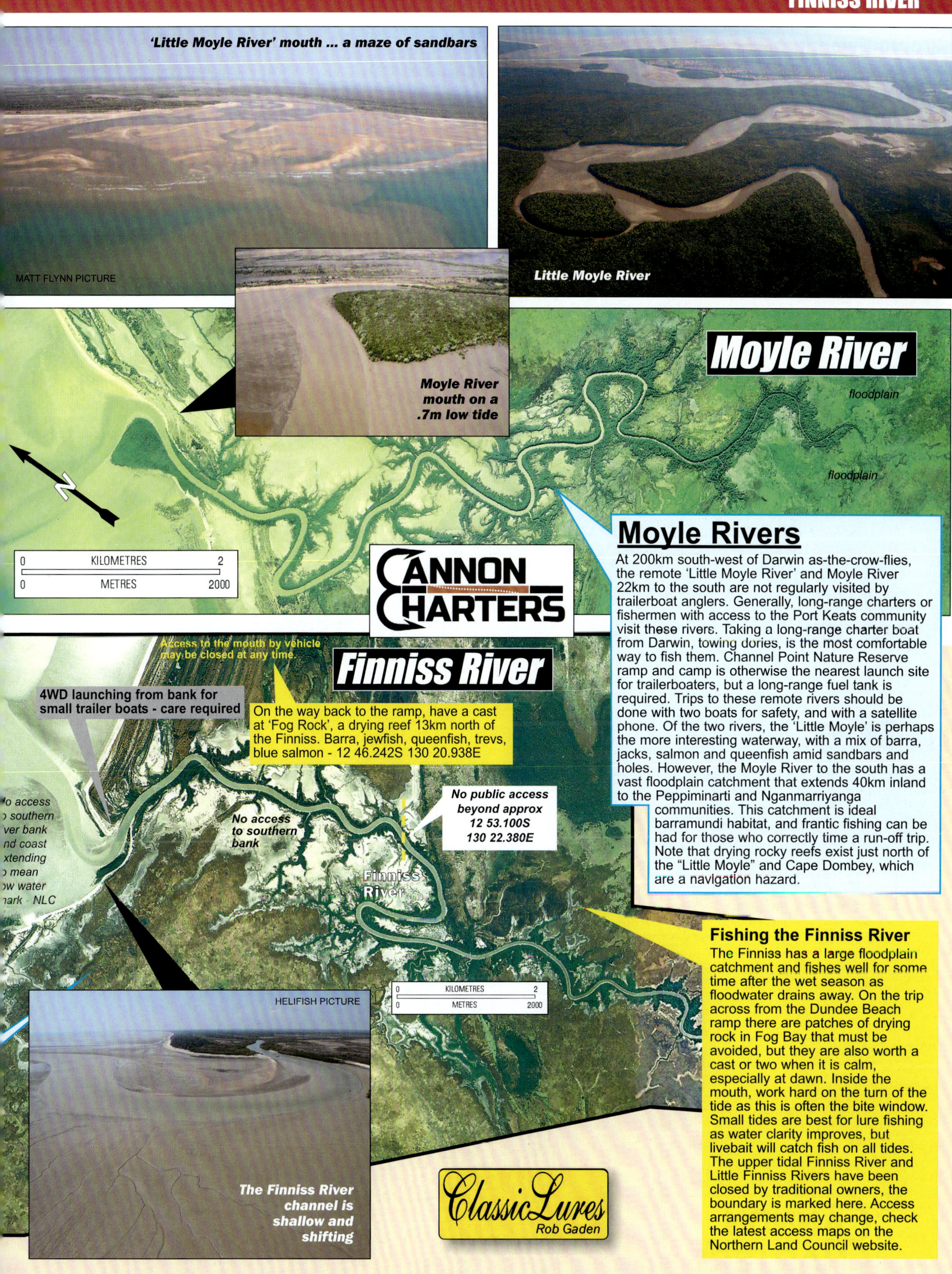

Moyle Rivers

At 200km south-west of Darwin as-the-crow-flies, the remote 'Little Moyle River' and Moyle River 22km to the south are not regularly visited by trailerboat anglers. Generally, long-range charters or fishermen with access to the Port Keats community visit these rivers. Taking a long-range charter boat from Darwin, towing dories, is the most comfortable way to fish them. Channel Point Nature Reserve ramp and camp is otherwise the nearest launch site for trailerboaters, but a long-range fuel tank is required. Trips to these remote rivers should be done with two boats for safety, and with a satellite phone. Of the two rivers, the 'Little Moyle' is perhaps the more interesting waterway, with a mix of barra, jacks, salmon and queenfish amid sandbars and holes. However, the Moyle River to the south has a vast floodplain catchment that extends 40km inland to the Peppiminarti and Nganmarriyanga communities. This catchment is ideal barramundi habitat, and frantic fishing can be had for those who correctly time a run-off trip. Note that drying rocky reefs exist just north of the "Little Moyle" and Cape Dombey, which are a navigation hazard.

Fishing the Finniss River

The Finniss has a large floodplain catchment and fishes well for some time after the wet season as floodwater drains away. On the trip across from the Dundee Beach ramp there are patches of drying rock in Fog Bay that must be avoided, but they are also worth a cast or two when it is calm, especially at dawn. Inside the mouth, work hard on the turn of the tide as this is often the bite window. Small tides are best for lure fishing as water clarity improves, but livebait will catch fish on all tides. The upper tidal Finniss River and Little Finniss Rivers have been closed by traditional owners, the boundary is marked here. Access arrangements may change, check the latest access maps on the Northern Land Council website.

Groote Eylandt

This is a true remote location, being 130km from the nearest public launch site at Port Roper, which is a remote spot in itself. Numbulwar Aboriginal community is the nearest mainland settlement. There are facilities at the mining township of Alyangula. Aboriginal access to the island and mainland are managed by different organisations. To fish Groote, visitors need a permit from **www.anindilyakwa.com.au**, or can join a tourist operation, or stay on a long-distance boat and fish outside the mean low water mark. The NLC manages access to the mainland coast. **Groote Eylandt Game and Sportfishing Club** has annual competitions, it has a Facebook page. Charters are available. While a difficult area logistically, this region has superb fishing and scenery. It has proven shallow-water sailfish grounds, and good shallow-water reef fishing. The adjacent mainland coast has barramundi fishing, permitted within the intertidal zone in the NLC Registration Access Area.

Key to Map

Hotspots

1. Mackerel, sailfish near shoals.
2. Shallow-water sailfish ground. Look for bait schools. Best in September/October.
3. Mixed fishing around Cumberlege Reef, including big mackerel and trevally, and reef fish.
4. Anchorages. Queenfish, GTs.
5. Excellent mixed fishing around Bombard Reef. Plenty of queenfish and trevally inshore.
6. Useful anchorage. Ciguatera risk area.

7&7&7. Barra around coastal rocks September-November. Approach quietly and cast shallow-running lures.

8. Jacks and barra along rock edges. Also monster barracuda, trevally and queenfish.
9. Reef fish on neap tides.
10. Queenfish, trevally around Cape Barrow.
11. Brady Rock (lighthouse) has big mackerel.
12. Proven sailfish area.
13. Pelagic fish off South Point.
14. Shallow reef - trout and goldies.
15. Big mackerel, tuna, also marlin and sailfish.
16. Proven billfish area, troll contour line.
17. Woody Island surrounded by good reef, coral trout and snapper.
18. Vicinity of Wedge Rock - troll for mackerel, trevally, queenfish.
19. Tuna schools in this area.

20 and 20. Prolific tuna fishing areas.

Launch sites

The nearest public launch site on the mainland is at the Roper River mouth, 130km from Groote Eylandt. Some visiting crews barge boats in to the island from Darwin. **Local tides have up to about 1.5m movement. Tidal predictions for Milner Bay are available.**

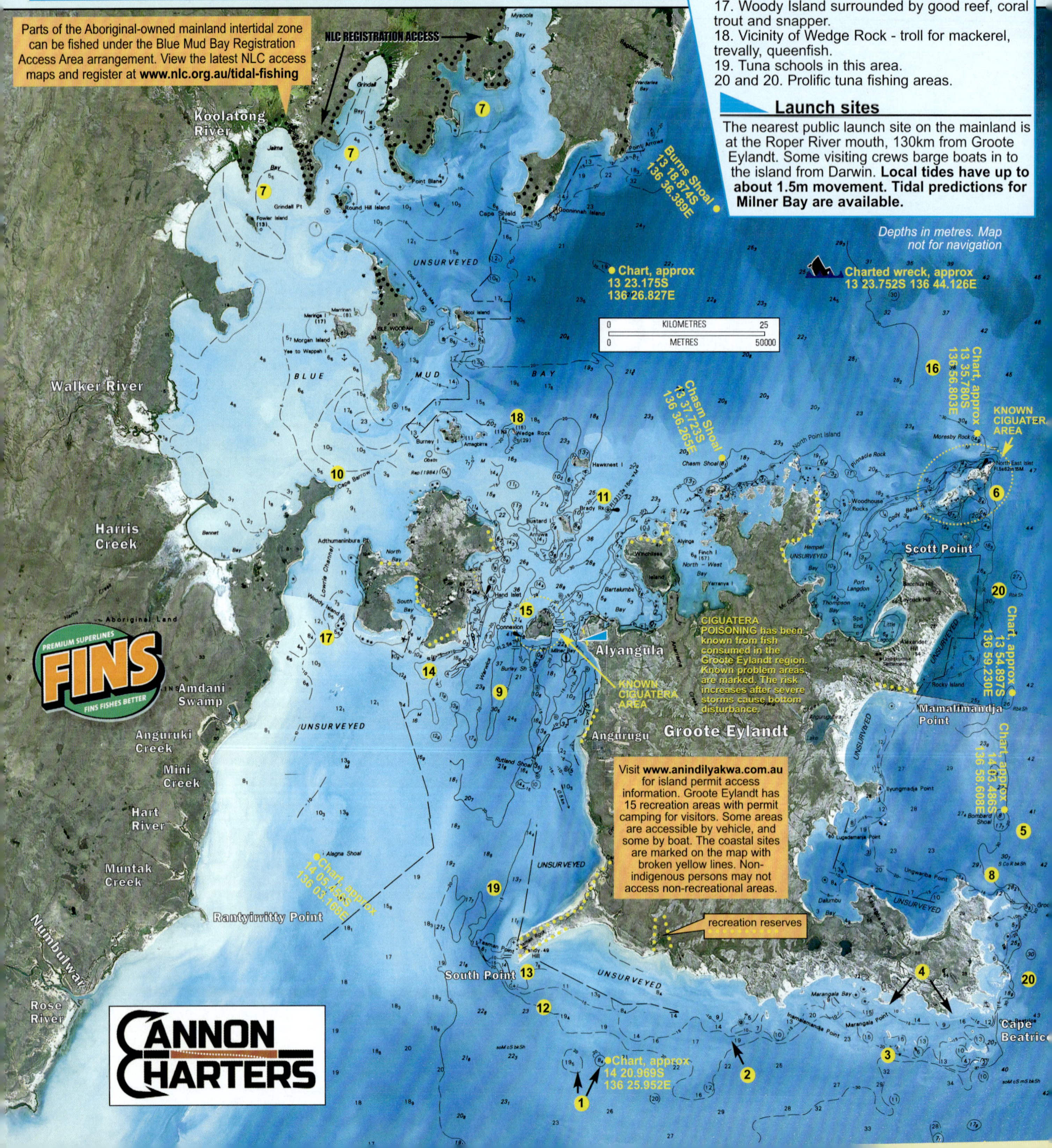

Parts of the Aboriginal-owned mainland intertidal zone can be fished under the Blue Mud Bay Registration Access Area arrangement. View the latest NLC access maps and register at **www.nlc.org.au/tidal-fishing**

Depths in metres. Map not for navigation

CIGUATERA POISONING has been known from fish consumed in the Groote Eylandt region. Known problem areas are marked. The risk increases after severe storms cause bottom disturbance.

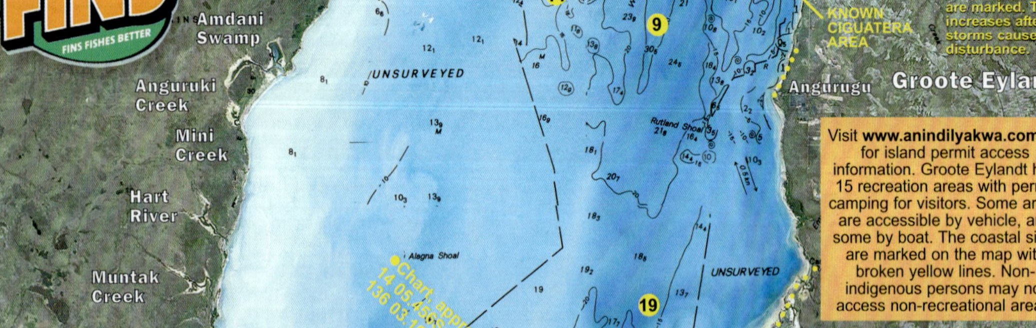

Visit **www.anindilyakwa.com.au** for island permit access information. Groote Eylandt has 15 recreation areas with permit camping for visitors. Some areas are accessible by vehicle, and some by boat. The coastal sites are marked on the map with broken yellow lines. Non-indigenous persons may not access non-recreational areas.

recreation reserves

Tiwi creeks

A Melville Island creek on the east side of the southern Apsley Strait entrance, near Cockle Point, at approx 11 47.386S 130 41.070E

A creek 5km east of Apsley Strait entrance at approx 11 48.111S 130 43.305E

A Tiwi circumnavigation

Bathurst and Melville Islands are Aboriginal land 74km north of Darwin. The south side of the islands and Apsley Strait can be fished. A Tiwi camping permit is available which gives access to three coastal camps. The north coast is closed to fishing, as are two NT Government reef fish protection areas. Otherwise, seaward of the mean low water mark, anglers may fish around the islands. A circumnavigation an exciting adventure for a well organised crew.

Mal Miles of Darwin Bluewater Charters said that by the time he circumnavigated Melville Island and explored creeks (before north coast fishing was restricted), he had done 900km. Boaters can refuel at Pirlangimpi/Garden Point store, on Apsley Strait, but call (08) 8978 3962 first. Fuel may also be available at Wurrumiyanga at the southern end of Apsley Strait.

When to go: Dry season winds drop away in the Build-up months of late Sept/Oct, but thunderstorms can occur at this time. Another good time is just after the Wet, about April/May, before dry season winds kick in.

The launch pad: Leaders Creek Fishing Base near Gunn Point is the ideal launch site. Once out of Leaders Creek it is a short jump across to Melville, but don't try it if the wind is over 15 knots. The tide rips in the strait are nasty.

First stop: A permit beach camp is at Robertson Creek, on Melville's south, about 45km north of Leaders Creek. The creeks have barra, salmon, queenfish, jacks and mud crabs. The camp floods on tides over 6.8m.

Conder Point: Further up the coast is Conder Point. Just offshore is a drop-off with snapper and jewfish. Further out, almost 6nm south of Conder Point, is Hunt Patch. The Deep nearby looks good on paper, but rarely produces.

Camp Point: Moving north-east, 10nm from Conder, is Camp Point, with a permit beach camp. Just out from the point is snapper country. The creeks in Cobham Bay, just west of Camp Point, have salmon, barra, golden snapper and jacks. Sandbars at creek mouths prevent access from half tide down. The eastern creek is shallow for most of its length.

Soldier Point: Departing Camp Point the coast starts tapering north and, around Cape Keith and Soldier Point, you are at the eastern tip of the island. Soldier Point is treacherous, being in a constriction that drains Van Diemen Gulf.

Tinganoo Bay: Just north of Soldier Point, this is a safe-haven, if you cop a bad day. Tiwi people request that minimal time is spent here. In a circumnavigation, travelling from Camp Point, you must now camp on your boat.

Quanipiri Point: North of Tinganoo Bay is Quanipiri Point, scary on a bad day. The water can be dirty, hiding reefs, so stay wide. Quanipiri and Yuanti Bays are safe havens, and shallow. The Tiwis request a minimal stay.

Johnston River: An official Tiwi anchorage. From here, you will head west to the Snake Bay anchorage. There is a hazardous headland, Point Jahleel. After that, you are in sheltered Brenton Bay and the Johnston River mouth anchorage.

Jessie River area: Between Johnston River and Snake Bay. Mackerel and snapper are on the reefs, but fishing in the river is not permitted.

Goose Creek: Andranangoo River mouth is 13km west of the Jessie River. Fishing in the river is not permitted.

Karslake Island: The reefs off Karslake have painted crays, but a safer bet is further along the coast at Cook Reef. Crocodiles and sharks.

Marie Shoal: Situated 40km north-west of Cape Van Diemen, rising from 55m to 8m at approx 10 54.30S, 130 05.40E. Clear water, fantastic fishing.

Apsley Strait: Back at Melville, the rest of the trip is easier if you return via Apsley Strait. Go around Bathurst Island only if you have ample fuel, or have arranged for fuel. Apsley Strait is over 74km in length and has great creeks, with jewfish and snapper off Garden Point. Exit the southern end of Apsley at high tide, as there are sandbars near Buchanan Island.

Twin creeks 10km north-west of Melville Island's Cape Gambier, at approx 11 52.559S 130 53.422E

A creek north of Conder Point, on the southern Melville coast, at approx 11 43.389S 131 17.321E

The first creek north-east of Cape Gambier, at approx 11 55.241S 130 59.271E

PIC E

The second creek north-east of Cape Gambier, at approx 11 54.399S 130 59.870E

This creek is immediately west of the creek pictured in 'G'

This creek is 3.5km west of Muranapi Point, at approx 11 53.217S 131 01.051E

Robertson Creek, on the south side of Melville Island, has a beach campsite available for use by permit. The creek mouth is at approx 11 50.082S 131 05.029E

This creek is just south-west of Conder Point, on the southern coast of Melville Island, at approx 11 44.862S 131 14.190E

Tiwi Islands
Killalure By Lance Butler
Marie Shoal 10 54.434S 130 05.655E
'Sister Marie' 10 54.362S 130 09.616E
Parry Shoal 11 12.245S 129 42.387E
'Big Reef' 11 13.178S 129 49.765E
Moss Shoal 11 08.297S 129 54.710E
Seagull Island
This area is surrounded by dangerous currents. Sandbars between the island and the main island are exposed at low tide.
reef fish
Cape Van Diemen
trolling
Reef 11 08.838S 130 29.457E
Reef 11 11.278S 130 29.638E
Aboriginal land extends to the mean low water mark, but may be extended a further 2km in some circumstances. Watch for changes at www.tiwilandcouncil.com
rocks at creek mouth and inside
Piper Head
'Airforce Creek'
beware shallow entrances
Cook Reef 11 15.727S 130 35.710E
Purumpenelli Point
Unsurveyed
11 21.962S
130 04.863E
Deception Point
Brace Point
'Bluewater Creek'
Pirlangimpi (Garden Point)
Shark Bay
Snake Bay
Brown Point
Johnson Point
Milikapiti
closure line
Dudwell Creek
rockbar inside this creek
Apsley Strait has strong currents, sandbars and shallow reef. It is most easily navigated during the day at high tide.
No fishing allowed in northern zone
Red border marks an NT Government no fishing zone
creek
Rocky Point
hazardous reef
flats at creek mouths
flats
Gullala Inlet
rocks
11 31.854S
129 59.400E
11 38.623S
Rancoo Creek
Kanunga Point
Apsley Strait
Permit fishing allowed in Apsley Strait
FINS
Gordon Bay
Cape Helvetius
Ranku
Port Hurd
No fishing allowed in this zone
Catfish Creek and lagoon
God's Creek
Perakary Creek
wreck exposed low tide
Tungunupu Creek
Cape Fourcroy
RED CLIFFS
Yinanapi Point
Mangutuwu Point
Shaggy's Camp (Tinkanrow)
This permit camp is in Apsley Strait on Bathurst Island. Like the two camps on Melville Island it has a roofed corrugated iron shelter, barbecue, and water tank. The water is not for drinking.
GPS 11 41.143S 130 30.765E
Wurrumiyanga
Takamprimili Creek
Taradiri Creek
Buchanan Island
Sacred Site
Use a chart when negotiating the entrance to Apsley Strait
Unsurveyed
Tiwi fishing permits allow fishing the coast and creeks south of this line, and also within the Apsley Strait
KILOMETRES
METRES
Hazardous area - currents and waves
Inadequate

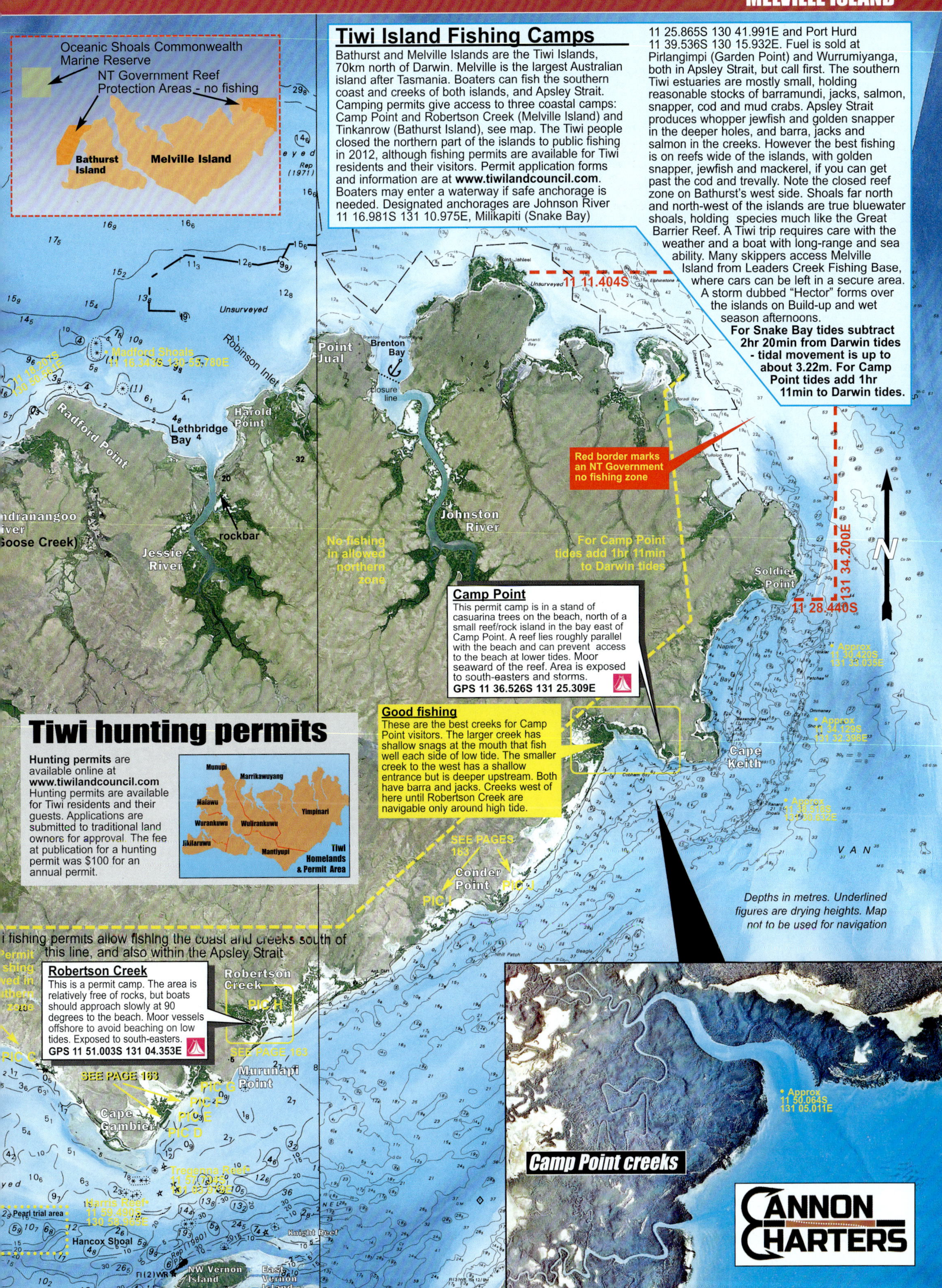

Tiwi Island Fishing Camps
Bathurst and Melville Islands are the Tiwi Islands, 70km north of Darwin. Melville is the largest Australian island after Tasmania. Boaters can fish the southern coast and creeks of both islands, and Apsley Strait. Camping permits give access to three coastal camps: Camp Point and Robertson Creek (Melville Island) and Tinkanrow (Bathurst Island), see map. The Tiwi people closed the northern part of the islands to public fishing in 2012, although fishing permits are available for Tiwi residents and their visitors. Permit application forms and information are at www.tiwilandcouncil.com. Boaters may enter a waterway if safe anchorage is needed. Designated anchorages are Johnson River 11 16.981S 131 10.975E, Milikapiti (Snake Bay) 11 25.865S 130 41.991E and Port Hurd 11 39.536S 130 15.932E. Fuel is sold at Pirlangimpi (Garden Point) and Wurrumiyanga, both in Apsley Strait, but call first. The southern Tiwi estuaries are mostly small, holding reasonable stocks of barramundi, jacks, salmon, snapper, cod and mud crabs. Apsley Strait produces whopper jewfish and golden snapper in the deeper holes, and barra, jacks and salmon in the creeks. However the best fishing is on reefs wide of the islands, with golden snapper, jewfish and mackerel, if you can get past the cod and trevally. Note the closed reef zone on Bathurst's west side. Shoals far north and north-west of the islands are true bluewater shoals, holding species much like the Great Barrier Reef. A Tiwi trip requires care with the weather and a boat with long-range and sea ability. Many skippers access Melville Island from Leaders Creek Fishing Base, where cars can be left in a secure area. A storm dubbed "Hector" forms over the islands on Build-up and wet season afternoons.
For Snake Bay tides subtract 2hr 20min from Darwin tides - tidal movement is up to about 3.22m. For Camp Point tides add 1hr 11min to Darwin tides.
Oceanic Shoals Commonwealth Marine Reserve
NT Government Reef Protection Areas - no fishing
Bathurst Island
Melville Island
Unsurveyed
11 11.404S
Madford Shoals 11 16.343S 130 55.780E
Robinson Inlet
Point Jual
Brenton Bay
closure line
Harold Point
Lethbridge Bay
Radford Point
rockbar
Jessie River
Johnston River
No fishing in allowed northern zone
For Camp Point tides add 1hr 11min to Darwin tides
Red border marks an NT Government no fishing zone
131 34.200E
Soldier Point
11 28.440S
Camp Point
This permit camp is in a stand of casuarina trees on the beach, north of a small reef/rock island in the bay east of Camp Point. A reef lies roughly parallel with the beach and can prevent access to the beach at lower tides. Moor seaward of the reef. Area is exposed to south-easters and storms.
GPS 11 36.526S 131 25.309E
Good fishing
These are the best creeks for Camp Point visitors. The larger creek has shallow snags at the mouth that fish well each side of low tide. The smaller creek to the west has a shallow entrance but is deeper upstream. Both have barra and jacks. Creeks west of here until Robertson Creek are navigable only around high tide.
Tiwi hunting permits
Hunting permits are available online at www.tiwilandcouncil.com Hunting permits are available for Tiwi residents and their guests. Applications are submitted to traditional land owners for approval. The fee at publication for a hunting permit was $100 for an annual permit.
Munupi
Marrikawuyang
Malawu
Wurankuwu
Wulirankuwu
Yimpinari
Jikilarruwu
Mantiyupi
Tiwi Homelands & Permit Area
Cape Keith
SEE PAGES 163
Conder Point
PIC I
PIC J
Depths in metres. Underlined figures are drying heights. Map not to be used for navigation
fishing permits allow fishing the coast and creeks south of this line, and also within the Apsley Strait
Robertson Creek
This is a permit camp. The area is relatively free of rocks, but boats should approach slowly at 90 degrees to the beach. Moor vessels offshore to avoid beaching on low tides. Exposed to south-easters.
GPS 11 51.003S 131 04.353E
Robertson Creek
PIC H
SEE PAGE 163
Murunapi Point
SEE PAGE 163
Cape Gambier
PIC C
Hancox Shoal
NW Vernon Island
East Vernon Island
Approx 11 50.064S 131 05.011E
Camp Point creeks
CANNON CHARTERS

WWW.COBOURGFISHINGSAFARIS.COM.AU
Cobourg offers great fishing and scenery
Not to be used for navigation. Depths in metres.
Orontes Ree
Marine P
Chart, approx 11 05.593S 131 55.344E
Chart, approx 11 05.896S 132 00.944E
Vashon Head
Wanaraij Point
Allaru Island
PRIVACY ZONE
Araru Point
Lingi Point
Blue Mud Bay
Midjari Point
RESORT ZONE
Seven Spirit Bay
Low P
Trepang Bay
PRIVACY ZONE
Marine Park
For Cape Don tides subtract 20min from Darwin tides
Popham Bay
Ardigbiyi Point
NO FISHING ZONE
Alcaro Bay
Cape Don
jetty
NO FISHING ZONE
KILOMETRES
METRES
CANNON CHARTERS
PREMIUM SUPERLINES
FINS
FINS FISHES BETTER
Shark Bay
Chart, approx 11 21.714S, 130 49.206E
Fitzpatrick Shoal
Unsurveyed
Shamrock Bay
Marine Park
Unsurveyed
Map
Cobourg Marine Park sanctuary zone - red area includes islands and Black Rock but not Mini Mini estuary system
FISHING AND OUTDOOR WORLD
Est 1972

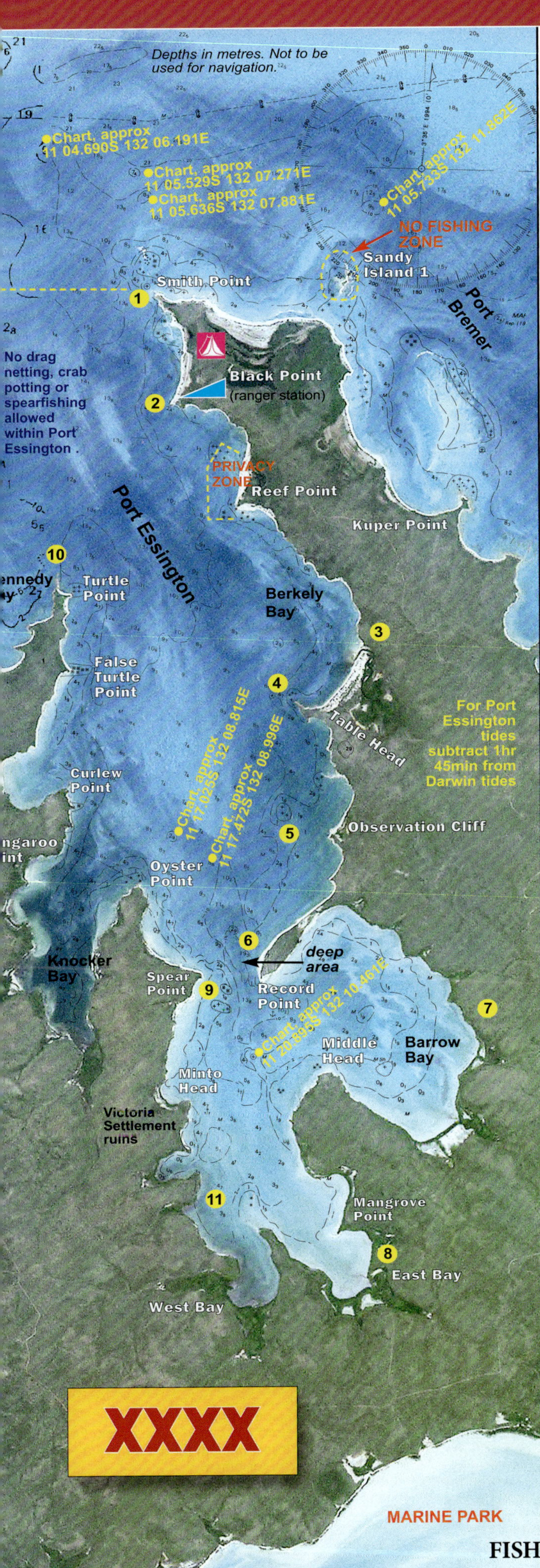

Cobourg Peninsula

The peninsula is 200km north-east of Darwin as the crow flies, or 570km by road. It can be reached by light plane or long-range boat from Darwin, or by driving in on the unsealed road via Kakadu NP and Cahills Crossing over the East Alligator River. The peninsula forms Garig Gunak Barlu National Park (formerly Gurig NP). Entry to the park is by permit, and camping is limited to the dry season, May to October. Fishing tends to be best early in the dry season, but there is often calmer boating weather in the late dry season. Visitors should take in everything they need, including spare parts. Vehicles may have to negotiate corrugations. Driving in, the tides at Cahills Crossing are about six hours behind Darwin tides and big tides or heavy rain may prevent vehicles crossing. Follow the signs on the unsealed road. At publication a fee of $232.10 applied per vehicle for up to five adult passengers for up to seven nights. Showers, composting toilets, barbecues, tables and limited bore water was provided. No powered sites are available, but generators are allowed in one camping area. The fishing around the peninsula is in relatively clear, sandy waters with shallow reefs. Offshore shoals have mostly tricky snapper, flag, coral trout, golden snapper and cod. Pelagic fish are reliable and include barracuda, mackerel, queenfish and various species of trevally. There are some jacks, barramundi and mud crabs in the small tidal creeks. Vashon Head, between Cape Don and Port Essington, has shallow reef, with the remains of the *Australian* wreck at about 11 06.600S and 131 59.100E. Care must be taken when navigating because the area is shallow, with drying reefs. Within the Cobourg Marine Park some no-fishing zones apply. Fishermen travelling from Darwin by sea stay wide of Cape Don in rough weather, as the current rip around the point causes rough seas. Big crocodiles are not as numerous in this area as some parts of the NT, but they *are* there, as are box jellyfish and stonefish.

For permits, visit www.nt.gov.au/leisure/parks-reserves/permits-for-parks/permits-for-cobourg-peninsula-garig-gunak-barlu-national-park For other information phone the ranger station on (08) 8979 0244.

Port Essington

This large bay is on the northern side of Cobourg Peninsula. There are coastal camp sites available by permit at Smith Point, with one area for gensets and one for quiet campers. There is a sealed boat ramp at Black Point, with the ranger available on VHF16. Port Essington's relatively clear, shallow waters offer good fishing opportunities, but barramundi are not a prominent feature. The main species on the shallow reefs and headlands are trevally, queenfish, mackerel and barracuda. Reef fish are best out wider at Orontes Reef, while creeks along the shores of southern Port Essington have mainly jacks, trevally and occasional barra. Tiger squid are common and hunt the shallows, and lobsters (painted crays) are also abundant. Lobsters can be taken by hand on inshore reefs at night, but watch for crocodiles. Special rules apply to Port Essington - no spearfishing, drag netting or crab pots are allowed.

Key to Map

Hotspots

Cobourg waters are within a marine park. Some no-fishing and outstation privacy zones apply.

General points: jacks are found in the bay and on near-shore reefs, as well as within creeks. Mud crabs, barramundi and salmon are best at the southern end of Port Essington, with jewfish in deep water near Spear Point. Queenfish, mackerel, trevally, coral trout, tricky snapper and cod are found throughout the seaward area. Tiger squid hunt the shallows.

1. Reefy headland, bommies nearby.
2. Fish Black Point at high tide.
3. Fish creek mouth on outgoing tide for trevally, queenfish. Jacks in creek.
4. Table Head has deep water with reef fish and barracuda. Good trolling.
5. Reef holds various species, especially sweetlip and coral trout.
6. Fish deep water on west side of this sandbar. Bait schools move up and down the west shore and queenfish, trevally and mackerel feed on them.
7. Barrow Bay has flats fishing for barra on incoming tides, pole or wade through shallow water. This bay is good for mud crabs (no pots allowed).
8. East Bay Creek for barra, West Bay Creek for jacks and small snapper.
9. Spear Point reef holds jewfish and loads of catfish.
10. Pelagic fish, cobia. Jewfish in deep water near Turtle Head
11. Excellent salmon fishing with jacks around the rocks to the north.
12. Golden snapper on spring tides.
13. Shallow clear creek holds jacks.
14. Large spring-fed creek holds good barra and jacks.
15. Allaru Island is a sand quay with surrounding reef. Big queenfish, trevally and barracuda. Beware rising tide as waves come over top of reef.
16. Creek. Fish on big tides for jacks, trevally.
17. Cape Don bommies hold big pelagic fish.
18. Queenfish, trevally along edges.
19. Clear creeks on west side of peninsula hold mostly jacks, queenfish and trevally. Barra fishing starts in the less clear creeks further south-east (off the chart) in the Mini Mini system.

GPS waypoints

a. Orontes Reef: 11 03.309S, 132 04.705E: reef fish - cobia, mackerel, lobsters.

Wrecks

A. The *Australian*. Approximate position is 11 06.600S and 131 59.100E.

Tidal movement at Cape Don is up to about 2.58m. For Port Essington tides subtract 1 hour and 45 minutes from Darwin times. For Cape Don tides subtract 20 minutes from Darwin times.

Estuaries & islands

The Mini Mini system is a labyrinth of mangrove creeks and islands tucked under the southern side of Cobourg Peninsula inside Endyalgout Island. It is an exciting remote fishing location.

The intertidal waters were marked as a restricted area on NLC maps at publication, however changes to arrangements were mooted. Check access status at **www.nlc.org.au/tidal-fishing** before planning a trip.

Boating access can be via the mouth of the South or East Alligator Rivers, but it is a long run and Van Diemens Gulf's shallow waters are subject to big tides and can turn up a horrendous chop.

The easiest option is to take a long-range charter boat from Darwin, with dinghies in tow to explore the creeks.

There are so many creeks and drains in the Mini Mini system it would take years to fish them all properly.

Every tidal drain is worth a cast. The fish are often found in slight holes, or eddies, or where bait has gathered. At times big golden snapper move in and are caught in shallow water.

North of the Mini Mini on the other side of Cobourg Peninsula is a different network of islands.

The largest is Croker, with New Year, Oxley, Lawson, Grant, Valencia and McCluer islands just off Croker's eastern coastline. Each island has its own character. These islands and the intertidal waters are Aboriginal-owned. Visitors can fish below the mean low water mark outside of Aboriginal waters.

Situated 37km east of Cape Croker, New Year Island is a tiny island with a lighthouse in the middle.

It has a coral beach on its southern corner and is fringed by coral reef. A troll along the coral drop-off along the side of the island is a sure bet for all sorts of big fish. Lumps show at depths around 30m.

A hotspot is the northern end, trolling the current lines 100m off the breaking reef out to the deep blue. The 50m deep drop-off here has been aptly named "The Wall". Big macks own "The Wall".

If you troll wider off the northern tip you will find tuna, sailfish and black marlin.

For those keen on a snorkel, the bommies have lobsters. Crocs are a threat however. And sharks.

The best anchorage is on the south-western tip but it doesn't offer much protection.

About 19km south of New Year Island is McCluer Island. It is larger than New Year, being about 5.5km long, and has safer anchorages. Its western coast has a smattering of reefs just offshore.

The northern tip of the island's fringing reef is loaded with sportfish. GTs, queenies, barracuda and mackerel patrol the reef. The south-western corner produces pelagic fish.

Coral trout can be lure-caught over the bommies.

About 19km north-east of McCluer Island is Hogmaney Shoal. It has big spaniards, tuna and billfish. Fish the northern end of Hogmaney for snapper.

Travelling another 9.25km south-west from McCluer Island is Grant Island.

Grant is a little higher than the other islands and is large enough to offer good shelter from strong winds, with the pick of the anchorages again being in the south-west corner.

There are lobster bommies around the north-western headland. Troll this headland for big GTs.

Oxley and Lawson Islands are some 13km north-west of Grant Island. Between Oxley and Lawson is a deep channel that often has a strong current.

All sorts of pelagics hang here and there are usually birds working the bait schools. The west side looks just right for a bonefish or two.

Just to the west of Oxley and Lawson Islands, heading towards Croker Island, the depth drops dramatically. Tuna, macks and billfish show up here.

Just offshore from Cape Croker is a multitude of reefs, stretching almost 10km out to sea. The current rips off the cape, but on a good day you'll catch great fish, including big golden snapper, trevally and cod.

If you wish to camp or land on the islands or fish the intertidal waters you will need a Northern Land Council permit. Check the latest access status at **www.nlc.org.au/tidal-fishing** before fishing.

Visit in October and November for the calmest weather, or April and early May before the south-easters kick in.

Hotspots

Key to Map

1. Launch site on Aboriginal land - a Northern Land Council permit is required to enter this area by road. Nearest public launch site is on the East Alligator River.
2. A ledge towards the south bank is the size of a couple of house blocks and rises from 9m to 5m. Incoming tides will usually produce trevally, grunter and big jewfish on bait and lures.
3. This shallow creek exits over shallow flats and good-sized threadfin salmon are found here at low tide.
4. Barramundi on upper tide in calm weather.
5. At spring low tide, rocks are seen on the point. If the water is dirty, barra from this corner of the island gather here. It is shallow, watch the prop.
6. An extensive low reef system runs from here back in the direction of the South Alligator. As the tide rises, move the boat over the flats - casting into the dirty water line will produce GTs and big queenfish. At high tide, cast the rocks for barramundi.
7. There is a small creek behind an oyster-encrusted rock wall. It fishes for barra at high tide. At half tide you will not exit, and must travel out the other end of the system. There are all the species in this creek, including huge groper.
8. The southern side of this creek has a shallow delta before it drops into the creek. On neap tides, the tree trunks in the water are a congregation area for barra.
9. Sandbar drop-off at southern tip of Valencia Island has big queenfish and trevally.

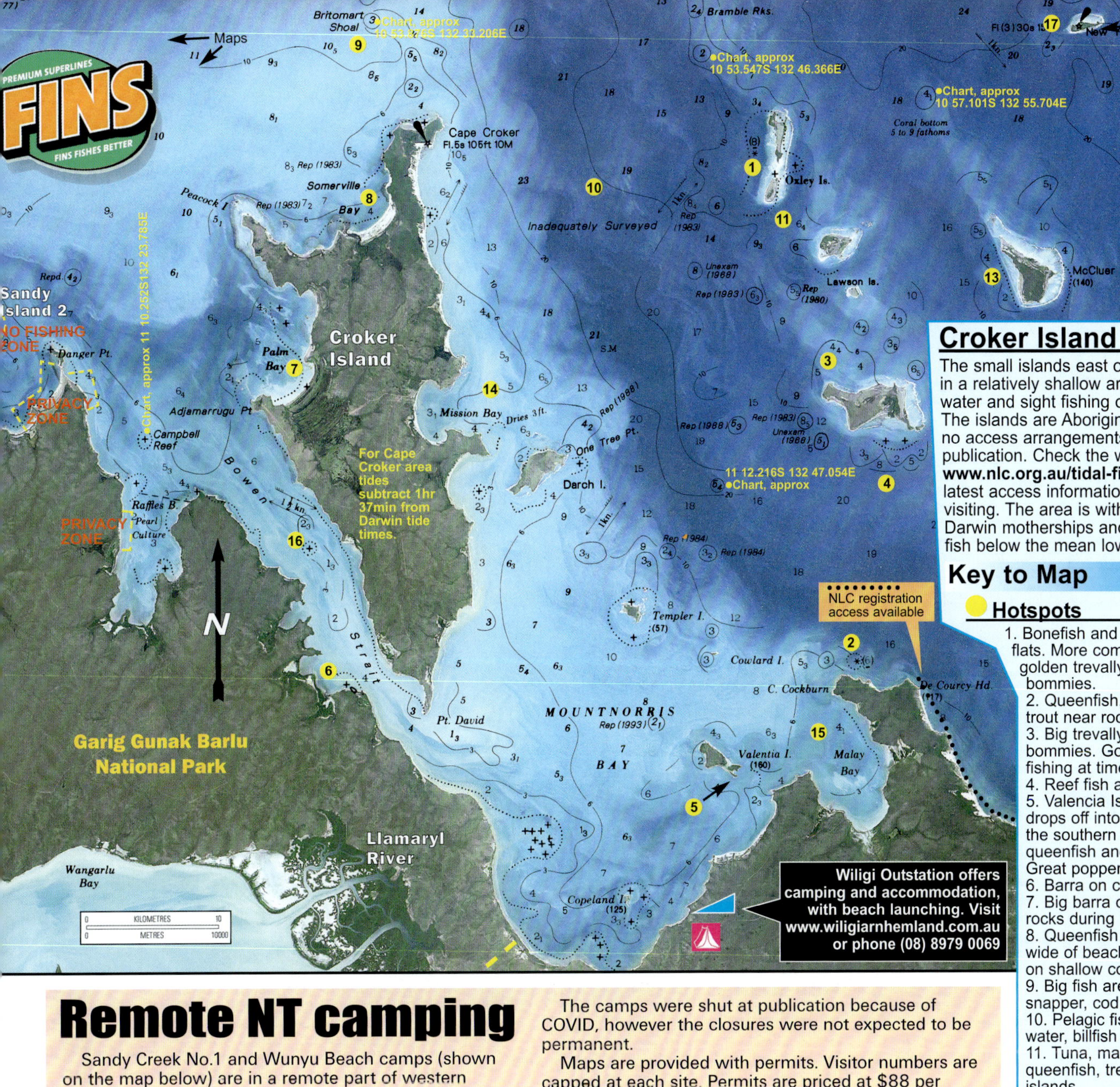

Croker Island Region

The small islands east of Croker are in a relatively shallow area, with clear water and sight fishing opportunities. The islands are Aboriginal land, with no access arrangements in place at publication. Check the website **www.nlc.org.au/tidal-fishing** for the latest access information before visiting. The area is within reach of Darwin motherships and boaters can fish below the mean low water mark.

Key to Map

Hotspots

1. Bonefish and permit over flats. More common are golden trevally. Trout on bommies.
2. Queenfish, trevally, small trout near rocks.
3. Big trevally around bommies. Good popper fishing at times.
4. Reef fish along edges.
5. Valencia Island sandbar drops off into deep water at the southern end, queenfish and trevally. Great popper fishing.
6. Barra on coastal rocks.
7. Big barra on coastal rocks during Build-up.
8. Queenfish and trevally wide of beach, coral trout on shallow coastal reefs.
9. Big fish area - mackerel, snapper, cod, trevally.
10. Pelagic fish in deep water, billfish potential.
11. Tuna, mackerel, queenfish, trevally between islands.
12. Troll southern edge drop-off for mackerel and trevally. Lobsters.
13. Sight fishing on edges.
14. Fish near rocky shores. Good in calm weather, sight fishing.
15. Bay is shallow, fly fishing for trevally, queenfish, jacks and occasional barra. Chance of bonefish, permit.
16. Trevally and barracuda.
17. Reef fish on west side, tricky snapper, coral trout, cod, cobia, big barracuda. Prolific milkfish area.
18. Mackerel, cobia, sailfish around shoal.

Launch sites

Nearest launch sites are Black Point in Garig Gunak Barlu NP, and Wiligi (private). Large boats travel by sea from Darwin (about 330km).

For Cape Croker tides subtract 1hr 37min from Darwin tide times.

Remote NT camping

Sandy Creek No.1 and Wunyu Beach camps (shown on the map below) are in a remote part of western Arnhem Land, publicly accessible through an Aboriginal recreational permit system.

Sandy Creek

Map not for navigation

Approximate camp locations are shown - the NLC wants people to refer to the map that is supplied with permits

North Goulburn Island
Bottle Rocks
Sims Island
Macquarie Strait
South Goulburn Island
Laterite Point
Wunyu Beach
Aurari Bay
White Rocks
White Point
Ross Point
Anuru Bay
Waminari Bay
Wangularni Bay
King River
Angularli Creek
Marligur Creek
Angarlban Creek
NLC registration access available
no access

The camps were shut at publication because of COVID, however the closures were not expected to be permanent.

Maps are provided with permits. Visitor numbers are capped at each site. Permits are priced at $88 per vehicle for either venue for up to five days.

Visitors must bring all they need and remove their rubbish. To book a permit, call the Northern Land Council in Jabiru on (08) 8938 3000.

The reward for the long drive in over corrugated roads is access to waters that are not heavily fished.

Sandy Creek has a bank launch, with some jacks, queenfish and mud crabs.

Shallow coastal reefs have coral trout, tricky snapper, tuskfish, trevally, queenfish, mackerel and lobsters.

The channel between the Goulbourn Islands has better reef fishing.

Wiligi Outstation (shown on the map above) provides private access to the remote mainland coast and islands in this region.

The outstation has accommodation and camp sites, with beach launching for visitors' boats, and boat hire.

The water in this area is relatively clear, with sight-fishing opportunities for queenfish, trevally and more.

Depths in metres. Underlined figures are drying heights. Maps not for navigation

Useful waypoints within 4km of Gove wharf

Dundas/Wargarpunda Point shallow rock, close in, 12 11.740S, 136 40.489E
Snapper Shoal, 1.2km west of West Woody Islet, 12 11.036S, 136 39.558E
West Woody lump one, 1.3km N/W of cargo wharf, 12 11.666S, 136 39.802E
West Woody lump two, 1.7km N/W of cargo wharf, 12 11.593S, 136 39.889E
West Woody lump three, 3.7km north of cargo wharf, 12 10.380S, 136 40.133E
Wargarpunda Point shallow bommie, 1.5km north of point, 12 10.315S, 136 41.523E
Wargarpunda Point shoal, 2km north of point, 12 09.835S, 136 41.046E

Getting there

The Central Arnhem Road to Gove Peninsula is passible by 4WD vehicle during the dry season. It leaves the Stuart Highway 52km south of Katherine. The first 30km is sealed. After that the road is corrugated, with loose gravel and patches of bulldust. There are river crossings that flood after heavy rain. It is 710km from Katherine, and there are two fuel stops, the first being 240km from Katherine at Mainoru Outback Store, 500km south of Nhulunbuy, and another at Bulman, payable by card. Be sure to carry enough fuel if towing. The road is not suitable for caravans, and only sturdy off-road camper trailers are permitted. Boat trailers must be strong and set up properly or damage is likely. Travellers must have a Northern Land Council permit to use the Central Arnhem Road and to enter land outside the Nhulunbuy town lease. Nhulunbuy can also be reached by air from Cairns or Darwin. There are fishing charters and hire boats available. The town has a camper-trailer park at Walkabout Lodge with powered sites, and amenities. Only bush camping is available in the outlying recreation areas managed by Dhimurru. Some tracks to recreation areas are sandy and may require tyre deflation, so carry a portable compressor. The East Arnhem region is a 'dry' area, including Nhulunbuy and the nearby communities of Gunyangara (Ski Beach) and Yirrkala. With the exception of some recreation areas, drinking in public places is prohibited. Visitors must obtain a liquor permit to buy alcohol and drink in a home or recreation area.

CIGUATERA POISONING is known from fish consumed in the Nhulunbuy region. Known problem areas are marked. The risk increases after severe storms, which cause bottom disturbance.

Launch sites

1. Perkins Wharf ramp (two ramps and pontoon)
2. Gove Yacht Club (mid-tide up)
3. East Woody Creek (high tide)
4. Yirrkala, permit needed.
5. Dalywoi Creek (most tides)

Local tides have up to about 2.5m movement.

Nhulunbuy

The Gove Peninsula is a bluewater paradise, with scenic headlands, white sand beaches and shallow coral reef. Offshore are numerous rocky islands. Small to medium black marlin and sailfish are regularly caught. Reef fish and spanish mackerel are the main target for local fishos. The shallow waters are generally clear and there is local interest in spearfishing, despite the numerous sharks and crocodiles. Boat hire and charters are available for people who fly in. Dhimurru Land Corporation permits give access to some great coastal fishing areas, with Cape Arnhem and surrounds being scenic and well worth a cast or two. Gove Fishing Club is active and has regular competitions, visit www.govefishingclub.org.au

Key to Map

Hotspots

1. Wirawawoi Beach: queenfish, mackerel, trevally. Banu Banu Lodge at nearby Bremer Island does fishing tours.
2. East Woody Creek: jacks, whiting, flathead, bream, mud crabs.
3. The sandspit - queenfish, trevally, tuna.
4. Nabalco Reef has queenfish, trevally, mackerel when it is too rough to go outside.
5. Giddy River entrance: barramundi, salmon.
6. Daliwuy Creek: most estuary fish, queenfish.
7. Isolated beaches and headlands off Cape Arnhem. Good fishing off rocks and inside headlands at times. Rising tide best. Trevally, mackerel and queenfish, some coral trout. Access is by 4WD along a soft sand track. The Bauxite Shelf rock ledge has excellent light tackle landbased sportfishing.
8. Queenfish and trevally around rocks. Tricky snapper, coral trout, trevally and mackerel on shoals and reefs. Excellent fishing in calmer weather. Note the ciguatera areas, usually a concern after rough weather.
9. Red emperor, coral trout and tricky snapper on reefs. Troll islets for mackerel. Billfish and black marlin are regularly sighted out wider.
10. Port Bradshaw is spectacular and has good light tackle sportfishing for queenfish, trevally, jacks, giant herring. Possible bonefish and permit.

Permit access

Most Gove Peninsula recreation areas are managed by Dhimurru Aboriginal Corporation. These spots include spectacular beaches and headlands, and some creeks and rivers. Activities include fishing, boating, camping and exploring. Destinations are signposted. Visit **www.dhimurru.com.au** for more information.

The following areas need a general Dhimurru permit:
Nanydjaka (Cape Arnhem)
Garanhan (Macassan Beach)
Guwatjurumurru (Giddy River)
Ganami (Wonga Creek)
Banambarrnga (Rainbow Cliff)
Wirrwawuy (Cape Wirawawoi)
Wupurr (Melville Bay)
Wathawuy (Latram River and Goanna Lagoon)
Gapuru (Memorial Park)
Lombuy (Crocodile Creek)
Ganinyara (The Granites)
Daliwuy (Daliwoi Bay)
Baringura (Little Bondi)
Dhamitjinya (East Woody Island)
Nhumuy (Turtle Beach)
Rangura (Caves Beach)
Lurrupukurru (Oyster Beach)
Gumuniya (Buffalo Creek)
Gadalathami (Town Beach)
Yarrapay (Rocky Point)

The following areas need a special Dhimurru permit:
Wanuwuy (Cape Arnhem)
Ganami
Gapuru
Mananggaymi
Cato River

The following areas need a Yirrkala Dhanbul Aboriginal Corporation permit, phone (08) 8987 3433:
Ganarrimirri (Shady Beach), Garrai (Rocky Bay Beach) and Witimurru (Yirrkala boat ramp)

To visit Gowupu (Catalina Boat Ramp) you need a permit from the NLC.

Most intertidal waters on this map can be fished under the Blue Mud Bay Registration Access Area arrangement.

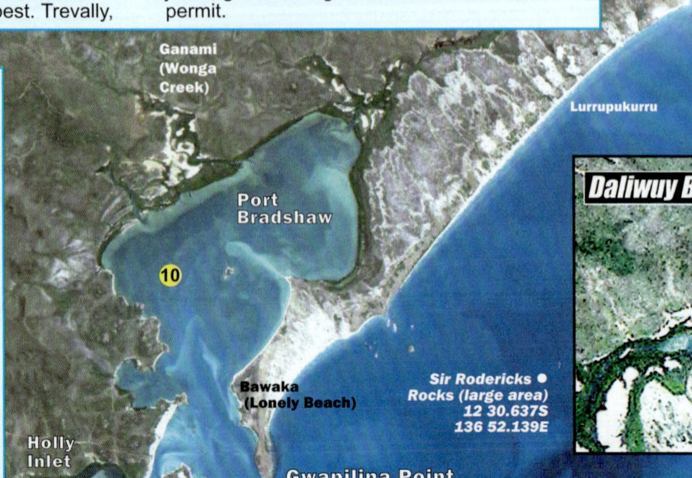

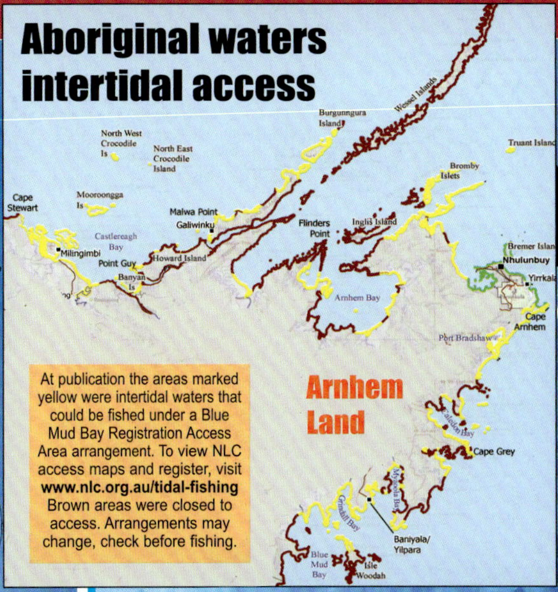

Aboriginal waters intertidal access

At publication the areas marked yellow were intertidal waters that could be fished under a Blue Mud Bay Registration Access Area arrangement. To view NLC access maps and register, visit **www.nlc.org.au/tidal-fishing** Brown areas were closed to access. Arrangements may change, check before fishing.

North-East Arnhem Land

The Wessel, Bromby and English Company Islands are among Australia's final frontiers for fishing explorers. The best time to visit is just before and after the wet season (Oct/Nov and Mar/Apr), as these periods usually have calmer weather. Mid-year conditions are cooler, but with south-east winds. Prevalent species are spanish mackerel, coral trout, and various cod and emperor. Sharks are abundant. The tides are smaller here than much of the NT coastline, and with no major river nearby the water is generally clear. While it might be tempting to swim or spearfish around the islands, saltwater crocodiles exist throughout.

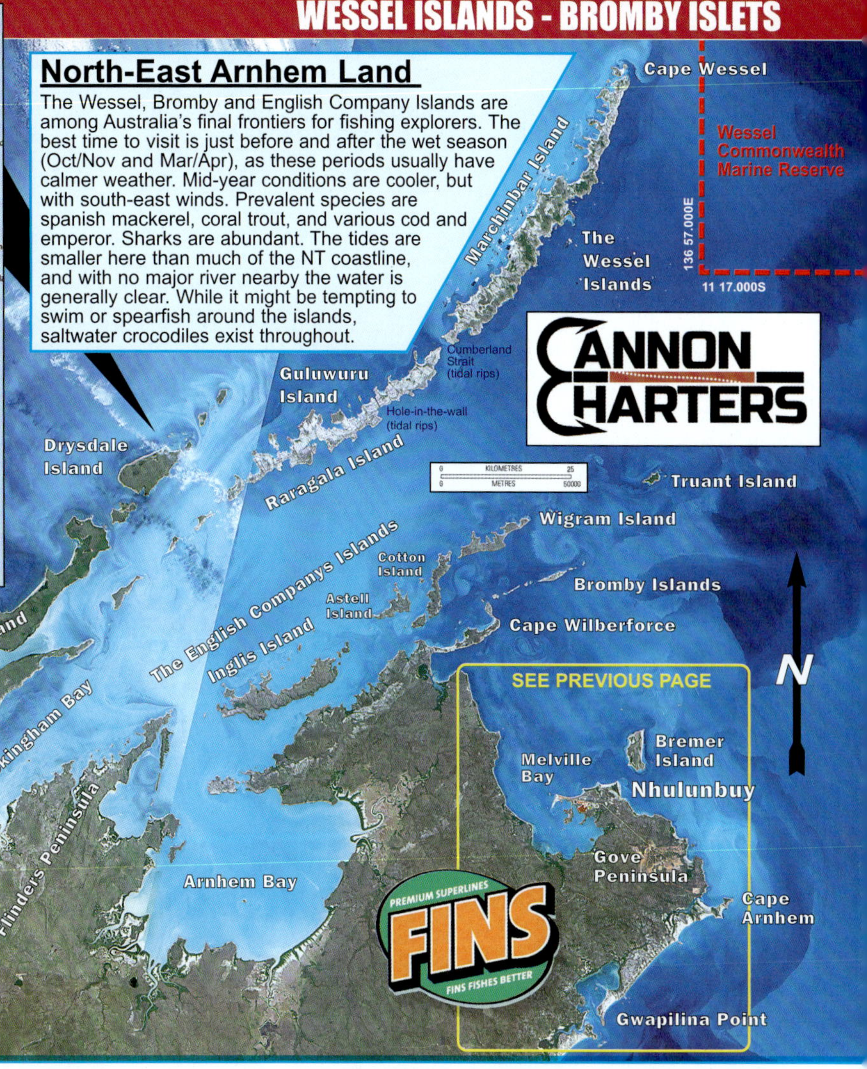

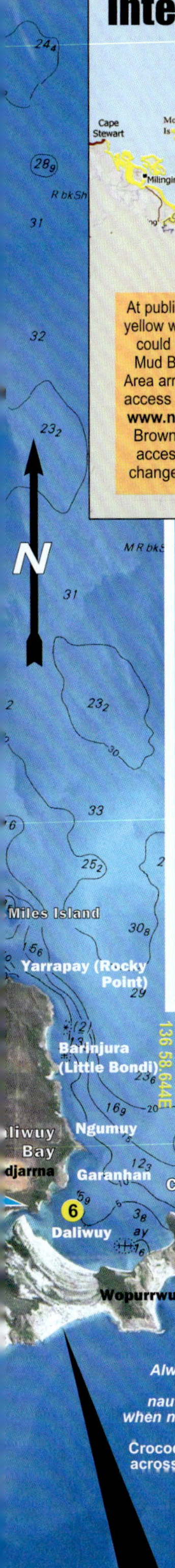

Always use a complete nautical chart when navigating.

Crocodiles exist across northern Australia

Remote shoals and islands

Remote shoals well wide of the Territory coast produce fishing much like that of the Great Barrier Reef.

Huge mangrove jacks, nannygai, red emperor, maori sea perch, wahoo, rankin cod, robinsons sea bream, footballer trout, various jobfish, sailfish and black marlin are taken.

Darwin charter companies go wide during the calm Build-up weather from October to December. Large trailer boats also make the journey.

A remote shoal is **Flat Top Bank**, 110km north-west of Fog Bay's Lodge of Dundee. Flat Top produces good fish, but the best spots are fairly small and there are sharks and, perhaps surprisingly, catfish.

About 37km north of Flat Top is **Newby Shoal.** Other spots off Melville Island include **Evans Shoal, Marie Shoal**, **Goodrich Bank** and the **Bathurst Trench**, which is a proven billfish ground.

NT islands differ greatly. Some are in clear blue water, surrounded by coral and sandflats, while others are part of turbid mangrove deltas.

Some islands have unusual geography, while others are flat.

Here's just a few ...

Sir Edward Pellew Group: These islands at the mouth of the McArthur River delta west of the NT/Qld border offer excellent fishing for barramundi and jewfish. Coral trout, cod, nannygai, mackerel and grunter are also caught. Camping is available. See pages 200-201.

The islands can be reached safely in good weather from the King Ash Bay fishing club on the McArthur River.

Vernon Islands: The sea runs through channels of rock in the strait between Cape Hotham, east of Darwin, and Melville Island, leaving the nearly verticle-sided Vernon Islands and associated reefs. The channels between are around 50m deep.

On the mainland there are two large rock channels at Gunn Point called the Blue Holes, with more blue holes in the rocky reef plateau around the islands.

At high tide there is not much to see at the Vernons as water inundates the mangroves, but at low tide the area is fascinating.

The Vernons are easily reached in good weather from Leaders Creek Fishing Base.

Croker region: The seas around the small islands near

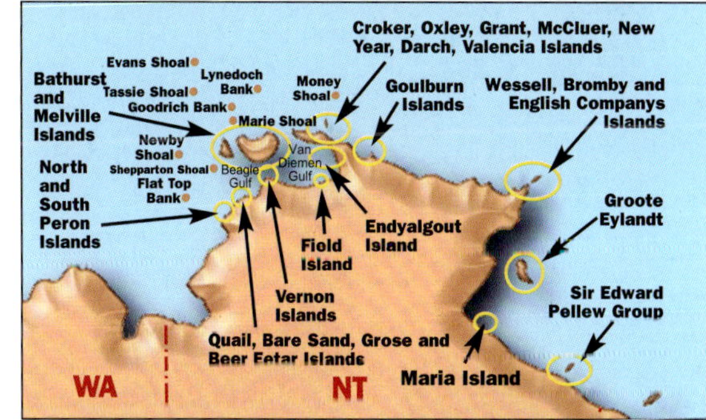

Croker Island, 260km north-east of Darwin, are an exciting long-range destination from Darwin. The islands include Grant, Lawson, Oxley, McCluer, New Year, Templer, Darch and Valentia. All are different. Oxley is surrounded by sandflats and bommies. New Year is fringed by coral reef. Valencia has a steep-sided sandbar on its south edge.

Tiwi Islands: Bathurst and Melville Islands north of Darwin are the largest NT islands, big enough to accommodate large river systems, although the largest rivers, on the north side, are off limits. Permits are available for fishing/camping on southern creeks.

Groote Eylandt: There is unlimited reef fishing here, with sailfish, and mainland barra hotspots nearby.

Peron Islands: The Peron Islands off Channel Point, south-west of Darwin, are a popular spot, easily accessible from Channel Point Nature Reserve.

Bynoe Harbour islands: These are the playground for Darwin trailerboaters. The islands are surrounded by shallow reefs and sand, with reef and pelagic fish.

There is an anchorage at Bare Sand Island, where people camp near the beach.

Note that many NT islands are Aboriginal land down to the mean low water mark.

The best places to

Choosing a Top End barramundi fishing destination requires a bit of planning.

Your ideal location depends on priorities. You may have family travelling with you, or you might be a keen angler chasing a trophy fish.

Are you fishing the dry season or wet season?

Serious fishos will find the best barramundi fishing across the Top End during the warm, rainy months of the Wet, and also during the notorious Build-up, which starts in October.

Unlike Queensland, the NT does not have a summer closed season for barramundi.

If you want a shot at winning a Million Dollar Fish (MDF) tagged barramundi prize, you must fish the open period, usually between October and March.

The wet season is a special time up north, when you see the real Top End. While it is true that flooding can cut off road access, floodwaters usually subside soon after rain events, and at this time cricket score catches of fish can be made.

You can even catch barra from flooded roadsides.

Shady Camp on the NT's Mary River

Do keep an eye on the weather bureau website, as severe thunderstorms and cyclones are a thing during the tropical summer.

Family fishos may prefer visiting the Top End in the cooler weather of dry season.

Barramundi can be caught at this time, but the fishing is usually a little slower.

Second decision - location.

MDF fish are released in waterways across the Top End.

If you are travelling with family you can't go past the Daly River, with its bankside tourist parks.

The Daly is a great producer of fish in all sizes and is home to the NT's two biggest barra competitions.

The Daly's banks have shady spots to pull up a boat and fish, and the river fishes well in the Wet and Dry, barring major floods. There are sandbars, rockbars and tree stumps that catch the unwary, but most boaters find the Daly easy to navigate, especially after a big wet season, which lifts the river level.

Another great family location is centred around Corroboree Park Tavern, on the Top End's famous "barra highway", the Arnhem Hwy.

The tavern, which has accommodation and campgrounds, is within easy driving distance of prime tidal and freshwater barramundi locations.

These include Corroboree Billabong, Hardies Lagoon, the Rock Hole and legendary Shady Camp, which has both tidal and freshwater fishing right next to the campground.

The NT's freshwater locations provide fishing without the hassle of tidal influence, with mornings, afternoons and night providing cooler conditions and greater fish activity.

For those who enjoy bush camping, with a chance of landing a wild trophy barra, the mighty Roper River is worth

catch barramundi

considering. Port Roper at the river mouth has big saltwater barra. You can pitch a tent there, but the only infrastructure is a boat ramp.

Midway along the Roper's tidal section is Tomato Island campground, with great amenities and pleasant dry season fishing that switches on and off with tide changes.

One Top End river has a lodge located on a mid-stream island. The Adelaide River's Goat Island Lodge offers lunch, cold drinks and cabin accommodation in the heart of barramundi country.

The Adelaide River is easy to navigate until just before Goat Island, when the rockbars start.

Proceeding upstream, there are several major rockbars, as shown in this book, and it is this area that produces good dry season barra fishing, and loads of cherabin.

Above Goat Island, the river is picturesque, and very different from the river at the Arnhem Hwy bridge, with plenty of shade and snags.

Kakadu National Park has many barramundi hotspots that can be fished during a daytrip from Darwin. Kakadu's South and East Alligator Rivers are

Top End saltwater barramundi

SHANE COMPAIN

worth a visit towards the end of the wet season.

The floodplains are a sight to behold when filled with water, although the fishing doesn't usually fire until the floodwater starts falling below the banks.

The last of the wet season sees a run of big barra.

During the dry season the tidal sections of these two rivers become problematic, being shallow and turbid, with many sandbars to catch the unwary.

At this time the rivers above the tidal limit form landlocked freshwater holes after floodwaters subside.

The Kakadu waterholes on the upper South Alligator and Wildman Rivers are scenic barramundi locations.

Don't be tempted to swim or loiter on the banks, as big crocodiles are abundant.

Secluded camping can be had in the eastern Top End on isolated waterways such the Towns, Limmen and Robinson Rivers, and Rosie Creek at Lorella Springs Station.

The fishing in these tidal rivers can be good, but you'll need to be self-sufficient, and access is only possible when the road is open after the Wet.

The McArthur River, near the Queensland border, has great facilities at the King Ash Bay fishing club.

The lower river is a labyrinth of tidal channels, opening out to the Sir Edward Pellew Islands

In the western Top End, near the WA border, Keep River has remote bush campsites on tidal water, in rocky surroundings.

The wide but shallow Victoria River is a tricky waterway to fish, best visited on neap tides when the water clears. The Vic's escarpment scenery makes a visit particularly enjoyable.

Next to Katherine township, the river has barra and sooty grunter, and Nitmiluk (Katherine Gorge) fishes well.

Flying in and out of Darwin for a fishing trip is an option.

The NT has many professional fishing guides who know where fish are likely to be in prevailing conditions. Most guides are based in Darwin, but offer day trips or extended expeditions to spots far afield.

Bluewater charters are also available, and they can take single bookings, or large groups.

The Daly

The Daly and Katherine rivers together form Australia's most iconic barramundi waterway.

The Daly is picturesque and prolific.

Most fishos stick to the tidal Daly River between the tourist parks and Hares Rockbar, arguably the river's best spot.

There is adventure for those willing to travel far. With planning and care navigating the tidal flats in the lower river, trailerboaters can fish the lower Daly and Anson Bay's coastal creeks.

Exciting spots in the lower Daly include the creeks inside Palmerston Island, the Reynolds River, and the coast near Red Cliff, which has rock patches that hold large barramundi, cod and snapper.

At the southern end of Anson Bay is Cape Ford, with hordes of big snapper.

To the north of Anson Bay are the Peron Island grounds and Bateman Shoal, which have reef fish, sailfish and mackerel, as well as cod, jacks, barra and snapper around the foreshores.

The ledge near Channel Point community is famous for big jewfish.

To explore the lower Daly, you need plenty of fuel and water. Ideally, travel with a satellite phone and second boat.

For those with boats, the Daly from the tidal limit at the main crossing near the police station, downstream to Alligator Head, is the best barramundi water.

This stretch is known for its green water and floodplain creeks, which flow after wet season floods.

About 2km downstream from the Daly Pub on the left-hand side opposite the Naiuyu Community are the Mission Creeks. There are two creeks about 200m apart. The mouths produce barra.

About 400m below Mango Farm on the right side, is Tommys Creek. The mouth produces good fish.

Bamboo Creek (not to be confused with another Bamboo Creek in the non-tidal section) can be fished from the bank and is popular during the Wet. The mouth, when flowing hard, produces big fish, especially at night.

Creeklets flow in along this section of the river during the wet season.

Try all these. The creek 400m up from Wooliana is also worth a try.

Along the river opposite the public ramp, a couple of creeks flow in. Fish the mouths.

Browns Creek fishes well near the mouth and just upstream around the rockbar. About 500m upstream on the right side is a 9m hole, a good spot.

Charlies Creek produces fish in the run-off. Fish the colour change at the mouth, and the left-hand edge downstream to the rock ledge on the next right-hand bend.

This section produces great fishing when the river drops down to normal height. From Charlies, fish the snags on the right side to the rock ledge.

A kilometre below Charlies is the Golden Mile. This runs to the rockbar. Troll either side close to logs with deep lures, or baitfish snags.

About 2km downstream is the main rockbar. Navigate with care. Troll from the rockbar upstream hugging the right bank to the next bend.

About 2km downstream is No Fish Creek. This is good in the run-off, at the colour change. When the water recedes, fish the change of tide. Bumpy bottom just upstream of the creek mouth fishes well.

Just downstream are the "S-bends". This stretch has big fish. Troll big lures on the tide change, and follow the tide upstream. Also fish snags and eddies.

Downstream about 4km on the right is Diesel Creek. Cast lures in the run-off at colour changes.

Another 2km down is Elizabeth Creek, a great run-off creek.

From the mouth troll along the snags to First Cliffs. This is a good area.

The small stretch between Elliott Creek and Hares Rockbar is one of the best spots in the river after a good wet season.

Further downstream are creeks all the way to Alligator Head. In the run-off most of these creeks empty a huge volume of water, with great fishing.

From Alligator Head the river changes. The high banks disappear and the river widens and gives way to semi-open country. This area is good in the Wet when the river is high upstream, but note the seasonal closure below Moon Billabong.

The next big creeks are Clearskin and Clear Creek. Pushing up Clear Creek in the run-off takes you to floodplain, with birds, bait and fish. From Clear Creek to the mouth of the Daly are many sandbars.

Note that during spring tides the Daly has a tidal bore. If tied up short or fishing under branches the bore can swamp small boats.

The freshwater section above the main crossing should not be ignored.

The non-tidal Daly can be accessed from here and higher up at Dorisvale and Oolloo crossings on roads that come off the Stuart Highway.

The area immediately above the main crossing, from the mouth of Heywood Creek down to Chilling Creek, has some deep rock holes, as well as scattered rocks, best fished early in the year.

Heywood Creek is about 10km above the crossing. Bait fishing the mouth of the creek with a float is effective. If the creek is flowing hard, venture up the creek, casting into snags.

The creek divides about 2km upstream, an ideal place to live bait with a cherabin.

About 8km upstream from the crossing is Chilling Creek mouth. Bait fishing the eddy close to the downstream bank produces good fish. Spangled perch, mullet or cherabin under floats are preferred baits.

Casting a lure up the creek and around the mouth and river edges is worth a try.

There are deep rocky holes in this stretch, and a series of small creeks running in to the main stream.

A large rock hole 500m above the crossing holds big fish. Fish lures close to the rock edge for better results.

The main crossing can be rewarding for landbased fishos at night, after early rain. A lot of big fish are caught there.

It is one of the top spots to fish if you do not have a boat, but the crocodile danger is real.

Katherine: the Top End's barra base

This small town is centrally located to three of the Top End's great barramundi rivers.

Within reach are the Roper River to the east, the Victoria River to the south-west, and the Daly River to the north-west.

All are about a three-hour drive from Katherine.

During and just after the Wet, which is the run-off season, the rivers tend to "fire" at different times, depending where rain falls.

By timing trips carefully you can hit each river when it is at its best, the water level falling after rain.

For a successful Top End barra fishing holiday, plan time off in late March/April. At this time the rivers usually start receding, although late rain may occur.

It is impossible to predict when each river will be at its prime, but the longer a river is in flood, the better it will be when it drops.

When a river is falling fast, clear water flows in from side creeks, and the barra feed in the channels and mouths on the bait that has built up during flooding. A call to the local tackle shop, Katherine Rod and Rifle, will reveal how the rivers are fishing.

If you plan to fish all the rivers at the end of the wet season, the first stop might be the Victoria River, because its drains the fastest.

Having fished the Vic, you could then drive to the Roper River, where the feeder creeks run for longer. After that, hit the Daly River, which fishes well into the dry season.

The Katherine River, which is technically the upper Daly, can have good barra fishing at the weirs and crossings, but timing is critical for spots like the Low Level Crossing and Knotts Crossing.

Katherine Gorge (Nitmiluk), is a series of 13 gorges separated by small rapids. It is a great spot for canoes. Barra are caught mainly by casting lures into the rapids between gorges after rain, but trolling the gorges can produce fish. Try casting small lures to snags and rocks. In the dry season, fish can be found in holes along the river. Sooty grunter are also caught, taking small baits and lures. Cherabin are caught in traps.

Good starting places are along Giles St next to the township (walk down the hill to the river), the Donkey Camp Hole and the small pools and rapids off Cossack Road.

Downstream of the town, the 50K Hole was to be reopened to public access in 2019.

The Flora River, with an access road off the Victoria Hwy, has picturesque water fishable by cartopper. The Flora runs clear and the fish can be hard to tempt.

Katherine has accommodation and many retail and service outlets.

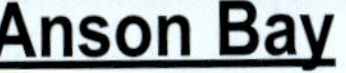

Anson Bay

The Daly River mouth and Anson Bay are for the adventurous fisho. There are remote creeks and reefs. The public camp and ramp at Channel Point makes dry season access easy enough, with the alternatives being a long boat trip down the Daly River, dodging the tidal flats, or travelling by sea or air from Darwin, or from Fog Bay's Dundee Beach. The boat trip down the Daly to the mouth is worthwhile when floodplain creeks are flowing as you can try each one. The bay's creeks and coastal rocks have barra and salmon, best during and just after the Wet, and during the Build-up. The area around Red Cliff has produced many big barra. Cape Ford has reef fish, particularly golden snapper. This region has big tides and strong currents.

At publication the intertidal waters of southern Anson Bay were a Permit-free Area. The two Peron Islands were a Restricted Area. The intertidal waters around Cape Scott and south to Dooley Bay were part of the Blue Mud Bay Registration Access Area. To view NLC access maps and register visit **www.nlc.org.au/tidal-fishing**

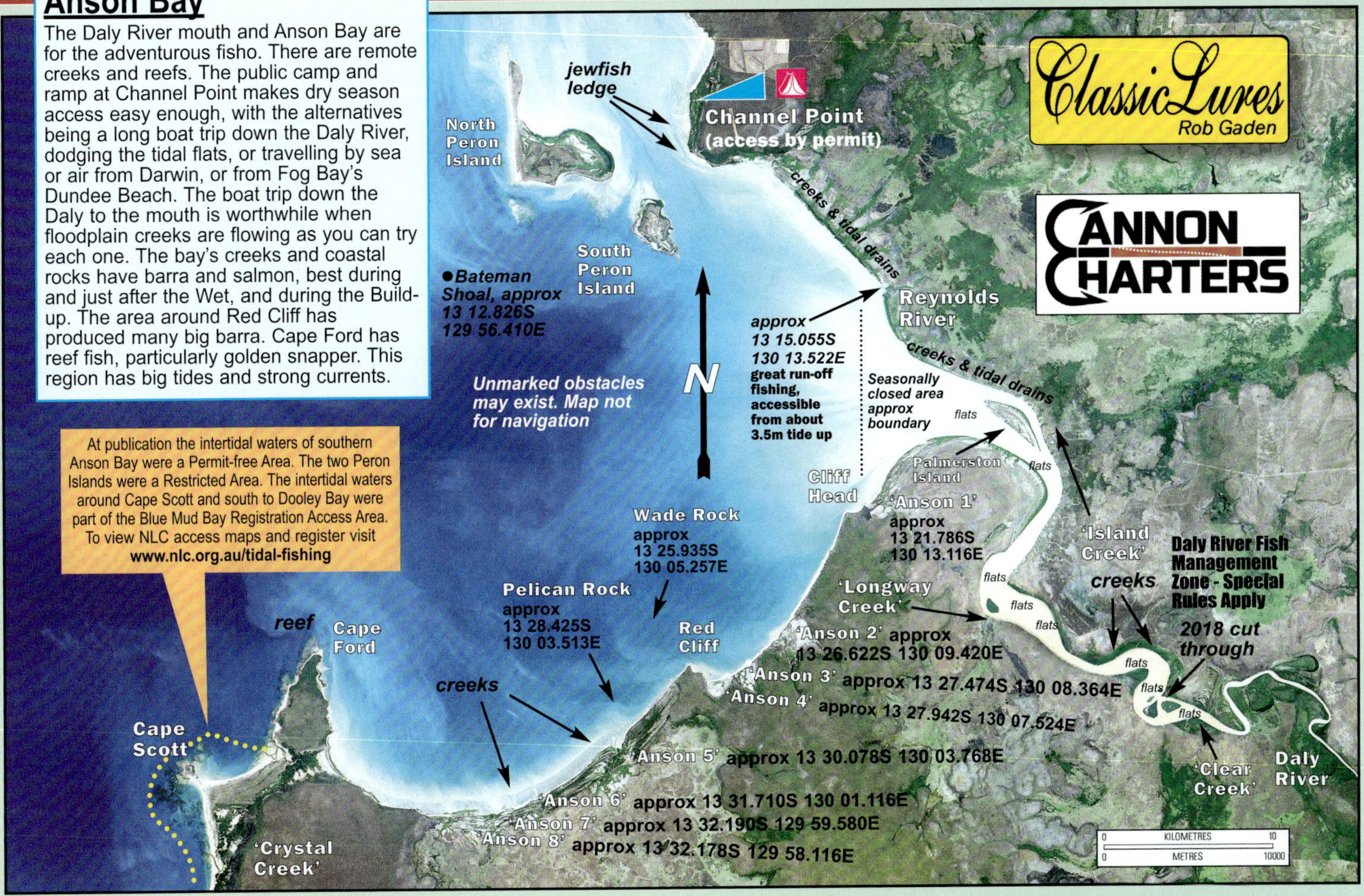

Canoes are available for hire at Nitmiluk during the dry season. These are suitable for fishing, but keep valuables in waterproof containers and take plenty of drinking water. For best results, fish the small rapids between the gorges with lures just after the Wet. During the Dry, fish the snags.

Darwin 320km

Warm spring enters river just upstream of railway bridge - good spot for barramundi. Take road to Springvalo Homestead

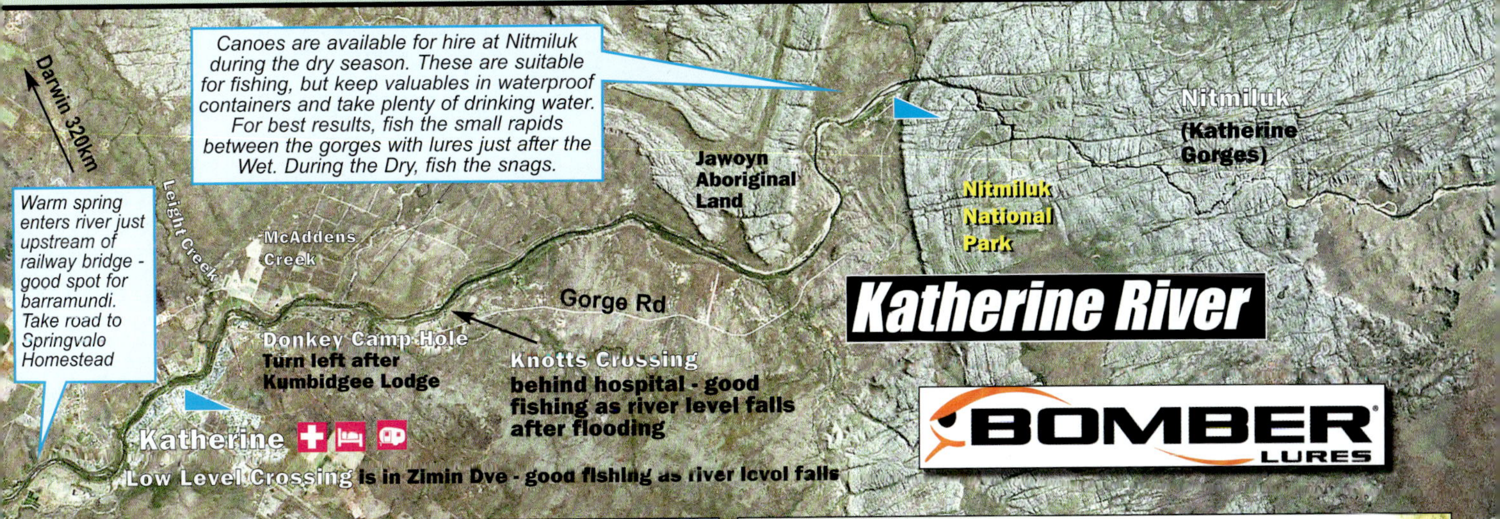

Jawoyn Aboriginal Land

Nitmiluk (Katherine Gorges)

Nitmiluk National Park

Leight Creek

McAddens Creek

Gorge Rd

Katherine River

Donkey Camp Hole Turn left after Kumbidgee Lodge

Knotts Crossing behind hospital - good fishing as river level falls after flooding

Katherine

Low Level Crossing is in Zimin Dve - good fishing as river level falls

Nitmiluk (Katherine Gorge)

Katherine River Low Level crossing

VLASSCO

Unmarked obstacles, including rocks and sunken trees, may exist in all waterways

'Croc Creek' The Cattle Yard Moon Billabong

'Cleanskin Creek' Alligator Point

'Clear Creek' 'Grassy Creek' 'Waterush Creek'

'Waterfall Creek' 'Reidys Creek' 'Lookout Creek'

'Hidden Creek' 'Second Cliffs' 'Catfish Creek' Hare's Rockbar 'Elliott Creek'

'First Cliffs Creek' 'Little Elizabeth Creek' rocks

SEE MAPS PAGE 178

'Diesel's Creek' billabong 'Elizabeth Creek' rocks sandbar The S-bend 'No Fish Creek'

troll bumps upstream of creek

creek rocks

MAJOR HAZARD Large rockbar approx 13 37.150 130 33.214, stay on west side, good fishing area

rocks 13 38.327S 130 34.193E

The Golden Mile (popular trolling area)

Browns Creek deep hole rocks 'Charlies Creek' rocks major sandbar near low water

The early incoming tide is a prime time to fish. Upriver tidal differences on Darwin tide times are (very approximate) two hours after Darwin at Clear Creek, four hours after Darwin at Elizabeth Creek, five hours at the S-bend, and opposite Darwin times at Browns Creek

shallow

Tidal variation at mouth: add approx 20 minutes to Darwin tides

Numerous sandbanks

TIDAL BORE ON BIG TIDES

CROCODILES INHABIT NORTHERN WATERWAYS

Alligator Point

AERIAL PHOTO

Daly River is closed to fishing downstream from dotted line from October 1 to January 31

S-Bend

Tidal variation at Browns Creek approx opposite scheduled Darwin tides

Browns Creek

crossing

Hazards

Low water level increases the chance of hitting obstacles. Major sandbars are at Browns Creek and below Alligator Head. There are rockbars and submerged timber dumped by wet season floods. Sub-surface stumps come and go each year. Look for disturbed waterflow. All marks are approximate. See maps on Page 178 for rockbar maps. This is not a complete list of hazards.

Main Rockbar
13 37.150S 130 33.214E
follow west bank

Wooliana Rocks
13 40.340S 130 38.672E
13 40.830S 130 38.539E

Rocks below Banyan Farm
13 41.691S 130 40.136E

Bottom of S-bends Rockbar
Rocks 13 36.439S 130 33.599E

Golden Mile Rocks
13 38.327S 130 34.198E

Rocks 2km below crossing
Rocks 13 45.139S 130 41.454E
Rocks 13 45.163S 130 41.620E
Rocks 13 45.318S 130 41.878E
Rocks 13 45.367S 130 41.993E
Rocks 13 45.557S 130 42.197E
Rocks 13 45.656S 130 42.261E

Mango Farm Sandbar
13 44.679S 130 41.108E

Browns Creek Sandbar
(varies each year, can be impassible at low tide, if so, try going around inside Browns Creek)
13 40.762S 130 36.628E

Rocks 8km above crossing
13 48.810S 130 42.929E

River levels

Fishermen can monitor the Daly and other NT river levels on the internet courtesy of numerous Bureau of Meteorology flood warning stations. The Daly has several stations along its length. Starting from near the Daly Crossing (tidal barrier) and heading upstream, some of the most important for fishermen are ...

Daly River Police Station
Mt Nancar
Beeboom Crossing
Theyona Station
Dorisvale Crossing
Katherine Railway Bridge

A falling river usually brings on the best barramundi fishing.

Daly Creek GPS

Fish River
13 56.790S 130 51.539E
Second Rapids
13 56.590S 130 50.420E
Tarpon Creek
13 54.550S 130 49.960E
Landslide Creek
13 54.640S 130 48.069E
First Rapids
13 53.680S 130 48.070E
Timber Creek
13 53.260S 130 44.620E
Island Creek
13 52.001S 130 44.190E
Mystery Creek
13 50.010S 130 43.980E
Fizzer Creek
13 50.630S 130 43.978E
Hayward Creek
13 49.050S 130 44.150E
Chilling Creek
13 49.340S 130 43.260E
Rockbar
13 48.810S 130 42.929E
Sandy Creek
13 46.140S 130 43.400E
Daly Crossing
13 46.029S 130 42.620E
Mission Creek
13 45.039S 130 41.101E
Yellowback Creek
13 44.991S 130 41.039E
Tommys Creek
13 44.010S 130 41.201E
Bamboo Creek
13 40.097S 130 39.502E
Public Ramp
13 40.750S 130 38.590E
Browns Creek
13 40.762S 130 36.624E
Charlies Creek
13 41.012E 130 35.352E
No Fish Creek
13 36.249S 130 34.070E
Diesel Creek
13 35.548S 130 31.635E
Elizabeth Creek
13 34.559S 130 31.149E
Little Elizabeth Creek
13 34.450S 130 31.090E
Elliott Creek
13 33.470S 130 31.635E
First Cliffs Creek
13 33.226S 130 30.963E
Catfish Creek
13 32.610S 130 30.069E
Lookout Creek
13 33.101S 130 30.899E
Hidden Creek
13 32.610S 130 30.079E
Reed Creek
13 30.692S 130 27.969E
Waterfall Creek
13 30.691S 130 27.659E
Alligator Creek
13 30.081S 130 28.424E
Moon Outlet
13 28.790S 130 27.411E
Mudflat Creek
13 28.310S 130 26.369E
Croc Creek
13 28.919S 130 24.758E
Little Cleanskin Creek
13 30.160S 130 25.660E
Cleanskin Creek
13 30.340S 130 25.640E
Waterrush Creek
13 30.440S 130 25.149E
Grassy Creek
13 30.310S 130 24.709E
Clearwater Creek
13 29.829S 130 23.529E
Blackwater Creeks
13 30.040S 130 22.629E

Use WGS 84 datum

Darwin Weipa Map Borroloola Karumba

Special Daly River Regulations

Fish possession limits

*Max. size limit of 90cm for barramundi, overall length, one fish over 90cm allowed.
*Max. size limit of 90cm for king threadfin, fork length, one fish over 90cm allowed.
*Maximum of three barramundi per person.
*Minimum size limit of 55cm for barramundi, overall length.
*Vessel limit of one barramundi over 90cm, overall length.
*Maximum of three king threadfin per person.
*Vessel limit of one king threadfin over 90cm, fork length.

Crustacean special possession limits

*Combined personal possession limit of 30 freshwater crustaceans, including a maximum personal possession limit of 10 cherabin.
*Total combined vessel limit of 90 freshwater crustaceans, including a maximum vessel possession limit of 30 cherabin with three or more people on board.
*You must release female freshwater crustaceans with a cluster of eggs under the abdomen. Females with eggs are said to be 'berried'.

Seasonal closure: Between October 1 and January 31 you must not fish, have a barramundi or a fishing line with a hook, lure or bait attached in the Daly River seasonal closure area below the Moon Billabong outlet to a north-south line drawn roughly between Cliff Head and Reynolds River at the Daly mouth.

The Daly

This is the Top End's premier barramundi river, home to the Barra Nationals and Barramundi Classic competitions in April/May. The Daly is popular because it holds a good stock of fish, and can fish well all year. It has several bankside tourist parks near the extent of tidal influence but the river is otherwise in its natural state. The best fishing is during and just after the wet season, usually at the mouths of floodplain run-off creeks, but many fish are caught trolling and casting to likely spots. The key is to find bait congregations, or locate fish with sonar. After the floodplain run-off has gone, the river continues to fish well during the "greenwater" period. One of the most popular areas is from Elizabeth Creek to Hare's Rockbar. During the wet season, when the river is high, anglers travel downstream, beyond Alligator Head. Anglers who find mullet schools will usually find big barramundi with them. During the dry season fishermen cast livebaits into snags and eddies. Cherabin are easily caught in traps. There is landbased fishing in the vicinity of Bamboo Creek and the main crossing near Daly River Police Station around high tide when the river has risen slightly, but beware crocodiles. Upstream of the main crossing, there is freshwater fishing for smaller barra and sooty grunter. Access further upstream (off map) is at Oolloo Crossing and Claravale Crossing, reached from turn-offs on the Stuart Highway. The Daly was closed to netting in 1988 and competition catches subsequently increased. The wet season now determines annual fishing quality. Special rules apply when fishing the Daly River.

Getting there

Turn off the Stuart Highway at sign-posted turn-offs at Adelaide River township (120km from Darwin) or, from Katherine, near Hayes Creek. Turn onto Dorat Road, then Daly River Road, and proceed about 70km. A 4WD vehicle is not required, although flooding can prevent access.

Launch sites

The public ramp is downstream from Woolianna, useable on most tides. Most tourist parks have private ramps. Some people launch at the crossing at high water, but it is not recommended. In flood the bridge can impede access.

Public launch site  Private launch site 

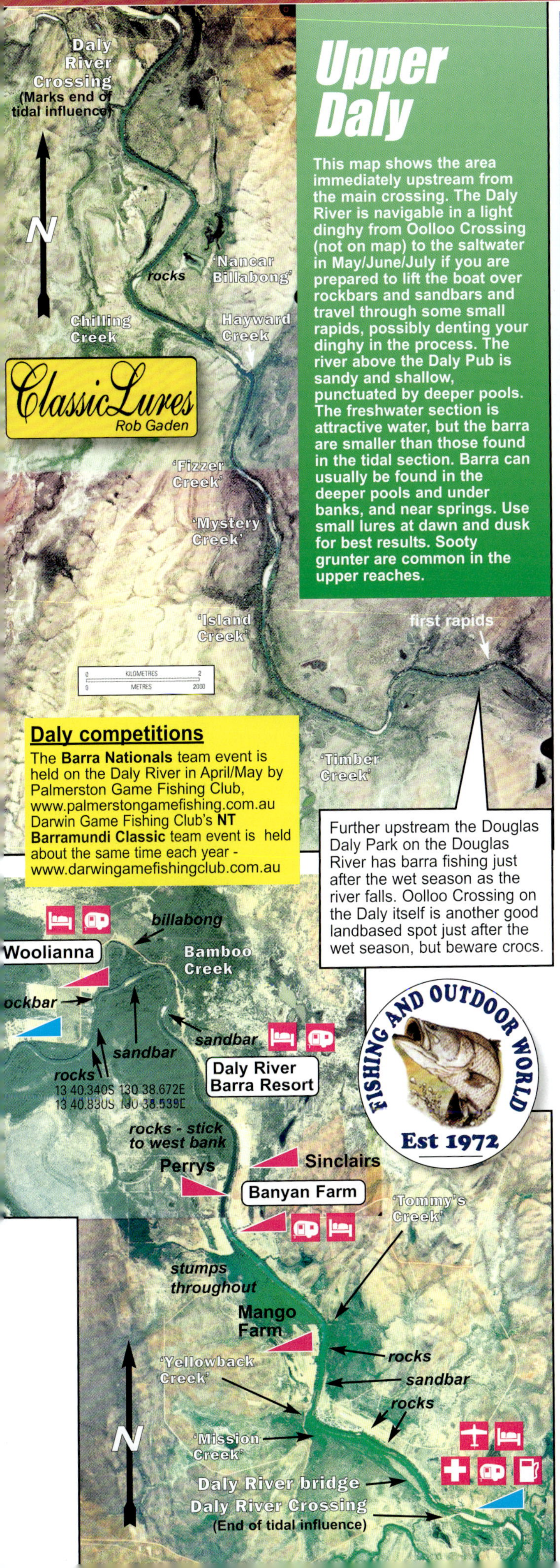

Upper Daly

This map shows the area immediately upstream from the main crossing. The Daly River is navigable in a light dinghy from Oolloo Crossing (not on map) to the saltwater in May/June/July if you are prepared to lift the boat over rockbars and sandbars and travel through some small rapids, possibly denting your dinghy in the process. The river above the Daly Pub is sandy and shallow, punctuated by deeper pools. The freshwater section is attractive water, but the barra are smaller than those found in the tidal section. Barra can usually be found in the deeper pools and under banks, and near springs. Use small lures at dawn and dusk for best results. Sooty grunter are common in the upper reaches.

Daly River Crossing (Marks end of tidal influence)
N
rocks
'Nancar Billabong'
Chilling Creek
Hayward Creek
'Fizzer Creek'
'Mystery Creek'
'Island Creek'
first rapids
'Timber Creek'
KILOMETRES 0 2
METRES 0 2000

Classic Lures
Rob Gaden

Daly competitions

The **Barra Nationals** team event is held on the Daly River in April/May by Palmerston Game Fishing Club, www.palmerstongamefishing.com.au Darwin Game Fishing Club's **NT Barramundi Classic** team event is held about the same time each year - www.darwingamefishingclub.com.au

Further upstream the Douglas Daly Park on the Douglas River has barra fishing just after the wet season as the river falls. Oolloo Crossing on the Daly itself is another good landbased spot just after the wet season, but beware crocs.

billabong
Woolianna
Bamboo Creek
ockbar
sandbar
sandbar
rocks
13 40.340S 130 38.672E
13 40.830S 130 38.539E
Daly River Barra Resort
rocks - stick to west bank
Perrys
Sinclairs
Banyan Farm
'Tommy's Creek'
stumps throughout
Mango Farm
rocks
sandbar
rocks
'Yellowback Creek'
N
'Mission Creek'
Daly River bridge
Daly River Crossing (End of tidal influence)

FISHING AND OUTDOOR WORLD
Est 1972

Daly's best fishing rockbars

These maps depict some of the best fishing rockbars on the Daly River. These spots consistently produce big barramundi, as well as good catches of smaller fish.

The swirling eddies, snags, rocks and sandbars of the Daly S-bend are a natural stopping point for mullet and barramundi.

Barra Nationals champion Shane Compain said the beauty of the S-bend was that it usually had a spot to fish at any stage of the tide.

"The S-bend area is a one-stop shop, it is a fish attractant - you've got creeks, rockbars, snags and back eddies," he said.

"It changes all the time with the tide and flooding.

"There are so many features you can usually fish it at any time.

"Heading downstream, just before the S-bend, you have the No Fish Creek lumps and No Fish Creek itself, which are famous spots.

"Then into the S-bend on the outside of the sweeping bend there is a back eddy that often fishes well at mid-tide on the outgoing tide.

"The fish will be there on the sounder and you have to wait for them to bite. They are often really good fish.

"The straight itself is where you go if other spots aren't working, with fish resting near the snags.

"And there are some big fish caught there.

"Fast-trolling the area below the lower sandbar works well for some.

"The top sandbar has a more distinct drop-off and and is a better spot that can fish well, especially at night.

"Some people throw big rubber lures off that sandbar during competitions."

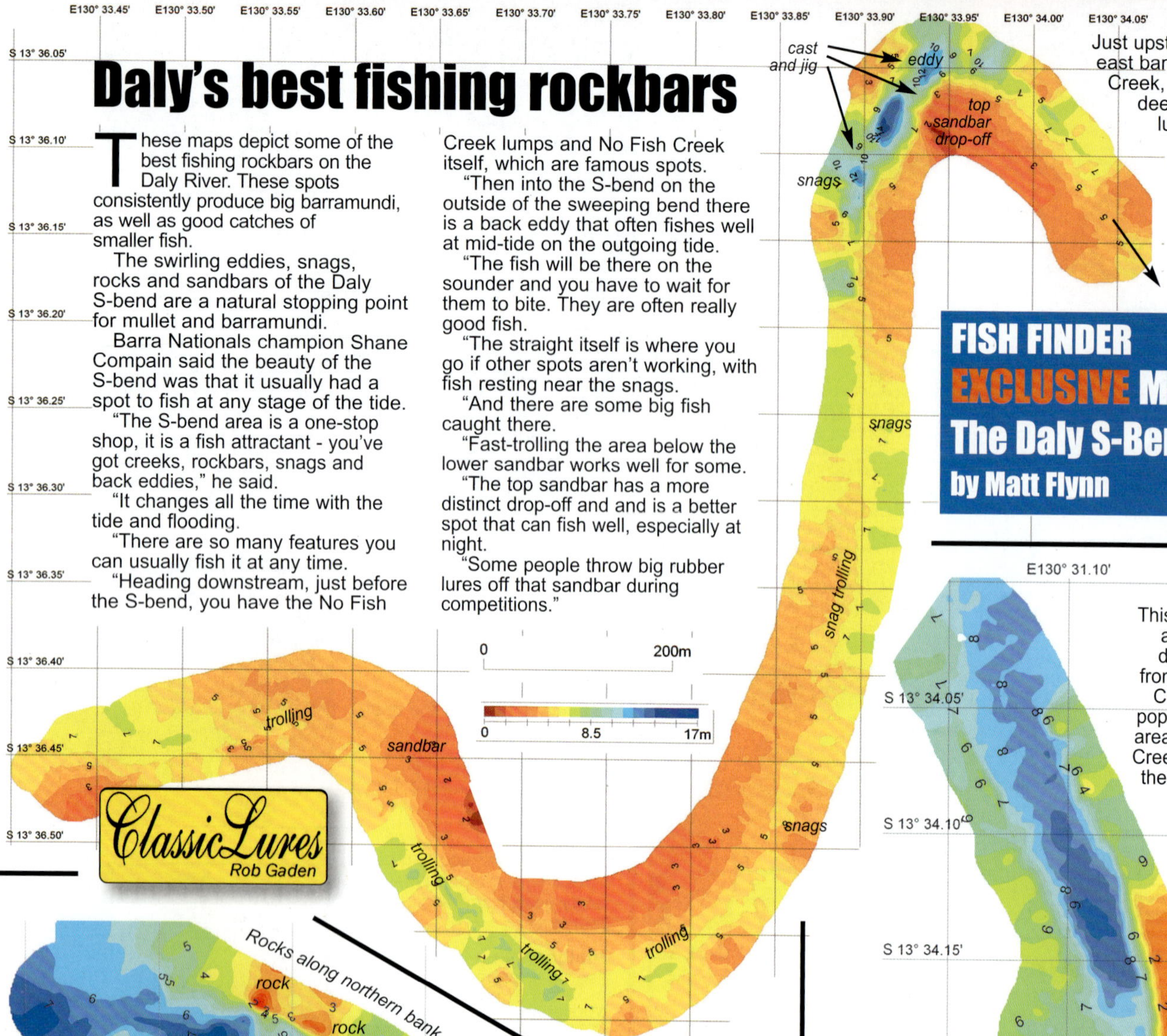

Just upstream on the east bank is No Fish Creek, which has a deep rockbar or lumpy bottom slightly upstream of the creek mouth. The creek and rockbar produce barra.

FISH FINDER EXCLUSIVE MAPS
The Daly S-Bend
by Matt Flynn

This rockbar is about 750m downstream from Elizabeth Creek. It is a popular trolling area. Elizabeth Creek is one of the better run-off creeks.

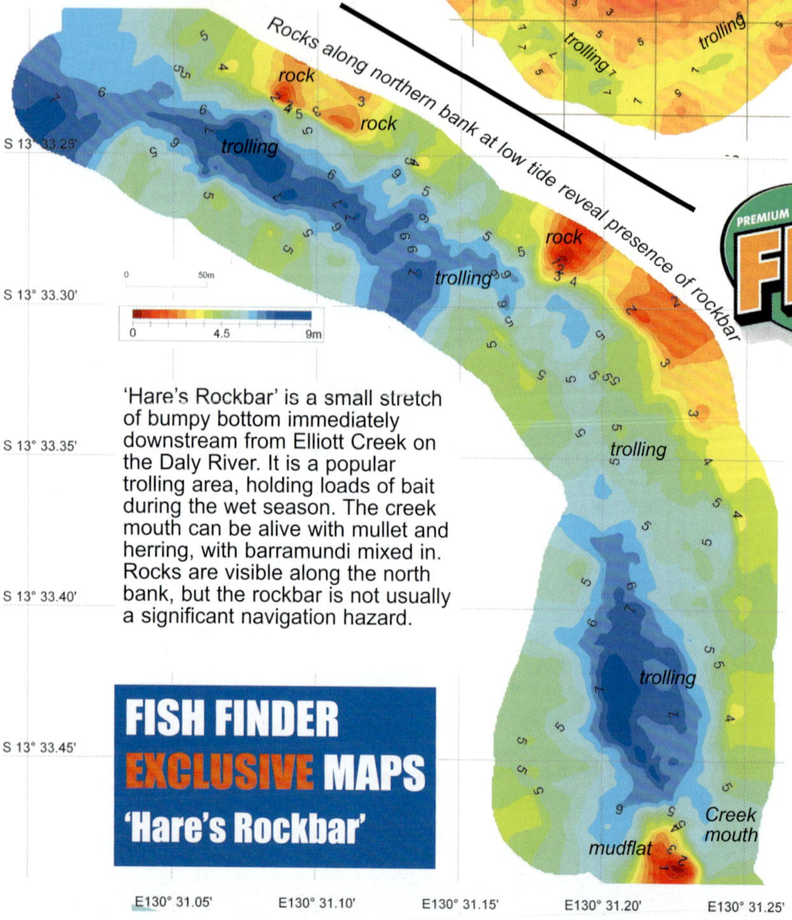

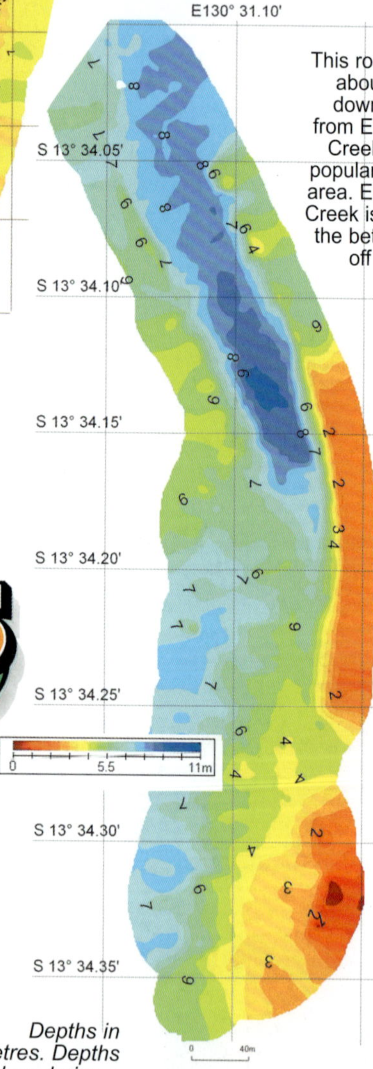

'Hare's Rockbar' is a small stretch of bumpy bottom immediately downstream from Elliott Creek on the Daly River. It is a popular trolling area, holding loads of bait during the wet season. The creek mouth can be alive with mullet and herring, with barramundi mixed in. Rocks are visible along the north bank, but the rockbar is not usually a significant navigation hazard.

FISH FINDER EXCLUSIVE MAPS
'Hare's Rockbar'

Depths in metres. Depths taken during a neap tide with some floodwater

Maps are for fish-finding purposes only. Not for navigation

FISH FINDER EXCLUSIVE MAPS
'Lizzy Rockbar'

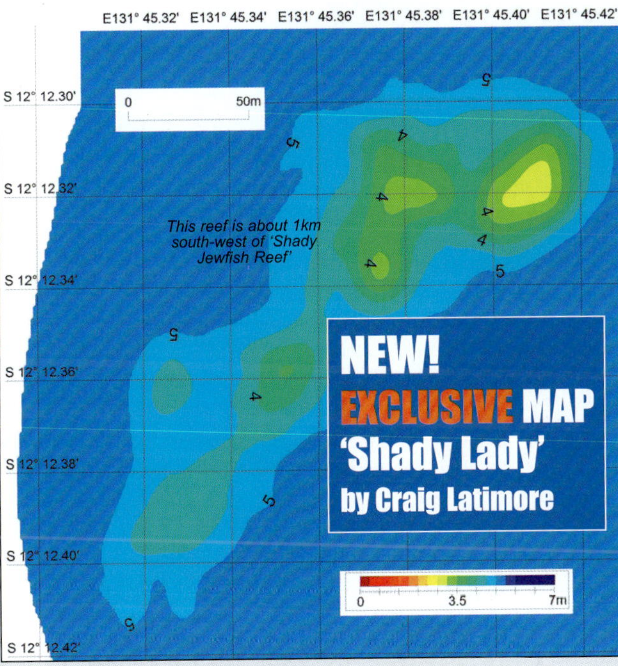

Swim Creek after wet season rain ... note the floodwater behind the creek

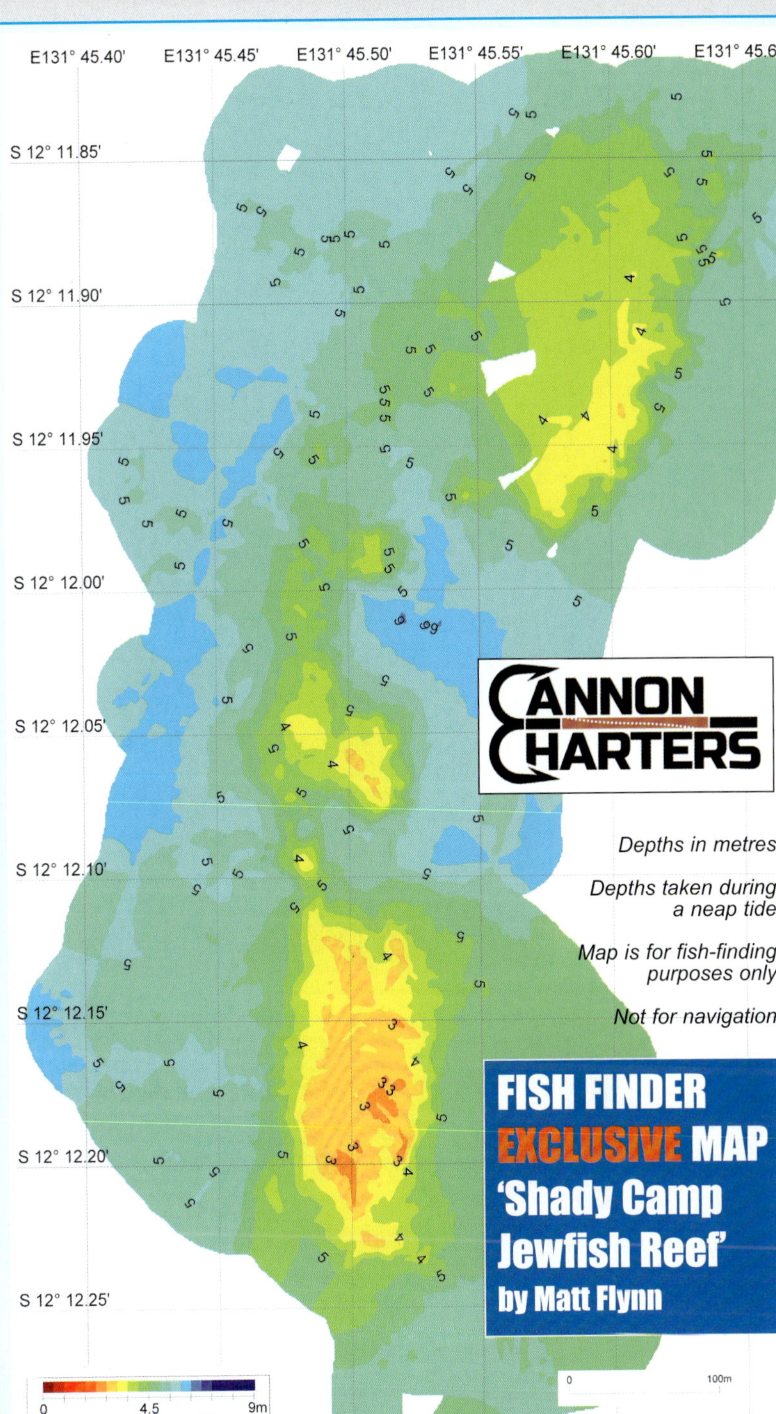

Shady Jewfish Reef

This shallow rocky reef in Chambers Bay fishes well for large black jewfish, blue salmon, golden snapper and cod. Two nearby reefs are shown above left. The reefs, 8km north of Sampan Creek mouth, are fed by a vast wetland that pours wet season floodwater into Chambers and nearby Finke Bays. The reefs are about a 48km run from the launch site at Shady Camp barrage, so take plenty of fuel and extra drinking water in case of a breakdown. The turn of the tide fishes best on these reefs. Be sure to have fresh bait as fish can sometimes be picky. The complicating factor when fishing this area is timing your launch and retrieve at Shady Camp, because all-tide access at the ramp is available only during wet season flooding. Otherwise, launching must be above about 4m of tide. Add about 4.5 hours to Darwin tides for tides at Shady Camp barrage. Be at the ramp earlier than required as the outgoing tide drains away fast. A full day on the water usually includes barramundi fishing at Sampan or Tommycut mouths or on the smaller coastal creeks, then a trip out to the reefs, then more barramundi fishing on the way home, with a final cast or two at the barrage. The access road off the Arnhem Highway is partly sealed. The unsealed section can be rough and gets get boggy and slippery after heavy rain, but usually remains open. Shady Camp is 110km as-the-crow-flies east of Darwin. The access road is signposted off the Arnhem Hwy.

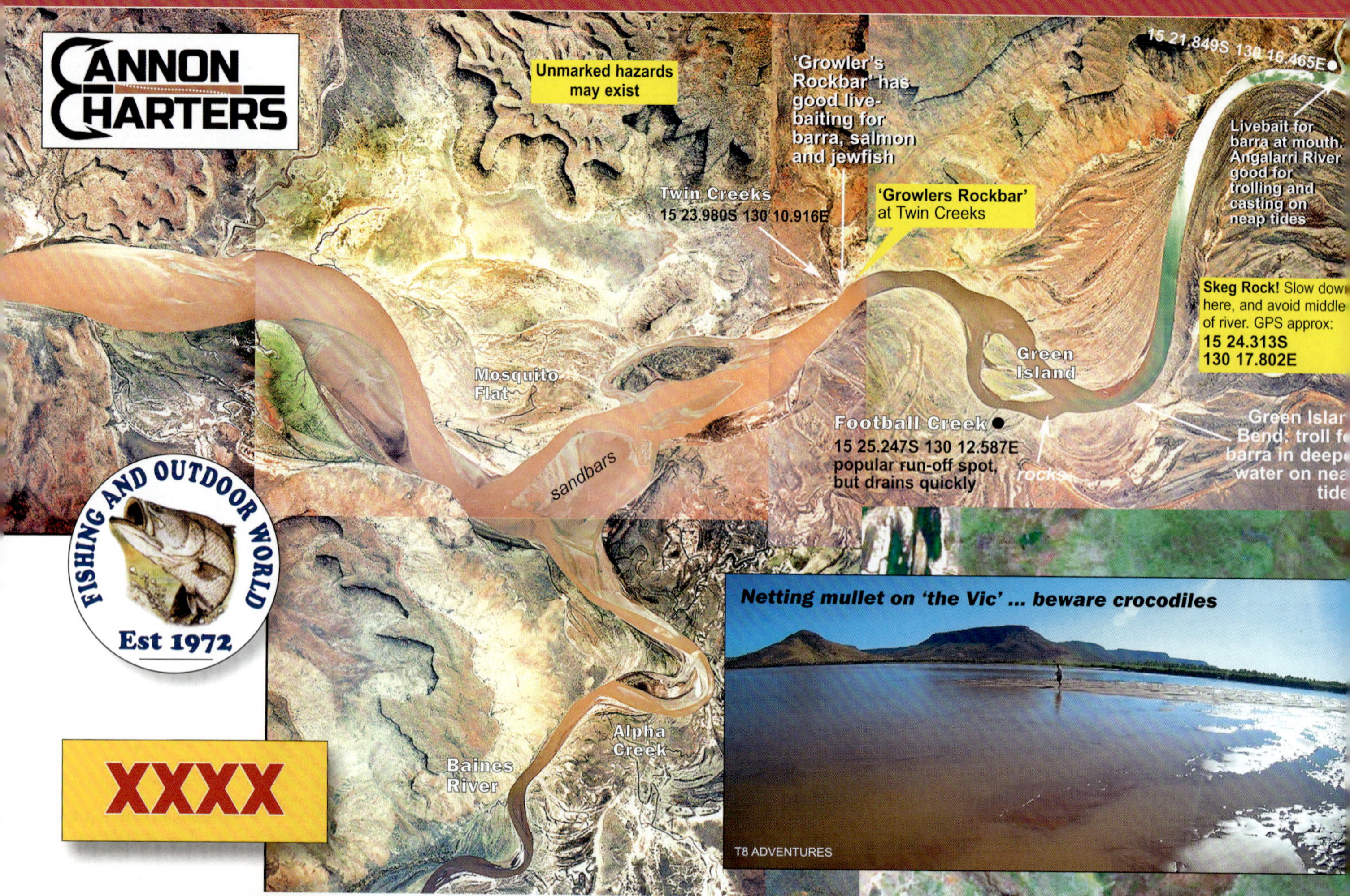

Unmarked hazards may exist

'Growler's Rockbar' has good live-baiting for barra, salmon and jewfish

15 21.849S 130 16.465E

Twin Creeks
15 23.980S 130 10.916E

'Growlers Rockbar' at Twin Creeks

Livebait for barra at mouth. Angalarri River good for trolling and casting on neap tides

Skeg Rock! Slow down here, and avoid middle of river. GPS approx: 15 24.313S 130 17.802E

Mosquito Flat

Green Island

Football Creek
15 25.247S 130 12.587E
popular run-off spot, but drains quickly

rocks

Green Island Bend: troll for barra in deeper water on neap tides

sandbars

Alpha Creek

Baines River

Netting mullet on 'the Vic' ... beware crocodiles

T8 ADVENTURES

Victoria River

The mighty "Vic" is 560km long and more than 3km wide in places, with 56 tributaries, most of which are dry outside of the wet season. Despite its size the Vic is shallow, with large, shifting sandbanks, and rocky areas. Visitors are wise to do their first trip on a rising tide. Local fishermen restrict their efforts mostly to neap tides because the water is clearer, and the fishing better. Navigate the Vic on an incoming tide and find an area to fish through the low tide. Most fishing takes place in the section between Timber Creek and the Baines River. The river has barramundi, threadfin salmon, jewfish, mud crabs and plenty of catfish. Livebait fishing is the norm, but lures work well in the wet season run-offs and during neap tides. Mud crabs move upstream as the dry season progresses. Places to fish include the steep west bank leading up to Sandy Island, the steep bank opposite Pelican Point, Angalarri River mouth, "Skeg Rock", and "Growler's Rockbar" at Twin Creeks. Most local anglers do not travel further downstream than Lobby Creek. "Skeg Rock" claims propellers because it sits almost midstream. Slow down well before you reach it. "Growler's Rockbar' comes out of Twin Creeks and is two rockbars. Cast lures or baits between the rocks for barra. Lobby Creek has a large rock formation nearby. "Football Creek" inside Green Island is a popular wet season run-off spot. The Baines River is shallow but offers good fishing, with some huge barra caught there. Like most of the Vic's tributaries, it has a swag of submerged timber to catch propellers. The Vic has a short-lived wet season run-off because its catchments are small and rocky. During the Wet, fish immediately after flooding as the water drops away quickly. Katherine Rod and Rifle proprietor Warren de With's Vic strategy is: "Be at the right spot at low tide. If you see fish on the sounder at half-tide and they aren't biting, don't leave. Wait for the tide to drop and turn." Locals say it is difficult to calculate variations against Darwin tide times. Landbased fishing can be had at Policeman's Point near Timber Creek, keeping in mind the crocodile danger, as well as at Big Horse Creek boat ramp, which has a wet season run-off creek nearby. Further upstream (off map), Dashwood Crossing and Humbert River Crossing have barramundi after wet season rain. For competition anglers, the river hosts the Big Horse Creek Barramundi Classic and Timber Creek Classic competitions.

Getting there

From Katherine, take the Victoria Hwy for 250km to Big Horse Creek boat ramp, which has camping. 4WD is not required. If going far downstream travel with another boat. There is a ramp on the upper non-tidal Vic at the roadhouse bridge (off map, 120km upstream). Freshwater fishing can also be had using a 4WD bank launch via a turn-off west of the roadhouse. **For river mouth tides, use Darwin tide times. Tides upstream are hard to predict.**

Big Horse Barra Classic

This event is held on the Victoria River out of Timber Creek each year, usually around the end of April.

The event has a huge spread of prizes across a wide range of categories, making it a top event for both family fishermen and serious anglers.

In 2021 the 33rd Classic had 299 competitors, with 92 teams. There were 164 barra, 11 jewfish, 45 salmon and 107 catfish entered. The biggest barra entered was 111cm.

The 2020 event was cancelled.

A total of 343 fishos tried their luck in 2019, comprising 98 teams. There were 136 barra caught. The biggest barra was 100cm and won its captor $4000.

The event is organised by Katherine Game Fishing Club, visit them at **www.kgfc.com.au** or on Facebook.

Low tide on a southern arm of the Fitzmaurice River, north of the Victoria River

Revised Barra Life History

According to the familiar barramundi life history model, first described by Darryl Grey in the late 1980s, barramundi migrate from saltwater spawning grounds into freshwater as juveniles and live there for three to four years, growing to 50cm to 80cm before heading back to saltwater to spawn as maturing males, where they later become female fish. This theory did not take into account that occasional metre-plus fish are caught in freshwater locations and that many young fish are found in estuaries. Studies have since identified three distinct groups of barramundi, each with their own migration strategy. The model includes Grey's classic life history, but also recognises an estuarine group that doesn't migrate into freshwater, and a group that lives in freshwater for up to a decade or so, where they develop female gonads before migrating to saltwater to spawn. This may explain why some metre-plus barramundi are caught from freshwater locations. Further research is looking at why barramundi behave in different ways, and whether some contingents grow faster than others.

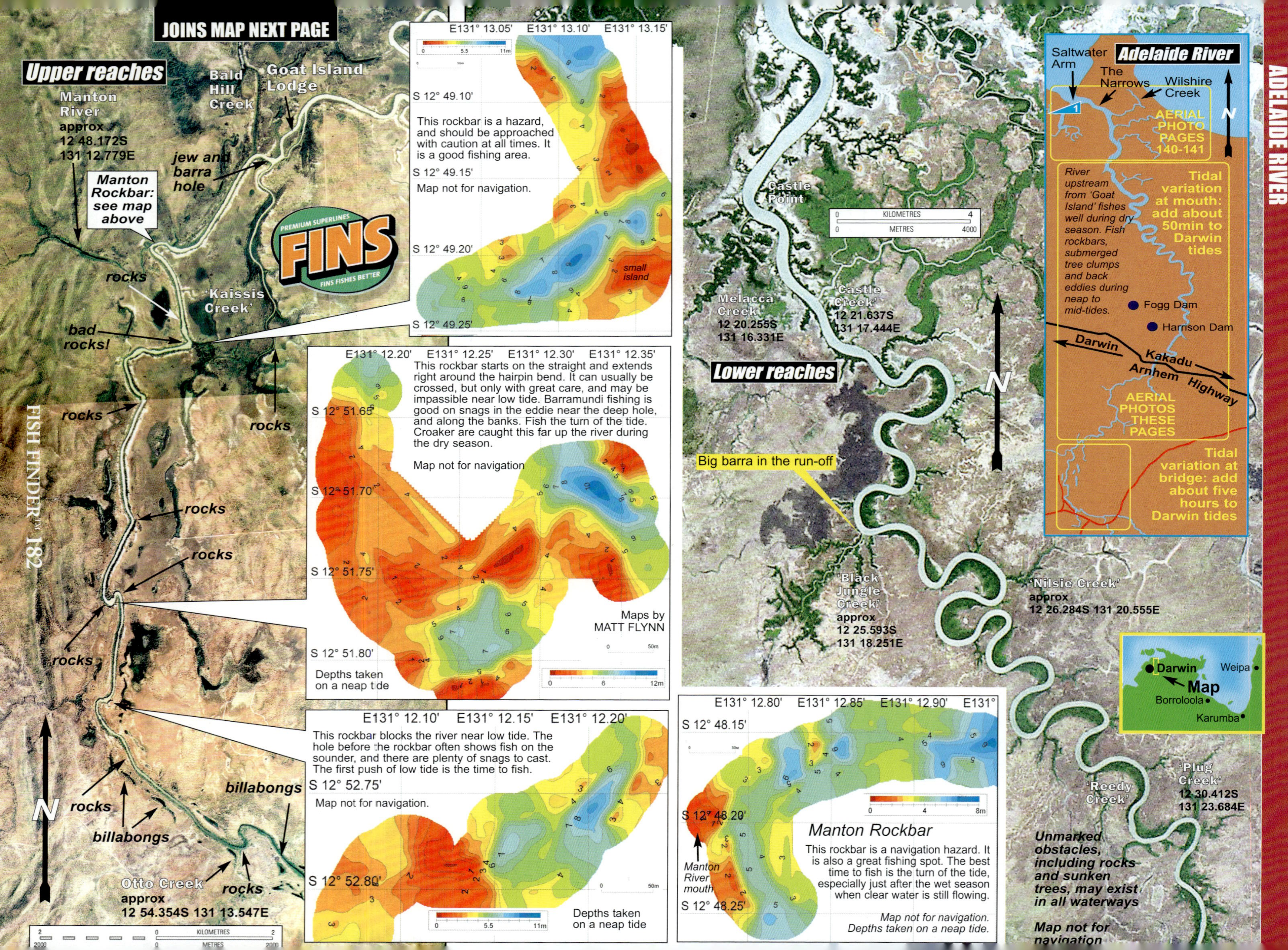
JOINS MAP NEXT PAGE
Upper reaches
Manton River approx 12 48.172S 131 12.779E
Manton Rockbar: see map above
Bald Hill Creek
Goat Island Lodge
jew and barra hole
rocks
'Kaissis Creek'
bad rocks!
rocks
rocks
rocks
rocks
rocks
rocks
billabongs
billabongs
rocks
Otto Creek approx 12 54.354S 131 13.547E
N
KILOMETRES
METRES
PREMIUM SUPERLINES
FINS
FINS FISHES BETTER
E131° 13.05' E131° 13.10' E131° 13.15'
S 12° 49.10'
This rockbar is a hazard, and should be approached with caution at all times. It is a good fishing area.
S 12° 49.15'
Map not for navigation.
S 12° 49.20'
S 12° 49.25'
small island
E131° 12.20' E131° 12.25' E131° 12.30' E131° 12.35'
This rockbar starts on the straight and extends right around the hairpin bend. It can usually be crossed, but only with great care, and may be impassible near low tide. Barramundi fishing is good on snags in the eddie near the deep hole, and along the banks. Fish the turn of the tide. Croaker are caught this far up the river during the dry season.
Map not for navigation
S 12° 51.65'
S 12° 51.70'
S 12° 51.75'
S 12° 51.80'
Depths taken on a neap tide
Maps by MATT FLYNN
E131° 12.10' E131° 12.15' E131° 12.20'
This rockbar blocks the river near low tide. The hole before the rockbar often shows fish on the sounder, and there are plenty of snags to cast. The first push of low tide is the time to fish.
S 12° 52.75'
Map not for navigation.
S 12° 52.80'
Depths taken on a neap tide
Castle Point
KILOMETRES 0 4
METRES 0 4000
Melacca Creek 12 20.255S 131 16.331E
'Castle Creek' 12 21.637S 131 17.444E
Lower reaches
N
Big barra in the run-off
'Black Jungle Creek' approx 12 25.593S 131 18.251E
'Nilsie Creek' approx 12 26.284S 131 20.555E
'Reedy Creek'
'Plug Creek' 12 30.412S 131 23.684E
Unmarked obstacles, including rocks and sunken trees, may exist in all waterways
Map not for navigation
E131° 12.80' E131° 12.85' E131° 12.90' E131°
S 12° 48.15'
S 12° 48.20'
S 12° 48.25'
Manton River mouth
Manton Rockbar
This rockbar is a navigation hazard. It is also a great fishing spot. The best time to fish is the turn of the tide, especially just after the wet season when clear water is still flowing.
Map not for navigation. Depths taken on a neap tide.
Adelaide River
Saltwater Arm
The Narrows
Wilshire Creek
N
AERIAL PHOTO PAGES 140-141
River upstream from 'Goat Island' fishes well during dry season. Fish rockbars, submerged tree clumps and back eddies during neap to mid-tides.
Tidal variation at mouth: add about 50min to Darwin tides
Fogg Dam
Harrison Dam
Darwin
Kakadu
Arnhem Highway
AERIAL PHOTOS THESE PAGES
Tidal variation at bridge: add about five hours to Darwin tides
Darwin
Weipa
Map
Borroloola
Karumba

Adelaide River

This is the nearest big river to Darwin. The tidal river runs through a series of looping bends downstream from the Arnhem Hwy bridge boat ramp, making it a long 95km trip to the mouth. During the wet season, when the river is high and falling, the feeder creeks produce bursts of good barramundi fishing, including some large fish, but the river is notoriously fickle. Fishing tends to be best from late February. The run-off does not last long once the rain stops. The river has good feeder creeks upstream of the Arnhem Hwy bridge to well above Goat Island. Downstream, Black Jungle Creek mouth is the best run-off spot. During the dry season the river above Goat Island is attractive water, almost on par with the iconic Daly River, with overhanging trees, snags, rockbars and reasonably clear water, unlike the turbid water of downstream. The upstream rockbars usually fish on the turn of the tide. Just after the wet season, during the greenwater period, and on neap tides, bump lures over rockbars and cast to eddies, snags and undercut banks. Sooty grunter, saratoga and cherabin inhabit the upper river. Goat Island Lodge is an excellent base to fish the upper river, being at the start of the rockbar country. The unsealed Marrakai Road off the Stuart Hwy crosses the freshwater reaches, while the far upper reaches cross the Stuart Hwy at Adelaide River township. There is good fishing at the river mouth in Saltwater Arm and the Wilshire Creeks (see pages 140-141), best on neap tides during and after the wet season, and in the early Build-up before storm rain dirties the water. The river mouth has jewfish on shallow reefs, fishable during neap tides. The mouth is most easily accessed by Saltwater Arm public ramp. The river is closed to netting. It is famous for its 'jumping crocodile' cruises. Fortunately the crocodiles tend to ignore small boats, but anyone landing a fish should take care.

Getting there

The Arnhem Hwy bridge ramp is about 65km from Darwin. The ramp is best used during the top half of the tide, unless the river is high from rain. The car park sometimes floods during the wet season. The Saltwater Arm and Leaders Creek ramps can be reached by turning off the Stuart Highway down the Howard Springs Road, then a further 45km down the unsealed Gunn Point Road to the sign-posted turn-off. **For the bridge ramp, add about five hours to Darwin tides. Tides times upstream at Goat Island are roughly reverse of Darwin tide times.**

Launch sites

1. Saltwater Arm, sealed ramp, turn-off is on Gunn Point Road (see pages 140-141). Add 50 min to Darwin tides.
2. Arnhem Hwy Bridge, concrete ramp, useable mid tide up. Add five hours to Darwin tides.

Main Adelaide River rockbars GPS waypoints in WGS84 (other unmarked rockbars and hazards may exist), travelling upstream:

12 46.678S, 131 15.579E
12 46.817S, 131 15.290E
12 46.964S, 131 15.137E
12 46.757S, 131 14.606E
12 51.761S, 131 12.294E
12 51.740S, 131 12.184E
12 52.783S, 131 12.164E
12 54.094S, 131 13.589E
12 54.132S, 131 13.538E
12 54.196S, 131 13.546E
12 54.354S, 131 13.610E
12 54.755S, 131 14.566E

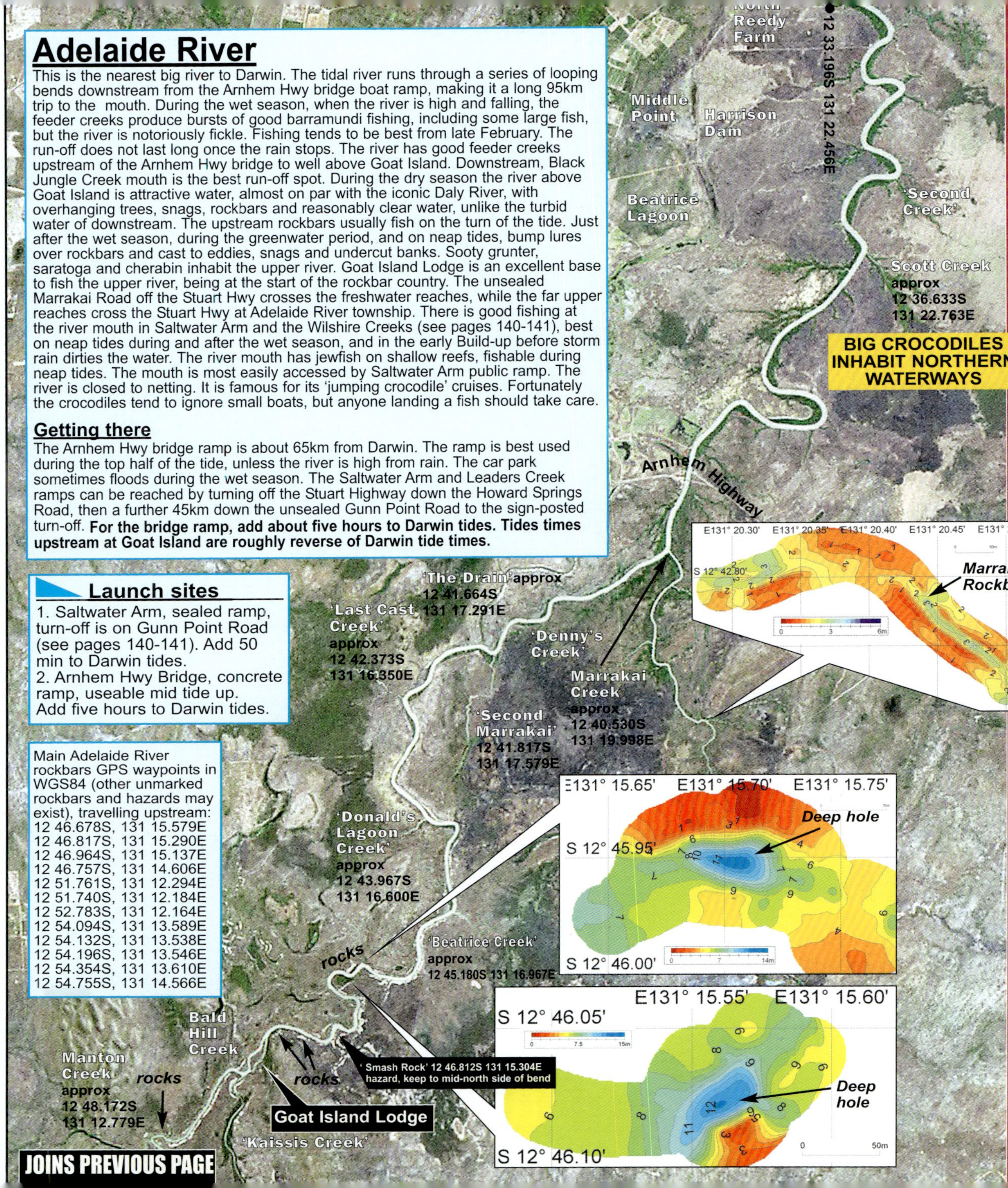

North Reedy Farm
12 33.196S 131 22.456E
Middle Point
Harrison Dam
Beatrice Lagoon
'Second Creek'
Scott Creek approx 12 36.633S 131 22.763E

BIG CROCODILES INHABIT NORTHERN WATERWAYS

Arnhem Highway
'The Drain' approx 12 41.664S 131 17.291E
'Last Cast Creek' approx 12 42.373S 131 16.350E
'Denny's Creek'
Marrakai Creek approx 12 40.530S 131 19.998E
'Second Marrakai' 12 41.817S 131 17.579E
E131° 20.30' E131° 20.35' E131° 20.40' E131° 20.45' E131° 20.50'
S 12° 42.80'
Marrakai Rockbar
'Donald's Lagoon Creek' approx 12 43.967S 131 16.600E
'Beatrice Creek' approx 12 45.180S 131 16.967E
rocks
E131° 15.65' E131° 15.70' E131° 15.75'
S 12° 45.95'
S 12° 46.00'
Deep hole
Bald Hill Creek
Manton Creek approx 12 48.172S 131 12.779E
rocks
'Smash Rock' 12 46.812S 131 15.304E hazard, keep to mid-north side of bend
Goat Island Lodge
'Kaissis Creek'
E131° 15.55' E131° 15.60'
S 12° 46.05'
S 12° 46.10'
Deep hole

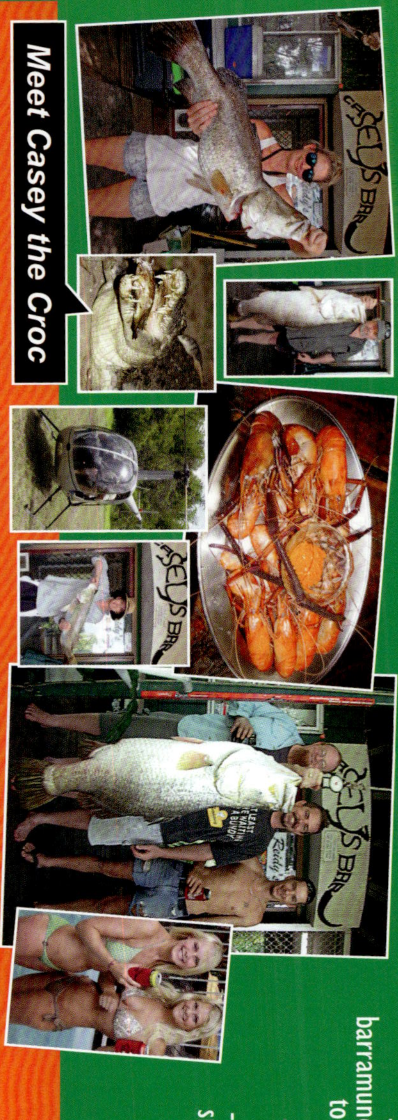

JOINS PREVIOUS PAGE

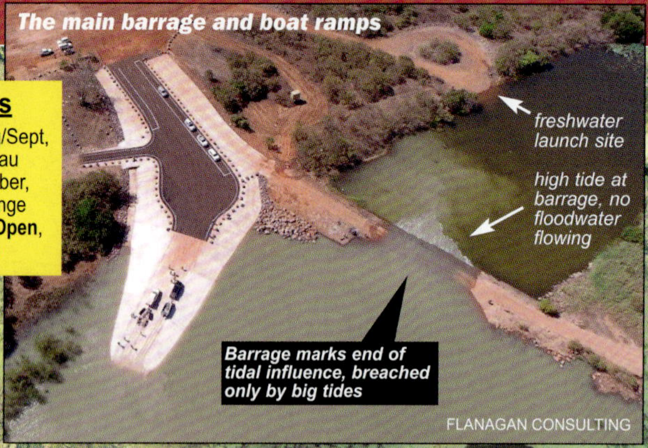

The main barrage and boat ramps
freshwater launch site
high tide at barrage, no floodwater flowing
Barrage marks end of tidal influence, breached only by big tides
FLANAGAN CONSULTING

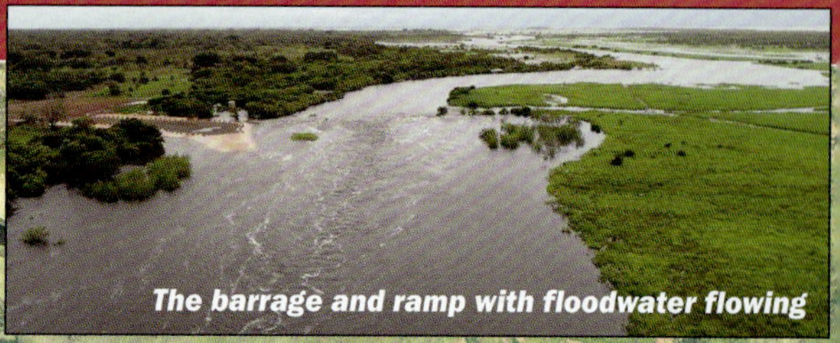

The barrage and ramp with floodwater flowing

Mary River Competitions

Corroboree Park Challenge, Aug/Sept, www.palmerstongamefishing.com.au
Secret Women's Business, October, www.facebook.com/swbbarrachallenge
Territory Freshwater Fly Fishing Open, May, www.darwinflyrodders.org.au

Large crocodiles are COMMON. Fish with care, and don't stand near or in the water

Mini barrage

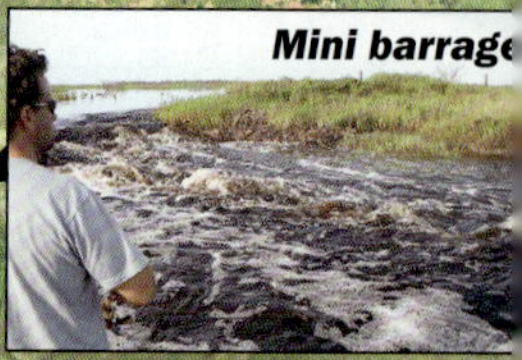

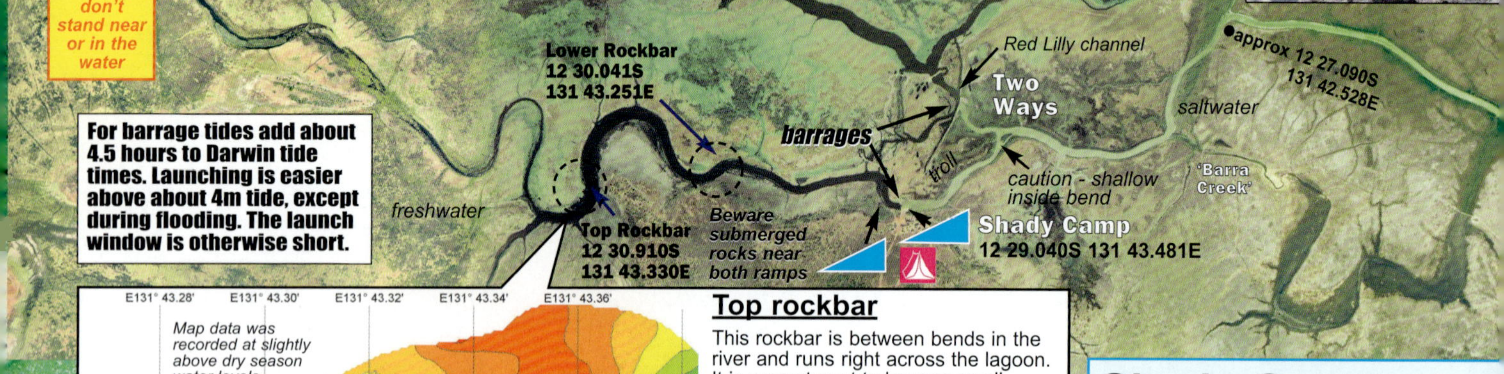

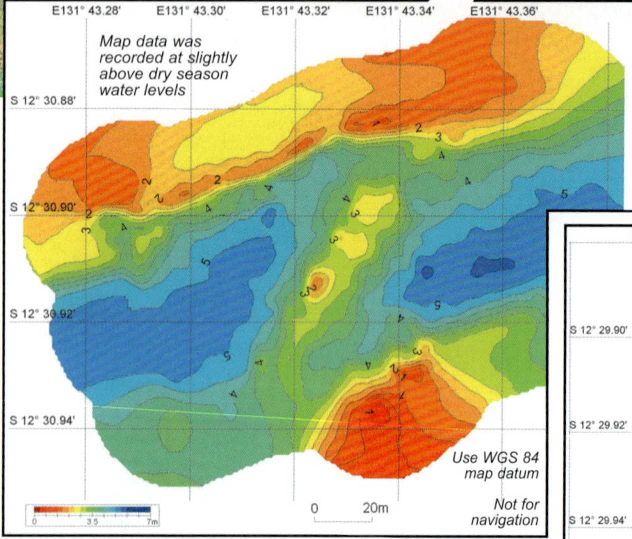

Barrages accessible during flooding - good fishing approx 12 27.134S 131 42.040E
Red Lilly channel
Two Ways
approx 12 27.090S 131 42.528E
saltwater
Lower Rockbar 12 30.041S 131 43.251E
barrages
troll
caution - shallow inside bend
'Barra Creek'
freshwater
Top Rockbar 12 30.910S 131 43.330E
Beware submerged rocks near both ramps
Shady Camp 12 29.040S 131 43.481E

For barrage tides add about 4.5 hours to Darwin tide times. Launching is easier above about 4m tide, except during flooding. The launch window is otherwise short.

E131° 43.28'
E131° 43.30'
E131° 43.32'
E131° 43.34'
E131° 43.36'
Map data was recorded at slightly above dry season water levels
S 12° 30.88'
S 12° 30.90'
S 12° 30.92'
S 12° 30.94'
Use WGS 84 map datum
Not for navigation
0 20m
0 3.5 7m

Top rockbar

This rockbar is between bends in the river and runs right across the lagoon. It is a great spot to bounce small rubber lures during the day. It often fires after dark, when poppers and fizzers work well. In warm weather the insects can be unkind, and the area has many large crocodiles.

E131° 43.22'
E131° 43.24'
E131° 43.26'
E131° 43.28'
Map data was recorded at slightly above dry season water levels
Maps may include some interpolation of data
Use WGS 84 map datum
Not for navigation
S 12° 29.90'
S 12° 29.92'
S 12° 29.94'
S 12° 29.96'
S 12° 29.98'
S 12° 30.00'
S 12° 30.02'
S 12° 30.04'
S 12° 30.06'
S 12° 30.08'
S 12° 30.10'
0 3 6m
0 20m

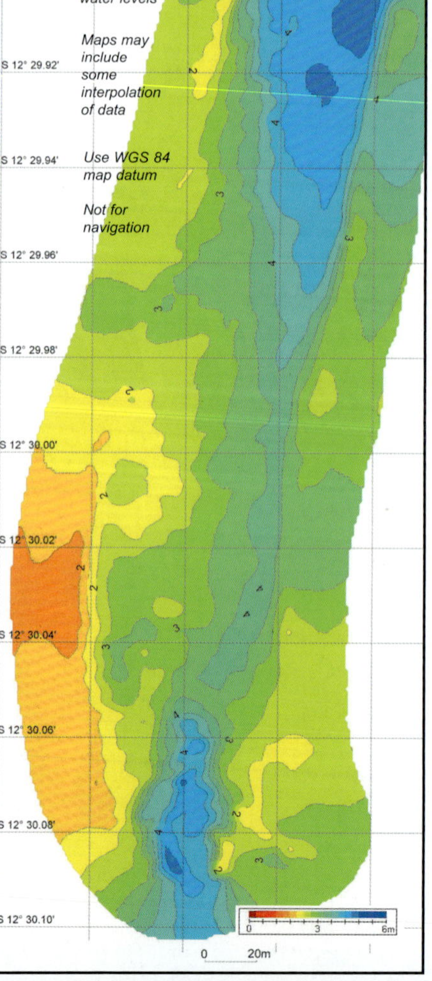

Lower rockbar

Troll lures over the rocks. If the lures are bouncing on rocks, you are in with a good chance of hooking a barra. Work the area on the far bank around the bend and along the front of the lilies. The near bank also has good structure, with a snaggy bottom just out from the bend with the tree on it. This area is worked quite hard by barramundi guides, so it must be good!

Maps created by SHANE DOEVY charting software

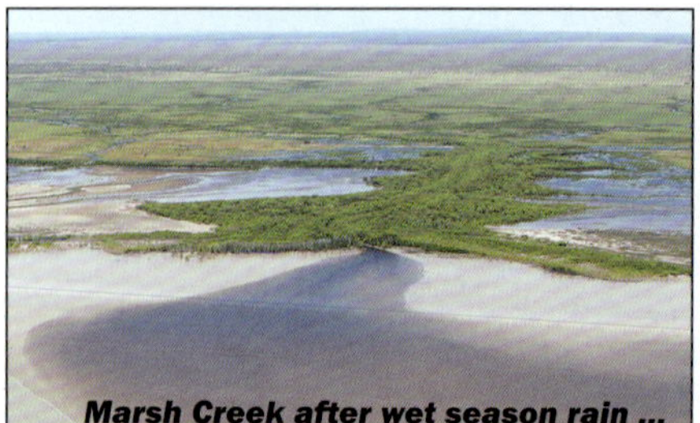

Marsh Creek after wet season rain ... entry into the creek up to a barrage is possible on the upper tide

Calm weather, clear water

There is barramundi fishing to be had in Chambers and Finke Bays in the dry season, after floodwaters stop flowing. The secret is to pick calm weather and neap tides for maximum water clarity. Launch at the barrage or Stuart Tree Fishing Camp, and troll the river mouth channels into the bay, or head around to Point Stuart and fish the rocks. Mud drains can be fished on outgoing tides. Barramundi fishing improves into the Build-up. Offshore, jewfish, blue salmon and snapper are on the reefs in the dry season. Big threadfin salmon are common in Chambers Bay and bite all year. For those with long-distance boats, rarely fished reefs exist throughout Van Diemen Gulf. Admiralty Chart AUS308 depicts the area.

Shady Camp

This is arguably the Top End's leading barramundi fishing region. The creeks flowing into Chambers and Finke Bays are outlets for vast wetlands that begin near Cape Hotham and extend east into Kakadu. The area is a fertile nursery, with many large barramundi and threadfin salmon. The shallow coastal reefs have big jewfish and golden snapper. The coast is reached by road via two points: Shady Camp, where boats are launched for the trip downstream into Chambers Bay, and from Stuart's Tree Fishing Camp on the Finke Bay foreshore. Both are tide dependent. The barrage near the boat ramp is a concrete structure that helps separate the Mary River's freshwater from tidal saltwater. It offers reliable landbased barramundi fishing on big tides and is popular despite abundant large crocodiles. Another large barrage lies 1km to the north-west, and there are earth barrages on creeks throughout the catchment. Some of the Top End's biggest barramundi are landed each year from the main barrage through to the coast, and further afield at Wildman River. Fishermen plan their trips for the wet season, when water levels are dropping after flooding. Fishing is generally poor when water is over the floodplain as the fish spread out. Trophy fish are caught trolling the deep Sampan and Tommycut mouths during neap tides, but the smaller creek mouths along the coast tend to produce big barramundi on the biggest tides. The creeks have barrages on the floodplains that can be accessed during big tides and/or flooding, and big catches can be expected on a good day, with barra 'boofing' around the boat. Night fishing off the barrage is popular, despite the real crocodile danger. Some crews overnight in their boats, braving wet season storms and the bugs typical of healthy aquatic habitat. Since a 2012 gill net ban in Chambers and Finke Bays, big threadfin salmon have become abundant.

Freshwater

The freshwater side of the barrage is a lily-lined waterway that usually fishes best in the Build-up, as the weather begins to warm. The waterhole is about 4km long, and has two rockbars that fish well in the early morning and evening. The first rockbar is almost 3km up the lagoon, stretching half way across (see maps left), and can be found by trolling the western bank and watching the sounder. The second rockbar is about 500m from the end of the lagoon, and starts on a slight bend. Troll with lures that dive deep enough to nudge the rocks. Poppers work well at night.

SAMPAN CREEK - TOMMYCUT CREEK - MARSH CREEK - SWIM CREEK - CARMOR CREEK - LOVE CREEK
Darwin
Map
Weipa
Borroloola
Karumba
'Dead Forest'
Melaleuca forests in this catchment began dying in the 1970/80s with saltwater inundation. The area will eventually become mangrove forest.
barrage approx 12 24.203S 131 40.204E
Sampan and Tommycut Creek mouths are accessible on most tides, but all other creeks require at least 6m+ of tide for easy boating access
'Dead Forest 2'
Tommycut Creek
Chambers Bay
Troll channel edges and inside mouth
12 20.250S 131 41.880E approx
troll
approx 12 19.751S 131 41.967E
'Dead Forest 1'
Cutting turn-off is approx 12 22.698S 131 42.312E - now usually impassible
barrage approx 12 24.249S 131 41.635E
The Cutting (now blocked)
KILOMETRES
METRES
Former cutting turn-off 12 24.546S 131 43.464E now impassible
The Mary River wetlands are changing fast. Sampan Creek mouth was 30m wide in the 1940s, and is now 150m+ and widening. Rising sea levels are inundating the area, as revealed by the dead melaleuca forests.
Tommycut Creek mouth after wet season rain. This is a popular trolling spot during the wet season
Offshore: Chambers Bay and Finke Bay has shallow reefs where jewfish, blue salmon and golden snapper are caught. See Page 179 for the maps.
GPS Marks
Jewfish Reef - See Page 179
12 11.175S 131 45.678E
12 11.875S 131 45.598E
12 12.160S 131 45.480E
12 11.089S 131 45.708E
12 10.641S 131 45.704E
Single bommie south of reef
12 12.631S 131 45.861E
Finke Snapper Reefs, out from Stuart's Tree Fishing Camp
12 11.293S 131 56.296E
12 12.171S 131 56.231E
12 12.021S 131 56.409E
12 13.265S 131 56.337E
Point Stuart Reefs
12 09.948S 131 53.912E
12 09.831S 131 54.337E
12 09.747S 131 54.129E
Regulations: Special rules apply in the Mary River Management Zone, which includes Shady Camp barrage, Sampan and Tommycut waterways, and some of the adjacent sea area.
Getting there
From Darwin, follow the Arnhem Hwy and turn left at the signposted turn-off about 120km from Darwin. There is a long stretch of unsealed road, which is usually passable in the wet season, but it gets slippery and potholed. The boating access points are an excellent concrete ramp just below Shady Camp barrage on the Mary River, a freshwater unsealed ramp above the barrage, and a coastal ramp at Stuart's Tree Fishing Camp at Finke Bay. All roads are signposted. On the saltwater side of the barrage, wet season floodwater provides a longer tidal launch window. Without floodwater, there is a launch limitation of about 4m of tide. Be at the ramp earlier than required as the outgoing tide drains fast. Add about 4.5 hours to Darwin tides for barrage tide times. Shady Camp has tent sites and toilets. Stuart's Tree has cabins and camping and is nearer Wildman River mouth, Finke Bay and Point Stuart reefs. The exposed Stuart's Tree coastal launch requires above about 4.5m of tide and suitable seas.
FISHING AND OUTDOOR WORLD Est 1972
CRAIG'S FISHING WAREHOUSE
Classic Lures Rob Gaden
approx 12 22.201S 131 46.150E
N
Sampan Creek
12 18.721S 131 46.384E approx
HOT TIP: Fish the coastal creeks immediately after a monsoonal event, even if flooding means you have to drive in via the Kakadu Hwy.
The wetlands drain to the sea through creek outlets in the wet season. Of these coastal creeks, only Tommycut and Sampan Creek mouths can be negotiated at low tide. The smaller creeks can be found by moving along the mangroves on a rising tide and looking for colour change from floodwater run-off. The small creek mouths fish from the top of the tide down to when boats must leave or be stranded on the mudflat. Exploring the creeks at high tide can be well worthwhile.
Sampan Creek mouth during the wet season. The corners are good at half tide, and trolling the colour change works during the wet season
Mary River Management Zone approximate boundary
All co-ordinates are approximate - careful navigation required at all times
Cape Hotham
N
Chambers Bay
For Point Stuart tides add 1hr 53min to Darwin times
shallow mudflat with sandy beach
Marsh Creek mouth 12 16.799S 131 33.246E
Wet season run-off creeks at 12.16.914S 131.35.412E 12.17.021S 131.36.224E 12.17.053S 131.37.845E
Tommycut Creek mouth 12 16.866S 131 42.060E
jewfish reefs page 179
Sampan Creek mouth 12 16.098S 131 46.500E
Swim Creek mouth 12 14.718S 131 49.836E
Point Stuart
Thrings Creek 12 13.845S 131 54.206E
Finke Bay
Carmor Creek 12 17.068S 131 58.774E
Love Creek 12 17.663S 132 00.952E
Wildman River mouth 12 18.098S 132 03.856E
Chambers Bay
Marsh barrage 12.17.680S 131.33.205E
To Shady Camp
Stuart's Tree Fishing Camp (08) 8978 8863
Adelaide River

Mary River Bridge Lagoon

This is a long freshwater pool on the Mary River that flows under the Arnhem Highway bridge. There is a concrete boat ramp and picnic reserve at the bridge. Most barramundi caught here are just over legal size, with the occasional big fish. The lagoon usually fishes best during the wet season when the water level is settling after rain, and also during the Build-up when barra become more active, but dry season fishing is pleasant and can be worthwhile. There are run-offs upstream and downstream that fish well immediately after a wet season flood, the best being an obvious outlet on the east bank well downstream of the Hardies Creek junction (GPS mark provided). Some fishermen do well trolling the bridge pool at night, despite the turbid brown water, and barramundi seem to have no problem finding lures trolled in the dark with an electric motor. While the hole under the bridge is deep, there are shallow, sandbanks and rocky areas above and below the bridge, so careful navigation is required. It is particularly shallow from the Hardies junction downstream. Mary River Management Zone fishing rules apply at the Mary River Bridge Lagoon, Corroboree, Hardies, Rock Hole and Shady Camp.

A Corroboree access channel

OREBOUND IMAGES

Getting there

Follow the Arnhem Hwy past the Corroboree Park Tavern and the Hardies Lagoon turn-off until you get to the bridge. Camping is not permitted at the bridge reserve.

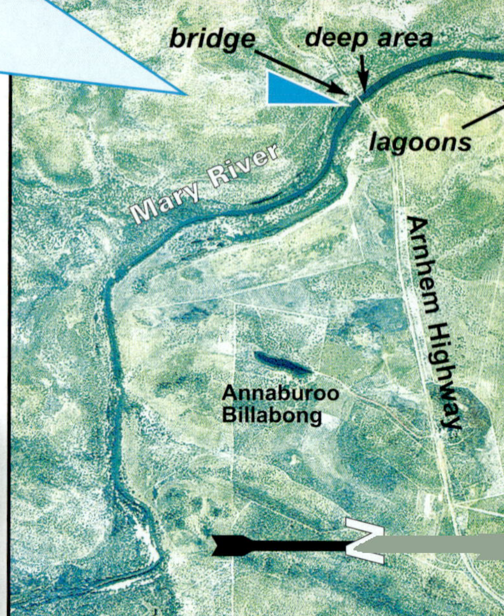

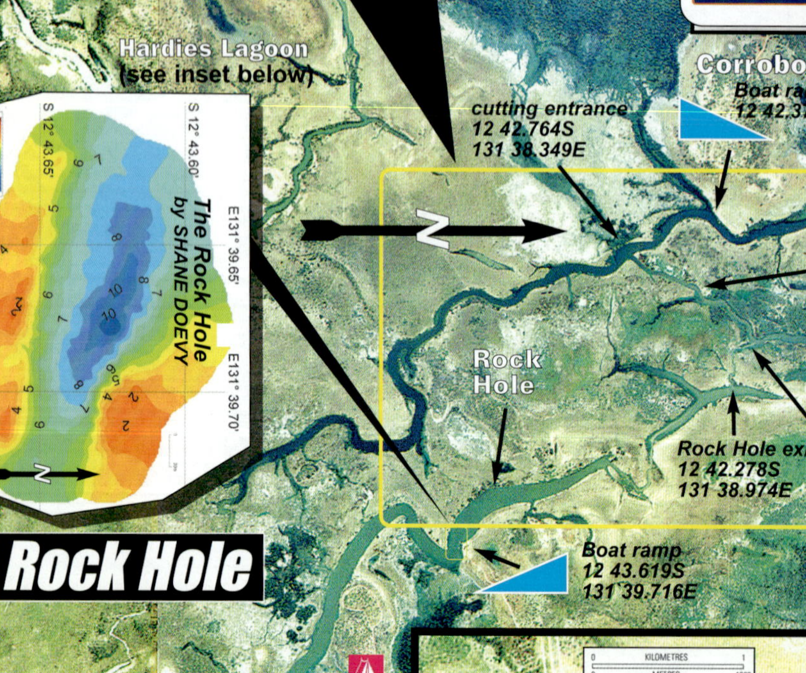

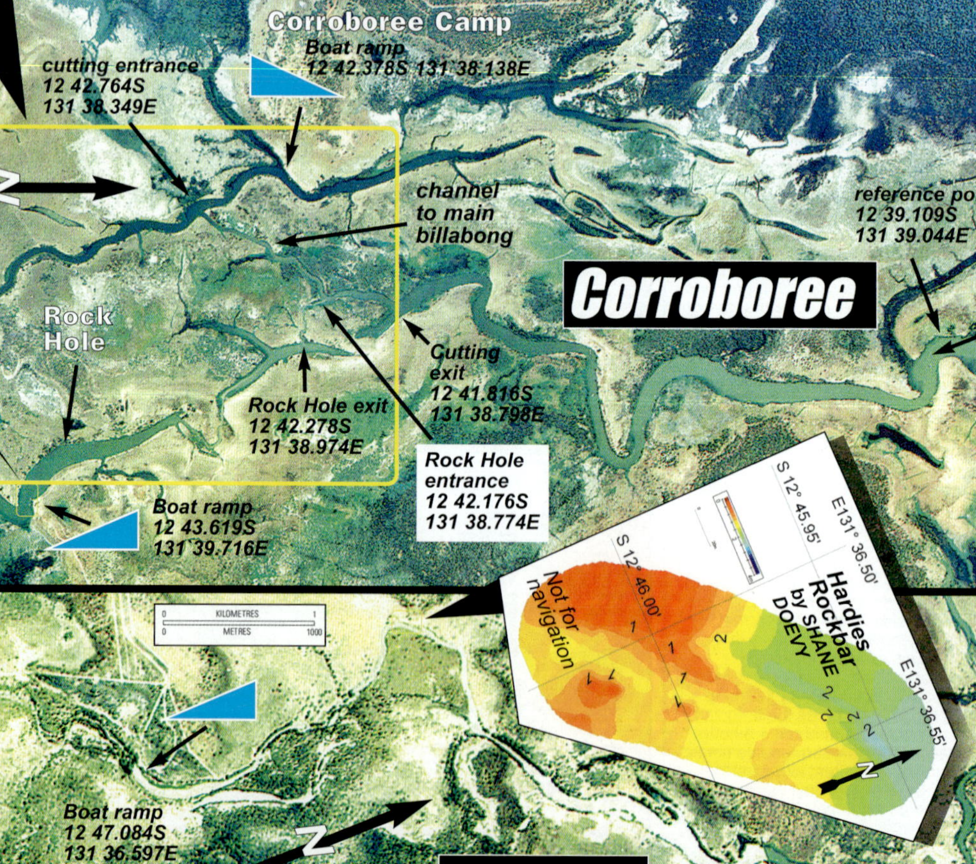

Corroboree & Hardies

Barramundi enthusiasts flock to Corroboree, the Rock Hole and Hardies waterholes, all part of the Mary River wetlands, a catchment of 8000sqkm, home to 34 species of fish, 250 species of birds, saltwater and freshwater crocodiles, feral pigs, buffalo and more. The water here flows through to Shady Camp during the wet season, exiting the sea mostly through Sampan and Tommycut Creek mouths. Corroboree is the largest freshwater hole at about 30km long. A narrow channel, often navigable, leads to the smaller Rock Hole. The Hardies Creek waterhole lies upstream, but the channel through is impassible. This area has premium fly and lure casting water for barramundi and saratoga. Locate barramundi in snags with sonar, and work them with lures. In cool weather, look for them warming up on shallow weedbeds. If you see barra in open water, it usually means they are feeding. Saratoga are caught by casting small weedless lures, flies or poppers into the lilies. Tarpon are active on the surface when floodwaters ebb. Night fishing works well with barramundi, while saratoga are best at dawn. The best time to fish is during the early Build-up. To avoid heat, fish mornings and afternoons. Fishermen who get in early after the wet season find good fishing, although abundant bait means barra can be well fed. Cool dry season days are pleasant but often slow. Annual lily cover varies - a strong wet season will rip out most of the lilies, but they cover much of the water after a poor Wet. The more weed that is removed the better, as fish then have fewer places to hide. The turn-off is just after the Corroboree Park Tavern, about 100km from Darwin, with a 30km access road. There is a formed ramp.

Hardies Creek

This smaller lagoon is accessed by a separate signposted road off the Arnhem Hwy and is usually not accessible by boat from Corroboree. It has a ramp and camping area.

Rock Hole

This is usually accessible by boat via a narrow channel from Corroboree. It can otherwise be reached by a signposted road off the Shady Camp road. The Shady Camp turn-off is on the Arnhem Hwy about 45km east of the Corroboree turn-off, with 35km more to the Rock Hole.

Facilities

Corroboree Park Tavern on the Arnhem Hwy has accommodation and camping and is an ideal rest point to fish the "barramundi highway". This area is part of the Mary River Management Zone and special rules apply.

Lily cover in Top End waterholes varies annually from open water to almost complete cover as shown. Prior wet season scouring largely determines how much weed exists the following dry season.

South Alligator River

This is a shallow, turbid and strongly tidal river that fishes best when clear wet season floodwater is flowing. Tidal influence stretches to the floodplain 20km above the Arnhem Hwy bridge. Further upstream the river forms dry season waterholes, the best known of which is Yellow Water, accessible from Cooinda, see Page 190. The tidal section has good run-off barramundi fishing, with floodplain creeks providing bursts of action, usually on the early run-out tide. During the wet season the floodplains fill with water and big barra move up the river, along with smaller fish moving down from the unlocked billabongs. During the wet season an "inland sea" of floodwater can form, pouring off the banks through dozens of miniature waterfalls, a spectacular sight. When there is too much water on the floodplain and the fish are spread out, fishermen go far downstream. During flooding, Brooke Creek at the river entrance produces trophy fish, as do the oyster rocks on the opposite side of the river from Brooke Creek. When the water drops below floodplain level, barra become an easy target as they congregate along the riverbanks, on rockbars, inside feeder creeks, in eddies, and at colour changes. Upstream of the bridge, the rockbar just inside Nourlangie Creek, the Nourlangie Creek upstream junctions, and the rockbar far upstream near Leichardt Creek, are prime hotspots. The rockbar barra usually bite on the turn of the tide. The few rockbars on the river can be covered in silt after a poor wet season or two. Much of the river dries dry at low tide. During the dry season, fishing in the tidal water is limited to neap tides when the water is clearer. Good shallow-water reef fishing for golden snapper and jewfish is had around Field Island at the mouth, with barra and salmon in the island's creeks - see Page 190. Special fishing rules apply in Kakadu.

Getting there

The boat ramp is just off the Arnhem Hwy, about 220km from Darwin. The ramp turn-off is near the Arnhem Hwy bridge. There are no camping facilities at the ramp. It is best to make the 80km trip downriver to the mouth on a rising tide as many sandbanks lie hidden and stranding is possible. A first exploration is best done with another boat. Boat retrieval at the ramp can be tricky when the tide is flowing fast. Areas upstream have been closed for aquatic weed control. These are sign-posted or roped off. To the west, camping is available near West Alligator Head, with fishermen driving in to Pococks Beach (4WD, dry season only) and launching from the beach at high tide.

Competitions

Kakadu-based Alligator Fishing Club NT holds competitions in this area ... visit them on Facebook.

Take care when fishing the Alligator rivers during a falling tide. Strong currents and shallow sandbanks make the river treacherous.

Beatrice Reef
(Chart, approx 11 53.269S 132 31.145E)

SEE PAGE 190

Field Island

Barron Island

West Alligator Head

Dries 12 ft.

Cunningham Channel

sand and mud

wreck

rock ledge

Brooke Creek mouth fishes well for big barra during wet season, 12 12.260S 132 24.959E

West Alligator River (no fishing)

mudbars

numerous mudbanks

mudbank

creek

N

KILOMETRES 0 4
METRES 0 4000

'Rookery' 12 25.687S 132 24.698E

Munmarlary Landing

Tidal variation at mouth: add about 2hr 40min to Darwin times

Tidal variation at bridge: add about 4.5 hours to Darwin times

rocks 12 36.087S 132 26.315E

'Culvert Creek'

Jabiru

Arnhem Highway

Darwin

SEE AERIAL PHOTO

floodplain

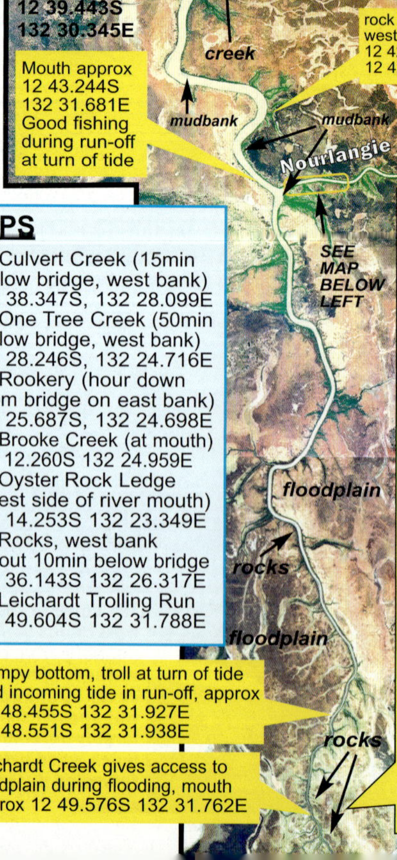

Nourlangie Creek

Creek flows clear during the wet season.

Unmarked obstacles, including rocks, sunken trees, mudbanks and more, may exist in all waters in this book

Arnhem Highway bridge - ramp at 12 39.443S 132 30.345E

Mouth approx 12 43.244S 132 31.681E Good fishing during run-off at turn of tide

rock ledges on eastern bank extend west into river, nav hazards, approx 12 42.421S 132 31.578E 12 42.540S 132 31.541E

Good run-off fishing at upper junctions

SEE MAP BELOW LEFT

rocks

East Alligator River barramundi

TYLERB

GPS

- Culvert Creek (15min below bridge, west bank) 12 38.347S, 132 28.099E
- One Tree Creek (50min below bridge, west bank) 12 28.246S, 132 24.716E
- Rookery (hour down from bridge on east bank) 12 25.687S, 132 24.698E
- Brooke Creek (at mouth) 12 12.260S 132 24.959E
- Oyster Rock Ledge (west side of river mouth) 12 14.253S 132 23.349E
- Rocks, west bank about 10min below bridge 12 36.143S 132 26.317E
- Leichardt Trolling Run 12 49.604S 132 31.788E

Nourlangie rockbar, navigation hazard with excellent barramundi fishing during run-off, approx 12 43.162S 132 31.998E

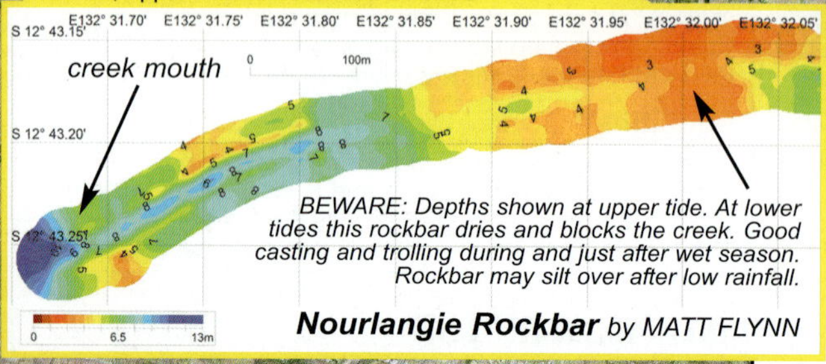

creek mouth

BEWARE: Depths shown at upper tide. At lower tides this rockbar dries and blocks the creek. Good casting and trolling during and just after wet season. Rockbar may silt over after low rainfall.

Nourlangie Rockbar by MATT FLYNN

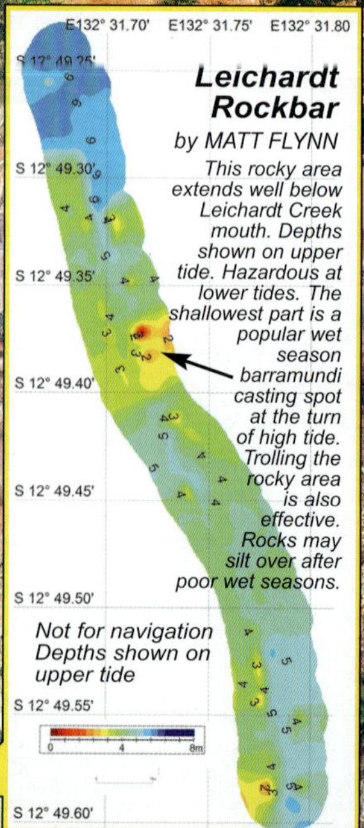

Bumpy bottom, troll at turn of tide and incoming tide in run-off, approx 12 48.455S 132 31.927E 12 48.551S 132 31.938E

Leichardt Creek gives access to floodplain during flooding, mouth approx 12 49.576S 132 31.762E

Leichardt Rockbar by MATT FLYNN

This rocky area extends well below Leichardt Creek mouth. Depths shown on upper tide. Hazardous at lower tides. The shallowest part is a popular wet season barramundi casting spot at the turn of high tide. Trolling the rocky area is also effective. Rocks may silt over after poor wet seasons.

Not for navigation Depths shown on upper tide

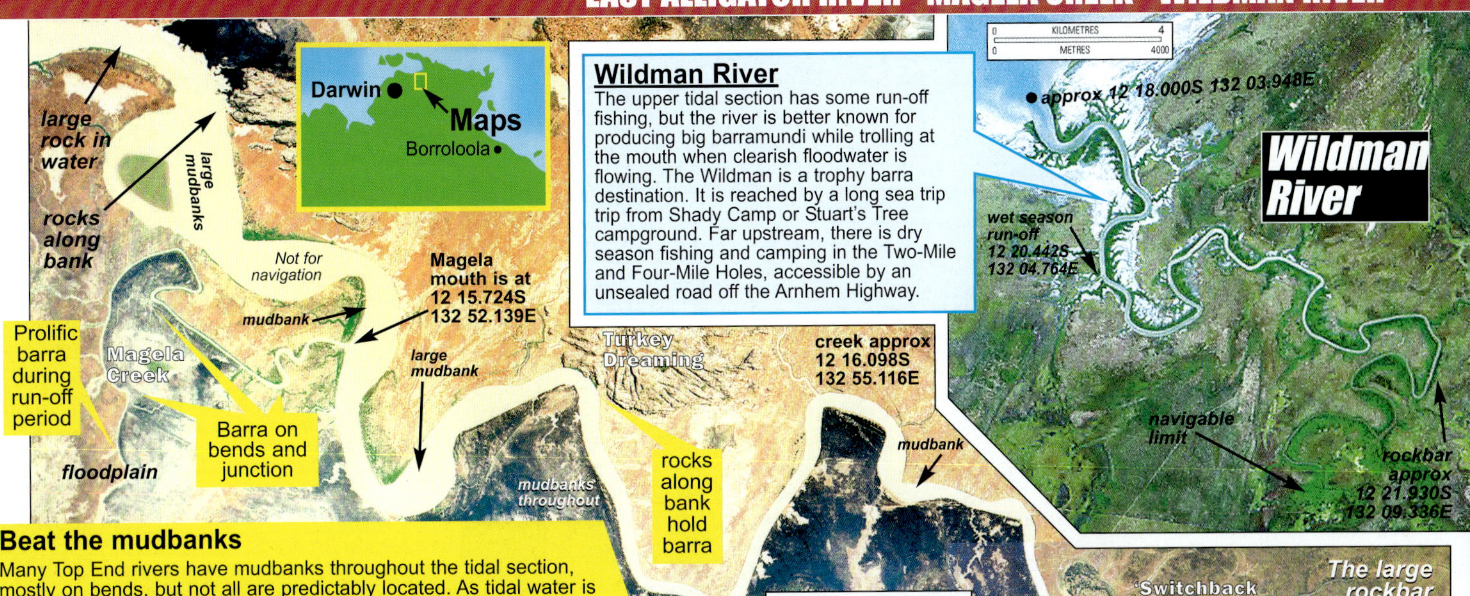

Wildman River

The upper tidal section has some run-off fishing, but the river is better known for producing big barramundi while trolling at the mouth when clearish floodwater is flowing. The Wildman is a trophy barra destination. It is reached by a long sea trip trip from Shady Camp or Stuart's Tree campground. Far upstream, there is dry season fishing and camping in the Two-Mile and Four-Mile Holes, accessible by an unsealed road off the Arnhem Highway.

Beat the mudbanks

Many Top End rivers have mudbanks throughout the tidal section, mostly on bends, but not all are predictably located. As tidal water is usually turbid, finding the channel is not always easy. Before an inaugural trip, explore low-tide Google Earth imagery. Travel on a rising tide so you can quickly refloat your boat if you become stuck.

Negotiating floodplain creeks

It is relatively easy to steer at slow speed when pushing against the current into a flowing floodplain creek. Leaving the creek is harder, especially when the tide flows out, as the boat moves fast and steering is more difficult. Being caught on timber in a strong flow can capsize a boat. If in doubt, stay out.

'Switchback Creek' approx 12 17.766S 132 57.024E

mudbanks

creek

mudbank

rocks along bank

The large rockbar 1.8km downstream from Cahills Crossing is navigable only on the upper tide or during flooding. Plan trips downstream accordingly.

N

12 19.897S 132 57.678E

Unmarked obstacles, including rocks, sunken trees, mudbanks and more, may exist in all waters in this book

run-offs

Cannon Hill

lagoon

'Twin Creeks' 12 22.872S 132 58.490E

Shaded, snaggy tidal stretch good for casting and trolling, but tidal ramp only useable at mid-tide up. Fish rockbar on rising tide.

rockbar

mudbanks throughout

rockbar approx 12 24.622S 132 58.117E

Cahills Crossing (diminishes tidal influence)

To Cobourg Peninsula

'Secret lagoon' - entrance is 12 27.553S 132 58.704E

East Alligator River

This river has tidal barramundi fishing, with a backdrop of escarpment country. Great fishing happens immediately below Cahills Crossing near the Merl public campsite. The secret to great fishing on "The East" is to get your boat in early after flooding, as soon as the Magela Creek road crossing is passable. This may require a 4WD vehicle with a snorkel as the road after the crossing will be flooded. There are run-offs a short distance below Cahills Crossing. The stretch just below the crossing is ideal for trolling and casting for barramundi during the run-off, on an incoming tide. The barrage area itself has produced barramundi to 120cm. The 40km trip downstream to Magela Creek, or 60km to "Second Magela Creek", can be more rewarding in terms of fish numbers. These creek mouths run clear after flooding, and produce good fishing. When there is sufficient tide, fishermen can travel up Magela Creek where the waterway winds through the floodplain and narrows. Barramundi will be present in numbers. Travelling downstream, the main river becomes wide but shallow, with many mudbanks making navigation difficult near low water. A large rockbar 1.8km below the crossing (see MAP 1) can only be negotiated during flooding or on the upper tide. Above Cahills Crossing, the freshwater section is shallow and sandy, with barra sitting under snags during the day, and feeding during the evening, or when big tides breech the crossing. There are boat ramps above and below Cahills Crossing, near the Merl public camp site. Big crocodiles inhabit the East Alligator River and its tributaries and they loiter in numbers around the crossing. The road continues over the crossing to Aboriginal land and Garig Gunak Barlu NP.

Special rules apply in Kakadu, see page 190.

Getting there

Follow the Arnhem Hwy about 260km from Darwin and take the Ubirr turn-off near Jabiru. A 4WD is not needed in the dry season. Magela Creek crossing is impassible when flooded, and the floodwater over the road on the other side is deeper.

East Alligator Rockbar by SHANE DOEVY

E132° 58.10' E132° 58.15' E132° 58.20'

S 12° 24.65'

Depths shown at upper tide ... rockbar can be passed on upper tide or during flooding

Kakadu NP

The national park has fishable waterholes off the Arnhem and Kakadu Highways, most being part of the South Alligator River and Wildman River systems. The waterholes join during the wet season. They are naturally restocked with barramundi each year, unless there is low rainfall. The barra fishing varies from year to year, but saratoga, archer fish, tarpon, sleepy cod and longtom are consistent. Night fishing is good, and offers respite from heat. The access tracks are unsealed, except at Yellow Water, and usually open quite late in the dry season. Camping is allowed. Some launch sites are off the bank and require 4WD. Big crocodiles live in the smallest waterholes, and on the beaches, so do not take risks. Four-Mile Hole on the Wildman is perhaps the most popular of the billabongs for fishing.

Getting there

Kakadu National Park is on the sealed Arnhem Hwy (from Darwin) and the Kakadu Hwy (from Katherine). 4WD may be needed in some areas.

Facilities

(Only Home Billabong and Yellow Water have wet season access)

	Boat hire	Van site	Camping	Launch site	Ramp
Alligator Billabong			•	•	
Baroalba Billabong			•		
Bucket Billabong			•	•	
Four-Mile Hole			•	•	
Two-Mile Hole			•	•	
Jim Jim Billabong		•	•		
Malabanbandju Billabong		•	•		
Mardugal Billabong		•	•		•
Muirella Park Billabong		•	•		•
Red Lily Billabong			•	•	
Sandy Billabong			•		
West Alligator Head			•	•	
Yellow Water			•		•
East Alligator (off map)			•		•

Fuel is sold at Aurora Kakadu, Cooinda Gagudju Lodge, and at Jabiru. Fuel sold at Jabiru is the Opal variety

Some Kakadu NP Fishing Rules

*You may possess up to three barramundi between 55cm and 90cm. One fish may be over 90cm. *Only a rod and reel or handline with a single hook or lure. *Nets, traps and pots are not allowed. *Crabs are protected. *Items used for fishing outside the park may only be transported through Kakadu NP along Oenpelli Rd, Old Jim Jim Rd, the Arnhem and Kakadu Highways and the South and East Alligator rivers downstream of boat access. *No livebaiting. *Waterways upstream of Kakadu Highway are closed, except Sandy and Jim Jim billabongs. *West Alligator River is closed to fishing *South Alligator River is closed between 'the forks' or 'the rapids' about 24km upstream of Arnhem Highway and 2km north of Fisherman's Gully on Yellow Water.

ASHLEA BECKETT

An exceptionally large billabong barramundi

How to fish Field Island

This island has a combo of barramundi and reef fishing. There are mangrove-lined creeks, shallow rocky reefs, and wet season run-offs. Most boaters launch at the highway ramp and make the long trip downstream. The alternative is taking a dry season 4WD track to West Alligator Head, and launching off the beach.

At the mouth of the South Alligator River, Field Island has excellent fish-holding grounds, but boaters should be wary, as these shallow waters have strong currents and quickly turn nasty.

The river's tidal current flows hard, especially with floodwater pushing down, and sandbanks in the river, hidden by turbid water, add further interest for skippers. A trip downstream is best done on a rising tide, so you can refloat off a mudbank.

Field Island is surrounded by drying reef, with channels. Snapper and jewfish are the main catch.

Creeks 1-7: The creeks have snags, holes and rocks with barra, jacks, snapper, jew on a rising tide. They offer refuge from weather, but are difficult to enter near low tide.

Creek 3 to Turtle Beach: Good casting and trolling along this stretch, with trevally, queenfish, barra. Occasional snapper and jacks.

Field Island Holes: Located between Field and Barron Islands. These have jewfish and snapper. Anchor on the edge of holes where the floor rises.

Brooke Creek: Great run-off creek during and just after wet season. Mouth approx 12 12.235S 132 24.960E. Also **Little Brooke Creek:** Mouth approx 12 09.465S 132 26.147E.

Field Island

Creek 4
Creek 3
Creek 5
Creek 6
Creek 7
Creek 1
Turtle Beach
Creek 2
N

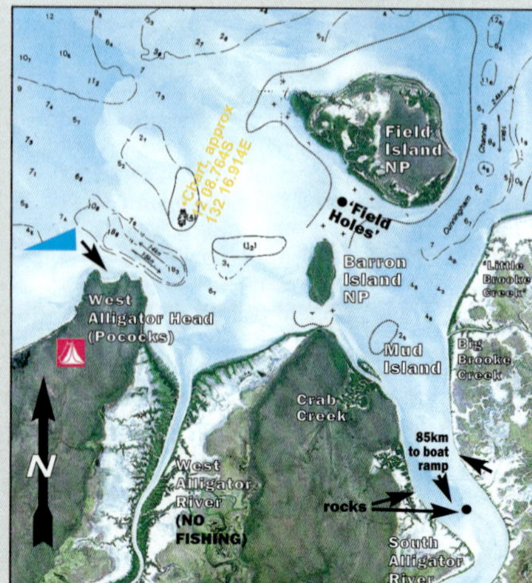

The Roper's rockbars

The Roper River flows east through one of the NT's biggest catchments, emptying into the Gulf of Carpentaria through a mouth 2.6km wide.

The river is perennial, with springs pushing freshwater over Roper Bar crossing into the tidal water all year.

During a big wet season, enough water leaves the Roper River mouth to turn the surrounding sea fresh out to Maria Island and beyond.

Because of the Gulf's odd tides, Roper River tides are often hard to predict, changing on a whim if the wind blows across the Gulf.

Being far from major population centres, the Roper River does not get fished hard, though it is popular with dry season campers.

Being lightly fished, perennial, vast, and pristine, it is hardly surprising that the Roper produces some of the Territory's biggest barramundi.

There is about 145km of tidal water between Roper Bar and the mouth.

The river's character and accessibility changes significantly when wet season floodwaters flow.

Public access to the tidal water is via three points:
1. Roper Bar boat ramp at the tidal limit.
2. Tomato Island (Munbililla) public ramp in the middle reach.
3. Port Roper ramp at the mouth.

Access to the freshwater section above Roper Bar is difficult, as most of it runs through pastoral and Aboriginal land.

This rockbar is on the first bend below Roper Bar. It is a shelf with vertical sides, so no warning is given on the sounder

Shallow rock bottom out from Roper Bar boat ramp at dry season water levels. Roper Bar is visible above

For those driving in from the Stuart Highway, the Roper Highway bitumen ends about 40km before Roper Bar, and the unsealed section is often corrugated. Corrugations can also be expected if driving in from the south.

Be sure your vehicle and trailer is in good condition and you have spares.

The Roper Highway can be cut by wet season flooding, but in recent years bridges have reduced the impact of flood events.

Roper Bar crossing was built on a rockbar that marks the tidal limit.

There is a van park and store at Roper Bar, but local services are limited.

Ngukurr, on the northern riverbank, is the nearest large community.

The Roper Bar boat ramp is a few metres downstream from the crossing, on the southern bank.

For southerners driving up from Borroloola, access to the Roper is

●Continued next page

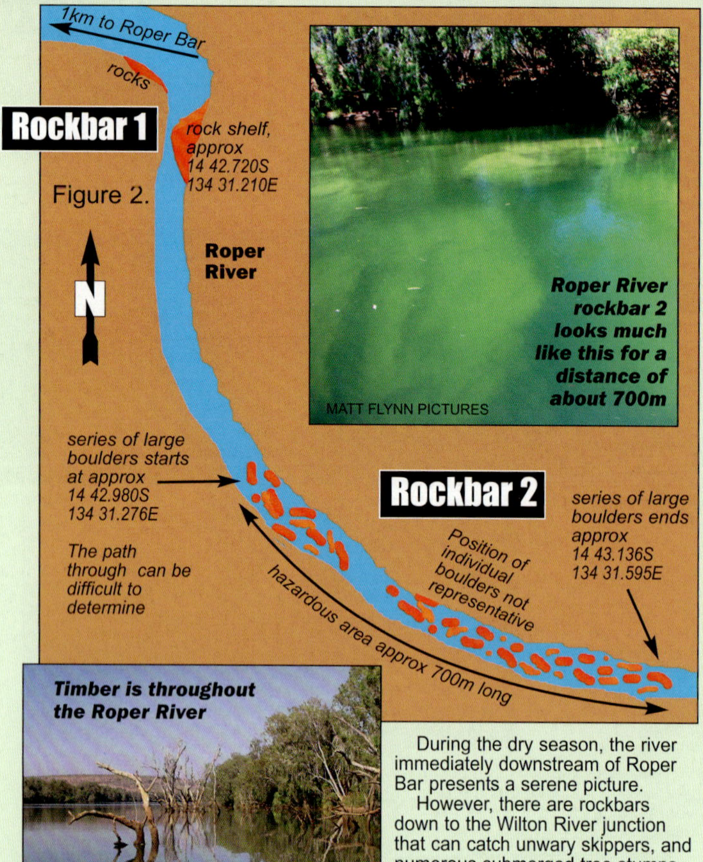

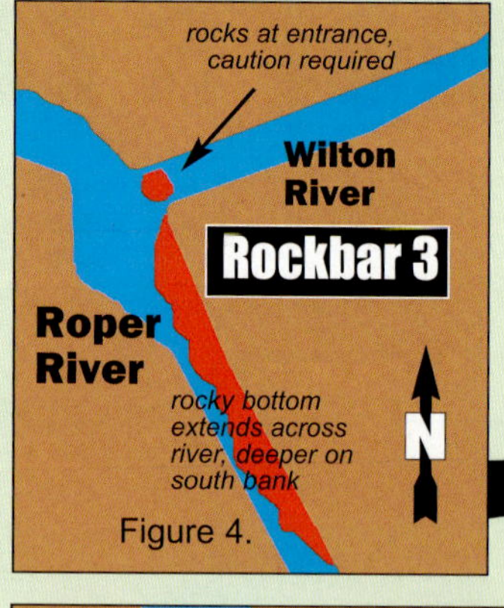

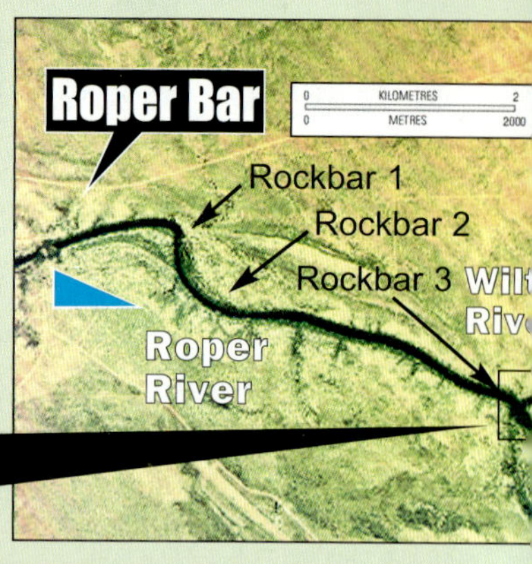

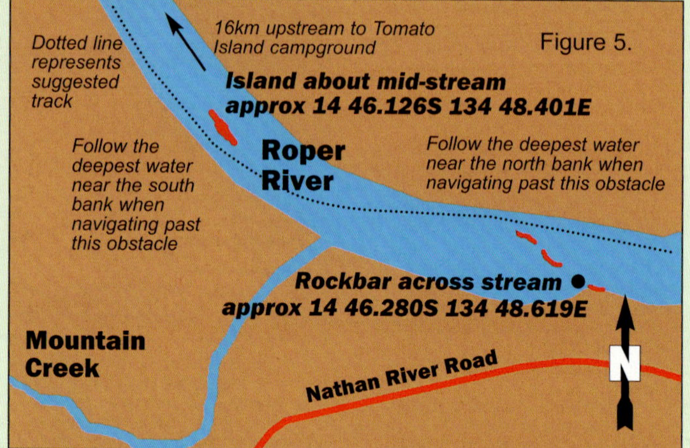

strictly dry season only as there are river crossings along the Savannah Way (Nathan River Rd) that rise quickly after rain.

Most fishos coming up from south use Limmen NP's Tomato Island ramp and camp, which has a large ablution block and barbecues.

Port Roper at the Roper mouth has only rough bush camping and a concrete ramp, but it offers the best chance of landing trophy barra from the mouths of the tidal creeks.

Boating from Roper Bar

For those who launch at Roper Bar ramp during the low water levels of the dry season, the first navigation hazard lies just out from the ramp. The shallow rocky bottom rises up gently, and can catch a propeller.

NT Fisheries says Roper Bar ramp should be used on tides above 2.5m.

It is hard to predict Roper tides, so this information may be difficult to implement.

During the dry season, the river immediately downstream of Roper Bar presents a serene picture.

However, there are rockbars down to the Wilton River junction that can catch unwary skippers, and numerous submerged tree stumps.

During the wet season, the river at Roper Bar is usually a torrent, but high enough to cover most hazards.

Keen fishermen get in early when the road opens to take a boat far downstream to the floodplain run-offs.

Post wet season launching is usually done from the side of Roper Bar crossing itself, launching into the fast-moving floodwaters.

For good run-off fishing, launch at the bar or, if the road is open, further downstream at Tomato Island campground, and take the boat far downstream to where the floodplain creeks are flowing in.

After a decent wet season, side creeks will be flowing clear run-off into the river, and barra won't be far away.

Roper Bar crossing is a popular landbased location during the wet season, when metre-plus barramundi are taken as the river rises and falls.

The presence of crocodiles makes this a risky place to be casting a lure, let alone battling the strong current.

Despite this, many people do it, and big barramundi are caught.

The rockbars

Skippers should have no trouble negotiating the rockbars Roper Bar by using our maps and making careful observations on the water.

Hitting submerged timber is the greater concern as new stumps and trunks appear each year.

Keep in mind that the maps and GPS marks provided are only a guide, and you'll have to use your eyes and common sense to navigate safely.

Rockbar 1 - The Shelf

This one is a cracker. See Figures 1 and 2. The rock shelf, at about 14 42.720S 134 31.210E, projects out from the north-eastern bank on the outside of the first sharp corner downstream from Roper Bar, about 1km from the launch site. Travelling downstream, you take the inside of the bend to avoid the shelf, but be wary of another small rock shelf close to the inside bank just before the bend. The channel through is narrow, but usually deep enough to navigate.

This rockbar has almost vertical sides, with very little warning slope, particularly on the downstream side.

Fortunately the water is usually fairly clear in the dry season, so keep your eyes open as you approach.

If you get out of your boat to walk the rockbar when it is dry, be wary of crocodiles. This spot always looks like it is worth a cast or two, but fishing is better further downstream.

Bait fishing with cherabin is effective in this upper section and is a relaxing way to spend a dry season afternoon, surrounded by Territory wildlife.

Timber can be fished with jigs. Bigger tides bring on the action.

Rockbar 2 - The Stones

This is another cracker, and a very different beast from Rockbar 1. See Figure 2. Rockbar 2 begins about 500m downstream from Rockbar 1.

This is about 1.6km downstream from Roper Bar.

This rockbar is a series of large boulders extending along a 700m stretch of river.

Some of the boulders have large gaps between. The stones are submerged on most tides.

Boats can usually find a way through at low tide, but care is required. High tide passage is recommended. When the water is clear you can see the boulders.

Heading downstream, the rockbar starts about 14 42.980S 134 31.276E and ends about 14 43.136S 134 31.595E. Once you have cleared this rockbar, you have a fairly clear run to the junction of the Wilton River, where you'll encounter Rockbar 3.

Rockbar 3 - The Wilton

Heading upstream, this patch of rocks rises up fairly slowly. See Figure 4. The rocks extend from the upstream end about 14 43.761S 134 33.133E to about 14 43.911S 134 33.228E at the downstream end.

If coming up from downstream, the rocks start about 600m from the Wilton mouth.

There is also a rockbar at the mouth of the Wilton River itself, which can usually be negotiated with care.

The Point

This is a small rocky point that extends into the water at approx 14 44.519S 134 33.612E on the north (in this case eastward) bank.

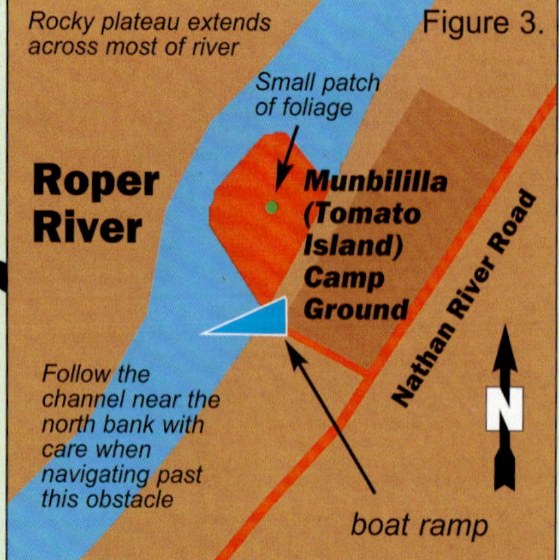

You'd be unlucky to hit this one, but take care near it nonetheless, particularly at low water. Worth a cast or two before passing by.

'Young Australian' wreck

A rocky island lies 1.25km upstream of the Tomato Island boat ramp at approx 14 45.145S 134 40.850E. It is seen long before any navigational threat poses.

Despite its apparent visibility, this hazard sunk the *Young Australian* steamer in 1873.

The heavy steel parts of the wreckage are still clearly visible.

A rock point extends from the island directly towards the shore for a few metres, and then drops away.

This can be a good fishing spot for barramundi, but expect it to be popular during the dry season as it is close to Tomato Island camp.

Be there at the turn of the tide to catch the bite window.

Tomato Island

This is a large rock shelf that lies next to the popular Munbililla (Tomato Island) campground. This is one of the Roper River's more significant navigation hazards. See Figure 3.

A tiny island of foliage on the rock shelf in no way hints at the size of the hazard, which often lies just under water, ready to catch unwary boaters.

Nonetheless, it is easy to navigate past if you follow the deep water on the north bank. During the dry season there are usually boats moored near the ramp at approx 14 44.779S 134 41.430E, near the rock shelf.

Hazards downstream of Tomato Island ...

Mission Island

This island is about 8.4km downstream from Tomato Island at 14 44.969S 134 44.932E. The island is clearly visible. It can be a good place to fish. Navigate past carefully on the north bank.

Mountain Creek

This creek is 16km downstream of Tomato Island. See Figure 5.

There is an island about 400m upstream of the Mountain Creek junction at approx 14 46.126S 134 48.401F. Navigate past in the deeper water on the south bank, but don't relax, as there is a major rockbar just 500m downstream at about 14 46.280S 134 48.619E. Navigate past carefully in the deeper water on the north bank. The rockbar can be a good fishing spot.

Island Creek - Hawks Nest

A small island lies about 130m out from a creek mouth on the south bank of the Roper River, 4km downstream of Kangaroo Island, at about 14 49.160S 135 02.194E. This is a good fishing area during and just after the wet season, trolling the rocks.

Other hazards

Aside from the rockbars described, the Roper River is a relatively easy river to navigate.

Submerged timber is a hazard in most Territory rivers waters because new pieces are washed in or moved during each wet season. There's not much you can do to avoid hitting submerged timber when going at speed, although disturbances on the surface may give away its presence.

Carry extra split pins and a spare prop as insurance.

Barra from shore

There are many places you can enjoy fishing from the land up north, keeping in mind the presence of crocodiles, marine stingers and stonefish. Here's a list of Northern Territory landbased fishing spots.

1. Buffalo Creek, Shoal Bay. Fish from near the boat ramp and just downstream at the exposed rockbar at night during the week when it is quiet. Best at first push of low tide. Good fishing from beach above ramp. Salmon on deadbaits on early rising tide, barra on livebait. Crocodiles are a risk.

2. Lee Point, Shoal Bay. Mackerel, queenfish and trevally at high tide on Darwin side of rocks. Also whiting and bream. Submerged rock patches on the Shoal Bay side are good on a low tide in calm weather for queenfish and barra.

3. Channel Island. Take the track opposite where you turn to the boat ramp. It is a fairly easy 25-minute walk, requiring crossing a tidal area. The fishing spot is a beach with rocks at each end, facing the city. The rocks to the south are best. Best tide is a low under 2m at noon. Arrive four hours after low tide. Barra, queenfish, trevally and more. The area around Channel Island bridge also has good neap tide fishing over a rough rock bottom.

4. Elizabeth River boat ramp and nearby rockbar. All-tide pontoon, with low-tide rockbar platform just downstream. Beware crocodiles.

5. Stokes Hill Wharf, Darwin. Jewfish, trevally, queenfish, barra, cod. Mackerel and tuna pass by in the dry season. Barra, baitfish and squid under lights at night. Fishing platform at start of wharf. End of the wharf is a no-fishing area.

6. Mandorah Wharf. Great spot for mackerel, queenfish, trevally, sharks. Barra around pylons. Reached by ferry from Darwin's Cullen Bay. Destined to have surrounding rock walls if a planned upgrade is completed by 2024.

7. Mandorah to Charles Point foreshores. Some areas are accessible. Check the Kenbi Land Claim map at the NLC website. Good beach and rock fishing on upper tide for blue salmon, queenfish, cod, barra. Jacks on headlands on incoming tide.

8. Harbour rock walls. Cullen Bay, Larrakeyah, East Arm boat ramp, Dinah Beach, Deckchair Cinema. Barra, queenfish, milkfish, bream, cod, jacks, crabs at high tide, best at night. Dinah Beach ramp pontoon has barra on the first push of the low tide late at night after boaters have gone home.

9. East Point rocks. Barra, queenfish, milkfish, salmon. Different areas fish at different stages of tide. Seaward rock ledge fishable at low tide. Ludmilla Creek side has a small ledge about 100m out with barra near low tide at dawn.

10. East Point mangrove boardwalk. Gate is at Lake Alexander playground carpark. The jetty is useable up to about 5m tide, after which it submerges. At low tide you can walk the flat.

11. Nightcliff jetty and rock groyne. queenfish, trevally, mackerel, tuskfish. Squid in dry season. Fires up when bait schools lob. Beware rising tide on rocks. Suburban foreshore rocks have barra in calm weather.

12. Rapid Creek. Rock ledge at mouth and rockbar 300m upstream from bridge off the bike path, barra, salmon, jacks.

RHONDA LEBROCQUE

The rocky shores near Dundee Beach boat ramp are prime spots to catch big barramundi at high tide

13. Leanyer drain. During wet season this drain has barra, tarpon.

14. Howard River rockbar. Entry via track through Howard River Reserve in dry season. Great barra spot, best at night. High croc risk.

15. Southport boat ramp. The high rocky bank is a useful landbased spot. Small snapper, barra, jacks, bream, salmon.

16. Darwin River rockbar. Heading to Mandorah on the Cox Peninsula Rd, the track is a turn right just before the bridge. Drive 100m and turn left. Fish rising tide after heavy rain.

17. Blackmore River rockbar. Heading to Mandorah on the Cox Peninsula Rd, the track is a turn right just past the bridge. Drive 450m and turn right. Fish a rising tide after rain.

18. Manton Dam. The dam wall spillway area usually has barra during flooding. The culvert on the road to the boat ramp has the odd fish during flooding.

19. Gunn Point Beach. Whiting, queenfish. Barra, salmon at creek.

20. Dundee Barra Rocks Sth. Just south of the Lodge of Dundee. Barra at high tide at dawn when calm.

21. Dundee Barra Rocks Nth. Walk from the lodge north along the beach about 2km to the rock ledges. High tide queenfish, trevally, salmon, barra. Walk another 1.5km north to a creek with a great rockbar. Another 1.5km further is a good beach rock formation. Calm weather only.

22. Finniss River mouth. 4WD on beach from Stingray Head (private access - may be closed at any time). Soft sand. Fish off beach at river mouth. Beware big crocs. Barra, salmon, jewfish.

23. Crab Claw Island, Bynoe Harbour. At low tide visitors staying at the resort can walk the "Highway to Heaven" sandspit at low tide to a large flat rock. Fish at low tide for queenfish, trevally, jacks and barra. Watch out for the incoming tide. Beware crocodiles.

24. Hardies Lagoon on Mary River system, off Arnhem Hwy. People fish for barra from the bank here, but this is serious big-crocodile country. Turn-off is signposted.

25. Shady Camp Barrage. A famous landbased spot, with the chance of hooking trophy barra on either side. Best on big tides, and when it has just dropped after wet season rain. Extreme crocodile danger - take no chances. Turn-off signposted off Arnhem Hwy.

26. Daly River Crossing. Big barra when river rises and falls from wet season rain. Best at night. Abundant crocodiles throughout river.

27. Bamboo Creek, Daly River. During the wet season Bamboo Creek mouth produces big barra.

28. Pococks Beach, Kakadu NP: Take the rough track in to West Alligator Head. Barramundi and more off the beach at high tide. Beware crocodiles.

29. Cahills Crossing. This is the road crossing on the East Alligator River. Big barra are caught around the crossing and from near the boat ramp at high tide. Big crocodiles.

30. Policeman's Point, Victoria River. Rock ledge produces big barra, usually after wet season rain. The Victoria Hwy runs along some of the river and there are fishable spots. Beware crocodiles.

31. Big Horse Creek boat ramp, Victoria River. This has a run-off creek near it, big barra in Wet.

32. Keep River. Reached by unsealed road from Kununurra, WA. There is bank fishing from near the track that runs along the tidal section. Beware crocodiles.

33. Katherine River crossings. Fish weirs and rockbars when floodwater is dropping. Best spots are Donkey Camp weir, Knotts Crossing, Low Level Crossing, and Galloping Jacks rockbar on Cossack Rd. Beware crocodiles.

34. Roper Bar crossing, Roper River. Good fishing after rain when river is falling back to near normal levels. Big barra and big crocodiles.

35. Mataranka Crossing. Barra after rain. Beware crocodiles.

36. McArthur River. The crossing near Borroloola is good after flooding. Downstream, fish from the bank at camp sites near King Ash Bay. Crocodiles.

37. Limmen River. The bank can be fished near some of the riverside fishing camps, high tide only. Crocodiles.

38. Towns River. Campers catch some good fish from the shoreline rock ledge next to the campsite. Beware crocodiles.

Roper River

This is a big-fish river, producing barramundi of more than 120cm each year. It is closed to commercial barra netting and sees relatively low recreational fishing pressure, as it is far from major centres. There is an annual influx of dry season campers. The main catchment of the Roper begins near Mataranka. The freshwater river meanders east, much of it as a broken watercourse fed by springs. At Leichardt's Roper Bar Crossing the tidal influence begins. The river flows ultimately through a 2.6km wide river mouth into the Gulf of Carpentaria. Most of the river is easy to navigate, but there are some significant hazards. There is excellent run-off fishing for barramundi just after the wet season, when road access allows, particularly in the lowe reaches. The trick is to drive to the Roper as soon as the Roper Highway opens after the wet season, launch at Roper Bar, which will be flooded and running fast, and go far downstream to the floodplain creeks. In recent years, Blackfella Creek has produced the best fishing,

A tiny island marks the presence of the Tomato Island rock shelf. The rock area is huge and often lies just under the surface. Follow the channel on the north bank with care. Munbililla (Tomato Island) camp boat ramp is visible on the right and INSET below

This outcrop 1.3km upstream of Tomato Island is where the Young Australian steamer wreck lies (above)

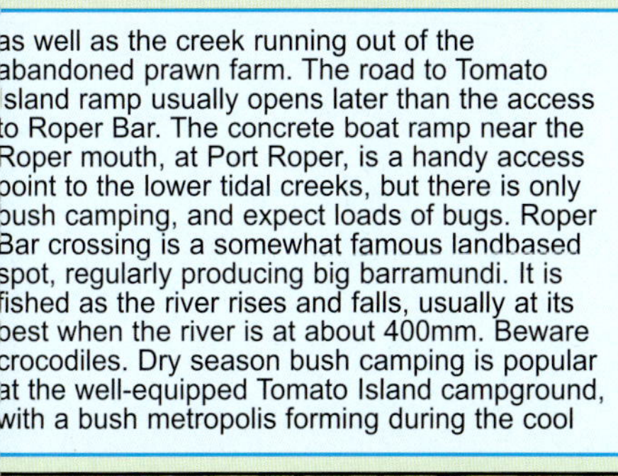

as well as the creek running out of the abandoned prawn farm. The road to Tomato Island ramp usually opens later than the access to Roper Bar. The concrete boat ramp near the Roper mouth, at Port Roper, is a handy access point to the lower tidal creeks, but there is only bush camping, and expect loads of bugs. Roper Bar crossing is a somewhat famous landbased spot, regularly producing big barramundi. It is fished as the river rises and falls, usually at its best when the river is at about 400mm. Beware crocodiles. Dry season bush camping is popular at the well-equipped Tomato Island campground, with a bush metropolis forming during the cool months, but the people soon disappear when the weather warms up from late August/September, ironically just as barramundi activity starts to increase.

Launch sites

A. Concrete ramp at Roper Bar near camping area. Beware shallow rocky ground immediately out the front of the ramp.
B. Launch site behind Roper Bar Park and Store.
C. Tomato Island - good concrete ramp but steep, large rock plateau lies immediately downstream. Campground has showers, toilets, barbecues.
Map at bottom - Port Roper ramp near river mouth.

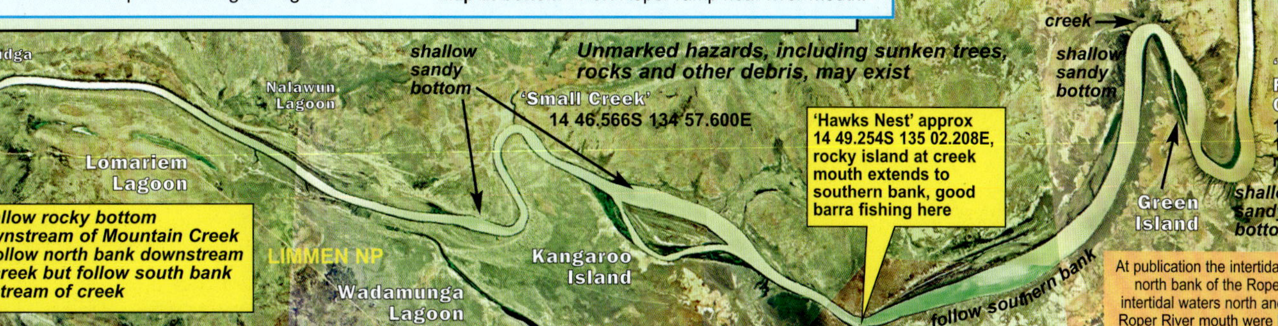

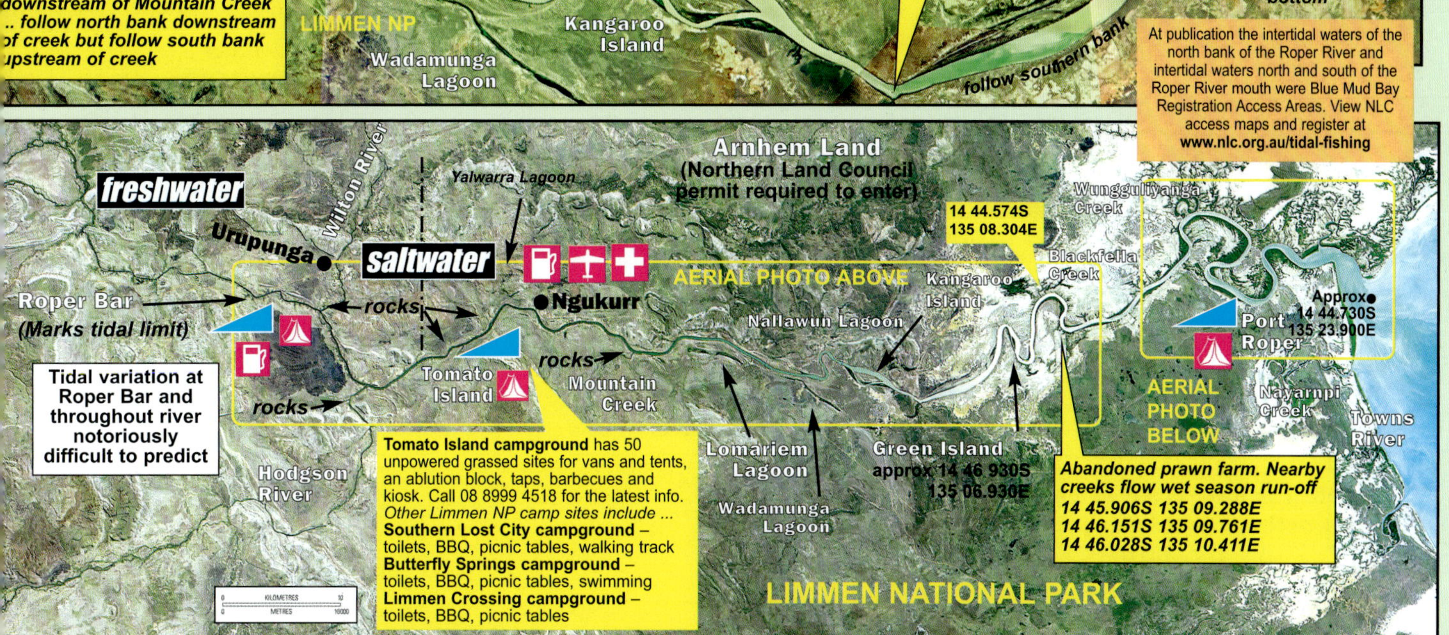

Roper Mouth

N

Phelp River

14 40.818S 135 16.236E

Painnyilatya Creek

Entrance of last creek before the river mouth is a popular big fish spot 14 43.283S 135 23.874E

14 42.738S 135 22.284E

Port Roper ramp is at 14 45.313S 135 19.124E useable most tides, bush camping only

Check at www.nlc.org.au for the latest access arrangements to the lower Roper River and Gulf of Carpentaria coastline

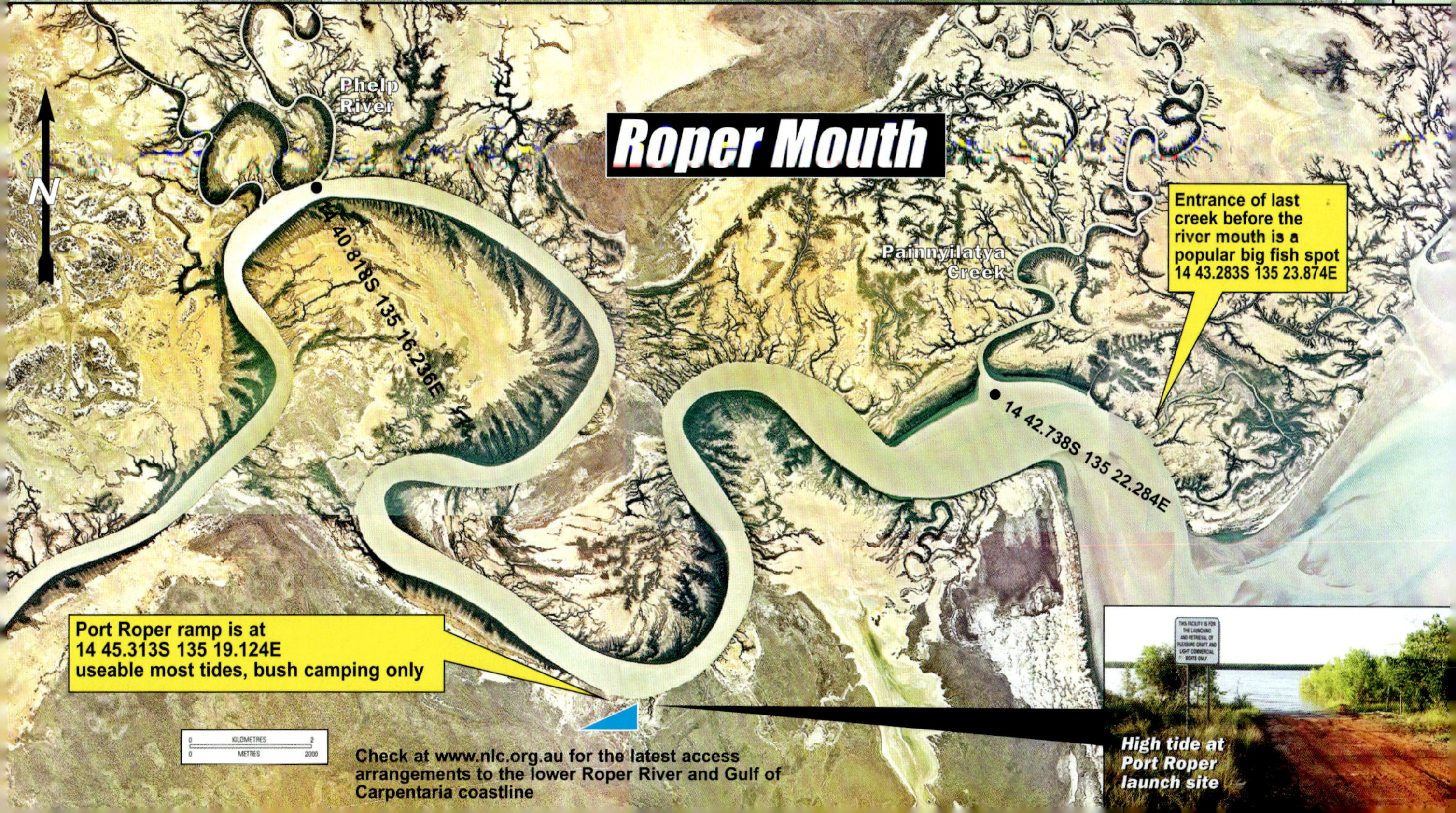

High tide at Port Roper launch site

Towns River at low tide approx 10km below the camp

MATT FLYNN PICTURE

No warranty is supplied or implied as to the suitability of this or any other supplied data for any particular purpose.

BOAT RAMP	S15 02.095	E135 13.156
ISLAND 1	S15 00.916	E135 14.491
ISLAND 2	S14 58.015	E135 18.210
ROCKS001	S15 02.124	E135 13.116
ROCKS002	S15 00.846	E135 14.616
ROCKS003	S15 00.835	E135 14.641
ROCKS004	S14 59.261	E135 17.875
ROCKS005	S14 58.667	E135 17.725
ROCKS006	S14 58.645	E135 17.747
ROCKS007	S14 58.222	E135 17.802
ROCKS008	S14 58.171	E135 17.834
ROCKS009	S14 57.961	E135 18.062
ROCKS010	S14 57.943	E135 18.395

N

14 57.66S
135 19.300E
Approx

Approx
14 56.816S
135 22.933E

approx
14 54.608S
135 25.969E

Very shallow at low tide

At publication the intertidal waters north and south of Towns River mouth were Blue Mud Bay Registration Access Areas. To register visit **www.nlc.org.au/tidal-fishing**

KILOMETRES 0 5
METRES 0 5000

Erossing

Towns River

Towns launch site, looking upstream ...

'BUZZDOG 'PICTURE

Moored at the camp

Towns River

This river is located conveniently between the Roper and Limmen Bight Rivers in Limmen National Park. It is well worth exploring. The Towns has a camping area with ablution block and a firm natural launch site near the camping area. There are not many snags in the Towns, so fishermen should approach what few snags are seen with caution, as there is usually a fish on them. The upper river has jacks, barra and mud crabs. After the wet season, crabs will be found well downstream in the saltwater, moving upstream as the dry season progresses. The river has rocky patches near the campsite, and just downstream. It becomes very shallow with drying sandbars a few kilometres down from the camp. A trip to the mouth should be done on a rising tide. Fishing at creek mouths and mud drains on the dropping tide is the standard method for catching barra. Use small lures as the average size of Towns fish tends to be a little smaller than on bigger rivers. Access to the Towns is during the dry season as the coastal road becomes impassible after wet season rains. You will need to be self sufficient here, as the nearest retail outlet is at Roper Bar, and there are no repair services. A tow out to Mataranka or Katherine will cost plenty.

Robinson River at Seven Emu Station, and the riverside bush camp (INSET BELOW)

VINCE BROZEK PICTURES

Savannah Way - the barramundi track

The eastern Top End is an exciting area, being far from population centres and therefore receiving low fishing pressure.

Fishos who explore the coast will find creeks and reefs that rarely see a boat.

Major rivers along along the Savannah Way road are the Roper, Limmen, McArthur, Wearyan and Robinson.

The central feature of this area for travellers is Limmen National Park.

There are several camping areas within and near the park of interest to fishermen.

These are Munbililla, also called Tomato Island, on the Roper River, Towns River, Lorella Springs Station, Limmen Bight Station and Seven Emu Station.

The road in from both the Queensland and NT side is subject to closures from wet season flooding.

Call Parks and Wildlife in Katherine (08 8973 8888) or Nathan River Ranger Station (08 8975 9940) for road info.

Call Katherine Rod and Rifle (08 8972 1020) for fishing information on the Territory side. The Roper's Munbililla (Tomato Island) campground has full ablution facilities and a ranger station.

South of the Roper, the relatively small Towns River, has bush camping near the river, also with an ablution block.

South again is the Limmen Bight River, which offers a wild bush camping experience along the riverbank.

The sites are unimproved, next to tidal water, and boats can be moored nearby at some of the campsites.

Centre Island tides provide approximate tide times to plan your Limmen trip.

You must be self sufficient when travelling and camping along the Savannah Way, and have a vehicle and trailer set up for rough, corrugated roads.

Fuel is at Borroloola, King Ash Bay, Robinson River Community and Roper Bar.

Roper Bar Park and Store had reopened at publication, after a prolonged closure.

The Limmen fishing camp supplies fuel in jerry cans.

Tank water is available at the Limmen camp if there has been enough rain. Call first.

A plus when fishing this region is that the NT does not have a barramundi closed season.

Best floodways for barramundi

During heavy wet season rain, barramundi swim upstream and downstream, crossing flooded roads and swimming through drains and under bridges.

The best fishing is usually at dawn and dusk, and at high tide.

Culverts are not a place for children, as passing cars and crocodiles are a real risk, and the water is often turbulent.

Small lures work best, presented on a light trace. Most barra will be small, but big ones show up. Expect to catch loads of tarpon.

Here's some of the best NT culverts.

1. Darwin metro - Leanyer drain: the drain beside the waterpark produces wet season barra.

2. Howard River Bridge: on the beginning of the Gunn Point road. Popular in the Wet.

3. Old Bynoe Rd has places to fish 5km and 16km from the Stuart Hwy. Neither are red hot, but are worth a look after heavy rain.

4. Pioneer Dve has a culvert in Pioneer River headwaters. Swimmers use it (risky), but at dusk and night there are barra.

5. Elizabeth Valley Rd: Head down the Stuart Hwy and pass Noonamah Pub. The next turn left is Elizabeth Valley Rd, with the culvert about 500m down the road. This is a reliable culvert, but with limited parking. Traffic passes at speed. Good fishing usually coincides with high tide. Don't swim here. Another culvert is upstream on **Weaver Rd**.

6. Hopewells Rd: Head down Cox Peninsula Rd past the Territory Wildlife Park. Hopewells Rd is on the left, with a short drive to the bridge. There is parking and clear banks, but many prefer fishing the bridge area. Dawn and dusk.

7. Meades Rd: Going down Cox Peninsula Rd, take the turn-off to the Litchfield Pub. Past the pub, Meades Rd is to the right. Follow the road a few kilometres until it takes a sharp turn left. Where it turns left, a small road runs to the right over a Blackmore River culvert. Fish off the culvert or the bank.

Scott Creek culvert in flood

8. Reedbeds Rd: Head down Darwin River Rd, take the first road left and then follow it until you reach an intersection. This is Reedbeds Rd. Turn right at Reedbeds Rd for a short trip to the crossing. Best when water is just over the road.

9. Cox Peninsula bridges: The area around Blackmore and Darwin River bridges have fish during flooding.

10. Beatrice Hill: This spot on the Arnhem Hwy, shortly before the Adelaide River bridge, is a place to sit and watch intense floodplain bait activity. Mimosa has choked it and killed it as a once-famous barra culvert.

10. Scott Creek Crossing: Heading from Darwin towards Corroboree Park Tavern on the Arnhem Hwy the second dirt road to the left into the national park takes you to Scott Creek Crossing. This is a reliable place to fish in flood, but gets busy. The Scott Creek crossing on the Stuart Hwy has barra when flooded over the road.

11. Arnhem Hwy road bridges: All well worth a look during and after heavy rain. The West Alligator River is a no-fishing zone.

12. Kakadu Hwy bridges: The "Three Bridges" across the highway at Nourlangie are good spots when floodwater is running.

13. 'Culvert Creek', South Alligator River: The creek on the Darwin side of the river is good after flooding. Fish move up with the tide. Cars fly past and crocs stalk you at night.

14. Daly River, Bamboo Creek: Next to where it flows into the Daly, famous for big fish after heavy rain.

15. Magela Creek, East Alligator River: A good spot at dawn and dusk when high. Crocs!

16. Tortilla Flats, Adelaide River: Fish when water is level with bridge.

17. White Creek on Whitehead Rd: Fish when water is just under bridge.

18. Manton Dam entry roads: The culvert half way in on the boat ramp road fires when the water is rising. The separate road to the dam wall has a walking track to the spillway, a great spot when it is flowing.

19. Marrakai Rd: Head past the Manton Dam turn-off and turn left at the sign. The unsealed road crosses the Adelaide River. Not strictly a culvert, but can fish well. Big crocs!

*** *In the wet season,* ***river crossings, weirs and rockbar barriers*** *are good places to fish during flooding. Shady Camp barrage, Roper Bar, Mataranka Crossing, the Daly River crossings, McArthur River crossing, Cahills Crossing, the Katherine River's Knotts Crossing and Low Level are just some. The Victoria River's Big Horse Creek ramp has landbased fishing next to a small run-off creek, and at Policeman Point. Further upstream, the Vic's Dashwood Crossing and the Humbert River crossing have barra after flooding.*

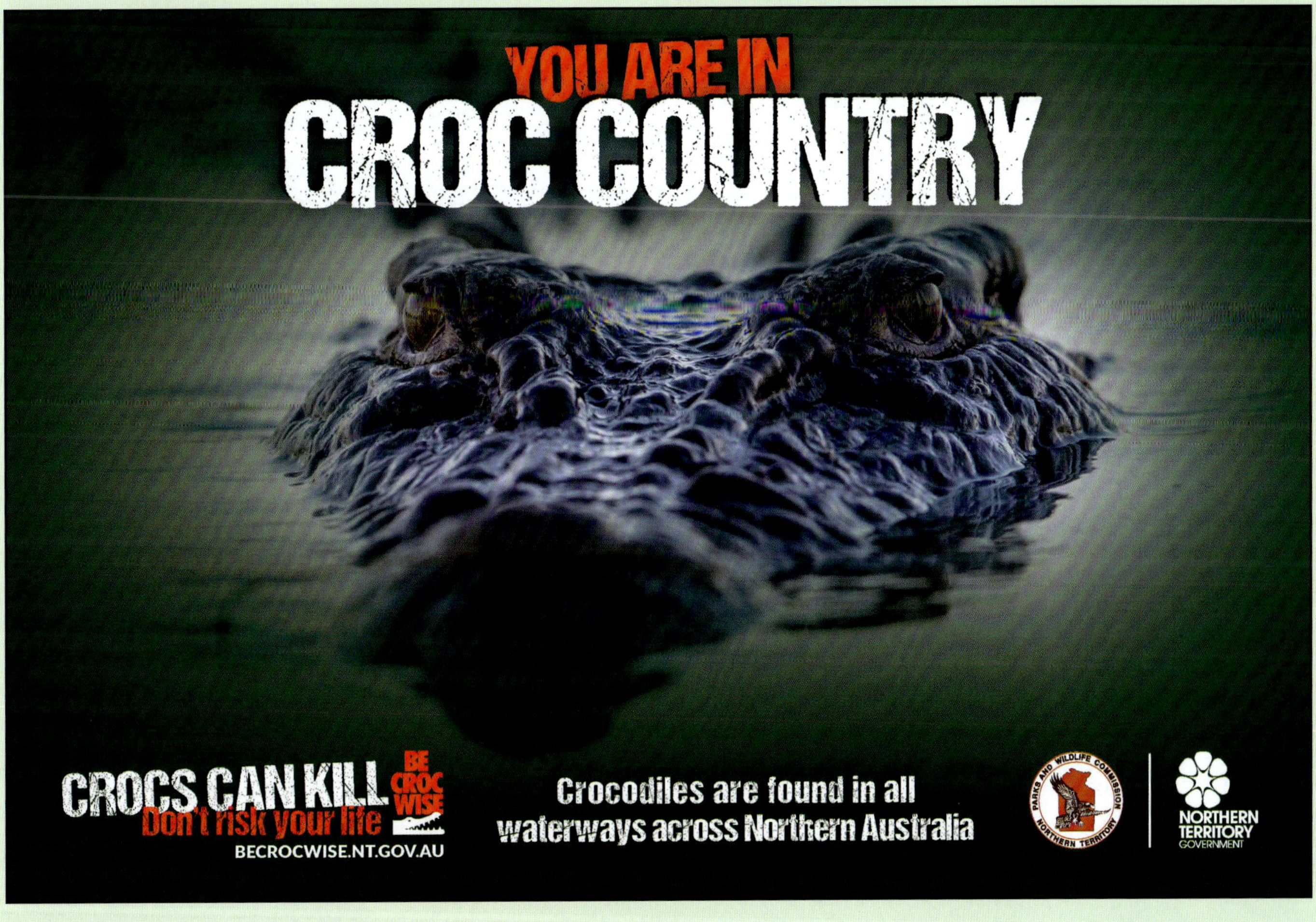

Regional facilities

	Ice	Boat hire	Accomm	Camping	Launch site	Hard ramp
Limmen Camp			•	•	•	
King Ash Bay F.C.	•		•	•	•	•
Lorella Springs Station			•	•	•	
Manangoora Station				•	•	
Seven Emu Station				•	•	
Towns River				•	•	

NT station camps

The eastern Top End has wilderness camps for fishermen where you can hear barramundi feeding at night not far from where you sleep.

Strong camper trailers, cartopper boats and large 4WDs are recommended. Caravans can be brought in, but are not recommended.

Fishing is best when the weather warms in September and October, before rain makes the tracks impassible, but there's plenty to catch in the cooler months, including mud crabs.

East of Borroloola, Manangoora Station (08 8975 9549) offers access to the tidal **Wearyan River.** There are bush camps and three bank launch sites, the nearest to Vanderlin Island. There are no toilets, showers or rubbish collection. There is bore water but no drinking water. The cost is $150 per vehicle for stays of six to 14 days, or $25 a day for shorter stays.

Seven Emu Station (08 8975 9904 - www.sevenemustation.com.au) offers access to **Robinson River** tidal water. The cost is $50 per vehicle per day. Seven Emu is accessible by 4WD only. There is a rough track to the **Calvert River** for serious off-roaders.

For the adventurous boater, shoals exist well wide of Robinson River that rarely see a boat. Admiralty chart AUS304 reveals some of them and GPS marks are provided on Page 202.

Access to this area by road is generally from April, depending on late wet season rainfall.

Robinson River Aboriginal Community, 50km off the Savannah Way, has fuel and supplies. Do not bring in alcohol. Phone 08 8975 9791.

Wollogorang Station closed access to **Tully** and **Massacre Inlets** in 2005. The station has since changed hands three times, but it remains to be seen if it will reopen to tourism.

To the north **Lorella Springs Station** (www.lorellasprings.com.au) offers access to wild **Rosie Creek**. A 4WD track leads to tidal water 80km from the homestead.

The creek launch and camp is about 13km from the sea, useable on the upper tide.

The creek has many rockbars that must be traversed at high tide to reach the sea. There are jacks, cod and mostly smaller barra. Big queenfish frequent the creek mouth.

Also available at Lorella is **Wuraliwuntya Creek**, and a track to the coast for beach launching. There are many tracks on the station and camping is allowed throughout. There is also accommodation and a bar. Fish may not be taken from the station.

Lorella is 135km from Cape Crawford, 180km from Borroloola, and 275 km from Roper Bar.

Further north is Limmen Bight Station (08 8975 9844), which has riverside bush camping, basic cabins, a shop and a launch site on the **Limmen Bight River's** tidal reaches (see next page).

Keep in mind this area's isolation. Medical help is distant and full self-sufficiency is required.

Rosie Creek mouth on Lorella Station

VINCE BROZEK PICTURE

Limmen Bight River

The upper tidal section, well above the fishing camp, is rocky, with mangrove jacks, cod and some barramundi. Heading downstream from the ramp, the river is broad, sandy and shallow, with drying sandbars, mangrove forests and some side creeks. The downstream section generally has the best fishing, with barramundi, queenfish and threadfin salmon. Reliable barra fishing is had at creek mouths near the mouth. The water is usually clear enough to see the many sandflats, but sometimes there is no clear channel through the shallows, so a light boat that can be dragged is an advantage at low tide. For those who go far upstream, the rockbar that stretches across the Cox River holds barra when it is flowing into the tidal water. Rocky islands should be approached quietly for a cast, as barra and jacks loiter around the edges. Access to the tidal water is from Steve Barrett's Limmen Fishing Camp, with bankside campsites located between 32km and 26km from the river mouth. The only retail item is fuel, sold in 20L lots. Drinking water is usually available, but not guaranteed. The camp is closed in the wet season. Phone (08) 8975 9844.

Getting there

Expect sometimes severe corrugations. Trailers must be strong and set up for rough roads. Do not leave heavy items in a boat while towing the Savannah Way.

Key to Map

Hotspots

1. Big barra at entrance of last small creek before the river mouth, on north bank. Water can be quite clear and the fish shy, so use large live mullet for bait.
2. Barra at creek mouths, first outgoing tide, cast lures to corners of creek mouths and just inside. Also good casting along north bank, watch for visible barra.
3 and 3. Barra in discoloured water where inlet behind island flows out during outgoing tide. Mud crabs throughout.
4. Shortcut to the creek to the north blocked at the time of writing, might wash out again after a big wet season.
5. Good trolling along river banks in Nathan River at times, rocky areas upstream good for jacks.
6. Cast lures at rocky islands for jacks and barra, approach quietly, best in early mornings.
7. Mostly jacks from here upstream, use small lures or livebait. Very careful navigation required, cartoppers only recommended. Cox River rockbar is well worth a look when flowing.
8. Bream and jacks over rocks.

Launch sites

A. Firm bank launch at Limmen Fishing Camp, OK for big boats from about mid tide up. Cartoppers can be launched from some of the campsites and moored near the camps. Beware crocodiles. River is shallow throughout, with many drying sandbars downstream and some hazardous rocky areas upstream.

Limmen Bight River just upstream of 'The Narrows'

Limmen Fishing Camp ramp

MATT FLYNN PICTURE

Limmen Bight River at low tide, near the fishing camps

Check at www.nlc.org.au for the latest access arrangements to the Limmen Bight River and Gulf of Carpentaria coastline

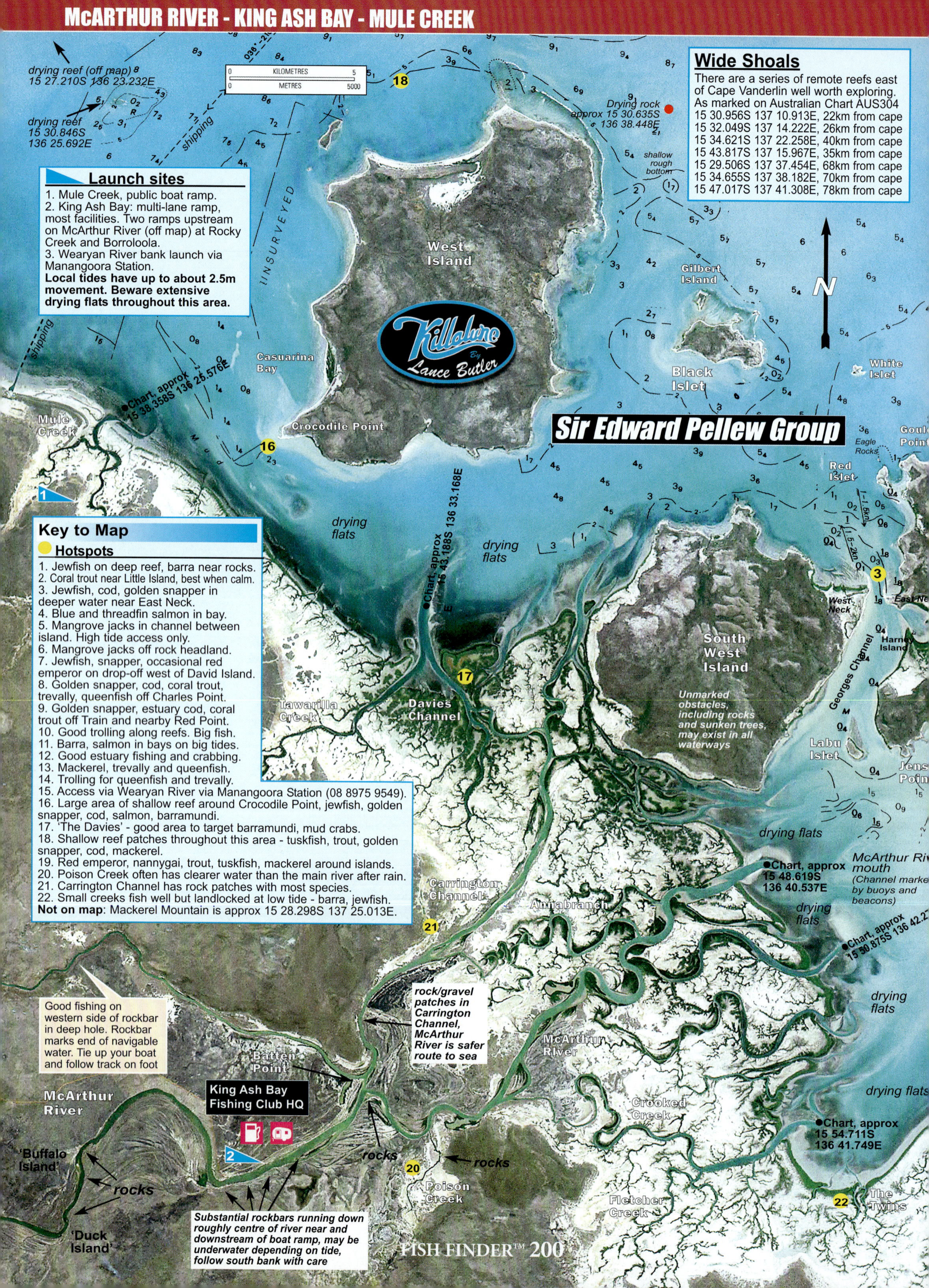

McARTHUR RIVER - KING ASH BAY - MULE CREEK
drying reef (off map)
15 27.210S 136 23.232E
drying reef
15 30.846S
136 25.692E
KILOMETRES
METRES
Launch sites
1. Mule Creek, public boat ramp.
2. King Ash Bay: multi-lane ramp, most facilities. Two ramps upstream on McArthur River (off map) at Rocky Creek and Borroloola.
3. Wearyan River bank launch via Manangoora Station.
Local tides have up to about 2.5m movement. Beware extensive drying flats throughout this area.
West Island
Casuarina Bay
Crocodile Point
Chart, approx 15 38.358S 136 25.576E
Mule Creek
UNSURVEYED
shipping
Drying rock approx 15 30.635S 136 38.448E
shallow rough bottom
Wide Shoals
There are a series of remote reefs east of Cape Vanderlin well worth exploring. As marked on Australian Chart AUS304
15 30.956S 137 10.913E, 22km from cape
15 32.049S 137 14.222E, 26km from cape
15 34.621S 137 22.258E, 40km from cape
15 43.817S 137 15.967E, 35km from cape
15 29.506S 137 37.454E, 68km from cape
15 34.655S 137 38.182E, 70km from cape
15 47.017S 137 41.308E, 78km from cape
N
Gilbert Island
Black Islet
White Islet
Killalane By Lance Butler
Sir Edward Pellew Group
Eagle Rocks
Red Islet
West Neck
East Neck
Harney Island
Georges Channel
Labu Islet
South West Island
Unmarked obstacles, including rocks and sunken trees, may exist in all waterways
Chart, approx 15 43.188S 136 33.168E
drying flats
Key to Map
Hotspots
1. Jewfish on deep reef, barra near rocks.
2. Coral trout near Little Island, best when calm.
3. Jewfish, cod, golden snapper in deeper water near East Neck.
4. Blue and threadfin salmon in bay.
5. Mangrove jacks in channel between island. High tide access only.
6. Mangrove jacks off rock headland.
7. Jewfish, snapper, occasional red emperor on drop-off west of David Island.
8. Golden snapper, cod, coral trout, trevally, queenfish off Charles Point.
9. Golden snapper, estuary cod, coral trout off Train and nearby Red Point.
10. Good trolling along reefs. Big fish.
11. Barra, salmon in bays on big tides.
12. Good estuary fishing and crabbing.
13. Mackerel, trevally and queenfish.
14. Trolling for queenfish and trevally.
15. Access via Wearyan River via Manangoora Station (08 8975 9549).
16. Large area of shallow reef around Crocodile Point, jewfish, golden snapper, cod, salmon, barramundi.
17. 'The Davies' - good area to target barramundi, mud crabs.
18. Shallow reef patches throughout this area - tuskfish, trout, golden snapper, cod, mackerel.
19. Red emperor, nannygai, trout, tuskfish, mackerel around islands.
20. Poison Creek often has clearer water than the main river after rain.
21. Carrington Channel has rock patches with most species.
22. Small creeks fish well but landlocked at low tide - barra, jewfish.
Not on map: Mackerel Mountain is approx 15 28.298S 137 25.013E.
Tawarilla Creek
Davies Channel
Carrington Channel
Anabranch
Chart, approx 15 48.619S 136 40.537E
McArthur River mouth
(Channel marked by buoys and beacons)
Chart, approx 15 50.875S 136 42.2
Good fishing on western side of rockbar in deep hole. Rockbar marks end of navigable water. Tie up your boat and follow track on foot
rock/gravel patches in Carrington Channel, McArthur River is safer route to sea
Batten Point
King Ash Bay Fishing Club HQ
McArthur River
'Buffalo Island'
'Duck Island'
rocks
Crooked Creek
Poison Creek
Fletcher Creek
Chart, approx 15 54.711S 136 41.749E
The Twins
Substantial rockbars running down roughly centre of river near and downstream of boat ramp, may be underwater depending on tide, follow south bank with care
FISH FINDER™ 200

NORTH ISLAND NP - VANDERLIN ISLAND - WEARYAN RIVER
PREMIUM SUPERLINES
FINS
FINS FISHES BETTER
GPS
* denotes drying reef, approach with extreme care and beware breaking waves
*Gulch Reef 15 37.603S 136 48.695E
*Heriot Reef 15 29.110S 136 55.298E
*Vanderlin Rocks 15 33.169S 137 01.072E
*Hervey Rocks 15 30.979S 136 54.897E
Urquhart East 15 30.365S 137 00.148E
A. Shallow wreck. Mast no longer visible. Approx 15 41.060S 136 50.406E
Heriot Reef
Pearce Island
Rose Point
Cape Pellew
Urquhart Island
Paradice Bay
Hervey Rocks
North Island
(Barranyi National Park)
Watson Island
Skull Island
Red Bluff
Vanderlin Rocks
Cape Vanderlin
Stevens Rocks
Turtle Island
Wheatley Island
Observation Island
Long Reef
Gulch Reef
Crab Rocks
David Island
Walker Point
Rose Bay
Sand Islet
Three Hummock Point
Kedge Point
Quince Islet
Phil Point
It is about 46km by sea from Cape Vanderlin to 'Mackerel Mountain' (not on map)
Centre Island
Rocky Island
Geranium Bay
Lake Eames (freshwater)
Charles Point
It is about 35km by sea from Jensen Point to Cape Vanderlin
Barclay Point
Survey Bay
Vanderlin Island
Little Island
Brown Islet
Train Point
Victoria Bay
Steepcut Rock
Combs Point
ClassicLures
Rob Gaden
Daisy Islet
Red Point
Jimmy Islet
Jolly Islet
Webinger Point
Small Islet
Ulbara Point
It is about 41km by water from the McArthur River King Ash Bay boat ramp to Jensen Point
King Ash Bay and Barranyi (North Island) National Park
King Ash Bay Fishing Club on the McArthur River is a seasonal fishing metropolis accessed from Borroloola via a gravel road. It is about a 60 minute run from the ramp down the McArthur River or Carrington Arm to the sea. The McArthur channel is the safest to navigate, but there are rocks midstream near and just downstream of the ramp. Sea conditions vary, with mainly south-east winds in the dry season and north-west winds and storms during the Wet. Drying tidal flats are a distinct hazard throughout this area. Barranyi (North Island) NP is a superb base to explore out wide, with great fishing around the islands, and arguably even better outside. The island is owned by Yanyuwa people and is leased to the NT Government as a park. The island is 30km from McArthur River and Carrington Channel entrances. There is drinking water, campsites and barbecues at Paradice Bay. The island has sandy beaches, with good fishing around the rocks. Boat fishing produces golden snapper, jewfish, blue salmon, coral trout, tuskfish, pikey bream, jacks and tricky snapper, with red emperor and nannygai on deeper reefs. At the time of writing public access was not available to other islands. Crocodiles inhabit this region, including on island beaches.
Stokes Bay
Clarkson Point
shallow
SEE PAGE 198
drying flats
Goat Point
Pelican Spit
Little Vanderlin Island
Sharker Point
rocks
drying flats
shallow
Chart, approx 15 54.691S 136 51.541E
Darwin
Map
Weipa
Borroloola
Karumba
Lousey Creek
Wearyan River
(Manangoora Station)
Tides in this region have up to about 2.5m movement
Fat Fellows Creek

Wearyan, Robinson, and Calvert Rivers

These three Northern Territory rivers, close to the Queensland border, are for fishermen who like wilderness and basic bush camping. They can be included in an extended fishing tour with the McArthur, Limmen, Towns and Roper Rivers. The Wearyan, Robinson and Calvert all require 4WD. There are camps but no facilities. Expect to catch barramundi, salmon and mud crabs, with queenfish, trevally and grunter at the creek mouths and golden snapper, coral trout, tuskfish, black jewfish and mackerel on coastal shoals. Robinson River is accessible via Seven Emu Station (08 8975 9904 - www.sevenemustation.com.au). There are bank launch sites and bush camping. The Seven Emu road is usually open in April, depending on rain, and a creek crossing is required. Access to **Wearyan River** is via Manangoora Station (08 8975 9549). It has bush camp sites and a launch site into tidal water, giving access to the Vanderlin Islands. To the east of the Wearyan mouth are small tidal systems that can fish well. Wide of Robinson and Calvert Rivers are rarely fished reefs for adventurous trailerboaters who have sufficient fuel and experience.

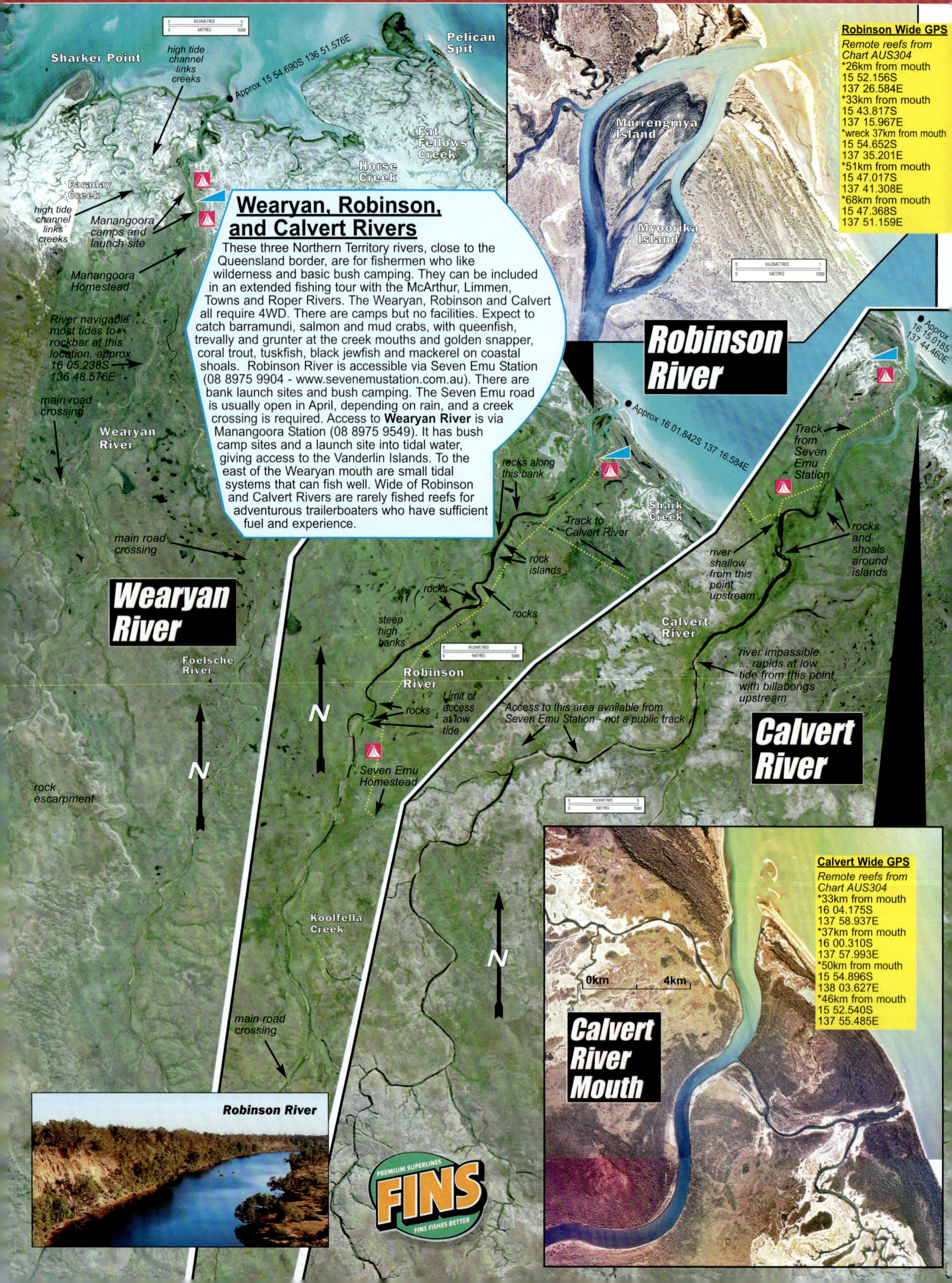

Robinson Wide GPS

Remote reefs from Chart AUS304

*26km from mouth
15 52.156S
137 26.584E

*33km from mouth
15 43.817S
137 15.967E

*wreck 37km from mouth
15 54.652S
137 35.201E

*51km from mouth
15 47.017S
137 41.308E

*68km from mouth
15 47.368S
137 51.159E

Calvert Wide GPS

Remote reefs from Chart AUS304

*33km from mouth
16 04.175S
137 58.937E

*37km from mouth
16 00.310S
137 57.993E

*50km from mouth
15 54.896S
138 03.627E

*46km from mouth
15 52.540S
137 55.485E

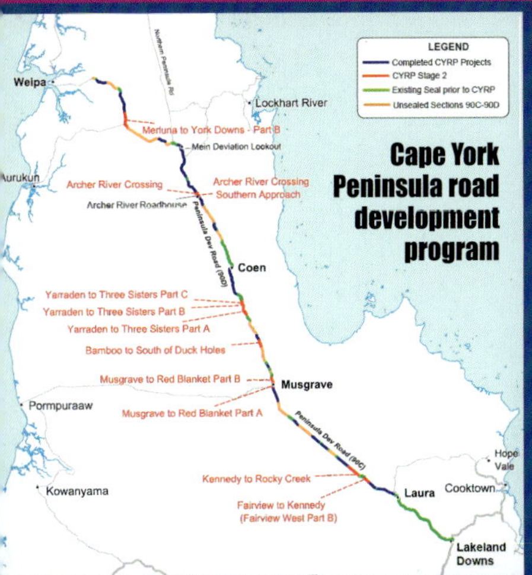

Regulations

Some Qld regulations are in this book. Visit **www.daf.qld.gov.au/fisheries/recreational** for complete Queensland fishing regulations.

Queensland aerial imagery within is © The State of Qld (Department of Natural Resources and Mines). The department gives no warranty in relation to the data (including accuracy, reliability, completeness or suitability) and accepts no liability (including without limitation, liability in negligence) for any loss, damage or costs (including consequential damage) relating to any use of the data.

Cape York Peninsula road development program

LEGEND
Completed CYRP Projects
CYRP Stage 2
Existing Seal prior to CYRP
Unsealed Sections 90C-90D

Weipa, Lockhart River, Merluna to York Downs - Part B, Mein Deviation Lookout, Aurukun, Archer River Crossing, Archer River Roadhouse, Archer River Crossing Southern Approach, Coen, Yarraden to Three Sisters Part C, Yarraden to Three Sisters Part B, Yarraden to Three Sisters Part A, Bamboo to South of Duck Holes, Musgrave to Red Blanket Part B, Musgrave, Pormpuraaw, Musgrave to Red Blanket Part A, Hope Vale, Kennedy to Rocky Creek, Kowanyama, Laura, Cooktown, Fairview to Kennedy (Fairview West Part B), Lakeland Downs

A project began in 2014 to seal large sections of the notoriously corrugated and dusty Peninsula Development Road between Laura and Weipa. Stage 2 was to be under way in 2023, after which 145km would remain unsealed. A separate Community Access Roads Program is improving the Northern Peninsula Road to Bamaga, and the roads to Pormpuraaw, Aurukun and Lockhart River. Long stretches of corrugations can be expected at times and a 4WD vehicle towing a sturdy dual-axle boat trailer is still the best choice for touring the peninsula.

Coral Fin Fish Closures

Queensland has coral reef fin fish closure dates at peak spawning times.
Closure dates - 2022 to 2023
October 22-26, 2022 - November 21-25, 2022
October 12-16, 2023 - November 10-14, 2023
The boundary is roughly marked with a yellow broken line on this map.
A seasonal closure for **snapper and pearl perch** applies from July 15 to August 15.

Rock Lobster Closure

A closed season applies to tropical rock lobster (family Panuliridae) usually from midnight October 1 to midnight December 31 in Queensland tidal waters: north of latitude 14°S, south of Cape York and east of longitude 142 31.816E in the Gulf of Carpentaria, shoreward of the 25nm line and south of latitude 10°48' S. A size limit of 11.5cm min. tail, 9cm min. carapace applies to the painted crayfish (*Panulirus ornatus*).

Many other fishing regulations apply in Queensland.

FADS - see Page 322

Fish Attracting Devices (FADS) are deployed in South-East Queensland waters, off the Gulf of Carpentaria's Weipa, and in some dams.

Alcohol Restrictions

Alcohol is restricted in 19 Queensland communities - Aurukun, Cherbourg, Doomadgee, Hope Vale, Kowanyama, Lockhart River, Mapoon, Mornington Island, Napranum, Northern Peninsula Area, Palm Island, Pormpuraaw, Woorabinda, Wujal Wujal and Yarrabah. Get more info at **www.qld.gov.au/firstnations/community-alcohol-restrictions/remote-discrete-communities**

GBRMPA Marine Park Zones

Some Great Barrier Reef Marine Park zones are shown in this book. Some zoning GPS co-ordinate data is included ... detailed data can be downloaded at **www.gbrmpa.gov.au**
YELLOW ZONES - fishing, with restrictions. **GREEN, PINK and ORANGE ZONES** - no fishing. Other restrictions may apply. **Other zones may exist in some areas.**

Cape York, page 224-225
Bamaga/Seisia, Jardine River, pages 222-225
Jackey Jackey, Escape River, pages 226-227
Jackson River to Crystal Creek, pages 220-221
Wenlock River, Pennefather River, pages 218-219
Lockhart River, page 228
Weipa, pages 216-217
Aurukun, page 215
Princess Charlotte Bay, Lakefield, Bathurst Bay, pages 230-235
Kirke, Love Rivers, pages 214
Mitchell, Coleman, Edward, Kendall, Holroyd Rivers, pages 212-213
Port Stewart, page 229
Nassau, Staaten, Gilbert, Smithburne Rivers, pages 208-211
Cooktown, pages 236-237
Port Douglas, Daintree, Mossman, pages 238-242
Burdekin region, pages 264-269
Bowen-Dingo Beach, region, pages 269-271
Whitsunday Islands, page 272-273
Cairns, pages 243-246
Innisfail, pages 247-250
Proserpine, pages 274-277
Mackay, region, pages 276-287
Cape Palmerston, Notch Point, West Hill region, pages 288-289
Lower Gulf, pages 204-207
Broad Sound, Shoalwater Bay, Stanage, pages 290-295
Hinchinbrook, pages 251-253
Ingham, Palm Islands page 254
Yeppoon, Rockhampton, Fitzroy River, pages 296-300
Gladstone, pages 301-303
Rodd Peninsula, Turkey Beach, Pancake Creek, Baffle Creek, Town of 1770, pages 304-305
Townsville, pages 255-263
Bundaberg, Burnett River, Hervey Bay, Sandy Strait pages 306-311
Qld and NSW stocked dams, pages 374-384
Noosa, pages 312-313
Sunshine Coast, Bribie Island pages 314-315
Moreton Bay, pages 316-319

Torres Strait, Seisia, Jardine River National Park, CORAL FINFISH CLOSURE AREA APPROX BOUNDARY, Shelburne Bay, Mapoon, Temple Bay, Weipa, N, Iron Range National Park, Chilli Beach, Lloyd Bay, Great Barrier Reef, Aurukun, Mungkan Kaanju National Park, Kulla National Park, Coen, Cape Keerweer, Princess Charlotte Bay, Bathurst Bay, Cape Melville National Park, Lakefield National Park, Pormpuraaw, KILOMETRES 0 100, METRES 0 100000, Kowanyama, Cooktown, Daintree National Park, Mossman, Port Douglas, Julatten, Mareeba, Cairns, Atherton, Great Barrier Reef, Marlin fleet base, Innisfail, Extent of imagery, Ayr, Cape Upstart, Bowen, Dingo Beach, Airlie Beach, Whitsunday Group, Proserpine, Seaforth, Mackay, Sarina, To Borroloola, Betinck Island, Sweers Island, Karumba, Burketown, Clairview, St Lawrence, Broad Sound, Stanage, Shoalwater Bay, Lucinda, Townsville, Yeppoon, Rockhampton, Port Alma, Curtis Island, Gladstone, Extent of imagery, Bundaberg, Hervey Bay, Maryborough, Caloundra, Brisbane

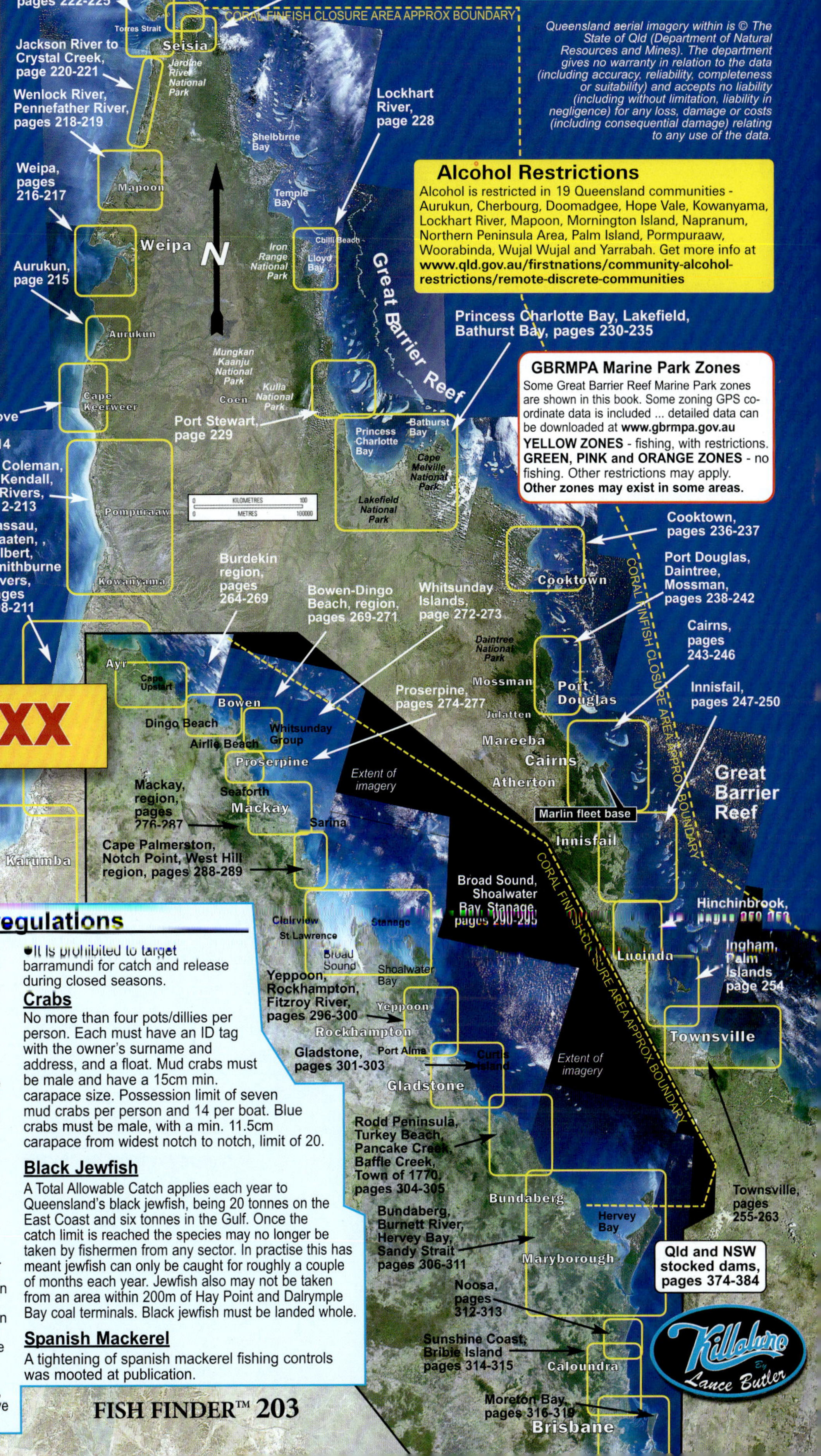

Some Queensland fishing regulations

- In tidal waters, up to three fishing lines are permitted with a total of six hooks. A fly, lure, bait jig or gang hook is considered equal to one hook. The angler must be present with the line(s) at all times.
- Cast nets may be used in tidal waters only. They must not exceed 3.7m from the point of rope attachment to the net lead line or the bottom of the lowest pocket. Mesh size must not exceed 28mm.
- Queensland has annual closed seasons for barramundi, one for the Gulf of Carpentaria and one for the East Coast. Both seasons unfortunately coincide with arguably the best fishing period, being the summer. The NT has no closed season.
- Barramundi minimum size: 58cm, maximum size 120cm, possession limit of 5, with a limit of 10 per boat with two or more persons on board.
- The East Coast barramundi closed season is midday Nov 1 to midday Feb 1, except in and from waterways upstream of Awoonga, Burdekin Falls, Callide, Eungella, Fairbairn, Fred Haigh (Lake Monduran), Kinchant, Koombooloomba, Lenthalls, Peter Faust, Teemburra, Tinaroo and Wuruma dams.
- The Gulf of Carpentaria barramundi closed season is from midday Oct 7 to midday Feb 1 (possession on boats allowed to midday Oct 17). Does not apply in East Leichhardt, Belmore, Corella, Julius, Fred Tritton and Moondarra dams, and waterways upstream.
- A possession limit of one barramundi applies during the closed season in the dams mentioned. The fish may be greater than 120cm. Fishers may continue to fish once they have reached their limit. Outside the closed season, in the dams mentioned, a take and possession limit of five applies and may include one barra of 120cm+.
- It is prohibited to target barramundi for catch and release during closed seasons.

Crabs

No more than four pots/dillies per person. Each must have an ID tag with the owner's surname and address, and a float. Mud crabs must be male and have a 15cm min. carapace size. Possession limit of seven mud crabs per person and 14 per boat. Blue crabs must be male, with a min. 11.5cm carapace from widest notch to notch, limit of 20.

Black Jewfish

A Total Allowable Catch applies each year to Queensland's black jewfish, being 20 tonnes on the East Coast and six tonnes in the Gulf. Once the catch limit is reached the species may no longer be taken by fishermen from any sector. In practise this has meant jewfish can only be caught for roughly a couple of months each year. Jewfish also may not be taken from an area within 200m of Hay Point and Dalrymple Bay coal terminals. Black jewfish must be landed whole.

Spanish Mackerel

A tightening of spanish mackerel fishing controls was mooted at publication.

Albert River boat ramp

BURKETOWN BARRAMUNDI FISHING ORGANISATION

River camp sites

Burketown, 140km west of Normanton, is on the Albert River. There is one public boat ramp, a landing, and camping areas with bankside access for fishermen.

Aboriginal corporation Gangalidda Garawa Services Pty Ltd provides paid campsites along the tidal Albert River.

Each campground has multiple campsites. They are ...

Dean's Creek (Dean's Landing). A flat, open area 12km from Burketown, with landings for small boats. Launching here shortens the time to reach the river mouth. However visitors can not cross the track gutters after a high tide as they are boggy. Dry season only. Four campsites.

Bridge to Bottle Heap. This has camping and day-use sites and is the nearest camping area to Burketown. There are two access points 1km and 2.5km from the town. The significant sites are Old Bridge, the Old Crossing (a usually submerged rockbar) and the Bottle Heap. The Old Bridge is a day-use area with picnic tables, toilets and fishing off the old bridge. The Old Crossing is visible on the lowest tides, and can provide excellent fishing. The Bottle Heap marks the entrance to The Loop, the original channel of the Albert River, on the east side of Burketown. There are 10 sites, with shade and near toilets.

The Wharf. This is a flat, open area 6km from Burketown on a bitumen road. There is a concrete ramp, toilets and pontoon. There are seven campsites. Given the presence of big crocodiles, fishing from the pontoon is risky.

Meatworks: Northeast of Burketown. Accessible to all vehicles, but secluded. There are historical sites found in this area, which is at the lower north end of The Loop. Sites are shaded, many with riverbank access for landbased fishing.

Gangalidda Garawa camping fees are from $35 a night per vehicle. Get permits at www.burketown.com.au/plan/camping

Elsewhere, the Leichardt River's upper reaches have numerous rockbars with good fishing. If you can't get entry permission from Armraynald Station, phone (07) 4748 5526, then go by boat via the Albert River ramp and either through the connecting channel, or via the mouth. Be sure to take enough fuel and water.

Boaters can launch at Albert River and visit other rivers by sea, when conditions allow.

Offshore, Wellesley and Bountiful Island groups offer light-tackle sportfishing. Sweers Island Resort is a good base for boaters.

A popular wet season pastime is fishing for barramundi in the floodwaters at the local road crossings and culverts, but watch for crocodiles and passing vehicles, not to mention rising floodwaters.

Fishing quality

Fishing in the lower Gulf of Carpentaria and its rivers fluctuates with the wet seasons. This area will fire up with a good wet season or two, so keep an eye on the weather reports.

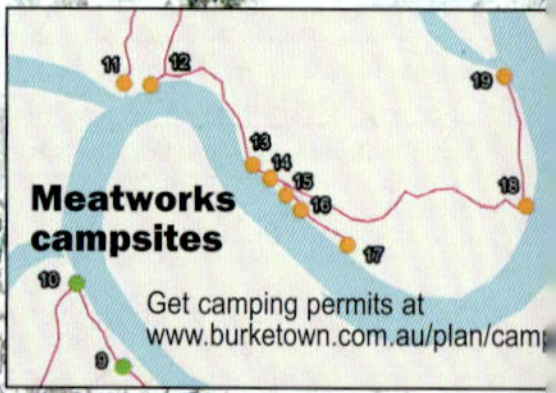

Meatworks campsites

Get camping permits at www.burketown.com.au/plan/camp

Albert River ramp

Gin Arm Creek

Nicholson River

Escott

Burketown

old channel 'The Loop'

Bottle Heap campsites

Albert River is navigable about 25km upstream. Beware many submerged trees

bridge

Albert River GPS

Location	GPS
Boat ramp	17 44.035S 139 35.553E
Hole at mouth of Twin Creeks	17 43.868S 139 38.198E
Creek 1, downstream from junction of saltwater arm and mouth	14 42.377S 139 38.589E
Creek 3	17 40.094S 139 41.290E
Creek 4	17 40.197S 139 43.328E
Ballast grounds	17 38.000S 139 42.946E
Hole	17 37.584S 139 43.269E
Landsborough Channel hole	17 37.675S 139 44.578E
Small creek	17 43.882S 139 38 952E

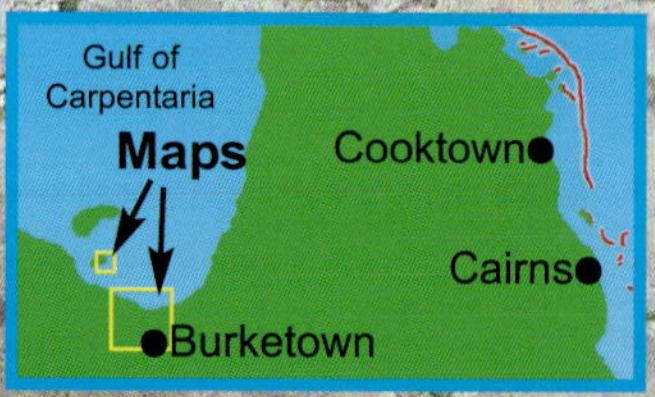

Gulf of Carpentaria

Maps

Cooktown

Cairns

Burketown

World Barramundi Fishing Championships

This event is held out of Burketown at Easter, with about $20,000 in prizes and trophies. For more information phone 0418 711 734 or visit Burketown Barramundi Fishing Organization Inc on Facebook

Hotspots

1. Deep holes hold jewfish, salmon, grunter. Best on early incoming tide.
2. Rockbars hold grunter, bream, salmon. Live bait for barra at low tide.
3. Troll rockbar with deep lures for barra.
4. Bank fishing at Dean's Creek campsites. Beware corocdiles. Deep hole in this area holds jewfish.
5. Fish old crossing just after wet season. Channels and snags, good barra during wet season. Big barra on live bait on most upstream snags. Crocodiles.
6. Fish billabong inlet during and just after Wet. Note that most small creeks will flow clearer water into the main river during and just after the wet season. Fish colour changes for barra.
7. There are several rockbars in the upper reaches of Gin Arm Creek. Upper reach is the site of the former Escott Lodge.

Key to Map

8. Fish river mouths and channel edges for grunter, barra and golden salmon. Good crabbing on flats at times.
9. Sandbars, gutters near Gore Point hold salmon.
10. Good crabbing in small creeks - most creeks on this coast are fishable through the tide, but entry and exit is only possible near high tide.
11. Hole at mouth of Pandanus Creek has jewfish.

Launch sites

1. Public ramp, Truginini Rd, useable on most tides, sharp drop at bottom at low tide. Jetty nearby with wheelchair access.
2. Dean's Landing - bank launch for small boats, best on upper tide, a shorter run from here to the river mouth than the public ramp.

8

Chart, approx 17 30.289S 139 36.382E

11 Pandanus Creek

Chart, approx 17 32.141S 139 38.853E

Vast tidal flats - take care to avoid being stranded on a diminishing tidal cycle, or you could be stuck for a week

Map not for navigation. Unmarked hazards may exist

N

Chart, approx 17 34.345S 139 45.398E

Chart, approx 17 34.591S 139 47.652E

Chart, approxx 17 38.643S 139 56.449E

KILOMETRES 0 5

METRES 0 5000

Wharf campsites

20 21 22 23 24 25 26

Deans Creek campsites

Camps 27, 28, 29 have boat landings

BEWARE CROCODILES

holes

1

rocks

Landsborough Channel joins Albert and Leichardt Rivers. Navigable at most tides

10

Gore Point

9

Rockbar at low tide 3

2

Leichardt River

Albert River

Disaster Inlet

Wharf campsites

jetty

Dean's Creek campsites

2

4

Bottle Heap campsites

Saltwater Arm channel generally clear of hazards, but watch for submerged trees

Saltwater Arm

Horseshoe Island

Douglas Island

Margaret Island

Albinia Island

Allen Island

Sweers Island

Investigator Road

Betinck Island

reef

Sweers Island Resort

Sweers Island

N

KILOMETRES

METRES

Trophy barra, mud crabs and more

Karumba is the gateway to western Cape York's remote barramundi rivers, home to huge barramundi and a popular grunter fishery. Blue and threadfin salmon and mud crabs are seasonally abundant, depending mainly on wet season rainfall.

A good wet season supercharges the fishing. Floods bring great fishing and crabbing to the lower Gulf of Carpentaria, and the local commercial prawn catch also benefits.

The gulf port of Karumba, 72km by sealed road from Normanton, has two boat ramps and a van park. The lower Norman River is not netted.

Jewfish can be caught off the beach at Karumba Point. A small army of visitors chase grunter in the dry season, with the season usually ending in September. Mackerel are found offshore in winter.

Offshore structure is hard to find, but if you do find some bumps you will catch golden snapper and jewfish. Big jewfish and snapper are best around Karumba in October/September.

A popular overnight trip from Karumba is the 48km journey to the anchorage in the Smithburne River. Travel between the mainland and Pelican Island at high tide. Grunter and salmon are caught out front, with jewfish in the hole at the mouth, and mixed species in the river.

Normanton: Access to the Norman River is via a concrete ramp, serviceable by 2WD most of the year. Very low tides can be a problem when launching and retrieving large boats. Rockbars start about 2km upstream from the bridge and continue to Glenore Crossing about 65km further up. Downstream from the town there are several rockbars for about 10km, then several mud and sandbars. Tidal water extends up to the weir at Glenore, with freshwater above the weir. Fishing is allowed at the weir with permission from the council, but no boats are permitted.

Fishermen stand a good chance of catching barramundi by trolling the rocky tidal stretches with a shallow lure, or livebaiting in front of the many creek and gutter mouths.

The ***Baffle Group*** of islands within the Norman River is great for variety. Fishing the sandbars and creek mouths turns up barra, salmon and queenfish. Landbased fishing is available within walking distance of the town or upstream via tracks off the old Croydon Road. Watch for crocs.

Not far over the Norman River bridge is a lagoon, where locals catch livebait using cast nets. This spot is good for flicking a lure in the run-off period. Near Normanton the upstream reaches of Walker's Creek and the Gilbert River to the north of Normanton are reasonable freshwater spots, but there are no boat ramps.

Walker's Creek is easily accessible as the crossing is on the sealed road between Normanton and Karumba. There is limited access to the Leichardt, Flinders and Bynoe Rivers on the Normanton Burketown Road. These and other waterways can be reached by sea along the coast and are worth fishing.

Gulf rivers are shallow and constantly changing. They should be navigated on an upper rising tide. Coastal mudflats often extend far to sea and pose a long-term stranding threat on a diminishing tidal cycle.

Plan your trips for high water.

Map not for navigation. Unmarked hazards may exist.

17 35.585S 140 35.476E approx, Chart

17 35.585S 140 35.476E approx, Chart

17 38.619S 140 27.508E Chart, approx

KILOMETRES 0 5
METRES 0 5000

Spring Creek

Flinders River

The Tides

The lower Gulf region has one tide a day punctuated by a double-tide period about every 14 days, which lasts 2-5 days. During the double tide, the water tends to clear. During the one-tide-a-day cycle the variation is usually high tides of 2m-4m to low tides of .5m-1.5m. The double tide variation is a maximum of 1m, with a low of usually less than .5m. Strong winds pushing water up or down the Gulf will affect tide heights and times. The southern Gulf coastline is difficult in northerly winds. Avoid the shallow river mouths in bad weather, and the extensive coastal mudflat. For Normanton tide times, add about six hours to Karumba times.

Karumba Channel at low tide

Passage north at half tide
queenfish, mackerel, trevally
grunter along channel edges
barra on rising tide
Passage north at full tide
Karumba
salmon along mangrove edges at high tide
trolling
INSET MAP A

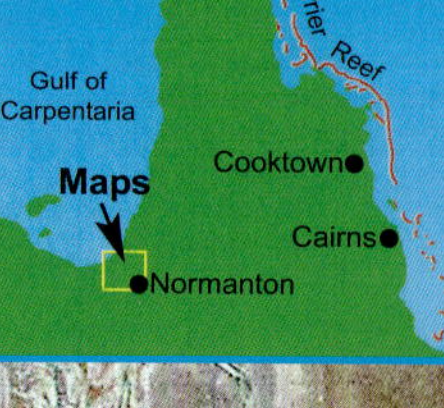

Hotspots

1. Channel markers hold golden snapper, grunter and jewfish. Spanish mackerel on furthest markers. Lumps are hard to find close to Karumba - an artificial reef would do well.
2. Troll channel edges for barramundi. Grunter and salmon on bait.
3. Mangrove edges holds loads of blue salmon near high tide. Mangroves yield most estuary fish on bait and lures.
4. Many big barra are taken by trolling along the town bank from the mouth downstream.
5. Jewfish in deep holes throughout river.
6. Good fishing for salmon, bream, barra and grunter around Baffle Islands.
7. Good fishing at bankside rocks.
8. The old bridge is a fishing platform, fish at night for barra. Jigging around the pylons is effective. Salmon and other estuary fish also present. Also try the town wharf. The floodplains on the north side of the bridge (The Corduroy) have barra in the Wet and can be caught casting from the road. During the wet season try any local flooded causeways/culverts.
9. Extensive lagoon area is useful for collecting baitfish.
10. Tidal water extends up to Glenore Crossing weir (just upstream off map). Only landbased fishing is permitted at the weir, which fishes well for barramundi after flooding.
11. Barramundi on Flinders and Bynoe River causeways on Savannah Way during flooding. Head west from Normanton toward Burketown for 30km. There is also a 4WD track going north between Bynoe and Little Bynoe causeways to the junction of the rivers. This is a good fishing area near high tide, but drains at low tide.
12. Upper Flinders River at Walkers Bend on Burke Development Rd. Barra best immediately after wet season.

Key to Map

Launch sites

1. Karumba, Gilbert St, off Yappar St, in Karumba township.
2. Karumba Point Boat Ramp - Palmer St, toilets.
3. Normanton public boat ramp, Landsborough St, most tides.
4. Walkers Bend - small boats off the causeway into Flinders River.

Karumba tides have up to about 4.9m movement.

Wrecks

Three wrecks are marked on charts wide of Karumba. The nearest is approx 17 17.925S 140 21.045E, 52km n-w of Norman River mouth. The next is approx 16 56.924S 140 17.117E, 81km n-w of river mouth. The third is approx 16 48.598S 140 51.647E, 74km north of river mouth.

Home of Prawns

The northern prawn trawl fishery works the coastal waters of the Gulf of Carpentaria. The fishery was proven up in the 1960s, after concentrations of prawns were found in depressions in the seabed offshore from Smithburne River. Several species of prawn are now harvested. White banana prawns form huge schools that can be located by plane. They are mainly caught during the day on the east side of the Gulf, with the highest catches taken offshore from mangrove forests, which are the nursery ground for juvenile banana prawns. Brown and grooved tiger prawns are taken mostly from the southern and western Gulf, and off Arnhem Land. Tiger prawns are found on seagrass beds, which serve as their nursery habitat. Two species of endeavour prawns are by-catch when trawling for tiger prawns. Other by-catch includes scampi, squid, bugs and scallops, as well as finfish, sharks and rays. The fishery has two seasons: a banana prawn season from April 1 to June 15, and a tiger prawn season, from August 1 to November 30. Catch rates are monitored and the season length is adjusted if required. Prawn catches peaked in the 1970s and underwent a decline in the 1990s from overfishing. Management has since improved but only the white banana prawn catch has proved resilient, the total catch of this species remaining steady or even increasing slightly, fluctuating with rainfall. Catches of other species stabilised around 1990s lows and have not markedly increased.

Impact on fishing

It is perhaps lucky the white banana prawn has recovered from overfishing, as its juvenile life among mangroves means it is a key food for the estuary fish recreational fishermen target. One can only speculate how the life cycles of all commercial prawn species affect Gulf fish and fishing. Some fish likely follow prawn schools at certain times of the year. Also, an abundance of young prawns can make estuary fish harder to catch as they gorge on the easy feed. Threadfin salmon can be fixated on juvenile prawns. Annual rain has been a predictor of the banana prawn catch, and rainfall also affects overall fishing quality in northern Australia. The phrase “a drought on land means a drought at sea” has proved true.

Smithburne River

It was an area outside the Smithburne River that yielded the first significant trawl that established the Gulf prawn fishery in the 1960s, a clue to the productive fishery that exists in this area. The Smithburne produces barramundi, grunter, cod, threadfin and blue salmon, with occasional jewfish. Queenfish and trevally also show up. Big tides get the fish biting. Drop livebaits into low-tide holes, and when the water clears, try trolling and casting lures. For barramundi, fish mud drains in rivers on the runout tide. Mullet strips fished in deeper areas will pick up grunter, but also attract catfish, rays and sharks. A large mudflat extends from shore at low tide, take care to avoid stranding. Take plenty of fuel and drinking water in this remote area.

Key to Map

Hotspots

1. Grunter on channel edges out from mouth. Salmon and barramundi tend to work the flats edge on the outer south side. Also queenfish and trevally.
2. Barramundi at creek mouth on north bank.
3. Barramundi inside first bend on south bank.
4. Barramundi at second creek mouth on north bank, and also just upstream of bend.
5. Mud crabs throughout.
6. Fish along both channel edges. Salmon, queenfish, trevally, barramundi.
7. Barramundi, salmon before first bend on north bank.
8. Barramundi, salmon at first creek mouth and mud drains on north bank.
9. Troll this bank.
10. Fish the drains on outgoing tide for barra. Mud crabs throughout.
11. Most species, especially blue salmon, along mangrove edge at or near high tide.
12. Grunter along channel edges.
13. Most species in deep area inside mouth.
14. These small creeks are worth a look at high tide - salmon, barramundi, mud crabs.

Launch sites

Nearest boat ramp is at Karumba, which has two public boat ramps, useable most tides. Beware the vast low-tide flat along coast as it is possible to be stuck for days if stranded on a descending tide cycle.

Weipa Camping Ground

Where The Bush Meets The Beach

Beachfront | Grassed Sites | Swimming Pool | Sunsets
Self Contained Cabins | Souvenirs | Ice | Local Tours
Barramunchies Takeaway | Helicopter Flights

* 13 acres of lush green lawns abounding in shady trees on the shores of beautiful Western Cape with plenty of shady grassed sites, both powered and unpowered.

* Accommodation ranges from beachfront self-contained villas to budget accommodation. All the accommodation includes linen, towels, air conditioning and tea & coffee making facilities. The self-contained cabins have kitchenettes and private ensuites and the beachfront villas include all of the above plus a washing machine, dryer and beach views.

* Cool off and relax in the large saltwater swimming pool or see the office for souvenirs, bait, ice, maps, cold drinks and ice creams or ask our friendly staff about the popular Helicopter flights, Fishing charters, Local tours and Barramunchies Takeaway.

* The Weipa Fishing Lodge offers 5 individual ensuited rooms and has stunning views. Accommodating 15 people at any one time and has features such as LCD TVs in all rooms, laundry facilities, function facilities and a private chef on request.

P: 07 4069 7871 | **E:** reception@campweipa.com.au
Lot 172, Kerr Point Road | PO Box 652, Weipa QLD 4874
www.campweipa.com.au

Weipa Camping Ground | #weipacampingground

Helicopter Flights

SCENIC FLIGHTS
HELI - FISHING & MORE

HEARTLAND HELICOPTERS

Bookings and Enquiries - Weipa Camping Ground Reception

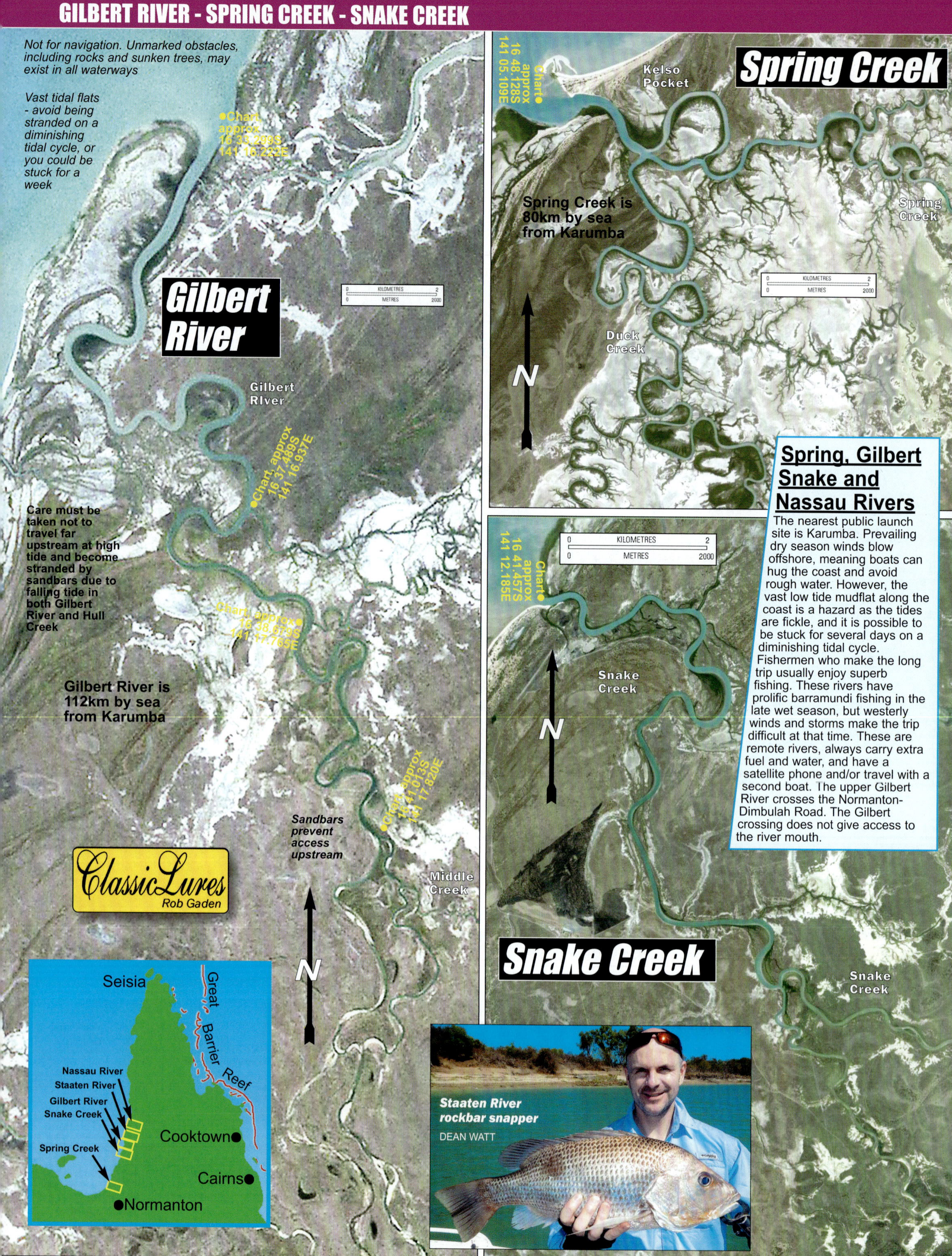
Not for navigation. Unmarked obstacles, including rocks and sunken trees, may exist in all waterways
Vast tidal flats - avoid being stranded on a diminishing tidal cycle, or you could be stuck for a week
●Chart, approx 16 33.299S 141 16.222E
Gilbert River
KILOMETRES 0 2
METRES 0 2000
Gilbert River
●Chart, approx 16 37.489S 141 16.837E
Care must be taken not to travel far upstream at high tide and become stranded by sandbars due to falling tide in both Gilbert River and Hull Creek
Chart, approx 16 38.679S 141 17.765E
Gilbert River is 112km by sea from Karumba
●Chart, approx 16 41.013S 141 17.820E
Sandbars prevent access upstream
Middle Creek
N
ClassicLures
Rob Gaden
Seisia
Great Barrier Reef
Nassau River
Staaten River
Gilbert River
Snake Creek
Spring Creek
Cooktown
Cairns
Normanton
Spring Creek
Chart● approx 16 48.128S 141 05.109E
Kelso Pocket
Spring Creek is 80km by sea from Karumba
Spring Creek
KILOMETRES 0 2
METRES 0 2000
Duck Creek
N
Spring, Gilbert Snake and Nassau Rivers
The nearest public launch site is Karumba. Prevailing dry season winds blow offshore, meaning boats can hug the coast and avoid rough water. However, the vast low tide mudflat along the coast is a hazard as the tides are fickle, and it is possible to be stuck for several days on a diminishing tidal cycle. Fishermen who make the long trip usually enjoy superb fishing. These rivers have prolific barramundi fishing in the late wet season, but westerly winds and storms make the trip difficult at that time. These are remote rivers, always carry extra fuel and water, and have a satellite phone and/or travel with a second boat. The upper Gilbert River crosses the Normanton-Dimbulah Road. The Gilbert crossing does not give access to the river mouth.
KILOMETRES 0 2
METRES 0 2000
Chart● approx 16 41.457S 141 12.185E
Snake Creek
N
Snake Creek
Snake Creek
Staaten River rockbar snapper
DEAN WATT

Nassau River

Old landing piles in water

Oxbow Creek

Nassau River is 185km by sea from Karumba

N

Chart, approx 15 54.452S 141 23.256E

Killarney Creek

Station Creek navigable to about 5km upstream near: rocks prevent further access

Station Creek

Hotspots

1 & 2. High-tide flats fishing for barra, threadfin and blue salmon when calm.
3. Front Rocks Rockbar - large barra, threadfin and golden snapper.
4. Weedy rocky bottom here has golden snapper.
5. Crabbers Camp Rockbar - barra, golden snapper.
6. Pete's Rockbar - barra, threadfin and blue salmon.
7. The Nest - gravelly lumps, cast or troll for big barra.
8. One Tree - rocky bottom, barra, threadfin, jacks.
9. Watty's Rocks - rocky bottom has barra, threadfin.
10. Blow Hole - deep edge on north bank - large barra.
11. Vanrook Creek - fish the many snags for barra.
12. Inkerman Creek - fish the many snags for barra.
13. 'Snaggy Island' - barra.
14. Large snags hold barra.
15. Fish eddies for barra.
16. Billabongs hold saratoga and barramundi.

Launch sites

1. Private ramp for campers. This is the nearest launch site to many western cape rivers.

Staaten River barramundi
DEAN WATT

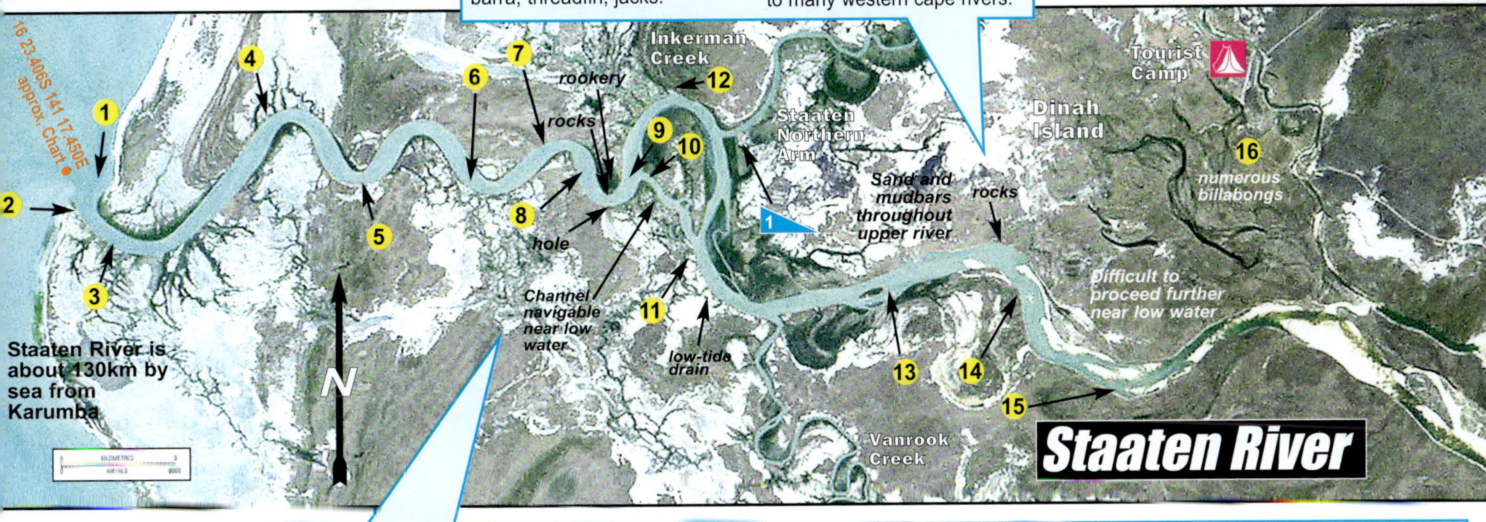

Staaten River

The river can be navigated 17km upstream until sand and rockbars prevent further access. The river branches 11km up from the mouth, rejoining 25km upstream, forming the 5200ha Dinah Island, a grazing lease. The Staaten has a large floodplain catchment. The lower river has a reasonably small tidal variation which, combined with its sandy bottom, gives good water clarity, great for lure and fly fishing. Dinah Island has billabongs with saratoga and barra. **Trolling:** A large portion of time should be spent deep trolling this river for potentially multiple captures of metre barra. Neap tides are best, with the smallest tide and the following two days the best producers. However, fish will show on rockbars throughout the tide cycle. Going from one rockbar to the next is the key, until you find feeding fish. The presence of baitfish and swarms of prawns are a good indicator. **The Nest** and **Front Rocks** are the pick of the bunch. Troll the treeless bank at The Nest to locate the fish among the large gravel lumps. Use deep-diving lures. **Pete's Bar** is a huge area of rock nearly spanning the river, just below **The Nest**. Barra and threadfin will hide among the jagged rock, although rarely schooling up. It is a matter of picking them off one at a time over this large area. Troll against the tide to help avoid loosing gear. Classic Barra 20+ and Halco Scorpion 5m and 8m are a good choice of lure. Keep the troll speed slow, making sure your lure is as far back as you dare and bumping along the bottom. Work the lure with jerks of the rod tip. For soft plastics in these areas go for large models dragged along the bottom where the fish are holding. **Casting:** There are many snags, drains and eddies to lob lures at. Target these features during larger tides when the bait is more concentrated. Fishing the flats at the river mouth over the high tide can be good sport in the clear water. Getting a lure into the mangrove gaps also scores fish. The run-out tide is the time to target snags, drains and eddies. There are plenty of snaggy feeder creeks to explore with either Inkerman Creek or Vanrook Creek a good place to start on your way upstream. Medium hardbody lures can be worked through structure. During a run-in tide it is worth slowly working high up Vanrook Creek. This area is great for snag bashing, and the sandbars create eddies that hold fish. Any pockets of slack water are worth a few casts and you soon recognise likely spots after a few hookups. Plot a track with your GPS unit on the way up, as there are stumps and shallow water. Watch the tide so you don't spend a day on a sandbar.

Dinah Island

The island's billabongs are usually well stocked with saratoga and barra, depending on the previous wet season. Weedless plastics, large spinnerbaits or fly all work well. The billabongs fire at first and last light. Most can be fished from land, keeping in mind crocodiles. Saratoga over 70cm are common and metre-plus barra are landed each year. The biggest billabongs have been given names - **Picnic, Plane 1 & 2, Pump and Eastern Billabongs** hold year round populations of fish. The billabongs also hold cherabin and the **Lodge Billabong** has redclaw. The causeway that gives access to the island is another option early in the year when there is plenty of flow from tide or freshwater run-off. From March through to about July you should always be able to rustle up quality barra. When the area reverts to tidal saltwater the best time is at the change of high tide. Tides are hard to predict at the causeway so its a matter of observing and planning. Concentrate fishing on the upstream side.

Seasons

The best times are April-June, and Oct-Nov, when the water temperatures are high and the big barra are aggressive. The fish can still be tempted in the cooler months. I only had one week out of a season when we struggled to find fish because of a cold snap. The billabongs fish well throughout the year. If the wind is favourable late in the season, it is worth throwing the swag in the boat and shooting 60km up the coast for an overnighter at Nassau River. This river is littered with rockbars and snags, chockers with barra and golden snapper that have never seen a lure.

Getting There

From Cairns it is a 700km drive east. From Karumba, by sea, it is 130km.

By former Staaten River fishing guide DEAN WATT

Staaten River barramundi

DEAN WATT PIC

Chart approx 15 03.676S 141 38.460E

See next page for Coleman River camping details

Malaman Creek

The Breakthrough

Coleman River

North Arm

Mitchell River

Chart approx 15 11.726S 141 35.081E

Map not for navigation. Unmarked hazards may exist on all maps

N

Bull Crossing and Wonya Creek camps

Boats can be moored next to camp sites

Bull Crossing

Mitchell River

Surprise Creek

Shelfo Camp just of map

No fishing South Mitchell River

South Mitchell River

Kilpatrick Creek

The South Mitchell River and waterways joining it are closed to fishing to where it joins Surprise Creek

15 29.749S 141 28.722E approx, Chart

Topsy Camp

Topsy Creek

Magnificent Creek

Kowanyama

Kowanyama

The Mitchell River catchment begins near Cairns, running to sea 268km north of Karumba through its own channel and side channels to the South Mitchell and Coleman River. The fishing potential is huge, with barramundi, grunter, salmon, jewfish and mud crabs the main catch. Kowanyama provides permits for four bush camping areas, available from June 1 to the end of the Gulf barra season. Each area has four sites, each taking up to three vehicles. All camps need 4WD. Fishing is not allowed in the South Mitchell.

1. Topsy Creek: tidal, good fishing, crabbing. Boats can be moored next to camps.

2. Shelfo Crossing (off map): on the Mitchell freshwater.

3. Bulls Crossing: shallow access to Mitchell River.

4. Surprise/Wonya Creek: top of the tidal reach on a branch of the Mitchell River. Also gives access to Wonya/Surprise Creeks. Boats can be moored next to camps.

Camp bookings are essential. Bookings open February 1. Dogs, hunting and alcohol not permitted. Book at www.kowcamp.com. For more information phone 07 4060 5224, fax 07 4060 5226. Fuel and groceries are at Kowanyama store, open Monday-Fridays 8.30-4pm and on Saturdays until 11am. There is a post office and EFTPOS. For camping on **Coleman River**, with access by boat to the Mitchell River via North Arm, see Pormpuraaw on the next page.

CHAPMAN RIVER - MUNGKAN CREEK - EDWARD RIVER - HOLROYD RIVER - KENDALL RIVER
Balurga Creek
Edward River
Wreck marked on nautical chart 14 45.438S 141 31.999E, 444km from Edward River
14 46.323S 141 34.162E approx, Chart
Mitchell River freshwater crossing at Dunbar ... fishing is best after flooding
NIC WILSON
Holroyd River
EVAN KRALL
Kendall River freshwater
Mouth approx 14 10.020S 141 35.711E
Kendall River
Kendall River
Kuchendoopen Outstation
Jardine River
Crystal Creek
Cotterell River
Doughboy River
MacDonald River
Jackson River
Skardon River
Wenlock & Ducie River
Pennefather River
Archer, Watson & Ward Rivers
Kendall & Holroyd Rivers
Edward River & Chapman Rivers
Mitchell and Coleman Rivers
Seisia
Weipa
Aurukun
Love & Kirke Rivers
Pormpuraaw
Kowanyama
Cooktown
Cairns
Great Barrier Reef
Kendall River
The Kendall and Holroyd Rivers open into a single mouth. There is a private hunting and fishing tourist operation between the two rivers that is not associated with the Pormpuraaw Shire Council camps. The Holroyd has some floodplain that provides run-off fishing after prolonged rain.
N
Holroyd River
Holroyd River
Mungkan River
Chart approx 14 51.167S 141 35.146E
N
Shoal marked on nautical chart 14 58.942S 141 28.570E, 17km from Pormpuraaw
Pormpuraaw
22km to Coleman River mouth, 33km to Mitchell River mouth
Chart approx 14 54.242S 141 36.238E
Pormpuraaw
Chapman River
Pormpuraaw
This Aboriginal community, 70km as the crow flies north of Kowanyama, offers bush camps on tidal water. The sites are:
Chapman River - toilets and showers, town water, shady trees, concrete boat ramp - 2km south of town, one site with a maximum six vehicles.
Mungkan River - toilets and showers, bore water, shady trees, shell boat ramp - 7km north of town, one site with a maximum six vehicles.
Coleman River - bush toilets, pump at waterhole 3km from camp sites, limited shade 40km south of town, eight sites with a maximum four vehicles each.
The Coleman River camps have a launch site that gives access to the Mitchell River by water via The Breakthrough and North Arm. The Chapman River has a sealed ramp, while Mungkan River has firm sand.
Camping bookings open February 1, with camping starting May 1. The camping season closes with the barra season. Maximum four vehicles per site. A maximum of 25 people is allowed at the beach camps. Phone (07) 4060 4155 for bookings or email ranger@pormpuraaw.qld.gov.au. Strict alcohol regulations apply. There is a store, fuel outlet, post office, bank and police station within 1km of the beach camps. All campsites require 4WD and campers may not enter until roads are sufficiently dry. The Chapman River offers good crabbing, with the first high bank in from the mouth worth trolling for barra and jacks. Mungkan River has barra, salmon, grunter and mud crabs. North of Pormpuraaw the Edward River has good fishing - try along the cliffs on the north bank about 1km up from the mouth.

Seisia
Great Barrier Reef
Next Page
Weipa
Aurukun
Maps
Kowanyama
Cooktown
Cairns

N

KILOMETRES 0 2
METRES 0 2000

Kirke River

shallow and drying areas ... explore on an incoming tide

pontoon
mudflat
barra and salmon
mudflat
Kirke River
13 54.561S 141 28.120E mouth approx
Cape Keerweer
Shifting flats at mouth

Maps not for navigation

Unmarked hazards may exist

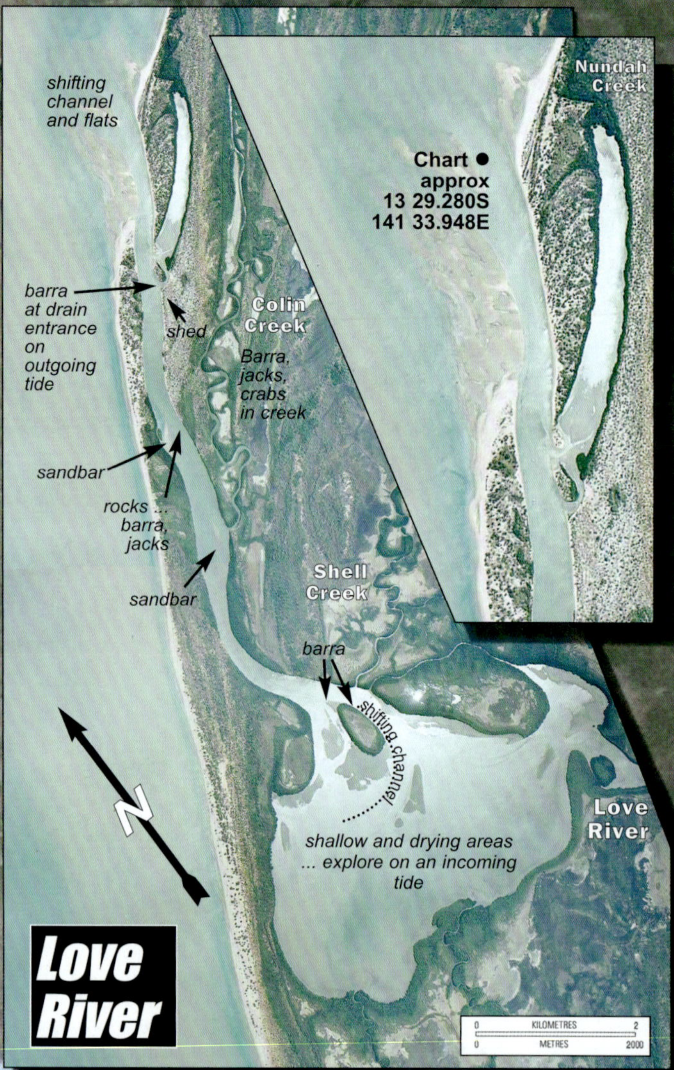

shifting channel and flats
Nundah Creek
Chart approx 13 29.280S 141 33.948E
barra at drain entrance on outgoing tide
shed
Colin Creek
Barra, jacks, crabs in creek
sandbar
rocks ... barra, jacks
sandbar
Shell Creek
barra
shifting channel
N
shallow and drying areas ... explore on an incoming tide
Love River

Love River

KILOMETRES 0 2
METRES 0 2000

Kirke River

This is one of the more unusual waterways on Cape York Peninsula. The Kirke, and nearby Love River, are probably among the least visited barramundi fishing spots in Australia. Both rivers are reached by sea, as land access is restricted by geography (swamps) and land tenure. Weipa is 90km north of the Love River mouth, and 100km north of the Kirke. These distances can only be covered by adequately prepared trailer boats. In the dry season boaters can avoid most chop from easterly or south-easterly winds by hugging the coast, keeping in mind the extensive low-tide mudflat and shallows. Enough fuel must be carried to allow for the sea journey and exploration within the rivers. The lower section of Love River is much the same as other rivers on the western side of the peninsula, being sandy at the mouth.

There is a small rock outcrop on the Love River's east side where good fishing can be had, with barra, jacks and even jewfish on lures. Travelling up from the mouth, the river opens up into a wide, shallow lake. This lake holds barra, salmon and mullet. It is shallow and should be navigated only near high tide.

Entry to the Kirke River 70km south of the Love is usually fairly straightforward, but the river becomes very shallow in the upper reaches. The upper river opens into a lake similar to the Love River, but much larger. The fertility of this lake and wetland is probably what produces the big barra the river is known for. Baitfish thrive. The narrow river channel leading into the lake concentrates the fish and is a good place to fish.

Aurukun

This Aboriginal community is at the mutual mouth of three large river systems, the Archer River to the south, the Watson River to the east and the Ward River to the north. The estuary is wide and shallow, with much of it drying near low water. The region is dotted with small lagoons, most of which vanish in the late dry season. Given that Weipa's publicly accessible estuaries to the north are closed to commercial netting, not many fishermen make the long sea trip to Aurukun. However the vast estuary is enticing and high-quality fishing can be expected. If you wish to enter Aurukun by road and use the town launch site, make an application, including where you want to go, and the number of boats/people, to the Aurukun Shire Council. More information is on the website www.aurukun.qld.gov.au, or phone (07) 4060 6800. Aurukun is strictly alcohol-free. Wuungkam Lodge offers accommodation, phone (07) 4060 6814 or email accommodation@aurukun.qld.gov.au

Key to Map

Hotspots

1. Queenfish, trevally, barracuda off beach.
2. Barra on rising tide. Explore the Archer River channels on a rising tide.
3. No netting in Watson River. Good crabbing.
4. Barra, milkfish. Very shallow. Many crocs.

Launch sites

The nearest public launch site is Weipa, 110km by sea. **For Archer River tides, use Weipa tides times plus 20 minutes. Local tides have up to about 2.12m movement.**

Weipa FADs and billfish

FADs were deployed wide of Albatross Bay in 2015. They proved to be a success, with sailfish, black marlin, mahi mahi and tripletail caught. **FADs are known to move position**, so check the marks with Qld Fisheries online before fishing. The FADs are marked with yellow buoys as shown.

FAD G1: Weipa 12 58.959S 141 17.009E, 67km from Weipa, 30m
FAD G2: Weipa 12 54.711S 141 22.625E, 54km from Weipa, 30m
FAD G3: Weipa 12 48.671S 141 23.665E, 46km from Weipa, 30m
FAD G4: Weipa 12 49.903S 141 32.594E, 33km from Weipa, 21m

Weipa Fishing Classic

The Weipa Fishing Classic is held mid-year attracting 1000+ competitors. For more information visit www.weipafishingclassic.com

Launch sites

1. Evans Landing - all-tide concrete ramp with boat-washing facilities and pontoon.
2. Rocky Point - need at least one metre of tide to launch here. Veer to south-west around shallow mudbank when tide is low. Boat-washing facilities.
3. Mission Bridge (south-western side) - beach launching off firm sand. Best when tide is below 1.9m.
4. Andoom Creek (north-western side of bridge) - bauxite ramp on creek bank, steep but firm. Good on all tides, no washing facilities.
5. Betridges Landing (Pine River) - firm, but can become washed out. Best on mid to high tide.

Local tides have up to about 2.68m movement.

Weipa GPS marks

9-Mile Reef 12 57.502S 141 26.624E
Mostly mackerel, queenfish and tuna
Tuskie 12 27.415S 141 35.775E
Tuskfish, barcheek trout, flag.
Westminster Reef 12 43.280S 141 44.001E
Queenfish, trevally, mackerel, tuna.
Fairway Lead 12 41.861S 141 41.353E
Mixed species, beware ships.
Three-Mile A 12 58.034S 141 29.385E
Three-Mile B 12 57.171S 141 28.035E
Mack Attack 12 57.488S 141 26.608E
Spanish mackerel, tuna.

Camping and grog

Alcohol is not permitted in much of this area on Napranum land. Mapoon land has fewer alcohol restrictions. Be sure to know the rules for each place you visit as heavy fines apply.

Key to Map

1. Wallaby Island: barramundi, cod, jacks around rocks on rising tide. grunter on rubble further out.
2. Kerr Point: shallow rocky reef good trolling for cod, golden snapper, golden trevally.
3. Gonbung Point: fish off the shore on run-in tide for grunter, best at the end of the wet season. In a boat, find the edge of the channel for grunter, jewfish on top of tide. Big jewfish, grunter and queenfish off the Evans Landing wharf, best April to July.
4. Deep water area: best at night on moving tide for tarpon, queenfish, golden snapper and jew. Accessible only by boat. Port authority security zones apply around shipping wharves.
5. Grandma's Creek: barra, salmon at mouth, low tide.
6. Roberts Creek: barramundi, jacks and cod in the upper reaches along the mangroves.
7. Urquhart Point: fish rocks for barramundi, jacks, queenfish and trevally. Queenfish, trevally, giant herring, longtail tuna and mackerel in the channel.
8. Wooldrum (Triluck) Creek: queenfish and golden trevally at mouth, barra, jacks, cod along rocky edges.
9. Shipping channel leads: the channel marker posts hold trevally, golden snapper, tripletail and queenfish, while bait schools in the channel attract mackerel, tuna and cobia. Big jew at night on low tide on outer posts.
10. Andoomajettie Point: rocks hold barramundi, golden snapper, jacks, cod, coral trout and threadfin salmon. Cast to the shallow rocks, troll quietly over deeper areas.
11. Andoom Creek: can be fished from shore near road bridge and at Red Beach. Barra, grunter, salmon and queenfish. Sheltered boat ramp on northern side.
12. Mission River Bridge: good shore fishing from southern end for grunter, golden snapper, salmon and barra on ebb tide. North-eastern point good for barramundi on run-in tide. Fish holes under bridge for jewfish, grunter and more.
13. The "Y" - fish the deep hole (in the middle of the river) golden snapper, blue salmon, cod and queenfish.
14. Shellgrit bank: grunter and queenfish in the channel, barra, salmon at the gutter mouths on ebb tide.
15. First rockbar (keep to north bank to avoid it): troll here for barra, golden snapper, cod and golden trevally.
16. Second rockbar (keep to northern bank to avoid it): fish holes for golden snapper, cod and bream.
17. Hey Point: troll for queenfish, barracuda, cod, trevally.
18. Lower Hey River: Fish the gutters and creek mouths for barramundi, king salmon and queenfish.
19. Rocks - beware! Golden trevally, queenfish, salmon.
20. Upper Hey: creeks fish well for barramundi, jacks, golden snapper, grunter and blue salmon.
21. Westminster: shallow rocks, bommies. Trolling and bottom fishing for most species.
22. Rainforest: shallow rocks and bommies. Good trolling and bottom fishing for golden snapper, cod, coral trout and mackerel.
23. Shallow rocks and bommies, species as for 22.
24. Boyd Point: trolling here for queenfish, trevally, longtail tuna and mackerel.
25. Pera Head: fish the rocky outcrops for trevally, queenfish, cobia, and mackerel. Shallow reef area about 1km south west, dries on low tides - bottom fish here for golden snapper, red emperor, cod and coral trout. Troll for mackerel, queenfish, trevally, cobia and tuna. Big tides best.
26. Thud Point: fish shallow reefs for coral trout, jacks, cod, stripies. Troll for queenfish, trevally, macks.
27. Pine River mouth: hole fishes well at slack water for golden snapper, grunter, cod and queenfish.
28. Crawford Creek: lure-casting and live-baiting for barramundi, jacks, cod and queenfish.
29. Paul's Creek: hard to get into on low tides. Barramundi, jacks, cod and grunter.
30. Duyfken Point: rocks at the end of the wet fish for barramundi. Troll the reef areas for coral trout, golden snapper, cod, mackerel and queenfish.
31. Jantz Point: extensive reef produces golden snapper, coral trout, stripies, cod, mackerel, cobia, trevally, queenfish.
32. Janssen Shoal: deeper reef can fish well for golden snapper, jewfish and grunter.

Tides

Tides in the Weipa area fluctuate about 2.5m on the spring tides, but there is usually only one large tide a day. In summer, the lower low tide happens at night meaning the tide is high all day on most occasions. From April to October, the lower low tide happens in daylight.

Pennefather River

The Pennefather River (see inset map above) was the site of the first recorded European landing in Australia, by Willem Jantz in the *Duyfken* in 1606. Today it is an ideal river for some easy remote area adventure, being a short drive off the Mapoon road, 75km from Weipa. Follow the track to the beach, or follow the sandy track north to the mouth. There is good camping at the river mouth on the south bank, with a sandy beach launch. There is a long rock shelf along the southern bank east of the camp and this is easy to walk along and fish. Keep in mind that large saltwater crocodiles are present in this and other local waterways. Permits can be obtained from Napranum Shire Council (07) 4069 7855 www.napranum.qld.gov.au or Weipa Newsagency (07) 4069 7235. Alcohol is not permitted at all Napranum sites.

Mapoon

This community is 80km north of Weipa. Visitors can camp, fish and launch boats at the impressive mutual mouth of the Wenlock and Ducie Rivers at Cullen Point. Trailerboats can also be launched at Cloughs Landing on the Wenlock. Janie Creek launch is suitable for small boats. Visitor permits are obtained online from Mapoon Aboriginal Corporation at www.mapoon.qld.gov.au, and also at the store. Mapoon has fewer alcohol restrictions than nearby Napranum land sites.

Janie Creek

**This site was closed at publication, check with Mapoon Aboriginal Shire Council before planning a trip.*

This sandy creek has bank launching on the upper tide, with reefs 2km seaward of the mouth. The creek has barra, jacks, cod and salmon. The mouth is shallow, with scattered rocks that are a boating hazard. Shallow reef out front has tuskfish, golden snapper, cod, trevally, queenfish and flag. Big mackerel turn up so float a livebait out. The camp is reached by driving towards Cullen Point and turning left at the sign. Drive south along the beach until you reach the creek.

Cullen Point

Basic camps are available with toilets and showers, with nearby 4WD boat launching. This gives access to the almost 4km-wide river mouth, a huge estuary that produces big barramundi, grunter, salmon and mud crabs. Expect big waves when wind and tide are opposed, with an outgoing tide and northerly wind producing the worst conditions. The sheer scale of fishable water can be bewildering for a newcomer, but typical barramundi tactics of fishing mud drains on outgoing tides, finding bait schools, and livebaiting holes can bring success anywhere in the system. Nemaleta Creek opposite Cullen Point has fish-holding rocks near the mouth, and deep holes on bends upstream. Rock patches throughout produce golden snapper, cod, grunter, jacks and more. Shallow reef outside such as Kerr Reef, 18.5km n-w of Cullen Point, has mostly tuskfish, cod, flag and snapper, with spanish mackerel in the dry season.

Wenlock River

This river begins in the ranges south-west of Portland Roads and flows to sea through the mouth at Mapoon. The freshwater reaches can be accessed at Moreton Telegraph Station Crossing. The freshwater has sooty grunter, catfish, saratoga, sharks and sawfish. About 70km north of Weipa is Stones Crossing and a nearby barrage (both off map), with good barra fishing at times. Check the height before driving across, it is not normally negotiable until late July.

Kerr Reef lies 18.5km north-north-west of Cullen Point at 11 48.673S 141 51.071E

Boating access

*Cloughs Landing is a rough launch site, use on upper tide.
*Batavia Landing has pleasant bush camping next to river.
*Stones Crossing (off map) is 70km from Weipa, east of the Mapoon road, with campsites on the south bank. The turn-off to the crossing is 36km north of Weipa. About 20km after the turn-off is a turn left to the old barrage. About 15km later is the turn-off to the rocky river crossing.

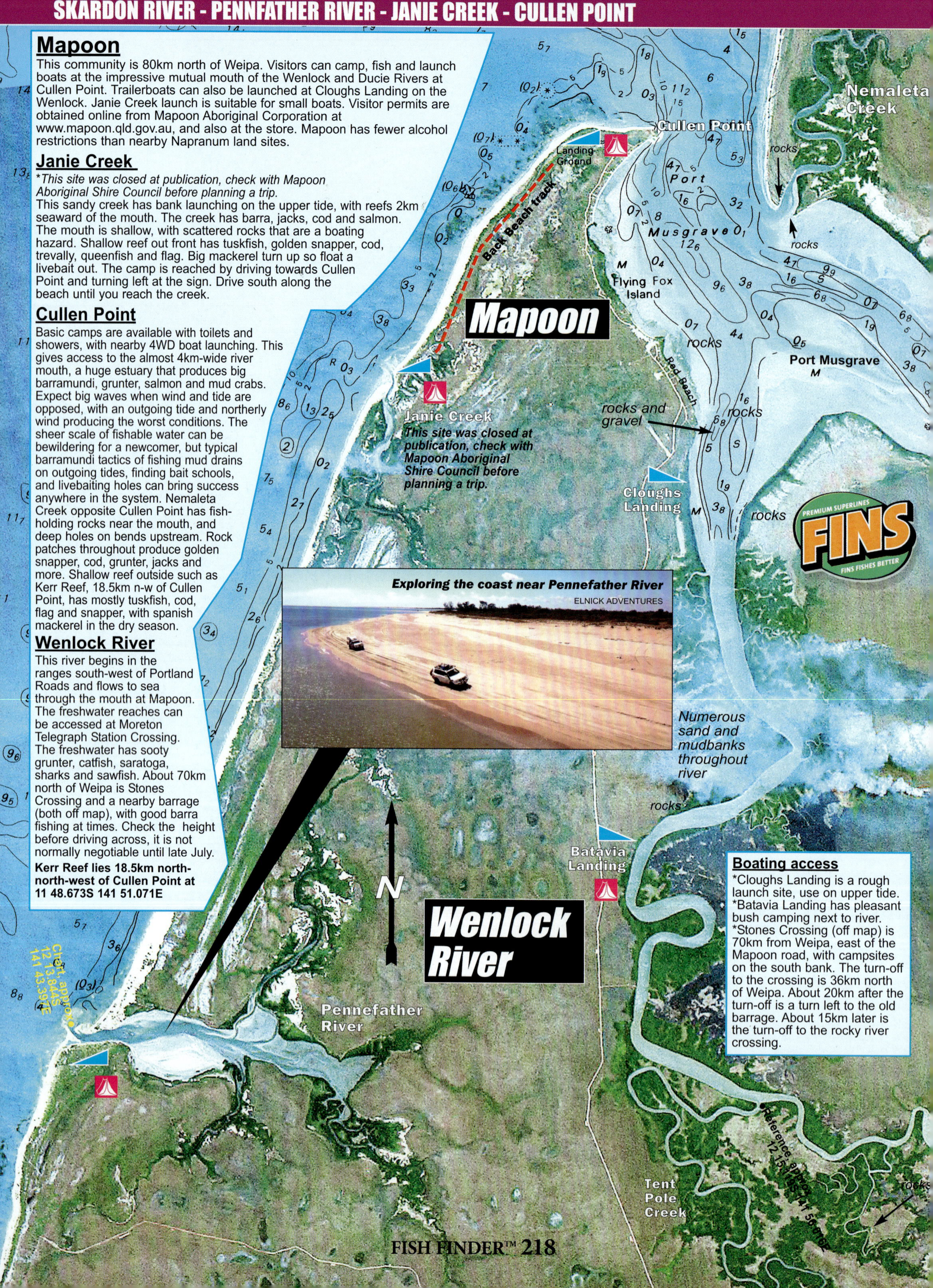

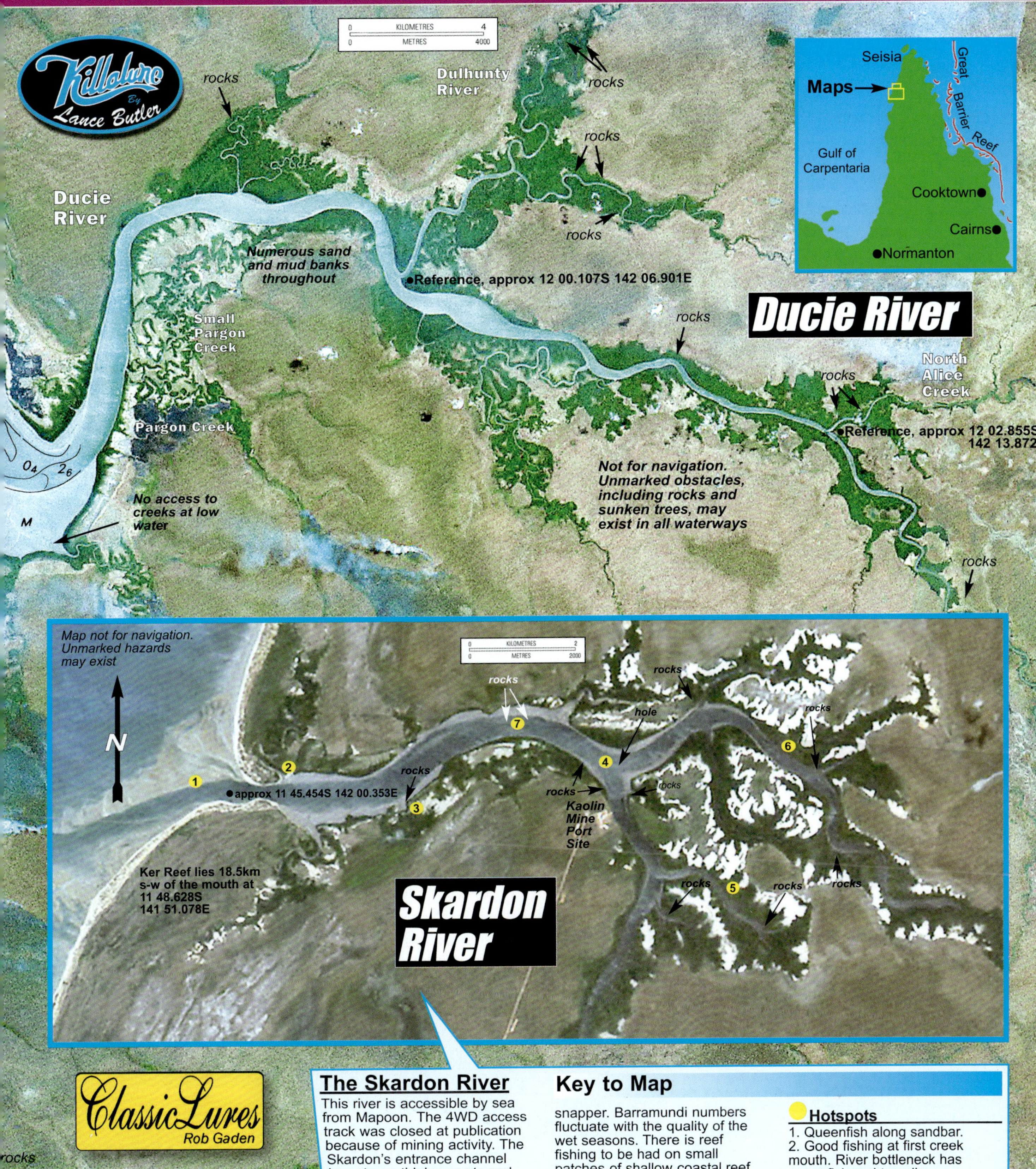

The Skardon River

This river is accessible by sea from Mapoon. The 4WD access track was closed at publication because of mining activity. The Skardon's entrance channel has strong tidal currents and standing waves of 1m+ are not uncommon, so approach during an incoming or still tide. Upstream there are rock patches that are navigation hazards. Rockbars on the north bank rise out of deep water and can catch unwary skippers. Most of the rock patches fish well for jacks, cod and golden snapper. Barramundi numbers fluctuate with the quality of the wet seasons. There is reef fishing to be had on small patches of shallow coastal reef between the Skardon and Jackson Rivers, which is 10km to the north. Kerr Reef is 18km s-w of the Skardon mouth and usually fishes well, especially for dry season mackerel, GPS approx 11 48.673S 141 51.071E. Closer in try 11 48.293S 141 55.421E. Like most north-western cape rivers the Skardon is quite clear, which is good for lure and fly fishing.

Key to Map

Hotspots

1. Queenfish along sandbar.
2. Good fishing at first creek mouth. River bottleneck has queenfish and trevally.
3. Fishing rising tide at rocks for cod, jacks and barra.
4. Deep hole holds jewfish.
5. Barra, crabs in mud drains.
6. Barra, crabs in mud drains.
7. Cod, jacks, snapper.

Launch sites

It is 28km by sea from Mapoon's Cullen Point, and another 10km to the Jackson River. The camping area was closed at publication.

'Number Two' creek mouth

Doughboy River mouth

SEAFARIS

Jackson River

This is a sandy and relatively clear waterway, usually with a reasonable entrance channel. Expect it to chop up on the outgoing tide. The river is home to jacks, giant herring, golden trevally, queenfish, cod and some barramundi. The Jackson has fishable water at low tide but much of the river dries. Low tide holes are worth livebaiting for barramundi but large shovelnose sharks often get to the baits first. Mud crabs are usually easy to find. There is freshwater upstream of the final fork, with saratoga and some barramundi.

Key to Map

Hotspots

1. Queenfish, trevally in bottleneck.
2. Barramundi, jacks in first creek.
3. Queenfish, barra, trevally, giant herring, cod near large rock.
4. Barra in channel near outflowing creeklet at low tide.
5. Barra along deep banks.
6. Barra and jacks.
7 and 7. Barra, cod and jacks around high tide, mud crabs.

Launch sites

Nearest launch sites are Mapoon (35km) or Weipa (150km). The Cotterell River is 70km by boat from Mapoon's Cullen Point, The Doughboy is 60km, the McDonald is 50km, the Jackson is 35km, and the Skardon 25km.

Crystal Creek mouth

McDonald River flats

SEAFARIS

McDonald River

This sandy, relatively clear river has mainly queenfish and golden trevally around the entrance, with tarpon, cod, barra, jacks and mud crabs upstream. Much of the McDonald dries at low tide. Fishing here can be "feast or famine". Plan your trip carefully with the tides and avoid the outgoing tide during westerly winds. The entrance channel changes.

Crystal Creek & No. 2
These relatively short tidal waterways are sandy and clear, with substantial drying flats extending to sea from the mouths. The lower rivers have mainly queenfish, golden trevally, giant herring and salmon, with cod, jacks, barramundi and mud crabs upstream. The river mouths are just 3.6km apart. Like all the north-west Cape waters, these sandy rivers hold many rays, sawfish and shovelnose sharks, and they can often be seen in the shallows. Woody Wallis Island is 30km from the mouth of Number 2, with good reef and pelagic fishing nearby, but the trip should only be attempted in good weather. Crab Island off Slade Point has queenfish, trevally and mackerel. The island is a turtle nursery. Beware large saltwater crocodiles throughout. Avoid the river mouths on an outgoing tide in westerly weather and steer well clear of the coastal flats on a falling tide.
Cotterell & Doughboy Rivers
These are relatively small, shallow waterways. The mouths are best tackled in calm weather. They have mostly jacks, queenfish, giant herring, tarpon and golden trevally, with occasional barramundi, and mud crabs upstream. The water is usually quite clear, well suited to lure fishing.
Key to Map
Hotspots
1. Queenfish, trevally, barracuda along edges. Most estuary fish in deep hole at mouth.
2. Barramundi along west bank.
3. Tarpon, queenfish, golden trevally along edges.
4. Jacks, cod, bream, mud crabs.
Launching
Crystal Creek is about a 55km run from Seisia, or 100km from Mapoon's Cullen Point. Beach access to this coast via the Vrilya Point 4WD track has been closed so entry to these waterways is only by sea. The Cotterell mouth is about 80km by sea from Seisia and 75km from Mapoon. Carry extra fuel to allow for strong currents and bad weather.
Cotterel River mouth
SEAFARIS
Cotterell River
Doughboy River
approx 11 21.838S 142 06.921E
approx 11 27.503S 142 05.247E
hole
rocks
access through creek at high tide
N
KILOMETRES 0 2
METRES 0 2000
Crystal Creek
Also called 'Number 1'
Crystal Creek
Reefs offshore at approx 11 15.014S 142 05.994E and 11 16.011S 142 05.912E
approx 11 05.227S 142 08.997E
approx 11 07.452S 142 09.106E
Map not for navigation. Unmarked hazards may exist on all maps
Hotspots
1. Barra and jacks in deep water near creek mouths.
2. Queenfish and trevally in channel. Cast for flathead and other fish along edges on ricing tide. Small tidal sandy lagoon near camp site has barra and queenfish on early morning and late afternoon high tide. Deep water bait fishing in the channel can yield surprises such as golden snapper and grunter, but large shovelnose and other rays are a problem. Beware crocs.
3. Deep channel edge good for queenfish, trevally, golden snapper.
4. Barra, jacks along deep banks.
5. Hole at junction. Freshwater upstream in Crystal Creek.
Look for baitfish and feeding birds. Cast near feeding rays as predatory fish will loiter nearby to eat scraps.
'Number Two'
KILOMETRES 0 2
METRES 0 2000

Hotspots

1. Quoin Islet: great spot on the runout tide for queenfish, trevally, tuna and mackerel.
2. A brilliant fish producer. Fish the bay from the Captain Cook Monument down. Look for birds feeding over bait. Use chrome lures and poppers for surface action. All pelagic species, best fishing in September to December.
3. Mutee Head south to Jardine: queenfish, trevally along current lines in summer with big mackerel and tuna in winter. Big sharks are abundant at times.
4. Jardine River: live bait holes at mouth for barra, salmon, queenfish.
5. Woody Wallis and Red Wallis Island: giant trevally, queenfish, mackerel, sailfish, coral trout, tuna. The islands offer little protection, so fish in good weather.
6. Crab Island: queenfish, trevally, salmon, mackerel in surrounding waters. A turtle rookery.
7. Crystal Creek (also called Number One) - see previous pages.
8. River Number 2: as for No 7.
9. Vrilya Point access track has been closed, future plans unknown.
10. Seisia jetty and nearby islands: jetty is still one of the great fishing spots on the Cape. Many species caught here, including barra. Sardines can be caught with a cast net or jig in large numbers. Be prepared, with heavy line and a drop gaff. Islets behind Red Island and Parau Island are worth a fish and easily reached from Seisia by boat.
11. Two small creeks hold salmon, barra. Best just before wet season.
12. Jetty holds large school of sardines (herrings). Queenfish, trevally and mackerel.
13. Ledge on north side of Friday Island - sweetlip, tuskfish, trout.
14. Coral trout on lures along reef drop-offs. Mixing currents and steep reefs - take care.
15. At the front of Peak Point locate the deep hole which goes from 10m to 25m deep and extends for about 70m. Golden snapper, sweetlip (best April/May) and mackerel and queenfish. Pressure waves and currents here at times.

Key to Map

Launch sites

1. Seisia jetty ramp, useable most tides.
2. Mutee Head and Jardine River, small boat sand launching, tyre deflation required. Upper tide.
3. Cowal Creek, Injinoo, Ware St.

*** Vrilya Point access was closed at publication.

Local tides have up to about 3.26m movement.

The Tip

Large sections of the road between Laura and Weipa have been sealed, making the notoriously rough Cape York Peninsula road trip a little easier.

Driving to the Tip is now safer and less damaging to vehicles and trailers, but long unsealed sections remain, so be sure your vehicle and trailer are prepared for corrugations. Many tracks off the main road still require 4WD.

This area is run by the Northern Peninsula Area Regional Council (NPARC).

The council operates a vehicular ferry over the Jardine River and sells camping permits that cover land around the Tip, which is good fishing country. Ferry and camping tickets can be bought at the council website www.nparc.qld.gov.au.

The Jardine River Ferry operates between 8am and 12pm and closes for lunch. It reopens from 1pm to 5pm. It runs seven days a week, except for some public holidays. Phone (07) 4090 4100 or (07) 4090 4120 for info or email jardineferry@nparc.qld.gov.au

There is accommodation and/or camping at Loyalty Beach, Punsand Bay, Alau Beach, Seisia and Somerset.

Loyalty Beach has a beachside restaurant, which serves local fish.

Fishermen can fly in to Bamaga and fish with a guide, or hire a boat from Cape York Ice and Tackle or Loyalty Beach.

Note that the once-popular Vrilya Point, which gives access to western coastal creeks, has been publication.

Bamaga: Bamaga is the main centre at the Tip. It is closest to the Jackey Jackey launch site on Fishbone Creek. On the coast, Seisia has a jetty that is a hot fishing spot. Local campgrounds have beachfront sites with fishing nearby. Don't underestimate the local beaches at high tide - livebait can produce golden snapper, queenfish, trevally, blue salmon and more. There are also two tidal creeks east of Punsand Bay.

Seisia: The jetty offers good fishing because it is a structure in a bare sand channel between Red Island and the mainland. The pylons hold schools of herring which attract queenfish, trevally, mackerel and barracuda. Other catches include barra, cod, wolf herring, giant herring and squid. The jetty is popular and can get crowded when the fish are on. Good arrow squid runs happen in the wet season.

Jardine River: The Jardine River mouth is 19km by water from Seisia, or by sandy 4WD track from Mutee Head. This sandy river flows constant freshwater, even late in the dry season. However

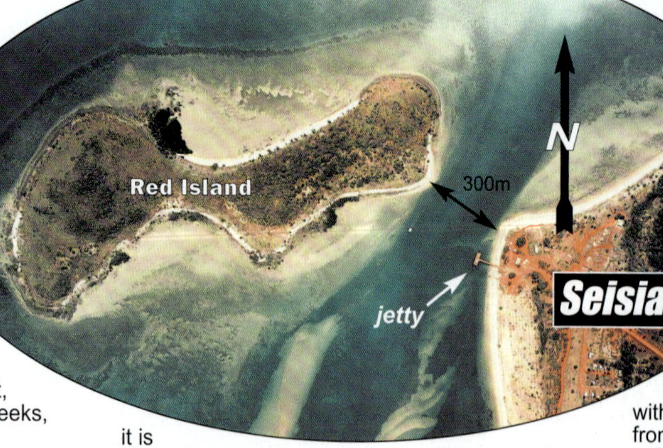

it is shallow and access is only easy at mid-tide up. Barramundi can usually be caught in the lower reaches, with live baiting the deeper holes the best method. There is a good hole at the mouth of the arm to the west of the river mouth. Upstream, the freshwater holds barra, saratoga and sooty grunter. Cast to snags. Barra fishing is best before and after the wet season. In cold weather trevally, queenfish and salmon action in the lower reaches makes up for the slower barra.

Coastal Reefs: There are numerous reefs near Seisia. In calm weather the 37km trip west to Red and Woody Wallis islands is the best offshore option. These rocky outcrops hold mackerel and barracuda, as well as endless shoals of trevally, plus coral trout and emperor. Troll past the rocks, or if it is calm get in close and cast lures. If the wind is blowing it is safer and more comfortable to head the 15km north to Quoin Islet, taking into the account the shallow areas. Expect mackerel, trevally and queenfish. Look for feeding birds.

Torres Strait Islands: The trip across Endeavour Strait should only be made during good weather and on neap tides. Fishermen must have enough time to be able to delay their return trip if the weather turns bad. There are reefs in this area that rise straight up out of deep water, and the pressure-waves caused by currents pushing between the reefs and islands can be eye-opening. Thursday Island is the main centre in the group, with hotels, accommodation and charters. Thursday and Horn Islands have jetties that hold fish, while two small creeks on Horn Island (see map) offer reasonable fishing.

Other Areas: Coastal creeks on the upper western peninsula were once accessible by 4WD track from Vrilya Point. This track has been closed.

To fish the western creeks, the trip by sea from Seisia is about 50km sea trip (one way) to Crystal Creek (also dubbed "Number One") and Number Two. These creeks do not have the same freshwater flow as the Jardine but do produce jacks, blue salmon and queenfish, with some barra. This area is relatively protected from s-e winds, but not westerlies.

The Tip: The northern tip of Australia, Cape York, is reached via the Pajinka road, and a short walk. The former tourist building is in disrepair but the nearby Tip has deep drop-offs and reefs for fishing. Coral trout, trevally and golden snapper are found along the edges. Pelagic fish are often seen feeding just off the rocks and in the channel between Eborac Island.

Somerset: Sandy tracks lead to beaches around Somerset, where cartoppers can be launched. However, the eastern tip's coast is exposed to south-easters. To the south is the Jackey Jackey and Escape River system, arguably the best fishing area near The Tip.

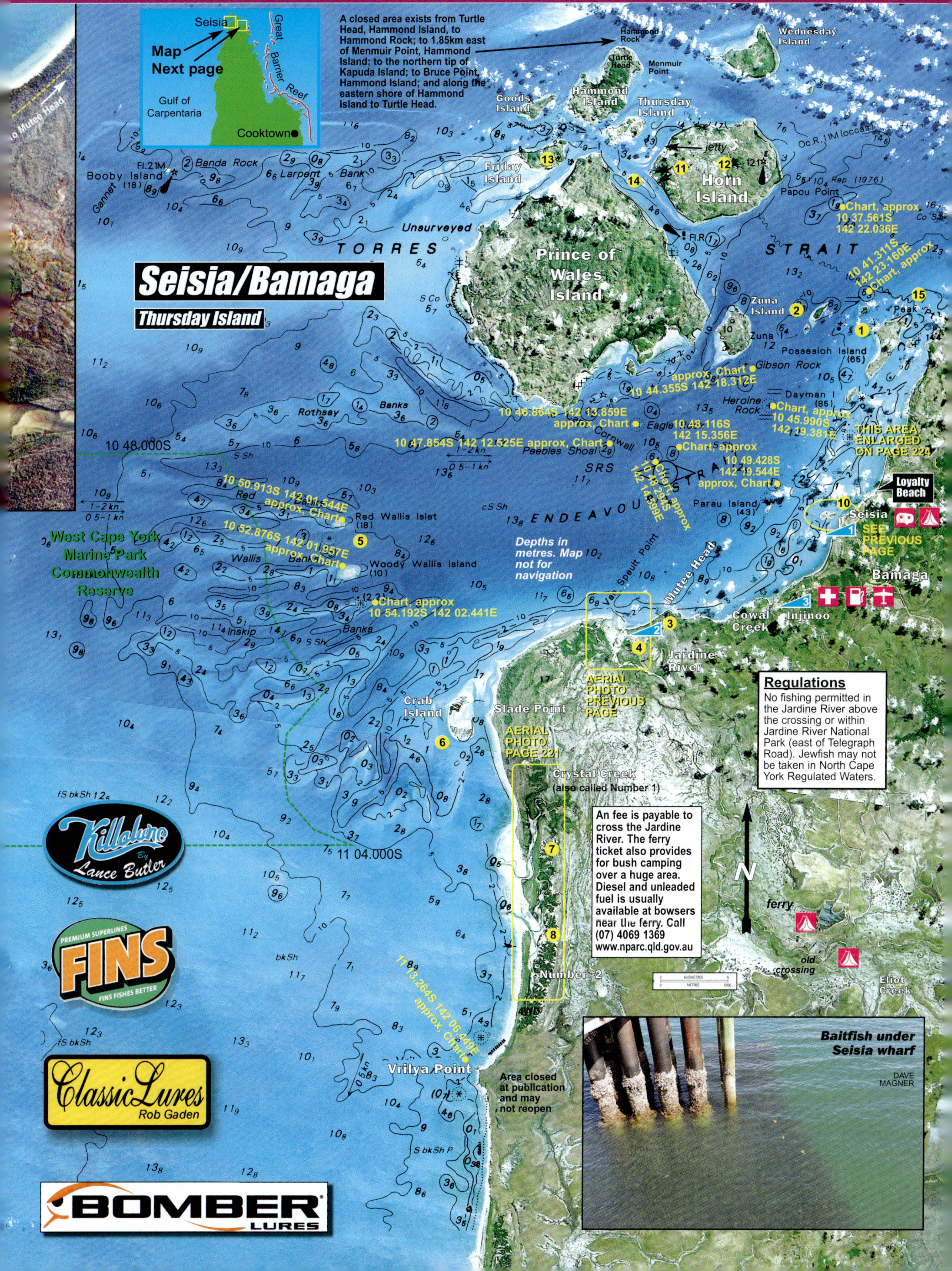

Seisia/Bamaga

Thursday Island

A closed area exists from Turtle Head, Hammond Island, to Hammond Rock; to 1.85km east of Menmuir Point, Hammond Island; to the northern tip of Kapuda Island; to Bruce Point, Hammond Island; and along the eastern shore of Hammond Island to Turtle Head.

Map Next page

Seisia

Gulf of Carpentaria

Great Barrier Reef

Cooktown

Depths in metres. Map not for navigation

West Cape York Marine Park Commonwealth Reserve

Hammond Rock

Turtle Head

Menmuir Point

Wednesday Island

Goods Island

Hammond Island

Thursday Island

Friday Island

Horn Island

Prince of Wales Island

Booby Island

Banda Rock

Larpent Bank

Unsurveyed

TORRES STRAIT

Zuna Island

Possesion Island

Gibson Rock

Dayman I

Heroine Rock

Rothsay Banks

Peebles Shoal

Eagle

Cornwall

ENDEAVOUR STRAIT

Parau Island

Red Wallis Islet

Woody Wallis Island

Wallis Banks

Inskip Banks

Crab Island

Slade Point

Van Spoult Point

Mutee Head

Jardine River

Cowal Creek

Injinoo

Seisia

Loyalty Beach

Bamaga

Crystal Creek (also called Number 1)

Number 2

Vrilya Point

Eliot Creek

ferry

old crossing

Chart, approx 10 37.561S 142 22.036E

10 41.311S 142 23.160E Chart, approx

approx, Chart 10 44.355S 142 18.312E

10 46.864S 142 13.859E approx, Chart

10 47.854S 142 12.525E approx, Chart

10 48.116S 142 15.356E Chart, approx

Chart, approx 10 45.990S 142 19.381E

10 49.428S 142 19.544E approx, Chart

10 48.294S 142 14.390E approx Chart

10 50.913S 142 01.544E approx, Chart

10 52.876S 142 01.957E approx, Chart

Chart, approx 10 54.192S 142 02.441E

11 13.264S 142 06.449E approx, Chart

10 48.000S

11 04.000S

THIS AREA ENLARGED ON PAGE 224

SEE PREVIOUS PAGE

AERIAL PHOTO PREVIOUS PAGE

AERIAL PHOTO PAGE 221

Area closed at publication and may not reopen

Regulations

No fishing permitted in the Jardine River above the crossing or within Jardine River National Park (east of Telegraph Road). Jewfish may not be taken in North Cape York Regulated Waters.

An fee is payable to cross the Jardine River. The ferry ticket also provides for bush camping over a huge area. Diesel and unleaded fuel is usually available at bowsers near the ferry. Call (07) 4069 1369 www.nparc.qld.gov.au

Baitfish under Seisia wharf

DAVE MAGNER

Remote beaches that can surprise

Seisia boat ramp is the gateway to the islands and reefs of the strait, but cartopper fishos can launch from beaches through to Somerset. Landbased fishos may find the beaches surprisingly good at high tide, with big fish such as trevally, queenfish and golden snapper cruising through, especially at night. Use livebait for best results and be wary of crocodiles. While Torres Strait is semi-protected by its islands, the current flows hard and it gets rough. Reefs, sandflats and standing waves keep skippers on their toes. Careful boaters who pick their weather and use a nautical chart or plotter with care should have no problem. Boat hire is available at Cape York Ice and Tackle in Bamaga, which means you don't have to tow your boat in over corrugations on the peninsula road. There are alternatives to driving. Visitors can fly in and take a mothership, or have their vehicle ferried to Weipa or Seisia from Karumba. Motherships work the peninsula coast from Seisia, anchoring in river mouths along the way. This is perhaps the best way to experience remote Cape York fishing. The late wet season can be an excellent time to fish, especially for barramundi, but it may not be possible to enter by road at this time. During the Wet, visitors can fly in or take the ferry. If driving in during the dry season, the choice of taking the easier Bypass Road to the tip or following the Old Telegraph Road and tackling the creek crossings is a personal decision. Some motorists enjoy the challenge of the Old Telegraph Road (track). A 4WD vehicle must have high clearance for this route and it is best not to use the track early after the wet season. Call ahead to check conditions. From a fishing perspective, fishermen should travel to the Tip early or late in the tourist season. Late in the year the winter crowds have left and warm weather stirs barramundi into action. The weeks following the wet season (about April) are good, but access can be difficult over crossings and boggy sections.

Cape York

Local reefs have coral trout, cod and tricky snapper, and hordes of trevally. South-east winds limit dry season fishing. Cartoppers can be launched from beaches around Somerset in calm weather, but the western coast is more sheltered. Mackerel are best in the winter (Jun/Sep), usually taken on the troll. Queenfish are often abundant.

Key to Map

Hotspots

1. Mid Rock: (approx 10 40.587S 142 35.869E) trevally, mackerel, queenfish. Calm weather only.
2. Troll around Cape and Eborac Islands for pelagic fish. Reef fish on drop-offs. Hole east side of Eborac has golden snapper, nannygai, cod.
3. Alpha Rock (approx 10 36.690S 142 30.955E) troll for big trevally, mackerel, cobia. Reef fishing in deeper water.
4. Quetta Rock (10 40.208S 142 37.814E). Pelagics.
5. Punsand Bay beach can surprise at high tide. Queenfish, trevally, mackerel, even golden snapper (fingermark). Nicely sheltered from dry season south-easters.
6. Albany Rock: troll for pelagic fish.
7. Sana Rock: pelagic fish.
8. Two tidal creeks produce barra, salmon, jacks and mud crabs. Walk in from Pajinka or Punsand Bay.
9. Mew River is a large tidal creek with barramundi, jacks crabs. Access by boat.
10. Mackerel in dry season, reasonably sheltered from south-easters.

Wrecks

A. Charted wreck, approx 10 38.989S 142 30.531E.
B. Charted wreck, historic site, approx 10 39.858S 142 37.450E.

Launch sites

1. Injinoo, creek ramp.
2. Seisia public ramp.
3. Punsand Bay private launch.
4. Cartopper beach launching.
5. Fishbone Ck, off Jackey Jackey.

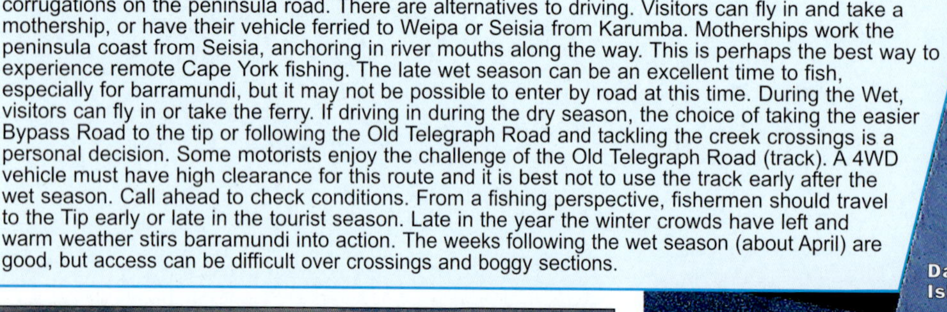

Looking over Red Island towards Seisia

Ussher and Sadd Point

These scenic spots (located off our main map) are on the east coast south of Escape River on a 60km 4WD track through the Jardine River Resource Reserve. The signposted turn-off is on the main road to Bamaga. Sadd Point is 12km south-east of Escape River mouth, with a camping area in shady rainforest near a clear, sandy creek mouth with white sand beach. This is a national park camping area and pre-booking is required. It is a beautiful spot, but fishing can be problematic because the coast is exposed to south-east winds. Being sandy and clear, the creek has mainly queenfish, jacks, trevally and giant herring, with occasional barra. There are patches of reef along the coast with coral trout, tricky snapper, flag, trevally and cod. Tern Islet, 6km north of Sadd Point, is part of a reefy area that extends 3km from shore. Shortland Reef is 16km north of Sadd Point.

Sadd Point

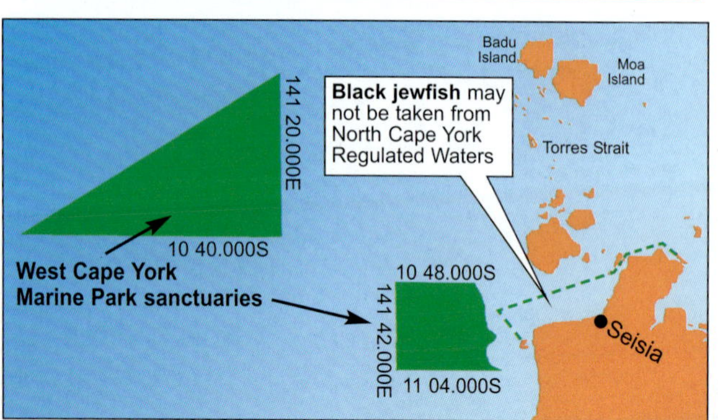

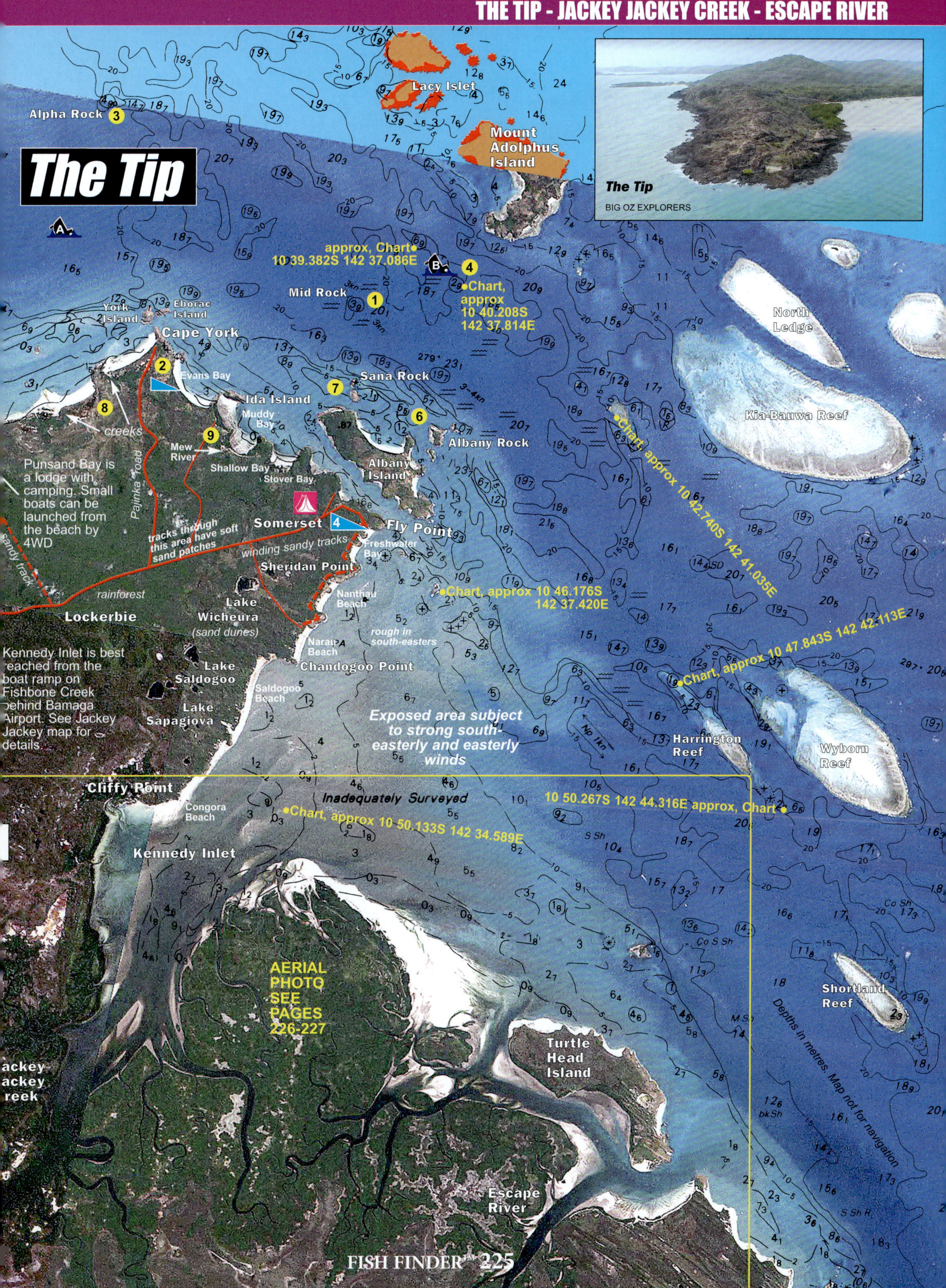
The Tip
Alpha Rock 3
Lacy Islet
Mount Adolphus Island
The Tip
BIG OZ EXPLORERS
approx, Chart 10 39.382S 142 37.086E
4 Chart, approx 10 40.208S 142 37.814E
Mid Rock 1
York Island
Eborac Island
Cape York
2 Evans Bay
Sana Rock
7
Ida Island
Muddy Bay
6
Albany Rock
8
creeks
9
Mew River
Shallow Bay
Stover Bay
Albany Island
Punsand Bay is a lodge with camping. Small boats can be launched from the beach by 4WD
Pajinka Road
tracks through this area have soft sand patches
Somerset
4
Fly Point
Freshwater Bay
winding sandy tracks
Sheridan Point
sandy track
rainforest
Lockerbie
Lake Wicheura
(sand dunes)
Nanthau Beach
Chart, approx 10 46.176S 142 37.420E
Chart, approx 10 42.740S 142 41.035E
North Ledge
Kia-Bauwa Reef
Chart, approx 10 47.843S 142 42.113E
rough in south-easters
Narau Beach
Chandogoo Point
Kennedy Inlet is best reached from the boat ramp on Fishbone Creek behind Bamaga Airport. See Jackey Jackey map for details.
Lake Saldogoo
Lake Sapagiova
Saldogoo Beach
Exposed area subject to strong south-easterly and easterly winds
Harrington Reef
Wybon Reef
Cliffy Point
Congora Beach
Inadequately Surveyed
Chart, approx 10 50.133S 142 34.589E
10 50.267S 142 44.316E approx, Chart
Kennedy Inlet
AERIAL PHOTO SEE PAGES 226-227
Shortland Reef
Turtle Head Island
Depths in metres. Map not for navigation
Jackey Jackey Creek
Escape River

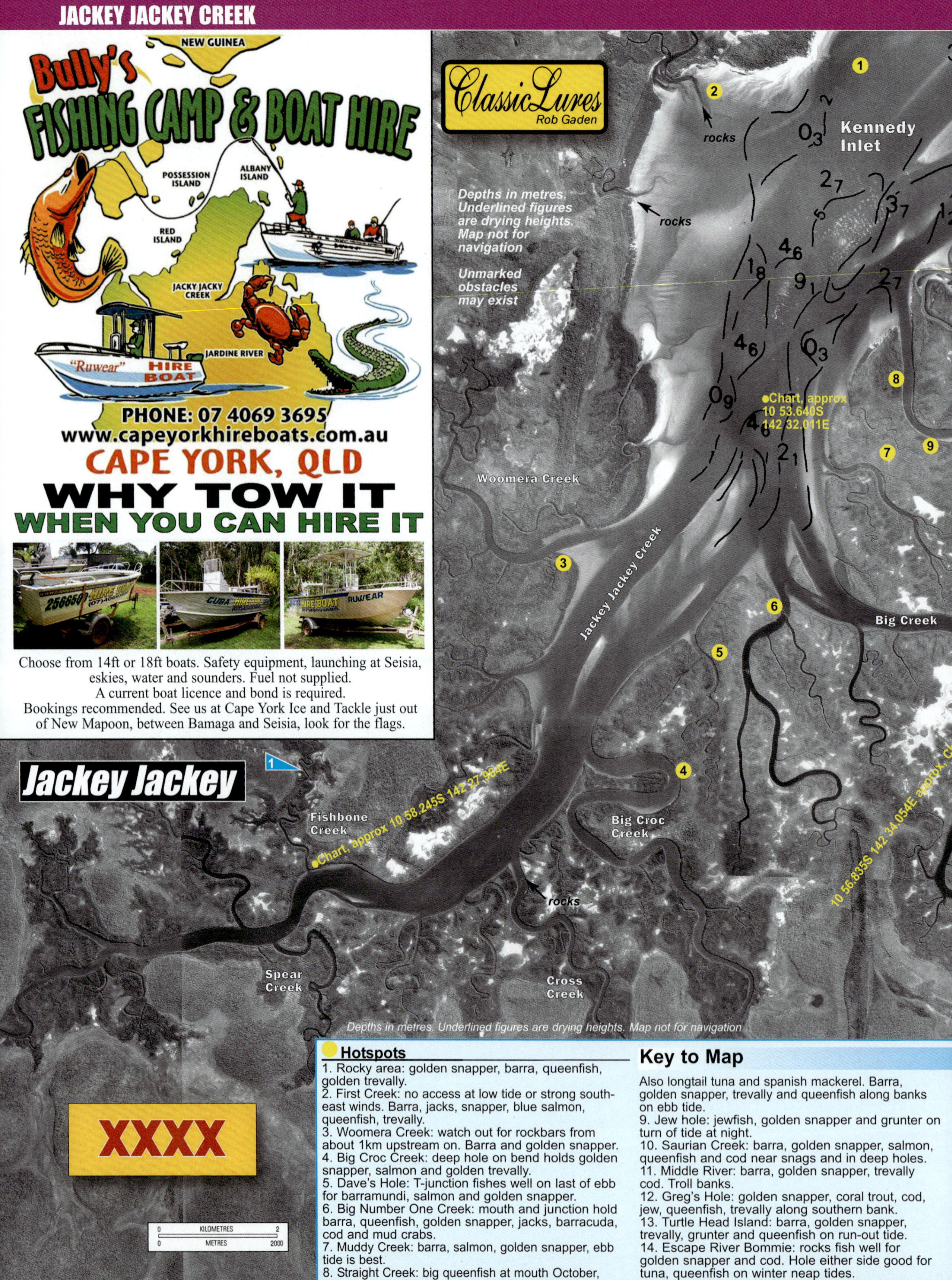

Hotspots

1. Rocky area: golden snapper, barra, queenfish, golden trevally.
2. First Creek: no access at low tide or strong south-east winds. Barra, jacks, snapper, blue salmon, queenfish, trevally.
3. Woomera Creek: watch out for rockbars from about 1km upstream on. Barra and golden snapper.
4. Big Croc Creek: deep hole on bend holds golden snapper, salmon and golden trevally.
5. Dave's Hole: T-junction fishes well on last of ebb for barramundi, salmon and golden snapper.
6. Big Number One Creek: mouth and junction hold barra, queenfish, golden snapper, jacks, barracuda, cod and mud crabs.
7. Muddy Creek: barra, salmon, golden snapper, ebb tide is best.
8. Straight Creek: big queenfish at mouth October, November. Grey mackerel in August, September.

Key to Map

Also longtail tuna and spanish mackerel. Barra, golden snapper, trevally and queenfish along banks on ebb tide.
9. Jew hole: jewfish, golden snapper and grunter on turn of tide at night.
10. Saurian Creek: barra, golden snapper, salmon, queenfish and cod near snags and in deep holes.
11. Middle River: barra, golden snapper, trevally cod. Troll banks.
12. Greg's Hole: golden snapper, coral trout, cod, jew, queenfish, trevally along southern bank.
13. Turtle Head Island: barra, golden snapper, trevally, grunter and queenfish on run-out tide.
14. Escape River Bommie: rocks fish well for golden snapper and cod. Hole either side good for tuna, queenfish on winter neap tides.
15. Barra, snapper, jacks, trevally, queenfish.

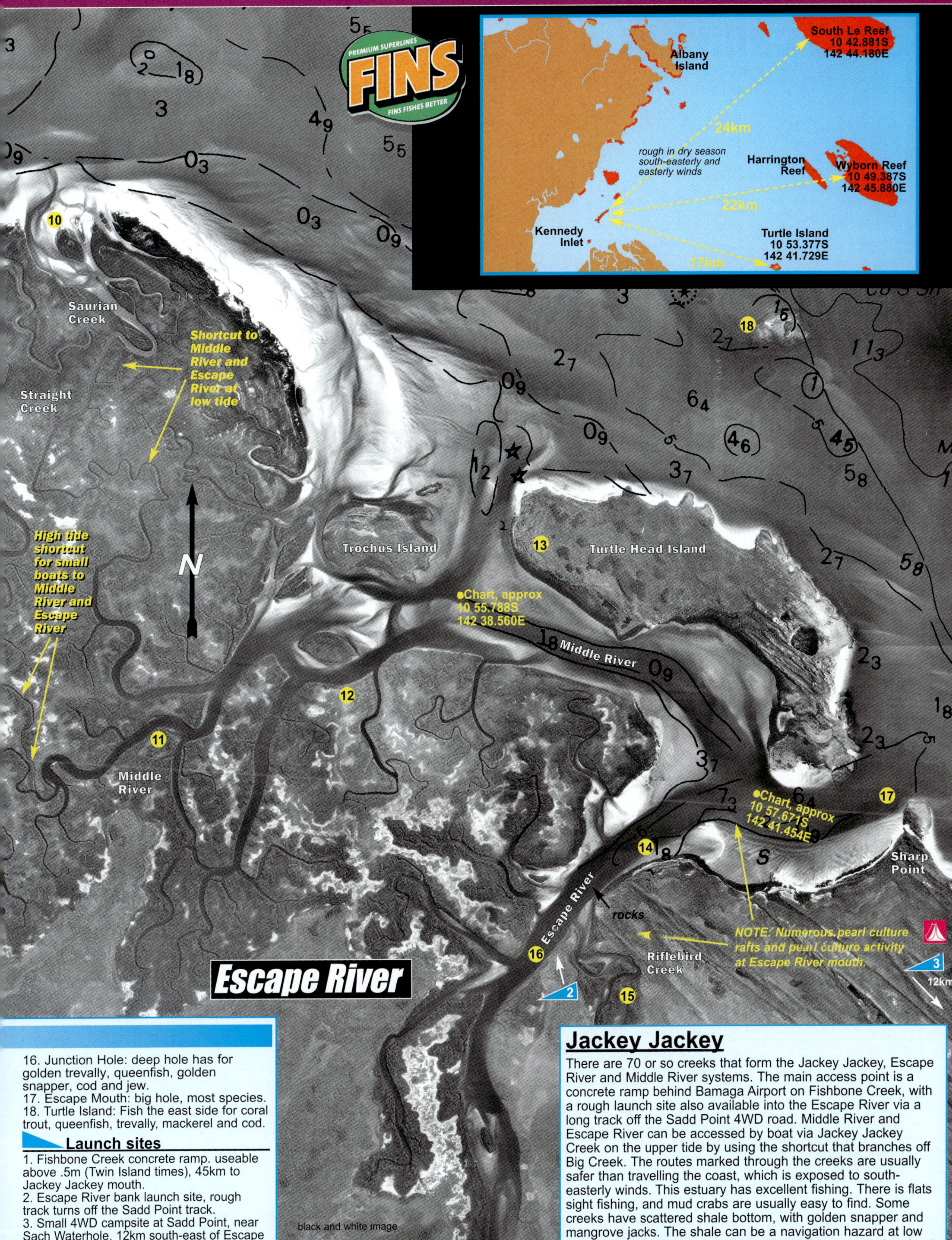

16. Junction Hole: deep hole has for golden trevally, queenfish, golden snapper, cod and jew.
17. Escape Mouth: big hole, most species.
18. Turtle Island: Fish the east side for coral trout, queenfish, trevally, mackerel and cod.

Launch sites

1. Fishbone Creek concrete ramp. useable above .5m (Twin Island times), 45km to Jackey Jackey mouth.
2. Escape River bank launch site, rough track turns off the Sadd Point track.
3. Small 4WD campsite at Sadd Point, near Sach Waterhole, 12km south-east of Escape River. Beach boat launching. Beware crocodiles in lake and creek near the camp.

Jackey Jackey

There are 70 or so creeks that form the Jackey Jackey, Escape River and Middle River systems. The main access point is a concrete ramp behind Bamaga Airport on Fishbone Creek, with a rough launch site also available into the Escape River via a long track off the Sadd Point 4WD road. Middle River and Escape River can be accessed by boat via Jackey Jackey Creek on the upper tide by using the shortcut that branches off Big Creek. The routes marked through the creeks are usually safer than travelling the coast, which is exposed to south-easterly winds. This estuary has excellent fishing. There is flats sight fishing, and mud crabs are usually easy to find. Some creeks have scattered shale bottom, with golden snapper and mangrove jacks. The shale can be a navigation hazard at low tide. Reefs offshore have coral trout, tuskfish, nannygai and red emperor, if you can get past the trevally and sharks.

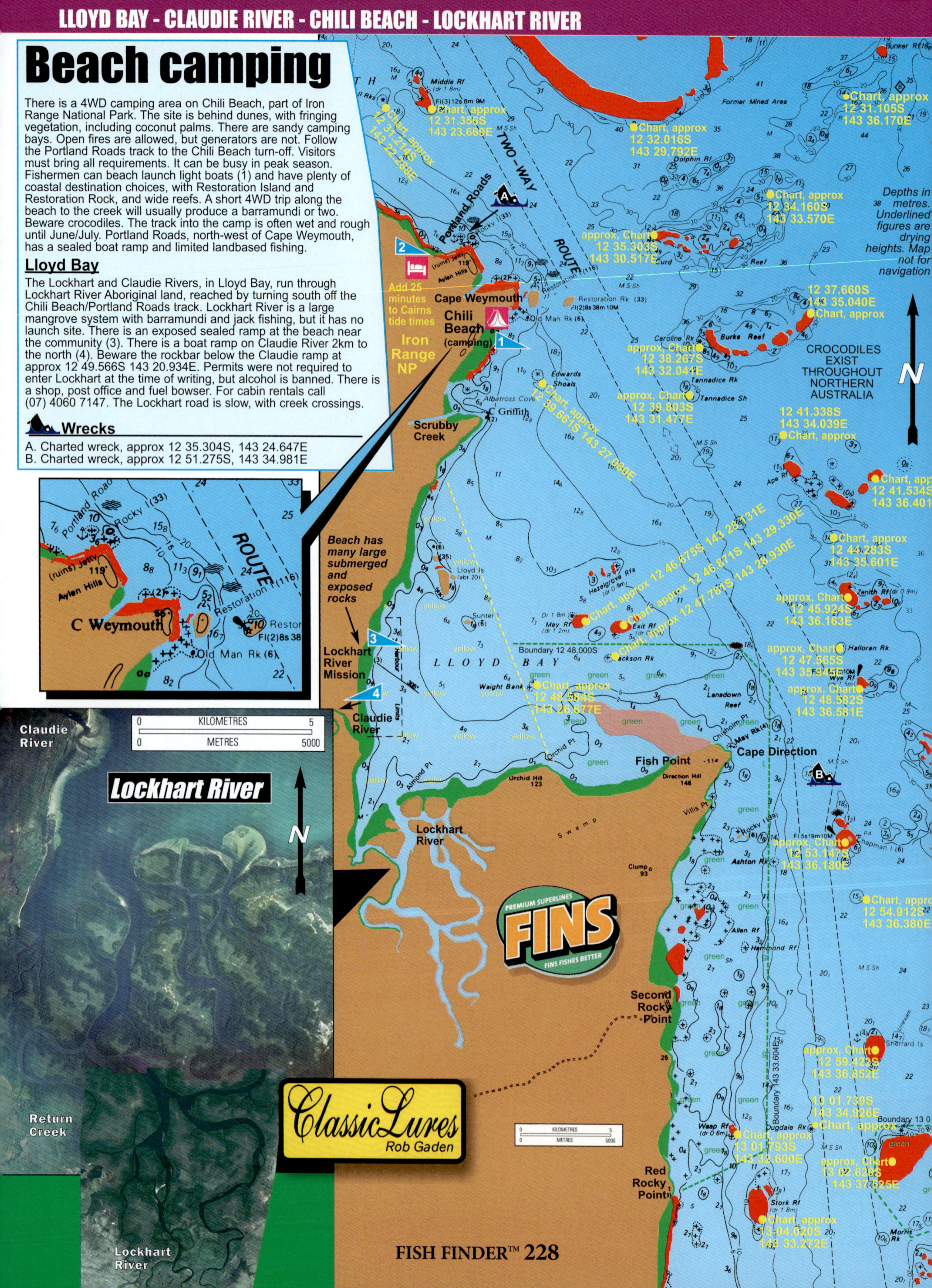
Beach camping
There is a 4WD camping area on Chili Beach, part of Iron Range National Park. The site is behind dunes, with fringing vegetation, including coconut palms. There are sandy camping bays. Open fires are allowed, but generators are not. Follow the Portland Roads track to the Chili Beach turn-off. Visitors must bring all requirements. It can be busy in peak season. Fishermen can beach launch light boats (1) and have plenty of coastal destination choices, with Restoration Island and Restoration Rock, and wide reefs. A short 4WD trip along the beach to the creek will usually produce a barramundi or two. Beware crocodiles. The track into the camp is often wet and rough until June/July. Portland Roads, north-west of Cape Weymouth, has a sealed boat ramp and limited landbased fishing.
Lloyd Bay
The Lockhart and Claudie Rivers, in Lloyd Bay, run through Lockhart River Aboriginal land, reached by turning south off the Chili Beach/Portland Roads track. Lockhart River is a large mangrove system with barramundi and jack fishing, but it has no launch site. There is an exposed sealed ramp at the beach near the community (3). There is a boat ramp on Claudie River 2km to the north (4). Beware the rockbar below the Claudie ramp at approx 12 49.566S 143 20.934E. Permits were not required to enter Lockhart at the time of writing, but alcohol is banned. There is a shop, post office and fuel bowser. For cabin rentals call (07) 4060 7147. The Lockhart road is slow, with creek crossings.
Wrecks
A. Charted wreck, approx 12 35.304S, 143 24.647E
B. Charted wreck, approx 12 51.275S, 143 34.981E
Portland Roads
TWO-WAY ROUTE
Cape Weymouth
Add 25 minutes to Cairns tide times
Chili Beach (camping)
Iron Range NP
Scrubby Creek
Griffith
Edwards Shoals
Restoration Rk
Old Man Rk (6)
Former Mined Area
Burke Reef
Depths in metres. Underlined figures are drying heights. Map not for navigation
CROCODILES EXIST THROUGHOUT NORTHERN AUSTRALIA
N
C Weymouth
Aylen Hills
Beach has many large submerged and exposed rocks
Lockhart River Mission
Claudie River
LLOYD BAY
Boundary 12 48.000S
Lanedown Reef
Fish Point
Cape Direction
Direction Hill 146
Orchid Hill 123
Lockhart River
Swamp
Second Rocky Point
Red Rocky Point
KILOMETRES 0 5
METRES 0 5000
Lockhart River
Claudie River
Return Creek
Lockhart River
PREMIUM SUPERLINES FINS
FINS FISHES BETTER
ClassicLures Rob Gaden

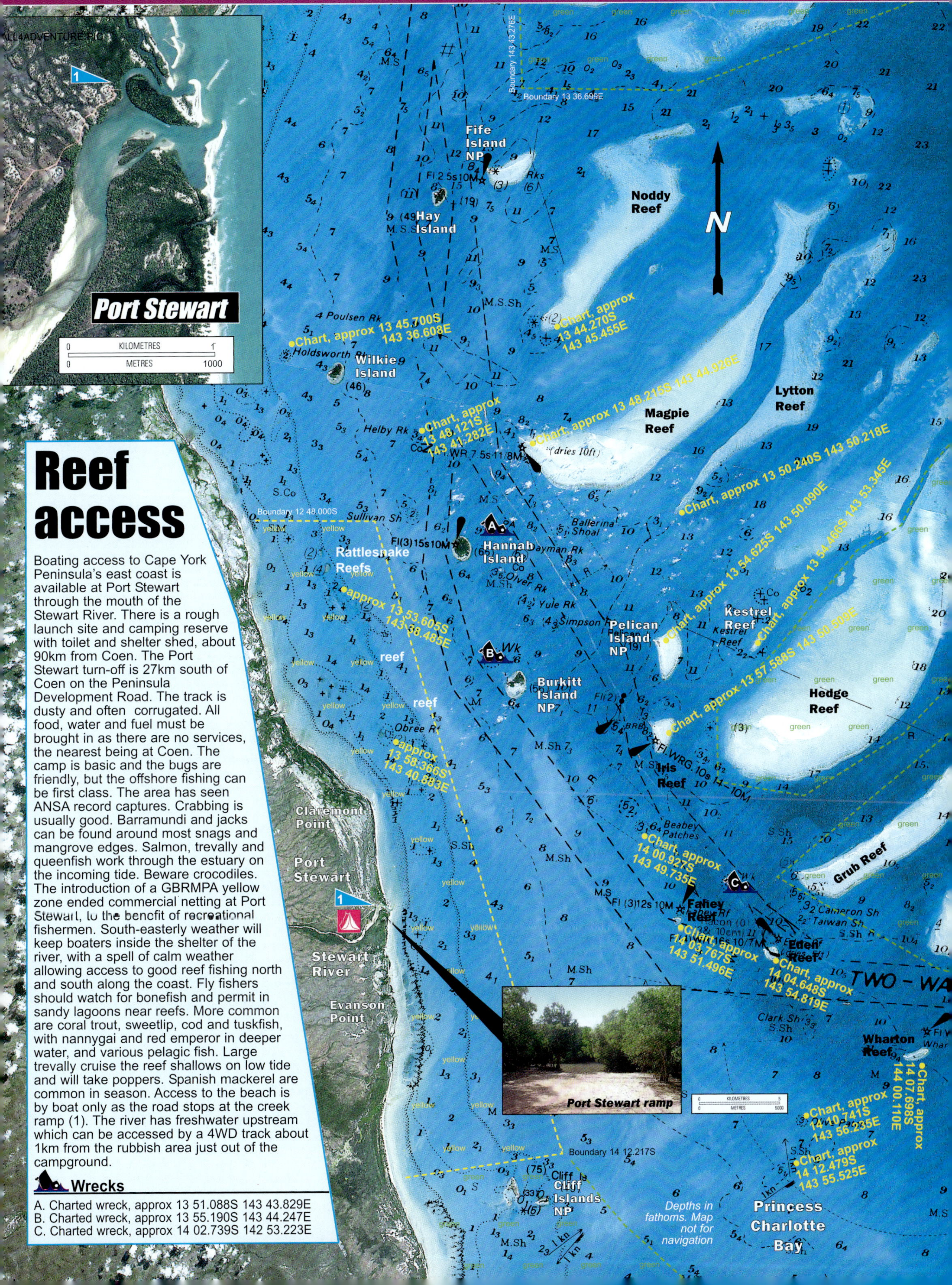

Reef access

Boating access to Cape York Peninsula's east coast is available at Port Stewart through the mouth of the Stewart River. There is a rough launch site and camping reserve with toilet and shelter shed, about 90km from Coen. The Port Stewart turn-off is 27km south of Coen on the Peninsula Development Road. The track is dusty and often corrugated. All food, water and fuel must be brought in as there are no services, the nearest being at Coen. The camp is basic and the bugs are friendly, but the offshore fishing can be first class. The area has seen ANSA record captures. Crabbing is usually good. Barramundi and jacks can be found around most snags and mangrove edges. Salmon, trevally and queenfish work through the estuary on the incoming tide. Beware crocodiles. The introduction of a GBRMPA yellow zone ended commercial netting at Port Stewart, to the benefit of recreational fishermen. South-easterly weather will keep boaters inside the shelter of the river, with a spell of calm weather allowing access to good reef fishing north and south along the coast. Fly fishers should watch for bonefish and permit in sandy lagoons near reefs. More common are coral trout, sweetlip, cod and tuskfish, with nannygai and red emperor in deeper water, and various pelagic fish. Large trevally cruise the reef shallows on low tide and will take poppers. Spanish mackerel are common in season. Access to the beach is by boat only as the road stops at the creek ramp (1). The river has freshwater upstream which can be accessed by a 4WD track about 1km from the rubbish area just out of the campground.

Wrecks

A. Charted wreck, approx 13 51.088S 143 43.829E
B. Charted wreck, approx 13 55.190S 143 44.247E
C. Charted wreck, approx 14 02.739S 142 53.223E

Port Stewart

Port Stewart ramp

Chart, approx 13 45.700S 143 36.608E
Chart, approx 13 44.270S 143 45.455E
Chart, approx 13 48.121S 143 41.282E
Chart, approx 13 48.215S 143 44.926E
Chart, approx 13 50.240S 143 50.218E
Chart, approx 13 54.625S 143 50.090E
Chart, approx 13 54.466S 143 53.345E
approx 13 53.605S 143 38.485E
Chart, approx 13 57.588S 143 50.698E
approx 13 58.366S 143 40.883E
Chart, approx 14 00.927S 143 49.735E
Chart, approx 14 03.767S 143 51.496E
Chart, approx 14 04.648S 143 54.819E
Chart, approx 14 07.698S 144 00.110E
Chart, approx 14 10.741S 143 56.235E
Chart, approx 14 12.479S 143 55.525E

Fife Island NP, Hay Island, Wilkie Island, Hannah Island, Burkitt Island NP, Pelican Island NP, Cliff Islands NP, Noddy Reef, Magpie Reef, Lytton Reef, Kestrel Reef, Hedge Reef, Iris Reef, Grub Reef, Fahey Reef, Eden Reef, Wharton Reef, Rattlesnake Reefs, Claremont Point, Port Stewart, Stewart River, Evanson Point, Princess Charlotte Bay

Depths in fathoms. Map not for navigation

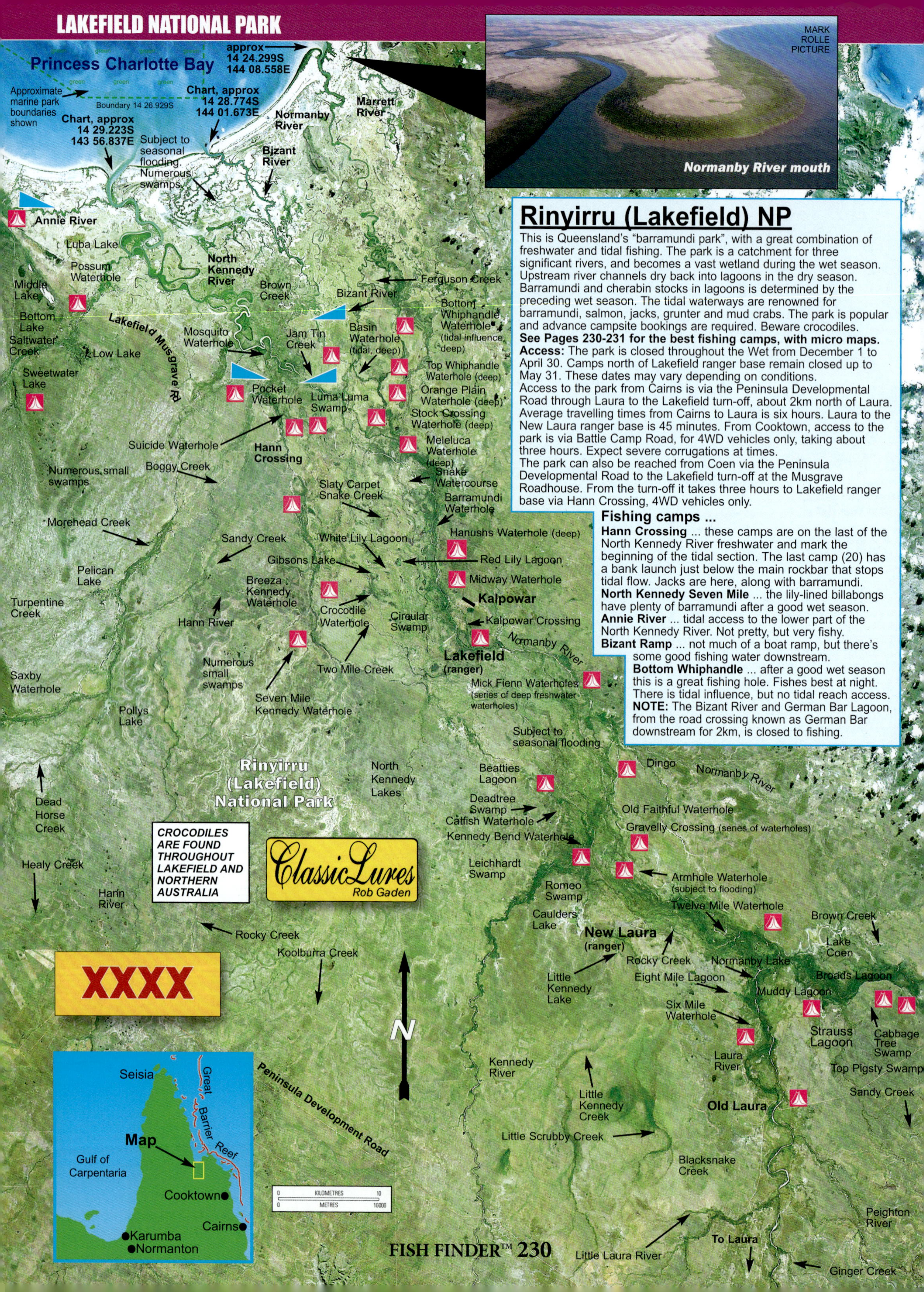

Rinyirru (Lakefield) NP

This is Queensland's "barramundi park", with a great combination of freshwater and tidal fishing. The park is a catchment for three significant rivers, and becomes a vast wetland during the wet season. Upstream river channels dry back into lagoons in the dry season. Barramundi and cherabin stocks in lagoons is determined by the preceding wet season. The tidal waterways are renowned for barramundi, salmon, jacks, grunter and mud crabs. The park is popular and advance campsite bookings are required. Beware crocodiles.

See Pages 230-231 for the best fishing camps, with micro maps.

Access: The park is closed throughout the Wet from December 1 to April 30. Camps north of Lakefield ranger base remain closed up to May 31. These dates may vary depending on conditions.

Access to the park from Cairns is via the Peninsula Developmental Road through Laura to the Lakefield turn-off, about 2km north of Laura. Average travelling times from Cairns to Laura is six hours. Laura to the New Laura ranger base is 45 minutes. From Cooktown, access to the park is via Battle Camp Road, for 4WD vehicles only, taking about three hours. Expect severe corrugations at times.

The park can also be reached from Coen via the Peninsula Developmental Road to the Lakefield turn-off at the Musgrave Roadhouse. From the turn-off it takes three hours to Lakefield ranger base via Hann Crossing, 4WD vehicles only.

Fishing camps ...

Hann Crossing ... these camps are on the last of the North Kennedy River freshwater and mark the beginning of the tidal section. The last camp (20) has a bank launch just below the main rockbar that stops tidal flow. Jacks are here, along with barramundi.

North Kennedy Seven Mile ... the lily-lined billabongs have plenty of barramundi after a good wet season.

Annie River ... tidal access to the lower part of the North Kennedy River.

Bizant Ramp ... not much of a boat ramp, but there's some good fishing water downstream.

Bottom Whiphandle ... after a good wet season this is a great fishing hole. Fishes best at night. There is tidal influence, but no tidal reach access.

NOTE: The Bizant River and German Bar Lagoon, from the road crossing known as German Bar downstream for 2km, is closed to fishing.

Lakefield's Tidal Rivers

At 537,000 hectares, Lakefield is Queensland's second largest national park. Rivers weave their way through most of it. In a big wet season, the catchments join to form an inland sea. A strong monsoon usually brings good fishing the following dry season as the rivers fall back into their channels, but it also means access tracks will take longer to dry out. While the dry season lagoons and freshwater holes have good fishing, serious fishermen work the tidal sections, as well as Princess Charlotte Bay itself. A lot of travelling on corrugated roads is required. The launch sites into the tidal water of the big rivers are marginal, and best done by 4WD at the top of the tide. The Annie River access in particular can only be tackled when the track has dried out. To access the Annie River landing take the Lilyvale Rd at Musgrave. It is 60km to the landing, and a further 14km by water to the mouth of the North Kennedy River. It is a much longer trip downstream to the sea from the Bizant and North Kennedy (Hanns Crossing) launch sites, being 51km by river from the launch below Hann crossing, and 27km from the Bizant launch. If doing an overnighter in the boat or near a river bank, sleep with mozzie domes, and stay well out of reach of Lakefield's many big crocodiles.

Fishing

Those who explore will usually be well rewarded. Fish holes and eddies at river bends and creek mouths, rock patches and submerged timber. Outside the river mouths are vast shallow flats and shallow channels, take care on an outgoing tide as stranding is possible. Cast lures to the mouths of tidal mud drains. The saltwater sections of these rivers have barramundi, threadfin and blue salmon, black jewfish and grunter. There's also pesky whiting, bream and flathead if you can be bothered when there are more exciting fish around. Big mud crabs are usually abundant, but their numbers vary each year.

Barra camps

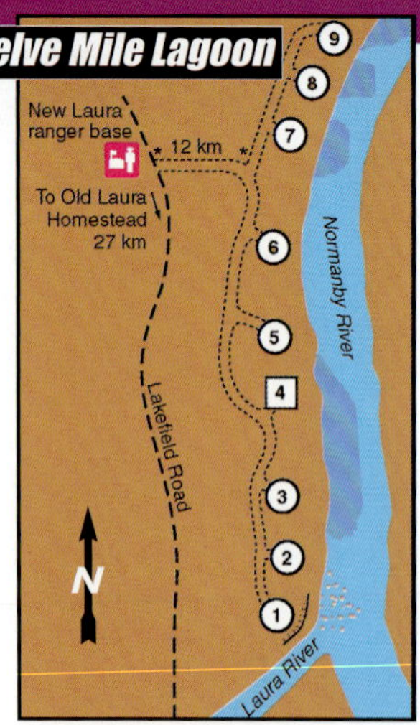

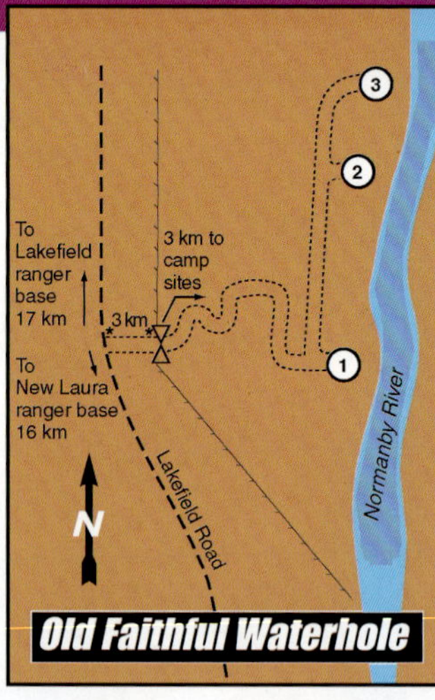

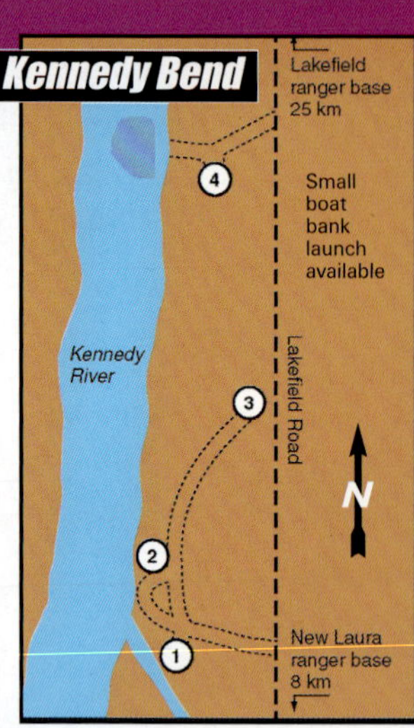

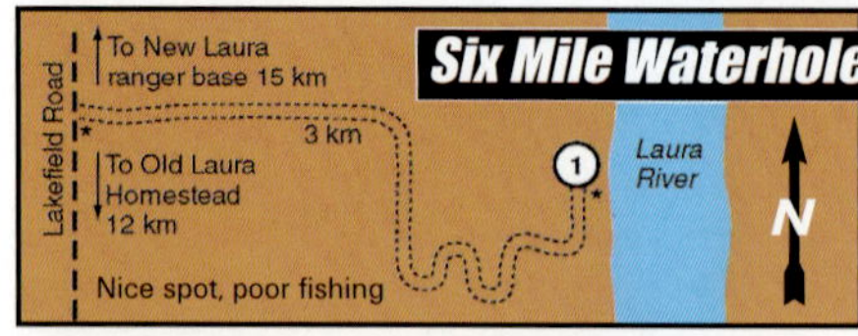

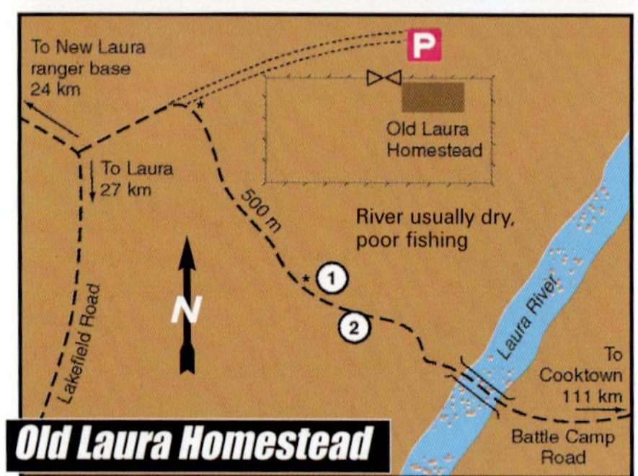

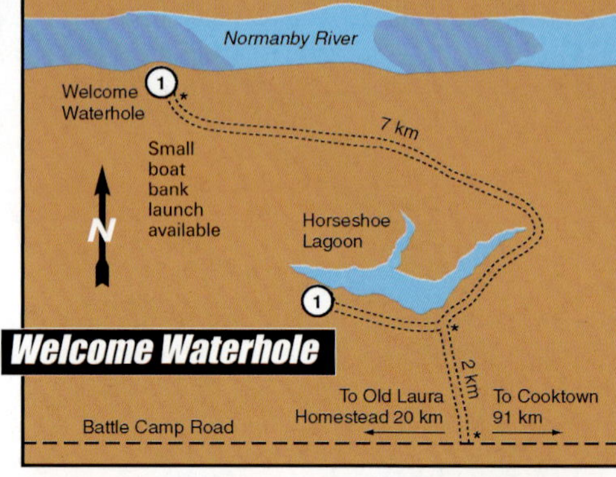

WITH its campsites set along a vast network of tropical rivers, lagoons and tidal estuaries, Lakefield National Park is famous for barramundi fishing.

This 530,000ha park extends 160km north from Laura to the mangrove-fringed waters of eastern Princess Charlotte Bay, and takes in much of the floodplain and savanna woodland of Laura Basin.

Each wet season the watercourses spread across floodplains. This triggers breeding on a grand scale for fish and wildlife, but also stops road access from about December to April.

Thus visitation is limited to the dry season months, when the dry landscape is in stark contrast to the lush Wet.

It is during the Dry that Lakefield's many permanent freshwater holes serve as an oasis for wildlife and sportfishermen alike.

The focus on Lakefield has traditionally been barramundi, but the tidal rivers have good fishing for most species. Bank fishing is suited to the smaller freshwater holes and the rapids between waterbodies, not forgetting the very real crocodile threat. A boat greatly increases options, and is essential for tidal areas because of mangrove vegetation.

Car-toppers and boats of about 4m on sturdy trailers are ideal for Lakefield.

Most freshwater holes are less than 3km long, while tidal sections extend for 20km or more. Where it is necessary to launch over a river bank, a cartopper is ideal.

Barra are most responsive in the immediate post wet season period, April and May, and during the Build-up months from late August through to October, keeping in mind Queensland's closed season.

The cooler water conditions associated with winter sees a slowdown with barramundi, especially in the freshwater. In tidal areas the barra remain more active.

There is however a greater diversity of fish in the saltwater, along with mud crabs.

Getting there: Because of the rough road conditions, access by 4WD is recommended.

However, a sturdy 2WD with good ground clearance can normally travel as far north as Bizant and the nearby Hann Crossing. The only reliable 2WD access into Lakefield and the most common entry route is via the Peninsula Development Road from Cairns, with the turn-off 2km north of Laura. Drive time from Cairns to New Laura Ranger Station is about six hours for the 360km. Lakefield Ranger Station is another 45 minutes further north.

Access via Cooktown from the east is along the scenic but often corrugated Battlecamp Road, with the 150km trip to New Laura taking two and a half hours.

Care should be taken at the Normanby and Laura River crossings early in the Dry, with dust holes and corrugations late in the Dry.

Coming from the north involves turning east off Peninsula Development Road at Musgrave down the Marina Plains road. Drive time for the 110km to Lakefield Ranger base is two hours.

These dates may vary depending on weather and road conditions.

Note: *All camping areas south of Lakefield ranger base are closed from December 1 to May 31. These include Dingo Waterhole, Horseshoe Lagoon, Kalpowar Crossing, Kennedy Bend, Mick Fienn Waterhole, Old Faithful Waterhole, Old Laura Homestead, Six Mile Waterhole, Twelve Mile and Welcome Waterhole.*

All camping areas north of Lakefield ranger base are closed from December 1 to June 30. These include: Sweetwater Lake, Annie River, Five Mile Creek, Saltwater Crossing, Bizant River, Brown Creek, Basin Hole, Top Whiphandle Waterhole, Bottom Whiphandle Waterhole, Orange Plain Waterhole, Hann Crossing, Hanush's Waterhole, Melaleuca Waterhole and Midway Waterhole.

Booking camps: The maximum length of stay is 21 nights. Bookings can be made up to six months in advance. Online bookings well in advance are recommended as demand is strong. Visit www.parks.des.qld.gov.au to book online. A tag must be displayed at campsites.

There are self-service kiosk camping permit booking facilities at Rinyirru (Lakefield) NP (CYPAL), Kutini-Payamu (Iron Range) NP (CYPAL) and Atambaya (Heathlands) at Heathlands Resources Reserve, as well as Coen and Cooktown QPWS offices.

Facilities: In keeping with its remote location and semi-wilderness qualities, Lakefield remains almost undeveloped, featuring an abundance of bush campsites, many alongside picturesque waterholes.

Many anglers select a base camp, and then move around to work other areas.

Kalpowar Crossing, 3km from the main Lakefield ranger base, is the only developed camp, with cold showers, toilets, and lush grassed campsites adjacent to the magnificent Normanby River. Both this location and the Hann Crossing have toilet blocks.

Park visitors need to be self sufficient, as there are no stores or services in the park. Fuel and some mechanical and tyre repairs are at Laura, and Hann River and Musgrave Roadhouses. Cooktown has far more services.

Waterholes: It is impossible to recommend one location over another, as many produce good fishing at times, and all possess unique scenery and character. Most of the freshwater holes are less than 3km long.

Barramundi are most responsive in the post wet season period up until late May, so those who have access to a mothership and come in from the sea before park roads and campsites open will experience the best fishing.

The onset of cooler weather sees barra quieten down, but they are still caught.

Redclaw and large freshwater prawns are usually abundant in freshwater holes.

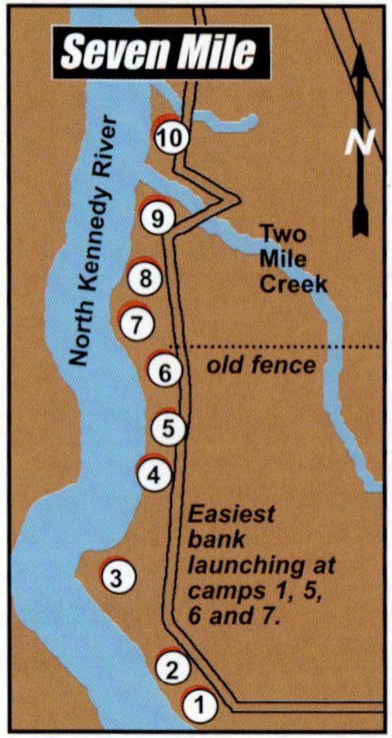

The Rivers: In detailing these areas, it is difficult to single out one location over another - they all produce excellent fishing.

Normanby River: This is Lakefield's longest river, with towering paperbarks, corypha palms and river gums. The 12-Mile Hole is 15km east of New Laura Ranger Station, featuring large deep holes separated by shallow water down from the Laura River junction. Designated campsites are spread along the length of the permanent water.

Further downstream, Gravelly Crossing and Old Faithfull adjoin each other, although the camp sites for each have different road access.

Gravelly Crossing features a series of smaller waterholes, while Old Faithfull is a more substantial body of water.

Dingo Waterhole is similar to Gravelly Crossing with only a couple of camp sites, but it offers excellent bank fishing if you are prepared to walk. It generally fishes better early in the season (April/May). Accessed from the same track, Mick Finn Waterhole features a couple of longer deeper holes, and like most of the Normanby Holes, is a fish producer.

Kalpowar Crossing waterhole is a long, deep and scenic stretch, suited to boat fishing.

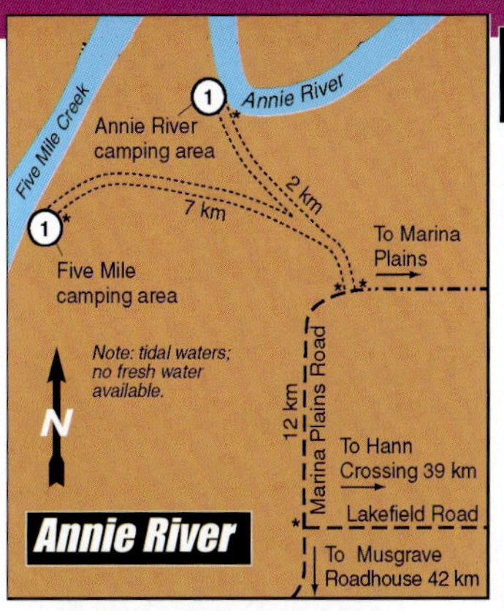

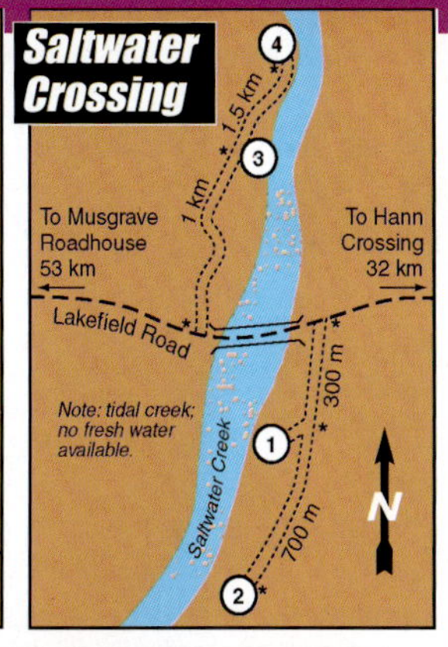

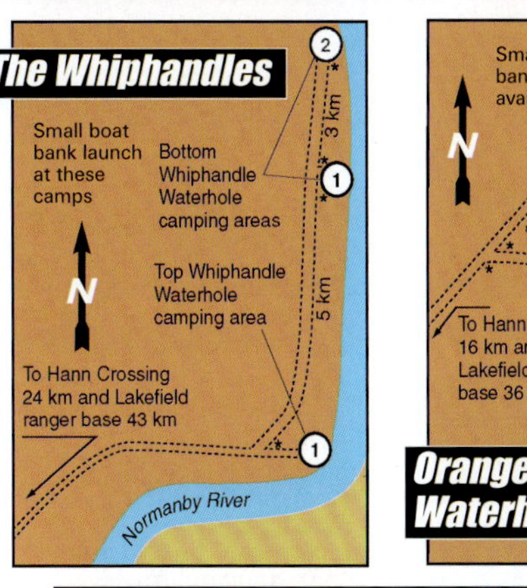

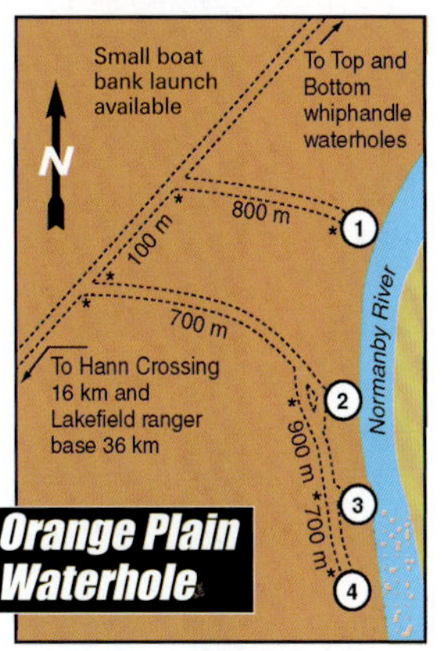

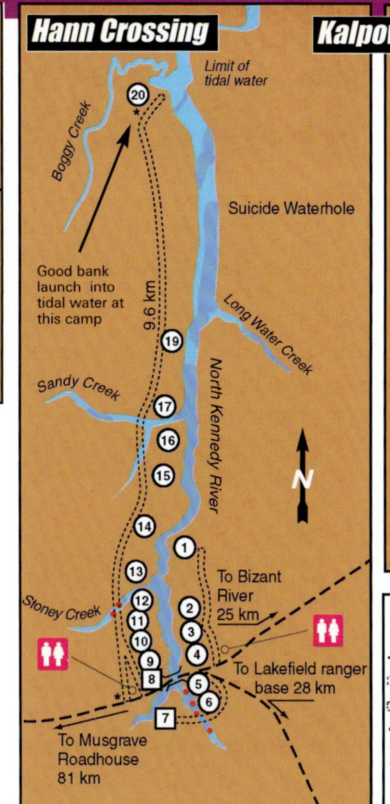

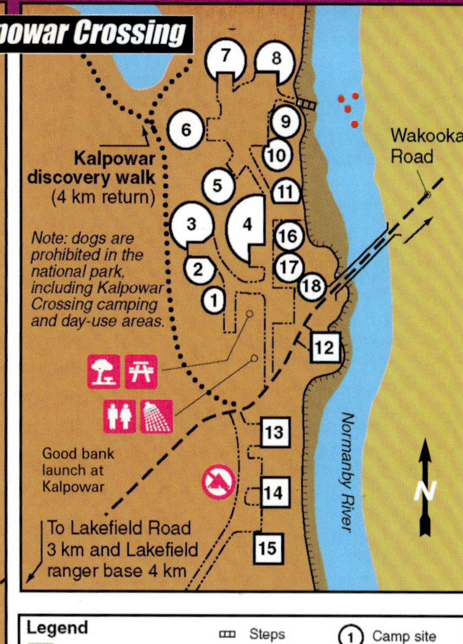

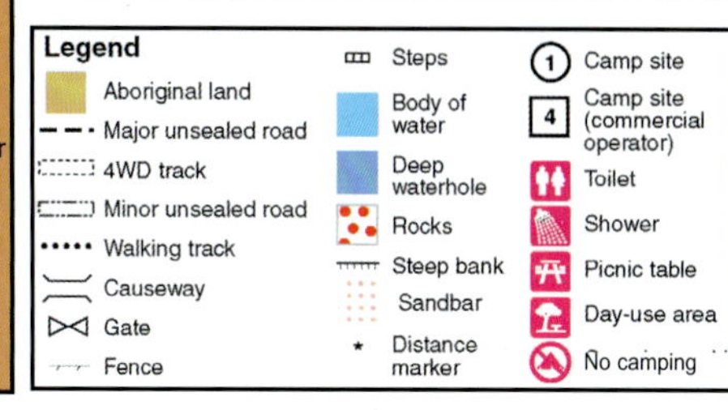

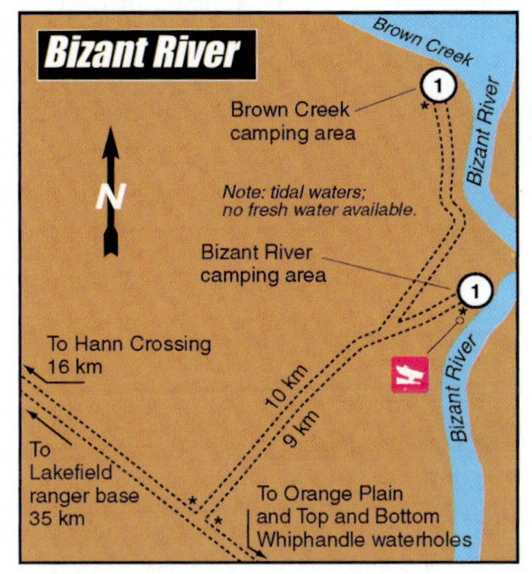

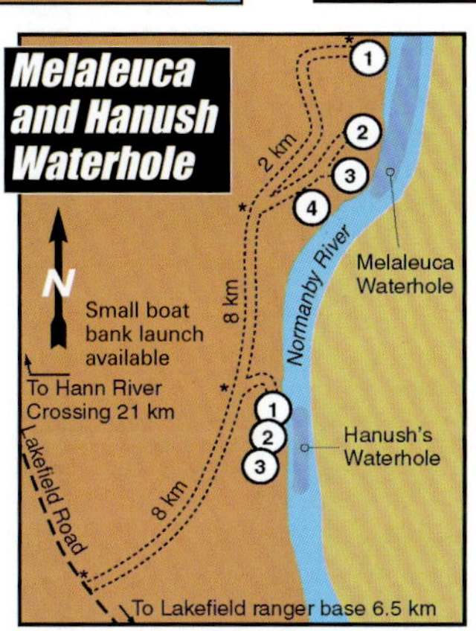

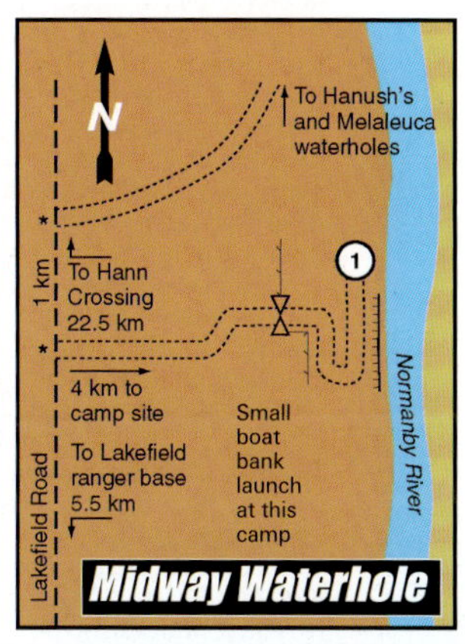

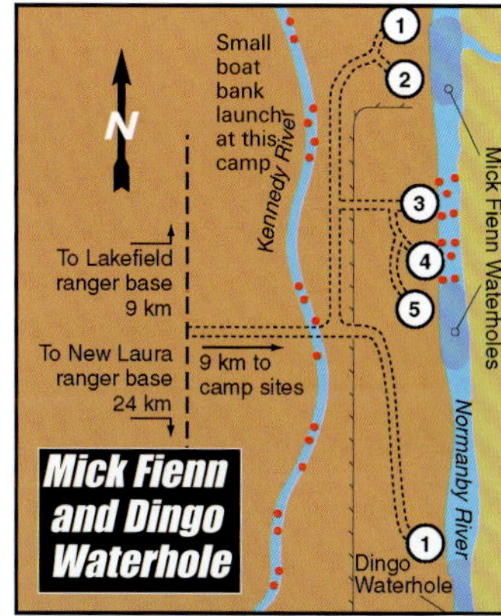

Bathurst Bay

BARRY LYON PICTURE

Coastal track in Cape Melville NP

HY CHEN

Trolling with deep divers is the best method. Early in the season the downstream rapids and pools can be productive. Midway and Hanush's Holes are shorter, but still substantial bodies of water, with good shady campsites.

Another big waterhole, on a "distributary" of the Normanby River (which in the Wet drains into the North Kennedy), is Melaleuca. This is best fished by boat, but care needs to be taken with submerged snags and a rockbar about 300m upstream from the north end of the hole.

Orange Plain, and Top and Bottom Whiphandle are smaller but deep holes set in beautiful shady gallery rainforest in the northern park. There scope to walk the pools.

Tidal movement is present at Bottom Whiphandle and further tidal water access is available downstream adjacent to Ferguson Creek. Most years, access to all Normanby holes downstream from Kalpowar Crossing is not possible until May/June because of boggy conditions. For those with 2WD or limited time, Kennedy Bend and Catfish Hole are close to the road between New Laura and Lakefield. Both offer good-sized fish and classic scenery.

Bizant River: The Bizant River, in the north-east part of the park, has no accessible freshwater fishing, but a basic boat ramp and campsite on the tidal section opens up the saltwater. Golden snapper and jewfish live in the holes, and barramundi too.

There are rockbars downstream between the boat ramp and Browns Creek, and upstream from the ramp. The upper part of the tidal stretch is a fish sanctuary.

North Kennedy River: The river rivals the Normanby for overall fishing diversity and its tidal reaches are more readily accessible.

Most notable of the holes are the adjoining Seven Mile and Breeza Kennedy Waterholes, west of Lakefield Ranger Station, and the Hann Crossing and Suicide Waterholes downstream.

Bank fishing is possible, especially at Hann Crossing, but a boat is recommended.

Nearby Mosquito Waterhole features brackish water, however good access to the tidal parts of the North Kennedy River is afforded by a boat ramp on Jam Tin Creek to the north of Bizant Ranger Station.

Beware a series of rockbars within Jam Tin Creek itself. These prevent boating traffic at low tide, and can be a navigation hazard at any time if you go over them in the wrong spot.

Jam Tin Creek and the North Kennedy fish well for the same species as the Bizant, not forgeting grunter in winter. Salmon are usually common in Jam Tin Creek. More campsites are at the top of the tidal influence, with barra and jacks in upstream freshwater.

Saltwater Creek, in the north-west of the park, is another North Kennedy tributary, and with freshwater and limited tidal water fishing.

The furthest camp below Hann Crossing has a bank launch into tidal water. Excellent jack and barra fishing can be had around the rocks near the launch site.

Beach camps

The Bathurst Bay area is one of Queensland's most diverse and ruggedly attractive remote fishing and camping destinations.

The "bay" stretches in a broad curve some 22km from Bathurst Heads to reach its eastern boundary at the impressive boulder fields of Cape Melville National Park.

Interspersed along this uninhabited coastline are sandy beaches, craggy sandstone and granite boulder headlands, inshore fringing reefs and mangrove forests, and small tidal streams, the largest being Muck River.

Unlike nearby Princess Charlotte Bay, there is a deficiency in sizable estuaries.

For fishermen, this is compensated by the presence of the nearby Flinders Islands, the smaller Rocky Islets, Pipon Reef, and shoals.

In favourable weather, small-boat anglers can enjoy excellent fishing around these locations for a wealth of pelagic and reef species.

In practical terms, the poor road access and the "bay's" isolation from the main settlements on Cape York means that the area is only suitable for adventurous, self-reliant anglers.

The dry season south-east trade winds are a major factor affecting fishing and boating on eastern Cape York, and can blow with a ferocity that has to be seen to be believed.

Bathurst Bay Coastal Route

The coastal route to Bathurst Bay from Cooktown via Starcke Station is about 240km and takes 10 to 12 hours driving time. It is rougher and slower than the inland route.

About 120km north of Cooktown, a short track eastwards leads to the mouth of the Starcke River, not shown on our maps. There is a concrete ramp and camping area near the mouth.

There is good tidal river fishing, excellent crabbing, and mosquitoes and sandflies.

A Green Zone sanctuary lies immediately outside, so fishing is restricted to the river unless you go 10km or so offshore.

About 3km north of the abandoned outstation at Wakooka, on the main Bathurst Bay road, another track heads about 7km into the top of Wakooka Creek. This is a small but productive system.

Once again, the adjacent coastal waters are a Green Zone, which prohibits fishing.

The tracks mentioned require 4WD and are slow and rough, featuring washouts, potholes, gullies, detours, bulldust and sand.

Mud holes will also be encountered early in the dry season.

It is essential that travellers carry vehicle recovery gear and a compressor, as reducing tyre pressure is required for sandy stretches.

Those intending to camp at Wakooka Creek or the Starcke mouth should carry drinking water.

Bathurst Bay visitors can normally replenish their supplies from the spring creek at the foot of Melville Range in all but the driest of years.

The nearest fuel and supplies can be purchased at Musgrave, Laura and Cooktown, with the latter two towns offering more services.

When boating in remote areas, carry extra fuel and water.

Camping permits for national parks are available from Lakefield or Cooktown, the latter for Cape Melville only. Or go online.

When camping along rivers, sites should be set away from the water to minimise crocodile risk. Don't wade or swim.

Fish frames should never be buried on the beach, as the smell attracts crocodiles.

Take your rubbish with you. The rubbish left behind by some visitors threatens future access.

And don't hack into the beachfront Wongai trees at Cape Melville, these are the best shade trees in the north.

However the coastal alignment at Bathurst Bay means that except for the far west near Bathurst Head, the south-easter is sweeping off the land, which means inshore waters remain calm for reasonable boat travel, although tents and tarps must be well pegged and lashed down.

When a gap develops between high pressure systems, or during the warmer dry season months when the more benign northerlies begin to blow, boaters are typically blessed with glassy seas in the morning, followed by a stiff afternoon north-east sea breeze.

Access

As with all remote Cape York areas, 4WD travel into Bathurst Bay is limited to the dry season months.

Typically, this varies according to the extent and severity of each monsoon season, as nature inevitably dictates.

Exceptionally heavy wet seasons may see the road only open as late as July or early August.

Late in the year it is getting hot and stormy, and although the evening lightning shows can be spectacular from the shady beachside camps, any widespread storm activity can close the access tracks.

QPWS rangers at Cooktown or Lakefield, the Police, and the Cook Shire can provide timely information on road conditions.

Cooktown and Laura offer the last opportunity to top up fuel and food supplies, and limited tucker supplies are also available at Coen or Musgrave if you are coming down from the northern Cape.

The coast at the eastern end of Bathurst Bay is accessed by two different 4WD tracks. Both join at Wakooka Outstation for the last section to the beach.

The 225km coastal route from Cooktown is rough. The first 80km to the old Starcke Station is reasonable, but the balance is mostly washouts, ruts, eroded creek crossings, sand and bulldust stretches.

Depending upon conditions, this route will take up to 12 hours, and may have muddy sections early in the dry season.

Heading north on this route, there is a concrete boat ramp on the lower Starcke River, but the adjacent coastline is shallow and a Green Zone applies along the coast out to about 12km seaward, the only nearby exception being Pethebridge Islets.

Further north on the track, Jeannie River crossing is steep and may require a winch.

Carry water for the road trip, as water supplies along the way are unreliable.

The 265km inland route from Lakeland Downs (on the Cooktown road) travels through Laura and into Lakefield NP.

From here the track crosses the Normanby River, threads northwards through Kalpowar and swings east at the junction with the Bathurst Heads road immediately after crossing a small log bridge.

Extreme care should be taken at Barramundi Creek crossing a few kilometres past this junction – early in the dry it is deep and boggy. Further down the track, lower tyre pressures for sandy stretches. Creating new diversions just causes damage and creates more soft sand.

The last 45km from Wakooka to the beach typically takes two hours.

Camping and fishing

The camp sites in eastern Bathurst Bay are within Cape Melville National Park.

All camping in Cape Melville NP must be booked in advance.

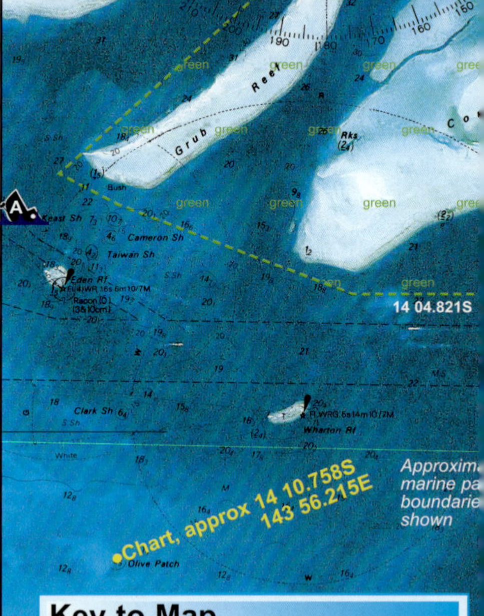

Key to Map

Hotspots

1. Rivers and river mouths hold large grunter, jewfish, trevally, queenfish.
2. Excellent mangrove jack fishing.
3. Rockbar on south side of mouth has barra.
4. Grunter, barramundi, salmon.
5. Big barramundi off rocks, best in warm, calm weather. Also queenfish, trevally.
6. Reef and pelagic fish near islands.
7. Queenfish, trevally around rocks.
8. High tide fishing off beach for queenfish, trevally. Fish small creeks along beach on first outgoing tide.
9. River mouth has barra, salmon, queenfish.

Launch sites

1. Bizant River, upper tide, rocks upstream. For PCB river mouths, add about 30 minutes to Cairns tides.
2 and 3. Melville NP beach launch, from about half tide up.
4. Ninian Bay beach launch.

Wrecks

A. Approx 14 02.739S, 143 53.242E, 17m.
B. Shallow wreck, approx 14 12.568S, 144 13.135E.
C. Shallow wreck, approx 14 06.696S, 144 30.098E.
D. Wreck, approx 14 07.706S, 144 34.664E, 20m

Local tidal movement is up to about 3m.

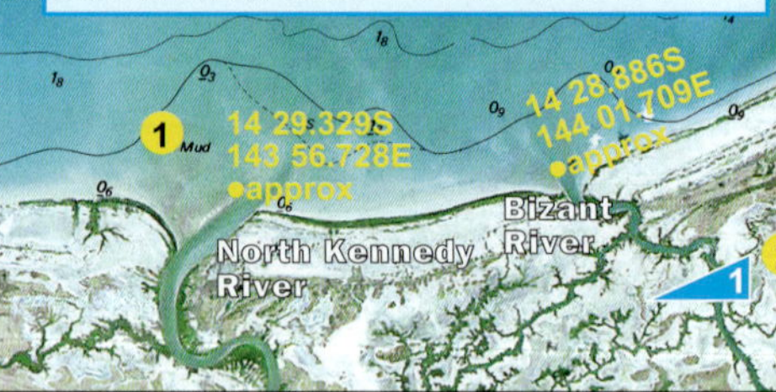

Campers must purchase an e-permit before arriving at the camping areas.

Self-registration is not available and there is no mobile phone coverage on site.

To obtain an e-permit, visit www.qpws.usedirect.com/qpws/

There is a self-service kiosk with camping permit booking facilities at Lakefield NP, Iron Range NP, and Heathlands Regional Park ranger bases, as well as QPWS Coen and Cooktown offices. Credit card and camping credits are accepted but no cash facilities are available.

Cape Melville NP has beautiful shady camp sites under gnarly groves of Wongai trees, with a view seawards that often features passing turtles, dolphins, manta rays and dugong, and an inland backdrop of a mountain range comprised of giant, jumbled granite boulders.

The Wongais, a native of Cape York, are very slow growing and campers should avoid trampling young plants, as these will eventually grow to provide new shady camps in future.

Fifty metres inland from where the beach is first reached, a track heads east for 4km to a clear creek where water supplies can be replenished.

A branching track crosses this creek and continues eastward towards the cape, with a number of campsites along this picturesque coastline.

The beaches can fish well for grunter, salmon, barramundi, cod, trevally, queenfish, trevally, and flathead, and night fishing can be productive, keeping in mind crocodiles.

Around the headlands and fringing reefs, the species list expands to mackerel, golden snapper, tuna, jacks, cobia, and maori sea perch. Out wider, the Flinders Islands group, Rocky Islets, Pipon Reef and the adjacent Pipon and Oswald Shoals are home to coral trout, sweetlip, red emperor and nannygai, however good weather is needed to reach these locations safely.

Bathurst Bay is zoned yellow by the GBRMPA, which allows recreational fishing but precludes gill netting.

This measure guarantees healthy stocks of barramundi and salmon.

Crocodiles

As with all areas of coastal Cape York Peninsula, Bathurst Bay has a crocodile population.

Each creek supports mostly smaller crocodiles, while larger animals patrol the coastline. An attack on a person happened after a big crocodile was attracted to fish frames buried on the beach by previous campers.

Burying fish frames, or throwing them out at the water's edge, is dangerous because it entices crocodiles to hang around and even travel up beaches near campsites.

Being opportunistic feeders, they will grab anything along the way that is edible, including people.

As anywhere in the North, camp well back from the water.

Take fish frames and other food remains out to sea where they won't attract giant reptiles.

Also take care when landing fish as crocodiles are invariably attracted to the struggles. Don't swim in any local creek or waterhole.

Marine stingers and stonefish are also abundant in these waters.

River & reef

Cooktown is famous for bluewater fishing, and wind. It can be a trick to get out during the tourist season as trade winds can blow with little respite.

When the wind eases, it is game on. Cooktown's proximity to the Great Barrier Reef puts some of Australia's best fishing on offer, with red emperor, nannygai, coral trout, cod and big reef-dwelling mangrove jacks.

The outside edge of the famous Ribbon Reefs is home to big bluespot trout, dogtooth tuna, giant trevally and green jobfish.

Giant trevally over 50kg are hooked, but less often landed.

For those who can't go wide, the inshore reefs fish well at times, and the local wharf and nearby rock-wall foreshore regularly produces big fish, including barramundi.

Fishing the inshore reefs is generally best in winter. Large spanish mackerel, spangled emperor, jacks, golden snpper (fingermark), tuskfish and barcheek trout are all caught from headland reefs such as Amos Bay, Archers Point, Graves Point, and north to South Bedford and Cape Flattery.

Broken bottom and rubble patches between the reefs, and wrecks, are home to saddle-tailed sea perch (nannygai). Fish over 80cm are common, with numerous fish cracking 90cm.

The reefs can be fished using soft plastics and jigs, surface poppers, stick baits, trolled lures and or simple cut baits.

One of the best black marlin fisheries in the world is 56km offshore at the Ribbon Reefs. From September to December these reefs produce more 1000lb black marlin than any other place in Australia, and possibly the world. Other species include sailfish, mahi mahi, wahoo and monster mackerel.

Headland spearfishing is good if you don't mind the tiger sharks and crocodiles.

The tidal movement in Cooktown is not huge, with average tides around the 2m to 2.5m mark. Water clarity in the Endeavour River is usually good, except during the wet season.

Endeavour River: The upper ramp near Marton township has protection from wind, and with plenty of parking. Follow the signs to the Cooktown Airport on the road, heading towards Hopevale. After you see the sign for Marton, turn right just before you enter the township onto Starke Road. Continue for 500m and turn into Slaughter Yard Road. From this road you will see the boat ramp on the right.

Endeavour River
WARICK GRUBB

Cooktown foreshore
WARICK GRUBB

The upper sections of the North and South Arms of the Endeavour River run through a mixture of tropical rainforest that looks similar to the Daintree, Russell and Mulgrave Rivers.

Catching barra and jacks from under the fan palms is an awesome experience.

Herring (sardines), garfish and mullet bait can be caught in the tidal river, and one of the best spots is downstream from the wharf. Blue and brown herring show up in the cast net, and the river jacks seem to prefer the blue ones.

From mid-year (June, July, August) herring school near the wharf in the Endeavour River and mackerel are usually onto them. Many are caught from the jetty and foreshore rocks at the mouth, and jacks, golden snapper and trevally are all a chance here and further upstream.

Pikey bream, flathead and whiting are common, with grunter, tarpon and queenfish also showing up.

Barramundi are best in warm, calm weather. Use livebait at night for best results.

Annan River: The Annan tends to clean up faster after rain than the Endeavour.

There is a launch site at the bridge, and the river is best navigated from half tide up, as it is shallow. It tends to fish better with cleaner water pushing in with the tide.

There is deep water upstream of the bridge that can fish well for golden snapper and jacks. Beware the many rockbars.

Key to Maps

Hotspots

Endeavour River ...
1. Along beach: whiting, flathead, trevally, queenish towards high tide.
2. Wharf: mackerel, trevally, barramundi, jacks, cod, bait herring. Foreshore rocks fish well on upper tide using lures or bait. Good all year, best in Dec/Jan.
3. Jacks, bream, trevally, bait herring.
4. Above sand slides: barramundi, jacks, tarpon.
5. Grunter and whiting.
6. Golden snapper and jacks.
7. Four Mile Creek: rocks near old rail line, barra and jacks.
8. Bank access: bream, trevally, jacks, grunter.
9. North Arm islands hold barra and jacks.
10. North Arm snags hold barra, jacks, trevally.
11. Shingle bar and rocks in this area.
12. Numerous rockbars above bridge.

Annan & Esk River - 1. Queenfish, jacks, grunter.
2. Saltwater Creek: jacks, bream, mud crabs.
3. Grunter and jacks.
4. Rockbar: jacks, barra, bream and cod.
5. Flathead, barra, queenfish on channel edge.
6. Rocks: jacks and bream.
7. Deep bank: golden snapper, jacks, tarpon.
8 and 8. Barra, jacks.
9. The river becomes shallow after this point.

Launch sites
1. Endeavour River. Use Cairns tide times.
2. Endeavour River, 4WD ramp.
3. Annan River: ramp on north side of bridge.

Wrecks
A. Charted wreck, approx 15 12.023S, 145 20.637E
B. Charted wreck, approx 15 17.718S, 145 21.544E.
Local tides have up to about 2.9m movement.

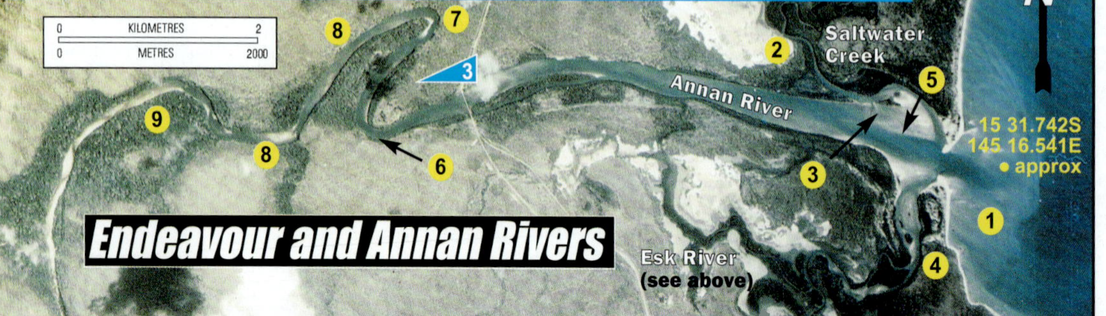

Both the Annan and Endeavour can fish well for barramundi after prolonged wet season rain, but the rain doesn't fall hard every year.

Esk River: The Esk runs off the Annan's south bank near the mouth.

This small river is strewn with rocks and snags, with great lure-casting for jacks, cod, salmon and barra.

The sandbar at the mouth usually has big queenfish and trevally.

McIvor River: The McIvor north of Cooktown is traversable by boat from the mouth up to a rockbar about 3km above the junction of the Morgan River tributary.

The river mouth is broad but shallow.

About 3km upstream are deep areas around an island which fish well for golden snapper and grunter. Barra can be caught by walking and casting above the rockbar, keeping in mind the crocodiles.

The reef outside the McIvor mouth should be fished in calm weather.

Morgan River: There is a launch site on the Morgan River on a 4WD track from Cooktown.

An alternate route is driving from Hopevale to Elim and then along the beach at low tide to the mouth, for which you will need permission from Hopevale, phone (07) 4060 9133.

North of Cooktown: The Starke River (off map) is a three-hour drive. A 4WD is required. The river has a concrete boat ramp with bush camping.

The coastline is a continuous Green Zone for 10km or so outside the river, but the nearby Pethebridge Islets can be fished and are within easy reach.

Coquet Island, 28km north of the mouth, has big pelagic fish, mainly on the north-west end.

Nearby Wilson Rock has monster trevally on big tides, with much the same at Miles Reef and Newton Island.

Port Douglas to Cape Tribulation

This area offers river fishing in tropical rainforest surroundings. For boaters, it is just a 30km run from Dayman Point ramp to Batt Reef, a major structure. There are inshore grounds which fish well for tuskfish, trout, cod, grass emperor and flag, especially when the water is slightly discoloured after rough weather. A coastal Green Zone restricts fishing north of Cape Tribulation along the famous Cape Tribulation road. The Low Islands are also part of a large marine sanctuary. The main species in the tidal creeks are flathead, whiting, bream, jacks, salmon and barra, along with queenfish and trevally. There are jungle perch and sooty grunter in the freshwater rainforest reaches of coastal streams.

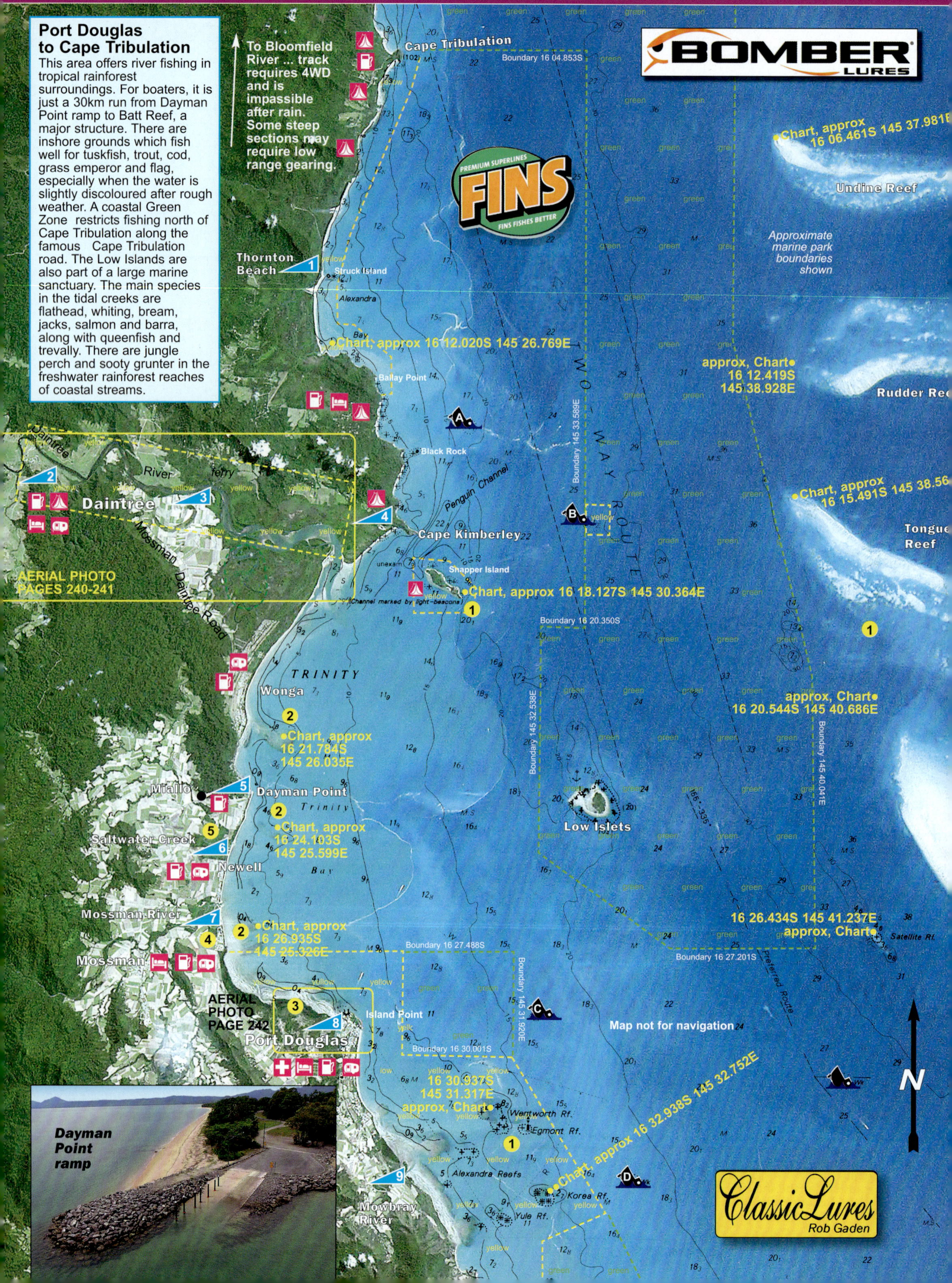

To Bloomfield River ... track requires 4WD and is impassible after rain. Some steep sections may require low range gearing.

Cape Tribulation

Boundary 16 04.853S

BOMBER LURES

FINS

Chart, approx 16 06.461S 145 37.981E

Undine Reef

Approximate marine park boundaries shown

Thornton Beach

Struck Island

Alexandra

Bay

Chart, approx 16 12.020S 145 26.769E

Ballay Point

approx, Chart 16 12.419S 145 38.928E

Rudder Reef

Black Rock

Daintree River

Daintree

ferry

Penguin Channel

Two Way Route

Boundary 145 33.589E

Chart, approx 16 15.491S 145 38.56

Tongue Reef

Cape Kimberley

Snapper Island

Mossman Daintree Road

AERIAL PHOTO PAGES 240-241

Chart, approx 16 18.127S 145 30.364E

(Channel marked by light-beacons)

Boundary 16 20.350S

Trinity

Wonga

Chart, approx 16 21.784S 145 26.035E

Boundary 145 32.538E

approx, Chart 16 20.544S 145 40.686E

Boundary 145 40.041E

Miallo

Dayman Point

Trinity Bay

Chart, approx 16 24.103S 145 25.599E

Saltwater Creek

Newell

Low Islets

Mossman River

Chart, approx 16 26.935S 145 25.326E

Mossman

Boundary 16 27.488S

16 26.434S 145 41.237E approx, Chart

Satellite Rf.

Boundary 16 27.201S

Boundary 145 31.920E

AERIAL PHOTO PAGE 242

Island Point

Port Douglas

Boundary 16 30.001S

Map not for navigation

Dayman Point ramp

16 30.937S 145 31.317E approx, Chart

Wentworth Rf.

Egmont Rf.

Chart, approx 16 32.938S 145 32.752E

Alexandra Reefs

Korea Rf.

Yule Rf.

Mowbray River

N

Classic Lures Rob Gaden

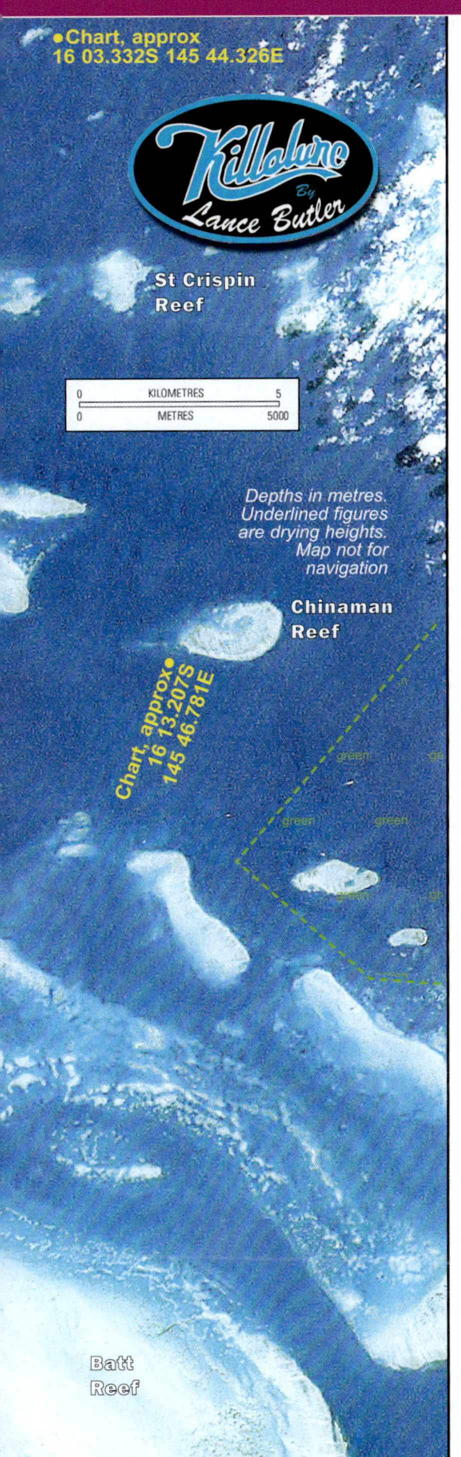

Wet tropics

For those travelling Queensland's north, the Daintree region is where the cane farms end and wild tropical sportfishing begins.

North of the Daintree, the last major settlement is Cooktown.

Boats need only travel a few kilometres to sea to catch coral trout, nannygai, emperor and more.

The Daintree region has plenty of fishing space, but visitors should note the Green Zones that run along the coast.

Daintree River: This is the largest river in the region and has a steady flow of freshwater all year.

Motorists cross the Daintree River by ferry to proceed up to Cape Tribulation and the Bloomfield track.

The South Arm of the Daintree River near the mouth is closed to fishing.

Jungle perch, mostly small barra and sooty grunter inhabit the freshwater reaches of the Daintree.

Fishos appreciate the rainforest setting and wildlife, including many crocodiles.

Launching is done near the ferry crossing and at the Daintree township ramp, both on sealed roads. Both ramps can be used during most tides.

The lower river has extensive mud and sandflats, but is fairly easy to navigate.

At the mouth good fishing is had for trevally and queenfish, especially in winter, with barra in warm weather. Grunter, whiting, flathead, salmon and prawns are often abundant.

Small creeks near the mouth are worth fishing, arguably best for boaters on the last of the run-out tide and the first two hours of the run-in tide.

For bait fishing a good spot is the Ballast Heap. As you approach the mouth of the river you see two shacks on the left side. About 500m from here are submerged rocks. Use your sounder.

The species usually caught here are barramundi, mangrove jacks, cod and golden snapper.

Another popular spot is opposite the boat ramp near the ferry on the run-out tide. About 5km upstream from the ferry boat ramp, the bankside vegetation starts to change and there are weedbeds. The weedbeds hold barra, which bite best in warm weather. Cast shallow lures.

There are several incoming creeks in the upper reaches which have limited wet season run-offs, including the Douglas junction just above the township.

Upstream the river narrows and jungle perch and sooty grunter take over.

Shaded pockets and grassy edges are the spots to fish. Small lures catch most fish.

Visitors can drive along the river above Daintree township and walk to the bank in places, but respect private property.

There are two crossings above the township.

Daintree offshore: The reefs around Snapper Island have coral trout, sweetlip, golden snapper and pelagic fish. There is a campsite on the island, which requires a parks permit. Cape Kimberley has rock fishing.

Just 22km east of the river mouth, Tongue Reef is a large, complex reef with many coral bommies that hold trout and lobsters (painted crays).

Batt Reef to the south has a long, deep southern wall, ideal for trolling up big pelagic fish.

Bloomfield River: The river, about 20km north of Cape Tribulation (north of the accompanying map), is in a yellow zone and therefore has no commercial fishing.

Bitumen stops at Cape Tribulation and 4WD access to the Bloomfield River is difficult to impossible in the wet season, with flowing creeks, soft sections and steep climbs.

The river has a concrete ramp just north of the tiny Ayton settlement. The other launch site, a sandbar at the mouth, is for 4WD.

Just inside the Bloomfield mouth is a hole which produces fish on live bait at the turn of tide.

Lure fishing is best along the deep banks, snags and creek junctions. Jacks, cod, trevally and queenfish are in the saltwater reaches.

There are gravel bars upstream that can be a hazard at low tide, but the upper river is pretty and worth exploring. Above the causeway there are a few jungle perch, sooty grunter and jacks, but this is a busy tourist area.

Mossman River and Saltwater Creek: These two small tidal waterways produce most estuary fish, and mud crabs.

Livebaiting is the best way to fish the creeks.

There is much the same tidal fishing in Dixon Inlet at Port Douglas. See Port Douglas detail on Page 242.

Mossman River has sooty grunter and jungle perch in the freshwater section.

Mowbray River: The Mowbray River 7.4km south of Port Douglas has a launch site near the main road and is good for jacks, golden snapper and mud crabs. It has a reef at the mouth which can fish well when the wind isn't blowing.

The best fishing near the reef is often after windy weather or a storm.

Key to Map

Launch sites

1. Thornton Beach ramp.
2. Daintree township, good concrete ramp into upper Daintree River.
3. Daintree River ferry crossing, single-lane concrete ramp. Beware ramp drop-off at low tide, and crocodiles.
4. Cape Kimberley high tide beach launch, easy access to Snapper Island.
5. Dayman Point, just south of Wonga Beach on Cook Hwy. Concrete ramp with small rock wall, poor in a northerly. Good access to offshore reefs.
6. Saltwater Creek, bank launch for small boats.
7. Mossman River, ramps at Newell and Cooya, best for small boats. Sea entrance is shallow, use on upper tide.
8. Port Douglas, three-lane sheltered ramp with most facilities nearby.
9. Mowbray River, unsealed launch site.

Crocodiles exist in these waters.
Local tides move up to about 3.11m

Hotspots

1&1. Smorgasboard of reefs east of Daintree River mouth. It is just 22km from the river mouth to giant Tongue Reef. For cartoppers, reefs near Cape Kimberley/Snapper Island have coral trout, grass sweetlip, cod, mackerel, queenfish, trevally and lobsters. Note Green Zone.
2, 2 and 2. Cod, queenfish, trout, tuskfish, trevally. Dayman Point boat ramp has a small rock wall suitable for landbased fishing.
3. Muddy Creek, some estuary fish, mud crabs.
4. Mossman River has most estuary fish, mud crabs. Fish mangrove edges and low tide holes.
5. Saltwater Creek at Newell had a fishing platform under construction in late 2021, jacks, whiting, flathead, salmon, barra and mud crabs.

Wrecks

A. Charted wreck, approx 16 14.020S, 145 30.585E
B. Charted wreck, approx 16 16.388S, 145 33.727E
C. Charted wreck, approx 16 28.516S, 145 32.444E
D. Charted wreck, approx 16 32.519S, 145 35.005E

Daintree River

The flats from Port Douglas to Daintree River are home to trevally, queenfish, sharks, snub-nosed dart (permit), tarpon, salmon and even bonefish. Look for fish working bait. Anglers can fish from shore at the Daintree River mouth by driving to Wonga Beach. Walk the beach at high tide and cast lures or baits. Some anglers target flathead and whiting, others chase queenfish and trevally. The tidal Daintree fishes well for barramundi at times, with sooty grunter, jacks and jungle perch upstream. The sealed road gives good rainy season access.

Barron River

This river leads upstream to Barron Falls about 18km from the mouth, and further on to Tinaroo Dam. The relatively short stretch of tidal river is quite deep and produces some large fish. Locals say the Barron River is under-rated as a trophy barra river, with 120cm+ fish caught by those in the know. For barra, try fishing at night on the run-out tide at the highway bridge. Further downstream there is a rock wall on the southern bank where barra are caught by trolling and casting lures near low tide. This wall also produces jacks, golden snapper and trevally. The mouth of the river has sandflats and on the run-in tide in the cooler months trevally and queenfish can be seen tearing up baitfish, when poppers and skipping lures work well. Whiting and flathead are also caught.
The river mouth can be reached by road by taking Machan's Beach turn-off from the highway. Pikey bream are common in the river, especially in rocky areas above the old bridge. Upstream the river narrows and becomes brackish. Above the falls the freshwater section contains jungle perch and sooty grunter. The lower river is easy to navigate but care is required upstream. Care is needed entering Thomatis Creek, where there are submerged rocks and trees, and concrete blocks under the bridge. Bankside access is readily available for landbased fishing, but crocodiles are present.

Key to Map

Hotspots

1. Trevally, permit, queenfish, whiting, bream, flathead along edge, best on winter mornings.
2. Fish along deep bank with live bait. Barra, salmon, whiting, flathead and more.
3, 3 and 3. Good fishing on run-out tide at mouths.
4. Barra near pylons at night under airport lights.
5. Bait fishing area for grunter, bream.
6. Barra after extended rain, jungle perch upstream.
7. Bream, cod, grunter off old bridge, which has been converted into a jetty for fishing. Pylons downstream hold fish, especially at night.
8. Deep hole holds fish. Good snags for lure castng just inside Redden Creek.

Launch sites

1. Barron River, Christensen St, all tides.
2. Barron River, Greenbank Rd, all tides.
3. Thomatis Creek, Acacia St, mid-upper tide.

Local tides have up to about 3.1m movement.

Daintree River

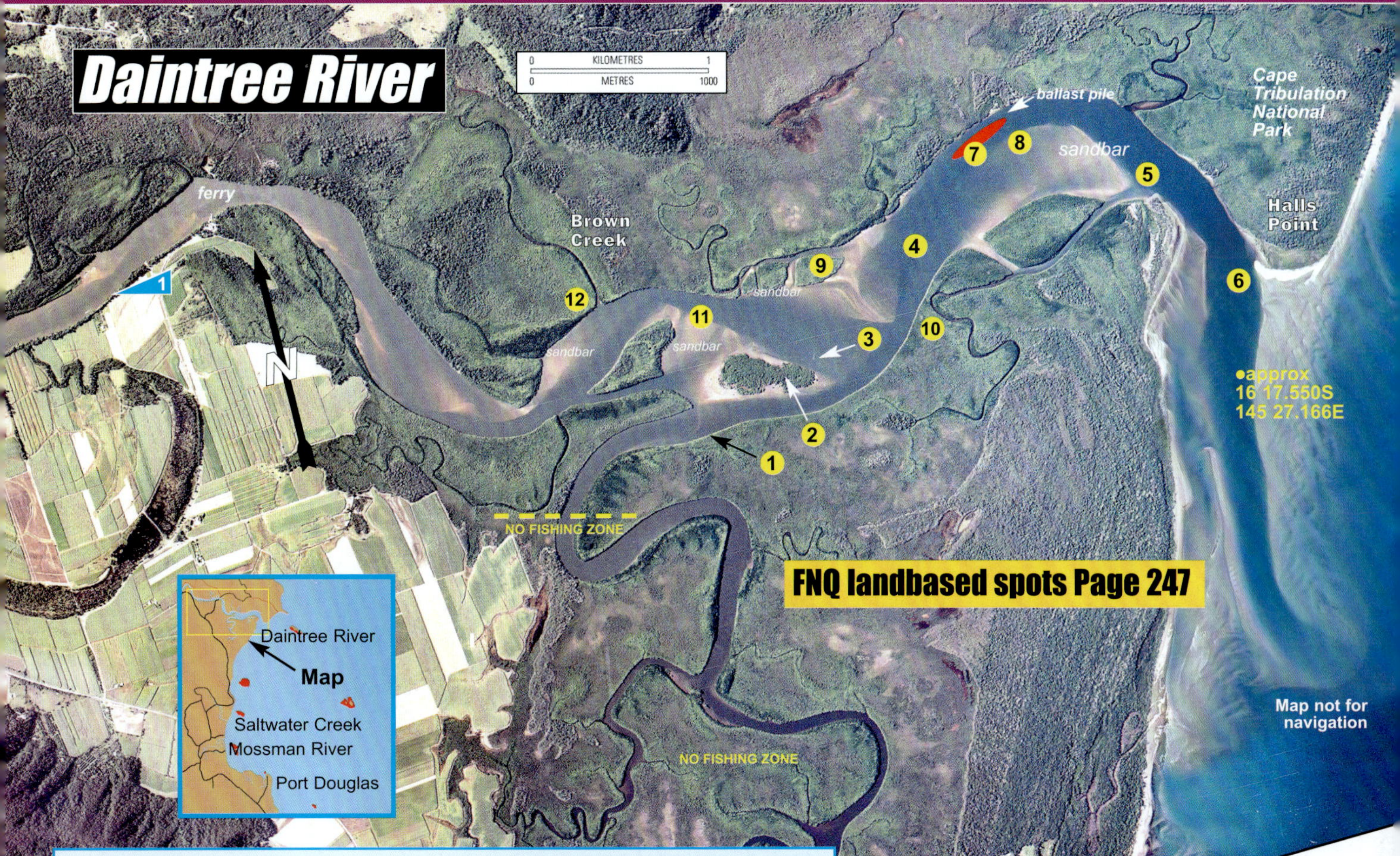

0 KILOMETRES 1
0 METRES 1000

ferry
Brown Creek
ballast pile
sandbar
Cape Tribulation National Park
Halls Point
N
●approx 16 17.550S 145 27.166E
NO FISHING ZONE
NO FISHING ZONE
Map not for navigation

Daintree River
Map
Saltwater Creek
Mossman River
Port Douglas

FNQ landbased spots Page 247

Key to Map

Hotspots

1. Snags here and along southern bank. Fish last of run-out tide. Good spot for mud crabs.
2. Right next to mangroves/island, best on big tide, first of run-out.
3. Fish drop-off on last of run-out, grunter.
4. Gutter near mangroves, grunter, queenfish.
5. Sand gutter just metres from bank. last run-out first run-in, bait and predators.
6. Sandbar gutters (use sounder) big queenfish and trevally.
7. Ballast piles, rock patches in deep water: good on slow tides for most estuary fish.
8. Drop-off, use sounder, queenfish, grunter.
9. Sandbar drop-off, most species.
10. Deep snags along bank.
11. Sandbar, deep, queenfish, GTs, grunter.
12. Last of run-out tide, grunter and trevally.
13. Sooty grunter, jungle perch, barramundi in the freshwater, use small lures and light leaders. Bream, jacks as you go downstream.

Launch sites

1. Concrete ramp with pontoon on south bank about 500m from ferry crossing.
2. All-tide concrete ramp at township.

Largemouth nannygai

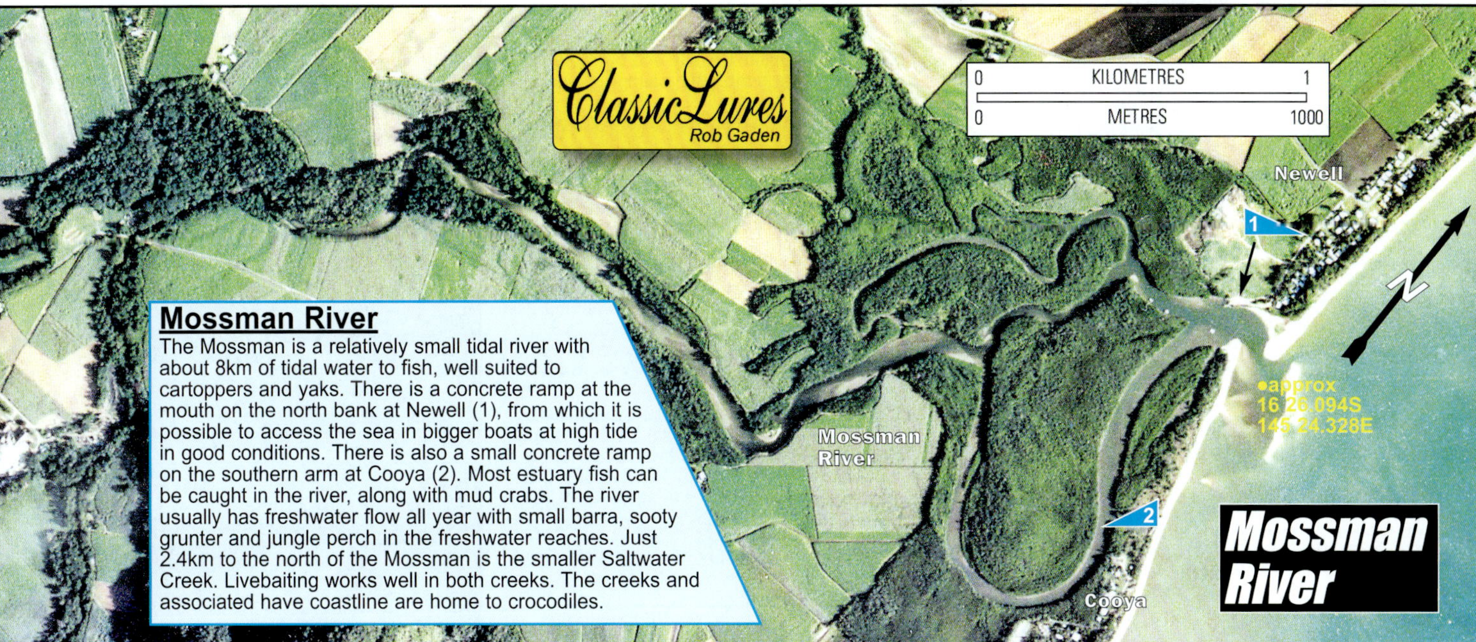

Map not for navigation

Port Douglas foreshore at the entrance to the inlet

Port Douglas

Dicksons Inlet is the major feature here, with the mangrove-lined estuary producing good fishing for barramundi, salmon and mud crabs. Around the many pylons are jacks, grunter, bream, cod and golden snapper. Further up the estuary, on big tides, work lures at mud drains as the tide falls. Morey Reef, near the mouth of Dicksons Inlet, has queenfish, trevally and some reef fish. The headland rocks are well worth fishing on a rising tide in calm weather, with trophy barramundi always a chance, as well as passing pelagic fish. The beach produces queenfish and blue salmon at high tide. Just 3.3km to the west is Muddy Creek, which winds back towards Dicksons Inlet. This creek has jacks, salmon, barramundi, bream, grunter and mud crabs. There are holes and usually some fallen trees. Entry is by boat through the mouth near high tide. Out the front of the creek fishermen catch sand crabs and mud crabs. To access Muddy Creek, leave Port Douglas ramp on a rising tide. Fish the top of the tide, and as soon as the tide starts to run out, leave, or your boat may become stranded. Just 9km south-east of Port Douglas are several shallow reefs located wide of the Mowbray River mouth. These produce mainly tuskfish, cod, bar-cheeked trout and tricky snapper. Note that there is a GBRMPA sanctuary zone east of Port Douglas. The town marina has boat hire.

Key to Map

Hotspots

General tip: jacks and golden snapper in summer. Trevally, queenfish, grunter in winter.

1. Headland rocks, via Rex Smeal Park: In calm weather catch queenfish, trevally and barramundi on lures. Also blue and threadfin salmon, golden snapper, grunter.
2. Flathead, whiting, grunter over flats. Queenfish during cooler months.
3. Good fishing in deep water near mouth.
4. Deep hole: golden snapper, grunter.
5. Deep water: golden snapper, grunter.
6. Barra, jacks at junctions on outgoing tide.
7. South end of 4-Mile Beach: On calm days fish the incoming tide for trevally, queenfish, dart, whiting, salmon and blacktip sharks.
8. Fish around pylons. Shipwreck Wharf behind St Mary's Church has bream and grunter. Marina rock wall fishes well, but fishing in marina is prohibited. Bream, grunter, jacks, snapper, barra.

Reefs and wrecks

Wentworth Reef (dries) 16 31.013S 145 31.406E, 8.5km
Egmont Reef (dries) 16 31.311S 145 32.242E, 10km
Alexandra Reefs (dries) 16 31.942S 145 30.623E, 12km
Korea Reef (dries) 16 33.029S 145 32.804E, 8km
Charted wreck 16 32.539S 145 35.004E, 15km
Charted wreck 16 30.052S 145 40.423E, 23km
Chartes wreck 16 28.524S 145 32.462E, 8.6km

Launch sites

1. Port Douglas, three lanes, OK for large boats.

Local tidal movement is up to about 3.1m.

Palm Cove jetty between Cairns and Port Douglas

Mackey Creek ramp

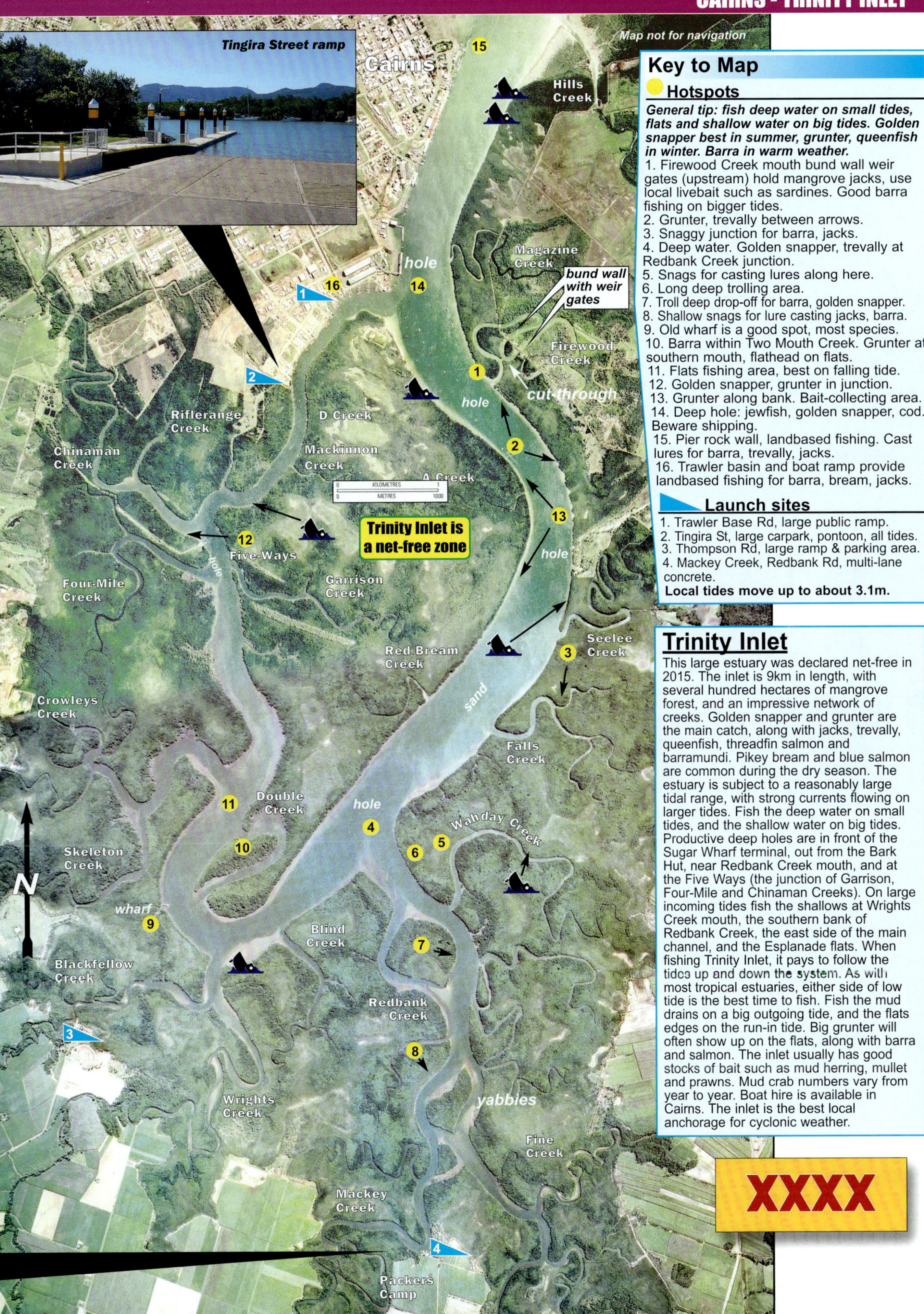

Key to Map

Hotspots

General tip: fish deep water on small tides, flats and shallow water on big tides. Golden snapper best in summer, grunter, queenfish in winter. Barra in warm weather.

1. Firewood Creek mouth bund wall weir gates (upstream) hold mangrove jacks, use local livebait such as sardines. Good barra fishing on bigger tides.
2. Grunter, trevally between arrows.
3. Snaggy junction for barra, jacks.
4. Deep water. Golden snapper, trevally at Redbank Creek junction.
5. Snags for casting lures along here.
6. Long deep trolling area.
7. Troll deep drop-off for barra, golden snapper.
8. Shallow snags for lure casting jacks, barra.
9. Old wharf is a good spot, most species.
10. Barra within Two Mouth Creek. Grunter at southern mouth, flathead on flats.
11. Flats fishing area, best on falling tide.
12. Golden snapper, grunter in junction.
13. Grunter along bank. Bait-collecting area.
14. Deep hole: jewfish, golden snapper, cod. Beware shipping.
15. Pier rock wall, landbased fishing. Cast lures for barra, trevally, jacks.
16. Trawler basin and boat ramp provide landbased fishing for barra, bream, jacks.

Launch sites

1. Trawler Base Rd, large public ramp.
2. Tingira St, large carpark, pontoon, all tides.
3. Thompson Rd, large ramp & parking area.
4. Mackey Creek, Redbank Rd, multi-lane concrete.

Local tides move up to about 3.1m.

Trinity Inlet

This large estuary was declared net-free in 2015. The inlet is 9km in length, with several hundred hectares of mangrove forest, and an impressive network of creeks. Golden snapper and grunter are the main catch, along with jacks, trevally, queenfish, threadfin salmon and barramundi. Pikey bream and blue salmon are common during the dry season. The estuary is subject to a reasonably large tidal range, with strong currents flowing on larger tides. Fish the deep water on small tides, and the shallow water on big tides. Productive deep holes are in front of the Sugar Wharf terminal, out from the Bark Hut, near Redbank Creek mouth, and at the Five Ways (the junction of Garrison, Four-Mile and Chinaman Creeks). On large incoming tides fish the shallows at Wrights Creek mouth, the southern bank of Redbank Creek, the east side of the main channel, and the Esplanade flats. When fishing Trinity Inlet, it pays to follow the tides up and down the system. As with most tropical estuaries, either side of low tide is the best time to fish. Fish the mud drains on a big outgoing tide, and the flats edges on the run-in tide. Big grunter will often show up on the flats, along with barra and salmon. The inlet usually has good stocks of bait such as mud herring, mullet and prawns. Mud crab numbers vary from year to year. Boat hire is available in Cairns. The inlet is the best local anchorage for cyclonic weather.

PALM COVE - TRINITY BEACH - RUSSELL HEADS

Depths in metres. Underlined figures are drying heights. Map not for navigation

16 38.105S approx. Chart
145 56.033E

Chart approx
16 44.606
146 05.396

Chart, approx
16 47.565S
146 03.415E

XXXX

Key to Map

Hotspots

1. Landbased spots include Yorkeys Knob rock walls, Taylors Point and popular Palm Cove jetty.
2. Moon River (creek inside Yorkeys Knob): barra and jacks. Mouth can be fished on foot. Lure-cast for barra off rock walls.
3 and 3. Frankland Islands area has big mackerel usually from May-Sept.
4. Queenfish, trevally, tarpon, whiting, flathead at river mouths.
5. Barra at junction.
6. Jungle perch, tarpon. Bank access for landbased fishing, but beware crocs.
7. Arlington Reef and Oyster Reef: mackerel along drop-offs and coral trout, emperor, cod and other reef fish in shallower water.
8. Channel markers: mackerel, cobia, golden snapper, trevally. Channel edges have grunter, salmon.
9. Mackerel in deep water off headland and at back of Fitzroy Island in winter. Large golden snapper off King Point in summer, use live or fresh squid.

Wrecks

A. Charted wreck, approx 16 39.012S, 145 44.254E, 21m deep.
B. Charted wreck, approx 16 40.641S, 145 42.436E, 12m.
C. Charted wreck, shallow, approx 16 42.549S, 145 40.709E, 8m.
D. Charted wreck, shallow, approx 16 45.387S, 145 41.635E.
E. Charted wreck, approx 16 46.549S, 145 56.851E, 33m.
F. Charted wreck, approx 16 57.540S, 146 03.780E, 26m.
G. Charted wreck, 15m *FV Lorana*, approx 17 09.467S 146 23.073E, 50m.

Launch sites

1. Yorkeys Knob marina (Moon River).
2. Barron River. Ramps off Greenbank and Christensen roads, useable most tides, see page 240. Also Acacia St in Thomatis Creek.
3. Trinity Inlet, see page 243. Multiple ramps, useable all tides.
4. Mulgrave River. Sealed ramp, amenities, boat hire, all tides.
5. Second Beach, Yarrabah Rd, concrete, upper tide.

Local tidal movement is up to about 3.1m.

SEE NEXT PAGE
AERIAL PHOTO PAGE 240
AERIAL PHOTO PAGE 243
AERIAL PHOTO PAGE 246

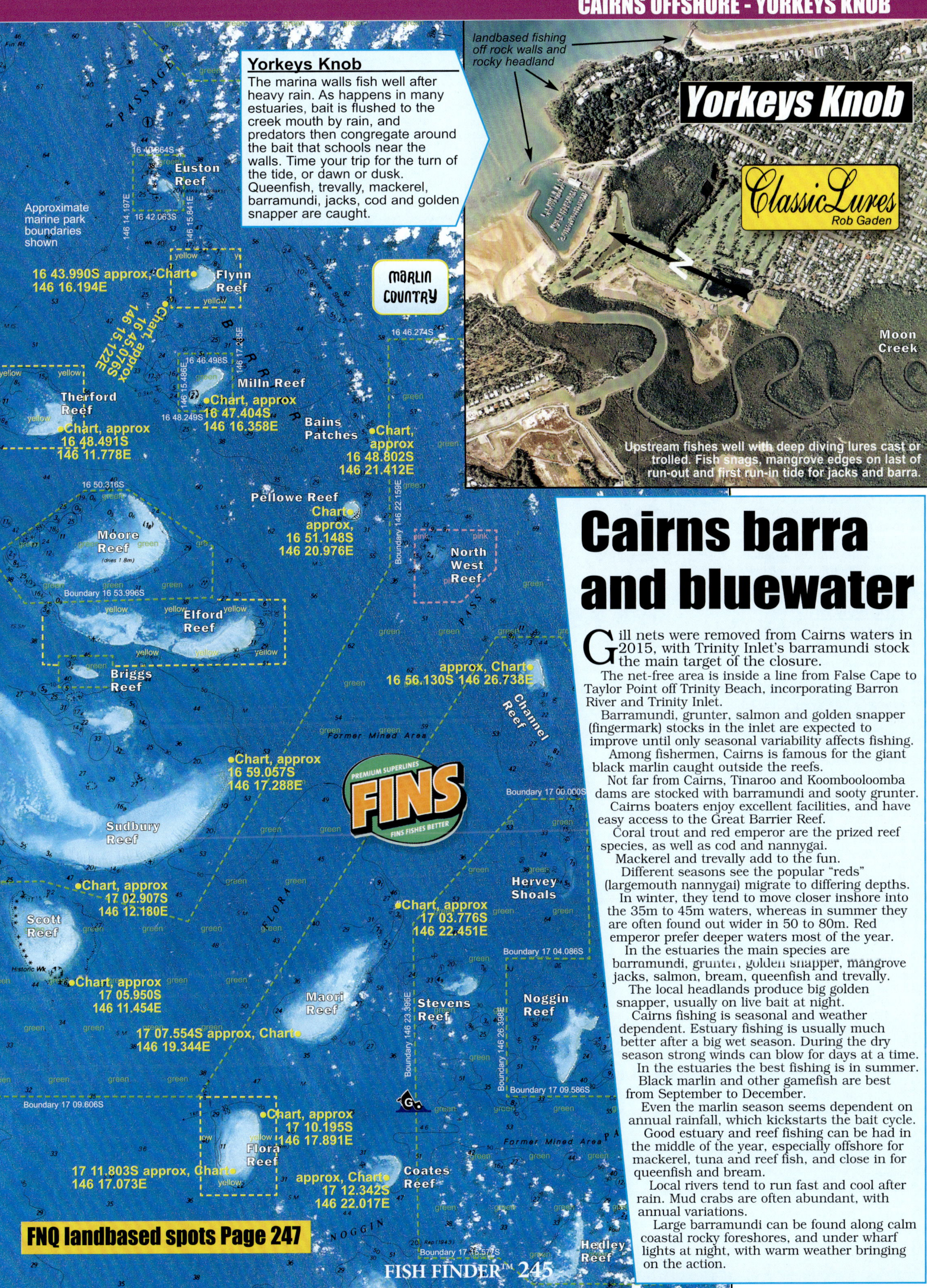

FNQ landbased spots Page 247

Cairns barra and bluewater

Gill nets were removed from Cairns waters in 2015, with Trinity Inlet's barramundi stock the main target of the closure.

The net-free area is inside a line from False Cape to Taylor Point off Trinity Beach, incorporating Barron River and Trinity Inlet.

Barramundi, grunter, salmon and golden snapper (fingermark) stocks in the inlet are expected to improve until only seasonal variability affects fishing.

Among fishermen, Cairns is famous for the giant black marlin caught outside the reefs.

Not far from Cairns, Tinaroo and Koombooloomba dams are stocked with barramundi and sooty grunter.

Cairns boaters enjoy excellent facilities, and have easy access to the Great Barrier Reef.

Coral trout and red emperor are the prized reef species, as well as cod and nannygai.

Mackerel and trevally add to the fun.

Different seasons see the popular "reds" (largemouth nannygai) migrate to differing depths.

In winter, they tend to move closer inshore into the 35m to 45m waters, whereas in summer they are often found out wider in 50 to 80m. Red emperor prefer deeper waters most of the year.

In the estuaries the main species are barramundi, grunter, golden snapper, mangrove jacks, salmon, bream, queenfish and trevally.

The local headlands produce big golden snapper, usually on live bait at night.

Cairns fishing is seasonal and weather dependent. Estuary fishing is usually much better after a big wet season. During the dry season strong winds can blow for days at a time.

In the estuaries the best fishing is in summer.

Black marlin and other gamefish are best from September to December.

Even the marlin season seems dependent on annual rainfall, which kickstarts the bait cycle.

Good estuary and reef fishing can be had in the middle of the year, especially offshore for mackerel, tuna and reef fish, and close in for queenfish and bream.

Local rivers tend to run fast and cool after rain. Mud crabs are often abundant, with annual variations.

Large barramundi can be found along calm coastal rocky foreshores, and under wharf lights at night, with warm weather bringing on the action.

Barra stocking

Cairns waterways, including Barron River, Trinity Inlet and the Russell/Mugrave system, were stocked with tagged barramundi between 2002 and 2009. The results showed that over the next decade, the Barron and Trinity fish stayed in or close to their respective systems. The Russell/Mulgrave fish were far more likely to wander. A small number of fish from both areas were recaptured 30km or more from their release point. All the long-distance travellers went south, the furthest location being the Johnstone River.

Island Camping

Camping is on Russell and High Islands only. Campers must be self-sufficient and use marked sites. Permits are required for High Island. Russell Island is a Commonwealth island and a free camping permit must be obtained. Visit www.parks.des.qld.gov.au for more information.

Russell and Mulgrave Rivers

This is a prime fishing area near Cairns, with the rainforest mountain catchment visible nearby and the scenic Frankland Islands and High Island just offshore. The two rivers receive an average rainfall close to the highest in Australia, running plenty of clear water to the dual mouth in the wet season. The catchment doesn't hold rain for long, with the best barramundi run-off fishing often just two or three days after a prolonged downpour. The Mulgrave tends to fish earlier after rain. The north bank of the river mouth has been eroded, with mangrove trees and old roots along the bank, a good place to target golden snapper, barra, bream, jacks and cod. In the dry season, saltwater makes its way further upstream and so do the marine fish. Smaller barramundi are caught far upstream and bigger fish are found near the mouth. Sooty grunter and jungle perch are in the upper reaches. There is a run of queenfish at the mouth from July until September. Big mackerel can be caught just offshore, usually from about June to September. The rocky Frankland Islands and High Island are great places to fish or moor for a break, keeping in mind the northern Green Zone. Large golden snapper are caught off High Island in summer, using live or freshly caught squid for bait. Barra can be caught from most local rocks in warm, calm weather, usually around high tide. Hire boats are available on the Mulgrave, as well as secure trailer storage. Care is required when navigating the rivers as they are shallow and there are snags and sandbars.

Key to Map

Hotspots

1. The mouth's T-junction is a popular spot. Aug/Sept is best for queenfish and big trevally, which patrol the edges of sandbars and channels. Use poppers or livebaits.
2. The Golden Mile ... deep bank with snags. The northern bank is eroded and fallen mangroves create snags. Most species caught here. Use sonar to find snags holding fish.
3. Bait-collecting area. Fishes on big tides.
4. Barra on weedbeds.
5. Mackerel (over 30kg) on livebaits, best in Sept. Golden snapper.
6. Shallow rocks: 10kg+ golden snapper in shallow water, most other species.
7. Jacks, grunter, barra, trevally in holes.
8. Rocks have bream and jacks. Snags along bank.
9. Big barra off rocks.
10. Queenfish, trevally on flats.

Launch sites

1. Deeral ramp, Mulgrave River, Ross Rd, all tides. Toilets and washdown. Limited parking. Inundated by peak tides/flooding. Car storage for extended trips.
2. Bellenden Ker, Russell River Rd. Turn onto Russell River Rd 6.5km south of Deeral. Toilets, washdown, jetty. Limited parking. Inundated by peak tides/flooding.

For High Island tides subtract 8min from Cairns tide times. Local tides have up to about 3m movement.

Koombooloomba Dam

This stocked dam, 60km south-west of Innisfail, is a hydro-electric impoundment. Its crystal clear water sets it apart from other dams. The rainforest catchment lets few nutrients into the dam, and that's probably why the water is so clear. Large barramundi and sooty grunter can be seen swimming below the boat and along shorelines. The barramundi are often fairly thin, but they fight hard. Sooties are the main catch. The dam, on the Tully River, averages 12m deep, but is deeper in places. It is 40km from Ravenshoe along the Tully Falls Road, which begins on the outskirts of Ravenshoe. The road requires care after rain and may become impassible. There is a boat ramp and camping area. Water levels fluctuate quickly because of heavy rain and hydro releases.

Johnstone River

This river passes through Innisfail, 90km south of Cairns. Johnstone barramundi respond well to the usual fishing techniques, with warm weather best for success. Like the short mountain-fed Russell/Mulgrave system to the north, barra fishing slows down when heavy rainfall cools the river, but it soon picks up again. The Johnstone's upstream reaches are among the best for sooty grunter and jungle perch. The river has rocky outcrops and care is required when navigating. Jewfish and big barramundi are caught in the deeper areas near the mouth, and there are quality jacks around the rocks. A Johnstone barra tagged in January 1995 at 50.5cm was recaptured in February 2010, 15 years later, at 117.5cm long, having grown at a rate of 4.4cm a year, and recaptured just 14km downstream. The river was stocked with barramundi until 2009.

FNQ landbased fishing spots

CAPE YORK PENINSULA

Anywhere you camp near water will likely yield fish, but crocodiles are ever-present. Use local livebait such as mullet or herring for best results.

1. Seisia Jetty. This small jetty has a legendary reputation. It gets busy, but there's usually fish to be caught, especially at night. Barramundi, queenfish, trevally, mackerel and giant barracuda are regular visitors, and there's plenty of herring around the pylons for bait.

2. Cape beaches. Many are just a mudflat at low tide, but a livebait lobbed from the sand at high tide will take barra, salmon, queenfish, trevally and even golden snapper. Don't be put off by a beach's lack of features, although it does help to fish a beach near a rocky area or creek mouth.

3. Chilli Beach. Take a 4WD from the camp site to the nearby tidal creek and fish off the bank for barramundi.

4. Jardine River mouth. Take a 4WD to the mouth from Mutee Heads and fish off the bank for barra, queenfish, trevally, barra and salmon.

5. Lakefield National Park. Most of the campsites are near waterholes. Access to tidal water is limited, and muddy banks mean it is only easily fishable at high tide. The first in after the wet season will do best in the freshwater holes. Barra are usually more abundant after a big wet season. Crocodiles are ever present. Big barramundi are caught off the beach at Bathurst Heads, as well as queenfish and trevally. See our Lakefield map.

6. Weipa. Many landbased spots. See our Weipa map on page 216-217. Beware crocodiles.

COOKTOWN-PORT DOUGLAS-CAIRNS

1. Cooktown. The wharf produces great fish, but be sure to use live sardines for bait. There are limited access points upstream along the tidal Endeavour River. The bridge over the Annan River produces fish at high tide. Archer Point has some rock fishing.

2. Daintree River mouth. Walk in from Wonga Beach. Usually lots of bait here after rain. Flathead, queenfish, salmon, trevally, barramundi, whiting.

3. Port Douglas. Shipwreck Wharf, behind St Mary's Church. Bream, grunter. **Rex Smeal Park,** off headland rocks in calm weather. Queenfish, trevally, barra. **Marina Road Wall,** no fishing in marina, but outside has bream, grunter, jacks, golden snapper, barra. **Southern Four Mile Beach,** fish calm incoming tides - trevally, queenfish, dart, whiting, salmon, barra.

4. Mossman River mouth. Walk in from Newell or Cooya. As for the Daintree.

5. Cairns Town Pier on the Esplanade. Any tide. Deep water. Most species.

6. The Esplanade. High tide over 2.5m for grunter, salmon, whiting, bream and whiting.

7. Barron River. Pontoon up from main bridge - jacks, barra, salmon, cod. Also **Barron River mouth at Machans Beach,** walk sandbar for whiting/bream in winter and flathead/grunter/trevally all year. Also barra.

8. Holloways Beach. Best at high tide. Salmon, jewfish, whiting, sharks.

9. Yorkeys Knob marina walls. Lure the rocks for barra, jacks, bream, cod.

10. Trinity Beach southern headland and Taylors Point. Good for barramundi just outside closed season. There are headlands on the way to Port Douglas, best in calm weather.

11. Suicide Bend headland near Ellis Beach. Barramundi.

12. Palm Cove Jetty. All tides. Better when it is calm and the water is clear. Plenty of bait around the jetty. Most species. Doggie mackerel in winter. Golden snapper and barra in warm weather.

13. South of Cairns is more difficult. There is no good landbased access at the tidal Russell and Mulgrave Rivers, but there is access upstream in the freshwater for sooty grunter/jungle perch. Beware crocodiles in all local waters.

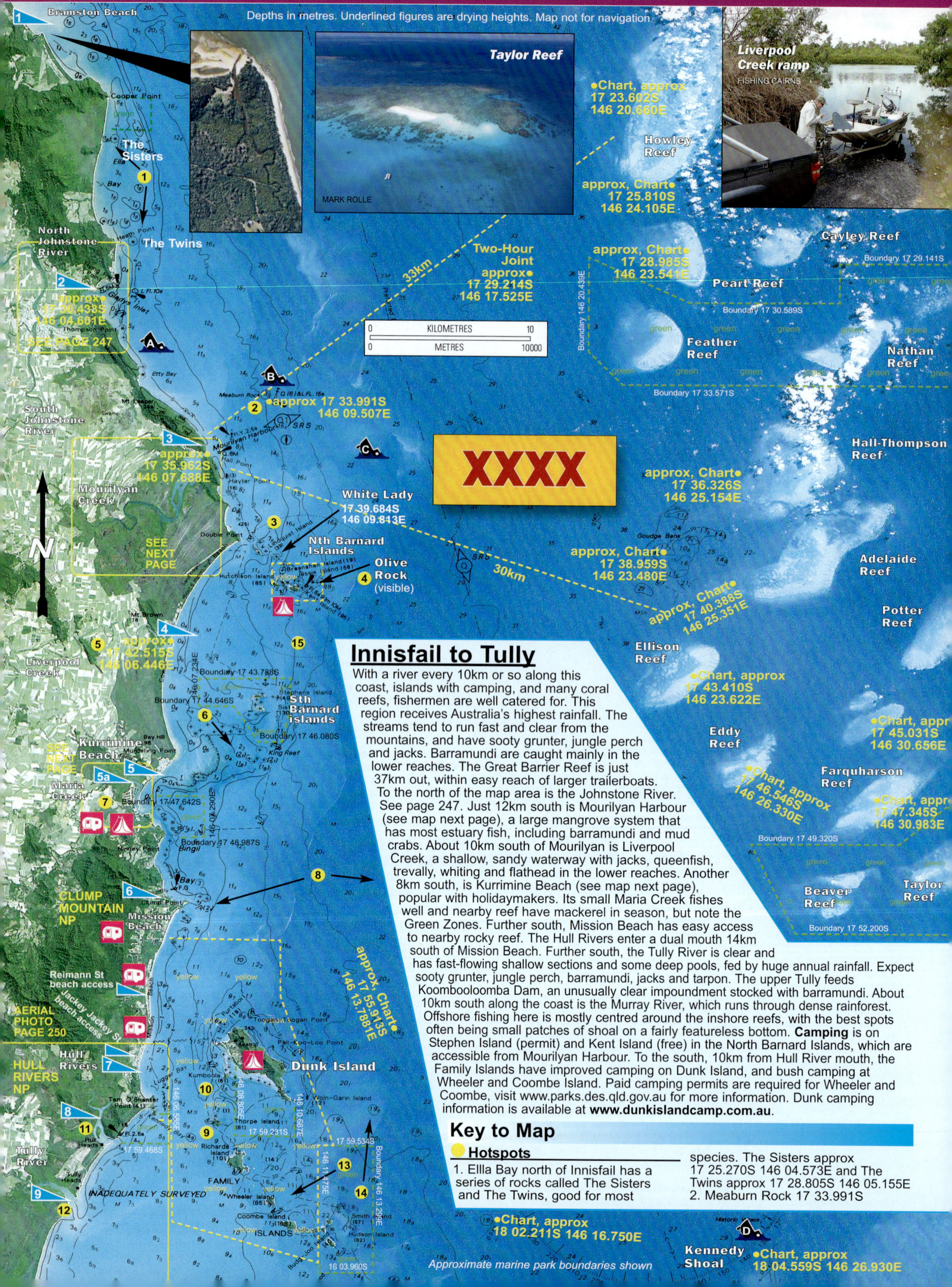

Depths in metres. Underlined figures are drying heights. Map not for navigation.

Innisfail to Tully

With a river every 10km or so along this coast, islands with camping, and many coral reefs, fishermen are well catered for. This region receives Australia's highest rainfall. The streams tend to run fast and clear from the mountains, and have sooty grunter, jungle perch and jacks. Barramundi are caught mainly in the lower reaches. The Great Barrier Reef is just 37km out, within easy reach of larger trailerboats. To the north of the map area is the Johnstone River. See page 247. Just 12km south is Mourilyan Harbour (see map next page), a large mangrove system that has most estuary fish, including barramundi and mud crabs. About 10km south of Mourilyan is Liverpool Creek, a shallow, sandy waterway with jacks, queenfish, trevally, whiting and flathead in the lower reaches. Another 8km south, is Kurrimine Beach (see map next page), popular with holidaymakers. Its small Maria Creek fishes well and nearby reef have mackerel in season, but note the Green Zones. Further south, Mission Beach has easy access to nearby rocky reef. The Hull Rivers enter a dual mouth 14km south of Mission Beach. Further south, the Tully River is clear and has fast-flowing shallow sections and some deep pools, fed by huge annual rainfall. Expect sooty grunter, jungle perch, barramundi, jacks and tarpon. The upper Tully feeds Koombooloomba Dam, an unusually clear impoundment stocked with barramundi. About 10km south along the coast is the Murray River, which runs through dense rainforest. Offshore fishing here is mostly centred around the inshore reefs, with the best spots often being small patches of shoal on a fairly featureless bottom. **Camping** is on Stephen Island (permit) and Kent Island (free) in the North Barnard Islands, which are accessible from Mourilyan Harbour. To the south, 10km from Hull River mouth, the Family Islands have improved camping on Dunk Island, and bush camping at Wheeler and Coombe Island. Paid camping permits are required for Wheeler and Coombe, visit www.parks.des.qld.gov.au for more information. Dunk camping information is available at **www.dunkislandcamp.com.au**.

Key to Map

Hotspots

1. Ellla Bay north of Innisfail has a series of rocks called The Sisters and The Twins, good for most species. The Sisters approx 17 25.270S 146 04.573E and The Twins approx 17 28.805S 146 05.155E
2. Meaburn Rock 17 33.991S

Approximate marine park boundaries shown

Mourilyan

This harbour has good estuary fishing at times, for mainly grunter, golden snapper, cod, queenfish, trevally and salmon. Barramundi are caught by patient anglers fishing with livebait. The deep area near the port is a jew hole, with a chance of big cod and snapper. Jacks are caught regularly in the upper reaches, with whiting and flathead over the flats. The headlands are most easily reached by boat and hold large barramundi in warm weather. Otherwise cod and golden snapper are the main catch. The islands to the south are mackerel and golden snapper hotspots.

Key to Map

Hotspots

1. Landbased fishing from headland through to the first creek. Boat ramp rock wall fishes well at times. Bream, jacks, barra, flathead.
2. Deep holes exist near port and mouth. Good for golden snapper, jewfish.
3. Grunter on drop-offs, whiting, flathead.
4. Queenfish, trevally off Hall Point, fishing by boat. Care needed here. Golden snapper at night on live squid.
5. Barra at junction on outgoing tide.
6. Deep bank good for grunter, jacks, barramundi.
7. Deep water between Double Point and Hutchison Island. Excellent fishing at times for mackerel. Golden snapper best at night.
8. Barra, grunter, salmon on flats at edges of islands.
9. Tidal run-off ... barramundi on outgoing tide.
10. Barra at junction.
11. Good fishing around coastal rocks at times on upper tide ... cod, coral trout, golden snapper. Barra during September/October. Calm weather fishing only by boat for most species.

Ramps

1. Concrete ramp with rock wall, useable most tides, but is exposed to prevailing winds and currents. **Local tidal movement is up to about 3.15m.**

146 09.525E is known locally as The Pinnacle: reef and pelagic fish.
3. White Lady bommie between Lindquist and Bresnshen Island, approx 17 39.684S 146 09.813E.
4. Exposed Olive Rock 200m off North Barnard Islands is described locally as the centre of the fishing universe. Big mackerel, trevally.
5. There are no major rockbars in the sandy Liverpool Creek. Some barra, many jacks, occasional mud crab. Small boats can get up to the highway where the river is not tidal. Above the highway, fishing is possible by canoe for sooty grunter and jungle perch. There is a landing 1.5km upstream from the mouth.
6. Plenty of reef near Kurrimine Beach, a township built around fishing. The inshore reefs, islands and the Great Barrier Reef make this area popular. The inshore has crayfish and is a favourite spot for grass sweetlip (called piggies), coral trout and golden snapper, with mackerel each year from April.
7. Maria Creek: Fish the bottom end for mostly whiting, flathead, jacks and some mud crabs.
8. Clump Point rocks hold barra just before the season closes. Offshore, west of Beaver Reef, marlin and sailfish are reliable in July/Aug.
9. Pelagic fish off rocky point.
10. Rocks along south-western corner of Dunk Island through to Thorpe Island and the shoals nearby hold mackerel. Also golden snapper and coral trout, with queenfish, trevally and mackerel near the reefs.
11. The Hull River has a ramp, mud crabs and whiting, and barra in warm months. Many sandbars and an all-tide channel at the mouth.
12. Tully River: jacks on snags.
13. Good bottom fishing and trolling around the islands.
14. Reef fish over shoals, fish the smallest patches and lumps.
15. There is an excellent run of spotted mackerel from the Barnard Islands to Dunk Island, which attracts anglers each year. Big mackerel at North Barnard Islands from June to September.

Wreck and reef

Of the wrecks in this region, 'The Crane' is most popular, being heavy machinery that fell off a barge. See 'Wrecks' below for GPS. Another hotspot is the 'Two-Hour Joint', an area of sand and shell lumps, on the 30m line, with mackerel and reef fish.

Two-Hour Joint
17 29.214S 146 17.525E

Out wide, fish the barrier reef edges and bommies for coral trout, and the deep rubble and holes between the reefs for nannygai and emperor.

Landbased fishing

Mourilyan rocks are accessible, with pelagics and the occasional jack. Clump Point has a rock wall and good rock fishing platforms, including on the southern side. Also, rock wall on south side of Hull River mouth.

Launch sites

1. Bramston Beach, exposed.
2. Johnstone River, good concrete ramps, most tides (see page 247).
3. Mourilyan Harbour, concrete ramp, exposed to some weather.
4. Launch off bank at creek mouth near Cowley Beach, or 1.5km upstream off Cowley Beach Rd.
5. Kurrimine Beach beach ramp - locals use tractors to launch and retrieve boats.
5a. Ramp on north bank of Maria Creek.
6. Clump Point, all-weather ramp with rock wall and pontoon.
7. Exposed ramp at South Mission Beach, Kennedy Esp. Beach access to north at Jackey Jackey St and Reimann St.
8. Hull River mouth, all-weather concrete site.
9. Tully River, via Vipiana Creek.

Wrecks

A. Charted wreck, approx 17 32.456S 146 05.654E
B. Charted wreck, approx 17 33.521S 146 09.725E
C. 'The Crane' ... reef fish, cobia 17 35.879S 146 12.912E
D. *Lady Bowen* wreck, approx 18 02.216S 146 25.849E

Hull River mouth

AUSSIE MARK

TULLY REALTY

Tully River mouth

TULLY REALTY

Hull Rivers

Tam O'Shanter Point

Tully River

Murray River

Bedford Creek

● Chart, approx 17 59.543S 146 04,541E

● Chart, approx 18 01.628S 146 03.011E

● Chart, approx 18 05.103S 146 01.625E

Unmarked hazards may exist. Maps not for navigation

This area is known for its run of spotted mackerel in July and August, with spanish mackerel mixed in. The fish school on shallow reefs and shoals. Spots worth trying are a couple of miles from the Hull River mouth and the east side of Dunk Island. Look for birds and boats.

Key to Map

Hotspots

1. No major rockbars reported in the Hull Rivers. Good crabbing, but heavily fished. Most estuary species. Comfortable landbased fishing at mouth on southern bank.
2. Tully River is shallow near the mouth and is only easily accessible for about the first 5km. The famous rapids start about 40km up from the mouth. The freshwater fishing here is among the best in North Queensland, with catches of 40 sooties and jungle perch possible in a day. Barramundi fishing in warm weather, with the Tully having both floodplain and mountain run-off.
3. Murray River: reasonably pristine waterway, with good fishing. **These three rivers have jacks and barra in warm weather, whiting in April, flathead all year (best in Dec), salmon in winter, mud crabs and grunter all year.

Launch sites

1 and 2. The **Hull Rivers** have three launch sites: one upstream on the north arm (1) and two all-tide boat ramps near the dual mouth on the south bank. Ramp pontoons available. The Hull River mouth is shallow.
3. The **Tully River** has access through Vipiana Creek. The track is off Costigan St in Tully Heads - about 1.2m of tide is needed to get out, small boats only. Upstream access is through private property: permission needed. The Tully mouth is shallow.
4 and 5. The **Murray River** has two launch sites: One is at Bedford Creek (4) on Bedford Creek Rd. The other is The Bluff landing 7km upstream from the mouth (5), on the southern bank, enter by Bluff Rd. A 4WD vehicle is recommended for both ramps.

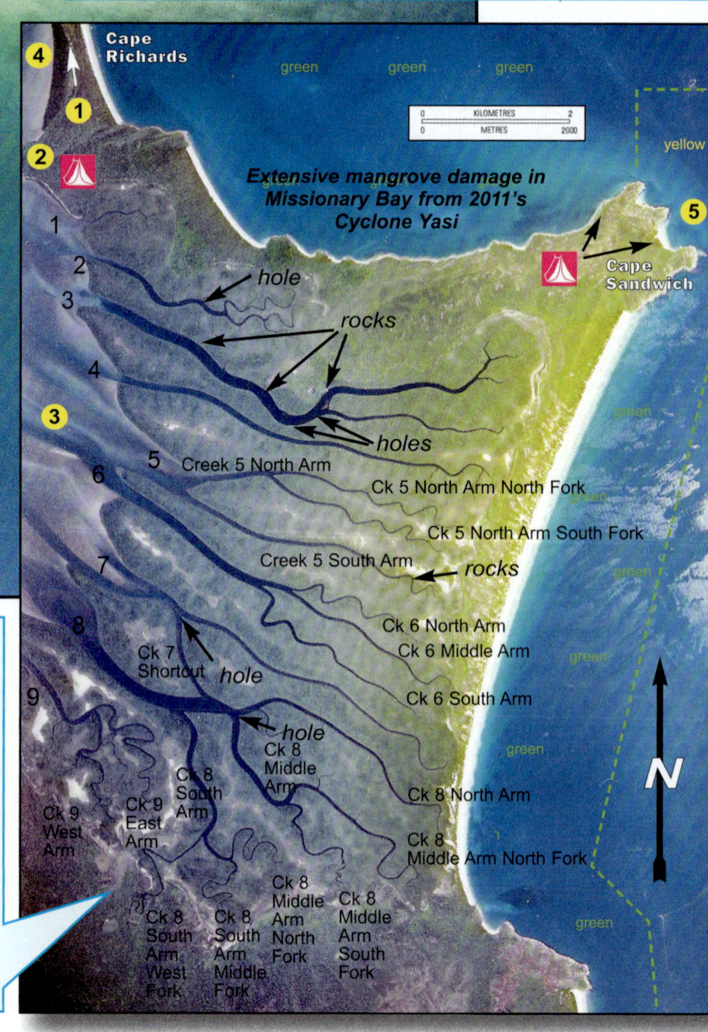

Missionary Bay

The flats and creeks of Missionary Bay on Hinchinbrook Island have good sight-fishing for golden trevally, queenfish, permit, barramundi and salmon. Entry into the creeks requires the upper tide, but deeper water is inside the creeks, allowing locked-in-at-low-tide fishing. The creeks have barramundi, cod, grunter and golden snapper, and mud crabs. Spotted and spanish mackerel make annual runs outside, with the biggest fish found around Cape Sandwich and the Brook Islands. The western tip of Goold Island is known for big spanish mackerel. The bay is exposed and trips require careful weather and tide planning.

Key to Map

Hotspots

1. Cape Richards rocks - golden snapper at night. Trevally, emperor, trout, mackerel in day. Same at Eva Island & Cape Sandwich.
2. Macusha Beach- camping by permit.
3. Creeks have most estuary fish, and mud crabs. Creeks 3 and 8 best for bottom fishing, Creek 2 has many drains & snags for barra, Creek 1 for crabs.
4. Reef fish, mackerel, trevally.
5. Reef fish out to Eva Island (2.6km to east, just off map).

Launch sites

1. See next page. Bay exposed to north-westerlies. Easier navigation at high tide.

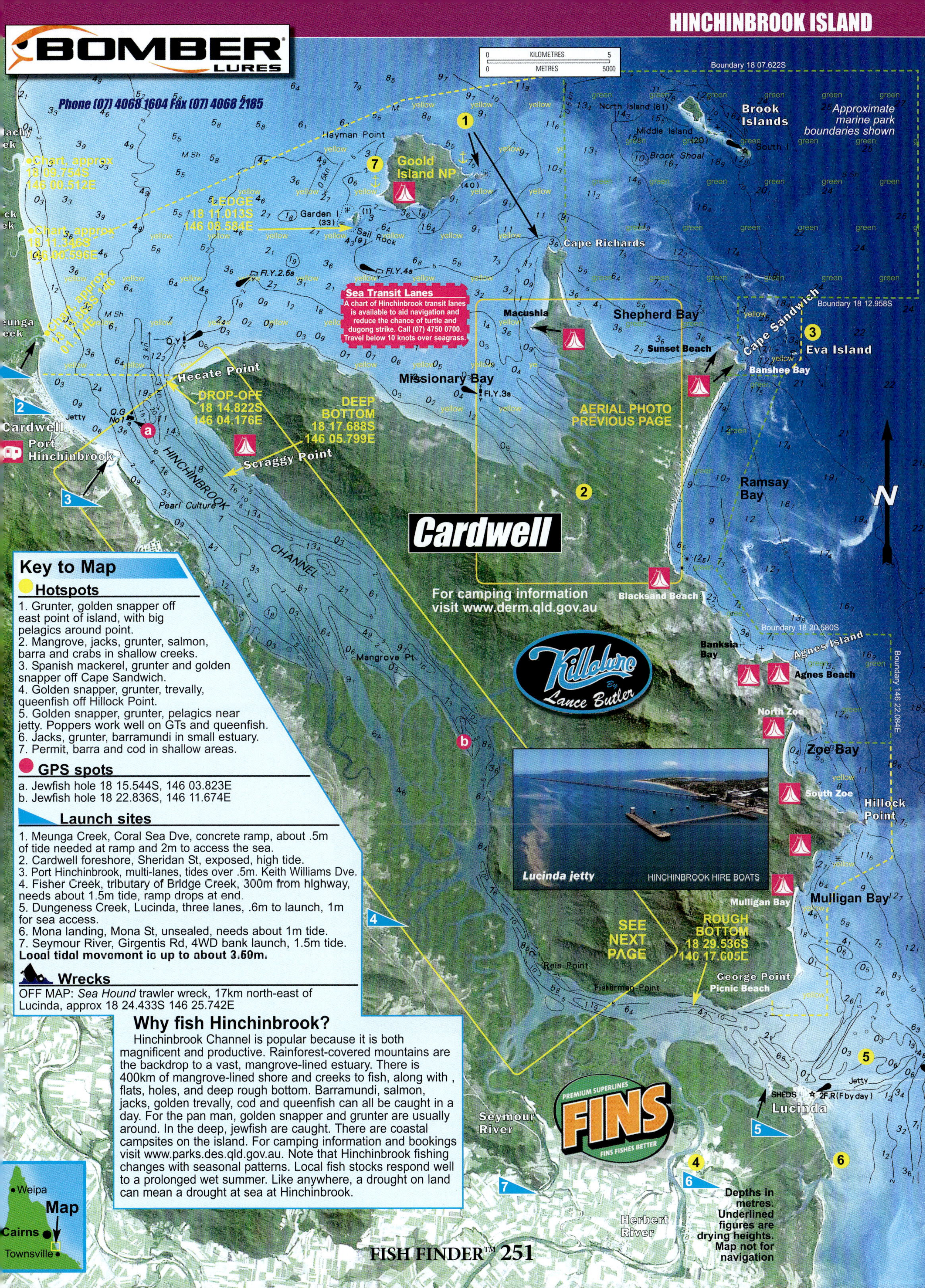

Key to Map

Hotspots

1. Grunter, golden snapper off east point of island, with big pelagics around point.
2. Mangrove, jacks, grunter, salmon, barra and crabs in shallow creeks.
3. Spanish mackerel, grunter and golden snapper off Cape Sandwich.
4. Golden snapper, grunter, trevally, queenfish off Hillock Point.
5. Golden snapper, grunter, pelagics near jetty. Poppers work well on GTs and queenfish.
6. Jacks, grunter, barramundi in small estuary.
7. Permit, barra and cod in shallow areas.

GPS spots

a. Jewfish hole 18 15.544S, 146 03.823E
b. Jewfish hole 18 22.836S, 146 11.674E

Launch sites

1. Meunga Creek, Coral Sea Dve, concrete ramp, about .5m of tide needed at ramp and 2m to access the sea.
2. Cardwell foreshore, Sheridan St, exposed, high tide.
3. Port Hinchinbrook, multi-lanes, tides over .5m. Keith Williams Dve.
4. Fisher Creek, tributary of Bridge Creek, 300m from highway, needs about 1.5m tide, ramp drops at end.
5. Dungeness Creek, Lucinda, three lanes, .6m to launch, 1m for sea access.
6. Mona landing, Mona St, unsealed, needs about 1m tide.
7. Seymour River, Girgentis Rd, 4WD bank launch, 1.5m tide.

Local tidal movement is up to about 3.60m.

Wrecks

OFF MAP: *Sea Hound* trawler wreck, 17km north-east of Lucinda, approx 18 24.433S 146 25.742E

Why fish Hinchinbrook?

Hinchinbrook Channel is popular because it is both magnificent and productive. Rainforest-covered mountains are the backdrop to a vast, mangrove-lined estuary. There is 400km of mangrove-lined shore and creeks to fish, along with , flats, holes, and deep rough bottom. Barramundi, salmon, jacks, golden trevally, cod and queenfish can all be caught in a day. For the pan man, golden snapper and grunter are usually around. In the deep, jewfish are caught. There are coastal campsites on the island. For camping information and bookings visit www.parks.des.qld.gov.au. Note that Hinchinbrook fishing changes with seasonal patterns. Local fish stocks respond well to a prolonged wet summer. Like anywhere, a drought on land can mean a drought at sea at Hinchinbrook.

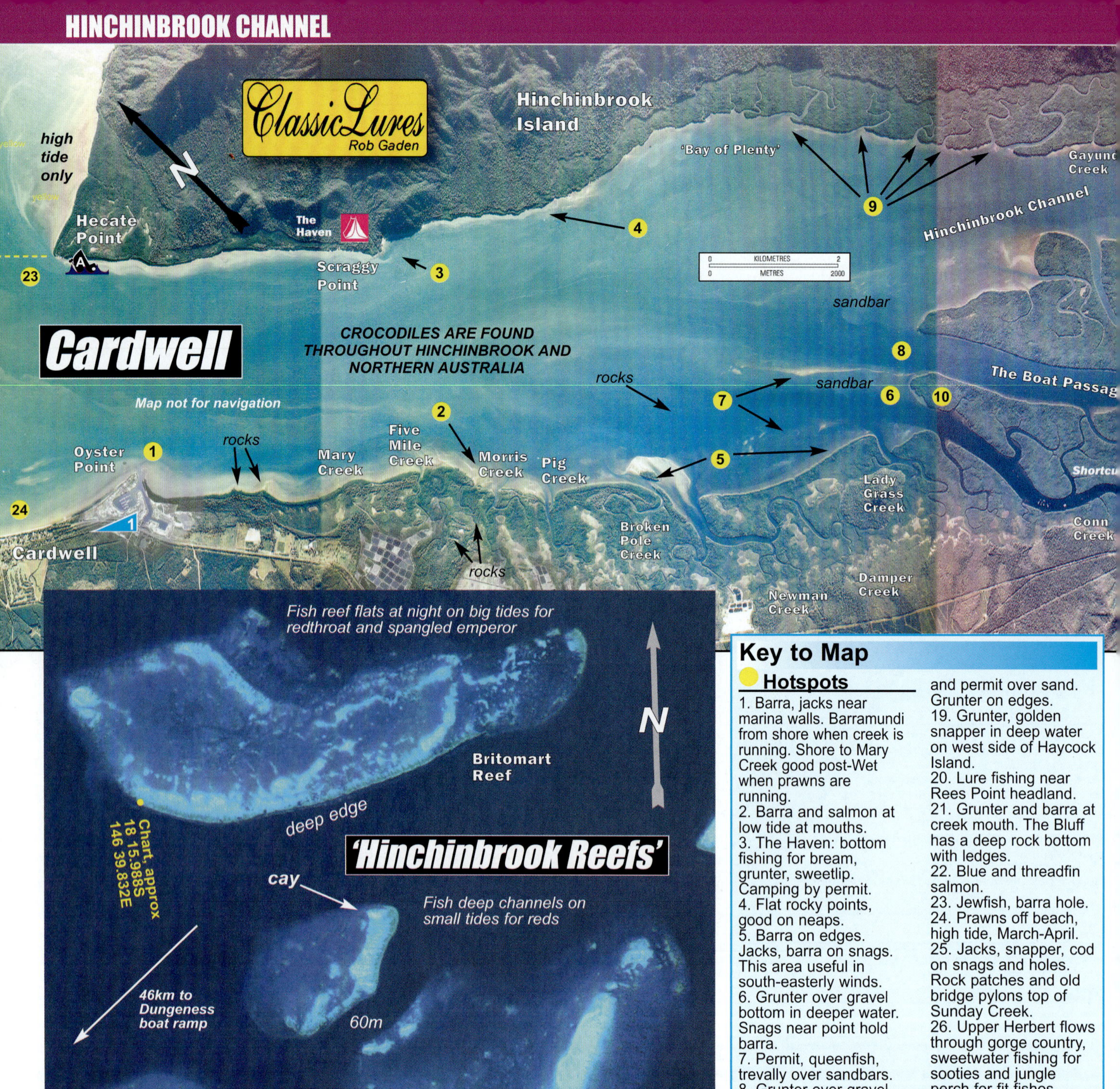

Key to Map

Hotspots

1. Barra, jacks near marina walls. Barramundi from shore when creek is running. Shore to Mary Creek good post-Wet when prawns are running.
2. Barra and salmon at low tide at mouths.
3. The Haven: bottom fishing for bream, grunter, sweetlip. Camping by permit.
4. Flat rocky points, good on neaps.
5. Barra on edges. Jacks, barra on snags. This area useful in south-easterly winds.
6. Grunter over gravel bottom in deeper water. Snags near point hold barra.
7. Permit, queenfish, trevally over sandbars.
8. Grunter over gravel.
9. Muddy creeks good for barra.
10. Deep holes and edges. No fishing near barramundi farm located upstream.
11. Mangrove jacks and barra. Golden snapper at rockbars marked nearby.
12. Permit, queenfish and trevally over sand. Bottom fishing and anchorage in creek.
13. Various species.
14. Useful deep water.
15. Deep arm, troll.
16. Seymour & Herbert mouths have trevally, queenfish, permit. Rockbar further up Seymour.
17. Mangrove jacks and grunter in channels.
18. Queenfish, trevally and permit over sand. Grunter on edges.
19. Grunter, golden snapper in deep water on west side of Haycock Island.
20. Lure fishing near Rees Point headland.
21. Grunter and barra at creek mouth. The Bluff has a deep rock bottom with ledges.
22. Blue and threadfin salmon.
23. Jewfish, barra hole.
24. Prawns off beach, high tide, March-April.
25. Jacks, snapper, cod on snags and holes. Rock patches and old bridge pylons top of Sunday Creek.
26. Upper Herbert flows through gorge country, sweetwater fishing for sooties and jungle perch for fit fishos.

Wrecks

A. Exposed wreck.

Launch sites

1. Port Hinchinbrook Marina, two lanes, use on tides above .5m.
2. Fischer's Creek, off Bridge Creek, just off highway, tides over 1.5m.
3. Dungeness Creek, Lucinda, five lanes, use over .5m tides, 1m for sea access. Caravan park nearby.
4. Taylor's Beach, Victoria Creek, 1m tide to launch, 1.5m for sea access.
5. Mona landing, Herbert River, Mona Rd, 1m tide.

Local tidal movement is up to about 3.59m.

Hinchinbrook Offshore

The nearest major reef from Dungeness boat ramp near Lucinda, at 20nm, is Bramble Reef. Many local fishermen head the extra few kilometres to the larger and more complex Britomart Reef. Britomart has an extensive plateau and reasonable shelter for anchoring. The many bommies have trout and lobsters, and deep water around the edges holds emperor, trout, nannygai, sweetlip and more. Britomart itself fishes best on big tides, although some fishermen prefer fishing the deep water between the reefs on small tides where hard bottom can produce fish such as nannygai - keep an eye on the sounder for fish. Closer to Dungeness, the *Sea Hound* trawler wreck is a popular spot, but busy on weekends. The *Sea Hound* is 9nm north-east of Lucinda, at approx 18 24.433S 146 25.742E. It has most local species, including big golden snapper.

snags
11
Palumah Creek
rocks
rocks
Mendel Creek
Deluge Inlet
12
anchorage
13
Benjamin Flats
rocks
gravel
14
Muller Creek
Bridge Creek
2
Waterfall Creek
Haycock islet
19
25
rock
Reis Point
Haycock Island
20
mudflat
16
gravel
Sunday Creek
rocks
rocks
Seymour River
15
rocks
Neames Inlet
17
Herbert River
SEE MAP BELOW
22
18
rock
rock
21
Bluff
Bluff Creek
George Point
3
Waterfall Creek
Seymour River and Hinchinbrook Channel at low tide
Weipa 
Cairns
Townsville
Map
Bowen
Mackay
Yeppoon
Bundaberg
Brisbane
Lucinda jetty ... excellent lure fishing for big trevally and queenfish
rocks
creek entry only above half tide, but fishable within at low tide
Groper Creek
Lucinda
3
causeway
Dungeness Creek
Gentle Annie Creek
16
Sea Transit Lanes
A chart of Hinchinbrook transit lanes is available to aid navigation and reduce the chance of turtle and dugong strike. Call (07) 4750 0700. Travel below 10 knots over seagrass.
KILOMETRES
METRES
Lucinda
4
Taylors Beach
5
Halifax
Victoria Creek
N
Herbert River
Seymour River
26
Herbert River freshwater
FISHING BY FOOT

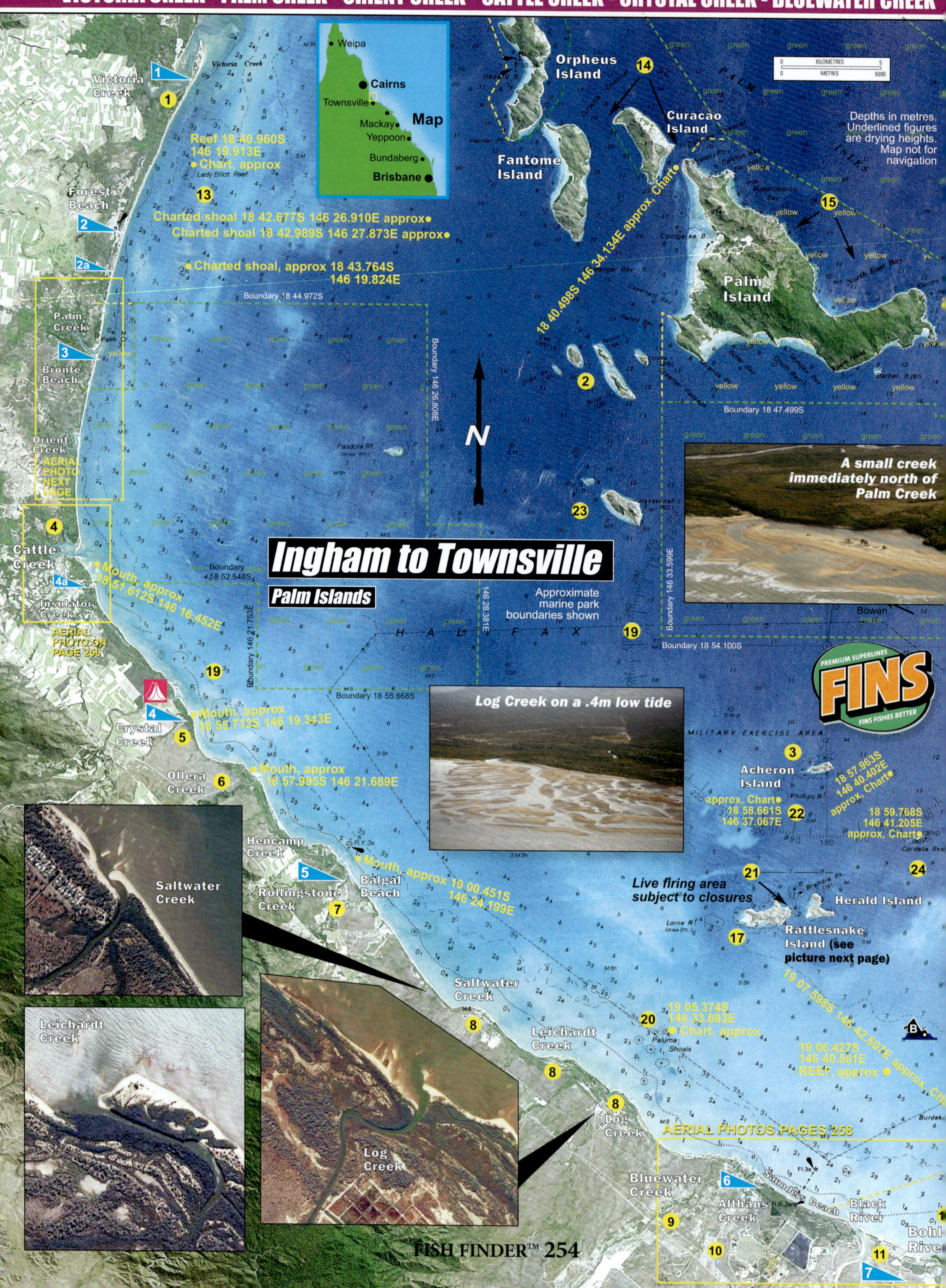
Ingham to Townsville
Palm Islands
Approximate marine park boundaries shown
Depths in metres. Underlined figures are drying heights. Map not for navigation
Weipa
Cairns
Townsville
Mackay
Yeppoon
Bundaberg
Brisbane
Map
Victoria Creek
Forest Beach
Palm Creek
Bronte Beach
Orient Creek
AERIAL PHOTO NEXT PAGE
Cattle Creek
Insulator Creek
AERIAL PHOTO ON PAGE 256
Crystal Creek
Ollera Creek
Hencamp Creek
Rollingstone Creek
Balgal Beach
Saltwater Creek
Leichardt Creek
Log Creek
Bluewater Creek
Althaus Creek
Black River
Bohl River
Orpheus Island
Fantome Island
Curacao Island
Palm Island
Acheron Island
Herald Island
Rattlesnake Island (see picture next page)
Reef 18 40.960S 146 19.913E
Chart, approx
Charted shoal 18 42.677S 146 26.910E approx
Charted shoal 18 42.989S 146 27.873E approx
Charted shoal, approx 18 43.764S 146 19.824E
18 40.498S 146 34.134E approx, Chart
Boundary 18 44.972S
Boundary 146 26.808E
Boundary 18 47.499S
Boundary 18 52.548S
Boundary 146 21.753E
Boundary 146 28.381E
Boundary 146 33.599E
Boundary 18 54.100S
Boundary 18 55.668S
Mouth, approx 18 51.612S 146 16.452E
Mouth, approx 18 55.712S 146 19.343E
Mouth, approx 18 57.995S 146 21.689E
Mouth, approx 19 00.451S 146 24.199E
18 57.963S 146 40.402E approx, Chart
approx, Chart 18 58.661S 146 37.067E
18 59.768S 146 41.205E approx, Chart
19 05.374S 146 33.693E Chart, approx
19 06.427S 146 40.581E REEF, approx
19 07.598S 146 42.607E approx, Chart
Live firing area subject to closures
MILITARY EXERCISE AREA
H A L I F A X
AERIAL PHOTOS PAGES 258
A small creek immediately north of Palm Creek
Log Creek on a .4m low tide
FINS
FINS FISHES BETTER
Saltwater Creek
Leichardt Creek
Log Creek

Palm Creek on a .4m low tide

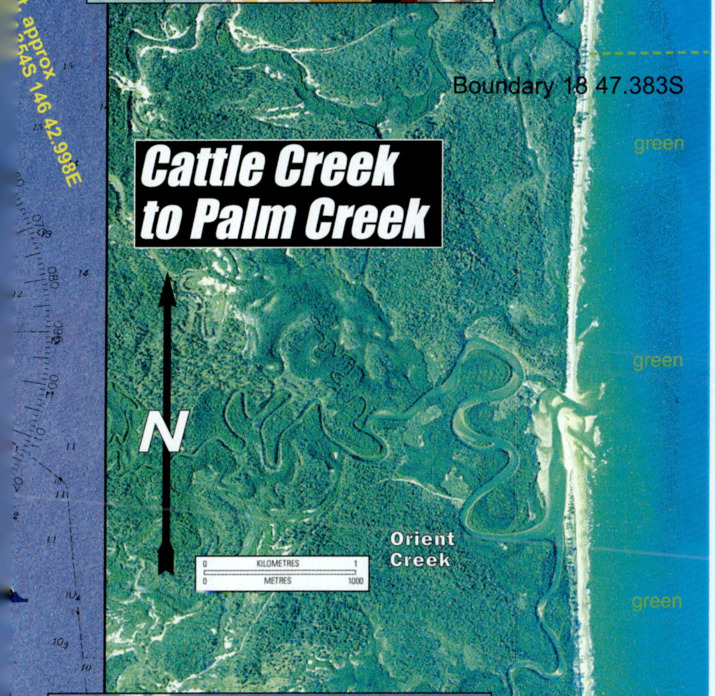

Cattle Creek to Palm Creek

Palm Creek

Bronte Beach

Boundary 18 47.383S

Orient Creek

Golden snapper (fingermark)

Ingham to Townsville

Shallow Halifax Bay has pelagic fish around the islands, mostly school mackerel, queenfish and tuna, with the chance of a big spaniard. The best pelagic fishing is usually on the bigger tides of the new and full moons. The bay is home to quality reef fish, which can be found by drifting over likely patches, or fishing the island bommies. There are golden trevally, queenfish and occasional permit sight fished when the water clears, and coral trout will take lures in the shallows. Most creeks are relatively small, with Cattle Creek the biggest and arguably most productive. To the south, Bluewater Creek and Bohle River produce some big barra and other estuary fish.

Key to Map

Hotspots

The coast from approx Cattle Creek to Orient Creek (see map) is a Green Zone. Fishing is permitted only in the creeks.

1. Victoria Creek: good fishing, most estuary species, one of the better creeks in this area.
2. Reef fish around islands.
3. Big spaniards in April and May off Acheron Island's rugged eastern side, also school mackerel, trevally, queenfish on north end. Best on big tides. Closed during defence firing, call RAAF on (07) 4752 1207 to check.
4. Cattle Creek is the best creek in this area. See previous pages.
5. Good fishing in Crystal Creek. Snags at river mouth, shallow reef outside. Upper reaches have jungle perch, sooties.
6. Ollera Creek - log landing, jacks, barra and crabs.
7. Rollingstone Creek gives best access to islands, with 1.3m tide required to get through mouth. Camping at mouth.

8, 8 & 8. Saltwater Creek easily reached at Toomulla for landbased fishing and beach launching. Good fishing at Leichardt and Log Creeks, which are more difficult to access.

9. Bluewater Creek, good fishing, flathead, whiting, bream.
10. Althaus (Deep) Creek, barra, crabs and jacks. Has run-off from a nickel refinery, so maybe not a food-fish creek.
11. Black River has rockbars, accessible by sea, barra, jacks, bream and whiting.
12. Bohle River has big barramundi. Good for grunter. Shalo bottom, Shallow at low tide. Rockbar near mouth, crabs year-round.
13. Lady Elliot Reef, shallow reef in Halifax Bay, need good weather to fish. School mackerel in winter.
14. Queenfish, trevally and mackerel in rips between islands. Coral trout on edges of Fantome and Curacoa Islands. Three campsites on Orpheus Island, best is south-west end near jetty, but no fishing from pier.
15. Coral trout.
16. Big mackerel, trevally and reef fish off Albino Rock, Paluma Rock, Chilcott Rock and Hayman Rock. Beware breaking waves. Palm Island has good reef fishing and diving.
17. Mackerel between islands, grunter in holes near Rattlesnake Island. Check with RAAF regarding live firing calendar, when the area is closed.
18. Big pelagic fish off Magnetic Island's West Point, reef fish.
19. Mackerel over shoals in winter. 18 55.343S 146 20.950E
20. Paluma Shoals, jewfish. Spaniards in April/May, then doggie mackerel.
21. Islands have coral trout, sweetlip, tuskfish. Queenfish, trevally in passage. Troll for spanish mackerel.
22. Phillips Reef: queenfish and trevally. Spanish mackerel on drifted baits. Coral trout.
23. Mackerel, mixed reef fish.
24. Queenfish, trevally, school mackerel, occasional jewfish.

Wrecks

A. Unidentified, approx 18 59.113S 146 43.669E.
B. Unidentified, approx 19 06.427S 146 40.553E
C. Unidentified, approx 19 07.113S 146 46.428E

Launch sites

1. Victoria Creek: Taylors Beach ramp on Boat Ramp Rd, Cassidy. Needs about 2.5m+ tide. Landing available on the upper creek.
2. Forest Beach: exposed beach ramp.

2a. 4WD bank launch into small creek south off Forest Beach.

3. Palm Creek - large creek has limited 4WD access to mouth, otherwise from Forest Beach.
4. Crystal Creek, Barrilgie Rd, turn-off is after fuel station, ramp on north bank near mouth, about 1.5m+ tide for sea access. Some bush camping north of ramp.

4a. Insulator Creek bank launch - 4WD sandy track from Crystal Creek.

5. Rollingstone Creek, Balgal, Crabb Dve, ramp, pontoon, most tides but about 1.5m+ tide needed to access sea.
6. Three ramps - north bank Althaus (Deep) Creek, Bluewater Rd, most tides. Also Saunders Beach side on south bank, Boat Ramp Rd. Third ramp upstream at Puruno Park. At least 1.5m tide needed to access sea.
7. Stony Creek (leads to Bohle River), Marina Dve, via Stony Ck: about .8m+ tide needed, 1.2m+ for sea access.
8. Pallarenda - exposed beach ramp, Cape Pallarenda Rd.

Local tides move up to about 3.78m.

Island camping

Palm Islands are Aboriginal land. Orpheus Island has camping at South Beach, Pioneer Bay and Yanks Jetty. Visitors must be self sufficient. No fishing allowed within 100m of Yanks Jetty.

Stony Creek ramp leads to Bohle River

Cattle Creek

This is one of the best creeks in the region, with an extensive wetland at the top of the creek. There are not many snags, but find a snag and you will likely catch fish. Entry is much easier with 1.5m+ of tide. Leaving the creek can be hazardous if the wind comes up, so the sea journey is not ideal for small boats. However, there is a bank launch at Insulator Creek via a 4WD track from Crystal Creek. Launching is usually from Forest Beach (north) or Crystal Creek (south).

Cattle Creek

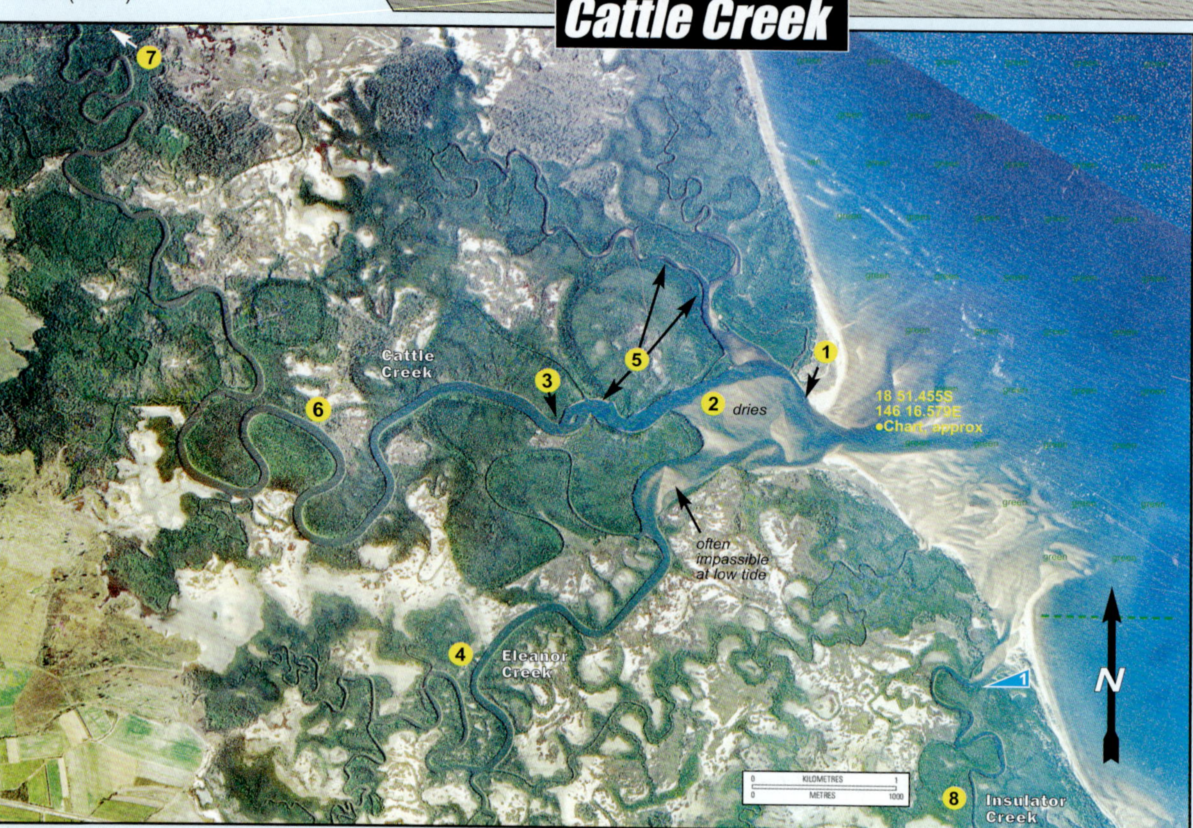

Hotspots

1. Bream, flathead, whiting, off beach.
2. Shallow flats - whiting, flathead and salmon.
3. Flathead and grunter.
4. Eleanor Creek - barra, jacks, cod, golden snapper, salmon. Casting and trolling.
5. Good area for mud crabs.
6. Mid-upper reaches - troll bends and snags. Barra, jacks, cod, golden snapper.

Key to Map

7. Brackish: Barra, tarpon in upper reaches.
8. Most species in Insulator Creek.

Launch sites

1. Driving from Townsville, turn right about 500m south of the Frosty Mango, at the fuel station. Follow the road through the cane farms, with Crystal Creek on the right. Launch at Crystal Creek boat ramp, or follow the 4WD track north for a rough bank launch at Insulator Creek. The track leads to Insulator Creek mouth, and to the bank on a small area of flats about 2km upstream. This 4WD access to the creek requires care. The mouth of Insulator Creek is shallow, but it is deeper upstream. Launch on the upper tide. To visit Cattle Creek by boat, work the tides carefully, because the sandflats at the mouth extend far out to sea.

Townsville GPS Marks

Coral trout
Fly Island
18 49.810S 146 31.865E
Hawkings Pt
19 11.200S 146 51.700E
Pallarenda
19 11.297S 147 02.998E

Spanish mackerel
Palm Island
18 46.684S 146 40.162E
Phillips Reef area
18 58.132S 146 38.467E
Liver Point wide
19 06.735S 146 46.799E
Salamander Reef
19 10.879S 147 03.516E

School mackerel
Rattlesnake Isle
19 01.110S 146 36.769E
Cleveland Bay
19 15.531S 146 56.481E
Lorne Reef
19 02.214S 146 35.001E

Gold spot cod
Orpheus Sth
18 42.920S 146 31.878E
Hawkings Pt
19 11.290S 146 51.702E
Red emperor & nannygai
Paluma Rock
18 45.100S 146 42.083E
Acheron East
18 58.004S 146 40.058E
Maggie Nth
19 00.392S 146 57.413E
Cape Cleveland West
19 10.538S 146 58.683E

Grunter
Spoil Ground
19 08.623S 146 45.215E
Launs Beach
19 14.488S 146 59.813E

Queenfish
Salamander Reef
19 10.916S 147 03.145E
Fingermark
Cordelia Rocks
18 59.646S 146 41.459E
Cordelia West
19 00.110S 146 43.500E
Middle Reef
19 12.066S 146 49.250E
Virago Shoals
19 12.607S 146 47.473E
Bungie Shoal
18 32.121S 146 29.456E
Burdekin Rock
19 07.589S 146 02.617E
Paluma Shoals
19 05.757S 146 03.382E

Townsville offers variety, with a great mix of species and habitat. There are seasonal billfish off Cape Bowling Green, shoals of big "reds" (nannygai and emperor), coral trout, and large spanish mackerel around the coastal reefs. There are wild and stocked barramundi in the local rivers. Big golden snapper (fingermark) are also caught. Despite being "dry tropics" the tidal creeks fish well, with grunter, three species of sand whiting, dusky and bar-tailed flathead, bream, jacks and more. The Ross River is stocked with barra, which can be caught from the bank above and below the Aplin, Gleesons and Black weirs. The best fishing is had near Aplin Weir, which is the bottom weir with tidal saltwater below. It fishes best when floodwater flows over the weir. The Ross River has freshwater prawns and yabbies. The rock walls around the mouth hold big barra, best in warm weather. The Lakes development in Hyde Park has barra and tarpon. Offshore, Magnetic Island is the main feature, with a 92km journey required to reach the Great Barrier Reef. Little and Big Broadhurst Reefs and Davies Reefs are among the most popular. The deep water between the reefs is home to schools of red emperor and nannygai. There are also closer grounds that hold "reds", just look for fish schools on the sounder. Shallow reefs near Cape Cleveland are renowned for giant spanish mackerel. Also in close are large black jewfish, grunter and golden snapper (fingermark). Townsville's outer channel leads hold fish - use live herring jigged from the pylons to catch tripletail, queenfish and mackerel. The west and south points of Magnetic Island offer great fishing, with golden snapper, coral trout and pelagic fish. West Point wide grounds have sharks, mackerel, cobia and reef fish. To the south, Magnetic Island has shallows where permit, trevally, queenfish and even barra can be sight-fished, with crayfish near reefs at night. Large barra are caught on the south side of Magnetic Island, usually on big tides. There are drying areas at low tide, with bommies. Banana prawns congregate on the west side of Magnetic Island in April/May on the full moon and the week before and after. Predators follow the prawns. Cleveland Bay is a nursery for sharks.

Townsville boat park

The Port of Townsville ... the rock walls hold many species

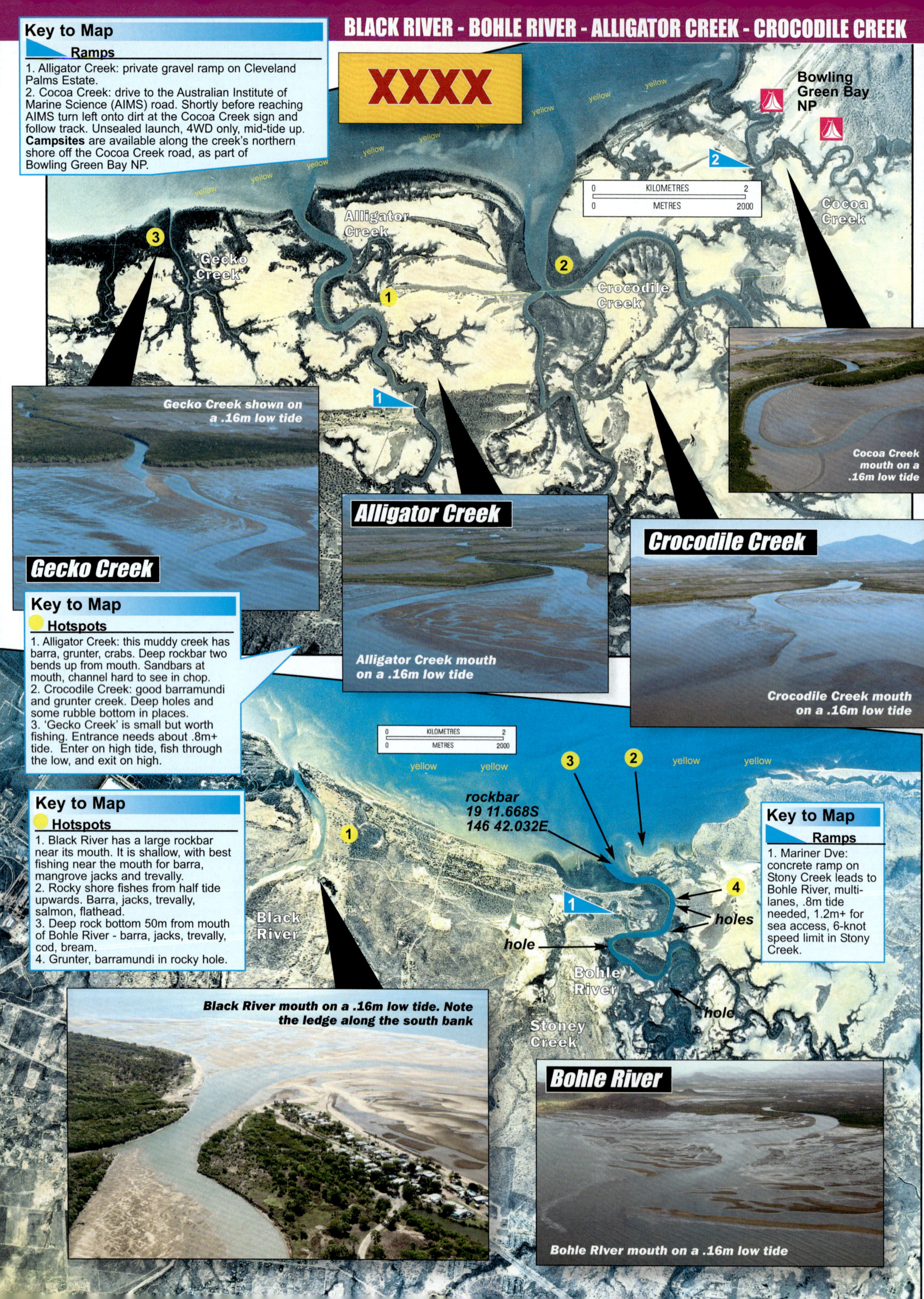

Key to Map
Ramps

1. Alligator Creek: private gravel ramp on Cleveland Palms Estate.
2. Cocoa Creek: drive to the Australian Institute of Marine Science (AIMS) road. Shortly before reaching AIMS turn left onto dirt at the Cocoa Creek sign and follow track. Unsealed launch, 4WD only, mid-tide up. **Campsites** are available along the creek's northern shore off the Cocoa Creek road, as part of Bowling Green Bay NP.

Cocoa Creek mouth on a .16m low tide

Gecko Creek shown on a .16m low tide

Gecko Creek

Alligator Creek

Alligator Creek mouth on a .16m low tide

Crocodile Creek

Crocodile Creek mouth on a .16m low tide

Key to Map
Hotspots

1. Alligator Creek: this muddy creek has barra, grunter, crabs. Deep rockbar two bends up from mouth. Sandbars at mouth, channel hard to see in chop.
2. Crocodile Creek: good barramundi and grunter creek. Deep holes and some rubble bottom in places.
3. 'Gecko Creek' is small but worth fishing. Entrance needs about .8m+ tide. Enter on high tide, fish through the low, and exit on high.

Key to Map
Hotspots

1. Black River has a large rockbar near its mouth. It is shallow, with best fishing near the mouth for barra, mangrove jacks and trevally.
2. Rocky shore fishes from half tide upwards. Barra, jacks, trevally, salmon, flathead.
3. Deep rock bottom 50m from mouth of Bohle River - barra, jacks, trevally, cod, bream.
4. Grunter, barramundi in rocky hole.

Key to Map
Ramps

1. Mariner Dve: concrete ramp on Stony Creek leads to Bohle River, multi-lanes, .8m tide needed, 1.2m+ for sea access, 6-knot speed limit in Stony Creek.

Black River mouth on a .16m low tide. Note the ledge along the south bank

Bohle River

Bohle RIver mouth on a .16m low tide

Townsville Wide

Townsville is 78km from the Great Barrier Reef. Shoals well inside the reef hold coral trout, redthroat emperor, nannygai, red emperor and pelagic fish. Cape Bowling Green has marlin and sailfish, tuna, wahoo, dorado and big mackerel. Tripletail are found around channel markers and flotsam. Local billfish events set the scene for fishos further south, who look to Bowling Green catches to assess the season ahead. There are many wrecks wide of Townsville. Some are trawlers that capsized after snagging nets. Charted co-ordinates for these are not always accurate, so searching is required, or go on a weekend and look for other boats.

Wreck co-ordinates in WGS84

A. *Kelgar* 18 38.554S 147 14.690E
B. *Moon Raker* 18 49.181S 147 10.937E
C. Charted 18 44.898S 147 28.013E
D. Charted 18 45.124S 147 27.232E
E. Charted 18 47.909S 147 26.963E
F. *Yongala*, protected, 19 18.259S 147 37.561E
G. *Elias E* 18 42.446S 147 19.368E
H. Plane 1 18 56.010S 147 10.188E
I. Plane 2 18 56.465S 147 09.043E
J. Wreck 18 59.113S 146 43.699E
K. *Pagamac* 18 43.313S 147 12.016E
L. Wreck 19 06.427S 146 40.553E
M. Plane 18 55.968S 147 10.263E
N. Wreck 19 04.950S 147 04.230E

Pelorus Island 18 14.194S 146 18.968E
Map not for navigation
Hinchinbrook Island
Britomart Reef 18 14.174S 146 41.593E
Pith Reef 18 12.720S 147 01.052E
Trunk Reef 18 21.929S 146 49.951E
Bramble Reef 18 24.517S 146 42.454E
Fore & Aft Reef 18 30.067S 147 01.981E
Lucinda 18 31.094S 146 20.179E
Pelorus Island
Calliope Channel 18 40.456S 146 41.806E
Palm Island
South East Cape 18 45.350S 146 34.057E
MORE ZONINGS APPLY: SEE OTHER MAPS OF THIS AREA
Reef GPS data taken with digital nautical chart
All waypoints are approximate. Many reefs have markers. Distances are as-crow-flies ... vessels at sea are likely to travel extra miles to reach each destination. Use a nautical chart when navigating.
John Brewer Reef 18 37.881S 147 03.274E
Helix Reef 18 37.473S 147 17.687E
Grub Reef 18 37.511S 147 25.966E
Lodestone Reef 18 41.593S 147 06.337E
Keeper Reef 18 44 822S 147 16 332E
foul ground
Centipede Reef 18 43.928S 147 32.019E
Davies Reef 18 49.576S 147 38.573E
18 52.938S 147 00.164E Shark Shoal
Map not for navigation
Big Broadhurst Reef
Little Broadhurst Reef 18 57.812S 147 42.004E
Cordelia Rocks 18 59.776S 146 41.126E
Lorne Reef (Rattlesnake Isle) 19 02.173S 146 34.995E
Shoals 18 58.909S 147 00.564E
Shoal 19 01.575S 147 24.020E
Pig Shoal 19 01.320S 147 33.463E
Approximate marine park boundaries shown
Morinda Shoal 19 08.494S 147 38.216E
Bowden Reef 19 02.046S 147 55.874E
Magnetic Island
Shoal 19 10.319S 147 06.591E
Cape Cleveland 19 10.731S 147 00.890E
Townsville 19 14.312S 146 49.975E
Shoals 19 15.068S 147 10.027E & 19 14.291S 147 08.027E
summer marlin grounds
Cape Bowling Green 19 17.588S 147 23.373E
Yongala Wreck
48km
41km
18.5km
42km
50km
79km
37km
22km
103km
KILOMETRES
METRES

Best launch sites

1. Port Hinchinbrook.
2. Dungeness Creek, Lucinda.
3. Forrest Beach (She-Oak St), via Allingham.
4. Althaus Creek and Bohle River.
5. Townsville Boat Park, multiple ramps, BBQs, toilets.
6. Morriseys, Barramundi Creek.
7. Barratta Creek, Jeroma.

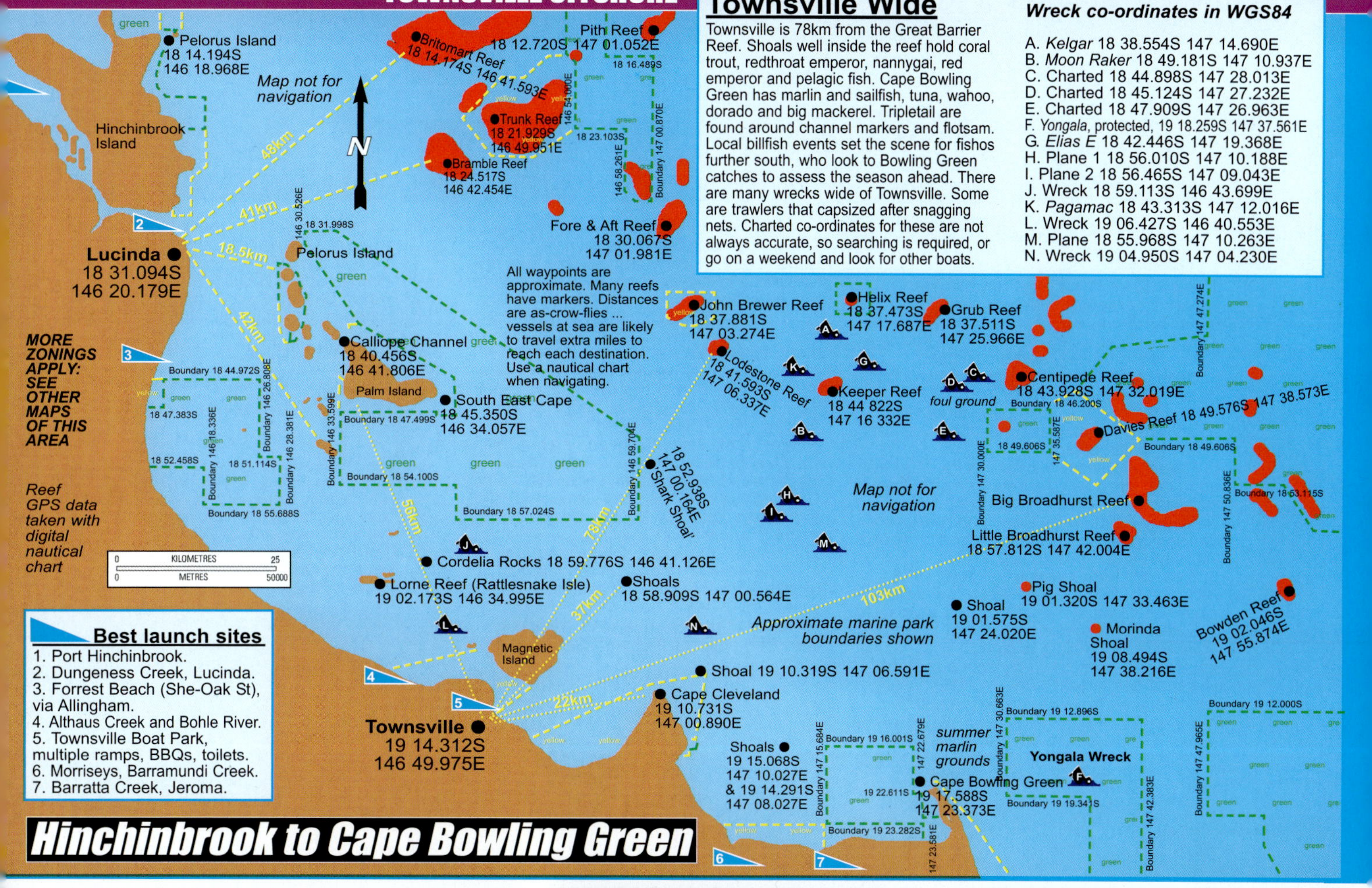

Hinchinbrook to Cape Bowling Green

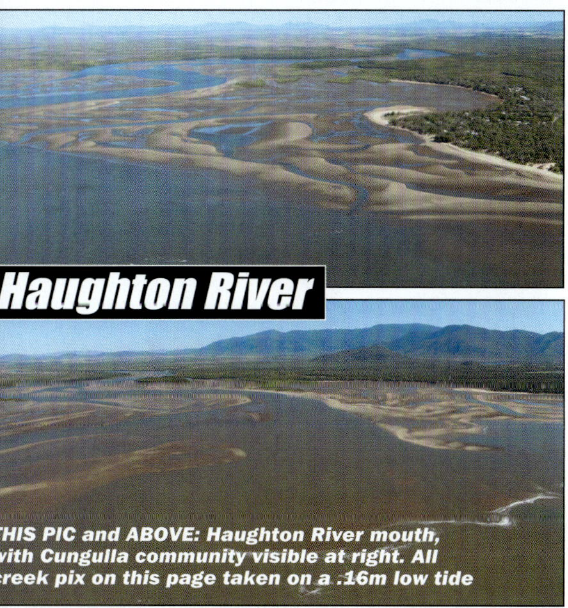

Haughton River

THIS PIC and ABOVE: Haughton River mouth, with Cungulla community visible at right. All creek pix on this page taken on a .16m low tide

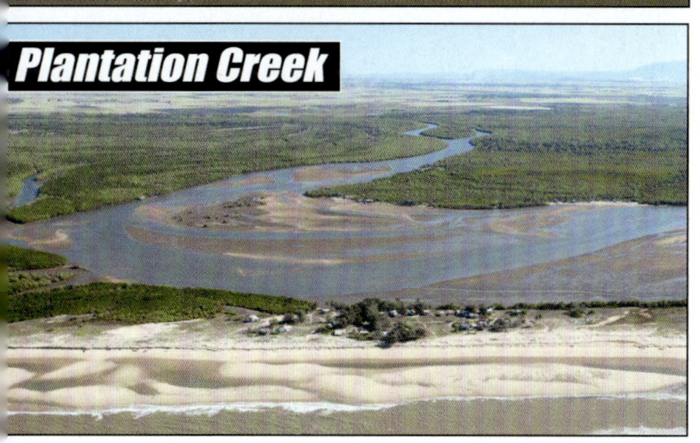

Plantation Creek

Magnetic Island

Lovers Bay
Horseshoe Bay
Balding Bay
Radical Bay
Huntingfield Bay
Wilson Bay
Joyce Bay
Norris Bay
Wreck approx 19 06.726S 146 46.804E
Golden snapper and other fish in West Point area on these marks 19 06.819S 146 46.736E 19 07.425S 146 46.695E 19 07.209S 146 46.659E
West Point holds big mackerel, cobia and sharks. Cobia best in April/May when multiple hook-ups are common. Fish often congregate within 100m of shore.
West Point
Gowrie Bay
Florence Bay
Arthur Bay
Young Bay
Bolger Bay
Whitfield Cove
Alma Bay
Geoffrey Bay
Bremner Point
Bright Point
Painted crayfish are readily available in Magnetic Island shallows and can be collected at night with a torch or spotlight. Full moon nights are best.
Sight fishing in this area for big barra ... quiet approach with electric motor is required. This area dries at low tide
Nelly Bay
Picnic Bay
Hawkings Point
Cockle Bay
Nobby Head
SS City of Adelaide wreck approx 19 10.515S 146 46.527E
KILOMETRES

Offshore Marks

Davies Reef Reds - sound around for bumps and fish 87km NE of Townsville 18 53.091S 147 33.358E
No Name Pinnacle 82km NE of Townsville 19 01.368S 147 33.527E
No Name Shoal 65km NE of Townsville 19 01.609S 147 24.020E

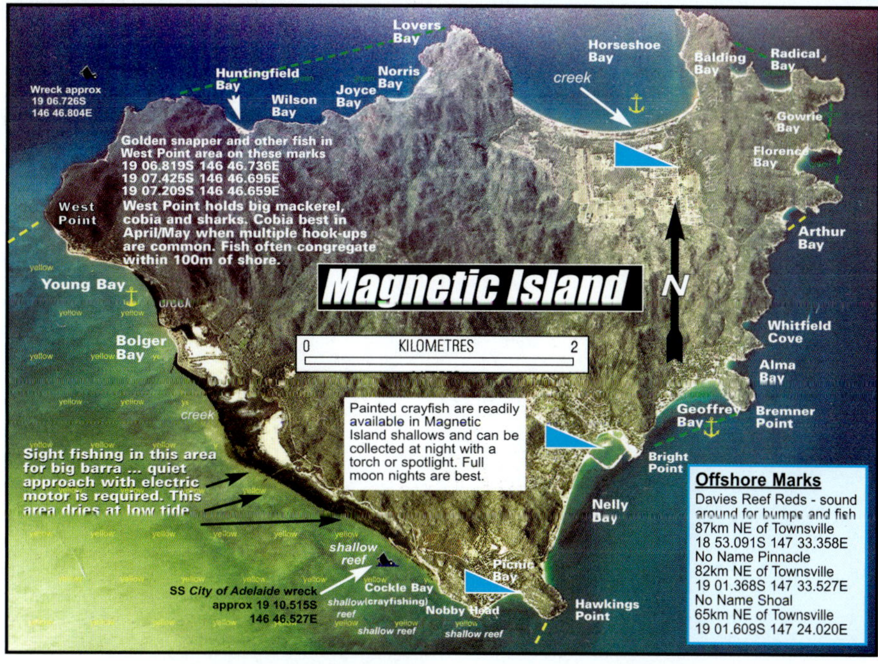

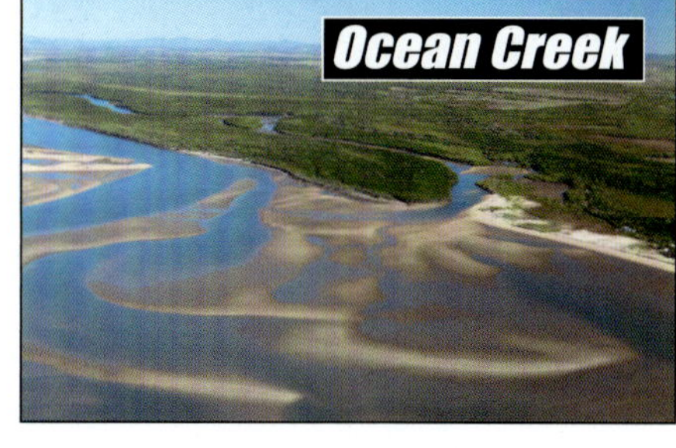

Ocean Creek

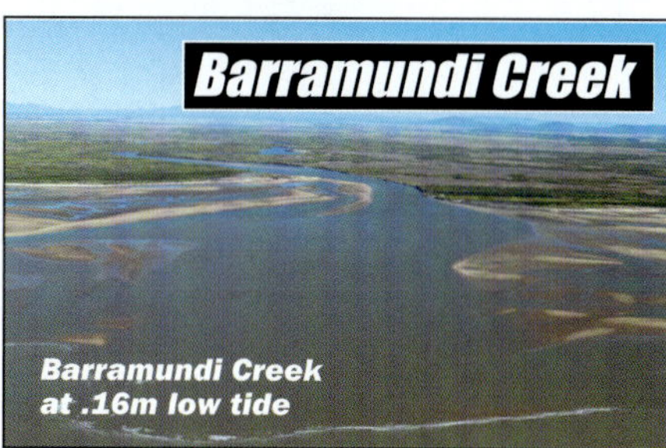

Barramundi Creek

Barramundi Creek at .16m low tide

Good fishing around islands, but area is periodically closed for defence exercises

Depths in metres. Underlined figures are drying heights. Map not for navigation

Approximate marine park boundaries shown

Key to Map

Hotspots

1. Black River has a large rockbar near its mouth. It is shallow, with best fishing near the mouth for barra, mangrove jacks and trevally.
2. Rocky shore fishes from half tide upwards. Barra, jacks, trevally, salmon, flathead.
3. Deep rock bottom 50m from mouth of Bohle River - barra, jacks, trevally, cod, bream.
4. Grunter, barramundi in deep rocky hole.
5. Shelly Beach: flathead, trevally, queenfish, salmon, whiting, barra.
6. Pallarenda: rocky shores fish from half tide up to half tide down. Queenfish, barra, salmon and flathead. Use shallow lures or live bait.
7. Kissing Point: rocky shore and rocky pool on low tide can be fished from land or by boat. Trevally, salmon, cod, bream.
8. Breakwall behind casino and Strand rock walls can be fished. Barra, jacks, cod, trevally, queenfish. Good at night. Cast lures along rocks.
9. Eastern breakwater can only be fished by boat. Big barra trolling at night.
10. Ross River mouth. The west side of the entrance has a rocky bank into deep water. Landbased barra, jacks, golden snapper.
11. Aplins Weir. There are another two weirs further upstream called Gleesons and Black. Every year 1m+ barra are caught in the river. Aplins has saltwater on downstream side and fishes best when floodwater flows.
12. Rooney's Bridge in city over Ross Creek. Fish from land or boat. Rockbar on south side. Barra, jacks, trevally, flathead.
13. Alligator Creek: muddy creek has barra, grunter. Deep rockbar two bends up from mouth. Sandbars at mouth, channel hard to see in chop.
14. Crocodile Creek: a good barramundi and grunter creek. Deep holes and rubble bottom.
15. Weedbeds out from creeks produce mackerel, trevally, grunter, queenfish, cobia.
16. West Point: spanish and school mackerel, cobia. Best June-Nov. Grunter and golden snapper on rubble off West and Liver Points.
17. Trevally, queenfish, school mackerel.
18. Channel leads hold bait schools with pelagic and reef fish. Furthest marker at approx 19 07.698S 146 54.368E has school, spotted and spanish mackerel, tuna, cod, queenfish, tripletail and nannygai. Winter best for big mackerel, school mackerel in summer. Clear water, use livebait for best results.
19. Pelagic fish at Burdekin Rock.
20. Grunter at 19 08.624S 146 45.215E.
21. Picnic Bay jetty: good bait-collecting area, with chance of quality fish off the end of jetty.
22. Reef flat: fish with care at high tide for golden trevally, occasional permit and more.
22. Middle Reef has trout and lobsters, plus passing pelagic fish. Yakkas and herring near end markers.

Wrecks

Offshore: Bomber 1, approx 18 56.010E, 147 10.188S, 52km. **Bomber 2**, approx 18 56.465E, 147 09.043E, 54km. Both broken up.

A. Liver Point wreck 19 06.869S 146 47.382E
B. Liver Point wreck 19 06.726S 146 46.804E
C. Barge wreck 19 10.624S 146 45.218E
D. *SS City of Adelaide* wreck 19 10.515S 146 49.528E

Herald I. (173)
Rattlesnake I. (396)
Lorne R (dries 3ft.)
Chart, approx 19 02.205S 146 35.098E
Chart, approx 19 05.374S 146 33.693E
Paluma Shoals
LUMP approx 19 06.958S 146 43.176E
Bay Rock (80)
Burdekin Rk
approx, Chart 19 07.598S 146 42.607E
West Pt
West Channel
Chart, approx 19 09.244S 146 38.942E
19 10.722S 146 39.088E Chart, approx
19 11.646S 146 42.159E Chart, approx
Bluewater Creek
Althaus (Deep) Creek
Black River
Bohle River

SEE PAGE 258

Althaus (Deep) Creek ramps

Althaus and Bluewater Creeks on a .4m low tide

Black River on a .4m low tide

Snapper Marks

Townsville is know for its big golden snapper (fingermark). These marks should produce them. Fresh or live bait is essential, although deep trolled lures sometimes work.

a. 'The Pipes'
19 06.429S 146 40.549E
snapper, grunter, mackerel .

b. 'The Barge'
19 08.619S 146 45.216E
big snapper and grunter

c. 'Fingermark Rock'
19 06.985S 146 46.737E
big snapper, grunter

Launch sites

1. Althaus/Deep Creek east bank, off Saunders Beach Rd: most tides. Toilets, barbecues.
2. Althaus/Deep Creek west bank, off Bluewater Rd: Ramp is opposite ramp No.1. Most tides.
3. Purono concrete ramp: take Purono Parkway Rd to the end. Most tides.
4. Bohle River, Mariner Dve: concrete ramp on Stony Creek, multi-lanes, .8m tide needed, 1.5m+ for sea access, 6 knot speed limit in Stony Creek.
5. Pallarenda, The Esplanade: sand-covered and exposed paver ramp, best on upper tide with 4WD.
6. Ross Creek, Sir Leslie Thiess Dve: two multi-lane ramps, pontoon, all tides, beware ferry wash.
7. Townsville Boat Park, huge public facility with multiple ramps, BBQs, toilets etc.
8. Ross River, Cameron St: single-lane, limited parking, upper tide.
9. Two concrete ramps off Barnacle St, pontoons.
10. Alligator Creek: private gravel ramp on Cleveland Palms Estate.
11. Cocoa Creek: take the Australian Institute of Marine Science (AIMS) road. Shortly before AIMS turn left onto dirt at the Cocoa Creek sign and follow the track. Unsealed launch, 4WD only, mid-tide up.

Local tides have up to about 3.78m movement.

Offshore GPS

Nannygai and emperor are often over flat hard bottom. Watch bottom hardness and look for fish.
*Shark Shoal, 50km from Townsville 18 52.938S 147 00.164E, big nannygai, just outside a Green Zone
*Nannygai ground, 33km N-E Magnetic Island, 19 00.392S 146 57.413E
*Magnetic Island shoals 18 58.909S 147 00.564E 18 59.124S, 147 00.506E
*West Point rubble 19 07.384S 146 46.692E
*Cape Cleveland wreck, 13km NNE of cape, approx 19 04.950S 147 04.230E

Ross River mouth on a .16m low tide ... the rock walls and flats make great barra habitat

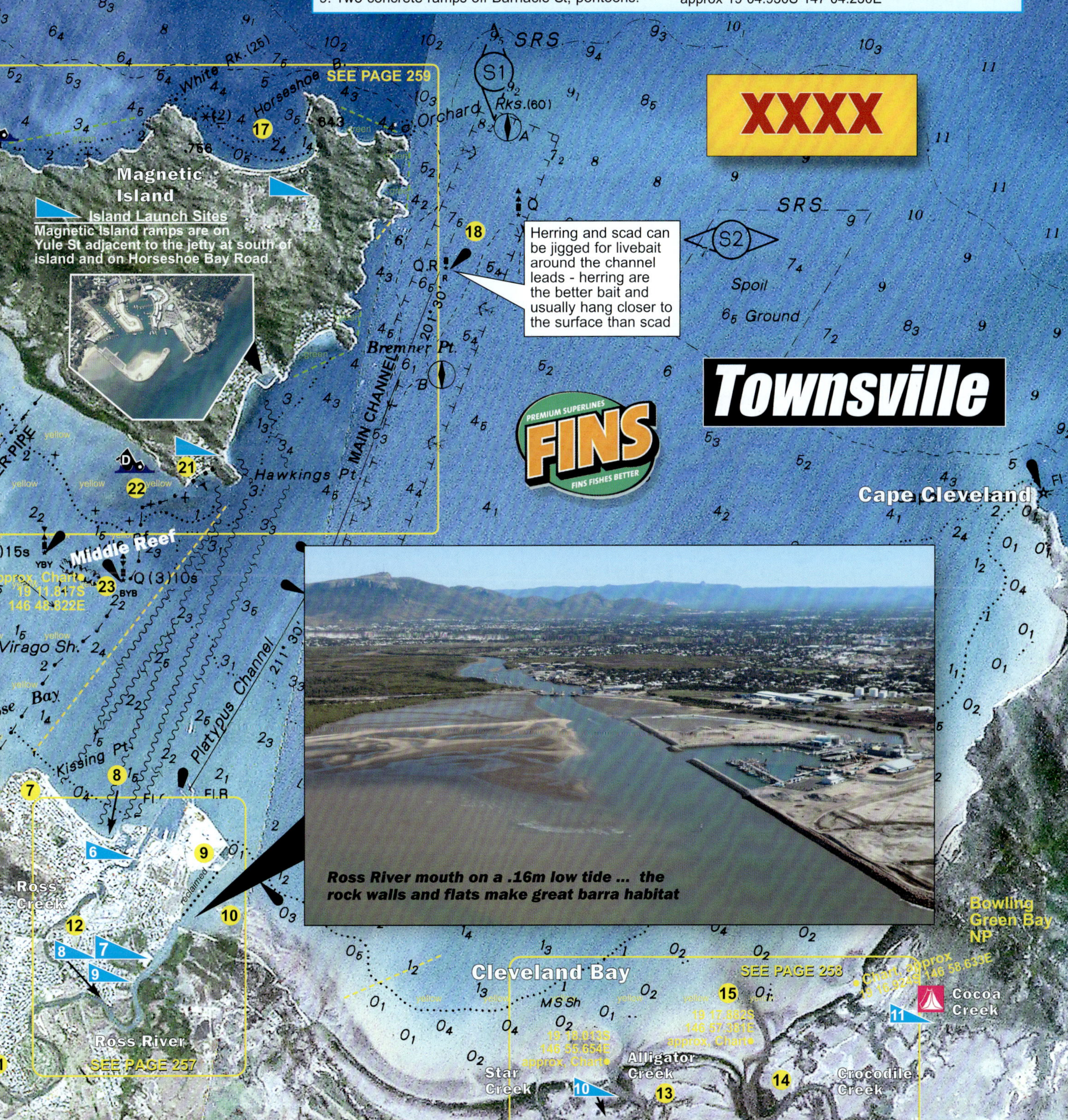

GPS

Cleveland West - rough bottom
19 10.533S 146 58.670E
Cleveland Nth Mackerel Patch (look for bait)
19 05.727S 147 06.843E
Bowling Green Mackerel Patch (look for bait)
19 08.857S 147 18.730E
Northern BGB Billfish
19 05.625 147 17 470E
Southern BGB Billfish
19 11.630S 147 32.544E
Haughton Shoals
19 17.903S 147 15.214E

Bowling Green Bay

The bay has many tidal rivers, creeks and inlets that produce salmon, barramundi, bream, grunter, flathead, whiting, golden snapper (fingermark), jacks, prawns and mud crabs. Fishing quality varies from season to season, with annual rainfall the key factor. Winter is best for bream, salmon and grunter, and warm weather for barramundi. Barra to 20kg have been caught in this area. The river mouths are generally shallow and difficult at low tide. There are landbased access points, but beware crocodiles.

Key to Map

Hotspots

1. Area near creek mouth has Parks and Wildlife permit campsites on east bank, 4WD access only. Mud landing suitable for cartoppers/yaks on upper reach's west bank, off rough track in dry conditions, turn off AIMS road.
2. Flathead, whiting, salmon, queenfish.
3. Haughton is a huge system with holes and snags throughout. River closed to netting. Landbased fishing near boat ramp. Run-offs upstream in floods. River has two weirs.
4. Barramundi Creek is another huge system with many snags, holes and rubble bottom areas. The 14m hole where Combe Creek enters is reliable.
5. Big barra in holes, good crabbing and estuary fish.
6. Barratta Creek is one of the better local crabbing areas. The creek has many holes, snags and sandbars. For landbased fishing use access tracks off Jerona Rd, or fish the rocks near the ramp on week days. Crocs.
7. Barra at low tide in hole near mouth.
8. Golden snapper over rough bottom.
9. Mud landing for cartoppers/yaks is on the upper reach's west bank, accessible only in dry conditions, turn off AIMs road.

Launch sites

1. Cocoa Creek, needs about 2.5m+ of tide. Track is off Cape Cleveland Rd.
2. Exposed ramp at Cungulla beach, shallow channel, upper tide only.
3. Follow sand track, leaving south end of Cungulla. Ramp into Doughboy Creek, needs .8m+ tide. Gives access to Haughton River on 1m+ tide.
4. Cromaty Creek, Boat Ramp Rd, via Giru, .6m+ tide to launch, 1.5m+ for sea access.
5. "Morrisseys" ramp, Morris Creek Rd via Hodel Rd, joins Barramundi Creek: all tides. 1m+ tide for sea access.
6. Barratta ramp, Jerona Rd: three lane .5m+ tide to launch, 1m+ sea access.

Bowling Green Bay

Bowling Green Offshore

There is an annual run of black marlin and sailfish. The marlin run from about July to October, with sailfish all year. The reefs just east of Cape Cleveland produce some huge spanish mackerel from April to September. There is also good bottom fishing, with shoals south-east of Cape Cleveland producing tricky snapper, redthroat emperor, cod, trout and more, as well as pelagic fish. Close to the cape, big jacks and jewfish are caught. Doggie and spotted mackerel move inshore during winter. Like anywhere, the fishing runs hot or cold - look for bait schools and big fish on sonar.

Key to Map

Hotspots

1. Salamander Reef, awash at high tide. Queenfish, best on runout tide, also mackerel, trevally. Golden snapper (fingermark) at night on tide turn. Pelagics best on big tides, big mackerel are usually caught in grounds just north of the reef.
2. 4-foot rock: Queenfish, mackerel, trevally, golden snapper.
3. 20-foot rock: Mackerel to 30kg. Slow-troll from rock through current lines towards shore with dead wolf herring. Best at dawn and dusk.
4. Bray Islet: golden snapper, grunter, mackerel.
5. Grunter, jewfish, mackerel off Cape Bowling Green. Barra, salmon in close.
6. Cape Bowling Green wide holds small marlin (July/Oct) with sailfish all year.
7. Shoal bottom produces mixed reef fish and mackerel.

Launch sites

Boats can launch from Townsville or from the rivers below. Cape Bowling Green tide times are the same as Townsville. **Local tidal movement is up to about 3.62m.**

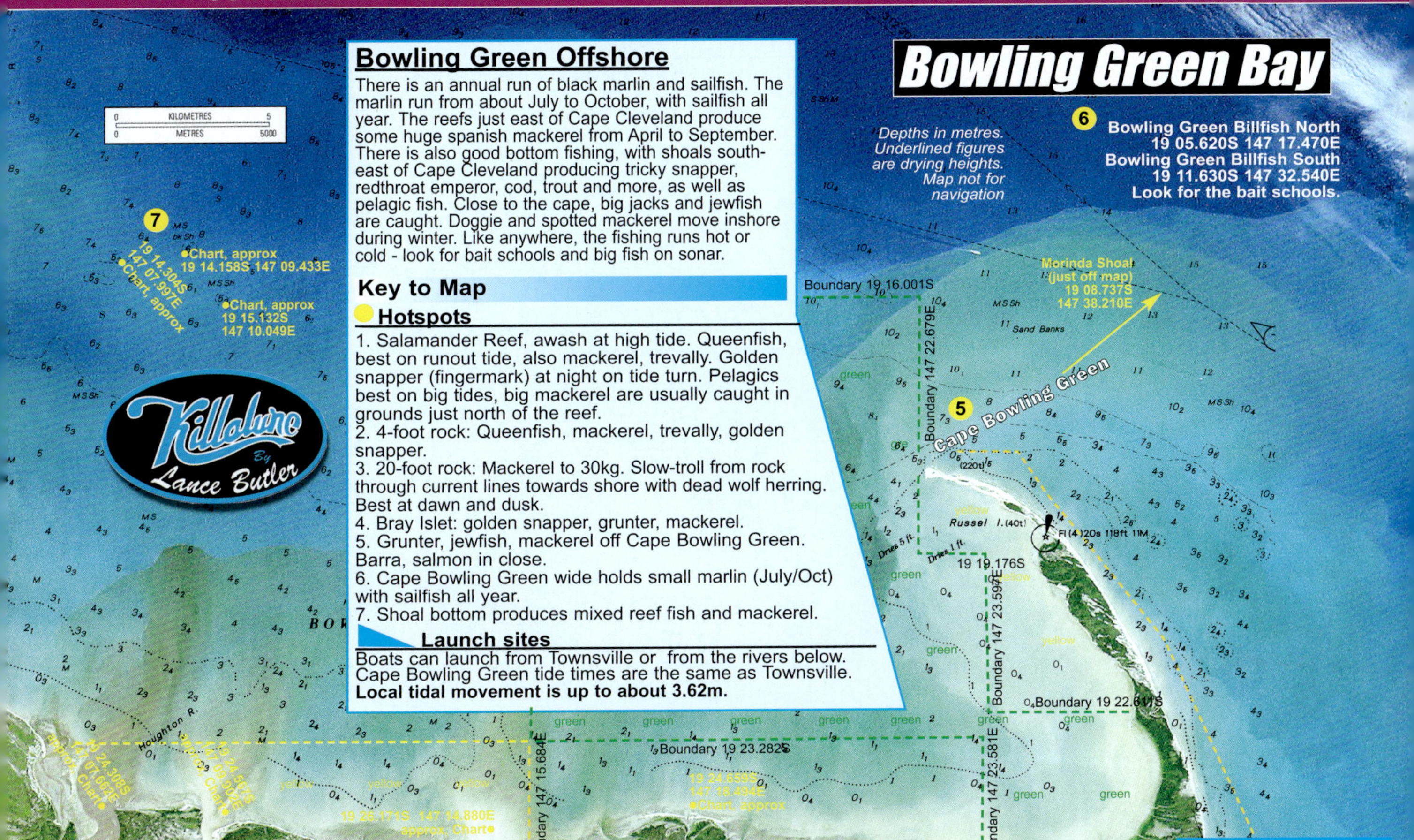

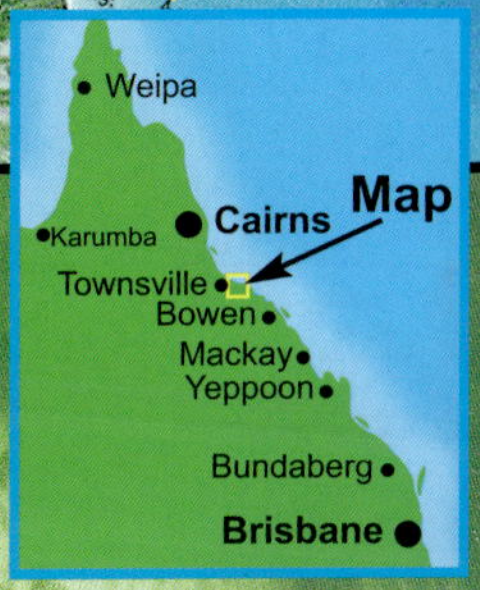

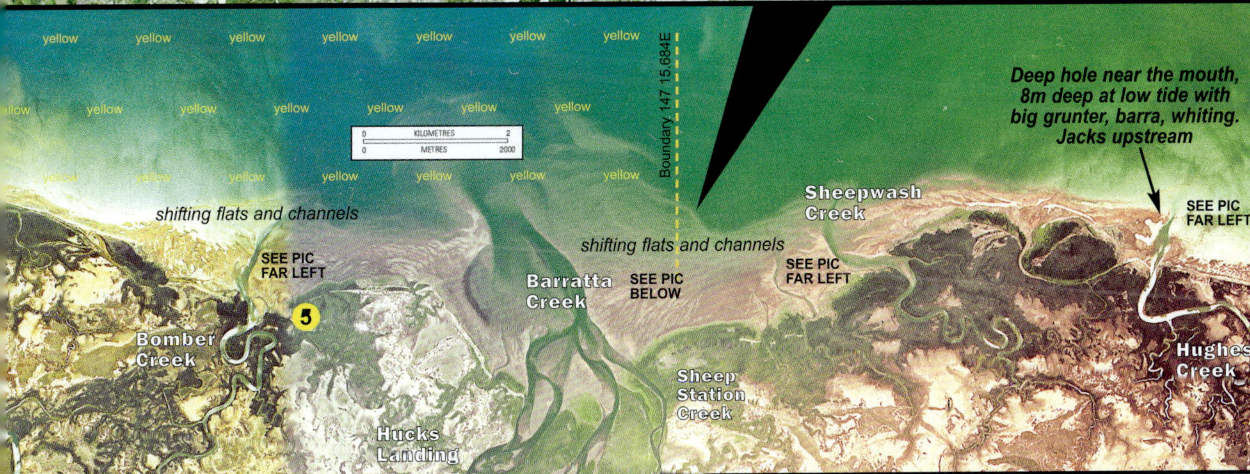

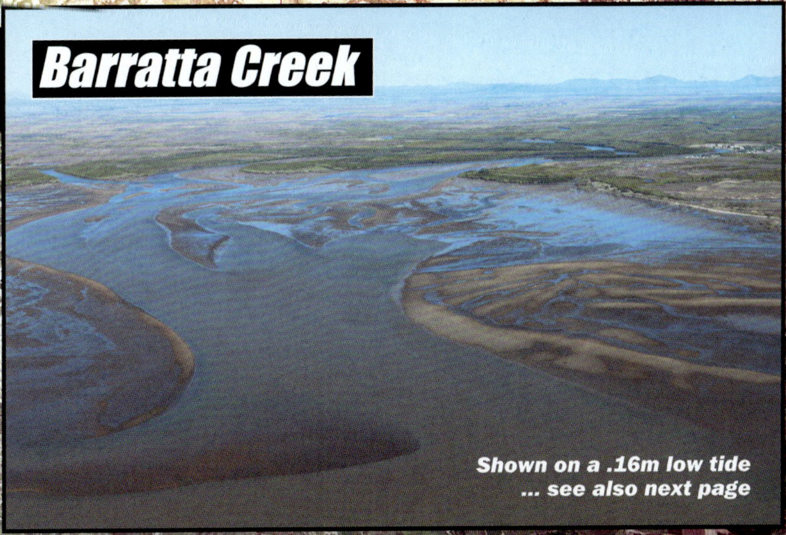

Shown on a .16m low tide ... see also next page

Wallaces and Wunjunga

This branch of the Burdekin delta is a popular fishing area with barra, jacks, salmon, bream, whiting and crabs. Try the marked snag areas. Near the mouth there are yabby beds around the two mud islands. The concrete boat ramp is accessed by turning left at Inkerman Hill and following the road. On the south side of this waterway on the beach there is basic 4WD camping near Wunjunga, where cartoppers can be beach launched.

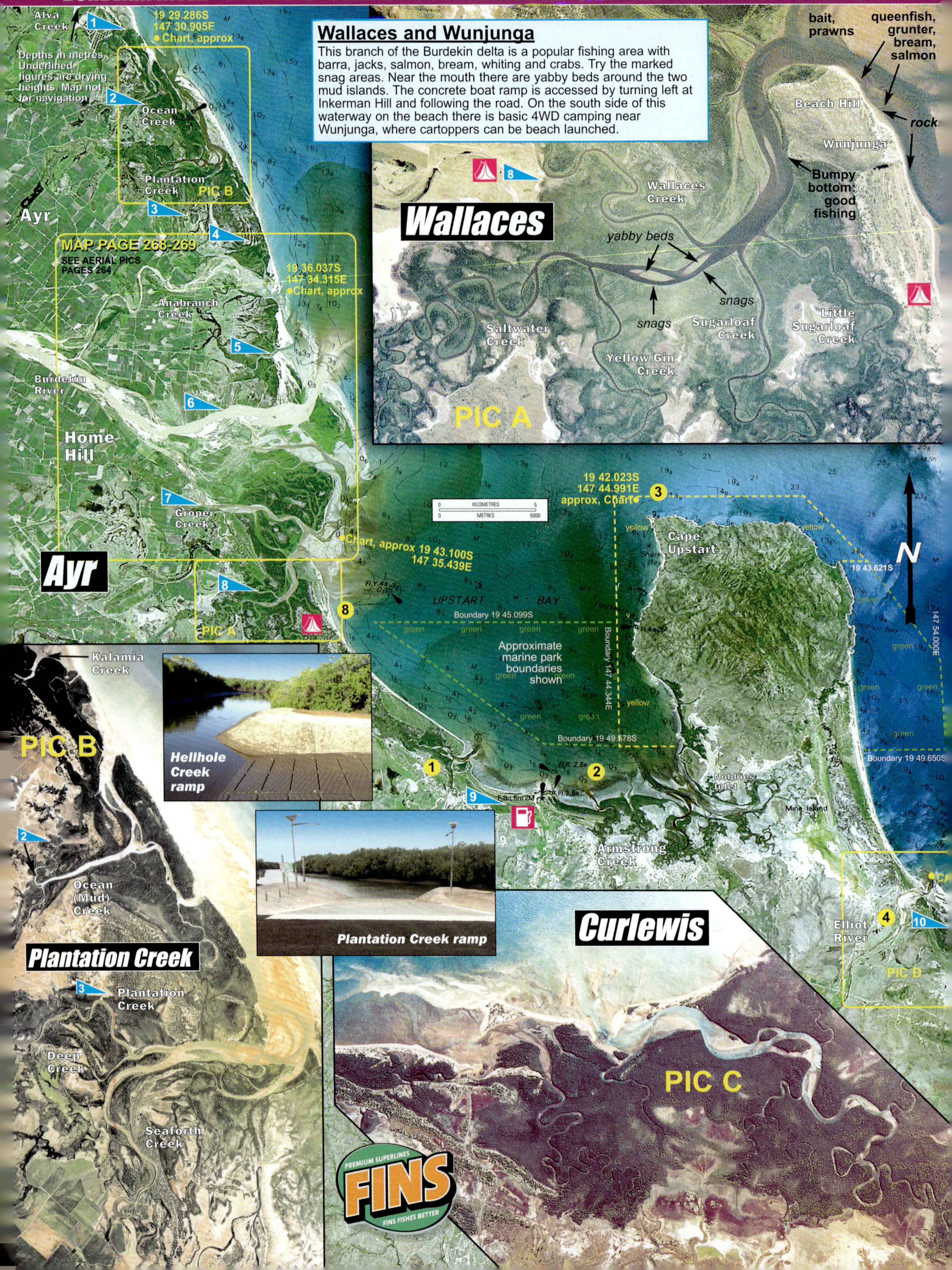

Hellhole Creek ramp

Plantation Creek ramp

Ayr to Bowen

Despite the Burdekin River's vast 130,000sqkm and 732km long catchment, the river mouth near Ayr is shallow and intermittent, with the bed under the highway bridge often just an expanse of dry sand. But when the Burdekin flows, it roars, flooding the delta and spewing sediment far out to sea. There is good fishing to be had in the tidal reaches, especially for blue salmon, trevally, queenfish and grunter. Whiting, flathead and mud crabs are common. Barramundi come on when the Burdekin Falls Dam wall upstream flows hard and barra migrate over the top. Bigger fish are generally caught by live-baiting holes at low tide. Prawns and crabs are abundant at times, and there are yabby beds on drying flats. For offshore anglers, Cape Upstart has deep water in close and is easily reached from Molongle Creek. Golden snapper are caught there at night, with tuskfish, grass sweetlip, cod and coral trout during the day, and pelagic fish. It is about 64km from Burdekin ramps to the Great Barrier Reef, but there are inshore patches. Some of the marked shoals include Pakhoi Bank at 19 26.343S 147 52.971E and Tink Shoal at 19 21.775S 147 51.651E. At Bowen, Nares Rock (approx 19 46.265S 148 21.511E) and nearby Holbourne Island at 26km and 33km NNE of Bowen are popular hotspots for mackerel and reef fish. Inland, the Bowen River Fish Stocking Association has released thousands of barra and sooty grunter into the Bowen and Broken river systems. Stocked barra move downstream during flooding, providing good saltwater fishing. Ocean and Plantation Creeks north of the Burdekin delta are other popular spots. Plantation Creek mouth is navigable only towards high tide.

Key to Map

Hotspots

1. Handy creek for whiting and flathead.
2. Best whiting spot within a day trip of Townsville. Big whiting, as well as occasional bonefish and permit over sand. This estuary has a vast seagrass bed out front. Also flathead, bream, grunter. Also yabbies, crabs, prawns.
3. Cape Upstart has deep water, with nannygai, golden snapper, emperor, trout and pelagic fish. Launch from Molongle Beach from half-tide up.
4. Elliot River has bream, whiting, flathead, jacks, golden snapper and cod. Beware shallow sandbanks and strong currents on big tides. Launch on upper tide. Camp Island has shallow reef on west side, deeper water on east side, with coral trout, cod sweetlip.
5. Mostly whiting, bream, flathead. Nearby launching area is on private property.
6. Abbott Point Jetty region: Big mackerel. Fishing near wharf is prohibited.
7. Whiting, flathead.
8. Fishing and camping near Wunjunga.
9. Whiting, yabbies, soldier crabs from beach.
10. Shoals around Nares Rock and island produce red emperor, nannygai at night.
11. Bowen Mackerel Patch 1 - 19 58.473S, 148 15.291E. Further offshore Mackerel Patch 2 at 19 55.350S 148 13.950E. Both produce mackerel from August to October each year.

Launch sites

1. Alva Creek, Lynch's Beach Rd, 16km from Ayr, gravel ramp, needs about 2m+ tide for sea access.
2. Ocean Creek, Peggy Bog Rd: 14km from Ayr, via Airdmillan, concrete, about .6m+ tide to launch and 1.5m+ for sea access.
3. Plantation Creek, Old Wharf Rd: ramps and pontoon, 2m+ tide needed for sea access.
4. Phillip's Landing: gravel ramp 25km from Ayr through gate on Phillip's Camp Rd, about 1.2m+ tide for sea access.
5. Hell Hole Creek, Hodder Rd, concrete, about 1m+ tide to launch, 1.5m+ sea access.
6. Kierle's Landing, Sandhills Rd. Gravel. About 1.5m tide to launch and 1m for sea access.
7. Groper Creek, Groper Creek Rd: two concrete ramps, jetty, van park, kiosk. Needs .5m+ tide to launch and 1m+ for sea access.
8. Wallace Landing, Peak Rd, on Yellow Gin Creek. Concrete, all-tide launch, .8m+ tide for sea access
9. Molongle Beach Rd, Molongle Creek, about 60km south of Home Hill, multi-lane ramp with facilities, .8m tide needed for sea access
10. Elliot River, bank landing.
11. Curlewis: private access.
12. Two ramps at Grays Bay.
13. Multiple ramps at Bowen boat harbour. Cartoppers/yaks only at Don River mouth.

Local tides have up to about 3.42m movement.

Wrecks

A. Charted wreck, approx 19 56.877S, 148 17.190E.
B. Charted wreck, approx 20 00.112S, 148 16.550E

ALSO, not marked on chart:
Wreck, approx 19 47.066S, 148 08.799E
C. Charted obstruction approx 19 55.895S 148 16.275E

Looking towards Beach Hill, Yellow Gin Creek and Groper Creek, the southern entrance to the Burdekin River, on a .16m low tide

The main entrance to the Burdekin River, looking across Peters Island

The Anabranch, or north entrance to the Burdekin River, with Ayr township in the distance

Groper Creek, showing the caravan park and launch site

The creek system on Rita Island

The seaward creek mouth on Rita Island

Burdekin River

Anabranch-Burdekin junction

Anabranch near the mouth

Townsville-Mackay landbased

Mackay Harbour rock wall
MONSTER FPV

The Strand foreshore, Townsville
NATHAN TANNER

TOWNSVILLE

1. Aplins Weir, Ross River. The final weir on the Ross River. Fishes best in the wet season when it is flowing. Fish the bottom side in the early morning and at night with livebait. Barra and jacks.

2. Blacks Weir, Ross River in Riverside. Blacks Weir is the top weir on the Ross River, with freshwater on both sides. Night fishing around the full moon. Shallow weedbeds and rockbars hold barramundi. Wet season best.

3. The Rock Pool, north end of the Strand, which is the main beachside road of Townsville. This spot fishes best through the cooler months of April to July and in the early mornings when the sea is calm. Golden trevally, mackerel, barra, tarpon and queenfish. Fishing along the rocks works best as fish cruise the edges.

4. The Breakwall, southern end of The Strand, is the main breakwall out to sea. It has plenty of area to fish. Good in the mornings. Barramundi are the main species, use soft plastics. Also cod, mangrove jacks, flathead and trevally. School mackerel on a morning high tide in winter.

5. Pallarenda Beach, the northern point of Rowes Bay. A great spot at high tide in the mornings and late afternoons for flathead, salmon, grunter and whiting. Winter best, from May/July. A great spot for the family.

6. Captains Creek, Rowes Bay, north of the Strand. Fishes best towards the end of the year, Sept - December. Main target species are flathead, tarpon, grunter and barra on livebaits and lures. This is a great afternoon and morning spot and on the runout tide around the new moon

7. The Strand Jetty. A high jetty Use bait jigs to catch livebait to target trevally, mackerel, queenfish and cod. Fishes best in the cooler months when the sea is calm. A big high tide around the full moon is ideal as there is more current, which seems to hold the baitfish and predators.

8. The Lakes, near Castletown shops. A great spot to lure barra, tarpon, jacks, giant herring and flathead. Fishes best in summer from October - Feburary and around the full and new moons when the tides are larger. Easy open banks and few snags.

9. Barratta Creek. Several bankside spots can be accessed on tracks off the Jerona Rd. Weather and tide dependent. Barra, jacks, mud crabs and more. Beware crocodiles.

MACKAY

1. North and south harbour breakwalls. Great fishing all year, with the warmer months between September and March seeing good catches of spanish, school, spotted and grey mackerel and longtail tuna. Floating live and dead baits or casting metal slugs and slices works. Large jewfish and golden snapper on live squid and soft plastics.

2. East Point. This is the mouth of the Pioneer River, with access via dirt road along Mulherin Dve. Large sandspit and rock wall fishes well all year, with Sept-May best for yellowtail, golden trevally, permit, queenfish and GTs. Best baits are live yabbies, green prawns. Metal slices and poppers for queenfish and GTs.

3. Palms. This is the upper reach of the Pioneer River, with deep holes and rockbars which are haven for mangrove jacks, barra and estuary cod. It can be fished all year, with best months Sept-Apr. May-Aug sees big whiting and bream caught below the Palms around the shingles and sandbars.

4. Bridge Road Fishing Platform. Commonly known as the old Hospital Bridge, this a great spot for young and old, used all year. Bread and butter species and mud crabs all year.

5. McReadys Creek. The rocky outcrops at the creek mouth provide livebaits and lure fishing for mangrove jack, barra, cod and queenfish from Sep/Apr, while the cooler months see large blue salmon taking baits along the shallow sandbars at the mouth along the beach.

6. Blacks Beach. Aug/May sees trevally, permit and mackerel on the bite. Best on the making tide with fresh yabbies or whole ganged pillies.

7. Dolphin Head. From October to April this is a fantastic area for large barra, fingermark, queenfish and jewfish. Best fished with lures around the bottom of the tide. Look for the weedbeds.

8. Reliance Creek. About a 20-minute walk south along Shoal Point Beach. The deep gutters inside the creek hold barra, jacks and golden snapper, while the rocky headlands at the mouth fish well for these plus king salmon. Best from September to April.

9. Belmunda Beach. A great camping area. Better on big tides. Sep/Apr sees king salmon, barra, flathead and queenfish. In winter, blue salmon and huge grunter.

10. Seaforth Beach. A great area when strong southerly winds blow, the rockbars at the mouth hold golden snapper, barra, jacks and cod. The main beach has bread and butter fish.

11. Constant Creek. The grass landing beside the boat ramp is an excellent fishing and camping area, the deep gutters along the creek hold barra, salmon, grunter, bream and flathead. Good crabbing.

12. Murray Creek. Great camping and fishing with big ledges and high banks, good for all bread and butter species. Sep/Feb threadfin salmon, barra and jacks. Blue salmon throughout winter.

13. Bakers Creek Ledge. Great fishing from Sep/Apr. Barra, threadfin salmon, queenfish. Use big livebaits (whiting, mullet) in the last three hours of the runout tide and first hour of making tide.

14. High Sands, McEwans Beach. This high sandbar at the mouth of McEwans Beach is a popular spot, with summer species being whiting and flathead. Winter species are whiting, bream, grunter and blue salmon.

15. Dunrock Ledge. Sandy Creek mouth is one of the most popular landbased spots. The summer months sees good schools of banana prawns. There are great yabby beds along the ledge. Many fish are caught here. Barra bite when prawns are running.

16. Grasstree Beach Creek. Sep/Feb. Great prawning creek, and the upper reaches around low tide have barra, jacks and golden snapper. Rocky foreshore has tuskfish - use big prawns.

17. Sarina Inlet. There are two boat ramps at the inlet, and most landbased anglers fish close to the ramps, though the rocky headlands produce better fish. Grunter, bream, flathead and golden snapper are common, with the odd tuskfish on fresh prawn.

18. Freshwater Point. Camping and fishing, the flat beach has rocky foreshores. From Aug/Feb best for barra, golden snapper, cod, mackerel.

19. Rocky Dam Creek. Great camping and landbased fishing, best Aug/May. Grunter, bream, threadfin salmon and barra. Plenty of mud crabs.

20. Cape Palmerston. The best camping area in the Mackay region, with large beaches, creeks and rocky headlands. All species in all sizes. 4WD is needed.

BURDEKIN RIVER - GROPER CREEK - ANABRANCH CREEK

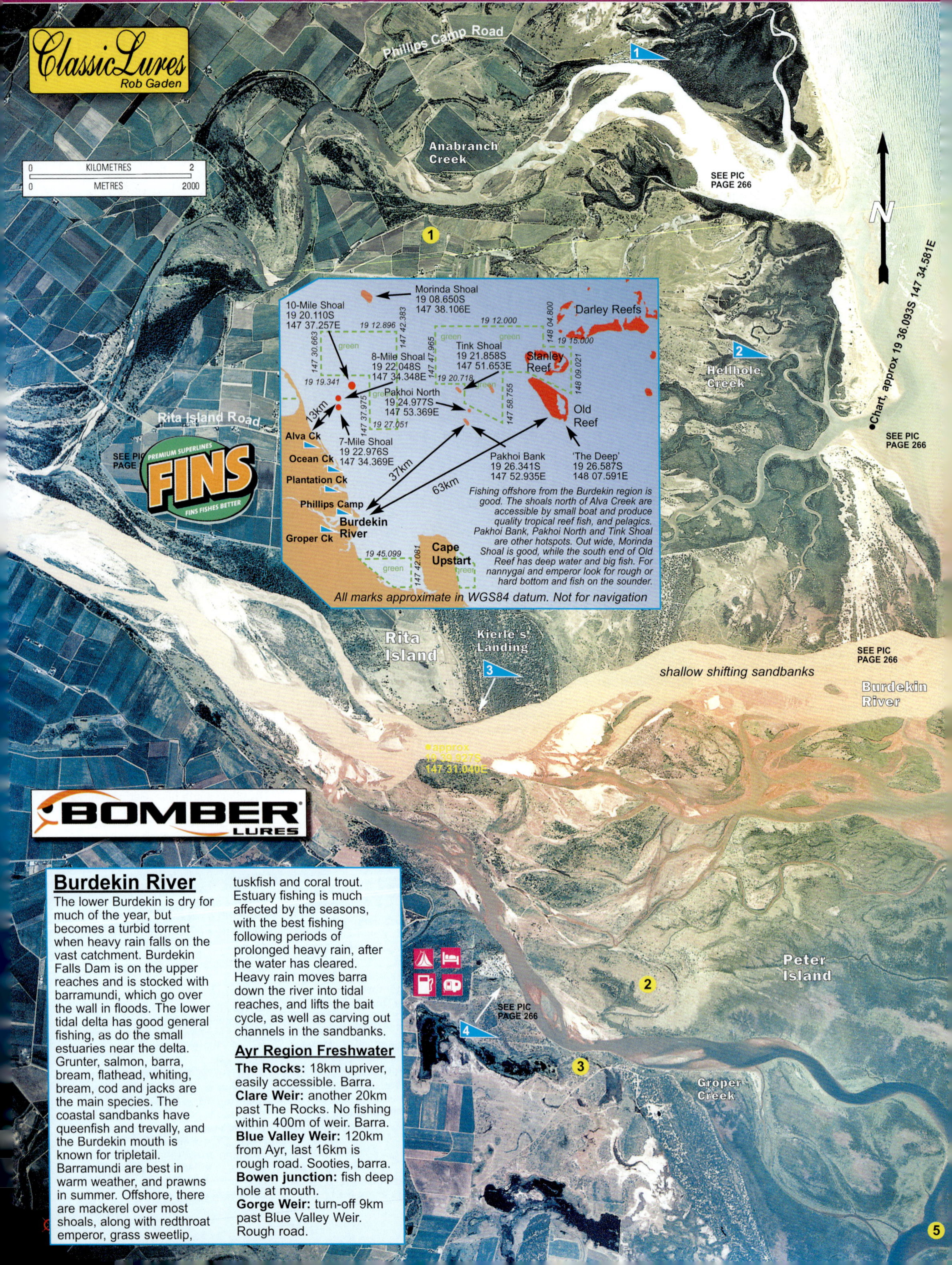

Classic Lures
Rob Gaden
Phillips Camp Road
Anabranch Creek
KILOMETRES 0 2
METRES 0 2000
SEE PIC PAGE 266
N
Chart, approx 19 38.093S 147 34.581E
1
2
Hellhole Creek
SEE PIC PAGE 266
Morinda Shoal
19 08.650S
147 38.106E
10-Mile Shoal
19 20.110S
147 37.257E
19 12.896
147 42.383
147 30.663
green
19 12.000
148 04.800
Darley Reefs
19 15.000
147 47.965
Tink Shoal
19 21.858S
147 51.653E
8-Mile Shoal
19 22.048S
147 34.348E
Stanley Reef
148 09.021
19 19.341
19 20.718
Pakhoi North
19 24.977S
147 53.369E
147 37.975
147 58.755
19 27.051
Old Reef
13km
Alva Ck
7-Mile Shoal
19 22.976S
147 34.369E
Ocean Ck
Plantation Ck
37km
63km
Pakhoi Bank
19 26.341S
147 52.935E
'The Deep'
19 26.587S
148 07.591E
Phillips Camp
Burdekin River
Groper Ck
19 45.099
147 42.081
Cape Upstart
Fishing offshore from the Burdekin region is good. The shoals north of Alva Creek are accessible by small boat and produce quality tropical reef fish, and pelagics. Pakhoi Bank, Pakhoi North and Tink Shoal are other hotspots. Out wide, Morinda Shoal is good, while the south end of Old Reef has deep water and big fish. For nannygai and emperor look for rough or hard bottom and fish on the sounder.
All marks approximate in WGS84 datum. Not for navigation
Rita Island Road
SEE PIC PAGE
FINS
PREMIUM SUPERLINES
FINS FISHES BETTER
Rita Island
Kierle's Landing
3
SEE PIC PAGE 266
shallow shifting sandbanks
Burdekin River
approx
19 39.927S
147 31.040E
BOMBER LURES
SEE PIC PAGE 266
4
2
3
Peter Island
Groper Creek
5

Burdekin River

The lower Burdekin is dry for much of the year, but becomes a turbid torrent when heavy rain falls on the vast catchment. Burdekin Falls Dam is on the upper reaches and is stocked with barramundi, which go over the wall in floods. The lower tidal delta has good general fishing, as do the small estuaries near the delta. Grunter, salmon, barra, bream, flathead, whiting, bream, cod and jacks are the main species. The coastal sandbanks have queenfish and trevally, and the Burdekin mouth is known for tripletail. Barramundi are best in warm weather, and prawns in summer. Offshore, there are mackerel over most shoals, along with redthroat emperor, grass sweetlip, tuskfish and coral trout. Estuary fishing is much affected by the seasons, with the best fishing following periods of prolonged heavy rain, after the water has cleared. Heavy rain moves barra down the river into tidal reaches, and lifts the bait cycle, as well as carving out channels in the sandbanks.

Ayr Region Freshwater

The Rocks: 18km upriver, easily accessible. Barra.
Clare Weir: another 20km past The Rocks. No fishing within 400m of weir. Barra.
Blue Valley Weir: 120km from Ayr, last 16km is rough road. Sooties, barra.
Bowen junction: fish deep hole at mouth.
Gorge Weir: turn-off 9km past Blue Valley Weir. Rough road.

Bowen

This area is renowned for its seasonal runs of grey, doggie, spotted and spanish mackerel. Fishing is mainly in winter at the Mackerel Patches, 5km and 8km north of Grays Bay ramp. Use the GPS marks or just look for the boats. August is often best for big spaniards. Bowen has shallow reefs around the islands and off Kings Beach. The larger bommies are home to coral trout, with golden snapper (fingermark) at night. The water is usually clear and divers can find lobsters (painted crays) easily. Gloucester Island is a 20km run to the east and has trout, lobsters, trevally, cobia and more. Mackerel, red emperor and nannygai are around Nares Rock, 28km north of Bowen, and the shoals near Holbourne Island, 33km north. Bowen has some creek fishing, with mainly bream, whiting, flathead and jacks. To the west, the 2.7km long Abbot Point jetty region is a 22km run from Grays Bay and produces big fish, including "unstoppables".

GPS marks

Mackerel Patch 1
19 55.559S 148 14.351E
Mackerel Patch 2
19 52.271S 148 12.545E
Winter Shoal - trout
20 04.507S 148 18.161E
Chyebassa Shoal
20 04.393S 148 20.221E
Southern Cross - trout
19 59.673S 148 16.311E
North Rock (dries)
19 58.157S 148 15.533E
Bradys Reef - west side of near Gloucester Island
20 03.347S 148 24.981E

Launch sites

1. Don River, yaks and cartoppers. 2.5m+ tide.
2. Grays Bay - exposed, 1m+ tide needed.
3. Bowen harbour - best local ramp, all tides.

*See ramp pix next page.

Bowen Family Fishing Classic

This huge event is held each September. In 2019 the total prize pool was $77,000. The 2020 and 2021 events were cancelled, but the Classic is expected to resume. Various categories allow everyone from family fishos to serious game fishermen to compete. For more information visit bowenfamilyfishingclassic.com.au

Key to Map

Hotspots

1. Anabranch River joins Burdekin River: most estuarine species, shallow in places.
2. Burdekin delta estuaries offer most species, with excellent whiting, bream and flathead. Many areas dry at low tide. Fish holes for barra in warmer months. Permit and queenfish over flats.
3. Groper Creek has a good boat ramp and caravan park. No reported rockbars, but there are usually some sunken trees. Popular prawning creek. Restocked with barra. Jacks, threadfin and blue salmon, bream, whiting and flathead. Golden snapper in spring/summer. Deep hole on first bend in from mouth and another upstream. Access to Burdekin at high water only. Groper Creek leads around to Yellow Gin Creek (also called Wallaces) which also has a boat ramp. Groper Creek is best avoided after heavy rain, as the water becomes sediment-loaded. Fishing quickly improves after rain.
4. Superb flathead and whiting fishing in calm weather. Also predatory fish such as barra, queenfish, trevally, permit.
5. Big grunter, golden snapper, barra, occasional jewfish.

Launch sites

1. Phillips Camp, gravel ramp, 25km from Ayr, poor after rain.
2. Hell Hole Creek (Hodder Road), need 1.5m+ tide for sea access.
3. Kierle's Landing: on the Rita Islands Road and Sandhills Road. Mid to high tide only.
4. Groper Creek: almost 30km from Ayr, two concrete ramps, need 1m+ tide for sea access.

Local tides have up to about 3.38m movement.

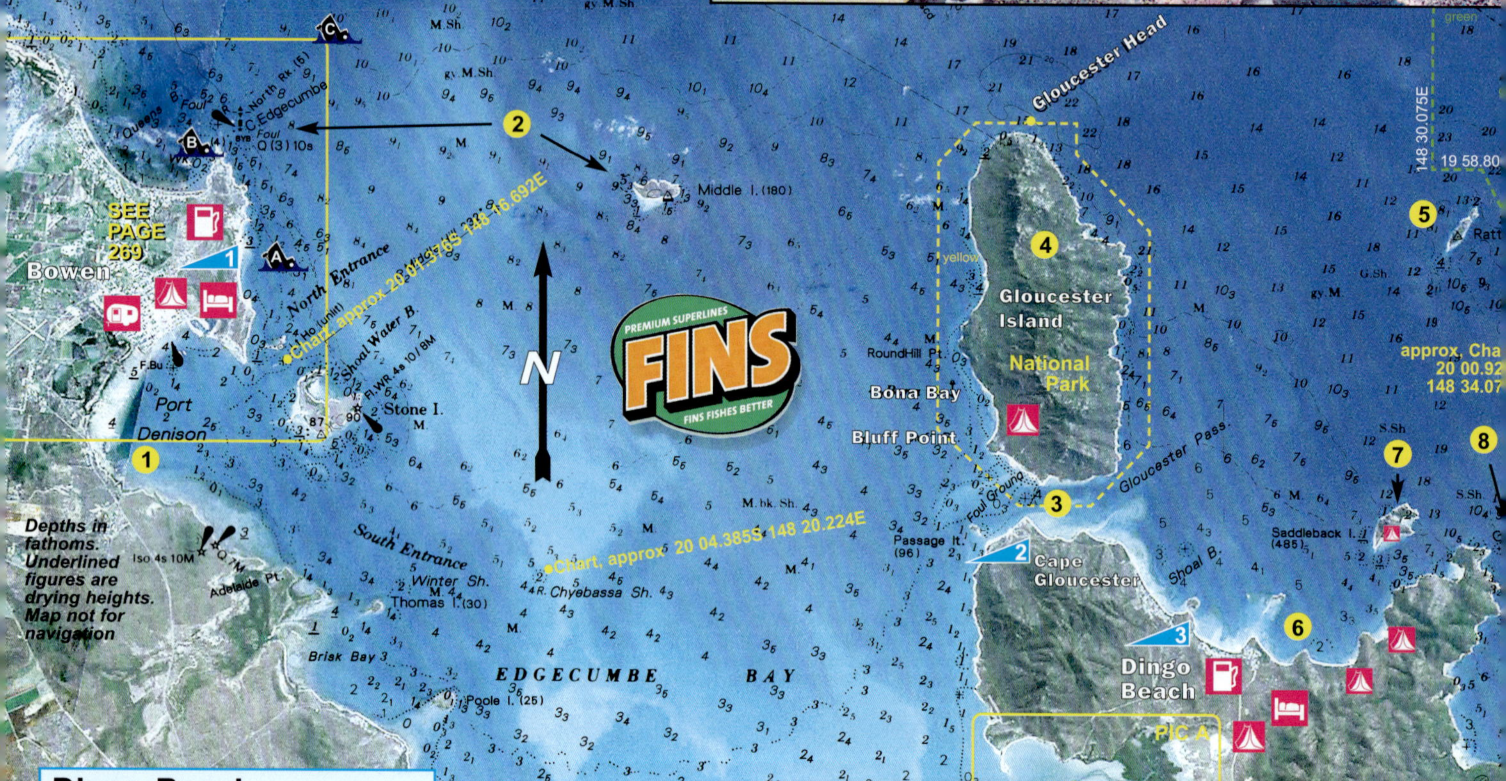

Bowen boat harbour ramp

Greys Bay ramp in Bowen

Whiting, flathead over flats

PIC A

Sinclair Bay

SEE PAGE 269

Depths in fathoms. Underlined figures are drying heights. Map not for navigation

Dingo Beach

This is the nearest launch site to reach the many islands in this region, which are otherwise a 20km sea run from Bowen. The 6km cruise from Dingo Beach to Gloucester Island is usually rewarded with good reef fishing around the drop-offs and bommies. Lobsters (painted crays) are common. The best chance of a barramundi is in the Longford and Gregory Creek systems, but the mouths are often silted and high tide may be needed to enter. Trevally, cod, coral trout and occasional permit lurk along the foreshores, with flathead and whiting in close. See also the Gloucester Island box at right. Boat hire and accommodation is available.

Key to Map

Hotspots

1. Whiting off beach - yabbies at low tide.
2. Mixed reef fish around island and off rock points, best at night. Mackerel.
3. Queenfish, trevally on big tide.
4. See Gloucester Island box at right.
5. Excellent reef fishing: trout, sweetlip, tuskfish, cod. Mackerel in season.
6. Islands can be reached from Dingo Beach. Shallow reef holds trout, sweetlip, golden trevally. Best at night for golden snapper. Some sight fishing. Jacks off headlands.
7. South-west edge has some bommies.
8. Reef fish, trevally, mackerel.
9. Mackerel, reef fish around islands.
10. Small creeks in coves. Crabs, jacks.
11. Trevally, occasional permit.
12. Reef fish off point, most species.
13. Mackerel, queenfish, trevally, trout off points and reefs.
14. Jewfish on Roseric Shoal. Mackerel on south tip of Double Cone Island.

Launch sites

1. Two ramps at Grays Bay and multi ramps in Bowen boat harbour.
2. Beach launch. Avoid in westerlies.
3. Dingo Beach, concrete ramp on beach, exposed.
4. Creek 4WD launch. On highway, turn after Dingo Creek bridge.

Wrecks

A. Off chart, 20 00.108S 148 16.565E
B. Off chart, 19 58.726S 148 15.269E
C. Off chart, 19 56.802S 148 17.231E
D. Off chart, 19 55.925S 148 16.269E

Dingo Beach tides, add about 50 min to Townsville times. Local tides have up to about 3.38m movement.

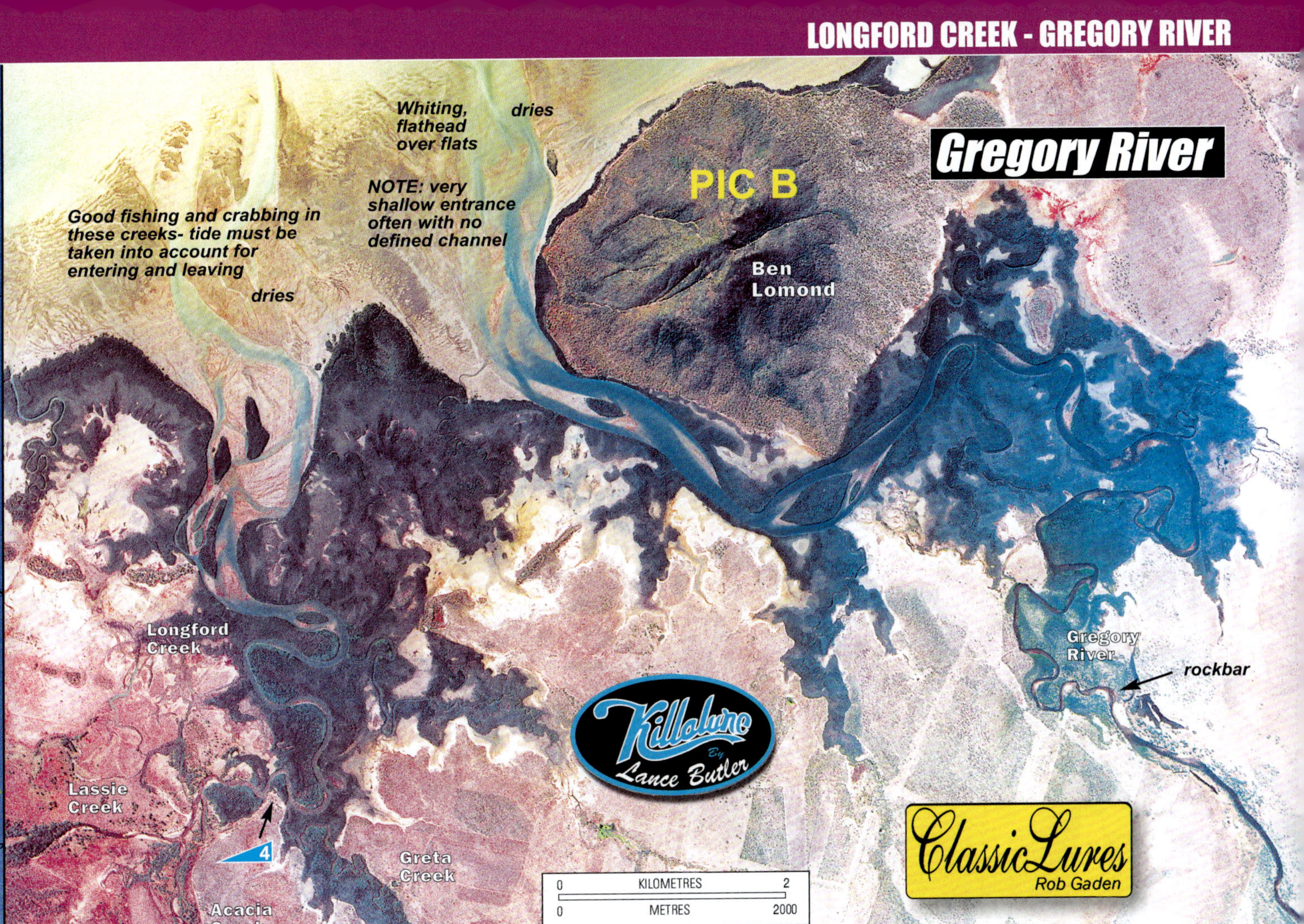

Gloucester Island

Gloucester Island is only a 6km run from Dingo Beach boat ramp, but in a boat it feels like a million miles away. The beauty of the area, and the great fishing, make it an ideal weekend destination. The island is a national park, in a GBRMPA yellow zone. Navigating is easy as the waters are deep and there are few surprises. The main area of concern is the shallow passage between the mainland and the island, which has strong currents and can get rough, and is tricky at low tide, with a rockbar at about 20 03.395S 148 28.168E. Navigate the deeper water on the island side of the passage. Camping is at Bona Bay on the south-west side. Fires are not permitted and there is no freshwater, but there is phone reception. The anchorage is deep and there are toilets and tables in the campground. The best fishing is usually on the east side of the island. There is another anchorage at East Side Bay. For those who wish to stay on land there is accommodation on the mainland near Dingo Beach.

Fishing

The north end of the island has strong tidal currents in deep water so bottom fishing must be done on neap tides or on the turn. Big grunter are a highlight, along with black jewfish, fingermark and largemouth nannygai. On big tides, large trevally can be jigged in the tidal rips. Big spanish mackerel also show up here and can be caught on the troll, jigging or with baits, along with cobia. Move along the eastern coast, fishing the best drop-offs, casting and jigging lures for mixed reef fish, including big barcheeked trout. The water is usually clear on neaps and divers can will find crayfish. Tiger squid can be jigged in close during the daytime, but spotlighting at night is the easier way to get them. Wide of East Side Bay is a reef with big golden snapper and grunter, at 19 59.450S 148 24.994E. It is good at night, and on neap tides. The west side of the island is usually the lee and fishes best on the south-west edge, with small pelagics in numbers, including queenfish and doggie mackerel. For endless trevally action try the shoal 3km off the southwest end at 20 03.380S 148 24.995E. Bottom fishing around Gloucester Island is best in the warmer months, with the various mackerel species best in winter.

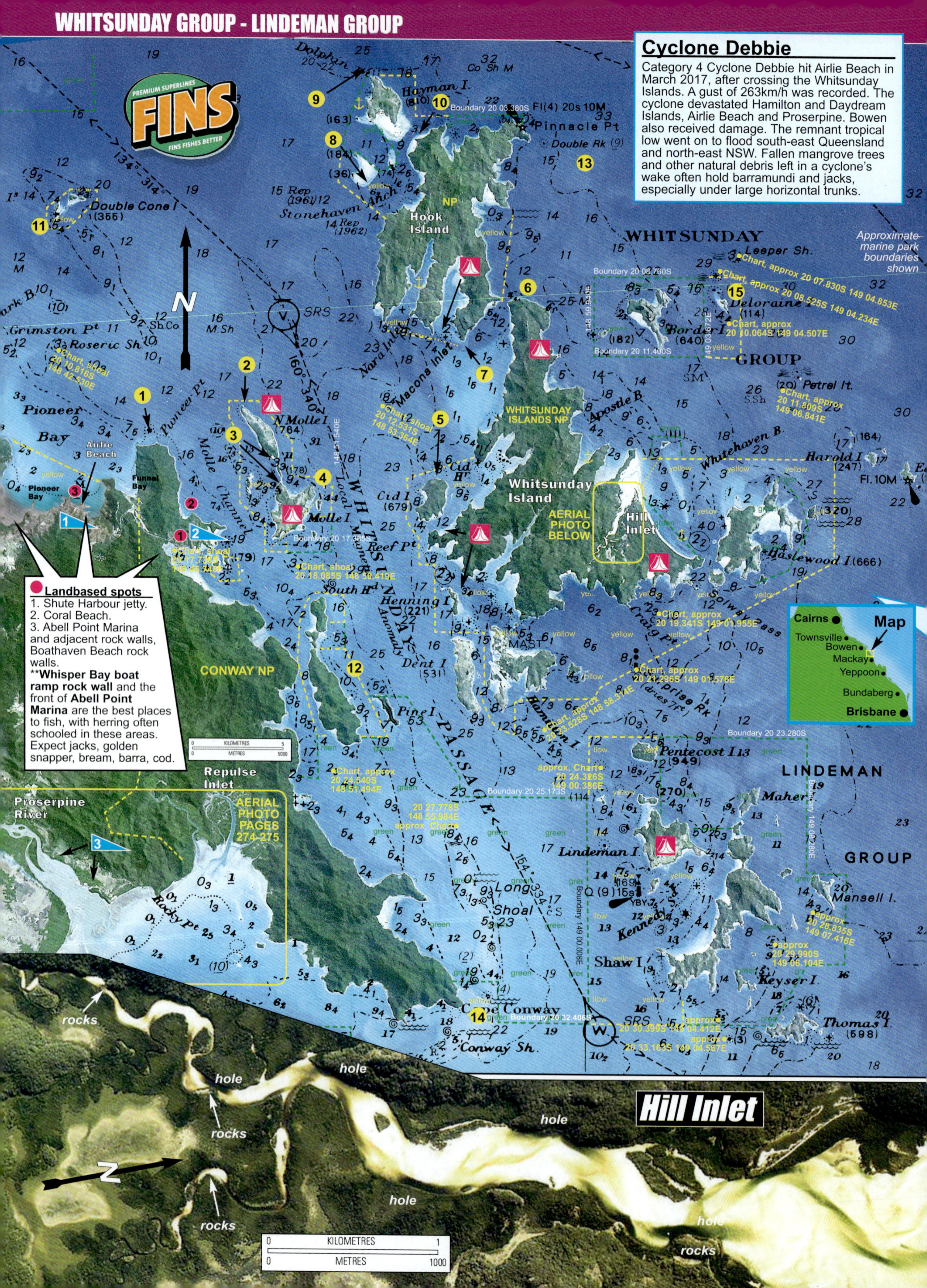

WHITSUNDAY GROUP - LINDEMAN GROUP
Cyclone Debbie
Category 4 Cyclone Debbie hit Airlie Beach in March 2017, after crossing the Whitsunday Islands. A gust of 263km/h was recorded. The cyclone devastated Hamilton and Daydream Islands, Airlie Beach and Proserpine. Bowen also received damage. The remnant tropical low went on to flood south-east Queensland and north-east NSW. Fallen mangrove trees and other natural debris left in a cyclone's wake often hold barramundi and jacks, especially under large horizontal trunks.
PREMIUM SUPERLINES
FINS
FINS FISHES BETTER
Landbased spots
1. Shute Harbour jetty.
2. Coral Beach.
3. Abell Point Marina and adjacent rock walls, Boathaven Beach rock walls.
**Whisper Bay boat ramp rock wall and the front of Abell Point Marina are the best places to fish, with herring often schooled in these areas. Expect jacks, golden snapper, bream, barra, cod.
Approximate marine park boundaries shown
Hook Island
Hayman I.
Pinnacle Pt
Double Rk
Stonehaven Anch
Nara Inlet
Macona Inlet
Whitsunday Island
WHITSUNDAY ISLANDS NP
AERIAL PHOTO BELOW
Hill Inlet
WHITSUNDAY GROUP
Leeper Sh.
Deloraine I.
Border I.
Petrel Pt.
Whitehaven B.
Harold I.
Haslewood I.
Solway Pass
Apostle B.
Cid H.
Cid I.
Molle I.
N Molle I.
Double Cone I.
Grimston Pt
Roseric Sh.
Pioneer Bay
Airlie Beach
Funnel Bay
Pioneer Pt
Molle Channel
Henning I.
Dent I.
South Hd
Reef Pt
Fitzalan Passage
Craig Pt
Esk I.
Pine I.
Hamilton I.
Surprise Rk
PASSAGE
CONWAY NP
Repulse Inlet
AERIAL PHOTO PAGES 274-275
Proserpine River
Rocky Pt
Long Shoal
Cape Conway
Conway Sh.
Lindeman I.
Pentecost I.
LINDEMAN GROUP
Maher I.
Mansell I.
Kennedy Is
Shaw I.
Keyser I.
Thomas I.
Map
Cairns
Townsville
Bowen
Mackay
Yeppoon
Bundaberg
Brisbane
KILOMETRES
METRES
Hill Inlet
rocks
hole

Dam, islands, river and reef

The Proserpine region has the Whitsunday Islands, Proserpine River and nearby Repulse Inlet, and Peter Faust Dam.

The dam is stocked with barramundi and produces many large, fat fish.

The redclaw fishery is legendary, although numbers fluctuate greatly.

The dam has a submerged timber forest on the western shore, and fishing this structure can be adrenalin-charged, with big fish flashing past lures, sometimes hitting, and then heading for the nearest snag.

Heavy line on powerful rods is required to win. There are also big sooty grunter.

ENDLESS OCEANS

Peter Faust Dam

The Proserpine River is one of the serious wild barramundi destinations on the East Coast, arguably second only to the mighty Fitzroy River at Rockhampton.

The Proserpine River is shallow and turbid and should only be navigated by newbies on a rising tide.

Expect to catch blue and threadfin salmon, pikey bream, mud crabs and barramundi. Be alert for crocodiles.

For landbased fishing, try the Airlie Beach rock walls for jacks, cod and barra.

Offshore, just a short run from the boat ramps at Shute Harbour and Airlie Beach, the Whitsunday Islands have great bluewater fishing.

Sandy beaches, coral reefs and shallow rocky headlands provide the backdrop while lure or bait fishing for resident reef fish and passing pelagics. The deep water of the outer islands produces spanish mackerel, cobia, black marlin and sailfish.

Red emperor, coral trout, sweetlip and nannygai are found on the reefs and rubble patches in between.

In close, jacks haunt the rocky foreshores, along with grunter, jewfish, trevally, queenfish, tarpon, giant herring, and occasional permit and bonefish.

The Great Barrier Reef is not a long trip from the outer Hayman Island (37km), but should only be visited in a suitable boat.

Good reef fishing can be had on the exposed boundaries of the islands.

The pinnacle off the north tip of Hayman Island produces big pelagic fish.

Fish inshore reefs at night with live squid for golden snapper.

Look for bommies for trout.

Lobsters (painted crayfish) are abundant in this region.

Numerous safe anchorages make this an enjoyable boating and overnighting location.

Hazards include shallow reefs and rocks, and strong currents between the islands. Night travel is not recommended.

The best anchorages are Blue Pearl Bay (Hayman Island), Butterfly Bay, Nara Inlet, Macona Inlet (Hook Island), Cid Harbour, Apostle Bay, Gulnare Inlet, Whitehaven Beach (Whitsunday Island), The Marina (Hamilton Island). Large tides must be taken into account when fishing this region.

Key to Map

Hotspots

1. Coral trout, other reef fish, mackerel off Pioneer Rocks.
2. Mackerel, queenfish and trevally off Hannah Point.
3. Mackerel, trevally at points.
4. Queenfish, mackerel, trevally and mixed reef fish off north-east point of Molle Island.
5. Queenfish, trevally, mackerel off north point of Cid Island.
6. Coral trout, red throat emperor, sweetlip in deep water off point.
7. As for number 6.
8. Mackerel, reef fish over reef bottom. Reef edge along Hook Island holds coral trout.
9. Mackerel, sailfish, marlin, cobia, trevally in current lines off point.
10. Mackerel rip between island.
11. Mackerel, queenfish, trevally off south end of Double Cone Islands. Reef fish off north edge.
12. Shallow reefs have mostly smaller reef fish in the day, better fish at night. Also golden trevally, queenfish, permit, jacks, barra.
13. Big pelagics around rock.
14. Grunter, jewfish, trout.
15. Troll east side of Deloraine Island for monster mackerel in winter. North and south end bommies have reef fish etc.

Launch sites

1. Abell Point Marina and Whisper Bay, all tides.
2. Shute Harbour, all tide.
3. Upper tide launch at river mouth. All-tide ramp upstream.

Local tides have up to about 4.06m movement.

DRONE VISION AUS

Airlie Beach foreshore

CHRIS NEWLYN

Shute Harbour

Spanish mackerel calendar

Spanish mackerel are usually in the greatest numbers off the Whitsundays from May to October.

Mackerel tend to congregate on different parts of the East Coast at different times.

The end of July is usually the start of the mackerel run along much of the East Coast, especially Townsville to Lucinda, however water temperature and currents play a role in their annual movements.

It is believed they have a northern migration on the inside of the Great Barrier Reef and then a southern movement on the outside of the reef.

Large numbers of mature spanish mackerel of 90cm or more (about two years of age) school on reefs off Townsville to spawn during the new moon in October and November. It is likely spawning occurs outside of these areas as far south as Yeppoon.

A large proportion of the entire commercial catch of spanish mackerel comes from areas around Rib and Bramble Reefs wide of Hinchinbrook in these two months alone.

While a large proportion of spanish mackerel migrate up and down the coast, there are groups of fish, known as "homers", that stay in an area, or on a reef system, all year.

For this reason, spaniards can be caught all year on most locations around the Great Barrier Reef.

Off Townsville, the larger fish tend to be found around the rocky headlands of Cape Upstart, Cape Bowling Green including Salamander Reef, and the Palm Island Group, usually mid-June to October.

May is generally the pick of the months to chase large spanish mackerel close to the coast, from the Gold Coast to Cape Upstart.

The smaller fish, to about 15kg, are often found on shoals off the Burdekin River, in Bowling Green Bay and behind Magnetic Island, from June through to October.

The reefs of Hinchinbrook's Lucinda (Bramble, Rib, Trunk) produce nice fish in October and November. The odd mackerel can also be found in Townsville's Cleveland Bay from July to November, particularly school or spotted mackerel.

Spaniards can be caught at night. Around the full moon is good.

Try hanging a bright light over the side of the boat to attract baitfish, then float a pilchard behind the boat until it is just outside the light shadow.

There doesn't appear to be any particular time when one bait or lure is preferred over another, it is best to see what is working on the day.

Early mornings and late arvo are always good times to fish, trolling deeper during the day.

Downriggers can work well.

Fish barriers removed

A Mackay-Whitsunday Fish Barrier Prioritisation study identified 3974 potential barriers to fish movement in streams. Of these, 171 were identified as substantially obstructing fish migration. Barriers were ranked according to the impact they had and the feasibility of rehabilitation. From this process a list of top priority barriers was developed. Several have since been replaced with structures that allow fish migration. Off-stream wetland barriers such as pondage pasture bund walls were also identified during the initial study, and a separate process to identify fixable wetland barriers was to be conducted. The work will improve wild fish stocks, especially for estuarine migrant species such as barramundi.

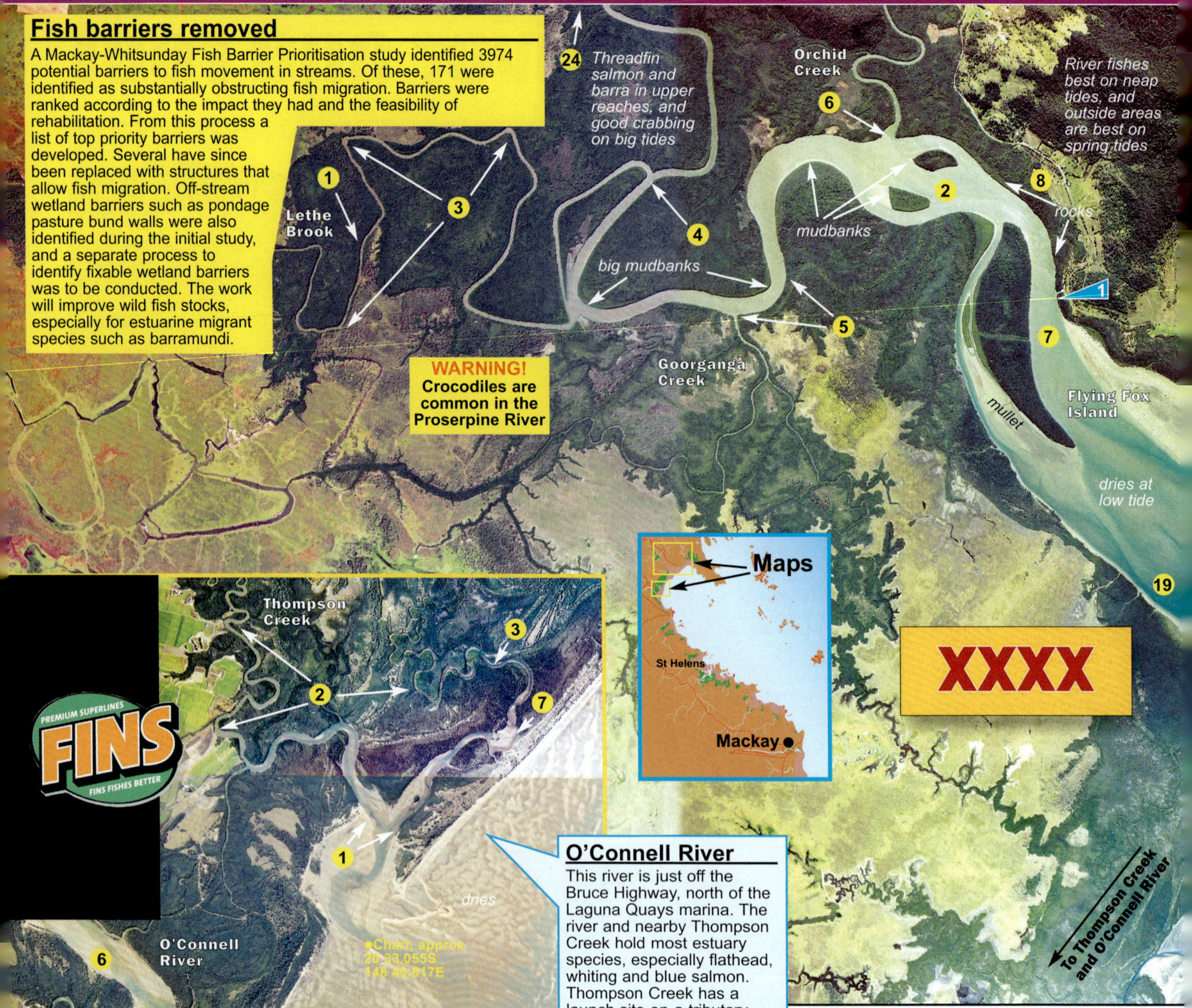

WARNING!
Crocodiles are common in the Proserpine River

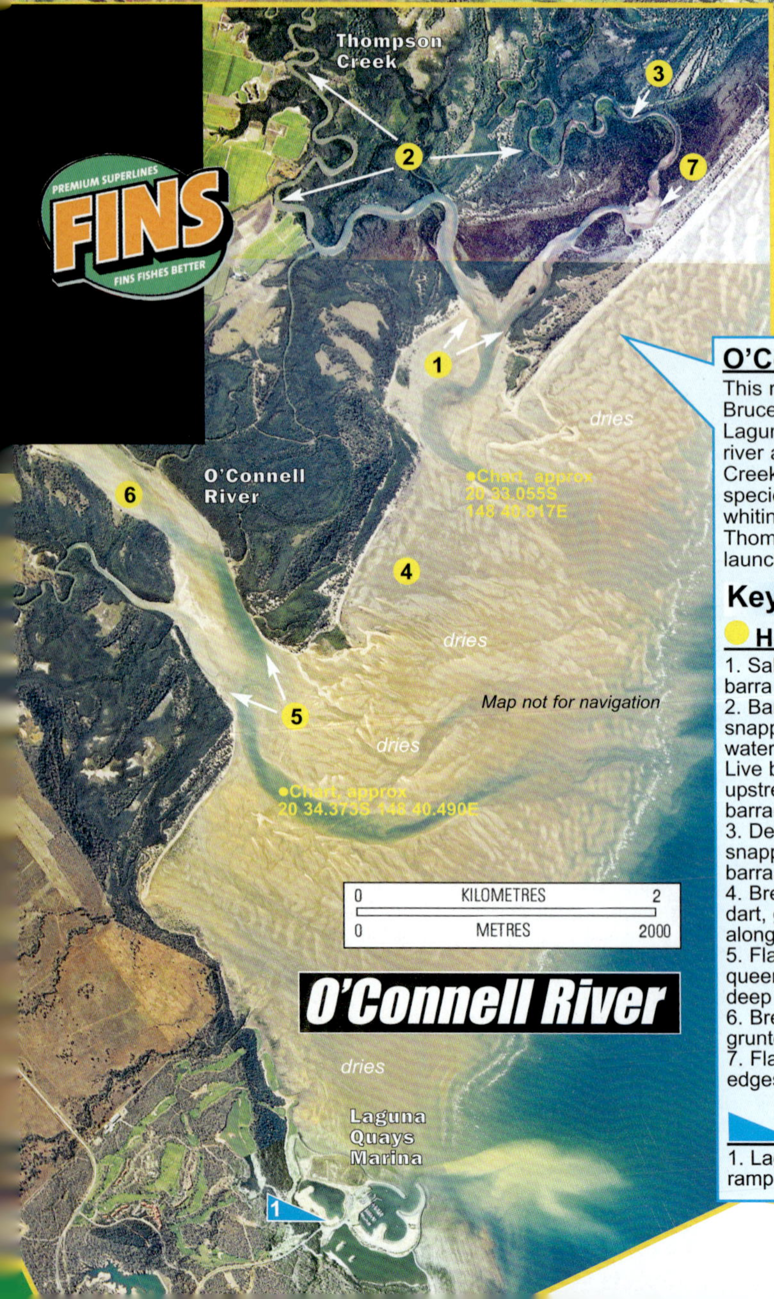

O'Connell River

This river is just off the Bruce Highway, north of the Laguna Quays marina. The river and nearby Thompson Creek hold most estuary species, especially flathead, whiting and blue salmon. Thompson Creek has a launch site on a tributary.

Key to Map

Hotspots

1. Salmon, grunter, salmon, barra along deep bank.
2. Barra, grunter, golden snapper, cod, jacks in deep water on outside of bends. Live bait best. Eddies around upstream S-bend holds barramundi on big tides.
3. Deep bend holds golden snapper, grunter, barramundi. Crabs.
4. Bream, whiting, flathead, dart, golden trevally, salmon along beach at high tide.
5. Flathead, whiting, trevally, queenfish and salmon on deep edges.
6. Bream, whiting, flathead, grunter, prawns.
7. Flathead along sandbar edges.

Launch sites

1. Laguna Quays marina ramp, all tides.

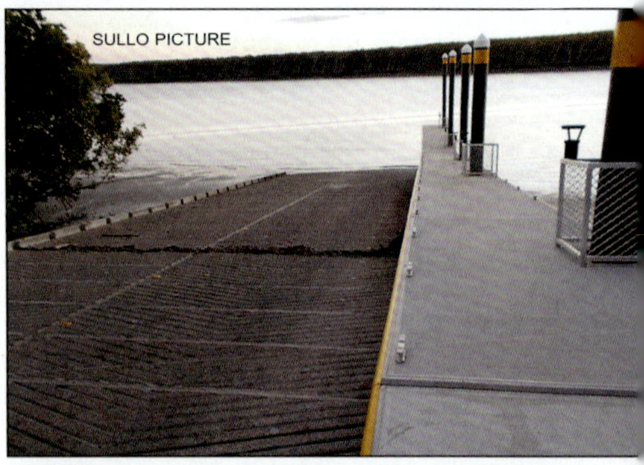
SULLO PICTURE

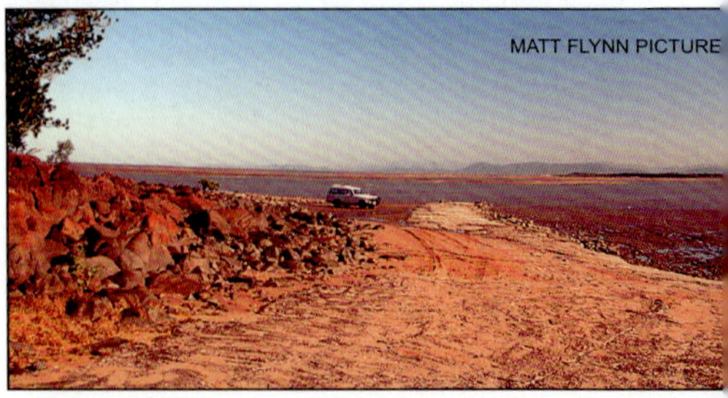
MATT FLYNN PICTURE

ABOVE: Proserpine River ramp. BELOW: An alternative launch site at the river mouth

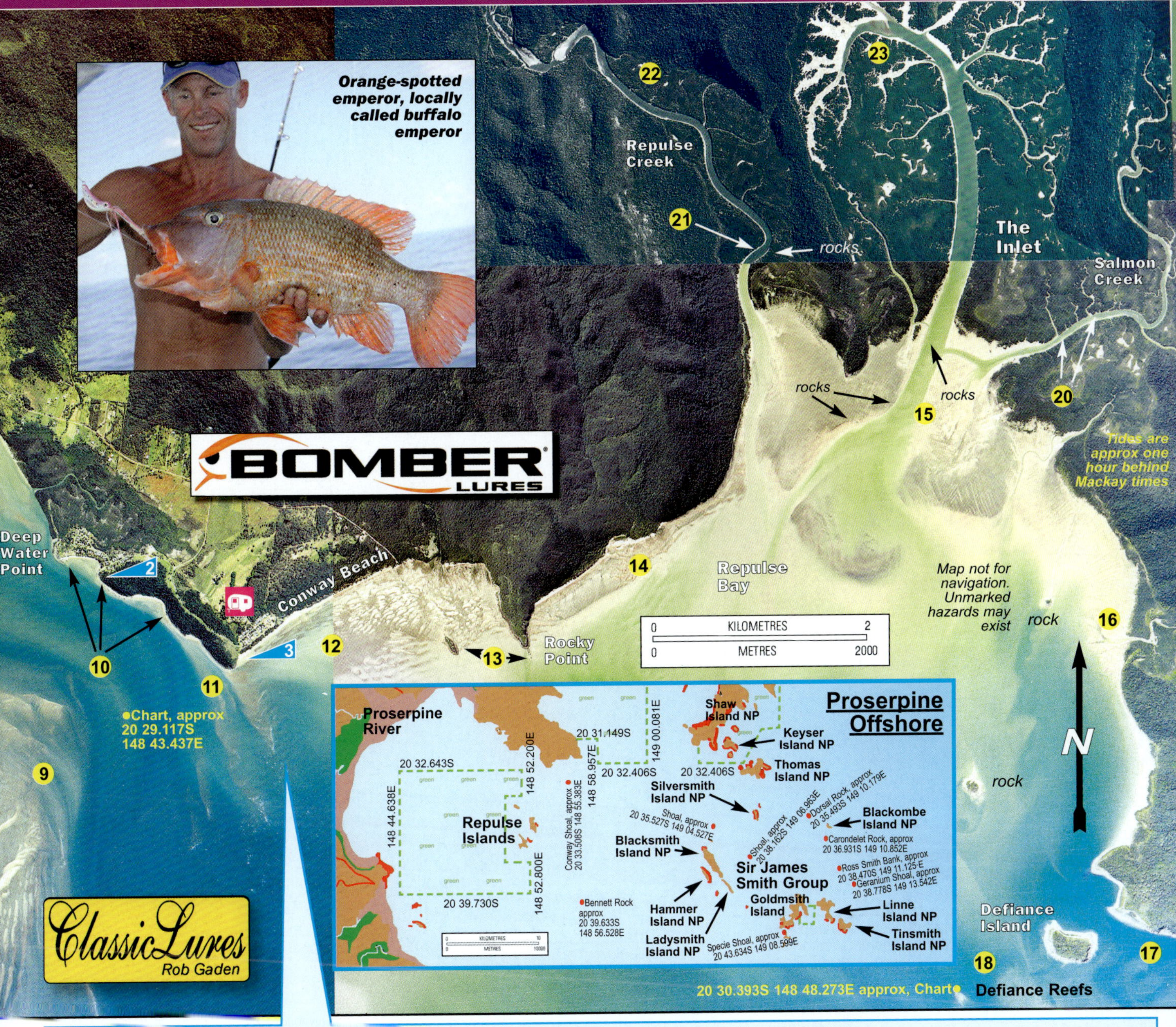

Key to Map

Hotspots

1. Troll for barra along straights at high tide, best after prolonged rain in warm weather.
2. Barra, salmon on flats edges around islands, incoming tide. Baitfish.
3. Estuary fish in holes on bends at high tide.
4. Junction hole, estuary fish on live bait.
5. Eddie at creek mouth holds barra and salmon, use live bait. Deep south bank on main river holds barra, salmon.
6. Barra, salmon, grunter.
7. Deep channel along east side of island good for trevally, salmon, grunter, barra. Small channel on west side of island holds prawns and mud crabs and is a useful area for collecting mullet for bait.
8. Area above boat ramp includes extensive oyster rocks, salmon, cod, big bream, grunter, whiting, jacks.
9. Creek drains have barra and salmon on falling tide. Good crabbing area after rain.
10. Cod, bream, whiting, grunter and barramundi along foreshore.
11. Fish headland rocks in calm weather.
12. Bream, whiting, salmon along beach at high tide. Beach launching available. Very good prawning area in season.
13. Trevally, barra and golden snapper off rocks at high tide.
14. Collect mullet at small inlet at high tide.
15. Good region for crabbing after heavy rain, best when it is calm
16. Barra, jacks and salmon. Watch flats edges for activity on first incoming tide.
17. Golden snapper, trout, tuskfish, cod just off headlands, also pelagics.
18. Mackerel and reef fish near rocks and over rough ground.
19. Barra, salmon, grunter along edge of deep channel with tide running out.
20. Barra on drains, falling tide.
21. Barra, salmon, jacks, snapper, crabs.
22. Most species. Good barra fishing on low tide gutters. Golden snapper at top of creek (off map) over deep rough bottom.
23. Mud crabs during dry weather.
24. Limited upstream bank access for landbased fishing off Glen Isla Rd.

Launch sites

1. Concrete ramp useable on most tides. Beware river mudbanks at low tide.
2. Upper tide launch, currents on big tides.
3. Beach launching area, high tide.

Proserpine

The Proserpine River's tidal water produces quality barramundi and mud crabs. Fishos can also try their hand at stocked Peter Faust Dam, on the upper river, where metre-plus fish are commonly caught. Across the bay, The flats and gutters of The Inlet and Repulse Creek fish well. Repulse Creek has rock patches which hold mixed species, including reef fish. Fish for barra and salmon where mud gutters drain into the channels. Barra are best in the warmer months, with blue and threadfin salmon and grunter in winter. Anglers who use livebait will be rewarded. Mullet, prawns, soldier crabs and yabbies are easily found. Mud crab availability varies from season to season. Prawning is best early in the year. This area has large tides. Lure fishing is best on neap tides when water clarity improves, but some tidal movement gets the fish biting. Repulse Bay is shallow and much of it dries. The mouth of the river is exposed to south-easters. To access the lower river, turn off Airlie Beach Rd onto the Conway Beach Rd. The larger structures of the Great Barrier Reef are a long way out, with Parker Reef being 111km out, followed by the Credlin Reefs at 130km, but good bluewater fishing is had around some of the inner islands and shoals. Golden snapper, cod, tuskfish, grunter and trout can be caught around rocky points and offshore spots such as Defiance Reefs, Conway Shoal and Bennett Rock. The reefs around the Repulse Islands are within a Green Zone.

Tides at the mouth are about one hour behind Mackay times. Local tides move up to about 5.18m.

Proserpine to Mackay

St Helens Beach and Seaforth were declared net-free in 2015. This followed the implementation of GBRMPA zones in 2003 that also restricted coastal netting. Large barramundi are now a regular catch in estuaries between the Proserpine River and Mackay, and king salmon (threadfin) and grunter stocks are good. This coastline is mostly shallow, with drying flats and mangrove creeks flushed by tides of up to around 6m. Barramundi, jacks, golden snapper (fingermark), cod, threadfin and blue salmon and mud crabs are all possible in a day, along with whiting, flathead and bream. The Great Barrier Reef is a long run out, but the many closer islands, shoals and rubble areas have coral trout, cod, emperor, tuskfish and mackerel. Big spanish and spotted mackerel move through in winter. Ribbon fish are about at the same time, and are the prime bait for big mackerel. Mud crabs and prawns vary in abundance from year to year. Big jacks inhabit the offshore reefs and are taken at night, with smaller jacks in the estuaries. Large golden snapper (fingermark) are taken on coastal reefs and headlands, best at night. Barramundi are around coastal rocks in calm, warm weather. Stocked barra escape from Proserpine's Peter Faust Dam during floods and enter the Proserpine River. Mackay fishermen have three dams stocked with barramundi. As this area has a large tidal movement, creek barramundi can be targeted at mud drains on the outgoing tides. Nippers are found on flats along this coast, and bait-sized mullet and herring are usually easy to find. Most tidal creeks are rocky in the upper reaches and careful navigation is required. Large tides must be taken into account when planning trips, and tidal currents and wind create rough conditions.

Key to Map

Hotspots

1. Reef, pelagic fish around islands.
2. Tuskfish, trout, cod on shallow reefs.
3. Reef, pelagic fish around islands.
4. Landbased fishing at Redcliffe Island, Seaforth, around Cape Hillsborough, and off Wedge Island. Both islands can be accessed from mainland near low tide, but are cut off by tide. A jewfish hole is north of Cape Hillsborough. Mackerel and ribbon fish in winter. Camping at Smalleys Beach.
5. Good reef fishing.
6. Big spanish mackerel around islands.
7. Blackwood Shoals - area of undulating bottom.
8. Trevally, mackerel, reef fish on patches.
9. Quality reef fish around patches. Usually worth travelling the long distance.

Wrecks

A. Charted wreck, approx 20 43.907S 149 10.624E

Launch sites

1. Laguna marina, silted up, poor at low tide.
2. Dempster Creek ramp, Midgeton.
3. St Helens and Murray Creek ramps.
4. Victor Creek and Seaforth Creek ramps.
5. Halliday Bay and Ball Bay beach launches. Also a creek launch inside Cape Hillsborough off Kippen Dve.
6. Constant Creek and Belmunda ramps.
7. Mackay Boat Harbour, multi-lanes.
8. Mackay's Pioneer River ramps - main ramp at River St, also under Mirani Bridge. Small-boat bank launch near Dumbleton Weir.

Mackay tides move up to about 6.4m. Big tides in this region must be considered for launching and retrieving boats, and navigating across shallow areas.

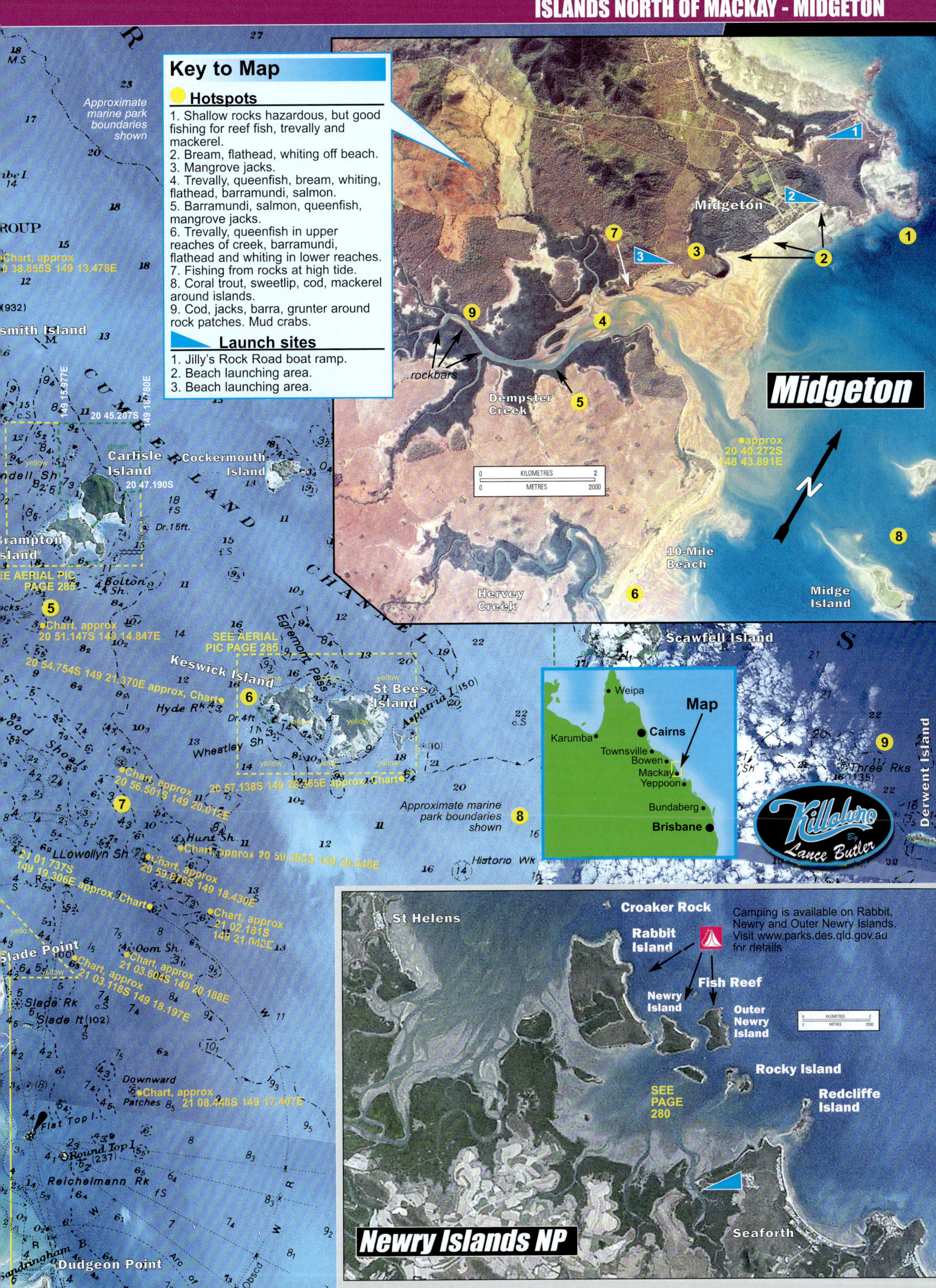
Key to Map
Hotspots
1. Shallow rocks hazardous, but good fishing for reef fish, trevally and mackerel.
2. Bream, flathead, whiting off beach.
3. Mangrove jacks.
4. Trevally, queenfish, bream, whiting, flathead, barramundi, salmon.
5. Barramundi, salmon, queenfish, mangrove jacks.
6. Trevally, queenfish in upper reaches of creek, barramundi, flathead and whiting in lower reaches.
7. Fishing from rocks at high tide.
8. Coral trout, sweetlip, cod, mackerel around islands.
9. Cod, jacks, barra, grunter around rock patches. Mud crabs.
Launch sites
1. Jilly's Rock Road boat ramp.
2. Beach launching area.
3. Beach launching area.
Midgeton
Midgeton
rockbars
Dempster Creek
Hervey Creek
10-Mile Beach
Midge Island
approx 20 40.272S 148 43.891E
Approximate marine park boundaries shown
Carlisle Island
Cockermouth Island
Brampton Island
Keswick Island
St Bees Island
SEE AERIAL PIC PAGE 285
Scawfell Island
Derwent Island
Slade Point
Dudgeon Point
Reichelmann Rk
Chart, approx 20 51.147S 149 14.847E
20 54.754S 149 21.370E approx, Chart
Chart, approx 20 56.501S 149 20.012E
20 57.138S 149 28.365E approx, Chart
Chart, approx 21 02.181S 149 21.042E
Chart, approx 21 03.604S 149 20.188E
21 03.118S 149 18.197E
Chart, approx 21 08.448S 149 17.407E
Map
Weipa
Karumba
Cairns
Townsville
Bowen
Mackay
Yeppoon
Bundaberg
Brisbane
Killaloe By Lance Butler
St Helens
Croaker Rock
Rabbit Island
Newry Island
Fish Reef
Outer Newry Island
Rocky Island
Redcliffe Island
Seaforth
SEE PAGE 280
Camping is available on Rabbit, Newry and Outer Newry Islands. Visit www.parks.des.qld.gov.au for details
Newry Islands NP

St Helens

This estuary was declared net-free in 2015. It is a challenging area, with drying flats and big tides, but with good fishing and crabbing. Many of the small side creeks have rock patches in the upper sections that fish on the upper tide. Cast to mud drains along the lower reaches on outgoing tides. Patches of deep rocky bottom in the creek channels fish well, and low-tide holes often hold barramundi and cod. Whiting, bream, grunter, salmon and flathead are the main catch off the beaches, with mackerel and reef fish on the shallow coastal rocks and shoals. Landbased fishing can be had off the beach near St Helens picnic area at high tide, and the rock outcrop to the west. Low Rock is just 4.3km off St Helens Beach at approx 20 49.376S 148 52.842E, and is also fished by boat from Seaforth. This rock holds mackerel in winter, along with big barracuda and trevally, with a chance of barramundi and queenfish in warm, calm weather. Another 2km out in deeper water is Croaker Rock at approx 20 49.154S 148 53.977E, a good spot for mackerel in winter months. Spanish mackerel are usually at their best through this region in July/August. Mud crabs are abundant, with annual variations. Take into account large tides when planning trips, with big tides bringing choppier conditions. Just 6km to the west are camp sites on Newry, Rabbit and Outer Newry Islands.

Marine stingers

Box jellyfish (pictured) are common in northern Australia, found from about Gladstone, Qld, to Exmouth, WA. They move close to shore in warmer months, but stings can happen all year. Box jellyfish move into the shallows in calm weather to feed on prawns and small fish. In murky conditions they are almost impossible to see. They have long tentacles that get caught in nets, anchor ropes and fishing line.

A bad sting can be fatal and children are vulnerable.

Tiny Irukandji jellyfish have a similar distribution, being particularly well recorded in Cairns, the Whitsundays and Broome, including inshore and offshore waters. The initial sting may be mild, but extreme full-body pain can follow. This delayed pain onset has been reported in other jellyfish species.

Stonefish are a common tropical hazard. They lie on the bottom, looking like a rock. They may be found around boat ramps. Their spines can penetrate shoes. The pain is excruciating.

Stingrays have a poisonous spine on their tail and fishermen are sometimes stung when wading. The pain can be severe.

Cone shells (several species) have a deadly sting, as does the tiny blue-ringed octopus.

Perhaps less well known is that anemones, seas slugs, coral and a variety of other fish can inflict bad stings.

Some types of coral are extremely toxic, and have made people sick inside homes where the coral has been kept in a fish tank and the coral washed or otherwise handled.

Be sure children do not pick up unidentified creatures.

Key to Map
Hotspots
Blue and threadfin salmon are caught throughout. 1. Whiting, bream, flathead off St Helens Beach. 2. Jacks, bream. 3. Prawns, baitfish. 4. Grunter, flathead, barra. 5. Barra, grunter in holes. Whiting over flats. 6. Barra in holes on outside of bends. Rock patches upstream fish fish at high tide. Mud crabs. 7. Barra, grunter on deep bends. 8. Barra, grunter, jacks. 9. Whiting, flathead over flat. 10. Flathead, grunter, bream off rocks at end of beach. 11. Hole on bend has barra. 12. Barra, grunter, jacks, crabs. 13. Troll deeper bank. 14. Deep hole. Rocky bottom upstream at shown GPS marks. 15. Mud crabs. 16. Troll deep bend. Mud crabs. 17. Barra, grunter, bream, flathead. 18. Mud crabs, grunter, barra. 19. 'The Shortcut' - barra. 20. Troll the deep bank. 21. Barra, whiting.
Launch sites
1. St Helens ramp, best above 1m tide.
2. Murray Creek ramp on Little Bogga Rd. All tides. Turn off the Bruce Hwy at the Mt Pelion turn-off. Tide difference about 2.5 hours after Mackay tide times. See also Victor Creek ramp to south at Seaforth, on next page.
Local tides move up to about 6m.
Mud Isle
NET FREE ZONE
Chart, approx 20 50.215S 148 51.957E
Low Rock 20 49.376S 148 52.842E
Map not for navigation
N
Killalure By Lance Butler
Mathers Creek
Premium Superlines FINS Fins Fishes Better
Home Creek
Mystery Creek
sandbars
St Helens Creek
Murray Creek
sandbar
sandbar
sandbars
drying rocky patches starting 5km upstream of ramp at 20 55.487S 148 51.345E 20 55.710S 148 51.220E hold grunter, bream, jacks, fingermark around high tide
ClassicLures Rob Gaden
rocks on south bank
rocks
rock
Murray Creek ramp
0 KILOMETRES 2
0 METRES 2000

Seaforth

Newry Island group is a 5km run from Victor Creek, with permit camping on Newry, Outer Newry and Rabbit Islands. The Smith Islands are 30km out, with permit camping on Goldsmith Island. The tidal creeks have blue and threadfin salmon, barra, grunter, jacks, golden snapper and mud crabs, with banana prawns in summer. The inner islands have fringing reefs and fish well for tuskfish, golden trevally, trout, cod and queenfish. Doggie, spotted and grey mackerel usually start running from May. Grounds around the outer islands produce all GBR species. Note the Green Zones. Local tidal movement is up to about 5.7m, with vast drying flats at low tide. Fish move into mangroves at high tide, fish draining gutters as the tide falls. Troll deep banks and rocky areas on neap or building tides when water clarity has improved. Whiting, bream, salmon and flathead are caught off beaches at high tide.

Key to Map

Hotspots

1. Low-tide gutter - salmon, flathead. Use shallow lures and quiet approach.
2. Junction hole has grunter, golden snapper and barra. Mud crabs, jacks, barra and grunter in upper reaches.
3. Barra and salmon on low tide gutters. Whiting and flathead over flat.
4. Excellent prawning on extensive flats from December to April.
5. Barra, salmon along edges.
6. Scattered rockbar near low tide. Jacks and barra.
7. Deeper water on bend has barra. Bait can be netted just upstream from ramp.
8. Grunter, golden snapper, crabs.
9. Queenfish, trevally and salmon around islands. Spotted and doggie mackerel on northern points in season, along with mixed reef fish.
10. Reef fish, mackerel, trevally, large golden snapper at night, odd jewfish.
11. Most estuary species inside Seaforth Creek mouth.
12. Good fishing in upper reaches, mostly on deep bends. Good family boating, but watch for sand/mudbars.
13. Jewfish off headland, mackerel, cod, some trout, mangrove jacks near rock. Whiting, flathead and occasional salmon and barra off beaches within headland.

Launch sites

1. Victor Creek. multi-lanes, pontoon, all tides, but 1.5m+ tide for sea access.
2. Seaforth Creek, bank launch.
3. Halliday Bay, exposed beach launch, best above 2.5m+ tide.

Victor Creek

This creek has the best launch site to access the Newry Islands, which have camp sites. The area has large tidal movement, which must be taken into account when planning trips. The water clears during neap (small) tides. Baitfish can usually be found in Victor Creek. There are yabby beds at low tide near the ramp, and banana prawns in summer. The channel markers are good for bream, golden snapper (fingermark), cod and grunter. The warmer months are best for barramundi, with pikey bream, queenfish and mud crabs in winter. Threadfin and blue salmon, flathead and whiting are usually available. Local headlands have barramundi in warm, calm weather. The main reef fish caught are tuskfish, grass sweetlip and cod, along with golden trevally. Some fishos head around to Mathers Creek (see St Helens map) at high tide to fish the deep hole out the front for barramundi and golden snapper. Crocodiles are found throughout this area.

Constant Creek

This area is subject to large tides, with drying flats that strand unwary boaters. Launching and travelling is easier at high tide. A day is best spent launching on the high and fishing the low and incoming tide, and heading back on the high. Fish rock patches on incoming tides, and mud drain outlets in creeks on falling tides. Low-tide holes on creek bends often hold good fish. Expect salmon, bream, jacks, barra, golden snapper, grunter and cod. Big threadfin are caught over the Sand Bay flats and in the channels on a rising tide, along with golden trevally and the odd permit. Whiting, bream and flathead are throughout. Bird Rock has queenfish, mackerel, barracuda and trevally on high tides. Mud crabs are usually good in the creeks, with prawns in summer. Constant Creek is known for its oyster rocks and snaggy banks. Careful navigation is required. Outside the bay lie the extensive Blackwood Shoals, with mackerel and reef fish at approx 20 55.961S 149 12.807E. A shoal lies off Green Island at 20 57.831S 149 09.517E. The island has a Green Zone off its western side, as does the north side of Cape Hillsborough to the north-east.

Key to Map

Hotspots

For trolling, fish neap or building tides for better water clarity.

1. Deeper water along bend - fish with livebait, barramundi and jacks. Whiting, salmon, flathead on sandspit at mouth.
2. Landbased fishing from first push in of tide.
3. Whiting, flathead, salmon.
4. Creek has mud crabs, grunter, baitfish, seasonal prawns.
5. Whiting, flathead, salmon on flats edges. Salmon on rising tide.
6. Good water for barra, salmon, jacks, grunter. Drop livebaits or fish low tide holes and gutters with lures.
7. Good trolling area along deep bank.
8. Deep bend, most fish.
9. Trolling, grunter on deadbait.
10. Mostly jacks, cod, bream. Many oyster rock patches, tricky navigation but good fishing. Fish holes on bends at low tide.
11. Barra, salmon.
12. Small holes. Good crabbing upstream.

Beware crocs in this area.

Launch sites

1. Landing Creek launch site off bank ... follow the Belmunda Rd. Stones and mud, better on upper tide.
2. Constant Creek - follow Howells Rd, off Seaforth Rd. Most tides. Rocks throughout creek.

Tides about 1hr after Mackay, up to 6m movement.

Wuruma Dam

This is on the Nogo River 48km north of Eidsvold. It is about 1800ha in area. The dam has fished well in years past, but low rainfall years can reduce the water level to almost zero. In good years, there are bass, barramundi, yellowbelly, silver perch and saratoga to be caught. Metre barra have been taken. Golden and silver perch tend to survive the droughts, but barra suffer. With high water levels the fishing improves. Troll small lures for bass and silver perch near the dam wall. There are toilets, shelters, barbecues and showers. There are no boating restrictions except when the dam is below 15 per cent full. There is a 200m clearance zone at the dam wall.

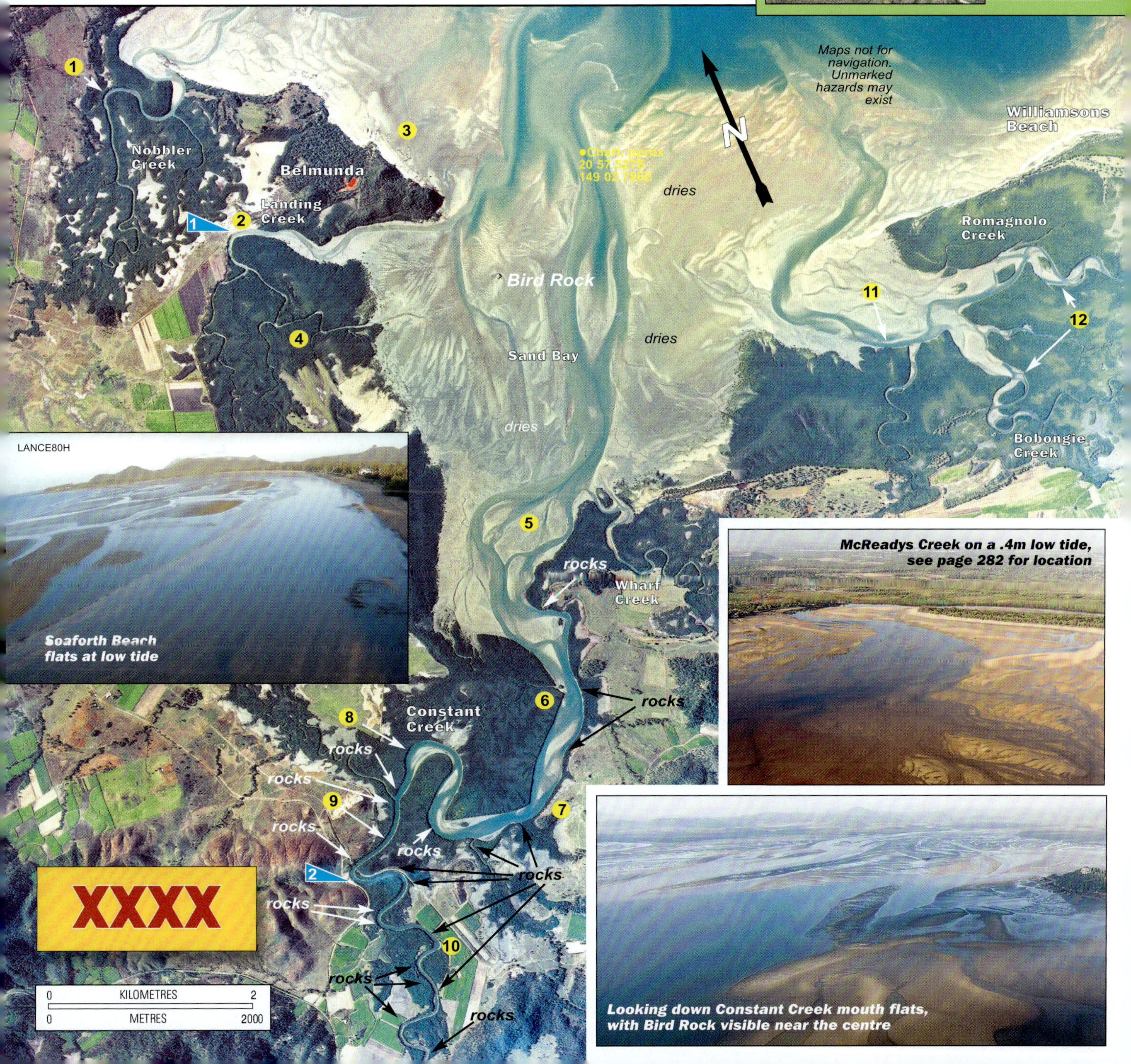

Maps not for navigation. Unmarked hazards may exist

Seaforth Beach flats at low tide

McReadys Creek on a .4m low tide, see page 282 for location

Looking down Constant Creek mouth flats, with Bird Rock visible near the centre

approx. Chart 21 06.306S 149 14.155E

Harbour Beach

Mackay Port

The V

Map not for navigation

Chart. approx 21 09.179S 149 13.453E

Pioneer Creek aerial pictures Page 285

Slade Point

Slade Bay

dries at low tide

rocks

Vines Creek

Basset Basin

Town Beach

Blacks Beach

McCreadys Creek - pic Page 281

Barnes Creek

Dolphin Heads

Bucasia Beach

Eimeo Creek

Forgan Smith Bridge

Pioneer River

Ron Camm Bridge

Fursden Creek

Hospital Bridge

KILOMETRES 0 2

METRES 0 2000

Pioneer River Artificial Reefs

Reef modules were installed within casting distance of **Bridge Road, Brisbane Street** and **Carlyle Street** piers in Pioneer River in 2021. Two types of reef units were used to provide habitat for sportfish, baitfish and crustaceans. Each habitat contains one 'Ledge and Cave' unit surrounded by four 'Pyramid' units. Fish livebaits at the turn of the tide for best results.

Mackay

Landbased anglers enjoy deepwater fishing off the marina's south wall. There is also good fishing off local beaches and river banks towards high tide. Mackay has three nearby stocked barramundi dams, large tidal creeks and estuaries, with easy boating access to several islands and reef grounds. For those with small boats, Mackay has shoal bottom in close. Boaters must take into account large tides and vast drying flats. Fishing can be good on big tides, but neap tide boating is easier. New areas should be explored on a rising tide to avoid stranding. Seas are rough when wind and tidal currents are opposed. Mackay's Pioneer River has good landbased access, with barramundi, blue and threadfin salmon, golden snapper, jacks, grunter, bream, whiting and flathead. Bank fishing is as good as anywhere near Balnagowan Bridge, and artificial reefs were installed off public

Key to Map

Hotspots

1. Lure-casting for barramundi in warm weather. Also bream, flathead, whiting.
2. Mackay Harbour rock wall has excellent fishing. The deep southern wall has most species, with a chance of a tuna, mackerel, cobia, shark or trout.
3. Rock walls throughout river mouth, most species. Best at night.
4. Basset Basin has yabby flats, good fishing for flathead and whiting.
5. Barra near bridge at night. Good yabby bed behind the rock walls across from the ramp in River St.
6. Pioneer River: River is shallow above River St boat ramp, but navigable on most tides downstream. Barramundi, queenfish, grunter and salmon, along with flathead, whiting and bream, are common, with barra best in the warmer months. Strong currents during big tides. Cod along rock walls, Abundant tarpon at times. Sardines (herring) are common in the river and ideal bait. River runs quite clear with best barra often taken at night.
7. Fish rock ledge by boat for whiting, flathead, barramundi. Enter Bakers Creek mouth on a rising tide to lessen risk of stranding. On opposite shore fish Far Beach on rising tide for whiting, flathead using local nippers.
8. Jacks, crabs, fish mid-tide up.
9. Landbased fishing at upper tide.
10. Sandy Creek: tides about three hours behind Mackay times. Nippers near McEwan's Beach, Dunrock and near mouth of Alligator Creek. Mainly bread and butter species.
11. Golden snapper, grunter, jacks, cod.
12. Whiting at high tide.
13. Queenfish, trevally.
14. Bream, jacks, barra, grunter through system and near big rockbar. Whiting and flathead from beach at mouth.
15. Threadfin salmon, flathead, whiting, crabs and prawns.

Offshore GPS waypoints

Downward Patches (shoals)
21 07.516S 149 17.344E, 9km to Mackay.
21 08.462S 149 17.417E, 9km to Mackay.
21 08.923S 149 17.371E, 7km to Mackay.
21 09.732S 149 17.189E, 7km to Mackay.
Booger's Shoal
21 03.586S 149 20.154E, 13km to Mackay.
Oom Shoal
21 03.160S 149 18.209E, 11km to Mackay.
Llewellyn Shoal
20 59.885S 149 18.564E, 13km to Mackay
Blackwood Shoals (huge area)
20 56.625S 149 15.219E, 15km to Mackay.

Alligator Creek on a .4 metre low tide

Bakers Creek on a .4m low tide

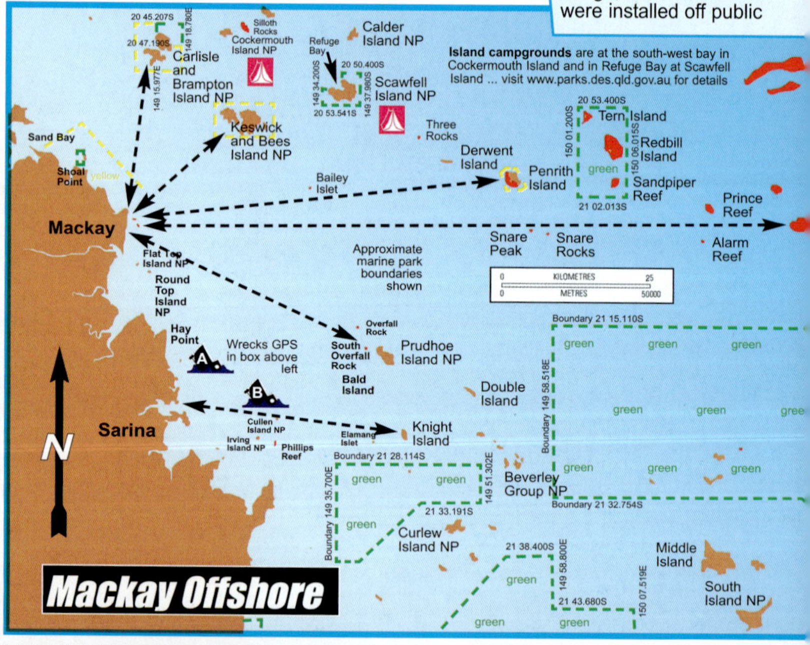

Sandy Creek on a .4m low tide

Mackay Offshore

Island campgrounds are at the south-west bay in Cockermouth Island and in Refuge Bay at Scawfell Island ... visit www.parks.des.qld.gov.au for details

Carlisle and Brampton Island NP

Calder Island NP

Scawfell Island NP

Keswick and Bees Island NP

Three Rocks

Derwent Island

Penrith Island

Tern Island

Redbill Island

Sandpiper Reef

Prince Reef

Snare Peak

Snare Rocks

Alarm Reef

Approximate marine park boundaries shown

Sand Bay

Shoal Point

Mackay

Bailey Islet

Round Top Island NP

Hay Point

Wrecks GPS in box above left

Prudhoe Island NP

Double Island

Knight Island

Sarina

Beverley Group NP

Curlew Island NP

Middle Island

South Island NP

Castrades Inlet on a .4m low tide

Illawong Beach on a .4m low tide

Key to Map

Launch sites

1. Eimeo Creek, Bucasia side, upper tide.
2. Eimeo Creek, Eimeo side, upper tide.
3. A McReadys Creek public ramp was being built at Seagull St at publication.
4. Marina, public ramp, all tides, pontoon.
5. Pioneer Creek ramp, end of River St, all tides, though river mouth is shallow.
6. Dunrock, Sandy Creek - turn to McEwan's Beach from highway, then turn at Chelona onto Dunrock road. Concrete, upper tides.
7. Sandy Creek, half tide up.
8. Bakers Creek, bank launch near main road.

Local tides move up to about 6.4m.

…ers in the river in …021. The far upper …ioneer River has …arra, sooty grunter, …leepy cod, jacks and …ngle perch. Mackay …eaches fish well for …hiting, flathead, …olden trevally, …ueenfish and …readfin salmon. …he harbour walls …roduce pelagic …nd reef fish, and …ome big …arramundi. …ewfish bite in the …arbour at night, try the …ay near the end of the …outh wall or the old …ontainer jetty. There are …athead and whiting near the old …oat ramp. Bait nippers are found …n the flats within most estuaries …nd are the ideal whiting bait, with …ve herring and mullet the best bait …or targeting predatory fish.

Continued on Page 285.

*Black jewfish may not be taken …rom an area within about 200m …round Hay Point and Dalrymple …ay coal wharves.

Wrecks

Victor Wreck (A)
21 20.188S 149 23.203E
Cullen Wreck (B)
21 22.941S 149 28.321E
Wreck 70km n-e Mackay
20 40.520S 149 42.113E

Shipping Channel marks

20 46.232S 149 45.503E
20 49.171S 149 48.081E
20 46.245S 149 45.365E
21 12.229S 149 55.889E
21 13.504S 149 58.058E

Reef and Shoal

Reichelmann Rock
21 11.314S 149 14.800E
Downward Patches
21 08.465S 149 17.408E
Oom Shoal
21 03.135S 149 18.206E
Oom North
21 01.746S 149 19.297E
Gould Shoal
21 03.604S 149 20.169E
Gould North
21 02.206S 149 21.078E
Spoil Ground
21 13.216S 149 17.309E
Llewellyn Shoal
20 59.888S 149 18.552E
Hunt Shoal
20 59.479S 149 20.134E
Fantome Rocks
20 51.230S 149 14.878E
Blackwood Shoals
20 56.192S 149 17.878E

Hazards

Dangerous Rf, 3km n-e Pioneer
21 07.987S 149 14.708E
Hay Pt Rock, 1.6km n-e harbour
21 16.660S 149 18.508E
Slade Rk, 2km nth harbour
21 05.221S 149 14.317E
Slade Island, reef east of island
21 05.881S 149 15.046E
Oyster Rock, 4km sth Pioneer
21 11.084S 149 13.474E

Reliance Creek

This creek is popular with Mackay fishermen, who catch mainly grunter, salmon, whiting and jacks. There is good crabbing and prawning at times. A cartopper or yak and 4WD is needed to drive in and fish.

Key to Map

Hotspots

1. Whiting, bream, flathead, salmon. Barramundi along edges on rising tide.
2. Good fishing and crabbing. Estuary fish throughout system, but biggest grunter are usually near the mouth. Barramundi.
3. Fish in holes on bends and junctions. Golden snapper, grunter, jacks. Mud crabs at top of creek arms on incoming tides.
4. Whiting, bream, flathead, salmon, queenfish, barramundi at high tide. Beach has worms, nippers and soldier crabs.

Launch sites

1. A 4WD trek over sand is required to access Reliance Creek via Shoal Point. Nearest proper launch site is at Eimeo, but access through Eimeo Creek mouth is from mid tide up. The shallow area at the front of Reliance Creek is difficult near low water.

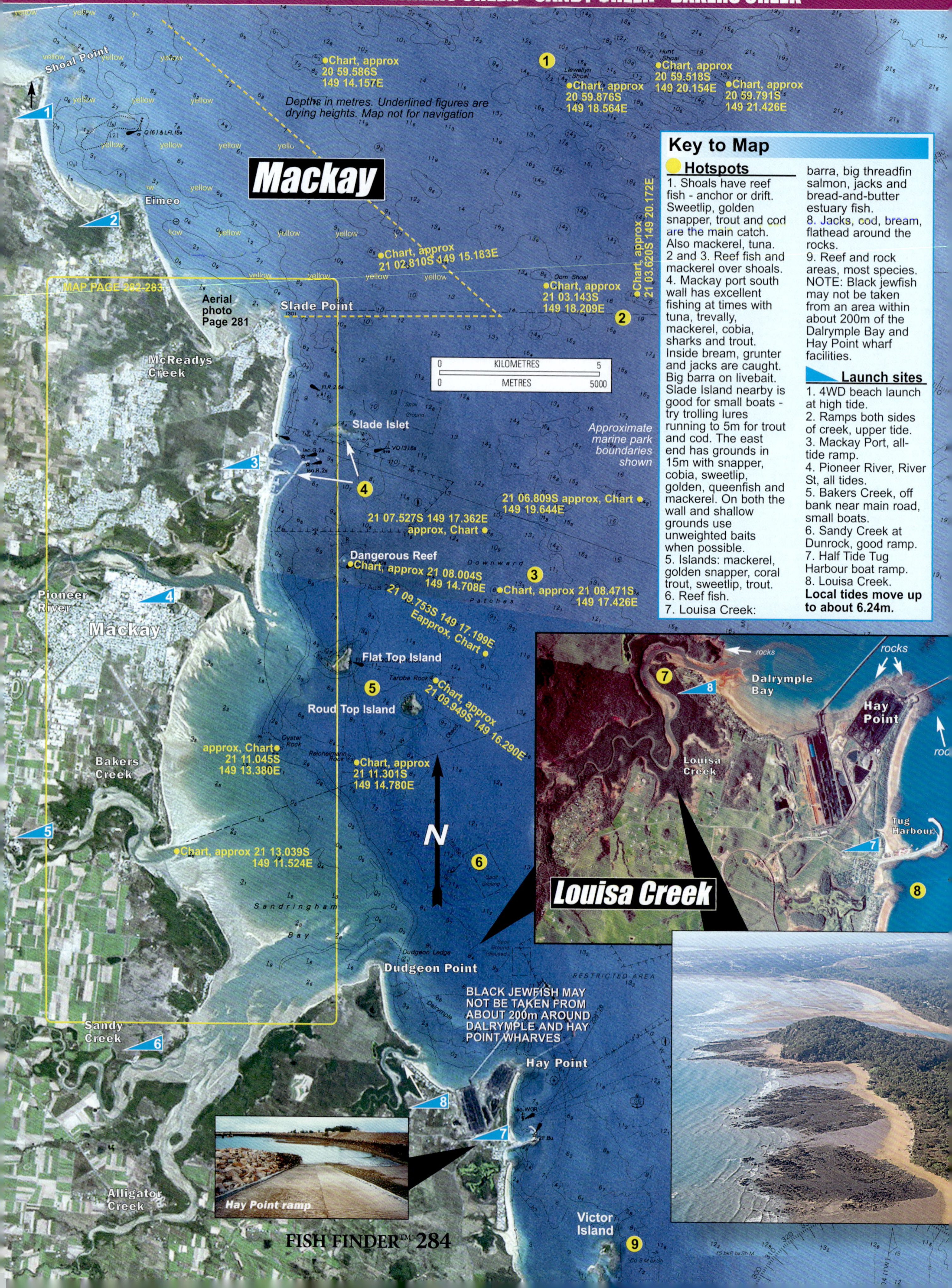

Mackay

Depths in metres. Underlined figures are drying heights. Map not for navigation

Key to Map

Hotspots

1. Shoals have reef fish - anchor or drift. Sweetlip, golden snapper, trout and cod are the main catch. Also mackerel, tuna.
2 and 3. Reef fish and mackerel over shoals.
4. Mackay port south wall has excellent fishing at times with tuna, trevally, mackerel, cobia, sharks and trout. Inside bream, grunter and jacks are caught. Big barra on livebait. Slade Island nearby is good for small boats - try trolling lures running to 5m for trout and cod. The east end has grounds in 15m with snapper, cobia, sweetlip, golden, queenfish and mackerel. On both the wall and shallow grounds use unweighted baits when possible.
5. Islands: mackerel, golden snapper, coral trout, sweetlip, trout.
6. Reef fish.
7. Louisa Creek: barra, big threadfin salmon, jacks and bread-and-butter estuary fish.
8. Jacks, cod, bream, flathead around the rocks.
9. Reef and rock areas, most species.

NOTE: Black jewfish may not be taken from an area within about 200m of the Dalrymple Bay and Hay Point wharf facilities.

Launch sites

1. 4WD beach launch at high tide.
2. Ramps both sides of creek, upper tide.
3. Mackay Port, all-tide ramp.
4. Pioneer River, River St, all tides.
5. Bakers Creek, off bank near main road, small boats.
6. Sandy Creek at Dunrock, good ramp.
7. Half Tide Tug Harbour boat ramp.
8. Louisa Creek.

Local tides move up to about 6.24m.

Chart, approx 20 59.586S 149 14.157E

Chart, approx 20 59.876S 149 18.564E

Chart, approx 20 59.518S 149 20.154E

Chart, approx 20 59.791S 149 21.426E

Chart, approx 21 02.810S 149 15.183E

Chart, approx 21 03.143S 149 18.209E

Chart, approx 21 03.620S 149 20.172E

21 06.809S approx, Chart 149 19.644E

21 07.527S 149 17.362E approx, Chart

Chart, approx 21 08.004S 149 14.708E

Chart, approx 21 08.471S 149 17.426E

21 09.753S 149 17.199E Eapprox, Chart

Chart, approx 21 09.949S 149 16.290E

approx, Chart 21 11.045S 149 13.380E

Chart, approx 21 11.301S 149 14.780E

Chart, approx 21 13.039S 149 11.524E

Shoal Point

Eimeo

MAP PAGE 282-283

Aerial photo Page 281

Slade Point

McReadys Creek

Slade Islet

Approximate marine park boundaries shown

Dangerous Reef

Downward Patches

Pioneer River

Mackay

Flat Top Island

Roud Top Island

Bakers Creek

Sandringham Bay

Dudgeon Point

Sandy Creek

Hay Point

Alligator Creek

Victor Island

KILOMETRES 0 5

METRES 0 5000

N

BLACK JEWFISH MAY NOT BE TAKEN FROM ABOUT 200m AROUND DALRYMPLE AND HAY POINT WHARVES

Louisa Creek

Dalrymple Bay

Hay Point

Tug Harbour

rocks

Hay Point ramp

Pioneer Creek just upstream of the town ramp

Pioneer River entrance on a .4m low tide

Camping on Mackay's islands

Smith Islands NP has permit camping at Roylen Bay, on the north-west side of Goldsmith Island, 45km north of Mackay. At 50km north-east of Mackay, South Cumberland Islands NP has permit camping at Scawfell Island's Refuge Bay and Cockermouth Island. Brampton Island's Western Bay and Dinghy Bay West have picnic tables and a toilet, but no camping. Private resorts on St Bees and Brampton Islands were in limbo at publication and any plans for camping or accommodation for boaters were not known.

To protect reefs there are two no-anchoring areas in South Cumberland Islands NP, off St Bees' northern point and Keswick Island's southern tip, marked by pyramid buoys. Anchoring is prohibited on the shore side of a line through these buoys.

Pioneer River mouth on a .4m low tide

● Continued from Page 283

For boaters, the best weather is from July to December.

South-east trade winds blow for much of the year, with northerlies in summer.

With big tides, any wind can whip up a sea, so pick your weather. With tides to 6m, the current can be fierce and heavy sinkers are needed to hold bottom.

Spanish mackerel are usually available but run best from June to October, and fish to 25kg are caught. Trolled lures, swimming gar and wolf herring work well.

Spotted, grey and doggie mackerel hit inshore grounds in winter. On rubble grounds, there's winter pink snapper, with tropical reef fish all year.

Keswick Island and St Bee's Islands are the nearest islands to the north-east, about 27km out, within range of trailerboats.

Further out are Brampton, Wigton, Calder, Scawfell and Derwent, to name a few, and a larger boat is needed to target these safely. Many have Green Zones.

Mackay's Keswick and Bees Islands have anchorages. Scawfell and Cockermouth Islands have permit camping.

For the tinnie crews, try the reef surrounding Taroba Rock, which is north-east of Flat Top and Round Top Island, easily accessible from Pioneer River mouth.

Great fishing can be had working the various islands' fringing reefs and points.

Try the lee side of the Whitsunday Islands north of Mackay for the more protected anchorages.

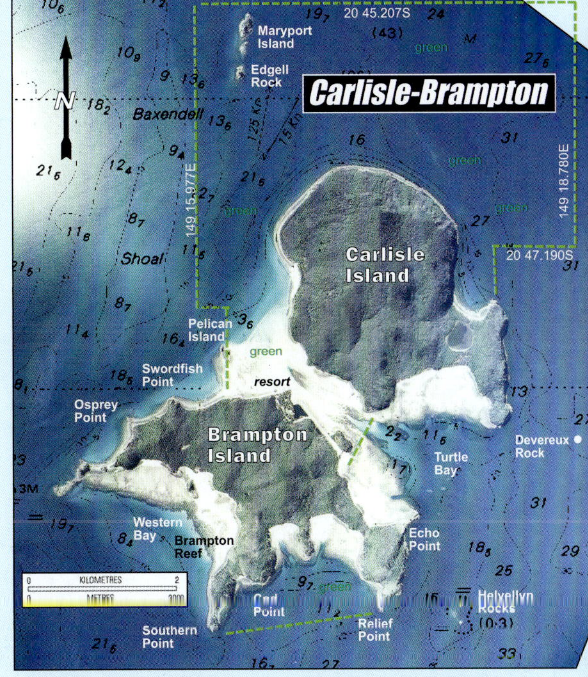

Stay the night, because fishing can be good, with grassy sweetlip and other fish coming into the shallows to feed.

There are day facilities at Brampton and some other islands.

The Great Barrier Reef has countless spots, but only big boats can safely fish here from Mackay.

Parker and Credlin Reefs are the closest at 84km. Crews can continue on to the remote outer reefs for 185km or more, but these are more suited to liveaboard boats.

The widest reefs have huge coral trout, red emperor and redthroat emperor, tuskfish and much more.

Spanish mackerel hit 30kg, and goldspot cod reach 20kg.

The inner islands and reefs get more pressure, but great fishing is still had.

Black marlin and sailfish are caught in the shipping channel wide of Scawfell and Calder Islands over summer, best from September to January. Troll skipping gar and lures at about six knots.

Mackay's best all-tide boat ramp is at Mackay marina, with a pontoon and good parking.

For dams, see pages 378-379. Fish the dams for barramundi in summer, or during warm weather.

To fish Mackay visit www.reefari.com

Pioneer River

Louisa Creek on a .4m low tide

Sarina

Big tides, drying flats and rocks make Sarina estuaries interesting to navigate, but there is good fishing for whiting, flathead, salmon, cod, jacks, golden snapper, grunter, bream, barramundi and crabs. Bait nippers are widely available. Mackerel, queenfish and trevally are reliable on the headlands and coastal reefs. The various islands and Phillips Reef about 19km out from Sarina (see next page) have winter school mackerel and pink snapper, and also trout, sweetlip and tuskfish, with spaniards best in spring. Local beaches have salmon, whiting and flathead, with a chance of golden trevally and queenfish.

Key to Map

Hotspots

1. Fish off the rocks for queenfish, trevally and salmon. Reefy areas offshore have trout, tiskfish, sweetlip and cod. Golden snapper and barra inshore at high tide.
2. Grunter, mud crabs, salmon and occasional barra upstream. Beware many rocks.
3. Whiting, flathead and bream near mouth. Rock midstream marked by beacon is worth a cast for flathead and bream.
4. Doggy mackerel in season. Golden trevally, barracuda, cod.
5. Rocks have barra and golden snapper, best for barra in calm weather. Also trevally, queenfish, dart, flathead, salmon, grunter.
6. Excellent area for bream, whiting and flathead.
7. Barra holes, also cod and jacks. Good hole next to large clay bank.
8. Rocky outcrops - care required: barra, cod, grunter, golden snapper, jacks and crabs.
9. Shallow channels and edges, good summer prawning and bait collecting.
10. Whiting, bream, flathead, queenfish, dart.
11. Good fishing off rocks and where rocks adjoin beaches for salmon, cod, jacks, golden trevally, tuskfish, barramundi and occasional golden snapper. Troll for queenfish, trevally, mackerel.
12. Salmon and grunter inside headland.

Launch sites

1. Steep boat ramp, rocks upstream, most tides.
2. Boat ramp, most tides.
3. Two ramps about 500m apart, mid to upper tide only.
4. Ramp near Freshwater Point. Useable about half tide up.
5. Armstrong Beach, beach launch at south end near high tide, avoid lower mudflat. Poor in easterlies.

Local tides have up to about up to about 6.75m movement.

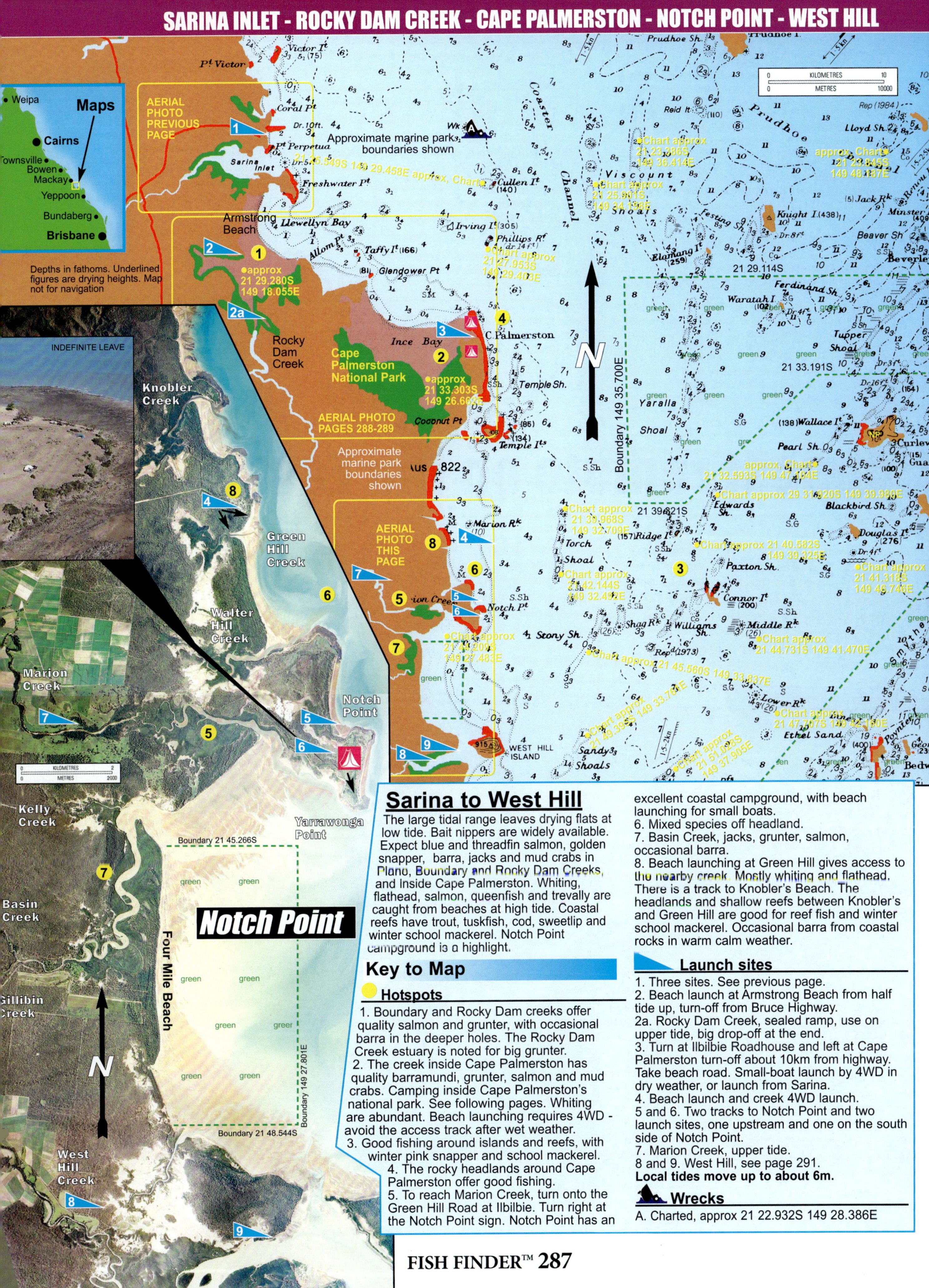

Sarina to West Hill

The large tidal range leaves drying flats at low tide. Bait nippers are widely available. Expect blue and threadfin salmon, golden snapper, barra, jacks and mud crabs in Plane, Boundary and Rocky Dam Creeks, and inside Cape Palmerston. Whiting, flathead, salmon, queenfish and trevally are caught from beaches at high tide. Coastal reefs have trout, tuskfish, cod, sweetlip and winter school mackerel. Notch Point campground is a highlight.

Key to Map

Hotspots

1. Boundary and Rocky Dam creeks offer quality salmon and grunter, with occasional barra in the deeper holes. The Rocky Dam Creek estuary is noted for big grunter.
2. The creek inside Cape Palmerston has quality barramundi, grunter, salmon and mud crabs. Camping inside Cape Palmerston's national park. See following pages. Whiting are abundant. Beach launching requires 4WD - avoid the access track after wet weather.
3. Good fishing around islands and reefs, with winter pink snapper and school mackerel.
4. The rocky headlands around Cape Palmerston offer good fishing.
5. To reach Marion Creek, turn onto the Green Hill Road at Ilbilbie. Turn right at the Notch Point sign. Notch Point has an excellent coastal campground, with beach launching for small boats.
6. Mixed species off headland.
7. Basin Creek, jacks, grunter, salmon, occasional barra.
8. Beach launching at Green Hill gives access to the nearby creek. Mostly whiting and flathead. There is a track to Knobler's Beach. The headlands and shallow reefs between Knobler's and Green Hill are good for reef fish and winter school mackerel. Occasional barra from coastal rocks in warm calm weather.

Launch sites

1. Three sites. See previous page.
2. Beach launch at Armstrong Beach from half tide up, turn-off from Bruce Highway.
2a. Rocky Dam Creek, sealed ramp, use on upper tide, big drop-off at the end.
3. Turn at Ilbilbie Roadhouse and left at Cape Palmerston turn-off about 10km from highway. Take beach road. Small-boat launch by 4WD in dry weather, or launch from Sarina.
4. Beach launch and creek 4WD launch.
5 and 6. Two tracks to Notch Point and two launch sites, one upstream and one on the south side of Notch Point.
7. Marion Creek, upper tide.
8 and 9. West Hill, see page 291.

Local tides move up to about 6m.

Wrecks

A. Charted, approx 21 22.932S 149 28.386E

Cape Palmerston

With relatively pristine habitat and being distant from major centres, the size of fish caught in this area is above average, particularly for flathead, bream, barramundi and mud crabs. The access track is partly soft sand but 4WD vehicles will not usually experience a problem. Campsites are provided in three areas. The best launching and camping for fishermen is arguably on the west side at Cape Creek. This is a steep but relatively firm sand launch. Fishing is good for barramundi, threadfin and blue salmon, bream, flathead, whiting and mud crabs. There are large tides and strong currents, and much of the creek empties at low tide. Crab pots must be placed carefully or will be lost. On big tides, fish outflowing mud drains and low-tide holes. On neap tides the water clears and trolling and sight-casting lures works well. Baitfish can usually be found, with herring and mullet in big schools. Small whiting are prolific. Offshore, there is plenty of broken bottom, with reef and pelagic fish easily found. Mackerel are best in winter, with Phillips Reef, just 10km north of the Cape Creek camp, and Cullen Reef 12.3km out, proven spots. The Windmill Bay beach launch is marginal. To get to Cape Palmerston, turn east from the Bruce Hwy at Ilbilbie towards Greenhill. After 7km turn left onto Cape Palmerston Rd. The park entrance is another 6.5km.

Key to Map

Hotspots

1. Estuary fish, visit from Armstrong Beach.
2. Whiting, flathead. Grunter, salmon, barra at Sandy Creek mouth.
3. Estuary fish, mud crabs, barra.
4. Whiting, flathead on flats. Crabs, barra, salmon in Dawson Creek.
5. Grunter, golden snapper, queenfish.
6. Shallow - mud crabs, estuary fish.
7. Crabs, estuary fish.
8. Land-based fishing near camp site: whiting, bream, grunter, barra.
9. Good fishing and crabbing.
10. Reef fish, mackerel in season.
11. Reef fish, mackerel in season.

Ramps

1. Windmill Bay beach launch near camp, about third tide up, calm weather only.
2. Bank launch on creek, about third tide up.
3. Creek bank launch, soft sand.
4. Armstrong Beach, upper tide.
5. Rocky Dam Creek landing, reached through Koumala, sign-posted at tram crossing north of town. 4WD needed after rain. Creek is navigable with care at low tide.

Local tides move up to about 6m.

Red emperor tips

In recent years boaters have been specifically targeting big red emperor on East Coast grounds. 'Reds' are found across Australia's north from Perth to Sydney. They are sometimes found in relatively shallow water, especially in the Far North, but the biggest ones are typically caught in deep waters around the Great Barrier Reef. A depth of 40m to 180m produces the biggest fish. The secret to finding red emperor is diligent use of sonar, covering a lot of ground in your search. Rough bottom around reefs, and rises and dips in the sea floor, are all worth exploring, as well as ledges, bommies and 'fern coral' grounds. Single big fish will show on a good sonar, as will schools of smaller fish. Drop baits or jigs when fish show. Spots that produce largemouth nannygai will usually have red emperor. Half the battle is getting big fish into the boat, as sharks have become familiar with boats on popular grounds, and it is not uncommon to lose multiple fish. Use heavy gear and get the fish in quick, and move if sharks are winning, do not waste valuable fish. Fresh squid or fish flesh baits work well on red emperor, and they will take most type of jigs.

Almost remote on the East Coast

Looking west from Cape Palmerston to Ince Bay ... note the plentiful broken bottom. INSET: Looking south from the cape

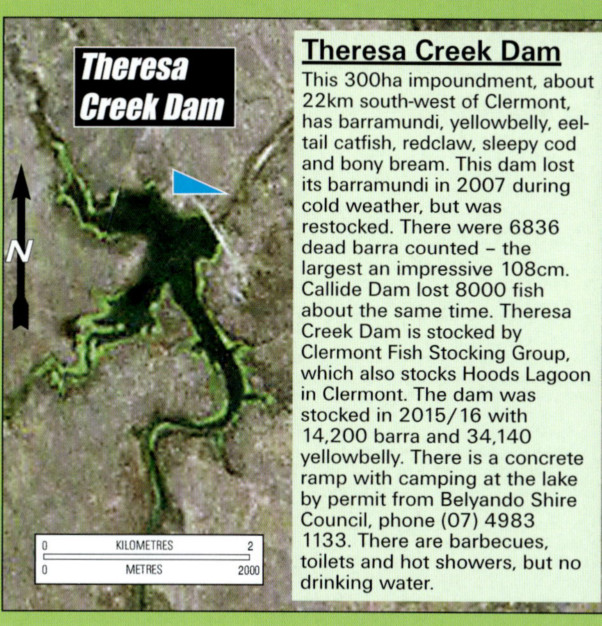

Theresa Creek Dam

This 300ha impoundment, about 22km south-west of Clermont, has barramundi, yellowbelly, eel-tail catfish, redclaw, sleepy cod and bony bream. This dam lost its barramundi in 2007 during cold weather, but was restocked. There were 6836 dead barra counted – the largest an impressive 108cm. Callide Dam lost 8000 fish about the same time. Theresa Creek Dam is stocked by Clermont Fish Stocking Group, which also stocks Hoods Lagoon in Clermont. The dam was stocked in 2015/16 with 14,200 barra and 34,140 yellowbelly. There is a concrete ramp with camping at the lake by permit from Belyando Shire Council, phone (07) 4983 1133. There are barbecues, toilets and hot showers, but no drinking water.

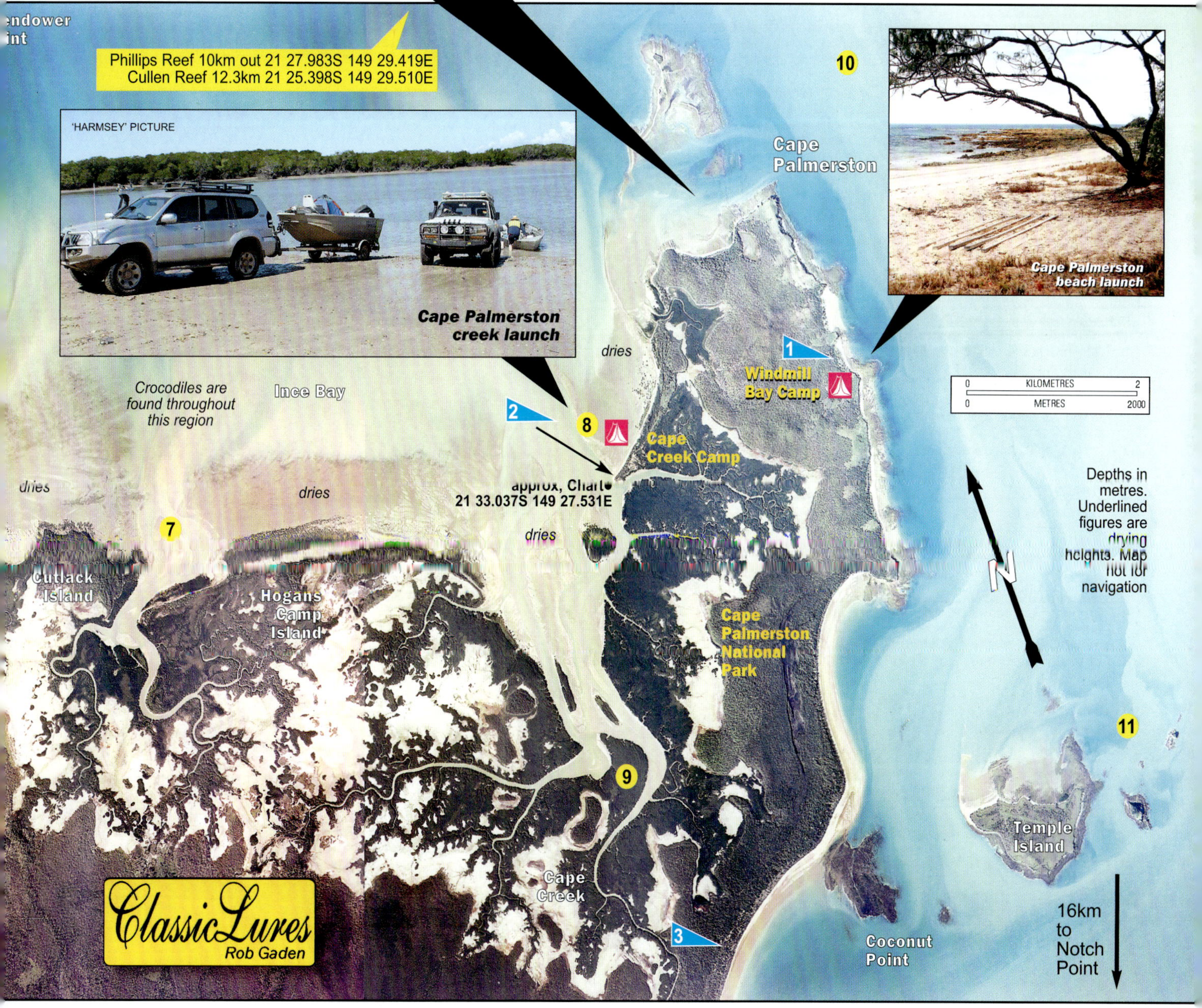

Phillips Reef 10km out 21 27.983S 149 29.419E
Cullen Reef 12.3km 21 25.398S 149 29.510E

'HARMSEY' PICTURE

Cape Palmerston creek launch

Cape Palmerston beach launch

Cape Palmerston
Windmill Bay Camp
Cape Creek Camp
Ince Bay
Crocodiles are found throughout this region
approx, Chart 21 33.037S 149 27.531E
Cutlack Island
Hogans Camp Island
Cape Palmerston National Park
Cape Creek
Temple Island
Coconut Point
16km to Notch Point

Depths in metres. Underlined figures are drying heights. Map not for navigation

Classic Lures Rob Gaden

Shoalwater Bay

By SHANE DOEVY

Lower Shoalwater Bay can only be publicly accessed by a long boat trip from Stanage.

Care must be taken when entering these waters, as they are naturally hazardous, and include the Shoalwater Bay Military Training Area.

Mariners should seek advice prior to entry, as live firing exercises are held.

The isolation of the area means fish and crab stocks are usually good.

The following spots are familar to me, but I have supplied co-ordinates using a map program, so marks are approximate.

The creek is marked as Spot 27 on page 293, at the far south-east end of Shoalwater Bay. Take care when navigating this creek and watch the tides.

Spot A 22 31.287S 150 29.228E
The point on the north-east side of the entrance to the creek has a rock ledge which protrudes some way out from the land mass and dries on lower tides. Blue salmon can be taken from the small beach in this area by casting lures on the incoming tides. Worth a troll along the rock ledge for a barra.

Spot B 22 34.597S 150 30.002E
The gravelly bottom around the island fishes well for bream and javelin fish (grunter). Exercise caution in this area at low tide as it poses a navigational hazard.

Spot C 22 35.589S 150 28.682E
Rockbar holds javelin fish, salmon and barra. Eddies form on the corners here and they hold barra. Mud bank on northern side holds good fish, use live bait on run-in tide.

Spot D 22 36.239S 150 28.678E
Large rock in centre of the river is a navigation hazard and should be negotiated with care. The deep water has barra, salmon, javelin fish and cod. The area can be fished from the shore from the rock shelf on the northern bank.

Spot E 22 36.238S 150 28.548E
Rocks on outside of the bend hold barra and salmon and javelin fish.

Spot F 22 36.348S 150 28.589E
Gravelly bottom holds school jewfish on a run-in tide. Fish lightly-weighted squid baits or live mullet for best results.

Island camps

The islands in and around Broad Sound are 150km from Mackay and Rockhampton, and therefore see low fishing pressure.

Broad Sound Islands National Park can only be visited by boat. Launch sites are at Stanage, Clairview and Carmila.

The water around the inshore islands is often turbid because of giant tides, but to the east are the clearer ocean waters of the Great Barrier Reef.

The park includes 48 islands, from Flock Pigeon Island near Clairview through to High Peak Island, one of the furthest islands from a Queensland port.

Sand and mudflats, seagrass meadows and mangroves make up the intertidal areas, with fringing reefs on some islands.

Bush camping is on High Peak, Flock Pigeon, Aquila, Hexham and Shields islands. There is a limit of six campers per island. There are no facilities. Seasonal closures may restrict entry. For details visit www.parks.des.qld.gov.au

This area requires trip planning because of big tides, drying reefs and flats, and strong currents. Broad Sound is swept by the biggest tides on the East Coast. The tides tend to concentrate fishing action into specific periods.

Some creeks have fishable holes at low tide.

West Hill (next page) has a good creek, but with poor boat launching. South of West Hill is the tiny community of Clairview, with Clairview Creek 10km south of the town.

The launch site at Clairview is exposed and dries at low tide.

Broad Sound creeks have barramundi, blue and threadfin salmon, grunter and big mud crabs, as well as flathead, bream and whiting.

Tidal bores occur in Broad Sound's lower creeks.

Take note of the Green Zones.

Broad Sound's Charon Point, between the Styx and Herbert Rivers, can be reached by a track from Marlborough.

Charon Point has a public reserve with camping and a 4WD boat launching site.

Another secluded base is St Lawrence. The township has a bank launch on St Lawrence Creek, and bank fishing.

East of Broad Sound is Shoalwater Bay, separated by a peninsula that ends at the tiny fishing town of Stanage.

St Lawrence

This tiny town is on the south bank of St Lawrence Creek, 6km east of the Bruce Highway, 183km north of Rockhampton. It was one of Queensland's first ports, but the fast-flowing tides of up to 7m+ eventually made the port unviable. The muddy habitat and tropical climate, with annual rainfall of 660mm and an average summer temperature of 35C, are well suited to barramundi, threadfin salmon and mud crabs. Good catches are made in better seasons, usually after a year or two of above-average rainfall, but the area is netted and anglers sometimes have to work hard to find good fish. St Lawrence Creek is shallow and the bigger tides can create tidal bores in the local rivers. It also gets rough when the tide flows against the wind. Fishermen must also avoid becoming stranded on drying flats during falling tides. The water is muddy on big tides, but this does not put the fish off. Smaller tides are safer for boaters and arguably better for lure fishing. Low-tide holes are worth livebaiting for barramundi. On a rising tide queenfish, barramundi and salmon will push bait into the shallows along sandflats and banks. Bank fishing and small-boat launching is possible near the St Lawrence railway bridge. The highway weir area is worth a look after heavy rain. The Waverley and Styx systems to the south provide much the same conditions, but Bund Creek ramp on the Waverley is covered in mud. The Styx is accessible from a rough launch site and campground at Charon Point, but there is a large Green Zone in the lower tidal section that greatly restricts fishing area.

Key to Map

Hotspots

1. Bank fishing near high tide. Also roadside access near highway weir.
2. Bank fishing near railway bridge on incoming tide
3. Low tide holes, livebait for barra and salmon.

Launch sites

1. The best bank launch is near the St Lawrence railway bridge, but only from about a third tide up. Bund Creek public ramp on Waverley Creek south of St Lawrence is covered in mud.

Tides in this area have up to about 10m movement. Beware tidal bores on big tides.

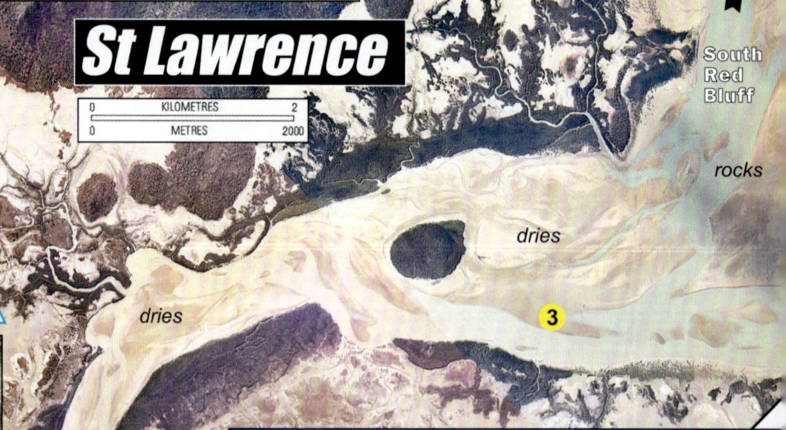

Styx River tidal bore

St Lawrence Creek weir just off the highway

St Lawrence Creek ... this is low tide at the bank launch near the railway bridge

Beware tidal bores in Broad Sound creeks on big tides

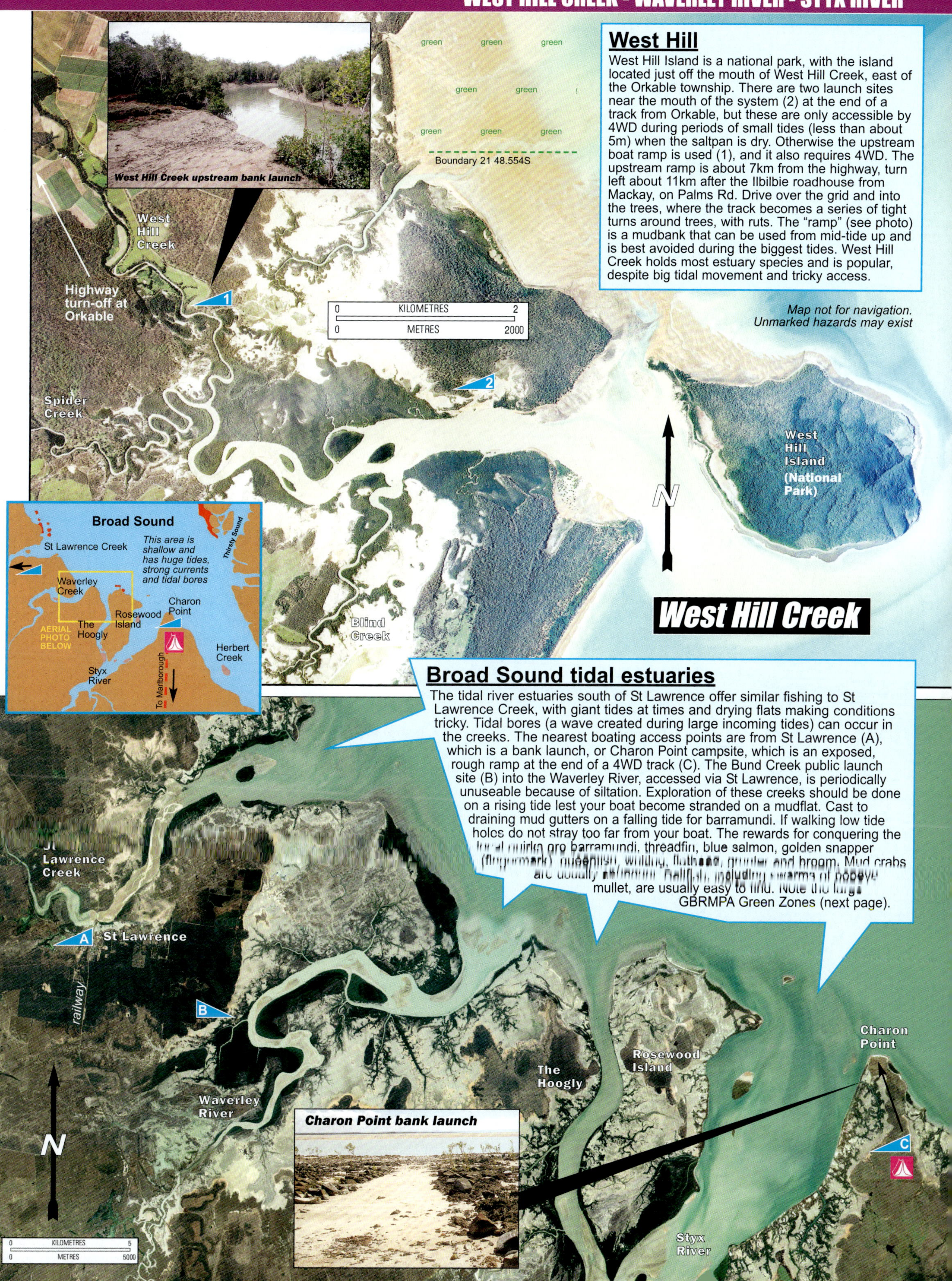

West Hill

West Hill Island is a national park, with the island located just off the mouth of West Hill Creek, east of the Orkable township. There are two launch sites near the mouth of the system (2) at the end of a track from Orkable, but these are only accessible by 4WD during periods of small tides (less than about 5m) when the saltpan is dry. Otherwise the upstream boat ramp is used (1), and it also requires 4WD. The upstream ramp is about 7km from the highway, turn left about 11km after the Ilbilbie roadhouse from Mackay, on Palms Rd. Drive over the grid and into the trees, where the track becomes a series of tight turns around trees, with ruts. The "ramp" (see photo) is a mudbank that can be used from mid-tide up and is best avoided during the biggest tides. West Hill Creek holds most estuary species and is popular, despite big tidal movement and tricky access.

Broad Sound tidal estuaries

The tidal river estuaries south of St Lawrence offer similar fishing to St Lawrence Creek, with giant tides at times and drying flats making conditions tricky. Tidal bores (a wave created during large incoming tides) can occur in the creeks. The nearest boating access points are from St Lawrence (A), which is a bank launch, or Charon Point campsite, which is an exposed, rough ramp at the end of a 4WD track (C). The Bund Creek public launch site (B) into the Waverley River, accessed via St Lawrence, is periodically unuseable because of siltation. Exploration of these creeks should be done on a rising tide lest your boat become stranded on a mudflat. Cast to draining mud gutters on a falling tide for barramundi. If walking low tide holes do not stray too far from your boat. The rewards for conquering the local creeks are barramundi, threadfin, blue salmon, golden snapper (fingermark), queenfish, whiting, flathead, grunter and bream. Mud crabs are usually abundant. Baitfish, including swarms of popeye mullet, are usually easy to find. Note the large GBRMPA Green Zones (next page).

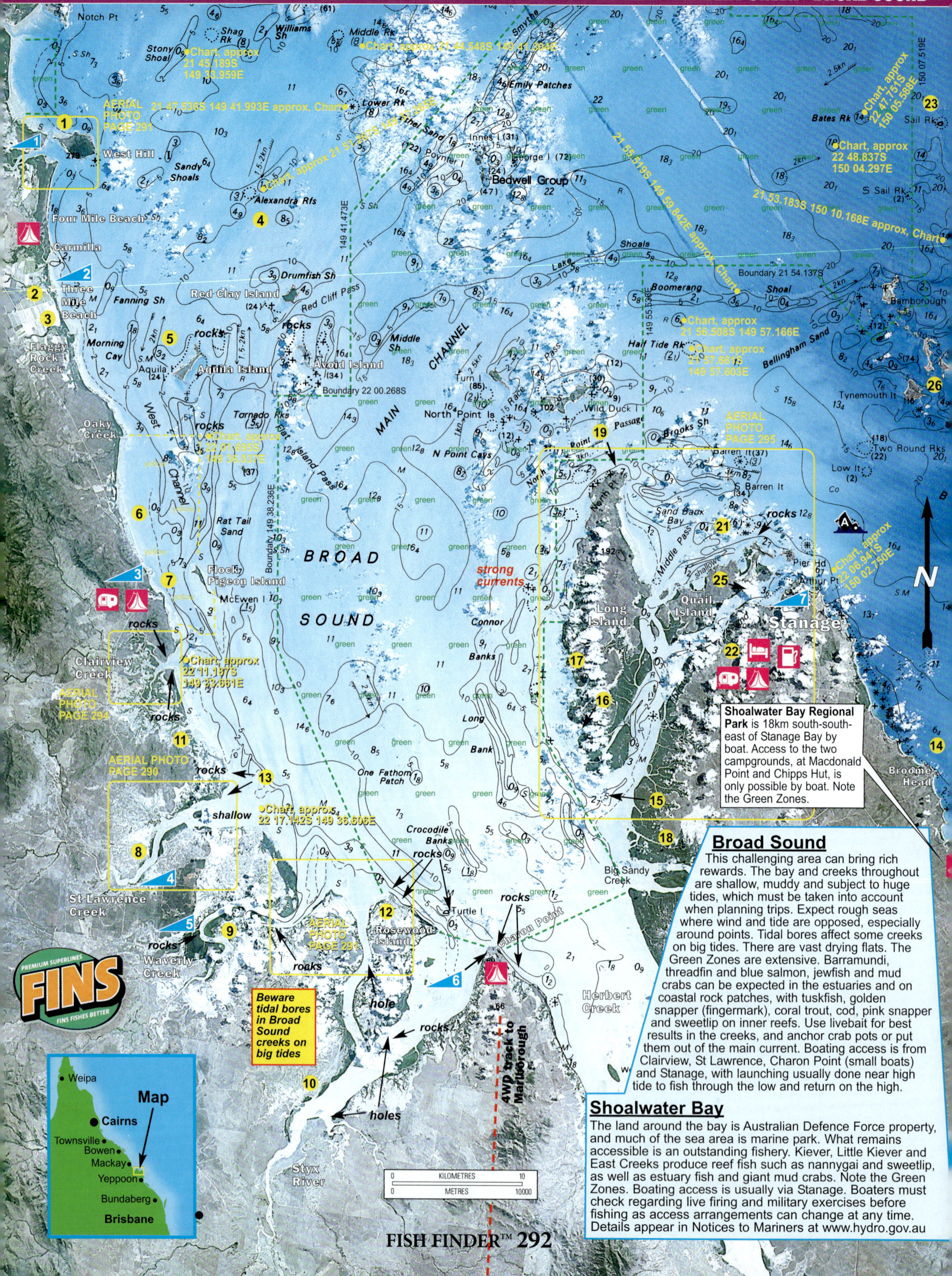

Shoalwater Bay Regional Park is 18km south-south-east of Stanage Bay by boat. Access to the two campgrounds, at Macdonald Point and Chipps Hut, is only possible by boat. Note the Green Zones.

Beware tidal bores in Broad Sound creeks on big tides

Broad Sound

This challenging area can bring rich rewards. The bay and creeks throughout are shallow, muddy and subject to huge tides, which must be taken into account when planning trips. Expect rough seas where wind and tide are opposed, especially around points. Tidal bores affect some creeks on big tides. There are vast drying flats. The Green Zones are extensive. Barramundi, threadfin and blue salmon, jewfish and mud crabs can be expected in the estuaries and on coastal rock patches, with tuskfish, golden snapper (fingermark), coral trout, cod, pink snapper and sweetlip on inner reefs. Use livebait for best results in the creeks, and anchor crab pots or put them out of the main current. Boating access is from Clairview, St Lawrence, Charon Point (small boats) and Stanage, with launching usually done near high tide to fish through the low and return on the high.

Shoalwater Bay

The land around the bay is Australian Defence Force property, and much of the sea area is marine park. What remains accessible is an outstanding fishery. Kiever, Little Kiever and East Creeks produce reef fish such as nannygai and sweetlip, as well as estuary fish and giant mud crabs. Note the Green Zones. Boating access is usually via Stanage. Boaters must check regarding live firing and military exercises before fishing as access arrangements can change at any time. Details appear in Notices to Mariners at www.hydro.gov.au

Hotspots

Allow for big local tides when planning trips.

1. West Hill ... drive 10 minutes south of the Ilbilbie Roadhouse and turn left at West Hill Road sign at crossroads. Bitumen turns to dirt and a saltpan leads to a mud ramp on north-west side of estuary. 4WD recommended. Whiting, bream, flathead, salmon, barra, jacks. Camping on south side of estuary.
2. Carmila Beach: from Bruce Hwy turn at Carmila service station. Turn left at seafront to boat ramp. Creek requires half tide up for comfortable fishing. Second creek about 1km south. Bream, whiting, flathead, grunter, salmon, barra. Campground at beach has large drying flat at low tide.
3. Flaggy Rock Creek: access from Carmila to the north, need at least half tide to enter creek. Fishing and camp site near mouth.
4. Good bottom fishing at Alexandra Reefs and North Patch for trout, cod and sweetlip. Poynter is the tallest of these islands, and has a good north-shore anchorage in southerly winds. In easterlies the best anchorage is on the north-west shore of Calliope Island. Beware shallow shoals to the west.
5. Flat Island Group: Avoid Island is surrounded by reef. Grunter, bream, cod.
6. Coastal creeks along the stretch all have shallow entrances. Deeper water is inside the creeks and holes can be fished at low tide.
7. See next page re Clairview. Sandbanks around Flock Pigeon Island have salmon, flathead, whiting, dart, queenfish, trevally. Deep channel inside island has golden snapper.
8. St Lawrence Creek, barra and salmon, mud crabs, tidal bore on big tides.
9. Waverley Creek: as for 8.
10. Styx River: barramundi, golden snapper, grunter, cod. Tidal bore on big tides.
11. Several coastal creeks, see Page 294. Also 'Barra Rock' outside Oyster Creek.
12. Most species around rocky foreshores.
13. Barra in low tide holes and channel.
14. Mackerel. Look for birds.
15. Flathead, queenfish, trevally.
16. Sight-fishing in sheltered inlets.
17. Most species around rocks here, but beware reef and strong currents on big tides.
18. Good crabbing in creeks.
19. Trevally, queenfish off rocky points. Fish north edge of Long island, south-east edges of Barren Islets, north-west of Turn Island.
20. Reef, pelagic fish on pinnacle drop-offs.
21. Queenfish, trevally, whiting, flathead. Good trolling close in.
22. Shallow, rising tide for whiting, flathead.
23. Mackerel, red emperor in winter, reef fish.
24 & 24. Cast lures over shallow reefs for coral trout, mackerel, GTs, cod, sweetlip. On big tides fish pressure points for pelagics. Nannygai, red emperor over rough ground.
25. Productive jewfish hole on far side from Stanage ramp, best between October and February, also cod, golden snapper.
26. Island has anchorages for exploring wider shoals. Coral trout in close.
27. Info for this creek is on Page 290.
28. 'Land of the Giants' - huge mud crabs, also reef fish in Kiever Creek, and estuary fish. Similar in nearby creeks.
29. Strong Tide Passage has excellent reef and pelagic fishing, big mud crabs in creeks. Work the tide changes.

Key to Map

Wrecks

A. Historic wreck of the Waverley, 22 05.013S 150 03.630E, 14m.

Launch sites

1. West Hill, upper tide.
2. Carmila, upper tide.
3. Clairview beach, exposed upper tide only, beware drying sandflat. Also a creek ramp 3.6km to the north off Colonial Dve on 'Sandfly Creek'.
4. St Lawrence Creek, bank launch near railway on unsealed road, south bank.
5. Waverley Creek public ramp in tributary Bund Creek, covered in mud. There is a 4WD landing further downstream on the Waverley.
6. 4WD road to Charon Point has bank launch, mid to upper tide only. Follow Bald Hills Road from Marlborough. Note Green Zone. Large campground at ramp site. Visit www.parks.des.qld.gov.au for details.
7. The drive to Stanage is about an hour on an unsealed road. Stanage has a sealed ramp. Also fuel, bait and tackle shop, pub and boats for hire. Ensure you have a seaworthy boat, a nautical chart and sufficient fuel to explore this region.

This area is subject to up to about 10m tidal movement. Beware dangerous tidal bores on big tides.

Basic bush camping is available on five islands within the Broad Sound Islands National Park.

These are High Peak, Flock Pigeon, Aquila, Hexham and Shields islands. Each island has just one campsite.

There is a limit of six campers per island and there are no facilities. Seasonal closures may restrict entry to protect breeding turtles and birds.

Camping permits are required and fees apply. Visit www.parks.des.qld.gov.au for details.

Shoalwater Bay is a weapons range.

There is no access by road within the defence land. For sea closure times call 07 4937 3030 or check Notices to Mariners at www.hydro.gov.au

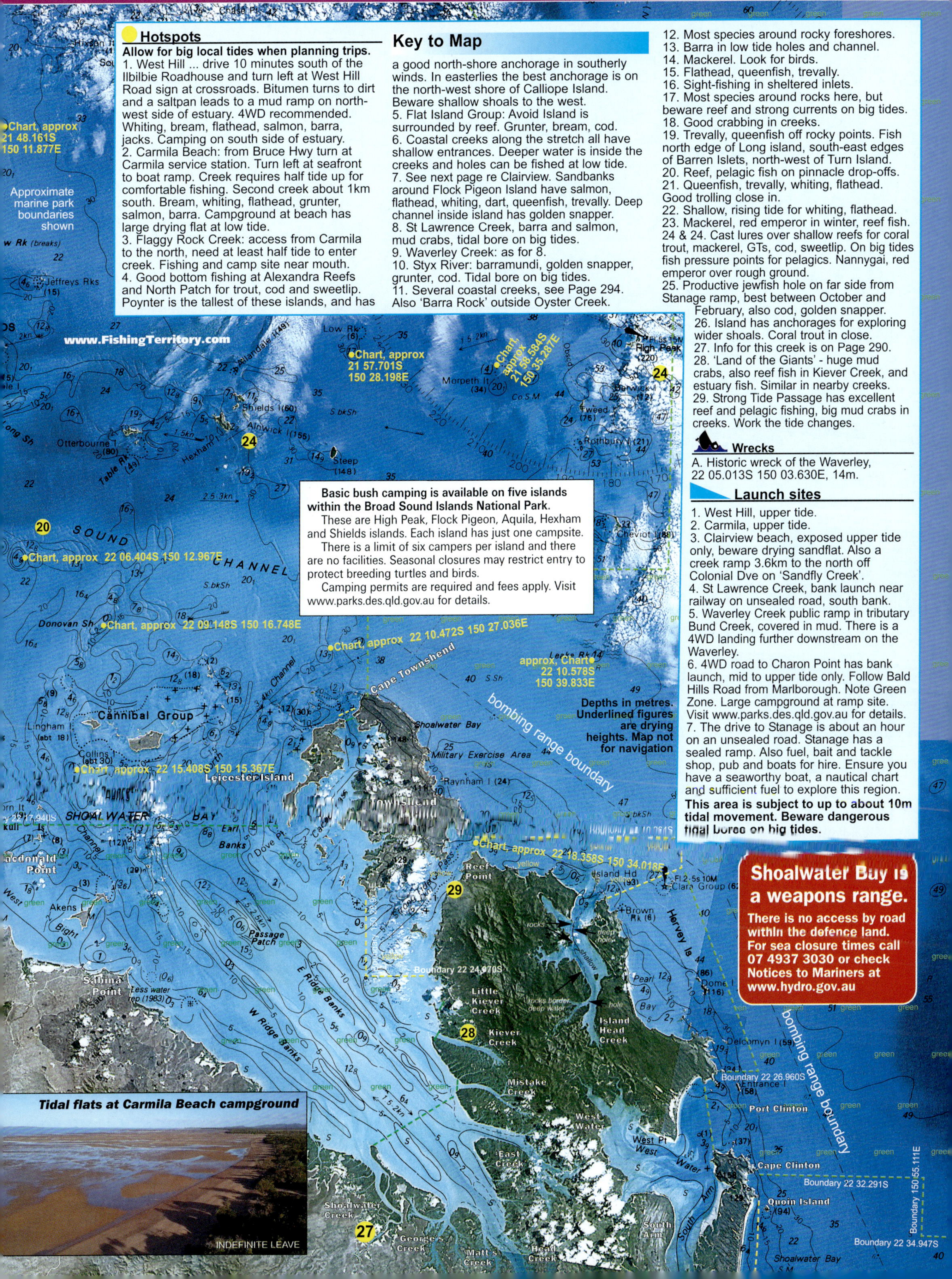

Depths in metres. Underlined figures are drying heights. Map not for navigation

Approximate marine park boundaries shown

Chart, approx 21 48.161S 150 11.877E

Chart, approx 21 57.701S 150 28.198E

Chart, approx 21 58.584S 150 35.287E

Chart, approx 22 06.404S 150 12.967E

Chart, approx 22 09.148S 150 16.748E

Chart, approx 22 10.472S 150 27.036E

approx, Chart 22 10.578S 150 39.833E

Chart, approx 22 15.408S 150 15.367E

Chart, approx 22 18.358S 150 34.018E

Boundary 22 24.670S

Boundary 22 26.960S

Boundary 22 32.291S

Boundary 22 34.947S

Boundary 150 55.111E

Sound Channel, Cannibal Group, Leicester Island, Shoalwater Bay, Cape Townshend, Townshend, Reef Point, Little Kiever Creek, Kiever Creek, Island Head Creek, Mistake Creek, West Water, East Creek, Shoalwater Creek, Port Clinton, Cape Clinton, Quoin Island, Sabina Point, Macdonald Point, Hervey Is, Military Exercise Area, bombing range boundary

www.FishingTerritory.com

Tidal flats at Carmila Beach campground

INDEFINITE LEAVE

CATTLE AND CLAIRVIEW CREEKS - BUNDOORA DAM

Clairview

This is a gateway into Broad Sound, a unique fishing and crabbing location. Careful trip planning is required as local launch sites can only be used on the upper tide, and a vast mudflat awaits those who miss the tide. Clairview and Cattle Creeks (shown above) are the largest tidal creeks easily accessible by boat from the Clairview ramp, with the sea entrance a 10km sea trip south of the caravan park. There are smaller creeks closer to Clairview. There is an exposed sealed boat ramp on the beach near the van park, with another sealed ramp into tiny 'Sandfly Creek' 3.5km to the north. Boaters usually launch on the incoming tide, fish the high tide and return while there is enough water to retrieve the boat. The creeks have jewfish, grunter, blue salmon, golden snapper, threadfin, jacks, barramundi and mud crabs. There are oyster rocks in the creeks. Most holes will yield jewfish and barramundi. Livebaiting is the best method, and mullet schools are not usually hard to find. Blue salmon and cod respond to dead baits. Because of the large tides a creek boating trip usual entails gathering bait near high tide, then fishing tidal drains/creeklets as the tide flows out and bait leaves the drains, attracting salmon and barramundi. Fish holes at low tide, then fish edges where bait is holding on the rising tide. Crab pots are best dropped on the earliest possible rising tide in spots where they won't be washed away by tidal currents. The small 'Oyster Creek', 5km south of Clairview Creek, fishes well but has a substantial rockbar that restricts upper access. Flock Pigeon Island is just 4km from the van park ramp, well within range of small boats. The reef at the south end of the island has mainly cod and blue salmon. For those with larger boats, Red Clay Island, 30km out, has coral trout and reef fish, including pink snapper. Most estuary fish bite all year, with threadfin salmon best in winter and barramundi in warm weather. Big salmon are caught from the beach near Clairview, as well as whiting and flathead. Mud crab abundance is usually good but varies from year to year, and the size is usually well above average.

Key to Map

Hotspots

1. Rock outcrop on south bank has holes around it, good at high tide for jewfish and blue salmon.
2. Shale bottom, grunter at high tide.
3. Deep bank with dead trees and snags, good barra spot.
4. Dangerous rocks that are just under the surface at high tide. Boats should stay clear of this area.
5. 'Shell Grit Beach' ... good livebait fishing off the beach for barra and other species.
6. Large rockbar in 'Oyster Creek' claims many propellers.
7. Salmon on incoming tide.
8. Good fishing and crabbing in Cattle Creek but numerous rockbars throughout. Good bream fishing on oyster rocks, and trolling over rockbars for most species.
9. Large hole produces many jewfish.
10. Barra and threadfin salmon close to bank on outgoing tide.
11. Reasonably deep anchorage.

Launch sites

1. The nearest launch site 10km away on Clairview beach. It is tide dependent, useable only near the top of the tide for larger boats. The ramp dries to a large mudflat, so plan trips carefully.

Stanage Wide GPS

Double Rocks Sth 22 05.301S 150 00.200E, 7km
Double Rocks Nth 22 05.030S 150 00.418E, 7km
Black Swan Rock 22 02.405S 150 00.018E, 11km
Half Tide Rock 21 57.812S 149 57.564E, 21km
Jeffreys Rocks 21 54.997S 150 13.630E, 34km
Jeffreys South 21 56.947S 150 13.957E, 30km
Glasgow Rock 21 53.233S 150 10.178E, 35km
South Sail Rock 21 51.044S 150 07.797E, 36km
Bates Rock 21 47.717S 150 05.653E, 43km
Bates South 21 48.957S 150 04.290E, 42km
Sail Rock 21 47.921S 150 09.234E, 42km

Long Island rocks (west side)

Comet Rock 22 04.810S 149 52.275E
Tail Rock 22 06.436S 149 51.548E
Boyle Reef 22 08.062S 149 50.257E
Gannet Rock 22 03.286S 149 52.820E

Stanage

This is one of the best fishing areas on Queensland's central coast, with a great mix of estuary and bluewater fishing. Stanage township and Thirsty Sound are at the end of a 100km road on a peninsula separating Broad Sound and Shoalwater Bay. The sign-posted turn-off is 175km north of Rockhampton on the Bruce Hwy. The unsealed section of the road is usually well maintained. Landbased fishermen can start at Porters Creek, reached by a track from the boat ramp, a good spot to collect bait and fish from the bank, with nearby camping.

Thirsty Sound, between Broad Sound and Shoalwater Bay, is a shallow area inside Quail and Long Islands, affected by strong currents. It enters Broad Sound to the west. Stanage is the gateway to many offshore islands and reefs, with tropical and southern species. Jewfish are best Oct-March, salmon and mackerel from June/Sept, and barra in warm weather. Reef fishing is all year. Large local tides mean crab pots must be well secured or they might wash away. Big male crabs are common around Stanage from Dec/July. Care is required navigating Thirsty Sound as it dries in places. The tidal run and shallow water ensures a big chop if wind and tide are opposed. There is beach and rock fishing near the township, with threadfin and blue salmon, cod and bream the main catch, along with jacks and barramundi. Prawns are in the gutters off Long Island from Dec/Feb. Some rockbars on the map can not be crossed from half-tide down. The Duke Islands are 22km north-east of Stanage and provide an anchorage for offshore exploration, with countless pinnacles, shoals and coral reefs with pink snapper, red emperor, coral trout, monster mackerel, cod, and more. For more info visit **www.stanagebay.com**

Hotspots

1. Barra off Long Island north point.
2. Big crabs in Long Island creeks.
3. Barra, salmon, grunter, crabs.
4. Barra, salmon around rocks.
5. Salmon Bay: blue and threadfin salmon, crabs in small creek.
6. Jewfish hole, usually fishes best from October to March.
7. Barra, salmon, grunter, jewfish and mud crabs in hole near Porters Creek mouth near high tide, on track behind boat ramp. Ledge inside mouth good for landbased fishing. Local beaches have salmon and whiting, best Aug/Sep.
8. Barramundi at tidal drains. Barra bite well in all the local creeks before and after summer rains.
9. Hole has barramundi, grunter, cod.
10. Good fishing in these creeks, barra, golden snapper, grunter, salmon, crabs.
11. Troll this coastline for mackerel when south-easter drops off.
12. Salmon and whiting at Alligator Beach.

Launch sites

1. Double-lane main ramp, half tide up. Bank launch nearby at Porters Creek for 4WD and dinghies, with nearby camping. NOTE: It is 15km from the entrance of Thirsty Sound to Charon Point, travelling across Broad Sound. Charon Point sits between the Styx and Herbert Rivers. Trip is not for small boats. Note large Green Zones in this area.

Stanage has up to about 7.5m tidal movement. Subtract 30min from Mackay tide times.

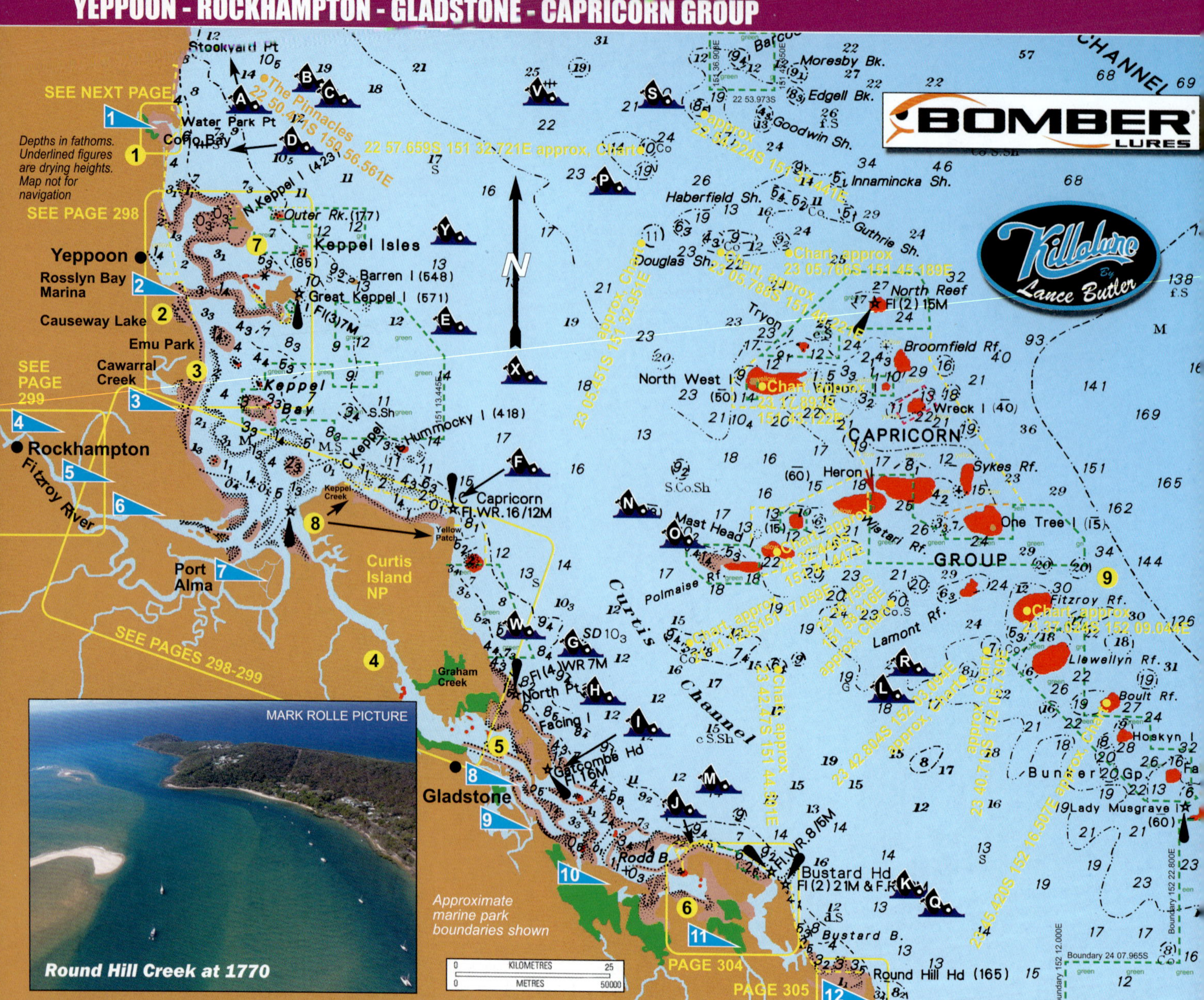

Curtis Coast

The Fitzroy River mouth and the estuarine labyrinth inside Curtis Island produce the biggest wild barramundi on the East Coast. The Fitzroy system also has big jewfish, threadfin and blue salmon, grunter, jacks, whiting, bream, cod and flathead. The river and estuary were declared a net-free zone in 2015. Offshore, the Keppel Islands produce spanish mackerel and reef fish. Gladstone Harbour has a mix of tropical and southern species. Outside the harbour, shoals extend out to the Great Barrier Reef. Gladstone's stocked Awoonga Dam is one of the better barramundi dams. Fish escape the dam in flooding and eventually leave the Boyne River to spread along the coast.

Key to Map

Hotspots

1. Good fishing in shallow Corio Bay and its creeks, see map on next page. Beach to the north has dart, flathead, whiting and sandworms.
2. Causeway Lake, land-based fishing. Big tides push through the causeway causing fish to gather - the bridge is the hotspot. Queenfish, trevally, big barracuda and even barra are caught, with jacks mostly upstream. The lake is shallow and night fishing is best. Morning or afternoons are OK for walking the banks. Ramp available.
3. Cawarral Creek includes three large creek arms. Large, mostly sandy system that produces good fishing and crabbing, including barramundi, queenfish and salmon. See page 298.
4. The shallow channel between Curtis Island and the mainland is a vast area of fertile mangroves, flats and smaller tidal channels and mud drains. See Gladstone section.
5. Gladstone: Calliope River and Boyne River and around the back of Boyne Island have good fishing and crabbing. Reef and pelagic fish outside from Rock Cod Shoals 23 41.123S 151 37.049E and 23 42.497S 151 44.446E to 56km out to Great Barrier Reef. Jewfish off city wharves. See Gladstone section for detail.
6. Estuary fish: whiting, crabs.
7. Keppel Islands: extensive reef areas and rocky points with good fishing and scenery.
8. Keppel Creek and Yellow Patch are great for whiting, also flathead, trevally, queenfish. Barra, jacks, crabs in creeks. Keppel Rocks at north of island hold barra, golden snapper.
9. Great Barrier Reef - huge range of tropical reef and pelagic fish.

Launch sites

1. Corbett's Landing Road - see ramp "A" next page. Take Byfield road from Yeppoon and turn right at sign 2km inside state forest. All-tides but rockbars above and below. Also, **Kellys Landing** ("B" on next page) where Waterpark Creek turns into Corio Bay. Track is rough, with wrong turns. Ramp dry at low tide. Also, **Fishing Creek** ("C" on next page), accessible through resort. Follow track to creek mouth, or take beach. Sandy launch.
2. Rosslyn Bay marina, big boat launch site for Keppel Islands etc.
3. All-tide ramp, north side of Cawarral Creek, Svendsen Rd, Zilzie. Also Keppel Sands & Emu Park at high tide.
4. Fitzroy River ramps, see page 299.
5. Nerimbra all-tide ramp, multi-lanes.
6. Thompsons Point, Thompsons Point Road, which turns off Emu Park Road. North bank of the river.
7. Port Alma, all-tide concrete ramp. Was to be relocated in 2019/20.
8. Calliope River and Auckland Inlet, multi-lane ramps.
9. Toolooa Bends, South Trees Inlet, concrete ramp.
10. Wild Cattle Creek, concrete ramp.
11. Turkey Beach, fairly sheltered but affected by current.
12. Town of 1770, Round Hill Creek.

Wrecks

Positions taken using digital charts. Accuracy may vary.

A. *Rama*, off Stockyard Point, grunter, black jew and large nannygai. Approx 22 48.887S 150 50.492E
B. Charted wreck, approx 22 49.965S 151 01.250E
C. Charted wreck, approx 22 51.886S 151 01.722E
D. Charted wreck, approx 22 57.981S 150 49.982E
E. Charted wreck, approx 23 12.095S 151 15.291E
F. *Joy Bird* concrete yacht, 23 27.883S 151 14.809E
G. *Bindari*, small profile left, 28m deep, approx 23 41.437S 151 23.563E, also steel yacht *Red Dolphin*, 23 41.483S 151 25.150E, 28m deep.
H. *Moreton Star*, wooden trawler, broken up, 25m deep, 23 45.504S 151 26.506E
I. Charted wreck, approx 23 52.663S 151 23.332E
J. Charted wreck, approx 23 58.290S 151 37.131E
K. *Cetacea* trawler, 28m deep, approx 24 03.042S 151 55.298E
L. *Barcoola* trawler, 41m deep, approx 23 46.917S 151 55.241E
M. *Nautilus* 48m iron barge, 27m deep, approx 23 53.228S 151 38.647E
N. *FV Melissa* approx 23 30.150S 151 25.816E
O. Charted wreck, approx 23 31.241S 151 33.728E
P. *Chromatt*, 18m fishing boat, approx 23 01.820S 151 24.340E
Q. *Tranquility* 15m boat, 30m deep, approx 24 04.682S 151 59.881E
R. *Shannon II* 40m trawler, 46m deep, approx 23 44.806S 151 59.232E
S. FV *Damarla* approx 22 52.455S 151 28.560E
T. Charted wreck, approx 22 47.842S 151 27.056E
U. Charted wreck, approx 22 47.573S 151 20.368E
V. Charted wreck, approx 22 52.155S 151 19.604E
W. Charted wreck in Green Zone, approx 23 39.394S 151 20.056E
X. FV *Linda Jane*, approx 23 17.804S 151 17.851E, 35m deep
Y. Charted wreck, approx 23 09.626S 151 15.438E

Tides in this area move up to about 5m.

Corio Bay

This shallow estuary 20km north of Yeppoon is the mutual mouth of Waterpark and Fishing Creeks. It was declared net-free in 2015. It dries at low tide, leaving shallow channels, the main entrance draining past a headland. Primary species are bream, whiting, salmon and flathead, best in July, August and September. Prawns are patchy. There is a fair chance of finding barramundi in warm weather. Mud crab numbers fluctuate from year to year. The bay is known for its whiting. Flathead can be prolific, and blue salmon schools provide furious action. There are fishable rockbars above Corbett's Landing. Queenfish, trevally and mackerel are at the bay's entrance, with grunter on rough ground outside. There are yabby banks in the bay and Fishing Creek. Waterpark Creek flows freshwater at the top. Greenslopes and Sandfly Creek are not accessible at low tide.

Ramps

Take the Byfield road and turn right at signpost 2km inside state forest.

A. **Corbett's Landing.** Take the Byfield road from Yeppoon and turn right at sign 2km inside state forest. Beware rockbars.

B. **Kellys Landing.** Track is rough, with wrong turns. Launch site dry at low tide.

C. **Fishing Creek.** Follow unsealed road to creek mouth, or take beach. Sandy launch, boggy.

Hotspots

1. Fish incoming tide with nippers or small mullet. Flathead, whiting, bream, queenfish, blue salmon.
2. Beach gutter produces flathead, dart, whiting.
3. Abundant salmon at times. Flathead, trevally. Access via boat or from Nine Mile Beach.
4. Flathead along channel edges, queenfish, salmon.
5. Flathead along channel edges, use lures or bait.
6. Black jewfish in deep water at night, queenfish.

For launch sites see key for Ramp 1 on previous page.

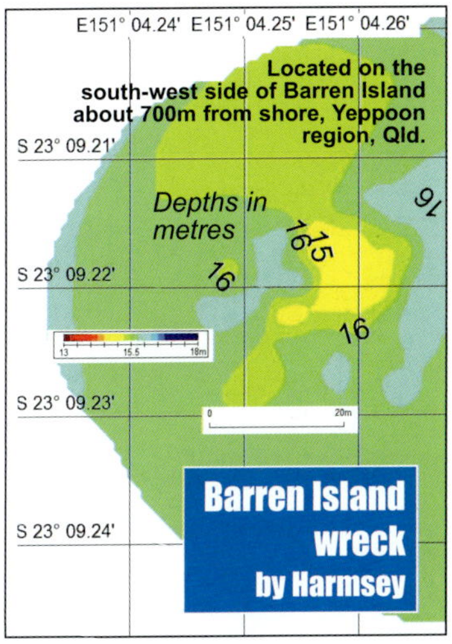

Waterpark Creek; Camping at nearby Red Rock; hole; rocks; Greenslopes Creek; Byfield NP; nippers; Nine Mile Beach; To Five Rocks; Corio Bay; Waterpark Point; Sandfly Creek; Deep Creek; Approximate marine park boundaries shown; Shifting channels and sandflats throughout; rocks approx 22 57.473S 150 46.707E; Chart, approx 22 56.804S 150 47.551E; holes; Sandy Point; Farnborough Beach; Fishing Creek

Map not for navigation. Unmarked hazards may exist on all maps

Corio Bay is a net-free zone

Barren Island wreck by Harmsey

Located on the south-west side of Barren Island about 700m from shore, Yeppoon region, Qld.

Depths in metres

Byfield National Park

A 4WD is needed for most of the park. The park has three access points. For entry through Byfield State Forest take a 30-minute drive north of Yeppoon via the sealed Yeppoon-Byfield Road. Follow signposts along the unsealed road to Waterpark Creek visitor area. The entrance to Byfield NP in Byfield State Forest is 10km east of Waterpark Creek visitor area. The 15km soft sand track from the entrance to the coast may take more than one hour. Intersections are marked. **Sandy Point** car park is accessible in conventional vehicles - travel 5km north of Yeppoon and turn right (eastward) at the roundabout. Continue for 10km on a sealed road past the Capricorn resort to the T-junction. Turn right and follow the gravel road for 10km to Sandy Point. Visitors can access the beach via a track from the carpark. Beach driving permits apply. **Waterpark Point** is part of Byfield NP on the north side of Corio Bay. This headland is accessible by boat. Small boats can be launched from the beach in the Sandy Point section. **Five Rocks** visitor area, 20km north of Corio Bay, has a campsite and good fishing. It requires 4WD.

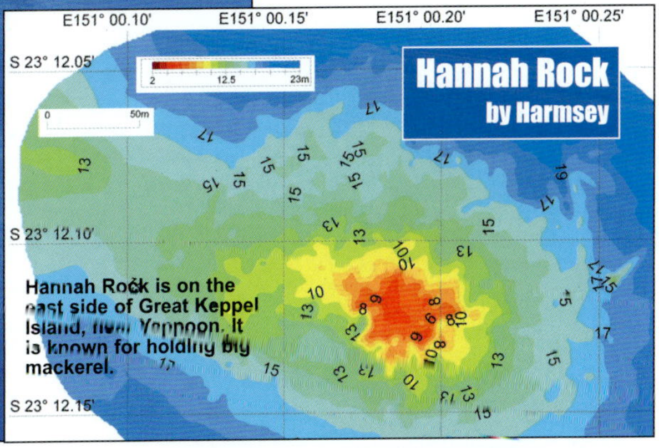

Great Keppel Island

great squid spot in winter on falling tide

troll end of peninsula for big spanish mackerel on big tides

ridge comes out from slane point, fish drop-off for reds and pelagics

Miall Island; Middle Island; Great Keppel Island; Bald Rock; Monkey Point; Halfway Island; Humpy Island

Hannah Rock by Harmsey

Hannah Rock is on the east side of Great Keppel Island, from Yeppoon. It is known for holding big mackerel.

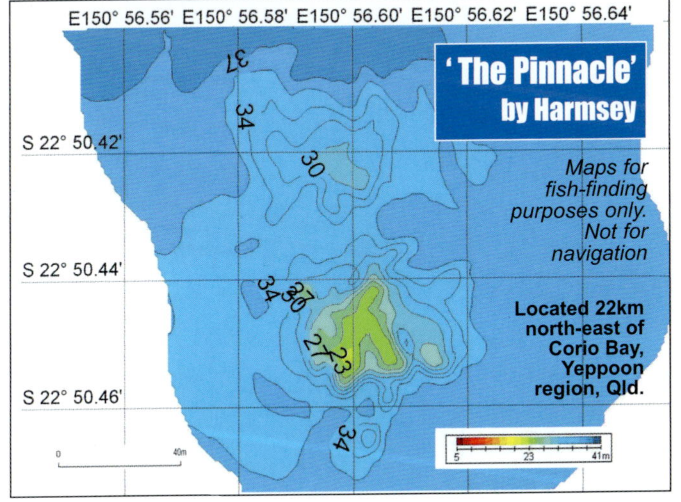

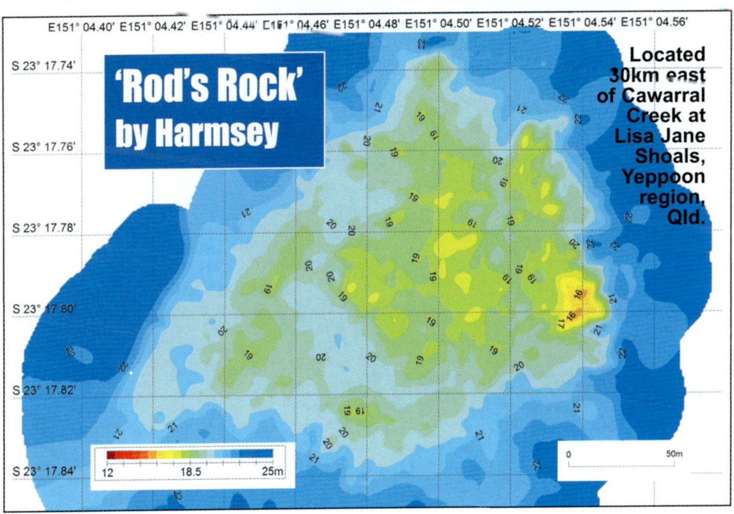

Cawarral Creek

Cawarral Creek is three creeks: Coorooman to the west, Cawarral to the north, and Emu Park Creek to the east. The system is closed to netting and most estuary species can be caught in season.

Hotspots

1. The Timbers - good area for grunter and blue salmon.
2. Prawn flats - after summer rains.
3. Yabbie banks .
4. Grunter patch.
5. The Junction.

Launch sites

1. Svendsen Rd, Zilzie, multi-lanes.
2. Keppel Sands, Taylor St, high tide.
3. Private toll ramp at Ranglewood Ranch (take the Kawana Crocodile Farm turn-off from the Emu Park road and look for the white arch entrance).

Beach Access

In Livingstone Shire, 4WD vehicles may use Farnborough Beach, north of the Bangalee beach access, and beaches in Byfield NP, Nine Mile Beach, and part of Five Rocks Beach.

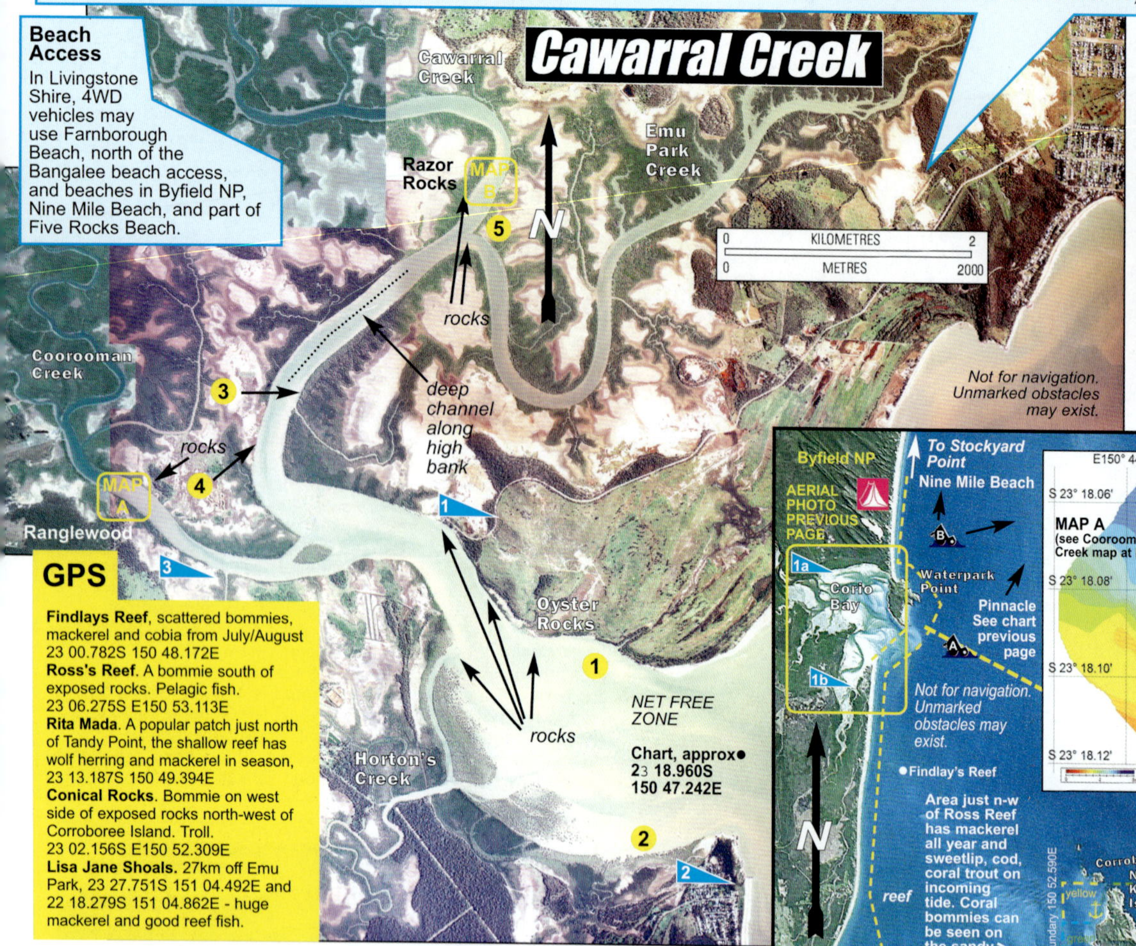

Cawarral Creek

Cawarral Creek
Emu Park Creek
Razor Rocks
MAP B
rocks
Coorooman Creek
deep channel along high bank
MAP A
Ranglewood
Oyster Rocks
NET FREE ZONE
Chart, approx 23 18.960S 150 47.242E
Horton's Creek
KILOMETRES 0 2
METRES 0 2000
Not for navigation. Unmarked obstacles may exist.

Five Rocks

Five Rocks
Walk out and spin for mackerel, trevally, queenfish
Byfield NP
Stockyard Point
Nine Mile Beach
Whiting here on rising tide

GPS

Findlays Reef, scattered bommies, mackerel and cobia from July/August 23 00.782S 150 48.172E

Ross's Reef. A bommie south of exposed rocks. Pelagic fish. 23 06.275S E150 53.113E

Rita Mada. A popular patch just north of Tandy Point, the shallow reef has wolf herring and mackerel in season, 23 13.187S 150 49.394E

Conical Rocks. Bommie on west side of exposed rocks north-west of Corroboree Island. Troll. 23 02.156S E150 52.309E

Lisa Jane Shoals. 27km off Emu Park, 23 27.751S 151 04.492E and 22 18.279S 151 04.862E - huge mackerel and good reef fish.

Yeppoon

Gill nets were removed from Corio Bay and Cawarral Creek in 2015. Blue and threadfin salmon and queenfish are easy to find, along with flathead, bream, jacks and grunter. Yeppoon is known for its mackerel, with reliable inshore grounds. Island edges, pinnacles and bommies produce grey, spotted and spanish mackerel, and cobia. Spanish mackerel to 30kg+ are caught, with ribbonfish (wolf herring) the proven big-fish bait. Mackerel show up all year, but are best from October to May. Fishing is usually best on big tides. Nannygai and red emperor move to coastal reefs after rain, presumably to feed on prawns, and are otherwise caught on deep grounds out wider. Coral trout, tuskfish, sweetlip, golden snapper and grunter are also caught in close. Corio Bay, Causeway Lake, Yeppoon Inlet and Cawarral Creek have grunter, bream, flathead and whiting. Barramundi, salmon and mud crabs are best in Cawarral Creek. Big barra are found on sheltered coastal rocks. The innside of Rosslyn Boat Harbour near the mangroves has seasonal prawns, as well as mullet, herring and gar for bait. Double Head and the boat harbour's extensive and easily accessible rock walls are good landbased spots. There is camping and 4WD beach access in Byfield NP at Corio Bay and Stockyard Point.

Wrecks

A. Scattered wreck about 3.7km from Corio Bay mouth at approx 22 57.568S 150 49.355E.

B. Off map, three charted wrecks. One off Stockyard Point, 16.6km from Corio Bay, approx 22 48.855S 150 50.375E. Two others 3.7km apart, 28km from Corio Bay, at approx 22 50.004S 151 01.210E, and 22 51.859S 151 01.718E.

C. See top of next page.

Launch sites

1a and 1b. See previous page.
2. Fig Tree Creek, off Yeppoon Inlet, Merv Anderson Park.
3. Rosslyn Bay marina, this is the best local launch site.
4. Causeway Lake, Resada Esplanade, south bank.
5. Emu Park beach ramp, Hill St, upper tide only.
6. Cawarral Creek, all-tides, Svendsen Rd, Zilzie. Also Coorooman Creek, see above.
7. Keppel Sands, Taylor St, upper tide only. Also nearby, Pumpkin Creek ramp, Limpus Ave.

Local tides have up to about 3.3m movement.

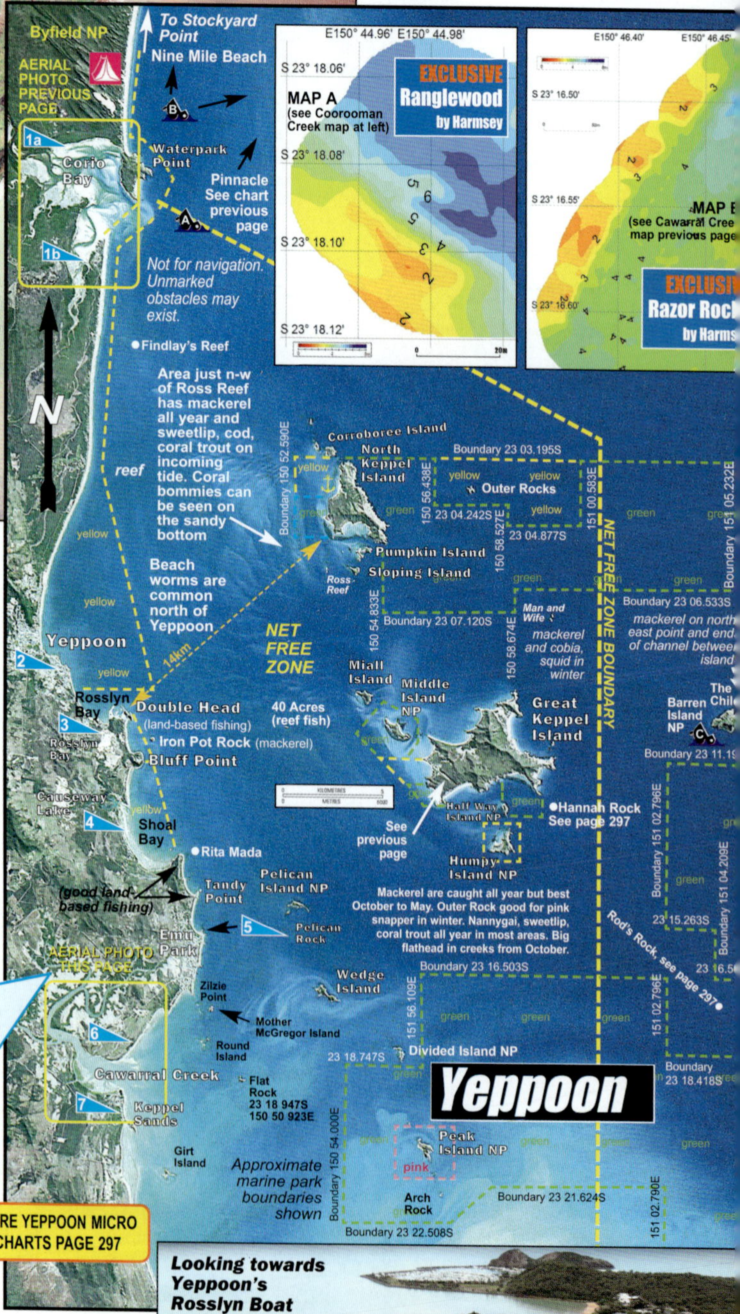

Yeppoon

Byfield NP
To Stockyard Point
Nine Mile Beach
AERIAL PHOTO PREVIOUS PAGE
Corio Bay
Waterpark Point
Pinnacle See chart previous page
Not for navigation. Unmarked obstacles may exist.
Findlay's Reef
Area just n-w of Ross Reef has mackerel all year and sweetlip, cod, coral trout on incoming tide. Coral bommies can be seen on the sandy bottom
Beach worms are common north of Yeppoon
NET FREE ZONE
Corroboree Island
North Keppel Island
Outer Rocks
Pumpkin Island
Sloping Island
Ross Reef
Man and Wife - mackerel and cobia, squid in winter
mackerel on north east point and end of channel between island
Yeppoon
Rosslyn Bay
Double Head (land-based fishing)
Iron Pot Rock (mackerel)
Bluff Point
40 Acres (reef fish)
Miall Island
Middle Island NP
Great Keppel Island
Barren Island NP
Causeway Lake
Shoal Bay
Rita Mada
See previous page
Halfway Island NP
Humpy Island NP
Hannah Rock See page 297
(good land-based fishing)
Tandy Point
Pelican Island NP
Pelican Rock
Emu Park
Mackerel are caught all year but best October to May. Outer Rock good for pink snapper in winter. Nannygai, sweetlip, coral trout all year in most areas. Big flathead in creeks from October.
AERIAL PHOTO THIS PAGE
Zilzie Point
Wedge Island
Mother McGregor Island
Round Island
Divided Island NP
Cawarral Creek
Keppel Sands
Flat Rock 23 18 947S 150 50 923E
Girt Island
Approximate marine park boundaries shown
Peak Island NP
Arch Rock
NET FREE ZONE BOUNDARY
Rod's Rock, see page 297

MAP A (see Coorooman Creek map at left)
EXCLUSIVE Ranglewood by Harmsey

MAP B (see Cawarral Creek map previous page)
EXCLUSIVE Razor Rock by Harmsey

MORE YEPPOON MICRO CHARTS PAGE 297

Looking towards Yeppoon's Rosslyn Boat Harbour

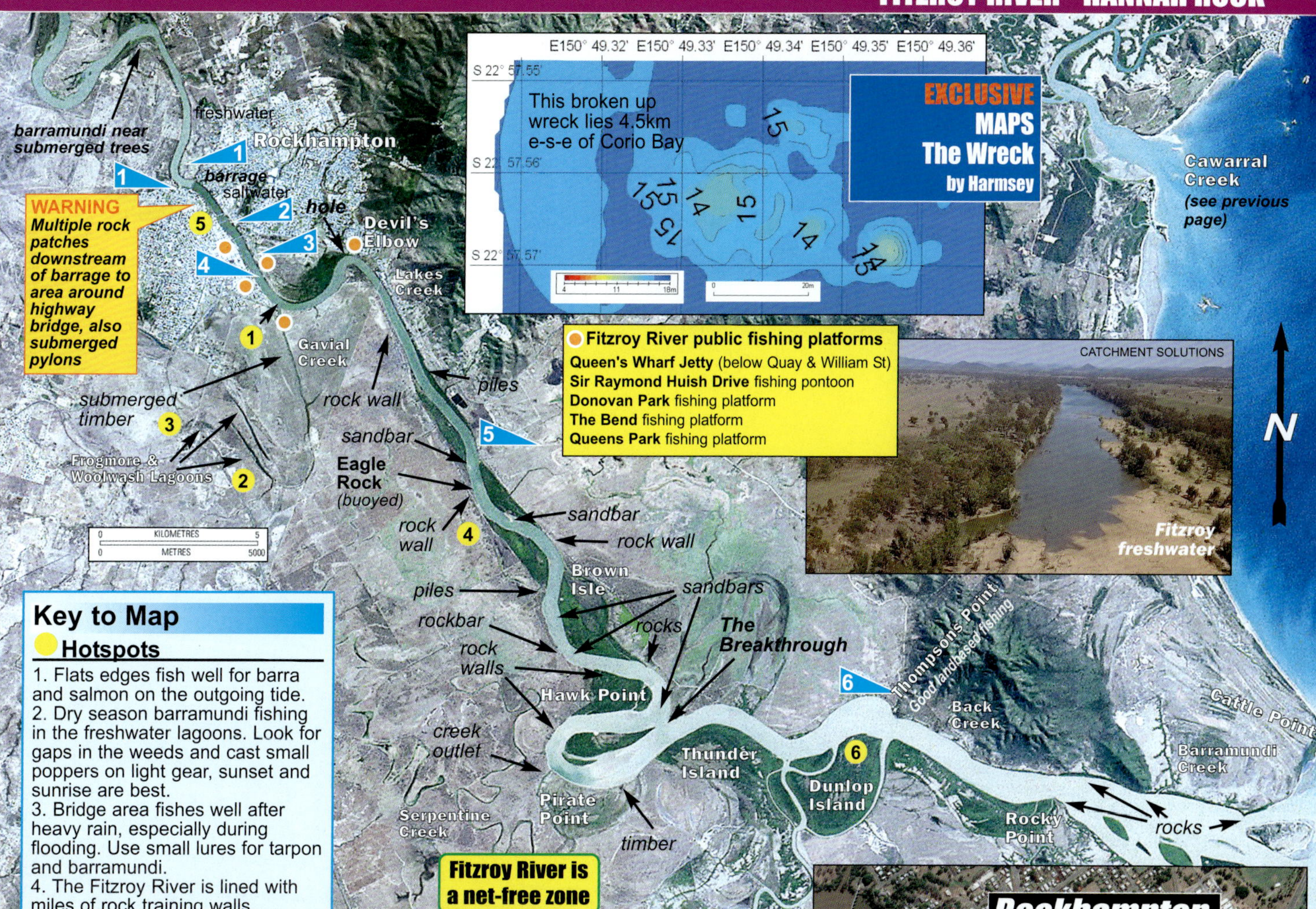

Key to Map

Hotspots

1. Flats edges fish well for barra and salmon on the outgoing tide.
2. Dry season barramundi fishing in the freshwater lagoons. Look for gaps in the weeds and cast small poppers on light gear, sunset and sunrise are best.
3. Bridge area fishes well after heavy rain, especially during flooding. Use small lures for tarpon and barramundi.
4. The Fitzroy River is lined with miles of rock training walls, remnants of an era when a clear shipping route was needed. The rock walls are now falling into disrepair but the fish don't mind. Mixed species can be caught trolling or casting lures, or anchor and fish baits. Also mud crabs.
5. In the CBD the remains of the old traffic bridge are a prime barramundi spot. Much of the bridge remains, including pavement and pylons. Extensive rockbars and holes exist between the highway bridge and barrage. areas, good spots to target big barramundi, jacks and cod, with barra to 120cm+ caught. Landbased fishos have several platforms to fish (see yellow box).
6. Fish mud drain outlets with lures as tide falls, barra, salmon, crabs.

Launch sites

1 & 1. Ramps in freshwater section above barrage, one on north bank, off Larcombe St, and one on south bank, off Ramsden St.
2. Old single-lane ramp next to highway bridge, poor security, now rarely used.
3. Town ramp, north bank, multi-lanes, pontoon, Callaghan Park, Robert Clark Drive.
4. Town ramp, south bank, multi-lanes, pontoon, off Quay St.
5. Nerimbera all-tide ramp, multi-lanes, St Christophers Chapel Rd.
6. Thompsons Point ramp on Thompsons Point Rd, off Emu Park Rd. Multi-lane concrete.

River mouth has tidal movement up to about 5.25m.

Rockhampton

The Fitzroy River and its vast lower estuary were declared net-free in 2015. This is now the most exciting wild barramundi destination on the East Coast, offering a real chance of 120cm+ fish. The Fitzroy mouth is a labyrinth of creeks, mangroves and tidal flats. Driving toward Port Alma, the intial impression is starkness, but the network of mangrove creeks could keep a fisherman busy for weeks. The river itself has deep water up to Rockhampton. The main species are barra, jewfish, threadfin and blue salmon, golden snapper (fingermark), grunter, estuary cod and mud crabs. There are also bread and butter fish like bream, whiting, and flathead. The Sunshine State's biggest barramundi and threadfin have been caught in the lower Fitzroy. The river's catchment is the second largest in Australia, after the Murray/Darling, but like many Australian rivers it often stops flowing and forms a chain of long pools. The catchment stretches from the Carnarvon Ranges in the west to the river mouth in Keppel Bay, bounded to the north by the Burdekin River catchment, another vast area. The Fitzroy is formed by the junction of the Dawson and Mackenzie rivers. The river is tidal until the city barrage, with more weirs upstream. It is about 40km from Rockhampton to the sea, and the river mouth is a kilometre wide. There are shallow sand, gravel and mudbars throughout, mostly on the insides of bends. The river is lined with man-made stone walls. These hold fish, especially where the walls have fallen into the river. Grunter are a favourite fish and a hotspot for them is 10km downstream from the city adjacent to the meatworks, fishing from November. Fishing in the city reach is as good as anywhere for barramundi around the rockbars and holes from the barrage down to the highway bridge. The lagoons on the south-western city outskirts, once home to mostly tarpon and spangled perch, have become reliable for barramundi since the netting closure. Big crocodiles inhabit this area, so don't take risks. Outside Curtis Island and into the bluewater, fishing is good out to the Capricorn group, which is the beginning of the Great Barrier Reef. At 100km+ it is a long run to the outer reefs, but there are many great spots to fish closer in, including rock and reef patches at the north end of Gladstone Island, and shoals and reef around Rundle Island, which produce big jewfish, spanish mackerel and much more.

Lures for the Fitzroy

Being a deep system, Fitzroy barra fishos tend to use diving and suspending lures. Lures that dive to 3m or 4m are popular. Vibes are versatile when fishing deep and are Fitzroy favourites because big threadfin (king) salmon like them. More typical shallow barramundi lures have their place when fishing flats, draining gutters and pocket eddies around rock walls. Aside from the rock walls and city rockbars and pylons, the river does not carry a lot of snags.

Rocky Barra Bash

The 2021 competition had a cash prize pool of more than $25,000 and a boat package valued at more than $30,000. Competitors fish the tidal reaches of the Fitzroy Delta Net Free Zones that extend through Rockhampton Regional Council and Livingstone Shire Council land. The three days of competition are held in October. The 'most metres' of barramundi wins $6000, with $3000 for second spot and $1500 for third, along with individual prizes for biggest fish. Visit the website **www.fitzroyriverbarrabash.com.au**

Lower Fitzroy River

The sportfishing potential of this vast network of tidal flats, creeks and mangrove shoreline was restored when gill nets were removed in 2015. Queensland's biggest barramundi and threadfin are caught here. Much fishing is done with livebaits dropped into holes, but trolling, casting tidal drains and fishing flats edges all work well. Barramundi bite best in warm weather, with blue salmon, jewfish, grunter, bream, whiting, crabs and prawns all year. Prawning is usually from February to May, depending on rain. A channel is marked through The Narrows - skippers should allow about 1.5m of tide plus the draft of the boat to get through. Travelling at high tide is easier. It is 96km to the Great Barrier Reef from the river mouth, or 61km from Gladstone, but inner islands and shoals offer good fishing, with the Bass Shoals and reefs around Rundle Island producing big jewfish, spanish mackerel and more, and Fairway Rock and Ship Rock near Hummocky Island known for big mackerel and reef fish. Spanish mackerel are caught all year, with school mackerel best in summer. Trophy barramundi can appear in numbers inside Curtis Island when Boyne River's Lake Awoonga floods and stocked fish escape and move downriver into Gladstone Harbour. **Local tides have up to about 5m movement.**

Camping

Curtis Island National Park has camping at Yellow Patch, Turtle Street and Joey Lees. Yellow Patch site is for boaters, and is near a large tidal creek system. Other sites can be reached 4WD, with a vehicular ferry from Gladstone. Permits are required and visitors must be self-sufficient. For details visit www.parks.des.qld.gov.au. Other Gladstone area camps include The Oaks on Facing Island, South End on Curtis Island, Workman's Beach at Agnes Water, and Lilley's Beach at Boyne Island.

Curtis Gas Project

Check the port authority website for the latest security zones. Gas ships have a secure zone. Boaters must not impede ships, anchoring is not permitted in the channel and boats must move well in advance of ships. Check the latest Notices for Mariners online at www.qld.gov.au/transport/boating/notices/about

Key to Map

Hotspots

1. Troll rock walls when water is clearish - barra, cod, jacks.
2. Mangrove-lined creek has good fishing and crabbing.
3. Salmon/grunter off cockle beach.
4. Bridge pylons hold fish.
5. Barra on flats edges on incoming tide in calm weather.
6. Good crabbing on big tides.
7. Good fishing in The Narrows.
8. Jewfish in creek mouth holes.
9. Shallow, sandy creeks have flathead and whiting. Mud crabs in upper reaches. Difficult or impossible access at low tide.
10. Pelagic fish, big mackerel around Fairway Rock, Ship Rock, reef off Cape Cape Capricorn.
11. Fish west side of Rundle Island for reef fish, including big jewfish. Summer mackerel and reef fish off north-east side. Jewfish best after heavy rain. Many rocks, approach island with care. Bass Shoals have reef fish on rising tide.
12. Flathead, whiting over flats.
13. Drops to deep water, reef fish.
14. Most species in this creek.
15. Rock wall at southern tip of Turtle Island fishes well.

GPS

*Jabiru Shoals, 24km from Fitzroy mouth, 23 21.114S 151 04.447E, 23 21.333S 151 05.036E, 23 21.910S 151 06.075 E

*Lisa Jane Shoals, 27km from Fitzroy mouth, 23 18.293S 151 04.861 E, 23 17.773S 151 04.482E, 23 17.586S 151 04.095E

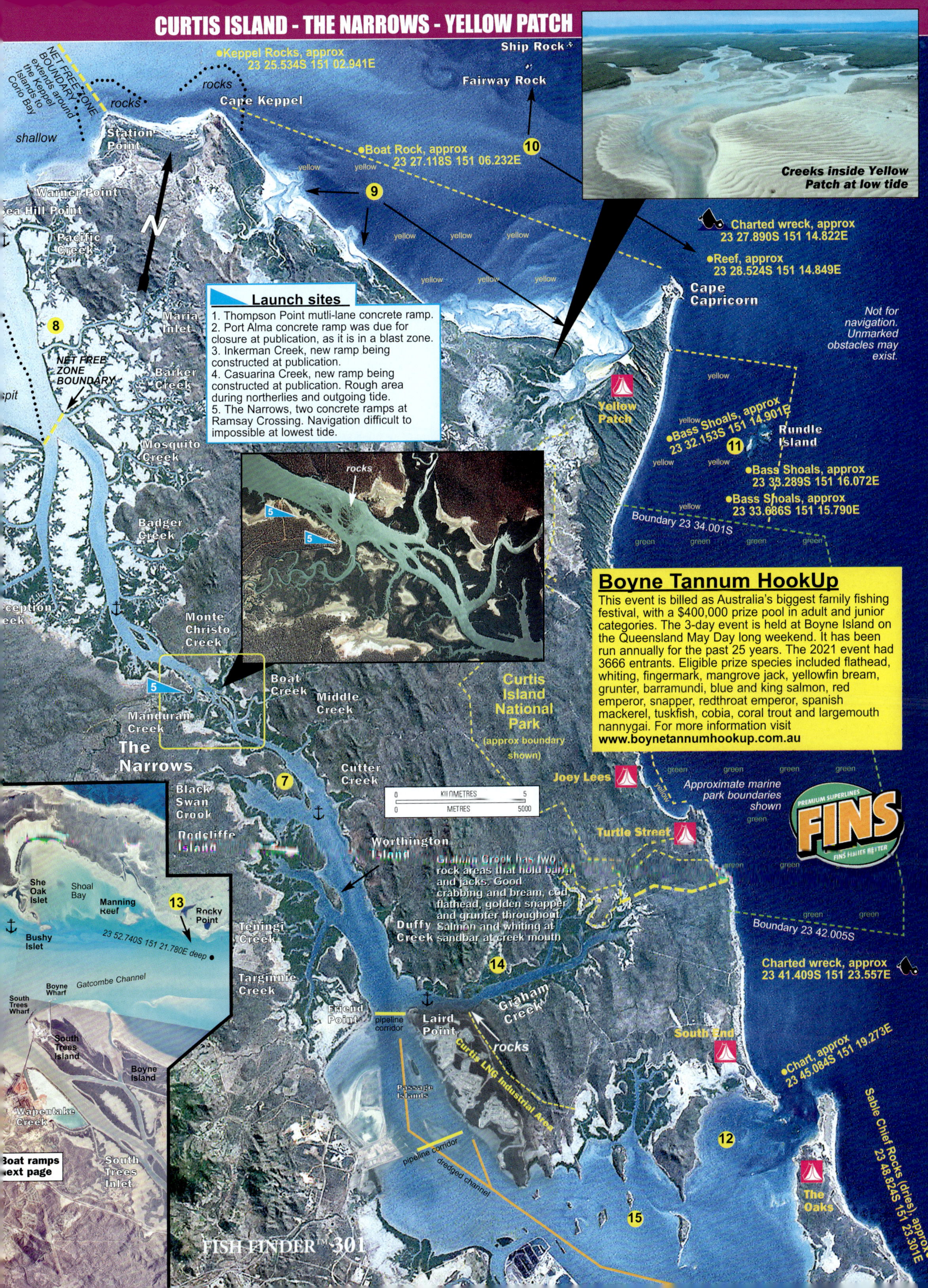

CURTIS ISLAND - THE NARROWS - YELLOW PATCH
Keppel Rocks, approx 23 25.534S 151 02.941E
Ship Rock
Fairway Rock
NET FREE ZONE BOUNDARY extends around the Keppel Islands to Corio Bay
rocks
rocks
Cape Keppel
shallow
Station Point
Boat Rock, approx 23 27.118S 151 06.232E
10
9
Creeks inside Yellow Patch at low tide
Warner Point
Sea Hill Point
Pacific Creek
N
Charted wreck, approx 23 27.890S 151 14.822E
Reef, approx 23 28.524S 151 14.849E
Cape Capricorn
Not for navigation. Unmarked obstacles may exist.
Launch sites
1. Thompson Point mutli-lane concrete ramp.
2. Port Alma concrete ramp was due for closure at publication, as it is in a blast zone.
3. Inkerman Creek, new ramp being constructed at publication.
4. Casuarina Creek, new ramp being constructed at publication. Rough area during northerlies and outgoing tide.
5. The Narrows, two concrete ramps at Ramsay Crossing. Navigation difficult to impossible at lowest tide.
8
Maria Inlet
NET FREE ZONE BOUNDARY
Barker Creek
spit
Yellow Patch
Bass Shoals, approx 23 32.153S 151 14.901E
Rundle Island
11
Bass Shoals, approx 23 33.289S 151 16.072E
Bass Shoals, approx 23 33.686S 151 15.790E
Boundary 23 34.001S
Mosquito Creek
rocks
5
5
Badger Creek
Boyne Tannum HookUp
This event is billed as Australia's biggest family fishing festival, with a $400,000 prize pool in adult and junior categories. The 3-day event is held at Boyne Island on the Queensland May Day long weekend. It has been run annually for the past 25 years. The 2021 event had 3666 entrants. Eligible prize species included flathead, whiting, fingermark, mangrove jack, yellowfin bream, grunter, barramundi, blue and king salmon, red emperor, snapper, redthroat emperor, spanish mackerel, tuskfish, cobia, coral trout and largemouth nannygai. For more information visit
www.boynetannumhookup.com.au
Monte Christo Creek
5
Boat Creek
Middle Creek
Manduran Creek
The Narrows
Curtis Island National Park
(approx boundary shown)
Cutter Creek
Joey Lees
Approximate marine park boundaries shown
FINS
7
Black Swan Creek
Redcliffe Island
0 KILOMETRES 5
0 METRES 5000
Worthington Island
Turtle Street
Graham Creek has two rock areas that hold barra and jacks. Good crabbing and bream, cod, flathead, golden snapper and grunter throughout. Salmon and whiting at sandbar at creek mouth
Duffy Creek
Teningi Creek
Targinnie Creek
14
Boundary 23 42.005S
Charted wreck, approx 23 41.409S 151 23.557E
She Oak Islet
Shoal Bay
Manning Reef
13
Rocky Point
23 52.740S 151 21.780E deep
Bushy Islet
Gatcombe Channel
Boyne Wharf
South Trees Wharf
South Trees Island
Boyne Island
Wapentake Creek
Boat ramps next page
South Trees Inlet
Friend Point
pipeline corridor
Laird Point
Graham Creek
rocks
Curtis LNG Industrial Area
South End
Chart, approx 23 45.084S 151 19.273E
Passage Islands
Sable Chief Rocks (dries), approx 23 48.824S 151 23.301E
12
pipeline corridor
dredged channel
The Oaks
15

Lake Lenthall

This is off the Bruce Highway at Torbanlea, via a 7km unsealed road. The dam was built on the Burrum River, south of Bundaberg, in 1984. The lake covers 400ha, with an average depth of 4m. It has barramundi, bass, yellowbelly and silver perch. Bass is the main species caught. This is one of the most southerly dams where barramundi can be caught. The boat ramp is a short way past the dam wall. The lake speed limit is four knots, with motors restricted to 6hp maximum. No camping is permitted, but Wongi State National Park has camps 16km away. The tidal Burrum River also has barramundi.

Lake Gregory

Also known as the Isis Balancing Storage, this small dam suits cartoppers and canoes. It is located between Bundaberg and Childers via the Isis Highway. Turn onto Voss Rd and right onto an unsealed track. Lake Gregory covers 200ha. The average depth is only 3m. It is stocked with bass and silver perch. Saratoga have been caught. This is a shallow weedy lake, especially around the edges, which makes trolling difficult. There is a 9m-deep area across from the unsealed launch site. Launching is near the dam wall. Camping is allowed, but there are no facilities.

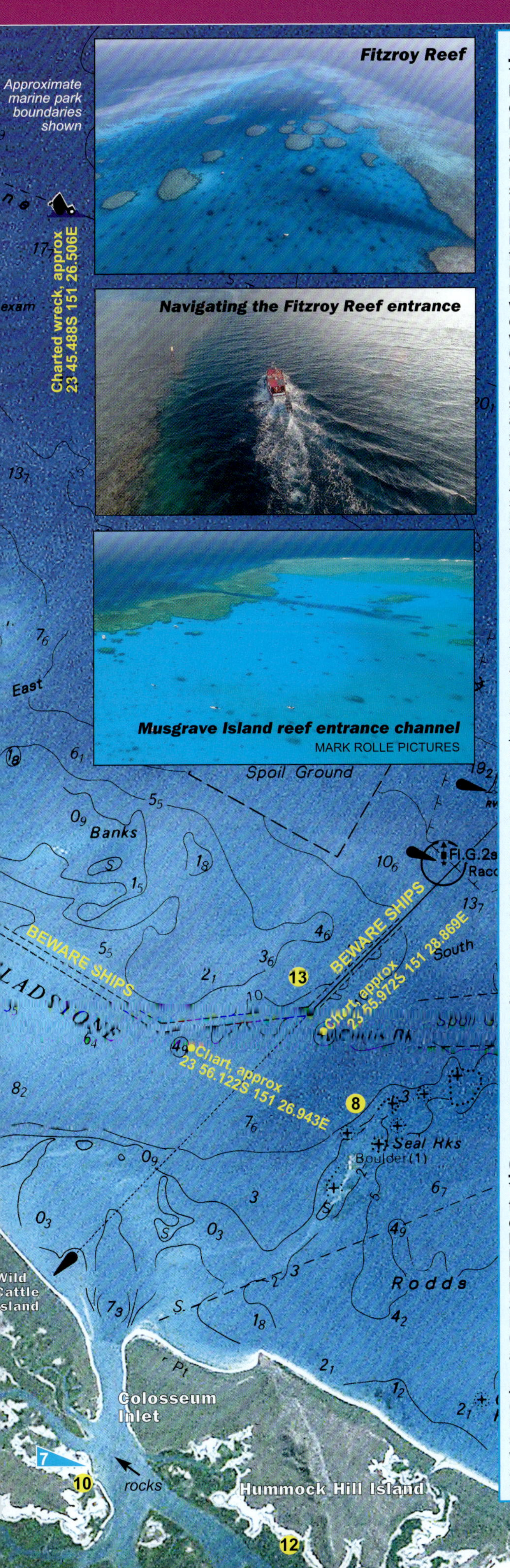

Fitzroy Reef

Navigating the Fitzroy Reef entrance

Musgrave Island reef entrance channel

MARK ROLLE PICTURES

Port of Gladstone

This industrial city has a large, complex harbour that adjoins the Fitzroy River estuary through a shallow channel behind Curtis Island. Barramundi are a prominent part of the fishery here, as are grunter and threadfin salmon. The harbour has ample sheltered water for small boats, and there are good landbased opportunities. A highlight for barra fishos is the shallow estuary inside Curtis Island, which goes through to the Fitzroy River mouth. Big barramundi and threadin salmon are a regular catch inside Curtis Island, along with jewfish, cod, bream, jacks and endless blue salmon. Flathead and whiting are common on the flats. Offshore, there is a mix of southern and tropical species, with emperor, sweetlip, cod, coral trout and pink snapper on the same reefs, along with kingfish, cobia and spanish mackerel. In the estuaries, southern and northern jewfish species co-exist, as do southern yellowfin and northern pikey bream. Gladstone's Lake Awoonga is an outstanding example of successful fish stocking, with trophy barramundi, but the far smaller Lake Tondoon (city botanic gardens), Lake Callemondah (behind the K Mart supermarket on the upper Auckland River), the Railway Dam on Glenlyon Road, Wilmott Lagoon (Mount Larcom) and the upper freshwater reaches of the Calliope River all have fish. During flooding, large barramundi go over the Awoonga dam wall and down the Boyne River into tidal waters along the coast, creating spectacular fishing as the fish spread along the coast. Big jewfish and barra live around wharf pylons, but fishos should note port security rules and exclusion zones. There is regular LNG gas shipping. Like anywhere, anchoring in the shipping channel is not permitted and skippers must keep watch for ships and move long before a ship draws near. During bigger tides, jewfish can be caught around natural structures, including gravel banks and sand that drops into deep water. Jewfish bite all year. Golden snapper (fingermark) and grunter are found around rocky reefs and rough ground.

Seasons

Barra, jacks, golden snapper, grunter, threadfin all year, summer best.
Blue salmon best April to September.
Mud crabs all year, best March/April.
Mackerel July to January inshore and March to July offshore.
Bream, flathead, cod all year.

Offshore

The Great Barrier Reef, about 63km from the port, is the big attraction, but there are closer grounds worth fishing.
Rock Cod Shoal - 23 41.039S 151 37.049E
Rock Cod Shoal East 1 - 23 42.330S 151 44.482E
Rock Cod Shoal East 2 - 23 42.079S 151 46.973E
Rock Cod Shoal West - 23 40.503S 151 34.160E
Shoal 64km east 23 50.624S 151 58.756E
Fitzroy inner shoal 23 42.787S 152 03.058E
Cabbage Patch between Masthead Island and Wistari Reef, 23 31.700S 151 49.600E

Wrecks

Charted co-ordinates supplied on Page 296. Most wrecks are small, such as trawlers, on sand, but with plenty of fish. To find a wreck, visit on a calm weekend - it is likely a boat will be on site, or drop a buoy at the mark and go round in expanding circles.

Key to Map

Hotspots

1. Deep hole holds jewfish, best in warmer months.
2. Big barra, queenfish and salmon, and crabs in river. Calliope River power station hot water outlet is a famous spot.
3. Landbased fishing off marina walls, access from park. Creek has most estuary fish, especially bream, jacks and cod. Look for barra under lights at night, use lures or livebait.
4. Flying Fox Creek has blue salmon in winter. Mud crabs best on bigger tides in late summer, also blue crabs. Some barra, jacks, cod, bream, whiting, flathead. Main creek navigable most tides. Use quiet approach in shallows. Best fishing using live bait at night. Crabs can be potted from bank upstream.
5. Channel has big jewfish, golden snapper and most other species, beware ships. Mackerel, cobia on channel markers.
6. Headlands have mackerel, queenfish in cooler months. Reef fish in calm weather.
7. Deep water estuary.
8. Good reef fishing off Seal Rocks, also queenfish, snub-nosed dart, trevally.
9. Rocks at Boyne River hold fish on upper tide, best at night. Land-based fishing under the bridge upstream, under lights. Area near ramp has nippers. Boyne River mouth is shallow at low tide, with sandbars and rocks. Blue salmon, bream, flathead on upstream gravel bars. Mud crabs throughout. Bream, whiting and flathead off Canoe Point.
10. Most estuary fish throughout Colosseum Inlet. Whiting and flathead from beach at high tide.
11. Land-based estuary fishing, flathead and whiting, fast current at times.
12. Estuary fishing: whiting, flathead.
13. Channel leads hold mackerel, jewfish, cobia,yellowtail kingfish.
14. Barra, whiting, flathead on flats.
15. South End rocks, reached by ferry, mixed species, camping.
16. Anabranch Bridge: estuary fish.
17. Yabby bed (look for reddish sand), whiting, flathead on rising tide.
18. Sable Chief Rocks to North Point, cod, tuskfish, trout.
19. Queenfish, trevally at mouth of South Trees. Barra, jacks, golden snapper and grunter around obstacles.
20. Jewfish, tarpon, barra, golden snapper and cod. Bait collecting at Barney Point beach. Gladstone Port Authority rules apply near wharves.
21. Bream, jacks, around rocks.
22. Expansive flats ... known locally as Flathead Heaven. Queenfish on poppers around Rat Island.
23. Calllope Camping Grounds - barra, flathead, mud crabs and bream downstream of weir at high tide.

Launch sites

1. Calliope River, off Hanson Rd, multi-lanes, most tides, pontoon.
2. Multi-lane ramp in Gladstone Marina.
3. Goodoon St, near yacht club, multi-lanes.
3a. Good ramp at east end of Morgan St. Small ramp at west end of Morgan St.
3b. Old landing off Baillie St.
4. Toolooa Bend, off Gladstone-Benaraby Rd, pontoon, tide restricted.
5. David Bray Park, off Wyndham Ave, multi-lanes, pontoon, good parking.
6. Wild Cattle Creek, concrete, upper tide.
7. Bank launch for small boats, high tide.
8. Curtis Island, two ramps at Southend.
9. Lions Park, off Tarcoola Dve, one lane.
10. Ibis Park, Tiller St, one lane.
11. Tannum Sands, bank launch via track.

Local tides move up to about 5.25m.

Turkey Beach

This is a weekend fishing area for Gladstone fishos, with three large estuaries. Turkey Beach can be reached by boat from Gladstone in good weather, but it is perhaps easier by road. Whiting and flathead are ever-present, mud crabs are reliable and barramundi are present. Pancake Creek to the east is sandy and usually clear, with quality whiting and flathead. The outermost of the three exposed rocks off Clew Point is a spanish mackerel hotspot. Big threadfin salmon and schools of blue salmon are a highlight in the estuaries. Spotted and grey mackerel visit the bays in season, often around August. Reef fish are found in close over scattered reef and coral. Nippers are plentiful in the estuaries and the best bait for big whiting on the flats and tuskfish on the reefs. Boaters can launch at Turkey Beach ramp and Pancake Creek causeway, which requires plenty of tide. Beware drying flats at low tide.

Key to Map

Hotspots

1. Drains have salmon on a falling tide. Occasional barramundi. On rising tide, grunter, whiting, bream, flathead, mud crabs, prawns.
2. Bream, whiting, flathead, mud crabs. Many areas drain out.
3. Deeper water holds most estuary species, live bait and trolling.
4. Fish around headland, Jansen Rock and over reef patches for slatey bream, trout, tuskfish, sweetlip, coral trout, cod. Pelagic fish also.
5. Large whiting and flathead along channel edges. Same in Jenny Lind Creek. Take care to avoid stranding.
6. Inner Rocks, Middle Rocks and Outer Rocks extend from coast to 4km out. Reef and pelagic fishing near rocks and over patches.

Launch sites

1. Turkey Beach, steep ramp, most tides. Locals usually launch off the nearby sand to avoid the current. Subtract about 30 minutes from Gladstone tides.
2. Launch at causeway over Pancake Creek. Turn off Bruce Hwy at Turkey Beach turn-off 35km south of Gladstone, travel 20km and turn right. Rising tide best, at least half tide required. Strong currents, it is easier if you have a helper or two. Or take the Middle Creek road through Eurimbula NP to the south, launch near high tide and travel up the creek to Pancake Creek - impassible at low tide.

The flats in this area are great fishing spots, but don't be stranded on a falling tide.

Baffle Creek

This relatively remote waterway has a mostly shallow tidal reach. It is known for jacks, but also has golden snapper (fingermark), blue and threadfin salmon, trevally, grunter, whiting, bream, flathead, mud crabs and prawns. Occasional barra and mulloway are caught. Livebait, including nippers, prawns, herring and pike, is easily found. Fishing quality is affected by seasonal rainfall. To catch jacks, find a rocky bank or submerged timber and use small lures or baits. Access through the mouth is best on a rising tide.

Key to Map

Hotspots

1. Tree stumps in mouth: jacks, barra.
2. Whiting and flathead on flats edges.
3. Grunter, bream, flathead.
4. Jacks, barra and cod.
5. Jacks, cod in shallow rocky reaches.
6. 4WD beach access - whiting, flathead.

OFF MAP: Two small creeks along the coast north and south of Baffle Creek, and are usually visited only by sea. Deep Water Creek to the north has rock holes upstream with mangrove jacks. Littabella Creek to the south (see page 308) has fishing and crabbing.

Launch sites

1. Winfield, concrete, all tides.
2. Rocky Point Rd, concrete, all-tides.
3. 3 and 4. Old ferry site, all tides.
5. Flat Rock, picnic area.

Baffle Creek

Deepwater and Mithell Creek (mutual mouth) 11km north of Baffle mouth at approx 24 26.088S 152 00.464E - upper reaches have mangrove jacks

Fingers Reef runs along coast just north of Baffle Creek - mixed reef fish

GPS Waypoints

With distances from Round Hill head ... all marks approximate.

*60km to the Great Barrier Reef and **Lady Musgrave Island**, has a safe anchorage, entrance at 23 53.467S 152 24.540E

*84km to Lady Elliot Island (green zone) 24 06.794S 152 42.821E

*Pinnacle at 24 06.794S 152 22.029E (48km), and mackerel over contours at 24 06.511S 152 03.073E (18.5km west) and 23 58.515S 152 01.818E (26km n-w).

*The Wides 23 49.940S 152 00.497E and 23 50.624S 151 58.756E (37km north)

*Boult Reef 23 44 100S 152 15.135E

*Lamont Reef 23 36.490S 152 00.970E

*Fitzroy Reef boat entrance 23 36.445S 152 09.440E

*Fitzroy inner shoal 23 42.787S 152 03.058E

*Banana Gutter 24 06.880E 152 11.100E

*18-Mile 24 07.630S 152 12.790E

*Mackerel Shoal 27km s-e 24 15.999S 152 06.925E

Wrecks

*The *Cetacea* and *Tranquility* wrecks are just 13km off Round Hill Head (see page 296).

Agnes Water and 1770

Round Hill Head near Agnes Water and 1770 has landbased fishing from the rocks, a short walk from the carpark, with large pelagic fish and reef fish caught. Expect mackerel, tuna, queenfish and trevally. Beach fishing produces dusky, sand and bartail flathead, whiting, dart, golden trevally and tailor. From April to September school and spotted mackerel move in close, sometimes within the creek. Coral trout, tuskfish, sweetlip and spanish mackerel are caught around the coral reefs, but it is the **big red emperor and nannygai** found on wider rubble grounds that attract many boaters to this area. Pink snapper and pearl perch are also caught on the reefs. The 1770 public ramp (1) is useable at all tides for small boats, but half tide up is best for big boats. Local national parks have estuary fishing for barra, jacks, flathead, bream, mud crabs and whiting. To reach Eurimbula National Park and **Eurimbula Creek**, drive out of Agnes Water along Round Hill Rd for 10km and turn at the sign. A 14km track leads to Bustard Bay camping area at Eurimbula Creek mouth. The track has sand in places but standard vehicles with high clearance usually get through. There are toilets and water at the camping area. Eurimbula Creek (a crab sanctuary) is OK for bank-launching dinghies but is not navigable at low tide. **Middle Creek** is reached via a turn-off 6km from Round Hill Rd (9km before the Bustard Bay camping area). The 4WD track is 12km, slow and impassable after heavy rain. **Deepwater National Park** offers 4WD access to the coast: from Agnes Water drive south along Springs Rd, turning on to Rocky Point Rd. The turn-off to Deepwater National Park is 1km down on the right and then another 2.5km by 4WD to the park. Tracks to the left give access to the beach, but before negotiating the steep drive down, check the track on foot. **Flat Rock** is a long shelf along the beach that produces reef and beach fish. **Middle Rock** has basic camping without facilities. **Wreck Rock** has several campsites, showers, toilets and water. It is accessible from the south by sealed road. Camping areas are popular in the holiday season with sites booked months ahead.

Key to Map

Hotspots

1. Flathead and whiting over the flats, bream and jacks near structure Salmon, trevally, queenfish, mackerel move in with tide following bait. Occasional barramundi in holes
2. Yabbie beds inside mouth, fish flats on incoming tide for whiting, flathead.
3. Channels on inland of islands hold salmon, jacks, barra.
4. Jacks in brackish reaches at top, move up with the tide.
5. Water between two rock patches called The Gateway, fish move into deep water on falling tide.
6. Rocks at mouth of Tanti Creek fish on outgoing tide for jacks, barra, salmon. Hole near rocks has salmon. Further upstream towards fork of Tanti Creek are rocky patches with jacks.
7. Whiting, flathead and nippers on flats at mouth of creek
8. Deep holes along north-eastern bank: grunter, salmon, barra and jacks
9. Small creeks along west bank with deep holes and scattered rock and mud. Cod, barra, jacks around rocks.
10. Prawns in Good Friday Creek about Jan/Feb. Prawns move out of creek on full moon early in the year. They gather in creeks days before the full moon.
11. Good fishing off point - pelagic, reef and estuary fish. Spotted and school mackerel around the Easter.
12. Mud crabs, jacks, salmon.

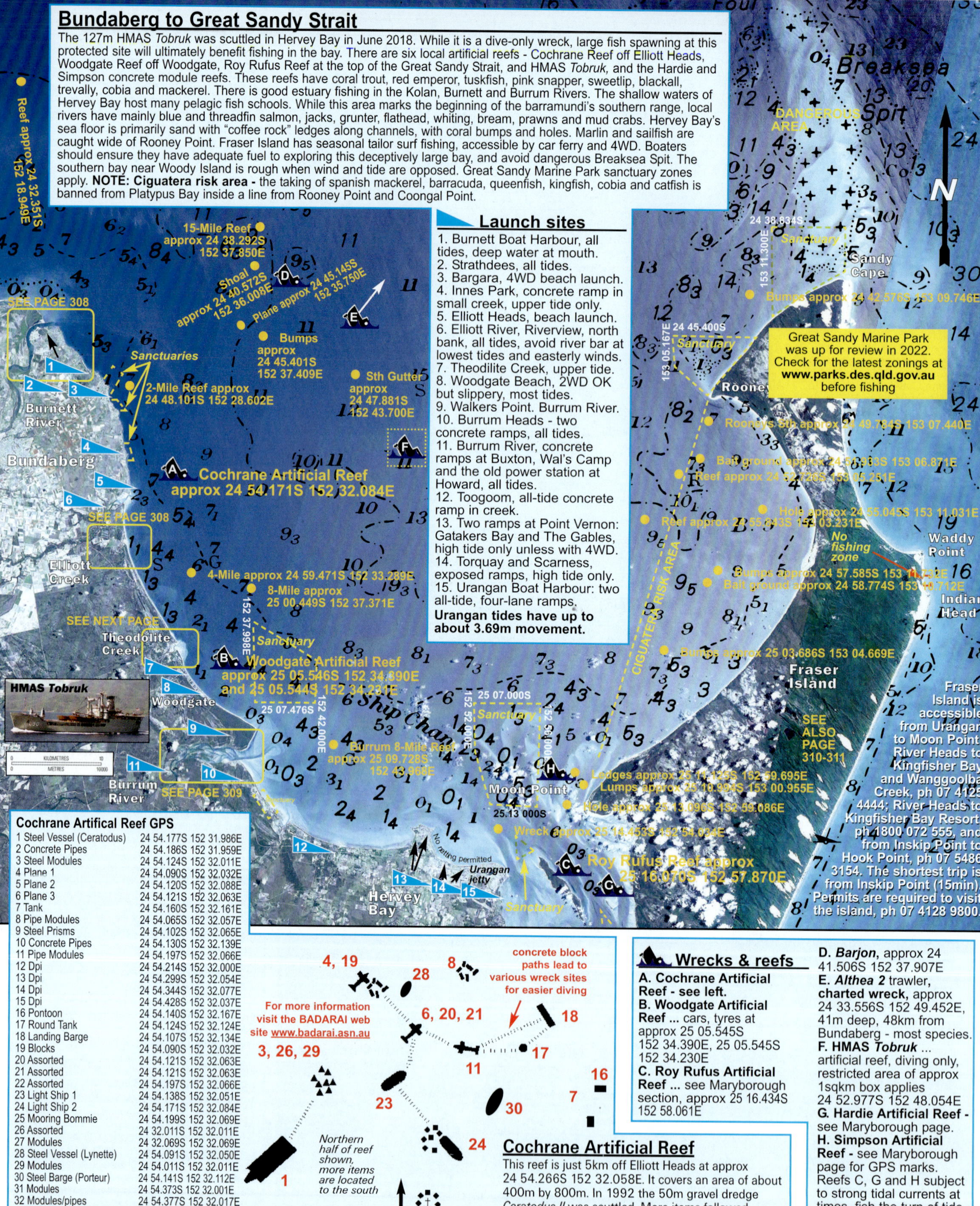

Bundaberg to Great Sandy Strait

The 127m HMAS *Tobruk* was scuttled in Hervey Bay in June 2018. While it is a dive-only wreck, large fish spawning at this protected site will ultimately benefit fishing in the bay. There are six local artificial reefs - Cochrane Reef off Elliott Heads, Woodgate Reef off Woodgate, Roy Rufus Reef at the top of the Great Sandy Strait, and HMAS *Tobruk*, and the Hardie and Simpson concrete module reefs. These reefs have coral trout, red emperor, tuskfish, pink snapper, sweetlip, blackall, trevally, cobia and mackerel. There is good estuary fishing in the Kolan, Burnett and Burrum Rivers. The shallow waters of Hervey Bay host many pelagic fish schools. While this area marks the beginning of the barramundi's southern range, local rivers have mainly blue and threadfin salmon, jacks, grunter, flathead, whiting, bream, prawns and mud crabs. Hervey Bay's sea floor is primarily sand with "coffee rock" ledges along channels, with coral bumps and holes. Marlin and sailfish are caught wide of Rooney Point. Fraser Island has seasonal tailor surf fishing, accessible by car ferry and 4WD. Boaters should ensure they have adequate fuel to exploring this deceptively large bay, and avoid dangerous Breaksea Spit. The southern bay near Woody Island is rough when wind and tide are opposed. Great Sandy Marine Park sanctuary zones apply. **NOTE: Ciguatera risk area -** the taking of spanish mackerel, barracuda, queenfish, kingfish, cobia and catfish is banned from Platypus Bay inside a line from Rooney Point and Coongal Point.

Launch sites

1. Burnett Boat Harbour, all tides, deep water at mouth.
2. Strathdees, all tides.
3. Bargara, 4WD beach launch.
4. Innes Park, concrete ramp in small creek, upper tide only.
5. Elliott Heads, beach launch.
6. Elliott River, Riverview, north bank, all tides, avoid river bar at lowest tides and easterly winds.
7. Theodolite Creek, upper tide.
8. Woodgate Beach, 2WD OK but slippery, most tides.
9. Walkers Point. Burrum River.
10. Burrum Heads - two concrete ramps, all tides.
11. Burrum River, concrete ramps at Buxton, Wal's Camp and the old power station at Howard, all tides.
12. Toogoom, all-tide concrete ramp in creek.
13. Two ramps at Point Vernon: Gatakers Bay and The Gables, high tide only unless with 4WD.
14. Torquay and Scarness, exposed ramps, high tide only.
15. Urangan Boat Harbour: two all-tide, four-lane ramps.

Urangan tides have up to about 3.69m movement.

Great Sandy Marine Park was up for review in 2022. Check for the latest zonings at **www.parks.des.qld.gov.au** before fishing

Fraser Island is accessible from Urangan to Moon Point; River Heads to Kingfisher Bay and Wanggoolba Creek, ph 07 4125 4444; River Heads to Kingfisher Bay Resort, ph 1800 072 555, and from Inskip Point to Hook Point, ph 07 5486 3154. The shortest trip is from Inskip Point (15min). Permits are required to visit the island, ph 07 4128 9800.

Cochrane Artifical Reef GPS

1 Steel Vessel (Ceratodus)	24 54.177S 152 31.986E
2 Concrete Pipes	24 54.186S 152 31.959E
3 Steel Modules	24 54.124S 152 32.011E
4 Plane 1	24 54.090S 152 32.032E
5 Plane 2	24 54.120S 152 32.088E
6 Plane 3	24 54.121S 152 32.063E
7 Tank	24 54.160S 152 32.161E
8 Pipe Modules	24 54.065S 152 32.057E
9 Steel Prisms	24 54.102S 152 32.065E
10 Concrete Pipes	24 54.130S 152 32.139E
11 Pipe Modules	24 54.197S 152 32.066E
12 Dpi	24 54.214S 152 32.000E
13 Dpi	24 54.299S 152 32.054E
14 Dpi	24 54.344S 152 32.077E
15 Dpi	24 54.428S 152 32.037E
16 Pontoon	24 54.140S 152 32.167E
17 Round Tank	24 54.124S 152 32.124E
18 Landing Barge	24 54.107S 152 32.134E
19 Blocks	24 54.090S 152 32.032E
20 Assorted	24 54.121S 152 32.063E
21 Assorted	24 54.121S 152 32.063E
22 Assorted	24 54.197S 152 32.066E
23 Light Ship 1	24 54.138S 152 32.051E
24 Light Ship 2	24 54.171S 152 32.084E
25 Mooring Bommie	24 54.199S 152 32.069E
26 Assorted	24 32.011S 152 32.011E
27 Modules	24 32.069S 152 32.069E
28 Steel Vessel (Lynette)	24 54.091S 152 32.050E
29 Modules	24 54.011S 152 32.011E
30 Steel Barge (Porteur)	24 54.141S 152 32.112E
31 Modules	24 54.373S 152 32.001E
32 Modules/pipes	24 54.377S 152 32.017E
33 Steel Vessel (Nirvana)	24 54.370S 152 32.032E
34 Balmers Bommie 1	24 54.354S 152 32.077E
35 Modules	24 54.357S 152 32.060E
36 Modules	24 54.345S 152 32.110E
37 Modules	24 54.381S 152 32.089E

4, 19
28
8
concrete block paths lead to various wreck sites for easier diving
For more information visit the BADARAI web site www.badarai.asn.au
6, 20, 21
18
3, 26, 29
11
17
16
7
23
30
24
1
Northern half of reef shown, more items are located to the south
N
11, 22, 25, 27
12

Cochrane Artificial Reef

This reef is just 5km off Elliott Heads at approx 24 54.266S 152 32.058E. It covers an area of about 400m by 800m. In 1992 the 50m gravel dredge *Ceratodus II* was scuttled. More items followed, including planes, two Fraser Island lightships, barges, concrete and steel modules, and pipes. Many fish visit and live on the reef, including huge groper, making it a valuable dive and fishing site.

Wrecks & reefs

A. Cochrane Artificial Reef - see left.

B. Woodgate Artificial Reef ... cars, tyres at approx 25 05.545S 152 34.390E, 25 05.545S 152 34.230E

C. Roy Rufus Artificial Reef ... see Maryborough section, approx 25 16.434S 152 58.061E

D. *Barjon*, approx 24 41.506S 152 37.907E

E. *Althea 2* trawler, **charted wreck,** approx 24 33.556S 152 49.452E, 41m deep, 48km from Bundaberg - most species.

F. HMAS *Tobruk* ... artificial reef, diving only, restricted area of approx 1sqkm box applies 24 52.977S 152 48.054E

G. Hardie Artificial Reef - see Maryborough page.

H. Simpson Artificial Reef - see Maryborough page for GPS marks.

Reefs C, G and H subject to strong tidal currents at times, fish the turn of tide.

OFF MAP. MV *Karma* barge, 26m deep, 18.5km n-e Baffle Creek, approx 24 23.877S 152 11.049E.

This creek is south of Bundaberg and just 9km north of Baffle Creek. The northern end follows Deepwater Rd. Whiting, bream, flathead, jacks, trevally and queenfish are the main catch.

Stocked dams

Lake Gregory near Bundaberg is a small bass fishery, with 50cm+ fish caught regularly. It also has saratoga. See page 302. Lake Monduran, on the Kolan River, is renowned for its big barramundi. It is affected by drought and floods, so check status before fishing. Some fish escape into the Kolan River and spread out along the coast. See Page 379 for more info.

Bundaberg fishing seasons

Garfish and trevally are all year. **Bream** are best in winter. **Flathead** are all year, best in early summer. **Summer whiting** between September-May, best on spring tides. **Winter whiting** from May to June. **Queenfish** from October to May. **Tuna** between March and May. **Spotted and grey mackerel** start spring, with **spaniards** best from Dec-May but available all year. **School mackerel** best in August. **Jewfish, grunter** all year, best after floods. **Herring (baitfish) and squid** all year. **Barra** in warm weather. **Blue salmon** best in winter. **Banana prawns** at Burnett River mouth from Nov-Apr. **Threadfin** all year, best in summer. **Mud and sand crabs** from Dec-Apr. **Pink snapper** March-May. **Red emperor, sweetlip and coral trout** all year.

Woodgate

This town is on the Bruce Hwy about half way between Gin Gin and Maryborough. It is relatively protected by Fraser Island. There is a ramp inside Thedolite Creek (A) and on The Esplanade (B). Woodgate is known for whiting, but mud and sand crabs, queenfish, flathead and bream are caught from boat and beach, with mackerel and reef fish are on Woodgate Artificial Reef. One Mile Reef runs along coast to north.Accommodation is at the local van park and motel. There are national park camps 8km south on Walkers Point Rd.
HOTSPOTS: 1 & 2. Whiting, bream and flathead in low-tide holes and on flats edges. 2. Big whiting in upper creek holes 3. Bream, jacks, mud crabs.

Key to Map

Hotspots

1. Good fish on tree stumps near Kolan River mouth. Big flathead in Sept/Oct on pilchards/mullet. Whiting.
2. Mangrove jacks and grunter.
3. Prawns, mud crabs.
4. Prawns, mud crabs in mangrove estuary. Booyan Bridge has bait around pylons, also salmon, jacks, bream, grunter, flathead.
5. Jacks, barra in upper reaches.
6. Beach fishing: queenfish, whiting, bream, flathead, trevally. Big flathead and crabs in Moore Park Creek.
7. Burnett River has a deep all-weather channel. Rock walls and wharves inside mouth have salmon, grunter, jewfish, cod, trevally, winter bream.
8. Threadfin and blue salmon. Prawns reliable in Rubyana Creek.
9. Rocky area - barra, jacks, flathead. Bream in winter. Prawns at Splitters Creek mouth. Downstream near rail bridge bream, salmon, jewfish.
10. Barramundi, salmon.
11. Upstream reaches - barra, jacks.
12. Rock fishing - easy access along most foreshore for range of species.
13. Elliott River has rock island near mouth. Tailor, mackerel around rocks. Jacks and more upstream at Shark's Nest. Jacks in upper reaches. Cochrane Artificial Reef 5km offshore.
14. Whiting, flathead. Jacks upstream. Reef fish, mackerel at One Mile Reef.

Launch sites

1. Miara Caravan Park, upper tide.
2. Concrete ramp, all tides.
3. Ramp near barrage, upper tide.
4. Burnett Heads Boat Harbour, all tides.
5. Strathdees, River Rd, all tides.
6. Edina St, all tides.
6a. Sharon, Rustic Rd.
6b. Branyan, Sandy Hook Rd, multi-lanes, picnic area.
7. Bargara, 4WD launch, Burkitt St.
8. Innes Park, concrete ramp in small creek, upper tide only.
9. Elliott Heads, upper tide beach launch.
10. Elliott River, Riverview, north bank, Peagam St, all tides, avoid bar at low tides and easterly wind.
11. Fairymead Rd, multi-lanes.
12. Kalkie ramp, McGills Rd, multi-lanes, picnic area.

The Jack Coast

The creeks of the Bundaberg coast are mostly sandy and have reasonably clear water. As the aerial pictures show, they largely drain out at low tide, leaving channels, holes and a sandbar at the mouth. These creeks are known for jacks, as well as threadfin and blue salmon, queenfish, dart, bream, flathead, whiting and occasional barra. The clear water requires careful presentation of lures and baits on light leaders.

Key to Map (Elliott River)

Hotspots

1. 3-Mile Reef and Cochrane Artificial Reef offshore: mackerel in September, best early morning - also cod, sweetlip, trout.
2. Trolling around rocks at mouth best at turn of bottom of tide at dawn for queenfish, mackerel and reef fish including pink snapper.
3. About 1km out from Coonarr Creek mouth is a rubble bottom that holds pink snapper.
4. Deep hole along bend called Sharks Nest: popular fishing spot, jacks, bream, cod, salmon.
5. Fish nipper beds for whiting on incoming tide.

Launch sites

1. Beach launch. 2. Sealed ramp, all tides.

Key to Map (Burnett River)

Hotspots

1. Shoal 13km out, approx 24 38.704 152 23.384E.
2. Dredge spoil grounds at 24 43.616S 152 26.223E and 24 42.158S 152 28.367E, 4km and 9km from mouth respectively. Move around to find patches. Mackerel in Sept/Oct. Rises on Aus 818 chart further out at 24 41.529S 152 34.294E and 24 40.517S 152 36.057E, 18.5km and 22km respectively.
3. Winter bream on rock walls. Light boats can be pulled over wall into adjacent estuary, good for prawns in Feb/Mar, also jacks, whiting, flathead, bream.
4. Big barra and threadfin salmon near wharf.
5. Deep water south of ferry crossing holds jewfish, blue salmon, threadfin, barra, cod, jacks.
6. Deep water along north bank holds big bream in winter, also blue salmon, threadfin, jacks, cod, barra.
7. Kirbys Wall: manmade rock wall good for bream, cod, jacks, blue salmon, crabs.

Launch sites

1. Two ramps at Burnett Heads Boat Harbour.
2. Ramp on Strathdees Rd, off Port Road.
3. Off Fairymead Rd, good ramp with parking.
4. Bundaberg town ramps upstream.

Key to Map (Litabella Creek)

Hotspots

Good crabbing and fishing throughout Litabella Creek. Access is only available by sea or by gaining permission to traverse private property.

1. Jacks, flathead along deep edges.
2. Jacks, bream, salmon, barra in holes.
3. Jacks, bream, salmon, barra in holes.
4. Cod, jacks, barra on rock patches. Mud crabs.

Key to Map (Kolan River)

Hotspots

The Kolan River mouth is a good spot for flathead, with many big ones caught.

1. Drive on beach from Moore Park by 4WD. Fish drop-off, dart, flathead, queenfish, whiting.
2. Fish gutters on outgoing tide for flathead.
3. Mangrove jacks, mud crabs and flathead.
4. Barramundi along gutter on run-out tide.
5. Bridge pylons have jacks, trevally, flathead.

Launch sites

1. Miara Caravan Park.
2. Baillies Road, off Booyan Road.

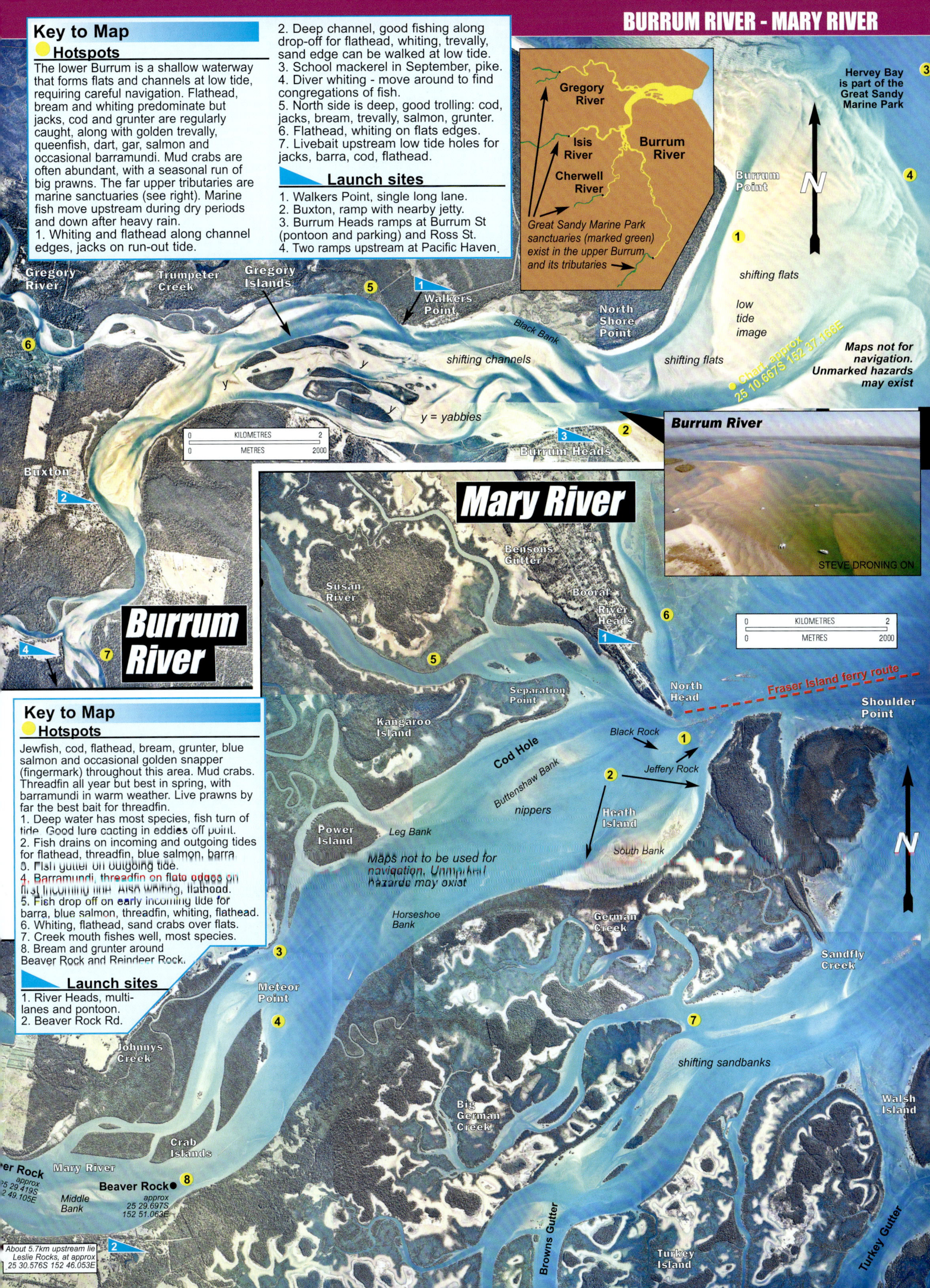
Key to Map
Hotspots
The lower Burrum is a shallow waterway that forms flats and channels at low tide, requiring careful navigation. Flathead, bream and whiting predominate but jacks, cod and grunter are regularly caught, along with golden trevally, queenfish, dart, gar, salmon and occasional barramundi. Mud crabs are often abundant, with a seasonal run of big prawns. The far upper tributaries are marine sanctuaries (see right). Marine fish move upstream during dry periods and down after heavy rain.
1. Whiting and flathead along channel edges, jacks on run-out tide.
2. Deep channel, good fishing along drop-off for flathead, whiting, trevally, sand edge can be walked at low tide.
3. School mackerel in September, pike.
4. Diver whiting - move around to find congregations of fish.
5. North side is deep, good trolling: cod, jacks, bream, trevally, salmon, grunter.
6. Flathead, whiting on flats edges.
7. Livebait upstream low tide holes for jacks, barra, cod, flathead.
Launch sites
1. Walkers Point, single long lane.
2. Buxton, ramp with nearby jetty.
3. Burrum Heads ramps at Burrum St (pontoon and parking) and Ross St.
4. Two ramps upstream at Pacific Haven.
Gregory River
Isis River
Cherwell River
Burrum River
Great Sandy Marine Park sanctuaries (marked green) exist in the upper Burrum and its tributaries
Hervey Bay is part of the Great Sandy Marine Park
Burrum Point
N
shifting flats
low tide image
Maps not for navigation. Unmarked hazards may exist
Chart approx 25 10.667S 152 37.166E
Gregory River
Trumpeter Creek
Gregory Islands
Walkers Point
Black Bank
North Shore Point
shifting channels
shifting flats
y = yabbies
Burrum Heads
Buxton
Burrum River
Burrum River
STEVE DRONING ON
Mary River
Bensons Gutter
Booral
River Heads
Susan River
Separation Point
North Head
Fraser Island ferry route
Shoulder Point
Kangaroo Island
Cod Hole
Buttenshaw Bank
Black Rock
Jeffery Rock
nippers
Heath Island
South Bank
Power Island
Leg Bank
Maps not to be used for navigation. Unmarked Hazards may exist
Horseshoe Bank
German Creek
Sandfly Creek
N
Key to Map
Hotspots
Jewfish, cod, flathead, bream, grunter, blue salmon and occasional golden snapper (fingermark) throughout this area. Mud crabs. Threadfin all year but best in spring, with barramundi in warm weather. Live prawns by far the best bait for threadfin.
1. Deep water has most species, fish turn of tide. Good lure casting in eddies off point.
2. Fish drains on incoming and outgoing tides for flathead, threadfin, blue salmon, barra.
3. Fish gutter on outgoing tide.
4. Barramundi, threadfin on flats edges on first incoming tide. Also whiting, flathead.
5. Fish drop off on early incoming tide for barra, blue salmon, threadfin, whiting, flathead.
6. Whiting, flathead, sand crabs over flats.
7. Creek mouth fishes well, most species.
8. Bream and grunter around Beaver Rock and Reindeer Rock.
Launch sites
1. River Heads, multi-lanes and pontoon.
2. Beaver Rock Rd.
Meteor Point
Johnnys Creek
shifting sandbanks
Walsh Island
Big German Creek
Crab Islands
Mary River
Beaver Rock
approx 25 29.697S 152 51.063E
Middle Bank
About 5.7km upstream lie Leslie Rocks, at approx 25 30.576S 152 46.053E
Browns Gutter
Turkey Island
Turkey Gutter

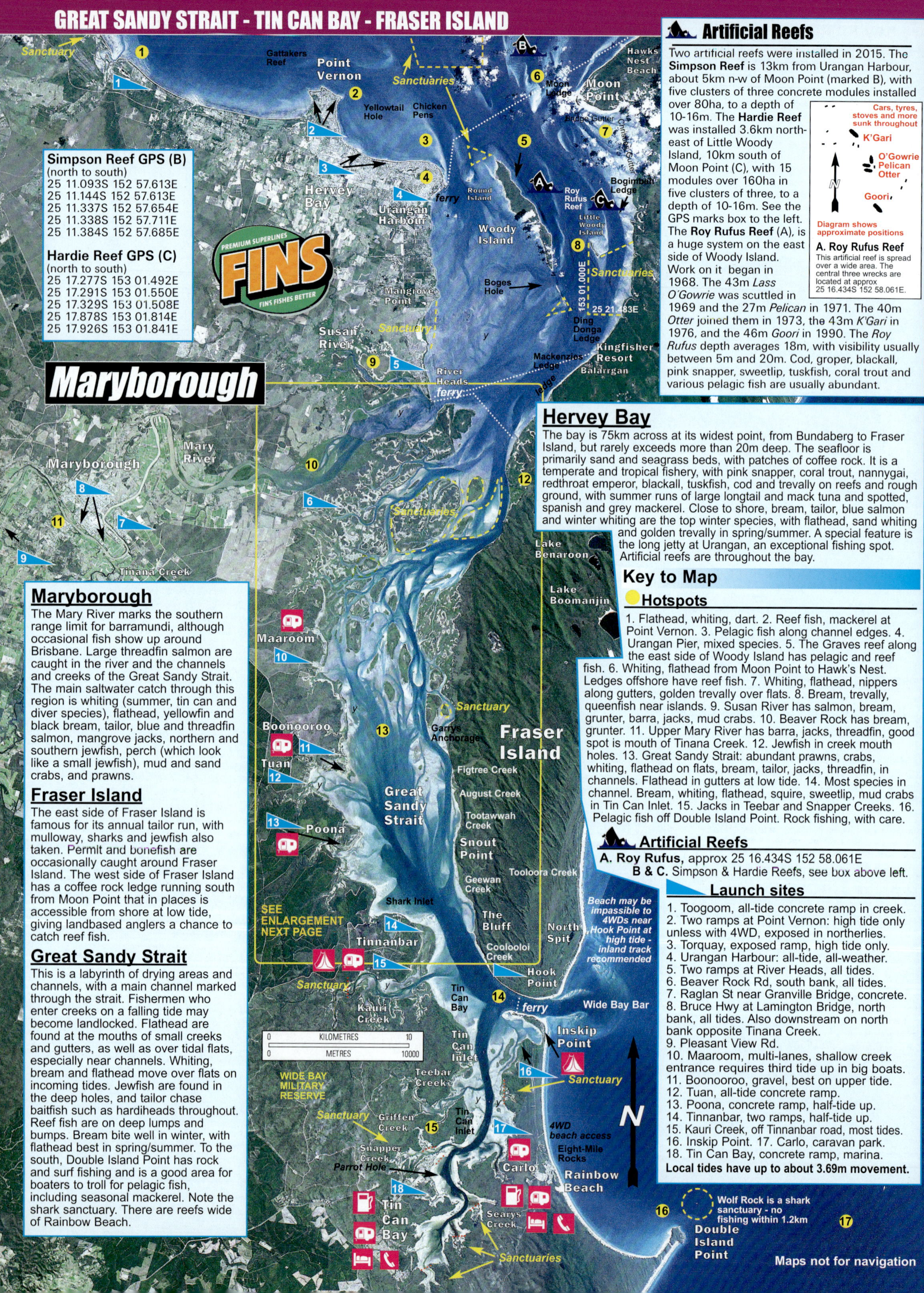

Simpson Reef GPS (B)
(north to south)
25 11.093S 152 57.613E
25 11.144S 152 57.613E
25 11.337S 152 57.654E
25 11.338S 152 57.711E
25 11.384S 152 57.685E

Hardie Reef GPS (C)
(north to south)
25 17.277S 153 01.492E
25 17.291S 153 01.550E
25 17.329S 153 01.508E
25 17.878S 153 01.814E
25 17.926S 153 01.841E

Artificial Reefs

Two artificial reefs were installed in 2015. The **Simpson Reef** is 13km from Urangan Harbour, about 5km n-w of Moon Point (marked B), with five clusters of three concrete modules installed over 80ha, to a depth of 10-16m. The **Hardie Reef** was installed 3.6km north-east of Little Woody Island, 10km south of Moon Point (C), with 15 modules over 160ha in five clusters of three, to a depth of 10-16m. See the GPS marks box to the left. The **Roy Rufus Reef** (A), is a huge system on the east side of Woody Island. Work on it began in 1968. The 43m *Lass O'Gowrie* was scuttled in 1969 and the 27m *Pelican* in 1971. The 40m *Otter* joined them in 1973, the 43m *K'Gari* in 1976, and the 46m *Goori* in 1990. The *Roy Rufus* depth averages 18m, with visibility usually between 5m and 20m. Cod, groper, blackall, pink snapper, sweetlip, tuskfish, coral trout and various pelagic fish are usually abundant.

A. Roy Rufus Reef
This artificial reef is spread over a wide area. The central three wrecks are located at approx 25 16.434S 152 58.061E.

Hervey Bay

The bay is 75km across at its widest point, from Bundaberg to Fraser Island, but rarely exceeds more than 20m deep. The seafloor is primarily sand and seagrass beds, with patches of coffee rock. It is a temperate and tropical fishery, with pink snapper, coral trout, nannygai, redthroat emperor, blackall, tuskfish, cod and trevally on reefs and rough ground, with summer runs of large longtail and mack tuna and spotted, spanish and grey mackerel. Close to shore, bream, tailor, blue salmon and winter whiting are the top winter species, with flathead, sand whiting and golden trevally in spring/summer. A special feature is the long jetty at Urangan, an exceptional fishing spot. Artificial reefs are throughout the bay.

Key to Map

Hotspots

1. Flathead, whiting, dart. 2. Reef fish, mackerel at Point Vernon. 3. Pelagic fish along channel edges. 4. Urangan Pier, mixed species. 5. The Graves reef along the east side of Woody Island has pelagic and reef fish. 6. Whiting, flathead from Moon Point to Hawk's Nest. Ledges offshore have reef fish. 7. Whiting, flathead, nippers along gutters, golden trevally over flats. 8. Bream, trevally, queenfish near islands. 9. Susan River has salmon, bream, grunter, barra, jacks, mud crabs. 10. Beaver Rock has bream, grunter. 11. Upper Mary River has barra, jacks, threadfin, good spot is mouth of Tinana Creek. 12. Jewfish in creek mouth holes. 13. Great Sandy Strait: abundant prawns, crabs, whiting, flathead on flats, bream, tailor, jacks, threadfin, in channels. Flathead in gutters at low tide. 14. Most species in channel. Bream, whiting, flathead, squire, sweetlip, mud crabs in Tin Can Inlet. 15. Jacks in Teebar and Snapper Creeks. 16. Pelagic fish off Double Island Point. Rock fishing, with care.

Artificial Reefs

A. Roy Rufus, approx 25 16.434S 152 58.061E
B & C. Simpson & Hardie Reefs, see box above left.

Launch sites

1. Toogoom, all-tide concrete ramp in creek.
2. Two ramps at Point Vernon: high tide only unless with 4WD, exposed in northerlies.
3. Torquay, exposed ramp, high tide only.
4. Urangan Harbour: all-tide, all-weather.
5. Two ramps at River Heads, all tides.
6. Beaver Rock Rd, south bank, all tides.
7. Raglan St near Granville Bridge, concrete.
8. Bruce Hwy at Lamington Bridge, on north bank, all tides. Also downstream on north bank opposite Tinana Creek.
9. Pleasant View Rd.
10. Maaroom, multi-lanes, shallow creek entrance requires third tide up in big boats.
11. Boonooroo, gravel, best on upper tide.
12. Tuan, all-tide concrete ramp.
13. Poona, concrete ramp, half-tide up.
14. Tinnanbar, two ramps, half-tide up.
15. Kauri Creek, off Tinnanbar road, most tides.
16. Inskip Point. 17. Carlo, caravan park.
18. Tin Can Bay, concrete ramp, marina.

Local tides have up to about 3.69m movement.

Maryborough

The Mary River marks the southern range limit for barramundi, although occasional fish show up around Brisbane. Large threadfin salmon are caught in the river and the channels and creeks of the Great Sandy Strait. The main saltwater catch through this region is whiting (summer, tin can and diver species), flathead, yellowfin and black bream, tailor, blue and threadfin salmon, mangrove jacks, northern and southern jewfish, perch (which look like a small jewfish), mud and sand crabs, and prawns.

Fraser Island

The east side of Fraser Island is famous for its annual tailor run, with mulloway, sharks and jewfish also taken. Permit and bonefish are occasionally caught around Fraser Island. The west side of Fraser Island has a coffee rock ledge running south from Moon Point that in places is accessible from shore at low tide, giving landbased anglers a chance to catch reef fish.

Great Sandy Strait

This is a labyrinth of drying areas and channels, with a main channel marked through the strait. Fishermen who enter creeks on a falling tide may become landlocked. Flathead are found at the mouths of small creeks and gutters, as well as over tidal flats, and especially near channels. Whiting, bream and flathead move over flats on incoming tides. Jewfish are found in the deep holes, and tailor chase baitfish such as hardiheads throughout. Reef fish are on deep lumps and bumps. Bream bite well in winter, with flathead best in spring/summer. To the south, Double Island Point has rock and surf fishing and is a good area for boaters to troll for pelagic fish, including seasonal mackerel. Note the shark sanctuary. There are reefs wide of Rainbow Beach.

Hotspots

1. Island ledge: Coral bream, tailor, blackall, barra, jacks, grunter, cod.
2. Jewfish over deep reef, slack tide.
3. Whiting, flathead, golden trevally.
4. Bream, flatheads, mud crabs.
5. Whiting, flathead on flats edges.

Fraser Island
INDEFINITE LEAVE

Closed waters

Waters and shore between 400m north of Waddy Point and 400m south of Indian Head are closed to fishing from noon August 1 to noon September 30 each year

Maps not for navigation

Best surf fishing is dawn and dusk, but tailor will bite both day and night in good conditions

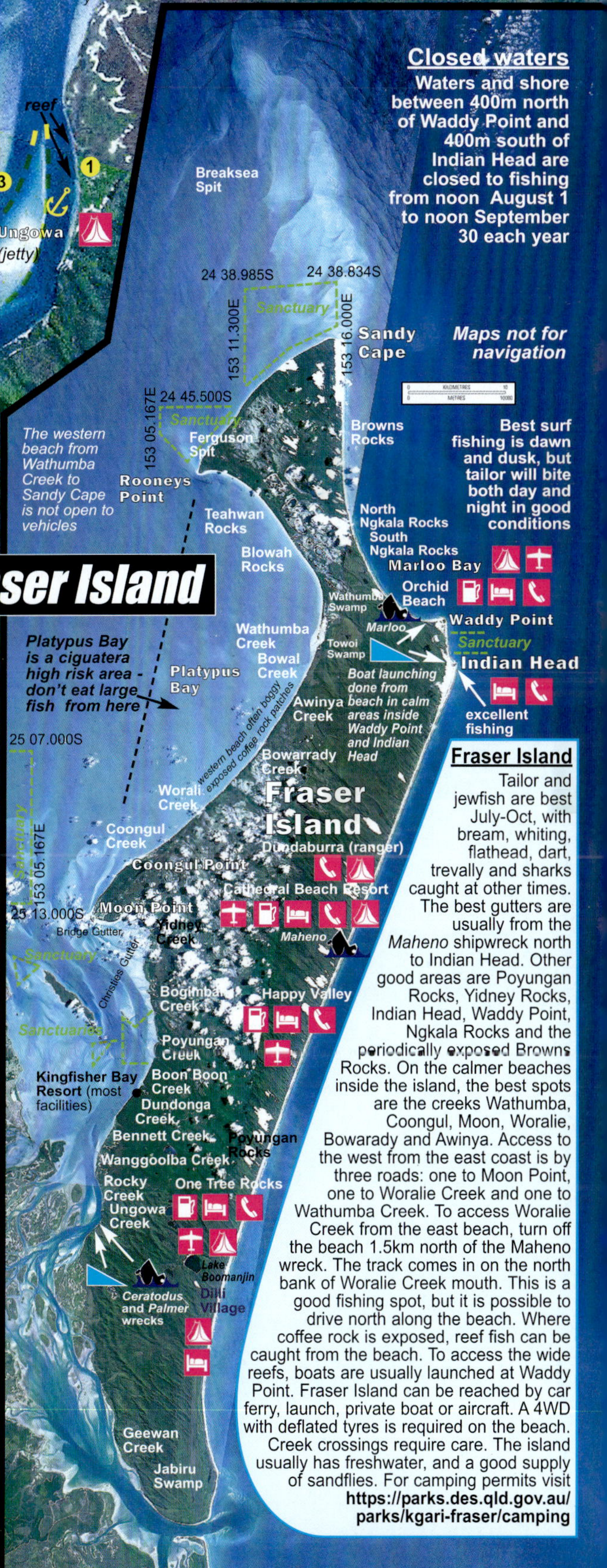

The western beach from Wathumba Creek to Sandy Cape is not open to vehicles

Platypus Bay is a ciguatera high risk area - don't eat large fish from here

Boat launching done from beach in calm areas inside Waddy Point and Indian Head

excellent fishing

Launch sites on previous page

Great Sandy Marine Park was up for review in 2022. Check for the latest zonings at **www.parks.des.qld.gov.au** before fishing

Fraser Island

Fraser Island

Tailor and jewfish are best July-Oct, with bream, whiting, flathead, dart, trevally and sharks caught at other times. The best gutters are usually from the *Maheno* shipwreck north to Indian Head. Other good areas are Poyungan Rocks, Yidney Rocks, Indian Head, Waddy Point, Ngkala Rocks and the periodically exposed Browns Rocks. On the calmer beaches inside the island, the best spots are the creeks Wathumba, Coongul, Moon, Woralie, Bowarady and Awinya. Access to the west from the east coast is by three roads: one to Moon Point, one to Woralie Creek and one to Wathumba Creek. To access Woralie Creek from the east beach, turn off the beach 1.5km north of the Maheno wreck. The track comes in on the north bank of Woralie Creek mouth. This is a good fishing spot, but it is possible to drive north along the beach. Where coffee rock is exposed, reef fish can be caught from the beach. To access the wide reefs, boats are usually launched at Waddy Point. Fraser Island can be reached by car ferry, launch, private boat or aircraft. A 4WD with deflated tyres is required on the beach. Creek crossings require care. The island usually has freshwater, and a good supply of sandflies. For camping permits visit **https://parks.des.qld.gov.au/parks/kgari-fraser/camping**

NOOSA RIVER - LAKE COROIBA - LAKE COOTHARABA

Noosa

The tidal estuary is best known for whiting, flathead and bream, but it also has tailor, mulloway, threadfin salmon, mangrove jacks and bass. Shallow Lake Cootharaba and the upper Noosa River have bass, with most fish taken above the mouth of Lake Cootharaba. The area accessible by 4WD from Harry's Hut (1) or by water from Boreen Point has long been a drawcard for Brisbane fishermen. This is part of Great Sandy National Park's Cooloola Recreation Area. There are several campsites north of Harry's Hut. Visit https://parks.des.qld.gov.au/parks/cooloola/ for site details. Camping permits must be booked in advance. The deep channels through the lakes (2, 5) have bream, whiting, flathead, tailor, school mulloway, jacks and luderick. Threadfin salmon are caught in the channel that links Lake Cootharaba and Cooroiba (3), and large prawns are a regular catch in the same area. A popular spot is the deep hole on the first bend heading north (4) after Lake Coroiba. There is another hole further north opposite the camping area near John's Landing. Lake Coroiba (5) has flathead and whiting, while the lower Noosa River (6) has most species on a seasonal basis - mangrove jacks and whiting are best in summer, bream and tailor are best in winter. Teewah Beach (7) can be accessed by 4WD after catching the Tewantin Ferry to the north bank and then driving down Maximillian Road and The Cutting. The beach offers good fishing in the ever-changing gutters for bream, tailor, dart, whiting and occasional mulloway. Noosa Head (8 - see next page) has some deepwater rock fishing platforms where tailor, kingfish and large mulloway are taken, and the associated beaches fish well for bream, dart, mulloway and tailor in season. Mackerel schools visit the area in summer.

Offshore

Noosa Bar is constantly shifting and crossings must be done with care, best on the top of the tide. Noosa has several reefs within 5km, and another set of reefs about 15km out. A mix of tropical and temperate species is caught on a seasonal basis, including coral trout, cobia, sweetlip, red emperor, cod, snapper, tuskfish, yellowfin tuna and spanish mackerel. Small black marlin visit the reefs.

Launch sites

1. Canoe launching.
2. Canoe launching.
3. Ramp at Boreen Point.
4. John's Landing - private.
5. Doonella St, Tewantin.
6. Two Noosaville ramps in Gympie Tce.

Far offshore GPS

*Barwon North, 35m, 46km from bar, approx 26 28.170S 153 32.247E

*17m steel trawler wreck, position approx 26 17.970S 153 43.502E, 61km e-n-e of Noosa Head.

Ciguatera

This is poisoning from eating tropical sea fish that have become toxic. It is quite common in Australia, but can be avoided. Ciguatoxin is well known in three areas, being southern Queensland between Caloundra and Bustard Head, particularly in Hervey Bay; between Bowen and Port Douglas; and in the Northern Territory near Nhulunbuy and Groote Eylandt. It can occur elsewhere. The narrow-barred or spanish mackerel is often responsible in southern Queensland, but many reef fish can carry it, including coral trout. Toxic fish seem to be more prevalent in an area after a big storm, such as when a cyclone has disturbed the seabed, possibly because the organism that creates the toxin thrives on newly exposed surfaces. To avoid ciguatera, eat only a small fish portion (30g or less) at the first serving. It is wise to not eat large fish, but small fish can cause poisoning. Some people test fish on a cat or dog by feeding it first and waiting 12 hours, but this is inhumane. Symptoms include nausea, vomiting, diarrhoea, abdominal cramps, altered pulse, reduced blood pressure, headache, itching, temperature reversal, and more. Seek medical help if symptoms appear. The poison is stored in body tissues and sufferers can be sensitive to a second dose.

Noosa River entrance

Noosa

Beach and rock fishermen can find a sheltered spot around the headland in most conditions. Hells Gate and Devils Kitchen give access to deep water for those who can safely negotiate the rocks from the access path. Fishing within the Noosa estuary tends to be better after storms, when the water is discoloured. When the water is clear, fish at night and use light tackle and the freshest baits, such as live nippers.

Hotspots

1. Munna Beach and sandspit best on falling tide for whiting, flathead. Deep water near jetty has mulloway at night, turn of tide.
2. Munna Bridge holds baitfish and jacks, trevally, bream, tailor. Mulloway at night.
3. Fish drop-offs on run-out tide for flathead. Other species at night.
4. Lions Park has family fishing for bream, whiting. Other species at dusk and dawn.
5. Island side of Sheraton Bridge has bank fishing around the pylons for jacks, trevally, bream and cod.
6. Woods Spit has bream, whiting and flathead during the day and jewfish along the drop-off at night.
7. Walking track gives access to good water - best on falling tide.
8. River mouth has carpark with variety of fishing, best near high tide. Rock wall holds luderick, tailor and bream in winter. Whiting along foreshores and mulloway, bream and trevally in deeper water.
9. Rock wall has luderick, bream, big tailor and occasional mulloway. Best in morning and evening at high tide.
10. Whiting and flathead along edges of flats. Bream in deeper water.
11. Jacks and bream throughout canal system. Look for deeper holes and structure. Mud crabs always a chance. Bull sharks in all the canals.
12. Pylons around Weyba bridges hold most species. Easy bank access.
13. Little Cove is sheltered but popular with surfers. Fish for bream, flathead, dart and whiting at dusk and dawn on weekdays.
14. Sheltered rocks - bream, tailor.
15. Rocks drop into deep water - bream, tailor, kingfish and mulloway.
16. Winch Cove produces some reef fish, especially after prolonged rough weather, and mulloway/tailor.
17. The area from Fairy Pools to Hells Gate has deep water. Big mulloway, kingfish, trevally, cobia, sharks.
18. Difficult climb, but big fish are taken here on heavy gear.
19. Mulloway along deep beach/rocks.
20. Sunshine Beach gutters have dart, tailor, bream, whiting.

Key to Map

Launch sites

1. Two ramps in Gympie Tce.

Add about an hour to Main Beach tides for tide times inside estuary. Noosa tides have up to about 2.08m movement.

Borumba Dam

This 500ha impoundment is 11km from Imbil, just a 45-minute drive from Noosa. The dam is on a tributary of the Mary River. It has been stocked with yellowbelly, silver perch, mary river cod bass and saratoga. Saratoga have formed a breeding population. There is a camping area below the dam wall. The water is usually clear and the fish can be shy at times, but the fishing is usually quite good. This dam is well suited to fly fishing. The upper arms have plenty of submerged timber.

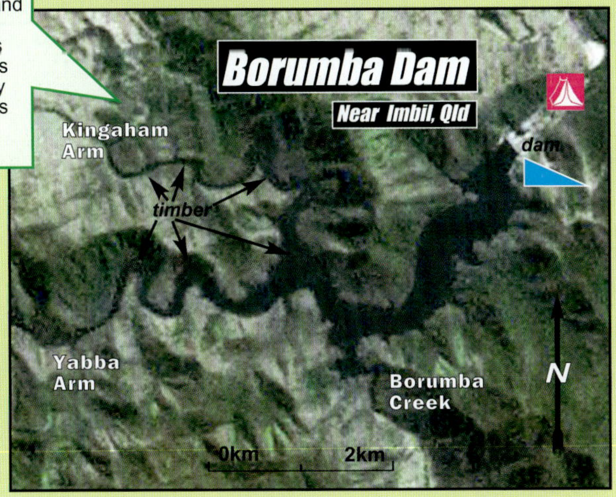

Borumba Dam
Near Imbil, Qld

26

Chardon's Reef approx 26 24.807S 153 13.049E

STEVE DRONING ON

Devil's Kitchen on the Noosa headland

22

Caloundra-Mooloolaba

Caloundra, at the northern end of Pumicestone Passage, has a headland and surf beaches. North of Caloundra there are rock platforms at Point Cartwright and Point Arkwright. South of Point Arkwright, Yaroomba Beach is one of the better spots, being sheltered from summer northerlies. Bream, dart, whiting and flathead are caught all year, with mulloway in the gutters and around the rocks. For boaters, the Mooloolah River has a safe entrance. Reef fishing out of Mooloolaba starts just 10 minutes away and extends to sea for 46km in patches, with snapper, pearl perch, cobia, yellowtail kingfish, sweetlip, mackerel and tuskfish. The rivers have whiting, flathead, bream and jacks. Occasional barramundi captures have been reported over the years.

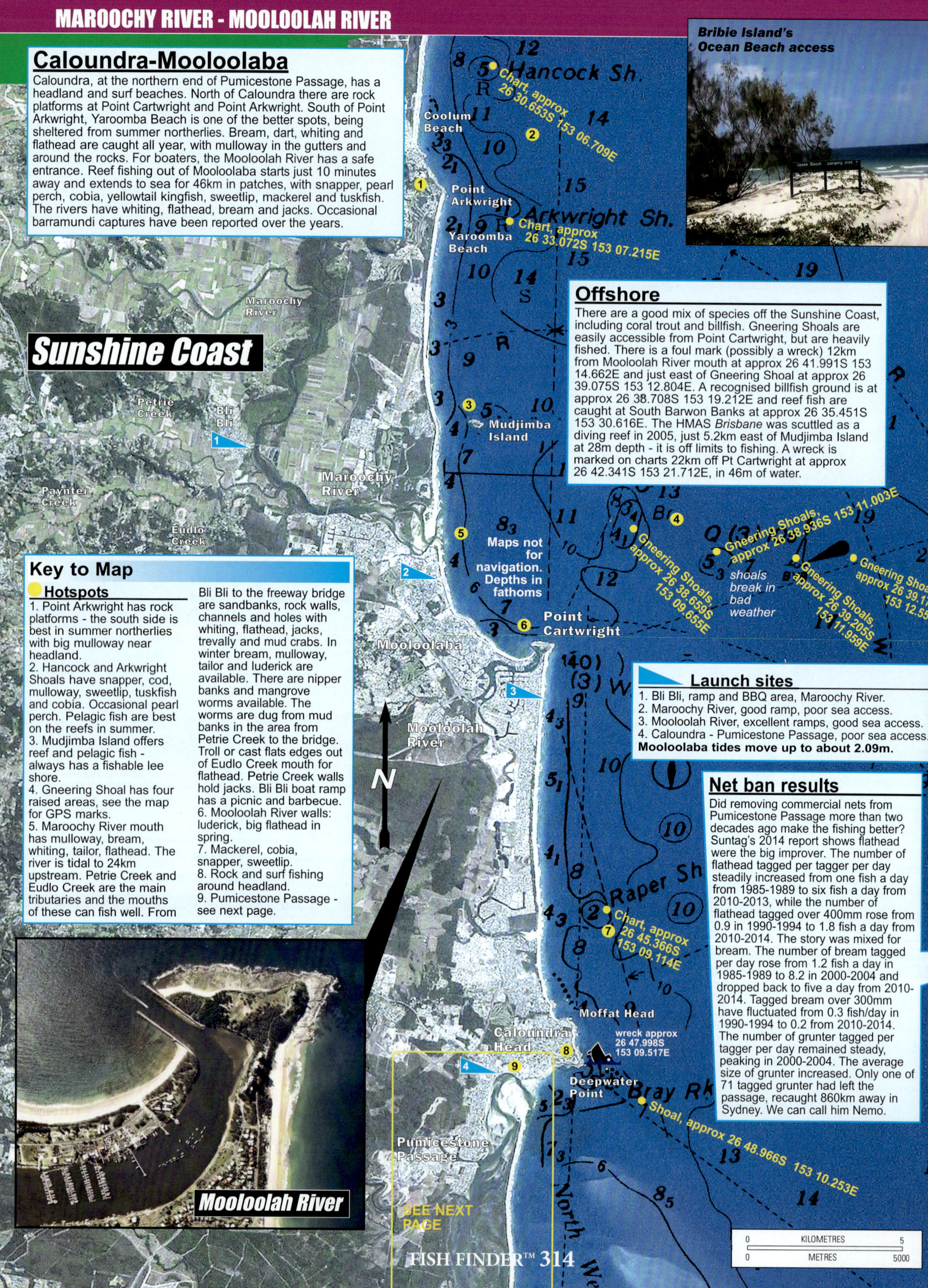

Offshore

There are a good mix of species off the Sunshine Coast, including coral trout and billfish. Gneering Shoals are easily accessible from Point Cartwright, but are heavily fished. There is a foul mark (possibly a wreck) 12km from Mooloolah River mouth at approx 26 41.991S 153 14.662E and just east of Gneering Shoal at approx 26 39.075S 153 12.804E. A recognised billfish ground is at approx 26 38.708S 153 19.212E and reef fish are caught at South Barwon Banks at approx 26 35.451S 153 30.616E. The HMAS *Brisbane* was scuttled as a diving reef in 2005, just 5.2km east of Mudjimba Island at 28m depth - it is off limits to fishing. A wreck is marked on charts 22km off Pt Cartwright at approx 26 42.341S 153 21.712E, in 46m of water.

Key to Map

Hotspots

1. Point Arkwright has rock platforms - the south side is best in summer northerlies with big mulloway near headland.
2. Hancock and Arkwright Shoals have snapper, cod, mulloway, sweetlip, tuskfish and cobia. Occasional pearl perch. Pelagic fish are best on the reefs in summer.
3. Mudjimba Island offers reef and pelagic fish - always has a fishable lee shore.
4. Gneering Shoal has four raised areas, see the map for GPS marks.
5. Maroochy River mouth has mulloway, bream, whiting, tailor, flathead. The river is tidal to 24km upstream. Petrie Creek and Eudlo Creek are the main tributaries and the mouths of these can fish well. From Bli Bli to the freeway bridge are sandbanks, rock walls, channels and holes with whiting, flathead, jacks, trevally and mud crabs. In winter bream, mulloway, tailor and luderick are available. There are nipper banks and mangrove worms available. The worms are dug from mud banks in the area from Petrie Creek to the bridge. Troll or cast flats edges out of Eudlo Creek mouth for flathead. Petrie Creek walls hold jacks. Bli Bli boat ramp has a picnic and barbecue.
6. Mooloolah River walls: luderick, big flathead in spring.
7. Mackerel, cobia, snapper, sweetlip.
8. Rock and surf fishing around headland.
9. Pumicestone Passage - see next page.

Launch sites

1. Bli Bli, ramp and BBQ area, Maroochy River.
2. Maroochy River, good ramp, poor sea access.
3. Mooloolah River, excellent ramps, good sea access.
4. Caloundra - Pumicestone Passage, poor sea access.

Mooloolaba tides move up to about 2.09m.

Net ban results

Did removing commercial nets from Pumicestone Passage more than two decades ago make the fishing better? Suntag's 2014 report shows flathead were the big improver. The number of flathead tagged per tagger per day steadily increased from one fish a day from 1985-1989 to six fish a day from 2010-2013, while the number of flathead tagged over 400mm rose from 0.9 in 1990-1994 to 1.8 fish a day from 2010-2014. The story was mixed for bream. The number of bream tagged per day rose from 1.2 fish a day in 1985-1989 to 8.2 in 2000-2004 and dropped back to five a day from 2010-2014. Tagged bream over 300mm have fluctuated from 0.3 fish/day in 1990-1994 to 0.2 from 2010-2014. The number of grunter tagged per tagger per day remained steady, peaking in 2000-2004. The average size of grunter increased. Only one of 71 tagged grunter had left the passage, recaught 860km away in Sydney. We can call him Nemo.

Bribie Island

Inside the island is a network of mangroves, flats and channels called Pumicestone Passage. The passage runs from Caloundra south to Moreton Bay. It includes 30km of fishable area, free of commercial nets, all just an hour by road north of Brisbane. There are deep channels, shallow gutters, sandbanks, mudbanks, creeks, mangrove islands, snags and weedbeds, and in any wind there is usually a sheltered spot to fish. This is one of the best SEQ winter bream grounds. It also produces quality flathead, whiting, mulloway, grunter and jacks. Cod, trevally and sweetlip are found in the deeper section of the southern passage in summer. There are bait grounds with nippers and soldier crabs. Flathead and whiting are best in summer, with bream and luderick in winter. Crabbers will find blue swimmer and mud crabs. Places to try are Coochin Creek, Hussey Creek, Tripcony Bight and Glass Mountain Creek. The secret to this area is to fish light and present the freshest possible bait, or tiny lures, on light tackle, as the fish can be finicky. Morning and afternoon are best.

Bream usually start in late May and run though until late August, with the best bream are taken at night. Best baits are mullet fillet and gut, nippers, prawns and chicken gut, which is a curiously popular bait around Brisbane. At Lime Pocket, there is deep water with big winter bream and some tailor - use fish fillets or pillies for bait. Work the smaller channels around the Pocket with lures for flathead and bream. From Lime Pocket across the bottom of Thooloora Island is a large sandbank and gutter along the edge of the Island. Work the gutter on a high tide for bream. To catch quality whiting dig mangrove worms out of the mud. A prime big-whiting spot is the mouth of Hussey Creek from September to March. From the top down to the edge of Thooloora Island is ideal flathead ground. Work up and down along the bank edges and the channel. Cast lures to the sand patches between weed. The oyster leases at Cowie Bank and Mission Point are also worth a look. A strong tide can be a deterrent to flathead - try to fish out of the current. Reliable spots are Elimbah Creek, Ningi Creek, Gallagers Gutter, Poverty Creek and the Stockyards. The deep channels that run down to the Bribie Bridge are good for both fish and blue crabs. The deep water at the southern bridge holds big fish - you can hook anything around the pylons. **Camping:** Bribie Island Recreation Area has coastal camps, some accessible by 4WD and others by boat. Fees apply. Camping is not permitted on the dunes, the northern spit or on the islands. Fresh water is not provided at camping areas. Fires are not permitted on the Ocean Beach site. At Mission Point and Poverty Creek, camping areas with fireplaces are provided but it is illegal to collect local firewood.

Camping areas accessible by 4WD vehicle include:
Gallaghers - no facilities. **Poverty Creek** – grass and shade. Toilets, picnic tables and fireplaces. **Ocean Beach** – 16km north of beach access point on North St, Woorim. Camps behind dunes. No toilets.
Camping and picnic areas accessible only by boat:
Mission Point - toilets, picnic tables and fireplaces are provided. **Lions Park** - this is a picnic area only. **Lighthouse Reach** - picnic area only.

Launch sites

1. Kings Beach, Esplanade.
2. Bulcock Beach, Maloja Ave.
3. Golden Beach, Lamerough Pde.
4. Golden Beach, Raleigh St.
5. Golden Beach, June St.
6. Donnybrook, Esplanade.
7. Meldale, Way St.
8. Toorbul, Moffat Esp.
9. Toorbul, Esplanade.
10. Toorbul, Freeman Rd.
11. Toorbul, First Ave.
12. Banksia Beach, Solander Esp.
13. Bellara, Marine Pde.
14. Ningi, Kal-ma-kuta Dve.
15. Ningi, Spinnaker Sound Marina.
16. Bongaree, Welsby Pde.

Local tides move up to about 1.6m. Currents in the passage can be quite strong.

Oyster Reefs

Trial shellfish reefs were installed in two areas in 2017/18 to rebuild shellfish stocks. The reefs are shown as yellow triangles on the map. Buoys mark each spot. A doubling of fish numbers was reported. Species seen were whiptails, silver biddies, stripeys, tuskfish, goatfish, wrasse, leatherjackets, happy moments, moses perch, tarwhine, bream, morwong, coralfish, cardinalfish and tawny nurse sharks. Don't anchor in the trial area.

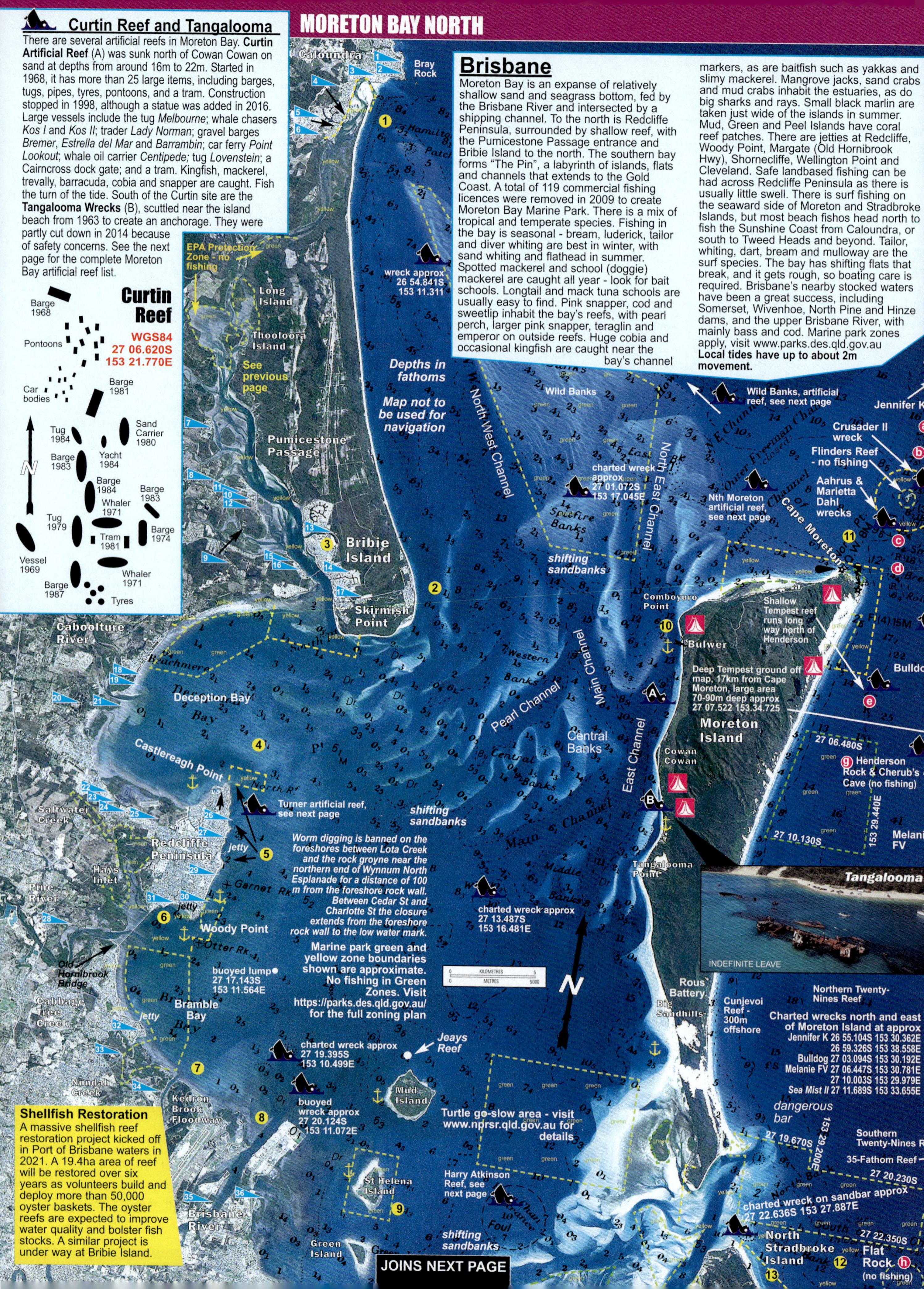

Curtin Reef and Tangalooma

There are several artificial reefs in Moreton Bay. **Curtin Artificial Reef** (A) was sunk north of Cowan Cowan on sand at depths from around 16m to 22m. Started in 1968, it has more than 25 large items, including barges, tugs, pipes, tyres, pontoons, and a tram. Construction stopped in 1998, although a statue was added in 2016. Large vessels include the tug *Melbourne*; whale chasers *Kos I* and *Kos II*; trader *Lady Norman*; gravel barges *Bremer*, *Estrella del Mar* and *Barrambin*; car ferry *Point Lookout*; whale oil carrier *Centipede*; tug *Lovenstein*; a Cairncross dock gate; and a tram. Kingfish, mackerel, trevally, barracuda, cobia and snapper are caught. Fish the turn of the tide. South of the Curtin site are the **Tangalooma Wrecks** (B), scuttled near the island beach from 1963 to create an anchorage. They were partly cut down in 2014 because of safety concerns. See the next page for the complete Moreton Bay artificial reef list.

Brisbane

Moreton Bay is an expanse of relatively shallow sand and seagrass bottom, fed by the Brisbane River and intersected by a shipping channel. To the north is Redcliffe Peninsula, surrounded by shallow reef, with the Pumicestone Passage entrance and Bribie Island to the north. The southern bay forms "The Pin", a labyrinth of islands, flats and channels that extends to the Gold Coast. A total of 119 commercial fishing licences were removed in 2009 to create Moreton Bay Marine Park. There is a mix of tropical and temperate species. Fishing in the bay is seasonal - bream, luderick, tailor and diver whiting are best in winter, with sand whiting and flathead in summer. Spotted mackerel and school (doggie) mackerel are caught all year - look for bait schools. Longtail and mack tuna schools are usually easy to find. Pink snapper, cod and sweetlip inhabit the bay's reefs, with pearl perch, larger pink snapper, teraglin and emperor on outside reefs. Huge cobia and occasional kingfish are caught near the bay's channel markers, as are baitfish such as yakkas and slimy mackerel. Mangrove jacks, sand crabs and mud crabs inhabit the estuaries, as do big sharks and rays. Small black marlin are taken just wide of the islands in summer. Mud, Green and Peel Islands have coral reef patches. There are jetties at Redcliffe, Woody Point, Margate (Old Hornibrook Hwy), Shorncliffe, Wellington Point and Cleveland. Safe landbased fishing can be had across Redcliffe Peninsula as there is usually little swell. There is surf fishing on the seaward side of Moreton and Stradbroke Islands, but most beach fishos head north to fish the Sunshine Coast from Caloundra, or south to Tweed Heads and beyond. Tailor, whiting, dart, bream and mulloway are the surf species. The bay has shifting flats that break, and it gets rough, so boating care is required. Brisbane's nearby stocked waters have been a great success, including Somerset, Wivenhoe, North Pine and Hinze dams, and the upper Brisbane River, with mainly bass and cod. Marine park zones apply, visit www.parks.des.qld.gov.au **Local tides have up to about 2m movement.**

Shellfish Restoration

A massive shellfish reef restoration project kicked off in Port of Brisbane waters in 2021. A 19.4ha area of reef will be restored over six years as volunteers build and deploy more than 50,000 oyster baskets. The oyster reefs are expected to improve water quality and bolster fish stocks. A similar project is under way at Bribie Island.

JOINS PREVIOUS PAGE

Seasonal availability

The main seasons are winter (bream, luderick, tailor, jewfish, snapper) and summer (mackerel, flathead, sweetlip, crabs, prawns, freshwater fish). Both summer and winter whiting species are caught.

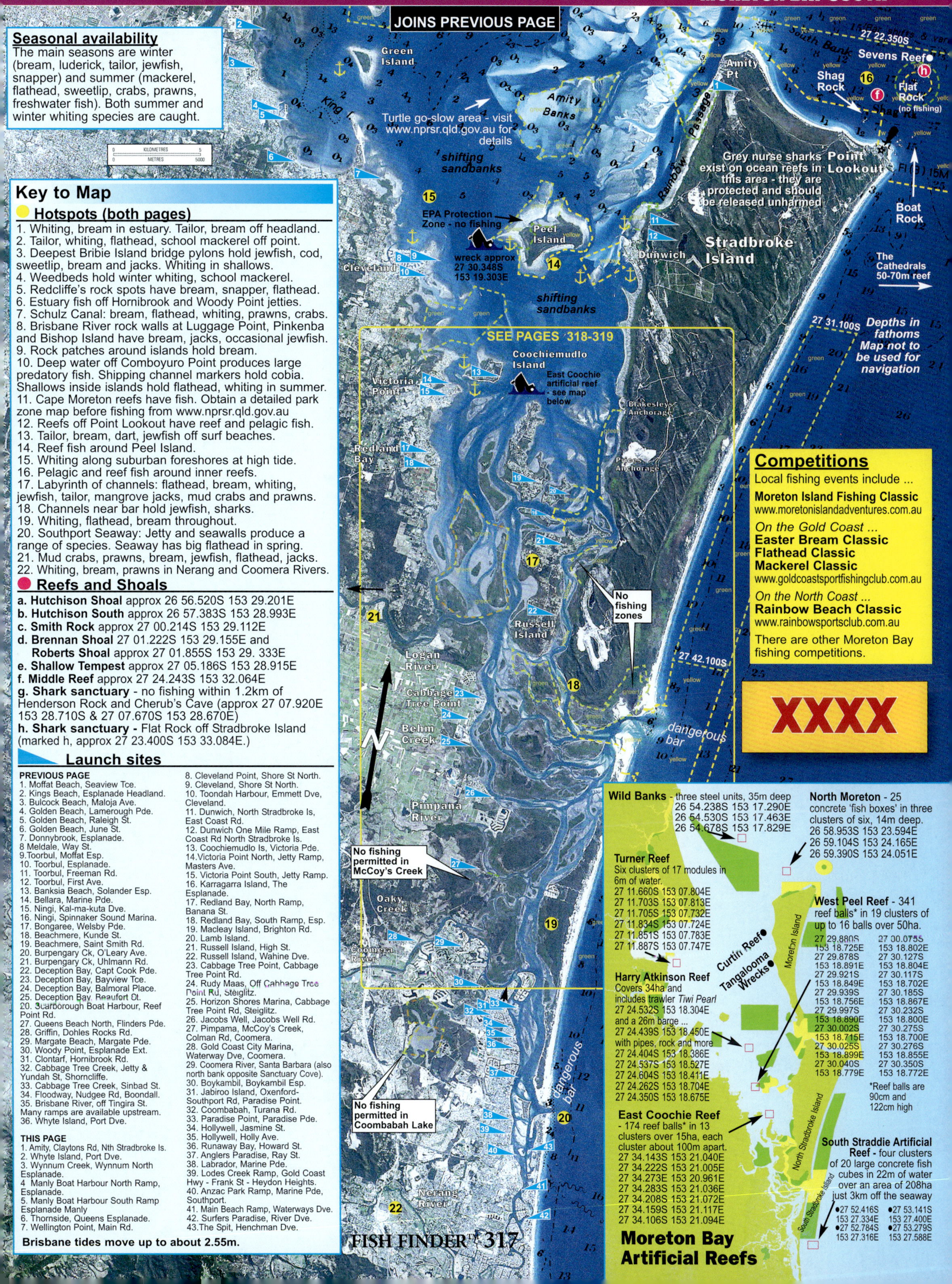

Key to Map

Hotspots (both pages)

1. Whiting, bream in estuary. Tailor, bream off headland.
2. Tailor, whiting, flathead, school mackerel off point.
3. Deepest Bribie Island bridge pylons hold jewfish, cod, sweetlip, bream and jacks. Whiting in shallows.
4. Weedbeds hold winter whiting, school mackerel.
5. Redcliffe's rock spots have bream, snapper, flathead.
6. Estuary fish off Hornibrook and Woody Point jetties.
7. Schulz Canal: bream, flathead, whiting, prawns, crabs.
8. Brisbane River rock walls at Luggage Point, Pinkenba and Bishop Island have bream, jacks, occasional jewfish.
9. Rock patches around islands hold bream.
10. Deep water off Comboyuro Point produces large predatory fish. Shipping channel markers hold cobia. Shallows inside islands hold flathead, whiting in summer.
11. Cape Moreton reefs have fish. Obtain a detailed park zone map before fishing from www.nprsr.qld.gov.au
12. Reefs off Point Lookout have reef and pelagic fish.
13. Tailor, bream, dart, jewfish off surf beaches.
14. Reef fish around Peel Island.
15. Whiting along suburban foreshores at high tide.
16. Pelagic and reef fish around inner reefs.
17. Labyrinth of channels: flathead, bream, whiting, jewfish, tailor, mangrove jacks, mud crabs and prawns.
18. Channels near bar hold jewfish, sharks.
19. Whiting, flathead, bream throughout.
20. Southport Seaway: Jetty and seawalls produce a range of species. Seaway has big flathead in spring.
21. Mud crabs, prawns, bream, jewfish, flathead, jacks.
22. Whiting, bream, prawns in Nerang and Coomera Rivers.

Reefs and Shoals

a. Hutchison Shoal approx 26 56.520S 153 29.201E
b. Hutchison South approx 26 57.383S 153 28.993E
c. Smith Rock approx 27 00.214S 153 29.112E
d. Brennan Shoal 27 01.222S 153 29.155E and **Roberts Shoal** approx 27 01.855S 153 29. 333E
e. Shallow Tempest approx 27 05.186S 153 28.915E
f. Middle Reef approx 27 24.243S 153 32.064E
g. Shark sanctuary - no fishing within 1.2km of Henderson Rock and Cherub's Cave (approx 27 07.920E 153 28.710S & 27 07.670S 153 28.670E)
h. Shark sanctuary - Flat Rock off Stradbroke Island (marked h, approx 27 23.400S 153 33.084E.)

Launch sites

PREVIOUS PAGE

1. Moffat Beach, Seaview Tce.
2. Kings Beach, Esplanade Headland.
3. Bulcock Beach, Maloja Ave.
4. Golden Beach, Lamerough Pde.
5. Golden Beach, Raleigh St.
6. Golden Beach, June St.
7. Donnybrook, Esplanade.
8 Meldale, Way St.
9.Toorbul, Moffat Esp.
10. Toorbul, Esplanade.
11. Toorbul, Freeman Rd.
12. Toorbul, First Ave.
13. Banksia Beach, Solander Esp.
14. Bellara, Marine Pde.
15. Ningi, Kal-ma-kuta Dve.
16. Ningi, Spinnaker Sound Marina.
17. Bongaree, Welsby Pde.
18. Beachmere, Kunde St.
19. Beachmere, Saint Smith Rd.
20. Burpengary Ck, O'Leary Ave.
21. Burpengary Ck, Uhlmann Rd.
22. Deception Bay, Capt Cook Pde.
23. Deception Bay, Bayview Tce.
24. Deception Bay, Balmoral Place.
25. Deception Bay, Beaufort Ct.
20. Scarborough Boat Harbour, Reef Point Rd.
27. Queens Beach North, Flinders Pde.
28. Griffin, Dohles Rocks Rd.
29. Margate Beach, Margate Pde.
30. Woody Point, Esplanade Ext.
31. Clontarf, Hornibrook Rd.
32. Cabbage Tree Creek, Jetty & Yundah St, Shorncliffe.
33. Cabbage Tree Creek, Sinbad St.
34. Floodway, Nudgee Rd, Boondall.
35. Brisbane River, off Tingira St. Many ramps are available upstream.
36. Whyte Island, Port Dve.

THIS PAGE

1. Amity, Claytons Rd, Nth Stradbroke Is.
2. Whyte Island, Port Dve.
3. Wynnum Creek, Wynnum North Esplanade.
4 Manly Boat Harbour North Ramp, Esplanade.
5. Manly Boat Harbour South Ramp Esplanade Manly
6. Thornside, Queens Esplanade.
7. Wellington Point, Main Rd.
8. Cleveland Point, Shore St North.
9. Cleveland, Shore St North.
10. Toondah Harbour, Emmett Dve, Cleveland.
11. Dunwich, North Stradbroke Is, East Coast Rd.
12. Dunwich One Mile Ramp, East Coast Rd North Stradbroke Is.
13. Coochiemudlo Is, Victoria Pde.
14.Victoria Point North, Jetty Ramp, Masters Ave.
15. Victoria Point South, Jetty Ramp.
16. Karragarra Island, The Esplanade.
17. Redland Bay, North Ramp, Banana St.
18. Redland Bay, South Ramp, Esp.
19. Macleay Island, Brighton Rd.
20. Lamb Island.
21. Russell Island, High St.
22. Russell Island, Wahine Dve.
23. Cabbage Tree Point, Cabbage Tree Point Rd.
24. Rudy Maas, Off Cabbage Tree Point Rd, Steiglitz.
25. Horizon Shores Marina, Cabbage Tree Point Rd, Steiglitz.
26. Jacobs Well, Jacobs Well Rd.
27. Pimpama, McCoy's Creek, Colman Rd, Coomera.
28. Gold Coast City Marina, Waterway Dve, Coomera.
29. Coomera River, Santa Barbara (also north bank opposite Sanctuary Cove).
30. Boykambil, Boykambil Esp.
31. Jabiroo Island, Oxenford-Southport Rd, Paradise Point.
32. Coombabah, Turana Rd.
33. Paradise Point, Paradise Pde.
34. Hollywell, Jasmine St.
35. Hollywell, Holly Ave.
36. Runaway Bay, Howard St.
37. Anglers Paradise, Ray St.
38. Labrador, Marine Pde.
39. Lodes Creek Ramp, Gold Coast Hwy - Frank St - Heydon Heights.
40. Anzac Park Ramp, Marine Pde, Southport.
41. Main Beach Ramp, Waterways Dve.
42. Surfers Paradise, River Dve.
43.The Spit, Henchman Dve.

Brisbane tides move up to about 2.55m.

Turtle go-slow area - visit www.nprsr.qld.gov.au for details

EPA Protection Zone - no fishing

wreck approx 27 30.348S 153 19.303E

Grey nurse sharks exist on ocean reefs in this area - they are protected and should be released unharmed

The Cathedrals 50-70m reef

Depths in fathoms Map not to be used for navigation

SEE PAGES 318-319

East Coochie artificial reef - see map below

No fishing zones

No fishing permitted in McCoy's Creek

No fishing permitted in Coombabah Lake

Competitions

Local fishing events include ...

Moreton Island Fishing Classic
www.moretonislandadventures.com.au

On the Gold Coast ...
Easter Bream Classic
Flathead Classic
Mackerel Classic
www.goldcoastsportfishingclub.com.au

On the North Coast ...
Rainbow Beach Classic
www.rainbowsportsclub.com.au

There are other Moreton Bay fishing competitions.

Moreton Bay Artificial Reefs

Wild Banks - three steel units, 35m deep
26 54.238S 153 17.290E
26 54.530S 153 17.463E
26 54.678S 153 17.829E

North Moreton - 25 concrete 'fish boxes' in three clusters of six, 14m deep.
26 58.953S 153 23.594E
26 59.104S 153 24.165E
26 59.390S 153 24.051E

Turner Reef
Six clusters of 17 modules in 6m of water.
27 11.660S 153 07.804E
27 11.703S 153 07.813E
27 11.705S 153 07.732E
27 11.834S 153 07.724E
27 11.851S 153 07.783E
27 11.887S 153 07.747E

Harry Atkinson Reef
Covers 34ha and includes trawler *Tiwi Pearl*
27 24.532S 153 18.304E
and a 26m barge ...
27 24.439S 153 18.450E
with pipes, rock and more
27 24.404S 153 18.386E
27 24.537S 153 18.527E
27 24.604S 153 18.411E
27 24.262S 153 18.704E
27 24.350S 153 18.675E

West Peel Reef - 341 reef balls* in 19 clusters of up to 16 balls over 50ha.

27 29.880S 153 18.725E	27 30.075S 153 18.802E
27 29.878S 153 18.891E	27 30.127S 153 18.804E
27 29.921S 153 18.849E	27 30.117S 153 18.702E
27 29.939S 153 18.756E	27 30.185S 153 18.867E
27 29.997S 153 18.890E	27 30.232S 153 18.800E
27 30.002S 153 18.715E	27 30.275S 153 18.700E
27 30.025S 153 18.899E	27 30.276S 153 18.855E
27 30.040S 153 18.779E	27 30.350S 153 18.772E

*Reef balls are 90cm and 122cm high

Curtin Reef

Tangalooma Wrecks

East Coochie Reef - 174 reef balls* in 13 clusters over 15ha, each cluster about 100m apart.
27 34.143S 153 21.040E
27 34.222S 153 21.005E
27 34.273E 153 20.961E
27 34.283S 153 21.036E
27 34.208S 153 21.072E
27 34.159S 153 21.117E
27 34.106S 153 21.094E

South Straddie Artificial Reef - four clusters of 20 large concrete fish cubes in 22m of water over an area of 208ha just 3km off the seaway

•27 52.416S 153 27.334E	•27 53.141S 153 27.400E
•27 52.784S 153 27.316E	•27 53.279S 153 27.588E

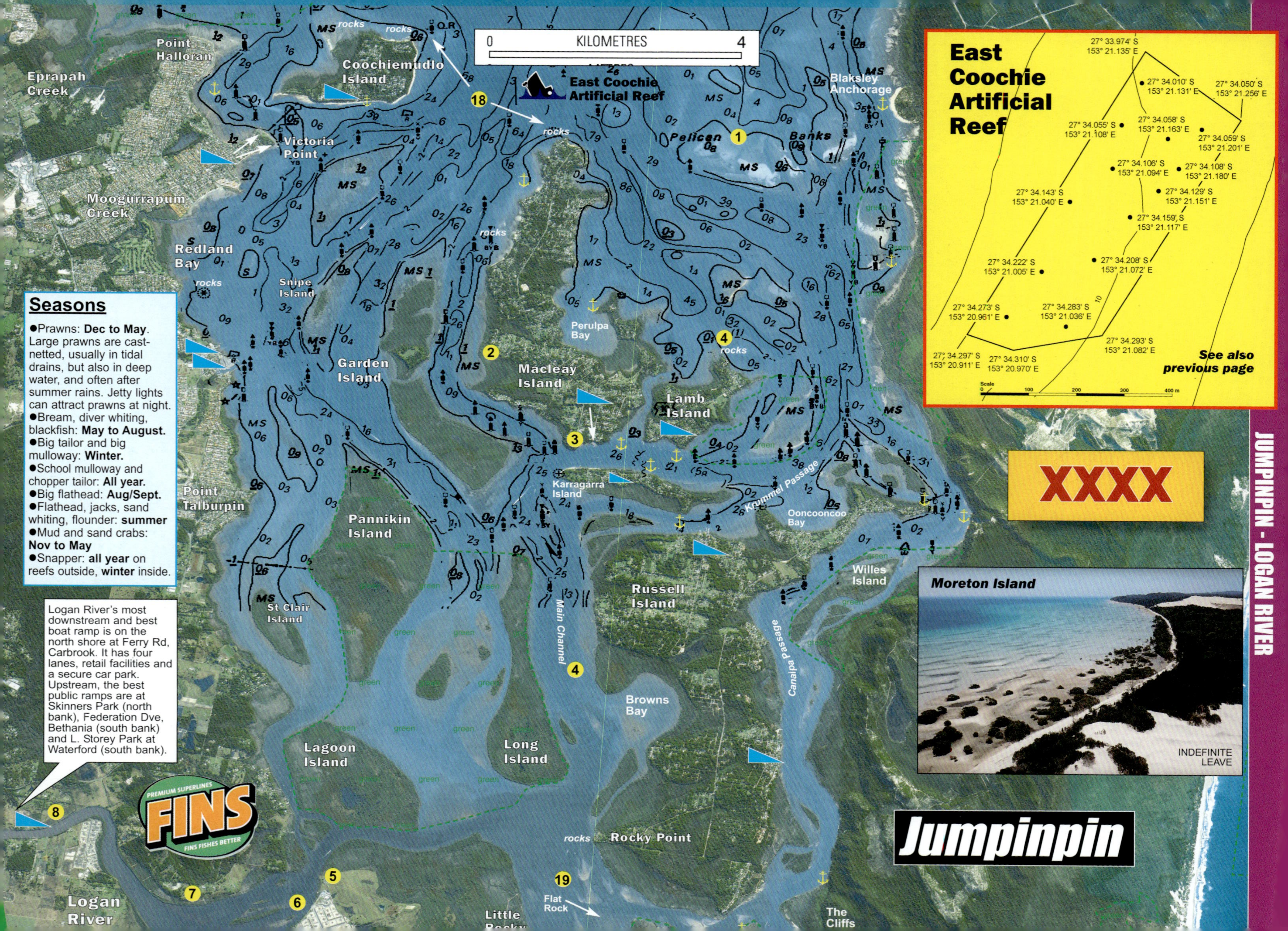
KILOMETRES
0
4
East Coochie Artificial Reef
Point Halloran
Eprapah Creek
Coochiemudlo Island
Victoria Point
Moogurrapum Creek
Redland Bay
Snipe Island
Garden Island
Macleay Island
Perulpa Bay
Lamb Island
Karragarra Island
Krummel Passage
Ooncooncoo Bay
Pelican
Banks
Blaksley Anchorage
Willes Island
Russell Island
Canaipa Passage
Main Channel
Browns Bay
Rocky Point
Flat Rock
Little Rocky
The Cliffs
Pannikin Island
St Clair Island
Point Talburpin
Long Island
Lagoon Island
Logan River
rocks
MS
green
Seasons
●Prawns: Dec to May. Large prawns are cast-netted, usually in tidal drains, but also in deep water, and often after summer rains. Jetty lights can attract prawns at night.
●Bream, diver whiting, blackfish: May to August.
●Big tailor and big mulloway: Winter.
●School mulloway and chopper tailor: All year.
●Big flathead: Aug/Sept.
●Flathead, jacks, sand whiting, flounder: summer
●Mud and sand crabs: Nov to May
●Snapper: all year on reefs outside, winter inside.
Logan River's most downstream and best boat ramp is on the north shore at Ferry Rd, Carbrook. It has four lanes, retail facilities and a secure car park. Upstream, the best public ramps are at Skinners Park (north bank), Federation Dve, Bethania (south bank) and L. Storey Park at Waterford (south bank).
FINS
PREMIUM SUPERLINES
FINS FISHES BETTER
East Coochie Artificial Reef
27° 33.974' S
153° 21.135' E
27° 34.010' S
153° 21.131' E
27° 34.050' S
153° 21.256' E
27° 34.055' S
153° 21.108' E
27° 34.058' S
153° 21.163' E
27° 34.059' S
153° 21.201' E
27° 34.106' S
153° 21.094' E
27° 34.108' S
153° 21.180' E
27° 34.143' S
153° 21.040' E
27° 34.129' S
153° 21.151' E
27° 34.159' S
153° 21.117' E
27° 34.222' S
153° 21.005' E
27° 34.208' S
153° 21.072' E
27° 34.273' S
153° 20.961' E
27° 34.283' S
153° 21.036' E
27° 34.293' S
153° 21.082' E
27° 34.297' S
153° 20.911' E
27° 34.310' S
153° 20.970' E
See also previous page
Scale
100
200
300
400 m
XXXX
Moreton Island
INDEFINITE LEAVE
Jumpinpin

Southern Moreton Bay

This maze of channels, mangroves, flats and islands in southern Moreton Bay, is collectively named after the Jumpinpin Bar that separates North and South Stradbroke Islands. 'The Pin' has an annual winter run of bream (May to August), big summer dusky flathead (August to November), as well as summer whiting to 40cm. Chopper tailor and school mulloway all year. Diver whiting are a small winter species that school on weedbanks. Mud and sand crabs are best in the warmer months. Locals chase big bream with dead baits of mullet gut, chicken gut, pilchards, prawns and fish strips. The water in some areas is clear, especially in winter, when stealth techniques and night fishing give the best results. Try fishing during the week when fewer boats are about. Mulloway are found in deeper areas in the channels, often near structure, but they also congregate around river mouths and outside the bar when rain pushes bait from upper reaches. Jacks, bream, cod and bull sharks are found in the nearby canal estates. Several varieties of trevally are caught. Barramundi are occasionally caught in the Logan River. Navigation of this region is tricky because of the flats, and first-timers should explore on a rising tide as it is then easier to get a boat off a sandbar. The area around the hazardous Jumpinin Bar constantly changes. While the islands appear large at first glance, the raised area of most is limited, with mangrove flats making up the bulk. A popular overnight spot for fishing boats is The Bedroom, an anchorage on South Stradbroke near the bar that allows easy access to the surf beach - some facilities are provided there. 'The Pin' maintains good fishing despite the pressure it receives.

Key to Map

Hotspots

1. Pelican Banks have diver whiting in winter. Use tiny hooks and prawn or squid baits.
2. Sand crabs in channel on west side of island.
3. Mulloway and snapper in deep water off point.
4. Bream along Lamb Island north shore rocks.
5. Marks Rocks on the south bank of the Logan River mouth is a popular mulloway location. The upper river has mulloway, whiting, jacks, bream, mud crabs and prawns. Night fishing works best.
6. Aggeston Sands has big whiting in summer. Nippers at the mangrove islands on south bank.
7. Crumbling bank has deep snags - use livebait for jacks, bream and cod.
8. Limited land-based access on a rock point off Riedel Rd is the closest access to the river mouth. Better access is upstream (off map) on the south bank at the park off Alberton Rd. There is also a jetty at Wharf Rd, Eagleby, and a boardwalk under the Pacific Hwy Bridge. There are pontoons at Alexander Clark Park. Bream in winter; whiting, flathead, small mulloway, occasional jacks and mud crabs in summer, plus sharks, catfish, pikey eels and rays.
9. Big tailor and mulloway are taken from the surf beaches. Access by boat can be had by mooring inside Shelter Island, the spit or near Swan Bay, and walking to the surf.
10. Chopper tailor schools in winter - look for birds. Big tailor always a chance. Big mulloway and flathead are taken in the deep water on the bottom at the turn of the tide, or by drift fishing on smaller tides. Strong currents in this area.
11. Big flathead along sandbank channel outlet edge in summer.
12. Bream and flathead in two small inlets. Bream around Crusoe Island mud lumps.
13. Good bream fishing around the mud clumps on Crusoe Island eastern foreshore.
14. Steep edges and point of Short Island are famous mulloway apots - fish turn of tide and smaller tides.
15. Blackfish and mulloway.
16. Reefs offshore from Jumpinpin start at 10km out, then 20km and 25km, running north to south along the coast.
17 and 18. Flathead and whiting along flatheads and channel drop-offs.
18. Snapper off islands' northern ends.
19. The area around the powerlines is a popular fishing spot for most local species.

Launch sites

This area is well served with boat ramps. Weekends are busy. The relatively small tidal range to about 2.5m makes launching and retrieving easy. Jumpinpin Bar is hazardous and changing. Speed limits apply in many areas.

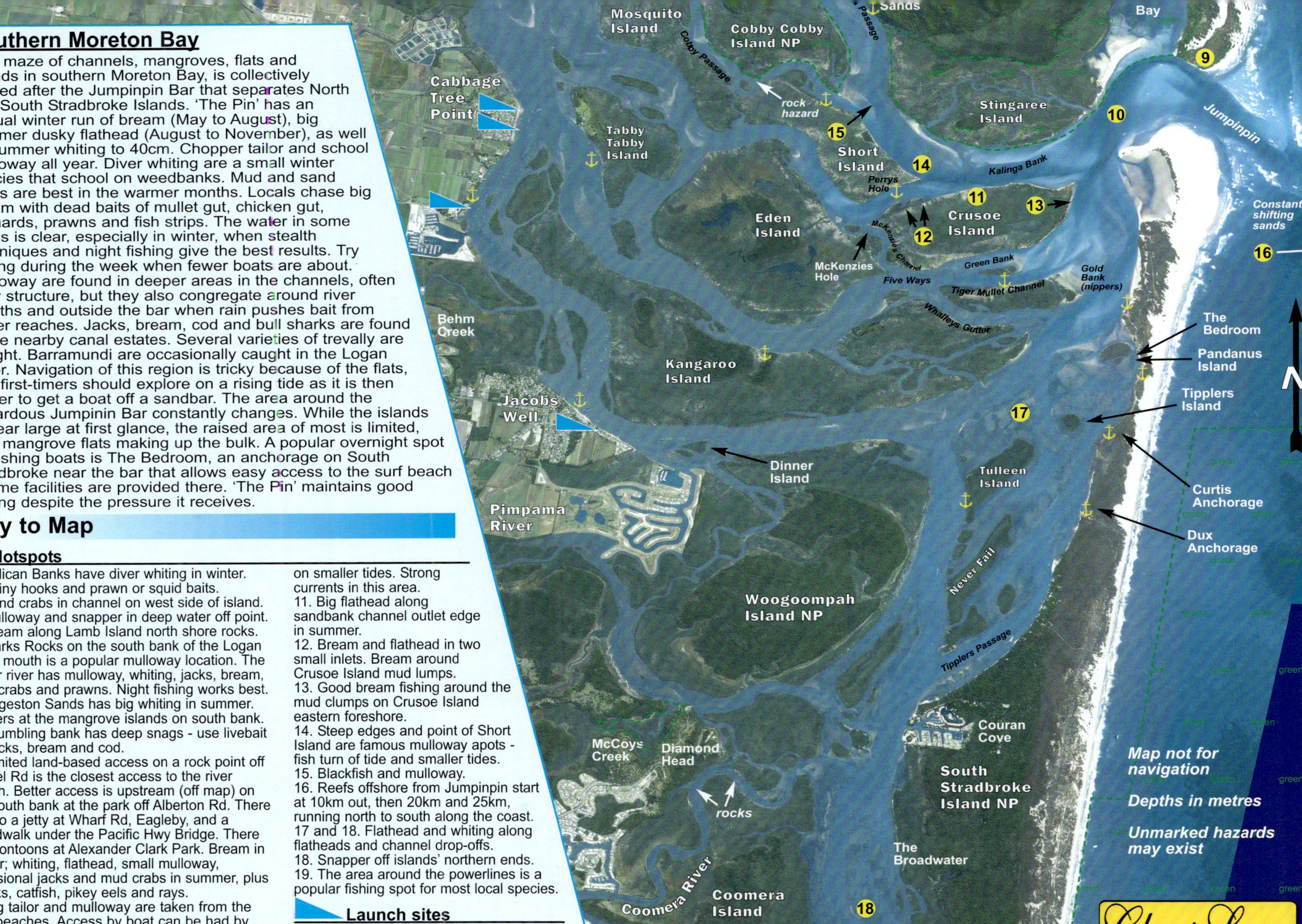

Key to Map

Hotspots

Note: You need a fishing licence to fish across the border in NSW.

1. Burleigh Head - north bank has tailor and bream. Rock groynes on south bank and along Palm Beach have tailor, tarwhine, luderick in winter. Palm Beach Reef has spotted mackerel in summer. On big tides Tallebudgera Creek has bream, whiting, flathead, luderick, jacks, tarwhine, queenfish, trevally, tarpon, giant herring and occasional mud crab.
2. Currumbin Rock south of creek has mackerel in season. Big flathead at creek mouth in spring. Currumbin Creek fishes as for Tallebudgera Creek.
3. Elephant Rock (north) and Flat Rock (south) have tailor, dart, bream, flathead, tarwhine on edges.
4. Snapper Rocks - bonito, tailor and tuna off rocks between Rainbow Bay and Point Danger.
5. (Next page) Tweed River's north and south walls have bitumen paths, for easy fishing access. Fish turn of tide. Bream, tailor, luderick, flathead, mulloway.
6. Next page: Deeper water follows west side. Footpath follows river. Flathead, bream, whiting.
7. Rock fishing at Fingal Head. Rock gaff etc needed.
8. Luderick, jacks on bridge pylons and southern bank. Downstream, Terranora Inlet has Foysters Jetty off Mingjungbal Dve. Upstream, Cobaki Creek/Terranora Creek has Pioneer Jetty, Kennedy Dve.
9. Tidal fishing extends to weir. Bass stocked upstream.
10. Good fishing at Cudgen Creek walls. Luderick at bridge.
11. Most species off Norries Head - road follows coast. Permit required to drive on beach.
12. Hastings Point has tailor, bream and luderick. Hole on beach north of creek has whiting, bream, tailor, mulloway. Creek has luderick in winter, some jacks in summer. Luderick near bridge on incoming tide. Nippers in creek.
13. Schnapper Rock near Pottsville has tailor, bream in winter, occasional snapper and mulloway. Pottsville Beach usually has good gutters. Mooball Creek has whiting, jacks. Black Rocks (south of map) is out of casting range but beach has tailor, bream, dart, mulloway - carpark nearby.
14. Barneys Point Bridge has a fishing jetty next to it.

Wrecks and reef

For micro charts of Nine Mile Reef, South Reef, Windarra Bank, Black Rock - see pages 325.

Four charted wrecks s-e of Tweed, approx marks ...

1. 28 16.374S 153 43.297E 20km from Tweed mouth
2. 28 19.041S 153 41.532E 21km from Tweed mouth
3. 28 23.049S 153 38.228E 25km from Tweed mouth
4. 28 27.593S 153 35.949E 32km from Tweed mouth

Tweed Offshore Artificial Reef

This was installed in October 2020 just 7.5km s-s-e of the Tweed River mouth, in 25m of water. It produces a broad range of tropical and temperate pelagic and demersal fish.

The reef consists of a central steel structure 10m high by 14m wide, surrounded by 32 concrete modules in eight clusters of four, spread over roughly 7ha.

A. 28 13.428S 153 35.473E

Clarrie Hall Dam

The dam wall was built on Doon Doon Creek in 1982 on a tributary of the upper Tweed River. The waterway holds 16,000 mega-litres when full and is the main off-river water storage for Tweed Shire. The dam is stocked with bass and there is an annual fishing competition. Facilities include electric and wood barbecues, shelters, picnic tables and chairs, toilets and playground. There are access points near the dam wall and at Crams Farm. The dam is only open in daylight hours. A NSW fishing licence is required. Midginbil Hill Farm Resort (02 6679 7158) has accommodation nearby.

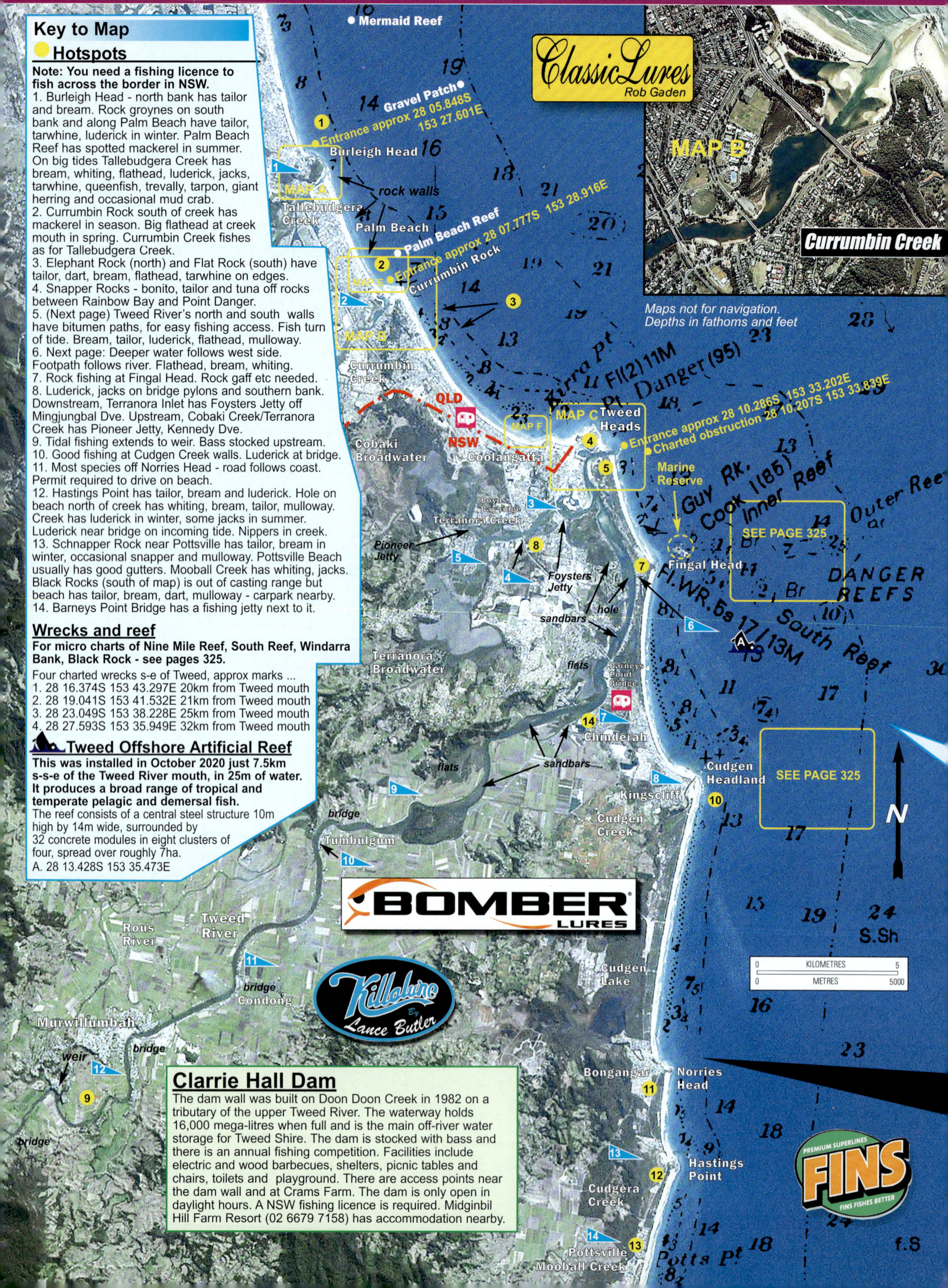

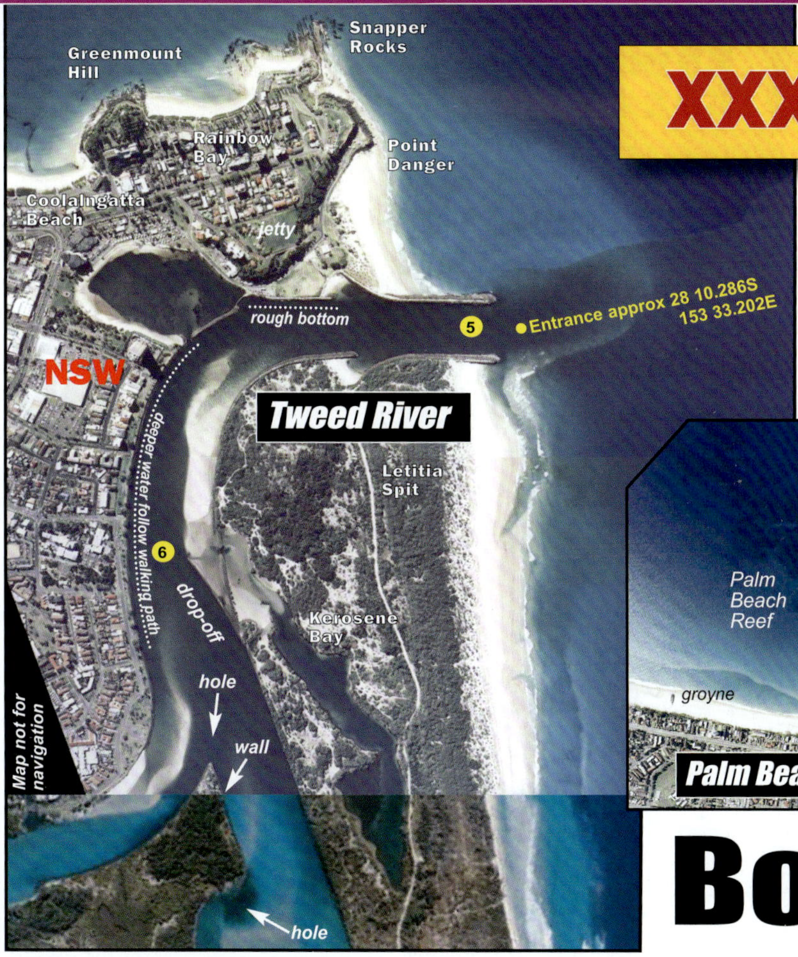

Border reefs

Launch sites

1. Ramps in Tallebudgera and Little Tallebudgera Creeks at Awoonga Ave, 19th Ave, Murlong Cres and TE Peters Dve. Cross bar in perfect conditions only.
2. Currumbin Ck ramps at Duringan St and Thrower Dve. Also RSL in Currumbin Ck Rd. Bar crossing in ideal conditions only.
3. Ray Pascoe Park, Kennedy Dve, twin lanes, all tides, into Terranora Creek.
4. Off Dry Dock Rd, all tides, into Terranora Creek.
5. The Lakes Drive, opposite Davey's Island, one lane, all tides.
6. Fingal Boat Harbour, all tides. A shallow ramp is further south at old boat harbour.
7. Chinderah, Oxley Park, poor at low tide.
8. Cudgen Creek, Kingscliffe, Marine Pde. Good, but bar is poor.
9. Opposite Dodds Island.
10. Riverside Dve, multi-lanes, all tides.
11. Off McLeod St, Condong, all tides.
12. Commercial Rd, all tides.
13. Gravel launch near Cudgora Creek bridge. Bar crossing only at high tide in perfect conditions. Beware rocks.
14. Overall Dve, into Mooball Creek.

Tweed Heads tides have up to about 1.74m movement.

The Tweed River, Fingal Head and reefs near Cook Island are focal points of this region. The town of Tweed Heads at the Tweed River mouth marks the NSW/Queensland border.

Starting at Burleigh Heads and moving south, Tallebudgera and Currumbin Creeks are suited to casting from canoe or cartopper.

The Tweed River is a more serious venue. The main arm of the river is about 60km long, tidal to a weir 2km upstream of Murwillumbah.

Significant Tweed tributaries are Cobaki Broadwater, Terranora Broadwater, Terranora Creek, Bilambil Creek, Rous River and Bilambil Creek.

The Tweed entrance walls have deep water, with bream, tarwhine, tailor, luderick, mulloway, jacks, flathead and whiting. Mulloway are best during flooding when bait is pushed downriver.

Large flathead appear in the river in spring, as do queenfish. In summer, spotted mackerel, sweetlip, cod, jacks, flathead, grunter, whiting and small mulloway are caught.

Squid are all year, while prawns are best in March-April just after the full moon, and mud crabs in summer. Winter sees bream biting hard, as well as mulloway, tailor and hairtail. For rockhoppers, Fingal Head, Cudgen, Norries and Hastings Point all have rock fishing. Fingal is probably best.

The nearby surf beaches produce tailor, bream, dart, whiting and mulloway.

Vehicles are not allowed on beaches in the Tweed Shire, but there are coastal access points along the roads.

Offshore: The Tweed River usually gives safe sea access and there are three major reefs to explore within 9.25km south-east of the mouth.

Of these the Nine Mile Reef, east of Cook Island, is most popular, and nearby South Reef. Fidos also fishes well. Further south are Windarra Bank and Black Rocks reefs. See page 325 for our exclusive maps of these reefs.

The Nine Mile is 7.4km out from the coast, with strong currents usually hitting the steep north face.

This reef rises to about 8m but averages 12m to 24m. The rubble bottom is at 40m. This reef and others in the area can break, so take care.

Wahoo, cobia, kingfish and dolphin fish are popular targets. Cobia of more than 40kg have been landed.

Mack tuna, longtail and yellowfin tuna are all caught.

The Tweed region has wider grounds variously called The Canyons, as well as reef areas named after their depths.

Calendar: July is usually good for boating with light westerly winds.

In winter striped marlin and yellowfin tuna can be taken on the wide grounds.

Also in winter, reef fish such as pink snapper, teraglin, mulloway, pearl perch and tuskfish are biting. The best action is usually early morning and late afternoon.

From July-Sept, yellowtail kingfish frequent the Nine Mile, with fish over 14kg common. September usually brings the biggest kingfish, to 30kg.

Samson fish and amberjacks are generally caught all year.

The best game fishing in this area is in summer. Trolling and livebaiting around bait schools works well.

The presence of bait is often associated with rain in the Tweed River.

Black marlin inhabit the inshore reefs from January to April. At the Nine Mile, wahoo appear any time from January to September, but March to June is best.

Cobia are all year, but best in spring/summer. Spanish mackerel are best on the Nine Mile from Feb to May.

Mackerel tuna are thick all year, with occasional striped tuna, and small yellowfin in autumn/winter.

Marks off Stradbroke, Tweed, Ballina and Yamba

Cathedral 27 30.650S 153 36.565E
Reef 27 33.903S 153 35.916E
Nth Strad 36s 27 36.581S 153 36.626E
Reef 27 39.971S 153 42.602E
The Pin 36s 27 46.384S 153 36.506E
The Pin 50s 27 39.699S 153 43.275E
The Pin 50s 27 42.371S 153 43.790E
Sullies 27 41.225S 153 33.605E
Cottons 27 44.021S 153 33.138E
Sth Strad 36s 27 52.720S 153 37.681E
Sth Strad Rf 27 57.508S 153 31.009E
Southport 18s 27 57.009S 153 28.499E
Southport 24s 28 00.838S 153 31.668E
Southport 36s 27 59.331S 153 38.582E
Southport 42s 28 01.600S 153 41.505E
Southport 50s 28 00.895S 153 45.970E
The Hole 27 59.581S 153 29.853E
Nine Mile Sth 28 11.976S 153 37.733E
Tweed 36s 28 07.503S 153 37.260E
Tweed 36s 28 08.750S 153 41.475E
Tweed 36s 28 10.790S 153 42.010E
Tweed 36s 28 11.853S 153 36.802E
Tweed 50s 28 08.489S 153 46.479E
Tweed 50s 28 09.111S 153 46.391E
Tweed 50s 28 12.635S 153 46.611E
Brunswick Rf 28 30.943S 153 34.058E
Windarra Bank 28 27.440S 153 41.402E
Ballina Reef 28 52.979S 153 39.650E
Ballina Wide 28 55.986S 153 46.751E
Ballina Wide 28 55.497S 153 46.293E
Ballina Sth 28 55.383S 153 41.049E
Evans Rf 28 56.051S 153 44.023E
Evans Ledge 28 56.050S 153 44.024E
Black Rock 29 13.184S 153 29.921E
Black Rock 29 13.513S 153 25.978E
Yamba 50s 29 18.567S 153 43.310E
Yamba Shoal 29 19.787S 153 32.452E
Knob Reef 29 19.532S 153 22.790E
The Pinnacle 29 28.174S 153 40.455E

Bundaberg to Brisbane

The family fisherman is well catered for fishing spots along this coastline, with bread and butter species like bream, whiting and flathead freely available, with a chance of big threadfin salmon and even barramdundi.

BUNDABERG

1. Burnett River - Town Reach. In the heart of town, there are many spots to choose from. A river walk has been built along the southern bank of the river below Quay St. Most of the piers and jetties are private property but there is a purpose-built fishing platform below Alexandra Park. There are numerous access points along the walk which allow anglers to get a bait into the water. Flathead are the common catch for bait anglers but bream, jacks and blue salmon also take fresh or live baits. On the north side of the river, floods have opened up large sections of the bank around the Lions Park boat ramp for land-based anglers. At times, schools of small trevally, tarpon and blue salmon push up the river and feed here. The outgoing tide seems to be the best time to toss a lure, with small metals and jigs popular, and soft plastics.

2. Kirby's Wall. Heading downstream the next major feature of interest to land-based anglers is Kirby's Wall, which can be accessed off McGills Road. This low rock wall juts out into the main river channel and is exposed a couple of hours either side of low tide. Just be sure not to stay too long as the wall goes under at high tide. Bream are the main target, using light lines and unweighted baits of squid, pilchard or prawn. Lure fishing can also be successful, with soft plastics. For the more adventurous, mangrove jacks hang around rocky structure and jewfish have been taken. At times, schools of small trevally and queenfish smash baitfish off the surface.

3. Burnett River Mouth. The Burnett Heads Marina and nearby rock walls are some of the most productive land-based fishing locations in the Bundaberg region. The low rock walls provide easy access to deep, clean water at the mouth of the Burnett River and produce a wide range of fish, including tuna and mackerel. Barramundi are encountered here. Anglers can soak a bait of pilchard or prawn for bream, or a more substantial livebait such as a poddy mullet or herring for flathead and other predators. Night can be productive as big winter bream move in around the rocks. Squid can be taken under the lights of the jetties. Lure fishermen do well at dawn and dusk (particularly over high tide) as schools of pelagic fish enter the river mouth. In summer school mackerel are a common catch and mackerel tuna also visit the river. In winter, tailor and pike are the main catch. Metal spoons cast out and retrieved rapidly are the best option for most of the pelagic fish. Bank anglers can also access the bottom section of the river near Port Bundaberg (on the large sandbar) and at the ferry crossing at Strathdees. There is a boat ramp at Strathdees, which is where the cable ferry crosses the river. There is plenty of space in this section of river, with ample rocky bank to fish. Flathead, bream and cod are the main species but pelagic fish do push this far upstream, so it can be worth tossing a lure.

4. Along the Bundaberg seafront, there are some fishable locations, but most of the shoreline between Burnett Heads and Bargara is shallow and rocky. Additionally, some sections are Green Zones. The local beaches are not highly recommended as most are shallow and featureless. They rarely hold fish for any length of time. The possible exceptions include Moore Park Beach to the north of Bundaberg and Coonarr Beach to the south. Both produce whiting but catches are typically moderate. Schools of tailor patrol beaches during the cooler months and can provide a surprise in the surf. Almost directly below the township of Burnett Heads, tuna and mackerel can be taken off the rocks in the warmer months. Spinning is the main game. There are several platforms and access requires only a short walk in most cases. The same applies to the rocks at Elliott Heads (where allowed) and tuna occasionally herd baitfish up to the rocks. Be aware of the Green Zones.

5. Elliott River. This offers pleasant fishing. There is a pontoon at Riverview, giving anglers the chance to dangle a line in the clear waters of the Elliott. The park area just upstream of the new ramp also provides plenty of bank access for a casual fishing trip. Catches are typically modest, with bartailed flathead, whiting and bream the mainstays. Occasional mangrove jacks (mainly at night) can spice things up, with small queenfish and trevally invading the river at times.

Flathead are a popular LB target

6. Kolan River. This has reasonable fishing off the bank in several places. If you have a 4WD, you can drive up along the beach from Moore Park and fish the mouth. This produces tailor and queenfish in the cooler months. Flathead, trevally and even permit are taken here as well. Alternatively, anglers drive to Mira and fish off the north bank. Bream, flathead and grunter are taken from the boat ramp area at Miara, while the caravan park is next to the water and staying there opens up a lot more water to fish. The area is tidal and shallow but don't let that put you off as there are snaggy stretches of bank near the mouth which produce good fishing.

BRISBANE

For landbased fishing, most Brisbane anglers leave the shallow shores of Moreton Bay and head north to the Sunshine Coast, Noosa and Fraser Island, or south to the Gold Coast and northern NSW, where surf beaches and headlands beckon. But there are worthwhile spots near the city, especially on the Redcliffe Peninsula. The fishing is seasonal, with tailor and bream best from July to October, and jacks, flathead, dart and whiting best in summer. Good fishing can be had all year.

1. Fraser Island. The surf fishing is famous, with tailor, bream, dart and sharks the main catch, with occasional mulloway and mackerel. A 4WD is required. Access is by ferry. See the Fraser section of this book.

2. Noosa Heads. Excellent rock fishing, with whiting and flathead in the nearby Noosa River. See the Noosa section of this book.

3. Bribie Island. The beaches within the passage and on the sea side provide good fishing. Small mackerel are caught from Skirmish Point. Whiting, bream and flathead are the main catch in the passage.

4. Brisbane River, Pinkenba rock wall. It's a fair walk out from the nearest parking area to this crumbling rock wall, but there are plenty of bream and the occasional mangrove jack and threadfin salmon. Unfortunately it has become a heavily littered area.

5. Brisbane River freshwater. Access points upstream have bass and cod, which are also stocked into the superb Wivenhoe and Somserset dams that lie upstream.

6. Shorneclife Jetty, Sandgate. Pike, bream, whiting, squid, catfish, rays.

7. Redcliffe/Scarborough beaches. Many of the relatively calm beaches have rocky reef within casting range. The rocky points fish well, especially at night. Quality bream and flathead are quite common, and snapper, cod and tailor show up. Woody Point and Redcliffe have jetties with sand crabs, bream and flathead.

8. Moreton Island. Good surf fishing on the inside and outside beaches. The sheltered inside beaches have flathead and whiting, while anything can show up in the gutters on the surf side.

9. Nudgee Canal. The lower section has whiting, bream, flathead and sand and mud crabs.

10. Canal estate rock walls. From southern Brisbane through to the Gold Coast are numerous canal estates. The rock walls are good fishing spots. Bream and jacks are the main target but it is surprising how many different species make their way through the canals, including bull sharks, mulloway, mud crabs, jacks and trevally.

11. Tweed Heads to Pottsville. Excellent surf and rock fishing with easy access to beaches, headlands and river rock walls. The roads follow much of the coast. Look for gutters. Tailor, flathead, bream, dart, mulloway and whiting. The Tweed River has easy landbased access near the mouth, with mulloway, bream, luderick, jacks and flathead.

QLD FADS

Three types of Fish Aggregating Devices, or FADs, are installed all year in South-East Queensland locations. There are also four FADS off Weipa in North Queensland. **Surface FADs** consist of one 800mm cone-shaped marker buoy and marine lantern. **Sub-surface SFADs** consist of six 300mm floats and aggregators positioned a minimum 25m below the surface. **All-water AFADs** consist of one 800mm cone-shaped marker buoy, a mid-water 300mm buoy, aggregators and a 1.6 tonne pyramid anchor. Mahi mahi (dolphinfish) are commonly found on FADs, along with tuna, mackerel, tripletail, cobia, trevally, marlin and sailfish. Demersal fish such as nannygai, cod and coral trout are caught around All-water AFADS. Co-ordinates are in WGS 84, and include the distance from the nearest launch point and the FAD depth. Check FAD news with Qld Fisheries online before fishing as FADs may go missing, be relocated or undergo repairs.

Surface FADs

FAD 1: Gold Coast 24s 27 59.268S 153 31.747E, 11km from Gold Coast Seaway, 46m
FAD 2: Gold Coast 50s 27 55.790S 153 45.198E, 30kmm from Gold Coast Seaway, 85m
FAD 3: Gold Coast 36s 27 48.408S 153 37.472E, 22km from Gold Coast Seaway, 68m
FAD 4: Stradbroke offshore 27 17.029S 153 37.672E, 18km from South Passage Bar, 83m
FAD 5: Moreton offshore 27 05.797S 153 34.177E, 26km from Comboyuro Point, 89m
FAD 6: Bribie offshore 26 55.735S 153 31.775E, 22km from Comboyuro Point, 100m
FAD 7: Mooloolaba 26 35.908S 153 19.686E, 19km from Mooloolaba, 55m
FAD 7B: Mooloolaba 26 34.999S 153 18.665E, 19km from Mooloolaba, 56m
FAD 7C: Mooloolaba 19km 26 35.099S 153 20.727E, 19km from Mooloolaba, 56m
FAD 8: Mooloolaba east 26 34.259S 153 33.796E, 45km from Mooloolaba, 101m
FAD 9: Noosa 26 15.558S 153 19.754E, 26km from Noosa, 55m
FAD 10: Double Island offshore 25 53.075S 153 21.907E, 30km from Wide Bay Bar, 57m
FAD 11: Gold Coast 36s 28 03.047S 153 39.480E, 30km from Gold Coast seaway, 65m
FAD 12: Gold Coast 36s 27 56.040S 153 38.331E, 20km from Gold Coast seaway, 64m
FAD 12B: Gold Coast 36s 27 55.462S 153 37.571E, 20km from Gold Coast seaway, 64m
FAD 12C: Gold Coast 36s 27 55.029S 153 38.267E, 20km from Gold Coast seaway, 64m
FAD 13: Gold Coast 50s 27 44.368S 153 44.314E, 37km from Gold Coast Seaway, 86m
FAD 14: Gold Coast 36s 27 40.460S 153 36.166E, 33km from Gold Coast Seaway, 66m
FAD 15: Point Lookout offshore 27 23.448S 153 40.623E, 22km from South Passage bar, 104m
FAD 16: Moreton offshore 27 11.097S 153 36.894E, 24km from South Passage bar, 108m
FAD 17: Cape Moreton offshore 26 59.654S 153 33.585E, 9km from Cape Moreton, 108m
FAD 18: Wide Caloundra 26 44.758S 153 27.189E, 33km from Mooloolaba, 60m
FAD 19: Mooloolaba 33km 26 36.144S 153 25.765E 32km from Mooloolaba, 49m
FAD 20: Noosa 26 22.700S 153 14.300E, 17km from Noosa, 52m
FAD 21: Fraser Island offshore 25 41.269S 153 22.616E, 32km from Wide Bay bar, 51m

Submerged FADS

SFAD 1A: Gold Coast continental shelf 27 55.542S 153 53.764E, 29km from Gold Coast Seaway, 256m
SFAD 1B: Gold Coast continental shelf 27 54.555S 153 54.108E, 29km from Gold Coast Seaway, 273m
SFAD 1C: Gold Coast continental shelf 27 55.425S 153 54.765E, 48km from Gold Coast Seaway, 306m
SFAD 2A: Point Lookout continental shelf 27 25.720S 153 49.764E, 35km from South Passage Bar, 250m
SFAD 2B: Point Lookout continental shelf 27 24.894S 153 50.489E, 37km from South Passage Bar, 258m
SFAD 2C: Point Lookout continental shelf 27 25.738S 153 51.278E, 37km from South Passage Bar, 290m
SFAD 3A: Cape Moreton continental shelf 27 01.074S 153 45.918E, 41km from Comboyuro Point, 269m
SFAD 3B: Cape Moreton continental shelf 27 00.412S 153 46.696E, 43km from Comboyuro Point, 280m
SFAD 3C: Cape Moreton continental shelf 27 01.088S 153 47.563E, 43km from Comboyuro Point, 295m
SFAD 4A: Mooloolaba continental shelf 26 40.491S 153 40.111E, 54km from Mooloolaba, 233m
SFAD 4B: Mooloolaba continental shelf 26 39.887S 153 40.786E, 54km from Mooloolaba, 244m
SFAD 4C: Mooloolaba continental shelf 26 40.709S 153 41.170E, 55km from Mooloolaba, 252m
FAD F1: Rooney Point, Fraser Island 24 48.296S 153 05.638E, 57km from Urangan, 34m
FAD F2: Fraser Island offshore 24 37.897S 153 24.348E, 15km from Sandy Cape, 54m
FAD F3: Fraser Island offshore 24 58.062S 153 32.673E, 20km from Waddy Point, 54m
FAD B1a: Bundaberg offshore 24 39.163S 152 32.925E, 19km from Burnett Heads, 25m
FAD B1b: Bundaberg offshore 24 39.265S 152 33.012E, 19km from Burnett Heads, 25m
FAD B1c: Bundaberg offshore 24 39.355S 152 32.922E, 19km from Burnett Heads, 25m
FAD B1d: Bundaberg offshore 24 39.280S 152 32.835E, 19km from Burnett Heads, 25m

North Queensland FADS

FAD G1: Weipa 12 58.959S 141 17.009E, 67km from Weipa, 30m
FAD G2: Weipa 12 54.711S 141 22.625E, 54km from Weipa, 30m
FAD G3: Weipa 12 48.671S 141 23.665E, 46km from Weipa, 30m
FAD G4: Weipa 12 49.903S 141 32.594E, 33km from Weipa, 21m

More artificial reefs and 30 estuary fishing havens

New South Wales' recreational fishermen are well catered for with no-net fishing havens, an ongoing artificial reef program and more than 30 offshore FADs.

NSW may look small on the map, but it has 1460km of coastline.

There are first-class surf beaches, rock fishing platforms that produce tuna and billfish, along with trout and native fish in the rivers and impoundments.

At publication there were offshore reefs near Sydney, Shoalhaven, Port Macquarie, Merimbula, Newcastle and Wollongong. The newest reefs are off Batemans Bay, Jervis Bay and Tweed Heads. The offshore reefs have attracted baitfish such as yakkas and mado, which attract predators like kingfish, mulloway and snapper.

Shoalhaven Reef footage shows it covered in salmon and tailor.

For the tinny brigade, there are sheltered-water reefs in Lake Macquarie, Lake Conjola, Merimbula Lake, St George's Basin, Botany Bay and Bellinger River. These reefs are made from clusters of concrete "reef balls".

NSW has 30 well-established recreational fishing havens, gazetted way back in 2002.

The havens, including bays, rivers and tributaries, tidal creeks and canals, have no commercial fishing. Reefs and havens were funded by a recreational fishing licence fee.

The fees collected are used in part to stock native fish in dams, including yellowbelly, bass, cod and, most recently, estuary perch.

Some stocked trout waters are open all year.

The Great Dividing Range tablelands follows the coast and forms an unbroken series of plateaus varying in width from 50km to 160km.

This range forms the watershed where both coastal and inland rivers begin.

The western rivers are home to yellowbelly, bass, cod and other native species.

Trout live mainly in the cold high country streams and lakes.

There is a mix of temperate and sub-tropical species caught off the coast.

For boaters, the Continental Shelf is within 26km to 56km in most areas, with blue, black and striped marlin and swordfish all available.

NSW has marine parks, and in some areas no fishing or bait collecting is allowed. Many zones are outlined in this book.

Many NSW river mouths have dangerous bar crossings. Skippers must check conditions before crossing a coastal bar.

NSW FADS

Fish Aggregating Devices (FADs) are installed off NSW from September to June. Mahi mahi (dolphinfish), tuna, mackerel, tripletail, cobia, trevally, marlin and sailfish are caught. Co-ordinates are in WGS 84, and include the distance from the nearest launch point, and the depth. Check with NSW Fisheries before fishing as FADs may go missing or be relocated.

1. Tweed Heads 28 09.730 153 41.000 Tweed Heads, 13km, 64m
2. Byron Bay 28 36.723 153 42.758 Brunswick Heads, 17.5km, 70m
3. Ballina 28 54.430 153 41.189 Richmond River, 14km, 70m
4. Evans Head 29 06.400 153 36.200 Evans River, 17km, 50m
5. Yamba 29 36.755 153 29.187 Clarence River, 23.5km, 65m
6. Wooli 29 52.703 153 26.117 Wooli River, 16km, 65m
7. Coffs Harbour 30 14.858 153 21.605 Coffs Harbour, 21km, 85m
8. Nambucca 30 39.622 153 08.934 Nambucca - 13km, 60m
9. South West Rocks 30 50.534 153 11.803 Macleay River, 16.5km, 104m
10. Hat Head 31 00.636 153 07.795 Korogoro Creek, 7.5km, 85m
11. Port Macquarie 31 24.567 153 04.725 Hastings River, 16km, 90m
12. Laurieton 31 39.601 152 56.235 Camden Haven,10km, 65m
13. Crowdy Head 31 47.000 152 55.200 Crowdy Head, 17km, 79m
14. Forster 32 13.211 152 40.680 Cape Hawke Harbour, 16.5km, 80m
15. Port Stephens 32 46.967 152 24.703 Tomaree, 22.5km, 120m
16. Port Stephens South 32 47.660 152 24.100 Tomaree, 22.5km, 130m
17. Newcastle 32 56.380 151 58.150 Hunter River, 19.1km, 95m
18. Swansea 33 10.005 151 48.976 Swansea Channel, 17km, 110m
19. Terrigal 33 30.032 151 38.592 Terrigal Skillion, 19km, 115m
20. Sydney North 33 35.700 151 34.600 Broken Bay, 22km, 105m
20a. Sydney North 33 35.700 151 34.930 Broken Bay, 22km, 105m
21. Sydney Harbour 33 47.021 151 22.700 Port Jackson, 8.5km, 50m
22. Sydney East 33 59.316 151 20.951 Botany Bay, 9.5km, 98m
23. Botany Bay Wide 33 59.672 151 26.743 Botany Bay, 18km, 140m
23a. Botany Bay Wide 33 59.672 151 27.068 Botany Bay, 18km, 140m
24. Sydney South 34 07.950 151 23.090 Port Hacking, 21km, 140m
25a. Sydney South 34 08.356 151 22.946 Port Hacking, 21km, 140m
26. Wollongong 34 27.321 151 04.308 Port Kembla Outer Harbour, 16km, 110m
27. Shellharbour 34 33.720 151 00.626 Shellharbour, 13km, 105m
28. Kiama 34 41.000 150 59.500 Kiama, 12km, 115m
29. Jervis Bay 34 57.750 150 58.500 Currarong, 13km, 110m
30. Ulladulla 35 22.732 150 41.776 Ulladulla Harbour, 22km, 120m
31. Batemans Bay 35 50.000 150 22.630 Batemans Bay 22km, 120m
32. Bermagui - details n/a at publication
33. Narooma 36 15.437 150 17.900 Wagonga Inlet 14km, 120m
34. Far South Coast 36 58.800 150 14.750 Eden 29km, 125m

FISH FINDER™ Map Coverage

N

Tweed Fishing Haven
4sqkm from the Tweed River mouth to Boyd's Bay Bridge and from Rocky Point east to Fingal Road, including canal states

Richmond Fishing Haven
8sqkm from the mouth of the Richmond River to Emigrant Creek

Clarence Fishing Haven
Four river locations – a 2km stretch at Middle Wall, around Romiaka Bridge and Oyster Channel Bridge, and the entrance of Saltwater Inlet

Bellinger/Kalang Rivers Fishing Haven

Deep Creek Fishing Haven

Hastings River Fishing Haven

Camden Haven River Fishing Haven
Down from Dunbogan and North Haven Bridges, including Gogleys Lagoon

Manning River Fishing Haven
Downstream from Ghinni Ghinni and Berady Creek, including Scotts Creek

Lake Macquarie Fishing Haven

Botany Bay Fishing Haven

St George's Basin Fishing Haven

Conjola Lake Fishing Haven

Narrawallee Inlet Fishing Haven

Tabourie River Fishing Havens

Tomaga River Fishing Haven

Bermagui River Fishing Haven

Pambula and Bega River Fishing Havens

Wonboyn River and Beach Fishing Havens

Burrill Lake Fishing Haven

Lake Brunderee and Tuross Lakes Fishing Havens

Little Lake Fishing Haven

Lake Dalmeny, Mummaga Lake, Nelson Lagoon Fishing Havens

Back Lagoon Fishing Haven

Towamba River and Back Lagoon Fishing Havens

Nullica and Yowaka River Fishing Havens

Split Rock Reservoir
Lake Keepit
Lake Glenbawn
Lake Burragorang
Lake Eucumbene
Lake Jindabyne

Tweed Heads, pages 320-321, 325
Byron Bay, Brunswick River, pages 325
Ballina, Richmond River, pages 326-327
Yamba, Clarence River, pages 328-329
Wooli River, Red Rock, page 330
Coffs Harbour, page 331
Nambucca Heads, Bellinger River, pages 332-333
Kempsey, Macleay River, South West Rocks, pages 334-335
Port Macquarie, Hastings River, pages 336-337
Taree, Camden Haven, pages 338-339
Forster-Tuncurry, pages 340-341
Myall Lake, page 341
Port Stephens, pages 342-343
Newcastle, pages 344-345
Lake Macquarie, pages 346-347
Tuggerah Lake, page 349
Hawkesbury River, pages 348-349
Broken Bay, pages 349-351
Sydney, Port Hacking, pages 349-355
Wollongong, pages 356
Nowra, page 357
Jervis Bay, page 358
Batemans Bay, page 359
Narooma, page 360
Bermagui, page 361
Merimbula, page 362
Eden, page 363

NSW & Qld stocked dams, pages 374-384

Coastal bar and surf webcams
www.coastalwatch.com/surf-cams-surf-reports/nsw

Nets and traps are banned in many areas. Check the NSW Fisheries website for details.
www.dpi.nsw.gov.au/fishing/recreational

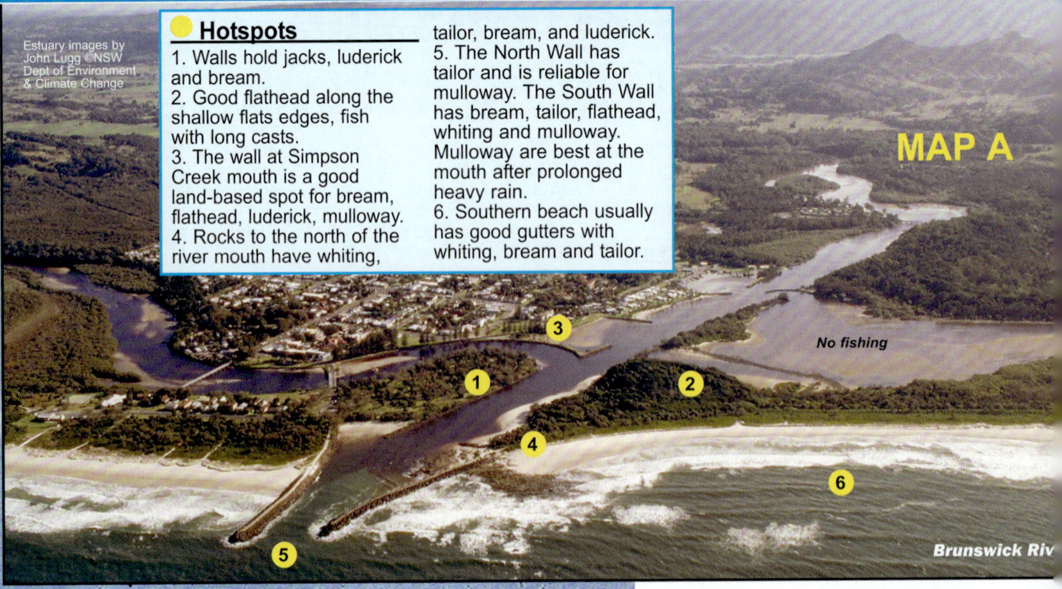

Hotspots

1. Walls hold jacks, luderick and bream.
2. Good flathead along the shallow flats edges, fish with long casts.
3. The wall at Simpson Creek mouth is a good land-based spot for bream, flathead, luderick, mulloway.
4. Rocks to the north of the river mouth have whiting, tailor, bream, and luderick.
5. The North Wall has tailor and is reliable for mulloway. The South Wall has bream, tailor, flathead, whiting and mulloway. Mulloway are best at the mouth after prolonged heavy rain.
6. Southern beach usually has good gutters with whiting, bream and tailor.

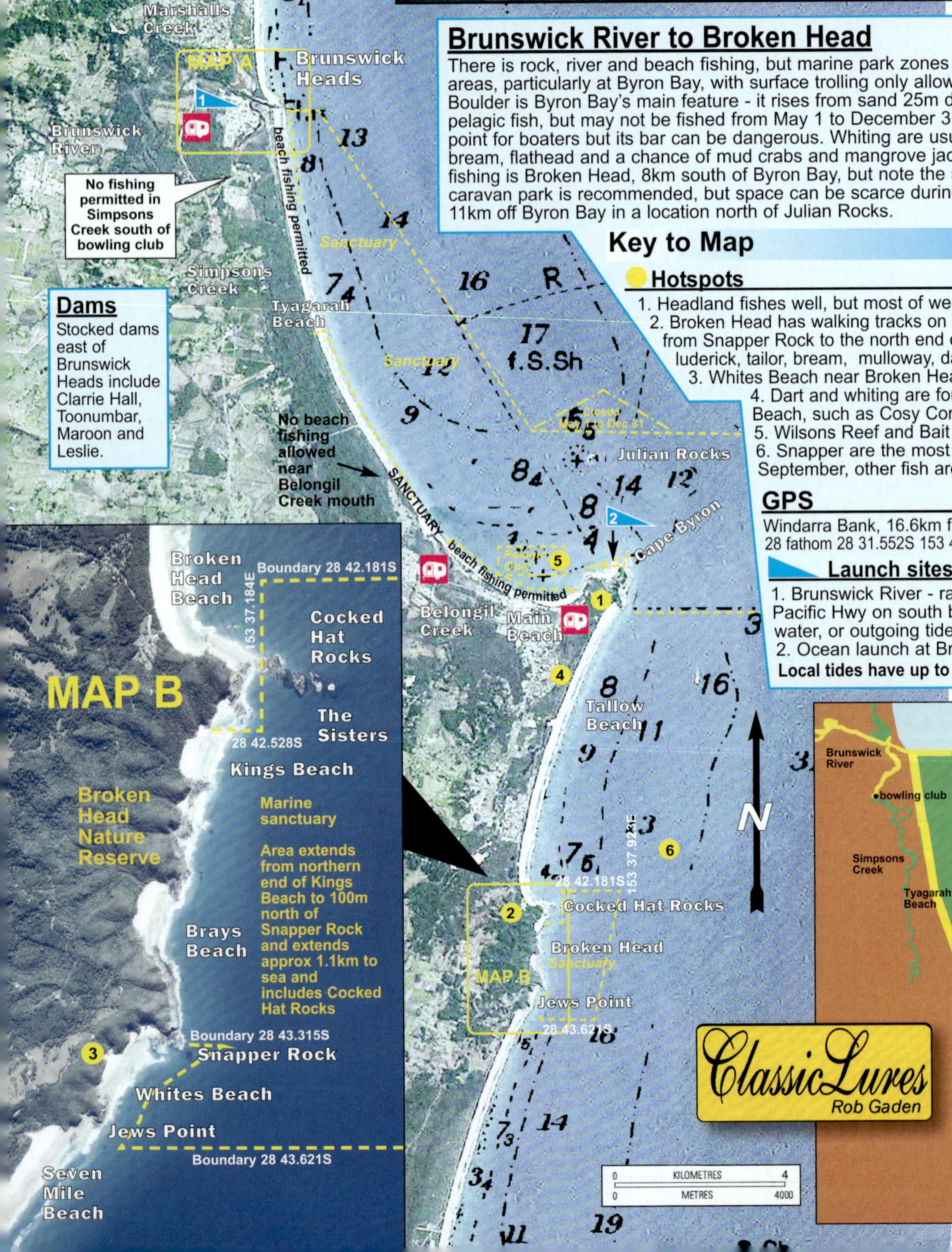

Dams

Stocked dams east of Brunswick Heads include Clarrie Hall, Toonumbar, Maroon and Leslie.

Brunswick River to Broken Head

There is rock, river and beach fishing, but marine park zones have shut fishermen out of many areas, particularly at Byron Bay, with surface trolling only allowed on some reefs. The Mackerel Boulder is Byron Bay's main feature - it rises from sand 25m deep up to 15m, and is home to pelagic fish, but may not be fished from May 1 to December 31. Brunswick River is a sea access point for boaters but its bar can be dangerous. Whiting are usually abundant in the river, with bream, flathead and a chance of mud crabs and mangrove jacks. The best spot for surf and rock fishing is Broken Head, 8km south of Byron Bay, but note the sanctuary zones. Broken Head's caravan park is recommended, but space can be scarce during holidays. A trawler wreck lies about 11km off Byron Bay in a location north of Julian Rocks.

Key to Map

Hotspots

1. Headland fishes well, but most of west side is marine park. Long walk.
2. Broken Head has walking tracks on the east face - fishing is not permitted from Snapper Rock to the north end of Kings Beach. The other ledges have luderick, tailor, bream, mulloway, dart, trevally and tarwhine.
3. Whites Beach near Broken Head is productive.
4. Dart and whiting are found on the protected parts of Tallow Beach, such as Cosy Corner.
5. Wilsons Reef and Bait Reef, trolling only.
6. Snapper are the most popular offshore catch, best about September, other fish are available.

GPS

Windarra Bank, 16.6km from Brunswick Heads - see next page.
28 fathom 28 31.552S 153 41.273E, 32 fathom 28 37.499S 153 42.693E

Launch sites

1. Brunswick River - ramps at Riverside Cres and Old Pacific Hwy on south bank, all tides. Avoid ocean bar at low water, or outgoing tide, or during swell.
2. Ocean launch at Brooke Dve, concrete ramp.

Local tides have up to about 1.89m movement.

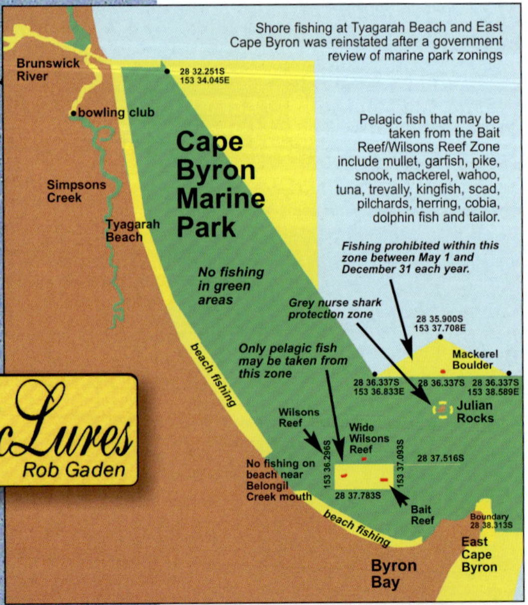

MAP B

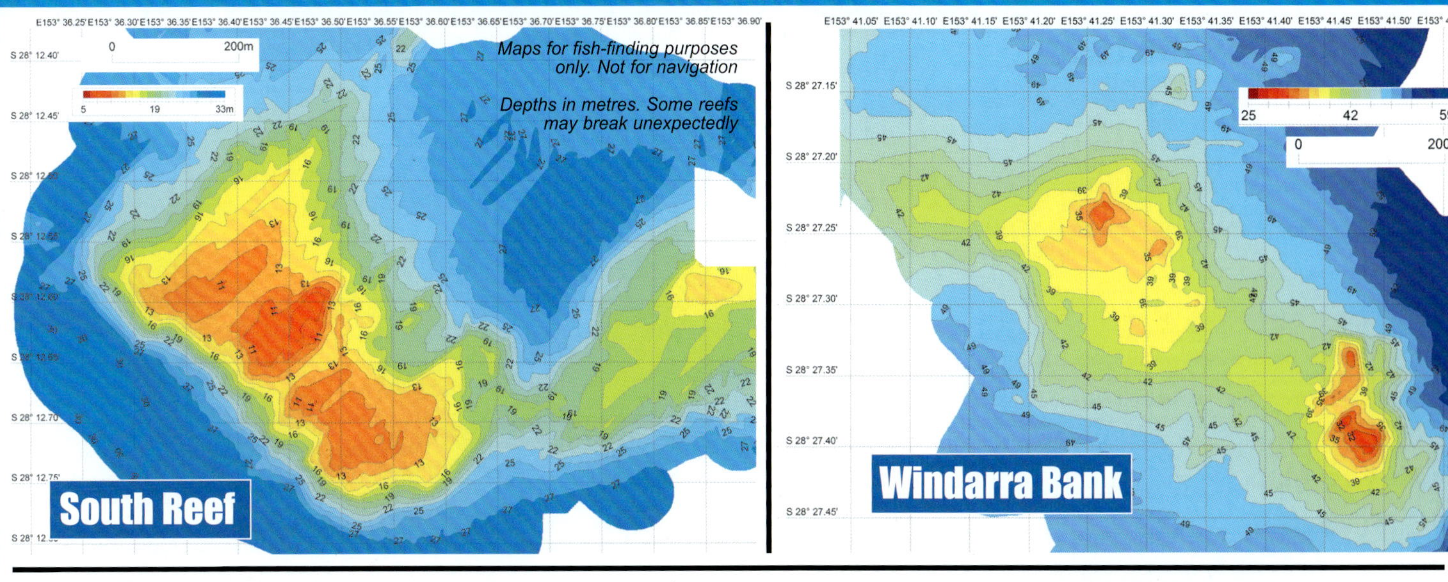

Tweed Reefs

The reefs east and south-east of Tweed Heads are within easy trailerboat range of the Tweed River mouth. These reefs are swept by changing ocean currents, which to some extent determine fishing quality. Boaters tend to target pelagic fish such as cobia, wahoo, dolphin fish, pink snapper, kingfish, mackerel tuna, striped tuna, yellowfin tuna, spanish and spotted mackerel, and mulloway. Small black marlin are a chance in season. The three reefs shown near Cook Island are more or less joined by areas of rough bottom, all of which is worth fishing. Care is required as some reefs break without warning. Winter is the calmer time of year and brings pink snapper, but summer brings the gamefish.

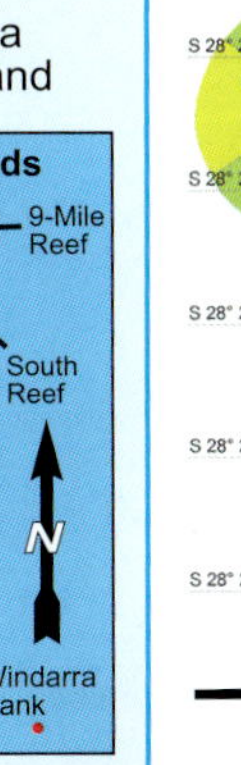

Brunswick Reefs

Windarra Bank is known for its summer pelagic fish, with small black marlin, yellowfin tuna, wahoo and spanish mackerel. Winter is dominated by kingfish, snapper and mulloway. When Windarra is firing it is an awesome fishery, but it can be frustrating, with fish life all over the sounder, but nothing biting. Black Rocks is known for mackerel in summer, with spanish mackerel and spotted mackerel making up the bulk of summer species. In winter good-sized snapper, tailor and occasional mulloway are caught.

Black Rocks

7 20 33m

0 200m

Maps for fish-finding purposes only. Not for navigation

Depths in metres. Some reefs may break unexpectedly

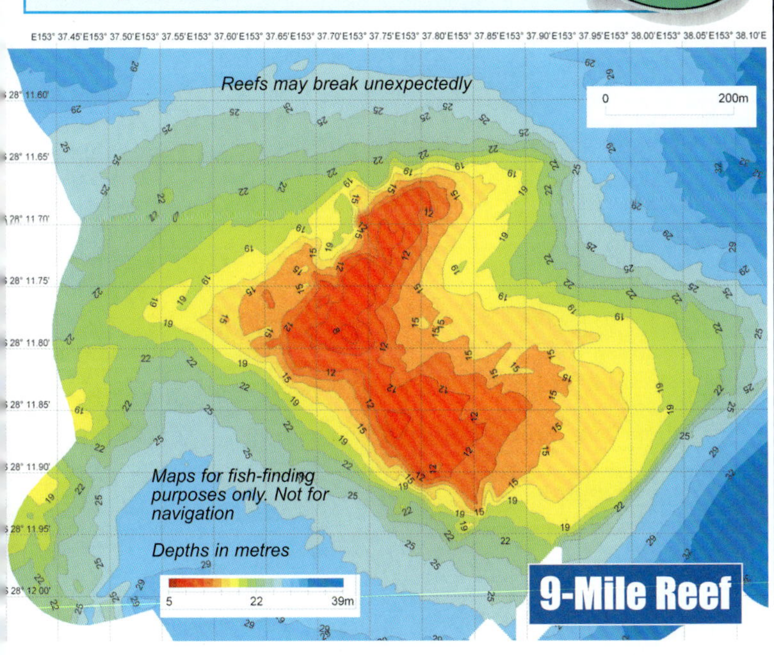

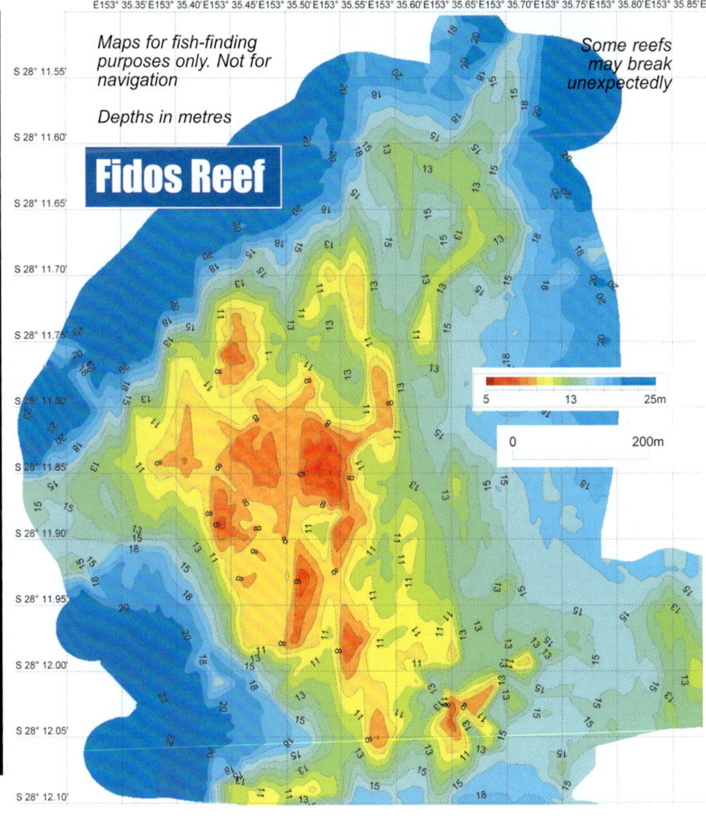

Ballina & Evans Head

Rock walls on the lower Richmond River provide the best fishing in this region. Bream, luderick, flathead, whiting, mulloway and tailor are caught.
There are estuary perch and bass upstream, and rain brings big mulloway to the river entrance. Most fishermen on extended stays base themselves at South Ballina. A vehicular ferry operates at Burns Point, or motorists can take the turn-off from Highway One, south of the Richmond River. This route follows the river's south bank. South Ballina has van parks, a seawall at the river mouth, and a great surf beach. The bar entrance is reasonable, but avoid outgoing tides and use only in suitable conditions. The Continental Shelf drop-off is about 24km wide. Bluewater fishing produces tropical and temperate species. Evans Head has good fishing in the river and off the sea entrance rock walls. Fishing around Lennox Head is somewhat restricted by Cape Byron Marine Park zones.

Key to Map

Hotspots

1. Bream, whiting, flathead off beach outside sanctuary. Boardwalk for disabled anglers. Bream in surf at Skennars Head, Black Head.
2. Missingham Bridge has bream, whiting, flathead, estuary perch. Fish change of tide. North Creek navigable in small boats - flathead, bream, whiting along flats edges. Best fishing at Munsey Point Bridge.
3. Seawalls have ample parking and are easy to walk: luderick, bream, whiting, dart, tailor and mulloway, with spanish mackerel, tuna in summer.
4. Porpoise Wall covers at high tide, bream, luderick, , whiting. Shallow south side has flathead, whiting.
5. Bream Hole out from River St ramp is crowded with boats during winter bream run. Best at night.
6. The Canal & Trawler Harbour - flathead & bream.
7. Flathead, school mulloway in holes.
8. Pimlico Island southern sandflat has large whiting. Flathead, bream and mulloway on edges.
9. Good crabbing in upper reaches.
10. Gutters and holes - 4WDs can visit the beach from track that passes South Ballina Holiday Park.
11. Upper Wilsons and Richmond Rivers, and Bungawalbin Creek, wild bass country. Plenty of snags and bankside timber. Best in spring.
12. Big bass in Emigrant Creek.
13. Spotted, spanish mackerel in summer on coast reefs.

Ballina GPS

Lennox 32 fathoms 28 49.622S 153 41.940E
Snapper 28 53.201S 153 39.751E
Snapper 28 55.049S 153 40.869E
Snapper, samson 28 55.252S 153 46.149E
Mulloway, kingfish 28 56.199S 153 43.919E
Pearl perch 28 57.469S 153 47.971E
Snapper 28 57.599S 153 38.871E
Teraglin, snapper 28 58.451S 153 37.469E
Ballina 42 fathoms 28 55.325S 153 46.285E
Ballina 42 fathoms 28 56.942S 153 46.346E
Pearl perch 28 59.614S 153 39.824E
Charted wreck 28 47.105S 153 40.506E
Charted wreck 28 52.836S 153 40.125E

Evans Head GPS

Sth Riordan 29 00.414S 153 30.163E
Nth Riordan 28 58.193S 153 31.472E
Sth Evans 29 12.769S 153 26.273E (breaks)
Nth Evans 29 10.345S 153 28.218E (breaks)
Far Sth Evans 29 14.922S 153 26.655E
Sth Sth Evans 29 13.997S 153 27.036E
Sth Evans Wide 29 14.332S 153 28.182E
Charted wreck 29 09.468S 153 37.290E
Charted wreck 29 11.015S 153 37.635E

Bass to and beyond Casino and Kyogle on the upper reaches

BASS COUNTRY

Bass to and beyond Lismore on the upper reaches

10 Wyrallah

Wilsons River

Richmond River

Luderick

FISHABOUT PICTURE

9 Coraki

Seelems Creek

11

Sandy Creek

Bungawalbin Creek

8 Woodburn

Launch sites

1. North Ballina: several ramps, best at North Creek Canal next to highway bridge, Ballina Quays off Riverside Dve, and River St.
2. South Ballina: two 4WD ramps at Mobbs Bay.
3. River St, multi-lanes, all tides.
3a. Keith Hall Lane, concrete, pontoon.
4. River St, East Wardell, one lane, all tides.
5. Off Broadwater Rd, Broadwater, one lane, all tides.
5a. Off highway, all tides.
6. Off Broadwater Rd, Dungarubba, one lane, all tides.
7. Rileys Hill Dock Rd, Rileys Hill, one lane, all tides.
8. Bank St, North Woodburn, one lane, all tides.
9. Richmond Tce, Coraki, one lane, all tides.
10. Wilsons River, Wyrallah Rd, multi-lanes, all tides.
Another two-lane ramp is on upper river at Lismore.
11. Evans River, ramps on Bundjalung Rd & Ocean Dve.
Local tides have up to about 1.76m movement.

Evans Head

This area is famous for its runs of pink snapper and spotted mackerel, but it also has good surf, rock and river fishing. There is offshore gamefishing for marlin, mahi mahi, wahoo and more, with the Continental Shelf about 37km out. The bar is hazardous. There is a caravan park on the Evans River.

Key to Map

Hotspots

1. Small beach is good for bream, mulloway and other surf species.
2. Airforce Beach often has a hole opposite the Surf Club with most species. 4WD access along beach by permit.
3. Whiting and flathead
4. Whiting and flathead.
5. Bream, flathead, mulloway, jacks.
6. The South Wall is worth a try for bream, whiting, tailor and flathead.
7. Half Tide Rock includes several rock platforms with most species: mulloway, bream, luderick, drummer, mackerel and tailor.
8. Mulloway, bream, drummer, tailor, luderick.
9. Snapper Rock's low ledge on the seaward side is dangerous in a swell, but in good weather produces bream, luderick, mulloway, and even mackerel and tuna.

Richmond River

The river starts high in the McPherson Range, flowing down through Kyogle, Casino, Coraki and entering the sea at Ballina. There is 114km of tidal water to about 4km downstream of Casino at a weir. The major tributary is Wilsons River, which has 115km of tidal water, and has NSW's wettest rain gauge at Rummery Park. These are serious bass rivers, popular with tournament fishos. Spring is prime time for bass as the fish move back upriver after spawning. The Richmond and Wilsons Rivers can be fished for much of their length for estuary fish during dry periods. Marine fish tend to move upstream during drought, and downstream after rain. Mulloway gather at the river mouth after heavy rain, awaiting flushed baitfish. Big floods can hurt nearby sea fishing, as tailor and mackerel move away from the flood plume, which may extend kilometres around the mouth. Floods have also caused fish kills, and efforts are being made to improve the river's catchment. The lower river at Ballina has a range of options. The rock walls have landbased fishing for luderick and bream in winter, and summer flathead. There is a good run of mud and sand crabs at times.

General tips

Tailor are present all year, with large whiting in spring/summer. Salmon and luderick in winter. Beach worms and pipis usually easy to find. mulloway are best at the river entrance rock walls after heavy rain.

Freshwater fishing

Picturesque Toonumbar Dam, on the Richmond tributary Iron Pot Creek near Kyogle, has bass fishing, with fast action down from the dam wall. Eastern cod were once abundant in the Richmond and Clarence River systems. The species declined in the 1930s and became almost extinct, surviving in remote tributaries. Stocking and habitat improvement have given hope for the species, which is protected. Carp are a pest in the upper Richmond River and must be destroyed if caught. Bass and estuary perch are found through much of the river.

4WD beach access

Vehicles can access Seven Mile Beach, Lennox Head, via Camp Drewe Road. Before taking a 4WD onto Seven Mile Beach you need to buy a permit at the automated kiosk located along Camp Drewe Road (payment by card only) or before you arrive via the EasyPark App. Fees for 2022 were day permit $20, 30-day permit $55, six-month permit $77, annual permit $132. Vehicles can also access a 4.6km stretch of Air Force Beach below the high tide mark north to the coffee rocks, this stretch is monitored by Richmond Valley Council. South Ballina Beach was closed to 4WD access in 2021.

Key to Map

Hotspots

See next page for main map.

1. Big flathead in early mornings.
2. 'T-Piece' is rock outcrop just north of tide gauge, luderick, mulloway at night.
3. Jew, tuna, mackerel, kingfish, luderick from south wall. Bream, mulloway, tailor from north wall.
4. Middle Wall has bream, luderick - best in winter. Best on north-east side.
5. Iluka Bay Wall: bream, mulloway.
6. Collis Wall - bream, mulloway, luderick on river side, flathead on shore side.
7. Luderick on gantry all year.
8. Bream, luderick, jacks.
9. Flathead along flats edges.
10. Flathead along flats edges.

Yamba

The Clarence River is the largest coastal NSW river, entering the sea at Yamba (south bank) and Iluka (north bank), with Grafton on the tidal reach. The Clarence commercial catch comprises more than 20 per cent of the total NSW estuarine commercial catch, and it is the major estuary for wild and farmed prawn production. The tidal river is in good condition despite the upper catchment being intensively farmed. Native freshwater fish, such as the Clarence River (eastern) cod and bass survive in inaccessible upstream gorges. Sand and mud crabs are caught in the tidal reach, as are estuary perch. To the south, the Sandon River is worth a visit, but fishing is restricted by marine park zones.

Tidal fishing: There is 109km of tidal water up to a rockbar at Copmanhurst. The lower Clarence fishes well all year, but the best time is June-Sept for the luderick and bream run. Rock walls, piers and bridges are good spots. Whiting, flathead and occasional mangrove jack bite through summer from September. The entrance rock walls are famous for mulloway during floods when bait moves downriver. Fishing off the walls is difficult during tidal run. Fishing in the upper tidal river around Grafton is affected by rain, with marine fish pushing upstream in dry periods.

Rock and surf: As well as the usual tailor, dart, drummer, flathead and bream, you will find mulloway, kingfish, salmon, groper, snapper and trevally.

Offshore fishing: Bluewater fishing is good all year. During winter, snapper move close to shore. Mulloway are also at onshore reefs at this time. Teraglin, tuskfish, kingfish and pearl perch are common, with cobia caught as the weather warms. From October through summer pelagic fish appear, including mackerel, northern bluefin and mackerel tuna. Oceanic leatherjackets are a popular winter table fish.

Freshwater fishing: Cod and bass are found in the upper Clarence, with Copmanhurst a good starting point. The upper river's gorges are for fit fishermen, with some areas only accessible by helicopter. The Nymboida and Mann Rivers have good bass fishing. Clarence bass are wild stock. They usually bite best on warm summer mornings and afternoons.

Local bait: Live herring are the best bait for bream, flathead and mulloway. Herring can be caught in the river, usually around pylons, on bait jigs. Pipis and beach worms are found on beaches. Prawns work on most species. "Black Magic" weed is found in local canefield drains and is good for luderick. It is sometimes sold at fishing shops.

Caravan parks: There are many van parks on the lower Clarence River, and three have boat ramps. These include the Blue Dolphin (Yamba Rd) with river frontage, ramp, jetty, boat hire and cabins. Across the river is The Anchorage (Marandowie Dr, Iluka). Another park with a ramp is Brown's Rocks Park (Goodwood Island, Clarence River). It is close to a submerged rock wall which is a fishing hotspot.

Boat ramps and tides: There are good ramps on both sides of the river. The best is at Iluka, with ample parking and fish cleaning area. It is busy during holidays. The Clarence River entrance is generally good but the outgoing tide creates pressure waves.

GPS

Double 29 11.282S 153 30.052E
S-E Kahors 29 11.474S 153 29.388E
Red Hill B 29 11.943S 153 29.747E
Red Hill A 29 12.250S 153 29.500E
Middle Evans 29 12.249S 153 26.321E
Bombie 29 12.940S 153 25.654E
Italian B 29 13.899S 153 27.701E
Italian A 29 14.128S 153 28.749E
Canyons A 29 29.425S 153 25.501E
Canyons B 29 29.425S 153 47.600E
N-E Corner 29 29.574S 153 25.501E
One Man 29 30.778S 153 24.34E
Redcliff 29 34.037S 153 23.328E

Charted wrecks

29 17.775S 153 28.491E, 19km from Yamba
29 19.272S 153 28.346E, 17km from Yamba
29 25.146S 153 24.582E, 6km from Yamba
29 28.695S 153 35.184E, 24km from Yamba

Yamba tides are fairly small, averaging about up to a metre movement, nonetheless strong currents flow in the river.

Summer

Whiting, bream, dart, flathead, mulloway, tailor, salmon, flounder, trevally, tuna, mackerel, crabs

Winter

Bream, mullet, mulloway, tailor, luderick, snapper, silver drummer, trevally, salmon

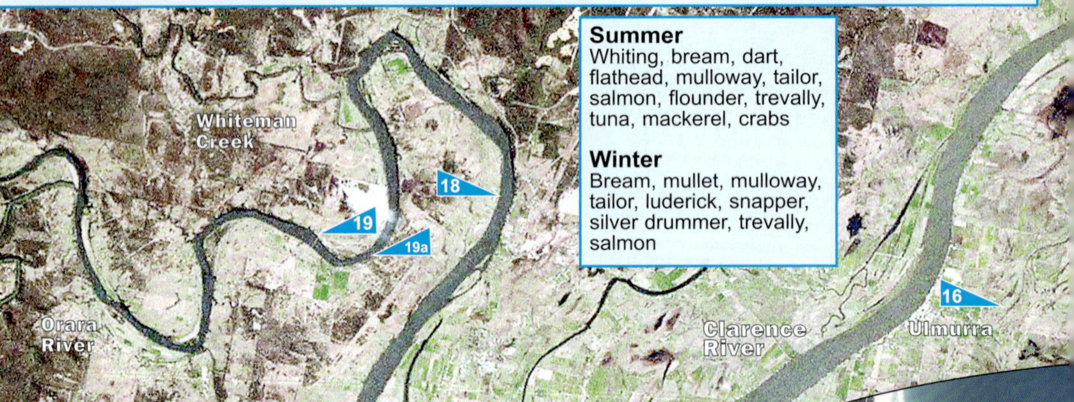

Tim the Bream

Yamba's **Tim the Bream** tagged fish competition has attracted up to 17,000 entrants. The event was first run in 1958. It was last held on the Clarence River in September 2018. A Rotary club spokesman said though recent years had been cancelled the event was likely to run again in future. In 2018 the tagged bream called Tim was worth $20,000, with 10 more bream worth $1000 each. There was a swag of prizes for other species of fish. Watch the Rotary Club of Yamba and local tackle shop Facebook pages for future developments.

Sandon River

Estuary images by John Lugg ©NSW Dept of Environment & Climate Change

Sandon

Note sanctuary zoning map on next page

Sandon River

MAP B

Launch sites

1. 4WD beach launch.
2. Four sites. Spencer St ramp north of bay is best, with jetty and all-tide access. Crown St and Marandowie Dve sites poor at low tide. Young St is firm sand.
3. Three launch sites. Harbour St has jetty; Yamba Rd has jetty, good parking; Witonga Dve has BBQ, ample parking. All tides.
4. Crystal Waters Reserve, Witonga Dve, multi-lanes, all tides.
5. Harwood Bridge, north bank, all tides.
6. Harwood Bridge, south bank, all tides.
7. Mcnaughton Place, all tides.
8. Two ramps on Lawrence Rd, all tides.
9. Chatsworth Rd, all tides.
10. Whitby Lane, Goodwood Island, all tides.
11. Fischers Lane, Chatsworth Island, shallow.
12. Old Ferry Rd, Ashby, all tides.
13. Bridge St, Lawrence, multi-lanes, all tides.
14. Weir Rd, Lower Southgate, all tides.
15. Ramps on either bank at bridge, all tides.
16. River St, Ulmarra, all tides.
17. Grafton ramps on north bank at Prince St, Fry St and Kirchner St. Ramp on south bank at Through St. All tides.
18. Perring Lane, Seelands, all tides.
19 & 19a. Both sides of river, Punt Lane & Old Punt Rd, all tides.
20. Lawrence St, Copmanhurst, all tides.
21. Lake Wooloweyah, Lakes Blvd.
22. Brooms Head beach launch.
23. Sandon River bank launch, shallow. Bar crossing is poor.
24. Coldstream Tce, Tucabia, all tides.

Local tides have up to about 1.74m movement.

Dams

Fishing dams west of Yamba include Pindari, Copeton, Beardy Waters and Coolmunda, all within 200-250km as the crow flies.

Hotspots

Key to Map

1. Shark Bay and 10-Mile Beach has 4WD access. There are camp sites to the north at Black Rock and south at Woody Head in Bundjalung National Park.
2. Woody Head has tailor, flathead, snapper, mulloway. Best in light easterly or northerly. Beach has bream, whiting. Frasers Reef has tailor and mulloway.
3. Iluka Bluff has big tailor and mulloway. Iluka Beach 4WD access by permit from Maclean Shire Council.
4. Outer rock walls have tailor, mulloway, bream, flathead. Luderick in winter. Tuna, mackerel in summer. Mulloway after rain.
5. Yamba Point - bream, mulloway.
6. Flat Rock and Miners Rock have tailor, mulloway, bream.
7. Green Point has bream, tailor and drummer. Angourie Point has whiting, tailor, snapper, mulloway.
8. One Man Rock - snapper, mulloway, tailor.
9. Shelley Beach has mulloway. Shelley Head has snapper, mulloway, tailor. Freeburn Rock Reef has tailor, mulloway, snapper.
10. Brooms Head has tailor, mulloway, snapper. Reef fish at Buchanans Rock.
11. Sandon River - good fishing after rain at mouth. Creek has bream, luderick, flathead, whiting, crabs. Rock fishing at Plover Island. Beware sanctuary zones.
12. Access to the Middle Wall, Collis Wall and Turkeys Nest is by boat, in winter luderick run here. Big flathead in the summer. Mulloway best after heavy rain on lures and bait.
13. Lake Wooloweyah, and Oyster and Romiaka Channels best after rain. Lake has flathead, bream, crabs. Luderick in channels.
14. Oyster Channel good for bream, luderick, mulloway.
15. Harwood Bridge and downstream: Flathead all year, mulloway in deep water along bank at Palmers Island. Browns Rocks and Goodwood Island have bream and flathead - deep southern bank good after rain. Fish all Clarence bridges.
16. The Broadwater: bream, mulloway, whiting, flathead.
17. Cowper: bream, flathead, mulloway.
18. Fishing around Grafton is affected by rain, as marine species move downstream.
19. Bass, cod in upper reaches.
20. Coldstream River has bass around Tucabia. Flathead and bream at junction.

MAP A

Wooli Wooli River

Estuary images by John Lugg ©NSW Dept of Environment & Climate Change

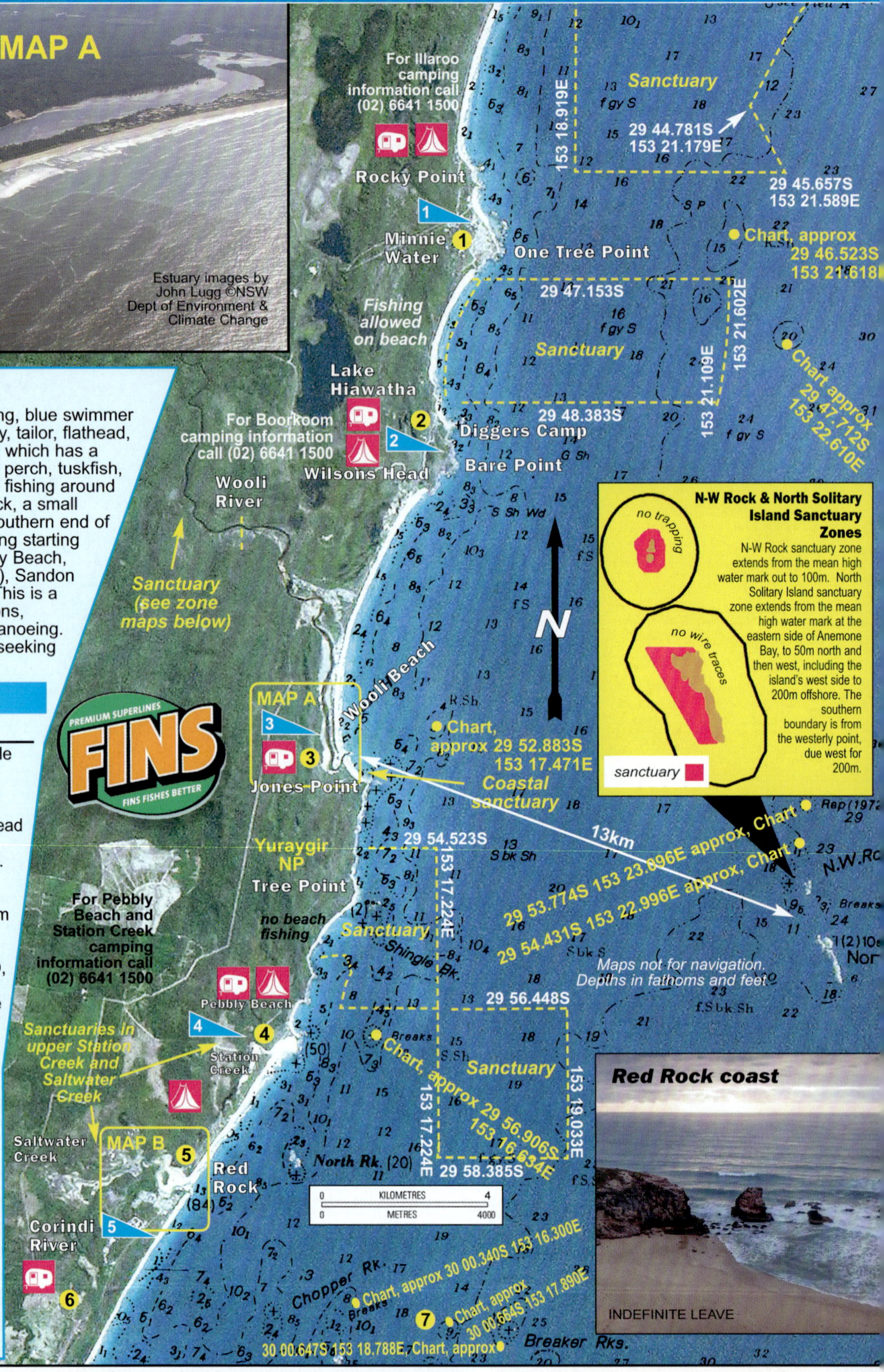

Wooli Wooli River

This river has good stocks of bream, flathead, whiting, blue swimmer and mud crabs. Note the sanctuary zones. Mulloway, tailor, flathead, jacks and luderick are taken from the entrance wall, which has a footpath. Nearby reefs have snapper, teraglin, pearl perch, tuskfish, amberjack, samson fish and kingfish. There is good fishing around the islands, but again note the park zones. Red Rock, a small fishing resort 13km north of Woolgoolga, is at the southern end of Yuraygir National Park. The park has coastal camping starting from just north of Red Rock at Station Creek, Pebbly Beach, Boorkoom (Wilsons Headland), Illaroo (Rocky Point), Sandon River, Lake Arragan, Red Cliff and Shelley Beach. This is a great natural setting for fishing, with beaches, lagoons, heathlands and swamps. The creeks are ideal for canoeing. There are long coastal bushwalking trails for those seeking a secluded fishing spot.

Key to Map

Hotspots

1. Bay with beach launching and rock platforms fishable near low tide for bream and drummer.
2. Good rock fishing off Diggers Camp.
3. Wooli River rock wall has footpath and fishes well, mulloway after rain, jacks in summer at night. Big flathead in spring/summer, salmon, luderick, bream in winter. Oyster racks have bream, flathead. Boat hire available. Nippers on flats near van park. Mud and blue crabs in river. Rockbar stops upper access, except for canoes. Beach accessible by 4WD. Good offshore fishing, 13km to North Solitary Island, but note park zones.
4. Station Creek access is via Barcoongere Forest Road into Yuraygir NP. There is beach access for 4WD, small boats can be launched in calm weather. Good fishing at rocks near Station Creek, tailor, bream, some mulloway. Tailor best in winter. Pebbly Beach has mulloway, bream, tailor. Access past Pebbly Beach is difficult and there is a sanctuary area.
5. Red Rock township beach has most species, including mulloway. Beach to north mostly has tailor and bream. The Corindi River has whiting and flathead, with mud crabs and mangrove jacks upstream, but beware large sanctuary zone.
6. Corindi Beach accessible by 4WD, bream, tailor.
7. Reefs, beware breaking waves, most species.

Launch sites

1. Beach launch in sheltered bay at Minnie Water.
2. Beach launch for small boats at Diggers Camp.
3. Wooli River ramps at Riverside Dve (all tides) and Wooli Rd (shallow). River bar crossing requires great care.
4. Beach launch near Station Creek campground.
5. Good ramp in Ford St, Corindi River, all tides.

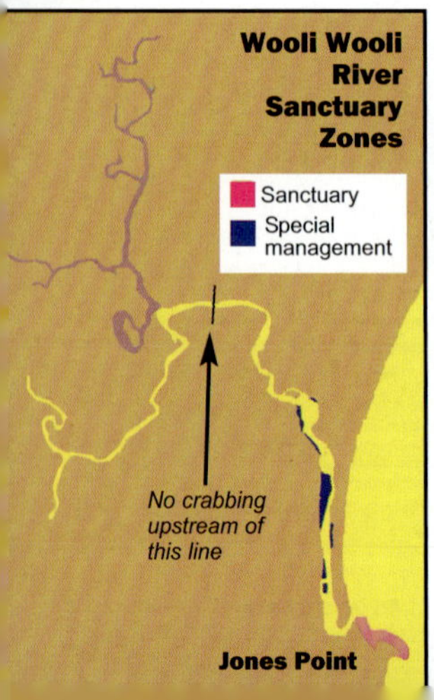

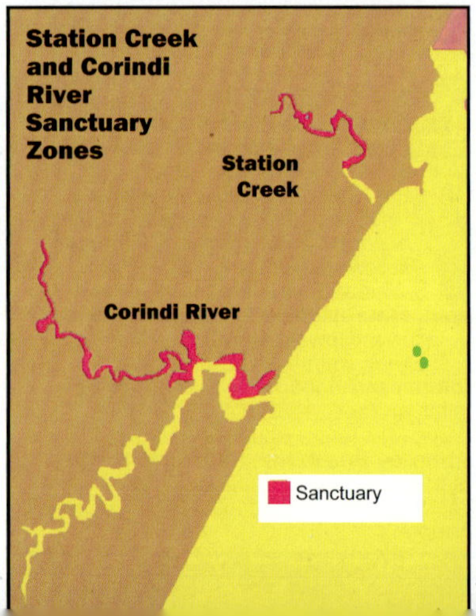

For Illaroo camping information call (02) 6641 1500

For Boorkoom camping information call (02) 6641 1500

For Pebbly Beach and Station Creek camping information call (02) 6641 1500

Sanctuary (see zone maps below)

Sanctuaries in upper Station Creek and Saltwater Creek

Fishing allowed on beach

no beach fishing

Coastal sanctuary

Maps not for navigation. Depths in fathoms and feet

N-W Rock & North Solitary Island Sanctuary Zones

N-W Rock sanctuary zone extends from the mean high water mark out to 100m. North Solitary Island sanctuary zone extends from the mean high water mark at the eastern side of Anemone Bay, to 50m north and then west, including the island's west side to 200m offshore. The southern boundary is from the westerly point, due west for 200m.

Red Rock coast

INDEFINITE LEAVE

Wooli Wooli River Sanctuary Zones

Sanctuary

Special management

No crabbing upstream of this line

Jones Point

Station Creek and Corindi River Sanctuary Zones

Station Creek

Corindi River

Sanctuary

MAP C

Coffs Harbour

The harbour gives safe big-boat access to gamefish such as black, blue and striped marlin, mako sharks, broadbill swordfish, sailfish, spearfish, tuna, wahoo, mahi mahi, mackerel and kingfish. Ocean kayak fishing is popular on the many inshore reefs from Corindi to Sawtell when snapper bite in close in daylight during dark moon phases in winter. Landbased fishos will find big bream and mangrove jacks along the harbour walls and wharf pylons. The north end of this map starts with Corindi Beach Caravan Park, which has surf fishing nearby. There is no 4WD beach access, but the van park is next to a hole with rock patches. Further south the township of Mullaway has a van park, with beach launching at Arrawarra Head. The rock headland at Mullaway is only easily fishable in calm weather. Further south, Look at Me Now Head, Moonee Beach, Diggers and McCauleys Heads are fishable spots. For boaters, spotted and spanish mackerel are locally best in summer, usually peaking March to May. Winter is best for snapper and pearl perch. Kingfish are best in winter-spring, with bream, tailor and luderick in winter. Northern fish such as spangled emperor are a regular late summer catch, along with tuskfish and maori cod. Tropical reef fish may appear more often with greater influxes of warm water. Coffs Creek, Boambee Creek and Bonville Creek have bream, whiting and flathead. Bass fishos can try the Bellinger River, just a half-hour drive south-west of Coffs Harbour. Before fishing this region, note the Solitary Islands Marine Park zones.

Key to Map

Hotspots

1. Mackerel in summer, tailor in winter, some reef fish.
2. Good fishing on east side of island for reef and pelagic fish.
3. Beach near van park has rocks, tailor and bream in day, mulloway and sharks at night. North of this hole are gutters with whiting, dusk and dawn.
4. Mullaway Headland has easy access and reasonable ledges. Ocean View and Mullaway beaches are shallow with whiting.
5. Woolgoolga Beach has tailor, bream, whiting. No 4WD on beach. Headland has tailor and mulloway.
6. Look at Me Now Head has tailor, bream, mulloway. Note sanctuaries at Diggers Point and Bare Bluff.
7. North side of Green Bluff is best. South end of Moonee Beach has most species, including mulloway. North end is a sanctuary.
8. Diggers Head off Charlesworth Bay Rd, deep water, most species.
9. Inshore reefs have snapper, mulloway, teraglin, cobia, kingfish all year. Samson appear with spanish mackerel in summer. Out wide from June-Sept are yellowfin tuna and striped marlin. On Continental Shelf from December to May are mackerel, wahoo, marlin, tuna and deepwater reef fish.
10. Boambee Beach has bream, tailor, mulloway, with 4WD access at northern end. Sawtell has two good creeks for bream, whiting, flathead and crabs.

Launch sites

1. Concrete and sand beach launch on north side of Arrawarra Headland, Second Ave, best at high tide.
2. Beach launch in Carrington St, Woolgoolga.
3. Sandy Beach Dve, beach launch.
4. Fiddaman Rd, Emerald Beach, beach launch.
5. Moonee Beach Rd, Moonee Creek, all tides.
6. Four-lane ramp on south side of Coffs boat harbour, Jordan Esp. Can be affected by swell. Ramps in Coffs Creek at Edgar St (shallow) and Melittas Ave.
7. Beach launch in Boronia St, Sawtell. Ramp in Bonville Creek at Lyons Rd, shallow. Bank launch at Boambee Creek Reserve.

Local tides have up to about 2m movement.

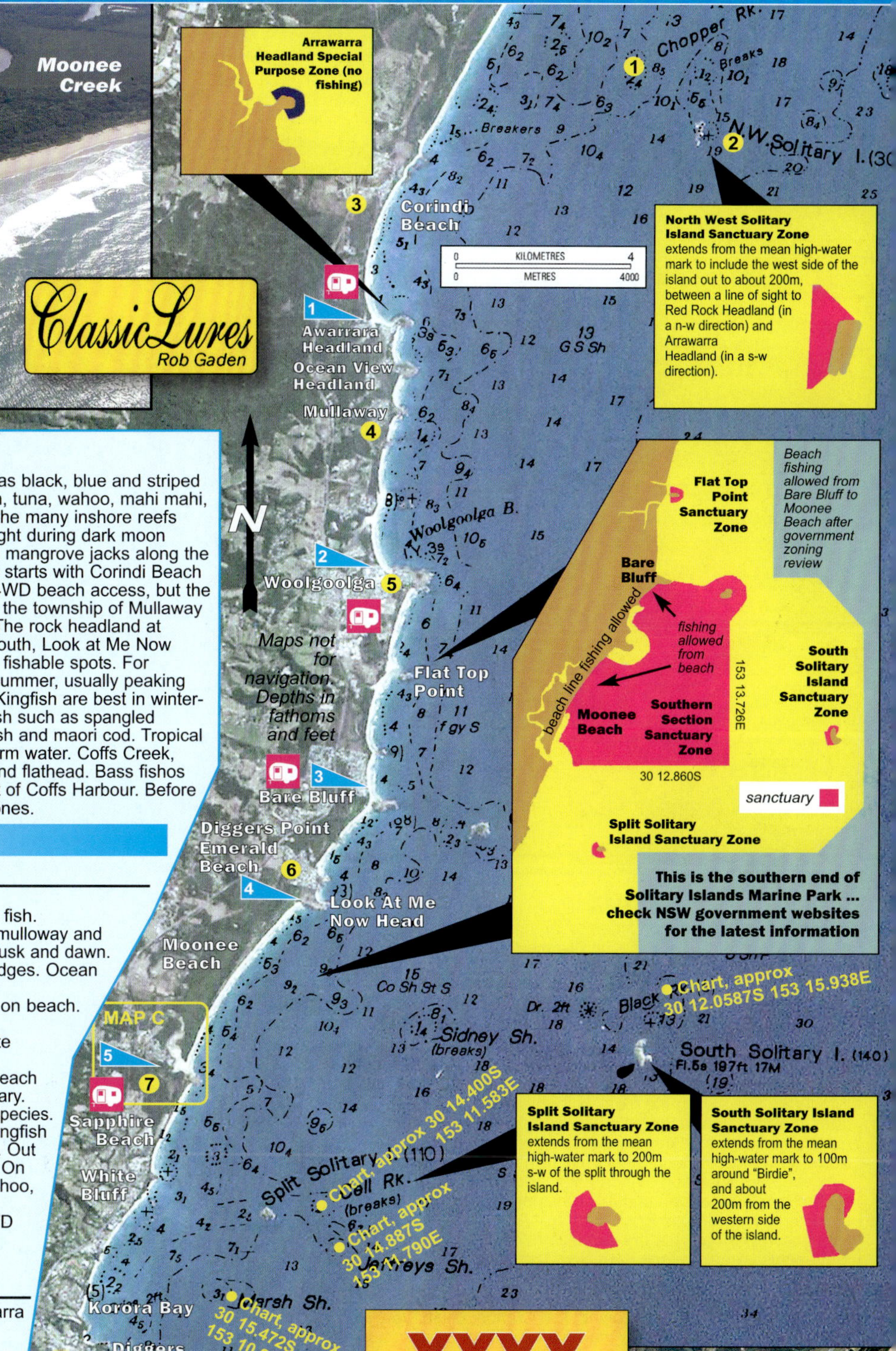

Arrawarra Headland Special Purpose Zone (no fishing)

North West Solitary Island Sanctuary Zone extends from the mean high-water mark to include the west side of the island out to about 200m, between a line of sight to Red Rock Headland (in a n-w direction) and Arrawarra Headland (in a s-w direction).

Beach fishing allowed from Bare Bluff to Moonee Beach after government zoning review

Flat Top Point Sanctuary Zone

Southern Section Sanctuary Zone

Split Solitary Island Sanctuary Zone

This is the southern end of Solitary Islands Marine Park ... check NSW government websites for the latest information

Split Solitary Island Sanctuary Zone extends from the mean high-water mark to 200m s-w of the split through the island.

South Solitary Island Sanctuary Zone extends from the mean high-water mark to 100m around "Birdie", and about 200m from the western side of the island.

Maps not for navigation. Depths in fathoms and feet

MAP D

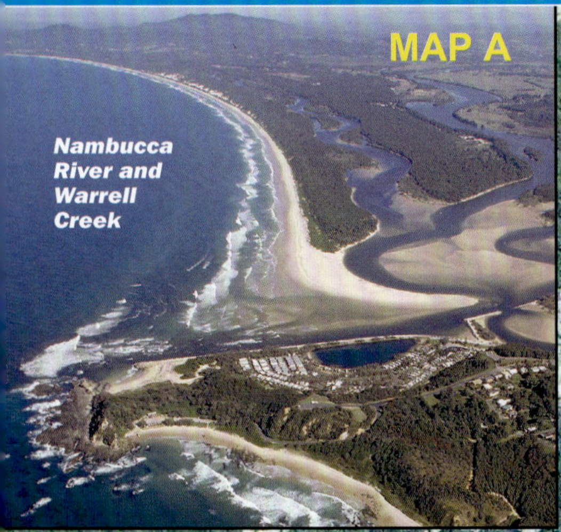

MAP A
Nambucca River and Warrell Creek

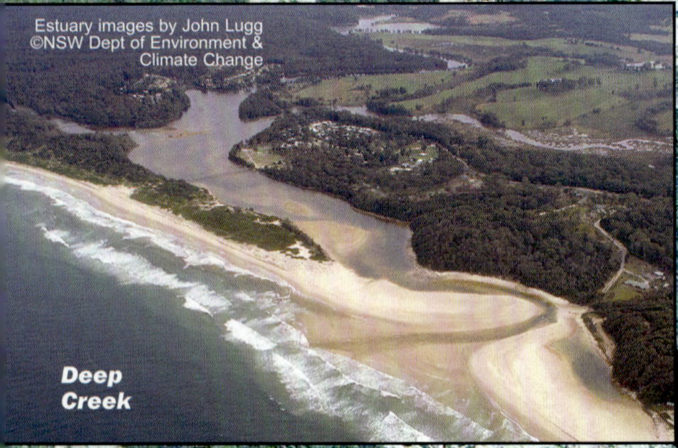

Estuary images by John Lugg ©NSW Dept of Environment & Climate Change
Deep Creek

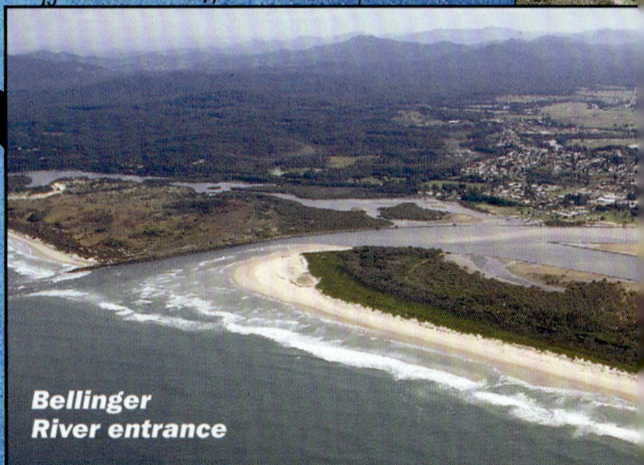

Bellinger River entrance

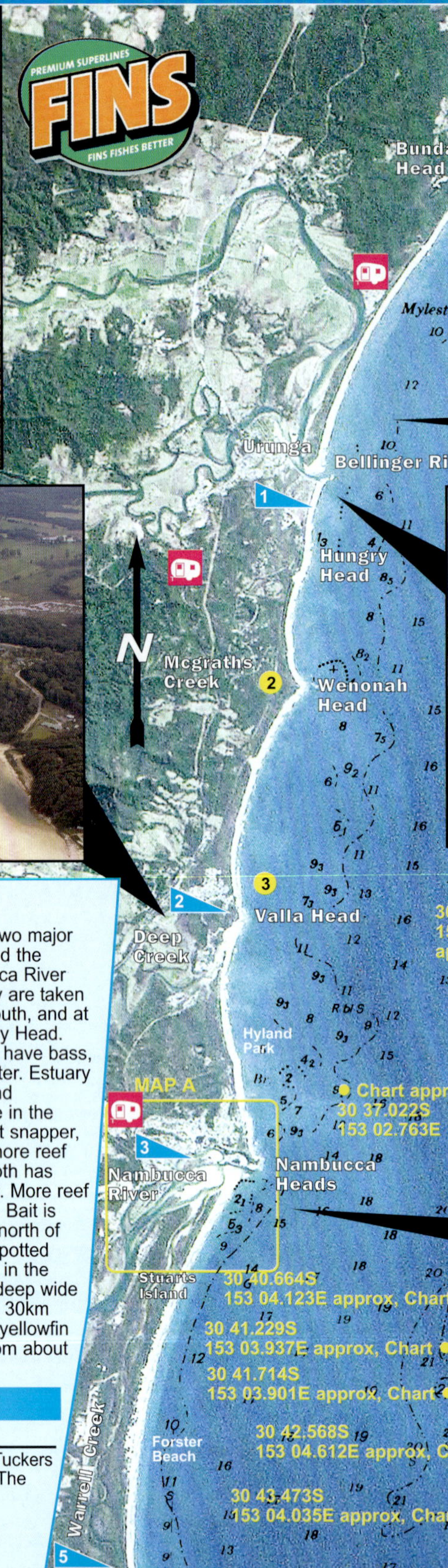

FINS
PREMIUM SUPERLINES
FINS FISHES BETTER
Bundagen Head
Mylestom
Charted shoal 17.5km from Bellinger mouth approx 30 26.313S 153 11.879E, also 30 25.266S 153 11.925E
Urunga
Bellinger River
Hungry Head
Mcgraths Creek
Wenonah Head
Valla Head
Deep Creek
30 36.333S 153 05.499E approx, Chart
30 36.681S 153 09.426E shoal off map
Hyland Park
Chart approx 30 37.022S 153 02.763E
Chart approx 30 37.650S 153 04.562E
MAP A
Nambucca River
Nambucca Heads
Stuarts Island
30 40.664S 153 04.123E approx, Chart
30 41.229S 153 03.937E approx, Chart
30 41.714S 153 03.901E approx, Chart
30 42.568S 153 04.612E approx, Chart
30 43.473S 153 04.035E approx, Chart
Forster Beach
Warrell Creek
Maps not for navigation. Depths in fathoms and feet
Scotts Head
30 45.592S 153 03.720E approx, Chart
30 48.009S 153 02.285E approx, Chart
Grassy Head
Agnes Irving 30 48.387S 153 00.299E
Bellinge
Bowravi
KILOMETRES
METRES

Nambucca Heads

The coast from Bundagen Head to Grassy Head has two major estuaries, the Bellinger River and Nambucca River, and the smaller Deep Creek. Warrell Creek flows into Nambucca River mouth. All have flathead, bream and whiting. Mulloway are taken at Nambucca wall and Wellington Rock at the river mouth, and at Hat Rock at Valla. There is landbased fishing at Grassy Head. The Nambucca River and tributaries above Macksville have bass, best Nov-March, with bass moving downstream in winter. Estuary perch are also in the river. In the bluewater, tropical and temperate fish are on the reefs, with most fishing done in the 30m to 50m depth range, about 22km offshore. Expect snapper, morwong, flathead, samson, cod and pearl perch. Inshore reef between Nambucca and Valla from 12m to 22m in depth has pink snapper, spangled emperor, flathead and kingfish. More reef exists from 38m to 43m and this runs north to Urunga. Bait is collected off Wellington Rock (14m to 17m deep) and north of Nambucca Bar opposite the surf club (12m to 18m). Spotted and spanish mackerel run from Nov-April. Hapuka are in the 120m-200m zone. A summer FAD is installed at 60m deep wide of Nambucca River. On the Continental Shelf drop-off, 30km east of Nambucca Heads, dolphin fish, wahoo, cobia, yellowfin tuna, striped, blue and black marlin and sailfish run from about December to May. Nambucca bar is dangerous.

Key to Map

Hotspots

1. North Beach and Bundagen Headland accessible via Tuckers Rock car park. 4WD permitted as far north as headland. The walk north to bay and creek worthwhile after rain.
2. Wenonah Head.
3. Valla Head. Large pelagic fish.
4. Reef and pelagic fish.
5. The main beach at Scotts Head has surf fishing.
6. Grassy Head has platforms into deep water, with a van park nearby. Boat fishing on nearby reefs.

Launch sites

1. Bellinger River has several ramps, some in van parks - see next page. Bellinger Bar should only be used in ideal conditions.
2. Deep Creek has a high-tide launch on Ocean View Dve. Also south side of Deep Creek Rd bridge. Bar not navigable.
3. Nambucca ramps at Gordon Park, the RSL carpark, Stuarts Island and along Riverside Dve near the V-wall. See next page. Gravel site on Pacific Hwy. Nambucca Bar is risky - consider using Shelly Beach ramp.
4. The surf club has a concrete ramp with pontoon in a sheltered beach area inside Scotts Head, and is the best local sea access.
5. Gumma campground has a bank launch into Warrell Creek.

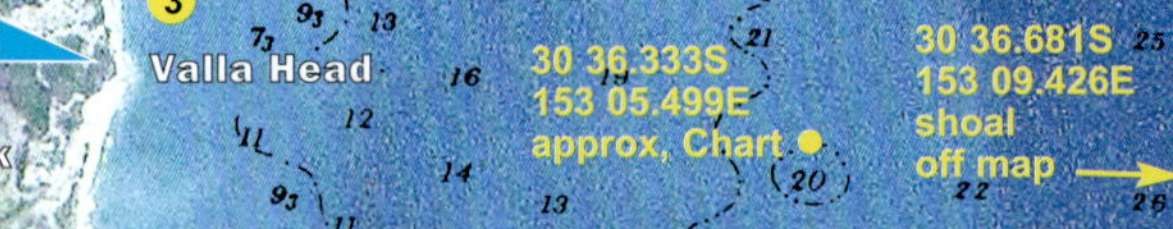

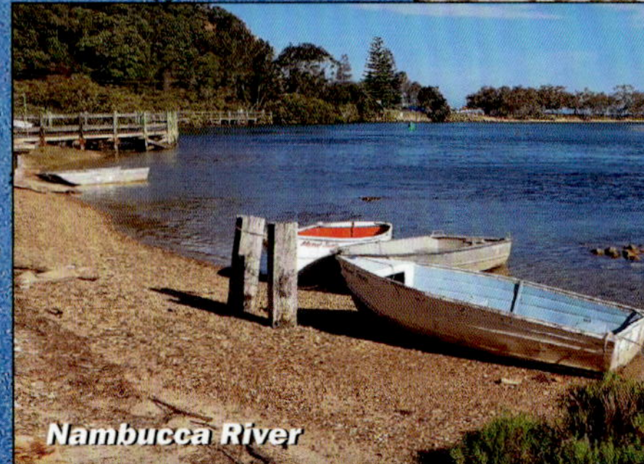

Nambucca River

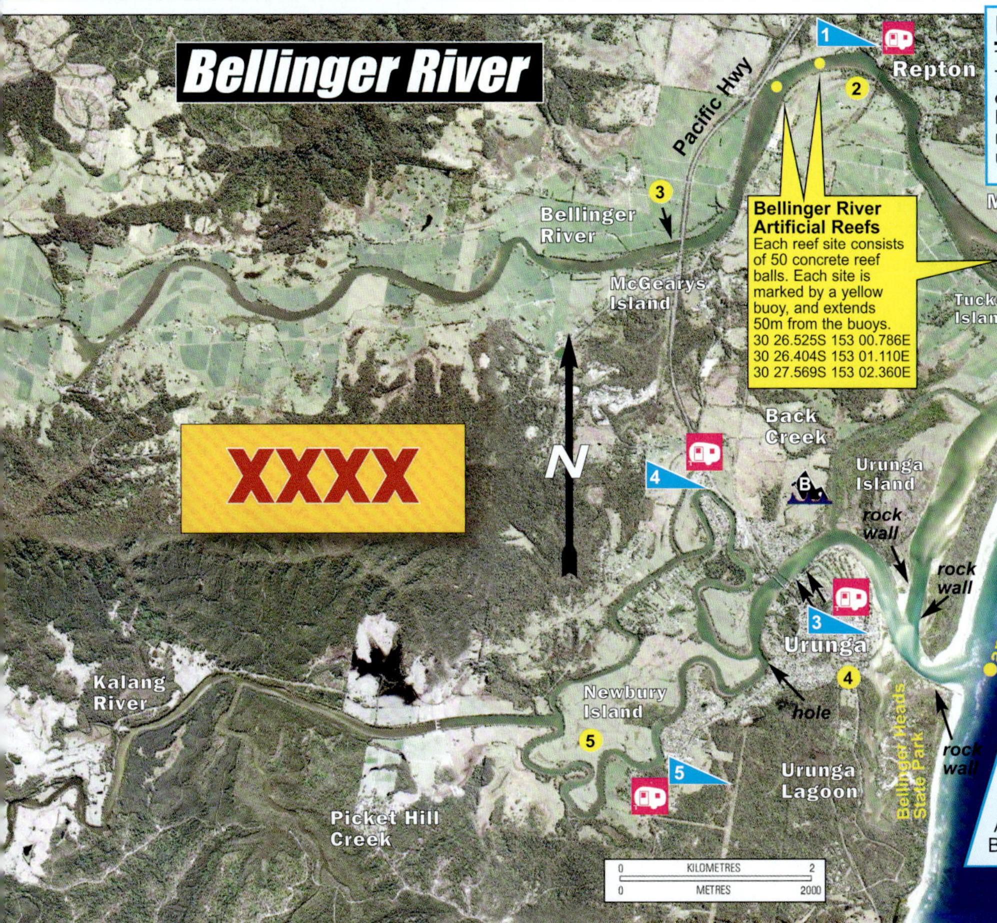

Urunga

The Bellinger and Kalang Rivers are a fishing haven. Tidal influence extends 20km upstream to Bellingen on the Bellinger River and 15km to Brierfield on the Kalang. The rivers are navigable by small boats to near the tidal limit. Canoe fishos will find bass water upstream of Bellingen, with the area between Thora and Gordonville Crossing (off map) having pools between gravel races that hold bass. Most estuary fish are found in the Bellinger's tidal section, with flathead, bream and whiting the main catch. The three artificial reefs are a good place to begin your efforts.

Key to Map

Hotspots

1. Tuckers Island flats edges have flathead, whiting. Nippers at low tide.
2. Deep water - bridge pylons have bream, flathead, luderick.
3. Bream north of island. Bass, bream above island, bass above Browns Crossing.
4. Rock wall near van park has most species. Urunga Lagoon has whiting, flathead, nippers.
5. Oyster leases around Newbury Island, bream flathead.

Launch sites

1. Repton ramp. Add an hour to Sydney tides.
2. Myleston, two single lane concrete ramps in Myleston Dve, all tides.
3. Urunga, two ramps, south bank, east of bridge.
4. Launch site at caravan park.
5. Launch sites at two caravan parks.
6. Unsealed ramp, south bank, Baker St, all tides.

Wrecks

A. Drogher paddle steamer remains in river.
B. Dredge wreck from 1930s.

Nambucca River

Nambucca Heads
jetty
walls
Nambucca River
Classic Lures Rob Gaden
Blackbutt Creek
Newee Creek
Watt Creek
Taylors Arm
Tilly Willy Creek
Macksville
Goat Island
Warrell Creek
Warrell Creek
Scotts Head
30 39.186S 153 00.867E approx
Maps not for navigation
INDEFINITE LEAVE

Nambucca

The Nambucca River has almost 30km of tidal water, but is only easily navigable to about 5km upstream at Macksville, with shallow gravel flats above. Most fishing takes place in the lower reaches. The bar is hazardous. The sandflats at the mouth offer sometimes excellent flathead and whiting fishing, with bream in the deeper sections. Luderick, tailor, drummer, garfish and mulloway are also taken. Warrell Creek enters the dual mouth opposite Nambucca Heads and is a good choice for fishermen who like wild surroundings. Bass live in the upper Nambucca River and Taylors Arm and estuary perch are taken in North Arm, South Arm, Warrell Creek and Taylors Arm. Mangrove jacks are caught on occasion.

Key to Map

Hotspots

1. Excellent fishing for tailor, luderick, bream, mulloway, occasional kingfish and snapper. Access is on foot via the rock wall.
2. Rock wall has mulloway, tailor and more. Only easily fishable at turn of tide. Walls inside river are easily accessible and have bream, flathead, luderick. Deep holes at ends of rock walls have jacks, mulloway, occasional hairtail.
3. Rock wall accessible only by boat, good fishing.
4. Mostly whiting and flathead in Warrell Creek.
5. Bream, occasional jack at Macksville bridges.
6. Bass above Blackbutt Creek, also in Taylors Arm.

Launch sites

1. Shelly Beach, sheltered cove. Concrete ramp, amenities.
2. Two good twin-lane ramps, one off Riverside Dve and one off Wellington Dve, all tides. Average high-tide ramp is located seaward off Wellington Dve. 2a. Stuarts Island ramp, off Riverside Dve. Good two-lane ramp, all tides.
3. Nambucca River Tourist Park ramp. 3a. Unsealed shallow site.
4. North Macksville: concrete ramp and toilets on north shore opposite bridge, off Ferry St, all tides.
5. Warrell Creek, Gumma Reserve, with camping.
6. Scotts Head, concrete ramp and pontoon. Best local sea access.
7. Newee Creek ramp (closed at publication), shallow at low tide.
8. Ramp at Pelican caravan park.
9. Launch site at Tilly Willy Creek rail bridge, off McKay St.
10. Bowraville concrete ramp, Wilson Rd.
11. Average concrete ramp at Congarinni Rd bridge, Macksville.

Macleay River

The upper river has some of Australia's best wild bass water. Estuary perch are in the lower reaches. There is 56km of tidal water up to near Dungay Creek. Inland, New England's high country trout streams are just a day-trip away. At South West Rocks and Hat Head the beach, rock and bluewater fishing is as good as it gets, but boating can be tricky because the river bar and shallow Back Creek access points are not ideal. There is 4WD access to beaches. Coastal reefs have tropical and temperate species. Sand and mud crabs are abundant in the lower river. Fish Rock, 2.3km south-east of Smoky Cape, is a prime inshore spot, especially for kingfish, but note that only lure fishing is permitted in Grey Nurse Shark zones. Boaters can target marlin, sailfish, spotted and spanish mackerel, wahoo, cobia, dolphin fish, kingfish and tuna. Christmas usually sees plagues of small kingfish, with big fish from July to December. Mulloway, bream and whiting are caught all year. Summer brings school mulloway action, along with big flathead, with reef fish such as snapper, pearl perch, morwong, pig fish, tuskfish, teraglin and longfin perch biting well for boaters. Winter is best for river luderick. Grassy Head Beach north of the river is good for surf mulloway.

Key to Map

Hotspots

1. Grassy Beach reached by 4WD from Grassy Head (off map) or a footbridge at Stuarts Point. Mulloway, whiting, big bream.
2. Continental Shelf starts about 25km out. Blue marlin and more.
3. South wall has a footpath and big fish. Strong tidal currents - fish turn of tide. Mulloway best after rain.
4. Good ledges off Laggers Point, mostly bream and tailor.
5. Green Island area has cobia, kingfish, snapper and more. Lure-only fishing in Grey Nurse Shark zone.
6. Black Rock has a hole at north end and lumps 200m south, with cobia, mulloway, snapper and kingfish. Fish Rock has kingfish and cobia, as well as seasonal sailfish and marlin. Spotted and spanish mackerel and small yellowfin tuna, and reef fish. Lure-only fishing in Grey Nurse Shark zone.
7. Smokey Beach has 4WD access and most surf fish. Creek mouth good after rain. Creek has whiting, bream, with big summer flathead.
8. Several platforms near and off the tip, with best spots dubbed Spinning Ledge and Death Hole. Both yield large pelagic fish, including marlin. Access to Death Hole is by ropes. Access to the island near the point is at low tide, with some worthwhile ledges to fish. Specialist tackle is needed for big fish. Bream and luderick anglers will find plenty of fish. Take extra care on the rocks.
9. Good ledges on mainland inside island, most species.
10. Rock ledges, most species. Walking track follows coast.
11. Mulloway, tailor in hole where Hungry Head joins beach and extends out to sea. Seaward platform also has tailor, drummer, mackerel, kingfish, cobia.
12. Killick Beach is reached off Pacific St, then Tourist Rd 12 on to Richardsons Crossing. This beach is renowned for mulloway, as well as tailor and bream.
13. Luderick in winter.
14. Flathead in Spencer Creek.
15. Jerseyville Bridge has mulloway, tailor, and cobia.
16. Good land-based fishing into deep water along Suez Rd. Mulloway, flathead.
17. Around deep junctions - mulloway at night.
18 and 18. Whiting, flathead, bream in upper reaches.
19. Upper Macleay River has bass. The road follows the river in places - take a canoe and enjoy the scenery. Trout are in the New England district highland rivers.

Launch sites

1. Macleay Arm has ramps at Fishermen's Reach (marked) and Stuarts Point to the north. Both are shallow near low tide.
2. New Entrance Rd, multi-lanes, all tides. Dangerous bar crossing, beware north-easters.
3. Back Creek ramp, shallow at low tide. Four-hour window.
4. Cardwell St, Trial Bay beach launch, shallow, restricted hours.
5. Jerseyville Bridge, Plummers Lane, all tides, pontoon.
5. Gladstone, both sides of Smithtown Bridge.
6. Summer Island Rd, all tides.
7. Riverside Dve, high tide only.
8. Main St, all tides.
9 & 9a. On opposite banks, Macleay St and Fredericton Ferry Rd, all tides.
10. Kempt St and Ramp St, all tides.
11. Greenhill Ferry Rd, all tides.
12. Hat Head Rd, shallow creek site.

Tidal variations from Sydney (Fort Dension tides): Kemps Corner, add about 30 minutes. Kempsey, add about 3.5 hours.

MAP C

Macleay River entrance

Offshore

Small black marlin can be caught in sheltered Trial Bay, less than 1km offshore. These fish usually run from December to February. Big cobia are also caught in close during summer. For bigger marlin, including blacks, striped and blues, the Continental Shelf is the place to fish and runs relatively close to the coast. The Shelf has yellowfin tuna, wahoo, striped, blue and black marlin, and sailfish, mostly from December to May. With its many inshore reefs and the presence of tropical and temperate reef and pelagic fish, this is a great bluewater fishing area.

Local fishing seasons

Small black marlin, Dec to Apr. Blue and striped marlin on Continental Shelf drop-off all year. Spotted mackerel Dec-June. Spanish mackerel late Jan-June. Cobia Dec-Aug. Dolphin fish Jan to June. Longtail and mack tuna Feb-Aug. Yellowtail kingfish all year, big fish in winter. Greenback tailor May-July. Offshore reef fish Jan-Oct. Mulloway all year. Yellowfin tuna/albacore Aug-Oct on the Continental Shelf. Flathead Nov-Feb. Luderick June-Aug. Bream, whiting and flathead can be caught all year. Freshwater bass, Oct-April.

Laggers Point
The Island
Little Smoky
MAP A
Green Island
Smoky Cape
Fish Rock
approx 30 56.443S 153 05.976E
Black Rocks
approx 30 57.038S 153 04.504E
Bass Country
19
Seven Oaks Drain
Frederickton
9
9a
Sherwood
11
Kempsey
10
tidal limit
bridge
Dungay Creek

Dams

Fishing dams west of Kempsey include Split Rock, Keepit Chaffey and Glenbawn, all within 230km as the crow flies.

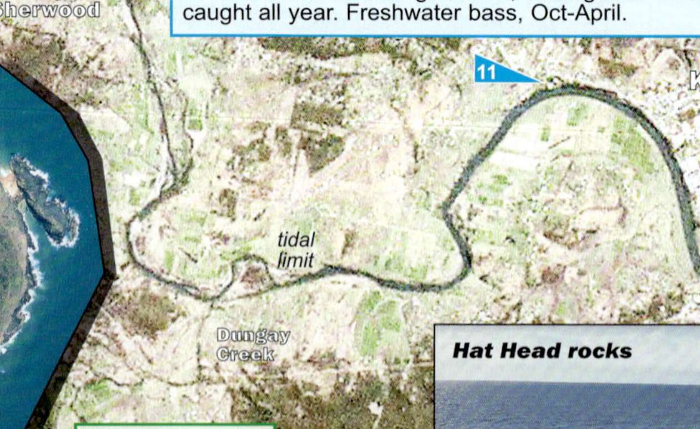

Hat Head rocks

South West Rocks coast
INDEFINITE LEAVE
Estuary images by John Lugg ©NSW Dept of Environment & Climate Change
Macleay Arm
Goat Island
MAP C
approx 30 52.385S 153 01.450E
rock walls
Shark Island
bridges
hole
Trial Bay
Laggers Point
Back Creek
South West Rocks
nippers
Little Smoky
Pelican Island
Spencers Creek
Hat Head National Park
Green Island
Grey nurse shark protection zones - special bait fishing rules apply
Smoky Cape
MAP A
Smoky Cape camping area, for details call (02) 6566 6168
Fish Rock
Black Rocks
Classic Lures
Rob Gaden
KILOMETRES
METRES
XXXX
Smoky Cape
INDEFINITE LEAVE
WARNING
Rock fishing is dangerous! Fish in good conditions only. If in doubt, don't!
Korogoro Head
bridge
Gladstone
Kinchella Creek
Belmore River
Korogoro Point
Hat Head
MAP B
Hungry Head
Hungry Gate camping area, for details call (02) 6566 6168
Belmore Swamp
Spinning Ledge
Death Hole
South Ledge
The Island
Gap Beach
Connors Beach
Connors Head
Hungry Head
FINS
Maps not for navigation. Depths in metres
Killick Beach

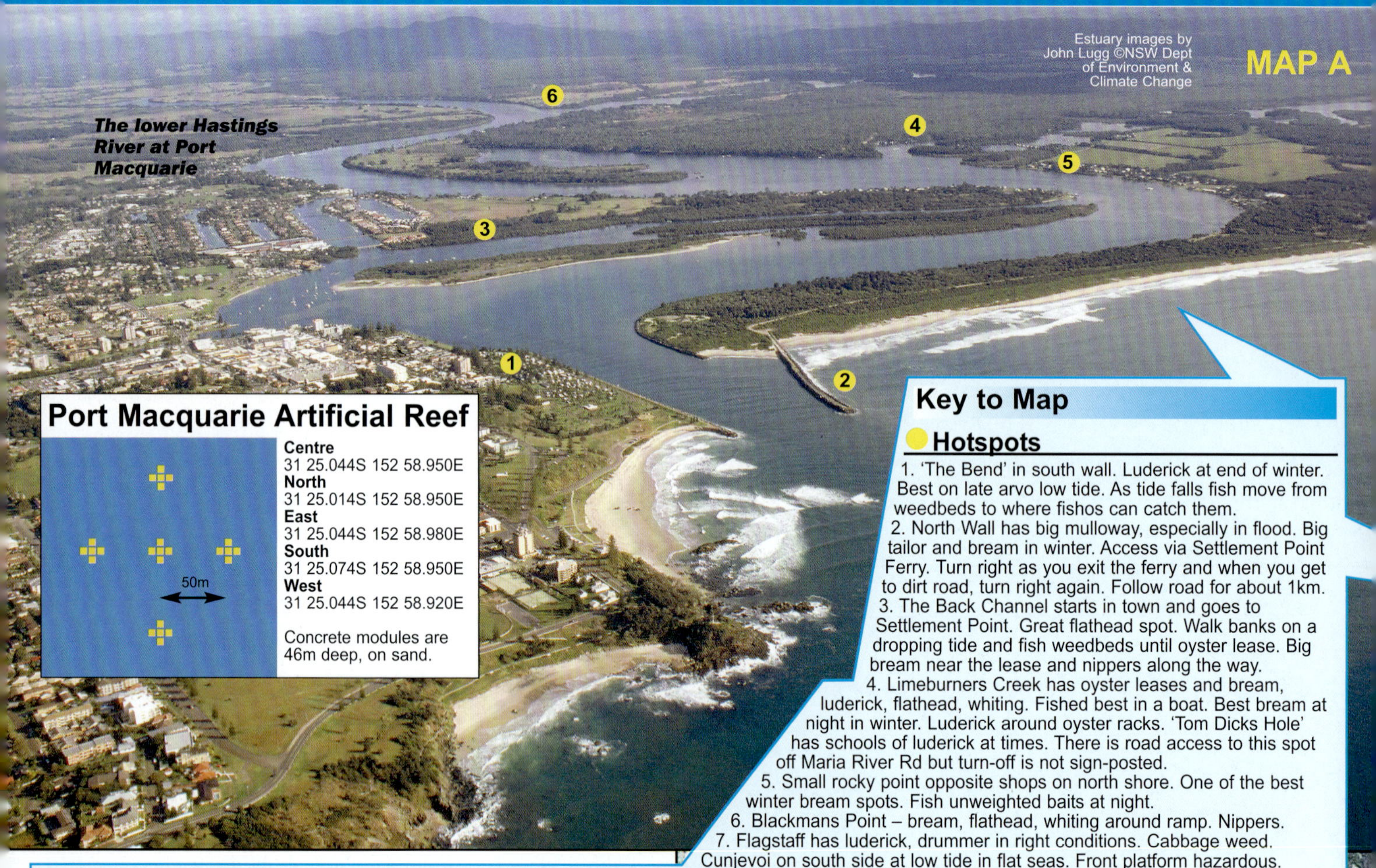

Estuary images by John Lugg ©NSW Dept of Environment & Climate Change

MAP A

The lower Hastings River at Port Macquarie

Port Macquarie Artificial Reef

Centre
31 25.044S 152 58.950E
North
31 25.014S 152 58.950E
East
31 25.044S 152 58.980E
South
31 25.074S 152 58.950E
West
31 25.044S 152 58.920E

50m

Concrete modules are 46m deep, on sand.

Key to Map

Hotspots

1. 'The Bend' in south wall. Luderick at end of winter. Best on late arvo low tide. As tide falls fish move from weedbeds to where fishos can catch them.
2. North Wall has big mulloway, especially in flood. Big tailor and bream in winter. Access via Settlement Point Ferry. Turn right as you exit the ferry and when you get to dirt road, turn right again. Follow road for about 1km.
3. The Back Channel starts in town and goes to Settlement Point. Great flathead spot. Walk banks on a dropping tide and fish weedbeds until oyster lease. Big bream near the lease and nippers along the way.
4. Limeburners Creek has oyster leases and bream, luderick, flathead, whiting. Fished best in a boat. Best bream at night in winter. Luderick around oyster racks. 'Tom Dicks Hole' has schools of luderick at times. There is road access to this spot off Maria River Rd but turn-off is not sign-posted.
5. Small rocky point opposite shops on north shore. One of the best winter bream spots. Fish unweighted baits at night.
6. Blackmans Point – bream, flathead, whiting around ramp. Nippers.
7. Flagstaff has luderick, drummer in right conditions. Cabbage weed. Cunjevoi on south side at low tide in flat seas. Front platform hazardous.
8. Rocky Beach, best in winter. Drummer, luderick, bream. Summer blue groper.
9. Nobby Head: Can only be fished by walking from north side. Large blowhole and cave on front side. Dangerous. Drummer, bream, tailor, mulloway.
10. Shellys Beach: Southern Point has drummer, bream, luderick, blue groper. Front platform dangerous. Track to left of toilet block goes to Miner's Beach, bream and drummer
11. Tacking Point: huge mulloway, drummer, bream, salmon, tailor. Front rock platform only fishable in flat seas. To north are The Pyramid and High Rock, big fish spots. Tough climb to High Rock. Long gaff is needed in this area. Dangerous.
12. Gulawah Beach has no 4WD access but there is a campground near the beach. Mostly tailor, bream.
13. Good fishing off Racecourse Head, island is accessible at low tide, most surf species.
14. Delicate Nobby: four rocks with access to three possible at low tide. Good for tailor, bream, some mulloway.
15. Camp next to creek - ledges off headland fishable with specialist gear. Beach launch, but no other access.
16. Point Plomer is a great spot with campsite, beach launch and rock platforms, with kingfish, mulloway. Queens Head to the south good for luderick, drummer.
17. North Beach reached by Settlement Point ferry. Surf fish, including salmon, tailor, mulloway.
18. South Wall has easy access and most species, including mulloway. Best at turn of tide. Luderick in winter. The town wharf also fishes well. North Wall reached by ferry - see No. 2 above.
19. Lake Cathie has school and tiger prawns, mud and blue crabs, nippers, garfish, whiting and flathead. Best conditions for prawns are at night around the new moon when they run for the sea on the runout tide. Bream and luderick in the channel. The lake opens to sea after heavy rain, when the beach usually fishes well.
20. River from Maria River junction to the bridge is good for flathead and whiting.
21. Mulloway in deep water at turn of tide, big flathead and whiting on edges.
22. Bass and bream in upper Maria and Wilson Rivers. The Maria good for surface bass fishing in summer.
23. Oxley Head and Sandy Point are best spots near Wauchope, big flathead, and bream and whiting. Wauchope region has garfish, bream and flathead. Fishing for natives farther upstream is better.
24. Oxley Hwy follows Hastings River - canoe fishing for bass. River has been stocked with bass. Also some estuary perch.

Port Macquarie

The Hastings and Maria Rivers have a prolific school mulloway fishery. There are also estuary perch, with bass in the upper river reaches, and big bream throughout. The main arm of the Hastings River is 120km long, with tidal water for 35km, to about 8km above Wauchope. The upper river runs through the Great Dividing Range. The mouth has big mulloway, especially after rain, but is tricky to fish by boat or land on an outgoing tide because of strong currents. The tidal river has mostly bream, flathead, whiting and luderick, with bream/luderick best in winter and flathead/whiting best in summer. Limeburner's Creek is suitable for small boats, with bream, luderick and flathead on oyster racks. The picnic area at the end of Settlement Point Road is a good family venue, as is Lake Cathie, with bream, whiting and flathead. Lake Cathie is one of the state's better prawning locations. There is ample offshore reef along the coast with temperate and tropical fish such as snapper, pearl perch, mulloway, cobia and kingfish. Spanish mackerel are seasonal and usually peak around Point Plomer in March/April. There is also an offshore artificial reef and summer FAD. Beaches from Town Beach to Lighthouse Beach have whiting, bream and tailor, with occasional mulloway.

Artificial Reef

A. The reef of 25 concrete 5m by 5m concrete modules was installed in 2016 in 46m of water 6.3km east of the Hastings River mouth. The centre is 31 25.044S 152 58.950E. See map above. A summer FAD is installed at approx 31 24.567S 153 04.725E, see NSW Fisheries website for latest position.

Launch sites

1. Off map, Killick Ck has a ramp at Crescent Head.
2. Beach launch at Big Hill Point.
3. Beach launch at Point Plomer.
4. Best launch sites are Short St, Buller St and Park St. All tides. Good ramp at Settlement Point on River Park Rd.
5. River Park Rd, all tides.
6. Fernbank Creek Rd, shallow.
7. Blackmans Point Rd, shallow.
8. Oakes Cres, shallow.
9. Rocks Ferry Rd, multi-lanes, all tides.
10. Cathie Creek, Evans St, all tides.

Local tides have up to about 1.6m movement.

XXXX
Classic Lures
Rob Gaden
FINS
FINS FISHES BETTER
Upstream
Port Macquarie has bass fishing in the rivers freshwater reaches. The Hastings River has bass above Beechwood, only a 25-minute drive from Port Macquarie. The Wilson River above Telegraph Point is about 25 minutes away and has good bass. Camden Haven River, 25 minutes south of Port Macquarie, has bass above Kendall. The Maria River is a good bass water, but access is more difficult.
Beach driving
Get beach driving permits from Hastings Council offices at Port Macquarie, Wauchope and Laurieton. Vehicles must display permits. Beach access points are *Point Plomer at northern end of North Beach *North Beach at intersection of Plomer Rd and North Shore Dve *Lighthouse Beach at southern end of Matthew Finders Dve * Lake Cathie, east of Dirah St and Middle Rock Rd *Grants Beach, north of North Haven *Dunbogan Garbage Tip Rd.
Port Macquarie Artificial Reef
Twenty concrete modules set in clusters, each module is 6.5m high, five of the modules have steel towers. Located in 46m.
See previous page.
Goolawah Beach
Racecourse Head
Delicate Nobby
Big Hill Point
31 16.680S
153 02.799E
shoal off chart
Flood mitigation canal
Limeburners Creek Nature Reserve
31 18.241S 153 00.328E approx, Chart
31 18.507S 152 59.274E approx, Chart
Saltwater Lake
Point Plomer
Queens Head
Maria River
Wilson River
North Beach
4 knot speed limit
Limeburners Creek
sandbar
nippers
oyster leases
Big Bay
Munns Channel
Little Rawdon Island
bridge
Caswell Channel
Rawdon Island
Hastings River
MAP A
Pelican Point
Town Beach
Diamantina Rocks
Oxleys Beach
Rocky Beach
Flynns Beach
Nobbys Beach
Nobby Head
Shelley Beach
Port Macquarie
Miner's Beach
Tacking Point
Chart approx 31 28.907S 152 57.096E
Wotonga Rock
Oxley Head
Sandy Point
Wauchope
King Ck
Lake Innes
Lake Innes Nature Reserve
Lighthouse Beach
KILOMETRES
METRES
Chart approx 31 31.570S 152 55.224E
Maps not for navigation.
Depths in metres
MAP B
Lake Cathie
Middle Rock Point
Shag Rock
Chart approx 31 32.376S 152 55.243E
31 33.547S 152 59.931E approx, Chart
Chart approx 31 33.859S 152 52.099E
N

Camden Haven and Manning Rivers

The lower Camden Haven River runs through the tidal Watson Taylor Lake, Queens Lake and Gogleys Lagoon. Further downstream, the river is easily accessible to landbased fishos via walls on both banks. Expect bream, flathead, whiting, luderick, tailor and mulloway. The river is a noted prawn and sand crab fishery, with the tidal lakes producing prawns on a dark moon in summer as they go to sea on outgoing tides. To the south, the Manning River is a good bass river and a great producer of estuary fish. The lower section is a complex estuary with two entrances, the main one at Harrington and another 12km south, called Farquhar Inlet. Farquhar Inlet closes at times. The Manning has tidal influence to Abbotts Falls, a gravel bar 54km from the mouth, and is navigable to Wingham, 30km from the entrance. The lower Manning has good landbased spots, with the main rock wall arguably best for big fish. Flathead and whiting are locally popular, but most estuary species show up. The river has shallows which can stand boaters, and the bar is hazardous. Coastal reef fishing is good, particularly off Diamond Head. There is beach and rock fishing at Diamond Head, Perpendicular Point and Bonny Hills, with drummer, luderick, bream, tailor and snapper. Perpendicular Point is a renowned spot with ledges over deep water producing tuna and kingfish, but specialist gear is needed to land big fish.

Key to Map

Hotspots

1. Good rock fishing off Grants Head, but difficult access. North Haven Beach to south has 4WD access at both ends. Southern end has mulloway after floods.
2. Northern rock wall produces plenty of fish, including mulloway, especially after rain. Winter tailor, bream, luderick. Turn of the tide best.
3. Lakes: whiting, flathead, prawns, crabs. Best for prawns at night around new moon as prawns head for the sea on the runout tide.
4. Stingray Ck has good north shore access. Luderick in channel and near bridge.
5. Perpendicular Point reached via walk from Pilot Beach carpark. High ledge out front has cobia, kingfish, mackerel, tuna - drop-gaff needed. Other ledges have tailor, drummer.
6. Lewis Rock is fishable via a walking track from headland lookout. Tailor, bream.
7. Good fishing in this stretch - try near bridge.
8. Diamond Head: camping and fishing for surf-rock species. Dunbogan Beach has 4WD access at Dunbogan and Diamond Head.
9. Crowdy Bay has an access track off Crowdy St.
10. Crowdy Head has excellent fishing platforms.
11. The 2km Harrington wall on the north bank fishes well. Nippers can be found on the flat. South bank's Manning Spit is reached by 4WD - the rock wall half way has mulloway. Upstream, try Pelican Bay oyster leases. Mud and sand crabs throughout.
12. Whiting on sandflats - other species when mouth breaks to sea.
13. Bream, flathead around bridge. Bass upstream.
14. The upper Manning is quality bass water. Excellent canoe fishing.

Launch sites

1. 4WD beach launch at Bartlett's Beach, Bonny Hills.
2. Ocean Dve, North Haven, shallow.
3. River St, Stingray Creek, all tides.
4. The Boulevard, all tides.
5. Ramps either side of river at Bay St and Laurie St.
6. Ramp at bridge, Ried St, all tides.
7. Sirius Dve, all tides.
8. Laurieton-Comboyne Rd, Camden Haven River, shallow.
9. 4WD beach launch, in ideal conditions only
10. Inside Crowdy Head, boat harbour, often affected by swell.
11. Beach St, multi-lanes, all tides.
12. Harrington Rd, all tides.
13. George Gibson Dve, all tides.
14. Mill St, Lansdowne, all tides.
15. Main Rd, all tides.
16. Ferry Rd, shallow.
17. River St, all tides.
18. Manning Point Rd, all tides.
19. Endeavour Pl, multi-lanes, all tides.
20. West End Ave, all tides.
21. Ramps both banks at Edinburgh Dve and Hutchinson St, all tides.
22. Unsealed, Petken Dve, all tides.
23. Farquhar St, all tides.

Local tides have up to about 1.41m movement.

Upstream

There are bass upstream of map limit near Charity Creek, Mt George, Cooplacurripa and Rocks Crossing, as far as the first big waterfall. Further upstream trout are found in the Manning and its tributaries, and other Barrington Tops waterways.

The COD GROUNDS Sanctuary is 9.25km south-east of Laurieton. No fishing is allowed within a 1km radius of 31 40.867S 152 54.617E

Grants Head

31 37.981S 152 54.407E shoal off map

Queens Lake

Stingray Creek

Camden Haven River

Laurieton

Dunbogan

MAP A, D

Perpendicular Point

Camden Head

Camden Haven

Dunbogan Beach

Charted wreck 31 39.915S 152 52.434E

31 41.449S 152 53.554E approx, Chart

31 42.614S 152 52.627E approx, Chart

31 42.754S 152 53.681E approx, Chart

Watson Taylors Lake

Diamond Head campground - call 02 6588 5555 for local NP office, or call 13000 PARKS to book a site, or book online. Permit needed for 4WD beach access. Most amenities.

Diamond Head

31 40.317S

152 53.983E

152 55.250E

Cod Grounds

Commonwealth Marine Sanctuary located approx 12km off Dunbogan Beach

31 41.417S

Crowdy Bay NP

Mermaid Reef

Chart approx 31 46.249S 152 48.265E

Crowdy Bay

Chart, approx 31 47.399S 152 49.737E

Chart, approx 31 48.377S 153 48.792E

Curphey Shoal (breaks with SE swell)

Chart, approx 31 48.206S 153 47.629E

Giles Shoal

Chart, approx 31 49.044S 152 45.884E

Crowdy Bay

Forde Rock

Crowdy Head

Great Swamp

MAP B

Manning River

Estuary image by John Lugg ©NSW Dept of Environment & Climate Change

MAP C

Farqhuar Inlet

Estuary image by John Lugg ©NSW Dept of Environment & Climate Change

KILOMETRES 0 4

METRES 0 4000

N

Landsdowne River

Cattai Creek

Mamboo Island

buoy marks old navigation marker

Ghinni Ghinni Creek

ballast (not marked)

hole

ballast (marked)

hole

Harrington

Mitchells Island

Chart, approx 31 52.806S 152 41.831E

Harrington Inlet

Manning Point

MAP B

Scotts Creek

Oxley Island

Farqhuar Inlet

MAP C

Chart, approx 31 57.238S 152 36.358E

Old Bar

Maps not for navigation. Depth in metres

Dennis Shoal approx 31 58.834S 152 37.667E

Shoal approx 31 58.989S 152 38.976E

Catch a $10,000 flathead

The month-long **Lower Manning Tagged Fish Roundup** sees a $10,000 flathead released into the river for recapture. More than 20 other flathead win smaller prizes. The prize pool has been around $18,000, said organiser Cliff Hoare, from the local Chamber of Commerce. Fish are released at Harrington, Manning Point and Coopernook in the Manning River. The event is usually held in January. For more information visit the competition website **www.harringtonandsurrounds.com.au**

MAP D

Camden Haven

Forster-Tuncurry

Wallis Lake and the associated Wallingat and Wallamba Rivers are superb fisheries. Surprise catches show up, including kingfish, but the lake is best known for big bream, usually found around the many oyster racks. A mix of temperate and tropical fish is caught offshore, including sailfish, coral trout, snapper, spangled emperor and tuskfish. This is roughly the southern limit for spotted and spanish mackerel, which may show up in late summer. At the north of the map is Khappinghat Creek, a usually landlocked waterway with a camp, launch site and bream fishing. Black and Red Heads rocks produce fish, but the nearby beaches do not usually have significant gutters. The main waterway into Wallis Lake, the Wallamba River, is tidal for 30km. The second major river, the Wallingat, runs through national park. The lake entrance walls are a prime fishing location, but the channel has strong currents. Tides diminish upstream from the sea entrance, with the mean spring range at Green Point within Wallis Lake being 0.3m, while 10km downstream at the mouth it is 1.5m. Fishing tends to be better in the more tidal areas. The Paddock, a large area of oyster leases and flats just above the bridge, has big flathead, bream and whiting, with tailor in the channels. Other good spots are the Breckenridge Channel, which runs along Little Street near the Forster CBD, and the area opposite the Boardwalk, which has big flathead in summer. The Boardwalk also has luderick, bream and whiting. Sand crabs, mud crabs and prawns are abundant in the lake at times, as are flounder, leatherjackets and pike. The Cooloongolook and Wang Wauk Rivers west of the lake system are tidal and worth fishing. Wallamba River has bass. The best surf fishing is at Seven Mile, Pacific Palms and Seal Rocks beaches. The protected Shelley and Elizabeth beaches are ideal for family fishing. For boaters, snapper are usually best on the wider 20-30 fathom grounds in winter, with the shallower gravel beds fishing in summer. Big kingfish are best April to July, with smaller fish in summer. Big flathead are best in summer, with bream and luderick all year but good in in autumn/winter. Mulloway are caught in the lower section after rain.

The Port Stephens-Great Lakes Marine Park covers part of this area and no-fishing zones apply - visit www.mpa.nsw.gov.au for detailed zoning information.

Estuary images by John Lugg ©NSW Dept of Environment & Climate Change

MAP A

Khappinghat Creek

Saltwater Beach

Diamond Beach

Red Head

Black Head

Hallidays Point

Chart approx 32 01.667S 152 36.012E

Chart approx 32 00.077S 152 35.638E

Chart approx 32 01.327S 152 35.357E

Chart approx 32 00.434S 152 35.165E

Chart approx 32 02.658S 152 34.794E

Chart approx 32 00.924S 152 34.339E

Chart approx 32 01.873S 152 34.056E

Chart approx 32 03.560S 152 33.783E

Chart approx 32 04.643S 152 33.674E

Check the annual Forster Fishing Carnival www.forsterfishingcarnival.com.au

Pacific Hwy

Nabiac

Wallamba River

Darawank

Nine Mile Beach

Chart approx 32 10.468S 152 30.665E

INDEFINITE LEAVE

Wallingat entrance north shore

Hotspots

1. Creek has bream, whiting, flathead. Best when mouth opens after rain. 4WD access off Old Soldiers Road.
2. Black Head reached via Hallidays Point Road off The Lakes Way. Average beach & rock fishing. Nine Mile Beach to the south reached by 4WD - best at ends.
3. Mulloway after rain. Big flathead in summer. Bream, whiting and luderick.
4. Tailor, drummer, luderick, snapper.
5. Seven Mile Beach: tailor, salmon, mulloway, bream. There is 4WD access from the north end at Jannies Corner and foot access from coast road. No 4WD south of Santa Barbara, near Tiona.
6. Booti Booti ledge has drummer, luderick. Elizabeth & Shelley beaches are sheltered. Charlotte Head has gamefish off the rocks.
7. Wallis Lake is best in more tidal areas. The Paddock above bridge fishes well, with the Boardwalk for landbased fishing. Lake has many oyster leases. Most fish, with prawns, sand and mud crabs.

Tuncurry

MAP C

MAP B

Bennetts Head

reef approx 32 10.928S 152 38.432

Forster

Burgess Beach

Boundary 32 12.516S

Cape Hawke

32 12.991S

Port Stephens Great Lakes MP Sanctuary

Janies Corner

Wang Wauk River

Cooloongolook River

Wallis Island

Wallingat River

Launch sites

1. Khappinghat Creek - no sea access. Shallow.
2. Beach launch inside Black Head, Main St, in calm only.
3. Point Rd, multi-lanes. Private ramp at van park.
4. Boat harbour, Mackerel Tce, multi-lanes, all tides.
5. Little St, shallow.
6. Elizabeth Pde, all tides.
7. Green Point, small boats.
8. Coomba Rd, all tides.
9. Lakes Way, Pacific Palms, all tides.
10. Beach launch inside headland, off Lakeside Cres, shallow.
11. Mimi St, all tides.
12. Robyn Rd, all tides.
13. Aquatic Rd, all tides.
14. Willow Point Rd, all tides.
15. Wharf St, all tides.

Local tides have up to about 1.8m movement.

Wallis Lake

This lake has a rich seagrass habitat with many oyster racks. Fish, crabs and prawns thrive. School and king prawns are caught with scoop nets at night in summer. Work a dark moon on an outgoing tide ... Breckenridge Channel is a good spot. A hand-hauled net works well on the flats along the eastern shore south of Greenpoint; hand-hauled nets are not allowed near the lake's entrance.

Coomba Park

Green Point

Booti Booti NP

Seven Mile Beach

Wallis Lake

Offshore

7-Mile Reef 7.4km sth Cape Hawke
32 16.080S 152 34.570E
32 16.150S 152 35.270E
5-Mile Reef 18.5km n-e Forster
32 05.150S 152 40.670E
32 05.400S 152 40.070E
32 05.270S 152 40.190E
Also, near Forster ...
Ballast 32 09.810S 152 33.190E
Barge 32 09.164S 152 32.386E
DC 16.6km n-e Forster
Reef 32 06.240S 152 39.250E
Blackhead 13km n-e Forster
Reef 32 04.350S 152 35.390E

N

KILOMETRES 0 4

METRES 0 4000

Smiths Lake

MAP D

Dams

Stocked dams west of Forster include Lake St Clair, Lostock Glenbawn and Liddell, all within 100-150km.

The Ruins

Booti Booti

Elizabeth Beach

Shelley Beach

Charlotte Head

Boomerang Beach

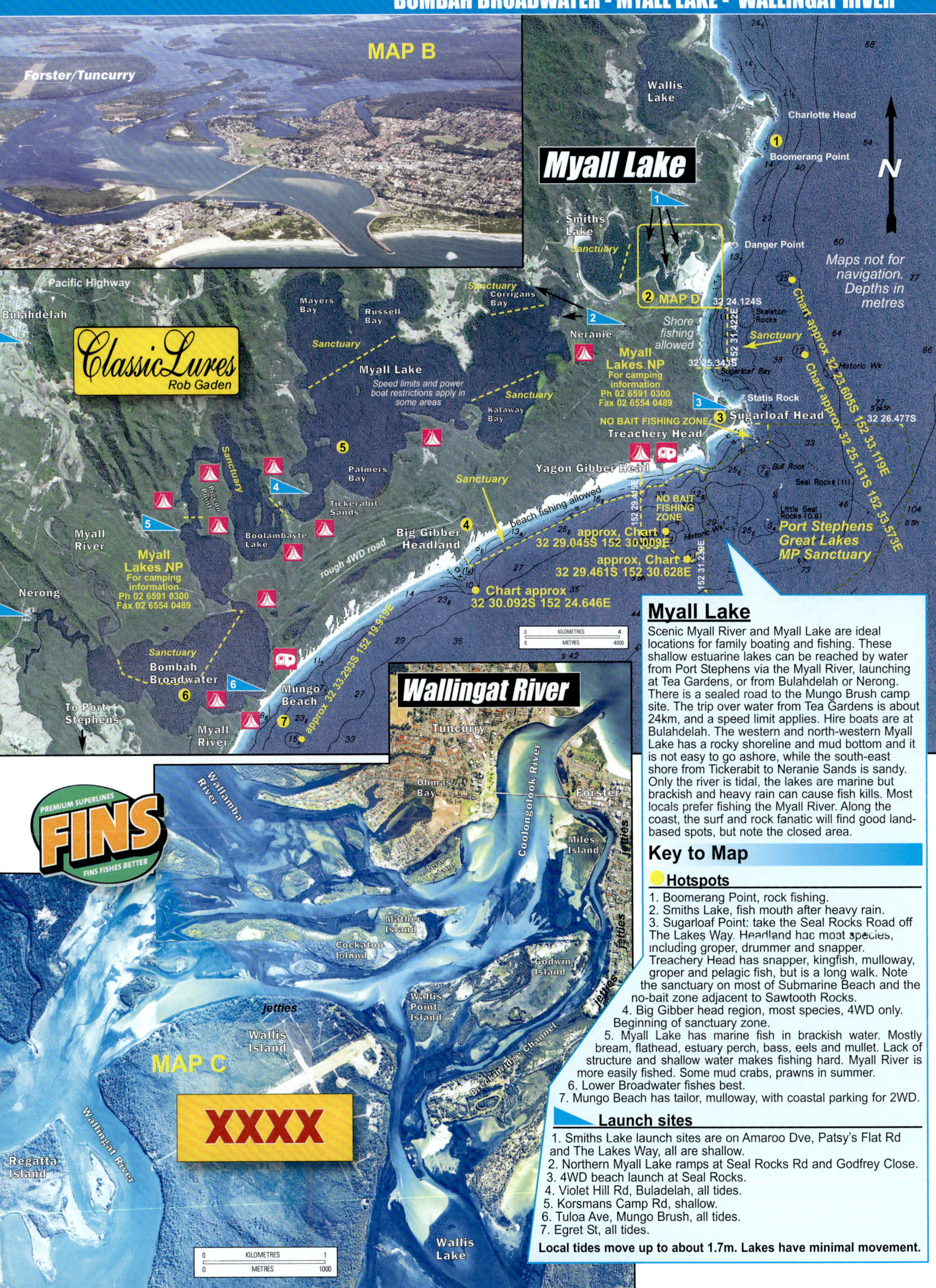

Myall Lake

Scenic Myall River and Myall Lake are ideal locations for family boating and fishing. These shallow estuarine lakes can be reached by water from Port Stephens via the Myall River, launching at Tea Gardens, or from Bulahdelah or Nerong. There is a sealed road to the Mungo Brush camp site. The trip over water from Tea Gardens is about 24km, and a speed limit applies. Hire boats are at Bulahdelah. The western and north-western Myall Lake has a rocky shoreline and mud bottom and it is not easy to go ashore, while the south-east shore from Tickerabit to Neranie Sands is sandy. Only the river is tidal, the lakes are marine but brackish and heavy rain can cause fish kills. Most locals prefer fishing the Myall River. Along the coast, the surf and rock fanatic will find good land-based spots, but note the closed area.

Key to Map

Hotspots

1. Boomerang Point, rock fishing.
2. Smiths Lake, fish mouth after heavy rain.
3. Sugarloaf Point: take the Seal Rocks Road off The Lakes Way. Headland has most species, including groper, drummer and snapper. Treachery Head has snapper, kingfish, mulloway, groper and pelagic fish, but is a long walk. Note the sanctuary on most of Submarine Beach and the no-bait zone adjacent to Sawtooth Rocks.
4. Big Gibber head region, most species, 4WD only. Beginning of sanctuary zone.
5. Myall Lake has marine fish in brackish water. Mostly bream, flathead, estuary perch, bass, eels and mullet. Lack of structure and shallow water makes fishing hard. Myall River is more easily fished. Some mud crabs, prawns in summer.
6. Lower Broadwater fishes best.
7. Mungo Beach has tailor, mulloway, with coastal parking for 2WD.

Launch sites

1. Smiths Lake launch sites are on Amaroo Dve, Patsy's Flat Rd and The Lakes Way, all are shallow.
2. Northern Myall Lake ramps at Seal Rocks Rd and Godfrey Close.
3. 4WD beach launch at Seal Rocks.
4. Violet Hill Rd, Buladelah, all tides.
5. Korsmans Camp Rd, shallow.
6. Tuloa Ave, Mungo Brush, all tides.
7. Egret St, all tides.

Local tides move up to about 1.7m. Lakes have minimal movement.

Karuah River

The section below the marine sanctuary usually has good stocks of bass. Tidal influence reaches as far as rocky rapids about 1km downstream from the bridge on Bucketts Way near Booral, with the sanctuary zone starting upstream of Allworth, with another zone in Little Branch Creek. Navigation around the island at Allworth must be done with great care as there are rocks. As in similar rivers, big bass can be found by working close to snags in the late afternoon and evening. The Myall River also produces bass. The lower Karuah has bream, flathead, whiting and mulloway.

NSW Oyster Reef Restoration

Restoration of NSW natural oyster reefs began around Port Stephens in 2019, including sites near Karuah and Myall River mouths. Construction began with 3000 tonnes of rock and 150 cubic metres of recycled oyster shell collected from oyster farms around Port Stephens. Oyster reefs once covered large areas in NSW estuaries but were lost to over-harvesting, dredging, pollution and disease. The new reefs are expected to improve water quality and bolster fish stocks.

Numerous wrecks, oyster racks and other structure in shallow Pindimar Bay, good for bream and flathead

Yacaaba Head at the entrance to Port Stephens

Myall River

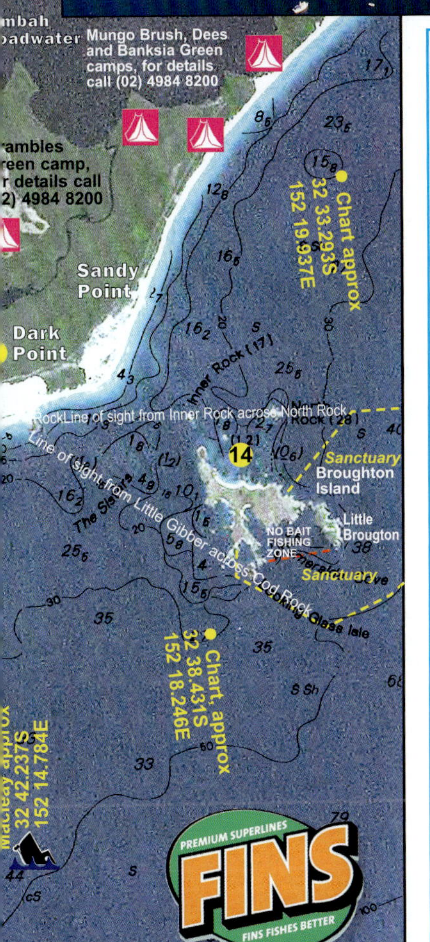

Port Stephens

The port is at the confluence of the Myall River, the Karuah River, Tilligerry Creek and the ocean. This is the largest NSW estuary, with mangroves of 23sqkm and saltmarsh of 8sqkm. It is NSW's biggest oyster-producing estuary and a major source of prawns and crabs. The port has two large basins, the lower section is marine, and the upper is a mud-settling area. East of Port Stephens are sandbeds which cover 275sqkm, extending inland 15km. The coast north includes beaches and rock platforms, with 4WD needed to reach many areas. This is a renowned gamefishing port, but there's also bass in the Karuah and Myall Rivers, and coastal snapper fishing in season. Locals say tailor and flathead are available most of the year, with salmon in winter. The Port Stephens-Great Lakes Marine Park extends from near Forster to Stockton Beach and includes parts of the Myall lakes. There are marine sanctuary areas, including the upper Karuah River. The Myall Lakes National Park includes the lakes and shoreline.

Key to Map

Hotspots

1. Dark Point is a good fishing spot. Access by 4WD from Hawks Nest or Mungo Brush. Most species, with bigger fish in winter. Upper Myall River has estuary fish, crabs (best in summer) and prawns (Sept-Mar). Luderick near pylons. Baitfish easily found.
2. 4WD permits give access to Hawks Nest beach up to Dark Point - an excellent fishing beach. Pipis and beachworms are available. Southern end best during rough weather. The Myall River bridge is a good spot for mulloway at the turn of the tide.
3. Yacaaba Headland - requires 4WD and long walk. Most species.
4. Tomaree Head reached through Tomaree Lodge carpark, end of Shoal Bay Rd - a hard walk. Gamefish and snapper. The north end has a popular spot called the Torpedo Tubes where big mulloway are caught. To the west, Little Beach has a platform for disabled fishos.
5. Beach has whiting, flathead and bream.
6. Fingal Bay is sheltered, especially at southern end, and has flathead and whiting. Boats can be launched at southern end.
7. Anna Bay - boat launching with some flathead, bream and whiting.
8. Boat Harbour is a good boat launch over firm sand. There is good rock and beach fishing, try Noamunga St and Kingsley Dve, as well as the walking track into Tomaree NP. Most species.
9. Access to Stockton Beach is off Gan Gan Rd south of the shopping centre. 4WD access is permitted by permit 21km south to Stockton Breakwall. The last remains of the *Sygna* wreck is at the Newcastle end approx 32 51.417S 151 50.680E. Stockton Beach produces most surf species, including runs of salmon. Big sharks patrol the beach.
10. Lower Port Stephens: flathead, whiting, bream and flounder from foreshores, with bream and luderick in the channels. Also blue crabs, and prawns December to March on dark moons. Nelson Head and Tomaree Head have mulloway. The channel out of Pindimar Bay has mulloway at turn of tide. Nelson Bay boat harbour walls have cobia and kingfish in summer. Pindimar Bay has whiting, flounder, bream, flathead - fish the small wrecks, pylons and oyster racks. The channel out of Soldier Point has mulloway at turn of tide. Land-based fishing on Soldier Point peninsula includes Salamander Wharf (most species, including blue crabs); Everitt Park boat ramp seawall (luderick, bream); Pearsons Park Jetty (nippers, flathead, whiting).
11. Swan Bay oyster leases have bream, whiting and flathead. Lemon Tree Passage produces good whiting. Tanilba Bay shores have bream. Snapper and Garden Islands have bream, flathead.
12. Tilligerry Creek: flounder, flathead, whiting, crabs, luderick.
13. Karuah River highway bridge has mulloway. North side of Wirrung Island has flathead. The two channels out of the river can fish and crab well.
14. Broughton Island 3km off the coast has good fishing, especially for snapper. Best anchorage is on southern side at Esmeralda Cove. Camping by Parks and Wildlife permit. Note marine park zones.
15. Inner islands have yellowtail kingfish, cobia, tailor, snapper.

Offshore

Port Stephens is renowned for producing big blue, black and striped marlin and huge sharks. Summer and autumn months are best when warm currents hit the offshore reefs between the coastal islands and Continental Shelf. Off Seal Rocks a chain of islands and reef meets a steep shelf edge that is a renowned fishing area. To the south-east the Newcastle-to-Norah Head canyons fire when the warm currents come in. Kingfish, yellowfin tuna, cobia and mackerel are also seasonally abundant.

Launch sites

Best ramps are Little Bay, Tea Gardens and Soldiers Point.

1. Marine Dve, all tides.
2. Marine Dve at bridge, all tides.
3. Moira Pde, all tides.
4. The Anchorage, shallow.
5. Lighthouse Rd, all tides.
6. Shoal Bay Rd, shallow.
7. Marine Dve, beach launch, shallow.
8. Graham St, all tides.
9. Pacific St, all tides.
10. Seaview Cres, shallow.
11. Mitchell Street, all tides.
12. Taylors Rd, shallow.
13. Cook Pde, all tides.
14. Beach Rd, all tides.
15. Bay St, shallow.
16. Peace Pde, shallow.
17. Bundabah St, all tides.
18. Stroud St, Allworth, all tides.
19. Bundabah Rd, all tides.
20. Curley Ave, all tides.
21. North Arm Cove.

Port Stephens tides are approx 45 min after Fort Denison times. Local tides have up to about 2m movement.

ClassicLures
Rob Gaden

Dams

Fishable dams west of Newcastle include Lake Windamere and Rylestone Reservoir, both about 180km as the crow flies. Some smaller private dams have bass and yellowbelly.

Newcastle

There is an all-year mulloway fishery, with big fish caught in the Hunter River off the entrance rock walls, and from the surf beaches. Mulloway are taken on lures at night under lights. The river mouth fishes best when heavy rain pushes baitfish down the river. Mulloway are slow in winter, but this time often produces the biggest fish. The river is used by coal carriers, which must be kept in mind when boating around the shipping channel. The entrance seawalls have footpaths, with fishing easier at the turn of the tide as current flow slackens. The lower river and local beaches have bream, luderick, salmon, mulloway and tailor in winter, with flathead, whiting, blue swimmer and mud crabs best in summer. Subtropical species such as mangrove jacks and spangled emperor appear occasionally in late summer, along with the odd spanish and spotted mackerel. The upper Hunter, Williams, Paterson and Allyn Rivers have bass, but enthusiasts make the trip to Lostock, St Clair and Glenbawn dams, which have more trophy-sized fish. Stockton Beach has historically made headlines for its white pointer and other large sharks seen in the surf. Tailor run at Stockton from December through to June, with salmon in winter.

Key to Map

Hotspots

1. Stockton Beach is renowned for tailor fishing. Beach vehicle access permitted. Southern rock wall best for mulloway after rain, but fishes at other times for bream, luderick, flathead, tailor.
2. Stockton Bridge is productive for bream, flathead and mostly small mulloway. Mud crabs upstream of bridge.
3. Seawall along river channel has mulloway, luderick, bream, tailor, flathead.
4. Southern rock wall is a big fish hotspot, but currents make fishing hard. Kingfish, mulloway and most other species. An indentation half way along is a good spot. Sheltered Horsehoe Beach near the base of the wall has flathead and whiting, while rock walls upstream have bream, tailor and luderick.
5. Queens Wharf is a family hotspot with the chance of mulloway. Nearby Lee Wharves fishable by boat when no ship is berthed.
6. The bridge at Throsby Creek holds good fish, with a land-based fishing area and a wharf. A large floating dock downstream is a good spot to collect yakkas.
7. Walsh Point has flathead and whiting on drop-off with mulloway in deeper water.
8,8 & 8. Bream, flathead, mulloway near pylons, also mud crabs.
9. Good stretch for mud crabs.
10. Land-based rock platforms and surf fishing at Redhead Beach.
11. Lake Macquarie is the largest saltwater lake in NSW, with an entrance to the sea through Swansea Channel.
12. Swansea Channel is a prime fishing area, but with strong currents. Most species, with reliable salmon in Salts Bay. See next page.
13. Caves Beach has a rough bottom, good for bream and flathead.
14. The rocks and headland at the southern end of Catherine Hill Bay have accessible fishing areas right around to Moonee Head, but some walking is involved. Access to the bay beach is via the surf club off Flowers Dve. Bream and tailor off the main beach with mulloway to the north of the conspicuous coal loader.
15. Excellent rock fishing on south side of Flat Rock Point.

Launch sites

(Map above)
1. Booth St, all tides.
2. Punt Rd, all tides.
3. Wharf Rd, all tides.
4. Tully St, multi-lanes, all tides.
5. Ferry Rd, shallow.
6. Tomago Rd, all tides.
7. Greenleaf Rd, all tides.

(Next page)
8. Hunter St, all tides.
9. Seaham Rd, all tides.
10. Queens Wharf Rd, Morpeth.
11. Torrence St, shallow.
12. Clarence Town ramps at Rifle St, Durham St and Limeburners Ck Rd, all tides, all west bank.
13. Tocal, all tides.

Tidal variations: Newcastle same as Fort Denison (Sydney) tides. Stockton Bridge, add approx 1 hour 30 minutes. Hexham - add approx 1 hour 45 min. to Fort Denison tides.

Newcastle and the Hunter River mouth

Estuary images by John Lugg ©NSW Dept of Environment & Climate Change

Samson fish
TOM CLANCY PICTURE
XXXX
KILOMETRES 0 4
METRES 0 4000
Stockton Beach
Aus 207
STOCKTON
GPS
48m Reef: 7.4km off Newcastle
32.58.609S 151.50.031E
The Cave: 3km off Swansea Hds
33.05.807 151.40.066
Dumping Ground: 4km off Newcastle
32.56.990S 151.49.245E
The Farm 1: 17km off Swansea
33.08.909S 151.49.162E
The Farm 2: 16.3km off Swansea
33.08.344S 151.49.678E
Fruitshed Reef: 8.2km off Swansea
33.01.751S 151.42.665E
Halfway Ballast
32.54.471S 151.49.735E
Kooragang Island
Sygna wreck 32 51.417S 151 50.680E
Charted reef approx 32 52.663S 151 50.627E
Charted wreck approx 32 53.348S 151 49.844E
Charted reef approx 32 53.370S 151 50.946E
Newcastle
MAP A
Yarra historic wreck approx 32 54.190S 151 48.194E
Davenport historic wreck approx 32 54.539S 151 47.762E
Charted obstruction approx 32 54.450S 151 55.530E
See map inset left for lower Hunter River boat ramps
Nobbys Head
Commodore wreck approx 32 55.330S 151 51.802E
Historic Wk
Spoil approx 32 57.126S 151 49.847E
Upstream
The Hunter, Williams, Allyn and Paterson Rivers have bass, with the upper reaches producing mostly small fish, and an occasional cracker. The Williams has one of the highest bass densities of NSW rivers, with Clarence Town and the Seaham Weir region good starting points for new visitors. Bass swim down the Hunter tributaries and school around Hexham to spawn, before going back in spring. The Hunter River has tidal influence for 63km up to 2km upstream of Oakhampton rail bridge. Williams River is tidal for 46km to Seaham Weir, 500m upstream from Jim Scott Bridge. The Paterson River is tidal for 74km to about 1km downstream from Gostwyck Bridge. The Allyn River flows from Barrington Tops, with seven minor tributaries entering before reaching its confluence with the Paterson River near Vacy, descending 640m over an 82km course.
Clarence Town
13 Tocal
12
Little Redhead Point
Depths in metres. Maps not for navigation
Paterson River
Wallaroo NP
tidal limit
11
Williams River
Pacific Highway
10
Redhead Point
KILOMETRES 0 5
METRES 0 5000
Maitland
Morpeth
10
Lake Windamere
This 1030ha impoundment, 230km west of Newcastle and 35km south of Mudgee on the Cudgegong River, is one of the better yellowbelly dams. The lake is long and narrow with both steep-sided banks and large shallow bays. There's plenty of timber and rocky shores. The lake is 55m at its deepest and averages 20m. It also has silver perch, rainbow and brown trout, carp, redfin and murray cod. It produces some big yellowbelly, best in warm weather. The lake has camp, kiosk, playground and laundry at Cudgegong Waters Park, where the ramp is located. Other popular dams for Newcastle fishos are Lostock, St Clair and Glenbawn. The upper Hunter River reaches also produce bass.
Hunter River
Grahamstown Lake
2800ha, av. depth 9m
9
8
N
Grahamstown Dam
Fishing is not permitted.
Bonnie Dundee wreck approx 33 03.331S 151 42.238E
Advance wreck approx 33 10.747S 151 42.216E
N
KILOMETRES 0 2
METRES 0 2000
Lake Windamere
Near Mudgee, NSW
Hexham
Fullerton Cove

Artificial Reefs

A. Lake Macquarie has an artificial reef system off Galgabba Point in 6m of water. There are six sites, comprising 600 hollow concrete reef balls, each 1m square, within a 3sqkm area. About 42 species are known to live on the reefs. There is also an offshore reef - see yellow box on next page. *The GPS supplied here is the central mark followed by four corner marks for each site.*

Site 1. 33 05.604S 151 36.612E
33 05.614S 151 36.616E
33 05.605S 151 36.602E
33 05.597S 151 36.607E
33 05.606S 151 36.624E

Site 2. 33 05.680S 151 36.738E
33 05.697S 151 36.738E
33 05.670S 151 36.748E
33 05.666S 151 36.739E
33 05.692S 151 36.728E

Site 3. 33 05.764S 151 36.790E
33 05.755S 151 36.787E
33 05.759S 151 36.782E
33 05.773S 151 36.791E
33 05.770S 151 36.799E

Site 4. 33 05.814S 151 36.891E
33 05.807S 151 36.885E
33 05.813S 151 36.877E
33 05.822S 151 36.899E
33 05.817S 151 36.905E

Site 5. 33 05.880S 151 36.879E
33 05.879S 151 36.870E
33 05.885S 151 36.874E
33 05.884S 151 36.888E
33 05.875S 151 36.881E

Site 6. 33 05.985S 151 36.942E
33 05.978S 151 36.949E
33 05.976S 151 36.942E
33 05.990S 151 36.933E
33 05.997S 151 36.942E

There are also some 'private' (illegal) artificial reefs in the lake.

Launch sites

Lake Macquarie is well served with launch sites. However many are in fair to poor condition and lack parking space. Some of the better ramps are:

1. Swansea Channel north shore, Bali St, good parking, suitable for large boats.
2. Lakeview Pde, off Makoro St, all tides. Closed at publication.
2a. Two good ramps at Wallarah St and Dobinson Dve, all tides.
2b. End of Naru St.
3. Croudace Bay in Thomas Halton Park, multi-lanes, suitable for large boats.
4. Ramps at Bath St and Wharf St, all tides.
5. Overhill Rd, all tides, has large jetty.
6. Rathmine, off Dorrington Rd, multi-lanes, all tides, good for large boats.
7. Nanda St, all tides.
8. Boyds Hole, The Esp, all tides.
9. Kullaroo Rd, all tides.
10. End of Dora St, exposed to wind, all tides.

Key to Map

Hotspots (both maps)

Bream, whiting squid, prawns, sand crabs, flathead and flounder are throughout lake.

1. Bike track follows shoreline from Warners Bay to Cockle Creek, good land-based fishing for bream, flathead. Great jetty at Speers Point.
2. Deep water off these points have most species.
3. Green Point Wharf
4. Salts Bay has reliable schools of salmon to 3kg, best May-Dec. Also big bream, tailor in this area.
5. Troll peninsula for flathead.
6. Most species found along

Charted lump approx 33 03.245S 151 41.372E

approx 33 05.154S 151 39.725E

Charted contour approx 33 07.465S 151 41.0515E

33 06.331S 151 42.229E

Galgabba Artificial Reef

MAP A NEXT PAGE

Depths in metres. Maps not for navigation

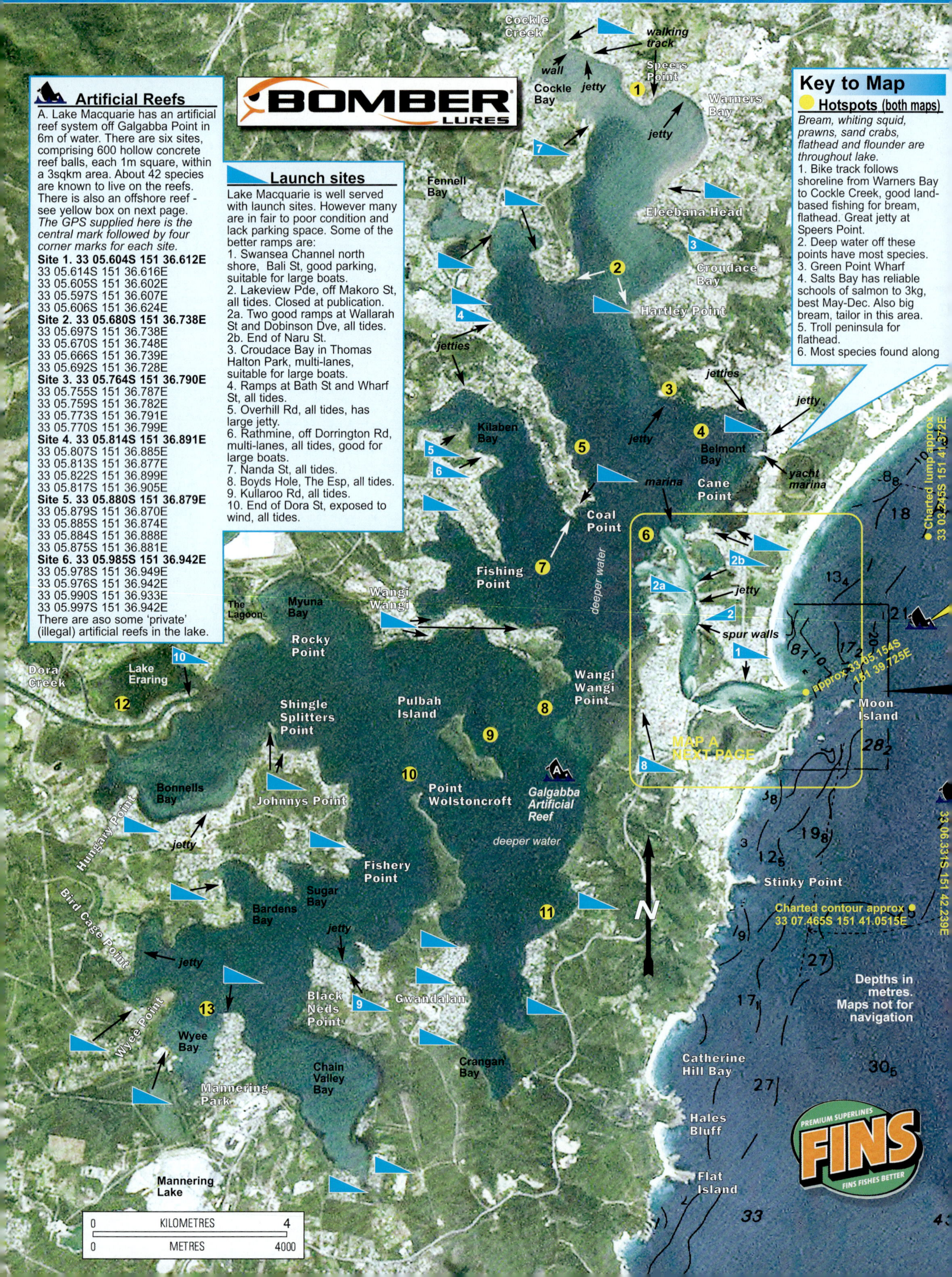

KILOMETRES 0 – 4
METRES 0 – 4000

deep drop-off. Mulloway from 60cm to 100cm on plastic vibes and jigs.
7. Bream, leatherjackets off rocky foreshores, jetties.
8. Deep water off point has tailor and mulloway.
9. Pulbah Island has most species including blue crabs and squid - deep water on north-east side has snapper and mulloway, southern end has whiting, flathead and flounder.
10. Most species, with blue crabs off point & east shore.
11. Cams Wharf.
12. Dora Creek, big bream - good lure casting area.
13. Mostly bream, whiting.
14. Rock walls south of boat ramp have flathead, bream, squid.

Newcastle Offshore Reef

This reef was installed in August 2019 just 3.5km north-east of the Swansea Bar, off Blacksmith's Beach, in 28m of water. There are two steel reef towers with a profile to 12m. Expect to catch kingfish, snapper, silver trevally, tailor, mulloway, yakkas and slimy mackerel.

33 04.300S 151 42.018E
33 04.380S 151 41.891E

Lake Macquarie

This huge estuary has 170km of shoreline and 11,000ha of water, with tidal influence through a bottleneck sea entrance at Swansea. The lake averages 9.7m deep. Commercial netting of the lake stopped in 2002. The main species caught are yellowfin bream, dusky flathead, tailor and sand whiting, but also expect luderick, snapper, tarwhine, silver trevally, blue crabs, flounder and prawns, Squid, mullet, slimy mackerel, yakkas and garfish are all in the lake and make ideal bait for mulloway. Look for mullet around shallow creek mouths. Slimy macks, whiting and flathead are best in summer/autumn, with other species available most of the year. Mulloway, kingfish and big tailor and flathead inhabit the entrance channel. Target mulloway by fishing livebait at night at the top of the tide over deep structure. Snapper also tend to inhabit deeper areas. Whiting are best in the shallows around Swansea, and Salts Bay hosts big schools of salmon. Tropical species such as dolphin fish, cobia, giant herring and bigeye trevally visit the lake, but this is unusual. Big sharks occasionally are seen cruising the shallow waters. There is usually somewhere sheltered to fish in almost any wind, but the lake can become rough, especially in a southerly. Skippers should watch for drying flats that can trap boats on a falling tide. Swansea Channel has an easily accessible wall along the entrance's north shore, but strong currents flow here despite relatively small local tides. The lake has an artificial reef of 180 concrete modules in six locations in 5m of water off Galgabba Point, first installed in 2005 and increased in size in 2009. There is an offshore artificial reef 3.5km north-east of Swansea Heads that attracts larger fish, including kingfish, snapper, mulloway and samson. Being shallow and clear, fish the lake with light tackle and fresh bait for best results. Week days and nights fish best when there is less boat traffic. Summer sees prawns run at night on an outgoing tide and dark moon. Bass are found in the lake's tributaries. Squid are often best at the channel entrance and near the bridge. Hire boats and canoes are available.

Key to Map

Hotspots

1. North wall reached via Ungala St and Grannys Pool carpark. The end of the wall is best, but it's a long walk and there is no smooth footpath. Most surf species.
2. The southern wall is easy to reach off Lambton Pde and easy to walk on. Mostly bream, flathead, luderick.
3. Spur rock wall fishes well for bream, flathead, luderick and squid. Sheltered water holds gar, flounder, whiting.
4. Sunken wall, visible at low tide. Bream, flathead.
5. Extensive rock wall along north shore has bream, luderick and flathead. This is a large area with easy access and parking.
6. Swansea Bridge holds most species, including kingfish and tailor. Heavy tackle may be required and heavy sinkers because of current flow. Black Ned's Bay to the south has nipper beds.
7. Channel edges have whiting, flathead. Bream, luderick on rock edges.
8. Channel drop-off has most species, including snapper and mulloway. Bream, luderick around Marks Point marina.
9. Flathead, whiting on edges.
10. Baitfish push in with tide and brings predator such as kingfish with them. The action can go as far up the channel as Marks Point.

Launch sites

See previous page for ramps. **Local tides have up to about 1.64m movement. Tidal movement is strong in the channel but minimal in the lake.**

Tuggerah Lakes

This chain of three tidal lakes has a common bottleneck sea entrance. Being just 120km north of Sydney, it is a popular destination. Some areas have heavy boat traffic and fishing can be best at night and early morning, and it gets busy when winter luderick are running. Green and late-season brown weed is available locally and is ideal luderick bait. The lakes are famous for prawns, taken in spring and summer on dark nights using lights and scoop nets. Sand crabs are also caught. Bream, luderick and whiting are the main catch, with some keeper flathead and tailor. Toukley and The Entrance bridges, and lower sections Wyong, Ourimbah, Narara and Erina creeks are flathead spots in summer, with Budgewoi channel the prime luderick spot. Heavy rain slows fishing in the lakes. There are wharves at Terilba Reserve on the north entrance shoreline, as well as Long Jetty. Most of the lake's rocky foreshores hold bream, easily accessible to landbased anglers. Bass are in Wyong Creek.

Key to Map

Hotspots

1. Good luderick fishing in channel.
2. Fast tidal flow through shallow entrance. Sometimes landlocked. Best access on south side at The Entrance Road reserve, which has a boat ramp. Many fishing spots along south shore. Bream, luderick near bridge at dawn. Luderick, flathead, whiting over flats. Sandbanks near entrance have prawns, whiting and flathead. Fishes best on outgoing tide. North bank channel of Pelican Island has flathead, with tailor at the drop-off into lake.
3. Creek entrance is a flathead spot.
4. Creek has bream. Bass upstream.
5. Prawns.
6. Power station hot water outlet, good when station is running. Otherwise, fish Tuggerah channel entrance wharves.
7. Furthest from sea, yet Lake Munmorah has snapper and tailor, but mostly bream, whiting. Little tidal push - use fine line.

Launch sites

1. Colongra Bay Rd, shallow.
2. Elizabeth Bay Dve, shallow.
3. Noela Pl, shallow.
4. Macleay Dve, shallow, jetty.
5. Ramps each side, all tides.
6. Narambi Rd, shallow.
7. Emu Dve, shallow.
8. Brundenell Ave, shallow.
9. Peel St, shallow.
10. Wallarah Rd, shallow.
11. Oakland St, shallow.
12. Wolseley Ave, all tides.
13. Wilfred Barrett Dve, all tides.
14. Tuggerah Pde, multi-lanes, all tides.
15. Marine Pde, shallow.
16. Tuggerah Pde, shallow.
17. Panorama Pde, sand launch.
18. Ramps each side of channel at Kalua Dve and Sunshine Ave, all tides.
19. Bald St, Norah Head beach launch.

Wiseman's Ferry

ferry wharf

KILOMETRES 0 5
METRES 0 5000

Mangro Creek

Hawkesbury River

Dharug NP

Colo River

bridge

ferry

Lower Portland

Hawkesbury River boat ramps are mostly privately owned by caravan parks and ski havens

Spen

Bass and estuary perch found throughout this area

Sackville

ferry

Ebenezer

Little Cattai Creek

Wilberforce

Cattai Creek

tidal limit

Hawkesbury River

Richmond

Windsor

Castlereagh

Excellent canoe fishing for bass from Castlereagh to Penrith

Penrith

Sydney Wide GPS Marks

Barrenjoey wide reef 33 35.870S 151 25.023E, reef fish
Boultons Reef approx 33 36.001S 151 22.262E, reef fish
Reggies 33 37.954S 151 22.221E, snapper, mulloway
Snapper approx 33 37.955S 151 22.222E, reef fish
Avalon Gutter approx 33 38.121S 151 21.399E, reef fish
Newport Reef approx 33 39.599S 151 20.233E, reef fish
Esmeralda Reef approx 33 39.521S 151 25.642E, reef fish
Rubble Reef approx 33 44.510S 151 21.980E, reef fish
Reef wide approx 33 44.452S 151 22.281E, reef fish
Reef close approx 33 44.371S 151 19.501E, reef fish
Reef 33 46.500S 151 21.800E, reef fish
Manly Reef approx 33 47.470S 151 17.399E, reef fish
Nth Head Bombora 33 48.990S 151 18.291E, reef fish

Broken Bay and Brisbane Water

This is Sydney's fishing playground, close enough for a day trip and with many spots accessible by public transport. Much of Broken Bay and the Hawkesbury River still has a natural feel despite its proximity to the city. The river has NSW's longest coastal catchment. Bass are the highlight in the upper Hawkesbury River, with big mulloway and bream the drawcard in the lower reaches, along with hairtail and pelagic fish near the sea entrance in Broken Bay. See Page 351 for detailed Hawkesbury information. **Brisbane Water is a shallow tidal estuary** north of Broken Bay, at the confluence of Narara and Coorumbine Creeks. There are many oyster racks. This estuary produces mostly bream, whiting and flathead, as well as prawns, crabs and occasional mulloway. It is shallow, averaging about 5m deep, and the water is clear, so careful bait or lure presentation on light gear, or night fishing, brings better results. Boaters chasing quality bream should fish holes such as those at The Rip bridge, or oyster racks such as those around Paddys Channel and Woy Woy. Oyster racks fish well on a rising tide, with bream moving out to weedbeds as the tide falls. Landbased anglers do well fishing the channel that runs through Woy Woy. Bream are best Jan-April, whiting are about all year, with luderick in winter.

Key to Map

Hotspots

1. Access Birdie Beach at surf club or Budgewoi road bays. Tailor, bream, salmon, mulloway best in winter.
2. Norah Head has good platforms, north-east side sheltered from southerlies, most species. Access via Bush St to the lighthouse and down stairs. Soldiers Point and Soldiers Beach to south are reliable.
3. Pelican Point has an outer reef: fish inside the reef or out on the shelf in calm weather with care. Access via surf club on Soldiers Point Dve.
4. North Entrance Beach has tailor and salmon in winter. Access off Wilfred Barrett Dve. Area near entrance has mulloway after flooding. Fish run-out tide.
5. Bream at Toowoon Bay.
6. Wamberal Beach is good for tailor and salmon in winter and sharks in summer. Wamberal Lagoon opens to sea on occasions - whiting, flathead.
7. Terrigal has a good headland, beach, lagoon and boat haven. The Skillion ledge is one of the best ledges near Sydney.
8. Avoca has a headland, lagoon and rock ledge. North Avoca headland has luderick and drummer, some tailor. South Avoca headland off Avoca Dve has all rock species, plus kingfish, cobia, tuna, mulloway. Avoca Beach is reliable. Avoca lagoon has bream, flathead, whiting when open to sea.
9. Copacabana and McMasters beaches have tailor, salmon in winter, with mulloway at lagoon entrance during floods.
10. Putty Beach: whiting, flathead in summer. Access via surf club on Beach Dve. Tallow Beach to south better for tailor, salmon. Mulloway when river floods. Access via Hawke Head Dve and foot track. West Reef fishes by boat - beware swells.
11. Box Head has tailor, salmon in winter and mulloway during flooding. Access via Hawke Head Dve and signposted walking track.
12. Fish each side of peninsula.
13. Cowan Creek, pristine and great fishing. Best spot for hairtail, check with tackle shops they are running. Mulloway, some pelagic fish, breams, squid.
14. Bream, whiting north of headland.

Launch sites

1. Inside Norah Head, Bald St. Best in southerly conditions, difficult in north or north-easterly winds.
2. Reasonably sheltered 4WD beach launch at Bateau Bay.
3. Terrigal Haven - launching for medium boats, affected by surge.
4. Patonga, ramp at east end of beach and west at end of point.
5. Dinghy launch, Sand Point.
6. Dinghy launch, Taylors Point
7. Pittwater Rd, multi-lanes.
8. Mooney Mooney Point, Peats Ferry Rd, multi-lanes, pontoon.
9. Liberator General San Martin Dve, all tides.
10. Bobbin Head Rd, all tides.
11. Wisemans Ferry Rd, all tides.
12. Old Northern Road, all tides.
13. River Rd, all tides.
14. Punt Rd and George St, all tides.
15. Bay Rd, multi-lanes, all tides.

Local tides have up to about 1.91m movement.

TUGGERAH LAKE - BROKEN BAY - BRISBANE WATER

FISHABOUT SYDNEY HARBOUR with Craig McGill

Key to Map

Hotspots

1. Most species near bridge rocks.
2. Fish flats edges for whiting, flathead, bream, flounder.
3. Edges of entrance channel and oyster leases fish well.
4. Crabs, whiting, flathead.
5. Most species in channel, fish the incoming tide.
6. Big bream in deep water.
7. Most species at bridge, mulloway at night, turn of tide.
8. Big flathead off point.
9. Ocean Beach has mulloway at night and after heavy rain.

Land-based: Woy Woy wharves, Ocean Beach, inside entrance sandbar, Anderson's wharf, Gosford railway bridge edges.

Long Reef Wreck Graveyard

SS *Bellubera* approx 33 42.705S 151 21.069E
Dee Why approx 33 42.938S 151 20.836E
Coolooli (out wider) approx 33 43.088S 151 20.953E
Doomba approx 33 42.971S 151 20.819E
Himma approx 33 43.121S 151 21.086E
Apollo approx 33 43.581S 151 21.049E
SS *Duckenfeld* 33 43.088S 151 19.453E

Best boat ramps are at Lions Park (Woy Woy) and Gosford (near the sailing club)

Depths in metres. Maps not for navigation

Collection of invertebrates from Bungan, Mona Vale, Narrabeen and Barrenjoey heads and Long reef not permitted

Undersea cables - no anchoring

Long Reef (large area) next page approx 33 44.710S 151 19.712E

Flint & Steel Reef PAGE 351

Chart approx 33 17.638S 151 37.284E
Chart, approx 33 17.439S 151 35.663E
Chart, approx 33 18.401S 151 34.599E
Chart approx 33 19.392S 151 34.099E
Chart, approx 33 19.804S 151 33.644E
Chart, approx 33 21.634S 151 32.352E
Chart, approx 33 24.042S 151 31.987E
Chart, approx 33 23.402S 151 30.752E
Chart, approx 33 25.139S 151 30.151E
Hall Caine wreck, approx 33 32.721S 151 25.402E
Chart, approx 33 32.892S 151 23.910E
Chart, approx 33 33.266S 151 22.111E
Valiant wreck approx 33 34.752S 151 20.736E
Birchgrove wreck approx 33 38.305S 151 22.719E
Trio wreck approx 33 40.921S 151 21.969E
SS Myola 33 45.671S 151 21.803E

Terrigal: Lord Ashley wreck, reef, The Haven (moorings), The Skillion Caves, The Skillion, reef

Wallarah Creek, Munmorah Lake, hole, Budgewoi Lake, rocks, shallow, Wyong Creek, Tuggerah Lake, Wyrrabalong National Park, Norah Head, Soldiers Point, Pelican Point, Chittaway Bay, jetties, The Entrance, KILOMETRES 0 4, METRES 0 4000

Wybung Head, Bird Island, Tuggerah Beach, Tuggerah Entrance, Toowoon Bay, Tuggerah Reef (breaks with SE swell), breaks with heavy swell, Shelly Bay, Bateau Bay, Yumbool Point, Forresters Beach, Wamberal Point, Terrigal Beach, Broken Head, The Skillion, Terrigal, lagoon, Avoca, Bulbararing Bay, Avoca Beach, Tudibaring Head, Copacabana Beach, McMasters Beach, Mourawaring Point, Bombi Point, Bouddi Point, MARINE RESERVE, Putty Beach, West Reef, East Reef, Historic Wk

Marlow, Mooney Mooney Creek, Wondabyne, Brisbane Water NP, Brisbane Water, Dangar Island, Brooklyn, Sydney-Newcastle Freeway, Juno Point, Broken Bay, Lion Island, Barrenjoey Head, Tallow Beach, BROKEN BAY, Cowan Creek, Ku-Ring-Gai Chase NP, Pittwater, Palm Beach, Little Head, Whale Beach, Careel Head, Bangalley Head, Avalon Beach, Bilgola Beach, Newport Beach, Little Reef, Bungan Head, Mona Vale, Turimetta Head, Narrabeen, Collaroy Beach, Dee Why Beach

The Broadwater, Brisbane Water, Cockle Broadwater, Woy Woy Bay, Lintern Channel, Pelican Island, Woy Woy Channel, Cockle Channel, Woy Woy Creek, The Rip, Hardies Bay, dangerous shallow entrance

You don't need a boat to enjoy great fishing

There are superb landbased fishing opportunities around Sydney, for both bread and butter species and gamefish. Here are some of the best spots.

Middle Head: Kingfish hold on the northern end where the reef hits the sand. They are best targeted with live squid. It's also a squid ground, over the kelp, at either end, but watch out for a couple of bommies that break in over about 1m swell. It's a great rock spot for tailor and drummer. Middle Head, although an inner harbour spot, is subject to ocean swells so exercise caution.

Obelisk Beach: The long rock platform at the southern end of the beach offers great shore and boat fishing. There is kelp in close but a good cast from the shore will put you onto a clean sand bottom with bream, flatties and even pelagics. The kelp produces squid, which means you have a ready bait supply at your feet. The open water of the beach can fire at times, with pelagics about when the bait is in. The sand makes for a good flattie drift.

Clifton Gardens: A great boat and shore spot. The jetty drops into 40 feet of water and produces kings and mulloway among the usual jetty inhabitants. There's a restricted zone around the navy jetty, but the white buoy to the north holds good kings. The drop-off towards midstream is a night mulloway spot. The rocks to the south offer the shore fisho deep water for kings, mulloway and luderick. An average cast lands you in 60 feet of water.

Bradley's Head: It's a great shore-based spot because commercial traffic makes it hard for boat fishos. You will pick up bream, luderick, flatties, salmon and tailor. On the downstream side is a big kelp bed good for squid.

Rushcutters and Double Bay: At times Rushcutters and Double Bay accumulate huge amounts of baitfish. This attracts pelagic fish, including some you wouldn't expect to be this far upstream, like samson and amberjack. The bottom also fishes well for whiting mulloway, bream and flatties. The southern end of Darling Pt is a great spot to bounce some plastics. Just off here is Clarke Island and Navy mooring buoys. This area also attracts huge clouds of bait. Kingies sit just under the buoys along with some huge tailor. On the bottom you will get mulloway, bream and the occasional keeper reddie.

Rose Bay: A great sand bottom location. The professional fishos used to pound it because of the clean bottom and this spot will benefit greatly now they are gone. The sandflat and the hole (known as the blue hole) in the south-east corner are great flattie and whiting grounds. You can wade the flats at low tide out to the edge of the hole. Watch for seaplanes landing.

Parsley and Vaucluse Bay and Bottle and Glass Point: Parsley bay jetty offers bream and flathead in summer and dory and trevally in winter. Mulloway too. Bottle and Glass Point offers good shore access and produces kingfish, bream, blackfish and squid. It's all good water in a southerly.

Camp Cove: There's squid at both ends of the beach, with lots of little cuttlefish on the southern corner. If you take your squid or cuttlefish to the rocky point at the southern end of the beach you might catch a big kingfish. This is the harbour's best shore-based spot for kingfish.

Spring Cove near Collins Beach: A good deep hole. It offers good shore access from the old gas works and produces both summer and winter fishing. It is a retreat in strong winds from the northern quadrant. You will find kings, salmon, bonito and flathead in summer and dory, drummer and groper in winter.

Cannae Point: A favorite harbour spot, producing winter and summer fishing and a mix of estuary and oceanic fish. It's the number one samson fish and morwong spot, and has produced great mulloway and thumping blue groper. An average cast will put you on the spot.

Fairlight Pt: This is another of North Harbour's great spots, and will produce pelagics, including samson fish. It is a great winter fishery. It's also a good yakka spot. It fishes well for blackfish. Difficult shore access. A similar spot with good shore access can be found on the adjacent point near Fairlight Pool. A good cast from here will put you onto sand next to reef. The stretch along the sand from Fairlight Point to Manly Aquarium is great for flatties off the shore.

North Harbour: Next stop is the sandbank drop-off up the back of North Harbour near the Davis Marina. This is a great flathead spinning spot and is accessible for both boat fishers and waders. It is also home to squid.

Washaway Beach: The first major feature you find heading north of Grotto is Washaway Beach. As the name implies, this beach washes away in a big storm. It's one of the reliable tailor spots in the harbour. It's often clouded with baitfish in summer, pushed onto shore by pelagics. Surface fish will attack from the top and bottom, and flatties and bream will work underneath - great lure fishing at this time. It has great shore access. Fish the beach or the rocks with the northern corner being most productive.

- **Fish Sydney with FISHABOUT TOURS**

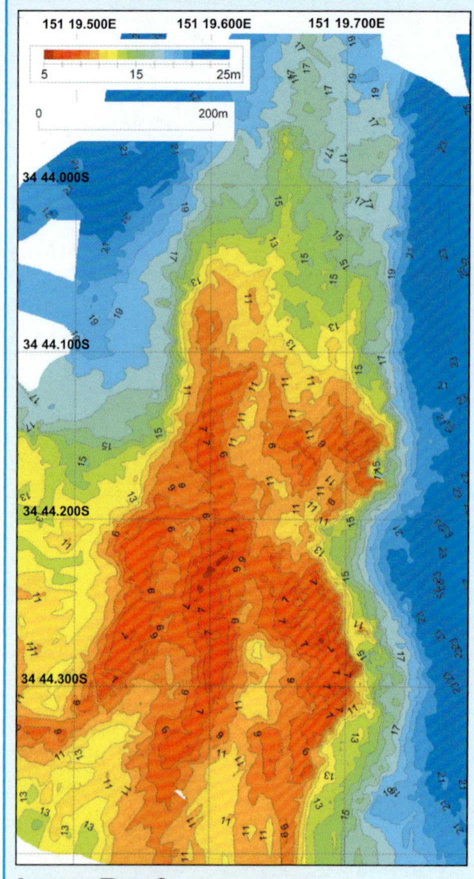

Long Reef

This is just 10km north of Sydney Heads, and is one of the better fishing reefs near Sydney. Boaters should look for baitfish schools over the reef, then drift out the baits. Big fish are hooked and lost here. Expect snapper, kingfish and more. Waves often break over the reef, so cautious boating is required.

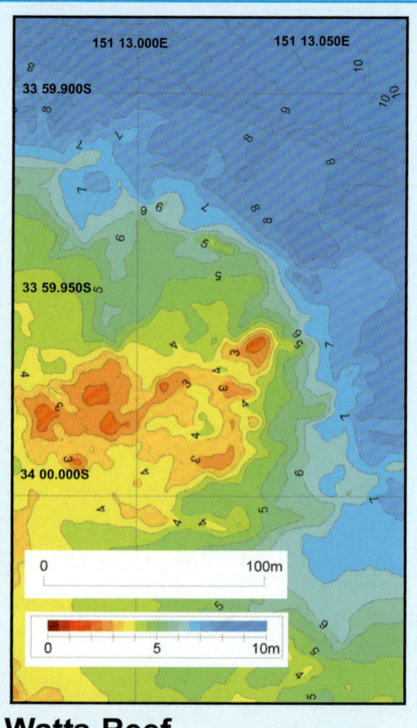

Watts Reef

In Botany Bay, on the other side of the shipping channel from Bare Island bommie, just off the Kurnell Peninsula, is Watts Reef. It is a shallow, broken reef covered in kelp. This is good habitat for squid. Catch them with jigs, and use them as livebait for kingfish or snapper. The reef is usually home to a nervous school of yellowtail (yakkas), which are often shadowed by kingfish. By anchoring and berleying in this area you can catch trevally, bream, flathead, snapper or mulloway. This spot is sheltered from the swell. A reasonably strong tidal current usually flows.

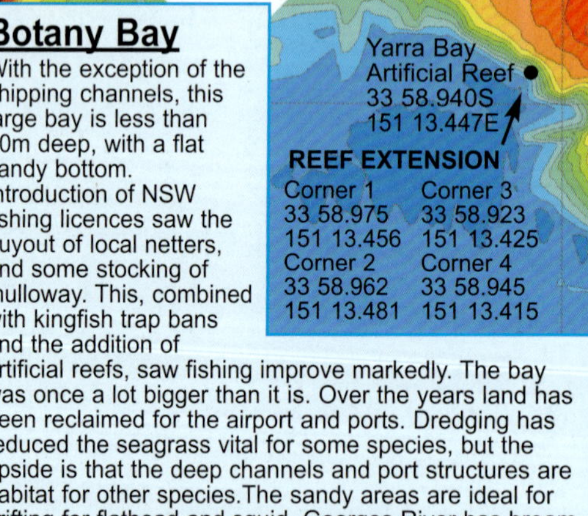

Botany Bay

With the exception of the shipping channels, this large bay is less than 10m deep, with a flat sandy bottom. Introduction of NSW fishing licences saw the buyout of local netters, and some stocking of mulloway. This, combined with kingfish trap bans and the addition of artificial reefs, saw fishing improve markedly. The bay was once a lot bigger than it is. Over the years land has been reclaimed for the airport and ports. Dredging has reduced the seagrass vital for some species, but the upside is that the deep channels and port structures are habitat for other species.The sandy areas are ideal for drifting for flathead and squid. Georges River has bream, flathead, whiting and mulloway. Towra Point Aquatic Reserve is a shallow mangrove swamp that holds juvenile fish and is a no fishing zone. The nearby oyster leases are good for bream. Molineaux Point, adjacent to the shipping channel, has a man-made containment wall consisting of a jumble of concrete blocks, where fish hide. It is a good spot to catch livebait (yakkas) and target kingfish, mulloway and tailor from boat or shore. La Perouse Peninsula and Bare Island are the more distinctive fishing spots within Botany Bay. There are caves and walls around Bare Island. The bommie just south of Bare Island is a large reef rising from sand, 14m to 4m. Anchor or drift for kingfish, mulloway, tailor, snapper, morwong and silver trevally. Be careful boating at the north end of the bommie as it breaks.

Mulloway and bass

The Hawkesbury River is on Sydney's doorstep, yet it produces mulloway to 30kg, trophy bream, flathead, blue swimmer and mud crabs, squid, octopus and prawns. There's also kingfish, hairtail, bass and estuary perch to be had.

Fish can be caught all year, but their habits change. Anglers who pay attention to seasonal changes and who use fresh bait and well presented lures will do well.

Bass and estuary perch: Bass and the similar estuary perch move upriver in summer and downriver in winter. Anglers who follow them sometimes catch 30 fish a day, to about 45cm.

Bass and estuary perch begin migrating down the river to spawn about May. In cold weather bass and perch school in deeper parts of the lower river.

Locate schools with a sounder and troll diving lures, or drop baits.

Use natural coloured lures in clear water and bright colours and golds in turbid water.

Bass start moving up the rivers about September. The upper reaches as far as Yarramundi usually fish from September. Bass and perch come up the river in a hungry mood after losing weight while spawning in winter.

Fish returning from salt water are sleek and silver compared with fish from the upper freshwater reaches.

Summer bass fishing is usually done in the upper reaches and the tributaries. Fishing is best when the barometer is high or rising.

Surface lures work in summer, usually at dawn and dusk. Strikes are often near cover. When the water temperature rises to 21C the fish feed aggressively.

While surface lures work best in the morning and evening, spinnerbaits are good around weedbeds. Night fishing for bass is also effective, especially on calm summer nights.

Big bass can usually be found around Yarramundi, as this area can only be reached by foot or canoes.

Large fish also come from the middle reaches where prawns are thickest.

Between Ebenezer and Lower Portland, bass fishing is best before skiiers arrive.

Between Wilberforce and Lower Portland there is good bass fishing along rock walls and heavy snags.

In winter schools of bass and estuary perch are found around Colo River and the snags on the lower Hawkesbury.

Bass can be caught on many baits - prawns, worms and even dough, which also produces mullet and carp. Plastic worms work well. Spinnerbaits with skirts or rubber tails are good around weedbeds.

Bass school at creek mouths flowing into the main river when spawning. They feed hard at this time - catch and release should be practised. Estuary perch feed on prawns, so imitate prawns if you want to catch them.

Fisheries studies show that the most successful bass spawnings happen in floods. Years of drought reduce catches.

Mixed bags: Bass, estuary perch, flathead and bream can be caught as far upstream as the Windsor and North Richmond bridges. At Wisemans Ferry mulloway, flathead, bream, estuary perch and mud crabs can be caught. Bait fishing with live or fresh prawns or squid work on mulloway, bream and flathead.

Mulloway: These range from juveniles to 30kg fish. Mulloway are about after rain. Lures work well around the bridges. Wisemans Ferry is a good area - catches of a dozen fish to 8kg are common, with the occasional monster. Juno Point and Brooklyn are best for big fish. Small mulloway travel far upstream about May, giving multi-fish sessions.

Flathead: Try casting into mangroves and jigging a lure down the mudflat to a drop-off. Flathead are good from Lower Portland to West Head and bag limits are easy.

Bream: Big fish are caught in winter, but will appear in summer. Sandworms and soft plastics work. Large bream are between Wisemans Ferry and Spencer. Expect fish to 2kg and 50cm in winter near Spencer. Fish the edges of holes. Rock walls and pylons hold big fish, especially on an incoming tide at night. Use fresh bait on unweighted lines.

Mud crabs: Try around Wisemans Ferry and Spencer - use traps baited with fish frames. Blue crabs are common in summer in the lower river.

Hairtail: Visit the lower reaches in winter. Use pilchards and live yakkas at various depths. Hairtail have sharp teeth and light wire traces are needed. Try a glowstick above the bait to attract fish.

Squid: Abundant in the lower reaches. Fish weedbeds in the day. The squid often seem to school so if you catch one throw another jig out quickly. Live squid is the ultimate jewfish and kingfish bait.

Luderick: Common around Wisemans Ferry in winter. They like the weed on rock walls. Use berley and stringy weed bait on an outgoing tide. Expect fish to 50cm.

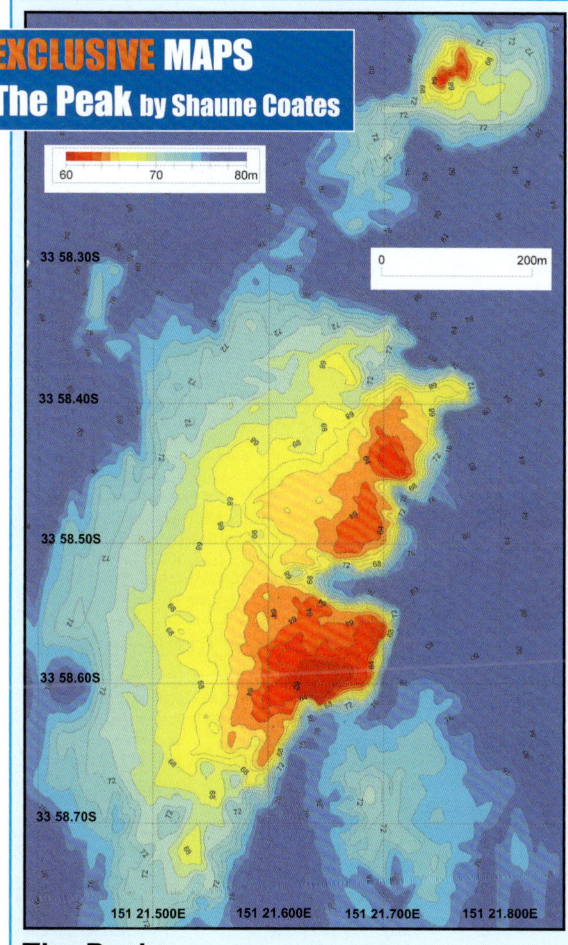

The Peak

Botany Bay is a popular launching spot for offshore game fishing. The Continental Shelf is 30km offshore and Browns Mountain, a seamount, is a further 10km. Closer in, at 12km north-west of Botany Heads is The Peak. It rises to 60m from a sandy plateau of around 85m. A few hundred metres to the east the bottom drops again to 110m. Marlin and tuna are caught in this area. In summer, dolphin fish are caught here and at the nearby Sydney East FAD. Buoy co-ordinates vary from year to year. Check the fisheries website for its location, as well as other FADs. At The Peak you can usually find kingfish schools on your sounder year-round, with winter producing bigger fish. Leatherjackets can be a problem, but they are good to eat. When they are not there you can anchor or drift for snapper or morwong.

www.dpi.nsw.gov.au/fishing/recreational/resources/fish-aggregating-devices

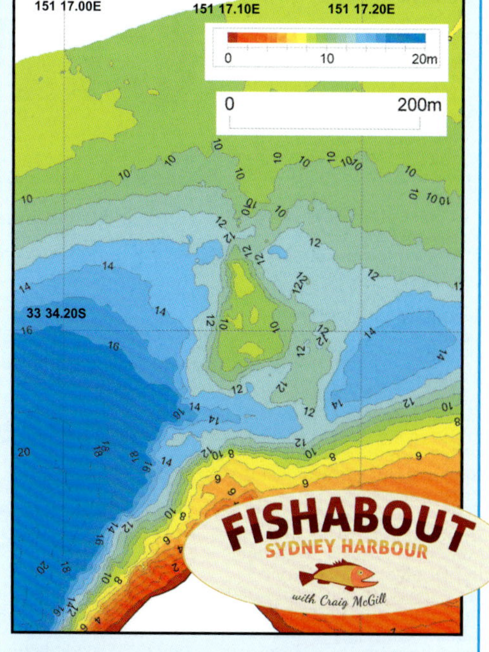

Flint and Steel

Broken Bay has a summer influx of pelagic fish, mainly salmon, kingfish, striped tuna, bonito and tailor. At times the bay is alive with thrashing fish and seagulls. **One of the better-known fishing spots is Flint and Steel Reef, shown above.** Big mulloway live here. Anchor and use just enough weight to get baits down. Livebait, especially squid, is best. Try week nights when traffic is less. Expect to also catch snapper, bream, flathead and tailor.

The mighty Hawkesbury

The Hawkesbury starts in the mountains near Goulburn. The river winds down through Sydney's western suburbs as the Nepean River to Windsor, where it becomes the Hawkesbury. From there it winds north to Wisemans Ferry. Somewhere between, depending on rain, the fresh merges with salt. From Wisemans Ferry she turns east and spills into Broken Bay and the South Pacific. When you consider Cowan, Pittwater, Berowra and Brisbane Waters are substantial waterways in their own right, the magnitude of the system becomes clear. Some of the less developed areas, especially around Cowan, and in the upper gorge country, are near pristine. Fishing options range from backpacking for bass and trout in the upper river through to chasing bluewater speedsters like tuna and kingfish in Broken Bay. Bass are the main fish in the fresh. There are also mullet, carp and rumours of murray cod and macquarie perch. Between the dam wall and Wisemans Ferry is where most bass anglers head, primarily in summer. Gorge country above Penrith offers scenery and small bass. The area from Penrith to Wisemans Ferry is floodplain country. The stretch from Wisemans Ferry to Spencer has estuary fish and is one of the more productive reaches. It is the least fished area because access is limited. Spencer to Broken Bay sees most pressure, but this section still turns on some of the best fishing. Big bream are caught around May. Mulloway to 30kg are landed. Blue swimmer crabs run in summer, along with mud crabs. Berowra Creek, branching off above the road bridges, is surrounded by steep hills and rocky ridges, offering all-weather fishing, superb scenery and limited boat traffic. Cowan Creek, branching off just inside the Hawkesbury mouth, offers all the benefits of Berowra in even more spectacular surroundings. This flooded valley has deep, clear water. As well as the usual estuary species, hairtail, john dory, tuna and blue groper are caught.

City fish

By CRAIG McGILL

Sydney fishing can be outstanding. Within a short drive of the CBD are Port Hacking and the Georges River, the Botany Bay Recreational Fishing Haven, the mighty Hawkesbury River, scenic Sydney Harbour, and offshore artificial reefs.

At least 53 fishable species are available.

Tropical species stray into Sydney waters. Mangrove jacks, giant trevally, giant herring, estuary cod and spangled emperor are caught.

There's even trout and bass in the hills.

In one creek the bass are as good as anywhere I've fished on the east coast.

There are brown and rainbow trout in the coastal range waterways.

The Coxs and Wollondilly Rivers and the rivers and dams near Lithgow, Oberon and Orange are the better trout spots. To the south are Burrinjuck and Wyangala dams, with trout, yellowbelly and murray cod.

Barrington Tops to the north is a rugged, scenic area with lots of small trout.

Glenbawn Dam, three hours north of Sydney, has huge yellowbelly.

Sydney has spectacular estuaries. There are protected deepwater bays and flooded valleys like Cowan Waters and Middle Harbour, as well as mangrove-lined, sandbank-studded waters in the upper Hawkesbury, Lane Cove, Parramatta and Georges Rivers.

In the more open areas such as Broken Bay and lower Sydney Harbour, summer sees an influx of baitfish which attracts pelagic fish. In all but the worst weather, kingfish, bonito, salmon, tailor, frigate mackerel, striped and mack tuna are available to trailerboaters.

Beach fishing: NSW surf beaches are the best in the country and Sydney is no exception. Sydney's northern suburbs have great beaches like Whale, Curl Curl, Narrabeen, and Palm.

In the winter months tailor are caught, with occasional salmon and silver trevally.

Things really start to pick up off the beaches in about November and continue through to May.

With the warmer northern currents whiting, bream, flathead and mulloway bite.

If you get the right bait, namely worms and pipis, of which the more secluded beaches hold better stocks, classic catches can be made.

Big mulloway can be caught on fresh or live bait.

Between Sydney and Jervis Bay to the south and Forster-Tuncurry to the north, just a couple of hours drive either way, are some of the best land-based game spots in the country.

The platforms to the north include classics such as The Ovens, South Avoca, Wybung, Tomaree, Seal Rocks and Charlotte Head.

Northern bluefin tuna are the mainstay, with black marlin, spanish mackerel and yellowtail kingfish as well.

Other areas include the rocks along Sydney's Royal National Park, Middle Head and the Kiama Blowholes. All are an easy daytrip. There is no shortage of scenic rock fishing for drummer, luderick, bream, tailor, mulloway, salmon, bonito and snapper.

Sydney's generally moderate weather means offshore grounds are accessible for all but a few weeks of the year. There is usually trouble-free offshore access through deep river and harbour entrances.

Offshore options are divided into three categories - out to the 30m grounds, then the middle 30m to 100m grounds, and wide from 100m to the Continental Shelf.

The closer reefs require skill to produce the goods but the river and harbour heads, islands and bombies and the flathead drifts produce well.

Trolling or baitfishing headlands in summer works well. Expect kingfish, bonito, tailor and bream.

The more recognised middle grounds, at roughly between 4km and 6km offshore, include Broken Bay wide, The Whale, Long Reef Wide, The Peak and the 4 and 6 mile.

It is these middle grounds that the more serious bottom fishers catch kingfish, snapper, morwong, trevally, mulloway, dory and jackets, to name a few. Pelagic fish include yellowfin tuna, dolphin fish, wahoo, sharks and marlin.

The wide grounds require a serious boat. Spots include the Peak Wide, Outer Long Reef and Broken Bay wide between 6km and 12km out, and the Shelf and Browns Mountain at 25km to 35km wide. These are the domain of big gamefish like blue, black and striped marlin, big yellowfin tuna and sharks including tigers, makos, whalers and whites.

Albacore and striped tuna are common in this area.

The wide grounds inside the shelf offer superb bottom fishing, but conditions must be right because of the depths where blue-eye trevalla, hapuku, bass groper, gemfish and deep sea perch live. Use modern thin lines, heavy leads and winches. Tides, currents and barometric pressure are the considerations for offshore trips. The best tide is between the run up and two hours after the high. Too much current makes anchoring and sinking baits difficult.

Bottom fish bite better on a high barometer or just before a major front. Summer months are best for offshore reef and surface fish.

There's a dip in species caught in winter, namely mulloway, tarwhine and teraglin, but they are replaced with dory and trevally. Winter is best for deep species like hapuku and blue-eye trevalla.

Many surface species move on in winter, with the exception of yellowfin and albacore, which peak at this time, along with mako and blue sharks.

Estuary images by John Lugg ©NSW Dept of Environment & Climate Change

The shipwrecks

Sydney Harbour has been described as the best harbour in the world. It covers 5500ha, with the deepest spot being 47m, between Dawes Point and Blues Point. Nonetheless, it has seen many shipping tragedies since the First Fleet arrived on January 26, 1788. The *Dunbar* was wrecked outside the dreaded Heads in 1858, killing 121. The *Catherine Adamson* lost 20 *after* she negotiated the Heads. In 1927 the liner *Tahiti* cut through a Sydney ferry, killing 40. In WWII a Japanese mini-sub sank the steamer *Kuttabul*, killing 19. Six vessels have been lost on Sow and Pigs Reef, one of the few real navigation hazards. There are more than 300 wrecks in the vicinity of the harbour, with 90 within the harbour. Many are in the Long Reef wreck graveyard outside the harbour. Only a few of the 300 wrecks have known remains, and only some interest divers and fishermen. Many are broken up or partly covered in sediment, but may still attract fish. Here's a few of interest ...

Valiant: A 23m tug that sank in 1981 east of Barrenjoey Head. It is at 27m, sitting upright on sand. Has kingfish and more.
SS Birchgrove Park: This 47m collier sank in 1956 and lies at 52m, on its side.
Trio: This 50m barge lies off Avalon Beach in 51m. It includes a concrete yacht hull being carried when it sank.
SS Duckenfeld: This collier hit Long Reef and sank in 1889. Some remains at 25m. A permit is required to dive it.
SS Dee Why: This 70m ferry was the first wreck scuttled at the Long Reef wreck graveyard, in 1976. It lies in 46m.
SS Bellubera: This 70m ferry was scuttled in 1980 near the *Dee Why*. It is in two pieces.
Coolooli: This 50m dredge sits high off the bottom in 48m. Has big mulloway and kingfish.
Himma: A 34m tug scuttled in 1980 in 48m of water.
Meggol: This 70m tanker started life in the navy as the *Doomba* and *Wexford*. Scuttled in 1976 just 20m from *Dee Why* in 49m.
SS Myola: This hull sank in 1919 and sits at 50m. Found in 1995.
Centurion: Only a little remains of this 63m vessel. Sits in 18m, on sand. Lots of fish.
Itata: Lies in Middle Harbour.
SS Centennial: This 66m hull sank in 1889 after a collision.
TSS Currajong: A 70m wreck 200m from shore in a busy part of the harbour, lying from 20m to 26m deep. Sank in 1910.
SS Royal Shepherd: A few pieces of this collier lie outside Sydney Heads at 27m. Sunk in 1890. Fish abundance varies.
Dunbar: This sank in 1858 and not much is left. The remains are just below the South Head signal station in 5m of water.
SS Annie Miller: A collier sunk north of Bondi Beach, in 45m of water. Lots of fish life.
TSS Belbowrie: This South Maroubra wreck lies 200m from the beach, off a rock platform. It sank in 1939. Pieces remain.
SS Tekapo: Steamship ran aground on way to Port Kembla. Remains lie at the point at the south of Maroubra Beach.
MV Malabar: Shallow wreck in pieces. Sank in 1931.
SS Kelloe: Sunk in 52m in 1902 after a collision. Broken up.
SS Minmi: The remains of this 80m collier lie inside Botany Bay's north head in less than 10m.
SS Hilda: Only pieces remain of this 37m hull. Sunk in 1893.
Wollomstrom: Tug sank in Gunnamatta Bay near the baths in less than 10m and is intact.
SS Tuggerah: On its side in 48m about 9.3km south of Port Hacking. Many fish.
SS Undola: Lies at 45m just 7.4km south-west of the *Tuggerah*. Great fish life.

Sydney Offshore Artificial Reef

The first NSW offshore artificial reef was deployed in October 2011. The structure was installed 1.2km east of The Gap (South Head) in 38m of water. It weighs more than 40 tonnes, and stands 12m at its highest point and is designed to remain intact for at least 30 years. Studies have shown the reef attracts baitfish such as scad, which in turn attract bigger fish such as kingfish. The reef can be found at 33 50.797S 151 17.988E

Sydney South Offshore Reef

A large offshore artificial reef was installed south of Sydney in 2017. It is accessible from Port Hacking and Port Botany. The reef is made of 36 concrete modules, 25 tonnes each, measuring 4m by 5m. Ten of the modules have vertical steel towers rising to 9m. Clusters of five modules are spread over two areas of 100sqm, on sand in 30m of water, 2.5km s-s-e of Jibbon Point. The reef, named after the late John Dunphy, has attracted a variety of fish, including kingfish, snapper and flathead.

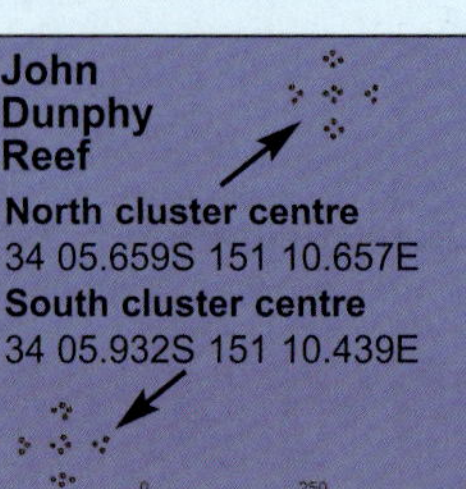

= public wharf
Strict speed limits apply on Sydney waterways
XXXX
Sydney
Long Reef PAGE 350
Long Reef Point
Collection of invertebrates from Long Reef or Dee Why Head not permitted
Dee Why Beach
Dee Why Head
No bait collecting in North Sydney Harbour
Curl Curl Beach
Manly Reservoir
Marine reserve
Bait
Sydney Harbour has little current and clear water, so fresh or live bait is often needed to make wary fish strike. Gar, yakkas and slimy macks are available - use berley to attract them. Freshly caught or live squid is best for mulloway and kingfish. Use light mono leaders.
Roseville Bridge
Bantry Bay
Sugarloaf Bay
Middle Harbour
Manly Beach
Manly Rock
Collection of invertebrates from Sydney Harbour not permitted
Chart, approx 33 47.785S 151 18.273E
Chart, approx 33 46.985S 151 20.956E
Lane Cove River
Parramatta River
Sailors Bay
Clontarf
Spring Cove
Sydney Harbour NP
North Harbour
North Head
trawler wreck approx 33 49.631S151 18.672E
Centurion wreck approx 33 49.047S 151 16.863E
South Head
Middle Head
Dunbar Head
No anchoring traffic regulations area
charted wreck approx 33 51.496S 151 20.718E
Annie Miller wreck approx 33 52.005S 151 17.936E
Maps not for navigation
Homebush Bay
Yaralla Bay
Morrisons Bay
Glades Bay
Brays Bay
Majors Bay
Burns Bay
Tambourine Bay
Woodford Bay
Long Bay
Quakers Hat Bay
Balmoral Beach
Hunters Bay
wrecks
Lavender Bay
Balls Head Bay
Berrys Bay
Neutral Bay
Mosman Bay
Shell Cove
Little Sirius Cove
Clifton Gardens
Taylors Bay
Obelisk Bay
Lady Bay
Camp Cove
Watsons Bay
Cockatoo Island
Goat Island
Hen and Chicken Bay
Five Dock Bay
Balmain
Harbour Bridge
Bradley's Head
Athol Bay
Shark Island
Sow and Pigs Reef
Steele Point
Hermit Bay
Garden Island
Clark Island
Darling Harbour
Iron Cove
Rushcutters Bay
Double Bay
Rose Bay
Collection of invertebrates from Bondi Beach rocks not permitted
KILOMETRES
METRES
North Bondi
Mackenzies Point
charted wreck approx 33 54.803S 151 19.561E
Shark Point
No bait collecting in reserve
Mistral Point
Maroubra Beach
Magic Point
Grey nurse shark protection zone
Collection of invertebrates from Long Bay not permitted
Malabar & Googlwai approx 33 58.209S 151 15.721E
Long Bay
Key to Map
Hotspots
1. Bantry Bay, most species.
2. Upstream of Roseville Bridge, estuary fish.
3. Near the Spit Bridge and Balmoral, most species. Land-based fishing off carpark. Good flathead drift, with chance of mulloway, kingfish.
4. Sow and Pigs Reef: excellent spot for most species. Exposed at low tide, breaking waves. Fish east side on run-in, west side on run-out. Best morning and afternoon. The large nav light eddies to the s-e and n-w hold kingfish.
5. Clifton Gardens, boat and jetty fishing, most species. Best shore fishing is at west end.
6. North Harbour, john dory, trevally and more.
7. Inside North Head, fish by boat or walk from carpark on North Head Scenic Dve. Good livebait (gar, yakkas) and fishing area.
8. Mangroves, beach, rocks near Roseville Bridge, estuary fish. Access via Waringah Rd
9. The Steps is a hole in Sugarloaf Bay - land-based and boat fishing for estuary fish, Via Eastern Valley Way.
10. Clontarf beach, most species. Via Spit Rd.
11. Cobblers Beach, most species. Military Rd.
12. Middle Head. Excellent land-based game spot. Exposed to swell. Via Military Rd.
13. Bradleys Head, most fish. Excellent all-round spot on early run-out tide. Access by boat or through national park (daylight hours).
14. Rose Bay, shallow weedbeds - squid, flathead with john dory near moorings.
15. Bottle and Glass Point, most species.
16. Inside South Head is best in rough weather. (Spots 14 to 16 reached via New South Head Rd.)
17. Land-based mulloway hotspot.
18. Pelagic and reef fish from entrance south.
19 & 20. Reef and rubble just north and south of entrance has most species, including snapper.
20. Good ledges near road, care required.
21. Bream fishing inside point in rough weather.
22. Rock groynes in bay are good land spots.
23. The three bridges are popular fishing spots.
24. Bream on oyster racks. Blue crabs throughout.
25. Cooks River mouth walls are land-based hotspots.
26. Merries Reef in close and Osborne Shoal out wide have most species. Anchor and berley.
Airport
The size and scope of security areas may change during times of heightened security risk
Security Zone
Botany Bay
deep
groynes
SEE PAGE 350 FOR REEF GPS DATA
drop-off
Artificial Reefs - see next page
Yarra Bay
Frenchmans Bay
bombora
Henry Head
busy shipping channel
do not anchor on seagrass - pink public moorings are supplied in many areas
moorings
Historic Wk
Georges River
Oatley Bay
Kyle Bay
Kogarah Bay
Dolls Point
Tom Ugly Bridge
Captain Cook Bridge
Oyster Bay
Sylvania Waters
Towra Point Reserve
sanctuary - no fishing
refuge
Weeney Bay
Quibray Bay
Inscription Point
Cape Banks
No bait collecting in reserve
Cape Solander
Woolooware Bay
Kurnell Peninsula
Botany Bay NP
No bait collecting in reserve
Cronulla Beach
Woniora approx 34 01.290S 151 15.603E
Collection of invertebrates from Inscription Point not permitted
Hilda, approx 34 02.376S 151 13.421E
No anchoring traffic regulations area
Artificial Reefs
Botany Bay has artificial reefs made from concrete 'reef balls'. See Page 350.
Bate Bay
Yowie Bay
Gymea Bay
Marine reserve
Burraneer Bay
Gunnamatta Bay
Port Hacking
Royal NP
Glaisher Point
Gooseberry Bay
Simpsons Bay
Cabbage Tree Point
The Basin
Jibbon Beach
Port Hacking Point
Collection of invertebrates from Cabbage Tree Point not permitted
Osborn Shoal
N
Launch sites
1. Roseville Ramp, Healey Way, multi-lanes, pontoon, NP fee applies. 2. Tunks Park, Brothers Ave - good ramp with pontoon. 3. Clontarf Beach, Clontarf Reserve - sandy, 4WD. Similar site on opposite shore 200m down from Spit Bridge - limited parking. 4. Little Manly Cove, North Harbour. 5. Lyne Park, into Rose Bay, off New South Head Rd. 6. Boat ramps at Greenwich Point and Manns Point. 7. Hawthorne Canal, Leichardt Park, next to bridge. 8. Woolwich Marina. 9. Taplin Park, turn off Lyons Rd. 10. Bayview Park, off Burwood Rd. 11. Kendall Bay, Cabarita Park, Cabarita Rd. 12. Kissing Point Park, off Delange Rd. West Ryde off Victoria Ave. 13. East side of John Whitton Bridge. 14. Yarra Bay Sailing Club. 15. Foreshore Dve, multi-lanes, pontoons. 16. Cooks River, Kyeemagh, Mutch Ave, multi-lanes, concrete to low water mark. 17. Ramsgate. 18. Blakehurst, Princes Hwy, Dover Park, Kogarah Bay, four ramps, firm sand at low tide. 19. Connells Point. 20. Oatley Bay. 21. Scylla Bay, Verona Range, shallow. 22. Tom Ugly Bridge, Princes Hwy, multi-lanes. 23. Hawkesbury Park, single lane, Moruya Ave. 24. Cronulla, Tonkin St, one lane, poor parking. 25. Burraneer Bay, Water St, one lane. 26. Dolans Bay - Wally's Wharf, Port Hacking Rd, two lanes, pontoon. 27. Yowie Bay Marina. 28. Gray's Point, Swallow Rock Dve, two lane shallow ramp. Usually ample parking. 29. Bonna Point, Prince Charles Pde, dual lane, shallow. 30. Bonnet Bay, Washington Dve. 31. Burnum Burnum, off River Rd. 32. Holts Point Place, one lane. 33. Oyster Bay, Connell Rd, one lane, shallow. 34. Prince Edward Park, small craft.
Wrecks
A. Centennial, historic wreck, approx 33 50.871S 151 15.003E
B. Currajong, good wreck but in busy part of harbour, approx 33 51.305S 151 14.936E
C. Charted wreck, approx 33 51.774S 151 14.562E
Artificial Reefs
D. Sydney Offshore Artificial Reef 33 50.797S, 151 17.988E 38m
E. John Dunphy Offshore Reef 34 05.659S 151 10.657E 30m 34 05.932S 151 10.439E 30m
Sydney tides move up to about 1.9m

Middle Harbour

Middle Harbour is a remarkable waterway. Garigal National Park keeps much of its upper towering foreshores free of development. The harbour is a flooded valley with a tiny catchment, so salinity is consistent. Its deepest point is 40m and it is home to oceanic and estuary species. The only obstacle to oceanic fish is the Hunter Bay shallows at Middle Harbour's mouth. This channel is about 3m deep, but it hasn't stopped blue groper, mulloway, kingfish, tuna, spotted mackerel and cobia from entering. The lower flats abound with nippers, the upper ones with cockles, squirt worms and black crabs, but you can't take invertebrates here for bait. The lower section, the stretch from Cobblers Beach to Clontarf drop-off, can be boiling with kingfish, salmon, tailor and bonito, usually in Nov/Dec. To fish, try the Clontarf drop-off. This bar goes from 5m to 23m over a run of only 50m. You can catch anything there. Deep water continues well upstream. The best spot in this stretch is across the mouth of Fisher Bay where an eddie concentrates bait.

Head upstream and keep left past Beauty Point into Long Bay, Quakers Hat Point and the adjacent bay hold good kings and are good in a southerly. Long Bay is good for dory in winter. Straight across from Quakers is an abrupt point called Fig Tree. This breaks the flow and has bream, mulloway, kingies and jackets. Back out into the main waterway and upstream towards the Roseville Bridge you find Seaforth Bluff on the right. This is a deep gnarly drop-off with a bit of rough stuff and has king and mulloway. If you head towards the middle of the river here you will find Middle Harbour's deepest water - 40m at high tide. Jump to the other shore to Powder Hulk Bay and you find VB Reef, with kingfish, mulloway, jackets, reddies and tailor. Find it by lining up the starboard markers on Seaforth Bluff with the one on Pickering Point and driving between the two. It comes up to about 20m from 26m. The upstream side of Pickering Point has king, jew and big flatties. Across from Pickering is Sugarloaf Bay. Both the upstream and downstream points hold king and jew. Just inside on the right is The Steps, a great hole for boat fishing and shore-based fishos' best chance of a king or jew west of the Spit Bridge. It is a dory hole in winter. The bay splits in two and up the back of these divisions are flats that fish well for flatties on the drop-off and bream on the flats at high tide.

The stretch from Seaforth Bluff to the 8-knot zone just downstream from Roseville ramp often has kings, salmon, bonito, frigates and tailor. Prime spots are the mouth of Bantry and Sugarloaf Bays and Seaforth Bluff across to Sailors Bay. Moving upstream on the right is Bantry Bay. The southern point and shore holds kings. The southeast shore has great bream and the drop-off on the flat up the end is a great flathead ground, with flats bream at high tide. The deep water in the middle has dory and squid. Bantry is also your best shot at a mid-winter king. Both Bantry and Sugarloaf Bay produce blue and mud crabs but the best muddies are above Roseville Bridge. The southern shore from Yeoland Point to Killarney Point is good for bream luring. Killarney Point, the start of the 8-knot zone, is prominent and the eddie it creates has scoured out a jew hole on the upstream side. You get pelagics up to this point. Roseville Bridge pylons have big jackets, mulloway, bream and flatties from shore. The mangroves and estuary start here and the first big tree stand on the left is a bream spot. Flick lures or black crabs into the shallows on high tide. Bream, flatties and jew can be lured from here up. It is shallow for the next 1km, especially towards the swimming area near Moores Creek. The creek enters on the left and has a sandbank at its mouth with bream and flatties. Watch your sounder as the next hole is a landbased mulloway spot. The Carroll Creek track follows the river. The next good spot is Gordon Creek and the stretch down to the power lines. Gordon Creek comes in on the left. The sandbank at the mouth extends three quarters across the main river, and has flatties and bream. Downstream is a good jew area. The last good hole is between Gordon Creek bank and The Narrows. At The Narrows the river halves. This short hole is your last cast for daytime jew. From The Narrows to Carroll Creek on the right is the last fishable stretch, with estuary perch. You can go upstream at high tide but only a canoe will get out at low tide.

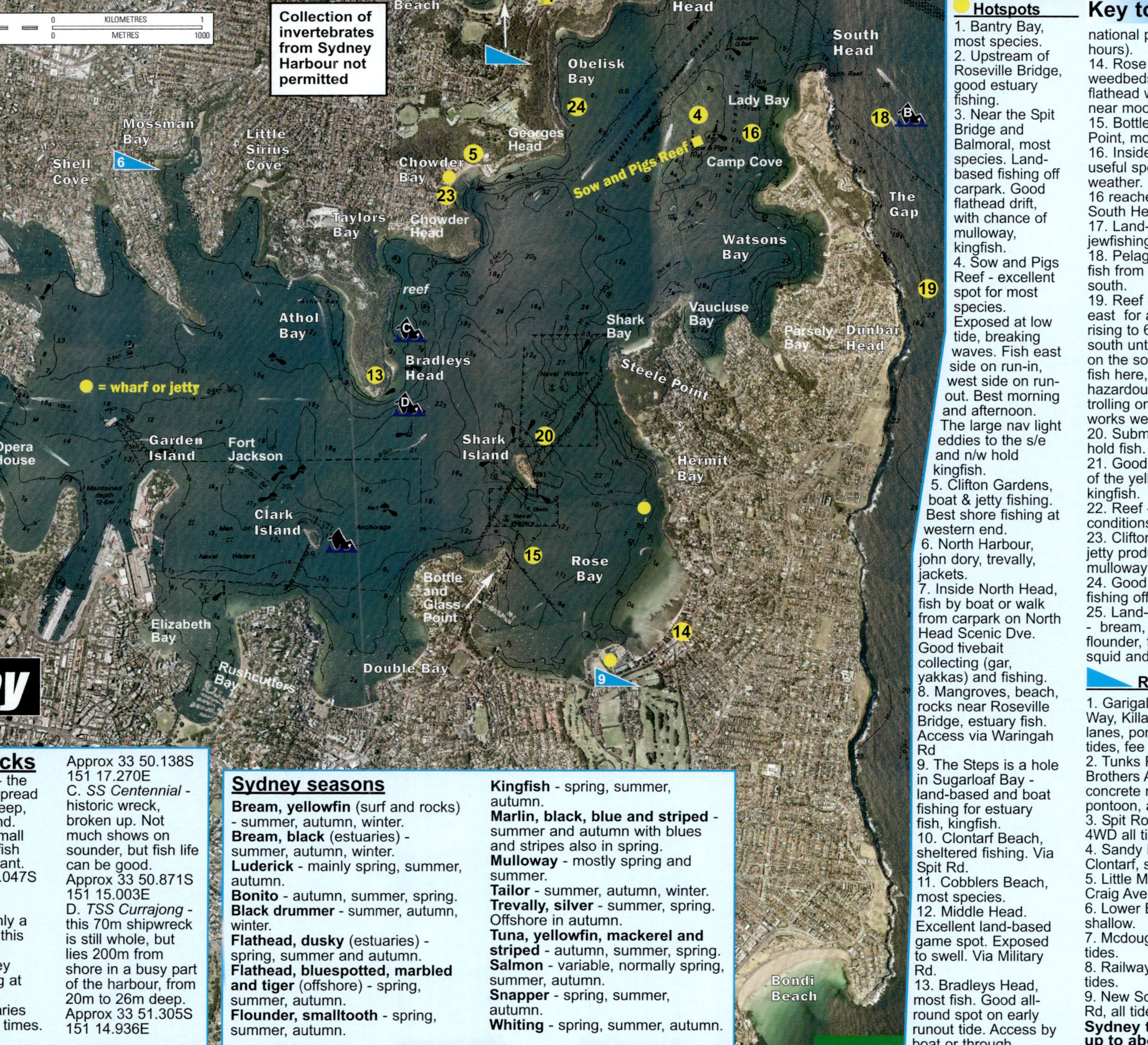

Wrecks

A. *Centurion* - the wreckage is spread out at 18m deep, resting on sand. Despite the small structure the fish can be abundant. Approx 33 49.047S 151 16.863E.

B. *SS Royal Shepherd* - only a few pieces of this collier remain outside Sydney Heads, resting at 27m. Fish abundance varies but is good at times. Approx 33 50.138S 151 17.270E

C. *SS Centennial* - historic wreck, broken up. Not much shows on sounder, but fish life can be good. Approx 33 50.871S 151 15.003E

D. *TSS Currajong* - this 70m shipwreck is still whole, but lies 200m from shore in a busy part of the harbour, from 20m to 26m deep. Approx 33 51.305S 151 14.936E

Sydney seasons

Bream, yellowfin (surf and rocks) - summer, autumn, winter.
Bream, black (estuaries) - summer, autumn, winter.
Luderick - mainly spring, summer, autumn.
Bonito - autumn, summer, spring.
Black drummer - summer, autumn, winter.
Flathead, dusky (estuaries) - spring, summer and autumn.
Flathead, bluespotted, marbled and tiger (offshore) - spring, summer, autumn.
Flounder, smalltooth - spring, summer, autumn.
Kingfish - spring, summer, autumn.
Marlin, black, blue and striped - summer and autumn with blues and stripes also in spring.
Mulloway - mostly spring and summer.
Tailor - summer, autumn, winter.
Trevally, silver - summer, spring. Offshore in autumn.
Tuna, yellowfin, mackerel and striped - autumn, summer, spring.
Salmon - variable, normally spring, summer, autumn.
Snapper - spring, summer, autumn.
Whiting - spring, summer, autumn.

Key to Map

Hotspots

1. Bantry Bay, most species.
2. Upstream of Roseville Bridge, good estuary fishing.
3. Near the Spit Bridge and Balmoral, most species. Land-based fishing off carpark. Good flathead drift, with chance of mulloway, kingfish.
4. Sow and Pigs Reef - excellent spot for most species. Exposed at low tide, breaking waves. Fish east side on run-in, west side on run-out. Best morning and afternoon. The large nav light eddies to the s/e and n/w hold kingfish.
5. Clifton Gardens, boat & jetty fishing. Best shore fishing at western end.
6. North Harbour, john dory, trevally, jackets.
7. Inside North Head, fish by boat or walk from carpark on North Head Scenic Dve. Good fivebait collecting (gar, yakkas) and fishing.
8. Mangroves, beach, rocks near Roseville Bridge, estuary fish. Access via Waringah Rd
9. The Steps is a hole in Sugarloaf Bay - land-based and boat fishing for estuary fish, kingfish.
10. Clontarf Beach, sheltered fishing. Via Spit Rd.
11. Cobblers Beach, most species.
12. Middle Head. Excellent land-based game spot. Exposed to swell. Via Military Rd.
13. Bradleys Head, most fish. Good all-round spot on early runout tide. Access by boat or through national park (daylight hours).
14. Rose Bay, shallow weedbeds - squid, flathead with john dory near moorings.
15. Bottle and Glass Point, most species.
16. Inside South Head, useful spot in rough weather. (Spots 14 to 16 reached via New South Head Rd.)
17. Land-based jewfishing.
18. Pelagic and reef fish from entrance south.
19. Reef ridge runs east for about 1km, rising to 6m. Travel south until it appears on the sounder. Big fish here, but hazardous, drifting and trolling only. Berley works well here.
20. Submerged pylons hold fish.
21. Good ground east of the yellow marker, kingfish.
22. Reef - good conditions only.
23. Clifton Gardens jetty produces kingfish, mulloway and more.
24. Good land-based fishing off rocks.
25. Land-based fishing - bream, tailor, flounder, flathead, squid and jackets.

Ramps

1. Garigal NP, Healey Way, Killarney, multi-lanes, pontoon, all tides, fee applies.
2. Tunks Park, Brothers Ave - concrete ramp with pontoon, all tides.
3. Spit Road, Mosman, 4WD all tides.
4. Sandy Bay Rd, Clontarf, sand, 4WD.
5. Little Manly Cove, Craig Ave, shallow.
6. Lower Boyle St, shallow.
7. Mcdougall St, all tides.
8. Railway Ave, all tides.
9. New South Head Rd, all tides.

Sydney tides move up to about 1.9m

Key to Map

Hotspots

1. Salmon, tailor, whiting, bream and mulloway.
2. Salmon, tailor, whiting, bream and mulloway.
3. Bulli and Thirroul Beaches have whiting, bream.
4. Bellambi has snapper grounds off Stanwell Park, Sandon Point, Thirroul Surf Club, at Bellambi bombora and Wollongong Five Islands, and flathead grounds north and south of ramp between Port Kembla and Windang Island. Snapper, morwong, pigfish, bream, groper on reefs.
5. From spring to autumn troll lures close to headlands and breakwall for kingfish, salmon, bonito, tailor, trevally, tuna. Ocean side of eastern Kembla harbour breakwall good by boat or from the rocks.
MM Beach is a popular salmon and bream beach.
6. Shallow lake has bream, whiting, flathead, flounder, luderick, chopper tailor, trevally, leatherjackets, blue swimmer crabs, prawns. Main channel from bridge to last navigation marker in lake is good flathead area, and the drop-off in the main part of the lake. Use squirt worms for whiting - look for holes in the sandflat and use a bait pump.
7. Bass Point Reserve: rock fishing platforms, most species. No fishing in Bushrangers Bay.
8. Kiama's Blowhole Point rocks produce marlin, tuna, kingfish, cobia, sharks, tailor, snapper. Squid on south side of the blowhole platform. In winter salmon, kingfish and bonito, with drummer and luderick in Blowhole rock pool area. Best beaches are Bombo, Surf, Kendall and East's - best in warmer months for whiting, dart, bream, flathead.

Launch sites

1. Headland Ave, beach launch.
2. Robert Cram Dve, two ramps. One is multi-lanes but shallow. Other is a beach ramp.
3. Wollongong boat harbour.
4. Port Kembla boat harbour, Foreshore Rd, fuel wharf facilities.
5. Two ramps, Northcliffe Dve.
6. Kanahooka Rd, all tides.
7. Fern St, shallow.
8. Reddel Pde, shallow.
9. Yallah Bay Rd, two ramps, all tides.
10. The Esplanade, all tides.
11. The Boulevarde, all tides.
12. Towns St, Shellharbour, all tides.
13. Bass Point Tourist Rd, all tides.
14. Three launch sites in creek, all shallow, poor sea access.
15. Kiama boat harbour, Terralong St, all tides.

Local tides have up to about 2m movement.

Wollongong

The 'Gong has surf beaches, headlands, rock walls at Port Kembla and Lake Illawarra, inshore reefs and islands, and deep reef fishing from only 13km out. There is an annual cuttlefish spawn between Stanwell Park and Kiama at the start of winter, which brings fish on. Birds give away the location of dead cuttlefish. Cast a bait into the action for snapper and trevally. Best whiting beaches are Thirroul, Bulli, Port Kembla, Windang and Warilla, but others fish well. Salmon and big mulloway are caught on the beaches in winter, with smaller fish in summer. Tailor are a regular catch. Summer gamefish include striped and black marlin and dolphin fish. Popular reef grounds are Bandit, Wollongong Reef, Five Islands and The Trap Reef, with bigger boats fishing out to the shelf for hapuku and morwong. Minamurra Creek has flathead, bream and whiting, but Shoalhaven River is a better location. Lake Illawarra has bream, whiting and flathead. Islands off Port Kembla have kingfish and yellowfin tuna. Summer is best for whiting, flathead, flounder and snapper. A steel tower artificial reef was installed 2.4km off Perkins Beach in 2019.

GPS

Flagstaff
34 26.156S 150 56.497E
34 26.286S 150 56.266E
34 26.435S 150 56.144E
Trap Reef
34 28.770S 151 03.730E
Flathead
34 29.997S 150 54.003E
Bass Point
34 35.141S 150 55.491E
34 35.317S 150 55.327E

Lake Illawarra entrance and Windang Island

Minnamurra River

Looking towards Windang Island and the sea entrance rock walls

Nowra

The Shoalhaven River has 50km of tidal water with two sea entrances, one permanently open at Crookhaven Heads and the other intermittently open at Shoalhaven Heads, 5km apart. Nowra is 18km up from the entrance. Shoalhaven River is shallow but has most estuary fish, with whiting, bream, luderick and flathead the main species. Mulloway, perch and bass can also be caught. Look for perch near the deeper rock walls. To the north the Gerringong area has good inshore boat fishing, with Werri Drift a flathead ground along Werri Beach, about 750m offshore. Gravel Patch is 2.5km off the northern point of Werri Beach and has morwong and flathead. The Crack in the Wall is almost 2km directly off Walkers Beach, with morwong and flathead. There is reef between Black Head and Werri Point. Local bass dams are Tallowa, Danjera and Flat Rock.

GPS

6-Mile Reef
34 41.980S 150 57.147E
4-Mile Reef
34 47.571S 150 52.451E
Kiama South
34 50.168S 150 55.798E
Kiama South 2
34 50.179S 150 54.780E
Kiama South 3
34 50.573S 150 54.340E

Key to Map

Hotspots

1. Werri Beach - changing gutters. Park along Pacific Ave. Salmon, tailor in winter, dawn & dusk. Summer bream, whiting and flathead. Bream best near rocky ends. Mulloway all year at night. Werri Beach's south headland, north side, adjacent to pool, has drummer, luderick and bream. Eastern platform has salmon, tailor, luderick, drummer. Boat harbour has fishable platforms, best on south side. Good squid area.
2. Walkers Beach reached via downhill walk over the golf course. Park at north end of course on Fern St. Salmon, tailor, mulloway.
3. Black Head has bream, snapper, kingfish, drummer, trevally, salmon, tailor. Park in Stafford St - tracks lead to the rocks. Access to point cut off at high tide. Crooked River has bream, flathead, prawns. Fish from shore, canoe or dinghy.
4. Seven Mile Beach has salmon, tailor in winter and bream, whiting in summer. Beach has pipis. Park in Burke Pde for access to Little and Seven Mile beaches, with access via tracks along Crooked River Rd, south of bridge.
5. Crookhaven River mouth - north shore bordering Comerong Island has flats and weed, with rock wall for land-based fishing accessible via ferry. Inner wall has luderick, outer wall tailor, bream, flathead, mulloway. South shore boat ramp provides sea access, with rocky shore to the entrance holding bream, luderick and trevally.
6. Lower Crookhaven has dense mangrove areas bordering extensive flats - whiting, bream, flathead.
7. The Canal is lined with rock walls. Walls on south bank have bream and luderick. Local oyster racks often hold good fish.
8. Flats at end of island have flathead, whiting, bream. Reef between island and bridge, north shore requires care - deep water next to it holds bream, luderick, jew. Bridge pylons hold fish. Upstream of bridge are rock walls with bream, flathead, whiting, mulloway, estuary perch.
9. Large flat on east end of island has big nippers. Good for whiting, flathead.
10. Upper river, Yalwal Creek and other tributaries (off map) hold bass. Coolendel is best access, and Tallowa Dam wall. Lake Yurrunga has bass, trout, macquarie perch - no combustion motors.
11. Sir John Young Banks - wahoo, tuna, kingfish, black marlin, flathead, snapper, pigfish. Beware breaking waves. Marlin to 100kg from January to March - north-east corner of banks is known as Main Hump; inside the banks is The Mud; and a nearby separate reef called The Block. Autumn is good for kingfish - jig the Main Hump or The Block or use deep livebaits.
12. Curleys Bay and other bays on south side are shallow and ideal for yak enthusiasts. Flats and oyster racks hold bream, flathead, mullet, garfish and luderick.
13. Broughton River at Berry has bass, estuary perch also found throughout system, flathead and whiting in lower reaches with marine fish moving up during dry spells.

Launch sites

1. Kiama boat harbour, all tides.
2. Gerringong boat harbour, good amenities but affected by swell from north-east.
3. Sand launch into Crooked River. Rare sea access.
4. River Rd, all tides.
5. Wharf Rd, all tides.
6. Hay Ave, shallow.
7. Back Forest Rd, all tides.
8. Collangata Rd, all tides.
9. Bolong Rd, all tides.
10. Fairway Dve, multilane, all tide.
11. Wharf Rd, all tides.
12. West St, into Shaws Ck, all tides.
13. Adelaide St, two lanes, all tides.
14. Halser Rd, all tides.
15. Wollumboola Lake, West Cres, shallow, unsealed.
16. Otranto Ave, all tides.
17. Prince Edward Ave, multi-lanes, good parking, all tides.
18. Private ramp at van park.

Local tides have up to about 1.9m movement.

Dams

Burrinjuck Dam lies 185km as the crow flies west of Nowra. This 5500ha dam has murray cod, macquarie perch, yellowbelly, silver perch, brown and rainbow trout, Atlantic salmon, redfin and carp. There are several tourist parks and boat ramps. The Goulburn trout district is 80km west of Nowra, with the Goulburn River and small Sooley and Pejar Dams arguably the main attractions.

Shoalhaven Offshore Artificial Reef
This was was installed in 2015. There are 20 concrete modules in five clusters of five modules per cluster, at a depth of 30m, over sand bottom. The centre is at 34 50.955S 150 47.731E. See reef layout map above left. Expect yakka, tailor, kingfish, trevally, snapper, morwong, salmon and mulloway.

Estuary images by John Lugg ©NSW Dept of Environment & Climate Change

Reef Off Beecroft

Beware breaking waves
a. 34 59.453S 150° 50.104E
Sir John Young Bank 1
b. 34 59.169S 150 51.814E
Sir John Young Bank 2
34 59.040S 150 52.342E

Currambene Creek sanctuary incorporates the creek upstream from a point west of Goodland Rd to the tidal limit, and part of the south bank near the mouth. Moona Moona Creek is a sanctuary from 50m above the road bridge to the tidal limit.

St Georges Reef

Made of hollow concrete reef balls.

Reef 1	35 07.303S	150 36.622E
Reef 2	35 07.491S	150 36.900E
Reef 3	35 07.396S	150 37.166E
Reef 4	35 07.314S	150 37.436E
Reef 5	35 07.314S	150 37.701E
Reef 6	35 07.271S	150 37.970E

St Georges Reef Expansion

Corner 1	35 07.563S	150 36.934E
Corner 2	35 07.516S	150 37.063E
Corner 3	35 07.488S	150 36.904E
Corner 4	35 07.446S	150 37.024E

Conjola Reefs

Artificial reefs of hollow concrete 'reef balls'.

Reef 1
35 15.632S 150 28.313E
Reef 2
35 15.628S 150 28.330E
Reef 3
35 15.668S 150 28.320E
Reef 4
35 15.664S 150 28.344E

Currambene Creek
Swan Lake
Lake Conjola
Burrill Lake
Sussex Inlet St Georges Basin

Jervis Bay

The bay is about three times the size of Sydney Harbour. It has some of Australia's best landbased fishing platforms. Point Perpendicular has one of the few landbased locations where yellowfin tuna and marlin are regularly caught. Currarong has excellent rock, beach and boat fishing. There are usually ample squid and bread and butter species available in the bay to keep holidaymakers busy. Note the marine park zonings and defence land. Offshore there are canyons along the Continental Shelf with blue, striped and black marlin. Yellowfin, bonito and albacore are the main tuna species seen. Gamefish are taken mainly in the warmer months. Hairtail show up in this region as far south as Ulladulla. Yellowtail kingfish and tailor numbers vary from year to year. St George's Basin is a Recreational Fishing Haven, with artificial reefs installed at a depth of 6.5m. Nearby Lake Conjola has a similar reef. Kayak and cartopper fishos will enjoy Burrill and Tabourie Lakes, which have mainly bream and flathead.

Key to Map

Hotspots

1. Rock fishing, gamefish in summer. Big Beecroft dangerous in swell. The Tubes on southern peninsula is more sheltered, but all need care. Walking, climbing required.
2. Boat fishing at Bombora Rock off Longnose Point in suitable conditions, approx 35 05.189S 150 46.537E.
3. Flathead, whiting, bream in creek - note sanctuary.
4. Hyams - turn right at car park and walk beach to gutters. Big whiting and bream in shallows.
5. Middle Ground, most fish.
6. St Georges Basin: big bream, whiting, crabs, flathead, prawns.
7. Swan Lake: as for 6.
8. Bream, prawns, crabs.
9. Ulladulla - rock & surf.
10. Burrill Lake - bream, prawns, crabs.
11. Shallow lake, top end is best. Burrill is better.

Launch sites

1. Yalwal St, beach ramp, and Warrain Cres, into creek.
2. Beach launch.
3. Rock shelf north end Honeymoon Bay, call (02) 4448 3411 for camp info.
4. Watt St, shallow.
5. Catherine St, nth bank of creek, Frank Lewis Way on sth bank.
6. Holden St, all tides.
7. Jervis Bay Rd, Murrays Beach, all tides.
8. Ramps at Sanctuary Point Rd, Naval Pde, Fisher St, all tides.
9. Ramps at Island Point Rd (shallow), The Basin Rd (sand), Basin View Pde (all tides), Boathaven Ave (sand, shallow).
10. Sussex Inlet ramps all on west side at Nielson Lane, River Rd, Sussex Rd (shallow), Lakehaven Dve (best ramp), Pacificana Dve (shallow).
11. Swan Lake, The Springs Rd, sand, shallow.
12. Berrara Ck, Lakeland Ave, sand.
13. Red Point Rd, beach launch, shallow, exposed.
14. Berringer Cres and York St (high tide only).
15. Ramps at Lake Conjola Entrance Rd and Aney St, shallow.
16. Ramps at Haviland St and Valley Dve, all tides.
17. Creek, Matron Porter Dve, high tide only.
18. Best ramp is north side of boat harbour, all tides. Two shallow sites on south side. Also Kings Pt via Ski Club.
19. Maria Ave (pontoon) and McDonald Pde.
20. Tabourie Caravan Park.

Local tides have up to about 2m movement.

Need more info? FISH FINDER recommends Ulladulla Fishing Centre, 12 Wason St, Ulladulla, phone (02) 4455 4344.

Maps not for navigation. Depths in fathoms

INDEFINITE LEAVE

Pretty Beach

Meroo Lake

Estuary images by John Lugg ©NSW Dept of Environment & Climate Change

Clyde River

Ulladulla coast

INDEFINITE LEAVE

Tomaga River

Shoalhaven Wide GPS
The Banks
34 56.950S
150 55.660E
The Block
34 58.440S
150 59.160E
Jervis Canyons
35 16.600S
150 55.400E
35 16.160S
151 00.400E
35 13.000S
150 51.600E

Batemans Wide GPS
BB Plateau
35 53.020S
150 36.020
BB Plateau 1
35 53.000S
150 36.000E
BB Plateau 2
35 56.020S
150 32.990E
BB Canyons
35 04.200S
150 26.250E

Ulladulla GPS
Conjola Bait Spot
35 17.860S
150 28.800E
Bannister Peak
35 19.050S
150 31.240E
Green Isle Snapper
35 17.280S
150 33.380E
Conjola Snapper
35 18.450S
150 31.640E
St Georges Plateau
35 15.680S
150 40.330E
Kingfish Ground
35 22.080S
150 32.170E
Morwong Reef
35 24.490S
150 29.120E
Tabourie Morwong
35 26.570S
150 26.350E
Hard Reef
35 26.800S
150 26.500E
Ulladulla Canyons
35 20.100S
150 52.300E
35 23.200S
150 49.800E

Pretty Beach - call (02) 4457 2019 for camping

Pebbly Beach - call (02) 4478 6023 for camping

Depot Beach - call (02) 4478 6582 for camping

Maps not for navigation. Depths in fathoms

Thanks to Compleat Angler in Batemans Bay for assistance.

Batemans Bay

Murramarang Beach near Bawley Point is the north end of Batemans Marine Park and the northern entry to Murramarang NP, which extends south to Batemans Bay. Beach 4WD access in the marine park is only to launch boats. Many beaches along this coast have camp sites. Batemans Bay, at the mouth of the Clyde River, gives safe access to the sea. The Continental Shelf drop-off is 35km out and has albacore, yellowfin and bluefin tuna, dolphin fish, mako sharks and marlin. The Clyde River has 43km of tidal water, extending to rapids 4km upstream of Shallow Crossing. In the estuary, oyster rafts hold big bream, with flathead, flounder and whiting in the shallows. The Clyde also has bass, estuary perch and luderick. Mulloway are at coastal outlets after rain, and within the Clyde River. In summer kingfish, marlin, yellowfin tuna and sharks are about, with snapper, morwong and flathead all year. Salmon, luderick and tailor are usually biting in winter.

Key to Map

Hotspots

1. Bawley Point: surf & rock fishing - small kingfish, tailor, luderick, drummer. Lake outlets hold mulloway after rain.
2. Good rock & surf fishing at Kiola, 4WD tracks. Snapper Point has kingfish, tuna, tailor, bream.
3. Pebbly Beach: great scenery. Bream, dart, whiting, tailor.
4. Lake has bream, whiting, flathead, blue crabs, prawns. Shore accessible via Lakesea Caravan Park with ramp at Durras Lake town. Much of upper lake is sanctuary. Ends of Durras Beach fishes well. Rock fishing at Wasp Head.
5. Oyster racks throughout lower river: bream, flathead and whiting on flats. Mulloway around bridge and in holes.
6. Flathead and whiting near bridge. Estuary fishing continues upstream to Cockwhy Creek, with bass from Cockwhy up.
7. Rock & beach fishing at Malua Bay, Mosquito Bay, Rosedale.
8. Tomaga River is a fishing haven - that means no gill nets. Bream, flathead, whiting and more. No fishing in Candlagan Creek.

Launch sites

1. Bawley Point, exposed, calm weather, upper tide.
2. Kioloa exposed, exposed, calm weather, upper tide.
3. Depot Beach Rd, shallow beach launch.
4. First St, shallow.
5. 4WD beach launch inside headland near Murramarang Resort.
6. Hibiscus Close, Maloneys Beach, 4WD sand launch.
7. Bay Rd, 4WD sand launch.
8. Wray St, all tides.
9. Princes Highway, all tides.
10. Hanging Rock Pl, multi-lanes, all tides.
11. George Bass Dve, all tides.
12. Lower Tomaga River, Kingston Pl, shallow.
13. Lower Tomaga River, Annetts Pde, all tides. Bar crossing requires care.
14. 4WD beach launching inside headland.

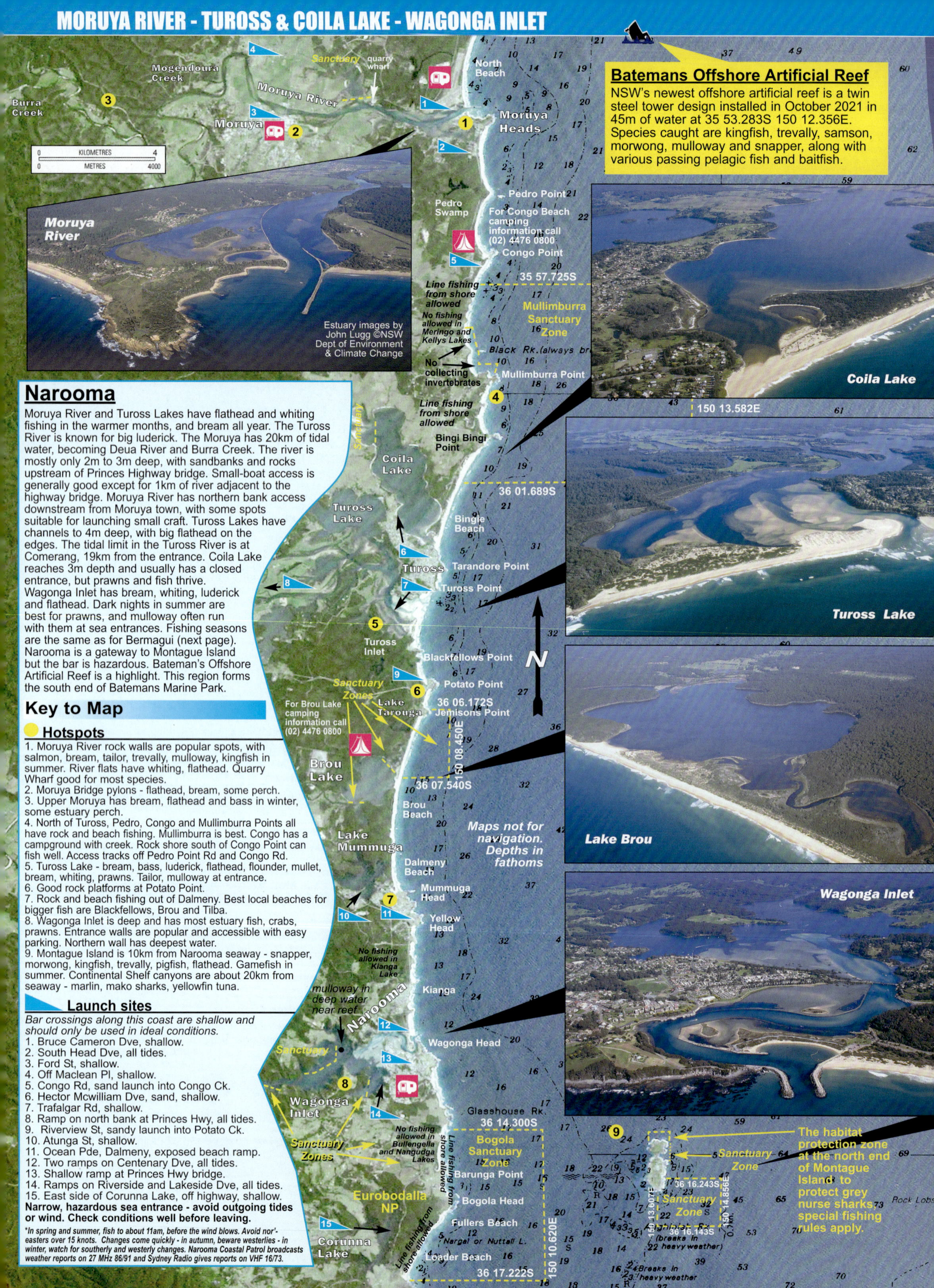

Narooma

Moruya River and Tuross Lakes have flathead and whiting fishing in the warmer months, and bream all year. The Tuross River is known for big luderick. The Moruya has 20km of tidal water, becoming Deua River and Burra Creek. The river is mostly only 2m to 3m deep, with sandbanks and rocks upstream of Princes Highway bridge. Small-boat access is generally good except for 1km of river adjacent to the highway bridge. Moruya River has northern bank access downstream from Moruya town, with some spots suitable for launching small craft. Tuross Lakes have channels to 4m deep, with big flathead on the edges. The tidal limit in the Tuross River is at Comerang, 19km from the entrance. Coila Lake reaches 3m depth and usually has a closed entrance, but prawns and fish thrive. Wagonga Inlet has bream, whiting, luderick and flathead. Dark nights in summer are best for prawns, and mulloway often run with them at sea entrances. Fishing seasons are the same as for Bermagui (next page). Narooma is a gateway to Montague Island but the bar is hazardous. Bateman's Offshore Artificial Reef is a highlight. This region forms the south end of Batemans Marine Park.

Key to Map

Hotspots

1. Moruya River rock walls are popular spots, with salmon, bream, tailor, trevally, mulloway, kingfish in summer. River flats have whiting, flathead. Quarry Wharf good for most species.
2. Moruya Bridge pylons - flathead, bream, some perch.
3. Upper Moruya has bream, flathead and bass in winter, some estuary perch.
4. North of Tuross, Pedro, Congo and Mullimburra Points all have rock and beach fishing. Mullimburra is best. Congo has a campground with creek. Rock shore south of Congo Point can fish well. Access tracks off Pedro Point Rd and Congo Rd.
5. Tuross Lake - bream, bass, luderick, flathead, flounder, mullet, bream, whiting, prawns. Tailor, mulloway at entrance.
6. Good rock platforms at Potato Point.
7. Rock and beach fishing out of Dalmeny. Best local beaches for bigger fish are Blackfellows, Brou and Tilba.
8. Wagonga Inlet is deep and has most estuary fish, crabs, prawns. Entrance walls are popular and accessible with easy parking. Northern wall has deepest water.
9. Montague Island is 10km from Narooma seaway - snapper, morwong, kingfish, trevally, pigfish, flathead. Gamefish in summer. Continental Shelf canyons are about 20km from seaway - marlin, mako sharks, yellowfin tuna.

Launch sites

Bar crossings along this coast are shallow and should only be used in ideal conditions.

1. Bruce Cameron Dve, shallow.
2. South Head Dve, all tides.
3. Ford St, shallow.
4. Off Maclean Pl, shallow.
5. Congo Rd, sand launch into Congo Ck.
6. Hector Mcwilliam Dve, sand, shallow.
7. Trafalgar Rd, shallow.
8. Ramp on north bank at Princes Hwy, all tides.
9. Riverview St, sandy launch into Potato Ck.
10. Atunga St, shallow.
11. Ocean Pde, Dalmeny, exposed beach ramp.
12. Two ramps on Centenary Dve, all tides.
13. Shallow ramp at Princes Hwy bridge.
14. Ramps on Riverside and Lakeside Dve, all tides.
15. East side of Corunna Lake, off highway, shallow.

Narrow, hazardous sea entrance - avoid outgoing tides or wind. Check conditions well before leaving.

**In spring and summer, fish to about 11am, before the wind blows. Avoid nor'-easters over 15 knots. Changes come quickly - in autumn, beware westerlies - in winter, watch for southerly and westerly changes. Narooma Coastal Patrol broadcasts weather reports on 27 MHz 86/91 and Sydney Radio gives reports on VHF 16/73.*

GPS

Lobster Reef
36 29.847S 150 06.437E
Cemetery - flathead
36 20.832S 150 07.198E
Camel Rock
36 22.450S 150 05.454E
The Kink - gamefish
36 18.000S 150 19.000E
4-Mile Reef
36 24.000S 150 08.400E
6-Mile Reef
36 24.440S 150 10.000E
12-Mile Reef
36 27.000S 150 15.000E
Bermagui Canyon - gamefish
36 17.175S 150 24.152E

Bermagui

This town has one of the safest NSW sea entrances, and the Continental Shelf is only 22km out. Everything from sand and tiger flathead to marlin and broadbill swordfish can be caught. The estuarine lakes along the coast have flathead, bream, luderick, whiting, mullet and garfish, with the smaller lakes fishing best when sea entrances are open. Wallaga, Wapengo and Bermagui River are all worthwhile. Four Mile, Six Mile and Twelve Mile reefs produce snapper, morwong, nannygai and flathead. Deeper reefs to 150m and beyond produce trumpeter, trevalla and gemfish, but expect strong currents. There are runs of kingfish, salmon and tailor along the coast. Timing is key. For snapper it is April to October, best in May, for marlin it is all year but best Dec-June (peak around Feb-Mar), yellowfin tuna are Nov-Aug (peak April-June), bluefin tuna are June-Aug, kingfish are all year, often best around April. Salmon, tailor and silver trevally run in winter. In the estuaries, whiting and flathead are best in summer, with bream all year. Offshore fishing changes with water temperature, prevailing currents and movement of baitfish. North of Bermagui, Mystery Bay is a quieter location with a launch site only 7km from Montague Island. Bass and estuary perch are available 30km west of Bermagui in Brogo Dam. Local fishing competitons are held, mostly run by Bermagui Big Game Anglers Club - **www.bbgac.com.au**

Key to Map

Hotspots

1. Lake Corunna has bream, flathead, whiting, flounder, garfish and mullet. Use nippers, prawns, and live mullet baits. Tailor when entrance is open.
2. Montague Island: see previous page.
3. Mystery Bay has landbased game fishing. Cliffs to north produce big kingfish, use live gar or squid. South end of the bay also has rock fishing. Surf beaches to south accessible by 4WD.
4. Tracks off 1080 Rd lead to good rock and beach fishing spots.
5. Wallaga Lake - to 10m deep in many areas, best in summer - flathead, bream, snapper, tailor and salmon. Entrance usually closed. Nippers on sandflats on both sides of bridge. Drift with live mullet or soft lures for big flathead. Bream in winter.
6. Bermagui River, shallow: luderick, flathead, flounder, bream, mullet - try midstream east of bridge. Use nippers or worms on rising tide. Offshore reefs at various depths; 4-Mile is east of Bermagui at 60m; the 6-Mile is south-east in 65m and the 12-Mile is further south-east at 120m. Brothers Reef is south in 50m and south of Bermagui there is reef off Goalen Head. Snapper, morwong, cod, wrasse, sharks, gurnard, mackerel, coutta and kingfish. 12-Mile Reef has trumpeter in summer. Flathead all year over sand to 120m deep, with prime grounds east of Mount Dromadery, between 28m to 40m. Other areas are Camel Rock in 40m, inside 4-Mile Reef at 50m, Beares Beach in 18m and Cuttagee Beach in 25m.
7. Rock and beach fishing: tailor, salmon, gummy sharks.
8. Good rock spots on south side of head. Mimosa Rocks NP walking tracks lead to good fishing spots. Camping with surf/rock fishing at Aragunnu Beach and Picnic Point.
9. Wapengo open to sea, has most estuary fish, with oyster racks throughout. Picnic Point camp site is nearest to ocean beach. Also Gillards Beach and Middle Beach camps on south side of lake. Salmon, tailor off rocks at lake entrance.

Launch sites

1. Lake Corunna, smaller boats only.
2. Mystery Bay: concrete ramp on beach. End drops off onto sand. Pull trailer out by rope if necessary - large jockey wheel helps. Useful site when local bars close.
3. Wallaga Lake, turn-off at Beauty Point for ramp and picnic area. Four van parks, with boat ramps and boat hire.
4. Bermagui - two ramps. Best is on south-east side near river mouth, off Lamont St, all tides. Other adjacent to bridge on south side, shallow.
5. Gravel/sand ramp beside oyster growers shed on eastern Wapengo Lake shore. Beware oyster leases throughout.

Local tides have up to about 2m movement. Add six minutes to Eden tide times.

Wallagoot Lake

Bega River

Merimbula Lake

Pambula Lake

Brogo Dam

This dam is on the Brogo River, a tributary of the Bega River. It has been stocked with thousands of estuary perch and bass. Estuary perch releases in 2017 and 2018 were the first undertaken in NSW, but bass have been stocked in the dam for two decades. The 100ha dam is up to 25m deep and boating is permitted.

Merimbula

Townships along the "Sapphire Coast" are located next to clear, sandy estuaries that offer pleasant fishing for holidaymakers with yaks or small boats. For trailerboaters, there are many inshore reefs. The Continental Shelf is just 37km offshore. Coastal reefs have snapper, morwong, kingfish, gummy shark, cod, flathead, leatherjackets, tailor, barracoutta and salmon. Warm summer currents bring yellowfin tuna, albacore and striped tuna; blue, black and striped marlin, broadbill swordfish, and mako and tiger sharks. Popular spots for reef fish are the 40 Fathom Reef, about 15km out from Merimbula, and the 70 Fathom Reef, at 28km. Deep reefs have trumpeter, morwong, leatherjackets, tiger flathead and nannygai. See the next page (Eden) for seasonal opportunities. The best estuaries are Nelson Lagoon, Bega River, Wallagoot Lake, Merimbula Lake and Pambula Lake, with mainly bream, whiting, flathead and luderick, along with estuary perch and bass. During flooding, mulloway are usually feeding at estuary outlets. There is landbased fishing off a walking track between Turingal Head and Kianinny Bay, with some of the best rock spots on the East Coast. An artificial reef was installed in Merimbula Lake in 2009, and an offshore reef in 2018.

Key to Map

Hotspots

1. Middle Lagoon Camp has estuary fishing, with surf and rocks a short drive away. Gillards Camp and Lagoon Camp have rock and beach fishing.
2. Nelson Lagoon is shallow and wadeable, with mostly flathead, bream, prawns. Mulloway at entrance after rain. Walking track to Moon Bay has surf and rock fishing.
3. Bega River flats hold flathead. Bream around snags, some estuary perch and mulloway. Bega River enters sea through Mogareka Inlet down from Hancock Bridge, the bridge being 500m from the entrance. The tidal limit is 11km upstream, half way to Bega. The river is navigable to tidal limit with depths to 15m.
4. Tathra - Continental Shelf is 20km out, with game fish. Best Nov/Dec to June with warm currents. Tathra wharf fishes well, beach is best at north end after floods, good headland.
5. Good rock platforms from Kianinny Bay to Turingal Head accessible by walking track in Bournda National Park.
6. Wallagoot Lake is up to 3m deep. North shore accessible from Wallagoot Lake Rd. Bournda NP camps on south bank. Prawns in summer. Opening is intermittent, yet snapper to 6kg have been caught, also bream and tailor.
7. Land-based spots: usually somewhere fishable in most seas. Tura Head is popular. Reefs run 2km east of Long Pt and Haystack Rock. Offshore hotspots are Long Reef, Horseshoe Reef and Lennards Island, with morwong, snapper, tiger flathead.
8. Great boat fishing. Land-based platforms on Fishpen Rd, upper tide. Mostly flathead, with black and yellowfin bream, luderick, mulloway on north-east side. Artificial reef has mulloway, snapper, bream. Fish ribbon weed edges for flathead.
9. Channel fishes best on falling tide, fish mouth on flood tide. Big black and yellowfin bream on oyster racks.
10. Hayock Rd gives access to good fishing at lake mouth, headland and Haycock Beach.
11. Severs Beach Access track leads to shallow beach which drops off sharply into channel.

** *Clear water in the lakes means light leaders should be used at all times. Fishing is often better after rain and during big tides.*

Launch sites

1. Ramp at bridge on Tathra-Bermagui Rd. Sea access in ideal conditions only.
2. Blackfellows Lake Rd, dirt, all tides.
3. Kianinny Bay ramp suitable for large boats. Good sea access.
4. Boat club, unsealed.
5. Hobart camp ground, dirt.
6. Lakewood Dve, all tides.
7. Arthur Kaine Dve, multi-lanes, all tides. Merimbula bar requires great care.
8. Pambula Lake, all tides.
9. Off Severs Beach Access track, canoe launch.

Local tides have up to about 2m movement.

A. Inshore Reef

An artificial reef was constructed in Merimbula Lake in 2009. It measures 1600sqm and contains 400 concrete reef balls.
Corner 1: 36 53.908S 149 53.139E
Corner 2: 36 53.918S 149 53.175E
Corner 3: 36 53.942S 149 53.105E
Corner 4: 36 53.948S 149 53.139E

B. Offshore Reef

Merimbula Offshore Artificial Reef 100m x 100m of modules in 30m of water. Approx position 36 54.867S 149 56.251E.

C. Wreck

C. Historic wreck, SS *Empire Gladstone* hit Haystack Rock in 1950. In 10m of water on south side of rock. Approx 36 57.043S 149 56.785E. Calm weather diving.

Estuary images by John Lugg ©NSW Dept of Environment & Climate Change

Nelson Lagoon

Towamba River

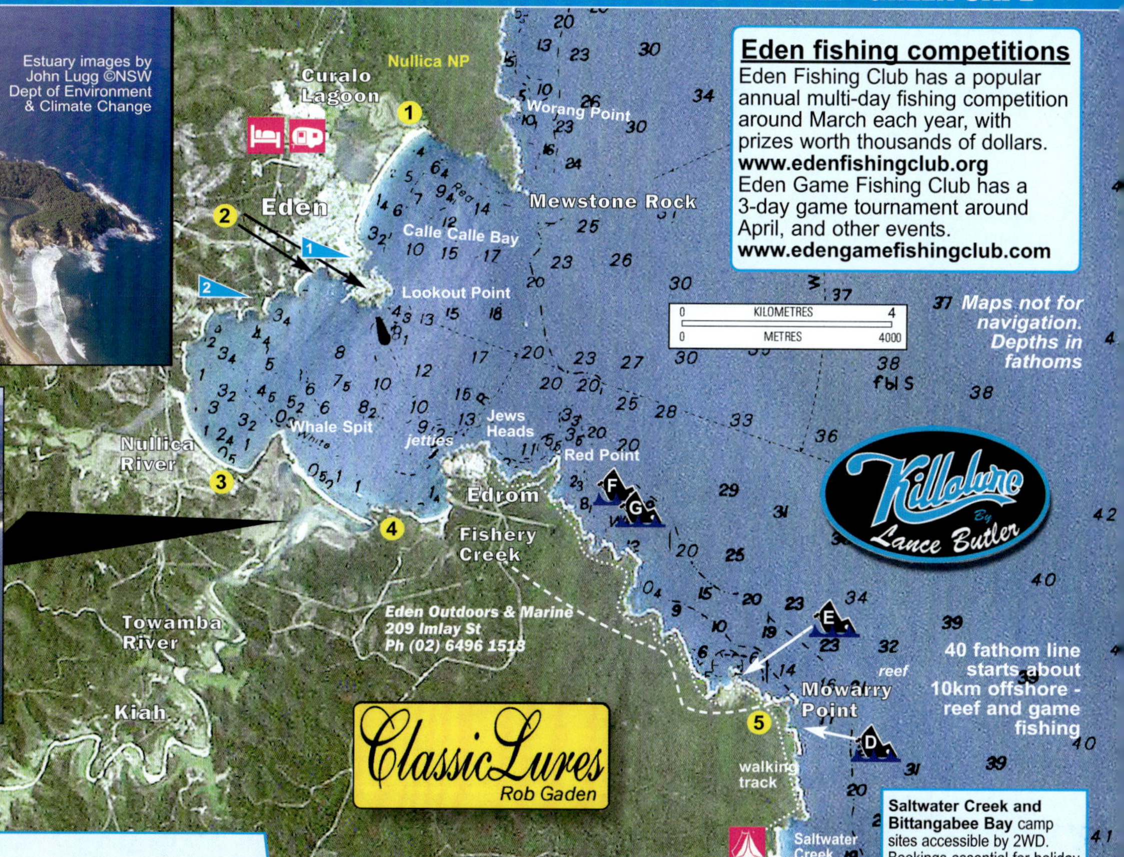

Wonboyn Lake entrance

Eden fishing competitions

Eden Fishing Club has a popular annual multi-day fishing competition around March each year, with prizes worth thousands of dollars.
www.edenfishingclub.org
Eden Game Fishing Club has a 3-day game tournament around April, and other events.
www.edengamefishingclub.com

Maps not for navigation. Depths in fathoms

40 fathom line starts about 10km offshore - reef and game fishing

Eden Outdoors & Marine 209 Imlay St Ph (02) 6496 1513

Saltwater Creek and Bittangabee Bay camp sites accessible by 2WD. Bookings essential for holiday periods. Easter bookings open Feb 1 and Christmas bookings on Aug 1. Apply by mail, fax or email.
Ph: (02) 6495 5000
Fax: (02) 6495 5055
FSCR@environment.nsw.gov.au
PO Box 656, Merimbula, NSW.

Eden

This scenic NSW fishing port, 50km north of the Victorian border, provides safe access to the sea. Blue, black and striped marlin and big sharks are within range of trailerboats, but it is schools of salmon, bonito, tailor, mulloway and kingfish that bring most fishos. Pelagic fish supported a local tuna cannery until 1999. Marlin fishing is best from December to May as warm currents move near shore, but trolling is good from mid-October to June for yellowfin tuna, albacore, dolphin fish and wahoo. Slow trolling with livebait works for striped and blue marlin in February/March. Reef fishing is excellent, with large areas of broken ground out from Green Cape, Mowarry Point and Disaster Bay. Snapper, morwong, leatherjackets, nannygai, flathead, barracoutta and school and gummy sharks are caught. There is usually somewhere in close to fish out of prevailing winds. Out wide, the deeper reefs have morwong, ling and hapuka. Kingfish are at Mowarry Point from October to June. Tailor are best from March to November. There are good spots for landbased fishing. The deepwater wharf is popular with families during holidays. Towamba River enters Twofold Bay through the permanently open but shallow Kiah Inlet, separated from the bay by a thin sand strip. Wonboyn Lake and its river system to the south has bream, flathead, flounder and more, with salmon, tailor and mulloway at the surf entrance. The lake has a resort with fishing facilities. Estuary outlets in this area have mulloway during floods, and they visit Twofold Bay in large schools. Estuary perch are caught in the rivers. Eden is busy during holiday periods.

Key to Map

Hotspots

1. Beach has tailor, salmon, bream, mulloway.
2. Wharf, rock wall, beach and rock fishing on Eden's Lookout Point peninsula. Wharf is most popular - slimy mackerel, yakkas, trevally, occasional kingfish, mulloway and more.
3. Sheltered beach has bream, whiting, flathead.
4. Reasonably safe rock fishing area.
5. Mowarry Point, via 4WD track from the Edrom road to Leatherjacket Bay. Long walk and climb to rock ledges. Plenty of reef offshore for boaters, in close and 10km out along 40 fathom line.
6. Bittangabee Bay - camping and beach launch. Rock fishing, snapper in bay, some bass in creek.
7. Disaster Bay surf beaches can be reached by car or by boat via Wonboyn River. Moor inside the estuary mouth on the north or south side and walk to the surf. North beach is less busy. Rock ledge on the south beach has salmon, tailor and bream.
8. Lower Lake Wonboyn is shallow but with strong tidal flow. Channel is marked, many sandbanks. Oyster leases line middle and lower lake. Middle lake is up to 5m deep, with the river to 10m deep, navigable to freshwater reaches. Flathead, whiting, luderick, tailor, estuary perch and bream, with to 10kg. Flathead best around 'Yellow Peg' area. Nippers near entrance. Bull Creek has flathead, bream and mullet small boats only. Fish the lake where the shallow entrance channels drop to deeper water. Mulloway best in summer on full moon nights. Lake Wonboyn resort pontoon has bream. Gar and mullet easily berleyed up. Lake tides about two hours behind sea tides.
9. The Pulpit and High Rock are superb platforms. The Pulpit is reached from the first track to the left past the track into City Rock. Park and climb down to the ledge. The left side has the best water but avoid the lower ledge. Nearby High Rock has deeper water - to the right of the car park, walk to the rocks below. At the bottom, turn left to reach a stone lying in a gap - climb the stone and the 3m climb up the back of the outer ledge then to High Rock on the left.
10. Green Cape ledges have bonito, kingfish, tuna, marlin, also luderick, drummer, snapper, tailor, salmon, barracoutta and groper. Trolling the coast is effective. Platform below cemetery reached by walking track from Lighthouse Road. Ledge is sloping and rugged but water is deep.
11. City Rock, named after the 1862 shipwreck *City of Sydney*. First track to right after leaving the forest area. Sheltered spot, yellowfin tuna and more. Some walking required. Wreck lies broken up in about 18m of water.

Wrecks

A. SS *City of Sydney* sank in 1862. Now just lots of small bumps near City Rock.
B. The SS *Ly-Ee-Moon* sunk in 1886. At 14m deep near graveyard with a second wreck.
C. SS *New Guinea* sunk in 1911. It is now broken up in 10m of water.
D. The 128-foot *Olive Cam* sank in 1954. Now just rubble in two shallow gullies.
E. *Lanercost* sank in 1872. Little is left.
F & G. Scuttled diving wrecks *Henry Bolte* 37 06.690S 149 57.790E and *Tasman Hauler* 37 06.556S 149 57.824E

Launch sites

1. Eden Harbour. 2. Quarantine Bay - best ramp.
3. Beach launch, camps at Bittangabee Bay.
4. Wonboyn Resort - private.
5. Public ramp. Lake's bar access only at high tide in absolute calm conditions.

Local tides have up to about 2m movement.

Victoria

This is a small state but with diverse aquatic habitat. Most fishing is done within Melbourne's two large, enclosed Port Phillip and Western Port bays, and in the Gippsland Lakes. Victoria's coast covers 2512km, some of it being rugged and difficult to access. Much of the state's northern border is the southern bank of the Murray River. Victoria has many lakes and streams, with both native fish and introduced trout. In recent times there has been a push towards stocking native fish, which resist climate extremes. Significant rivers in the state include the Ovens, Goulborn, Patterson, King, Loddon, Barwon, Rubicon, Snowy, Yarra, Mitta, Hopkins, Merri and Kiewa. The best lakes include Bullen Merri, Burrumbeet, Eildon, Eppalock, Hume, Mulwala and Purrumbete. In the sea, pink snapper, spotted and sand whiting, yelloweye mullet, black bream, luderick, garfish, flounder, flathead, salmon, silver trevally, estuary perch and squid are the main catch. In the surf, salmon prevail, with gummy and school sharks, mulloway, pink snapper and tailor. Gummy and school sharks are highly regarded. Mulloway and snapper move in close after storms. Offshore, pink snapper, flathead and kingfish are prime targets, with bluefin tuna, albacore and striped tuna on the surface. Mako and thresher sharks are chased by dedicated anglers. Victorian fishing have improved thanks to better management. Snapper are now often abundant around Melbourne, and big tuna have improved in the west. Kingfish are usually in good numbers. The state has limited commercial fishing in the Gippsland Lakes and Corio Bay, and increasing fish stocking, allowed boats with electric motors onto most freshwater reservoirs, and opening up Crown Land river frontage to camping and fishing.

Regulations: A recreational fishing licence covers Victoria's marine, estuarine and inland waters. Gear, size limits and bag restrictions apply. Fishers can use a maximum of two hooks. Set lines, cast nets, snares and mussel rakes are banned. Bait haul nets can be used in some areas. Victoria's intertidal zones are protected areas. From the intertidal zone fishermen may only collect bivalve shellfish such as pipis, scallops, mussels, oysters and squirters, and squid, octopus and cuttlefish, crabs, lobster, marine worms and burrowing shrimp. All other molluscs, including marine snails such as abalone, limpets, periwinkles and turbo shells must not be taken. Within Port Phillip Bay fishermen may only collect marine worms, burrowing shrimp, squid, octopus and cuttlefish from the intertidal zone. The use of a digging implement is prohibited in intertidal areas. Bait haul nets may not be used in Port Phillip Bay and Western Port, the North Arm and Cunningham Arm of Gippsland Lakes, some of the waters of Toorloo Arm and Nowa Nowa Arm of Lake Tyers, as well as Tamboon Inlet and Sydenham Inlet. Many water storages are closed to the public, and some small sections of specific freshwater locations are closed. Check with local water authorities before entering. Other fishing regulations apply throughout the state.

Seasons: In Port Phillip Bay, juvenile salmon are all year, while bream are best June to November. Flathead, garfish and spotted whiting are best in summer, with whiting through to April. Silver trevally and snapper are best October to May. Mullet are from April to October. Kingfish are best in summer. Squid are all year, best from June to October. Mulloway bite around Melbourne in winter.

Weather: Victoria's climate varies widely, despite the state's small size. The state's north-west is semi-arid temperate with hot summers, but the coast is temperate and cool. The Great Dividing Range produces a cooler, mountain climate in the state's centre. Winters along the coast are mild. The Alps in the north-east are the coldest part of Victoria. Rainfall increases from south to north, with more rain at high altitude. Rain is heaviest in the Otway Ranges and Gippsland in southern Victoria, and in the mountainous north-east. Rain is most frequent in winter, but summer rain is heavier. At Melbourne Airport the mean wind speed is between 20km/h and 24km/h through the year, with April, May and June being calmest and August and September windiest. Melbourne winds tend to blow northerly in winter and southerly in summer. Easterlies are uncommon. Winter fronts bring gales, and summer brings strong afternoon sea breezes. Victoria's tidal range is small, about 1m at Portland and under 2m at the NSW border.

Bait, lures and tackle: Pilchards, bluebait, prawns and squid are popular baits. Local bait can make all the difference. Lure fishing is popular, especially for salmon and kingfish, for which chrome slice lures are a good all-rounder. Bream and estuary perch are targeted with small minnows and soft plastics. Paternoster rigs are popular for bait fishing. In Victoria's estuaries, with small tides and often clear water, a light-tackle approach is crucial. Fishing is easier when the water dirties.

Special features: Some Victorian fishermen target the seasonal elephantfish run in Western Port between March and May. Large seven-gill sharks frequent both of Melbourne's bays. The volcanic crater that is Lake Purrumbete produces high growth rates in trout, and the lake is also stocked with chinook salmon, as is Lake Bullen Merri. Many estuaries have estuary perch, which may respond to baits presented on ultralight gear. Gummy sharks are a popular table fish, but the southern rock lobster (*Jasus edwardsii*) is the most desired seafood.

Marine parks and reserves: Victoria has state marine sanctuaries (see maps) that affect boaters and landbased fishermen.

Discovery Bay region marine sanctuary
38 20.000S 141 19.060E; 38 19.990S 141 24.080E; 38 22.750S 141 21.550E; 38 22.760S 141 18.250E

Merri River region marine sanctuary
38 23.920S 142 27.870E; 38 24.330S 142 28.270E
Merri River; bridge; Merri Island; breakwall; Middle Island

Marengo Reefs region marine sanctuary
38 46.510S 143 40.020E; 38 46.600S 143 40.190E; 38 46.710S 143 40.450E; 38 46.710S 143 40.160E; 38 46.790S 143 40.380E; 38 46.540S 143 39.970E

Point Addis region marine sanctuary
38 22.060S 144 17.100E; 34 24.190S 144 12.630E; 38 26.060S 144 16.950E; 38 28.130S 144 12.480E

Bunurong region marine sanctuary
38 40.000S 145 40.430E; 38 40.420S 145 37.960E; 38 43.490S 145 37.900E; 38 43.520S 145 40.380E

Twelve Apostles region marine sanctuary
38 38.860S 143 03.320E; 38 41.460S 143 01.610E; 38 42.010S 143 03.890E; 38 44.010S 143 11.170E; 38 45.770S 143 08.410E
shore fishing

Eagle Rock region marine sanctuary
38 28.020S 144 06.610E; 38 28.200S 144 06.460E; 38 28.280S 144 06.080E

Barwon Bluff region marine sanctuary
38 17.333S 144 30.350E; 38 17.600S 144 30.067E

The Arches region marine sanctuary
38 37.790S 142 59.720E; 38 37.780S 143 00.350E; 38 38.140S 143 00.220E; 38 38.150S 142 59.730E

SA; Vic; Discovery; Portland; Portland Bay; Port Fairy; Warrnambool; Cape Nelson; Lady Julia Percy Island; Hopkins River; Curdie Inlet; Port Campbell; Moonlight Head; Cape Otway; Aire River; Apollo Bay; Barham River; Lorne; Aireys Inlet; Torquay; Barwon River; Melbourne; Port Phillip Bay; Western Port Bay; Cape Schanck; Phillip Island; Cape Paterson; Cape Liptrap; Wa

Torquay Artificial Reef
Five modules in five clusters 3km out in 25m of water, with five FADs.
38 19.828S 144 22.500E
38 19.942S 144 22.600E
38 20.184S 144 22.320E
38 20.065S 144 22.225E

Catch the $80,000 cod

Victoria's **GoFish Nagambie** tournament put up an $80,000 first prize for the biggest murray cod caught over the event's three days. The second biggest cod won $15,000. Organisers said there was a total of $500,000 in prizes. Nagambie is on the Goulburn River. To enter, entrants snap a picture of their best fish using a phone app. GoFish organisers have also put together a **Western Port and Port Phillip Bay event**, held over three days. Check for the latest GoFish competition news at **https://gofishtournament.com.au**

Mallacoota: This large Inlet is the first major fishing area encountered heading south from NSW. The inlet is at the mouth of the Genoa River and Wallagaraugh Rivers, 23km off the Princes Hwy from Genoa. Mallacoota consists of top and bottom lakes, connected by a channel called **The Narrows**. The sea entrance is open only intermittently and is dangerous. Flathead, yellowfin and black bream, luderick, school and king george whiting, and tailor are the main catch, with estuary perch and bass in the upper reaches. Deeper areas have mulloway, small snapper and silver trevally. Deep areas worth exploring in a boat include Howe Bight, Baker Bight and The Narrows. Landbased fishos should try Captains Point and Mallacoota Wharf, Slipway Jetty and the Cow Paddock. The **Bottom Lake** is mostly fairly deep, with shallow areas at Goodwin Sands, Robertsons Bank, and around Goat and Horse Islands near the sea entrance. The main channel is marked by pylons. For bait, the flats have sandworms and nippers, with shrimp in weedy areas. The **Top Lake** is shallow and has big flathead and bream, with the chance of estuary perch, luderick and mulloway. Cape Horn has the deepest water, at about 12m. The **Genoa River** is shallow and has sandbanks with sandworms. The upstream area has winter bream, luderick, flathead and perch. The **Wallagaraugh River** is shallow but navigable for several kilometres. It produces bream. Landbased fishos should try the Gypsy Point Wharf. Surf fishos should try Entrance Beach, which drops into deep water, and Tip Beach (golf club turn-off).

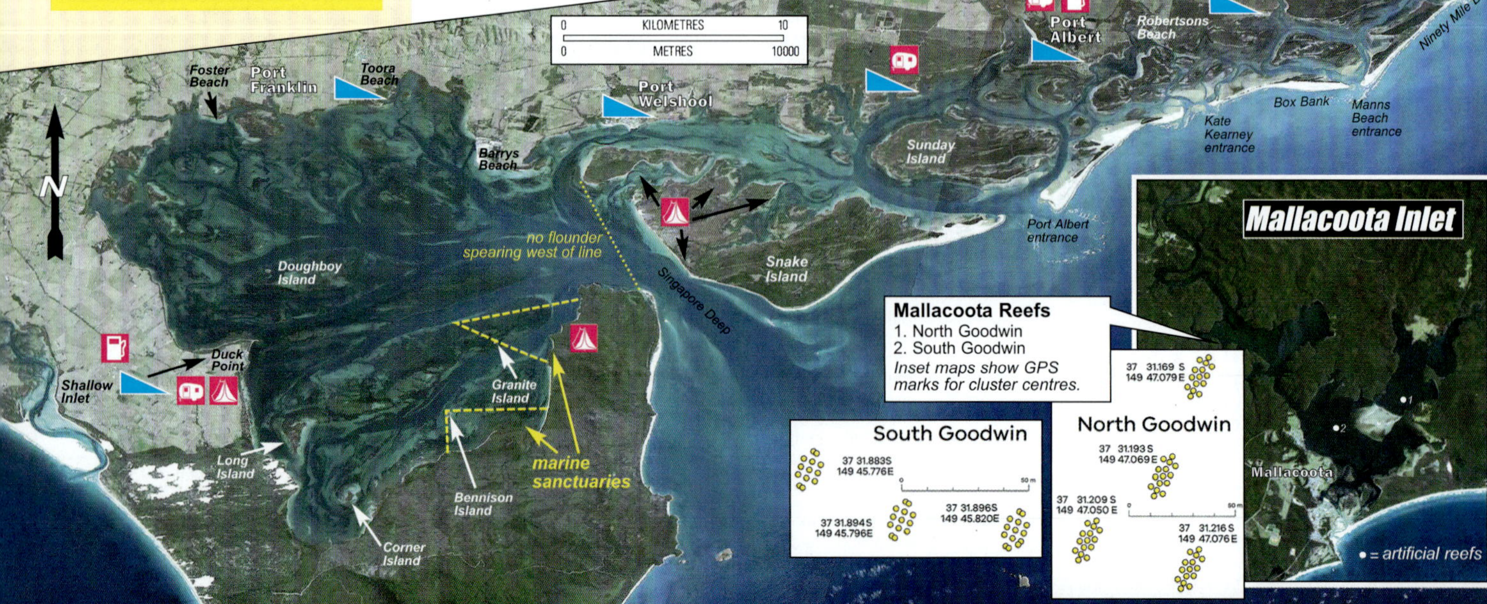

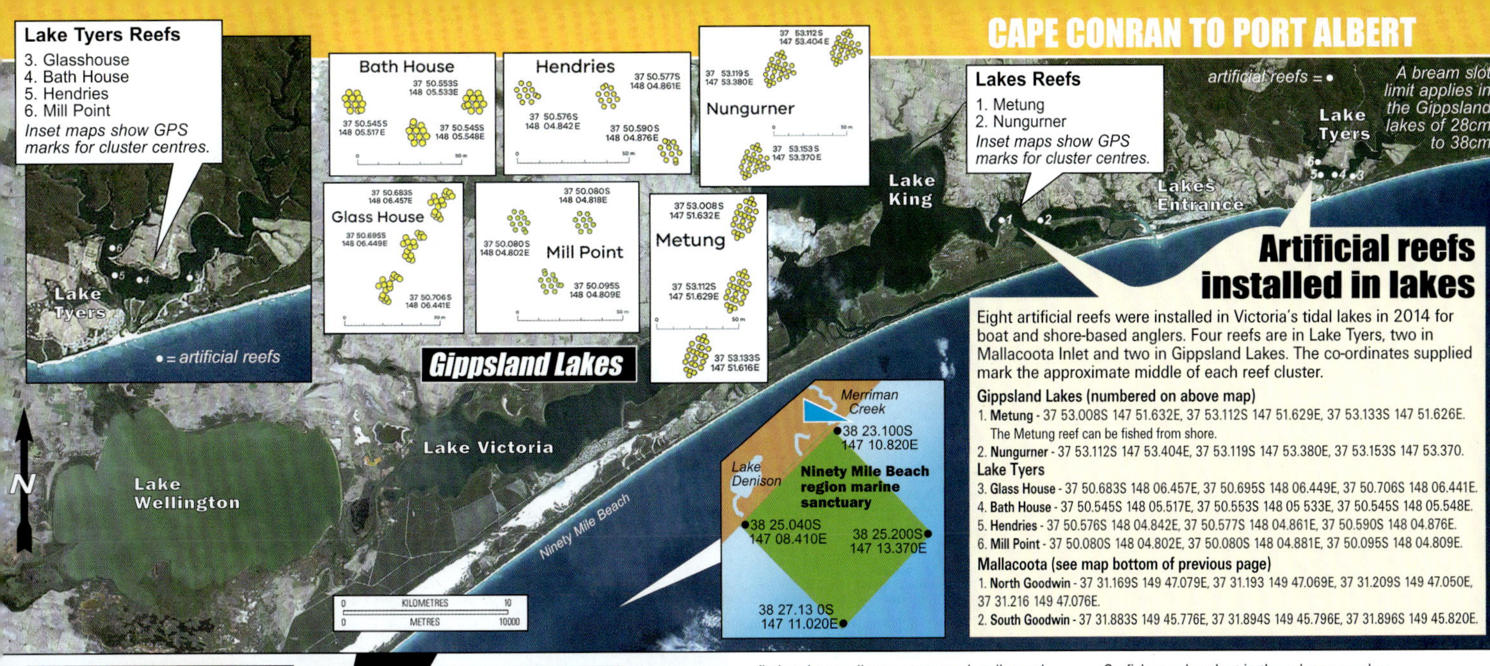

Artificial reefs installed in lakes

Eight artificial reefs were installed in Victoria's tidal lakes in 2014 for boat and shore-based anglers. Four reefs are in Lake Tyers, two in Mallacoota Inlet and two in Gippsland Lakes. The co-ordinates supplied mark the approximate middle of each reef cluster.

Gippsland Lakes (numbered on above map)

1. **Metung** - 37 53.008S 147 51.632E, 37 53.112S 147 51.629E, 37 53.133S 147 51.626E. The Metung reef can be fished from shore.
2. **Nungurner** - 37 53.112S 147 53.404E, 37 53.119S 147 53.380E, 37 53.153S 147 53.370.

Lake Tyers

3. **Glass House** - 37 50.683S 148 06.457E, 37 50.695S 148 06.449E, 37 50.706S 148 06.441E.
4. **Bath House** - 37 50.545S 148 05.517E, 37 50.553S 148 05 533E, 37 50.545S 148 05.548E.
5. **Hendries** - 37 50.576S 148 04.842E, 37 50.577S 148 04.861E, 37 50.590S 148 04.876E.
6. **Mill Point** - 37 50.080S 148 04.802E, 37 50.080S 148 04.881E, 37 50.095S 148 04.809E.

Mallacoota (see map bottom of previous page)

1. **North Goodwin** - 37 31.169S 149 47.079E, 37 31.193 149 47.069E, 37 31.209S 149 47.050E, 37 31.216 149 47.076E.
2. **South Goodwin** - 37 31.883S 149 45.776E, 37 31.894S 149 45.796E, 37 31.896S 149 45.820E.

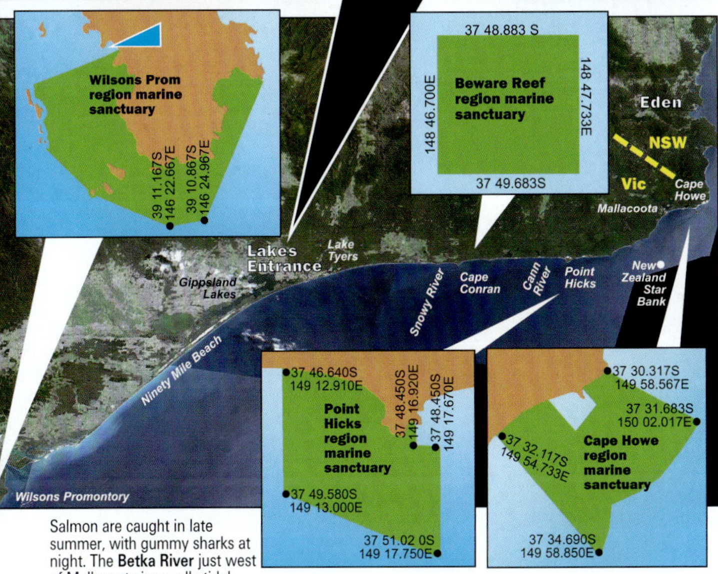

Salmon are caught in late summer, with gummy sharks at night. The **Betka River** just west of Mallacoota is usually tidal, with bream, luderick, salmon, mullet and trevally. There are estuary perch and eels upstream. Much of the downstream area is accessible for landbased fishing. There is a boat ramp 500m from the bridge. Sandworms, nippers and shrimp can be collected on the flats. Mulloway are best in summer at night, using livebait. Launch sites in this area include Mallacoota, Bastion Point, Karbethong and Gypsy Point.

Red River to Wingan Inlet: From Betka River, the Old Coast Road leads to a 4WD track past little Shipwreck Creek, to the larger Benedore River, which is often landlocked. It can be fished by cartopper or canoe for bream. Between Benedore River and Red River is Sandpatch Point, which has rock fishing on the east side. Further west, on a 4WD track, is Red River and Easby Creek. Access is on the East Wingan Rd off the Princes Hwy. The track forks off to Red River and Easby Creek. Both creeks can be fished by canoe or cartopper. **Red River** has limited bank access. When the sea access is open expect luderick, tailor, bream and whiting. **Easby Creek** produces big bream among the rock outcrops, some of which are fishable from shore. Surf fishing produces mullet, salmon and gummy sharks. **Wingan Inlet** is scenic, with a large estuary open to the sea. It has most estuary species, including perch. Wingan Rd access is on the west side of the estuary, where there is a camping area with jetty, toilets and barbecue. There is no launch site, so cartoppers or canoes only can be used. Landbased access is limited. Good surf fishing is a half-hour walk from the carpark, where big salmon, tailor, mulloway and sharks can be caught. Red Rocks on the east side of the inlet is a good spot. Prawns run in March/April. The 30km unsealed road to the inlet West Wingan Rd is marked on the Princes Hwy between Cann River and Genoa.

Thurra and Mueller Rivers: West of Wingan are the Thurra and Mueller Rivers, reached by taking the Tamboon Rd from Cann River on the Princes Hwy and turning left on the Point Hicks Rd. The Thurra is shallow 2km up from the mouth, then deepens for another 2km, where estuary perch and bass are caught. To reach Mueller River take the last track to the left before Thurra River bridge. The Mueller can be fished from shore for mullet, flathead and bream. Large bream, bass and perch can be caught upstream by cartopper. Camping is on the west side of both river estuaries. Surf fishing is reasonable. **Point Hicks Reserve rock fishing** is limited by the sanctuary zone, but the fishable east side has the most sheltered water. Expect salmon, snook, sweep and drummer.

Tamboon Inlet: The inlet is at the end of the Cann River, accessed at Furnells Landing launch site, 22km from Cann River township. Camping is at the north end of the inlet. Access downstream from the landing can be tricky, with rocky patches, but this is a good fishing area. Access upstream continues to waterfalls. The inlet entrance is rarely open. Upstream of the landing are estuary perch. Downstream, flathead and bream are caught, with salmon, tailor, trevally and luderick when the entrance opens. Prawns are about in late summer. The beach at the entrance has tailor, salmon, mulloway and sharks. An hour's walk takes you to **Clinton Rock**, which can fish well. The Tamboon side of the rock is deep and holds most rock species.

Sydenham Inlet: This is next to Bemm River township. The turn-off to the township is on the Princes Hwy between Cann River and Orbost. The inlet is shallow, with limited bankside access. The sea entrance opens occasionally. The inlet has quality bream and flathead, as well as estuary perch, tailor and luderick. The **Bemm River** has loads of snags, with estuary perch, bass and bream. The river is deeper than the inlet, with some bankside access. The river mouth into the inlet is shallow but the flats are a bait-pumping area. Bream and estuary perch are found in Swan and Mud lakes on the east side of the inlet. Surf beaches can be accessed by taking a boat to the entrance lagoon and walking. To the west there is a 4WD track leading to camping and beach fishing at Pearl Point, with salmon and sharks.

Cape Conran: The turn-off to Cape Conran is on the Princes Hwy at Cabbage Tree, or approach from Marlo to the west. The West Cape Rd leads to a boat ramp that gives access to flathead, kingfish and snapper grounds. The ramp is exposed to swell. There is camping at Banksia Bluff, with some rock fishing at Cape Conran and nearby East Cape. The track east leads to **Yeerung River**, which opens to sea on occasion. It has big bream and estuary perch.

Lake Corringle: This lake is at mouth of the Snowy and Brodribb Rivers. The Snowy River has good landbased fishing spots where you can fish near the car for bream and estuary perch. The **Brodribb River** has less bankside access, but good boat fishing. The shallow Lake Corringle has luderick. Marlo gives access to the lower estuary, with two boat ramps and a jetty. Most of the inlet is navigable and most species are caught, including mulloway. Prawns in late summer. Beach access is off Cape Conran Rd, with mulloway, salmon, tailor and gummy sharks.

Lake Tyers: This large estuary is 10km east of Lakes Entrance. The lake has two arms, one extending more than 20km north to Nowa Nowa, and the Toorloo Arm extending 6km to Cherry Tree. Snapper and silver trevally are caught, along with estuary fish. There are bass and estuary perch in the Nowa Nowa arm. Lake Tyers township has most facilities, including van parks, houseboats and boat hire. Boat ramps are at Nowa Nowa, Mill Point, Fishermens' Arm, at Lake Tyers opposite Mud Island, and on the west bank near the entrance. The sea entrance is often closed. Landbased fishos should try Long Point off Byrnes Track, and the surf beach adjacent to the entrance of Lake Bunga, as well as along the tracks off Lake Tyers House Road.

The Gippsland Lakes

This is a vast area of interconnected waterways served by a maintained sea entrance. A bream slot limit of 28cm-38cm applies in the lakes and tributaries. The lakes are fed by the Tambo, Mitchell and Nicholson Rivers. The sea opening is not safe for trailer boats, but the lakes produces enough fish to warrant staying inside. The main towns are Lakes Entrance, Kalimna, Metung and Paynesville. Boat ramps are at Eagle Point, Lakes Entrance (Marine Pde), Loch Sport (Charlies St and Seagull Dve), Hollands Landing, Marley Point, Nicholson River, Nungurner, Raymond Island, Seacombe, Metung, Shaving Point and Tambo River (Swan Reach and Johnsonville) and Wattle Point. Paynesville has boat ramps at King St, Newlands, the yacht club and the motel. **Lakes Entrance** township has most facilities, including boat hire, and North Arm has a good boat ramp. Garfish are abundant in these lower reaches, with bream and estuary perch upstream. Using lures helps avoid juvenile bream. **Landbased anglers** should try Eastern Beach off Eastern Beach Rd for salmon, tailor and mullet; Kalimna Jetty for bream, luderick, flathead, tailor and salmon; Kalimna Wall for luderick and bream; Nungurner Jetty and the north side of Reeve Channel; Fishermen's Wharf at Paynesville; the Crane Jetty at Shaving Point (mulloway); Raymond Island Jetty; Montague Point (bream and big flathead); Point Harrington spit (flathead and flounder); and Resides Jetty north of Point Scott. Artificial reefs have been installed in the lakes, see the maps for GPS marks. The **Tambo River** has good bream, with bankside fishing spots. Access is below the Princes Hwy Bridge via the Metung Rd and above the bridge via the Upper Tambo Rd. Downstream access is via McFarlanes Rd. Launch boats at the Johnsonville ramp. The river mouth into the lake is a great place for big bream, especially after rain. Marshalls Flat on the west bank is a popular landbased area, as is Rough Rd, off Metung Rd. The upper river fishes best in dry weather. Mulloway are caught. The **Nicholson River** has little landbased access, but the small area called The Pear Tree, on the west bank about 1.5km below the Princes Hwy bridge, is a good spot. A boat ramp is near the highway. Bream, luderick and flathead are throughout the river. The **Mitchell River** has a boat ramp at Eagle Point gives access to good spots such as The Cut, where the river flows into Jones Bay. Bream, estuary perch, flathead, mullet and garfish are caught. Landbased fishing is at East Riverbank Rd and at the jetty next to the Lucknow Bridge. The upper river's snags fish best in summer. **Lake King** fishes best after rain, which forces fish out of the rivers. **Eagle Point Bay** is good after rain when fish are flushed from Mitchell River. The same applies for Tambo Bay and Salt Creek near the Tambo River. Jones Bay is good for pumping bait, and fishes best after heavy rain. **Lake Wellington** is a large lake with an average depth of only 2.5m. It is fed by the Avon, Perry and Latrobe Rivers, and at the south-east end drains into Lake Victoria through McLennans Strait. There is no tidal influence. On the north shore, **Marley Landing**, which is 1km west of the Avon River entrance into the lake, gives access to the Avon River mouth, with flathead, whiting and bream. On the south bank, Bull Bay has a launch site on a track off Seacombe Rd. A boat ramp is at Seacombe at the top of the strait. The strait has bream and estuary perch, with luderick in autumn. The lake can become rough.

Lake Victoria is 25km long and 2.5km wide, with an average depth over 5m. It has little if any tidal influence. Water flows through McLennans Strait if wind or rain changes the lakes' levels. Bream, garfish, mullet, luderick, trevally, tailor, flounder and flathead are the main species. **Loch Sport** is the access point, reached from Sale or Rosedale on the Princes Hwy, then from Longford via Collier Hill from the South Gippsland Hwy. There is a jetty and good boat ramp. Holland's Landing on the north side of **McLennans Strait** has a van park. The 9km strait holds most species, including estuary perch. Jones and Blond Bays are good bream areas. Flathead and whiting are caught on the channel edges. Flounder spearing is popular in both lakes. **LaTrobe River** has carp, mullet and bream. The river is navigable from Lake Wellington to Sale, via the Thompson River, but is not popular. **Ninety Mile Beach** extends from Lakes Entrance to McLoughlins Beach in South Gippsland. In summer there are snapper, flathead and mulloway. Elephant fish and gummy sharks bite at night. Snapper are best in Oct/Nov, but bite all summer. Winter produces salmon. Good access, travelling south, with numerous coastal campsites, is at Paradise Beach, Golden Beach, Delray Beach, Seaspray - from Longford - and Woodside and Reeves Beaches further south. Fishing near **Merrimans Creek** mouth near Seaspray during flooding produces mulloway.

Corner Inlet

The South Gippsland region offers some of Victoria's best fishing, especially for larger snapper, whiting, flathead, kingfish and gummy sharks. The area that makes it great is the large Corner Inlet north of Wilsons Promontory, which extends east to **McLoughlins Beach** township. McLoughlins can be reached from Yarram on the South Gippsland Hwy. The jetty near the McLoughlins boat ramp is a good spot, and those who make the 3km walk to the sea entrance will find great surf fishing, with the chance of a snapper or large salmon. The inlet has large flathead, spotted whiting, big garfish, mullet and flounder. Nippers can be pumped on the flats and beach worms can be caught. Fishing is best in summer, with mainly trevally, salmon and tailor in winter. Robertsons Beach has good landbased fishing on the Tarra River channel at low tide, with big flathead and spotted whiting, and mulloway at night.
Port Albert is a great access point for boaters, and there are jetties that can be fished on the run-in tide for most species. The upper **Albert River** has estuary perch. Its mouth, called **Old Port**, produces occasional snapper, with flathead and whiting the usual catch. A reliable spot for big snapper is the Snake Channel inside Snake Island, fishing at night and at dawn. Big snapper are caught as far in as Old Port in Nov/Dec. On the western side of Snake Island is Singapore Deep, which drains much of the inlet. This channel reaches 34m depth and has strong currents. Fish the Singapore Deep on small tides for big snapper and gummy sharks. Don't ignore shallow areas through the inlet, as big flathead, whiting, squid and gar are common. **Port Welshpool** has an excellent boat ramp, which is near the best sea access from Corner Inlet, through Singapore Deep, though it is by no means a safe passage, with a runout tide and southerly swell quickly creating bad conditions. Big snapper live in the Deep, and a great many species are found just offshore, including kingfish around the islands, and thresher sharks. The Lewis Channel out of Port Welshpool is well marked, and can be fished by foot at low tide. Kingfish are a regular catch around the markers. At **Toora**, the boat ramp dries at low tide. Fishing around Toora Channel produces snapper and gummy sharks. Further to the west is **Yanakie**, which has a boat ramp useable from half tide up. The western inlet comprises sandflats and weedbeds drained by channels, with big flathead and whiting in summer. The channels run into Franklin Channel, which runs into Singapore Deep.

Wilsons Promontory:
Most of the area, including the coastal rocks and nearby islands, is a marine sanctuary, and can not be fished.

Shallow Inlet:
Immediately west of Wilsons Promontory is shallow inlet, accessible via Sandy Point township on Waratah Rd, and a small ramp on the north side on Lester Rd, where there is a van park. The southern bank has a sand boat launch. The channel has snapper, gummy sharks, trevally and salmon and flathead. Pipis and nippers are in the flats at low tide. Surf fishing is good at low tide at the mouth, with a 3km walk.

Waratah Bay:
Waratah Bay is off the South Gippsland Hwy, turning off at Meeniyan. Boat launching is off the beach. The bay has seagrass beds and sand patches which hold whiting and squid, with salmon and mullet from beaches. The rocks from Walkerville around to Cape Liptrap have kingfish in summer. Bear Gully just south of Bell Point has landbased fishing for whiting, salmon and flathead. There is a van park at Walkerville, with beach launching nearby. Rock fishing at Cape Liptrap is limited.

Tarwin River:
This is reached via Inverloch, along the Inverloch-Lower Tarwin Rd. There is a launch site on the south bank off Evergreen Rd. The river has mainly estuary perch, mullet and bream. There is good bank access. Bream, flathead, salmon and mullet can be taken in the lower reach, with a chance of mulloway.

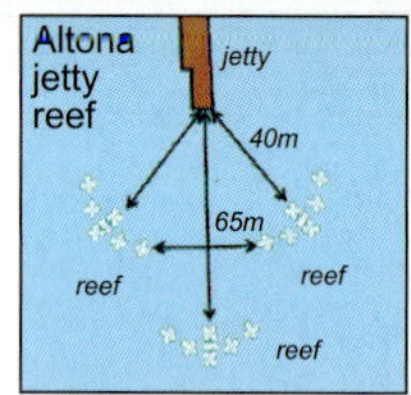

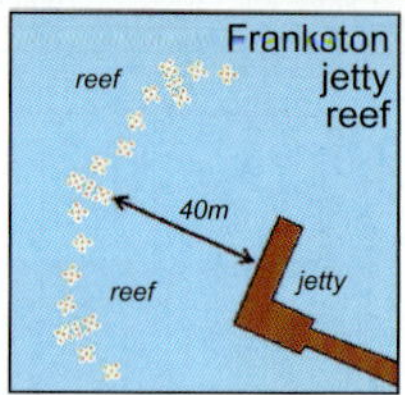

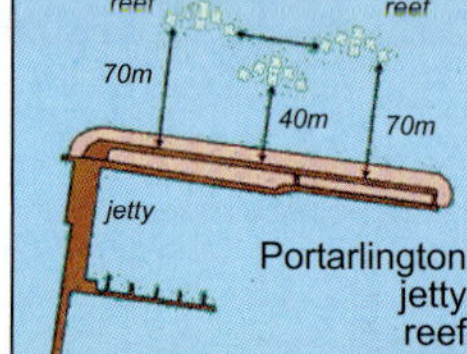
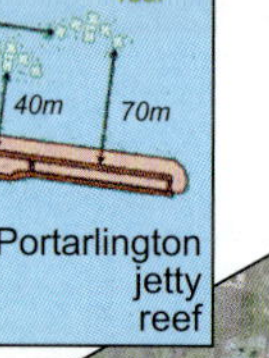

Andersons Inlet:
This shallow inlet is the mouth of the Tarwin River. It is drained primarily by a marked channel on the northern side. Mullet and estuary perch can be caught from jetties at Lower Tarwin off Evergreen Rd. The western end of the inlet near the sea entrance has bigger fish, with flathead, salmon, whiting and gummy shark. Mulloway are a chance near the inlet mouth. There are several sections of accessible beach near Venus Bay township, where pipis can be found at low tide. Surf fishing is good from June to September at high tide for salmon, mullet and tailor. There are three boat ramps; one near the sea entrance at Inverloch, one near Beacon Point on the south bank, and Mahers Landing on the north shore, which has a barbecue, toilet and fresh water. Near the sea entrance, Wyethers Beach has a camping area and fishing jetty. Fishing is best after heavy rain. The inlet creeks have estuary perch.

Cape Paterson:
There is a boat ramp reached from Surf Beach Pde near the caravan park. Offshore fishing is quite good. For landbased fishos, Undertow Bay has the best beach, but most fishos go to Kilcunda.

Kilcunda:
This beach produces excellent salmon and mullet fishing from April to August, and is easily accessible off the Powlett River road. There is a caravan park nearby. The river produces bream and estuary perch and has easy access upstream of the bridge. There are various rock ledges in this area that are fishable, none are particularly safe.

Western Port Bay:
This 45km long and 30km wide bay is a shallow maze of sandflats, seagrass and channels that run around French Island in the middle and Phillip Island at the entrance. Much of the north-eastern area is flats at low tide. The bay is best known for snapper, whiting and gummy sharks. There is an annual run of elephant fish in autumn between **Tortoise Head, Corinella and New Haven**. Squid are abundant at times. Fishing the bay requires working the tides, as on bigger tides the bay drains, leaving channels. Fishing can be good on the bigger tides, but a trip requires planning to ensure good fishing time at the chosen spot. The best boat ramps are at Hastings, Corinella and Stony Point. For big spotted whiting try **McHaffey's Reef** and **Cat Bay** in winter. Snapper are all year, with a big run in spring. Any rubble bottom may produce but note the marine sanctuary areas. For flathead, try the channel edges. Other species include kingfish, mulloway, salmon and snook. Mulloway are best in **Mosquito Channel, around Pelican Island, Elizabeth Island and near the Corinella hole**. Good landbased fishing can be had at **Stockyard Point, Lang Lang, Grantville Jetty, Tenby Point, Corinella Jetty and Settlement Point.** At the entrance to Western Port, Phillip Island is reached by a bridge and has its own boat ramps, with **landbased fishing at Cowes Jetty, San Remo Back Beach, Newhaven Jetty, Red Rock, Rhyll and Cat Bay.** The waters outside Western Port are renowned for sharks in summer, including makos, threshers, blues and whalers. There are tiger flathead grounds outside the bay, and striped tuna are abundant in summer.

Port Phillip Bay:
This is very different from its Western Port "sister" waterway. Port Phillip reaches 24m in depth, with half being less than 8m deep, however it is navigable almost throughout. There is 264km of shoreline. **The Rip** through the Heads is only 2km wide and flows hard, creating hazardous seas. It is a kingfish hotspot. The bay is best known for snapper, but also has spotted whiting, salmon, silver trevally, flathead, mullet, flounder, squid and garfish. Mulloway are caught by dedicated fishos, mostly in winter. There are good boat ramps, the best with regards to useability and parking being at Queenscliff, The Warmies, St Kilda Marine, Werribee River, Altona, Brighton, Mordialloc, Martha Cove, Indented Head and Rye Pier. Landbased fishing is best after heavy weather when snapper come in shallow while the water is discoloured, even during the day. At other times night is better. **Landbased snapper fishing can be had at Mornington Pier, Mount Martha Rocks, and St Leonards Pier.** For other species, travelling around the bay, Portsea Pier is a fine fishing spot, with good boat fishing grounds through to Sorrento. Blairgowrie has wading grounds for flathead and whiting, and the jetty has garfish and squid. The nearby shipping channel edges have snapper and flathead. Near Rye, Capel Sound is a large area at the end of Sorrento Channel and South Channel that has snapper and gummy sharks, with whiting, garfish and squid in the shallower areas. Rosebud is shallow, with flounder at night. The jetty has mainly garfish, squid and flathead. **Dromana to Safety Beach** is sheltered in a southerly and good for flounder, squid and whiting. **Mount Martha to Mornington** has deep water near shore and rocky foreshores where squid are prolific at times, with snapper in shallow after storms. Nunns Walk rock ledge below Strachans Rd has snapper in summer. **Mornington Pier** is one of the best bay jetties, with snapper biting in strong north-easters, with the chance of kingfish. **Frankston Pier** is good for snapper in Oct/Nov, and salmon in rough weather. The area from Seaford to Carrum has snapper after a south-westerly blow. **Patterson River** has bream and mullet, with mulloway in spring and summer. **Mordialloc jetty** has squid, whiting, flathead and garfish. **Rickets Point has a reef extending to Black Rock**, with snapper in spring and summer in the deeper water, along with most other species. **Half Moon Bay** has a jetty and a good reef for boat fishos. Big snapper are taken from the pier in Oct/Nov. **Sandringham Harbour** has a jetty and breakwall, with snapper in rough weather. Green Point has rock groynes that can fish well. Middle Brighton Pier produces snapper and loads of squid. From **Brighton to St Kilda** are grounds up to 15m deep with cunjevoi beds that hold snapper, with garfish and whiting. **Elwood Drain** is a great rough-bottom shallow area with snapper at night. **St Kilda rock wall** has snapper in spring and summer, and the pier produces some trevally, garfish and squid. Kerford Rd jetty is a better spot, while Lagoon Pier has occasional snapper and mulloway. The **Yarra River** has mulloway around bridge pylons at night. **Newport Power Station** has warm water outlets that attract fish. Breakwater Pier can be fished from a car. **Altona Bay** has shallow water with whiting, and snapper in Oct/Nov. **Altona Pier** produces mainly flathead. Point Cook jetty has good whiting fishing nearby for boaters. **Werribee River** can be

Shellfish Reefs

Shellfish reefs are being reconstructed in Port Phillip Bay to restore fish habitat and improve recreational fishing. Native flat oysters and mussels have been used to re-establish shellfish reefs at locations in 8-12m of water at Geelong, St Kilda (Hobsons Bay) and Chelsea.

Depths shown in metres
Map not for navigation

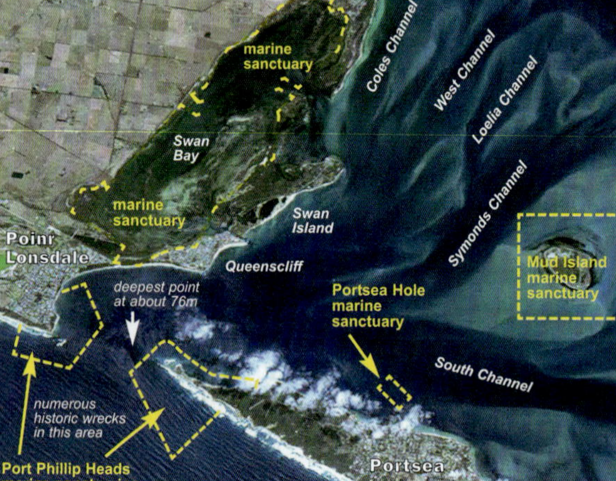

Port Phillip Artificial Reefs

Port Phillip Bay has three artificial reefs for boaters, installed in 2009. The reefs are made of concrete "pallet balls". They are 11m deep, about 2km out from Aspendale, Seaford and Frankston. Expect most local species, including snapper and squid.

Aspendale Far North Pallet Ball	38 02.152S	145 04.616E
Aspendale Far East Pallet Ball	38 02.168S	145 04.636E
Aspendale Far South Pallet Ball	38 02.184S	145 04.615E
Aspendale Far West Pallet Ball	38 02.167S	145 04.596E
Seaford Far North Pallet Ball	38 05.229S	145 05.954E
Seaford Far East Pallet Ball	38 05.246S	145 05.974E
Seaford Far South Pallet Ball	38 05.261S	145 05.953E
Seaford Far West Pallet Ball	38 05.245S	145 05.934E
Frankston Far North Pallet Ball	38 08.467S	145 05.480E
Frankston Far East Pallet Ball	38 08.483S	145 05.500E
Frankston Far South Pallet Ball	38 08.499S	145 05.479E
Frankston Far West Pallet Ball	38 08.482S	145 05.459E

Reefs built for jetty fishermen

Three artificial reefs have been built for Port Phillip's landbased anglers. They were installed in 2012 about 40m seaward of Frankston Jetty, and 40m to 70m seaward of Portarlington Jetty's rockwall section, and 40m to 65m off Altona Jetty. Each reef is made of concrete reef balls in three complexes. See the maps on the previous page. The reef modules are between 170kg and 340kg in weight and 50cm to 60cm in height, with openings. They are within casting distance of the jetties. A variety of fish are caught around the reefs, including snapper, trevally, whiting, flathead, leatherjackets and squid.

fished on the east side for big bream, as well as whiting and mullet. **Point Wilson** fishes well in the region of the long pier. Limeburners Bay is a sheltered spot for snapper in winter and spring, both landbased and by boat. **Rippleside Pier in Corio Bay** has garfish, flathead and whiting, as does **Griffins Gully Jetty.** The south bank of outer harbour near Moolap has spotted whiting in summer. On the Bellarine Peninsula, Grassy Point is a great whiting spot. **Clifton Springs Jetty** has been extended for fishing and **Portarlington** has a relatively new marina that is proving to be an excellent fishing spot for many species. At Indented Head, the **St Leonards Pier and rockwall** are good for fishing, while offshore the Governor Reefs have whiting and squid. **Swan Bay entrance** has big flathead in summer for boaters, with squid over the weedbeds. Most of Swan Bay is marine park. **Bell Reef** has a fishable low-tide platform under the lighthouse on Shortland Bluff. **Queenscliff Pier** produces mainly smaller fish. The Rip off Port Phillip Heads, accessed from Queenscliff ramp, has kingfish. Fish for kingfish in summer when the tide ebbs, usually about three hours after high or low tide. Jigging is popular. Whiting are caught near the **White Lady marker** off the northern tip of Swan Island but note the marine sanctuary boundary. The drop-off east of the marker has snapper. **Point Lonsdale Pier** can fish well at times, especially for big garfish, salmon and whiting, with snapper in spring. Artificial reefs are in the bay, see the maps.

West of Melbourne

Collendina Beach looks shallow and unappealing, yet produces big snapper and mulloway at low tide, fishing near the reef patches. **Ocean Grove Beach** is similar. Using waders and fishing a low tide works best.

Barwon River is shallow but famous for mulloway, most of which are caught in the lower reach below the golf course. The river channel is shallow at low tide and night fishing must be done quietly. Mulloway can be caught from the bridge near the mouth after heavy rain, especially in autumn and winter. Mullet, bream and small salmon are the usual catch. The spit and beach off Ocean Grove Rd on the east river mouth produces mulloway. The beach near Fishermen's Jetty near the mouth is good at low tide. The jetty at the bottom of Ozone Rd is a good spot on the early incoming tide. Boat fishermen should try the deep water at the end of Talbot Rd. The river has three boat ramps, the best being Ocean Grove on the east bank, but even this one is shallow. Upstream, shallow **Lake Connewarre** has bream, mullet and eels. The Barwon sea entrance is dangerous. West of **Barwon Heads**, Thirteenth Beach has salmon and gummy sharks. There are reef areas. At **Breamlea**, mullet, bream and estuary perch can be caught from **Thompson Creek** bank. Good surf fishing is off Vagg St. **Torquay** has an artificial reef of 25 concrete modules in clusters of five, installed in 2015. Each module is more than 4m high. The site is in 25m, 3km offshore. Expect flathead, snook, kingfish, snapper, barracoutta and more.

Anglesea to Cape Otway

This rugged coast has rock, surf and river fishing. Sea access for boaters is limited, with the safest point being Apollo Bay. Trout live in many of the streams. At **Anglesea** there is beach fishing near the van park, with rock fishing via a short walk to The Cove. A rising tide cuts access to the rock area. There is 4WD beach launching in good weather. **Anglesea River** has most estuary fish. Best fishing is between the bridge and river mouth between April and August. In summer, fish the upper river. There is vehicle access along both banks. Night fishing is best. Beach fishermen should try Hutt Gully reef at low tide. There are parking areas at the beach through to Urquharts Bluff. At **Airies Inlet**, Painkalac Creek has bream and estuary perch. Moggs Creek Beach is one of the best local beaches, with salmon, and Moggs Creek has bream. At **Lorne,** Jump Rock is a good rock fishing spot, just before Stony Creek, with salmon, whiting and snapper. There is a rock ledge that begins at the main road opposite Albert St. Lorne boat ramp is dangerous in a swell, which often comes in the afternoon. Lorne Pier is a great fishing spot. Travelling onward, **St George River** has river, rocks and beach fishing is available. Nearby **Back Point** has two rock platforms. The river has small salmon and mullet. **Cumberland River** is well worth a stop, with mullet, salmon and brown trout. Rocks near the river mouth produce small snapper at dusk and dawn. **Jamieson River** has rock fishing on the nearest rock platforms, but further on Artillery Rocks is better. **Wye River** is popular, with bream, mullet, salmon and brown trout. The rocky point under the radio installation produces snapper, flathead, salmon and whiting. **Grey River** has a sheltered reef near the river with snapper, flathead and whiting. **Apollo Bay** has a marina. There are good grounds south-east of Apollo Bay, within 2km of the boat ramp. Breaking waves over reefs must be considered, particularly at Henty Reef, and Bumbry Reef off the headland. Reefs also break about 2km off Cape Otway. Family fishos can try the beach at **Barham River** mouth, and the boat harbour. The outer wall is a good spot. Keen surf fishermen should try Marengo, which has big whiting. Local creeks have brown trout, particularly the **Barham**, which also has bream and estuary perch.

Cape Otway to the SA Border

This coastal strip has few safe access points for boaters, and fairly limited coastal access for landbased fishing. What is available is well worthwhile. **Aire River** has quality bream and some brown trout. It opens to sea intermittently. Small boats can be launched, or fish the east bank on foot after crossing the bridge. The Ford River tributary has trout. Bream fishing is at its best in the lower river when it opens to the sea. The surf beach requires a 20-minute walk, with the beach on the east side being best. Night fishing in the surf can produce big fish. **Johnanna Beach** is a steep beach with reefs and rips that produce big fish, mostly salmon and gummy sharks. Fish high tide for best results. Camping is permitted. Night fishing is best. **Gellibrand River** has bream, estuary perch and brown trout. There is easy foot access to the eastern bank. The steep beach at the mouth has snapper and mulloway. **Gibsons Steps**, 4.5km past Princetown, is signposted and has great surf fishing, but requires fitness to access. **Port Campbell** has a beach launch. The Fisherman's Jetty is a good spot for most species. Nearby rock fishing spots include The Arch, London Bridge and Newfield Bay. **Curdies Inlet** at Peterborough has bream and estuary perch. There are two boat ramps. When the river opens to the sea the fishing improves. **Warrnambool** hasa boat ramp inside a breakwater. Logans Beach has most surf species, especially at night. Offshore fishing is best in summer in the 30-60m range, and bluefin tuna have made a comeback in recent years. The **Hopkins River** has 8km of tidal water. It is known for big bream and school mulloway. It is stocked with trout and produces sea runners in season. The river has four boat ramps. Sandworms and nippers can be pumped at the mouth. Fish the lower river after rain and the upper river during dry spells. There is good landbased fishing outside the river mouth for surf species, including snapper and mulloway. The **Merri River** has bream, estuary perch, mullet and small mulloway, but is best known for trout. Sea run trout are caught in winter and spring. Boats can be launched at Drummond St and at the end of Russell St, but there is plenty of bank access, including a bike track. Fishing is not allowed downstream of the footbridge. **Port Fairy** has a protected boat ramp at the Moyne River mouth that provides good sea access, and there is no need to go far to find fish. However, Lady Julia Perry Island, 25km to the west is a popular run, producing variety, including queen snapper, a type of morwong. White sharks and large bluefin tuna inhabit these waters. Landbased fishos can try the **Moyne River** breakwater for most species. The river has quality bream, and silver trevally in winter. The Moyne is stocked with brown trout and produces sea runners. **Portland** has great fishing within Portland Bay and the harbour, and the boat ramp is a safe access point into the Southern Ocean. Fish the boat harbour for whiting, garfish and mullet. Minerva and Julia Reefs are about 3km offshore and produce snapper, kingfish and more. Mako and thresher sharks are caught just 5km or so offshore. Between the boat harbour and Snapper Point are grounds for snapper, flathead, whiting and mulloway. For landbased fishos, the rock wall along Dutton Way produces snapper after storms in spring, as well as salmon and whiting. The harbour rock walls have great fishing, with snapper and gummy sharks a good chance. The **Glenelg River** is a scenic waterway at Nelson, near the SA border. The river has big bream and school mulloway. The beach at the river mouth looks shallow but is a mulloway hotspot. Mulloway are usually in the estuary from near the river mouth to around the highway bridge. A boat is needed to fish the best places, with launch sites above and below the highway. Bream move far upstream in dry weather. There are estuary perch in the river, and mullet and juvenile salmon. Boat hire is available.

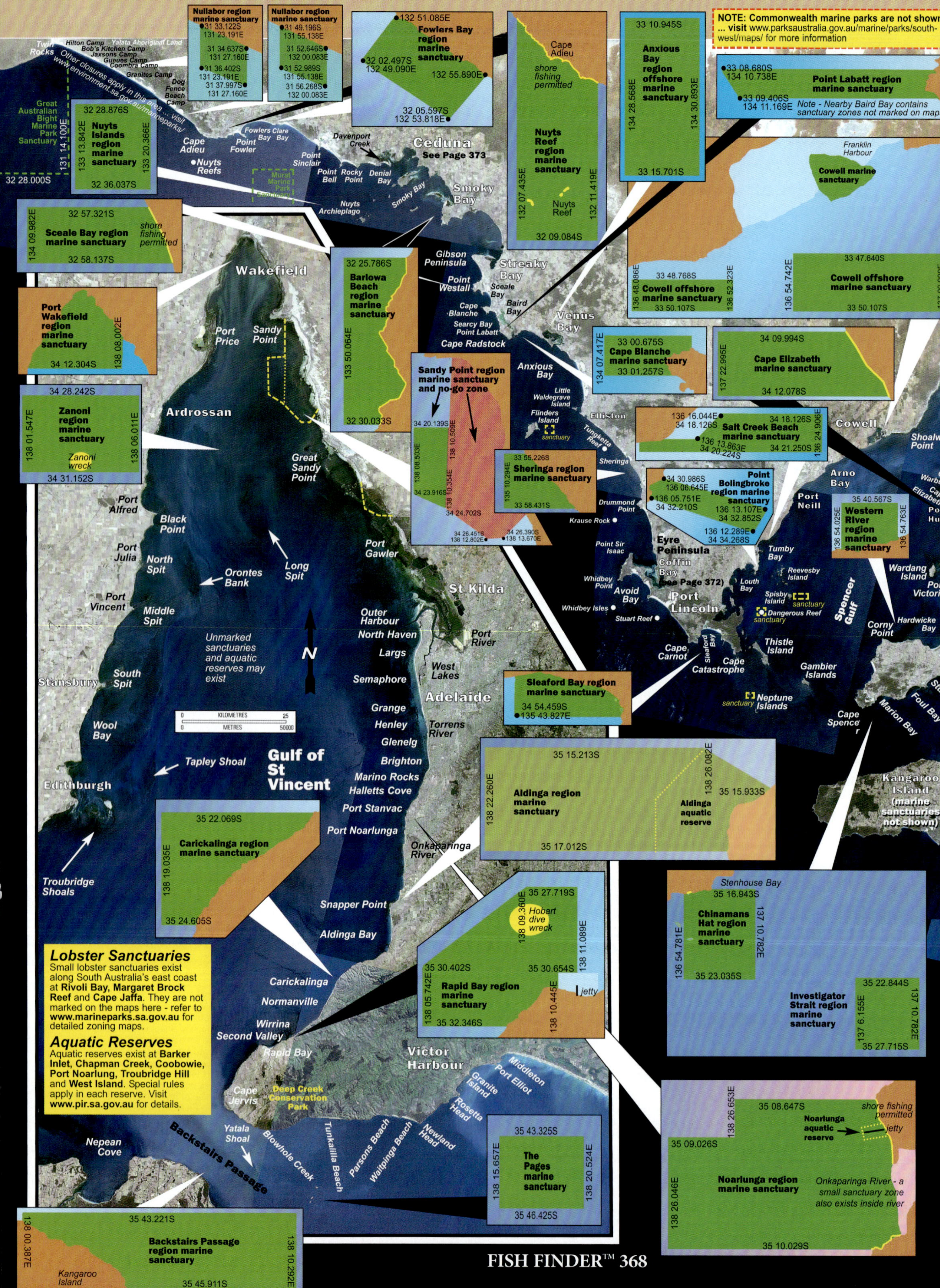

NOTE: Commonwealth marine parks are not shown ... visit www.parksaustralia.gov.au/marine/park/south-west/maps/ for more information
Nullabor region marine sanctuary
31 33.122S
131 23.191E
31 34.637S
131 27.160E
31 36.402S
131 23.191E
31 37.997S
131 27.160E
Nullabor region marine sanctuary
31 49.196S
131 55.138E
31 52.646S
132 00.083E
31 52.989S
131 55.138E
31 56.268S
132 00.083E
Fowlers Bay region marine sanctuary
132 51.085E
32 02.497S
132 49.090E
132 55.890E
32 05.597S
132 53.818E
Cape Adieu
shore fishing permitted
Nuyts Reef region marine sanctuary
132 07.435E
132 11.419E
Nuyts Reef
32 09.084S
Anxious Bay region offshore marine sanctuary
33 10.945S
134 28.568E
134 30.893E
33 15.701S
Point Labatt region marine sanctuary
33 08.680S
134 10.738E
33 09.406S
134 11.169E
Note - Nearby Baird Bay contains sanctuary zones not marked on maps
Franklin Harbour
Cowell marine sanctuary
Cowell offshore marine sanctuary
33 48.768S
136 48.086E
136 52.323E
33 50.107S
Cowell offshore marine sanctuary
33 47.640S
136 54.742E
137 00.999E
33 50.107S
Other closures apply in this area ... visit www.environment.sa.gov.au/marineparks/
Great Australian Bight Marine Park Sanctuary
32 28.000S
131 14.100E
Nuyts Islands region marine sanctuary
32 28.876S
133 13.842E
133 20.366E
32 36.037S
Cape Adieu
Nuyts Reefs
Point Fowler
Fowlers Bay
Clare Bay
Point Sinclair
Point Bell
Rocky Point
Denial Bay
Davenport Creek
Ceduna
See Page 373
Smoky Bay
Murat Marine Park Sanctuary
Nuyts Archipelago
Sceale Bay region marine sanctuary
32 57.321S
134 09.982E
shore fishing permitted
32 58.137S
Barlowa Beach region marine sanctuary
32 25.786S
133 50.064E
32 30.033S
Gibson Peninsula
Point Westall
Streaky Bay
Sceale Bay
Cape Blanche
Searcy Bay
Point Labatt
Baird Bay
Venus Bay
Cape Radstock
Anxious Bay
Wakefield
Port Wakefield region marine sanctuary
138 08.002E
34 12.304S
Port Price
Sandy Point
Sandy Point region marine sanctuary and no-go zone
34 20.139S
138 08.503E
138 10.509E
138 10.354E
34 23.916S
34 24.702S
34 26.451S
138 12.802E
34 26.390S
138 13.670E
Zanoni region marine sanctuary
34 28.242S
138 01.547E
138 06.011E
Zanoni wreck
34 31.152S
Ardrossan
Great Sandy Point
Cape Blanche region marine sanctuary
33 00.675S
134 07.417E
33 01.257S
Cape Elizabeth marine sanctuary
34 09.994S
137 22.995E
34 12.078S
Little Waldegrave Island
Flinders Island
sanctuary
Elliston
Tungketta Reef
Sheringa region marine sanctuary
33 55.226S
135 10.294E
33 58.431S
Sheringa
Salt Creek Beach marine sanctuary
136 16.044E
34 18.126S
34 18.126S
136 24.906E
136 13.863E
34 20.224S
34 21.250S
Cowell
Shoalwater Point
Point Bolingbroke region marine sanctuary
34 30.986S
136 06.645E
136 05.751E
34 32.210S
136 13.107E
34 32.852S
136 12.289E
34 34.268S
Arno Bay
Port Neill
Western River region marine sanctuary
35 40.567S
136 54.025E
136 54.763E
Port Alfred
Black Point
Port Julia
North Spit
Orontes Bank
Long Spit
Port Gawler
Port Vincent
Middle Spit
St Kilda
Outer Harbour
North Haven
Port River
Drummond Point
Krause Rock
Point Sir Isaac
Eyre Peninsula
Coffin Bay
(See Page 372)
Whidbey Point
Avoid Bay
Whidbey Isles
Stuart Reef
Port Lincoln
Louth Bay
Tumby Bay
Reevesby Island
Spilsby Island
sanctuary
Dangerous Reef
sanctuary
Spencer Gulf
Wardang Island
Port Victoria
Corny Point
Hardwicke Bay
Thistle Island
Gambier Islands
Cape Carnot
Sleaford Bay
Cape Catastrophe
Unmarked sanctuaries and aquatic reserves may exist
N
Largs
Semaphore
West Lakes
Stansbury
South Spit
Adelaide
Grange
Henley
Torrens River
Glenelg
Brighton
Marino Rocks
Halletts Cove
Port Stanvac
Port Noarlunga
Sleaford Bay region marine sanctuary
34 54.459S
135 43.827E
sanctuary
Neptune Islands
Cape Spencer
Marion Bay
Foul Bay
KILOMETRES
METRES
Wool Bay
Tapley Shoal
Gulf of St Vincent
Edithburgh
Aldinga region marine sanctuary
35 15.213S
138 22.260E
138 26.082E
35 15.933S
Aldinga aquatic reserve
35 17.012S
Kangaroo Island (marine sanctuaries not shown)
Carickalinga region marine sanctuary
35 22.069S
138 19.035E
35 24.605S
Troubridge Shoals
Onkaparinga River
Snapper Point
Aldinga Bay
Rapid Bay region marine sanctuary
35 27.719S
138 09.360E
Hobart dive wreck
138 11.089E
35 30.402S
35 30.654S
138 05.742E
jetty
138 10.445E
35 32.346S
Chinamans Hat region marine sanctuary
Stenhouse Bay
35 16.943S
136 54.781E
137 10.782E
35 23.035S
Investigator Strait region marine sanctuary
35 22.844S
137 6.155E
137 10.782E
35 27.715S
Carickalinga
Normanville
Wirrina
Second Valley
Rapid Bay
Cape Jervis
Deep Creek Conservation Park
Victor Harbour
Middleton
Port Elliot
Granite Island
Rosetta Head
Newland Head
Waitpinga Beach
Parsons Beach
Tunkalilla Beach
Blowhole Creek
Yatala Shoal
Backstairs Passage
Nepean Cove
The Pages marine sanctuary
35 43.325S
138 15.657E
138 20.524E
35 46.425S
Noarlunga region marine sanctuary
35 08.647S
138 26.653E
35 09.026S
Noarlunga aquatic reserve
shore fishing permitted
jetty
Onkaparinga River - a small sanctuary zone also exists inside river
138 26.046E
35 10.029S
Backstairs Passage region marine sanctuary
35 43.221S
138 00.387E
138 10.292E
Kangaroo Island
35 45.911S
Lobster Sanctuaries
Small lobster sanctuaries exist along South Australia's east coast at Rivoli Bay, Margaret Brock Reef and Cape Jaffa. They are not marked on the maps here - refer to www.marineparks.sa.gov.au for detailed zoning maps.
Aquatic Reserves
Aquatic reserves exist at Barker Inlet, Chapman Creek, Coobowie, Port Noarlunga, Troubridge Hill and West Island. Special rules apply in each reserve. Visit www.pir.sa.gov.au for details.

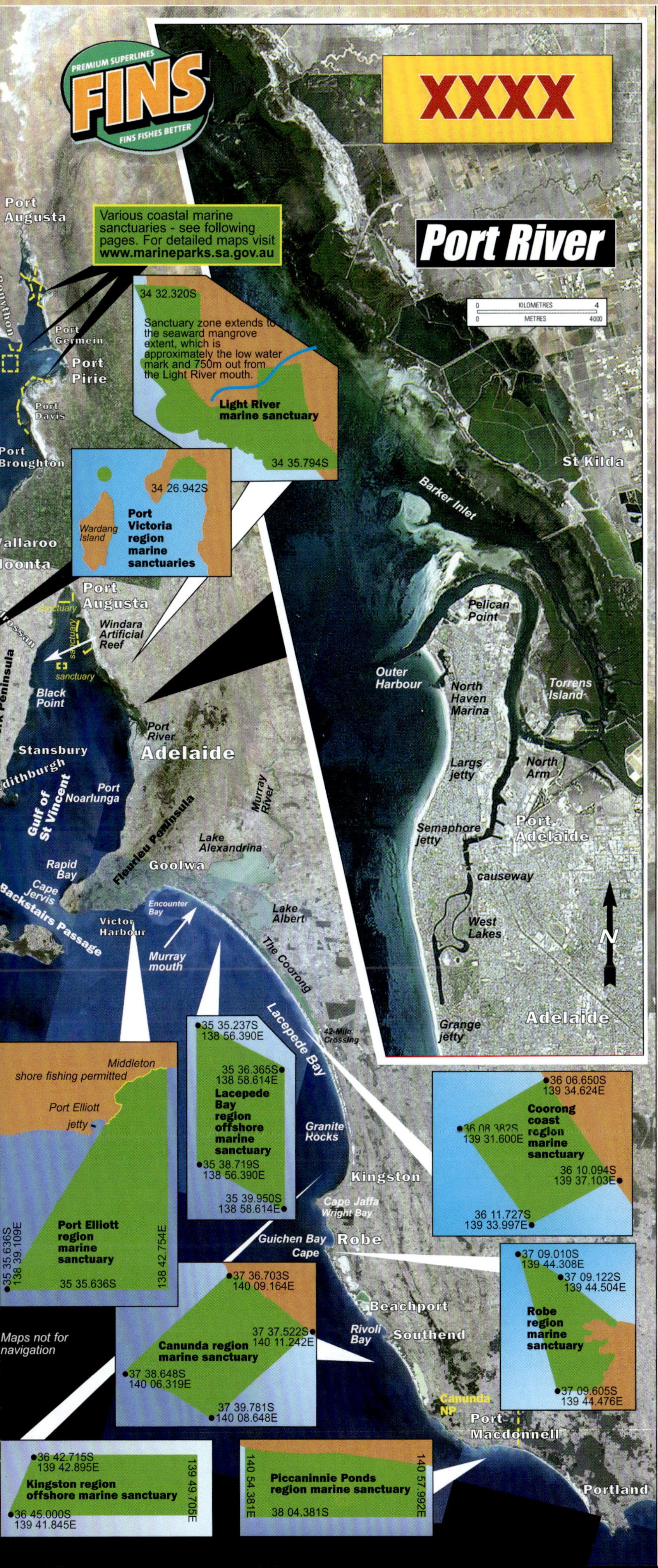

Port Macdonnell coast

Port River

Various coastal marine sanctuaries - see following pages. For detailed maps visit www.marineparks.sa.gov.au

Maps not for navigation

South Australia

Much of the state's fishing is from the many jetties and low-energy beaches within the two gulfs that form much of the SA coastline. The St Vincent and Spencer Gulfs' proliferation of jetties is matched elsewhere in Australia only by Victoria's Port Phillip Bay. Townships with a good fishing jetty invariably attract holidaymakers. The state's western coast is remote and wild, swept by the Southern Ocean. The Murray River empties into a surf beach 80km south-east of Adelaide. An annual bluefin tuna run and rock lobsters (crays) are big attractions. SA is blessed with many bread and butter fish, including spotted (KG) and yellowfin whiting, tommy ruff, snapper*, salmon, mullet, black bream, squid, sweep, blue swimmer and two-spot sand crabs and garfish. Adelaide itself has several metro jetties, and the Port River system. Squid are common in the gulfs, as is the world's largest cuttlefish species, which spawns near Whyalla. SA lacks marlin but has other large fish, including mulloway, kingfish, samson, mako, gummy and school sharks, and bluefin tuna. Other popular species are red mullet (goatfish), leatherjackets, flathead, flounder, snook and silver trevally. Wide reefs produce queen snapper (blue morwong), southern nannygai and harlequin fish. Remote reefs have blue groper. Bluethroat wrasse are common. Warm waters from WA's Leeuwin Current sometimes pass the state and bring tropical species, with mahi mahi visiting the gulfs on occasion. Boating facilities are generally excellent, with all-tide dual lane ramps the norm, usually with caravan parks nearby. Adelaide's Gulf of St Vincent is protected by Kangaroo Island, itself a popular location, but crossing Backstairs Passage requires care. Outside the gulfs, the Southern Ocean commands respect. The Murray River has golden perch (also called yellowbelly or callop), cod (protected), silver perch, redfin, tench and carp. Trout are in some dams and streams.

***Snapper restrictions in South Australia** include a ban on taking them from western and gulf waters (roughly north of Kangaroo Island) until January 31, 2023. South-East waters remained open with a bag limit of one fish. Statewide snapper fishing is likely to resume when stocks recover, therefore snapper spots continue to be listed in this book. Snapper may only be taken when and where permitted, check at **www.pirsa.sa.gov.au/fishing** before fishing.

Seasons - Winter is usually best for spotted (KG) whiting and coincides with good boating weather, but KGs show up all year. Winter is good for mulloway near Adelaide, while the west coast beaches fish well in summer. Bream bite best in winter, as do yellow-eye mullet, which move in close along beaches from autumn. The gulf blue crab run is in summer, with the biggest crabs taken in March. Salmon are winter fish on the surf beaches, but juvenile salmon (dubbed salmon trout in SA) bite all year. West coast beaches have big salmon all year. Squid are best in summer in clear water. Snapper* are best in spring and summer, and come in close during storms. Bluefin tuna appear off western SA before Christmas, reaching Port Lincoln about late February, and the eastern SA coast around March, depending on currents. The early season brings the biggest tuna, along with albacore.

Bait, lures and tackle - Cockles (pipis) and bungum (beach) worms are popular SA baits. These both live in the sand of surf beaches. Tubeworms are collected from muddy estuary flats, and are a prime bream bait. Bloodworms are available in season. Worms found in rotting seaweed on SA beaches are good for whiting. Maggots (gents) are used for garfish - breed them in rotting meat, then purge in bran. Mulloway are targeted with livebait. Local squid make good bait, particularly as fresh or live bait for mulloway and kingfish. Of the packet baits, prawns, bluebait, whitebait and pilchards work well on salmon, tommy ruffs, bream and snapper*. Pilchards presented on ganged hooks are ideal for big salmon. A shellfish called razorfish is a great whiting bait. It is found on tidal flats. Paternoster rigs are standard when beach and boat fishing in SA, using star sinkers and small long-shank hooks. For bream, running sinker or weightless rigs work. Gar and tommy ruffs are caught using float-fishing methods, and floats work when rock fishing for sweep. **Lures:** Small soft plastics and minnows work on bream. Chrome slices catch salmon, snook and silver trevally. Squid jigs are a must, including baited wire jigs set under a float.

Weather and tides - Autumn and winter have stable weather between gales, with more wind in spring and summer. Strong sea breezes blow in the warm months, and temperatures can soar to above 40C. April, May and June are the best boating months, although major storm fronts do come through. Keep an eye on forecasts. In the Southern Ocean a huge swell occurs, and boaters must beware breaking waves over reefs. Most of the state has a tidal range to about 2m, increasing to almost 4m in the upper reaches of the gulfs where the water mass is pushed into a smaller area. The gulfs have a tidal quirk called "dodge tides", a period of little movement and usually little fish activity. Port Lincoln has a localised tidal quirk of a one-tide day. Bigger tides tend to fish best. Avoid fishing dodge tides.

Special features - South Aussies "dab" garfish in the shallows at night. A spotlight and scoop net is used. Another pastime is raking blue crabs in the shallows. Crabs are also caught from jetties and boats with baited drop nets. Flounder are speared in shallows at night. SA's yellow-eye mullet are one of the few mullet that eat meat baits, and the autumn/winter run is prolific. Lobsters (crayfish) are caught mainly on the oceanic coast. Gummy and school sharks are popular food fish, and big rays, including the jumping cow-nosed ray and giant smooth rays, often steal baits.

Marine parks and reserves - The state has many marine sanctuaries. There are also small aquatic reserves, some not marked on the map here - each aquatic reserve has its own rules, and some allow fishing. Reserves are at Point Labatt (no entry), Cowleds Landing Whyalla (no fishing), Blanche Harbour (handspear only), Yatala Harbour (no fishing), Goose Island (no fishing), Coobowie (Area 1 line fishing, Area 2 no fishing), Troubridge Hill (rod and line only), St Kilda (crabbing only, and line fishing from breakwater), Barker Inlet, Port Noarlunga (rod and line only), Onkaparinga Estuary, Aldinga (no fishing), West Island (Area 1 - line only, Area 2 - no entry, Area 3 - no fishing), American River Inlet (no fishing), Seal Bay (Bales Beach - no fishing, Seal Bay - no entry), Bales Beach and Great Australian Bight (various zones).
*****Most Kangaroo Island sanctuaries are not in this book.**

Stocked waters - The first dam stocked was Warren Reservoir, in 2010. Since then, impoundment fishing has become more established, with murray cod, golden perch (yellowbelly) and silver perch stocked in Williamstown's Warren and South Para, Laura's Beetaloo, Spalding's Bundaleer Reservoir, Aroona Dam near Leigh Creek, Tod Reservoir near Port Lincoln, and Myponga Reservoir. Bundaleer has rainbow trout. Some have only shore-based fishing. More sites are planned. Redfin exist in many SA dams. Permits are required to fish. Visit **www.recfishsa.org.au/reservoir-fishing/**. Cod have been stocked in the Murray River, but only for seasonal catch and release fishing.

Port Macdonnell: There is surf, jetty, breakwall and rock fishing, as well as good offshore spots. Tommy ruffs are the main target on the jetty, with salmon and spotted whiting. The boat ramp is sheltered inside a 1km-long breakwall, which is a great fishing spot. Some boaters catch plenty inside the harbour. Pinchcut Reef lies 1km east of the jetty, and in calm weather the reef around Ruby Rock can be worth the 18km sea trip east, fishing outside of the sanctuary zone. Summer snapper* are caught in the surf near the rock outcrops. Some of SA's biggest tuna are caught offshore from March to July. The Continental Shelf lies just 30km south-south-west of the port, with tuna albacore, mako sharks and more. A marine sanctuary exists east of Port McDonnell.

- **Pinchcut Reef 38 03.390S 140 42.687E**

Cape Banks Beach: This beach fires in winter when it is rough and salmon move inside the reef. Beach-launching is possible in good conditions, and at nearby Red Rock Bay.

Nene Valley: Good beach fishing 16km west of Port MacDonnell for salmon, whiting and mullet. Beach launching in good weather. Nearby Livingstons Bay has quality garfish for boaters. Snapper* are caught on local reefs, with salmon visiting in winter. Snook in summer. Shallow beach launch at either end of bay.

Rivoli Bay: A great place for trailerboat fishing. Southend is at the southern end of the bay, with Beachport to the north. There is surf, rock, jetty and boat fishing at Southend. The boat ramp is exposed. The jetty is worthwhile for a range of species, including squid. Beachport has a good jetty covering a large expanse of shallow water, with most species, including occasional mulloway and trevally. Beachport's boat ramp is poor at low tide.

Ringwood Reef is almost 2km long and lies just 6km off Beachport, while West Rocks and Lipson Rock are 4km out. All produce snapper*, trevally, squid, sweep and even mulloway. Nearby Canunda National Park has beaches with mulloway (summer), salmon and mullet (winter) and gummy sharks.

- **West Rock 37 31.118S 140 01.577E**
- **Ringwood East 37 32.054S 140 02.473E**
- **Ringwood West 37 32.172S 140 01.746E**
- **'Three Mile' 37 31.513S 139 58.443E**
- **Lipson Rock 37 30.767S 140 02.303E**
- **Sherbert Rock 37 31.232S 140 03.839E**
- **De Mole Reef 37 29.661S 140 02.048E**

South of Robe: There is 4WD beach access through Little Dip Conservation Park. The fishing can be very good with trevally, mullet and salmon in winter, and mulloway and snapper* in summer. Good fishing is at West Beach, Evans Cave Beach, Back Beach, Domashenz Beach, The Boundary and Nora Creina. The Boundary is accessible by 2WD and produces salmon in winter, with mulloway and sharks in summer. Nora Creina is a protected bay where beach launching is possible. Great care is required boating outside the bay. Some beaches have soft sand and it is best to drive with a second vehicle, or walk in from the dunes.

Robe: Robe is a large town with most facilities. For family fishos, Lake Butler boat haven has school mulloway in summer, along with small salmon, mullet and bream through the year. There is a large rock wall outside the boat haven which produces most species, including garfish, flathead, whiting, squid and large mulloway. There is a good fishing jetty. Cape Dombey next to Robe has rock fishing, with a chance of snapper*. Robe's lakes have black bream, with boat launching near the jetty on Lake Battye. Mulloway are an occasional catch. For boaters, Guichen Bay has reef running north to south between Cape Thomas and Cape Dombey, with Baudin Rocks at the north end of the bay offering relatively sheltered fishing. Beware the shallow reefs outside and at South Point that may break unexpectedly, including the Black Pigs. Long Beach inside Guichen Bay is mostly firm for driving and has good mulloway fishing, as well as other surf species, including occasional snapper*. North of Guichen Bay is Wright Bay. This can be reached from the main road between Kingston and Robe or via 4WD access from Kingston to Cape Jaffa. The middle and northern ends are best for surf fishing, with big mulloway. Boaters will find snapper* at the north end of the bay, and most other species.

Cape Jaffa: This township has a good marina with sheltered boat launching, and excellent fishing nearby, including crayfish grounds. A big boat is not needed in good conditions because the outlying reefs and Cape Jaffa reduce the swells, providing somewhat sheltered fishing between Cape Jaffa and Kingston. The weed bottom holds loads of whiting, garfish, flathead snook and squid. Cape Jaffa has an excellent fishing jetty. For boaters, the substantial Margaret Brock Reef lies 7km west of Cape Jaffa, extending about 8km north and south. There is broken ground inside the reef through to the cape, with most species, including crayfish. Some reef areas break, including North Rock and South Breaker (see GPS). Outside the inner reefs, big snapper*, school sharks and more are caught. Cape Jaffa's beaches fish well, with the more sheltered spots providing garfish and flounder at night for dab netters and spearers. Summer brings good sea conditions in this area.

Kingston: This town has good facilities and sheltered boat launching, along with an excellent fishing jetty. Maria Creek has black bream, juvenile samon and mullet. For boaters, the weedbeds have whiting, mullet, garfish, flathead and squid. Flounder spearing is popular on the sheltered beaches. The jetty produces scores of tommy ruff and squid, along with mullet and occasional mulloway. Boats can be launched from the beach by 4WD through to Granite Rocks 19km north of Kingston on Long Beach. Nation Rock lies about 3km off Long Beach 17km north of Kingston (see GPS), but it can break unexpectedly. Long Beach becomes deep north of Granite Rocks and fishermen looking for mulloway concentrate on this section. Drive along the beach track and look for likely gutters. Travel with two vehicles because of soft sand patches. Long Beach can have piled weed and is fully exposed to the Southern Ocean. Mulloway are the main target, but salmon, snapper*, gummy sharks, school sharks and flathead are caught. The beach north of Tee Tree Crossing is closed to vehicles from October 24 to December 24. Camping is in marked areas. Cockles are available. A sanctuary exists along the beach between lattitudes 36 10.094S and 36 10.094S.

- **Nation Rock 36 40.912S 139 49.542E**
- **Granite Rocks 36 39.536S 139 51.068E**

Goolwa: The Murray River enters the ocean 12km south of Goolwa, and the river mouth is a famous spot for big mulloway. Goolwa itself is next to the Goolwa Channel that runs between Hindmarsh Island and the mainland. The river mouth is reached by 4WD along the Sir Richard Peninsula. Goolwa itself has a flat beach with mostly smaller fish. At the river mouth, when there is floodwater flowing, the big mulloway bite. A strong current makes wading dangerous. Baits and lures catch the big mulloway. A seal colony became established in recent years, making fishing difficult. The inland lakes hold Murray River fish, but mostly carp, and are not usually of great interest. The Coorong, which runs behind the ocean beach, has mullet, juvenile salmon and small mulloway.

Port Elliot: This small town just east of Victor Harbour has some landbased fishing, and a small jetty. The jetty has produced big mulloway at night. A marine sanctuary extends offshore from the east end of Horseshoe Bay, including nearby Pullen Island, but shore-based fishing is allowed.

Victor Harbour: This seaside town is one of Adelaide's great weekend fishing destinations. Being outside the shelter of the Gulf of St Vincent, the rugged coastline between 'Victor' and Cape Jervis has some deeper beaches and rock platforms and can produce bigger fish. Victor Harbour has a good, sheltered boat ramp but the ocean outside quickly becomes dangerous in poor weather. Granite Island is Victor Harbour's jewel for landbased fishos, being reached on foot via a long causeway over shallow weedbeds. It is a long walk so take a trolley if you fish with a lot of gear. The island's Screwpile Jetty is a short but at times productive spot that produces anything from salmon to snapper*, seven-gill sharks, barracoutta, mulloway, silver trevally and sharks. The snapper* and mulloway bite at night and dawn. Near the Screwpile Jetty is an ocean rock wall that shields the jetty. This rock wall produces just about anything, but should not be fished in a swell. The island's causeway is good for gar and squid. Victor Harbour's two rivers hold black bream, with a few trout upstream. Trailerboaters will find squid, gar, tommy ruff, juvenile salmon on the shallow reef grounds in the area. There is an anchorage inside Granite Island on the southern side. Nearby, at Rosetta Head, the Bluff Jetty is small but popular, and especially good for squid. Boaters who want to fish inshore should concentrate on the grounds between Granite Island and Wright Island.

Waitpinga Beach: This and nearby Parsons Beach are proper surf beaches, unlike the sheltered beaches of the Gulf of St Vincent. They are the most easily accessible surf beaches near Adelaide. Expect salmon and yellow-eye mullet in autumn and winter. Mulloway and gummy sharks are caught in spring and summer, along with occasional snapper* and tailor.

Blowhole Creek: Blowhole Creek beach is at the western boundary of Deep Creek Conservation Park. This is one of seven small beaches along a mostly steep-cliffed, inaccessible section of coast. Three beaches are in the Deep Creek Conservation Park and accessible, with the remainder backed by farmland. Access to Blowhole Creek beach is via a steep 4WD track to a carpark on a headland, or visitors can park at Cobblers Hill and walk 2km. The beach is at the base of a steep valley and fishos visiting this area must be fit and should travel light. A creek runs across the beach. Fishable rocks extend seaward. The western side of the beach has a good platform, and requires the least walking. The beach itself is small, only 120m wide. From the rocks the usual catch is big spotted whiting, tommy ruff, salmon trout and squid. Fishing the more remote rocks will often find bigger leatherjackets, sweep etc.

Tunkalilla Beach: This 5km-long beach is accessible from a carpark on a bluff above the western end of the beach. It is a long walk, especially on the way back. It should be fished in light weather, preferably a northerly. It has good salmon, with a mulloway or snapper* a chance at night in spring and summer. Sharks in summer.

Cape Jervis: At the end of Fleurieu Peninsula, this small community is the gateway to Backstairs Passage, home of big snapper*, and an embarking point for the Kangaroo Island car ferry. The Passage is not easily fished, being subject to strong currents and standing waves. Big sinkers are required. Note that The Pages island group in the passage includes a marine sanctuary and no-go zones. There is a sheltered boat ramp at Cape Jervis. The local jetty has big tommy ruffs in winter. Fisheries Beach off the road into Cape Jervis produces mostly smaller fish like mullet, juvenile salmon and tommy ruffs.

Win $12,000 in a carp competition

The SA Carp Frenzy at Barmera in 2021 saw $12,000 in prizes on offer, including a $3000 cash prize. Not only did entrants clean up with prizes, they removed 2277 feral fish from Lake Bonney, Chambers Creek and Loch Luna. The biggest carp caught was 80cm. Back in 2017, after a flood, 16,660 carp were caught during this great event. For information on future events **www.facebook.com/SACarpFrenzy**

Rapid Bay: Once famous for its huge ore-loading jetty, the pier fell into disrepair and was closed. A new, smaller jetty was built for public use. The new jetty is only half as long as the old one, but produces good fishing for garfish, tommy ruffs and occasionally silver trevally. Don't discount the beach at Rapid Bay, which has juvenile salmon, red mullet and school mulloway.

Second Valley: There is a tiny jetty that fishes well for squid and some gar and small snook, but it gets crowded. The nearby rocks drop into reasonably deep water in snaggy country. Boats can be launched at Wirrina 2km to the north.

Wirrina: This small cove has a marina which provides safe sea access for trailerboaters, with plenty of good fishing ground nearby. There is a small no-fishing zone extending around the marina itself. The wreck of the AV *Ulonga* lies 18km out in 39m of water offshore and holds big snapper*, silver trevally and yellowtail kingfish.

Normanville: There is good beach fishing here at times for mostly smaller fish, including mullet, sand whiting and flathead. Nearby Carickalinga Rocks has a large marine sanctuary extending outward. The Normanville ramp is an exposed beach launch and requires 4WD.

Myponga: Fish the rocks at the southern end of the beach for snapper*, salmon and big spotted whiting. The creek has bream. The local reservoir has redfin, native fish and occasional trout.

Port Noarlunga: The jetty extends out to a reef. Salmon move inside the reef in winter and the fishing can be exciting. In winter yellow-eye mullet bite in the shallows. There is a marine sanctuary at the end of the jetty, and another sanctuary in part of the nearby Onkaparinga River. The 'Onk' is a prime bream spot. The best known access is Perrys Bend. There is a closed season upstream of the main road from September 1 to November 30. The upper reaches contain trout and redfin, as does Mt Bold

Reservoir, but the river runs through private property and access is difficult, and the reservoir is off limits.

O'Sullivan Beach: There is a marine sanctuary here. While there is good fishing inshore for gar, whiting and red mullet, most fishos head out to the Stanvac barges, which have big snapper* in summer, usually best when there is a bit of chop. The former Port Stanvac industrial jetty area has become a boat fishing hotspot, with snapper*, kingfish, squid, leatherjackets and red mullet caught around the pylon debris. The nearby Port Stanvac breakwater is expected to be developed into a landbased fishing area.

Halletts Cove: There is rock fishing to be had for smaller fish, including leatherjackets, tommy ruff and squid, with the chance of other fish.

Adelaide Metro: The bread and butter fisho will be happy in Adelaide. Being within a protected gulf, the metro beaches are sedate compared with ocean beaches, and are popular for fishing and swimming, if you ignore the great white sharks. Adelaide's beaches tend to become shallower to the north, with the metro beaches ending at the Port River mouth, called Outer Harbour. Though Adelaide's metro beaches might not excite surf fishermen who chase big salmon and mulloway, there are quality yellowfin whiting to be had, as well as a mid-year mullet run, beach-going black bream, flathead, squid, juvenile

salmon (locally called salmon-trout), elephant fish and blue and sand crabs. Adelaide is arguably Australia's capital for jetty fishing. On the suburban jetties, squid, garfish and tommy ruff are caught, with bream around the pylons. Less well known is that big snapper* are taken from Adelaide's jetties, usually during or after rough weather in spring. This includes the somewhat maligned Brighton jetty, where the author saw several 10kg+ snapper* taken one stormy night. Drop-netting for crabs is popular, usually on the run-in tide at night. Semaphore has yellowfin whiting and mullet, with gar and tommies at night. Adelaide has excellent boating facilities, and a small tidal range, making boating easy. There are metro artificial and natural reefs that produce snapper*, but most boaters fish weed and sand patches and broken bottom for garfish, tommy ruff, snapper*, spotted whiting and snook. An SA favourite is a type of goatfish, locally called red mullet, which turns up on whiting grounds. Berley works well in Adelaide's shallow waters. Big mulloway are caught mostly at night within the Port River, sometimes in quite shallow water. The Port River's entrance, Outer Harbour, has a long rock wall which is a superb landbased fishing spot, though it lacks a footpath, which makes access perilous. On the north side of the Port River the shallows of St Kilda are home to a prolific blue crab run. Two-spot sand crabs also run in gulf waters. Adelaide fishos do miss out in a couple of areas. Adelaide fishos do not have metro access to gamefish, but there are plenty of sharks and rays, including the tasty gummy shark and jumping cownose ray. The city's Torrens River has carp, which are good sport. Adelaide's squid are big and abundant. For best results fish from a jetty at dawn or at night with a baited jig or artificial lure. In recent years kingfish have been turning up in numbers, even in the Port River, but snapper* stocks are down.

Windara Shellfish Reef

In 2017 a 20ha shellfish restoration reef was installed south of Ardrossan, 7km off the coast, in 10m of water, to bring back native shellfish, which have been lost from much of Yorke Peninsula's inshore seabed. The reef is a combination of concrete structures and limestone rock. It started as a 4ha site, and was expanded to 20ha. Only drift fishing is permitted, no anchoring. Corner co-ordinates for the more established 4ha section are ...

34 30.496S 137 53.953E
34 30.604S 137 53.949E
34 30.499S 137 54.083E
34 30.607S 137 54.079E

Adelaide seasons: Spotted whiting are caught all year but best in winter and spring. snapper* are best in spring and summer, with fish close inshore in rough weather. Snook and elephant fish are best in spring. Yellowfin whiting, snook and gar go well in summer. Juvenile salmon bite all year, and yellow-eye mullet run in very close along the beaches in autumn and winter. Prevailing summer winds are south-west to south-east, with strong onshore winds blowing in winter. April, May and June are the calmest months, between the gales. The maximum tidal variation is a little under 3m. Locally, there is a small tide every fortnight that lasts for about 36 hours, when the tidal flow drops to almost zero. These "dodge tides" are poor for fishing. Adelaide waters become turbid in rough weather. This is good for snapper* fishing, but squidding is best in clear water.

Adelaide Region GPS

Cabbage Patch approx 34 46.832S 138 23.843E
Buckets approx 34 46.388S 138 25.314E
Norma (Outer Harbour) approx 34 49.349S 138 25.111E
Outer Harbour Ballast approx 34 50.457S 138 19.346E
Grange Tyre Reef approx 34 54.895S 138 24.062E
Glenelg Dredge approx 34 58.719S 138 26.440E
Glenelg Barge approx 34 58.731S 138 26.464E
Glenelg Tyre Modules approx 34 58.911S 138 26.464E
Glenelg 'Fish City' approx 34 58.163S 138 28.832E
Glenelg Blocks (shallow) approx 34 58 406 S 138 30.494 E
Glenelg Rough Ground approx 34 57.773S 138 28.822E
Glenelg Mac's Ground approx 34 58.550S 138 27.084E
Milkies Reef approx 34 59.189S 138 27.241E
Somerton Reef (shallow) approx 34 59.184 S 138 29.266E
Claris Wreck approx 35 00.250S 138 21.089E
Brighton Reef approx 35 01.920S 138 28.220E
Seacliff Reef approx 35 02.264S 138 29:440E
Willunga Pinnacles approx 35 16.020S 138 26.003E
Stanvac Mooring Blocks approx 35 05.766S 138 26.404E
Stanvac Barges 1 approx 35 06.982E 138 24.544E
Stanvac Barge 2 approx 35 06.945S 138 34.637E
Stanvac Barge 3 approx 35 06.979S 138 24.597E
Stanvac Dump approx 35 06.210S 138 28.117E

West Lakes: This former marshland is now a canal estate. The lake is connected to the sea via pipes at the southern end, with a causeway into the Port River at the north end. West Lakes is full of black bream, including some stonkers. They can be hard to tempt, light line and live or fresh bait is essential. Mullet, mulloway, squid and garfish are in the system. Nearby beaches have yellowfin whiting in summer, which respond best to live worm baits.

Port River: The "river" is a saltwater inlet that wraps around Torrens Island. The river's North Arm wraps around Garden Island through to Barker Inlet. Known locally as "The Port", this whole area contains quality fish, including big winter mulloway. These must be targeted with livebaits, although lures will work. Only occasionally do they take deadbaits. Low tide at night is best for mulloway, although lure fishermen should try flicking under the three Port bridges' lights near high tide. Big snapper* were once taken in shallow water behind Torrens Island at night, but in recent years there have been few reports. The Port holds quality black bream. Lures get past the smaller bream, but small crab baits also work well. A boat really helps on "The Port" but there are some great landbased spots. Ask for the latest access details at the local tackle shop. Local tubeworms are an effective bait and can be dug at low tide through much of the Port, or buy them. Bloodworms are a seasonal favourite. Peeled prawns also work well.

Glenelg Shellfish Reef

In late 2020 a 5ha shellfish restoration reef was installed 1.3km w-n-w of Patawalonga Boat Haven, off the Adelaide suburb of Glenelg, in 5m of water. The reef was closed to fishing at publication to allow it to settle. Check the status before fishing. At publication another shellfish reef was being installed 18km to the south of the Glenelg site, off O'Sullivan's Beach. Corner co-ordinates for the Glenelg reef are ...

34 58.314S 138 29.787E
34 58.314S 138 29.955E
34 58.422S 138 29.787E
34 58.422S 138 29.955E

Outer Harbour: The entrance to the Port River is bordered by two giant rock walls, the southern one being accessible on foot. There is no footpath, so it's a long hop, skip and jump to the end. Anything is possible here - mulloway, snapper*, kingfish, salmon, zebra fish, drummer, sharks and rays. On the shallow side of the wall mainly flathead and leatherjackets are caught. The wharf at the base of the rock wall can not be fished, but there is a platform nearby. Nearby North Haven provides safe boat launching and also has rock walls.

North of Adelaide: The shallow coast north of Adelaide is a mecca for crabbers. Access points include Middle Beach, Thompson Beach, Port Parham and Webb Beach. The main town in the area is Two Wells. Crab raking is the usual method and bag limit catches are not uncommon. Fishermen will find yellowfin whiting in summer.

Port Wakefield: The shallow waters off Port Wakefield have spotted whiting, garfish, snook and squid. There is a good boat ramp in a creek that is requires some tide for easy entry. There are snapper* in summer, including big ones, but finding structure is hard. Blue crabs are abundant in summer, with the biggest crabs taken in March. There is a large marine sanctuary wide of Port Wakefield. Quality yellowfin whiting are caught on the rising tide. Spotted whiting caught in the upper Gulf are often small.

Price: This community on the upper western Gulf of St Vincent has two creeks with mostly juvenile fish. Launching by 2WD into Wills Creek is at high tide only if you don't have 4WD. The fishing is much as per Port Wakefield. Private (illegal) artificial reefs have been sunk and hold snapper* in summer.

Ardrossan: This town is best known among fishos for its great jetty, but it also has a large, ground-breaking artificial reef nearby. The Windara Shellfish Reef began as a 4ha reef made of 60 concrete reef balls, limestone, oyster shells and live native oysters. Phase two of construction in 2018 expanded the reef to 20ha. See the inset box for the GPS marks. Ardrossan otherwise has outstanding crabbing, squid, tommy ruff, gar and yellowfin whiting. There are good all-tide launching facilities, and a hopper barge artificial reef 15km offshore with summer snapper*.
● **Barge 34 31.815S 138 03.784E**

Black Point: This holiday community is on a wide shallow bay, and being on the west side of the gulf the winds are offshore in summer. The main catch in the shallow bay are yellowfin whiting, flathead, flounder, yellow-eye mullet, gar, squid and blue crabs. There are snapper* offshore, but finding ground, or someone's private artificial reef, can be difficult. The Black Point launch site is exposed, and dries as the tide falls. Nearby Port Julia has a small jetty that dries at low tide, and a basic launch site. Squid are caught off the point.

Port Vincent: The town has a marina with sheltered all-tide boat launching. Unlike many gulf towns, there is no jetty. The attraction for boaters is Orontes Bank about 15km offshore, which produces spotted whiting, gar, snapper* and squid. The whiting are generally bigger than those in the upper gulf. There is a blue crab run in summer. North Spit north of Port Vincent is a great low-tide location for blue crabs. Garfish dabbing is best on a dark night (no moon).

Stansbury: The jetty has spotted whiting at the far end, and garfish, yellowfin whiting, tommy ruff, snook and squid. There is a

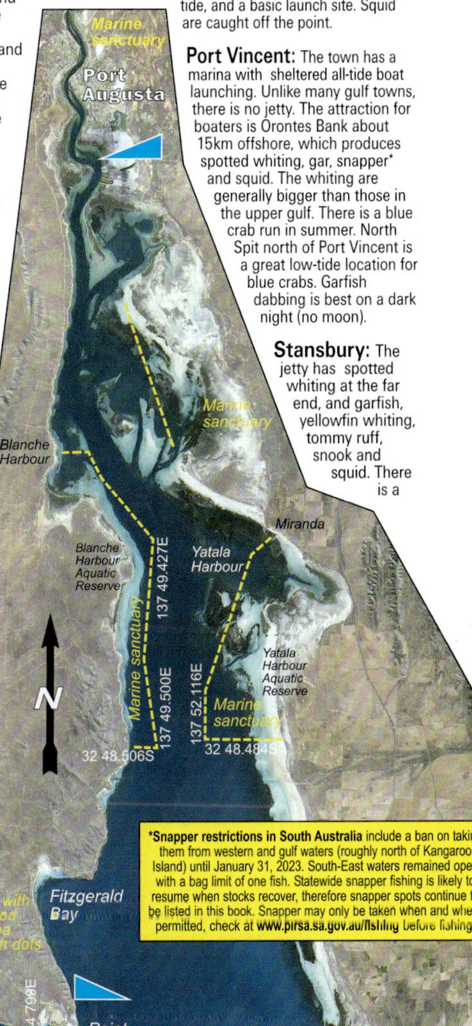

***Snapper restrictions in South Australia** include a ban on taking them from western and gulf waters (roughly north of Kangaroo Island) until January 31, 2023. South-East waters remained open with a bag limit of one fish. Statewide snapper fishing is likely to resume when stocks recover, therefore snapper spots continue to be listed in this book. Snapper may only be taken when and where permitted, check at **www.pirsa.sa.gov.au/fishing** before fishing.

summer run of blue crabs, usually raked around South Spit. The boat ramp is excellent. North of Stansbury are good squidding grounds.

Wool Bay: There is a short jetty which produces mostly squid, gar and tommy ruff. The launch site is poor and requires 4WD.

Port Giles: The long loading jetty here has produced big snapper* in years past. Otherwise, tommy ruff, slimy mackerel, chow, trevally, squid and gar are the main catch. The jetty is closed when grain is being loaded. The rocks to the north are known to produce snapper*, usually after a storm. South of Port Giles, Salt Creek Bay at Coobowie has yellowfin whiting, mullet and flounder. There is a tyre reef 3km off Giles Point.
- **Giles Tyre Reef 35 02.715S 137 47.483E**

Edithburgh: The small jetty here punches above its weight, with tommy ruffs, garfish, snook and squid. Night is best. The boat ramp is good. The spotted whiting are usually of a good size. There is snapper* and more at Troubridge Shoals, Tapley Shoal and Marion Reef for those with suitable boats. Currents can be strong and fishing is best done at the turn of the tide.

Marion Bay: This large bay is under the "foot" of Yorke Peninsula. It is one of two places where boats can be launched along the bottom end of the peninsula, the other being Pondalowie Bay. It is not an ideal launch site however, being exposed and only a single lane. Marion Bay jetty fishes well for squid, gar, tommy ruff and mullet. The beach is renowned for its autumn mullet run. Boaters who want to catch large spotted whiting should launch here and go 25km east to Foul Bay. The beaches from Marion Bay east to Troubridge Point produce big mulloway. Flathead are also caught. Charter operators visit distant hotspots. Offshore grounds here and further west have samson, morwong, harlequin fish, kingfish, trevally, snapper*, nannygai, sharks and more.

Stenhouse Bay: This is within Innes National Park. The jetty has produced kingfish, but is better known for autumn/winter mullet and salmon. Bush camping is available. Mulloway are caught in the bay. A sanctuary exists south of the bay, which limits boat fishing options.

Pondalowie Bay: This bay is also within Innes National Park. The beach launch provides access to exciting offshore grounds, but the weather must be right to contemplate fishing, and a swell can make launching impossible. The fishing, from Emmes Reef north-west to Wedge Island, can be superb. Wedge Island is inhabited, with holiday houses that can be hired. Many boaters fish the calmer waters between Wedge and North Island for whiting and snapper*. The beach on the north side has big flathead and salmon. Kingfish are common.

Browns Beach: Like many great salmon beaches, Browns has an outlying reef, and salmon move inside on a rising tide. Fishing is best in winter, but some salmon stay all year. This is a somewhat famous beach in SA. Walking is required, and a permit for Inness National Park. To the north, Dust Hole Beach has salmon in winter, big mulloway in summer, and mullet, flathead and sharks. It also requires walking, depending where gutters lie. North of the Dust Hole Beach is Daly Head and Gleesons Landing. Gleesons has 4WD access and a reasonably sheltered beach launch. Expect salmon, mullet, occasional mulloway.

Corny Point: This is at the north-west tip of Yorke Peninsula, with Berry Bay nearby and West beach to the immediate south. There is camping at Corny Point, from where you can walk off for a fish. West Beach is the last proper surf beach heading north along this coast, as beaches in the gulf are more sheltered. There is surf fishing at nearby Berry Bay for salmon and mullet. A caravan park is 4km east of the point, with a tractor for beach launching. Small boats can fish this reasonably sheltered area, expect garfish, whiting, tommy ruff, with snapper* offshore.

Point Turton: The marina here is suitable for large boats. The jetty produces the usual species, including yellowtail kingfish. This is a protected area in a southerly, but north-westerly winds make it rough. Whiting, snook, gar, flathead and flounder are caught in close. About 10km to the east, 4WD boat launching can be done at Hardwicke Bay. The same applies at Port Rickeby to the north, which also has a small jetty.

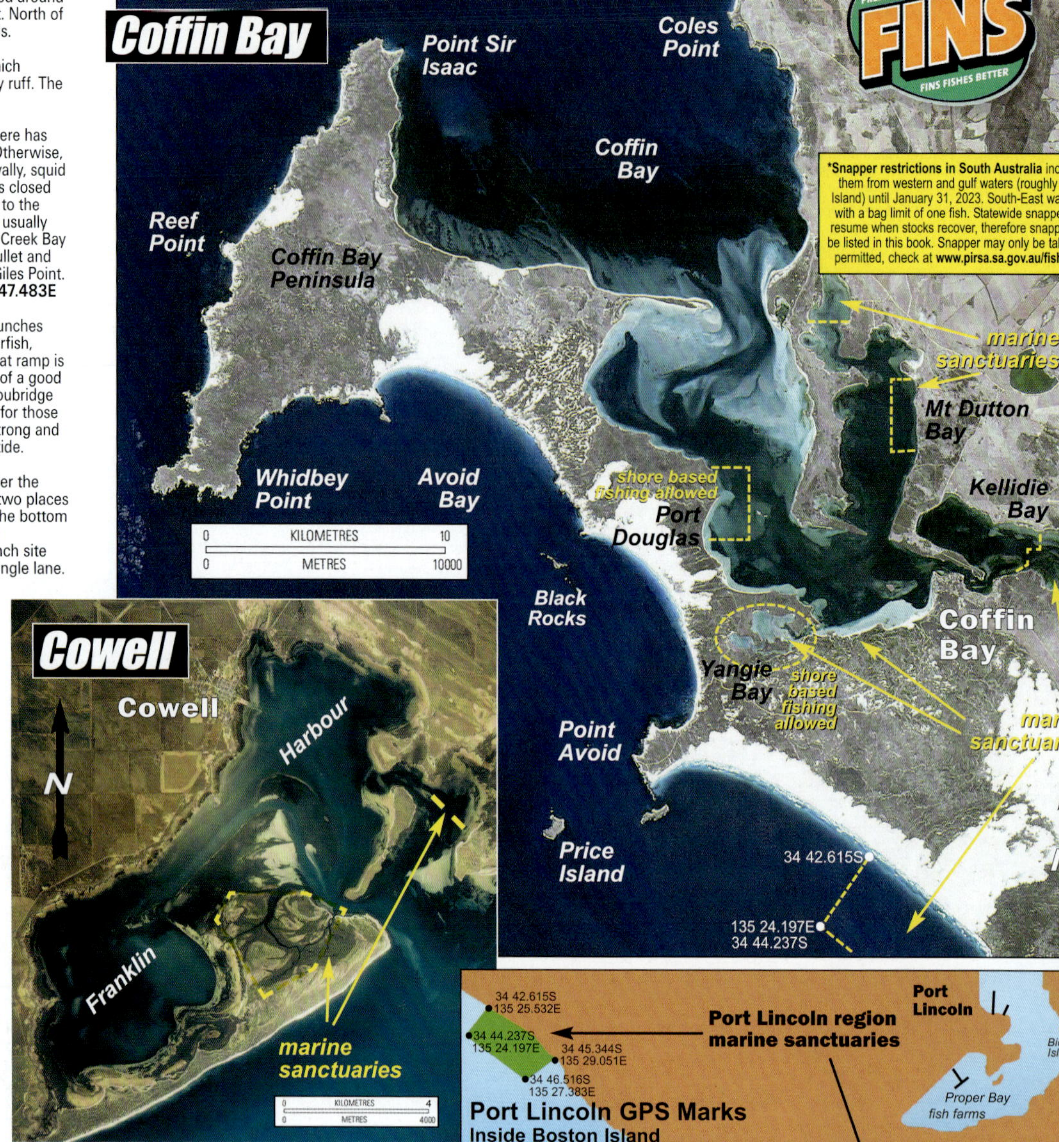

34 42.615S
135 25.532E
34 44.237S
135 24.197E
34 45.344S
135 29.051E
34 46.516S
135 27.383E

Port Lincoln region marine sanctuaries

Port Lincoln, Boston Island, Cape Donnington, Bickers Islands, Proper Bay fish farms, Spalding Cove, Port Lincoln NP, Sleaford Bay, Taylor Island

34 54.459S
135 43.827E

Port Lincoln GPS Marks

Inside Boston Island
Le Hunte Shoal 34 41.690S 135 52.571E
Bass Shoal 34 41.036S 135 52.905E
Sunken Brother 34 45.121S 135 56.732E

Outside Boston Island
Kangaroo Reef 34 40.171S 135 55.519E
Davidson Rock 34 40.765S 135 58.545E
Nowland Shoal 34 36.969S 135 59.118E
Penny Shoal 34 42.732S 136 06.226E
Jane Shoal 34 40.836S 136 07.223E

Port Victoria: This town has a sheltered all-tide ramp and long jetty. Wardang Island lies 10km offshore, with some protected water to fish. All the usual species are caught, with spotted whiting within and outside the bay. Flounder are speared in the bay. To the north, Balgowan has an exposed boat ramp.

Port Hughes: This town has excellent boating facilities inside a marina, although it is shallow at low tide. The long jetty fishes well for tommy ruff, gar and squid, with blue crabs and yellowfin whiting in summer. Whiting, snook and snapper* can be caught on the wide grounds. Tiparra Reef has a light and is good for gar, snook and squid, while snapper* fishos target the Steamer channel, which is a snapper* highway. There are whiting, squid and gar grounds in close. Gar dabbing is popular in northern Moonta Bay on a calm night.
- **Tiparra Reef 34 03.913S 137 23.494E**
- **Tiparra Wide 34 04.654S 137 18.261E**

Wallaroo: The town's long jetty fishes well, with snapper* caught at the end, usually after rough weather, as well as occasional kingfish. Otherwise it is best for gar, squid and blue crabs. The town has excellent boating facilities. Big snapper* have been reliable in years past on grounds about 10km out. There is an artificial reef of tyres 9km out, and *Jurassic Park*, which is a trophy snapper* spot (off limits at publication, check status before fishing). There are two small shoals within Wallaroo Bay.
- **Wallaroo Tyre Reef 33 51.411S 137 34.384E**
- **Moonta Shoal 33 53.883S 137 34.902E**
- **Riley Shoal 33 53.220S 137 34.951E**
- **Jurassic Park 33 54.700S 37 19.100E**

Port Broughton: The town has a long fishing jetty. Yellowfin whiting are caught using fine tackle and the freshest bait on an evening rising tide. Big snapper* are found on the *Illusion* and *Santa Anna* wrecks, but these were off limits at publication, check status before fishing. Plank Shoal also produces. The town's boating facilities are excellent but the entrance channel is shallow and winding. There is a car reef.
- **Car Reef 33 32.914S 137 51.483E**
- **Illusion 33 28.900S 137 32.600E**
- **Santa Anna 33 36.300S 137 36.300E**

Port Pirie: This smelter town has excellent boating facilities, with beach launching at nearby Port Germein. However, the discovery of heavy metal contamination in fish brought localised fishing closures. Check www.pirsa.sa.gov.au before fishing.

Port Augusta: The shallow waters of upper Spencer Gulf lead north to the town of Port Augusta. It is an unusual marine area, being shallow and sheltered from all winds except southerlies. The area around the now closed Port Augusta power station outlets still attracts kingfish. Fish or more than 50kg have been taken. Livebait and strong gear is needed. A rare local catch is the tropical dolphin fish (mahi mahi), brought in some years by warm currents. Big snapper* are caught in the channel, but most Adelaide snapper* fishos travel onward to Whyalla and Arno Bay. Otherwise, the waters here are best for yellowfin whiting, blue crabs, gar, bream and snook. Boating facilities are good. There is a tyre reef 20km south of Port Augusta.
- **Augusta Tyre Reef 32 39.914S 137 45.879E**

Whyalla: The new fishing jetty produces most species. This town for many years hosted the Australian Snapper* Fishing Championships. The big snapper* were found on private (illegal) reefs, at Fairway Bank, in the deep water between Fairway Bank and Eastern Shoal, and off Lowly Point, among other spots. There is landbased fishing at Lowly Point, with kingfish a chance. The town has excellent boating facilities. There is an annual run of giant cuttlefish. There are artificial reefs made of tyres 8km off Whyalla and 700m and 3.6km north of Point Lowly.
- **Whyalla Tyres 33 06.212S 137 36.381E**
- **Lowly Tyres Nth 32 58.010S 137 46.983E**
- **Lowly Tyres Sth 32 59.213S 137 47.581E**

Cowell: This town lies next to an almost fully enclosed bay called Franklin Harbour. The flats are home to quality yellowfin whiting. There are blue crabs in summer, along with gar, squid, flathead and flounder. The long jetty fishes well for gar, tommy ruff, squid and whiting. Boating facilities are good. A charted wreck lies 15km off Cowell, and Dillon Shoals lies 26km out.
- **Charted wreck 33 45.488S 137 02.231E**
- **Dillon Shoals 33 48.677S 137 07.725E**

Arno Bay: A marina provides safe access to nearby snapper* grounds. This is trophy snapper* country, the best known spot was the *Estelle Star* wreck 30km offshore (off limits at publication) and nearby ledges. Snapper* of more than 20kg

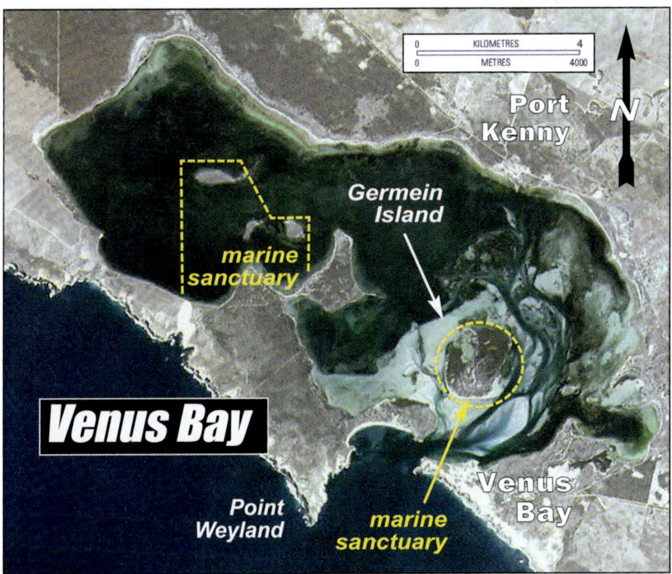

have been caught. Arno Bay beaches fish well and produce mulloway after rough weather.
● **Estelle Star 33 58.900S 136 50.900E**

Port Neill: There is a good boat ramp and jetty. Snapper* are on the inshore reefs in summer, with the wreck of the *Phoenix* being reliable. Spotted whiting are common, along with the usual gar, squid and snook. A hull has been installed as an artificial reef 3km off Port Neill.
● **Hull 34 06.616S 136 22.685E**

Tumby Bay: This town has a well-lit long jetty and good boating facilities inside a marina, giving safe access to the Sir Joseph Banks Group of islands. Most fish are caught around the islands, including very large spotted whiting, garfish and squid. Quality yellowfin whiting are caught within the bay, along with flathead and flounder. Kingfish are a chance on the jetty, as they are throughout much of the western Spencer Gulf, thanks to escapes from fish farms.

Louth Bay: This tiny town has only beach launching, but is popular because of its location. The jetty fishes well for gar and squid in the mornings. Garfish are dabbed in the sheltered waters of bay, and there are flathead and flounder. The Tod River has black bream in winter and small mulloway.

Port Lincoln: This is the largest town on Eyre Peninsula, with facilities for big boats. There are two fishing jetties. Port Lincoln Bay is shallow and has flounder, gar, flathead and yellowfin whiting. Offshore fishing produces just about all SA species, depending on how far you are willing to travel. A highlight is bluefin tuna, which often swim outside the aquaculture pens. More distant reefs hold samson fish, kingfish, tuna, blubig e groper, blue morwong and more. For those who want to fish the islands south of Port Lincoln there is a beach launch at Taylors Landing, giving access to the coastline of Taylor Island just 5km away. Further on lie the islands of Thorny Passage. Quality snapper* and spotted whiting are caught within the passage, with samson, nannygai and morwong on the deep reefs. This is not an ideal area for trailerboaters, with strong currents and the power of the Southern Ocean. Charter services are recommended to fish wide grounds. For surf and rock fishermen, Sleaford Bay south of Port Lincoln has big salmon. Rock platforms such as Millers Hole and Salmon Hole require a long gaff or drop gaff to land big fish. A tug hull was sunk in Boston Bay in 1990 as a reef.
● **Bronzewing Hull**
34 40.912S 135 52.482E

Coffin Bay: One of SA's best fishing locations. The bay is huge, with plenty of sheltered water for trailerboats, and excellent boating facilities. A highlight is a spring run of big yellowtail kingfish that move into shallow Kellidie Bay. These fish can be targeted in small boats and sight fishing is possible, one of the state's fishing highlights. Coffin Bay has most of the usual SA species, including flathead and flounder. The peninsula that forms Coffin Bay is Coffin Bay National Park. Avoid Bay forms most of the south side of this peninsula, and it has big salmon in winter. Beach launching is done at the south end of Avoid Bay. Point Isaac marks the north end of the bay and the deep water outside has samson, morwong and nannygai. Snapper* are caught from shore in the bay. North of Coffin Bay is rock and surf fishing at Coles Point, Greenly Beach, Convention Beach Drummond Point.

Elliston: Elliston is by a sheltered bay of only 2km width. Elliston is renowned for its 430m jetty, one of the state's great fishing platforms, recently upgraded with barbecues and a toilet. Fish dusk into the evening or early mornings for gar, tommy ruff and squid. Boat launching is on a relatively hard sand beach. A ramp located north of nearby Cape Finniss gives access to Waldegrave Islands and reefs beyond. Elliston is a good base to visit Locks Well and Sheringa beaches, two great salmon locations. There are almost 300 stairs carved into the cliff to access Locks Well beach, keep this in mind if you plan to keep fish. As well as salmon, the beaches produce big tommy ruffs and mullet.

Venus Bay: This 16km-wide bay is shallow, dissected in the middle by a marked channel from Port Kenny to the sea entrance at South Head. The bay fishes well for gar, flathead, squid, tommy ruff, juvenile salmon, flounder and yellowfin whiting. There are spotted whiting but these are usually small. The sea entrance is unsafe, especially so when wind and tide are opposed. There is a small jetty that fishes well, and a boat ramp. To the immediate south, Mt Carmel Beach produces salmon.

Baird Bay: This 19km-long bay is 30km west of Venus Bay. It is very shallow for most of its length, with a narrow sea entrance. It offers much the same species as Venus Bay. The bay is best known for a sea lion and dolphin free-swimming eco-tours. Boats are beach launched.

Sceale Bay: This open bay is 20km south of Streaky Bay. It is worth a visit for the scenery alone, with good rock, beach and boat fishing. Boaters will find morwong, nannygai, samson and blue groper, along with the usual spotted whiting and snapper*. Bluefin tuna pass well within range of trailer boats. There is a ramp at the bay's south end, with bush camping.

Streaky Bay: This is a large town with most facilities. There is a good launch site, and a jetty that produces most species, including snapper*. There is another jetty at nearby Haslam. The bay has big spotted whiting, snapper*, squid, blue crabs, snook, gar and more. Paddys Plains beach has mulloway, snapper*, salmon and mullet. Just 10km off Cape Bauer lies Olive Island, which is surrounded by reef.

Smoky Bay: This is a relatively protected bay with a long jetty that produces quality snook, gar, squid, whiting and tommy ruffs. There are razorfish beds, and garfish dabbing and flounder spearing are popular. For those who fish outside the protection of Eyre Island, there are numerous reefs. Franklin Island lies 30km out, covering an area 6km long. Smoky Bay has an all-tide boat ramp. Those with cartoppers or kayaks should try Acraman Creek, an inlet 15km south of Smoky Bay, with sheltered water and good fishing. There is an artificial reef made from tyres at the southern end of the bay, 8km north of the township.
● **Streaky Tyre Reef**
32 43.925S 134 14.813E

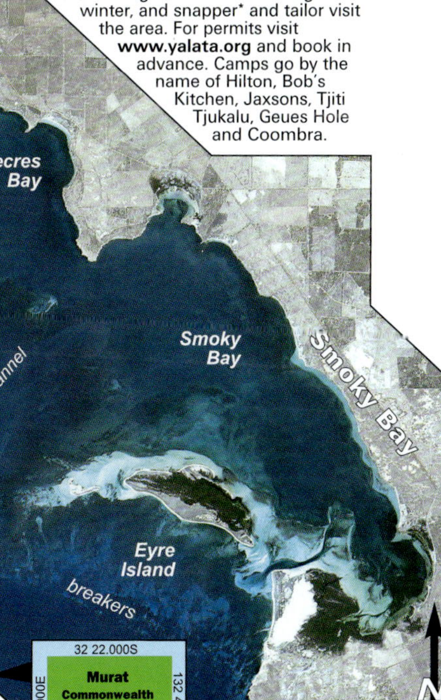

Ceduna: This is the last major SA town heading west, situated next to the relatively sheltered Denial Bay. There are three jetties within the bay and excellent launching facilities at Ceduna. The town jetty produces mainly squid, gar and tommy ruff in the mornings and evenings. The shipping jetty at Thevenard has a wider range of species, including occasional snapper*. The Denial Bay jetty, on the west side of the bay, produces crabs, snook, squid and tommy ruffs. For those with big boats, Nuyts Archipelago is a 54km run from Ceduna. This area provides incredible fishing, with anchorages at St Francis and Masillon Islands. Big samson, yellowtail kingfish, blue groper and bluefin tuna are caught around the islands, as well as the usual species. Denial Bay has an excellent run of summer blue crabs, as well as gar dabbing and flounder spearing. About 50km west of Ceduna, Point Bell offers good landbased rock fishing, with a chance of big yellowtail kingfish. Davenport Creek, which runs into Tourville Bay, is worth a look if you want sheltered fishing for a cartopper or canoe, with plenty of flounder, flathead, gar, squid and whiting in the shallow bay.

Point Sinclair: There is a huge jetty on the east side of the point, which produces big snook, garfish, tommy ruff and squid and occasional mulloway. Cactus Beach on the west side holds big salmon, but is best known as a surfing beach.

Fowlers Bay: This community has a jetty renowned for its squid, along with garfish, tommy ruff and snook. Launching is from the beach. There is reef close in off Point Fowler but conditions must be calm to fish it, with unexpected wave breaks are a possibility. Scott's Bay is on the west side of the Point Fowler peninsula and offers good surf fishing for big mulloway in summer, with salmon in winter. A 4WD is needed to reach the gutters.

Nullabor: Some of Australia's biggest mulloway come from the beaches of the Nullabor. This is not an area to be taken lightly, but the rewards are great. Visitors need 4WD vehicles and must be self-sufficient. Permits are available to stay at campsites behind the first dunes along the western end of the Nullabor coast, between the dingo fence and Twin Rocks, with public access available on the eastern end. Sanctuary areas apply to landbased fishos, as well as no-go zones for boaters - the no-go zone is much larger from May 1 to October 31 each year. Campers must be bring fresh water, refrigeration and shade. A compressor to reflate tyres after sand driving is essential. Alcohol is not permitted in the Aboriginal land area. Access to the best gutters requires either a good 4WD or quad bikes, as the distances are long. The months either side of Christmas are good for mulloway, fishing the big tides of the full and new moons. Use fresh or live bait and strong tackle. Day fishing at high tide works, with less chance of hooking sharks and rays than at night. Salmon are caught in winter, and snapper* and tailor visit the area. For permits visit **www.yalata.org** and book in advance. Camps go by the name of Hilton, Bob's Kitchen, Jaxsons, Tjiti Tjukalu, Geues Hole and Coombra.

Visit **www.water.bom.gov.au/waterstorage/awris/** for water storage levels of impoundments in all states

Hinze Dam

Lake Advancetown (Hinze Dam) is 10km west of Nerang on Queensland's Gold Coast. The dam was built in 1989 on the Nerang River. The lake has a surface area of 970ha and an average depth of 17m. It has been stocked with golden and silver perch, saratoga, mary river cod and bass. There is a natural population of eels and eel-tail catfish. The lake is best known for its quality bass, and these are the fish most commonly caught. Saratoga are also taken. Banded grunter have been illegally introduced and should be destroyed if caught. This dam is regarded as a good fly fishing destination because bass often come to the surface to feed on calm summer mornings and afternoons. Most rocky points are worth a cast. A good spot to start is The Hump just out from the eastern boat ramp. The bank south of the Pelican Point boat ramp is good for trolling and casting, and Ian's Island also fishes well. Live shrimp is a popular bait. Boaters may only use electric motors. Accommodation is 3km away at Advancetown, with no camping at the dam. The dam has three boat ramps and boat hire is available. Fishing licences are sold at the kiosk.

Picture courtesy LISA LINEHAN

Lake Mulwala when empty

Black Rocks
Trolling, best 24C to 28C
Kyffins Reserve
Mulwala Canal
Northern Bight
Late evening casting poppers
Good land-based fishing
Navigable channel is marked by beacons and does not necessarily follow old riverbed
Straight trolling run, fish edges
Late evening casting poppers
old riverbed
Good general fishing areas
marked channel
old riverbed
Murray River
Rams Head
Pierce Point
Yarrawonga
old riverbed
The Everglades
Lake Mulwala
Yarrawonga, NSW-Vic
Woodlands
Lure-casting around The Willows
Southern Bight
Spring Dve
ICONIC COD FISHERY
Ski Land
Majors Creek
Murray River
KILOMETRES 0 2
METRES 0 2000
Yellowbelly are in this area
Bundalong
Ovens River
N

Yellowbelly

TOM CLANCY PICTURE

Lake Mulwala

Mention Mulwala and fishermen think of murray cod. Lake Mulwala formed after Yarrawonga Weir was built on the Murray River in 1939 for irrigation. The lake has an area of 4400ha when full. It is now one of the few waterways where cod are the dominant native fish in catches. Most fish are fairly small, but a few of more than 1m taken each year. The lake's stocked yellowbelly can reach 5kg. Thousands of tree trunks are located just underwater and damaged propellers are common. The former river channel is lined with large dead red gums, while tributary channels usually have smaller trees, making it easy to find drop-offs. The river channel can exceed 10m deep and fish are found along the edges. The cleared section close to the weir has plenty of submerged timber on the lake floor and holds cod but the old river bed is hard to follow. The biggest cod tend to be taken in the deeper parts of the lake. Popular spots include the Yellow Trail, a tributary of the Murray that heads to Kyffins Reserve boat ramp from The Horseshoe. The Yellow Trail is marked with yellow paint and buoys at The Horseshoe and red and green paint on dead trees as you get deeper into it. The Yellow Trail is about 3m to 5m deep. Kyffins Reserve has plenty of submerged timber. Lures work best in warm weather. Yellowbelly will generally take the same lures as cod. Lure choice depends on fishing style - deep divers are needed to probe deep channels, but during balmy summer and autumn evenings poppers and ultra-shallow lures can work well and provoke exciting surface strikes. Always fish near cover such as willow trees or timber. Most shores on the lake are good for landbased fishing, especially those near the channel. The lake has carp, but numbers have fallen dramatically from historic levels. Trout appear from time to time. There are usually good numbers of shrimp and these can be caught in a bait trap. Other popular baits include bardi grubs, yabbies and worms. Mulwala is home to the Cod Classic annual event that attracts more that attracts up to 3500 anglers, with a $1m+ prize pool. Winning cod over the years have been around the metre mark. Visit **www.codclassic.com.au** for details. Below the Yarrawonga Weir, cod action can be good, and the rare trout cod, macquarie perch and silver perch are also caught. A Recreational Fishing Licence is required to fish Lake Mulwala.

Stocked impoundments guide

Check conditions first

Dams are periodically affected by drought or flood. Dams that reach low levels may suffer fish mortality. Floods may also adversely affect impoundment fish stocks. Ask about local conditions when planning a trip.

Not a complete list - other stocked waterways exist. Permits are required to fish most impoundments.

A selected list

Many dams and rivers are stocked with fish. North of Brisbane, the main species are barramundi, sleepy cod, sooty grunter and redclaw crayfish. Further south, bass, yellowbelly, cod, silver perch and saratoga prevail. From Inverell south, trout are stocked in some waters. Permits are usually required to fish stocked waters, available either near the site, or online.

Queensland

Sunwater storage levels
www.storagelevels.sunwater.com.au/win/reports/win_storages.htm

Awoonga Dam, Boyne River: 30km south of Gladstone, 3500ha, av. depth 8m, barramundi, yellowbelly, sooty grunter, redclaw, mullet, saratoga, sleepy cod, catfish, gar.
Barambah Lake, Barkers Creek: 12km from Murgon, 2200ha, av. depth 6m. Bass, mary river cod, yellowbelly, saratoga, silver perch, sleepy cod.
Belmore Lake, Belmore Creek: 4km west of Croydon, 118ha, av. depth 5m, barra, sooty grunter, sleepy cod.
Corella Dam, Corella Creek: 30km west of Cloncurry: 320ha, av. depth 5m, sooty grunter, sleepy cod, redclaw.
Callide Dam, Callide Creek: 12km east of Biloela, 1240ha, av. depth 11m, barra, yellowbelly, saratoga, silver perch, longtom.
Dalrymple Lake (Burdekin Falls Dam), Burdekin River: 80km south of Ravenswood: 22,400ha, av. depth 9m, barra, yellowbelly, sooty and leathery grunter, redclaw longtom.
East Leichardt Dam, East Leichardt River: 35km east of Mt Isa, 150ha, av. depth 8m, sooty grunter, archer fish, redclaw.
Eungella Dam, Broken River: 30km from Eungella, west of Mackay, 890ha, av. depth 15m, barra, saratoga, sooty grunter, bony bream. Barra to 20kg, sooties to 5kg.
Fairbairn Dam, Nogoa River: 20km east of Emerald, 18,000ha, av. depth 9m, barra, cod, saratoga, silver and yellowbelly, leathery grunter, redclaw. Barra below dam.
Hinze Dam, Nerang River: 8km south-west of Nerang, almost 1000ha, av. depth 17m, bass, mary river cod, yellowbelly, saratoga, silver perch. Boat hire. Excellent bass fishery.
Julius Lake, Leichardt River: 100km north of Mt Isa, 1420ha, av. depth 9m, barra, saratoga, sooty grunter, longtom, sleepy cod.
Kinchant Dam, Pioneer River: 30km west of Mackay, 920ha, av. depth 7m, barra, sleepy cod, sooty grunter. Small dam with huge barra.
Koombooloomba Dam, Tully River: 30km south-west of Ravenshoe, 1550ha, av. depth 13m, barra, sooty grunter. Clear water.
Mt Morgan Dam, Dee River: 3km east of Mt Morgan, 48ha, av. depth 15m, yellowbelly, silver perch, saratoga, redclaw. Max 4hp motors.
Monduran Lake, Kolan River: 20km north of Gin Gin off the Bruce Hwy, 5300ha when full but varies widely, av. depth 11m. Bass, silver perch, yellowbelly, sooty grunter, saratoga, barra.
Moondarra Dam, Leichardt River: 16km north-east of Mt Isa: 2375ha, av. depth 6m, barra, saratoga, archerfish, sleepy cod, sooty grunter, redclaw. Flows into Lake Julius.
Peter Faust Dam, Proserpine River: 30km north-west of Proserpine, 4350ha, av. depth 12m, barra, saratoga, sooty grunter, redclaw. Big barra are common.
Samsonvale Lake: 5km west of Petrie, North Pine River, 2200ha, av. depth 10m. Bass, yellowbelly, silver perch, mary river cod and saratoga. Limited entry by ballot - visit www.prfma.tripod.com/contact_us.htm
Somerset Dam, Stanley River: Near Esk/Kilcoy, above Lake Wivenhoe, 220km above Brisbane River mouth, 8100ha, av. depth 9m. Yellowbelly, silver perch, mary river cod, saratoga and bass.
Teemburra Dam, Pioneer River: 60km west of Mackay, 1040ha, av. depth 14m, barra, sooty grunter. Lots of timber.
Tinaroo Dam, Barron River: 15km north-east of Atherton, 3320ha, av. depth 13m, barra, saratoga, jacks, silver perch, gar, sleepy cod, sooty grunter, redclaw, tilapia. Known for huge barra.
Wivenhoe Dam, Brisbane River: 150km above Brisbane River mouth, 11,000ha (full), av. depth 11m. Yellowbelly, silver perch, mary river cod, saratoga, bass, redclaw and local native fish. No combustion engines.
Annan and Endeavour Rivers, Cooktown: stocked with barra and sooty grunter. Other species occur naturally.
Baralba Weir, Baralba: 295ha, av. depth 4m, barra, yellowbelly, silver perch, saratoga, sleepy cod.
Barron River, Cairns: stocked with barra. Other species occur naturally.
Bedford Weir, Mackenzie River: 30km north of Blackwater, 468ha, av. depth 5m, barra, yellowbelly, saratoga, sleepy cod.
Bowen River, Collinsville Weir: at Collinsville, 100ha, av. depth 2.5m, barra, sooty grunter, fork-tail catfish.
Brisbane River, 60km stretch from Lake Wivenhoe to Kholo Crossing: bass, mary river cod, yellowbelly, saratoga, ox-eye herring.
Burdekin River, Ayr: stocked with barra. Other species occur naturally. Best fishing at Gorge Weir and The Rocks, opposite the Burdekin Quarry Company.
Caboolture River Weir: 109ha, 5km from Caboolture, stocked with bass, gar, mullet, bank launch, non-combustion boats only.
Charters Towers Weir, Burdekin River: 15km north-east of Charters Towers, 213ha, av. depth 2.5m, barra, sooty and leathery grunter, yellowbelly, sleepy cod.
Fitzroy Barrage, Fitzroy River: Rockhampton, 1400ha, av. depth 5m, barra, yellowbelly, saratoga, sleepy cod.
Glebe Weir, Dawson River: 56km north of Taroom, 530ha, av. depth 3m, yellowbelly, silver perch, sleepy cod, saratoga.
Herbert River, Ingham: 150km stretch downstream of Herbert Falls is stocked with barra. Other species occur naturally.
Jericho Waterholes, Jericho: 10km stretch of Jordon River from Jericho Town Weir to Burgoyne Weir, barcoo grunter.
Johnstone River, Innisfail: stocked with barra. Other species occur naturally.
Moura Weir, Dawson River: Moura, 320ha, av. depth 2m, barra, yellowbelly, saratoga, sleepy cod.
Ross River, Townsville: stocked with barra. The river's weirs breach only in rare floods.
Russell-Mulgrave Rivers: just south of Cairns, well stocked with barra. Other species occur naturally. No weirs.

NSW

WaterNSW storage levels
www.waternsw.com.au/supply/regional-nsw/dam-levels

Chaffey Dam, Peel River: Yellowbelly, silver perch, catfish. Clear upper Peel has some trout. Limited public access to river between Chaffey Dam and junction of Peel and Namoi rivers below Keepit Dam. Lower Peel has cod, yellowbelly.
Clarrie Hall Dam, Doon Doon Creek (a Tweed River tributary): 4km from Uki, take the Nimbin/Kyogle road from Brisbane and turn off to Cram's Farm. A small but productive bass dam.
Copeton Dam, Gwydir River: 40km from Inverell via Gwydir Highway, 4600ha, many facilities. Access also from Bundarra and Bingara. Cod, yellowbelly, redfin. Upstream of lake, gorges - cod, yellowbelly. Trout below dam.
Glenbawn Dam, Hunter River: About 15km east of Scone, 2615ha, max. depth 85m, bass, cod, yellowbelly, silver perch, trout.
Keepit Dam, Namoi River: About 13km upstream from the Peel River junction, near Gunnedah. Yellowbelly, cod.
Lake Mulwala, Murray River: created by construction of Yarrawonga Weir, covers 4400ha. Great murray cod fishery, also yellowbelly. NSW licence is required to fish at Lake Mulwala.
Lake St Clair, Glennies Creek: north of Singleton, Barrington Tops National Park, 1620 ha, bass, yellowbelly, silver perch.
Lostock Dam, Paterson River: Near East Gresford, 220ha max. depth 30m, bass.
Pindari Dam, Severn River: about 60km from Inverell and 20km from Ashford. The lake covers 10sqkm, max. depth 85m, good cod water, with yellowbelly.
Toonumbar Dam, Iron Pot Creek: 30km west of Kyogle, 400ha, road requires 4WD after rain, good bass and cod.
Lake Eucumbene, Adaminaby, 14,500ha, av. depth 33m, brown and rainbow trout. Plenty of accommodation. Camping at Kosciuszko NP. Steep road in.
Lake Jindabyne, Jindabyne, 3035ha, av. depth 15m, brown trout and rainbow trout. Camping at Kosciuszko NP.
Blowering Dam, Tumut, 4300ha, max. depth 90m, murray cod, yellowbelly, silver perch, rainbow and brown trout, redfin, and macquarie perch*.
Burrinjuck Dam, 57km south-west of Yass, 5500ha, murray cod, macquarie perch*, yellowbelly, silver perch, rainbow and brown trout, Atlantic salmon, redfin.
*macquarie perch are protected.

Northern Territory

Manton Dam, 70km south of Darwin just off Stuart Hwy, stocked with barramundi. Also wild saratoga.
Durack Lakes, in suburban Palmerston, stocked with barramundi.

Western Australia

Lake Kununurra: formed in 1963 by the construction of the Ord Diversion Dam in Kununurra. The lake stretches for 55km upstream from the dam towards the larger Lake Argyle. Stocked with barra and now holding many 120cm+ fish, as well as wild sooty grunter and introduced redclaw crayfish.

Lake Kununurra

This man-made reservoir is located in the Ord River valley, formed in 1963 by the construction of the Ord Diversion Dam at Kununurra. The lake, looking more like a river on aerial imagery, stretches for 55km upstream of the Diversion Dam towards the far larger Lake Argyle. Lake Kununurra is stocked with barramundi and holds some huge fish, as well as native grunter and redclaw, with fishing set among picturesque country. In 2012, the WA government allocated $700,000 towards the stocking program, which had seen about 550,000 barramundi fingerlings released into the lake by 2016. Despite appearing to be eminently suitable, nearby Lake Argyle is not yet stocked with barramundi. It has a large population of silver cobbler (catfish).

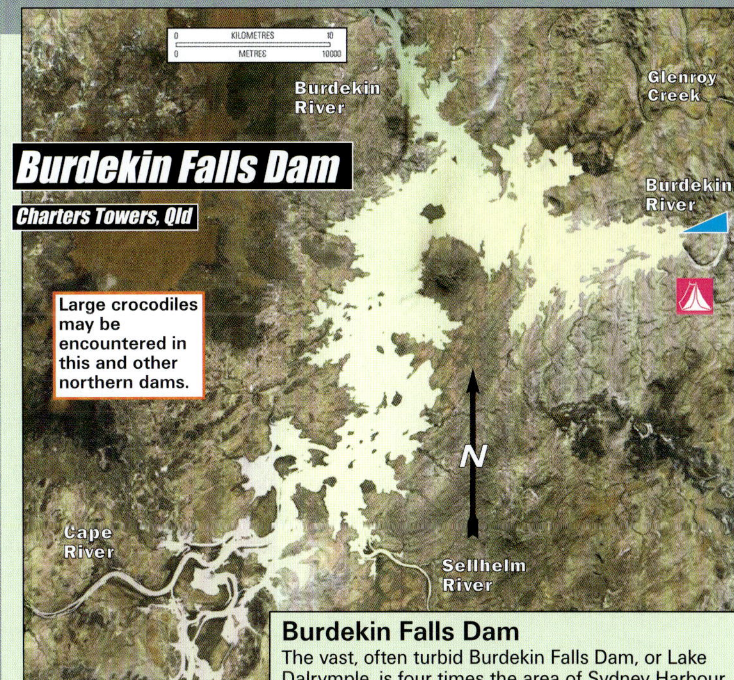

Burdekin Falls Dam

The vast, often turbid Burdekin Falls Dam, or Lake Dalrymple, is four times the area of Sydney Harbour. At 22,400ha, it is Queensland's largest lake, yet it has an average depth of only 9m. The dam is on a sealed road 130km from Townsville and 80km from Charters Towers, on the Burdekin River. Two species of grunter are caught, along with sleepy cod, archerfish, eel-tail and fork-tail catfish, eels, spangled perch, redclaw and a breeding stock of yellowbelly. Yellowbelly and sleepy cod are the main catch. Thousands of barramundi have been released but are not regularly taken, possibly because of the size of the lake and because big barra migrate over the wall during floods. Some migrating fish make it the 165km to the river mouth. Barra are found in the rocky pools of the Burdekin River after flooding. The dam is dirty after rain but this does not bother the fish. There is no foreshore camping, but there is a campsite near the dam wall with toilet, showers, laundry and barbecues. The dam contains large crocodiles.

Teemburra Dam

The wall was built in 1997 on the Pioneer River, 60km north-west of Mackay. The impoundment covers an area of 1080ha and has an average depth of 14m. It holds barramundi, sooty and banded grunter and spangled perch. Barramundi have shown fast growth rates and sooty grunter are prolific and large. The dam has loads of timber, weed and lilies. There is no camping and boat motors are limited to 25hp. Further west lies picturesque Eungella Dam, which has also fished well for large barramundi and sooties, but with the barra usually coming on later in the summer as Eungella is a cooler area.

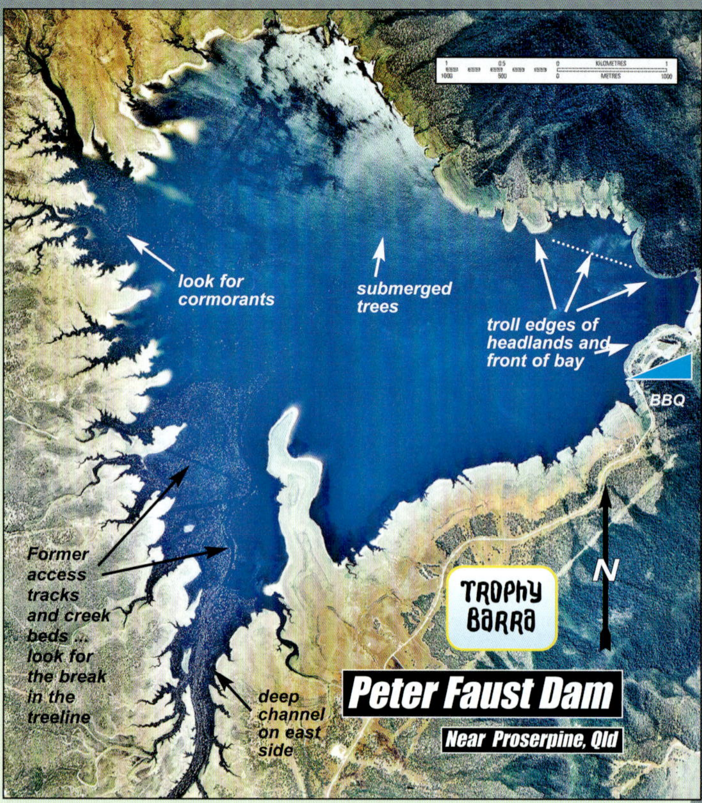

Peter Faust Dam

One of the great barramundi lakes. The dam was built in 1990 on the Proserpine River, 30km north-west of Proserpine. It covers 4350ha, with an average depth of 12m. There are barramundi, saratoga, sleepy cod, sooty grunter, spangled perch, eels and redclaw. Barra over 1m are common, as well as big sooty grunter. Redclaw numbers fluctuate. The barra can be hard to catch at times, possibly being "educated" by angling pressure. Cold weather does not always put the barra off, but warm weather is the best time to chase them. Most fishing is done on the timbered west side. There is no camping at the dam, with the nearest accommodation 2km away.

TOM CLANCY PICTURE

Tinaroo Falls Dam

This dam is famous for giant barra, partly because it was one of the first Queensland dams stocked. To catch the big barra you should fish early or late in warm weather when baitfish move and the big barra feed. Boat fishing is best but there is landbased fishing at the Yungaburra end. The barra can turn on and off in an hour so you have to be on your spot and fishing at the right time. Look for structure such as shallow weed, in-flowing creeks or timber, but also keep in mind that big barra move around and sometimes feed in open water. Thousands of sooty grunter fingerlings have been stocked in Tinaroo. These fish can be caught all day, but morning and evening is best. Use small lures for sooties. Fish near timber and expect to lose lures when these powerful fish dive for cover. About 4500 mangrove jacks were stocked from 1999 to 2002 and some may still be in the dam. More jacks are expected to be stocked in 2022/23. Tinaroo was formed by the damming of the Barron River in 1958 and covers 3320ha with an average depth of 13m. Over the years sooty grunter, sleepy cod, archer fish, bony bream, snub-nose gar, saratoga, silver perch, barramundi, redclaw and jacks have been stocked. The sooties have been caught to 7.5kg and barra to 35kg+, but very jacks have been caught. Redclaw vary in numbersr. The lake is in a relatively cool area of North Queensland and best fishing is usually between the first and last moon quarter in still, warm weather between November and March. Tinaroo has van parks, camping, barbecues, and a restaurant.

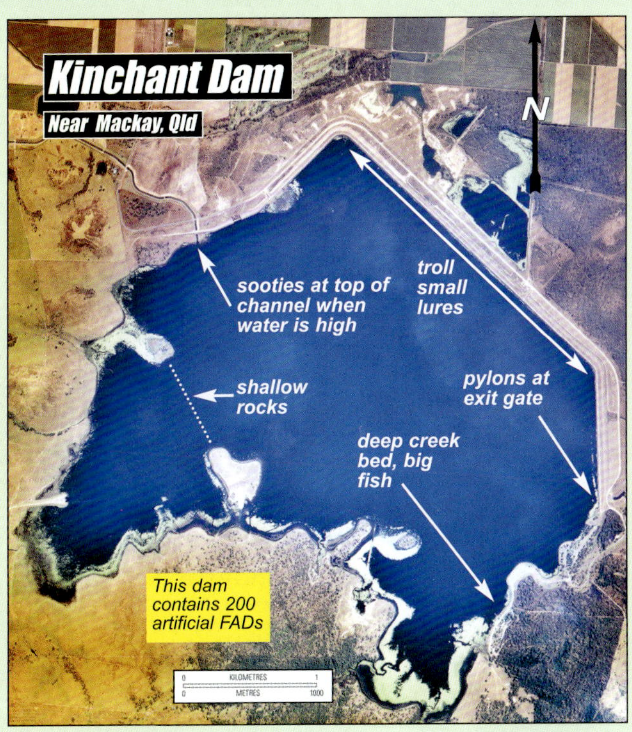

Kinchant Dam

The dam wall was built on the Pioneer River in 1977, 30km west of Mackay. The lake covers 920ha, with an average depth of 7m. This small dam holds barramundi, sleepy cod, sooty grunter, eeltail catfish, fork-tails, spangled perch and mouth almighty. Barramundi were introduced in 2000 and have done exceptionally well, with huge, fat fish caught. The somewhat featureless bottom has been enhanced with engineered FADS and these have been effective at aggregating fish. Large sooty grunter and sleepy cod are also caught. Teemburra and Eungella dams are more scenic, but Kinchant is well worth fishing.

Maps not for navigation. Unmarked obstacles may exist. Fishing and boating is usually not permitted close to and immediately downstream of spillway walls.

Eungella Dam

The dam wall was built in 1969, and the lake now covers 890ha, with an average depth of 15m. Being on top of the Clarke Ranges, west of Mackay, about 3000 feet above sea level, it is cooler than other regional dams. Subsequently, barramundi do not grow as quickly, but the dam has been stocked since 1994 and 1m+ fish are present. Big sooty grunter can be found around the many drowned trees, and sleepy cod have also been stocked. Fish this dam for barramundi only during warm weather. Camping fees apply and an honesty box is at the toilet and ablution block. Visitors should bring drinking water. The eastern end of Eungella Dam has large stands of dead timber. As with all dams, rotting trees should be treated with caution when limbs are high above the water - on windy days stay away, and don't drive up to trees at ramming speed. Note that the drive up the steep Clarke Range road is spectacular but it will test heavily-loaded vehicles.

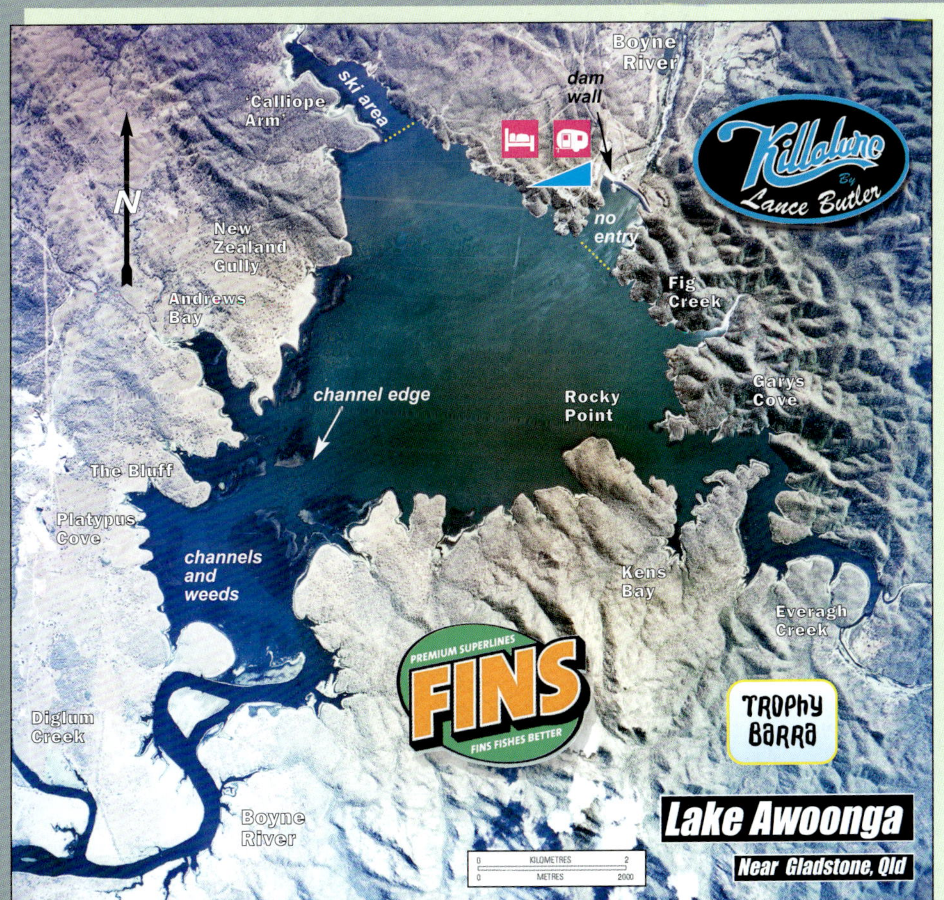

TOM CLANCY PICTURE

Awoonga Dam

One of Queensland's most exciting dams, with very barramundi to 135cm caught. A 36.5kg barramundi was taken in 2008. When the dam floods the big fish enter the Boyne River, and these barra move up and down the coast, providing exciting fishing. Thousands of fish escaped in 2011. Awoonga was first stocked with mangrove jacks in 2001/02, and some original fish may still exist. Subsequent jack stockings totalled 71,000 fish. This dam has been stocked with bream, sooty grunter, silver perch, mullet and yellowbelly, but barramundi, redclaw and fork-tailed catfish now predominate. The fish are bred at the Gladstone Area Water Board Fish Hatchery. The general rule for barra is to fish deep when the sun is up and where fish are seen on the sounder, and cast to timber and weedbeds in mornings and afternoons. Bony bream schools in summer often bring barramundi into the open lake. The redclaw population tends to fluctuate. Accommodation is at Lake Awoonga Caravan Park. The lake has toilets, picnic tables, barbecues, kiosk, playground, lookout, walking tracks and even a restaurant. Awoonga occasionally suffers from low water levels. Awoonga guide Rod Harrison warns that the lake gets rough, usually during the afternoon sea breeze.

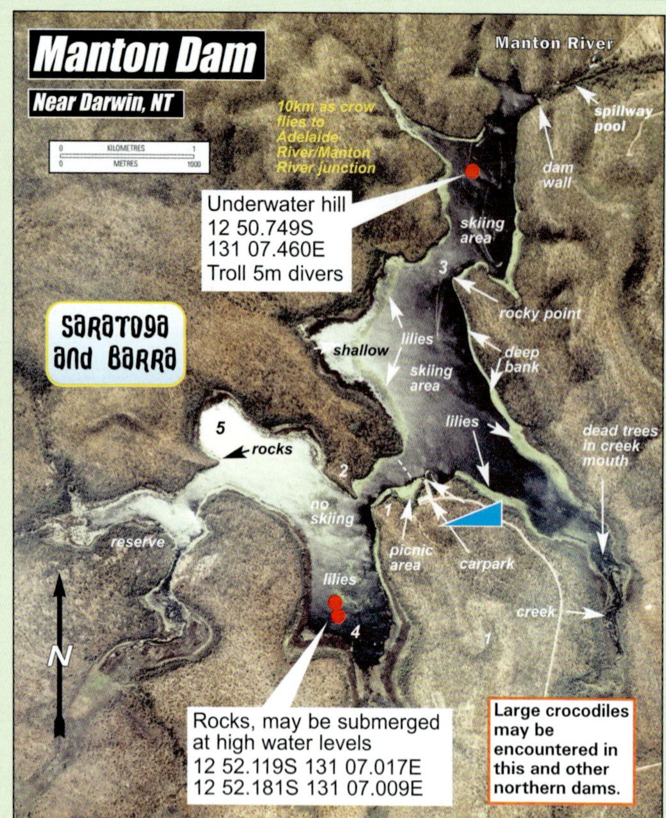

Maps not for navigation. Unmarked obstacles may exist. Fishing and boating is usually not permitted close to and immediately downstream of spillway walls.

Darwin's Manton Dam & Palmerston Lakes

Manton's wall was built on Manton Creek in 1942, a tributary of the Adelaide River just 70km south of the NT's Darwin. This is a small dam with an area of just 330ha. It is scenic, with hills, lily-lined banks and rocky points. It has been stocked with barramundi since the early 1990s. There were 40,000 fish released in April 2021. Metre fish have proved elusive and the dam is considered quirky, but those in the know catch fit 80cm to 90cm fish. Studies show the water stratifies, with little oxygen in the lower layer, meaning fishing should be done in the upper column. Night fishing is generally best, with the fish coming on the bite for short periods. If fish are visible in open water on sonar they are likely feeding. During the day, surface lures cast around the lilly pads and rocky points will produce barra. The dam has many big saratoga, which respond well to surface lures in the early morning. The park gates are usually left open overnight, but check the latest arrangements before fishing. Despite the occasional crocodile showing up, the dam is used by skiers, but the shallow and weed-filled southern arms are restricted for fishing only. Week-day fishing is best when there are fewer boats on the water. The much larger Darwin River Dam nearby is not open to fishing. Darwin's satellite city of Palmerston has suburban lakes that have been stocked with barramundi since 2012.

Lake Moondarra

Mt Isa Fish Stocking Group stocks Lake Moondarra, Lake Julius, Lake Corella and East Leichhardt Dam. Lake Moondarra has been an outstanding barramundi fishery at times, but it has suffered from floods, when barramundi migrate over the dam wall and swim downstream, if there is enough water to complete the journey. The lake's shallow and featureless nature, combined with the warmth of the Mt Isa region, initially made it an outstanding fishery, breaking a state record for the number of barra weighed in at a competition, and the dam once had a high "catch per unit effort", but this was not sustained. The lake has an area of 2375ha and average depth of 6m. Mt Isa Mines built the spillway on the West Leichhardt River in 1957, but stocking did not begin until 1985, with 30,000 sooty grunter added. Barramundi stocking began in 1994. Lake Julius lies downstream, and receives Moondarra's barramundi if enough water flows. Moondarra facilities include toilets, shelters, barbecues, drinking water and a ramp. There is no camping. The Lake Moondarra Fishing Classic is held around October each year.

Cania Dam

This 700ha dam near Monto averages 12m in depth. It has been stocked with yellowbelly, silver perch, bass and saratoga. The dam is an excellent saratoga fishery after an initial stocking of only 200 fish led to natural breeding. The dam is known for scenic rock escarpments and wildlife. As well as the usual submerged timber hazards Cania also has submerged rocks, and the lower the dam falls the more hazardous it becomes. The two shallow rock areas on the map should be avoided when the level is low. There is no camping at Cania but the Cania Gorge Tourist Park is nearby. The dam is near Cania Gorge National Park on a sealed road off the Burnett Hwy, 12km north of Monto or about 80km south of Biloela.

Lake Julius

The lake was formed in 1976 with a dam built across the Leichhardt River. The lake covers 1415ha when full and averages 9m deep. It is known for the size of its sooty grunter, at 50cm+. Like other lakes in the region, species include barramundi, fork-tailed catfish, mouth almighty, spangled perch, rainbow fish, bony bream, sleepy cod, long tom and archer fish. Lake Julius is a safe place to fish from a canoe, as only freshwater crocodiles have been seen in the lake. There are some landbased spots, but a boat provides a better chance of tangling with big sooties in the snags. The lake turnoff is 15km east of Mt Isa, then 90km to the dam along a gravel road. The road often has wandering stock, mostly at dusk and dawn. Camping is below the dam wall.

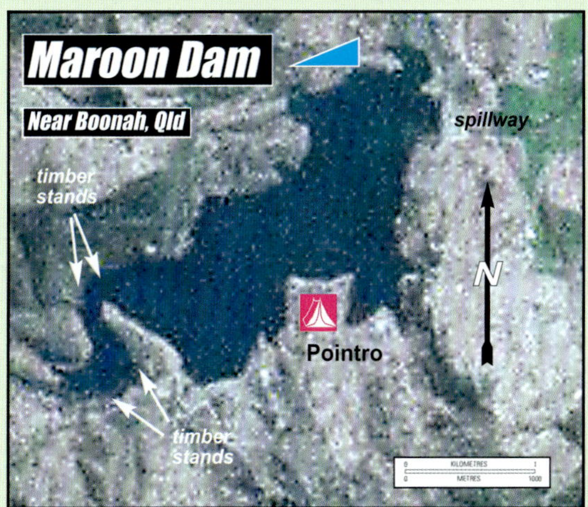

Maroon Dam

This is a small impoundment, having a surface area of just 350ha and an average depth of 9.6m. It is 25km south of Boonah on Burnett Creek, a tributary of the Logan River. Stocked species include yellowbelly, silver perch, mary river cod and bass. Bass are the main species caught. It has in years past been described as one of South-East Queensland's best freshwater fly and surface fishing dams, presumably because a lack of gar and bony bream has caused bass to feed on bugs and shrimp in the weedbeds, making them susceptible to fly. Maroon Dam has great fishing areas - lilies, overhanging trees, rock ledges and shallow bays with rafts of weed that harbour fish. At times weed blankets the dam. Best places to fish when weed is thick is near "The Rock" and in front of the dam wall. The dam is popular with waterskiiers at weekends. There are barbecues and picnic areas and canoes for hire. There are public camp sites at Pointro for tent-style camping. Call (07) 5463 6209 for details. A large high-set house is available for rent that will accommodate 40 people, call (07) 3263 3082. Pointro is at 532 Burnett Creek Rd on the southern shore of Maroon Dam, and has a bitumen road all the way from Boonah to the property entrance. A Stocked Impoundment Permit (SIP) is required to fish Lake Maroon.

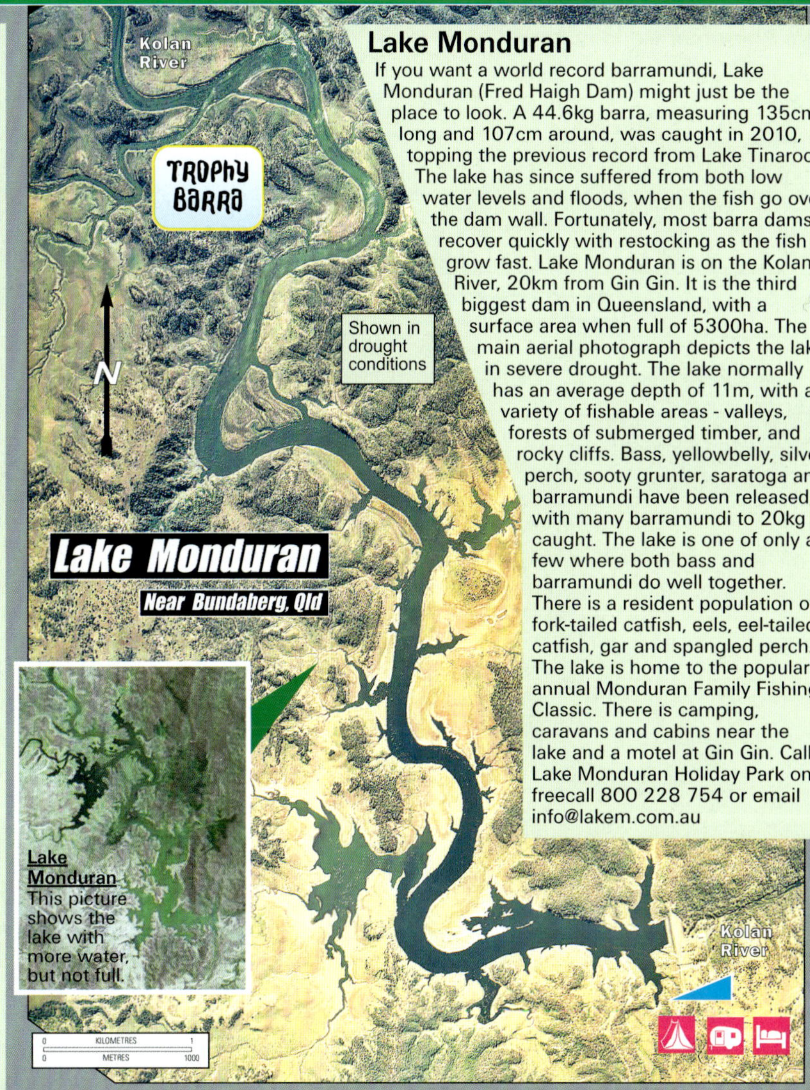

Lake Monduran This picture shows the lake with more water, but not full.

Lake Monduran

If you want a world record barramundi, Lake Monduran (Fred Haigh Dam) might just be the place to look. A 44.6kg barra, measuring 135cm long and 107cm around, was caught in 2010, topping the previous record from Lake Tinaroo. The lake has since suffered from both low water levels and floods, when the fish go over the dam wall. Fortunately, most barra dams recover quickly with restocking as the fish grow fast. Lake Monduran is on the Kolan River, 20km from Gin Gin. It is the third biggest dam in Queensland, with a surface area when full of 5300ha. The main aerial photograph depicts the lake in severe drought. The lake normally has an average depth of 11m, with a variety of fishable areas - valleys, forests of submerged timber, and rocky cliffs. Bass, yellowbelly, silver perch, sooty grunter, saratoga and barramundi have been released, with many barramundi to 20kg caught. The lake is one of only a few where both bass and barramundi do well together. There is a resident population of fork-tailed catfish, eels, eel-tailed catfish, gar and spangled perch. The lake is home to the popular annual Monduran Family Fishing Classic. There is camping, caravans and cabins near the lake and a motel at Gin Gin. Call Lake Monduran Holiday Park on freecall 800 228 754 or email info@lakem.com.au

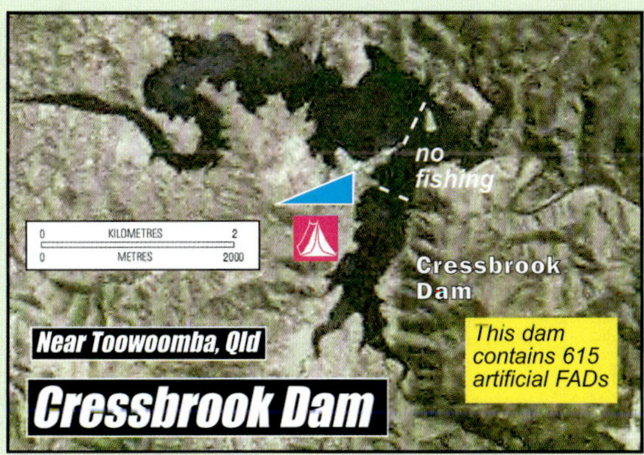

Cressbrook Dam

The dam was built in 1983 to supply Toowoomba with water. The impoundment has a surface are of 515ha, with an average depth of 16m. Lake Cressbrook is open to boating with an 8-knot speed limit, which means no water-skiers. The dam has several types of engineered FADS installed in the west and south arms, with the marks available on the Qld Fisheries website. There are spangled perch, eel-tailed catfish and eels, along with stocked bass, yellowbelly, silver perch, mary river cod, snub-nosed gar and saratoga. Bait fishing is popular but shrimps are scarce. Entry and camping fees apply. The bank near the camping area produces fish. Boating is not allowed at night. Cressbrook has a good walking track for fit fishermen. Nearby Lake Perseverance is not stocked, but further west Cooby Dam is stocked with golden and silver perch and cod. Cooby Dam is electric motors only, there is no camping.

Permits to fish both Cooby and Cressbrook are sold at Crow's Nest Shire Council, Emu Creek Road, Crow's Nest Crow's Nest Seafood and Tackle, New England Highway, Crow's Nest Hampton Store, Cnr New England Highway and Hampton Road, Hampton Shell Service Station, New England Highway, Highfields Meringandan Store, Main Street, Meringandan, Cabarlah Store, New England Highway, Cabarlah.

Callide Dam

Scenic Callide Dam, built in 1965, was one of the later Queensland impoundments stocked with barramundi, and fished well for them until a cold-weather fish kill in 2007. The dam, built to supply water to a power station, has an average depth of 10.5m and an area of 1240ha when full. Fishermen will find stocked saratoga, barramundi, yellowbelly and silver perch alongside native eel-tailed catfish, sleepy cod, spangled perch, gar and eels. The Callide Valley Native Fish Stocking Association runs a fish hatchery for this dam. Boating is not allowed within 200m of the spillway. The dam has boat ramps, toilets, tap water, picnic tables and a playground. Accommodation is 12km away in Biloela.

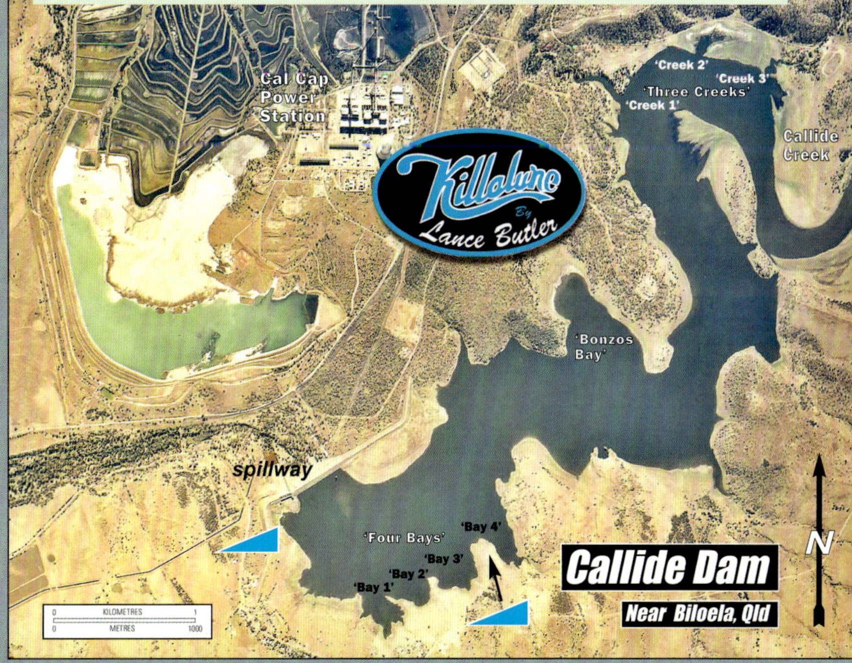

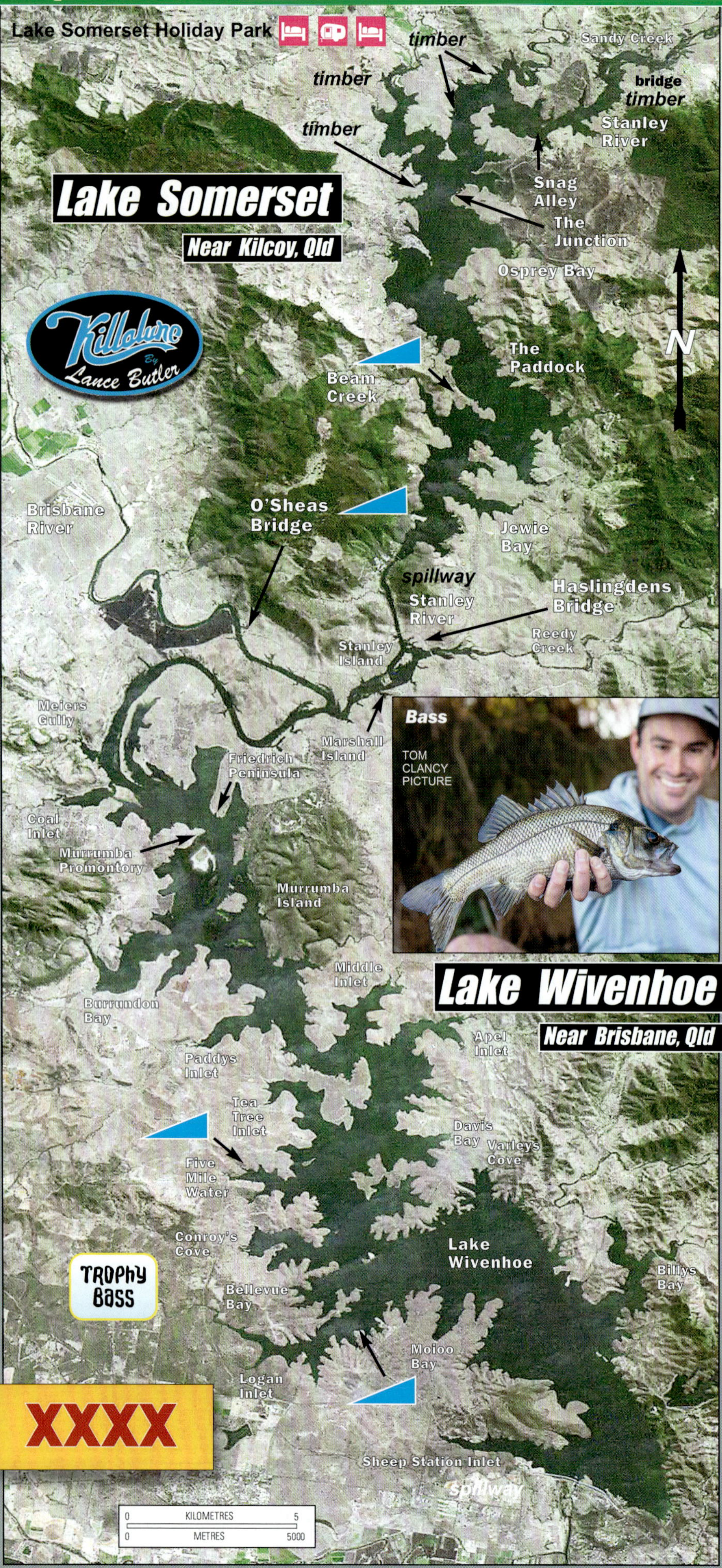

Lake Somerset Holiday Park
timber
timber
timber
Sandy Creek
bridge
timber
Stanley River
Snag Alley
The Junction
Osprey Bay
Lake Somerset
Near Kilcoy, Qld
Killalure By Lance Butler
The Paddock
N
Beam Creek
Brisbane River
O'Sheas Bridge
Jewie Bay
spillway
Stanley River
Haslingdens Bridge
Reedy Creek
Stanley Island
Meiers Gully
Bass
TOM CLANCY PICTURE
Marshall Island
Friedrich Peninsula
Coal Inlet
Murrumba Promontory
Murrumba Island
Middle Inlet
Lake Wivenhoe
Near Brisbane, Qld
Burrundon Bay
Apel Inlet
Paddys Inlet
Tea Tree Inlet
Davis Bay
Valleys Cove
Five Mile Water
Conroy's Cove
Lake Wivenhoe
TROPHY BASS
Bellevue Bay
Billys Bay
Moioo Bay
Logan Inlet
XXXX
Sheep Station Inlet
spillway
0 KILOMETRES 5
0 METRES 5000

Lake Wivenhoe & Lake Somerset

Lake Somerset dam, 25km from Esk, was built on the Stanley River, a Brisbane River tributary, in 1959. The impoundment has an impressive area of 4200ha, averaging just 9m deep. Bass, yellowbelly, silver perch, mary river cod, saratoga and snub-nosed gar have been stocked. There are also eel-tailed catfish, spangled perch, banded grunter, lungfish and redclaw. This is one of the most popular fishing spots in Queensland, home to a big competition each October. Camping is at Lake Somerset Holiday Park (www.lakesomerset.com.au) and Somerset Park Council Campgrounds (07) 5426 0108 or (07) 5424 4000. A SEQWCorp camping permit is required at both areas, available from the kiosk or ranger station next to the wall lookout. A SEQWCorp permit is required for trailer boats, phone (07) 5427 8100 for details. There is a six-lane ramp at Kirkleagh and a gravel ramp used during low water, and a ramp at The Spit near the dam wall. Ramp access is daylight only unless you are at Lake Somerset Holiday Park, phone ahead on (07) 5497 1093 to get a gate pin number before it opens at 7am. Lake Somerset flows into **Lake Wivenhoe,** 150km above the mouth of Brisbane River. This lake, built in 1985, covers almost 11,000ha when full, averaging 11m deep. Despite it's size Lake Wivenhoe is only for electric, paddle or sail powered boats. Wivenhoe has similar fish to Lake Somerset. Camping is at Captain Logans Camp (07) 5426 4729 and Lumley Hill. Boat launching is at Logans Inlet and Hamon Cove. The **Brisbane River** below Lake Wivenhoe has been stocked with bass and cod.

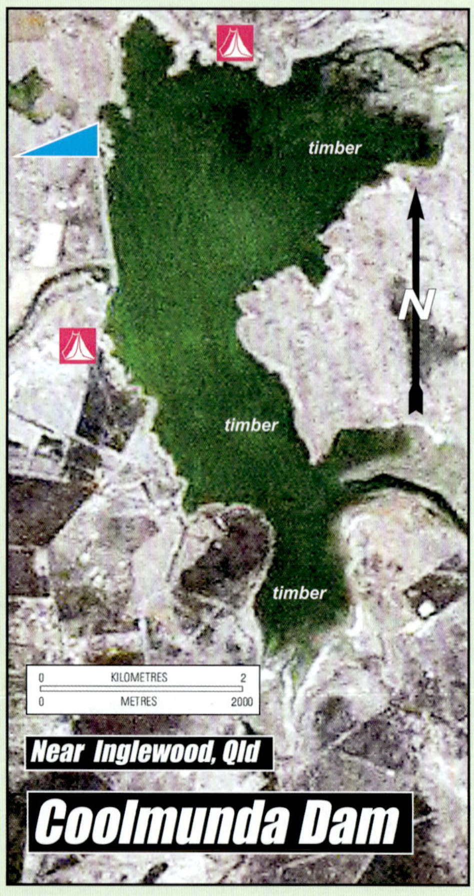

Coolmunda Dam

The dam, 14km from Inglewood, was built on Macintyre Brook in 1968. The lake has an average depth of only 4m or so, and an area of 1740ha. This small dam has been well stocked with yellowbelly and silver perch and murray cod, with yellowbelly making up half the total reported catch. Cod are caught quite regularly. The dam has many eel-tailed catfish. Carp are also caught. There is a concrete ramp. There is a SunWater camp site on the shoreline and Lake Coolmunda Caravan Park at the entrance to the lake, phone (07) 4652 4171.

Lake Barambah

Bjelke-Petersen Dam (Lake Barambah) was built in 1988 just 15km from Murgon, 250km north-west of Brisbane. The impoundment covers an area of 2200ha. It has been stocked with yellowbelly, silver perch, saratoga and bass. There are also eel-tailed catfish, spangled perch, sleepy cod and redclaw. The lake is popular with bass fishermen. Troll the timber in the upper region to locate schools, and then cast or jig, or try moving around while observing sonar and cast when you find fish. Accommodation is at Yallakool Tourist Park (07) 4168 4746, or at Murgon. There are two boat ramps, one at the dam wall and one at the camp site. The proximity of Lake Boondooma and Lake Barambah make this region popular. The lake hosts the Inland Fishing Classic in October and Golden Lure Championships in November.

Lake Boondooma

The dam, on the Boyne River 25km from Proston and 70km from Kingaroy, was built in 1983. The 2000ha impoundment has a mix of good fishing and scenery, with rocky headlands and gullies. The lake has mostly bare banks, but there is structure in the deeper water. The average depth is 11m. Boondooma has been stocked with bass, yellowbelly, silver perch, saratoga, murray cod and mary river cod. Eel-tail catfish and spangled perch are abundant. In 1994, almost 70,000 barramundi were released but few were recaptured. The lake is best known for bass and yellowbelly. Anglers should target the shallow weedbeds along the shore in the bays and the few timbered areas with small lures worked slowly. Bass schools can be found over structure such as channels (old creek beds), drop-offs and the tops of submerged hills. As in all impoundments, a good sounder makes finding fish easier. Boat launching is via a two-lane ramp at the foreshore camping area. Phone (07) 4168 9694 for camping details.

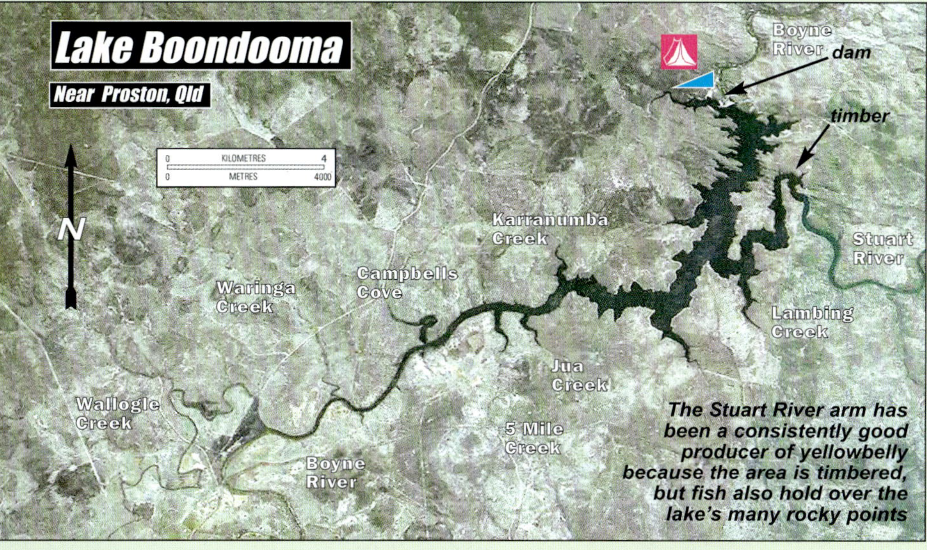

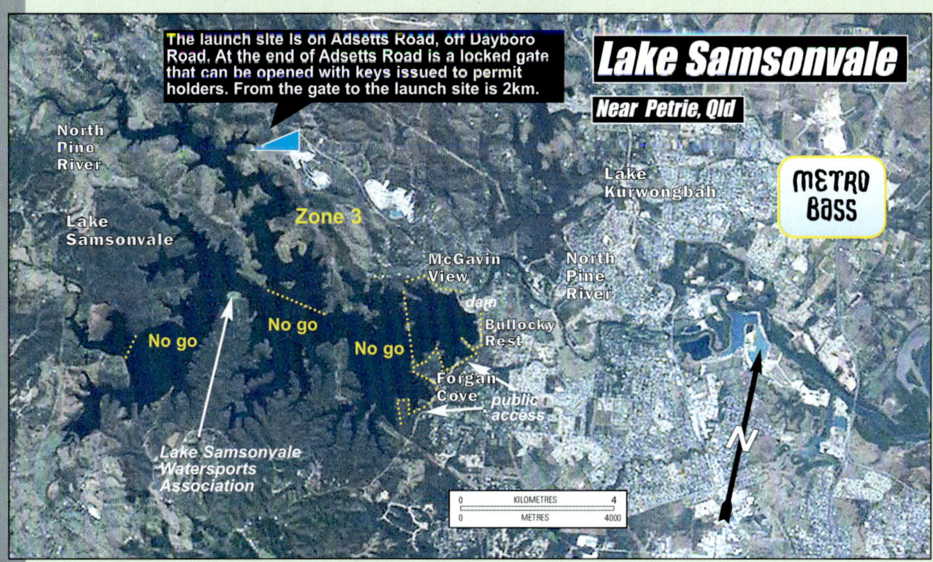

Lakes Samsonvale & Kurwongbah

North Pine Dam (Lake Samsonvale), west of Petrie, was built in 1976 on the North Pine River. The lake covers 2200ha, with an average depth of 10m. Bass, yellowbelly, mary river cod and saratoga are the stocked species, with the first stocking in 1991 There are also tilapia and redclaw. For years only landbased fishing was allowed from limited areas such as Bullocky Rest and McGavins View, but when boat anglers entered the lake on a limited entry permit system they found big bass and yellowbelly, well fed from the bony bream, snub-nosed gar and redclaw in the lake. Boating is in Zone 3 and only a limited number of permits are issued each year. For boating permit applications and maps visit www.prfma.com.au. Fads and other infrastructure have been installed in Zone 3. In 2018/19 there were 58,000 bass, 22,000 yellowbelly, 1000 cod and 27 adult saratoga stocked. **Lake Kurwongbah** has much the same species. It covers 367ha, with fishing restricted to two areas, the Mick Hanfling Park on Beeville Rd (picnic shelters, barbecues, toilets) and Kurwongbah Park, located on Dayboro Rd (shelter with picnic tables and barbecues). Canoes are allowed only within a designated area. Little **Lake Gaffney** is a closed educational fishery.

Maps not for navigation. Unmarked obstacles may exist. Fishing and boating is usually not permitted close to and immediately downstream of spillway walls.

Glenlyon Dam

This impoundment is 40km from Texas township, and 90km from Stanthorpe. It covers an area of 1800ha and has an average depth of just 4.3m. Yellowbelly are the main catch, but big murray cod attract many fishos. The lake has also been stocked with silver perch, and there are native eel-tailed catfish and spangled perch. Glenlyon has large areas of timber, particularly in the upper reaches of the creeks. The timber is thickest at the north end. The area in front of the limestone caves is popular - fish where large trees stand in front of the rocks. Further up and around the corner from the caves, on the western side, are steep rock banks which are worth trolling. Further up is a water tank on the west bank where there is submerged timber which often holds fish. About 2km up from the tank, on the east side, is a bay with weed beds and standing timber. When the depth at the base of the trees is 3m to 6m (about 20 per cent capacity) this spot produces fish. The lake does at times suffer from a low water level and weed growth, but fish are still caught. Glenlyon Dam Tourist Park (02) 6737 5266 has toilets, showers, barbecues, boat hire, phones, tennis court and playground. The kiosk has bait, tackle, ice, gas and petrol.

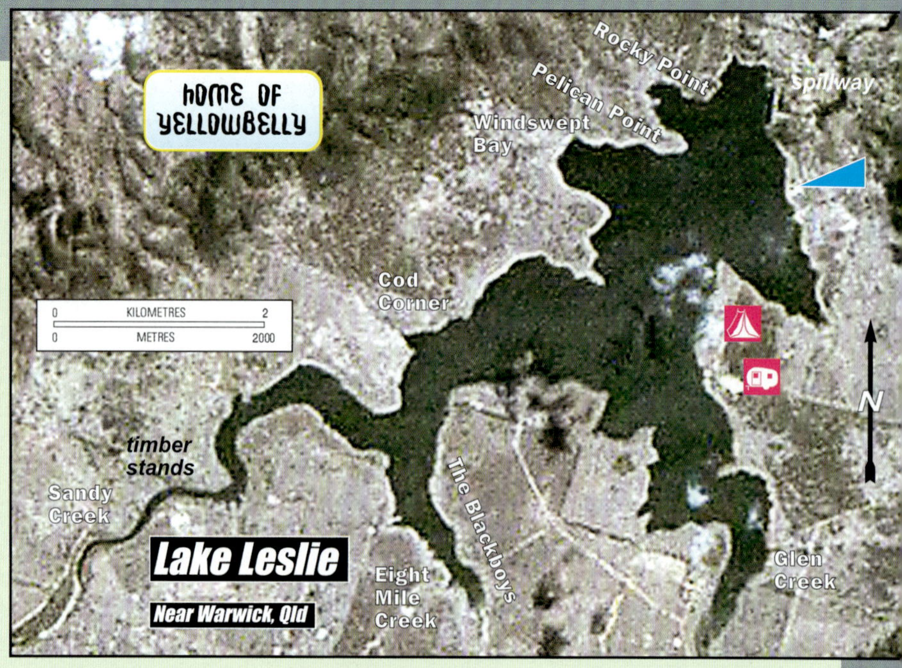

Lake Leslie

The impoundment was created in 1963 by a dam built on Sandy Creek, 15km from Warwick. The lake has a surface area of 1250ha, and an average depth of 8m when full. Lake Leslie is a popular spot, with yellowbelly, silver perch and murray cod. It also has native populations of spangled perch and eel-tailed catfish. It has been well stocked in years past and was once one of the best yellowbelly dams in Queensland. Big yellowbelly are regularly caught on lures. Silver perch are caught less often, usually on bait. Cod are an occasional catch. Lake Leslie has many rocks around the fringes and standing timber in the upper reaches of Sandy Creek - these areas are good places to start fishing. The lake has a range of facilities, including a shop. Lake Leslie Tourist Park has camping, boats and kayaks, phone (07) 4661 9116, or email info@lltp.com.au. Boats can be launched from a concrete ramp or the bank. Local streams have also been stocked with fish.

Lake Moogerah

This lake, 60km from Warwick, is regarded by some as the home of big bass. It is a medium-sized lake of 880ha, with an average depth of about 10m. The dam is below the junction of Coulsons and Reynolds Creeks. This is one of South-East Queensland's better impoundments. It has yellowbelly, silver perch, mary river cod, bass and saratoga. Waterskiers use the lake so fishing is usually done near the shoreline. The beginning of the standing timber is a good spot to start. Troll rocky points for bass following the shore line in 5m to 7m of water using lures that swim to this depth. Soft vibes can work well. Best times are early morning and late afternoon, but fish will bite through the day in warm weather. Good areas for trolling are the rocky points either side of the dam wall, and the rocky points leading to the gorge. Bait fishing with shrimp gets bass but lures and flies are effective. The gorge below the dam flows into Warrill Creek and then into the mighty Bremer and Brisbane Rivers. Moogerah Dam has at times suffered from low water. Launching is difficult when the water is low and a 4WD may be needed. Camping is at Lake Moogerah Caravan Park, phone (07) 5463 0141. A Stocked Impoundment Permit (SIP) is required.

Pindari Dam

This impoundment is on the Severn River in NSW's far north, about 60km from Inverell and 20km from Ashford. The dam, built in 1969, created the first big water storage in northern NSW, with the wall doubled in height in 1995. The lake covers 1050ha, half the size of Sydney Harbour, and has an impressive maximum depth of 85m. However it suffered from extremely low levels in 2019/20, and was recovering after refilling in 2021. In good years Pindari is a noted cod water, producing big fish. The dam is in rugged country with loads of rock structure. Casting to the drop-offs among huge granite boulders provokes some exciting hookups. The top of the dam is a popular area, with waterfalls after rain. Yellowbelly and silver perch are also caught, along with redfin. Below the dam the river has cod in rugged gorges, but bankside access is limited - use Jimagie and Ashford about 20km below the dam as access points. Visitors can also go picnicking, walking, sailing, swimming and waterskiing. There are boat ramps on Richard Tighe Scenic Dve, barbecues, bush sheds, tables and an amenities block. This region gets cold at short notice so prepare accordingly.

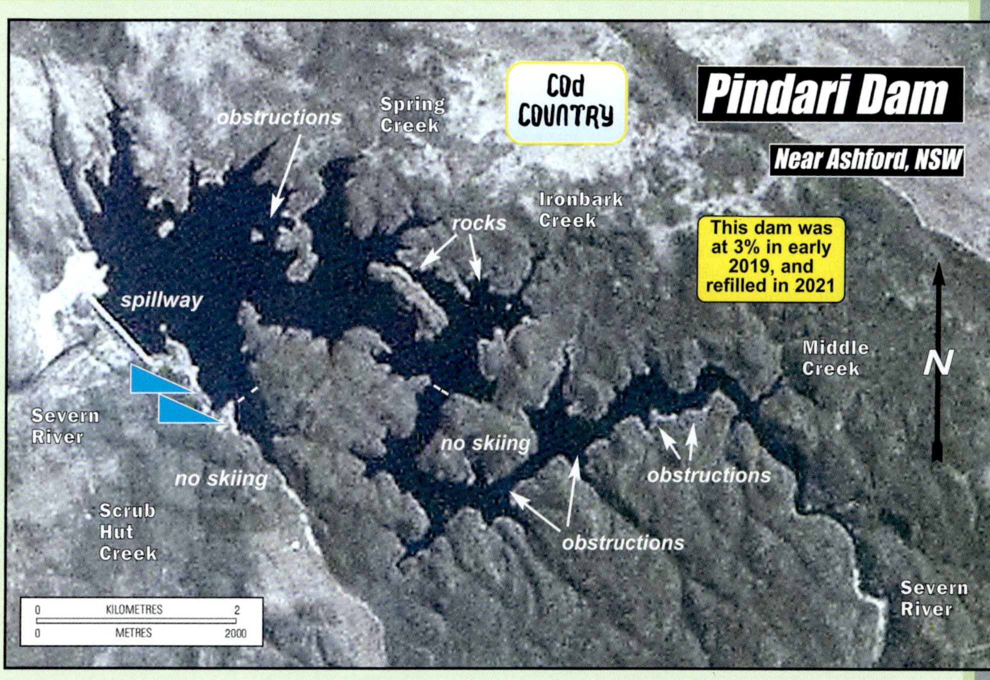

Lake Maraboon

Lake Maraboon, or Fairbairn Dam, is on the Nogoa River 20km east of Emerald in 1972. It has a huge area of nearly 15,000ha when full, but is quite shallow. The dam was first stocked in the 1980s. In 2017/18, 9000 barramundi, 39,500 yellowbelly and 7150 silver perch were released. A total of 252,514 barramundi and 489,412 yellowbelly have been stocked since 2009. After a slow start fat barramundi over 120cm are now being caught, making for an exciting fishery. The species list is yellowbelly, murray cod, saratoga, silver perch, leathery grunter, spangled perch, eels, eel-tail catfish, redclaw, barramundi and sleepy cod. Redclaw are usually abundant and popular with visitors. Yellowbelly are the next most common catch, but the big barramundi are now attracting a strong following. Cod may be breeding in the Nogoa River as they have been caught in the dam long after stocking ceased. For cod, fish around the rocky foreshores when water levels are high. Silver perch are usually hard to find. Like most big dams, Lake Maraboon fishes better for those who have time to explore, with the best fishing usually in the upper Nogoa River arm, where there are ample weedbeds, timber and channels, but this area is a long run from the boat ramp. It is perhaps easier to find barramundi in the town weir below the dam, but the dam produces the biggest fish. Like most big dams it can become rough. Lake Maraboon Holiday Park and boat ramp is near the dam wall. For details phone (07) 4982 3677 or fax (07) 4982 1932.

Copeton Dam

This is 40km from Inverell, near Tingha and Bundarra townships. It is a big impoundment, about 4600ha, or three times the size of Sydney Harbour. The dam was built on the Gwydir River in 1976 for irrigation. The water level can drop quickly, and this can affect the fishing. Copeton has cod, yellowbelly, silver perch, redfin and eel-tail catfish. Cod of 20kg are caught often enough for cod specialists to concentrate their efforts here. The north and south-east shores have large stands of timber that hold fish. The southern river entrance has rugged gorges and pools with cod and yellowbelly. Rock outcrops and timber stands are good places to fish. Cod can be caught all year, with yellowbelly best in spring and summer. Trout are found downstream of the dam in the Gwydir River and were once stocked in the dam. Copeton Waters State Park on the south side of the lake covers more than 900ha and has many good fishing and camping spots along the peninsula, and a boat ramp. Canoes and cartoppers can be launched at several locations with camping nearby. There are hot showers and amenities blocks in the park, making this an ideal family location. There is a kiosk and laundry and powered camping and caravan sites. Cabins, caravans, fuel and boat hire is available, along with barbecues, golf course, tennis courts, adventure playgrounds and waterslides. The Northern Shores Recreational Area on Auburn Vale Rd has barbecues, hot showers, powered van sites and camping, with two good boat ramps.

Lake Glenbawn

This is arguably the best big-bass impoundment in NSW. The dam wall was built on the Hunter River 15km from Scone in 1958. The wall was upgraded in 1986 and the lake now has a surface area of 2620ha and an impressive maximum depth of 85m. Because the lake is just two hours (160km) from Newcastle and three and half hours from Sydney, it is popular at weekends. Glenbawn is probably the nearest dam for Brisbane anglers to head south to catch trout. Bass and trout can be caught side by side, but bass are by far the main catch, with some yellowbelly. The lake is near Barrington Tops National Park, a high area known for its trout streams. Bass, murray cod, yellowbelly, silver perch, brown and rainbow trout have been stocked in the dam over the years, but this location is best known for big bass, with fish of more than 4kg landed. Glenbawn usually fishes best from early spring until early summer, and slows as the water gets hot, before improving again from late summer to early autumn. In winter, fish deep, but expect it to be cold. Look for sunlit shallows in winter and spring, and work the sonar to find fish. The lake has submerged timber, but sonar also reveals fish in open water. Through summer, watersports are popular, so weekday trips are recommended, although the lake's size means there is usually a quiet place to fish. Facilities include accommodation, powered camp and van sites, tent sites and cabins. There are barbecues, picnic areas and amenities blocks, tennis courts, playgrounds, a cricket oval, three-hole golf, and a functions hall. There is boat and canoe hire at the kiosk. The park office phone is (02) 6543 7193 fax (02) 6543 7422.

Fal Brook
Carrow Brook
N
TROPHY BASS
Reedy Cove
Richards Point
St Clair Island
spillway
Glennies Creek
Connell Inlet
Lake St Clair
Near Singleton, NSW
0 KILOMETRES 2
0 METRES 2000

Lake St Clair

This scenic impoundment is in the foothills of the Mount Royal Range in Barrington Tops National Park. The lake was created by damming Glennies Creek in 1983. The dam wall is 40km upstream from the Glennies Creek-Hunter River junction, 25km from Singleton. This huge lake has a storage capacity about half the volume of Sydney Harbour. It is 5km long and up to 3km wide. It supplies water for Singleton, as well as for irrigation and mining in the Hunter Valley. The dam wall is 67m high and the lake when full has a surface area of 1540ha. Upstream from Glennies Creek Dam, Fal Brook and Carrow Brook join to form Glennies Creek. Yellowbelly, silver perch and bass are stocked, and bass have thrived. The lake has only a small amount of standing timber, mostly near shore. Any foreshores near timber generally provide good landbased fishing, particularly on the southern bank. The bank below the road following the eastern shoreline is good in the early morning. Because the dam is in the hills it is reasonably protected and suitable for small boats and canoes, but weather-watching care is still required. Watersports are popular, with weekday fishing more peaceful. Facilities include powered and unpowered sites and lots of bush camping. Camping, barbecues, hot showers, toilets, boat ramp and a kiosk are available. Fees apply. Call Lake St Clair Park on (02) 6577 3370 for details. Fishing licences are sold by the lake caretaker.

Lake Keepit

This dam is in the New England region of northern NSW. It is reached via Oxley Highway, 60km west of Tamworth. The dam is on the Namoi River, 13km up from its junction with Peel River, between the towns of Gunnedah and Manilla, about 400km north of Sydney. The dam wall was built in 1961 and the lake covers 4370ha, to 48m deep. As it provides water for Walgett and irrigation water for Namoi Valley, and hydro-electricity, the lake often suffers low water levels. There are carp, murray cod, yellowbelly, silver perch, eel-tailed catfish and eels. During good times it is one of the better cod lakes, but carp and yellowbelly are the main catch. When levels are low rocky islands appear, and these can be a boating hazard. Lake Keepit Family Fishing Club runs a fishing competition each January. There are barbecues and picturesque picnic spots. There is bush camping, river camps, powered and unpowered sites, cabins and chalets, amenities blocks with laundry facilities, camp kitchen, a concrete boat ramp, swimming area, children's playgrounds, wading pool, BMX bike track, walking trails, skating bowl, five-hole golf course, tennis court, sailing club and a gliding club. Watersports are popular. Canoe hire is available. The park office is (02) 6769 7605 fax (02) 6769 7547. Email keepitsp@bigpond.com. The fishing club is (02) 6769 7693.

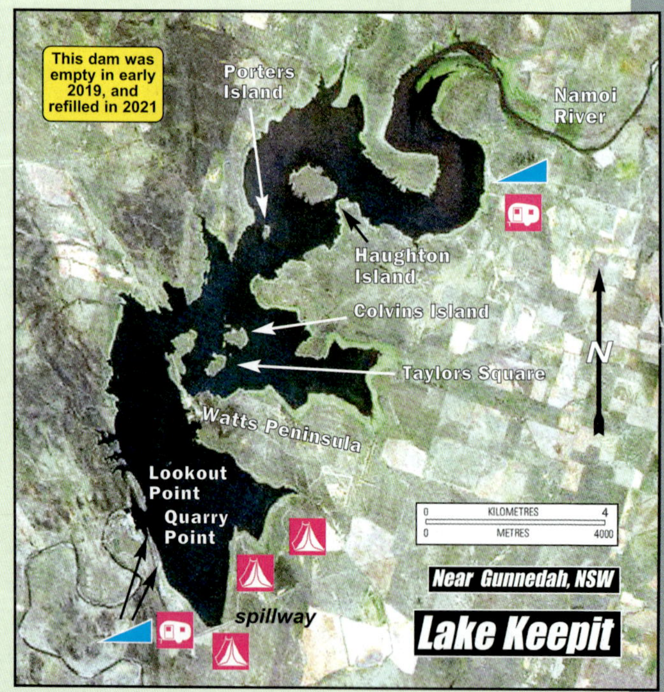